HALSBURY'S
Laws of England

FIFTH EDITION
2013

Volume 5

This is volume 5 of the Fifth Edition of Halsbury's Laws of England, containing the title
BANKRUPTCY AND INDIVIDUAL INSOLVENCY.

The title BANKRUPTCY AND INDIVIDUAL INSOLVENCY replaces the Fourth Edition title
BANKRUPTCY AND INDIVIDUAL INSOLVENCY, contained in volume 3(2) (2002 Reissue).
That volume has been completely replaced, and may now be archived.

For a full list of volumes comprised in a current set of Halsbury's Laws of England please
see overleaf.

Fifth Edition volumes:

1 (2008), 2 (2008), 3 (2011), 4 (2011), 5 (2013), 6 (2011), 7 (2008), 8 (2010), 9 (2012), 10 (2012), 11 (2009), 12 (2009), 13 (2009), 14 (2009), 15 (2009), 16 (2011), 17 (2011), 18 (2009), 19 (2011), 21 (2011), 22 (2012), 23 (2013), 24 (2010), 25 (2010), 26 (2010), 27 (2010), 28 (2010), 30 (2012), 31 (2012), 32 (2012), 33 (2013), 34 (2011), 35 (2011), 36 (2011), 39 (2009), 40 (2009), 41 (2009), 42 (2011), 43 (2011), 44 (2011), 45 (2010), 46 (2010), 48 (2008), 49 (2008), 50 (2008), 51 (2013), 52 (2009), 53 (2009), 54 (2008), 55 (2012), 56 (2011), 57 (2012), 60 (2011), 61 (2010), 62 (2012), 63 (2012), 64 (2012), 65 (2008), 66 (2009), 67 (2008), 68 (2008), 69 (2009), 70 (2012), 71 (2013), 72 (2009), 73 (2009), 74 (2011), 75 (2013), 76 (2013), 77 (2010), 78 (2010), 79 (2008), 80 (2013), 81 (2010), 82 (2010), 83 (2010), 84 (2013), 84A (2013), 85 (2012), 87 (2012), 88 (2012), 88A (2013), 89 (2011), 90 (2011), 91 (2012), 92 (2010), 93 (2008), 94 (2008), 96 (2012), 97 (2010), 98 (2013), 99 (2012), 100 (2009), 101 (2009), 102 (2010), 103 (2010)

Fourth Edition volumes (bold figures represent reissues):

1(1) (2001 Reissue), **8(1)** (2003 Reissue), **8(2)**, **12(1)**, **15(3)** (2007 Reissue), **15(4)** (2007 Reissue), **16(2)**, **17(2)**, **23(1)**, **23(2)**, 24, **39(1A)**, **39(1B)**, **44(2)**, 48 (2007 Reissue), 51, 52

Additional Materials:

Housing (*Housing Benefit*) containing vol **22** (2006 Reissue) paras 140–186; *Road Traffic* (*Tramways*) containing vol **40(3)** (2007 Reissue) paras 1532–1634; *Sentencing and Disposition of Offenders* (*Release and Recall of Prisoners*) containing vol **92** (2010) paras 761–820; *Specific Performance* containing vol **44(1)** (Reissue) paras 801–1000; *Tort* (*Conversion and Wrongful Interference with Goods*) containing vol **45(2)** (Reissue) paras 542–686

Fourth and Fifth Edition volumes:

2013 Consolidated Index (A–E), 2013 Consolidated Index (F–O), 2013 Consolidated Index (P–Z), 2014 Consolidated Table of Statutes, 2014 Consolidated Table of Statutory Instruments, etc, 2013 Consolidated Table of Cases (A–L), 2013 Consolidated Table of Cases (M–Z, ECJ Cases)

Updating and ancillary materials:

2013 Annual Cumulative Supplement; Monthly Current Service; Annual Abridgments 1974–2012

November 2013

HALSBURY'S
Laws of England

FIFTH EDITION

LORD MACKAY OF CLASHFERN
Lord High Chancellor of Great Britain
1987–97

Volume 5

2013

 LexisNexis®

Members of the LexisNexis Group worldwide

United Kingdom	LexisNexis, a Division of Reed Elsevier (UK) Ltd, Lexis House, 30 Farringdon Street, LONDON, EC4A 4HH, and London House, 20–22 East London Street, EDINBURGH, EH7 4BQ
Australia	LexisNexis Butterworths, Chatswood, New South Wales
Austria	LexisNexis Verlag ARD Orac GmbH & Co KG, Vienna
Benelux	LexisNexis Benelux, Amsterdam
Canada	LexisNexis Canada, Markham, Ontario
China	LexisNexis China, Beijing and Shanghai
France	LexisNexis SA, Paris
Germany	LexisNexis GmbH, Dusseldorf
Hong Kong	LexisNexis Hong Kong, Hong Kong
India	LexisNexis India, New Delhi
Italy	Giuffrè Editore, Milan
Japan	LexisNexis Japan, Tokyo
Malaysia	Malayan Law Journal Sdn Bhd, Kuala Lumpur
New Zealand	LexisNexis NZ Ltd, Wellington
Poland	Wydawnictwo Prawnicze LexisNexis Sp, Warsaw
Singapore	LexisNexis Singapore, Singapore
South Africa	LexisNexis Butterworths, Durban
USA	LexisNexis, Dayton, Ohio

FIRST EDITION	*Published in 31 volumes between 1907 and 1917*
SECOND EDITION	*Published in 37 volumes between 1931 and 1942*
THIRD EDITION	*Published in 43 volumes between 1952 and 1964*
FOURTH EDITION	*Published in 56 volumes between 1973 and 1987, with reissues between 1988 and 2008*
FIFTH EDITION	*Commenced in 2008*

A CIP Catalogue record for this book is available from the British Library.

ISBN 13 (complete set, standard binding): 9781405734394

ISBN 13: 9781405763561

ISBN 978-1-4057-6356-1

9 781405 763561

Typeset by Letterpart Limited, Caterham on the Hill, Surrey CR3 5XL
Printed and bound by CPI Group (UK) Ltd, Croydon, CR0 4YY
Visit LexisNexis at www.lexisnexis.co.uk

Editor in Chief

THE RIGHT HONOURABLE

LORD MACKAY OF CLASHFERN

LORD HIGH CHANCELLOR OF GREAT BRITAIN

1987–97

BANKRUPTCY AND INDIVIDUAL INSOLVENCY

Consultant Editors

RICHARD SHELDON, MA,
of Gray's Inn,
one of Her Majesty's Counsel

FELICITY TOUBE, BA, BCL,
of the Inner Temple,
one of Her Majesty's Counsel

The law stated in this volume is in general that in force on 1 October 2013,
although subsequent changes have been included wherever possible.

Any future updating material will be found in the Current Service and annual
Cumulative Supplement to Halsbury's Laws of England.

TABLE OF CONTENTS

Volume 5

BANKRUPTCY AND INDIVIDUAL INSOLVENCY

HOW TO USE HALSBURY'S LAWS OF ENGLAND

Volumes

Each text volume of Halsbury's Laws of England contains the law on the titles contained in it as at a date stated at the front of the volume (the operative date).

Information contained in Halsbury's Laws of England may be accessed in several ways.

First, by using the tables of contents.

Each volume contains both a general Table of Contents, and a specific Table of Contents for each title contained in it. From these tables you will be directed to the relevant part of the work.

Readers should note that the current arrangement of titles can be found in the Current Service.

Secondly, by using tables of statutes, statutory instruments, cases or other materials.

If you know the name of the Act, statutory instrument or case with which your research is concerned, you should consult the Consolidated Tables of statutes, cases and so on (published as separate volumes) which will direct you to the relevant volume and paragraph. The Consolidated Tables will indicate if the volume referred to is a Fifth Edition volume.

(Each individual text volume also includes tables of those materials used as authority in that volume.)

Thirdly, by using the indexes.

If you are uncertain of the general subject area of your research, you should go to the Consolidated Index (published as separate volumes) for reference to the relevant volume(s) and paragraph(s). The Consolidated Index will indicate if the volume referred to is a Fifth Edition volume.

(Each individual text volume also includes an index to the material contained therein.)

Additional Materials

The reorganisation of the title scheme of Halsbury's Laws for the Fifth Edition means that from time to time Fourth Edition volumes will be *partially* replaced by Fifth Edition volumes.

In certain instances an Additional Materials softbound book will be issued, in which will be reproduced material which has not yet been replaced by a Fifth Edition title. This will enable users to remove specific Fourth Edition volumes from the shelf and save valuable space pending the replacement of that material in the Fifth Edition. These softbound books are supplied to volumes subscribers free of charge. They continue to form part of the set of Halsbury's Laws Fourth Edition Reissue, and will be updated by the annual Cumulative Supplement and monthly Noter-Up in the usual way.

Updating publications

The text volumes of Halsbury's Laws should be used in conjunction with the annual Cumulative Supplement and the monthly Noter-Up.

The annual Cumulative Supplement

The Supplement gives details of all changes between the operative date of the text volume and the operative date of the Supplement. It is arranged in the same volume, title and paragraph order as the text volumes. Developments affecting particular points of law are noted to the relevant paragraph(s) of the text volumes. As from the commencement of the Fifth Edition, the Supplement will clearly distinguish between Fourth and Fifth Edition titles.

For narrative treatment of material noted in the Cumulative Supplement, go to the Annual Abridgment volume for the relevant year.

Destination Tables

In certain titles in the annual *Cumulative Supplement*, reference is made to Destination Tables showing the destination of consolidated legislation. Those Destination Tables are to be found either at the end of the titles within the annual *Cumulative Supplement*, or in a separate *Destination Tables* booklet provided from time to time with the *Cumulative Supplement*.

The Noter-Up

The Noter-Up is contained in the Current Service Noter-Up booklet, issued monthly and noting changes since the publication of the annual Cumulative Supplement. Also arranged in the same volume, title and paragraph order as the text volumes, the Noter-Up follows the style of the Cumulative Supplement. As from the commencement of the Fifth Edition, the Noter-Up will clearly distinguish between Fourth and Fifth Edition titles.

For narrative treatment of material noted in the Noter-Up, go to the relevant Monthly Review.

REFERENCES AND ABBREVIATIONS

ACT	Australian Capital Territory
A-G	Attorney General
Admin	Administrative Court
Admlty	Admiralty Court
Adv-Gen	Advocate General
affd	affirmed
affg	affirming
Alta	Alberta
App	Appendix
art	article
Aust	Australia
B	Baron
BC	British Columbia
C	Command Paper (of a series published before 1900)
c	chapter number of an Act
CA	Court of Appeal
CAC	Central Arbitration Committee
CA in Ch	Court of Appeal in Chancery
CB	Chief Baron
CCA	Court of Criminal Appeal
CCR	County Court Rules 1981 (SI 1981/1687) as subsequently amended
CCR	Court for Crown Cases Reserved
C-MAC	Courts-Martial Appeal Court
CO	Crown Office
COD	Crown Office Digest
CPR	Civil Procedure Rules 1998 (SI 1998/3132) as subsequently amended (see the Civil Court Practice)
Can	Canada
Cd	Command Paper (of the series published 1900–18)
Cf	compare
Ch	Chancery Division
ch	chapter
cl	clause

Cm	Command Paper (of the series published 1986 to date)
Cmd	Command Paper (of the series published 1919–56)
Cmnd	Command Paper (of the series published 1956–86)
Comm	Commercial Court
Comr	Commissioner
Court Forms (2nd Edn)	Atkin's Encyclopaedia of Court Forms in Civil Proceedings, 2nd Edn. See note 2 post.
Court Funds Rules 1987	Court Funds Rules 1987 (SI 1987/821) as subsequently amended
CrimPR	Criminal Procedure Rules 2010 (SI 2010/60) as subsequently amended
DC	Divisional Court
DPP	Director of Public Prosecutions
EAT	Employment Appeal Tribunal
EC	European Community
ECJ	Court of Justice of the European Community
EComHR	European Commission of Human Rights
ECSC	European Coal and Steel Community
ECtHR Rules of Court	Rules of Court of the European Court of Human Rights
EEC	European Economic Community
EFTA	European Free Trade Association
EWCA Civ	Official neutral citation for judgments of the Court of Appeal (Civil Division)
EWCA Crim	Official neutral citation for judgments of the Court of Appeal (Criminal Division)
EWHC	Official neutral citation for judgments of the High Court
Edn	Edition
Euratom	European Atomic Energy Community
Ex Ch	Court of Exchequer Chamber
ex p	ex parte
Fam	Family Division
Fed	Federal
Forms & Precedents (5th Edn)	Encyclopaedia of Forms and Precedents other than Court Forms, 5th Edn. See note 2 post.
GLC	Greater London Council
HC	High Court
HC	House of Commons
HK	Hong Kong
HL	House of Lords

IAT	Immigration Appeal Tribunal
ILM	International Legal Materials
INLR	Immigration and Nationality Law Reports
IRC	Inland Revenue Commissioners
Ind	India
Int Rels	International Relations
Ir	Ireland
J	Justice
JA	Judge of Appeal
Kan	Kansas
LA	Lord Advocate
LC	Lord Chancellor
LCC	London County Council
LCJ	Lord Chief Justice
LJ	Lord Justice of Appeal
LoN	League of Nations
MR	Master of the Rolls
Man	Manitoba
n	note
NB	New Brunswick
NI	Northern Ireland
NS	Nova Scotia
NSW	New South Wales
NY	New York
NZ	New Zealand
OHIM	Office for Harmonisation in the Internal Market
OJ	The Official Journal of the European Community published by the Office for Official Publications of the European Community
Ont	Ontario
P	President
PC	Judicial Committee of the Privy Council
PEI	Prince Edward Island
Pat	Patents Court
q	question
QB	Queen's Bench Division
QBD	Queen's Bench Division of the High Court
Qld	Queensland
Que	Quebec
r	rule
RDC	Rural District Council
RPC	Restrictive Practices Court

RSC..	Rules of the Supreme Court 1965 (SI 1965/1776) as subsequently amended
reg	regulation
Res	Resolution
revsd......................................	reversed
Rly..	Railway
s..	section
SA...	South Africa
S Aust.....................................	South Australia
SC...	Supreme Court
SI	Statutory Instruments published by authority
SR & O	Statutory Rules and Orders published by authority
SR & O Rev 1904	Revised Edition comprising all Public and General Statutory Rules and Orders in force on 31 December 1903
SR & O Rev 1948	Revised Edition comprising all Public and General Statutory Rules and Orders and Statutory Instruments in force on 31 December 1948
SRNI	Statutory Rules of Northern Ireland
STI..	Simon's Tax Intelligence (1973–1995); Simon's Weekly Tax Intelligence (1996-current)
Sask	Saskatchewan
Sch..	Schedule
Sess...	Session
Sing	Singapore
TCC	Technology and Construction Court
TS...	Treaty Series
Tanz..	Tanzania
Tas..	Tasmania
UDC..	Urban District Council
UKHL......................................	Official neutral citation for judgments of the House of Lords
UKPC	Official neutral citation for judgments of the Privy Council
UN	United Nations
V-C..	Vice-Chancellor
Vict...	Victoria
W Aust....................................	Western Australia
Zimb	Zimbabwe

NOTE 1. A general list of the abbreviations of law reports and other sources used in this work can be found at the beginning of the Consolidated Table of Cases.

NOTE 2. Where references are made to other publications, the volume number precedes and the page number follows the name of the publication; eg the reference '12 Forms & Precedents (5th Edn) 44' refers to volume 12 of the Encyclopaedia of Forms and Precedents, page 44.

NOTE 3. An English statute is cited by short title or, where there is no short title, by regnal year and chapter number together with the name by which it is commonly known or a description of its subject matter and date. In the case of a foreign statute, the mode of citation generally follows the style of citation in use in the country concerned with the addition, where necessary, of the name of the country in parentheses.

NOTE 4. A statutory instrument is cited by short title, if any, followed by the year and number, or, if unnumbered, the date.

TABLE OF STATUTES

TABLE OF STATUTORY INSTRUMENTS

TABLE OF CIVIL PROCEDURE

Civil Procedure Rules 1998, SI 1998/3132 (CPR)

Practice Directions supplementing CPR

TABLE OF EUROPEAN UNION LEGISLATION

TABLE OF
NON-STATUTORY MATERIAL

TABLE OF CASES

PARA

PARA

C

PARA

PARA

PARA

PARA

PARA

Decisions of the European Court of Justice are listed below numerically. These decisions
are also included in the preceding alphabetical list.

BANKRUPTCY AND INDIVIDUAL INSOLVENCY

1. INTRODUCTION

(1) IN GENERAL

1. Insolvency procedures. Insolvency procedures for individuals, companies and partnerships are in the main governed by regimes under the Insolvency Act 1986[1]. Some aspects of the procedures are broadly the same, such as the regulation of official receivers and insolvency practitioners[2], the European Regulation on Insolvency Proceedings[3] and cross-border proceedings[4]. In this title the emphasis is placed on those aspects of insolvency law that relate solely to individuals. Where the law applies also to companies and partnerships, this is set out in detail elsewhere in this work[5].

There are three types of procedure under the Insolvency Act 1986 which govern the administration of the affairs of insolvent individuals:

(1)   debt relief orders under Part 7A of the 1986 Act[6] under which a debtor may be discharged from his debts after one year;

(2)   voluntary arrangements under Part 8 of the 1986 Act[7] which contains provisions which apply when a proposal is made by a debtor for a composition in satisfaction of his debts or for a scheme of arrangement of his affairs; and

(3)   bankruptcy under Part 9 of the 1986 Act[8] which contains provisions relating to the bankruptcy of an individual.

The power to make a criminal bankruptcy order formerly conferred on the Crown Court[9] was abolished in 1989[10]. However, criminal bankruptcy orders made before that date are still governed by provisions contained in the Insolvency Act 1986[11].

As an alternative to the statutory procedures, a debtor may try to reach a compromise with his creditors under an informal arrangement, also known as a family arrangement or a debt management plan[12].

The Money Advice Service (previously known as the consumer financial education body) is specifically charged with assisting members of the public with the management of debt and providing debt advice[13].

1   In relation to individual insolvency see the Insolvency Act 1986 Pts 7A–11 (ss 251A–385) (referred to as 'the Second Group of Parts'). In relation to company insolvency see the Insolvency Act 1986 Pts 1–7 (ss 1–251) (referred to as 'the First Group of Parts'). The Third Group of Parts (ss 386–444) contains miscellaneous matters bearing on both company and individual insolvency.

2   See PARA 35 et seq; and COMPANY AND PARTNERSHIP INSOLVENCY vol 16 (2011) PARAS 9–57, 453–458.

3   See PARAS 41, 42; and COMPANY AND PARTNERSHIP INSOLVENCY vol 16 (2011) PARAS 58–82.

4   See PARAS 826–828; and COMPANY AND PARTNERSHIP INSOLVENCY vol 17 (2011) PARAS 1127–1208.

5   See notes 2–4. Insolvency procedures for insolvent partnerships (see PARA 851) include provisions for insolvency procedures in relation to individual members of the partnership.

6   Ie under the Insolvency Act 1986 Pt 7A (ss 251A–251X): see PARA 101 et seq.

7   Ie under the Insolvency Act 1986 Pt 8 (ss 252–263G): see PARA 43 et seq.

8   Ie the Insolvency Act 1986 Pt 9 (ss 264–371): see PARA 129 et seq.

9   Ie the power conferred by the Powers of Criminal Courts Act 1973 s 39 (repealed).

10 See the Criminal Justice Act 1988 ss 101(1), 171(1) (s 101(1) repealed); Criminal Justice Act 1988 (Commencement No 7) Order 1989, SI 1989/264, art 2, Schedule Pt II. Nothing in the Criminal Justice Act 1988 s 101(1) affects any criminal bankruptcy order made before 3 April 1989 or prevents the taking of any step following such an order: s 101(2) (repealed). 'Criminal bankruptcy order' means an order under the Powers of Criminal Courts Act 1973 s 39(1) (repealed): Insolvency Act 1986 s 385(1).

11	As from such day as the Secretary of State may by order made by statutory instrument appoint, the following provisions of the Insolvency Act 1986 are to be repealed: s 264(1)(d) and the word 'or' immediately preceding it (see PARA 130 head (6)); s 266(4) (see PARA 130 note 14); s 267(3) (see PARA 132 note 6); s 277 (see PARA 130 note 10); s 282(2) (see PARA 620 note 5); in s 293(1) (see PARA 261 note 2) the words 'does not apply where the bankruptcy order was made on a petition under s 264(1)(d) (criminal bankruptcy); and it'; s 297(1) (see PARA 321 note 6); s 327 (see PARA 600 note 1); s 341(4), (5) (see PARA 685 note 3); s 382(1)(c) (see PARA 508 note 7); in s 383(1)(a) (see PARA 574 note 2) the words from 'being' to 'question'; in s 385(1) (see above) the definition of 'criminal bankruptcy order'; and s 402 (official petitioner): Criminal Justice Act 1988 ss 171(1), 170(2), Sch 16. At the date at which this volume states the law no such day had been appointed.

In relation to criminal bankruptcy see also the Insolvency Rules 1986, SI 1986/1925, rr 6.230–6.234 (rr 6.232, 6.234 amended by SI 1987/1919; the Insolvency Rules 1986, SI 1986/1925, r 6.232 further amended by SI 2010/686).

12	Under such an arrangement the debtor requests the creditors to accept a lower payment, perhaps in monthly instalments. However, such arrangements are not legally binding and do not prevent a creditor from subsequently seeking a statutory remedy.

13	See the Financial Services Act 2000 s 3S (added by the Financial Services Act 2012 s 6(1)).

## 2.	Application of the statutory provisions.

The statutory provisions relating to the insolvency proceedings relating to individuals previously mentioned[1] are for the most part contained in the Insolvency Act 1986[2] which came into force on 29 December 1986[3] and in the Insolvency Act 2000[4]. The practice in such insolvency proceedings, so far as not laid down by those Acts, is regulated by rules, regulations and orders made under the Insolvency Act 1986[5] and by Practice Directions[6].

Subject to certain exceptions[7], nothing in the Insolvency Act 1986 relating to individual insolvency extends to Northern Ireland[8].

Her Majesty may, by Order in Council, direct that such of the provisions of the Insolvency Act 1986 as are specified in the Order, being provisions formerly contained in the Insolvency Act 1985, are to extend to any of the Channel Islands or any colony with such modifications as may be so specified[9].

1	See PARA 1.

2	See the Insolvency Act 1986 Pts 7A–11 (ss 251A–385). Parts 1–7 (ss 1–251) contain provisions relating to company insolvency: see COMPANY AND PARTNERSHIP INSOLVENCY vol 16 (2011) PARA 1 et seq. See also Pts 12–18 (ss 386–436B) which contain provisions bearing on both company and individual insolvency; and PARA 3 et seq.

3	Insolvency Act 1986 s 443; Insolvency Act 1985 (Commencement No 5) Order 1986, SI 1986/1924, art 3.

4	The Insolvency Act 2000 ss 3, 4, 12–14, Sch 3 contain provisions relating to personal insolvency; ss 1, 2, 9–11, Schs 1, 2 contain provisions relating to company insolvency; and ss 5–8, Sch 4 contain provisions relating to the disqualification of company directors.

5	See the Insolvency Practitioners Tribunal (Conduct of Investigations) Rules 1986, SI 1986/952; the Insolvency Practitioners (Recognised Professional Bodies) Order 1986, SI 1986/1764; the Insolvency Rules 1986, SI 1986/1925 (amended by SI 1987/1919; SI 1989/397; SI 1991/495; SI 1993/602; SI 1995/586; SI 1998/1129; SI 1999/359; SI 1999/1022; SI 2001/763; SI 2001/1149; SI 2001/3649; SI 2002/1307; SI 2002/2712; SI 2003/1730; SI 2007/1974; SI 2008/737; SI 2009/642; SI 2009/2472; SI 2010/686; SI 2011/785; SI 2012/2404); the Insolvency Proceedings (Monetary Limits) Order 1986, SI 1986/1996 (amended by SI 2004/547; SI 2009/465); the Administration of Insolvent Estates of Deceased Persons Order 1986, SI 1986/1999; the Insolvency (Amendment of Subordinate Legislation) Order 1986, SI 1986/2001 (amended by SI 1986/2245; SI 1987/1398); the Co-operation of Insolvency Courts (Designation of Relevant Countries and Territories) Order 1986, SI 1986/2123; the Insolvency Act (Guernsey) Order 1989, SI 1989/2409; the Insolvent Partnerships Order 1994, SI 1994/2421 (amended by SI 1996/1308; SI 2001/767; SI 2001/3649; SI 2002/1308); the Insolvency Regulations 1994, SI 1994/2507 (amended by SI 2000/485; SI 2001/762; SI 2001/3649; SI 2003/1633; SI 2004/472; SI 2005/512; SI 2007/3224; SI 2008/670; SI 2009/482; SI 2009/2748; SI 2011/2203); the Contracting Out (Functions of the Official Receiver) Order 1995, SI 1995/1386; the Co-operation of Insolvency Courts (Designation of

Relevant Countries) Order 1996, SI 1996/253; the Co-operation of Insolvency Courts (Designation of Relevant Country) Order 1998, SI 1998/2766; the Insolvency Practitioners Regulations 2005, SI 2005/524 (amended by SI 2007/3224; SI 2009/2748; SI 2009/3081); the Debt Relief Orders (Designation of Competent Authorities) Regulations 2009, SI 2009/457 (amended by SI 2009/1553).

As to fees see the Insolvency Proceedings (Fees) Order 2004, SI 2004/593 (amended by SI 2005/544; SI 2006/561; SI 2007/521; SI 2008/714; SI 2009/645; SI 2010/732; SI 2011/1167); the Department of Trade and Industry (Fees) Order 1988, SI 1988/93 (amended by SI 1990/1473; SI 1995/1294; SI 2001/3649); the Civil Proceedings Fees Order 2008, SI 2008/1053 (amended by SI 2008/2853; SI 2009/1498; SI 2011/586); and PARA 816.

6   *Practice Direction—Insolvency Proceedings* came into effect on 23 February 2012 and replaced all previous Practice Directions, Practice Statements and Practice Notes relating to insolvency proceedings (see para 2.1). It applies to practice and procedure in insolvency proceedings both in the High Court and in a county court. As to the status of Practice Directions see CIVIL PROCEDURE vol 11 (2009) PARA 12. In the Insolvency Rules 1986, SI 1986/1925, 'practice direction' means a direction as to the practice and procedure of any court within the scope of the Civil Procedure Rules: Insolvency Rules 1986, SI 1986/1925, rr 13.1, 13.13(6) (substituted by SI 1999/1022).

7   The following provisions of the Insolvency Act 1986 relating to individual insolvency extend to Northern Ireland: s 426 (see PARA 828); ss 426A, 426B, 427 (see PARA 722); s 428(3); s 439 and Sch 14 (in so far as they relate to enactments which extend to Northern Ireland): s 441(1) (amended by SI 2012/1544).

8   Insolvency Act 1986 s 441(2).

9   Insolvency Act 1986 s 442. The Insolvency Act 1986 (Guernsey) Order 1989, SI 1989/2409, has been made under this power.

3.   Crown application. The provisions of the Insolvency Act 1986 relating to individual insolvency[1] which derive from the Insolvency Act 1985[2] bind the Crown so far as affecting or relating to the following matters:

(1)   remedies against, or against the property of, companies or individuals[3];

(2)   priorities of debts[4];

(3)   transactions at an undervalue or preferences[5];

(4)   voluntary arrangements approved under Part 8 of the Insolvency Act 1986[6]; and

(5)   discharge from bankruptcy[7].

1   As to the provisions referred to see PARA 2 note 2.

2   Ie the Insolvency Act 1985 (repealed save for certain amending provisions): see the Insolvency Act 1986 s 438, Sch 12.

3   Orders made under the Insolvency Act 1986 s 236 (inquiry into company's dealings etc: see COMPANY AND PARTNERSHIP INSOLVENCY vol 17 (2011) PARA 637) bind the Crown: *Soden v Burns, R v Secretary of State for Trade and Industry, ex p Soden* [1996] 3 All ER 967, [1996] 1 WLR 1512. It is apprehended that the position is the same in respect of the Insolvency Act 1986 s 366 (inquiry into bankrupt's dealings and property): see PARA 305.

4   See PARA 587 et seq.

5   See PARA 678 et seq.

6   Ie under the Insolvency Act 1986 Pt 8 (ss 252–263G): see PARA 43 et seq.

7   Insolvency Act 1986 s 434. In the case of the administration in bankruptcy of the insolvent estate of a deceased person dying before the presentation of a bankruptcy petition, s 434 applies: Administration of Insolvent Estates of Deceased Persons Order 1986, SI 1986/1999, art 3(1), Sch 1 Pt II para 36. As to the administration in bankruptcy of the insolvent estates of deceased debtors see further PARA 830 et seq.

As to the issue of statutory demands by the Crown see PARA 161 note 2; as to the presentation of petitions by the Crown see PARA 164; as to discharge from bankruptcy see PARA 638 et seq; and as to the application to the Crown of the provisions of the Insolvency Act 1986 relating to company insolvency see COMPANY AND PARTNERSHIP INSOLVENCY vol 16 (2011) PARA 7.

4.   Punishment of offences. In many cases the Insolvency Act 1986 and the Insolvency Rules 1986 impose either imprisonment or a fine, or both, on individuals who fail to comply with the statutory requirements. Schedule 10 to the Insolvency Act 1986 and Schedule 5 to the Insolvency Rules 1986 have effect with respect to the way in which such offences are punishable on conviction[1].

In relation to an offence under a provision of the Insolvency Act 1986 or the Insolvency Rules 1986 specified in the first column of the appropriate Schedule (the general nature of the offence being described in the second column), the third column shows whether the offence is punishable on conviction on indictment, or on summary conviction, or either in the one way or the other[2].

The fourth column of the appropriate Schedule shows, in relation to an offence, the maximum punishment by way of fine or imprisonment under the appropriate statutory provision which may be imposed on a person convicted of the offence in the way specified in relation to it in the third column, that is to say on indictment or summarily, a reference to a period of years or months being to a term of imprisonment of that duration[3].

The fifth column shows, in relation to an offence for which there is an entry in that column, that a person convicted of the offence after continued contravention is liable to a daily default fine, that is to say, he is liable on a second or subsequent summary conviction of the offence to the fine specified in that column for each day on which the contravention is continued, instead of the penalty specified for the offence in the fourth column of the appropriate Schedule[4].

1   Insolvency Act 1986 s 430(1); Insolvency Rules 1986, SI 1986/1925, r 12.21(1).
        In the case of the administration in bankruptcy of the insolvent estate of a deceased person dying before the presentation of a bankruptcy petition, the Insolvency Act 1986 s 430 applies: Administration of Insolvent Estates of Deceased Persons Order 1986, SI 1986/1999, art 3(1), Sch 1 Pt II para 36. As to the administration in bankruptcy of the insolvent estates of deceased debtors see further PARA 830 et seq.
2   Insolvency Act 1986 s 430(2); Insolvency Rules 1986, SI 1986/1925, r 12.21(2).
3   Insolvency Act 1986 s 430(3); Insolvency Rules 1986, SI 1986/1925, r 12.21(3).
4   Insolvency Act 1986 s 430(4); Insolvency Rules 1986, SI 1986/1925, r 12.21(4).

5.   Meaning of 'associate'.   For the purposes of the Insolvency Act 1986, any question whether a person is an associate of another person is to be determined in accordance with the following provisions[1].

A person is an associate of an individual if that person is the individual's husband or wife or civil partner, or is a relative[2], or the husband or wife or civil partner of a relative, of the individual or of the individual's husband or wife or civil partner[3].

A person is an associate of any person with whom he is in partnership, and of the husband or wife or civil partner or a relative of any individual with whom he is in partnership; and a Scottish firm is an associate of any person who is a member of the firm[4].

A person is an associate of any person whom he employs or by whom he is employed[5].

A person in his capacity as trustee of a trust other than a trust arising under the Insolvency Act 1986[6], or a pension scheme or an employees' share scheme[7], is an associate of another person if the beneficiaries of the trust include, or the terms of the trust confer a power that may be exercised for the benefit of, that other person or an associate of that other person[8].

A company[9] is an associate of another company if:

(1)   the same person has control[10] of both, or a person has control of one and persons who are his associates, or he and other persons who are his associates, have control of the other; or

(2)   a group of two or more persons has control of each company, and the groups either consist of the same persons or could be regarded as consisting of the same persons by treating, in one or more cases, a member of either group as replaced by a person of whom he is an associate[11].

A company is an associate of another person if that person has control of it or if that person and persons who are his associates together have control of it[12].

1   Insolvency Act 1986 ss 435(1), 436(1) (numbered as such by SI 2009/1941). Any provision in the Insolvency Act 1986 s 435 that a person is an associate of another person is to be taken to mean that they are associates of each other: s 435(1). In the case of the administration in bankruptcy of the insolvent estate of a deceased person dying before the presentation of a bankruptcy petition, s 435 applies: Administration of Insolvent Estates of Deceased Persons Order 1986, SI 1986/1999, art 3(1), Sch 1 Pt II para 36. As to the administration in bankruptcy of the insolvent estates of deceased debtors see further PARA 830 et seq.

2   For these purposes, a person is a relative of an individual if he is that individual's brother, sister, uncle, aunt, nephew, niece, lineal ancestor or lineal descendant, treating any relationship of the half blood as a relationship of the whole blood and the stepchild or adopted child of any person as his child, and an illegitimate child as the legitimate child of his mother and reputed father; and references in the Insolvency Act 1986 s 435 to a husband or wife include a former husband or wife and a reputed husband or wife and references to a civil partner include a former civil partner and a reputed civil partner: s 435(8) (amended by the Civil Partnership Act 2004 s 261(1), Sch 27 para 122(1), (4); and SI 2005/3129). Stepchildren of civil partners are included: see the Civil Partnership Act 2004 ss 246, 247(1)(a), Sch 21 para 28. As to the meaning of 'reputed wife' see *Smurthwaite v Simpson-Smith* [2006] BPIR 1483, [2005] All ER (D) 275 (Apr).

3   Insolvency Act 1986 s 435(2) (substituted by the Civil Partnership Act 2004 Sch 27 para 122(1), (2)).

4   Insolvency Act 1986 s 435(3) (amended by the Civil Partnership Act 2004 Sch 27 para 122(1), (3)).

5   Insolvency Act 1986 s 435(4). For these purposes, any director or other officer of a company is to be treated as employed by that company: s 435(9).

6   Ie under the Insolvency Act 1986 Pts 7A–11 (ss 251A–385): see PARA 43 et seq.

7   See COMPANIES vol 14 (2009) PARA 169.

8   Insolvency Act 1986 s 435(5) (amended by SI 2009/1941). The exception in favour of trustees of a pension scheme applies even where all the beneficiaries of the scheme constitute a majority of trustees: *Re Thirty-Eight Building Ltd* [1999] 1 BCLC 416, [2000] BCC 260; *Re Thirty-Eight Building Ltd (in liquidation) (No 2), Simms v Saunders* [2000] 1 BCLC 201, sub nom *Re Thirty-Eight Building Ltd* [2000] BCC 422.

9   For these purposes, 'company' includes any body corporate, whether incorporated in Great Britain or elsewhere; and references to directors and other officers of a company and to voting power at any general meeting of a company have effect with any necessary modifications: Insolvency Act 1986 s 435(11). As to the meaning of 'body corporate' see COMPANY AND PARTNERSHIP INSOLVENCY vol 16 (2011) PARA 6. 'Great Britain' means England, Scotland and Wales: Union with Scotland Act 1706, preamble art I; Interpretation Act 1978 s 22(1), Sch 2 para 5(a). See further CONSTITUTIONAL LAW AND HUMAN RIGHTS vol 8(2) (Reissue) PARA 3.

10   For these purposes, a person is to be taken as having control of a company if: (1) the directors of the company or of another company which has control of it, or any of them, are accustomed to act in accordance with his directions or instructions; or (2) he is entitled to exercise, or control the exercise of, one-third or more of the voting power at any general meeting of the company or of another company which has control of it; and, where two or more persons together satisfy either of the above conditions, they are to be taken as having control of the company: Insolvency Act 1986 s 435(10). For these purposes, a beneficial owner of shares is entitled to exercise, or control the exercise of, voting power; cf a bare trustee of the shares who is required to vote in accordance with the direction of the beneficial holder: *Re Kilnoore Ltd (in liquidation)* [2005] EWHC 1410 (Ch), [2006] Ch 489, [2005] 3 All ER 730.

11   Insolvency Act 1986 s 435(6).

12   Insolvency Act 1986 s 435(7).

(2) BANKRUPTCY COURTS

6. Courts having jurisdiction. For the purposes of the provisions of the Insolvency Act 1986 relating to the insolvency or bankruptcy of individuals[1], the High Court and the county courts have jurisdiction throughout England and Wales[2]; and a county court has, in addition to its ordinary jurisdiction, all the powers and jurisdiction of the High Court, and the orders of the court may be enforced accordingly in the prescribed manner[3].

For the purposes of the provisions of the Insolvency Act 1986 relating to the insolvency or bankruptcy of individuals[4], jurisdiction is exercised:

(1)　by the High Court or the Central London County Court in relation to the proceedings which, in accordance with the Insolvency Rules 1986[5], are allocated to the London insolvency district[6]; and

(2)　by each county court[7] in relation to the proceedings which are so allocated to the insolvency district of that court[8].

1　Ie for the purposes of the Insolvency Act 1986 Pts 7A–11 (ss 251A–385).
2　Insolvency Act 1986 s 373(1). As from a day to be appointed, s 373(1) is amended to refer to the county court: see s 373(1) (amended by the Crime and Courts Act 2013 Sch 9 Pt 3 para 93(d)). At the date at which this volume states the law no such day had been appointed.

　　In the case of the administration in bankruptcy of the insolvent estate of a deceased person dying before the presentation of a bankruptcy petition, the Insolvency Act 1986 s 373 applies: Administration of Insolvent Estates of Deceased Persons Order 1986, SI 1986/1999, art 3(1), Sch 1 Pt II para 30. As to the administration in bankruptcy of the insolvent estates of deceased debtors see further PARA 830 et seq.
3　Insolvency Act 1986 s 373(2).
4　See note 1.
5　Ie the Insolvency Rules 1986, SI 1986/1925.
6　As to the allocation of proceedings to the London insolvency district see the Insolvency Rules 1986, SI 1986/1925, r 7.10ZA; and PARA 8. As to the meaning of 'the London insolvency district' see PARA 7 note 2.
7　As to the county courts having jurisdiction see PARA 7.
8　Insolvency Act 1986 s 373(3) (amended by SI 2011/761). As from a day to be appointed, the Insolvency Act 1986 s 373(3) is amended to substitute the reference to the Central London County Court with a reference to the county court; and head (2) in the text is substituted to read 'by the county court in relation to the proceedings which are so allocated to any other insolvency district': see s 373(3) (amended by the Crime and Courts Act 2013 Sch 9 Pt 3 para 93(e), (f)). At the date at which this volume states the law no such day had been appointed.

　　The Insolvency Act 1986 s 373(3) is without prejudice to the transfer of proceedings from one court to another in the manner prescribed by the Insolvency Rules 1986, SI 1986/1925 (see PARA 756); and nothing in the Insolvency Act 1986 s 373(3) invalidates any proceedings on the grounds that they were initiated or continued in the wrong court: s 373(4).

　　As to the appropriate courts in which bankruptcy proceedings are to be commenced see further PARA 164 (creditor's petition) and PARA 191 (debtor's petition).

　　In the Insolvency Act 1986, 'the court', in relation to any matter, means the court to which, in accordance with s 373 and the Insolvency Rules 1986, SI 1986/1925, proceedings with respect to that matter are allocated or transferred: Insolvency Act 1986 s 385(1). In the case of the administration in bankruptcy of the insolvent estate of a deceased person dying before the presentation of a bankruptcy petition, s 385 applies, with the modification that, at the end of the definition of 'the court', there are to be added the words 'and subject thereto 'the court' means the court within the jurisdiction of which the debtor resided or carried on business for the greater part of the six months immediately prior to his death': Administration of Insolvent Estates of Deceased Persons Order 1986, SI 1986/1999, Sch 1 Pt II para 33.

7. Insolvency districts. The Lord Chancellor may, with the concurrence of the Lord Chief Justice[1], by order designate the areas which are for the time being to be comprised in the London insolvency district[2] and the insolvency district of each county court[3]; and such an order may exclude any county court from having jurisdiction or confer jurisdiction on any county court which has not previously had that jurisdiction[4].

1   The Lord Chief Justice may nominate a judicial office holder to exercise his functions under the Insolvency Act 1986 s 374: s 374(5) (added by the Constitutional Reform Act 2005 s 15(1), Sch 4 para 187(1), (4)). As to the meaning of 'judicial office holder' see the Constitutional Reform Act 2005 s 109(4); and COURTS AND TRIBUNALS vol 24 (2010) PARA 961.

2   Subject to any order under the Insolvency Act 1986 s 374, the district which, immediately before 29 December 1986 (see PARA 2), was the London bankruptcy district became, on 29 December 1986, the London insolvency district: s 374(4)(a). The London insolvency district comprises the areas situated within the districts of the following county courts: Barnet; Bow; Brentford; Central London; Clerkenwell and Shoreditch; Edmonton; Lambeth; Mayor's and City of London; Wandsworth; West London; and Willesden: London Insolvency District (Central London County Court) Order 2011, SI 2011/761, art 2. Jurisdiction in relation to proceedings under the Insolvency Act 1986 Pts 7A–11 (ss 251A–385) that are allocated to the London insolvency district in accordance with the Insolvency Rules 1986, SI 1986/1925, are conferred on the Central London County Court: London Insolvency District (Central London County Court) Order 2011, SI 2011/761, art 3. As to the London insolvency district see also LONDON GOVERNMENT vol 71 (2013) PARA 280.
    A British warship, wherever it may be, is deemed part of the parish of Stepney and persons on it are within the London insolvency district: see *Fraser v Akers* (1891) cited in 35 Sol Jo 477; *Seagrave v Parks* [1891] 1 QB 551.

3   Subject to any order under the Insolvency Act 1986 s 374, any district which, immediately before 29 December 1986, was the bankruptcy district of a county court became, on 29 December 1986, the insolvency district of that court; and any county court which immediately before 29 December 1986 was excluded from having jurisdiction in bankruptcy is excluded, on and after 29 December 1986, from having jurisdiction for the purposes of Pts 7A–11: s 374(4)(b), (c). As to such insolvency districts and county courts see the Civil Courts Order 1983, SI 1983/713, art 9, Sch 3; and CIVIL PROCEDURE vol 11 (2009) PARA 58. As to alternative courts for debtors' petitions see PARA 191.

4   Insolvency Act 1986 s 374(1) (amended by the Constitutional Reform Act 2005 Sch 4 para 187(1), (2)). As from a day to be appointed, the Insolvency Act 1986 s 374(1) is amended to provide that the Lord Chancellor may, with the concurrence of the Lord Chief Justice, by order designate the areas which are for the time being to be comprised in the London insolvency district and the insolvency district, or districts, of the county court: see s 374(1) (amended by the Crime and Courts Act 2013 Sch 9 Pt 3 para 93(g)). At the date at which this volume states the law no such day had been appointed.
    An order under the Insolvency Act 1986 s 374 may contain such incidental, supplemental and transitional provisions as may appear to the Lord Chancellor and the Lord Chief Justice necessary or expedient (s 374(2)); and any such order must be made by statutory instrument and, after being made, must be laid before each House of Parliament (s 374(3)). In exercise of this power the London Insolvency District (Central London County Court) Order 2011, SI 2011/761, has been made; and by virtue of the Insolvency Act 1986 s 437, Sch 11 para 23, the Civil Courts Order 1983, SI 1983/713, Sch 3 continues to have effect.
    In the case of the administration in bankruptcy of the insolvent estate of a deceased person dying before the presentation of a bankruptcy petition, the Insolvency Act 1986 s 374 applies: Administration of Insolvent Estates of Deceased Persons Order 1986, SI 1986/1999, art 3(1), Sch 1 Pt II para 30. As to the administration in bankruptcy of the insolvent estates of deceased debtors see further PARA 830 et seq.

8.   **Allocation of proceedings to the London insolvency district.**   Proceedings relating to bankruptcy petitions and applications in relation to a debt relief order[1] are allocated to the London insolvency district[2] where:

(1)   the debtor is resident in England and Wales and within the six months immediately preceding the presentation of the petition or the making of the application the debtor carried on business within the area of the London insolvency district for the greater part of those six months, or for a longer period in those six months than in any other insolvency district;

(2)　　the debtor is resident in England and Wales and within the six months immediately preceding the presentation of the petition or the making of the application the debtor did not carry on business in England and Wales but resided within the area of the London insolvency district for the greater part of those six months, or a longer period in those six months than in any other insolvency district;

(3)　　the debtor is not resident in England and Wales but within the six months immediately preceding the presentation of the petition or the making of the application carried on business within the area of the London insolvency district;

(4)　　the debtor is not resident in England and Wales and within the six months immediately preceding the presentation of the petition or the making of the application did not carry on business in England and Wales but resided within the area of the London insolvency district;

(5)　　the debtor is not resident in England and Wales and within the six months immediately preceding the presentation of the petition or the making of the application the debtor neither carried on business nor resided in England and Wales[3].

Also allocated to the London insolvency district are:

(a)　　creditors' bankruptcy petitions presented by a minister of the Crown or a government department, in relation to which in any statutory demand on which the petition is based the creditor has indicated the intention to present a bankruptcy petition to a court exercising jurisdiction in respect of the London insolvency district, or the petition is presented[4] on the ground[5] that execution or other process issued in respect of the debt has been returned unsatisfied[6];

(b)　　bankruptcy petitions: (i) where the petitioner is unable to ascertain the place where the debtor resides or, if the debtor carries on business in England and Wales, both where the debtor resides and where the debtor carries on business; or (ii) where the debtor is a member of a partnership and either the partnership is being wound up by the High Court sitting in London, or a petition for the winding up of the partnership has been presented to the High Court sitting in London and at the time of the presentation of the bankruptcy petition, the petition for the winding of the partnership has not been finally disposed of[7]; and

(c)　　bankruptcy petitions based on criminal bankruptcy orders[8].

1　　Ie under the Insolvency Act 1986 s 251M (powers of court in relation to debt relief orders: see PARA 116) or s 251N (inquiry into debtor's dealings and property) (see PARA 118).

2　　As to the London insolvency district see also LONDON GOVERNMENT vol 71 (2013) PARA 280.

3　　Insolvency Rules 1986, SI 1986/1925, r 7.10ZA(a) (r 7.10ZA added by SI 2011/785).

4　　Ie under the Insolvency Act 1986 s 267(2)(c) (see PARA 132).

5　　Ie on the grounds specified in the Insolvency Act 1986 s 268(1)(b) (see PARA 133).

6　　Insolvency Rules 1986, SI 1986/1925, r 7.10ZA(b) (as added: see note 3).

7　　Insolvency Rules 1986, SI 1986/1925, r 7.10ZA(c) (as added: see note 3).

8　　Insolvency Rules 1986, SI 1986/1925, r 7.10ZA(d) (as added: see note 3). Bankruptcy petitions based on criminal bankruptcy orders are brought under the Insolvency Act 1986 s 264(1)(d) (see PARA 130 head (6)).

(3)　PERSONS SUBJECT TO BANKRUPTCY LAW

9.　Who may be made bankrupt. Subject to the statutory conditions, any individual within the jurisdiction of a bankruptcy court[1] owing a debt or debts, the amount of which, or the aggregate amount of which, is equal to or exceeds the bankruptcy level, the payment of which may be enforced against him personally, may be made bankrupt[2]. There is no distinction in English law between traders and non-traders as there is in some foreign jurisdictions[3].

1   As to bankruptcy courts see PARAS 6, 7.
2   See PARA 129 et seq.
3   Certain offences apply, however, only to persons carrying on a trade or business: see PARA 733 et seq.

10.   Married women.   Subject to the statutory conditions, a married woman is subject to bankruptcy law and to the enforcement of judgment debts and orders in the same way as if she were a single woman ('feme sole')[1].

1   See the Law Reform (Married Women and Tortfeasors) Act 1935 s 1(d); PARA 130 et seq; and MATRIMONIAL AND CIVIL PARTNERSHIP LAW vol 72 (2009) PARAS 204, 210.

11.   Persons who lack capacity to manage their affairs.   Incapacity is no bar to being made bankrupt; and the Insolvency Rules 1986 make specific provision with respect to persons who lack capacity to manage their affairs[1].

1   See the Insolvency Rules 1986, SI 1986/1925, Pt 7 Ch 7 (rr 7.43–7.46); and PARA 824.

12.   Foreigners and debtors residing abroad.   Subject to the statutory conditions[1], a foreign national or a British subject residing abroad may be made the subject of bankruptcy proceedings. The debt need not necessarily have been incurred within the jurisdiction, nor need the petitioning creditor have any territorial connection with England and Wales[2]. A bankruptcy petition may, with the permission of the court, be served outside England and Wales in such manner as the court may direct[3].

1   A bankruptcy petition may not be presented to the court in respect of a debtor who is not domiciled in England and Wales unless the debtor is personally present in England and Wales on the day on which the petition is presented, or at any time in the period of three years ending with that day the debtor: (1) has been ordinarily resident, or has had a place of residence, in England and Wales; or (2) has carried on business in England and Wales: see the Insolvency Act 1986 s 265(1)(b), (c); and PARA 131 heads (2), (3). See also Council Regulation (EC) 1346/2000 (OJ L160, 30.6.2000, p 1) on insolvency proceedings (see PARAS 41, 42 et seq). As to cross-border insolvency see PARAS 826–828.
2   As to creditors who may present a bankruptcy petition see PARA 141 et seq.
3   See the Insolvency Rules 1986, SI 1986/1925, r 6.14(6); and PARA 175. A statutory demand is not a document issued by the court and, therefore, permission to serve out of the jurisdiction is not required: *Practice Direction—Insolvency Proceedings* para 13.2.1. As to statutory demands generally see PARA 158 et seq.

13.   Minors.   The status of minority[1] as such is irrelevant to the exercise of bankruptcy jurisdiction. A minor may be adjudged bankrupt, or may present a petition against himself in respect of any debt or debts which are legally enforceable against him[2]. At common law[3] the general rule is that a minor's contracts are voidable at the instance of the minor[4], but contracts for necessaries[5] and contracts for education, apprenticeship and service[6] are enforceable, provided that they are beneficial to the minor[7].

Where a person ('the claimant') has entered into a contract with another ('the defendant'), and the contract is unenforceable against the defendant, or he repudiates it, because he was a minor when the contract was made, the court may, if it is just and equitable to do so, require the defendant to transfer to the claimant any property acquired by the defendant under the contract, or any property representing it[8]. Where a guarantee is given in respect of an obligation

of a party to a contract, and the obligation is unenforceable against him, or he
repudiates the contract, because he was a minor when the contract was made,
the guarantee is not for that reason alone unenforceable against the guarantor[9].

A minor may be made bankrupt on a debt due to the Crown in respect of tax
or excise duty[10].

1   The age of majority is 18 years: see the Family Law Reform Act 1969 s 1; and CHILDREN AND
    YOUNG PERSONS vol 9 (2012) PARA 1.
2   *Re Smedley* (1864) 10 LT 432; *Re Purser, ex p Stevenson* (1868) 19 LT 23; *Re Jones, ex p Jones*
    (1881) 18 ChD 109, CA (in all of which a bankruptcy order was refused as there was no legally
    enforceable debt against the minor); *R v Newmarket Income Tax Comrs, ex p Huxley* [1916]
    1 KB 788, CA; *Re A Debtor (No 564 of 1949), ex p Customs and Excise Comrs v Debtor*
    [1950] Ch 282, [1950] 1 All ER 308, CA (where the earlier decisions relating to bankruptcy
    jurisdiction over minors were reviewed); *Re Davenport, ex p Bankrupt v Eric Street
    Properties Ltd* [1963] 2 All ER 850, [1963] 1 WLR 817, CA (where the petitioning creditor's
    debt was not for necessaries and the bankruptcy order was annulled by the court in its discretion
    under the Bankruptcy Act 1914 s 29(1) (repealed and replaced by the Insolvency Act 1986
    s 282(1): see PARA 620)). A respondent who is a minor must have a litigation friend to conduct
    proceedings on his behalf unless the court orders otherwise: see CPR 21.2(2); CHILDREN AND
    YOUNG PERSONS vol 9 (2012) PARA 10; CIVIL PROCEDURE vol 11 (2009) PARA 222.
3   The Infants Relief Act 1874 was repealed by the Minors' Contracts Act 1987 ss 1(a), 4(2),
    which came into force on 9 June 1987: see s 5(2). Minors' contracts are now governed entirely
    by common law principles.
4   Such contracts remain binding on the other party, and will be valid against the minor unless he
    avoided the contracts during his minority or within a reasonable time after attaining his
    majority: *North Western Rly Co v M'Michael* (1850) 5 Exch 114.
5   'Necessaries' means goods suitable to the condition in life of the minor concerned and to his
    actual requirements at the time of the sale and delivery: see the Sale of Goods Act 1979 s 3(3);
    and SALE OF GOODS AND SUPPLY OF SERVICES vol 91 (2012) PARA 38. Where necessaries are sold
    and delivered to a minor, he must pay a reasonable price for them: see s 3(2); and SALE OF
    GOODS AND SUPPLY OF SERVICES vol 91 (2012) PARA 38. What is a reasonable price is a question
    of fact dependent on the circumstances of each particular case: see s 8(3); and SALE OF GOODS
    AND SUPPLY OF SERVICES vol 91 (2012) PARA 57.
        'Necessaries' also includes services: see *Huggins v Wiseman* (1690) Carth 110 (medical
    services); *Chapple v Cooper* (1844) 13 M & W 252 (funeral services); *Helps v Clayton* (1864)
    17 CBNS 553; *Re Jones (an infant)* (1883) 48 LT 188 (legal services).
        A minor's trading contracts are not contracts for necessaries: *Lowe v Griffith* (1835) 1 Hodg
    30; *Lovell and Christmas v Beauchamp* [1894] AC 607, HL; explained in *Re A Debtor (No 564
    of 1949), ex p Customs and Excise Comrs v Debtor* [1950] Ch 282, [1950] 1 All ER 308, CA.
6   As to contracts of apprenticeship and service see *Clements v London and North Western Rly Co*
    [1894] 2 QB 482 at 491, CA; and as to education see *Roberts v Gray* [1913] 1 KB 520
    (professional billiards playing).
7   The contract, even for necessaries, must be beneficial to the minor and will be unenforceable if
    it contains harsh and oppressive terms: *Flower v London and North Western Rly Co* [1894]
    2 QB 65, CA (contract for necessary carriage nevertheless voidable because of exemption
    clause in respect of liability for injury even if caused by negligence; but see now the Unfair
    Contract Terms Act 1977; and CONTRACT vol 22 (2012) PARA 408 et seq); *Buckpitt v Oates*
    [1968] 1 All ER 1145.
8   See the Minors' Contracts Act 1987 s 3(1); and CHILDREN AND YOUNG PERSONS vol 9 (2012)
    PARA 24. Nothing in s 3 is to be taken to prejudice any other remedy available to the claimant:
    s 3(2). It is apprehended that an order under s 3 would constitute a bankruptcy debt: see PARA
    508.
9   See the Minors' Contracts Act 1987 s 2; and CHILDREN AND YOUNG PERSONS vol 9 (2012) PARA
    14.
10 *R v Newmarket Income Tax Comrs, ex p Huxley* [1916] 1 KB 788, CA; *Re A Debtor (No 564
    of 1949), ex p Customs and Excise Comrs v Debtor* [1950] Ch 282, [1950] 1 All ER 308, CA.

14.   Diplomats.   An ambassador, a minister or a consul accredited by a foreign
government is exempt from local jurisdiction, and, even though a British subject,
may claim privilege from bankruptcy law[1]. This privilege attaches to a bona fide
member of the embassy even if he is a British subject, but not when his

appointment has been obtained for the purpose of using the privilege to defeat creditors[2]. The Attorney General's statement on the instructions of the Foreign and Commonwealth Office as to the status of a person claiming immunity from judicial process on the ground of diplomatic privilege is conclusive[3]. However, diplomatic privileges and immunities are now generally regulated by statute[4].

1   See *Macartney v Garbutt* (1890) 24 QBD 368; the Diplomatic Privileges Act 1964; and INTERNATIONAL RELATIONS LAW vol 61 (2010) PARA 265 et seq. Such immunity may be waived by the foreign state or by its head of mission: see *R v Madan* [1961] 2 QB 1, [1961] 1 All ER 588, CCA; and INTERNATIONAL RELATIONS LAW vol 61 (2010) PARA 283.
2   *Re Cloete, ex p Cloete* (1891) 8 Morr 195, CA.
3   *Engelke v Musmann* [1928] AC 433, HL.
4   See generally INTERNATIONAL RELATIONS LAW vol 61 (2010) PARA 265 et seq. They now extend to senior representatives of many international organisations.

15.   Corporations and companies.   No corporation, nor any association or company registered under the Companies Acts, is liable to bankruptcy proceedings[1].

1   A petition for a bankruptcy order may be presented against an individual only: see the Insolvency Act 1986 s 264; and PARA 130. As to the winding up of companies see COMPANY AND PARTNERSHIP INSOLVENCY vol 16 (2011) PARA 380 et seq.

16.   Members of Parliament.   Bankruptcy proceedings may be commenced against members of either House of Parliament, privilege of Parliament being no defence to a petition in bankruptcy[1].

1   See the Insolvency Act 1986 s 426A; and PARA 722. As to the disqualification of an individual from being a member of either House of Parliament see also PARLIAMENT vol 78 (2010) PARA 903.

17.   Partners.   Bankruptcy proceedings may be commenced against an individual who is a partner[1].

1   As to bankruptcy proceedings against partners and partnerships see COMPANY AND PARTNERSHIP INSOLVENCY vol 17 (2011) PARA 1209 et seq.

18.   Undischarged bankrupts.   Being adjudged bankrupt is no bar to further bankruptcy proceedings; and a second or subsequent bankruptcy order may be made in respect of liabilities incurred after the commencement[1] of the earlier bankruptcy[2].

1   As to the commencement of bankruptcy see PARA 209.
2   Under the Bankruptcy Act 1914 (repealed) the court had a discretion in such a case whether to make a receiving order which would lead to a further adjudication and might refuse to make such an order if it was satisfied that there would be no assets for administration under the subsequent bankruptcy: *Re Betts, ex p Betts* [1897] 1 QB 50, CA. However, the debtor's own affidavit that there was no prospect of assets was not enough: *Re Betts, ex p Betts*. The court has a similar discretion under the Insolvency Act 1986: see s 266(3); *Re Thulin* [1995] 1 WLR 165; and PARA 130. As to later bankruptcies see PARAS 489, 617–619.

2. INSTITUTIONS

(1) SECRETARY OF STATE

(i) Functions of the Secretary of State

19. Powers and duties of the Secretary of State. The Secretary of State[1] has various powers and duties in connection with individual insolvency. Such powers and duties concern primarily the administration and financial control of bankruptcy. The Secretary of State has wide powers to make rules and regulations[2]. He has power to inspect the records to be maintained by all insolvency practioners[3]; and he exercises a general surveillance over the records and accounts required to be maintained by trustees in bankruptcy, with power to carry out an audit of the accounts which must be submitted to him by trustees[4]. The Secretary of State is responsible for official receivers[5] and for the qualification of insolvency practitioners[6].

The Secretary of State must keep an account with the Bank of England, called the Insolvency Services Account, into which all moneys received by him in respect of insolvency proceedings must be paid[7]. He may, however, allow trustees to operate a local bank account instead of their paying moneys into the Insolvency Services Account[8].

The Secretary of State may by order prescribe amounts for the purposes of certain provisions of the Insolvency Act 1986[9]; and any such order may contain such transitional provisions as may appear to the Secretary of State necessary or expedient[10].

As soon as practicable after the end of each calendar year, the Secretary of State must prepare and lay before each House of Parliament a report about the operation during that year of the statutory provisions relating to the insolvency or bankruptcy of individuals[11] and about proceedings in the course of that year under the Deeds of Arrangement Act 1914[12].

1 In any enactment, 'Secretary of State' means one of Her Majesty's principal Secretaries of State: see the Interpretation Act 1978 s 5, Sch 1. The office of Secretary of State is a unified office, and in law each Secretary of State is capable of performing the functions of all or any of them: see CONSTITUTIONAL LAW AND HUMAN RIGHTS vol 8(2) (Reissue) PARA 355. For the purposes of the legislation relating to insolvency, the powers of the Secretary of State are exercised in practice by the Secretary of State for Business, Innovation and Skills: see the Secretary of State for Trade and Industry (New Departments) Order 1974, SI 1974/692 (lapsed); the Transfer of Functions (Trade and Industry) Order 1983, SI 1983/1127; the Secretaries of State for Children, Schools and Families, for Innovation, Universities and Skills and for Business, Enterprise and Regulatory Reform Order, SI 2007/3224; the Secretary of State for Business, Innovation and Skills Order 2009, SI 2009/2748; and TRADE AND INDUSTRY vol 97 (2010) PARA 802. Matters relating to trade were originally within the general jurisdiction of the Board of Trade which no longer meets (see CONSTITUTIONAL LAW AND HUMAN RIGHTS vol 8(2) (Reissue) PARA 505; TRADE AND INDUSTRY vol 97 (2010) PARA 802). Its effective head, the President of the Board of Trade, now exercises functions concurrently with the Secretary of State for Business, Innovation and Skills who uses both titles so that any reference to the Board of Trade now has effect as if it were, or included, a reference to the Secretary of State: see the Secretary of State for Trade and Industry Order 1970, SI 1970/1537, arts 2(1), 7(4); and TRADE AND INDUSTRY vol 97 (2010) PARA 802 et seq.

2 See the Insolvency Act 1986 s 412; and PARA 773.

3 See the Insolvency Practitioners Regulations 2005, SI 2005/524, reg 17; PARA 40; and COMPANY AND PARTNERSHIP INSOLVENCY vol 16 (2011) PARA 57.

4 See the Insolvency Regulations 1994, SI 1994/2507, reg 24; and PARA 387 et seq.

5 See PARA 35 et seq.

6 See PARA 40; and COMPANY AND PARTNERSHIP INSOLVENCY vol 16 (2011) PARAS 9–57.

7   See PARAS 22, 393 et seq.

8   See PARA 395.

9   Ie for the purposes of the Insolvency Act 1986 s 251S(4) (maximum amount of credit which a person in respect of whom a debt relief order is made may obtain without disclosure of his status: see PARA 123), s 273 (minimum value of debtor's estate determining whether immediate bankruptcy order should be made; small bankruptcies level: see PARA 203 note 4), s 313A (value of property below which application for sale, possession or charge to be dismissed: see PARA 414), s 346(3) (minimum amount of judgment, determining whether amount recovered on sale of debtor's goods is to be treated as part of his estate in bankruptcy: see PARA 703), s 354(1), (2) (minimum amount of concealed debt, or value of property concealed or removed, determining criminal liability under s 354: see PARAS 735, 736), s 358 (minimum value of property taken by a bankrupt out of England and Wales, determining his criminal liability: see PARA 744), s 360(1) (maximum amount of credit which bankrupt may obtain without disclosure of his status: see PARA 747), s 364(2)(d) (minimum value of goods removed by the bankrupt, determining his liability to arrest: see PARA 217 head (d)), Sch 4ZA paras 6–8 (maximum amount of a person's debts, monthly surplus income and property for purposes of obtaining a debt relief order: see PARA 106). References in Pts 7A–11 (ss 251A–385) to the amount prescribed for the purposes of any of those provisions, and references in those provisions to the prescribed amount, are to be construed accordingly: s 418(1).

10 Insolvency Act 1986 s 418(1), (2) (s 418(1) amended by the Enterprise Act 2002 s 261(6); and the Tribunal, Courts and Enforcement Act 2007 s 108(3), Sch 20 paras 1, 11). An order under the Insolvency Act 1986 s 418 must be made by statutory instrument subject to annulment in pursuance of a resolution of either House of Parliament: s 418(3). In exercise of the powers conferred by s 418, and by s 386(1), Sch 6 paras 9, 12 (see PARA 593), the Secretary of State has made the Insolvency Proceedings (Monetary Limits) Order 1986, SI 1986/1996 (amended by SI 2004/547; and SI 2009/465). In the case of the administration in bankruptcy of the insolvent estate of a deceased person dying before the presentation of a bankruptcy petition, the Insolvency Act 1986 s 418 applies: Administration of Insolvent Estates of Deceased Persons Order 1986, SI 1986/1999, art 3(1), Sch 1 Pt II para 36. As to the administration in bankruptcy of the insolvent estates of deceased debtors see further PARA 830 et seq.

11 Ie the provisions contained in the Insolvency Act 1986 Pts 7A–11 (ss 251A–385).

12 Insolvency Act 1986 s 379. In the case of the administration in bankruptcy of the insolvent estate of a deceased person dying before the presentation of a bankruptcy petition, s 379 applies: Administration of Insolvent Estates of Deceased Persons Order 1986, SI 1986/1999, art 3(1), Sch 1 Pt II para 30. As to proceedings under the Deeds of Arrangement Act 1914 see PARA 852 et seq.

20. Rules and regulations. With the concurrence of the Secretary of State and, in the case of rules that affect court procedure, with the concurrence of the Lord Chief Justice, the Lord Chancellor may make rules for the purpose of giving effect to the provisions of the Insolvency Act 1986 relating to the insolvency or bankruptcy of individuals[1].

The Secretary of State may[2], subject to the Insolvency Act 1986 and the Insolvency Rules 1986[3], from time to time make regulations with respect to so much of any matter that may be provided for in the rules as relates to the carrying out of the functions of the interim receiver[4], of the official receiver while acting as receiver and manager[5] or of a trustee of a bankrupt's estate including, without prejudice to the generality of the above, provision with respect to the following matters arising in individual insolvency:

(1)   the preparation and keeping by trustees, interim receivers and the official receiver, of books, accounts and other records[6], and their production to such persons as may be authorised or required to inspect them;

(2)   the auditing of trustees' accounts;

(3)   the manner in which trustees are to act in relation to the bankrupt's books, papers and other records, and the manner of their disposal by the responsible office-holder[7] or others;

(4)   the supply by the trustee to creditors and the creditors' committee[8] of

copies of documents relating to the insolvency and the affairs of the insolvent individual, on payment, in such cases as may be specified by the regulations, of the specified fee;

(5)   the manner in which insolvent estates[9] are to be distributed by trustees, including provision with respect to unclaimed funds and dividends;

(6)   the manner in which moneys coming into the hands of a trustee in the course of his administration are to be handled and invested, and the payment of interest on sums which, in pursuance of statutory regulations[10], have been paid into the Insolvency Services Account[11];

(7)   the amount, or the manner of determining the amount, to be paid to the official receiver by way of remuneration when acting as interim receiver or trustee[12].

Such regulations may confer a discretion on the court, make non-compliance with any of the regulations a criminal offence, and make different provision for different cases, including different provision for different areas, and may contain such incidental, supplemental and transitional provisions as may appear to the Secretary of State necessary or expedient[13].

1   See the Insolvency Act 1986 s 412(1); and PARA 773. Rules can also be made for the purpose of giving effect to Council Regulation (EC) 1346/2000 (OJ L160, 30.6.2000, p 1) on insolvency proceedings ('European Regulation on Insolvency Proceedings') (see PARAS 41, 42): see the Insolvency Act 1986 s 412(1); and PARA 773.
2   Ie pursuant to the Insolvency Act 1986 s 412(2), Sch 9 para 30: see PARA 773 note 2 head (38).
3   Ie the Insolvency Rules 1986, SI 1986/1925.
4   Ie under the Insolvency Act 1986 s 286: see PARA 219 et seq.
5   Ie under the Insolvency Act 1986 s 287: see PARA 229 et seq.
6   In the Insolvency Act 1986, except in so far as the context otherwise requires, 'records' includes computer records and other non-documentary records: s 436(1). In the case of the administration in bankruptcy of the insolvent estate of a deceased person dying before the presentation of a bankruptcy petition, s 436 applies: Administration of Insolvent Estates of Deceased Persons Order 1986, SI 1986/1999, art 3(1), Sch 1 Pt II para 36. As to the administration in bankruptcy of the insolvent estates of deceased debtors see further PARA 830 et seq.
7   'Office-holder' means in relation to insolvency proceedings any person who by virtue of any provision of the Insolvency Act 1986 or the Insolvency Rules 1986, SI 1986/1925, holds an office in relation to those proceedings: Insolvency Rules 1986, SI 1986/1925, r 13.9A (added by SI 2010/686).
8   As to the creditors' committee see PARA 326 et seq.
9   See PARA 830 et seq.
10   Ie made under the Insolvency Rules 1986, SI 1986/1925, r 12.1(1).
11   As to the Insolvency Services Account see PARAS 22, 393 et seq.
12   Insolvency Act 1986 Sch 9 para 30; Insolvency Rules 1986, SI 1986/1925, r 12.1(1) (amended by SI 1987/1919; SI 2001/763; SI 2009/642; and SI 2010/686). In the Insolvency Act 1986 'the trustee', in relation to a bankruptcy and the bankrupt, means the trustee of the bankrupt's estate: s 385(1). Any reference in the Insolvency Rules 1986, SI 1986/1925, r 12.1(1) to a trustee includes a reference to the official receiver when acting as a receiver and manager under the Insolvency Act 1986 s 287: Insolvency Rules 1986, SI 1986/1925, r 12.1(2).
13   Insolvency Rules 1986, SI 1986/1925, r 12.1(3) (amended by SI 1987/1919).

21.   Secretary of State's role in bankruptcies. If a meeting summoned to appoint a first trustee is held but no appointment of a person as trustee is made, it is the duty of the official receiver to decide whether to refer the need for an appointment to the Secretary of State; and, on such a reference, the Secretary of State must either make an appointment or decline to make one[1]. Where the appointment of any person as trustee fails to take effect or, such an appointment having taken effect, there is otherwise a vacancy in the office of trustee, the Secretary of State must either make an appointment or decline to make one, on a reference to him by the official receiver[2]. If a trustee is appointed by the Secretary of State, he may be removed by a direction of the Secretary of State[3].

If the official receiver, while he is the trustee, gives notice to the Secretary of State that the administration of the bankrupt's estate is for practical purposes complete, he has his release with effect from such time as the Secretary of State may determine[4]. A person other than the official receiver who has ceased to be the trustee has his release, in the case of a person who has been removed from office by a general meeting of the bankrupt's creditors that has resolved against his release, or by the court, or by the Secretary of State, or who has vacated office on ceasing to be qualified as an insolvency practitioner, from such time as the Secretary of State may, on application by that person, determine[5].

At any time when the official receiver is the trustee, the functions of the creditors' committee are vested in the Secretary of State. Where there is for the time being no creditors' committee and the trustee is a person other than the official receiver, the functions of the creditors' committee are similarly vested in the Secretary of State[6].

Where there is comprised in the bankrupt's estate property consisting of an interest in a dwelling house which is occupied by the bankrupt or by his spouse or former spouse and the trustee has been unable for any reason to realise that property, the trustee may not summon a final meeting unless (inter alia) the Secretary of State has issued a certificate to the trustee stating that it would be inappropriate or inexpedient for an application for an order charging such property for the benefit of the bankrupt's estate to be made in the case in question[7].

An appeal lies at the instance of the Secretary of State from any order of the court made on an application for the rescission or annulment of a bankruptcy order, or for a bankrupt's discharge[8].

An appeal[9] against a decision of the Secretary of State must be brought within 28 days of the notification of the decision[10].

1   See PARA 319.
2   See PARA 370.
3   See PARA 369.
4   See PARA 380.
5   See PARA 379.
6   See PARA 341.
7   See PARA 616.
8   See PARA 762.
9   Ie under the Insolvency Act 1986 or the Insolvency Rules 1986, SI 1986/1925.
10   See the Insolvency Rules 1986, SI 1986/1925, r 7.50; and PARA 769.

(ii) Insolvency Service Finance, Accounting and Investment

22. Insolvency Services Account. All money received by the Secretary of State[1] in respect of proceedings under the Insolvency Act 1986 as it applies to England and Wales must be paid into the Insolvency Services Account kept by the Secretary of State with the Bank of England; and all payments out of money standing to the credit of the Secretary of State in that account must be made by the Bank of England in such manner as he may direct[2].

Whenever the cash balance standing to the credit of the Insolvency Services Account is in excess of the amount which, in the opinion of the Secretary of State, is required for the time being to answer demands in respect of bankrupts' estates, he must notify the excess to the National Debt Commissioners[3], and must pay into the Insolvency Services Investment Account[4] the whole or any part of the excess as the Commissioners may require[5] in accordance with certain statutory provisions[6].

Whenever, in the Secretary of State's opinion, any part of the money so invested is required to answer demands in respect of bankrupts' estates, he must notify to the National Debt Commissioners the amount so required, and the Commissioners must thereupon repay to the Secretary of State such sum as may be required to the credit of the Insolvency Services Account; and, for that purpose, they may direct the sale of any such part of the securities in which the money has been invested as may be necessary[7].

1   As to the Secretary of State see PARA 19.
2   Insolvency Act 1986 s 403(1). As to the Bank of England see FINANCIAL SERVICES AND INSTITUTIONS vol 49 (2008) PARA 793. As to payment into and out of the account see PARAS 393, 394 respectively. In the case of the administration in bankruptcy of the insolvent estate of a deceased person dying before the presentation of a bankruptcy petition, s 403 applies: Administration of Insolvent Estates of Deceased Persons Order 1986, SI 1986/1999, art 3(1), Sch 1 Pt II para 36. As to the administration in bankruptcy of the insolvent estates of deceased debtors see further PARA 830 et seq.
3   As to the National Debt Commissioners see FINANCIAL SERVICES AND INSTITUTIONS vol 49 (2008) PARA 1332.
4   The Insolvency Services Investment Account is an account kept by the National Debt Commissioners with the Bank of England (see PARA 23): Insolvency Act 1986 s 403(2)(b).
5   Ie in accordance with the Insolvency Act 1986 ss 403(3)–410: see PARA 23 et seq.
6   Insolvency Act 1986 s 403(2).
7   Insolvency Act 1986 s 403(3).

23.   Insolvency Services Investment Account.   Any money standing to the credit of the Insolvency Services Investment Account[1], including any money received by the National Debt Commissioners[2] by way of interest on or proceeds of any investment, may be invested by the Commissioners in accordance with such directions as may be given by the Treasury, in any manner for the time being specified[3] in the Trustee Investments Act 1961[4].

1   As to the Insolvency Services Account see PARA 22.
2   As to the National Debt Commissioners see FINANCIAL SERVICES AND INSTITUTIONS vol 49 (2008) PARA 1332.
3   Ie specified in the Trustee Investments Act 1961 s 1, Sch 1 Pt II: see TRUSTS vol 48 (2007 Reissue) PARA 1017 et seq. Schedule 1 Pt II is repealed by the Trustee Act 2000 s 40(1), (3), Sch 2 Pt I para 1(1), Sch 4 Pt I as from 1 February 2001 (see s 42(2), (3)), except in so far as it is applied by or under any other enactment.
4   Insolvency Act 1986 s 404. In the case of the administration in bankruptcy of the insolvent estate of a deceased person dying before the presentation of a bankruptcy petition, the Insolvency Act 1986 s 404 applies: Administration of Insolvent Estates of Deceased Persons Order 1986, SI 1986/1999, art 3(1), Sch 1 Pt II para 36. As to the administration in bankruptcy of the insolvent estates of deceased debtors see further PARA 830 et seq.

24.   Investment or otherwise handling of funds; payment of interest.   The Lord Chancellor may, with the concurrence of the Secretary of State, make rules providing for the manner in which moneys received by the trustee of a bankrupt's estate in the course of carrying out his functions are to be invested or otherwise handled and providing for the payment of interest on sums which have been paid into the Insolvency Services Account[1].

Accordingly, where the cash balance standing to the credit of the bankrupt in the account in respect of that bankrupt kept by the Secretary of State is in excess of the amount which, in the opinion of the trustee[2], is required for the immediate purposes of the bankruptcy and should be invested, he may request the Secretary of State to invest the amount not so required in government securities, to be placed to the credit of that account for the benefit of the bankrupt[3]. When any of the money so invested is, in the opinion of the trustee, required for the immediate purposes of the bankruptcy, he may request the Secretary of State to raise such sum as may be required by the sale of such of those securities as may be necessary[4]. Where at any time after 1 April 2004 there are any monies standing to the credit of the estate of the bankrupt in the Insolvency Services Account, the estate is entitled to interest on those monies at the rate of 4.25% per annum[5].

All money received in respect of investments and interest earned under the above provisions must be paid into the Insolvency Services Account to the credit of the bankrupt[6]. Where a bankrupt's estate has become entitled to any sum by way of interest, the Secretary of State must certify that sum and the amount of tax payable on it to the National Debt Commissioners[7] who must pay, out of the Insolvency Services Investment Account[8], into the Insolvency Services Account the sum certified less the amount of tax certified and to the Commissioners for Her Majesty's Revenue and Customs[9] the amount of tax certified[10].

1   Insolvency Act 1986 s 412(1), Sch 9 para 21 (amended by the Insolvency Act 2000 s 13(1)). As to the Insolvency Services Account see PARA 22.

2   For these purposes, except where the context otherwise requires, 'trustee' means trustee of a bankrupt's estate including the official receiver when so acting: Insolvency Regulations 1994, SI 1994/2507, reg 3(1). However, in addition to the application of the provisions of Pt 3 (regs 19–31; see PARAS 387 et seq, 600) to the official receiver when acting as trustee, the provisions of Pt 3, other than reg 30 (see PARA 392) and reg 31 (see PARA 601) also apply to him when he is acting as receiver or manager under the Insolvency Act 1986 s 287 (see PARA 229 et seq); and the term 'trustee' is to be construed accordingly: Insolvency Regulations 1994, SI 1994/2507, reg 19(2).

3   Insolvency Regulations 1994, SI 1994/2507, reg 23A(1) (added by SI 2001/762). In cases where investments have been made at the request of the trustee in pursuance of the Insolvency Regulations 1994, SI 1994/2507, reg 23A(1) and additional sums to the amounts so invested, including money received under reg 23A(7), are paid into the Insolvency Services Account to the credit of the bankrupt, a request must be made to the Secretary of State by the trustee if it is desired that these additional funds should be invested: reg 23A(3) (added by SI 2001/762).

     Any request relating to the investment in, or sale of, as the case may be, Treasury Bills under the Insolvency Regulations 1994, SI 1994/2507, reg 23A(1), (2) or (3) must be made on a form obtainable from the Department for Business, Innovation and Skills or on one that is substantially similar; and any request relating to the purchase or sale, as the case may be, of any other type of government security made thereunder must be made in writing: regs 3(3), 23A(4) (reg 3(3) amended by SI 2009/2748; the Insolvency Regulations 1994, SI 1994/2507, reg 23A added by SI 2001/762). Any request made under the Insolvency Regulations 1994, SI 1994/2507, reg 23A(1), (2) or (3) is sufficient authority to the Secretary of State for the investment or sale, as the case may be: reg 23A(5) (added by SI 2001/762). As to the fee payable in relation to a request made by a trustee in bankruptcy for the purchase of government securities see the Insolvency Proceedings (Fees) Order 2004, SI 2004/593, Sch 2 para 2 Fee INV1 (amended by SI 2009/645).

4   Insolvency Regulations 1994, SI 1994/2507, reg 23A(2) (added by SI 2001/762). See also note 3.

5   Insolvency Regulations 1994, SI 1994/2507, reg 23A(6) (added by SI 2001/762; and substituted by SI 2004/472). Interest ceases to accrue from the date of receipt by the Secretary of State of a notice in writing from the trustee that in the opinion of the trustee it is necessary or expedient in order to facilitate the conclusion of the bankruptcy that interest should cease to accrue but interest starts to accrue again where the trustee gives a further notice in writing to the Secretary of State requesting that interest should start to accrue again: Insolvency Regulations 1994, SI 1994/2507, reg 23A(6A) (added by SI 2004/472). The Secretary of State may by notice published in the London Gazette vary the rate of interest and such variation has effect from the day after the date of publication of the notice in the London Gazette or such later date as may be specified in the notice: Insolvency Regulations 1994, SI 1994/2507, reg 23A(6B) (added by SI 2004/472).

6   Insolvency Regulations 1994, SI 1994/2507, reg 23A(7) (added by SI 2001/762).

7   As to the National Debt Commissioners see FINANCIAL SERVICES AND INSTITUTIONS vol 49 (2008) PARA 1332.

8   As to the Insolvency Services Investment Account see PARA 27.
9   As to the Commissioners for Her Majesty's Revenue and Customs see CUSTOMS AND EXCISE vol 31 (2012) PARA 921 et seq.
10 Insolvency Act 1986 s 406 (amended by the Insolvency Act 2000 s 13(2); and by virtue of the Commissioners for Revenue and Customs Act 2005 s 50(1)).

25.   Unclaimed dividends; undistributed balances.   The Secretary of State must from time to time pay into the Consolidated Fund[1] out of the Insolvency Services Account[2] so much of the sums standing to the credit of that account as represents:

(1)   dividends which were declared before such date as the Treasury may from time to time determine and have not been claimed; and

(2)   balances ascertained before that date which are too small to be divided among the persons entitled to them[3].

For these purposes, the sums standing to the credit of the Insolvency Services Account are deemed to include any sums paid out of that account and represented by any sums or securities standing to the credit of the Insolvency Services Investment Account[4].

The Secretary of State may require the National Debt Commissioners[5] to pay out of the Insolvency Services Investment Account into the Insolvency Services Account the whole or part of any sum which he is required so to pay out of that account under the above provisions; and the Commissioners may direct the sale of such securities standing to the credit of the Insolvency Services Investment Account as may be necessary for that purpose[6].

1   As to the Consolidated Fund see CONSTITUTIONAL LAW AND HUMAN RIGHTS vol 8(2) (Reissue) PARA 711.
2   As to the Insolvency Services Account see PARA 22.
3   Insolvency Act 1986 s 407(1). In the case of the administration in bankruptcy of the insolvent estate of a deceased person dying before the presentation of a bankruptcy petition, s 407 applies: Administration of Insolvent Estates of Deceased Persons Order 1986, SI 1986/1999, art 3(1), Sch 1 Pt II para 36. As to the administration in bankruptcy of the insolvent estates of deceased debtors see further PARA 830 et seq.
4   Insolvency Act 1986 s 407(2). As to the Insolvency Services Investment Account see PARA 23.
5   As to the National Debt Commissioners see FINANCIAL SERVICES AND INSTITUTIONS vol 49 (2008) PARA 1332.
6   Insolvency Act 1986 s 407(3).

26.   Adjustment of balances.   The Treasury may direct the payment out of the Consolidated Fund[1] of sums into the Insolvency Services Account[2] or the Insolvency Services Investment Account[3]. The Treasury must certify to the House of Commons the reason for any such payment[4]. The Secretary of State may pay sums out of the Insolvency Services Account into the Consolidated Fund[5]. The National Debt Commissioners may pay sums out of the Investment Account into the Consolidated Fund[6].

1   As to the Consolidated Fund see CONSTITUTIONAL LAW AND HUMAN RIGHTS vol 8(2) (Reissue) PARA 711.
2   As to the Insolvency Services Account see PARA 22.
3   Insolvency Act 1986 s 408(1) (s 408 substituted by the Enterprise Act 2002 s 272(2)). As to the Insolvency Services Investment Account see PARA 23. In the case of the administration in bankruptcy of the insolvent estate of a deceased person dying before the presentation of a bankruptcy petition, the Insolvency Act 1986 s 408 applies: Administration of Insolvent Estates of Deceased Persons Order 1986, SI 1986/1999, Sch 1 Pt II para 36. As to the administration in bankruptcy of the insolvent estates of deceased debtors see further PARA 830 et seq.
4   Insolvency Act 1986 s 408(2) (as substituted: see note 3).
5   Insolvency Act 1986 s 408(3) (as substituted: see note 3).
6   Insolvency Act 1986 s 408(4) (as substituted: see note 3).

27.   Annual financial statement; audit. The National Debt Commissioners[1] must for each year ending on 31 March prepare a statement of the sums credited and debited to the Insolvency Services Investment Account[2] in such form and manner as the Treasury may direct and must transmit it to the Comptroller and Auditor General[3] before the end of November next following the year[4].

The Secretary of State must for each year ending 31 March prepare a statement of the sums received or paid by him[5] in such form and manner as the Treasury may direct and must transmit each statement to the Comptroller and Auditor General before the end of November next following the year[6].

Every statement[7] must include such additional information as the Treasury may direct[8].

The Comptroller and Auditor General must examine, certify and report on every such statement and must lay copies of it, and of his report, before Parliament[9].

1   As to the National Debt Commissioners see FINANCIAL SERVICES AND INSTITUTIONS vol 49 (2008) PARA 1332.
2   As to the Insolvency Services Investment Account see PARA 23.
3   As to the Comptroller and Auditor General see CONSTITUTIONAL LAW AND HUMAN RIGHTS vol 8(2) (Reissue) PARAS 724–726.
4   Insolvency Act 1986 s 409(1). In the case of the administration in bankruptcy of the insolvent estate of a deceased person dying before the presentation of a bankruptcy petition, s 409 applies: Administration of Insolvent Estates of Deceased Persons Order 1986, SI 1986/1999, art 3 (1), Sch 1 Pt II para 36. As to the administration in bankruptcy of the insolvent estates of deceased debtors see further PARA 830 et seq.
5   Ie under the Insolvency Act 1986 s 403: see PARA 22.
6   Insolvency Act 1986 s 409(2).
7   Ie whether by the National Debt Commissioners or by the Secretary of State.
8   Insolvency Act 1986 s 409(3).
9   Insolvency Act 1986 s 409(4).

(iii) Individual Insolvency Register

28.   The individual insolvency register; the bankruptcy restrictions register; the debt relief restrictions register. The Secretary of State must create and maintain a register of matters relating to bankruptcies[1], debt relief orders[2] and individual voluntary arrangements[3] called the 'individual insolvency register'[4]. The bankruptcy restrictions register[5] and the debt relief restrictions register[6] must also be maintained in accordance with the statutory provisions[7]. The registers must be open to public inspection on any business day[8] between the hours of 9.00 am and 5.00 pm[9].

Where an obligation to enter information onto, or delete information from, the registers arises[10], that obligation must be performed as soon as is reasonably practicable after it arises[11].

1   As to bankruptcy orders see PARA 198 et seq.
2   As to debt relief orders see PARA 101 et seq.
3   As to individual voluntary arrangements see PARA 43 et seq.
4   Insolvency Rules 1986, SI 1986/1925, r 6A.1(1) (added by SI 2003/1730; and amended by SI 2009/642). For the purposes of the Insolvency Rules 1986, SI 1986/1925, Pt 6A (rr 6A.1–6A.8), the 'registers' means the registers referred to in r 6A.1(1), (2): r 6A.1(3) (added by SI 2003/1730). In practice, a single register, which amalgamates the individual insolvency register, the bankruptcy restrictions register and the debt relief restrictions registers, is kept and maintained by the Insolvency Service. As to the Insolvency Service see PARA 36.
5   As to the bankruptcy restrictions register see the Insolvency Act 1986 Sch 4A para 12; and PARA 656.

6 As to the debt relief restrictions register see the Insolvency Act 1986 s 251W; and PARA 105 note 6.

7 Insolvency Rules 1986, SI 1986/1925, r 6A.1(2) (added by SI 2003/1730; and substituted by SI 2009/642). See note 4. The relevant statutory provisions are those in the Insolvency Rules 1986, SI 1986/1925, Pt 6A.

8 'Business day' means any day other than a Saturday, a Sunday, Christmas Day, Good Friday or a day which is a bank holiday in any part of England and Wales under or by virtue of the Banking and Financial Dealings Act 1971 (see TIME vol 97 (2010) PARA 321): Insolvency Rules 1986, SI 1986/1925, r 13.13(1) (substituted by SI 1999/1022; and amended by SI 2010/686).

9 Insolvency Rules 1986, SI 1986/1925, r 6A.1(4) (added by SI 2003/1730).

10 Ie under the Insolvency Rules 1986, SI 1986/1925, Pt 6A.

11 Insolvency Rules 1986, SI 1986/1925, r 6A.1(5) (added by SI 2003/1730).

29. Entry and deletion of information relating to individual voluntary arrangements. Where a voluntary arrangement has been accepted by the debtor's creditors[1] and the Secretary of State has received the relevant information[2] and notices[3], then the Secretary of State must enter onto the individual insolvency register[4]:

(1) the name and address of the debtor;

(2) the date on which the arrangement was approved by the creditors;

(3) the debtor's gender;

(4) the debtor's date of birth;

(5) any name by which the debtor was or is known, not being the name in which the debtor has entered into the voluntary arrangement;

(6) as regards an arrangement other than a fast-track voluntary arrangement[5], the name and address of the supervisor;

(7) as regards a fast-track voluntary arrangement, that the official receiver is the supervisor and the address of the official receiver; and

(8) a statement whether the arrangement was completed in accordance with its terms or failed[6].

The Secretary of State must delete from the individual insolvency register all information concerning an individual voluntary arrangement where he receives notice[7] of the making of a revocation order in respect of the arrangement or he receives notice[8] of the full implementation or termination of the arrangement, and in either case a period of three months has elapsed from the receipt of the notice[9].

1 See PARA 62 et seq.

2 Ie the Secretary of State has received information under the Insolvency Rules 1986, SI 1986/1925, r 5.29(1) sent pursuant to r 5.29(3) (revoked; see now r 5.34(1)): see PARA 88.

3 Ie under the Insolvency Rules 1986, SI 1986/1925, r 5.34 (see PARA 88), r 5.45 (see PARA 97) or r 5.50 (see PARA 100).

4 As to the individual insolvency register see PARA 28.

5 Ie under the Insolvency Act 1986 s 263A: see PARA 90.

6 Insolvency Rules 1986, SI 1986/1925, r 6A.2A(1), (2) (r 6A.2A added by SI 2010/686). The Insolvency Rules 1986, SI 1986/1925, r 6A.2A(2) is subject to r 5.67 (see PARA 81), r 6A.3 (see the text and notes 7–9) and r 6A.8 (see PARA 34): r 6A.2A(5) (as so added). For transitional arrangements see the Insolvency Rules 1986, SI 1986/1925, r 6A.2A(3), (4) (as so added).

7 Ie under the Insolvency Rules 1986, SI 1986/1925, r 5.30(5) (see PARA 87) or r 5.46(4) (see PARA 99).

8 Ie under the Insolvency Rules 1986, SI 1986/1925, r 5.34(3) (see PARA 88) or r 5.50(3) (see PARA 100).

9 Insolvency Rules 1986, SI 1986/1925, r 6A.3 (added by SI 2003/1730; and amended by SI 2010/686).

30. Entry and deletion of information relating to bankruptcy orders. Where the official receiver[1] receives[2] a copy of a bankruptcy order[3] from the court, he must cause to be entered onto the individual insolvency register[4]:

(1) the matters with respect to the identification of the debtor[5] as they are stated in the bankruptcy petition;

(2) the date of the making of the bankruptcy order;

(3) the name of the court that made the order; and

(4) the court reference number as stated on the order[6].

The official receiver must cause to be entered onto the individual insolvency register as soon as reasonably practicable after receipt by him, the following information:

(a) the name, gender, occupation, if any, and date of birth of the bankrupt;

(b) the bankrupt's last known address;

(c) where a bankruptcy order or debt relief order has been made in the period of six years immediately prior to the day of the latest bankruptcy order made against the bankrupt (excluding for these purposes any bankruptcy order that was annulled or any debt relief order[7] that was revoked), the date of whichever is the latest of them;

(d) any name by which the bankrupt was known, not being the name in which he was adjudged bankrupt;

(e) the address of any business carried on by the bankrupt and the name in which that business was carried on if carried on in a name other than the name in which the bankrupt was adjudged bankrupt;

(f) the name and address of any insolvency practitioner appointed to act as trustee in bankruptcy[8];

(g) the address at which the official receiver may be contacted;

(h) the automatic discharge date[9]; and

(i) where a bankruptcy order is rescinded by the court[10], the fact that such an order has been made, the date on which it is made and, if different, the date on which it has effect[11].

Where the official receiver receives a copy of an order suspending the bankrupt's discharge[12] he must cause to be entered onto the individual insolvency register the fact that such an order has been made and the period for which the discharge has been suspended or that the relevant period has ceased to run until the fulfilment of conditions specified in the order[13].

Where a copy of a certificate[14] certifying the discharge of an order on the application of the official receiver or the trustee of a bankrupt's estate[15] is received by the official receiver, he must cause to be entered onto the individual insolvency register that the court has discharged the order and the new date of discharge of the bankrupt; but where the order discharging the order is subsequently rescinded by the court, the official receiver must cause the register to be amended accordingly[16].

Where a bankrupt is discharged from bankruptcy on the automatic discharge date[17] or on notice being given that investigation of the bankrupt's affairs is unnecessary or concluded[18], the official receiver must cause the fact and date of such discharge to be entered in the individual insolvency register[19].

The Secretary of State must delete from the individual insolvency register all information concerning a bankruptcy where:

(i) the bankruptcy order has been annulled[20] and a period of three months has elapsed since notice of the annulment was given to the Secretary of State;

(ii)   the bankrupt has been discharged from the bankruptcy and a period of three months has elapsed from the date of discharge;

(iii)   the bankruptcy order is annulled on the ground that it should not have been made[21] and 28 days have elapsed since notice of the annulment was given to the Secretary of State[22]; or

(iv)   the bankruptcy order is rescinded by the court[23], the Secretary of State has received a copy of the order made by the court and 28 days have elapsed since receipt of the copy of the order[24].

1   As to the official receiver see PARA 35 et seq.
2   Ie pursuant to the Insolvency Rules 1986, SI 1986/1925, r 6.34 (see PARA 201) or r 6.46 (see PARA 207).
3   As to bankruptcy orders see PARA 198 et seq.
4   As to the individual insolvency register see PARA 28.
5   Ie the matters listed in the Insolvency Rules 1986, SI 1986/1925, r 6.7 (see PARA 165) and r 6.38 (see PARA 192).
6   Insolvency Rules 1986, SI 1986/1925, r 6A.4(2) (added by SI 2003/1730). As to transitional provision see the Insolvency Rules 1986, SI 1986/1925, r 6A.4(1) (as so added). The Insolvency Rules 1986, SI 1986/1925, r 6A.4 is subject to r 6.235B (see PARA 165), r 6A.5 (see the text and notes 20–24) and r 6A.8 (see PARA 34): r 6A.4(7) (added by SI 2003/1730; and amended by SI 2010/686). The court may, on the application of the bankrupt or a creditor, order the official receiver to suspend action under the Insolvency Rules 1986, SI 1986/1925, r 6A.4(2), pending a further order of the court: see r 6.46(3) (amended by SI 1999/359; SI 2005/527; and SI 2010/686); and PARA 207.
7   As to debt relief orders see PARA 101 et seq.
8   See PARA 314 et seq.
9   Ie under the Insolvency Act 1986 s 279: see PARA 638.
10 See PARA 647.
11 Insolvency Rules 1986, SI 1986/1925, r 6A.4(3) (added by SI 2003/1730; and amended by SI 2009/642; and SI 2010/686). See note 6.
12 Ie pursuant to the Insolvency Rules 1986, SI 1986/1925, r 6.176(5) (see PARA 298) or r 6.215(8) (see PARA 641).
13 Insolvency Rules 1986, SI 1986/1925, r 6A.4(4) (added by SI 2003/1730). See note 6.
14 Ie pursuant to the Insolvency Rules 1986, SI 1986/1925, r 6.216(7): see PARA 642.
15 Ie under the Insolvency Act 1986 s 279(3): see PARA 640.
16 Insolvency Rules 1986, SI 1986/1925, r 6A.4(5) (added by SI 2003/1730). See note 6.
17 Ie under the Insolvency Act 1986 s 279(1): see PARA 638.
18 Ie under the Insolvency Act 1986 s 279(2): see PARA 638.
19 Insolvency Rules 1986, SI 1986/1925, r 6A.4(6) (added by SI 2003/1730). See note 6. In relation to bankruptcy orders made on or after 1 October 2013, the reference in the Insolvency Rules 1986, SI 1986/1925, r 6A.4(6) to the Insolvency Act 1986 s 279(2) (see the text to note 18) is omitted: see the Insolvency Rules 1986, SI 1986/1925, r 6A.4(6) (amended by SI 2013/2135).
20 Ie pursuant to the Insolvency Act 1986 s 261(2)(a), 261(2)(b) (see PARA 69), s 263D(3) (see PARA 95) or s 282(1)(b) (see PARA 620 head (2)).
21 Ie pursuant to the Insolvency Act 1986 s 282(1)(a): see PARA 620 head (1).
22 Ie under the Insolvency Rules 1986, SI 1986/1925, r 6.213(2): see PARA 631.
23 Ie under the Insolvency Act 1986 s 375: see PARA 761.
24 Insolvency Rules 1986, SI 1986/1925, r 6A.5 (added by SI 2003/1730; and amended by SI 2010/686).

31.   Entry and deletion of information relating to debt relief orders. The official receiver[1] must cause to be entered onto the individual insolvency register[2] as soon as reasonably practicable after the making of a debt relief order[3] the following information relating to the order or to the debtor in respect of whom it has been made:

(1)   as they are stated in the debtor's application: (a) the name, gender, occupation, if any, and date of birth of the debtor; (b) the debtor's last known address; (c) the name or names in which he carries or has carried

on business, if other than his true name; and (d) the nature of his business and the address or addresses at which he carries or has carried it on and whether alone or with others;

(2)   the date of the making of the debt relief order;

(3)   the reference number of the order;

(4)   the date of the end of the moratorium period[4]; and

(5)   where a bankruptcy order or a debt relief order has been made in the period of six years immediately prior to the date of the latest debt relief order made against the debtor, excluding for these purposes any bankruptcy order that was annulled or any debt relief order that was revoked, the date of whichever is the latest of them[5].

Provided that information concerning a debt relief order has not been validly deleted[6], the official receiver must also cause to be entered on the register in relation to the order:

(i)   where the moratorium period is terminated early, the fact that such has happened, the date of early termination and whether the early termination is on revocation of the debt relief order or by virtue of any other enactment;

(ii)   where the moratorium period is extended, the fact that such has happened, the date on which the extension was made, its duration and the date of the new anticipated end of the moratorium period; or

(iii)   where the debtor is discharged from all qualifying debts, the date of such discharge[7].

The Secretary of State must delete from the individual insolvency register all information concerning a debt relief order where the debt relief order has been revoked, or the debtor has been discharged from his qualifying debts, and a period of three months has elapsed from the date of revocation or discharge[8].

1   As to the official receiver see PARA 35 et seq.
2   As to the individual insolvency register see PARA 28.
3   As to debt relief orders see PARA 101 et seq.
4   As to the moratorium period see PARA 109.
5   Insolvency Rules 1986, SI 1986/1925, r 6A.5A(2) (added by SI 2009/642). The Insolvency Rules 1986, SI 1986/1925, r 6A.5A is subject to rr 5A.18, 6A.5B, 6A.8 (see PARAS 117, 34): r 6A.5A(1) (added by SI 2009/642; and amended by SI 2010/686).
6   Ie under the Insolvency Rules 1986, SI 1986/1925, r 6A.5B (see the text and note 8).
7   Insolvency Rules 1986, SI 1986/1925, r 6A.5A(3) (added by SI 2009/642). See note 5.
8   Insolvency Rules 1986, SI 1986/1925, r 6A.5B (added by SI 2009/642).

32.   Entry and deletion of information relating to bankruptcy restrictions orders and undertakings. Where an interim bankruptcy restrictions order[1] or a bankruptcy restrictions order[2] is made against a bankrupt, the Secretary of State[3] must enter onto the bankruptcy restrictions register[4]:

(1)   the name, gender, occupation, if any, and date of birth of the bankrupt;

(2)   the bankrupt's last known address;

(3)   a statement that an interim bankruptcy restrictions order or, as the case may be, a bankruptcy restrictions order has been made against him;

(4)   the date of the making of the order, the court and the court reference number; and

(5)   the duration of the order[5].

Where a bankruptcy restrictions undertaking[6] is given by a bankrupt, the Secretary of State must enter onto the bankruptcy restrictions register:

(a)   the name, gender, occupation, if any, and date of birth of the bankrupt;

(b)   the bankrupt's last known address;

   (c)   a statement that a bankruptcy restrictions undertaking has been given;

   (d)   the date of the acceptance of the bankruptcy restrictions undertaking by the Secretary of State; and

   (e)   the duration of the bankruptcy restrictions undertaking[7].

In any case where an interim bankruptcy restrictions order or a bankruptcy restrictions order is made or a bankruptcy restrictions undertaking has been accepted, the Secretary of State must remove from the bankruptcy restrictions register all information regarding that order or, as the case may be, undertaking after receipt of notification that the order or, as the case may be, the undertaking has ceased to have effect, or the expiry of the order or, as the case may be, undertaking[8].

1   As to interim bankruptcy restrictions orders see PARA 663 et seq.
2   As to bankruptcy restrictions orders see PARA 657 et seq.
3   As to the Secretary of State see PARA 19.
4   As to the bankruptcy restrictions register see PARA 28.
5   Insolvency Rules 1986, SI 1986/1925, r 6A.6(1) (added by SI 2003/1730; and amended by SI 2004/584). The Insolvency Rules 1986, SI 1986/1925, r 6A.6 is subject to rr 6.235B, 6A.7, 6A.8 (see PARAS 34, 165): r 6A.(3) (added by SI 2003/1730; and amended by SI 2010/686).
6   As to bankruptcy restrictions undertakings see PARA 668 et seq.
7   Insolvency Rules 1986, SI 1986/1925, r 6A.6(2) (added by SI 2003/1730; and amended by SI 2004/584).
8   Insolvency Rules 1986, SI 1986/1925, r 6A.7 (added by SI 2003/1730).

33.   Entry and deletion of information relating to debt relief restrictions orders and undertakings.   Where an interim debt relief restrictions order[1] or a debt relief restrictions order[2] is made against a debtor, the Secretary of State[3] must enter onto the debt relief restrictions register[4]:

   (1)   the name, gender, occupation, if any, and date of birth of the debtor;

   (2)   the debtor's last known address;

   (3)   a statement that an interim debt relief restrictions order or, as the case may be, a debt relief restrictions order has been made against him;

   (4)   the date of the making of the order and the order reference number; and

   (5)   the duration of the order[5].

Where a debt relief restrictions undertaking[6] is given by a debtor, the Secretary of State must enter onto the debt relief restrictions register:

   (a)   the name, gender, occupation, if any, and date of birth of the debtor;

   (b)   the debtor's last known address;

   (c)   a statement that a debt relief restrictions undertaking has been given;

   (d)   the date of the acceptance of the debt relief restrictions undertaking by the Secretary of State and reference number of the undertaking; and

   (e)   the duration of the debt relief restrictions undertaking[7].

In any case where an interim debt relief restrictions order or a debt relief restrictions order is made or a debt relief restrictions undertaking has been accepted, the Secretary of State must remove from the debt relief restrictions register all information regarding that order or, as the case may be, undertaking after receipt of notification that the order or, as the case may be, undertaking has ceased to have effect or the expiry of the order or, as the case may be, undertaking[8].

1   As to interim debt relief restrictions orders see PARA 126.
2   As to debt relief restrictions orders see PARA 125 et seq.
3   As to the Secretary of State see PARA 19.
4   As to the debt relief restrictions register see PARA 28.

5   Insolvency Rules 1986, SI 1986/1925, r 6A.7A(2) (added by SI 2009/642). The Insolvency
    Rules 1986, SI 1986/1925, r 6A.7A is subject to rr 5A.18, 6A.7B, 6A.8 (see PARAS 34, 117):
    r 6A.7A(1) (added by SI 2009/642; and amended by SI 2010/686).
6   As to debt relief restrictions undertakings see PARA 127.
7   Insolvency Rules 1986, SI 1986/1925, r 6A.7A(3) (added by SI 2009/642).
8   Insolvency Rules 1986, SI 1986/1925, r 6A.7B (added by SI 2009/642).

34.   Rectification of the registers.   Where the Secretary of State[1] becomes
aware that there is any inaccuracy in any information maintained on the registers
he must rectify the inaccuracy as soon as reasonably practicable[2].

Where the Secretary of State receives notice of the date of the death of a
person in respect of whom information is held on any of the registers, he must
cause the fact and date of the person's death to be entered onto the individual
insolvency register and, as the case may be, the bankruptcy restrictions register
or the debt relief restrictions register[3].

1   As to the Secretary of State see PARA 19.
2   Insolvency Rules 1986, SI 1986/1925, r 6A.8(1) (added by SI 2003/1730).
3   Insolvency Rules 1986, SI 1986/1925, r 6A.8(2) (added by SI 2003/1730; and substituted by
    SI 2009/642). As to the registers see PARA 28. As to the administration in bankruptcy of the
    insolvent estates of deceased debtors see further PARA 830 et seq.

(2) OFFICIAL RECEIVERS AND THE INSOLVENCY SERVICE

35.   Appointment of official receivers.   The official receiver, in relation to any
bankruptcy[1], individual voluntary arrangement[2], debt relief order or application
for such an order[3], is any person who is authorised[4] to act as the official receiver
in relation to that bankruptcy, individual voluntary arrangement, debt relief
order or application for such an order[5]. The Secretary of State appoints persons
to the office of official receiver, and determines salary and terms and conditions
of appointment[6]. Where a person holds the office of official receiver, the
Secretary of State must from time to time attach him either to the High Court or
to a county court having jurisdiction for the purposes of the provisions[7] dealing
with the insolvency of individuals and bankruptcy[8].

Subject to any directions[9] by the Secretary of State, an official receiver
attached to a particular court is the person authorised to act as the official
receiver in relation to every bankruptcy, individual voluntary arrangement, debt
relief order or application for such an order falling within the jurisdiction of that
court[10]. The Secretary of State must ensure that there is, at all times, at least one
official receiver attached to the High Court and at least one attached to each
county court having jurisdiction for the purposes of the provisions dealing with
the insolvency of individuals and bankruptcy, but he may attach the same official
receiver to two or more different courts[11].

The Secretary of State may appoint deputy official receivers and staff[12].

In the absence of the official receiver authorised to act in a particular case, an
officer authorised in writing for the purpose by the Secretary of State, or by the
official receiver himself, may, with the permission of the court, act on the official
receiver's behalf and in his place in any examination[13], and in respect of any
application to the court[14]. In case of emergency, where there is no official
receiver capable of acting, anything to be done by, to or before the official
receiver may be done by, to or before the registrar or district judge[15].

1   As to bankruptcy see PARA 129 et seq. The official receiver is also empowered to act in respect of
    any winding up: see the Insolvency Act 1986 s 399(1), (4); and COMPANY AND PARTNERSHIP

INSOLVENCY vol 16 (2011) PARA 453. Detailed provisions as to the appointment and duties of official receivers are set out in COMPANY AND PARTNERSHIP INSOLVENCY vol 16 (2011) PARA 453 et seq.

2   As to individual voluntary arrangements see PARA 43 et seq.

3   As to debt relief orders see PARA 101 et seq.

4   Ie by virtue of the Insolvency Act 1986 ss 399(2)–(7), 401: see the text and notes 6–12.

5   Insolvency Act 1986 s 399(1) (amended by the Enterprise Act 2002 s 269, Sch 23 paras 1, 14(a); and the Tribunals, Courts and Enforcement Act 2007 s 108(3), Sch 20 paras 1, 7). In the case of the administration in bankruptcy of the insolvent estate of a deceased person dying before the presentation of a bankruptcy petition, s 399 applies: Administration of Insolvent Estates of Deceased Persons Order 1986, SI 1986/1999, art 3(1), Sch 1 Pt II para 36. As to the administration in bankruptcy of the insolvent estates of deceased debtors see further PARA 830 et seq.

6   See the Insolvency Act 1986 s 399(2); and COMPANY AND PARTNERSHIP INSOLVENCY vol 16 (2011) PARA 453. Judicial notice must be taken of the appointment of official receivers: see the Insolvency Rules 1986, SI 1986/1925, r 10.1.

7   Ie the provisions contained in the Insolvency Act 1986 Pts 7A–11 (ss 251A–385). As to the courts having jurisdiction see PARAS 6, 7.

8   Insolvency Act 1986 s 399(3). As from a day to be appointed, s 399(3) is amended to provide that where a person holds the office of official receiver, the Secretary of State must from time to time attach him either to the High Court or to the county court: see s 399(3) (amended by the Crime and Courts Act 2013 Sch 9 Pt 3 para 93(h)). At the date at which this volume states the law no such day had been appointed.

9   Ie under the Insolvency Act 1986 s 399(6): see COMPANY AND PARTNERSHIP INSOLVENCY vol 16 (2011) PARA 453.

10   Insolvency Act 1986 s 399(4) (amended by the Enterprise Act 2002 s 269, Sch 23 paras 1, 14(b); and the Tribunals, Courts and Enforcement Act 2007 s 108(3), Sch 20 paras 1, 7).

11   Insolvency Act 1986 s 399(5). As from a day to be appointed, s 399(5) is amended to provide that the Secretary of State must ensure that there is, at all times, at least one official receiver attached to the High Court and at least one attached to the county court, but he may attach the same official receiver to both courts: see s 399(5) (amended by the Crime and Courts Act 2013 Sch 9 Pt 3 para 93(i)). At the date at which this volume states the law no such day had been appointed.

12   See the Insolvency Act 1986 s 401; and COMPANY AND PARTNERSHIP INSOLVENCY vol 16 (2011) PARA 457.

13   Ie under the Insolvency Act 1986 s 251N (see PARA 118), s 290 (see PARA 289 et seq) or s 366 (see PARA 305 et seq).

14   Insolvency Rules 1986, SI 1986/1925, r 10.2(1) (amended by SI 2009/642; and SI 2010/686). See also COMPANY AND PARTNERSHIP INSOLVENCY vol 16 (2011) PARA 458.

15   Insolvency Rules 1986, SI 1986/1925, r 10.2(2) (amended by SI 2010/686). As to the meaning of 'registrar' see PARA 786 note 2.

36.   The Insolvency Service. By order of the Secretary of State, with effect from 21 March 1990, the official receivers and their duties and functions were placed under the umbrella of the Insolvency Service which is an executive agency of the government.

The Insolvency Service maintains the individual insolvency register[1].

1   See PARA 28.

37.   Functions and status of official receiver. The primary function of the official receiver is to act as receiver and manager of the bankrupt's estate[1] pending the vesting of the estate in the trustee[2] and to carry out an investigation into the conduct and affairs of the bankrupt with a report of such investigation to the court if he thinks fit[3]. The official receiver has a number of functions conferred on him by the Insolvency Act 1986 in relation to bankruptcy and personal insolvency[4]; and a person holding the office of official receiver[5] is required to carry out such other functions as may from time to time be conferred on him by the Secretary of State[6].

In the exercise of the functions of his office a person holding the office of official receiver must act under the general directions of the Secretary of State and is also an officer of the court[7] in relation to which he exercises those functions[8].

The official receiver may apply to the court for directions in relation to any matter arising in insolvency proceedings[9].

Any property vested in his official capacity[10] in a person holding the office of official receiver vests, on his dying, ceasing to hold office or being otherwise succeeded in relation to the bankruptcy in question by another official receiver, in his successor without any conveyance, assignment or transfer[11].

1   As to the bankrupt's estate see PARA 211.
2   As to the trustee see PARA 314 et seq.
3   See PARA 252 et seq.
4   For various functions conferred on the official receiver under the Insolvency Act 1986 see ss 251B, 251C (application for a debt relief order: see PARAS 102, 105); s 251L (power to revoke or amend a debt relief order: see PARA 115); s 253(3) (application to the court for an interim order for a voluntary arrangement proposed by an undischarged bankrupt: see PARA 46); s 262(2) (challenge to the decision of a creditors' meeting summoned to consider a voluntary arrangement proposed by an undischarged bankrupt: see PARA 85); s 263B (approval of fast-track voluntary arrangement: see PARA 90); s 279(3) (application to suspend the running of the relevant period for the purposes of discharge where the bankrupt has failed or is failing to comply with obligations: see PARA 640); s 286(1) (appointment as the interim receiver of debtor's property after the presentation of a petition and before the making of a bankruptcy order: see PARA 219); s 287 (receiver and manager of bankrupt's estate pending the appointment of trustee: see PARA 229 et seq); s 288(3) (power to release the bankrupt from his obligation to submit a statement of affairs or to extend the period allowed for its submission: see PARAS 240, 244); s 289(1)–(4) (duty to investigate the conduct and affairs of every bankrupt and to report to the court if he thinks fit: see PARA 252); s 290 (application for, and taking part in, the public examination of the bankrupt: see PARA 289 et seq); s 293(1), (2) (duty to decide whether to summon a general meeting of creditors to appoint the first trustee and to give notice to the court and every creditor if he decides against summoning such a meeting: see PARAS 261, 316); s 293(3) (appointment as trustee where notice given to the court that he has decided against summoning a meeting of creditors to appoint a trustee: see PARAS 261, 321); s 294(2) (duty to summon a meeting to appoint a trustee where required to do so by one-quarter in value of the bankrupt's creditors: see PARAS 263, 317); s 295(1) (duty to decide whether to refer the need for the appointment of trustee to the Secretary of State where a general meeting of creditors fails to make appointment: see PARAS 265, 319); s 295(4) (appointment as trustee where he decides not to refer need for appointment to the Secretary of State or where the Secretary of State declines to make an appointment: see PARAS 265, 319, 321); s 296(1) (application by the official receiver to the Secretary of State to appoint a person as trustee in place of the official receiver: see PARA 319); s 300 (appointment as trustee when there is a vacancy in office: see PARA 370); ss 305–349A (general functions, duties and powers as trustee: see PARA 397 et seq); s 346 (involvement in enforcement procedures where execution is not completed before the commencement of bankruptcy: see PARA 703 et seq); s 365(1) (application to seize property comprised in the bankrupt's estate: see PARA 216); ss 366, 367 (application for a private examination: see PARA 305 et seq); s 369 (application for the production of documents by the inland revenue: see PARA 299 et seq); s 370 (application for the appointment of a special manager: see PARA 232); s 371 (application for the redirection of the bankrupt's letters: see PARAS 264, 468); s 372 (application as trustee or interim receiver for the continuation of essential supplies by utilities: see PARAS 226, 485); s 389B (power to act as nominee or supervisor in relation to a voluntary arrangement: see PARA 74); s 424 (application for an order where the debtor subsequently adjudged bankrupt has entered into a transaction to defraud creditors: see PARA 690 et seq); Sch 4ZB para 1 (application for debt relief restrictions order: see PARA 125).
5   Ie including persons appointed to act as the official receiver's deputy: see the Insolvency Act 1986 s 401(2): see COMPANY AND PARTNERSHIP INSOLVENCY vol 16 (2011) PARA 457.
6   Insolvency Act 1986 s 400(1). As to the exercise of functions see further s 400(2), (3); and COMPANY AND PARTNERSHIP INSOLVENCY vol 16 (2011) PARA 454. In the case of the administration in bankruptcy of the insolvent estate of a deceased person dying before the presentation of a bankruptcy petition, s 400 applies: Administration of Insolvent Estates of

Deceased Persons Order 1986, SI 1986/1999, art 3(1), Sch 1 Pt II para 36. As to the administration in bankruptcy of the insolvent estates of deceased debtors see further PARA 830 et seq.

7 See *Bottomley v Brougham* [1908] 1 KB 584; *Burr v Smith* [1909] 2 KB 306, CA. As to the application of the principles in *Re Condon, ex p James* (1874) 9 Ch App 609 to officers of the court see PARA 477. Where the official receiver acts in the course of bankruptcy proceedings and prepares reports for the purpose of such proceedings, any statements made in such reports are entitled to absolute privilege and the official receiver is immune from action in respect of them: *Mond v Hyde* [1999] QB 1097, [1998] 3 All ER 833, CA.

8 Insolvency Act 1986 s 400(2).

9 Insolvency Rules 1986, SI 1986/1925, r 10.3. For these purposes, 'insolvency proceedings' means any proceedings under the Insolvency Act 1986 or the Insolvency Rules 1986, SI 1986/1925: rr 13.1, 13.7.

10 See the Insolvency Act 1986 s 306; and PARA 398.

11 Insolvency Act 1986 s 400(3).

38.   Contracted out functions of official receiver. The Secretary of State has power by order to contract out any function of the official receiver[1].

Any function of the official receiver which is conferred by or under the insolvency legislation[2] may be exercised by, or by employees of, such person, if any, as may be authorised in that behalf by the official receiver, except for the following functions[3]:

(1)   the functions of the official receiver as interim receiver[4];

(2)   the receipt of any deposit which relates to a bankruptcy petition[5];

(3)   the chairing[6] of the first meeting of creditors[7] in a bankruptcy[8];

(4)   the making of an application to the Secretary of State for the appointment[9] of a person as trustee instead of the official receiver[10];

(5)   the taking of a decision whether or not to refer[11] to the Secretary of State the need for an appointment of a trustee in any case where at a meeting duly summoned[12] no appointment of a person as trustee is made[13];

(6)   the making of a reference[14] to the Secretary of State of the need for an appointment of a trustee where a vacancy has arisen and, in the period of 28 days beginning with the day on which the vacancy first came to the official receiver's attention, he has not summoned, and is not proposing to summon, a general meeting of creditors for the purpose of filling the vacancy[15];

(7)   the functions:

(a)   of a creditors' committee exercisable[16] by the official receiver; or

(b)   of the official receiver in relation to the hearing of an application to the court[17] by a bankrupt for a release or extension of time in respect of the statement of affairs[18];

(8)   the giving of notice to the Secretary of State[19] of the release of the official receiver as trustee[20];

(9)   consideration as to whether[21] a request by creditors for a meeting of creditors has been properly made in accordance with the Insolvency Act 1986[22];

(10)   the making or conduct of any application to the court:

(a)   to commit a bankrupt for contempt of court for failure to comply with an obligation imposed on him in relation to his statement of affairs[23], his duties in relation to the official receiver[24], his obligation to surrender control to the trustee[25], his duties in relation to the trustee[26] and in relation to the general control of the court[27]; or

(b)   for the suspension[28] of the discharge of a bankrupt[29];

(11)   the making or conduct of any application to the court to commit for contempt of court a person who has failed to attend[30] his public examination[31];

(12)   the making of a report to the court pursuant to the provisions relating to:

(a)   an investigation by the official receiver[32];

(b)   a report to the court on an application by a bankrupt for discharge from bankruptcy[33];

(c)   a report to the court etc on application by a bankrupt for release from his duty to submit a statement of affairs or for an extension of time[34];

(d)   a report[35] in support of an application for the suspension of the discharge of a bankrupt[36];

(13)   the making or conduct of an application to the court for a public examination[37] and the making or conduct of any application in relation to any public examination[38];

(14)   the making or conduct of an application to the court to relieve the official receiver from an obligation to make an application for a public examination duly[39] requested[40];

(15)   the taking part in a public examination or the questioning[41] of a bankrupt[42];

(16)   the making or conduct of an application to the court for the issue[43] of a warrant for the arrest of a debtor, an undischarged bankrupt or a discharged bankrupt, and for the seizure of any books, papers, records, money or goods in that person's possession, as the case may be[44];

(17)   the making or conduct of an application to the court for the transfer of bankruptcy proceedings from one court to another[45];

(18)   any function of the official receiver in relation to the hearing of an application by a bankrupt for permission to act as a director of, or directly or indirectly, to take part in or be concerned in the promotion, formation or management of, a company[46];

(19)   any function corresponding to one referred to in heads (1) to (18) above which is exercisable by the official receiver by virtue of an application, with or without modifications, of any provision of the insolvency legislation to insolvent partnerships[47].

A function which may be so contracted out, and which involves the exercise of a right of audience[48] in relation to any proceedings before a court, may only be exercised subject to the condition that such right of audience may not be exercised by any person other than a person who has a right of audience[49] in relation to the proceedings in question[50].

1   See the Deregulation and Contracting Out Act 1994 ss 69, 71, 72, 73, 79; and COMPANY AND PARTNERSHIP INSOLVENCY vol 16 (2011) PARA 455. See the Contracting Out (Functions of the Official Receiver) Order 1995, SI 1995/1386.

2   For these purposes, 'the insolvency legislation' means the Insolvency Act 1986, the Companies Act 1985, the Company Directors Disqualification Act 1986 and any subordinate legislation made under any of those Acts and any regulations made under the Insolvency Rules 1986, SI 1986/1925, r 12.1 (see PARA 20): Contracting Out (Functions of the Official Receiver) Order 1995, SI 1995/1386, art 2(1).

3   Contracting Out (Functions of the Official Receiver) Order 1995, SI 1995/1386, art 3(1). As to the contracting out of the official receiver's functions in relation to corporate insolvency proceedings see COMPANY AND PARTNERSHIP INSOLVENCY vol 16 (2011) PARA 456.

4   Contracting Out (Functions of the Official Receiver) Order 1995, SI 1995/1386, art 3(1), Schedule para 1(c). The functions of the official receiver as interim receiver are those under the Insolvency Act 1986 s 286: see PARA 218 et seq.
5   Contracting Out (Functions of the Official Receiver) Order 1995, SI 1995/1386, Schedule para 2. As to the deposit payable on the presentation of a bankruptcy petition see PARA 168.
6   Ie by virtue of the Insolvency Rules 1986, SI 1986/1925, r 6.82: see PARA 268.
7   Ie as defined in the Insolvency Rules 1986, SI 1986/1925, r 6.79(7): see PARA 263.
8   Contracting Out (Functions of the Official Receiver) Order 1995, SI 1995/1386, Schedule para 3(b).
9   Ie under the Insolvency Act 1986 s 296(1): see PARA 319.
10 Contracting Out (Functions of the Official Receiver) Order 1995, SI 1995/1386, Schedule para 4(b).
11 Ie pursuant to the Insolvency Act 1986 s 295(1): see PARA 319.
12 Ie summoned under the Insolvency Act 1986 s 293 or s 294: see PARAS 316, 317.
13 Contracting Out (Functions of the Official Receiver) Order 1995, SI 1995/1386, Schedule para 5(b).
14 Ie pursuant to the Insolvency Act 1986 s 300(4): see PARA 370.
15 Contracting Out (Functions of the Official Receiver) Order 1995, SI 1995/1386, Schedule para 6.
16 Ie the functions exercisable under the Insolvency Rules 1986 r 6.166(2): see PARA 341.
17 Ie under the Insolvency Rules 1986, SI 1986/1925, r 6.62(2): see PARA 244.
18 Contracting Out (Functions of the Official Receiver) Order 1995, SI 1995/1386, Schedule para 8(a), (b)(iii).
19 Ie pursuant to the Insolvency Act 1986 s 299(2): see PARA 380.
20 Contracting Out (Functions of the Official Receiver) Order 1995, SI 1995/1386, Schedule para 10.
21 Ie pursuant to the Insolvency Rules 1986, SI 1986/1925, r 6.83(2): see PARA 269.
22 Contracting Out (Functions of the Official Receiver) Order 1995, SI 1995/1386, Schedule para 11(c).
23 Ie under the Insolvency Act 1986 s 288: see PARA 240.
24 Ie under the Insolvency Act 1986 s 291: see PARA 239.
25 Ie under the Insolvency Act 1986 s 312: see PARA 408.
26 Ie under the Insolvency Act 1986 s 333: see PARA 343.
27 Ie under the Insolvency Act 1986 s 363: see PARA 215.
28 Ie pursuant to the Insolvency Act 1986 s 279(3): see PARA 640.
29 Contracting Out (Functions of the Official Receiver) Order 1995, SI 1995/1386, Schedule para 12.
30 Ie under the Insolvency Act 1986 s 290: see PARA 289 et seq.
31 Contracting Out (Functions of the Official Receiver) Order 1995, SI 1995/1386, Schedule para 13(b).
32 Ie pursuant to the Insolvency Act 1986 s 289(1)(a): see PARA 252.
33 Ie pursuant to the Insolvency Act 1986 s 289(1)(b): see PARA 252.
34 Ie pursuant to the Insolvency Rules 1986, SI 1986/1925, r 6.62(5): see PARA 244.
35 Ie pursuant to the Insolvency Rules 1986, SI 1986/1925, r 6.215(2): see PARA 641.
36 Contracting Out (Functions of the Official Receiver) Order 1995, SI 1995/1386, Schedule para 14(b), (c), (e), (f).
37 Ie under the Insolvency Act 1986 s 290(1): see PARA 289 et seq.
38 Contracting Out (Functions of the Official Receiver) Order 1995, SI 1995/1386, Schedule para 15.
39 Ie pursuant to the Insolvency Act 1986 s 290(2): see PARA 290.
40 Contracting Out (Functions of the Official Receiver) Order 1995, SI 1995/1386, Schedule para 16.
41 Ie pursuant to the Insolvency Act 1986 s 290(4)(a): see PARA 293.
42 Contracting Out (Functions of the Official Receiver) Order 1995, SI 1995/1386, Schedule para 17.
43 Ie pursuant to the Insolvency Act 1986 s 364: see PARA 217.
44 Contracting Out (Functions of the Official Receiver) Order 1995, SI 1995/1386, Schedule para 18(b).
45 Contracting Out (Functions of the Official Receiver) Order 1995, SI 1995/1386, Schedule para 20. As to the transfer of bankruptcy proceedings see PARA 756.
46 Contracting Out (Functions of the Official Receiver) Order 1995, SI 1995/1386, Schedule para 22(a). As to applications for permission see PARA 730.

47 Contracting Out (Functions of the Official Receiver) Order 1995, SI 1995/1386, Schedule para 24. As to insolvent partnerships see COMPANY AND PARTNERSHIP INSOLVENCY vol 17 (2011) PARA 1209 et seq.

48 For these purposes, 'right of audience' means the right to appear before and address a court including the right to call and examine witnesses: Courts and Legal Services Act 1990 s 119(1) (definition amended by the Access to Justice Act 1999 s 43, Sch 6 paras 4, 10(1), (2)); applied by the Contracting Out (Functions of the Official Receiver) Order 1995, SI 1995/1386, art 2(1).

49 The Contracting Out (Functions of the Official Receiver) Order 1995, SI 1995/1386, refers to a right of audience by virtue of the Courts and Legal Services Act 1990 Pt II (ss 17–70). This has been replaced by a right to carry out a reserved legal activity under the Legal Services Act 2007 Pt 3 (ss 12–26): see COURTS AND TRIBUNALS vol 24 (2010) PARA 612; LEGAL PROFESSIONS vol 65 (2008) PARA 509 et seq.

50 Contracting Out (Functions of the Official Receiver) Order 1995, SI 1995/1386, art 3(2), (3).

39. Remuneration and expenses. In respect of the performance by the official receiver of his functions under the Insolvency Act 1986[1], such fees are payable as the Lord Chancellor may, with the sanction of the Treasury, direct[2].

Any expenses[3] incurred by the official receiver, in whatever capacity he may be acting, in connection with proceedings taken against him in insolvency proceedings[4] are to be treated as expenses of the insolvency proceedings for this purpose[5]. In relation to any sums due to the official receiver in connection with insolvency proceedings other than proceedings relating to debt relief orders[6] or applications for debt relief orders, he has a charge on the bankrupt's estate or, as the case may be, the debtor's property[7].

1 Ie under the Insolvency Act 1986 Pts 7A–11 (ss 251A–385).
2 Insolvency Act 1986 s 415(1) (amended by the Tribunals, Courts and Enforcement Act 2007 s 108(3), Sch 20 para 9). In the case of the administration in bankruptcy of the insolvent estate of a deceased person dying before the presentation of a bankruptcy petition, the Insolvency Act 1986 s 415 applies: Administration of Insolvent Estates of Deceased Persons Order 1986, SI 1986/1999, art 3(1), Sch 1 Pt II para 36. As to the administration in bankruptcy of the insolvent estates of deceased debtors see further PARA 830 et seq.
   For the prescribed fees see the Insolvency Proceedings (Fees) Order 2004, SI 2004/593 (amended by SI 2005/544, SI 2006/561, SI 2007/521, SI 2008/714, SI 2009/645, SI 2010/732). As to the remuneration of liquidators see further COMPANY AND PARTNERSHIP INSOLVENCY vol 16 (2011) PARAS 498–500.
3 For these purposes, 'expenses' includes damages: Insolvency Rules 1986, SI 1986/1925, r 10.4(1).
4 As to the meaning of 'insolvency proceedings' see PARA 37 note 9.
5 Insolvency Rules 1986, SI 1986/1925, r 10.4(1). See also r 12.2; and PARA 588. In the event of a costs order being made in his favour following proceedings, the official receiver is in the same position as the Treasury Solicitor or a solicitor employed by a party to litigation and is accordingly entitled to the recovery of costs in respect of time expended by himself and his staff and is not limited to the recovery of disbursements: *Re Minotaur Data Systems Ltd, Official Receiver v Brunt* [1999] 3 All ER 122, [1999] 1 WLR 1129, CA.
6 As to debt relief orders see PARA 101 et seq.
7 Insolvency Rules 1986, SI 1986/1925, rr 10.4(2), 13.1, 13.8(b) (r 10.4(2) amended by SI 2009/642). As to the order of priority of the expenses of the bankruptcy see the Insolvency Rules 1986, SI 1986/1925, r 6.224; and PARA 590.

(3) INSOLVENCY PRACTITIONERS

40. Insolvency practitioners. The Insolvency Act 1986 introduced a system of licensing to ensure the professional competence and skill of insolvency practitioners in individual and corporate insolvency[1]. A person who is not an individual is not qualified to act as an insolvency practitioner[2]; nor is he qualified so to act if he is subject to one of the statutory exceptions[3].

A person is not qualified to act as an insolvency practitioner unless at that time:

(1)	he is authorised by virtue of membership of a recognised professional body[4], or he holds an authorisation granted by a competent authority[5];

(2)	he fulfils the prescribed requirements as to education and practical training and experience[6]; and

(3)	there is in force security for the proper performance of his functions[7].

A person acts as an insolvency practitioner in relation to an individual by acting:

(a)	as his trustee in bankruptcy or interim receiver of his property;

(b)	as trustee of a deed which is a deed of arrangement made for the benefit of his creditors;

(c)	where a voluntary arrangement in relation to the individual is proposed or approved and approved under the Insolvency Act 1986[8], as nominee or supervisor; or

(d)	in the case of a deceased individual to the administration of whose estate these provisions apply[9], as administrator of that estate[10].

Application may be made to a competent authority for authorisation to act as an insolvency practitioner[11]; and the authority may grant or refuse the application[12]. Where the competent authority proposes to refuse such an application or withdraw an authorisation, it must give the applicant or holder written notice of its intention to do so[13]; and the applicant may give written notice to the authority requiring the case to be referred to the Insolvency Practitioners Tribunal[14]. On such a reference, the tribunal must investigate the case and make a report to the competent authority stating what would in its opinion be the appropriate decision in the matter and the reason for that opinion; and it is the duty of the competent authority to decide the matter accordingly[15].

When acting in relation to any person, an insolvency practitioner must maintain, allow the inspection of and preserve prescribed records[16].

Where an individual who is acting as an office-holder[17] ('the outgoing office-holder') dies, retires from practice, or is otherwise unable or unwilling to continue in office, and it is expedient to transfer some or all of the cases in which the outgoing office-holder holds office to one or more office-holders ('the replacement office-holder') in a single transaction, then the court has the power to make a block transfer order, appointing a replacement office-holder in the place of the outgoing office-holder[18].

1	Provision relating to insolvency practitioners is set out in detail in COMPANY AND PARTNERSHIP INSOLVENCY vol 16 (2011) PARAS 9–57.

2	Acting without qualification is an offence: see the Insolvency Act 1986 s 389; and COMPANY AND PARTNERSHIP INSOLVENCY vol 16 (2011) PARA 11. Section 389 does not apply to a person acting in relation to a voluntary arrangement proposed or approved under Pt 8 (ss 252–263G) as nominee or supervisor if he is authorised so to act: see s 389A (added by the Insolvency Act 2000 s 4(1), (4)); and COMPANY AND PARTNERSHIP INSOLVENCY vol 16 (2011) PARA 12. As from a day to be appointed, s 389A is amended by the Enterprise and Regulatory Reform Act 2013 s 71, Sch 19 paras 1, 57: see PARA 130 note 17.

3	See the Insolvency Act 1986 s 390; and COMPANY AND PARTNERSHIP INSOLVENCY vol 16 (2011) PARA 14 et seq. As from a day to be appointed, s 390 is amended by the Enterprise and Regulatory Reform Act 2013 s 71, Sch 19 paras 1, 58: see PARA 130 note 17.

4	As to recognised professional bodies see the Insolvency Act 1986 s 391; and COMPANY AND PARTNERSHIP INSOLVENCY vol 16 (2011) PARA 15.

5	As to authorisation by a competent authority see the Insolvency Act 1986 s 392; and COMPANY AND PARTNERSHIP INSOLVENCY vol 16 (2011) PARA 16.

6	See the Insolvency Practitioners Regulations 2005, SI 2005/524, Pt 2 (rr 5–11); and COMPANY AND PARTNERSHIP INSOLVENCY vol 16 (2011) PARAS 19–23.

7   See the Insolvency Practitioners Regulations 2005, SI 2005/524, Sch 2; and COMPANY AND
    PARTNERSHIP INSOLVENCY vol 16 (2011) PARAS 24–25.
8   Ie under the Insolvency Act 1986 Pt 8: see PARA 43 et seq.
9   Ie in the case of a deceased individual to the administration of whose estate the Insolvency
    Act 1986 s 388 applies by virtue of an order under s 421: see PARA 830 et seq. In the case of the
    administration in bankruptcy of the insolvent estate of a deceased person dying before the
    presentation of a bankruptcy petition, s 388 applies: Administration of Insolvent Estates of
    Deceased Persons Order 1986, SI 1986/1999, art 3(1), Sch 1 Pt II para 36. As to the
    administration in bankruptcy of the insolvent estates of deceased debtors see further PARA 830 et
    seq.
10 Insolvency Act 1986 s 388(2) (amended by the Insolvency Act 2000 ss 4(1), (2)(b)). Nothing in
    the Insolvency Act 1986 s 388 applies to anything done by the official receiver (see PARA 35 et
    seq) (s 388(5)(a) (substituted by the Bankruptcy (Scotland) Act 1993 s 11(1))); nor to anything
    done in relation to insolvency proceedings under Council Regulation (EC) 1346/2000 (OJ L160,
    30.6.2000, p 1) on insolvency proceedings ('European Regulation on Insolvency Proceedings') in
    a member state other than the United Kingdom (Insolvency Act 1986 s 388(6) (added by
    SI 2002/1240)). As to the European Regulation on Insolvency Proceedings see PARAS 41, 42.
    'United Kingdom' means Great Britain and Northern Ireland: Interpretation Act 1978 s 5, Sch 1.
11 See the Insolvency Act 1986 s 392; and COMPANY AND PARTNERSHIP INSOLVENCY vol 16 (2011)
    PARA 16.
12 See the Insolvency Act 1986 s 393; and COMPANY AND PARTNERSHIP INSOLVENCY vol 16 (2011)
    PARA 17.
13 See the Insolvency Act 1986 s 394; and COMPANY AND PARTNERSHIP INSOLVENCY vol 16 (2011)
    PARA 32.
14 See the Insolvency Act 1986 ss 395, 396; and COMPANY AND PARTNERSHIP INSOLVENCY vol 16
    (2011) PARA 33 et seq. As to refusal or withdrawal without reference to the Tribunal see s 398;
    and COMPANY AND PARTNERSHIP INSOLVENCY vol 16 (2011) PARA 49.
15 See the Insolvency Act 1986 s 397; and COMPANY AND PARTNERSHIP INSOLVENCY vol 16 (2011)
    PARA 48.
16 See the Insolvency Practitioner Regulations 2005, SI 2005/524, Pt 4 (rr 13–17); and COMPANY
    AND PARTNERSHIP INSOLVENCY vol 16 (2011) PARAS 50–57.
17 As to the meaning of 'office-holder' see PARA 20 note 7.
18 See the Insolvency Rules 1986, SI 1986/1925, rr 7.10A–7.10D; and COMPANY AND
    PARTNERSHIP INSOLVENCY vol 17 (2011) PARA 1064, 1065. An application for a block transfer
    order may be made to the registrar or district judge for: (1) the transfer to the High Court of the
    cases specified in the schedule to the application; (2) the transfer of the cases back to the court
    from which they were transferred when a replacement office-holder has been appointed; (3) the
    removal of the outgoing office-holder by the exercise of powers under the Insolvency Act 1986
    s 298 (see PARA 363), the Insolvency Rules 1986, SI 1986/1925, r 7.10B(2) (see PARA 377) or the
    Insolvency Act 1986 s 263(5) (see PARA 76); (4) the appointment of a replacement office-holder
    by the exercise of any powers under s 298 (see PARA 363), s 303(2) (see PARA 342) or the
    Insolvency Rules 1986, SI 1986/1925, r 7.10B(2) (see PARA 377); and (5) such other order or
    direction as may be necessary or expedient in connection with any of the matters referred to
    above: r 7.10C(1)–(3) (added by SI 2010/686).

3. EUROPEAN REGULATION ON INSOLVENCY PROCEEDINGS

41. Introduction and scope. The European Regulation on Insolvency Proceedings[1] governs, between member states of the European Union (except Denmark)[2], matters of jurisdiction in relation to opening cross-border insolvency proceedings and judgments arising therefrom, and the recognition and enforcement of such judgments[3]. It also harmonises, to the extent that it applies, the law applicable to insolvency proceedings in member states[4], replacing (within its scope) the national rules of private international law. However, it does not provide uniform rules for the grounds on which insolvency proceedings may be opened in the individual member states; nor does it seek to harmonise or affect national insolvency rules and procedures, which continue to apply[5].

The European Regulation on Insolvency Proceedings applies to collective insolvency proceedings which entail the partial or total divestment of a debtor[6] and the appointment of a liquidator[7]. As regards the United Kingdom, insolvency proceedings for this purpose include winding up by or subject to the supervision of the court[8], creditors' voluntary winding up (with confirmation by the court)[9], administration[10], voluntary arrangements under insolvency legislation[11] and bankruptcy[12]. The European Regulation applies to both company and individual insolvency and the provisions are set out in detail elsewhere in this work[13].

1　Ie Council Regulation (EC) 1346/2000 (OJ L160, 30.6.2000, p 1) on insolvency proceedings. As to the history of the Regulation and its application to member states see further COMPANY AND PARTNERSHIP INSOLVENCY vol 16 (2011) PARA 58. A proposal has been made to amend the Regulation (see the Proposal for a Regulation of the European parliament and of the Council amending Council Regulation (EC) 1346/2000 on insolvency proceedings (2012/0360)) to which the United Kingdom has opted in (see HC Official Report (6th series), 15 April 2013, written ministerial statement col 1WS).

2　Denmark is not bound by or subject to the European Regulation on Insolvency Proceedings: Recital 33. In relation to the Regulation, the term 'member state' must be construed accordingly.

3　See the European Regulation on Insolvency Proceedings Recital 6.

4　See the European Regulation on Insolvency Proceedings Recital 23.

5　As to the national rules that apply to English proceedings see CONFLICT OF LAWS vol 19 (2011) PARA 774.

6　The European Regulation on Insolvency Proceedings applies to insolvency proceedings whether the debtor is a natural person or a legal person, a trader or an individual: Recital 9. This is to say that the Regulation applies to individual cross-border insolvency proceedings (bankruptcy and individual voluntary arrangements) as well as to corporate cross-border insolvency proceedings.

7　European Regulation on Insolvency Proceedings art 1.1. 'Liquidator' means any person or body whose function is to administer or liquidate assets of which the debtor has been divested or to supervise the administration of his affairs, and include, in the case of the United Kingdom, a supervisor of a voluntary arrangement, an official receiver and a trustee: European Regulation on Insolvency Proceedings art 2(b), Annex C. As to the powers and duties of the liquidator as so defined see COMPANY AND PARTNERSHIP INSOLVENCY vol 16 (2011) PARAS 67–69.

8　As to winding up see COMPANY AND PARTNERSHIP INSOLVENCY vol 16 (2011) PARA 386 et seq.

9　As to creditors' voluntary winding up see COMPANY AND PARTNERSHIP INSOLVENCY vol 17 (2011) PARA 904 et seq.

10　As to administration see COMPANY AND PARTNERSHIP INSOLVENCY vol 16 (2011) PARA 158 et seq.

11　As to company voluntary arrangements see COMPANY AND PARTNERSHIP INSOLVENCY vol 16 (2011) PARA 83 et seq. As to individual voluntary arrangements see PARA 43 et seq. A member state liquidator may apply to the court for conversion under the European Regulation on Insolvency Proceedings art 37 of a voluntary arrangement into a bankruptcy and must comply with the Insolvency Rules 1986, SI 1986/1925, rr 5.62–5.65 (added by SI 2003/1730; and amended by SI 2010/686). As to bankruptcy see PARA 129 et seq.

12 European Regulation on Insolvency Proceedings art 2(a). Annex A.
13 See COMPANY AND PARTNERSHIP INSOLVENCY vol 16 (2011) PARAS 58–82.

42.   Proceedings.   The European Regulation on Insolvency Proceedings[1] applies only to proceedings where the centre of the debtor's main interests[2] is located in a member state[3]. Insolvency proceedings[4] may be opened only in the courts[5] of the member state where the centre of a debtor's main interests is situated[6]. These proceedings are known as 'main proceedings' because they have universal scope and aim at encompassing all the debtor's assets[7]. Where the centre of a debtor's interests is situated in a member state, the courts of another member state have jurisdiction to open insolvency proceedings against a debtor only if he possesses an establishment within the territory of that other member state[8]. However, the effect of such proceedings is limited to those assets of the debtor which are situated in territory of the latter member state[9] and, where such proceedings are opened at a time when main proceedings have been opened, they are known as 'secondary proceedings' and must, in the case of individual insolvency proceedings in England and Wales, be bankruptcy proceedings[10].

In general, the law applicable to insolvency proceedings is that of the member state within whose territory such proceedings are opened and that law determines all the effects of the insolvency proceedings both procedural and substantive on the persons and legal relations concerned[11]. The Regulation does, however, specify conflict of laws rules on a number of specific insolvency-related issues[12].

The Regulation provides for mutual recognition of judgments relating to insolvency proceedings[13].

1   Ie Council Regulation (EC) 1346/2000 (OJ L160, 30.6.2000, p 1) on insolvency proceedings. See PARA 41.
2   As to the meaning of 'centre of main interests' see COMPANY AND PARTNERSHIP INSOLVENCY vol 16 (2011) PARA 59. See also Case C-396/09 *Interedil Srl v Fallimento Interedil Srl* [2012] Bus LR 1582, [2011] BPIR 1639, [2011] All ER (D) 195 (Oct). A debtor's centre of main interest falls to be determined at the date of the presentation of a bankruptcy petition rather than the date, if different, on which the petition is heard: *O'Donnell v Governor and Company of the Bank of Ireland* [2012] EWHC 3749 (Ch), [2013] NLJR 21, [2012] All ER (D) 257 (Dec). In cases where an individual has recently purported to change his centre of main interest to the United Kingdom, the court will carefully scrutinise the facts where the change appears to have been made for the purposes of forum shopping in order to ensure that the change has the necessary degree of permanence having regard to objective factors ascertainable by third parties, and if this is not established the court will dismiss the bankruptcy petition or, if already made, will annul the bankruptcy order: see *O'Donnell v Governor and Company of the Bank of Ireland*; *Die Sparkasse Bremen Ag v Armutcu* [2012] EWHC 4026 (Ch), [2013] BPIR 210; *Sparkasse Hilden Ratingen Verlbert v Benk* [2012] EWHC 2432 (Ch), [2012] BPIR 1258, [2012] All ER (D) 88 (Sep); *Irish Bank Resolution Corp Ltd v Quinn* [2012] BPIR 322; *Sparkasse Hannover v Korffer* [2011] BPIR 768. In a postscript to his judgment in *Re Eichler (a bankrupt) (No 2)* [2011] BPIR 1293, the Chief Bankruptcy Registrar stated that in the light of persistent abuse of the court's jurisdiction the bankruptcy court had developed the following practices when dealing with petitions where it had doubt about its jurisdiction: (1) before a bankruptcy order is made, a debtor may be required to file more detailed evidence than is required by the Insolvency Rules 1986, SI 1986/1925, r 6.38 (see PARA 192) and r 6.41 (see PARA 194) in order to establish that his centre of main interests is in England and Wales, exhibiting documentary evidence in support; (2) before making a bankruptcy order, the court may adjourn the petition and require that notice of the hearing be given to the debtor's creditors so that they may appear and make representations in opposition to the petition rather than have to apply after the order is made.
3   European Regulation on Insolvency Proceedings Recital 14. See PARA 41 note 2.
4   See PARA 41 text to notes 8–12.
5   'Court' means the judicial body or any other competent body of a member state empowered by national law to open insolvency proceedings or to take decisions in the course of such

proceedings: European Regulation on Insolvency Proceedings art 2(d). The expression should be given a broad meaning because the proceedings do not necessarily involve the intervention of a judicial authority: see Recital 10.

6 European Regulation on Insolvency Proceedings art 3.1. As to the debtor's centre of main interests see note 2.

7 European Regulation on Insolvency Proceedings Recital 12.

8 European Regulation on Insolvency Proceedings arts 3.2, 27. 'Establishment' is defined as 'any place of operations where the debtor carries out a non-transitory economic activity with human means and goods': art 2(h). See further COMPANY AND PARTNERSHIP INSOLVENCY vol 16 (2011) PARA 60. See also Case C-396/09 *Interedil Srl v Fallimento Interedil Srl* [2012] Bus LR 1582, [2011] BPIR 1639, [2011] All ER (D) 195 (Oct); *Re Olympic Airlines SA* [2013] EWCA Civ 643, [2013] 2 BCLC 171, [2013] All ER (D) 39 (Jun).

9 European Regulation on Insolvency Proceedings art 3.2.

10 European Regulation on Insolvency Proceedings arts 2(c), 3.3, Annex B. As to secondary proceedings see COMPANY AND PARTNERSHIP INSOLVENCY vol 16 (2011) PARAS 62–66. Territorial proceedings (namely, for individual insolvency proceedings in England and Wales, individual voluntary arrangements and bankruptcy) may be opened in a member state where the debtor has an establishment before the opening of main proceedings, but there are restrictions: see art 3.4; and COMPANY AND PARTNERSHIP INSOLVENCY vol 16 (2011) PARA 61. Once main proceedings are opened, the territorial proceedings become secondary proceedings and the courts with jurisdiction in the territorial proceedings may, at the instance of the liquidator in the main proceedings, convert, in the case of territorial proceedings in England and Wales relating to an individual, an individual voluntary arrangement into bankruptcy proceedings: European Regulation on Insolvency Proceedings art 37; Insolvency Rules 1986, SI 1986/1925, rr 5.62–5.64 (see PARA 41 note 11).

As to the co-ordination of proceedings see COMPANY AND PARTNERSHIP INSOLVENCY vol 16 (2011) PARA 61. As to the rights, powers and duties of liquidators (see PARA 41 note 7) and their role in coordinating proceedings, see COMPANY AND PARTNERSHIP INSOLVENCY vol 16 (2011) PARAS 67, 68. For the purposes of certain specified rules in the Insolvency Rules 1986, SI 1986/1925, a member state liquidator is deemed to be a creditor in connection with the giving of notices and providing copies of documents to member state liquidators, and their rights of participation in individual insolvency proceedings: see rr 6.238, 6.239 (both added by SI 2002/1307; the Insolvency Rules 1986, SI 1986/1925, r 6.238 amended by SI 2010/686).

Where a member state liquidator has been appointed in relation to the bankrupt, a member state liquidator is deemed to be a creditor for the purposes of the following provisions of the Insolvency Rules 1986, SI 1986/1925: r 6.73(1) (duty of official receiver: see PARA 253), r 6.75(1) (report of official receiver: see PARA 254), r 6.76(2) (report of official receiver: see PARA 255), r 6.79(2) (creditors' meeting: see PARAS 262, 263), r 6.81 (power to call creditors' meeting: see PARA 266), r 6.83 (requisitioned meetings: see PARA 269), r 6.93 (entitlement to vote: see PARA 286), r 6.94 (admission and rejection of proof: see PARAS 286, 287), r 6.96 (meaning of 'prove': see PARA 544), r 6.97 (supply of forms: see PARA 545), r 6.98 (contents of proof: see PARA 546), r 6.100 (cost of proving: see PARA 547), r 6.101 (inspection of proofs: see PARA 548), r 6.104 (admission and rejection of proofs for dividend: see PARA 550), r 6.105(1) (appeal against decision on proof: see PARA 551), rr 6.105(2), 6.106 (withdrawal or variation of proofs: see PARAS 551, 552), r 6.107(1) (expunging of proof: see PARA 553), r 6.108 (negotiable instruments etc: see PARA 585), r 6.109 (secured creditors: see PARA 575), r 6.110 (discounts: see PARA 556), r 6.111 (debts in foreign currency: see PARA 557), r 6.112 (payments of a periodical nature: see PARA 558), r 6.113 (interest: see PARA 559), r 6.114 (debt payable at future time: see PARA 560), r 6.126(1) (resignation of trustee: see PARA 358), r 6.136(1) (release of official receiver: see PARA 380), r 6.137(1) (final meeting: see PARA 381), r 6.142(1) (challenge to remuneration: see PARA 353), r 6.150(2) (creditors' committee: see PARA 327), r 6.160(3) (vacancy on creditors' committee: see PARA 340), r 6.172(3) (request for public examination: see PARA 291), r 6.212(1) (notice of annulment: see PARA 630) and r 6.217(3) (application by bankrupt for discharge: see PARA 643): r 6.238(1)–(3) (r 6.238 added by SI 2002/1307; the Insolvency Rules 1986, SI 1986/1925, r 6.238(3) amended by SI 2010/686). The Insolvency Rules 1986, SI 1986/1925, r 6.238(2), (3) are without prejudice to the generality of the right to participate referred to in the European Regulation on Insolvency Proceedings art 32(3) (exercise of creditor's rights): Insolvency Rules 1986, SI 1986/1925, r 6.238(4) (as so added). Without prejudice to the generality of the obligations imposed by the European Regulation on Insolvency Proceedings art 31 (duty to cooperate and communicate information), where the trustee is obliged to give notice to, or provide a copy of a document (including an order of court) to, the court or the official receiver, the trustee must give notice or provide copies, as the case may be, to the member state liquidator: Insolvency Rules 1986, SI 1986/1925, r 6.238(5), (6) (as so added).

In addition to r 6.238, where a member state liquidator has been appointed in main proceedings in relation to the bankrupt, the member state liquidator is deemed to be a creditor for the purposes of the following rules: r 6.18(3) (hearing of petition: see PARA 178), r 6.23(1) (notice of intention to appear: see PARA 180), r 6.28(4) (extension of time: see PARA 183), r 6.30(2) (substitution of petitioner: see PARA 185), r 6.31(1) (change of carriage of petition: see PARA 186) and r 6.218(4) (report of official receiver: see PARA 644): r 6.239(1)–(3) (r 6.239 added by SI 2002/1307). This is without prejudice to the generality of the right to participate referred to in the European Regulation on Insolvency Proceedings art 32 (exercise of creditor's rights): Insolvency Rules 1986, SI 1986/1925, r 6.239(4) (as so added).

11 See the European Regulation on Insolvency Proceedings art 4.1; and COMPANY AND PARTNERSHIP INSOLVENCY vol 16 (2011) PARA 70. As to the application of domestic law to the distribution of assets in secondary proceedings in England, see also *Re Alitalia Linee Aeree Italiane SpA* [2011] EWHC 15 (Ch), [2011] 1 WLR 2049, [2011] Bus LR 926.

12 See the European Regulation on Insolvency Proceedings arts 5–15; and COMPANY AND PARTNERSHIP INSOLVENCY vol 16 (2011) PARAS 71–81. In particular, the rights in rem of creditors and third parties in respect of assets belonging to the debtor are not affected: see art 5; and COMPANY AND PARTNERSHIP INSOLVENCY vol 16 (2011) PARA 72.

13 See the European Regulation on Insolvency Proceedings arts 16–26; and COMPANY AND PARTNERSHIP INSOLVENCY vol 16 (2011) PARA 82.

4. INDIVIDUAL VOLUNTARY ARRANGEMENTS

(1) THE PROPOSAL

43. Meaning of 'voluntary arrangement'; 'the proposal'; 'the nominee'; and 'the supervisor'. A voluntary arrangement under the Insolvency Act 1986[1] is a composition[2] in satisfaction of an individual's debts or a scheme of arrangement[3] of his affairs[4]. For the purposes of the provisions relating to voluntary arrangements[5], a proposal is a proposal to an individual's creditors which provides for some person ('the nominee') to act in relation to the voluntary arrangement either as trustee or otherwise for the purpose of supervising its implementation[6]. Once a voluntary arrangement is approved and takes effect, the person supervising its implementation is known as 'the supervisor' of the voluntary arrangement[7].

1   Ie under the Insolvency Act 1986 Pt 8 (ss 252–263G): see PARA 44 et seq.
2   A composition is an agreement between the compounding debtor and all or some of his creditors by which the compounding creditors agree with the debtor, and, expressly or impliedly, with each other, to accept from the debtor payment of less than the amounts due to them in full satisfaction of the whole of their claims: *Re Bradley-Hole (a bankrupt)* [1995] 4 All ER 865 at 886, [1995] 1 WLR 1097 at 1118, 1119. See also *March Estates plc v Gunmark Ltd* [1996] 2 BCLC 1 at 5, [1996] BPIR 439 at 442, 443; *Re Hatton* (1872) 7 Ch App 723 at 726; *Slater v Jones, Capes v Ball* (1873) LR 8 Exch 186 at 193, 194; *Re Griffith* (1886) 3 Morr 111 at 116.
3   A scheme of arrangement does not necessarily involve any compromise or release and this is particularly so for a scheme of arrangement which provides for a moratorium: *March Estates plc v Gunmark Ltd* [1996] 2 BCLC 1, [1996] BPIR 439. A scheme may take any form acceptable to the parties provided there is the necessary element of give and take (see *IRC v Adam & Partners Ltd* [2001] 1 BCLC 222, [2000] BPIR 986, CA); but the usual method is by assignment by the debtor of his property to a trustee for realisation and distribution of the proceeds of sale amongst the creditors rateably or in such proportion as they agree. Where the central proposal does not constitute an arrangement within the meaning of the statute, it cannot be remedied by a modification proposal before the meeting of creditors: *IRC v Bland* [2003] EWHC 1068 (Ch), [2003] BPIR 1274. As to the creditors' meeting see PARA 62 et seq. As to remote attendance at meetings see PARA 267. For the purposes of the provisions relating to voluntary arrangements, 'creditors' is not restricted to those persons who would have claims provable in the bankruptcy: see *Re T & N Ltd* [2005] EWHC 2870 (Ch), [2006] 3 All ER 697, [2006] 1 WLR 1728 (a case covering a company voluntary arrangement); c f *Child Maintenance and Enforcement Commission v Beesley* [2010] EWCA Civ 1344, [2011] 3 All ER 233, [2011] 1 WLR 1704. As to the position of student loans see the Education (Student Loans) (Repayment) Regulations 2009, SI 2009/470, reg 80; and EDUCATION vol 36 (2011) PARA 1249.
4   Insolvency Act 1986 s 253(1) (amended by the Insolvency Act 2000 Sch 3 paras 1, 3(a)). References in the Insolvency Act 1986 Pts 8–11 (ss 252–385) to a person's affairs include his business, if any: s 385(2). For these purposes, except in so far as the context otherwise requires, 'business' includes a trade or profession: s 436 (amended by the Tribunals, Courts and Enforcement Act 2007 Sch 13 para 85; SI 2002/1037; SI 2005/879; SI 2007/2194; and SI 2009/1941). As to the application of the Insolvency Act 1986 s 385 in the case of the administration in bankruptcy of the insolvent estate of a deceased person dying before the presentation of a bankruptcy petition see PARA 6 note 8.
    Where insolvency orders are made against an insolvent partnership and an insolvent member of that partnership in his capacity as such, an individual member of that partnership may be the subject of a voluntary arrangement under the Insolvency Act 1986 Pt 8 (ss 252–263G): see the Insolvent Partnerships Order 1994, SI 1994/2421, art 5; and COMPANY AND PARTNERSHIP INSOLVENCY vol 17 (2011) PARA 1234.
5   See note 1.
6   Insolvency Act 1986 s 253(1), (2) (s 253(1) as amended (see note 4); s 253(2) amended by the Insolvency Act 1986 Sch 3 paras 1, 3(b)). The nominee must be a person who is qualified to act as an insolvency practitioner, or authorised to act as nominee, in relation to the voluntary arrangement: s 253(2) (as so amended).
    The Insolvency Rules 1986, SI 1986/1925, Pt 5 (rr 5.1–5.68) (see PARA 46 et seq) apply in relation to a voluntary arrangement, except in relation to voluntary arrangements under the

Insolvency Act 1986 s 263A (see PARA 90), in relation to which only the Insolvency Rules 1986, SI 1986/1925, Pt 5 Chs 7, 10–14 (rr 5.35–5.50, 5.57–5.67) apply: r 5.1(1) (substituted by SI 2002/2712; and amended by SI 2003/1730; and SI 2010/686).

7   See the Insolvency Act 1986 s 263(2); and PARA 73 et seq.

44.   Who may propose an arrangement; false representations.   A proposal for a voluntary arrangement[1] may be made by the debtor[2]. If, for the purpose of obtaining the approval of his creditors to a proposal for a voluntary arrangement, the debtor makes any false representation or fraudulently does, or omits to do, anything, then, even if the proposal is not approved, he commits an offence and is liable on conviction on indictment to imprisonment for a term not exceeding seven years or a fine, or to both, or on summary conviction to imprisonment for a term not exceeding six months or a fine not exceeding the statutory maximum, or to both[3].

1   As to the meaning of 'voluntary arrangement' see PARA 43.
2   Insolvency Act 1986 s 253(1) (amended by the Insolvency Act 2000 Sch 3 paras 1, 3(a)). 'The debtor', in relation to a proposal for the purposes of the Insolvency Act 1986 Pt 8 (ss 252–263G) (see PARAS 43, 45 et seq), means the individual making or intending to make that proposal: s 385(1)(a). As to the application of s 385 in the case of the administration in bankruptcy of the insolvent estate of a deceased person dying before the presentation of a bankruptcy petition see PARA 6 note 8.
3   Insolvency Act 1986 s 262A (added by the Insolvency Act 2000 s 3, Sch 3 paras 1, 12); Insolvency Act 1986 s 430, Sch 10 (amended by the Insolvency Act 2000 Sch 3 paras 1, 16). See also PARA 4.

(2)   INTERIM ORDER

45.   Interim order of court.   In the case of a debtor[1], being an individual, the court may make an interim order[2] which has the effect that, during the period for which it is in force[3]:

(1)   no bankruptcy petition[4] relating to the debtor may be presented or proceeded with[5];

(2)   no landlord or other person to whom rent is payable may exercise any right of forfeiture by peaceable re-entry in relation to premises let to the debtor in respect of a failure by the debtor to comply with any term or condition of his tenancy of such premises, except with the leave of the court[6]; and

(3)   no other proceedings[7], and no execution or other legal process[8], may be commenced or continued and no distress may be levied against the debtor or his property[9] except with the permission of the court[10].

1   As to the meaning of 'debtor' see PARA 44 note 2.
2   Insolvency Act 1986 s 252(1). As to applications for interim orders see PARA 46 et seq.
3   As to the duration of an interim order see PARA 52.
4   As to bankruptcy petitions see PARA 129 et seq.
5   Insolvency Act 1986 s 252(2)(a).
6   Insolvency Act 1986 s 252(2)(aa) (added by the Insolvency Act 2000 Sch 3 paras 1, 2(a)).
7   'Other proceedings' includes the making of a charging order absolute over a debtor's property: *Clarke v Coutts & Co* [2002] EWCA Civ 943, [2002] BPIR 916, [2002] All ER (D) 98 (Jun).
8   An interim order cannot impede the operation of a confiscation order granted in criminal proceedings (see *R v Barnet Justices, ex p Phillippou* [1997] BPIR 134, DC) or an application to court by the prosecutor under the Drug Trafficking Act 1994 s 26(7) for the appointment of a receiver of the realisable property of a person against whom criminal proceedings have been instituted (*Re M (Restraint Order)* [1992] QB 377, [1992] 1 All ER 537); cf *Re Rhondda Waste Disposal Ltd* [2001] Ch 57, [2000] 3 WLR 1304, CA. See also *Smith (a bankrupt) v Braintree District Council* [1990] 2 AC 215, [1989] 3 All ER 897, HL.

9   As to the meaning of 'property' see PARA 412.

10   Insolvency Act 1986 s 252(2)(b) (amended by the Insolvency Act 2000 Sch 3 paras 1, 2(b)). The High Court is not excluded from exercising its jurisdiction to give permission to bring proceedings pursuant to the Insolvency Act 1986 s 252 by the county court having made an interim order in insolvency proceedings: *Hall v Van der Heiden* [2010] EWHC 537 (TCC), [2010] BPIR 585, [2010] All ER (D) 237 (Oct).

46.   Application for interim order.   Application to the court for an interim order may be made where the debtor[1] intends to make a proposal[2] to his creditors for a composition in satisfaction of his debts or a scheme of arrangement of his affairs[3]. Except in the case of an undischarged bankrupt[4], an application to the court must be so made to a court in which the debtor would be entitled to present his own petition in bankruptcy[5]. The application must contain sufficient information to establish that it is brought in the appropriate court[6]; and, in the case of an undischarged bankrupt, such an application must be made in the court having the conduct of his bankruptcy and must be filed with those bankruptcy proceedings[7]. The application may be made:

(1)   if the debtor is an undischarged bankrupt, by the debtor, the trustee[8] of his estate[9] or the official receiver[10]; and

(2)   in any other case, by the debtor[11];

but an application may not be made under head (1) above unless the debtor has given notice of the proposal to the official receiver and, if there is one, the trustee of his estate[12].

An application may not be made while a bankruptcy petition presented by the debtor is pending, if the court has appointed an insolvency practitioner[13] to inquire into the debtor's affairs[14] and report[15].

An application to the court for an interim order must be accompanied by a witness statement of the following matters:

(a)   the reasons for making the application;

(b)   particulars of any execution or other legal process or levying of any distress which, to the debtor's knowledge, has been commenced against him;

(c)   that he is an undischarged bankrupt or, as the case may be, that he is able to petition for his own bankruptcy;

(d)   that no previous application for an interim order has been made by or in respect of the debtor in the period of 12 months ending with the date of the witness statement;

(e)   that the nominee[16] under the proposal, naming him, is willing to act in relation to the proposal and is a person who is either qualified to act as an insolvency practitioner in relation to the debtor or is authorised to act as nominee in relation to him; and

(f)   whether the debtor has submitted to the official receiver either a document setting out the terms of the voluntary arrangement[17] or a statement of his affairs[18] and, if so, when and with what result[19].

A copy of the notice to the intended nominee[20], indorsed to the effect that he agrees so to act, and a copy of the debtor's proposal given to the nominee, must be attached to the witness statement[21].

On receiving the application and the witness statement, the court must fix a venue[22] for the hearing of the application[23]; and the applicant must give at least two business days'[24] notice of the hearing:

(i)   where the debtor is an undischarged bankrupt, to the bankrupt, the official receiver and the trustee, whichever of those three is not himself the applicant;

(ii)   where the debtor is not an undischarged bankrupt, to any creditor who, to the debtor's knowledge, has presented a bankruptcy petition against him; and

(iii)   in either case, to the nominee who has agreed to act in relation to the debtor's proposal[25].

1   As to the meaning of 'debtor' see PARA 44 note 2.
2   Ie under the Insolvency Act 1986 Pt 8 (ss 252–263G): see PARAS 43–45, 47 et seq.
3   Insolvency Act 1986 s 253(1) (amended by the Insolvency Act 2000 Sch 3 paras 1, 3(a)); see also PARA 43.
4   As to the meaning of 'bankrupt' see PARA 129. As to discharge from bankruptcy see PARA 638 et seq. In the case of the administration in bankruptcy of the insolvent estate of a deceased person dying before the presentation of a bankruptcy petition, s 381 applies: Administration of Insolvent Estates of Deceased Persons Order 1986, SI 1986/1999, art 3(1), Sch 1 Pt II para 30. As to the administration in bankruptcy of the insolvent estates of deceased persons see further PARA 830 et seq.
5   Insolvency Rules 1986, SI 1986/1925, r 5.8(1) (r 5.8 substituted by SI 2002/2712; Insolvency Rules 1986, SI 1985/1925, r 5.8(1) amended by SI 2010/686). A debtor's petition may be presented to the court only on the grounds that the debtor is unable to pay his debts: see the Insolvency Act 1986 s 272(1); and PARA 163.
6   Insolvency Rules 1986, SI 1986/1925, r 5.8(2) (as substituted: see note 5).
7   Insolvency Rules 1986, SI 1986/1925, r 5.8(3) (as substituted: see note 5).
8   As to the trustee see PARA 314 et seq.
9   For these purposes, 'estate', in relation to a bankrupt, is to be construed in accordance with the Insolvency Act 1986 s 283 (see PARA 211): s 385(1). As to the application of s 385 in the case of the administration in bankruptcy of the insolvent estate of a deceased person dying before the presentation of a bankruptcy petition see PARA 6 note 8.
10   As to the official receiver see PARA 35 et seq.
11   Insolvency Act 1986 s 253(3).
12   Insolvency Act 1986 s 253(4) (amended by the Insolvency Act 2000 Sch 3 paras 1, 3(c)).
13   Ie under the Insolvency Act 1986 s 273: see PARA 203. As to insolvency practitioners and their qualification see PARA 40; but see also PARA 43 note 6.
14   As to the meaning of references to a person's affairs see PARA 43 note 4.
15   Insolvency Act 1986 s 253(5). As from a day to be appointed s 253(5) is repealed by the Enterprise and Regulatory Reform Act 2013 s 71, Sch 19 paras 1, 2. At the date at which this volume states the law no such day had been appointed. As to the changes proposed by the Enterprise and Regulatory Reform Act 2013 see PARA 130.
16   As to the meaning of 'nominee' see PARA 43.
17   As to the meaning of 'voluntary arrangement' see PARA 43.
18   Ie the documents referred to in the Insolvency Act 1986 s 263B(1); see PARA 90.
19   Insolvency Rules 1986, SI 1986/1925, r 5.7(1) (r 5.7 substituted by SI 2002/2712; Insolvency Rules 1986, SI 1985/1925, r 5.7(1) amended by SI 2003/1730; and SI 2010/686).
20   Ie under the Insolvency Rules 1986, SI 1986/1925, r 5.4; see PARA 54.
21   Insolvency Rules 1986, SI 1986/1925, r 5.7(2) (r 5.7 as substituted (see note 19); r 5.7(2) amended by SI 2010/686).
22   For these purposes, references to the venue for any proceeding or attendance before the court, or for a meeting, are to the time, date and place for the proceeding, attendance or meeting or to the time and date for a meeting held in accordance with the Insolvency Act 1986 s 379A (see PARA 267) without any place being specified for it: Insolvency Rules 1986, SI 1986/1925, rr 13.1, 13.6 (r 13.6 amended by SI 2010/686).
23   Insolvency Rules 1986, SI 1986/1925, r 5.7(3) (r 5.7 as substituted (see note 19); r 5.7(3) amended by SI 2010/686).
24   As to the meaning of 'business day' see PARA 28 note 8.
25   Insolvency Rules 1986, SI 1986/1925, r 5.7(4) (r 5.7 as substituted (see note 19); r 5.7(4) amended by SI 2010/686).

47. Effect of application for interim order. At any time when an application for an interim order[1] is pending, no landlord or other person to whom rent is payable may exercise any right of forfeiture by peaceable re-entry in relation to premises let to the debtor[2] in respect of a failure by the debtor to comply with any term or condition of his tenancy of such premises, except with the leave of the court[3], and the court may forbid the levying of any distress on the debtor's property or its subsequent sale, or both, and stay any action, execution or other legal process[4] against the property or person of the debtor[5]. On proof that an application has been so made in respect of that individual, the court may either stay the proceedings or allow them to continue on such terms as it thinks fit[6].

1 Ie under the Insolvency Act 1986 s 253: see PARA 46.
2 As to the meaning of 'debtor' see PARA 44 note 2.
3 Insolvency Act 1986 s 254(1)(a) (amended by the Insolvency Act 2000 Sch 3 paras 1, 4(a)).
4 As to cases on the meaning of 'execution and other legal process' see PARA 45 note 8.
5 Insolvency Act 1986 s 254(1)(b) (amended by the Insolvency Act 2000 Sch 3 paras 1, 4(b)).
6 Insolvency Act 1986 s 254(2).

48. Cases in which interim order may be made. The court may not make an interim order on an application under the statutory provisions[1] unless it is satisfied:

(1) that the debtor[2] intends to make a proposal for a voluntary arrangement[3];

(2) that, on the day of the making of the application, the debtor was an undischarged bankrupt[4] or was able to petition for his own bankruptcy[5];

(3) that no previous application has been made by the debtor for an interim order in the period of 12 months ending with that day[6]; and

(4) that the nominee[7] under the debtor's proposal is willing to act in relation to the proposal[8].

The court may make an order if it thinks that it would be appropriate to do so for the purpose of facilitating the consideration and implementation of the debtor's proposal[9]; and, where the debtor is an undischarged bankrupt, the interim order may contain provision as to the conduct of the bankruptcy and the administration of the bankrupt's estate[10], during the period for which the order is in force[11]. An interim order may not, however, in relation to a bankrupt, make provision relaxing or removing any of the statutory requirements[12] unless the court is satisfied that that provision is unlikely to result in any significant diminution in, or in the value of, the debtor's estate for the purpose of the bankruptcy[13].

Subject to the statutory provisions[14], an interim order[15] ceases to have effect at the end of the period of 14 days beginning with the day after the making of the order[16].

1 Ie under the Insolvency Act 1986 s 253: see PARA 46.
2 As to the meaning of 'debtor' see PARA 44 note 2.
3 Insolvency Act 1986 s 255(1)(a) (amended by the Insolvency Act 2000 Sch 3 paras 1, 5(a)). As to proposals for a voluntary arrangement see PARA 53 et seq.
4 As to the meaning of 'bankrupt' see PARA 129. As to discharge from bankruptcy see PARA 638 et seq.
5 Insolvency Act 1986 s 255(1)(b). A debtor's petition may be presented to the court only on the grounds that the debtor is unable to pay his debts: see s 272(1); and PARA 163. As from a day to be appointed, in s 255(1)(b) the words 'petition for his own bankruptcy' are replaced with 'make a bankruptcy application' by the Enterprise and Regulatory Reform Act 2013 s 71, Sch 19 paras 1, 3. At the date at which this volume states the law no such day had been appointed. As to the changes proposed by the Enterprise and Regulatory Reform Act 2013 see PARA 130.

6 Insolvency Act 1986 s 255(1)(c). It is not proper to use the jurisdiction to review under s 375 (see PARA 761) to circumvent the prohibition in s 255(1)(c) against second applications for an interim order within a 12-month period: *Hurst v Bennett (No 2)* [2002] BPIR 102.

7 As to the meaning of 'nominee' see PARA 43.

8 Insolvency Act 1986 s 255(1)(d) (amended by the Insolvency Act 2000 Sch 3 paras 1, 5(b), Sch 5).

9 Insolvency Act 1986 s 255(2). The exercise of the court's discretion under s 255(2) depends on whether the debtor's proposal is 'serious and viable': *Hook v Jewson Ltd* [1997] 1 BCLC 664, [1997] BPIR 100; and see *Re a Debtor (No 103 of 1994), Cooper v Fearnley* [1997] BPIR 20; *Davidson v Stanley* [2004] EWHC 2595 (Ch), [2005] BPIR 279, [2004] All ER (D) 441 (Oct); *Hurst v BDO Stoy Hayward LLP* [2006] EWHC 791 (Ch), [2006] BPIR 960, [2006] All ER (D) 104 (Apr). The court will not conduct a 'mini-trial' to assess whether the debtor's proposal is serious and viable but will leave it to the creditors to assess the position: *Shah v Cooper* [2003] BPIR 1018. The fact that the returns on a voluntary arrangement might be small is not, in itself, a good reason for dismissing the application for an interim order out of hand: *Knowles v Coutts & Co* [1998] BPIR 96. The court may refuse to make an interim order where the size of the nominee's fee is excessive: *Re Julie O'Sullivan* [2001] BPIR 534; and see *IRC v Adam & Partners Ltd* [2001] 1 BCLC 222, [2000] BPIR 986, CA; *Cadbury Schweppes plc v Somji* [2001] 1 WLR 615, sub nom *Somji v Cadbury Schweppes plc* [2001] 1 BCLC 498, CA (there is a requirement of good faith as between competing unsecured creditors and, therefore, secret deals or inducements to one or more creditors to vote in favour of a proposal are prohibited). As to the meaning of 'secured creditor' see PARA 574.

10 As to the meaning of 'estate' see PARA 46 note 9.

11 Insolvency Act 1986 s 255(3). Subject to s 255(5), (6) (see text to notes 12–16), the provision contained in an interim order by virtue of s 255(3) may include provision staying proceedings in the bankruptcy or modifying any provision in Pts 8–11 (ss 252–385) and any provision of the Insolvency Rules 1986, SI 1986/1925, in their application to the debtor's bankruptcy: Insolvency Act 1986 s 255(4). The Insolvency Act 1986 s 255(4) is the proper gateway for a bankrupt to seek to suspend his discharge from bankruptcy so as to enable him to put a proposal to his creditors: *Bramston v Haut* [2012] EWCA Civ 1637, [2013] 1 WLR 1720, [2012] All ER (D) 127 (Dec).

12 Ie any provision of the Insolvency Act 1986 Pts 8–11 (ss 252–385) or of the Insolvency Rules 1986, SI 1986/1925.

13 Insolvency Act 1986 s 255(5).

14 Ie the Insolvency Act 1986 ss 256–263G: see PARA 51 et seq.

15 Ie made on application under the Insolvency Act 1986 s 253: see PARA 46.

16 Insolvency Act 1986 s 255(6).

49. Hearing of application for interim order. Any of the persons who have been given notice of the hearing[1] may appear or be represented at the hearing of the application[2]. In deciding whether to make an interim order on the application, the court must take into account any representations made by or on behalf of any of those persons, in particular, whether an order should be made containing provision[3] as to the conduct of the debtor's bankruptcy and the administration of the bankrupt's estate[4]. If the court makes an interim order, it must fix a venue[5] for consideration of the nominee's report[6]; and the date for that consideration must be not later than that on which the interim order ceases[7] to have effect[8]. If, however, an extension of time is granted for filing the nominee's report[9], the court must, unless there appear to be good reasons against it, correspondingly extend the period for which the interim order has effect[10].

1 Ie under the Insolvency Rules 1986, SI 1986/1925, r 5.7(4): see PARA 46.

2 Insolvency Rules 1986, SI 1986/1925, r 5.9(1) (r 5.9 substituted by SI 2002/2712). In suitable cases the court will, as a matter of practice, normally be prepared to make an interim order without the attendance of any party, provided that there is no bankruptcy order in existence and, so far as is known, no pending petition: see *Practice Direction—Insolvency Proceedings* para 16.

3 Ie containing such provision as is referred to in the Insolvency Act 1986 s 255(3), (4): see PARA 48.

4   Insolvency Rules 1986, SI 1986/1925, r 5.9(2) (as substituted: see note 2). As to the meaning of
    'estate' see PARA 46 note 9.
5   As to the meaning of 'venue' see PARA 46 note 22.
6   As to the meaning of 'nominee' see PARA 43; and as to the nominee's report see PARA 57.
7   Ie under the Insolvency Act 1986 s 255(6): see PARA 52.
8   Insolvency Rules 1986, SI 1986/1925, r 5.9(3) (as substituted: see note 2). As to the duration of
    an interim order see PARA 52.
9   Ie under the Insolvency Act 1986 s 256(4): see PARA 58.
10 Insolvency Rules 1986, SI 1986/1925, r 5.9(4) (as substituted: see note 2).

50.   Making of interim order.   Where an interim order is made, at least two
sealed copies of the order must be sent by the court to the person who applied
for it; and that person must serve one of the copies on the nominee[1] under the
debtor's[2] proposal[3]. The applicant must also as soon as reasonably practicable
give notice of the making of the order to any person who was given notice of the
hearing[4] and was not present or represented at it[5].

1   As to the meaning of 'nominee' see PARA 43.
2   As to the meaning of 'debtor' see PARA 44 note 2.
3   Insolvency Rules 1986, SI 1986/1925, r 5.10(1) (r 5.10 substituted by SI 2002/2712). As to the
    prescribed form of interim order see r 5.10, Sch 4 Form 5.2 (r 5.10 as amended; Sch 4 Form 5.2
    amended by SI 2003/1730; SI 2009/642; and SI 2010/686).
4   Ie pursuant to the Insolvency Rules 1986, SI 1986/1925, r 5.7(4): see PARA 46.
5   Insolvency Rules 1986, SI 1986/1925, r 5.10(2) (r 5.10 as substituted (see note 3); r 5.10(2)
    amended by SI 2009/642). If an interim order is not made, there can be no valid voluntary
    arrangement: *Fletcher v Vooght* [2000] BPIR 435.

51.   Procedure where no interim order made.   Where a debtor[1], being an
individual:

(1)   intends to make a proposal for a voluntary arrangement[2], but an
      interim order has not been made[3] in relation to the proposal and no
      application for such an order is pending; and
(2)   if he is an undischarged bankrupt[4], has given notice of the proposal to
      the official receiver[5] and, if there is one, the trustee[6] of his estate,

then, unless a bankruptcy petition presented by the debtor is pending and the
court has appointed an insolvency practitioner[7] to inquire into the debtor's
affairs and report[8], the debtor must, for the purpose of enabling the nominee[9] to
prepare a report[10], submit to the nominee:

(a)   a document setting out the terms of the voluntary arrangement which
      the debtor is proposing; and
(b)   a statement of his affairs containing such particulars of his creditors and
      of his debts and other liabilities and of his assets as may be prescribed,
      and such other information as may be prescribed[11].

If the nominee is of the opinion that the debtor is an undischarged bankrupt,
or is able to petition for his own bankruptcy[12], the nominee must, within 14
days, or such longer period as the court may allow, after receiving the document
mentioned in head (a) above, submit a report to the debtor's creditors stating:

(i)   whether, in his opinion, the voluntary arrangement which the debtor is
       proposing has a reasonable prospect of being approved and
       implemented;
(ii)   whether, in his opinion, a meeting of the debtor's creditors should be
       summoned to consider the debtor's proposal; and
(iii) if, in his opinion, such a meeting should be summoned, the date on
       which, and time and place at which, he proposes the meeting should be
       held[13].

The court may:

(A)   on an application made by the debtor in a case where the nominee has
        failed to submit the report required by these provisions or has died; or

(B)   on an application made by the debtor or the nominee in a case where it
        is impracticable or inappropriate for the nominee to continue to act as
        such,

direct that the nominee is to be replaced as such by another person qualified to
act as an insolvency practitioner, or authorised to act as nominee, in relation to
the voluntary arrangement[14].

The court may, on an application made by the nominee, extend the period
within which the nominee is to submit his report[15].

1   As to the meaning of 'debtor' see PARA 44 note 2.
2   Ie under the Insolvency Act 1986 Pt 8 (ss 252–263G): see PARAS 43–50, 52 et seq.
3   As to the making of interim orders see PARA 45 et seq.
4   As to the meaning of 'bankrupt' see PARA 129. As to discharge from bankruptcy see PARA 638 et
    seq.
5   As to the official receiver see PARA 35 et seq.
6   As to the trustee see PARA 314 et seq.
7   Ie under the Insolvency Act 1986 s 273: see PARA 203. As to insolvency practitioners and their
    qualification see PARA 40; but see also PARA 43 note 6.
8   Insolvency Act 1986 s 256A(1) (s 256A added by the Insolvency Act 2000 Sch 3 paras 1, 7). As
    from a day to be appointed, the words 'unless a bankruptcy petition presented by the debtor is
    pending and the court has appointed an insolvency practitioner to inquire into the debtor's
    affairs and report' are omitted from s 256A(1) by the Enterprise and Regulatory Reform
    Act 2013 s 71, Sch 19 paras 1, 4. At the date at which this volume states the law no such day
    had been appointed. As to the changes proposed by the Enterprise and Regulatory Reform
    Act 2013 see PARA 130.
9   As to the meaning of 'nominee' see PARA 43.
10 Ie under the Insolvency Act 1986 s 256A(3): see text to notes 12, 13.
11 Insolvency Act 1986 s 256A(2) (s 256A as added (see note 8); s 256A(2) amended by
    SI 2010/18).
12 A debtor's petition may be presented to the court only on the grounds that the debtor is unable
    to pay his debts: see the Insolvency Act 1986 s 272(1); and PARA 163.
13 Insolvency Act 1986 s 256A(3) (s 256A as added (see note 8); s 256A(3) amended by
    SI 2010/18). As from a day to be appointed, in the Insolvency Act 1986 s 256A(3) the words
    'petition for his own bankruptcy' are replaced with 'make a bankruptcy application' by the
    Enterprise and Regulatory Reform Act 2013 Sch 19 paras 1, 4. At the date at which this volume
    states the law no such day had been appointed. See note 8.
        If the nominee has the opinions set out in heads (i), (ii) in the text, he must attach to the
    report his comments on the debtor's proposal and deliver within the same timeframe: (1) a copy
    of the report; (2) a copy of the nominee's comments attached to the report; (3) a copy of the
    debtor's proposals, with amendment, if any, authorised under the Insolvency Rules 1986,
    SI 1986/1925, r 5.3(3) (see PARA 53); (4) a copy or summary of any statement of affairs
    provided by the debtor; (5) a copy of the notice referred to in r 5.4(3) (see PARA 54); and (6) a
    statement that no application for an interim order under the Insolvency Act 1986 s 253 (see
    PARA 46) is to be made, to (a) each of the debtor's creditors of whose address the nominee is
    aware; (b) where the debtor is an undischarged bankrupt, the official receiver and the trustee, if
    any; and (c) any person who has presented a bankruptcy petition against the debtor: Insolvency
    Rules 1986, SI 1986/1925, r 5.14A(1), (2)(a), (3), (4) (r 5.14A substituted by SI 2010/686). If
    the nominee does not hold those opinions he must, within the same timeframe as submitting the
    report, deliver a copy of the report to each of the debtor's creditors of whose address he is aware
    and give the reasons for that opinion to the debtor: Insolvency Rules 1986, SI 1986/1925,
    r 5.14A(1), (2)(b), (5) (r 5.14A as so substituted).
        Where a report has been made under the Insolvency Act 1986 s 256A and the debtor is not
    an undischarged bankrupt, any application relating to a voluntary arrangement or a proposal
    for a voluntary arrangement must be filed in the court in which the debtor would be entitled to
    present the debtor's petition in bankruptcy under the Insolvency Rules 1986, SI 1986/1925,
    r 6.40A (see PARA 191): Insolvency Rules 1986, SI 1985/1925, r 5.14B(1) (r 5.14B substituted
    by SI 2010/686). As to the meaning of 'file in court' see PARA 57 note 13. Where the debtor is an
    undischarged bankrupt, the appropriate court is the court having the conduct of the debtor's

bankruptcy and any application must be filed with the bankruptcy proceedings: r 5.14B(2) (as so substituted). The report must contain sufficient information to identify the appropriate court in which to file an application: r 5.14B(3) (as so substituted). Where an application is made to the court in relation to any matter relating to a voluntary arrangement or a proposal for a voluntary arrangement, in addition to the documents in support of the application, the applicant must file in court such other documents required by the Insolvency Rule 1986, SI 1986/1925, Pt 5 (rr 5.1–5.68) as the applicant considers may assist the court in determining the application: r 5.14B(4) (as so substituted).

14 Insolvency Act 1986 s 256A(4) (as added: see note 8). Where the debtor intends to apply for the nominee to be replaced, he must give the nominee at least five business days' notice of the application: Insolvency Rules 1986, SI 1096/1925, r 5.14B(5) (as substituted: see note 13). As to the meaning of 'business day' see PARA 28 note 8. Where the nominee intends to apply to be replaced he must give the debtor at least five business days' notice of the application: r 5.14B(6) (as so substituted). The court must not appoint a replacement nominee unless a statement by the replacement nominee indicating consent to act is filed in court: r 5.14B(7) (as so substituted).

15 Insolvency Act 1986 s 256A(5) (as added: see note 8).

52. Duration of interim order; extension; and discharge.

An interim order[1] ceases to have effect at the end of the period of 14 days beginning with the day after the making of the order[2]. On an application made by the debtor[3] in a case where the nominee[4] has failed to submit a report[5], the court may direct that the interim order is to continue or, if it has ceased to have effect, is to be renewed, for such further period as the court may specify in the direction[6]. On the application of the nominee, the court may extend the period for which the interim order has effect so as to enable the nominee to have more time to prepare his report[7].

If the court is satisfied, on receiving the nominee's report, that a meeting of the debtor's creditors should be summoned to consider the debtor's proposal, the court must direct that the period for which the interim order has effect is to be extended, for such further period as it may specify in the direction, for the purpose of enabling the debtor's proposal to be considered by his creditors[8].

The court may discharge the interim order if it is satisfied, on the application of the nominee, that the debtor has failed to comply with his obligation[9] to submit to the nominee a proposal and statement of affairs or that for any other reason it would be inappropriate for a meeting of the debtor's creditors to be summoned to consider the debtor's proposal[10].

1 Ie an order made on an application under the Insolvency Act 1986 s 253: see PARA 46.
2 Insolvency Act 1986 s 255(6). Section 255(6) is subject to ss 256–263G (see PARA 55 et seq): s 255(6).
3 As to the meaning of 'debtor' see PARA 44 note 2.
4 As to the meaning of 'nominee' see PARA 43.
5 Ie as required by the Insolvency Act 1986 s 256: see PARA 57.
6 Insolvency Act 1986 s 256(3A) (added by the Insolvency Act 2000 Sch 3 paras 1, 6). As to the exercise of the court's jurisdiction to extend the period for which an interim order has effect see *Re Cove (a debtor)* [1990] 1 All ER 949 at 957, sub nom *Re a Debtor (No 83 of 1988)* [1990] 1 WLR 708 at 718.
7 Insolvency Act 1986 s 256(4). As to the nominee's report see PARA 57.
8 Insolvency Act 1986 s 256(5). As to the prescribed form of order extending the effect of an interim order see the Insolvency Rules 1986, SI 1986/1925, Sch 4 Form 5.3 (amended by SI 2002/2712). In suitable cases the court may be prepared to make a 'concertina' order without the attendance of either party, combining a 14-day interim order with a standard order on consideration of the nominee's report, extending the interim order to a date seven weeks after the date of the proposed meeting, directing the meeting to be summoned and adjourning to a date about three weeks after the meeting: see *Practice Direction—Insolvency Proceedings* para 16.1(3). However, the court's role in considering the nominee's report is not merely to rubber stamp the nominee's report recommending that a meeting of creditors be held. The court has to be satisfied that a meeting should be held: *Re a Debtor (No 140 IO of 1995)* [1996] 2 BCLC 429, sub nom *Re a Debtor (No 140 IO of 1995), Greystoke v Hamilton-Smith* [1997]

BPIR 24. Where the court has not yet directed a meeting but it takes place nonetheless, it is invalid: *Vlieland-Boddy v Dexter Ltd* [2003] EWHC 2592 (Ch), [2004] BPIR 235, [2003] All ER (D) 423 (Oct).

9   Ie under the Insolvency Act 1986 s 256(2): see PARA 55.

10   Insolvency Act 1986 s 256(6). The court may refuse to continue the interim order if it is satisfied that the creditors' meeting will serve no useful purpose because there is a strong probability that the debtor will be unable to obtain a majority vote in favour of his proposals: *Re Cove (a debtor)* [1990] 1 All ER 949, sub nom *Re a Debtor (No 83 of 1988)* [1990] 1 WLR 708.

(3) PROCEDURE ON THE PROPOSAL

53.   Preparation and contents of the proposal.   The debtor[1] must prepare for the intended nominee[2] a proposal on which, with or without amendments[3], to make his report[4].

The debtor's proposal must provide a short explanation why, in his opinion, a voluntary arrangement[5] is desirable, and give reasons why his creditors may be expected to concur with such an arrangement[6].

The following matters must be stated, or otherwise dealt with in the proposal[7]:

(1)   the following matters, so far as within the debtor's immediate knowledge:

    (a)   his assets, with an estimate of their respective values;

    (b)   the extent, if any, to which the assets are charged in favour of creditors;

    (c)   the extent, if any, to which particular assets are to be excluded from the voluntary arrangement[8];

(2)   particulars of any property, other than assets of the debtor himself, which is proposed to be included in the arrangement, the source of such property and the terms on which it is to be made available for inclusion[9];

(3)   the nature and amount of the debtor's liabilities, so far as within his immediate knowledge, the manner in which they are proposed to be met, modified, postponed or otherwise dealt with by means of the arrangement and, in particular:

    (a)   how it is proposed to deal with preferential creditors[10] and creditors who are, or claim to be, secured[11];

    (b)   how associates[12] of the debtor, being creditors of his, are proposed to be treated under the arrangement; and

    (c)   where the debtor is an undischarged bankrupt[13], whether, to the debtor's knowledge, claims have been made under the provisions dealing with transactions at an undervalue[14], preferences[15] or extortionate credit transactions[16]; and, where the debtor is not an undischarged bankrupt, whether there are circumstances which would give rise to the possibility of such claims in the event that he should be adjudged bankrupt;

and, where any such circumstances are present, whether, and if so how, it is proposed under the voluntary arrangement to make provision for wholly or partly indemnifying the insolvent estate[17] in respect of such claims[18];

(4)   whether any, and, if so, what, guarantees have been given of the debtor's debts by other persons, specifying which, if any, of the guarantors are associates of his[19];

(5)　the proposed duration of the voluntary arrangement[20];

(6)　the proposed dates of distributions to creditors, with estimates of their amounts[21];

(7)　how it is proposed to deal with the claims of any person bound[22] by the arrangement[23];

(8)　the amount proposed to be paid to the nominee as such by way of remuneration and expenses[24];

(9)　the manner in which it is proposed that the supervisor of the arrangement should be remunerated, and his expenses defrayed[25];

(10)　whether, for the purposes of the arrangement, any guarantees are to be offered by any persons other than the debtor, and whether, if so, any security is to be given or sought[26];

(11)　the manner in which funds held for the purposes of the arrangement are to be banked, invested or otherwise dealt with pending distribution to creditors[27];

(12)　the manner in which funds held for the purpose of payment to creditors, and not so paid on the termination of the arrangement, are to be dealt with[28];

(13)　if the debtor has any business, the manner in which it is proposed to be conducted during the course of the arrangement[29];

(14)　details of any further credit facilities which it is intended to arrange for the debtor, and how the debts so arising are to be paid[30];

(15)　the functions which are to be undertaken by the supervisor of the arrangement[31];

(16)　the name, address and qualification of the person proposed as supervisor of the voluntary arrangement, and confirmation that he is, so far as the debtor is aware, qualified to act as an insolvency practitioner in relation to him[32];

(17)　whether the European Regulation on Insolvency Proceedings[33] will apply and, if so, whether the proceedings will be main proceedings or territorial proceedings[34];

(18)　within the 24 months preceding the date on which the proposal is delivered to the nominee, whether a proposal for an individual voluntary arrangement in respect of the debtor was submitted: (a) to a meeting of the debtor's creditors for approval and, if so, whether the proposal was approved and the arrangement completed or whether the proposal was rejected or the arrangement was terminated and if so, in what respects it differs from the proposal in these provisions; (b) to the court in connection with an application for an interim order[35] and, if so, whether the interim order was made[36].

With the agreement in writing of the nominee, the debtor's proposal may be amended at any time up to the delivery of the nominee's report[37].

1　As to the meaning of 'debtor' see PARA 44 note 2.
2　As to the meaning of 'nominee' see PARA 43.
3　Ie with or without amendments to be made under the Insolvency Rules 1986, SI 1986/1925, r 5.3(3): see text to note 37.
4　Ie to the court under the Insolvency Act 1986 s 256 (see PARA 57) or to the debtor's creditors under s 256A (see PARA 51): Insolvency Act 1986 s 256(2)(a); Insolvency Rules 1986, SI 1986/1925, r 5.2 (substituted by SI 2002/2712; amended by SI 2010/686).
5　Ie under the Insolvency Act 1986 Pt 8 (ss 252–263G): see PARAS 43–52, 54 et seq.
6　Insolvency Rules 1986, SI 1986/1925, r 5.3(1) (r 5.3 substituted by SI 2002/2712).
7　It is important that the matters referred to in the Insolvency Rules 1986, SI 1986/1925, r 5.3(2) (see text to notes 8–36) are addressed comprehensively because the nominee must bring a critical

eye to the debtor's statements of assets and liabilities and must assess whether the proposal contains the necessary matters which must be contained in the proposal according to the Insolvency Rules 1986, SI 1986/1925: see *Re a Debtor (No 222 of 1990), ex p Bank of Ireland* [1992] BCLC 137.

8   Insolvency Rules 1986, SI 1986/1925, r 5.3(2)(a) (as substituted: see note 6).
9   Insolvency Rules 1986, SI 1986/1925, r 5.3(2)(b) (as substituted: see note 6).
10 As to the meaning of 'preferential creditor' see PARA 62 note 13.
11 As to the meaning of 'secured creditor' see PARA 574.
12 As to the meaning of 'associate' see PARA 5.
13 As to the meaning of 'bankrupt' see PARA 129. As to discharge from bankruptcy see PARA 638 et seq.
14 Ie under the Insolvency Act 1986 s 339: see PARA 678 et seq.
15 Ie under the Insolvency Act 1986 s 340: see PARA 678 et seq.
16 Ie under the Insolvency Act 1986 s 343: see PARA 697 et seq.
17 For these purposes, references to 'the insolvent estate' are, in relation to a bankruptcy or a petition for bankruptcy, the bankrupt's estate or, as the case may be, the debtor's property: Insolvency Rules 1986, SI 1986/1925, rr 13.1, 13.8(b) (r 13.8(b) amended by SI 2009/642).
18 Insolvency Rules 1986, SI 1986/1925, r 5.3(2)(c) (as substituted: see note 6).
19 Insolvency Rules 1986, SI 1986/1925, r 5.3(2)(d) (as substituted: see note 6).
20 Insolvency Rules 1986, SI 1986/1925, r 5.3(2)(e) (as substituted: see note 6).
21 Insolvency Rules 1986, SI 1986/1925, r 5.3(2)(f) (as substituted: see note 6).
22 Ie by virtue of the Insolvency Act 1986 s 260(2)(b)(ii); see PARA 69.
23 Insolvency Rules 1986, SI 1986/1925, r 5.3(2)(g) (as substituted: see note 6).
24 Insolvency Rules 1986, SI 1986/1925, r 5.3(2)(h) (as substituted: see note 6).
25 Insolvency Rules 1986, SI 1986/1925, r 5.3(2)(j) (as substituted: see note 6). As to the supervisor see PARA 73 et seq; and as to his fees, costs, charges and expenses see PARA 82.
26 Insolvency Rules 1986, SI 1986/1925, r 5.3(2)(k) (as substituted: see note 6).
27 Insolvency Rules 1986, SI 1986/1925, r 5.3(2)(l) (as substituted: see note 6).
28 Insolvency Rules 1986, SI 1986/1925, r 5.3(2)(m) (as substituted: see note 6).
29 Insolvency Rules 1986, SI 1986/1925, r 5.3(2)(n) (as substituted: see note 6).
30 Insolvency Rules 1986, SI 1986/1925, r 5.3(2)(o) (as substituted: see note 6).
31 Insolvency Rules 1986, SI 1986/1925, r 5.3(2)(p) (as substituted: see note 6).
32 Insolvency Rules 1986, SI 1986/1925, r 5.3(2)(q) (r 5.3 as substituted (see note 6); r 5.3(2)(q) amended by SI 2010/686). As to insolvency practitioners and their qualification see PARA 40; but see also PARA 43 note 6.
33 Ie Council Regulation (EC) 1346/2000 (OJ L160, 30.6.2000, p 1) on insolvency proceedings. As to the European Regulation on Insolvency Proceedings see PARAS 41, 42.
34 Insolvency Rules 1986, SI 1986/1925, r 5.3(2)(r) (as substituted: see note 6).
35 Ie under the Insolvency Act 1986 s 253: see PARA 46.
36 Insolvency Rules 1986, SI 1986/1925, r 5.3(2)(s) (r 5.3 as substituted (see note 6); r 5.3(2)(s) added by SI 2010/686). As to the making of interim orders see PARA 45 et seq.
37 Insolvency Rules 1986, SI 1986/1925, r 5.3(3) (r 5.3 as substituted (see note 6); r 5.3(3) amended by SI 2010/686). The nominee's report is made to the court under the Insolvency Act 1986 s 256 (see PARA 57) or to the debtor's creditors under s 256A (see PARA 51).

54.   Notice to intended nominee, official receiver and trustee. The debtor[1] must give to the intended nominee[2] written notice[3] of his proposal[4]; and the notice, accompanied by a copy of the proposal, must be delivered either to the nominee himself, or to a person authorised to take delivery of documents on his behalf[5]. If the intended nominee agrees to act, he must cause a copy of the notice to be indorsed to the effect that it has been received by him on a specified date[6]. The copy of the notice so indorsed must be returned by the nominee as soon as reasonably practicable to the debtor at an address specified by him in the notice for that purpose[7]. Where the debtor is an undischarged bankrupt[8] and he gives notice of his proposal to the official receiver[9] and, if any, the trustee[10], the notice must contain the name and address of the insolvency practitioner[11] who has agreed to act as nominee[12].

1   As to the meaning of 'debtor' see PARA 44 note 2.
2   As to the meaning of 'nominee' see PARA 43.

3   As to the giving of notices see PARA 808.
4   Insolvency Rules 1986, SI 1986/1925, r 5.4(1) (r 5.4 substituted by SI 2002/2712).
5   Insolvency Rules 1986, SI 1986/1925, r 5.4(2) (as substituted: see note 4).
6   Insolvency Rules 1986, SI 1986/1925, r 5.4(3) (as substituted: see note 4).
7   Insolvency Rules 1986, SI 1986/1925, r 5.4(4) (r 5.4 as substituted (see note 4); r 5.4(4) amended by SI 2009/642).
8   As to the meaning of 'bankrupt' see PARA 129. As to discharge from bankruptcy see PARA 638 et seq.
9   As to the official receiver see PARA 35 et seq.
10 As to the trustee see PARA 314 et seq.
11 As to insolvency practitioners and their qualification see PARA 40; but see also PARA 43 note 6.
12 Insolvency Rules 1986, SI 1986/1925, r 5.4(5) (as substituted: see note 4).

55.   Statement of affairs.   For the purpose of enabling the nominee to prepare his report[1], the debtor[2] must submit to the nominee[3] a document setting out the terms of the voluntary arrangement which the debtor is proposing[4] and a statement of affairs containing such particulars of his creditors and of his debts and other liabilities and of his assets as may be prescribed[5], and such other information as may be prescribed[6].

Where the debtor is an undischarged bankrupt[7], then, if he has already delivered a statement of affairs[8], he need not deliver a further statement unless so required by the nominee, with a view to supplementing or amplifying the former one[9]. In any other case, the debtor must, at the same time as the proposal is delivered to the nominee, deliver to the nominee a statement of his, the debtor's, affairs[10].

The statement must comprise the following particulars, supplementing or amplifying, so far as is necessary for clarifying the state of the debtor's affairs, those already given in his proposal:

(1)   a list of his assets, divided into such categories as are appropriate for easy identification, with estimated values assigned to each category[11];

(2)   in the case of any property on which a claim against the debtor is wholly or partly secured, particulars of the claim and its amount, and of how and when the security was created[12];

(3)   the names and addresses of the debtor's preferential creditors[13], with the amounts of their respective claims[14];

(4)   the names and addresses of the debtor's unsecured creditors[15], with the amounts of their respective claims[16];

(5)   particulars of any debts owed by or to the debtor to or by persons who are associates[17] of his[18];

(6)   such other particulars, if any, as the nominee may in writing require to be furnished for the purposes of making his report to the court, or to the debtor's creditors as the case may be, on the debtor's proposal[19].

The statement of affairs must be made up to a date not earlier than two weeks before the date of the notice[20] to the nominee[21]. The nominee may, however, allow an extension of that period to the nearest practicable date, not earlier than two months before the date of the notice to the nominee; and, if he does so, he must give his reasons in his report on the debtor's proposal[22]. The statement must be verified by a statement of truth made by the debtor[23].

1   Ie pursuant to the Insolvency Act 1986 s 256(1): see PARA 57.
2   As to the meaning of 'debtor' see PARA 44 note 2.
3   As to the meaning of 'nominee' see PARA 43.
4   Insolvency Act 1986 s 256(2)(a).
5   See the text to notes 11–19.

6   Insolvency Act 1986 s 256(2)(b). As to the disclosure of additional information for the assistance of the nominee see PARA 56. See also s 256A(2); and PARA 51.

     Where the court has made an interim order under s 252 (see PARA 45) in respect of an individual who subsequently dies, s 256 applies with the modification that, where the individual dies before he has submitted the document and statement referred to in s 256(2), the nominee must, after the death of the individual comes to his knowledge, give notice to the court that the individual has died, and, after receiving such notice, the court must discharge the order mentioned in s 256(1) (see PARA 57): s 256(1A), (1B); Administration of Insolvent Estates of Deceased Persons Order 1986, SI 1986/1999, art 3(1), Sch 1 Pt III para 1. As to the administration in bankruptcy of the insolvent estates of deceased persons see further PARA 830 et seq.

7   As to the meaning of 'bankrupt' see PARA 129. As to discharge from bankruptcy see PARA 638 et seq.

8   Ie under the Insolvency Act 1986 s 272 (debtor's petition: see PARA 163) or s 288 (creditor's petition: see PARA 240).

9   Insolvency Rules 1986, SI 1986/1925, r 5.5(1), (2) (r 5.5 substituted by SI 2002/2712; Insolvency Rules 1986, SI 1986/1925, r 5.5(1) amended by SI 2010/686).

10   Insolvency Rules 1986, SI 1986/1925, r 5.5(1) (as substituted: see note 9).

11   Insolvency Rules 1986, SI 1986/1925, r 5.5(3)(a) (as substituted: see note 9).

12   Insolvency Rules 1986, SI 1986/1925, r 5.5(3)(b) (as substituted: see note 9).

13   As to the meaning of 'preferential creditor' see PARA 62 note 13.

14   Insolvency Rules 1986, SI 1986/1925, r 5.5(3)(c) (as substituted: see note 9).

15   As to the meaning of 'secured creditor' see PARA 574.

16   Insolvency Rules 1986, SI 1986/1925, r 5.5(3)(d) (as substituted: see note 9).

17   As to the meaning of 'associate' see PARA 5.

18   Insolvency Rules 1986, SI 1986/1925, r 5.5(3)(e) (as substituted: see note 9).

19   Insolvency Rules 1986, SI 1986/1925, r 5.5(3)(f) (r 5.5 as substituted (see note 9); r 5.5(f) amended by SI 2010/686). As to the nominee's report to the court see PARA 57.

20   Ie under the Insolvency Rules 1986, SI 1986/1925, r 5.4: see PARA 54.

21   Insolvency Rules 1986, SI 1986/1925, r 5.5(4) (r 5.5 as substituted (see note 9); r 5.5(4) amended by SI 2010/686).

22   Insolvency Rules 1986, SI 1986/1925, r 5.5(4) (as substituted and amended: see notes 9, 21).

23   Insolvency Rules 1986, SI 1986/1925, r 5.5(5) (r 5.5 as substituted (see note 9); r 5.5(5) amended by SI 2010/686).

56.   Additional disclosure for assistance of nominee. If it appears to the nominee[1] that he cannot properly prepare his own report[2] on the basis of information in the debtor's proposal[3] and statement of affairs[4], he may call on the debtor[5] to provide him with:

(1)   further and better particulars as to the circumstances in which, and the reasons why, he is insolvent or, as the case may be, threatened with insolvency[6];

(2)   further and better particulars of any proposals[7] which have been submitted by the debtor[8];

(3)   particulars of any previous proposals[9] which have been made by the debtor at any time[10];

(4)   any further information with respect to his affairs[11] which the nominee thinks necessary for the purposes of his report[12].

The nominee may call on the debtor to inform him whether and in what circumstances he has at any time been concerned in the affairs of any company, whether or not incorporated in England and Wales, which has become insolvent, or been adjudged bankrupt[13], or entered into an arrangement with his creditors[14].

For the purpose of enabling the nominee to consider the debtor's proposal and prepare his report on it, the latter must give the nominee such access to his accounts and records as the nominee may require[15].

1   As to the meaning of 'nominee' see PARA 43.

2   As to the nominee's duty to report to the court see PARA 57.
3   As to the meaning of 'proposal' see PARA 43.
4   As to the statement of affairs see PARA 55.
5   As to the meaning of 'debtor' see PARA 44 note 2.
6   Insolvency Rules 1986, SI 1986/1925, r 5.6(1)(a) (r 5.6 substituted by SI 2002/2712).
7   Ie of the kind, and within the period, referred to in the Insolvency Rules 1986, SI 1986/1925, r 5.3(2)(s): see PARA 53.
8   Insolvency Rules 1986, SI 1986/1925, r 5.6(1)(aa) (r 5.6 as substituted (see note 6); r 5.6(1)(aa) added by SI 2010/686).
9   Ie other than those referred to in the Insolvency Rules 1986, SI 1986/1925, r 5.3(2)(s): see PARA 53.
10 Ie under the Insolvency Act 1986 Pt 8 (ss 252–263G): see PARAS 43–55, 57 et seq: Insolvency Rules 1986, SI 1986/1925, r 5.6(1)(b) (r 5.6 as substituted (see note 6); r 5.6(1)(b) amended by SI 2010/686).
11 As to the meaning of 'affairs' see PARA 43 note 4.
12 Insolvency Rules 1986, SI 1986/1925, r 5.6(1)(c) (as substituted: see note 6).
13 As to the meaning of 'bankrupt' see PARA 129.
14 Insolvency Rules 1986, SI 1986/1925, r 5.6(2) (as substituted: see note 6). As to arrangements with creditors see PARA 852 et seq.
15 Insolvency Rules 1986, SI 1986/1925, r 5.6(3) (r 5.6 as substituted (see note 6); r 5.6(3) amended by SI 2010/686).

57.   Nominee's report on debtor's proposal.   Where an interim order has been made on an application under the statutory provisions[1], the nominee[2] must, before the order ceases to have effect[3], submit a report to the court stating:

(1)   whether, in his opinion, the voluntary arrangement which the debtor[4] is proposing has a reasonable prospect of being approved and implemented[5];

(2)   whether, in his opinion, a meeting of the debtor's creditors should be summoned to consider the debtor's proposal[6]; and

(3)   if, in his opinion, such a meeting should be summoned, the date on which, and time and place at which, he proposes the meeting should be held[7].

The nominee must deliver two business copies of his report to the court not less than two days before the interim order ceases to have effect[8]; and with his report the nominee must deliver a copy of the debtor's proposal, with amendments, if any, authorised under the statutory provisions[9], and a copy or summary of any statement of affairs provided by the debtor[10].

If the nominee makes known his opinion that the debtor's proposal has a reasonable prospect of being approved and implemented, and that a meeting of the debtor's creditors should be summoned[11], his report must have annexed to it his comments on the debtor's proposal; and, if his opinion is otherwise, he must give his reasons for that opinion[12]. The court must upon receipt of the nominee's report cause it to be indorsed with the date on which it is filed in court[13] and returned to the nominee[14].

Where the debtor is an undischarged bankrupt[15], the nominee must send to the official receiver[16], and the trustee if any[17], a copy of the debtor's proposal, a copy of his, the nominee's, report and his comments accompanying it, if any, and a copy or summary of the debtor's statement of affairs[18]; and, where the debtor is not an undischarged bankrupt, the nominee must send a copy of each of those documents to any person who has presented a bankruptcy petition[19] against the debtor[20]. At the hearing by the court to consider the nominee's report any of the persons given notice[21] of the application for an interim order may appear or be represented[22].

1 Ie under the Insolvency Act 1986 s 253: see PARA 46. As to the importance of this requirement see *Bramston v Haut* [2012] EWCA Civ 1637, [2013] 1 WLR 1720, [2012] All ER (D) 127 (Dec).
2 As to the meaning of 'nominee' see PARA 43.
3 As to the duration of interim orders see PARA 52.
4 As to the meaning of 'debtor' see PARA 44 note 2.
5 Insolvency Act 1986 s 256(1)(a) (amended by the Insolvency Act 2000 Sch 3 paras 1, 6(a)).
6 Insolvency Act 1986 s 256(1)(aa) (added by the Insolvency Act 2000 Sch 3 paras 1, 6(a)). For the purpose of enabling the nominee to prepare his report, the debtor must submit to the nominee: (1) a document setting out the terms of the voluntary arrangement which the debtor is proposing; and (2) a statement of his affairs containing such particulars of his creditors and of his debts and other liabilities and of his assets as may be prescribed, and such other information as may be prescribed: Insolvency Act 1986 s 256(2); see also PARA 55. As to the statement of affairs see PARA 55.
7 Insolvency Act 1986 s 256(1)(b).
8 Insolvency Rules 1986, SI 1986/1925, r 5.11(1) (r 5.11 substituted by SI 2002/2712; the Insolvency Rules 1986, SI 1986/1925, r 5.11(1) amended by SI 2010/686).
9 Ie authorised under the Insolvency Rules 1986, SI 1986/1925, r 5.3(3): see PARA 53.
10 Insolvency Rules 1986, SI 1986/1925, r 5.11(2) (as substituted: see note 8).
11 Ie under the Insolvency Act 1986 s 257: see PARA 59. In forming his opinion, the nominee must satisfy himself that the debtor's position has not been misrepresented, that the proposal has real chances of implementation and that the proposal contains no manifest unfairness: see *Re a Debtor (No 140 IO of 1995)* [1996] 2 BCLC 429, sub nom *Re a Debtor (No 140 IO of 1995)*, Greystoke v Hamilton-Smith* [1997] BPIR 24; see also *Mourant & Co Trustees Ltd v Sixty UK Ltd (in liquidation)* [2010] EWHC 1890 (Ch), [2011] 1 BCLC 383, [2010] 2 EGLR 125; *Tradition (UK) Ltd v Ahmed* [2008] EWHC 2946 (Ch), [2009] BPIR 626, [2008] All ER (D) 72 (Dec). Where a nominee falls below the required professional standard in making his report, he may be liable for the costs of proceedings arising from his conduct: *Re a Debtor (No 222 of 1990), ex p Bank of Ireland (No 2)* [1993] BCLC 233.
12 Insolvency Rules 1986, SI 1986/1925, r 5.11(3) (as substituted: see note 8).
13 For these purposes, 'file in court' and 'file with the court' mean deliver to the court for filing: Insolvency Rules 1986, SI 1986/1925, rr 13.1, 13.13(3) (r 13.13(3) amended by SI 2003/1730).
14 Insolvency Rules 1986, SI 1986/1925, r 5.11(4) (as substituted: see note 8).
15 As to the meaning of 'bankrupt' see PARA 129. As to discharge from bankruptcy see PARA 638 et seq.
16 As to the official receiver see PARA 35 et seq.
17 As to the trustee see PARA 314 et seq.
18 Insolvency Rules 1986, SI 1986/1925, r 5.11(6) (as substituted: see note 8).
19 As to bankruptcy petitions see PARA 129 et seq.
20 Insolvency Rules 1986, SI 1986/1925, r 5.11(7) (as substituted: see note 8).
21 Ie under the Insolvency Rules 1986, SI 1986/1925, r 5.7(4): see PARA 46.
22 Insolvency Rules 1986, SI 1986/1925, r 5.13(1) (r 5.13 substituted by SI 2002/2712). The Insolvency Rules 1986, SI 1986/1925, r 5.10 (see PARA 50) applies to any order made by the court at the hearing: r 5.13(2) (as so substituted).

58. Failure to submit report; replacement of nominee. On the application of the nominee[1], the court may extend the period for which the interim order has effect[2] so as to enable the nominee to have more time to prepare his report[3].

On an application made by the debtor[4] in a case where the nominee has failed to submit a report[5] or has died, or on an application made by the debtor or the nominee in a case where it is impracticable or inappropriate for the nominee to continue to act as such, the court may direct that the nominee is to be replaced as such by another person qualified to act as an insolvency practitioner[6], or authorised to act as nominee, in relation to the voluntary arrangement[7]. On an application made by the debtor in a case where the nominee has failed to submit the report, the court may direct that the interim order is to continue or (if it has ceased to have effect) be renewed, for such further period as the court may specify in the direction[8].

Where the debtor intends so to apply to the court for the nominee to be replaced, he must give to the nominee at least five business days'[9] notice of his application[10]. No appointment of a replacement nominee will be made by the court unless there is filed in court[11] a statement by the replacement nominee indicating that he consents to act and is qualified to act as an insolvency practitioner or is an authorised person in relation to the debtor[12].

1　As to the meaning of 'nominee' see PARA 43.

2　As to the duration of interim orders see PARA 52.

3　See the Insolvency Act 1986 s 256(4); and PARA 52. As to the nominee's report see PARA 57.

4　As to the meaning of 'debtor' see PARA 44 note 2.

5　Ie as required by the Insolvency Act 1986 s 256: see PARA 57.

6　As to insolvency practitioners and their qualification see PARA 40; but see also PARA 43 note 6.

7　Insolvency Act 1986 s 256(3) (substituted by the Insolvency Act 2000 Sch 3 paras 1, 6(b)).

8　Insolvency Act 1986 s 256(3A) (added by the Insolvency Act 2000 Sch 3 paras 1, 6(b)).

9　As to the meaning of 'business day' see PARA 28 note 8.

10　Insolvency Rules 1986, SI 1986/1925, r 5.12(1) (r 5.12 substituted by SI 2002/2712; the Insolvency Rules 1986, SI 1986/1925, r 5.12(1) amended by SI 2010/686).

11　As to the meaning of 'file in court' see PARA 57 note 13.

12　Insolvency Rules 1986, SI 1986/1925, r 5.12(2) (r 5.12 as substituted (see note 10); r 5.12(2) amended by SI 2010/686).

59. Summoning of meetings. If the court is satisfied, on receiving the nominee's report[1], that a meeting of the debtor's creditors should be summoned to consider the debtor's proposal, the court must direct that the period for which the interim order has effect[2] is to be extended, for such further period as it may specify in the direction[3], for the purpose of enabling the debtor's proposal to be considered by his creditors in accordance with the statutory provisions[4]. The court may, however, discharge the interim order if it is satisfied, on the application of the nominee, that the debtor has failed to comply with his obligation to submit to the nominee a proposal and statement of affairs[5] or that for any other reason it would be inappropriate for a meeting of the debtor's creditors to be summoned to consider the debtor's proposal[6].

Where it has been reported to the court[7] or to the debtor's creditors[8] that a meeting of the debtor's creditors should be summoned, the nominee or his replacement[9] must, unless the court otherwise directs, summon that meeting for the time, date and place proposed in the report[10]. The persons summoned to the meeting are every creditor of the debtor of whose claim and address the person summoning the meeting is aware[11].

If in his report the nominee states that in his opinion a meeting of creditors should be summoned to consider the debtor's proposal, the date on which the meeting is to be held must be:

(1)　in a case where an interim order has not been obtained, not more than 28 days from that on which the nominee received the document and statement[12];

(2)　in a case where an interim order is in force, not less than 14 days from that on which the nominee's report is filed in court[13] nor more than 28 days from that on which the report is considered[14] by the court[15].

Notices calling the meeting must be sent by the nominee at least 14 days before the day fixed for it to be held, to all the creditors of the debtor of whose address the nominee is aware[16]. Each such notice must specify:

(a)　in a case where an interim order has not been obtained, the court to which application must be made[17]; or

(b)   in a case where an interim order is in force, the court in which the
       nominee's report on the debtor's proposal has been filed[18],
and must state the effect of the provisions dealing with requisite majorities of
creditors at the meeting[19]; and with it there must be sent, unless attached to the
nominee's report[20]:

(i)   a copy of the proposal[21];

(ii)   a copy of the statement of affairs[22] or, if the nominee thinks fit, a
       summary of it, the summary to include a list of the creditors and the
       amounts of their debts; and

(iii) the nominee's report with the comments on the proposal annexed to
       it[23].

1   As to the nominee's report see PARA 57. A meeting summoned by the nominee before the court
    has positively considered whether one should be called is not a meeting validly convened under
    the Insolvency Act 1986 s 257 (see text to notes 7–11): *Vlieland-Boddy v Dexter Ltd* [2003]
    EWHC 2592 (Ch), [2004] BPIR 235, [2003] All ER (D) 423 (Oct).
2   As to the duration of interim orders see PARA 52.
3   As to the court's jurisdiction to extend the period for which an interim order has effect see *Re
    Cove (a debtor)* [1990] 1 All ER 949 at 957, sub nom *Re a Debtor (No 83 of 1988)* [1990]
    1 WLR 708 at 718.
4   Insolvency Act 1986 s 256(5). The statutory provisions referred to are ss 257–263G (PARA 60 et
    seq): s 256(5). See further PARA 67 note 8. As to remote attendance at meetings see PARA 267.
5   Ie the obligation under the Insolvency Act 1986 s 256(2): see PARA 55.
6   Insolvency Act 1986 s 256(6).
7   Ie under the Insolvency Act 1986 s 256: see PARA 57.
8   Ie under the Insolvency Act 1986 s 256A: see PARA 51.
9   Ie under the Insolvency Act 1986 s 256(3)(a) (see PARA 58) or s 256A(4) (see PARA 51).
10 Insolvency Act 1986 s 257(1) (amended by the Insolvency Act 2000 Sch 3 paras 1, 8(a), (b)). A
    person summoning a meeting may allow a meeting to be conducted and held in such a way that
    persons who are not present together at the same place may attend it: Insolvency Act 1986
    s 379A (added by SI 2010/18).
        Where the court has made an interim order under the Insolvency Act 1986 s 252 (see PARA
    45) in respect of an individual who subsequently dies, s 257 applies with the modification that,
    where the individual dies before a creditors' meeting has been held, then no such meeting may be
    held and, if the individual was at the date of his death an undischarged bankrupt, the personal
    representative must give notice of the death to the trustee of his estate and the official receiver:
    Administration of Insolvent Estates of Deceased Persons Order 1986, SI 1986/1999, art 3(1),
    Sch 1 Pt III para 2. As to the administration in bankruptcy of the insolvent estates of deceased
    persons see further PARA 830 et seq.
11 Insolvency Act 1986 s 257(2). For these purposes, the creditors of the debtor who is an
    undischarged bankrupt include: (1) every person who is a creditor of the bankrupt in respect of
    a bankruptcy debt; and (2) every person who would be such a creditor if the bankruptcy had
    commenced on the day on which notice of the meeting was given: s 257(3). As to the meaning of
    'creditors' more generally see PARA 43 note 3; and *Re Debtor (No 48810 of 1996), JP v Debtor*
    [1999] 2 FCR 637, [1999] 1 FLR 926, [1999] BPIR 206.
12 Ie the document and statement as set out in the Insolvency Act 1986 s 256A(2): see PARA 51.
13 Ie under the Insolvency Rules 1986, SI 1986/1925, r 5.11: see PARA 57. As to the meaning of
    'file in court' see PARA 57 note 13.
14 Ie under the Insolvency Rules 1986, SI 1986/1925, r 5.13: see PARA 57.
15 Insolvency Rules 1986, SI 1986/1925, r 5.17(1) (r 5.17 substituted by SI 2002/2712; the
    Insolvency Rules 1986, SI 1986/1925, r 5.17(1) amended by SI 2010/686).
16 Insolvency Rules 1986, SI 1986/1925, r 5.17(2) (r 5.17 as substituted (see note 15); r 5.17(2)
    amended by SI 2010/686). As to provisions dealing with the giving of notice see PARA 808.
17 Ie under the Insolvency Rules 1986, SI 1986/1925, r 5.14B(1) or (2) as the case may be: see PARA
    51.
18 Ie under the Insolvency Rules 1986, SI 1986/1925, r 5.8: see PARA 46.
19 Ie the effect of the Insolvency Rules 1986, SI 1986/1925, r 5.23(2)–(4) (see PARA 64): r 5.17(3)
    (r 5.17 as substituted (see note 15); r 5.17(3) amended by SI 2010/686).
20 Ie in accordance with the Insolvency Rules 1986, SI 1986/1925, r 5.14A; see PARA 51.
21 As to the proposal see PARA 53 et seq.
22 As to the statement of affairs see PARA 55.

23 Insolvency Rules 1986, SI 1986/1925, r 5.17(3A) (r 5.17 as substituted (see note 16); r 5.17(3A) added by SI 2010/686).

(4) CONSIDERATION OF THE PROPOSAL

(i) Meeting of Creditors

60. Summoning of meeting; proxies. In fixing the venue[1] for the creditors' meeting, the nominee must have regard to the convenience of creditors[2]. The meeting must be summoned for commencement between 10.00 and 16.00 hours on a business day[3]; and with every notice summoning the meeting there must be sent out forms of proxy[4].

1 As to the meaning of 'venue' see PARA 46 note 22.
2 Insolvency Rules 1986, SI 1986/1925, r 5.18(1) (r 5.18 substituted by SI 2002/2712).
3 Insolvency Rules 1986, SI 1986/1925, r 5.18(2) (as substituted: see note 2). As to the meaning of 'business day' see PARA 28 note 8.
4 Insolvency Rules 1986, SI 1986/1925, r 5.18(3) (as substituted: see note 2). Proxies sent by facsimile are acceptable: see *Re a Debtor (No 2021 of 1995), ex p IRC v Debtor, Re a Debtor (No 2022 of 1995), ex p IRC v Debtor* [1996] 2 All ER 345, [1996] 1 BCLC 538. A creditor is entitled to amend a proxy between meetings if there is an adjournment: see *Re Cardona, IRC v Cardona* [1997] BCC 697, [1997] BPIR 604. As to the prescribed form of proxy see the Insolvency Rules 1986, SI 1986/1925, r 5.18(3), Sch 4 Form 8.1. The provisions relating to proxies are the same as those which apply to meetings in a bankruptcy: see PARA 276 et seq; but see also PARA 61. As to remote attendance at meetings see PARA 267.

61. Chairman of the meeting. The nominee[1] must be the chairman of the creditors' meeting[2]. If, however, for any reason the nominee is unable to attend, he may nominate another person to act as chairman in his place; but a person so nominated must be a person qualified to act as an insolvency practitioner[3] in relation to the debtor[4]; an authorised person in relation to the debtor; or an employee of the nominee or his firm who is experienced in insolvency matters[5].

The chairman may not, by virtue of any proxy held by him, vote to increase or reduce the amount of the remuneration or expenses of the nominee or the supervisor[6] of the proposed arrangement, unless the proxy specifically directs him to vote in that way[7].

1 As to the meaning of 'nominee' see PARA 43.
2 Insolvency Rules 1986, SI 1986/1925, r 5.19(1) (r 5.19 substituted by SI 2002/2712).
3 As to insolvency practitioners and their qualification see PARA 40; but see also PARA 43 note 6.
4 As to the meaning of 'debtor' see PARA 44 note 2.
5 Insolvency Rules 1986, SI 1986/1925, r 5.19(2) (as substituted: see note 2).
6 As to the supervisor see PARA 73 et seq.
7 Insolvency Rules 1986, SI 1986/1925, r 5.20 (substituted by SI 2002/2712). As to the position where the chairman uses a proxy contrary to this provision see PARA 64 text and notes 19–21.

(ii) Decisions of Meetings; Voting Rights and Majorities

62. Decisions of creditors' meetings. A creditors' meeting summoned[1] to consider the proposal must decide whether to approve the proposed voluntary arrangement[2]; and the meeting may approve the proposed voluntary arrangement with modifications[3], but may not do so unless the debtor[4] consents to each modification[5]. The modifications subject to which the proposed voluntary arrangement may be approved may include one conferring the functions proposed to be conferred on the nominee[6] on another person qualified to act as an insolvency practitioner[7] or authorised to act as nominee in relation to the voluntary arrangement[8]; but they must not include any modification by which the proposal ceases to be a proposal[9] for a voluntary arrangement[10].

A meeting so summoned may not approve any proposal or modification which affects the right of a secured creditor[11] of the debtor to enforce his security, except with the concurrence of the creditor concerned[12]. Nor may the meeting approve any proposal or modification under which:

(1)   any preferential debt[13] of the debtor is to be paid otherwise than in priority to such of his debts as are not preferential debts; or

(2)   a preferential creditor of the debtor is to be paid an amount that bears to the debt a smaller proportion than is borne to another preferential debt by the amount that is to be paid in respect of that other debt;

but the meeting may approve such a proposal or modification with the concurrence of the preferential creditor concerned[14].

Subject to the above provisions, the meeting must be conducted in accordance with the Insolvency Rules 1986[15]; but an approval given at a meeting is not invalidated by any irregularity at or in relation to the meeting[16].

1   Ie the meeting summoned under the Insolvency Act 1986 s 257: see PARA 59.
2   Insolvency Act 1986 s 258(1). Where the court has made an interim order under s 252 (see PARA 45) in respect of an individual who subsequently dies, s 258 applies: Administration of Insolvent Estates of Deceased Persons Order 1986, SI 1986/1999, art 3(1), Sch 1 Pt III para 3. As to the administration in bankruptcy of the insolvent estates of deceased persons see further PARA 830 et seq.
3   For these purposes, except in so far as the context otherwise requires, 'modifications' includes additions, alterations and omissions; and cognate expressions are to be construed accordingly: Insolvency Act 1986 s 436. As to the application of s 436 in the case of the administration in bankruptcy of the insolvent estate of a deceased person dying before the presentation of a bankruptcy petition see PARA 20 note 6. If a proposal is rejected at the meeting, it cannot be approved at a subsequent meeting: *Re Symes (a debtor), Kent Carpets Ltd v Symes* [1995] 2 BCLC 651, [1996] BPIR 169. A voluntary arrangement cannot be modified after approval, unless all creditors consent or there is a provision for modification in the original proposal: *Raja v Rubin* [2000] Ch 274, [1999] 3 All ER 73, CA; and see *Re Broome (a debtor), Thompson v Broome* [1999] 1 BCLC 356, sub nom *Horrocks v Broome* [1999] BPIR 66; *Re Alpa Lighting Ltd* [1997] BPIR 341.
4   As to the meaning of 'debtor' see PARA 44 note 2.
5   Insolvency Act 1986 s 258(2). The debtor's consent is a condition precedent for the approval of the proposal subject to any proposed modification: *Re Plummer* [2004] BPIR 767.
6   As to the meaning of 'nominee' see PARA 43.
7   As to insolvency practitioners and their qualification see PARA 40; but see also PARA 43 note 6.
8   Insolvency Act 1986 s 258(3) (amended by the Insolvency Act 2000 Sch 3 paras 1, 9).
9   Ie a proposal such as is mentioned in the Insolvency Act 1986 Pt 8 (ss 252–263G): see PARAS 43–61, 63 et seq.
10 Insolvency Act 1986 s 258(3) (as amended: see note 8).
11 As to the meaning of 'secured creditor' see PARA 574. Dependent upon the terms of the arrangement, a secured creditor waives his rights as such by agreeing to participate in an individual voluntary arrangement and accepting a dividend: *Khan v Permayer* [2001] BPIR 95 cf *Whitehead v Household Mortgage Corpn plc* [2002] EWCA Civ 1657, [2003] 1 All ER 319, [2003] 1 WLR 1173 (where the court refused to imply a term to such effect).
12 Insolvency Act 1986 s 258(4).
13 For these purposes, 'preferential debt' has the meaning given by the Insolvency Act 1986 s 386 (see PARA 591); and 'preferential creditor' is to be construed accordingly: s 258(7).
14 Insolvency Act 1986 s 258(5). Goods seized under a writ of fieri facias constitute security: see *Peck v Craighead* [1995] 1 BCLC 337, sub nom *Re a Debtor (No 10 of 1992), Peck v Craighead* [1995] BCC 525; cf the Insolvency Act 1986 s 346(5), (6) (cited in PARAS 703, 704). A right of re-entry is not security: *Razzaq v Pala* [1997] 1 WLR 1336, [1997] BPIR 726; and see *Christopher Moran Holdings Ltd v Bairstow* [2000] 2 AC 172, sub nom *Re Park Air Services plc, Christopher Moran Holdings Ltd v Bairstow* [1999] 1 All ER 673, HL; *Re Lomax Leisure Ltd* [2000] Ch 502, [1999] 3 All ER 22, [1999] 2 BCLC 126.
15 Insolvency Act 1986 s 258(6). See also PARAS 60, 61, 63 et seq.

16 Insolvency Act 1986 s 262(8). Section 262(8) is subject to the right to challenge decisions under s 262 (see PARAS 84–86): s 262(8). Where the court has made an interim order under s 252 (see PARA 45) in respect of an individual who subsequently dies, s 262 applies with the modification that it ceases to apply on or after the death of the individual: Administration of Insolvent Estates of Deceased Persons Order 1986, SI 1986/1999, Sch I Pt III para 4.

63.   Voting rights.   Subject to the following provisions, every creditor who has notice of the creditors' meeting[1] is entitled to vote at the meeting or any adjournment of it[2]. A creditor's entitlement to vote is calculated as follows:

(1)   where the debtor[3] is not an undischarged bankrupt[4] and an interim order is in force, by reference to the amount of the debt owed to him as at the date of the interim order[5];

(2)   where the debtor is not an undischarged bankrupt and an interim order is not in force, by reference to the amount of the debt owed to him at the date of the meeting[6]; and

(3)   where the debtor is an undischarged bankrupt, by reference to the amount of the debt owed to him as at the date of the bankruptcy order[7].

A creditor may vote in respect of a debt for an unliquidated amount or any debt whose value is not ascertained, and for the purposes of voting, but not otherwise, his debt shall be valued at £1 unless the chairman agrees to put a higher value on it[8].

At the creditors' meeting the chairman must ascertain the entitlement of persons wishing to vote and admit or reject their claims accordingly[9]. A claim may be rejected in whole or in part[10]. The chairman's decision on entitlement to vote is, however, subject to appeal to the court by any creditor, or by the debtor[11]. If the chairman is in doubt whether a claim should be admitted or rejected, he must mark it as objected to and allow votes to be cast in respect of it, subject to such votes being subsequently declared invalid if the objection to the claim is sustained[12]. If on an appeal the chairman's decision is reversed or varied, or votes are declared invalid, the court may order another meeting to be summoned, or make such other order as it thinks just; but the court's power to make such an order is exercisable only if it considers that the matter is such as to give rise to unfair prejudice or a material irregularity[13].

An application to the court by way of appeal against the chairman's decision may not be made after the end of the period of 28 days beginning with the first day on which: (a) where the creditors' meeting was summoned[14] pursuant to a report to the debtor's creditors[15], the notice of the result of the meeting[16] has been given[17]; or (b) where the creditors' meeting was summoned pursuant to a report to the court[18], the report[19] is made to the court[20]. The chairman is not, however, personally liable for any costs incurred by any person in respect of an appeal under the above provisions[21].

1   As to the creditors to be given notice of the meeting see PARA 59.
2   Insolvency Rules 1986, SI 1986/1925, r 5.21(1) (r 5.21 substituted by SI 2002/2712). A creditor who votes must vote for all his debts not just for those included in the debtor's proposal: *Re Hoare* [1997] BPIR 683.
3   As to the meaning of 'debtor' see PARA 44 note 2.
4   As to the meaning of 'bankrupt' see PARA 129. As to discharge from bankruptcy see PARA 638 et seq.
5   Insolvency Rules 1986, SI 1986/1925, r 5.21(2)(a) (as substituted: see note 2).
6   Insolvency Rules 1986, SI 1986/1925, r 5.21(2)(b) (as substituted: see note 2).
7   Insolvency Rules 1986, SI 1986/1925, r 5.21(2)(c) (as substituted: see note 2).
8   Insolvency Rules 1986, SI 1986/1925, r 5.21(3) (as substituted: see note 2). 'Agrees' does not require bilateral concurrence between the chairman of the creditors' meeting and the creditor, merely that the chairman should be willing to place a value on the unliquidated or unascertained

claim of the creditor: *Doorbar v Alltime Securities Ltd* [1996] 2 All ER 948, [1996] 1 WLR 456, CA. As to what is required of the chairman see *Re a Debtor (No 222 of 1990), ex p Bank of Ireland* [1992] BCLC 137; *Re Newlands (Seaford) Educational Trust (in administration), Chittenden v Pepper* [2006] EWHC 1511 (Ch), [2007] BCC 195, [2006] BPIR 1230. As to the meaning of 'debt for an unliquidated amount or any debt whose value is not ascertained' see *Revenue and Customs Comrs v Portsmouth City Football Club Ltd (in administration)* [2010] EWHC 2013 (Ch), [2010] BPIR 1123, [2010] All ER (D) 58 (Aug). As to secured creditors and preferential creditors see PARA 62; and as to debts secured by bills of exchange see PARA 64.

9   Insolvency Rules 1986, SI 1986/1925, r 5.22(1) (r 5.22 substituted by SI 2002/2712). There is no right to vote in respect of an unassessed bill of costs: *Re Wisepark Ltd* [1994] BCC 221.
10   Insolvency Rules 1986, SI 1986/1925, r 5.22(2) (as substituted: see note 9).
11   Insolvency Rules 1986, SI 1986/1925, r 5.22(3) (as substituted: see note 9). As to the mode of appeal and the procedure see the text to notes 14–20; and PARA 761 et seq.
12   Insolvency Rules 1986, SI 1986/1925, r 5.22(4) (as substituted: see note 9).
13   Insolvency Rules 1986, SI 1986/1925, r 5.22(5) (as substituted: see note 9). The court hearing an appeal against the chairman's decision may consider further evidence which was not before the chairman: *Re a Debtor (No 574 of 1995)* [1998] 2 BCLC 124 at 128, sub nom *National Westminster Bank plc v Scher* [1998] BPIR 224 at 227; *Power v Petrus Estates Ltd* [2008] EWHC 2607 (Ch), [2009] 1 BCLC 250, [2009] BPIR 141; *Re Shruth Ltd* [2005] EWHC 1293 (Ch), [2006] 1 BCLC 294, [2007] BCC 960.
14   Ie under the Insolvency Act 1986 s 257: see PARA 59.
15   Ie a report pursuant to the Insolvency Act 1986 s 256A(3): see PARA 51.
16   Ie the notice required by the Insolvency Act 1986 s 259(1)(a): see PARA 67.
17   Insolvency Rules 1986, SI 1986/1925, r 5.22(6)(a) (as substituted: see note 9).
18   Ie a report pursuant to the Insolvency Act 1986 s 256(1)(aa): see PARA 57.
19   Ie the report required by the Insolvency Act 1986 s 259(1)(b): see PARA 67.
20   Insolvency Rules 1986, SI 1986/1925, r 5.22(6)(b) (as substituted: see note 9).
21   Insolvency Rules 1986, SI 1986/1925, r 5.22(7) (as substituted: see note 9); cf *Re a Debtor (No 222 of 1990), ex p Bank of Ireland (No 2)* [1993] BCLC 233.

64.   Requisite majorities.   At the creditors' meeting, a resolution is passed when a majority, in value, of those present and voting in person or by proxy[1] have voted in favour of it[2], except for a resolution approving a proposal or modification[3], which is passed when a majority of three-quarters or more, in value, of those present and voting in person or by proxy have voted in favour of it[4].

In the following cases there is to be left out of account a creditor's vote in respect of any claim or part of a claim:

(1)   where written notice of the claim was not given, either at the meeting or before it, to the chairman[5] or the nominee[6];

(2)   where the claim or part is secured[7];

(3)   where the claim is in respect of a debt wholly or partly on, or secured by, a current bill of exchange or promissory note, unless the creditor is willing:

(a)   to treat the liability to him on the bill or note of every person who is liable on it antecedently to the debtor[8], and against whom a bankruptcy order[9] has not been made, or in the case of a company, which has not gone into liquidation[10], as a security in his hands; and

(b)   to estimate the value of the security and, for the purpose of entitlement to vote, but not for any distribution under the arrangement, to deduct it from his claim[11].

Any resolution is invalid if those voting against it include more than half in value of the creditors, counting in these latter only those:

(i)   who have notice of the meeting[12];

(ii)   whose votes are not to be left out of account under the above provisions; and

(iii)   who are not, to the best of the chairman's belief, associates[13] of the debtor[14].

It is for the chairman of the meeting to decide whether a vote is to be left out of account[15] or a person is an associate of the debtor[16] and, in relation to the second of these two cases, the chairman is entitled to rely on the information provided by the debtor's statement of affairs[17] or otherwise in accordance with the rules relating to voluntary arrangements[18].

If the chairman uses a proxy to vote for an increase or reduction in the amount of the remuneration or expenses of the nominee or supervisor[19] where the proxy does not specifically direct him so to vote[20], his vote with that proxy does not count towards any majority under the above provisions[21].

An appeal against the decision of the chairman under the above provisions lies to the court[22].

1   As to the applicable provisions relating to proxies see PARA 60 note 4.
2   Insolvency Rules 1986, SI 1986/1925, r 5.23(1) (r 5.23 substituted by SI 2002/2712; Insolvency Rules 1986, SI 1986/1925, r 5.23(1) substituted by SI 2010/686).
3   As to the modifications which are permissible see PARA 62.
4   Insolvency Rules 1986, SI 1986/1925, r 5.23(2) (r 5.23 as substituted (see note 2); r 5.23(2) substituted by SI 2010/686).
5   As to the chairman of the meeting see PARA 61.
6   As to the meaning of 'nominee' see PARA 43. For the purposes of this rule, written notice must be given by the creditor seeking to vote: *Roberts v Pinnacle Entertainment Ltd* [2003] EWHC 2394 (Ch), [2004] BPIR 208, [2003] All ER (D) 347 (Oct) (sending of proxy by the creditor to the chairman constituted the giving of notice for the purposes of the vote).
7   As to the meaning of 'secured creditor' see PARA 574. Where a debt is partly secured, the creditor is entitled to vote for that part of the debt which is not secured: *Re a Debtor (Nos 31/32/33 of 1993), Calor Gas Ltd v Piercy* [1994] 2 BCLC 321, [1994] BCC 69.
8   As to the meaning of 'debtor' see PARA 44 note 2.
9   As to bankruptcy orders see PARA 198 et seq.
10   As to the meaning of 'go into liquidation' see COMPANY AND PARTNERSHIP INSOLVENCY vol 16 (2011) PARA 10.
11   Insolvency Rules 1986, SI 1986/1925, r 5.23(3) (as substituted: see note 2).
12   As to the creditors to be given notice of the meeting see PARA 59.
13   As to the meaning of 'associate' see PARA 5.
14   Insolvency Rules 1986, SI 1986/1925, r 5.23(4) (as substituted: see note 2).
15   Ie in accordance with the Insolvency Rules 1986, SI 1986/1925, r 5.23(3): see text to notes 5–11.
16   Ie for the purposes of the Insolvency Rules 1986, SI 1986/1925, r 5.23(4)(c): see head (iii) in the text.
17   As to the debtor's statement of affairs see PARA 55.
18   Insolvency Rules 1986, SI 1986/1925, r 5.23(5) (as substituted: see note 2).
19   As to the supervisor see PARA 73 et seq.
20   Ie contrary to the Insolvency Rules 1986, SI 1986/1925, r 5.20: see PARA 61.
21   Insolvency Rules 1986, SI 1986/1925, r 5.23(6) (as substituted: see note 2).
22   Insolvency Rules 1986, SI 1986/1925, r 5.23(7) (as substituted: see note 2). The applicable provisions regarding such an appeal are rr 5.22(5)–(7) (see PARA 63): r 5.23(7).

65.   Proceedings to obtain agreement on the proposal. On the day on which the creditors' meeting is held, it may from time to time be adjourned[1]. If on that day the requisite majority[2] for the approval of the voluntary arrangement, with or without modifications[3], has not been obtained, the chairman[4] may, and must if it is so resolved, adjourn the meeting for not more than 14 days[5]. If there are subsequently further adjournments, the final adjournment may not be to a day later than 14 days after that on which the meeting was originally held[6]. Once only in the course of a meeting the chairman may, without an adjournment, declare it suspended for any period up to an hour[7]. If following any final adjournment of the meeting the proposal, with or without modifications, is not agreed to, it is deemed rejected[8].

1   Insolvency Rules 1986, SI 1986/1925, r 5.24(1) (r 5.24 substituted by SI 2002/2712).
2   As to the requisite majorities see PARA 64.
3   As to the modifications which are permissible see PARA 62.
4   As to the chairman of the meeting see PARA 61.
5   Insolvency Rules 1986, SI 1986/1925, r 5.24(2) (as substituted: see note 1). If the meeting is adjourned under r 5.24(2), notice of the fact must be given by the chairman as soon as reasonably practicable to the court: r 5.24(4) (r 5.24 as so substituted; r 5.24(4) amended by SI 2009/642). If a proposal is rejected at the meeting, it cannot be approved at a subsequent meeting: *Re Symes (a debtor), Kent Carpets Ltd v Symes* [1995] 2 BCLC 651, [1996] BCC 137. As to the power to adjourn the meeting see *Tradition (UK) Ltd v Ahmed* [2008] EWHC 2946 (Ch), [2009] BPIR 626, [2008] All ER (D) 72 (Dec).
6   Insolvency Rules 1986, SI 1986/1925, r 5.24(3) (as substituted: see note 1).
7   Insolvency Rules 1986, SI 1986/1925, r 5.24(4A) (r 5.24 as substituted (see note 1); r 5.24(4A) added by SI 2010/686).
8   Insolvency Rules 1986, SI 1986/1925, r 5.24(5) (as substituted: see note 1).

66.   Resolutions to follow approval.   If the voluntary arrangement is approved, with or without modifications[1], a resolution must be taken by the creditors, where two or more individuals are appointed to act as supervisor[2], on the question whether acts to be done in connection with the arrangement may be done by any one of them, or must be done by both or all[3].

If at the creditors' meeting a resolution is moved for the appointment of some person other than the nominee[4] to be supervisor of the arrangement, there must be produced to the chairman[5], at or before the meeting, that person's written consent to act, unless he is present and then and there signifies his consent, and his written confirmation that he is qualified to act as an insolvency practitioner[6] in relation to the debtor[7] or is an authorised person in relation to the debtor[8].

1   As to the modifications which are permissible see PARA 62.
2   As to the supervisor see PARA 73 et seq.
3   Insolvency Rules 1986, SI 1986/1925, r 5.25(1) (r 5.25 substituted by SI 2002/2712; Insolvency Rules 1986, SI 1986/1925, r 5.25(1) amended by SI 2010/686).
4   As to the meaning of 'nominee' see PARA 43.
5   As to the chairman of the meeting see PARA 61.
6   As to insolvency practitioners and their qualification see PARA 40; but see also PARA 43 note 6.
7   As to the meaning of 'debtor' see PARA 44 note 2.
8   Insolvency Rules 1986, SI 1986/1925, r 5.25(2) (as substituted: see note 3).

67.   Report of creditors' meeting.   After the conclusion of the creditors' meeting[1], the chairman of the meeting[2] must give notice of the result of it[3] to all those who were sent notice of the meeting[4] and any other creditor of whose address the chairman is aware and, where the debtor[5] is an undischarged bankrupt[6], the official receiver[7] and the trustee if any[8]. Where the meeting was summoned[9] pursuant to a report from the nominee stating that it was his opinion that a creditors' meeting should be summoned to consider the debtor's proposal[10], the chairman must prepare a report of the meeting[11] and file it in court[12] within four business days of the meeting being held[13]. The court must cause the report to be endorsed with the date of filing[14].

The report must:

(1)   state whether the proposal for a voluntary arrangement was approved or rejected and, if approved, with what, if any, modifications[15];

(2)   set out the resolutions which were taken at the meeting, and the decision on each one;

(3)   list the creditors, with their respective values, who were present or
       represented at the meeting, and how they voted on each resolution;

(4)   state whether in the opinion of the supervisor: (a) the European
       Regulation on Insolvency Proceedings[16] applies to the voluntary
       arrangement; and (b) if so, whether the proceedings are main
       proceedings or territorial proceedings; and

(5)   include such further information, if any, as the chairman thinks it
       appropriate to make known to the court or the debtor's creditors as the
       case may be[17].

If the report is that the meeting has declined, with or without modifications,
to approve the voluntary arrangement[18], the court may discharge any interim
order which is in force in relation to the debtor[19]. In a case where no interim
order has been obtained the court must not consider the chairman's report unless
an application is made to the court[20].

1 Ie in accordance with the Insolvency Act 1986 s 257 (see PARA 59); and the Insolvency
   Rules 1986, SI 1986/1925, Pt 5 Ch 5 (rr 5.17–5.24) (see PARA 59 et seq).
2 As to the chairman of the meeting see PARA 61.
3 Insolvency Act 1986 s 259(1)(a).
4 As to the creditors to be given notice of the meeting see PARA 59.
5 As to the meaning of 'debtor' see PARA 44 note 2.
6 As to the meaning of 'bankrupt' see PARA 129. As to discharge from bankruptcy see PARA 638 et
   seq.
7 As to the official receiver see PARA 35 et seq.
8 Insolvency Rules 1986, SI 1986/1925, r 5.27(4) (r 5.27 substituted by SI 2002/2712; Insolvency
   Rules 1986, SI 1986/1925, r 5.27(4) amended by SI 2010/686). As to the trustee see PARA 314 et
   seq. The notice must be sent: (1) where the creditors' meeting was summoned under the
   Insolvency Act 1986 s 257 (see PARA 59) pursuant to a report to the court under s 256(1)(aa)
   (see PARA 57), as soon as reasonably practicable after a copy of the chairman's report is filed in
   court; (2) where the creditors' meeting was summoned under s 257 pursuant to a report to
   creditors under s 256A(3) (see PARA 51), within four business days of the meeting being held:
   Insolvency Rules 1986, SI 1986/1925, r 5.27(4A) (r 5.27 as substituted; r 5.27(4A) added by
   SI 2010/686). As to the meaning of 'file in court' see PARA 57 note 13. As to the meaning of
   'business day' see PARA 28 note 8.
9 Ie under the Insolvency Act 1986 s 257: see PARA 59.
10 Ie a report to the court under the Insolvency Act 1986 s 256(1)(aa): see PARA 57.
11 Insolvency Rules 1986, SI 1986/1925, r 5.27(1) (as substituted: see note 8).
12 Insolvency Act 1986 s 259(1)(b).
13 Insolvency Rules 1986, SI 1986/1925, r 5.27(3) (r 5.27 as substituted (see note 8); r 5.27(3)
   amended by SI 2010/686).
14 Insolvency Rules 1986, SI 1986/1925, r 5.27(3) (r 5.27 as substituted (see note 8); r 5.27(3) as
   amended (see note 13)).
15 As to the modifications which are permissible see PARA 62.
16 Ie Council Regulation (EC) 1346/2000 (OJ L160, 30.6.2000, p 1) on insolvency proceedings. As
   to the European Regulation on Insolvency Proceedings see PARAS 41, 42.
17 Insolvency Rules 1986, SI 1986/1925, r 5.27(2) (r 5.27 as substituted (see note 8); r 5.27(2)
   amended by SI 2010/686).
18 Ie the arrangement proposed under the Insolvency Act 1986 s 256: see PARA 53.
19 Insolvency Act 1986 s 259(2). Where the court has made an interim order under s 252 (see PARA
   45) in respect of an individual who subsequently dies, s 259 applies: Administration of Insolvent
   Estates of Deceased Persons Order 1986, SI 1986/1999, art 3(1), Sch 1 Pt III para 3. As to the
   administration in bankruptcy of the insolvent estates of deceased persons see further PARA 830
   et seq.
       As to the prescribed form of alternative order to be made at the hearing to consider the
   chairman's report see the Insolvency Rules 1986, SI 1986/1925, Sch 4 Form 5.4 (substituted by
   SI 2003/1730; amended by SI 2010/686). In suitable cases the court will normally be prepared
   to make a final order on consideration of the chairman's report without attendance if the
   chairman's report has been filed and complies with the Insolvency Rules 1986, SI 1986/1925,

r 5.27(1) (see text to note 11). The order will record the effect of the chairman's report and may discharge the interim order: *Practice Direction—Insolvency Proceedings* para 16.1(4); and see para 16.2.
20 Insolvency Rules 1986, SI 1986/1925, r 5.27(5) (as substituted: see note 8).

68.   Reports to the Secretary of State. As soon as reasonably practicable, and in any event within the period of 14 days, after a report[1] that the creditors' meeting has approved the voluntary arrangement has been filed in court[2] or sent to the creditors as the case may be, the chairman[3] of the creditors' meeting must send to the Secretary of State[4] the following information:

(1)   the name and address of the debtor[5];

(2)   the date on which the arrangement was approved by the creditors;

(3)   the name and address of the supervisor[6];

(4)   the debtor's gender;

(5)   the debtor's date of birth; and

(6)   any name by which the debtor was or is known, not being the name in which the debtor has entered into the voluntary arrangement[7].

A person who is appointed to act as supervisor of an individual voluntary arrangement, whether in the first instance or by way of replacement of another person previously appointed[8], must as soon as reasonably practicable give written notice to the Secretary of State of his appointment; and, if he vacates office as supervisor, he must as soon as reasonably practicable give written notice of that fact also to the Secretary of State[9].

1   As to the report of the creditors' meeting see PARA 67.
2   As to the meaning of 'file in court' see PARA 57 note 13.
3   As to the chairman of the meeting see PARA 61.
4   As to the Secretary of State see PARA 19. The Secretary of State must maintain an individual insolvency register including certain information on voluntary arrangements: see the Insolvency Rules 1986, SI 1986/1925, rr 6A.1–6A.3; and PARA 28 et seq.
5   As to the meaning of 'debtor' see PARA 44 note 2.
6   As to the supervisor see PARA 73 et seq.
7   Insolvency Rules 1986, SI 1986/1925, r 5.29(1) (r 5.29 substituted by SI 2002/2712; Insolvency Rules 1986, SI 1986/1925, r 5.29(1) amended by SI 2010/686). As to the fee payable on the registration of an individual voluntary arrangement, Fee IVA1, see the Insolvency Proceedings (Fees) Order 2004, SI 2004/593, Sch 2 para 2 (amended by SI 2009/645).
8   Ie under the Insolvency Act 1986 s 256(3)(a) (see PARA 58) or s 258(3) (see PARA 62).
9   Insolvency Rules 1986, SI 1986/1925, r 5.29(2) (r 5.29 as substituted (see note 7); r 5.29(2) amended by SI 2009/642).

(5) EFFECT OF APPROVAL

69.   Effect of approval. Where the meeting of creditors[1] approves the proposed voluntary arrangement, with or without modifications[2], the approved arrangement:

(1)   takes effect as if made by the debtor[3] at the meeting; and

(2)   binds every person who[4] was entitled to vote[5] at the meeting, whether or not he was present or represented at it, or would have been so entitled if he had had notice[6] of it, as if he were a party to the arrangement[7].

Any interim order in force in relation to the debtor immediately before the end of the period of 28 days beginning with the day on which the report with respect to the creditors' meeting was made to the court[8] ceases to have effect at the end of that period[9]. Where proceedings on a bankruptcy petition have been stayed by an interim order which so ceases to have effect, that petition is deemed, unless the court otherwise orders, to have been dismissed[10].

1   Ie summoned under the Insolvency Act 1986 s 257: see PARA 59.

2   As to the modifications which are permissible see PARA 62.

3   As to the meaning of 'debtor' see PARA 44 note 2.

4   Ie in accordance with the Insolvency Rules 1986, SI 1986/1925.

5   As to the rules relating to entitlement to vote see PARA 63.

6   As to the rules relating to notice of the meeting see PARA 59. The reasons why a creditor did not have notice of the meeting do not restrict the binding effect of approval: *Re T & N Ltd* [2006] EWHC 842 (Ch), [2006] 1 WLR 2831, [2006] BPIR 1268. If, when the arrangement ceases to have effect, any amount payable under the arrangement to a person bound as a party to the arrangement by virtue of being someone who would have been entitled to vote had they had notice of the meeting has not been paid, and the arrangement did not come to an end prematurely, the debtor at that time becomes liable to pay that person the amount payable under the arrangement: Insolvency Act 1986 s 260(2A) (added by the Insolvency Act 2000 Sch 3 paras 1, 10). A voluntary arrangement approved by a creditors' meeting summoned under the Insolvency Act 1986 s 257 (see PARA 59) comes to an end prematurely if, when it ceases to have effect, it has not been fully implemented in respect of all persons bound by the arrangement by virtue of s 260(2)(b)(i) (see the text to note 7): s 262C (added by the Insolvency Act 2000 Sch 3 paras 1, 10).

7   Insolvency Act 1986 s 260(1), (2) (s 260(2) amended by the Insolvency Act 2000 Sch 3 paras 1, 10). Approval of the arrangement gives rise to a form of statutory contract: see *Davis v Martin-Sklan* [1995] 2 BCLC 483, [1995] BCC 1122. Thus, whether a voluntary arrangement has the effect of releasing a jointly liable co-debtor depends on whether, as a matter of construction of the voluntary arrangement, it constitutes an absolute release in relation to all the joint debtors or a release with a reservation: *Johnson v Davies* [1999] Ch 117, [1998] 2 All ER 649, CA. The fact that a mortgagee makes a claim and accepts a dividend does not require it to be treated as having elected to abandon its security for any part of the mortgage debt that is secured: *Whitehead v Household Mortgage Corpn plc* [2002] EWCA Civ 1657, [2003] 1 All ER 319, [2003] 1 WLR 1173. Creditors whose debts are caught by the voluntary arrangements will have no further claim to interest on those debts: *El Ajou v Stern* [2006] EWHC 3067 (Ch), [2007] BPIR 693, [2006] All ER (D) 11 (Dec). A term of a voluntary arrangement excluding or limiting an employee's statutory rights is not void under the Employment Rights Act 1996 s 203 (restrictions on contracting-out: see EMPLOYMENT vol 39 (2009) PARA 126): *Re Britannia Heat Transfer Ltd (in admin)* [2007] BCC 470, [2007] BPIR 1038. Limitation periods will not run in respect of debts caught by the voluntary arrangement: *Tanner v Everitt* [2004] EWHC 1130 (Ch), [2004] BPIR 1026, [2004] All ER (D) 192 (May).
    The Deed of Arrangement Act 1914 (see PARA 852 et seq) does not apply to the approved voluntary arrangement: Insolvency Act 1986 s 260(3). Where the court has made an interim order under s 252 (see PARA 45) in respect of an individual who subsequently dies, s 260 applies with the modification that it ceases to apply on or after the death of the individual: Administration of Insolvent Estates of Deceased Persons Order 1986, SI 1986/1999, art 3(1), Sch I Pt III para 4. As to the administration in bankruptcy of the insolvent estates of deceased persons see further PARA 830 et seq.

8   Ie under the Insolvency Act 1986 s 259: see PARA 67.

9   Insolvency Act 1986 s 260(4). Section 260(4) applies except to such extent as the court may direct for the purposes of any application under s 262 (see PARAS 84–86): s 260(4).

10 Insolvency Act 1986 s 260(5).

70. Effect on undischarged bankrupt. Where the creditors' meeting approves the proposed voluntary arrangement[1], with or without modifications, and the debtor is an undischarged bankrupt[2], the court must annul the bankruptcy order[3] on an application made: (1) by the bankrupt; or (2) where the bankrupt has not made an application within the prescribed period[4], by the official receiver[5]. Such an application may not be made at any time before the end of the period of 28 days beginning with the day on which the report of the creditors' meeting was made to the court[6], or at any time when an application challenging the decision of the meeting[7] or an appeal in respect of such an application is pending or at any time in the period within which such an appeal may be brought[8].

Where the above provisions apply the court may give such directions about the conduct of the bankruptcy and the administration of the bankrupt's estate as it thinks appropriate for facilitating the implementation of the approved voluntary arrangement[9].

1　See PARA 69.
2　As to the meaning of 'bankrupt' see PARA 129. As to discharge from bankruptcy see PARA 638 et seq. For these purposes, 'undischarged bankrupt' includes a bankrupt who has been discharged between the approval of the arrangement and his application to annul: *Re Johnson* [2006] BPIR 987.
3　As to bankruptcy orders see PARA 198 et seq; and as to the annulment of bankruptcy orders see PARA 620 et seq.
4　As to the prescribed period see PARA 623.
5　Insolvency Act 1986 s 261(1), (2) (s 261 substituted by the Enterprise Act 2002 Sch 22 para 1). As to the official receiver see PARA 35 et seq. As to the application see PARAS 71–72. Where the court has made an interim order under the Insolvency Act 1986 s 252 (see PARA 45) in respect of an individual who subsequently dies, s 261 applies with the modification that it ceases to apply on or after the death of the individual: Insolvent Estates of Deceased Persons Order 1986, SI 1986/1999, Sch I Pt III para 4. As to the prescribed form of alternative orders to be made at the hearing to consider the chairman's report see the Insolvency Rules 1986, SI 1986/1925, Sch 4 Form 5.4 (substituted by SI 2003/1730; and amended by SI 2010/686).
6　Ie not within the period specified in the Insolvency Act 1986 s 262(3)(a): see PARA 85.
7　Ie an application under the Insolvency Act 1986 s 262: see PARAS 84–86.
8　Insolvency Act 1986 s 261(3) (as substituted: see note 5).
9　Insolvency Act 1986 s 261(4) (as substituted: see note 5).

71. Application by bankrupt to annul bankruptcy order. Where a bankrupt applies for an annulment of a bankruptcy order[1], the application to the court must specify the statutory provision under which it is made[2]. The application must be supported by a witness statement[3] stating: (1) that the voluntary arrangement has been approved at a meeting of creditors[4]; (2) the date of the approval by the creditors; and (3) that the 28 day period for applications to be made[5] has expired and no applications or appeal remain to be disposed of[6].

The application and supporting witness statement must be filed in court[7]; and the court must give to the bankrupt notice of the venue[8] fixed for the hearing[9].

The bankrupt must give notice of the venue, accompanied by copies of the application and witness statement to the official receiver, any trustee who is not the official receiver, and the supervisor of the voluntary arrangement[10] not less than five business days[11] before the date of the hearing[12].

The official receiver, the supervisor of the voluntary arrangement and any trustee who is not the official receiver may attend the hearing or be represented and call to the attention of the court any matters which seem to him to be relevant[13].

Where the court annuls a bankruptcy order, it must send sealed copies of the order of annulment[14] to the bankrupt, the official receiver, the supervisor of the voluntary arrangement and any trustee who is not the official receiver[15].

Where the official receiver has notified creditors of the debtor's bankruptcy, and the bankruptcy order is annulled, he must, as soon as reasonably practicable, notify them of the annulment[16].

1　Ie under the Insolvency Act 1986 s 261(2)(a): see PARA 70 head (1). As to bankruptcy orders see PARA 198 et seq; and as to the annulment of bankruptcy orders see PARA 620 et seq.
2　Insolvency Rules 1986, SI 1986/1925, rr 5.51, 5.52(1) (rr 5.51, 5.52 added by SI 2003/1730).
3　As to the meaning of 'witness statement' see PARA 161 note 7.

4   See PARA 69.

5   Ie the 28 day period in the Insolvency Act 1986 s 262(3)(a) for applications to be made under
    s 262(1): see PARA 84.

6   Insolvency Rules 1986, SI 1986/1925, r 5.52(2) (added by SI 2003/1730; and amended by
    SI 2010/686).

7   As to the meaning of 'file in court' see PARA 57 note 13.

8   As to the meaning of 'venue' see PARA 46 note 22.

9   Insolvency Rules 1986, SI 1986/1925, r 5.52(3) (added by SI 2003/1730; and amended by
    SI 2010/686).

10 As to the supervisor see PARA 73 et seq.

11 As to the meaning of 'business day' see PARA 28 note 8.

12 Insolvency Rules 1986, SI 1986/1925, r 5.52(4) (added by SI 2003/1730; and amended by
    SI 2010/686).

13 Insolvency Rules 1986, SI 1986/1925, r 5.52(5) (added by SI 2003/1730).

14 As to the prescribed form of order of annulment see the Insolvency Rules 1986, SI 1986/1925,
    Sch 4 Form 5.7 (added by SI 2003/1730; substituted by SI 2004/584; and amended by
    SI 2009/642; and SI 2010/686). In an order under the Insolvency Act 1986 s 261(2)(a), (b) (see
    PARA 70) or s 263D(3) (see PARA 95) the court must include provision permitting vacation of the
    registration of the bankruptcy petition as a pending action, and of the bankruptcy order, in the
    register of writs and orders affecting land: Insolvency Rules 1986, SI 1986/1925, r 5.60(1)
    (r 5.60 added by SI 2003/1730). The court must as soon as reasonably practicable give notice of
    the making of the order to the Secretary of State: Insolvency Rules 1986, SI 1986/1925,
    r 5.60(2) (as so added). The former bankrupt may in writing within 28 days of the date of the
    order require the Secretary of State to give notice of the making of the order; and as soon as
    reasonably practicable the notice must be gazetted and advertised in the same manner as the
    bankruptcy order to which it relates was advertised: r 5.60(3) (as so added; and substituted by
    SI 2009/642). As to the meaning of 'gazetted' see PARA 165 note 12. In addition to the standard
    contents (see PARA 165 note 12), the notice must state: (1) the name of the former bankrupt; (2)
    the date on which the bankruptcy order was made; (3) that the bankruptcy order has been
    annulled; (4) the date of the annulling order; and (5) the grounds of the annulment: Insolvency
    Rules 1986, SI 1986/1925, r 5.60(3A) (added by SI 2010/686). Where the former bankrupt has
    died, or is a person who lacks capacity to manage his affairs (see PARA 824), the references to
    him in the Insolvency Rules 1986, SI 1986/1925, r 5.60(3) is to be read as referring to his
    personal representative or, as the case may be, a person appointed by the court to represent or
    act for him: r 5.60(5) (as so added; and amended by SI 2005/527).

15 Insolvency Rules 1986, SI 1986/1925, r 5.52(6) (added by SI 2003/1730). Where a bankruptcy
    order is annulled under s 261(2)(a), (b) (see PARA 70) or s 263D(3) (see PARA 95), this does not
    of itself release the trustee from any duty or obligation, imposed on him by or under the
    Insolvency Act 1986 or the Insolvency Rules 1986, SI 1986/1925, to account for all his
    transactions in connection with the former bankrupt's estate: r 5.61(1) (added by SI 2003/1730).
    The trustee must submit a copy of his final account to the Secretary of State as soon as
    reasonably practicable after the court's order annulling the bankruptcy order; and he must file a
    copy of the final account in court: Insolvency Rules 1986, SI 1986/1925, r 5.61(2) (as so added).
    The final account must include a summary of the trustee's receipts and payments in the
    administration, and contain a statement to the effect that he has reconciled his account with that
    held by the Secretary of State in respect of the bankruptcy: r 5.61(3) (as so added). The trustee
    is released from such time as the court may determine, having regard to whether r 5.61(2) has
    been complied with: r 5.61(4) (as so added).

16 Insolvency Rules 1986, SI 1986/1925, r 5.53(1) (r 5.53 added by SI 2003/1730). Expenses
    incurred by the official receiver in giving such notice are a charge in his favour on the property
    of the former bankrupt, whether or not actually in his hands: Insolvency Rules 1986,
    SI 1986/1925, r 5.53(2) (as so added). Where any property is in the hands of a trustee or any
    person other than the former bankrupt himself, the official receiver's charge is valid subject only
    to any costs that may be incurred by the trustee or that other person in effecting realisation of
    the property for the purpose of satisfying the charge: r 5.53(3) (as so added).

72.   Application by official receiver to annul bankruptcy order.   Where the
official receiver applies for an annulment of a bankruptcy order[1], the application
to the court must specify the statutory provision under which it is made[2]. The
official receiver may not make the application before the expiry of the period of
42 days beginning with the day on which: (1) where the creditors' meeting was

summoned pursuant to a report to a court[3], the nominee filed the report of the creditors' meeting with the court; or (2) where the creditors' meeting was summoned pursuant to a report to the debtor's creditors[4], the result of the creditors' meeting was notified to the creditors[5].

The application must be supported by a report stating the grounds on which it is made; and must also state that the time period for application[6] has expired and that the official receiver is not aware that any application or appeal remains to be disposed of[7].

The application and the report must be filed in court and the court must give to the official receiver notice of the venue[8] fixed for the hearing[9]. The official receiver must give notice of the venue, accompanied by copies of the application and the report to the bankrupt not less than five business days[10] before the date of the hearing[11].

Where the court annuls a bankruptcy order, it must send sealed copies of the order of annulment[12] to the official receiver, any trustee who is not the official receiver, the supervisor of the voluntary arrangement[13] and the bankrupt[14].

Where the bankruptcy order is annulled, the official receiver must notify all creditors of whose address the official receiver is aware of the annulment[15].

1 Ie under the Insolvency Act 1986 s 261(2)(b): see PARA 70 head (2). As to bankruptcy orders see PARA 198 et seq; and as to the annulment of bankruptcy orders see PARA 620 et seq.

2 Insolvency Rules 1986, SI 1986/1925, rr 5.54, 5.55(1) (rr 5.54, 5.55 added by SI 2003/1730).

3 Ie where the creditors' meeting was summoned under the Insolvency Act 1986 s 257 pursuant to a report to a court under s 256(1)(aa): see PARA 57.

4 Ie the creditors' meeting was summoned under the Insolvency Act 1986 s 257 pursuant to a report to the debtor's creditors under s 256A(3): see PARA 51.

5 Insolvency Rules 1986, SI 1986/1925, r 5.55(2) (added by SI 2003/1730; and substituted by SI 2010/686).

6 Ie the time period in the Insolvency Rules 1986, SI 1986/1925, r 5.55(2): see the text to notes 3–5.

7 Insolvency Rules 1986, SI 1986/1925, r 5.55(3) (added by SI 2003/1730).

8 As to the meaning of 'venue' see PARA 46 note 22.

9 Insolvency Rules 1986, SI 1986/1925, r 5.55(4) (added by SI 2003/1730).

10 As to the meaning of 'business day' see PARA 28 note 8.

11 Insolvency Rules 1986, SI 1986/1925, r 5.55(5) (added by SI 2003/1730; and amended by SI 2010/686).

12 As to the prescribed form of order of annulment see the Insolvency Rules 1986, SI 1986/1925, Sch 4 Form 5.7 (added by SI 2003/1730; substituted by SI 2004/584; and amended by SI 2009/642; and SI 2010/686). As to the requirement to give notice of the order see the Insolvency Rules 1986, SI 1986/1925, r 5.60; and PARA 71 note 14.

13 As to the supervisor see PARA 73 et seq.

14 Insolvency Rules 1986, SI 1986/1925, r 5.55(6) (added by SI 2003/1730). The trustee must submit a final account before being released: see the Insolvency Rules 1986, SI 1986/1925, r 5.61; and PARA 71 note 15.

15 Insolvency Rules 1986, SI 1986/1925, r 5.56(1) (r 5.56 added by SI 2003/1730; the Insolvency Rules 1986, SI 1986/1925, r 5.56(1) amended by SI 2010/686). Expenses incurred by the official receiver in giving such notice are a charge in his favour on the property of the former bankrupt, whether or not actually in his hands: Insolvency Rules 1986, SI 1986/1925, r 5.56(2) (as so added). Where any property is in the hands of a trustee or any person other than the former bankrupt himself, the official receiver's charge is valid subject only to any costs that may be incurred by the trustee or that other person in effecting realisation of the property for the purpose of satisfying the charge: r 5.56(3) (as so added).

(6) IMPLEMENTATION OF THE ARRANGEMENT; THE SUPERVISOR

73. The supervisor. Where a voluntary arrangement approved by the meeting of creditors[1] has taken effect[2], the person who is for the time being carrying out, in relation to the voluntary arrangement, the functions conferred by virtue of the approval on the nominee[3], or his replacement[4], is to be known as the supervisor of the voluntary arrangement[5].

The supervisor may apply to the court[6] for directions in relation to any particular matter arising under the voluntary arrangement[7].

1 Ie the meeting summoned under the Insolvency Act 1986 s 257: see PARA 59.
2 As to when a voluntary arrangement takes effect see PARA 69.
3 As to the meaning of 'nominee' see PARA 43.
4 Ie under the Insolvency Act 1986 s 256(3) (see PARA 58), s 256A(4) (see PARA 51) or s 258(3) (see PARA 62).
5 Insolvency Act 1986 s 263(1), (2) (s 263(2) amended by the Insolvency Act 2000 Sch 3 paras 1, 13(a)). As to the supervisor's duty to register certificates relating to the security to be provided by him see COMPANY AND PARTNERSHIP INSOLVENCY vol 16 (2011) PARA 28; and as to the appointment of supervisors by the court see PARA 76.
6 As to the mode of application and the procedure see PARA 786 et seq.
7 Insolvency Act 1986 s 263(4). As to the supervisor's power to present a petition for a bankruptcy order see PARA 130.

74. Supervisor to be insolvency practitioner. A person who acts as supervisor of a voluntary arrangement[1] must be qualified to act as an insolvency practitioner[2] in relation to the individual or must be authorised so to act[3]. The official receiver is authorised to act as nominee or supervisor in relation to a voluntary arrangement provided that the debtor is an undischarged bankrupt when the arrangement is proposed[4].

1 Ie under the Insolvency Act 1986 Pt 8 (ss 252–263G): see PARAS 43–73, 75 et seq; but see PARA 43 note 6.
2 As to insolvency practitioners and their qualification see PARA 40; but see PARA 43 note 6.
3 Insolvency Act 1986 ss 388(2)(c), 389A(2) (s 388 substituted, and s 389A added, by the Insolvency Act 2000 s 4(1), (2)(b), (4)). Nothing in the Insolvency Act 1986 s 388 applies to anything done (whether in the United Kingdom or elsewhere) in relation to insolvency proceedings under Council Regulation (EC) 1346/2000 (OJ L160, 30.6.2000, p 1) on insolvency proceedings ('European Regulation on Insolvency Proceedings') in a member state other than the United Kingdom: Insolvency Act 1986 s 388(6) (added by SI 2002/1240). As to the European Regulation on Insolvency Proceedings see PARAS 41, 42.
4 See the Insolvency Act 1986 s 389B (added by the Enterprise Act 2002 s 264(1), Sch 22 para 3).

75. Control by the court. If the debtor[1], any of his creditors or any other person is dissatisfied by any act, omission or decision of the supervisor[2], he may apply to the court[3]; and on such an application the court may:

(1) confirm, reverse or modify any act or decision of the supervisor;
(2) give him directions; or
(3) make such other order as it thinks fit[4].

The supervisor may apply to court for directions in relation to any particular matter arising under the voluntary arrangement[5].

1 As to the meaning of 'debtor' see PARA 44 note 2.
2 As to the supervisor see PARAS 73, 74, 76 et seq.
3 As to the mode of application and the procedure see PARA 786 et seq.
4 Insolvency Act 1986 s 263(3). Section 263 provides a self-contained procedure allowing the court to deal with complaints about a supervisor's conduct and, therefore, there is no private law right of action for creditors for breach of statutory duty against a supervisor: *King v Anthony* [1998] 2 BCLC 517, [1999] BPIR 73, CA; and see *Heritage Joinery (a firm) v Krasner*

[1999] BPIR 683; *Pitt v Mond* [2001] BPIR 624. Where the court has made an interim order under the Insolvency Act 1986 s 252 (see PARA 45) in respect of an individual who subsequently dies, s 263 applies with the modification that, where the individual dies after a voluntary arrangement has been approved, then in s 263(3), for the words 'debtor, any of his' there are to be substituted the words 'personal representative of the deceased debtor, any of the deceased debtor's'; and the supervisor must give notice to the court that the individual has died: Administration of Insolvent Estates of Deceased Persons Order 1986, SI 1986/1999, art 3(1), Sch I Pt III para 5. As to the administration in bankruptcy of the insolvent estates of deceased persons see further PARA 830 et seq.

5   Insolvency Act 1986 s 263(4). See eg *Davis v Martin-Sklan* [1995] 2 BCLC 483, [1995] BCC 1122. As to the effect on a voluntary arrangement where a bankruptcy order is made see further PARA 89. The court cannot authorise a supervisor to recover disbursements in excess of that permitted by a cap specified in the arrangement: *Re Block Transfer by Kaye and Morgan, Re Murphy* [2010] EWHC 692 (Ch), [2010] BPIR 602; see also PARA 82.

76.   Appointment of supervisor by the court.   Whenever it is expedient to appoint a person to carry out the functions of the supervisor[1] and it is inexpedient, difficult or impracticable for an appointment to be made without the assistance of the court, the court may make an order appointing a person who is qualified to act as an insolvency practitioner[2] or authorised to act as supervisor, in relation to the voluntary arrangement, either in substitution for the existing supervisor or to fill a vacancy[3].

Such power is exercisable so as to increase the number of persons exercising the functions of the supervisor or, where there is more than one person exercising those functions, so as to replace one or more of those persons[4].

1   As to the supervisor see PARA 73.
2   As to insolvency practitioners and their qualification see PARA 40; but see also PARA 43 note 6.
3   Insolvency Act 1986 s 263(5) (amended by the Insolvency Act 2000 Sch 3 paras 1, 13(b)). The Insolvency Act 1986 s 263(5) is without prejudice to the Trustee Act 1925 s 41(2) (power of court to appoint trustees of deeds of arrangement: see PARA 873): Insolvency Act 1986 s 263(5) (as so amended). As to deeds of arrangements under the Deeds of Arrangement Act 1914 generally see PARA 852 et seq. For a further power of the court to appoint a supervisor see the Insolvency Act 1986 s 273(2); and PARA 203. The court has jurisdiction to appoint a new supervisor to one or more voluntary arrangements as part of a 'composite' application replacing an insolvency practitioner in relation to all appointments held by him: see *Supperstone v Auger* [1999] BPIR 152; *Re Equity Nominees Ltd* [1999] 2 BCLC 19, [2000] BCC 84. The power to make a substitute appointment is sufficiently wide to enable the court to order an appointment on a temporary basis: *Clements v Udal* [2002] 2 BCLC 606, [2001] BCC 658, [2001] BPIR 454. As to block transfer rules see the Insolvency Rules 1986, SI 1986/1925, rr 7.10A–7.10D; and PARA 377.
4   Insolvency Act 1986 s 263(6).

77.   Hand-over of property to supervisor; transactions defrauding creditors. As soon as reasonably practicable after the approval of the voluntary arrangement, the debtor[1] or, where the debtor is not an undischarged bankrupt[2], the official receiver[3] or the debtor's trustee[4], must do all that is required for putting the supervisor[5] into possession of the assets included in the arrangement[6].

Where the debtor is an undischarged bankrupt, the supervisor must, on taking possession of the assets, discharge any balance due to the official receiver[7] and, if other, the trustee[8] by way of remuneration or on account of fees, costs, charges and expenses properly incurred and payable[9] and any advances made in respect of the insolvent estate[10], together with interest on such advances at the specified rate[11] at the date of the bankruptcy order[12]. Alternatively, where the debtor is an undischarged bankrupt, the supervisor must, before taking possession, give the official receiver or the trustee a written undertaking to discharge any such balance out of the first realisation of assets[13]. Where the debtor is an undischarged bankrupt, the official receiver and, if other, the trustee has a charge on the assets included in the voluntary arrangement in respect of any sums due as above until they have been discharged, subject only to the deduction from realisations by the supervisor of the proper costs and expenses of realisation; and any sums due to the official receiver take priority over those due to a trustee[14]. The supervisor must from time to time out of the realisation of assets discharge all guarantees properly given by the official receiver or the trustee for the benefit of the estate, and must pay all their expenses[15].

The supervisor has power to apply to the court for an order under the provisions relating to transactions defrauding creditors where the victim of the transaction is bound by a voluntary arrangement[16].

1   As to the meaning of 'debtor' see PARA 44 note 2.
2   As to the meaning of 'bankrupt' see PARA 129. As to discharge from bankruptcy see PARA 638 et seq.
3   As to the official receiver see PARA 35 et seq.
4   As to the trustee see PARA 314 et seq.
5   As to the supervisor see PARA 73 et seq.
6   Insolvency Rules 1986, SI 1986/1925, r 5.26(1) (r 5.26 substituted by SI 2002/2712; Insolvency Rules 1986, SI 1986/1925, r 5.26(1) amended by SI 2009/642).
7   As to the official receiver's fees, costs, charges and expenses see PARA 39.
8   As to the trustee's fees, costs, charges and expenses see PARA 348 et seq.
9   Ie under the Insolvency Act 1986 or the Insolvency Rules 1986, SI 1986/1925.
10 As to the meaning of 'the insolvent estate' see PARA 53 note 17.
11 Ie the rate specified in the Judgments Act 1838 s 17: see FINANCIAL SERVICES AND INSTITUTIONS vol 49 (2008) PARA 1307.
12 Insolvency Rules 1986, SI 1986/1925, r 5.26(2) (as substituted: see note 6).
13 Insolvency Rules 1986, SI 1986/1925, r 5.26(3) (as substituted: see note 6).
14 Insolvency Rules 1986, SI 1986/1925, r 5.26(4) (as substituted: see note 6). The charge does not extend to the fees, costs and expenses of a trustee in bankruptcy received after the date when the supervisor takes possession of the assets: *Rooney v Cardona* [1999] BPIR 954.
15 Insolvency Rules 1986, SI 1986/1925, r 5.26(5) (as substituted: see note 6).
16 See the Insolvency Act 1986 s 424(1)(b); and PARA 690 head (2). As to transactions defrauding creditors generally see PARA 688 et seq.

78.   Power to ensure continuation of essential supplies by utilities.   Where on any day ('the relevant day') a voluntary arrangement proposed by an individual is approved[1], and if a request is made by or with the concurrence of the supervisor[2] and for the purposes of any business[3] which is or has been carried on by the individual, by a firm or partnership of which the individual is or was a member, or by an agent or manager for the individual or for such a firm or partnership[4] for the giving after the relevant day of:

(1)   a supply of gas by a gas supplier[5];
(2)   a supply of electricity by an electricity supplier[6];
(3)   a supply of water by a water undertaker; or
(4)   a supply of communications services[7] by a provider of a public electronic communications service[8],

the supplier:

(a)   may make it a condition of the giving of the supply that the supervisor personally guarantees the payment of any charges in respect of the supply; but
(b)   must not make it a condition of the giving of the supply that any outstanding charges in respect of a supply given to the individual before the relevant day are paid[9].

1   Ie under the Insolvency Act 1986 Pt 8 (ss 252–263G): see PARAS 43–77, 79 et seq: s 372(1)(b).
2   The provisions of the Insolvency Act 1986 s 372 apply also where: (1) a bankruptcy order is made against an individual (see PARAS 258, 485) or an interim receiver of an individual's property is appointed (see PARA 226); or (2) a deed of arrangement is made for the benefit of an individual's creditors (see PARA 874); and in such cases references to 'the supervisor' should be read as references to the official receiver, the trustee in bankruptcy, the interim receiver or the trustee under the deed of arrangement, as the case may be: see s 372(1). As to the supervisor see PARA 73 et seq. In the case of the administration in bankruptcy of the insolvent estate of a deceased person dying before the presentation of a bankruptcy petition, the Insolvency Act 1986 s 372 applies: Administration of Insolvent Estates of Deceased Persons Order 1986, SI 1986/1999, art 3(1), Sch 1 Pt II para 30. As to the administration in bankruptcy of the insolvent estates of deceased persons see further PARA 830 et seq.
3   As to the meaning of 'business' see PARA 43 note 4.
4   Insolvency Act 1986 s 372(3).
5   Ie within the meaning of the Gas Act 1986 Pt 1 (ss 1–48): see ENERGY AND CLIMATE CHANGE vol 42 (2011) PARA 266.
6   Ie within the meaning of the Electricity Act 1989 Pt I (ss 1–64): see ENERGY AND CLIMATE CHANGE vol 43 (2011) PARA 539.
7   For these purposes, 'communications services' do not include electronic communications to the extent that they are used to broadcast or otherwise transmit programme services within the meaning of the Communications Act 2003 (see TELECOMMUNICATIONS vol 97 (2010) PARA 16): Insolvency Act 1986 s 372(5)(c) (substituted by the Communications Act 2003 Sch 17 para 82(1), (3)(b)).
8   Insolvency Act 1986 s 372(4) (amended by the Water Act 1989 Sch 25 para 78(1); the Gas Act 1995 Sch 4 para 14(3); the Utilities Act 2000 Sch 6 para 47(1), (3)(a); and the Communications Act 2003 Sch 17 para 82(1), (3)(a)).
9   Insolvency Act 1986 s 372(2).

79. Supervisor's accounts and reports. Where the voluntary arrangement authorises or requires the supervisor[1]:

(1)   to carry on the debtor's[2] business[3] or to trade on his behalf or in his name;

(2)   to realise assets of the debtor, or where the debtor is an undischarged bankrupt[4], belonging to the estate[5]; or

(3)   otherwise to administer or dispose of any funds of the debtor or the estate,

he must keep accounts and records of his acts and dealings in and in connection with the arrangement, including, in particular, records of all receipts and payments of money[6].

The supervisor must, in respect of each period of 12 months ending with the anniversary of the commencement of the arrangement, send within two months of the end of that period a report on the progress and prospects for the full implementation of the voluntary arrangement to the debtor and all those of the debtor's creditors who are bound by the arrangement[7] and of whose address the supervisor is aware[8], unless an obligation to send a final report[9] arises in that period of two months[10].

1   As to the supervisor see PARA 73 et seq.
2   As to the meaning of 'debtor' see PARA 44 note 2.
3   As to the meaning of 'business' see PARA 43 note 4.
4   As to the meaning of 'bankrupt' see PARA 129. As to discharge from bankruptcy see PARA 638 et seq.
5   As to the meaning of 'estate' see PARA 46 note 9.
6   Insolvency Rules 1986, SI 1986/1925, r 5.31A(1), (2) (r 5.31A added by SI 2010/686). The supervisor must also preserve any such accounts and records which were kept by any other person who has acted as supervisor of the arrangement and are in the supervisor's possession: Insolvency Rules 1986, SI 1986/1925, r 5.31A(3) (as so added). As to the records to be kept by insolvency practitioners generally see COMPANY AND PARTNERSHIP INSOLVENCY vol 16 (2011) PARAS 50–57.

7　As to the persons who are bound by the voluntary arrangement see PARA 69 head (2).
8　Insolvency Rules 1986, SI 1986/1925, r 5.31A(4) (as added: see note 6). The report must include or be accompanied by an abstract of receipts and payments required to be recorded by virtue of r 5.31A(2) or, where there have been no such receipts and payments, a statement to that effect: r 5.31A(6) (as so added).
9　Ie under the Insolvency Rules 1986, SI 1986/1925, r 5.34: see PARA 88.
10　Insolvency Rules 1986, SI 1986/1925, r 5.31A(5) (as added: see note 6).

80. Production of accounts and records to the Secretary of State. The Secretary of State[1] may at any time during the course of the voluntary arrangement or after its completion require the supervisor[2] to produce for inspection his records and accounts in respect of the arrangement and copies of abstracts and reports[3]. The Secretary of State may require production either at the premises of the supervisor or elsewhere; and it is the duty of the supervisor to comply with any requirement imposed on him under these provisions[4].

The Secretary of State may cause any accounts and records produced to him under the above provisions to be audited; and the supervisor must give to the Secretary of State such further information and assistance as he needs for the purpose of his audit[5].

1　As to the Secretary of State see PARA 19.
2　As to the supervisor see PARA 73 et seq.
3　Insolvency Rules 1986, SI 1986/1925, r 5.32(1) (r 5.32 substituted by SI 2002/2712; Insolvency Rules 1986, SI 1986/1925, r 5.32(1) amended by SI 2010/686). The copies of abstracts and reports are those prepared in compliance with the Insolvency Rules 1986, SI 1986/1925, r 5.31A (see PARA 79): r 5.32(1).
4　Insolvency Rules 1986, SI 1986/1925, r 5.32(2) (as substituted: see note 3).
5　Insolvency Rules 1986, SI 1986/1925, r 5.32(3) (as substituted: see note 3).

81. Provision of information. A person ('the relevant person') who has acted or is acting as a nominee[1] in respect of a proposed voluntary arrangement, or a supervisor[2] in respect of a voluntary arrangement must supply a statement free of charge on request in writing by the debtor and, where the proposal has been approved, any creditor of the debtor in respect of the arrangement[3].

The statement must cover the period beginning with the date of the appointment of the relevant person as nominee or supervisor, as the case may be, and ending (1) with the date next before the date of making the request on which the relevant person has completed any period as nominee or supervisor, or both, which is a multiple of six months; or (2) where the relevant person has ceased to act as nominee or supervisor, the date upon which the person so ceased[4].

The statement must comprise the following details:
(a)　the total number of hours spent on the voluntary arrangement by the relevant person whether as nominee or supervisor, or both, and any staff assigned to the voluntary arrangement during that period;
(b)　for each grade of individual so engaged, the average hourly rate at which any work carried out by individuals in that grade is charged; and
(c)　the number of hours spent by each grade of staff during that period[5].

No request under these provisions may be made where more than two years has elapsed since the relevant person ceased to act in any capacity in relation to the proposal or any voluntary arrangement arising out of the approval of the proposal[6]. Any statement required to be provided to any person must be supplied within 28 days of the date of the receipt of the request by the person required to supply it[7].

In any case where disclosure or continuing disclosure to other persons (whether to the public generally or to specific persons) of the current address[8] or whereabouts of a debtor might reasonably be expected to lead to violence against the debtor or against a person who normally resides with the debtor as a member of the debtor's family, the court may, on the application of the debtor, the supervisor, the official receiver[9] (whether acting as a supervisor or otherwise) or the Secretary of State[10], order that:

(i) details of the debtor's current address be removed from any part of the court file of the proceedings in relation to the debtor which is open to inspection and be kept on a separate file not open to inspection;

(ii) the details in respect of the debtor to be entered onto the individual insolvency register[11] in respect of an individual voluntary arrangement must not include details of the debtor's current address; and

(iii) any notice published by the Secretary of State of the making of any order permitting vacation of the registration of a bankruptcy petition[12] must not include details of the bankrupt's address[13].

Where the court makes such an order, it may further order that the details in respect of the debtor to be entered onto the individual insolvency register must instead include such other details of the debtor's addresses or whereabouts as the court thinks just, including details of any address at which the debtor has previously resided or carried on business[14].

The court, on the application of the nominee, the debtor or any person appearing to it to have an interest, may direct that specified information may be omitted from any statement of affairs required to be sent to the creditors where the disclosure of such information would be likely to prejudice the conduct of the voluntary arrangement or might reasonably be expected to lead to violence against any person[15].

1 As to the meaning of 'nominee' see PARA 43.
2 As to the supervisor see PARA 73 et seq.
3 Insolvency Rules 1986, SI 1986/1925, r 5.66(1), (2) (rr 5.66, 5.67, 5.68 added by SI 2010/686).
4 Insolvency Rules 1986, SI 1986/1925, r 5.66(3)(a) (as added: see note 3).
5 Insolvency Rules 1986, SI 1986/1925, r 5.66(3)(b) (as added: see note 3).
6 Insolvency Rules 1986, SI 1986/1925, r 5.66(4) (as added: see note 3).
7 Insolvency Rules 1986, SI 1986/1925, r 5.66(5) (as added: see note 3).
8 For this purpose, 'current address' means, in relation to any debtor, the address of the debtor's current place of residence and any address at which the debtor currently carries on business; and 'debtor' means a debtor who has entered into an individual voluntary arrangement: Insolvency Rules 1986, SI 1986/1925, r 5.67(2) (as added: see note 3).
9 As to the official receiver see PARA 35 et seq.
10 As to the Secretary of State see PARA 19.
11 Ie under the Insolvency Rules 1986, SI 1986/1925, r 6A.2A (see PARA 29).
12 Ie as referred to in the Insolvency Rules 1986, SI 1986/1925, r 5.60 (see PARA 71).
13 Insolvency Rules 1986, SI 1986/1925, r 5.67(1), (3) (as added: see note 3). In any case where an application is made in respect of a debtor under or by virtue of r 5.67, the application must be accompanied by a witness statement referring to r 5.67 and containing sufficient evidence to satisfy the court that r 5.67(1) applies to or in respect of that debtor: r 5.67(5) (as so added). As to the meaning of 'witness statement' see PARA 161 note 7.
14 Insolvency Rules 1986, SI 1986/1925, r 5.67(4) (as added: see note 3).
15 Insolvency Rules 1986, SI 1986/1925, r 5.68 (as added: see note 3).

82. Fees, costs, charges and expenses. The fees, costs, charges and expenses that may be incurred for any purposes of the voluntary arrangement are:

(1) any disbursements made by the nominee[1] prior to the approval of the arrangement, and any remuneration for his services as such agreed between himself and the debtor[2], the official receiver[3] or the trustee[4];

(2) any fees, costs, charges and expenses which are sanctioned by the terms

of the arrangement or would be payable, or correspond to those which would be payable, in the debtor's bankruptcy[5].

1 As to the meaning of 'nominee' see PARA 43.
2 As to the meaning of 'debtor' see PARA 44 note 2.
3 As to the official receiver see PARA 35 et seq.
4 As to the trustee see PARA 314 et seq.
5 Insolvency Rules 1986, SI 1986/1925, r 5.33 (substituted by SI 2002/2712). As to the fees, costs, charges or expenses payable in a bankruptcy see PARA 590. The court cannot authorise a supervisor to recover disbursements in excess of that permitted by a cap specified in the arrangement: *Re Block Transfer by Kaye and Morgan, Re Murphy* [2010] EWHC 692 (Ch), [2010] BPIR 602.

(7) PROSECUTION OF DELINQUENT DEBTORS

83. Prosecution of delinquent debtors. Where a voluntary arrangement approved by a creditors' meeting which has been duly summoned[1] has taken effect[2] and it appears to the nominee[3] or supervisor[4] that the debtor[5] has been guilty of any offence in connection with the arrangement for which he is criminally liable, he must forthwith:

(1) report the matter to the Secretary of State[6]; and
(2) provide the Secretary of State with such information and give the Secretary of State such access to and facilities for inspecting and taking copies of documents, being information or documents in his possession or under his control and relating to the matter in question, as the Secretary of State requires[7].

Where a prosecuting authority[8] institutes criminal proceedings following any such report, the nominee or, as the case may be, supervisor must give the authority all assistance in connection with the prosecution which he is reasonably able to give[9]; and the court may, on the application of the prosecuting authority, direct a nominee or supervisor to comply with that requirement if he has failed to do so[10].

1 Ie under the Insolvency Act 1986 s 257: see PARA 59.
2 As to when a voluntary arrangement takes effect see PARA 69.
3 As to the meaning of 'nominee' see PARA 43.
4 As to the meaning of 'supervisor' see PARA 43.
5 As to the meaning of 'debtor' see PARA 44 note 2.
6 As to the Secretary of State see PARA 19.
7 Insolvency Act 1986 s 262B(1), (2) (s 262B added by the Insolvency Act 2000 Sch 3 paras 1, 12).
8 For these purposes, 'prosecuting authority' means the Director of Public Prosecutions or the Secretary of State: Insolvency Act 1986 s 262B(3) (as added: see note 7). As to the Director of Public Prosecutions see CRIMINAL PROCEDURE vol 27 (2010) PARAS 23, 33 et seq.
9 Insolvency Act 1986 s 262B(3) (as added: see note 7).
10 Insolvency Act 1986 s 262B(4) (as added: see note 7).

(8) CHALLENGE OF DECISIONS; REVOCATION OR SUSPENSION OF THE ARRANGEMENT

84. Grounds for challenge. An application to the court[1] may be made by any of certain specified persons[2], on one or both of the following grounds, namely:

(1) that a voluntary arrangement approved by a creditors' meeting[3] unfairly prejudices[4] the interests of a creditor[5] of the debtor[6];
(2) that there has been some material irregularity[7] at or in relation to such a meeting[8].

1   As to the mode of application and the procedure see PARA 786 et seq.
2   Ie the persons specified in the Insolvency Act 1986 s 262(2): see PARA 85.
3   Ie a meeting summoned under the Insolvency Act 1986 s 257: see PARA 59.
4   Inadequate investigation by the nominee of the debtor's affairs will not amount to unfair prejudice: *Re a Debtor (No 574 of 1995)* [1998] 2 BCLC 124, sub nom *National Westminster Bank plc v Scher* [1998] BPIR 224. The precise boundary of unfair prejudice is unclear: *Cadbury Schweppes plc v Somji* [2001] 1 WLR 615, sub nom *Somji v Cadbury Schweppes plc* [2001] 1 BCLC 498, CA. In determining whether an arrangement is unfairly prejudicial, the prejudice must arise from the arrangement itself. The fact that all creditors are treated in the same way is not necessarily conclusive of the absence of unfair prejudice. A creditor with rights under the Third Persons (Rights against Insurers) Act 1930 (see PARA 433; and INSURANCE vol 60 (2011) PARA 651 et seq) could be unfairly prejudiced if the effect of the arrangement was to remove his rights: *Sea Voyager Maritime Inc v Bielecki (t/a Hughes Hooker & Co)* [1999] 1 All ER 628, [1999] 1 BCLC 133. The existence of differential treatment in an arrangement is not by itself sufficient to prove unfair prejudice; the court must consider all the circumstances: *Re a Debtor (No 101 of 1999)* [2001] 1 BCLC 54, [2000] BPIR 998; and see *Re a Debtor (No 488 IO of 1996), JP v Debtor* [1999] 2 BCLC 571, [1999] 2 FCR 637 (a wife can be unfairly prejudiced where she is bound by an arrangement to accept a dividend in satisfaction of a matrimonial debt which would otherwise not be discharged in a bankruptcy), approved in *Child Maintenance and Enforcement Commission v Beesley* [2010] EWCA Civ 1344, [2011] 3 All ER 233, [2011] 1 WLR 1704; *Re Naeem (a bankrupt) (No 18 of 1988)* [1990] 1 WLR 48 (landlord not unfairly prejudiced by an arrangement because he retained a right of forfeiture, even though claim for rent is compromised); *IRC v Wimbledon Football Club Ltd* [2004] EWHC 1020 (Ch), [2005] 1 BCLC 66, [2004] BPIR 700 (no unfair prejudice from less favourable treatment); *Revenue and Customs Comrs v Portsmouth City Football Club Ltd (in administration)* [2010] EWHC 2013 (Ch), [2010] BPIR 1123, [2010] All ER (D) 58 (Aug) (no unfair prejudice from football creditor rules); *Prudential Assurance Co Ltd v PRG Powerhouse Ltd* [2007] EWHC 1002 (Ch), [2007] Bus LR 1771, [2008] 1 BCLC 289; *Mourant & Co Trustees Ltd v Sixty UK Ltd (in liquidation)* [2010] EWHC 1890 (Ch), [2011] 1 BCLC 383, [2010] BPIR 1264 (unfair prejudice to landlord).
5   The Child Maintenance and Enforcement Commission is not capable of being a creditor entitled to participate in and be bound by an individual voluntary arrangement because it is not capable of compromising liability in respect of arrears of child support, which is an implied requirement under the Insolvency Act 1986 Pt 8 (ss 252–263G): *Child Maintenance and Enforcement Commission v Beesley* [2010] EWCA Civ 1344, [2011] 3 All ER 233, [2011] 1 WLR 1704.
6   As to the meaning of 'debtor' see PARA 44 note 2.
7   A material irregularity in the debtor's proposal or statement of affairs could constitute a material irregularity for the purposes of the Insolvency Act 1986 s 262(1)(b): see head (2) in the text. Material irregularity is not confined to irregularities in the manner the meeting is convened or conducted: *Re a Debtor (No 87 of 1993) (No 2)* [1996] 1 BCLC 63, [1996] BCC 80. A secret deal with one or more of a debtor's creditors, even if not offered by the debtor himself, can amount to a material irregularity: *Cadbury Schweppes plc v Somji* [2001] 1 WLR 615, sub nom *Somji v Cadbury Schweppes plc* [2001] 1 BCLC 498, CA. The test for material irregularity is whether, objectively assessed, the error or omission is likely to make a material difference to the way in which the creditors consider and assess the terms of a proposal: *Monecor (London) Ltd v Ahmed* [2008] BPIR 458, [2008] All ER (D) 22 (Mar); *IRC v Fender* [2003] BPIR 1304, [2003] All ER (D) 148 (Jul). See also *Tradition (UK) Ltd v Ahmed* [2008] EWHC 2946 (Ch), [2009] BPIR 626, [2008] All ER (D) 72 (Dec); and *Kapoor v National Westminster Bank* [2011] EWCA Civ 1083, [2012] 1 All ER 1201, [2011] BPIR 1680.
8   Insolvency Act 1986 s 262(1). Where the court has made an interim order under s 252 (see PARA 45) in respect of an individual who subsequently dies, s 262 applies with the modification that it ceases to apply on or after the death of the individual: Administration of Insolvent Estates of Deceased Persons Order 1986, SI 1986/1999, art 3(1), Sch 1 Pt III para 4. As to the administration in bankruptcy of the insolvent estates of deceased persons see further PARA 830 et seq.

85. Who may apply and when. The persons who may apply to the court[1] are:

(1)   the debtor[2];

(2)   a person entitled[3] to vote at the creditors' meeting, or who would have been so entitled if he had had notice of it[4];

(3)   the nominee[5] or his replacement[6]; and

(4)   if the debtor is an undischarged bankrupt[7], the trustee[8] of his estate[9] or the official receiver[10].

Such an application may not be made, however, after the end of the period of 28 days beginning with the day on which the report of the creditors' meeting was made[11] to the court[12] or, in the case of a person who was not given notice of the creditors' meeting, after the end of the period of 28 days beginning with the day on which he became aware that the meeting had taken place[13]. Subject to those provisions, an application made by a person who would have been entitled to vote at the meeting had he had notice of it[14] on the ground that the arrangement prejudices his interests may be made after the arrangement has ceased to have effect, unless it has come to an end prematurely[15].

1   Ie under the Insolvency Act 1986 s 262: see PARA 84.
2   Insolvency Act 1986 s 262(2)(a). As to the meaning of 'debtor' see PARA 44 note 2. Where the court has made an interim order under s 252 (see PARA 45) in respect of an individual who subsequently dies, s 262 applies with the modification that it ceases to apply on or after the death of the individual: Administration of Insolvent Estates of Deceased Persons Order 1986, SI 1986/1999, art 3(1), Sch 1 Pt III para 4. As to the administration in bankruptcy of the insolvent estates of deceased persons see further PARA 830 et seq.
3   Ie in accordance with the Insolvency Rules 1986, SI 1986/1925.
4   Insolvency Act 1986 s 262(2)(b) (substituted by the Insolvency Act 2000 Sch 3 paras 1, 11(1)(a)). See also note 2. As to the creditors to be given notice of the meeting see PARA 59.
5   As to the meaning of 'nominee' see PARA 43.
6   Insolvency Act 1986 s 262(2)(c) (amended by the Insolvency Act 2000 Sch 3 paras 1, 11(1)(b)). See also note 2. As to the nominee's replacement see the Insolvency Act 1986 s 256(3) (see PARA 58), s 256A(4) (see PARA 51) and s 258(3) (see PARA 62).
7   As to the meaning of 'bankrupt' see PARA 129. As to discharge from bankruptcy see PARA 638 et seq.
8   As to the trustee see PARA 314 et seq.
9   As to the meaning of 'estate' see PARA 46 note 9.
10   Insolvency Act 1986 s 262(2)(d). See also note 2. As to the official receiver see PARA 35 et seq.
11   Ie under the Insolvency Act 1986 s 259: see PARA 67.
12   Insolvency Act 1986 s 262(3)(a) (amended by the Insolvency Act 1986 Sch 3 paras 1, 11(2)(a)). The court has jurisdiction to extend the time for making an application under the Insolvency Act 1986 s 262: *Tager v Westpac Banking Corpn* [1997] 1 BCLC 313, [1997] BPIR 543; cf *Re Bournemouth & Boscombe Athletic Football Club Co Ltd* [1998] BPIR 183. As to factors to be considered by the court when exercising its discretion to extend the period within which an application can be made see *Warley Continental Services Ltd v Johal* [2004] BPIR 353, (2002) Times, 28 October.
13   Insolvency Act 1986 s 262(3)(b) (added by the Insolvency Act 1986 Sch 3 paras 1, 11(2)(b)). See also note 2.
14   Ie an application made by a person falling within the Insolvency Act 1986 s 262(2)(b)(ii): see text to note 4.
15   Insolvency Act 1986 s 262(3) (amended by the Insolvency Act 2000 Sch 3 paras 1, 11(2)). As to arrangements coming to an end prematurely see the Insolvency Act 1986 s 262C; and PARA 69 note 6.

86.   Powers of the court. Where, on an application challenging the decision of a creditor's meeting[1], the court is satisfied as to either of the specified grounds[2], it may do one or both of the following, namely:

(1)   revoke or suspend any approval given by the meeting[3];
(2)   give a direction to any person for the summoning of a further meeting of the debtor's[4] creditors to consider any revised proposal he may make or, in a case where there has been some material irregularity at or in relation to the meeting[5], to reconsider his original proposal[6].

Where, at any time after giving a direction under head (2) above for the summoning of a meeting to consider a revised proposal, the court is satisfied that the debtor does not intend to submit such a proposal, the court must revoke the direction and revoke or suspend any approval given at the previous meeting[7]. Where the court gives such a direction, it may also give a direction continuing or, as the case may require, renewing, for such period as may be specified in the direction, the effect in relation to the debtor of any interim order[8].

In any case where the court, on an application made with respect to a creditors' meeting, gives a direction under head (2) above or revokes or suspends an approval under the above provisions[9], the court may give such supplemental directions as it thinks fit and, in particular, directions with respect to:

(a) things done since the meeting under any voluntary arrangement approved by the meeting; and

(b) such things done since the meeting as could not have been done if an interim order had been in force in relation to the debtor when they were done[10].

Except in pursuance of the above provisions[11], an approval given at a creditors' meeting[12] is not invalidated by any irregularity at or in relation to the meeting[13].

1 Ie under the Insolvency Act 1986 s 262(1)–(3): see PARAS 84, 85.
2 Ie the grounds mentioned in the Insolvency Act 1986 s 262(1): see PARA 84.
3 Insolvency Act 1986 s 262(4)(a). As to the procedure where an order of revocation or suspension is made see PARA 87. Where the court has made an interim order under s 252 (see PARA 45) in respect of an individual who subsequently dies, s 262 applies with the modification that it ceases to apply on or after the death of the individual: Administration of Insolvent Estates of Deceased Persons Order 1986, SI 1986/1999, art 3(1), Sch 1 Pt III para 4. As to the administration in bankruptcy of the insolvent estates of deceased persons see further PARA 830 et seq.
4 As to the meaning of 'debtor' see PARA 44 note 2.
5 If it appears to the court that sufficient creditors (in value) would at any further meeting vote against the proposal, the court may decline to order a further meeting: *Re a Debtor (No 222 of 1990), ex p Bank of Ireland* [1992] BCLC 137. When deciding whether to order a further meeting of creditors, the court ought to balance the heinousness of the irregularities that gave rise to the revocation against the interests of creditors: *IRC v Duce* [1999] BPIR 189. The test to be applied when considering the question whether to direct a further meeting to consider revised proposals is equivalent to that employed when considering whether to make an interim order, ie whether the proposal is serious and viable: *Re a Debtor (No 101 of 1999) (No 2)* [2001] BPIR 996.
6 Insolvency Act 1986 s 262(4)(b).
7 Insolvency Act 1986 s 262(5). See also note 3.
8 Insolvency Act 1986 s 262(6).
9 Ie under the Insolvency Act 1986 s 262(4)(a) or (5): see text to notes 1–3, 7.
10 Insolvency Act 1986 s 262(7). As to the court's jurisdiction to award costs against a nominee/chairman as a result of breaches of duty on an application under s 262 see *Harmony Carpets v Chaffin-Laird* [2000] BCC 893, [2000] BPIR 61. See also *Re a Debtor (No 222 of 1990), ex p Bank of Ireland (No 2)* [1993] BCLC 233.
11 Ie the Insolvency Act 1986 s 262(1)–(7): see text to notes 1–10; and PARAS 84, 85.
12 Ie a meeting summoned under the Insolvency Act 1986 s 257: see PARA 59.
13 Insolvency Act 1986 s 262(8).

87. Procedure following revocation or suspension. Where the court makes an order of revocation or suspension of the voluntary arrangement[1], the person who applied for the order must serve sealed copies of it:

(1) where the debtor[2] is an undischarged bankrupt[3], on the debtor, the official receiver[4] and the trustee[5];

(2) in any other case, on the debtor; and

(3) in either case, on the supervisor[6] of the voluntary arrangement[7].

If the order includes a direction by the court[8] for any further creditors' meeting to be summoned, notice must also be given[9], by the person who applied for the order, to whoever is, in accordance with the direction, required to summon the meeting[10]. Where the debtor is an undischarged bankrupt, the trustee or, if there is no trustee, the official receiver, and in any other case, the debtor, must:

(a) as soon as reasonably practicable after receiving a copy of the court's order, give notice of it to all persons who were sent notice of the creditors' meeting[11] which approved the voluntary arrangement or who, not having been sent that notice, are affected by the order;

(b) within five business days[12] of their receiving a copy of the order, or within such longer period as the court may allow, give notice to the court whether it is intended to make a revised proposal to creditors, or to invite reconsideration of the original proposal[13].

The person on whose application the order of revocation or suspension was made must, within five business days after the making of the order, give written notice of it to the Secretary of State[14], and must, in the case of an order of suspension, within five business days of the expiry of any suspension order, give written notice of such expiry to the Secretary of State[15].

1 Ie under the Insolvency Act 1986 s 262: see PARAS 84–86.
2 As to the meaning of 'debtor' see PARA 44 note 2.
3 As to the meaning of 'bankrupt' see PARA 129. As to discharge from bankruptcy see PARA 638 et seq.
4 As to the official receiver see PARA 35 et seq.
5 As to the trustee see PARA 314 et seq.
6 As to the supervisor see PARA 73 et seq.
7 Insolvency Rules 1986, SI 1986/1925, r 5.30(1), (2) (r 5.30 substituted by SI 2002/2712).
8 Ie under the Insolvency Act 1986 s 262(4)(b): see PARA 86 head (2).
9 As to the mode of giving notice see PARA 808.
10 Insolvency Rules 1986, SI 1986/1925, r 5.30(3) (as substituted: see note 7).
11 As to the creditors to be given notice of the meeting see PARA 59.
12 As to the meaning of 'business day' see PARA 28 note 8.
13 Insolvency Rules 1986, SI 1986/1925, r 5.30(4) (r 5.30 as substituted (see note 7); r 5.30(4) amended by SI 2009/642; and SI 2010/686).
14 As to the Secretary of State see PARA 19.
15 Insolvency Rules 1986, SI 1986/1925, r 5.30(5) (r 5.30 as substituted (see note 7); r 5.30(5) amended by SI 2010/686).

(9) COMPLETION OR TERMINATION OF THE ARRANGEMENT

88. Completion or termination of the arrangement. Not more than 28 days after the final completion or termination of the voluntary arrangement, the supervisor[1] must send to all creditors of the debtor[2] who are bound by the arrangement[3], and to the debtor, a notice that the arrangement has been fully implemented or, as the case may be, terminated[4]. With the notice there must be sent to each of those persons a copy of a report by the supervisor summarising all receipts and payments made by him in pursuance of the arrangement, and explaining any difference in the actual implementation of it as compared with the proposal as approved by the creditors' meeting or, in the case of termination of the arrangement, explaining the reasons why the arrangement has not been implemented in accordance with the proposal as approved by the creditors' meeting[5].

The supervisor must, within the 28 days mentioned above, send to the Secretary of State[6] and, where the creditors' meeting was summoned[7] pursuant to a report by the nominee stating that it was his opinion that a creditors' meeting should be summoned to consider the debtor's proposal[8], file with the court[9] a copy of the notice to creditors, together with a copy of the report[10]; and he must not vacate office until after he has complied with these provisions[11].

On application[12] by the supervisor, the court may extend the periods of 28 days referred to above[13].

1   As to the supervisor see PARA 73 et seq.
2   As to the meaning of 'debtor' see PARA 44 note 2.
3   As to the persons bound by the voluntary arrangement see PARA 69 head (2).
4   Insolvency Rules 1986, SI 1986/1925, r 5.34(1) (r 5.34 substituted by SI 2002/2712).
5   Insolvency Rules 1986, SI 1986/1925, r 5.34(2) (as substituted: see note 4).
6   As to the Secretary of State see PARA 19.
7   Ie under the Insolvency Act 1986 s 257: see PARA 59.
8   Ie pursuant to a report under the Insolvency Act 1986 s 256(1)(aa): see PARA 57.
9   As to the meaning of 'file with the court' see PARA 57 note 13.
10 Insolvency Rules 1986, SI 1986/1925, r 5.34(3A) (r 5.34 as substituted (see note 4); r 5.34(3A) added by SI 2010/686).
11 Insolvency Rules 1986, SI 1986/1925, r 5.34(3) (r 5.34 as substituted (see note 4); r 5.34(3) substituted by SI 2010/686).
12 As to the mode of application and the procedure see PARA 786 et seq.
13 Insolvency Rules 1986, SI 1986/1925, r 5.34(4) (r 5.34 a substituted (see note 4); r 5.34(4) amended by SI 2010/686).

(10) EFFECT OF BANKRUPTCY ON THE ARRANGEMENT

89. Effect of bankruptcy on voluntary arrangement. Where a voluntary arrangement has been approved by the debtor's[1] creditors[2] and a bankruptcy order[3] is made against the debtor prior to final completion of the voluntary arrangement[4], the order has the effect of bringing the voluntary arrangement to an end[5]. Where a voluntary arrangement provides for moneys or other assets to be paid or transferred or held for the benefit of creditors under a voluntary arrangement, a trust of those moneys or assets is created for those creditors. The effect of the bankruptcy of the debtor on a trust created by the voluntary arrangement depends on the provisions of the voluntary arrangement relating thereto. If the voluntary arrangement does not so provide, the trust will continue notwithstanding the bankruptcy and must take effect according to its terms. The creditors under a voluntary arrangement may prove in the bankruptcy for so much of their debt as remains after payment of what has been or will be recovered under the trust[6].

1   As to the meaning of 'debtor' see PARA 44 note 2.
2   Ie pursuant to the Insolvency Act 1986 s 258: see PARA 98 et seq.
3   As to bankruptcy orders see PARA 198 et seq.
4   As to final completion of the arrangement see PARA 88.
5   *Re NT Gallagher & Son Ltd (in liquidation), Shierson v Tomlinson* [2002] EWCA Civ 404, [2002] 3 All ER 474, [2002] 1 WLR 2380 (a case concerning a company voluntary liquidation but the reasoning expressly extends to individual voluntary arrangements).
6   *Re NT Gallagher & Son Ltd (in liquidation), Shierson v Tomlinson* [2002] EWCA Civ 404, [2002] 3 All ER 474, [2002] 1 WLR 2380. For earlier cases on individual voluntary arrangements see also *Davis v Martin-Sklan* [1995] 2 BCLC 483, [1995] BCC 1122; *Re McKeen (a debtor)* [1995] BCC 412; *Re Bradley-Hole (a bankrupt)* [1995] 4 All ER 865, [1995] 1 WLR 1097.

(11) FAST-TRACK VOLUNTARY ARRANGEMENTS

90. Availability. Where an individual debtor[1] intends to make a proposal to his creditors for a voluntary arrangement and: (1) the debtor is an undischarged bankrupt[2]; (2) the official receiver[3] is specified in the proposal as the nominee[4] in relation to the voluntary arrangement; and (3) no interim order[5] is applied for[6], the debtor may submit to the official receiver a document setting out the terms of the voluntary arrangement which the debtor is proposing[7], and a statement of his affairs containing such particulars as may be prescribed of his creditors, debts, other liabilities and assets and such other information as may be prescribed[8].

1   As to the meaning of 'debtor' see PARA 44 note 2.
2   As to the meaning of 'bankrupt' see PARA 129. As to discharge from bankruptcy see PARA 638 et seq.
3   As to the official receiver see PARA 35 et seq.
4   As to the meaning of 'nominee' see PARA 43.
5   Ie an interim order applied for under the Insolvency Act 1986 s 253: see PARA 46.
6   Insolvency Act 1986 s 263A (added by Enterprise Act 2002 Sch 22 para 2). The Secretary of State may by order amend the Insolvency Act 1986 so as to extend the provisions of ss 263B to 263G to some or all cases other than those specified in s 263A: Enterprise Act 2002 s 264(2)–(4). At the date at which this volume states the law no such order had been made. As to the Secretary of State see PARA 19.
7   Insolvency Act 1986 s 263B(1)(a) (s 263B added by Enterprise Act 2002 Sch 22 para 2).
8   Insolvency Act 1986 s 263B(1)(b) (as added: see note 7). Where a debtor submits documents to the official receiver under s 263B(1), no application for an interim order under s 253 (see PARA 44) may be made in respect of the debtor until the official receiver has: (1) made arrangements as described in s 263B(2) (see PARA 92); or (2) informed the debtor that he does not intend to make arrangements, whether because he does not think the voluntary arrangement has a reasonable prospect of being approved and implemented or because he declines to act: s 263B(5) (as so added). As to the prescribed particulars see PARA 91.

91.   Contents of proposal. The debtor's[1] proposal[2] must be accompanied by any fee payable[3] to the official receiver[4] for acting as nominee[5] and contain: (1) a statement that the debtor is eligible to propose a voluntary arrangement; (2) a short explanation why, in his opinion, a voluntary arrangement is desirable, and give reasons why his creditors may be expected to concur with such an arrangement; and (3) a statement that the debtor is aware that he commits an offence[6] if, for the purpose of obtaining the approval of his creditors to his proposal, he makes any false representation, or fraudulently does, or omits to do, anything[7].

The proposal must be authenticated[8] by the debtor and must state, or otherwise deal with:

(a)   so far as within the debtor's immediate knowledge:
   (i)   his assets, with an estimate of their respective values;
   (ii)   the extent, if any, to which the assets are charged in favour of creditors; and
   (iii) the extent, if any, to which particular assets are to be excluded from the voluntary arrangement[9];

(b)   particulars of any property, other than assets of the debtor himself, which is proposed to be included in the voluntary arrangement, the source of such property and the terms on which it is to be made available for inclusion[10];

(c)   the nature and amount of the debtor's liabilities, so far as within his immediate knowledge, the manner in which they are proposed to be met, modified, postponed or otherwise dealt with by means of the voluntary arrangement and, in particular:
   (i)   how it is proposed to deal with preferential creditors[11] and creditors who are, or claim to be, secured[12];

    (ii)   how associates[13] of the debtor, being creditors of his, are proposed to be treated under the voluntary arrangement; and

    (iii)   whether, to the debtor's knowledge, claims have been made relating to transactions at an undervalue[14], preferences[15] or extortionate credit transactions[16], or whether there are circumstances giving rise to the possibility of such claims,

and, where any such circumstances are present, whether, and if so how, it is proposed under the voluntary arrangement to make provision for wholly or partly indemnifying the insolvent estate[17] in respect of such claims[18];

(d)   whether any, and if so what, guarantees have been given of the debtor's debts by other persons, specifying which, if any, of the guarantors are associates of his[19];

(e)   the proposed duration of the voluntary arrangement[20];

(f)   the proposed dates of distributions to creditors, with estimates of their amounts[21];

(g)   how it is proposed to deal with the claims of any person who is bound by the arrangement[22];

(h)   an estimate of the fees and expenses that will be incurred in connection with the approval and implementation of the voluntary arrangement[23];

(i)   whether, for the purposes of the voluntary arrangement, any guarantees are to be offered by any persons other than the debtor, and whether, if so, any security is to be given or sought[24];

(j)   the manner in which funds held for the purpose of payment to creditors, and not so paid on the termination of the voluntary arrangement, are to be dealt with[25];

(k)   the functions which are to be undertaken by the supervisor[26] of the voluntary arrangement[27];

(l)   an address of the official receiver to which correspondence with the official receiver is to be sent[28], to be supplied to the debtor on request[29];

(m)   the names and addresses of all the debtor's creditors so far as within his immediate knowledge[30]; and

(n)   whether the EC Regulation[31] will apply and, if so, whether the proceedings will be main proceedings[32] or territorial proceedings[33].

1   As to the meaning of 'debtor' see PARA 44 note 2.
2   Ie submitted under the Insolvency Act 1986 s 263B(1): see PARA 90. For these purposes, 'proposal' means the document setting out the terms of the voluntary arrangement which the debtor is proposing: Insolvency Rules 1986, SI 1986/1925, r 5.36 (substituted by SI 2003/1730).
3   As to the official receiver's fees, costs and expenses see PARA 95.
4   As to the official receiver see PARA 35 et seq.
5   Insolvency Rules 1986, SI 1986/1925, r 5.37(1)(a) (r 5.37 substituted by SI 2003/1730). As to the meaning of 'nominee' see PARA 43.
6   Ie an offence under the Insolvency Act 1986 s 262A: see PARA 44.
7   Insolvency Rules 1986, SI 1986/1925, r 5.37(1)(b) (as substituted: see note 5). As to transactions defrauding creditors generally see PARA 688 et seq.
8   As to authentication see PARA 158 note 2.
9   Insolvency Rules 1986, SI 1986/1925, r 5.37(2)(a) (r 5.37 as substituted (see note 5); r 5.37(2) amended by SI 2010/686).
10 Insolvency Rules 1986, SI 1986/1925, r 5.37(2)(b) (as substituted and amended: see notes 5, 9).
11 As to the meaning of 'preferential creditors' see the Insolvency Act 1986 s 258(7); and PARA 591 note 2.
12 As to secured creditors see PARA 574.
13 As to the meaning of 'associate' see PARA 5.
14 Ie under the Insolvency Act 1986 s 339: see PARAS 678–679.

15 Ie under the Insolvency Act 1986 s 340: see PARA 681.
16 Ie under the Insolvency Act 1986 s 343: see PARA 697 et seq.
17 As to the meaning of 'the insolvent estate' see PARA 53 note 17.
18 Insolvency Rules 1986, SI 1986/1925, r 5.37(2)(c) (as substituted and amended: see notes 5, 9).
19 Insolvency Rules 1986, SI 1986/1925, r 5.37(2)(d) (as substituted and amended: see notes 5, 9).
20 Insolvency Rules 1986, SI 1986/1925, r 5.37(2)(e) (as substituted and amended: see notes 5, 9).
21 Insolvency Rules 1986, SI 1986/1925, r 5.37(2)(f) (as substituted and amended: see notes 5, 9).
22 Insolvency Rules 1986, SI 1986/1925, r 5.37(2)(g) (as substituted and amended: see notes 5, 9).
    The reference to a person bound is to a person bound by virtue of the Insolvency Act 1986
    s 263D(2)(c): see PARA 95.
23 Insolvency Rules 1986, SI 1986/1925, r 5.37(2)(h) (as substituted and amended: see notes 5, 9).
24 Insolvency Rules 1986, SI 1986/1925, r 5.37(2)(j) (as substituted and amended: see notes 5, 9).
25 Insolvency Rules 1986, SI 1986/1925, r 5.37(2)(k) (as substituted and amended: see notes 5, 9).
26 As to the meaning of 'supervisor' see PARA 43.
27 Insolvency Rules 1986, SI 1986/1925, r 5.37(2)(l) (as substituted and amended: see notes 5, 9).
28 Insolvency Rules 1986, SI 1986/1925, r 5.37(2)(m) (as substituted and amended: see notes 5, 9).
29 Insolvency Rules 1986, SI 1986/1925, r 5.37(3) (as substituted: see note 5).
30 Insolvency Rules 1986, SI 1986/1925, r 5.37(2)(n) (as substituted and amended: see notes 5, 9).
31 Ie Council Regulation (EC) 1346/2000 (OJ L160, 30.6.2000, p 1).
32 As to the meaning of 'main proceedings' see PARA 175 note 9.
33 Insolvency Rules 1986, SI 1986/1925, r 5.37(2)(o) (as substituted and amended: see notes 5, 9).
    'Territorial proceedings' means proceedings opened in accordance with Council Regulation (EC)
    1346/2000 (OJ L160, 30.6.2000, p 1) art 3(2), (4) and falling within the definition of insolvency
    proceedings in art 2(2) and set out in Annex A under the heading 'United Kingdom'.

92.   Official receiver's decision. Where the official receiver[1] receives a proposal for a voluntary arrangement[2], he must, within 28 days of its receipt, serve a notice on the debtor[3] stating: (1) that he agrees to act as nominee[4] in relation to the proposal[5]; (2) he declines to act as nominee in relation to the proposal, specifying reasons for his decision[6]; or (3) on the basis of the information supplied to him, he is unable to reach a decision as to whether to act and specifying what further information he requires[7].

As soon as reasonably practicable after the official receiver agrees to act as nominee[8] and if he thinks that the voluntary arrangement proposed has a reasonable prospect of being approved and implemented[9], he must send to the creditors[10] and any trustee[11] who is not the official receiver:

(a)   a copy of the proposal[12]; and

(b)   a notice inviting creditors to vote to approve or reject the debtor's proposal and stating that:

   (i)   if a majority of three-quarters or more in value of creditors who vote[13] approve the proposal, the official receiver will, as soon as reasonably practicable, notify the Secretary of State[14] that the proposal has been approved[15];

   (ii)   under the provisions relating to the revocation of a voluntary arrangement[16]: (A) the debtor, a person who was entitled to participate in the arrangements[17], any trustee who is not the official receiver, or the official receiver, has 28 days from the date the official receiver notifies[18] the Secretary of State that the proposal has been approved to apply to the court to have the proposal set aside[19]; (B) a creditor, who was not made aware of the arrangements[20] at the time when they were made, has 28 days from the date on which he becomes aware of the voluntary arrangement, to apply to have the proposal set aside[21]; and

   (iii) creditors cannot propose modifications to the debtor's proposal[22]; and

(c)   for the creditors, a copy of the voting form in relation to a proposal for a voluntary arrangement[23] for their use[24].

Such notice must include a date specified by the official receiver as the final date on which he will accept votes from creditors, being a date not less than 14 days and not more than 28 days from the date of the notice[25].

As soon as is reasonably practicable after the implementation of the arrangements set out above, the official receiver must notify the Secretary of State whether the proposed voluntary arrangement has been approved or rejected[26].

1   As to the official receiver see PARA 35 et seq.
2   Ie a proposal in accordance with the Insolvency Rules 1986, SI 1986/1925, r 5.37: see PARA 91.
3   As to the meaning of 'debtor' see PARA 44 note 2.
4   As to the meaning of 'nominee' see PARA 43.
5   Insolvency Rules 1986, SI 1986/1925, r 5.38(1)(a) (r 5.38 substituted by SI 2003/1730).
6   Insolvency Rules 1986, SI 1986/1925, r 5.38(1)(b) (as substituted: see note 5).
7   Insolvency Rules 1986, SI 1986/1925, r 5.38(1)(c) (as substituted: see note 5). Where the debtor supplies the information requested, the official receiver, within 28 days of the receipt of the information, must serve a notice on the debtor in accordance with the Insolvency Rules 1986, SI 1986/1925, r 5.38(1): r 5.38(2) (as so substituted).
8   Ie in accordance with the Insolvency Rules 1986, SI 1986/1925, r 5.38: see text to notes 1–7.
9   Insolvency Act 1986 s 263B(2) (s 263B added by the Enterprise Act 2002 Sch 22 para 2).
10 For these purposes, a person is a 'creditor' only if he is a creditor of the debtor in respect of a bankruptcy debt, and the official receiver is aware of his claim and his address: Insolvency Act 1986 s 263B(3) (as added: see note 9).
11 As to the trustee see PARA 314 et seq.
12 Insolvency Act 1986 s 263B(4)(a) (as added: see note 9); Insolvency Rules 1986, SI 1986/1925, r 5.39(1)(a) (r 5.39 added by SI 2003/1730).
13 As to creditors' votes see PARA 93.
14 As to the Secretary of State see PARA 19.
15 Insolvency Act 1986 s 263B(4)(b) (as added: see note 9); Insolvency Rules 1986, SI 1986/1925, r 5.39(1)(b)(i) (r 5.39 as added (see note 12); r 5.39(1)(b)(i) amended by SI 2010/686). As to approval of a voluntary arrangement see PARA 94.
16 Ie the Insolvency Act 1986 s 263F: see PARA 99.
17 Ie arrangements pursuant to the Insolvency Act 1986 s 263B(2): see text to note 9.
18 Ie under the Insolvency Act 1986 s 263C: see text to note 26.
19 Ie on the grounds set out in the Insolvency Act 1986 s 263F(1): see PARA 99.
20 Ie arrangements pursuant to the Insolvency Act 1986 s 263B(2): see text to note 9.
21 Insolvency Rules 1986, SI 1986/1925, r 5.39(1)(b)(ii) (r 5.39 as added (see note 12); r 5.39(1)(b)(ii) amended by SI 2010/686). See also note 12.
22 Insolvency Act 1986 s 263B(4)(c) (as added: see note 9); Insolvency Rules 1986, SI 1986/1925, r 5.39(1)(b)(iii) (as added: see note 12).
23 Ie the voting form in relation to a proposal for a voluntary arrangement under the Insolvency Act 1986 s 263A: Insolvency Rules 1986, SI 1986/1925, Sch 4 Form 5.6.
24 Insolvency Rules 1986, SI 1986/1925, r 5.39(1)(c) (as added: see note 12).
25 Insolvency Rules 1986, SI 1986/1925, r 5.39(2) (as added: see note 12).
26 Insolvency Act 1986 s 263C (s 263C added by the Enterprise Act 2002 Sch 22 para 2).

93.   Creditors' votes.   Any creditor who is sent a notice[1] by the official receiver[2] is entitled to vote for the approval[3] or rejection of the proposal[4]. A creditor's entitlement to vote is calculated by reference to the amount of debt at the date of the bankruptcy order[5]. A creditor may vote in respect of a debt for an unliquidated amount or any debt whose value is not ascertained, and for the purposes of voting, but not otherwise, his debt is to be valued at £1 unless the official receiver agrees to put a higher value on it[6]. The official receiver has the power to admit or reject a creditor's claim for the purpose of his entitlement to vote, such power being exercisable with respect to the whole or part of the claim[7] and subject to appeal to the court by any creditor or the debtor[8].

All creditors who wish to vote must send notice[9] to the official receiver, at the address specified in the notice, of their decision whether to accept or reject the debtor's proposal[10]. Such notification may be sent by a representative of a creditor if it is accompanied by a written authority for that representation authenticated by the creditor[11].

1   Ie a notice sent pursuant to the Insolvency Act 1986 s 263B and the Insolvency Rules 1986, SI 1986/1925, r 5.39: see PARA 92.
2   As to the official receiver see PARA 35 et seq.
3   As to the approval of a voluntary arrangement see PARA 94.
4   Insolvency Rules 1986, SI 1986/1925, r 5.41(1) (r 5.41 added by SI 2003/1730).
5   Insolvency Rules 1986, SI 1986/1925, r 5.41(2) (as added: see note 4). As to bankruptcy orders see PARA 198 et seq.
6   Insolvency Rules 1986, SI 1986/1925, r 5.41(3) (as added: see note 4).
7   Insolvency Rules 1986, SI 1986/1925, r 5.42(1) (r 5.42 added by SI 2003/1730).
8   Insolvency Rules 1986, SI 1986/1925, r 5.42(2) (as added: see note 7). As to the meaning of 'debtor' see PARA 44 note 2. If on appeal the official receiver's decision is reversed or varied, or votes are declared invalid, the court may order another vote to be held or make such order as it thinks just, and such power of the court is exercisable only if it considers that the circumstances giving rise to the appeal are such as give rise to unfair prejudice or material irregularity: r 5.42(3) (as so added). As to cases on what constitutes unfair prejudice or material irregularity see PARA 84 notes 4, 7. An application to the court by way of appeal against the official receiver's decision must not be made after the end of the period of 28 days beginning with the day on which the official receiver is required by the Insolvency Act 1986 s 263C (see PARA 92) to notify the Secretary of State: Insolvency Rules 1986, SI 1986/1925, r 5.42(4) (r 5.42 as so added; r 5.42(4) amended by SI 2010/686). As to the Secretary of State see PARA 19. The official receiver is not liable for any costs incurred by any person in respect of an appeal under the Insolvency Rules 1986, SI 1986/1925, r 5.42: r 5.42(5) (as so added).
9   As to the notice see the Insolvency Rules 1986, SI 1986/1925, Sch 4 Form 5.6.
10 Insolvency Rules 1986, SI 1986/1925, r 5.40(1) (r 5.40 substituted by SI 2003/1730).
11 Insolvency Rules 1986, SI 1986/1925, r 5.40(2) (as substituted: see note 10).

94. Approval of voluntary arrangement. A proposal[1] is approved by the creditors if three-quarters or more in value of the creditors who vote approve it[2]. In the following cases there is to be left out of account a creditor's vote in respect of any claim or part of a claim:

(1)   where the claim or part is secured[3];
(2)   where the claim is in respect of a debt wholly or partly on, or secured by, a current bill of exchange or promissory note, unless the creditor is willing: (a) to treat the liability to him on the bill or note of every person who is liable on it antecedently to the debtor[4], and against whom a bankruptcy order[5] has not been made, or in the case of a company, which has not gone into liquidation, as a security in his hands; and (b) to estimate the value of the security and, for the purpose of entitlement to vote, but not of any distribution under the arrangement, to deduct it from his claim[6].

A proposal is not approved if those voting against it include more than half in value of the creditors, counting in the latter only those who gave notice to the official receiver[7]; whose votes are not to be left out of account under heads (1) and (2) above[8]; and who are not, to the best of the official receiver's belief, associates[9] of the debtor[10].

1   Ie a proposal in accordance with the Insolvency Rules 1986, SI 1986/1925, r 5.37: see PARA 91.
2   Insolvency Rules 1986, SI 1986/1925, r 5.43(1) (r 5.43 added by SI 2003/1730; Insolvency Rules 1986, SI 1986/1925, r 5.43(1) amended by SI 2010/686).
3   Insolvency Rules 1986, SI 1986/1925, r 5.43(2)(a) (as added: see note 2). As to the meaning of 'secured creditor' see PARA 574.
4   As to the meaning of 'debtor' see PARA 44 note 2.

5   As to bankruptcy orders see PARA 198 et seq.
6   Insolvency Rules 1986, SI 1986/1925, r 5.43(2)(b) (as added: see note 2).
7   Insolvency Rules 1986, SI 1986/1925, r 5.43(3)(a) (r 5.43 as added (see note 2); r 5.43(3) added by SI 2004/584). Ie in accordance with the Insolvency Rules 1986, SI 1986/1925, r 5.40; see PARA 93.
8   Insolvency Rules 1986, SI 1986/1925, r 5.43(3)(b) (as added: see notes 2, 7).
9   As to the meaning of 'associate' see PARA 5. It is for the official receiver to decide whether, under the Insolvency Rules 1986, SI 1986/1925, r 5.43, a person is an associate of the debtor for the purpose of r 5.43(3)(c) and in relation to this he is entitled to rely on the information provided by the debtor's statement of affairs or otherwise in accordance with the Insolvency Rules 1986, SI 1986/1925, Pt 5 (rr 5.1–5.68): r 5.43(4) (r 5.43 as added: (see note 2); r 5.43(4) added by SI 2004/584).
10 Insolvency Rules 1986, SI 1986/1925, r 5.43(3)(c) (as added: see notes 2, 7).

95.   Implementation of voluntary arrangement.   Where the official receiver[1] notifies[2] the Secretary of State[3] that a proposed voluntary arrangement has been approved[4]: (1) the voluntary arrangement takes effect, binds the debtor[5], and binds every person who was entitled to participate in the arrangements[6]; (2) the court must annul the bankruptcy order[7] in respect of the debtor on an application made by the official receiver[8]; and (3) the court may give such directions about the conduct of the bankruptcy and the administration of the bankrupt's estate[9] as it thinks appropriate for facilitating the implementation of the approved voluntary arrangement[10].

The fees, costs and expenses in respect of the performance by the official receiver of his functions in relation to the bankruptcy and those of the trustee[11] who is not the official receiver, including those in connection with the employment of agents, are a first charge on any sums realised under the terms of the voluntary arrangement, and those of the official receiver in relation to the voluntary arrangement are a second charge[12].

1   As to the official receiver see PARA 35 et seq.
2   Ie under the Insolvency Act 1986 s 263C: see PARA 92.
3   As to the Secretary of State see PARA 19.
4   Insolvency Act 1986 s 263D(1) (s 263D added by the Enterprise Act 2002 Sch 22 para 2; Insolvency Act 1986 s 263D(1) amended by SI 2010/18). As to approval of a voluntary arrangement see PARA 94.
5   As to the meaning of 'debtor' see PARA 44 note 2.
6   Insolvency Act 1986 s 263D(2) (as added: see note 4). The arrangements referred to are those made under s 263B(2) (see PARA 92). Section 263 (see PARA 73 et seq) applies to a voluntary arrangement which has effect by virtue of s 263D(2) as it applies to a voluntary arrangement approved by a creditors' meeting: s 263E (added by the Enterprise Act 2002 Sch 22 para 2). The Insolvency Act 1986 s 262B has effect in relation to a voluntary arrangement which has effect by virtue of s 263D(2) (for which purposes the words 'by a creditors' meeting summoned under s 257' are to be disregarded): s 263G(2) (s 263G added by the Enterprise Act 2002 Sch 22 para 2).
7   As to bankruptcy orders see PARA 198 et seq.
8   Insolvency Act 1986 s 263D(3) (as added: see note 4). Such an application may not be made: (1) during the period specified in s 263F(3) (see PARA 99) during which the voluntary arrangement can be challenged by application under s 263F(2) (see PARA 99); (2) while an application under s 263F is pending; or (3) while an appeal in respect of an application under s 263F is pending or may be brought: s 263D(4) (as so added). As to the application to annul the bankruptcy order see PARA 96.
9   As to the meaning of 'estate' see PARA 46 note 9.
10 Insolvency Act 1986 s 263D(5) (as added: see note 4). Section 262A (see PARA 44) has effect in relation to obtaining approval to a proposal for a voluntary arrangement under s 263D: s 263G(1) (added by the Enterprise Act 2002 Sch 22 para 2). The Deeds of Arrangement Act 1914 does not apply to the voluntary arrangement: Insolvency Act 1986 s 263D(6) (as added: see note 4). A reference in the Insolvency Act 1986 or another enactment to a voluntary arrangement approved under Pt 8 (ss 252–263G) includes a reference to a voluntary arrangement which has effect by virtue of s 263D: s 263D(7) (as added: see note 4).

11 As to the trustee see PARA 314 et seq.
12 Insolvency Rules 1986, SI 1986/1925, r 5.48 (added by SI 2003/1730).

96. Application by official receiver to annul bankruptcy order. Where the official receiver[1] applies for an annulment of a bankruptcy order[2], the application to the court must specify the statutory provision under which it is made[3]. The application must be made within 21 days of the expiry of the relevant period[4]; and must be supported by a report stating the grounds on which it is made and a statement by the official receiver that he is not aware that any application or appeal[5] remains to be disposed of[6]. The report must be accompanied by a copy of the proposal for the voluntary arrangement[7].

The application, together with the report and the documents in support, must be filed in court[8] and the court must give to the official receiver notice of the venue[9] fixed for the hearing[10]. The official receiver must give notice of the venue, accompanied by copies of the application and the report, to the bankrupt not less than five business days[11] before the date of the hearing[12].

Where the court annuls a bankruptcy order, it must send sealed copies of the order of annulment[13] to the official receiver and the bankrupt[14].

Where the official receiver has notified creditors of the debtor's bankruptcy, and the bankruptcy order is annulled, he must, as soon as reasonably practicable, notify them of the annulment[15].

1 As to the official receiver see PARA 35 et seq.
2 Ie under the Insolvency Act 1986 s 263D(3): see PARA 95. As to bankruptcy orders see PARA 198 et seq; and as to the annulment of bankruptcy orders see PARA 620 et seq.
3 Insolvency Rules 1986, SI 1986/1925, rr 5.57, 5.58(1) (rr 5.57, 5.58 added by SI 2003/1730).
4 Insolvency Rules 1986, SI 1986/1925, r 5.58(2) (added by SI 2003/1730). The relevant period is the period set out in the Insolvency Act 1986 s 263D(4): see PARA 95 note 8.
5 Ie under the Insolvency Act 1986 s 263F: see PARA 99.
6 Insolvency Rules 1986, SI 1986/1925, r 5.58(3) (added by SI 2003/1730).
7 Insolvency Rules 1986, SI 1986/1925, r 5.58(4) (added by SI 2003/1730). As to the proposal see PARA 91.The Insolvency Rules 1986, SI 1986/1925, r 5.58(4) refers also to a copy of the report to the court under the Insolvency Act 1986 s 263C but the report has now been replaced by a requirement to notify the Secretary of State (see s 263C (amended by SI 2010/18); and PARA 92).
8 As to the meaning of 'file in court' see PARA 57 note 13.
9 As to the meaning of 'venue' see PARA 46 note 22.
10 Insolvency Rules 1986, SI 1986/1925, r 5.58(5) (added by SI 2003/1730).
11 As to the meaning of 'business day' see PARA 28 note 8.
12 Insolvency Rules 1986, SI 1986/1925, r 5.58(6) (added by SI 2003/1730; and amended by SI 2010/686).
13 As to the prescribed form of order of annulment see the Insolvency Rules 1986, SI 1986/1925, Sch 4 Form 5.8 (added by SI 2003/1730; substituted by SI 2004/584; and amended by SI 2009/642; and SI 2010/686). As to the requirement to give notice of the order see the Insolvency Rules 1986, SI 1986/1925, r 5.60; and PARA 71 note 14.
14 Insolvency Rules 1986, SI 1986/1925, r 5.58(7) (added by SI 2003/1730). The trustee must submit a final account before being released: see the Insolvency Rules 1986, SI 1986/1925, r 5.61; and PARA 71 note 15.
15 Insolvency Rules 1986, SI 1986/1925, r 5.59(1) (r 5.59 added by SI 2003/1730). Expenses incurred by the official receiver in giving such notice are a charge in his favour on the property of the former bankrupt, whether or not actually in his hands: Insolvency Rules 1986, SI 1986/1925, r 5.59(2) (as so added). Where any property is in the hands of a trustee or any person other than the former bankrupt himself, the official receiver's charge is valid subject only to any costs that may be incurred by the trustee or that other person in effecting realisation of the property for the purpose of satisfying the charge: r 5.59(3) (as so added).

97. Notice of appointment as supervisor. Where the official receiver[1] is appointed to act as supervisor[2] of a voluntary arrangement, he must, as soon as reasonably practicable, give written notice of his appointment to the Secretary of

State[3], and all creditors of whose address the official receiver is aware, and the trustee[4], if any, who is not the official receiver[5]. If the official receiver vacates office as supervisor he must, as soon as reasonably practicable after doing so, give written notice of that fact to the Secretary of State[6].

1   As to the official receiver see PARA 35 et seq.
2   As to the meaning of 'supervisor' see PARA 43.
3   As to the Secretary of State see PARA 19.
4   As to the trustee see PARA 314 et seq.
5   Insolvency Rules 1986, SI 1986/1925, r 5.45(1) (r 5.45 added by SI 2003/1730; Insolvency Rules 1986, SI 1986/1925, r 5.45(1) amended by SI 2010/686).
6   Insolvency Rules 1986, SI 1986/1925, r 5.45(2) (r 5.45 as substituted (see note 5); r 5.45(2) amended by SI 2010/686).

98.   Supervisor's accounts and reports. The supervisor[1] must keep accounts and records of the supervisor's acts and dealings in, and in connection with, the arrangement including in particular records of all receipts and payments of money[2].

The supervisor must in respect of each period of 12 months ending with the anniversary of the commencement of the arrangement send within two months of the end of that period a report on the progress and prospects for the full implementation of the voluntary arrangement to the debtor[3] and all those of the debtor's creditors who are bound by the voluntary arrangement[4] of whose address the supervisor is aware[5], unless an obligation to send a final report[6] arises in that two-month period[7].

1   As to the meaning of 'supervisor' see PARA 43.
2   Insolvency Rules 1986, SI 1986/1925, r 5.47A(1) (r 5.47A added by SI 2010/686). The supervisor may employ agents in connection with the realisation of any assets subject to the terms of the voluntary arrangement: Insolvency Rules 1986, SI 1986/1925, r 5.49 (substituted by SI 2003/1730).
3   As to the meaning of 'debtor' see PARA 44 note 2.
4   As to who is bound by the voluntary arrangement see PARA 95.
5   Insolvency Rules 1986, SI 1986/1925, r 5.47A(2) (as added: see note 2).
6   Ie under the Insolvency Rules 1986, SI 1986/1925, r 5.50: see PARA 100.
7   Insolvency Rules 1986, SI 1986/1925, r 5.47A(3) (as added: see note 2).

99.   Revocation of a fast-track voluntary arrangement. The court may make an order revoking a voluntary arrangement[1] on the ground that it unfairly prejudices[2] the interests of a creditor of the debtor[3], or that a material irregularity[4] occurred in relation to the arrangements made[5] for deciding whether to approve a voluntary arrangement[6]. Such an order may be made only on the application of the debtor, a person who was entitled to participate[7] in the arrangements made for deciding whether to approve a voluntary arrangement, the trustee[8] of the bankrupt's estate[9], or the official receiver[10]. An application for an order revoking a voluntary arrangement may not be made after the end of the period of 28 days beginning with the date on which the official receiver notifies[11] the Secretary of State[12] that the proposed voluntary arrangement has been approved[13], unless being made by a creditor who was not made aware of the arrangement for voting, who may make an application within 28 days beginning with the date on which he becomes aware of the voluntary arrangement[14].

Where the court makes an order for revocation of a voluntary arrangement[15], and the person who applied for the order is:

(1)   the debtor, he must serve a sealed copy of the order on the supervisor[16] and any trustee of his estate who is not the official receiver[17];

(2)   the supervisor, he must serve a sealed copy of the order on the debtor, and any trustee who is not the official receiver[18];

(3)   a trustee who is not the official receiver, he must serve a sealed copy of the order on the debtor and the supervisor[19]; and

(4)   a creditor, he must serve a sealed copy of the order on the debtor, the supervisor and any trustee who is not the official receiver[20].

The supervisor must, as soon as reasonably practicable after receiving a copy of the order, give notice of it to all persons who were sent a copy of the debtor's proposal[21] and all other persons who are affected by the order[22]. The person on whose application the order was made must, within five business days[23] after the making of the order, give written notice of it to the Secretary of State[24].

1   Ie an arrangement which has effect by virtue of the Insolvency Act 1986 s 263D(2): see PARA 95.
2   As to what constitutes unfair prejudice see PARA 84 note 4.
3   As to the meaning of 'debtor' see PARA 44 note 2.
4   As to what constitutes material irregularity see PARA 84 note 7.
5   Ie under the Insolvency Act 1986 s 263B(2): see PARA 92.
6   Insolvency Act 1986 s 263F(1) (s 263F added by the Enterprise Act 2002 Sch 22 para 2).
7   As to who is entitled to participate see PARA 92.
8   As to the trustee see PARA 314 et seq.
9   As to the meaning of 'estate' see PARA 46 note 9.
10   Insolvency Act 1986 s 263F(2) (as added: see note 6). As to the official receiver see PARA 35 et seq.
11   Ie under the Insolvency Act 1986 s 263C; see PARA 92.
12   As to the Secretary of State see PARA 19.
13   Insolvency Act 1986 s 263F(3) (s 263F as added (see note 6); s 263F(3) amended by SI 2010/18).
14   Insolvency Act 1986 s 263F(4) (as added: see note 6).
15   Ie under the Insolvency Act 1986 s 263F (see text to notes 1–14): Insolvency Rules 1986, SI 1986/1925, r 5.46(1) (r 5.46 added by SI 2003/1730).
16   As to the meaning of 'supervisor' see PARA 43.
17   Insolvency Rules 1986, SI 1986/1925, r 5.46(2)(a) (as added: see note 15).
18   Insolvency Rules 1986, SI 1986/1925, r 5.46(2)(b) (as added: see note 15).
19   Insolvency Rules 1986, SI 1986/1925, r 5.46(2)(c) (as added: see note 15).
20   Insolvency Rules 1986, SI 1986/1925, r 5.46(2)(d) (as added: see note 15).
21   Ie under the Insolvency Rules 1986, SI 1986/1925, r 5.39: see PARA 92.
22   Insolvency Rules 1986, SI 1986/1925, r 5.46(3) (as added: see note 15).
23   As to the meaning of 'business day' see PARA 28 note 8.
24   Insolvency Rules 1986, SI 1986/1925, r 5.46(4) (as added: see note 15).

100.   Completion or termination of a fast-track voluntary arrangement. Not more than 28 days after the final completion or termination of the voluntary arrangement, the supervisor[1] must send to all creditors of the debtor[2] who are bound by the arrangement[3], and to the debtor, a notice that the voluntary arrangement has been fully implemented, or, as the case may be, terminated[4]. With the notice there must be sent to each of those persons a copy of a report by the supervisor summarising all receipts and payments made by him in pursuance of the voluntary arrangement[5], and explaining any difference in the actual implementation of it compared with the proposal as approved[6] by the creditors[7]. The supervisor must, within the 28 days mentioned above, send to the Secretary of State[8] a copy of the notice, together with a copy of the report, and he must not vacate office until after such copies have been sent[9].

1   As to the meaning of 'supervisor' see PARA 43.
2   As to the meaning of 'debtor' see PARA 44 note 2.
3   As to creditors bound by the arrangement see PARA 95.
4   Insolvency Rules 1986, SI 1986/1925, r 5.50(1) (r 5.50 added by SI 2003/1730; Insolvency Rules 1986, SI 1986/1925, r 5.50(1) amended by SI 2010/686). The court may, on application by the supervisor, extend the period of 28 days: Insolvency Rules 1986, SI 1986/1925, r 5.50(4).

5 As to the supervisor's accounts and reports see PARA 98.
6 As to approval of a voluntary arrangement see PARA 94.
7 Insolvency Rules 1986, SI 1986/1925, r 5.50(2) (as added: see note 4).
8 As to the Secretary of State see PARA 19.
9 Insolvency Rules 1986, SI 1986/1925, r 5.50(3) (as added: see note 4).

5. DEBT RELIEF ORDERS

(1) APPLICATION FOR A DEBT RELIEF ORDER

101. Debts in respect of which orders can be made. An individual who is unable to pay his debts may apply for a debt relief order[1] to be made in respect of debts which are for a liquidated sum payable either immediately or at some certain future time and which are not excluded debts[2] ('qualifying debts')[3]. Excluded debts are:

(1)　any fine[4] imposed for an offence and any obligation, including an obligation to pay a lump sum or to pay costs, arising under an order made in family proceedings[5] or any obligation arising under a maintenance assessment[6];

(2)　any obligation arising under a confiscation order[7];

(3)　any debt or liability to which a debtor[8] is or may become subject in respect of any sum paid or payable to the debtor as a student by way of loan[9] and which he receives before or after a debt relief order is made in respect of him;

(4)　any debt which consists in a liability to pay damages[10] for negligence, nuisance or breach of a statutory, contractual or other duty, or to pay damages by virtue of provisions relating to product liability[11], being in either case damages in respect of the death or personal injury[12], including any disease or other impairment of physical or mental condition, to any person; and

(5)　any obligation arising from a payment out of the social fund[13] by way of crisis loan or budgeting loan[14].

1　'Debt relief order' means an order made by the official receiver under the Insolvency Act 1986 Pt 7A (ss 251A–251X): Insolvency Act 1986 s 251X(1) (s 251X added by the Tribunals, Courts and Enforcement Act 2007 s 108(1), Sch 17). As to the official receiver see PARA 35 et seq.

2　'Excluded debt' is to be construed in accordance with the Insolvency Act 1986 s 251A (see the text to notes 3–14): s 251X(1) (as added: see note 1).

3　Insolvency Act 1986 ss 251A(1), (2), 251X(1) (s 251A added by the Tribunals, Courts and Enforcement Act 2007 Sch 17; Insolvency Act 1986 s 251X as added (see note 1)). A debt is not a qualifying debt to the extent that it is secured: Insolvency Act 1986 s 251A(3) (as so added).

4　For these purposes, 'fine' has the meaning given by the Insolvency Act 1986 s 281(8) (see PARA 650 note 5): Insolvency Rules 1986, SI 1986/1925, r 5A.2 (added by SI 2009/642).

5　For these purposes, 'family proceedings' has the meaning given by the Insolvency Act 1986 s 281(8) (see PARA 650 note 9): Insolvency Rules 1986, SI 1986/1925, r 5A.2 (as added: see note 4). See *Child Maintenance and Enforcement Commission v Beesley* [2010] EWCA Civ 1344, [2011] 3 All ER 233, [2011] 1 WLR 1704 (liability to pay child support).

6　Ie a maintenance assessment made under the Child Support Act 1991 (see CHILDREN AND YOUNG PERSONS vol 9 (2012) PARA 573 et seq).

7　Ie a confiscation order made under the Drug Trafficking Offences Act 1986 s 1 (repealed), the Criminal Justice (Scotland) Act 1987 s 1 (repealed), the Criminal Justice Act 1988 s 71 (repealed) or the Proceeds of Crime Act 2002 Pts 2–4 (ss 6–239) (see SENTENCING AND DISPOSITION OF OFFENDERS vol 92 (2010) PARA 390 et seq).

8　As to the meaning of 'debtor' see PARA 102 note 4.

9　'Loan' means a loan made pursuant to regulations made under the Teaching and Higher Education Act 1998 (see EDUCATION) or the Education (Student Loans) Act 1990 (see EDUCATION vol 36 (2011) PARA 1247), or the Education (Student Loans) Act 1990 as it continues in force by virtue of any savings made, in connection with its repeal by the Teaching and Higher Education Act 1998, by an order made under the Teaching and Higher Education Act 1998 s 46(4), including any interest on the loan and any penalties or charges incurred in connection with it: Insolvency Rules 1986, SI 1986/1925, r 5A.2 (as added: see note 4).

10　As to damages see generally DAMAGES.

11 Ie the Consumer Protection Act 1987 Pt 1 (ss 1–9) (see CONSUMER PROTECTION vol 21 (2011) PARA 642 et seq).

12 As to damages for personal injury see DAMAGES vol 12(1) (Reissue) PARA 878 et seq.

13 Ie the social fund under the Social Security Contributions and Benefits Act 1992 s 138(1)(b) (repealed). As to the social fund see SOCIAL SECURITY AND PENSIONS vol 44(2) (Reissue) PARAS 228–236.

14 Insolvency Act 1986 s 251A(4) (as added: see note 3); Insolvency Rules 1986, SI 1986/1925, r 5A.2 (as added (see note 4); and amended by SI 2010/686; and SI 2012/469).

102. Making of application. An application for a debt relief order[1] must be made to the official receiver[2] through an approved intermediary[3] and must include:

(1)　a list of the debts to which the debtor[4] is subject at the date of the application[5], specifying the amount of each debt[6] including any interest, penalty or other sum that has become payable in relation to that debt on or before that date, and the creditor to whom it is owed[7];

(2)　details of any security held in respect of any of those debts[8];

(3)　the following information:

　(a)　the debtor's surname, forenames and occupation, if any;

　(b)　the debtor's gender and date of birth;

　(c)　the debtor's places of residence[9] during the three years preceding the date of the application;

　(d)　any name or names used by the debtor for any purpose, if different from that given under head (3)(a) above;

　(e)　the name, address and nature of any business[10] carried on by the debtor, including any business carried on by: (i) a firm or partnership of which the debtor is a member; (ii) an agent or manager for the debtor or for such firm or partnership;

　(f)　any other liabilities, including those imposed by an order of the court[11], to which the debtor is subject;

　(g)　the address of the creditor to whom each debt is owed;

　(h)　the total amount of the debtor's monthly income from any source[12];

　(i)　the sources of that income and the amount from each source;

　(j)　particulars of the expenditure which the debtor claims is necessary to meet the monthly reasonable domestic needs of the debtor and his or her family, including the object and the amount of that expenditure;

　(k)　the total amount available from any source to meet the claimed monthly reasonable domestic needs of the debtor and his or her family; and

　(l)　particulars of the debtor's property[13] and its total estimated value[14];

(4)　statements as to:

　(a)　whether or not the debtor at the date of the application: (i) has given a preference to any person during the period of two years prior to and ending with the application date[15]; (ii) has entered into a transaction[16] with any person at an undervalue during the period of two years prior to and ending with the application date; (iii) is domiciled[17] in England and Wales; (iv) at any time during the period of three years ending with the application date was ordinarily resident[18], had a place of residence or carried on business, in England and Wales; (v) is an undischarged bankrupt[19]; (vi) is subject to a debt relief order; (vii) has been subject to a debt relief order in the six years preceding the date of the application; (viii) is subject to an interim order or a voluntary arrangement[20]; or (ix) is subject to a bankruptcy restrictions order or undertaking[21] or debt relief restrictions order or undertaking[22]; and

(b)   whether at the date of the application: (i) a bankruptcy petition[23] has been presented by the debtor or by a creditor against the debtor; (ii) a bankruptcy petition has been presented by the debtor, but the court has referred the debtor for the purpose of making an application for a debt relief order; (iii) any debt management arrangements[24] are in force in respect of the debtor; and (iv) any other legal action has been taken against the debtor in respect of any of the debtor's existing debts[25].

In the application the debtor must also: (A) consent to checks being made by the official receiver for the purpose of verifying that the debtor complies with the conditions to which the making of a debt relief order is subject[26]; (B) state that the debtor is unable to pay his or her debts; (C) request a debt relief order; and (D) indicate the date on which the application is completed[27].

The debtor must submit to the approved intermediary such information and such documents by reference to which the information in the application, including information about each debt, the amount of the debt and the name and address of the creditor, may be substantiated[28].

An application for a debt relief order must be completed and sent to the official receiver in electronic form[29] and by electronic means[30], and an application so sent will be treated as not having been submitted unless and until its receipt has been acknowledged by the official receiver in the same form and by the same means[31].

An application is not to be regarded as having been made until it has been submitted to the official receiver and any fee required in connection with the application[32] has been paid to the specified person[33].

1   As to the meaning of 'debt relief order' see PARA 101 note 1.

2   As to the official receiver see PARA 35 et seq.

3   Insolvency Act 1986 s 251B(1) (s 251B added by the Tribunals, Courts and Enforcement Act 2007 s 108(1), Sch 17). As to the approved intermediary see PARA 103.

4   'Debtor' means: (1) in relation to an application for a debt relief order, the applicant; and (2) in relation to a debt relief order, the person in relation to whom the order is made: Insolvency Act 1986 ss 251X(1), 385(1)(za) (s 251X added by the Tribunals, Courts and Enforcement Act 2007 s 108(1), Sch 17; the Insolvency Act 1986 s 385(1)(za) added by the Tribunals, Courts and Enforcement Act 2007 Sch 20 Pt 1 paras 1, 5(1), (2)).

5   Where at the application date any payment was accruing due, the debt consists of so much as would have fallen due at that date, if accruing from day to day: Insolvency Rules 1986, SI 1986/1925, r 5A.3(10) (r 5A.3 added by SI 2009/642). As to the meaning of 'application date' see note 15. A debtor may include a debt of which payment is not yet due at the date of the application, provided that it is for a liquidated sum payable at some certain future time: Insolvency Rules 1986, SI 1986/1925, r 5A.3(11) (as so added).

6   In making the application, the debtor must in every case deduct from the amount of the debt all trade and other discounts which are available to the debtor, except any discount for immediate, early or cash settlement: Insolvency Rules 1986, SI 1986/1925, r 5A.3(6) (as added: see note 5). Where a debt was incurred or is payable in a currency other than sterling, the amount of the debt must be converted into sterling at the official exchange rate prevailing on the application date: r 5A.3(7) (as so added). The official exchange rate is the middle exchange rate on the London foreign exchange market at the close of business, as published for the date in question or, in the absence of any such published rate for the date in question, such rate as the official receiver determines: r 5A.3(8) (as so added). As to the meaning of 'application date' see note 15.

Where a debt consists of unpaid payments of a periodical nature, the amount of the debt consists of any amounts due and unpaid up to the date of the application: r 5A.3(9) (as so added).

7   Insolvency Act 1986 s 251B(2)(a) (as added: see note 3). For these purposes references to a creditor specified in a debt relief order as the person to whom a qualifying debt is owed by the debtor include a reference to any person to whom the right to claim the whole or any part of the debt has passed, by assignment or operation of law, after the date of the application for the order: s 251X(2) (as added: see note 4). As to the meaning of 'qualifying debts' see PARA 101.

8   Insolvency Act 1986 s 251B(2)(b) (as added: see note 3).

9   As to the meaning of 'residence' see PARA 131 note 5.

10   As to the meaning of 'business' see PARA 43 note 4.

11   As to the meaning of 'court' see PARA 6 note 8.

12   As to the determination of the debtor's monthly surplus income see PARA 106 note 23.

13   As to the meaning of 'property' see PARA 412.

14   Insolvency Act 1986 s 251B(2)(c) (as added: see note 3); Insolvency Rules 1986, SI 1986/1025, r 5A.3(1), (2) (r 5A.3 added by SI 2009/642). As to the debtor's property see PARA 106 note 25.

15   'Application date', in relation to a debt relief order or an application for a debt relief order, means the date on which the application for the order is made to the official receiver: Insolvency Act 1986 s 251X(1) (as added: see note 4).

16   As to the meaning of 'transaction' see PARA 678 note 2.

17   As to the debtor's domicile see PARA 131 note 4.

18   As to the meaning of 'ordinary residence' see CONFLICT OF LAWS vol 19 (2011) PARA 359. See also PARA 131 note 5.

19   As to the meaning of 'bankrupt' see PARA 129. As to discharge from bankruptcy see PARA 638 et seq.

20   Ie an interim order or a voluntary arrangement under the Insolvency Act 1986 Pt 8 (ss 252–263G): see PARA 43 et seq.

21   As to bankruptcy restrictions orders and undertakings see PARA 657 et seq.

22   'Debt relief restrictions order' and 'debt relief restrictions undertaking' mean an order made, or an undertaking accepted, under the Insolvency Act 1986 Sch 4ZB (see PARA 125 et seq): s 251X(1) (as added: see note 4). As to debt relief restrictions orders and undertakings see PARA 125 et seq.

23   As to the meaning of 'bankruptcy petition' see PARA 129.

24   As to debt management arrangements see PARA 108 note 15.

25   Insolvency Act 1986 s 251B(2)(c) (as added: see note 3); Insolvency Rules 1986, SI 1986/1025, r 5A.3(1), (3) (as added: see note 14).

26   As to such checks and conditions see PARA 106.

27   Insolvency Act 1986 s 251B(2)(c) (as added: see note 3); Insolvency Rules 1986, SI 1986/1025, r 5A.3(1), (4) (as added: see note 14).

28   Insolvency Act 1986 s 251B(3)(c) (as added: see note 3); Insolvency Rules 1986, SI 1986/1025, r 5A.3(1), (5) (as added: see note 14).

29   An application is completed in electronic form if it is an application which is created, and sent, by electronic means (see note 30): Insolvency Rules 1986, SI 1986/1925, r 5A.4(2)(b) (r 5A.4 added by SI 2009/642).

30   Insolvency Rules 1986, SI 1986/1925, r 5A.4(1) (as added: see note 29). An application is sent by electronic means if it is sent initially and received at its destination by means of electronic equipment for the processing, which expression includes digital compression, or storage of data and entirely created, transmitted, conveyed and received by wire, by radio, by optical means or by other electromagnetic means but does not include electronic facsimile transmission or mobile telephonic text messaging: r 5A.4(2)(a) (as so added). In the event of any malfunction or error in the operation of the electronic form or means referred to, the official receiver must notify the competent authorities and approved intermediaries: (1) that approved intermediaries may, for a specified period, complete and send applications in hard copy form; and (2) of the postal address to which such applications are to be sent and any terms or conditions to which their use is subject: r 5A.4(4) (as so added). An application in hard copy form, means an application completed and sent on paper and capable of being read (but is not the product of an electronic facsimile transmission): r 5A.4(2)(c) (as so added).

31   Insolvency Rules 1986, SI 1986/1925, r 5A.4(3) (as added: see note 29).

32   Ie required by an order made under the Insolvency Act 1986 s 415, which will specify the person to whom the fee is payable: see PARA 825.

33   Insolvency Act 1986 s 251B(4) (as added: see note 3).

103.   The approved intermediary.   An approved intermediary is an individual for the time being approved by a competent authority[1] to act as an intermediary between a person wishing to make an application for a debt relief order and the official receiver[2].

The approved intermediary, as and when requested by a debtor[3] who proposes to make an application for a debt relief order through him or her, must create an application for a debt relief order in the name of the debtor[4].

The approved intermediary through whom the application for a debt relief order is to be made may assist the debtor: (1) to identify what information is required to complete the application; (2) based upon the documentation and information supplied by the debtor, to ascertain whether: (a) the debtor appears to have debts not exceeding £15,000[5]; (b) the debtor's surplus income does not exceed £50[6]; and (c) the value of the debtor's property[7] does not exceed £300[8]; and (3) to ensure that the application, if any, is completed in full[9].

The approved intermediary must draw the debtor's attention to: (i) all the conditions to which an application for, and the making of, a debt relief order is subject[10]; (ii) the possible consequences of the making by the debtor of any false representation or omission in the debtor's application[11]; and (iii) the fact that verification checks[12] will be made for the purpose of verifying that the debtor complies with the conditions to which the making of a debt relief order is subject and the requirement for the debtor to consent to such checks being made[13].

If and when instructed to do so by the debtor, the approved intermediary must send the application to the official receiver on behalf of the debtor[14].

An approved intermediary may not charge a debtor any fee in connection with an application for a debt relief order[15] and is not liable to any person in damages for anything done or omitted to be done when acting, or purporting to act, as an approved intermediary in connection with a particular application by a debtor for a debt relief order[16], unless the act or omission was in bad faith[17].

1   As to competent authorities see PARA 104. A competent authority may approve an individual to act as an intermediary between a person wishing to make an application for a debt relief order and the official receiver if the individual makes an application to a competent authority to be approved as an intermediary and it appears to the competent authority that the individual is a fit and proper person to act as intermediary between a person wishing to make an application for a debt relief order and the official receiver: Insolvency Act 1986 s 251U(4)(c), (10) (s 251U added by the Tribunals, Courts and Enforcement Act 2007 Sch 17); Debt Relief Orders (Designation of Competent Authorities) Regulations 2009, SI 2009/457, reg 8. As to the meaning of 'debt relief order' see PARA 101 note 1. As to the official receiver see PARA 35 et seq. As to descriptions of individuals ineligible to be approved by a competent authority to act as intermediaries see the Insolvency Act 1986 s 251U(4)(b), (10) (as so added); and the Debt Relief Orders (Designation of Competent Authorities) Regulations 2009, SI 2009/457, reg 9. As to the process for applying for approval to act as an intermediary see the Insolvency Act 1986 s 251U(4)(c), (10) (as so added); and the Debt Relief Orders (Designation of Competent Authorities) Regulations 2009, SI 2009/457, reg 10.

    A competent authority must withdraw an approval to act as intermediary from any individual where the individual so requests or with the individual's consent, or where it becomes clear to the competent authority after approval that the individual: (1) was ineligible at the time of the approval; (2) has become ineligible for approval; (3) is at any time not or no longer a fit and proper person to act as intermediary; (4) has failed to comply with any provisions of the Insolvency Act 1986 Pt 7A (see PARA 101 et seq) or any rule, regulations or orders made under it, including the Debt Relief Orders (Designation of Competent Authorities) Regulations 2009, SI 2009/457; or (5) has furnished the competent authority with any false, inaccurate or misleading information, and the competent authority may from time to time request an approved intermediary to supply such information or evidence about that intermediary or his or her activities as may be required by that authority for the purpose of ensuring that the requirements of the Debt Relief Orders (Designation of Competent Authorities)

Regulations 2009, SI 2009/457, are being met: Insolvency Act 1986 s 251U(4)(d), (10) (as so added); Debt Relief Orders (Designation of Competent Authorities) Regulations 2009, SI 2009/457, reg 11.

2   Insolvency Act 1986 ss 251U(1), 251X(1) (s 251U as added (see note 1); s 251X added by the Tribunals, Courts and Enforcement Act 2007 s 108(1), Sch 17).

3   As to the meaning of 'debtor' see PARA 102 note 4.

4   Insolvency Act 1986 s 251U(6) (as added: see note 1); Insolvency Rules 1986, SI 1986/1925, r 5A.5(1) (r 5A.5 added by SI 2009/642).

5   As to the limit on the debtor's overall indebtedness see PARA 106. See also the Insolvency Proceedings (Monetary Limits) Order 1986, SI 1986/1996, art 3, Schedule Pt II (art 3 amended by SI 2009/465; the Insolvency Proceedings (Monetary Limits) Order 1986, SI 1986/1996, Schedule Pt II substituted by SI 2004/547; and amended by SI 2009/465).

6   As to the limit on the debtor's monthly surplus income see PARA 106. As to the meaning of 'monthly surplus income' see PARA 106 note 23. See also the Insolvency Proceedings (Monetary Limits) Order 1986, SI 1986/1996, art 3, Schedule Pt II (art 3 as amended, Schedule Pt II as substituted and amended (see note 5)).

7   As to the meaning of 'property' see PARA 412. As to the value of the debtor's property and the limit on it see PARA 106.

8   Insolvency Proceedings (Monetary Limits) Order 1986, SI 1986/1996, art 3, Schedule Pt II (art 3 as amended, Schedule Pt II as substituted and amended (see note 5)).

9   Insolvency Act 1986 s 251U(5)(a), (b) (as added: see note 1); Insolvency Rules 1986, SI 1986/1925, r 5A.5(2) (as added: see note 4).

10   As to such conditions see PARA 106.

11   As to the offence of false representations or omissions see PARA 119.

12   As to the verification checks see PARA 106.

13   Insolvency Act 1986 s 251U(6) (as added: see note 1); Insolvency Rules 1986, SI 1986/1925, r 5A.5(3) (as added: see note 4). As to such consent see PARA 102 head (A).

14   Insolvency Act 1986 s 251U(5)(c) (as added: see note 1); Insolvency Rules 1986, SI 1986/1925, r 5A.5(4) (as added: see note 4).

15   Insolvency Act 1986 s 251U(7) (as added: see note 1).

16   Insolvency Act 1986 s 251U(8) (as added: see note 1).

17   Insolvency Act 1986 s 251U(9) (as added: see note 1).

104.   Competent authorities.   The Secretary of State[1] may designate a body to be a competent authority for the purposes of approving individuals as approved intermediaries[2] if the body: (1) makes an application[3] to the Secretary of State to be designated as a competent authority[4]; (2) provides or ensures the provision of debt management or debt counselling services through intermediaries and the provision to those intermediaries of education, training and development, including continuing education, training and development, in debt management or debt counselling services[5]; and (3) it appears to the Secretary of State that it is a fit and proper body[6] to approve individuals to act as intermediaries between a person wishing to make an application for a debt relief order[7] and the official receiver[8].

The Secretary of State designates a competent authority by sending to the applicant body a letter of designation which must contain a statement that the applicant body as competent authority is designated to approve persons of any description ('unlimited designation') or a statement that the applicant body as competent authority is designated to approve persons only of a particular description ('limited designation') and the description of person to which the designation is limited[9].

The Secretary of State may at any time modify or withdraw an existing designation where a competent authority so requests or withdraws its consent, or withdraw an existing designation where it appears to the Secretary of State that a body: (a) is not or is no longer a fit and proper body to act as a competent authority; (b) has failed to comply with provisions relating to debt relief orders[10] or any rules, regulations or order made under them, including any failure to approve an intermediary, or failure to withdraw approval of any intermediary[11]; or (c) has furnished the Secretary of State with any false, inaccurate or misleading information[12].

The Secretary of State may from time to time request a competent authority to supply such information or evidence about itself and its activities as a competent authority, or any intermediary appointed by it or the activities of any such intermediary, as may be required by him for the purpose of ensuring that requirements[13] are being met[14].

1   As to the Secretary of State see PARA 19.
2   Insolvency Act 1986 s 251U(2) (s 251U added by the Tribunals, Courts and Enforcement Act 2007 s 108(1), Sch 17); Debt Relief Orders (Designation of Competent Authorities) Regulations 2009, SI 2009/457, reg 3(1). As to approved intermediaries see PARA 103.
3   As to the process for applying to be a competent authority see the Insolvency Act 1986 s 251U(4)(a), (10) (as added: see note 2); and the Debt Relief Orders (Designation of Competent Authorities) Regulations 2009, SI 2009/457, reg 4.
4   Insolvency Act 1986 s 251U(4)(a), (10) (as added: see note 2); Debt Relief Orders (Designation of Competent Authorities) Regulations 2009, SI 2009/457, reg 3(2)(a).
5   Insolvency Act 1986 s 251U(4)(a), (10) (as added: see note 2); Debt Relief Orders (Designation of Competent Authorities) Regulations 2009, SI 2009/457, reg 3(2)(b).
6   A body is not a fit and proper body qualified to act as a competent authority if it: (1) has committed any offence under any enactment contained in insolvency legislation; (2) has engaged in any deceitful or oppressive or otherwise unfair or improper practices, whether unlawful or not, or any practices which otherwise cast doubt upon the probity of the body; (3) has not carried on its activities with integrity and the skills appropriate to the proper performance of the duties of a body which purports to ensure the provision of, or to provide, debt management or debt counselling services to the public or of a competent authority; or (4) has entered into a company voluntary arrangement under the Insolvency Act 1986 Pt 1 (see COMPANY AND PARTNERSHIP INSOLVENCY vol 16 (2011) PARA 83 et seq): Debt Relief Orders (Designation of Competent Authorities) Regulations 2009, SI 2009/457, reg 5(2).
7   As to the meaning of 'debt relief order' see PARA 101 note 1.
8   Insolvency Act 1986 s 251U(4)(a), (10) (as added: see note 2); Debt Relief Orders (Designation of Competent Authorities) Regulations 2009, SI 2009/457, regs 3(2)(c), 5(1). As to the official receiver see PARA 35 et seq.
9   Insolvency Act 1986 s 251U(3), (4)(a), (10) (as added: see note 2); Debt Relief Orders (Designation of Competent Authorities) Regulations 2009, SI 2009/457, reg 6.
10 Ie the Insolvency Act 1986 Pt 7A: see PARA 101 et seq.
11 Ie in accordance with the Debt Relief Orders (Designation of Competent Authorities) Regulations 2009, SI 2009/457.
12 Debt Relief Orders (Designation of Competent Authorities) Regulations 2009, SI 2009/457, reg 7(1).
13 Ie the requirements under the Debt Relief Orders (Designation of Competent Authorities) Regulations 2009, SI 2009/457.
14 Debt Relief Orders (Designation of Competent Authorities) Regulations 2009, SI 2009/457, reg 7(2).

105. Duty of official receiver to consider and determine application. Where an application for a debt relief order[1] is made, the official receiver[2] may stay consideration of the application until he has received answers to any queries raised with the debtor[3] in relation to anything connected with the application[4].

The official receiver must determine the application by deciding whether to refuse it as authorised or required by the following provisions[5] or, if he does not refuse it, by making a debt relief order[6] in relation to the specified debts[7] he is satisfied were qualifying debts[8] of the debtor at the application date[9].

The official receiver may refuse the application if: (1) the application does not meet all the requirements imposed[10]; (2) any queries raised with the debtor have not been answered to the satisfaction of the official receiver within such time as he may specify when they are raised[11]; (3) the debtor has made any false representation or omission in making the application or on supplying any information or documents in support of it[12]; or (4) he is not satisfied that each of the specified conditions[13] is met[14]. The official receiver must refuse the application if he is not satisfied: (a) that the debtor is an individual who is unable to pay his debts[15]; (b) at least one of the specified debts was a qualifying debt of the debtor at the application date[16]; or (c) each of the prescribed conditions[17] is met[18].

If the official receiver refuses an application he must send a notice in writing to the debtor stating that the official receiver has decided to refuse the debtor's application, and the reason[19] for which it has been refused[20].

1 As to the meaning of 'debt relief order' see PARA 101 note 1.
2 As to the official receiver see PARA 35 et seq.
3 As to the meaning of 'debtor' see PARA 102 note 4.
4 Insolvency Act 1986 s 251C(1), (2) (s 251C added by the Tribunals, Courts and Enforcement Act 2007 s 108(1), Sch 17).
5 Ie by the Insolvency Act 1986 s 251C(4)–(7): see text to notes 10–20.
6 As to the making of a debt relief order see PARA 108. The Secretary of State must maintain a register of matters relating to debt relief orders, debt relief restrictions orders and debt relief restrictions undertakings: Insolvency Act 1986 s 251W (added by the Tribunals, Courts and Enforcement Act 2007 s 108(1), Sch 17). As to the Secretary of State see PARA 19. As to the keeping of the register see PARA 28. As to debt relief restrictions orders see PARA 125. As to debt relief restrictions undertakings see PARA 127.
7 'Specified debt' means a debt specified in the application: Insolvency Act 1986 s 251C(8) (as added: see note 4).
8 As to the meaning of 'qualifying debts' see PARA 101.
9 Insolvency Act 1986 s 251C(3) (as added: see note 4). As to the meaning of 'application date' see PARA 102 note 15. In considering an application for a debt relief order, the official receiver is exercising a judicial function: *R (on the application of Howard) v Official Receiver* [2013] EWHC 1839 (Admin), [2013] NLJR 20, [2013] All ER (D) 73 (Jul).
10 Insolvency Act 1986 s 251C(4)(a) (as added: see note 4). The requirements are those imposed by the Insolvency Act 1986 s 251B: see PARA 102.
11 Insolvency Act 1986 s 251C(4)(b) (as added: see note 4).
12 Insolvency Act 1986 s 251C(4)(c) (as added: see note 4).
13 Ie specified in the Insolvency Act 1986 Sch 4ZA Pt 2: see PARA 106.
14 Insolvency Act 1986 s 251C(6) (as added: see note 4).
15 Insolvency Act 1986 s 251C(5)(a) (as added: see note 4).
16 Insolvency Act 1986 s 251C(5)(b) (as added: see note 4).
17 Ie conditions prescribed by the Insolvency Act 1986 Sch 4ZA Pt 1: see PARA 106.
18 Insolvency Act 1986 s 251C(5)(c) (as added: see note 4).
19 As to the conditions for making a debt relief order see PARA 106.
20 Insolvency Act 1986 s 251C(7) (as added: see note 4); Insolvency Rules 1986, SI 1986/1925, r 5A.6 (added by SI 2009/642).

106. Conditions for making a debt relief order. The conditions that must be met before the official receiver[1] may make a debt relief order[2] are:

(1) the debtor[3] is domiciled[4] in England and Wales on the application date[5], or, at any time during the period of three years ending with that date, was ordinarily resident[6] or had a place of residence[7], or carried on business[8], in England and Wales[9];

(2) the debtor is not, on the determination date[10]: (a) an undischarged bankrupt[11]; (b) subject to an interim order or voluntary arrangement[12]; or (c) subject to a bankruptcy restrictions order[13] or a debt relief restrictions order[14];

(3) a petition for the debtor's bankruptcy[15]: (a) has not been presented by or, in the case of a creditor's petition for the debtor's bankruptcy, against the debtor before the determination date; (b) has been so presented, but proceedings on the petition have been finally disposed of before that

date; or (c) has been so presented and proceedings in relation to the petition remain before the court[16] at that date, but: (i) in the case of a debtor's petition for the debtor's bankruptcy, the court has referred the debtor[17] for the purposes of making an application for a debt relief order; or (ii) in the case of a creditor's petition for the debtor's bankruptcy, the person who presented the petition has consented to the making of an application for a debt relief order[18];

(4)   a debt relief order has not been made in relation to the debtor in the period of six years ending with the determination date[19];

(5)   the total amount of the debtor's debts on the determination date, other than unliquidated debts[20] and excluded debts[21], does not exceed £15,000[22];

(6)   the debtor's monthly surplus income[23], if any, on the determination date does not exceed £50[24]; and

(7)   the total value of the debtor's property[25] on the determination date does not exceed £300[26].

The official receiver may refuse an application for a debt relief order if the debtor has entered into a transaction with any person at an undervalue[27] or given a preference to any person[28] during the period between the start of the period of two years ending with the application date and the determination date[29].

1   As to the official receiver see PARA 35 et seq; and as to the duty of the official receiver to consider and determine an application see PARA 105.
2   As to the meaning of 'debt relief order' see PARA 101 note 1.
3   As to the meaning of 'debtor' see PARA 102 note 4.
4   As to the debtor's domicile see PARA 131 note 4.
5   As to the meaning of 'application date' see PARA 102 note 15.
6   As to the meaning of 'ordinary residence' see CONFLICT OF LAWS vol 19 (2011) PARA 359. See also PARA 131 note 5.
7   As to the meaning of 'residence' see PARA 131 note 5.
8   'Carrying on business' for these purposes includes the carrying on of business by a firm or partnership of which the debtor is a member and the carrying on of business by an agent or manager for the debtor or for such firm or partnership: Insolvency Act 1986 Sch 4ZA Pt 1 para 1(2) (Sch 4ZA added by the Tribunals, Courts and Enforcement Act 2007 s 108(2), Sch 18). As to the meaning of 'business' see PARA 43 note 4.
9   Insolvency Act 1986 Sch 4ZA Pt 1 para 1(1) (as added: see note 8). The checks prescribed for these purposes are verification checks made in, or with, either the electoral registers for the areas of England and Wales in which the debtor in, and at the date of, the debtor's application, claims to reside or to carry on business or to have resided or carried on business, the individual insolvency register, the bankruptcy restrictions register, the debt relief restrictions register or a credit reference agency: Insolvency Rules 1986, SI 1986/1925, r 5A.7(3) (r 5A.7 added by SI 2009/642). As to the individual insolvency register see PARA 28. As to the bankruptcy restrictions register see PARA 656. As to the debt relief restrictions register see PARAS 28, 105 note 6. For these purposes 'credit reference agency' means a person licensed to carry on a business comprising the furnishing of information relevant to the financial standing of individuals: Insolvency Rules 1986, SI 1986/1925, r 5A.7(1) (as so added).
10 'Determination date', in relation to a debt relief order or an application for a debt relief order, means the date on which the application for the order is determined by the official receiver: Insolvency Act 1986 s 251X(1) (s 251X added by the Tribunals, Courts and Enforcement Act 2007 Sch 17).
11 As to the meaning of 'bankrupt' see PARA 129. As to discharge from bankruptcy see PARA 638 et seq.
12 Ie an interim order or voluntary arrangement under the Insolvency Act 1986 Pt 8 (ss 252–263G): see PARA 43 et seq.
13 As to bankruptcy restrictions orders see PARA 657 et seq.
14 Insolvency Act 1986 Sch 4ZA Pt 1 para 2 (as added: see note 8). As to debt relief restrictions orders see PARA 125. The checks prescribed for these purposes, except for the purpose of

verifying that a debtor is not subject to an interim order, are verification checks made in one or more of the individual insolvency register, the bankruptcy restrictions register or the debt restrictions register: Insolvency Rules 1986, SI 1986/1925, r 5A.7(4), (5) (as added: see note 9).

15 Ie a petition under the Insolvency Act 1986 Pt 9 (ss 264–371): see PARA 130 et seq.

16 As to the meaning of 'court' see PARA 6 note 8.

17 Ie referred under the Insolvency Act 1986 s 274A(2): see PARA 203.

18 Insolvency Act 1986 Sch 4ZA Pt 1 paras 3, 4 (as added: see note 8). As from a day to be appointed, Sch 4ZA Pt 1 para 3 is substituted by the Enterprise and Regulatory Reform Act 2013 s 71, Sch 19 paras 1, 62: see PARA 130 note 17.

The checks prescribed for these purposes, and for the purpose of verifying that a debtor is not, on the determination date, subject to an interim order, are verification checks made in one or more of the individual insolvency register, county or other court records or a credit reference agency: Insolvency Rules 1986, SI 1986/1925, r 5A.7(6), (7) (as added: see note 9).

Where, prior to the determination of an application, a creditor's petition for bankruptcy has been presented against a debtor and the proceedings in relation to that petition remain before the court, if the petitioner, on the hearing of a creditor's petition for bankruptcy, consents to the making by the debtor of an application for a debt relief order in respect of the debt: (1) the court must: (a) refer the debtor to an approved intermediary for the purpose of making an application for a debt relief order in relation to the debtor and the debt noting the consent of the creditor on the order for referral; (b) stay the proceedings on the petition in relation to the debt on such terms and conditions as it thinks just; and (2) the debtor must send to the approved intermediary as soon as reasonably practicable after the making of the order of referral: (a) a sealed copy of the order; and (b) copies of the petition and, if any, of the creditor's statutory demand: r 5A.23(1), (2), (3) (r 5A.23 added by SI 2009/642; the Insolvency Rules 1986, SI 1986/1925, r 5A.23(3) amended by SI 2010/686). As to the approved intermediary see PARA 103. The approved intermediary must, on receipt of the order and the copies, as soon as reasonably practicable after the application for a debt relief order has been made, send them to the official receiver indorsed with the name of the debtor and the number of the application to which they relate: Insolvency Rules 1986, SI 1986/1925, r 5A.23(4) (as so added). If, following the reference by the court, a debt relief order is made in relation to the debt, the petition must be dismissed in relation to it unless the court otherwise directs: Insolvency Rules 1986, SI 1986/1925, r 5A.23(5) (as so added).

19 Insolvency Act 1986 Sch 4ZA Pt 1 para 5 (as added: see note 8). The checks prescribed for these purposes are verification checks made in one or more of the individual insolvency register, the bankruptcy restrictions register or the debt restrictions register: Insolvency Rules 1986, SI 1986/1925, r 5A.7(4), (5) (as added: see note 9).

20 For this purpose an unliquidated debt is a debt that is not for a liquidated sum payable to a creditor either immediately or at some future time: Insolvency Act 1986 Sch 4ZA Pt 1 para 6(2) (as added: see note 8).

21 As to the meaning of 'excluded debts' see PARA 101.

22 Insolvency Act 1986 Sch 4ZA Pt 1 para 6(1) (as added: see note 8); Insolvency Proceedings (Monetary Limits) Order 1986, SI 1986/1996, art 3, Schedule Pt II (art 3 amended by SI 2009/465; the Insolvency Proceedings (Monetary Limits) Order 1986, SI 1986/1996, Schedule Pt II substituted by SI 2004/547; and amended by SI 2009/465). The checks prescribed for these purposes are verification checks made with a credit reference agency: Insolvency Rules 1986, SI 1986/1925, r 5A.7(8) (as added: see note 9).

23 For this purpose 'monthly surplus income' is the amount by which a person's monthly income exceeds the amount necessary for the reasonable domestic needs of himself and his family: Insolvency Act 1986 Sch 4ZA Pt 1 para 7(2) (as added: see note 8). The spending of money on cigarettes may fall within 'reasonable domestic needs' but not the consumption of cannabis even if taken wholly or partly for medicinal purposes: _London Borough of Islington v Official Receiver_ [2012] BPIR 363. For these purposes, the income of a debtor comprises every payment in the nature of income which is from time to time made to him or to which he from time to time becomes entitled, including any payment in respect of the carrying on of any business or in respect of any office or employment and, despite anything in the Welfare Reform and Pensions Act 1999 (see PERSONAL AND OCCUPATIONAL PENSIONS vol 80 (2013) PARA 776 et seq), any payment under a pension scheme: Insolvency Act 1986 Sch 4ZA Pt 1 para 7(3) (as so added); Insolvency Rules 1986, SI 1986/1925, r 5A.8(1) (r 5A.8 added by SI 2009/642). In determining the monthly surplus income of a debtor, the official receiver must take into account any contributions made by any member of the debtor's family to the amount necessary for the reasonable domestic needs of the debtor or his or her family: Insolvency Act 1986 Sch 4ZA Pt 1 para 7(3) (as so added); Insolvency Rules 1986, SI 1986/1925, r 5A.8(2) (as so added).

24 Insolvency Act 1986 Sch 4ZA Pt 1 para 7(1) (as added: see note 8); Insolvency Proceedings (Monetary Limits) Order 1986, SI 1986/1996, art 3, Schedule Pt II (art 3 as amended, Schedule Pt II as substituted and amended (see note 22)). The checks prescribed for these purposes are verification checks made with a credit reference agency: Insolvency Rules 1986, SI 1986/1925, r 5A.7(8) (as added: see note 9).

25 As to the meaning of 'property' see PARA 412. For these purposes the official receiver must regard all property belonging to or vested in the debtor on the determination date and any property which is comprised in or treated as such property by virtue of the Insolvency Rules 1986, SI 1986/1925, rr 5A.10–5A.27 (see PARA 108 et seq) as a debtor's property: Insolvency Act 1986 Sch 4ZA Pt 1 para 8(2) (as added: see note 8); Insolvency Rules 1986, SI 1986/1925, r 5A.9(1) (r 5A.9 added by SI 2009/642). References to property, in relation to a debtor, include references to any power exercisable by him or her over or in respect of property except in so far as the power is exercisable over or in respect of property which is not, or is deemed not, for the time being to be the property of the debtor and cannot be exercised for the benefit of the debtor, and a power exercisable over or in respect of property is deemed to vest in the person entitled to exercise it at the time of the transaction or event by virtue of which it is exercisable by that person, whether or not it becomes exercisable at that time: Insolvency Act 1986 Sch 4ZA Pt 1 para 8(2) (as so added); Insolvency Rules 1986, SI 1986/1925, r 5A.9(2) (as so added). As to the meaning of 'transaction' see PARA 678 note 2. For these purposes, property belonging to or vested in the debtor so belongs or vests in him or her subject to the rights of any person other than the debtor, whether as a secured creditor of the debtor or otherwise, in relation thereto: Insolvency Act 1986 Sch 4ZA Pt 1 para 8(2) (as so added); Insolvency Rules 1986, SI 1986/1925, r 5A.9(3) (as so added). As to secured creditors see PARA 574 et seq. As to what the official receiver must disregard when determining the value of a debtor's property see r 5A.10 (added by SI 2009/642).

26 Insolvency Act 1986 Sch 4ZA Pt 1 para 8(1) (as added: see note 8); Insolvency Proceedings (Monetary Limits) Order 1986, SI 1986/1996, art 3, Schedule Pt II (art 3 as amended, Schedule Pt II as substituted and amended (see note 24)). The checks prescribed for these purposes are verification checks made with a credit reference agency: Insolvency Rules 1986, SI 1986/1925, r 5A.7(8) (as added: see note 9).

27 For this purpose a debtor enters into a transaction at an undervalue if: (1) he makes a gift to that person or he otherwise enters into a transaction with that person on terms that provide for him to receive no consideration; (2) he enters into a transaction with that person in consideration of marriage or the formation of a civil partnership; or (3) he enters into a transaction with that person for a consideration the value of which, in money or money's worth, is significantly less than the value, in money or money's worth, of the consideration provided by the individual: Insolvency Act 1986 Sch 4ZA Pt 2 para 9(2) (as added: see note 8). As to the meaning of 'transaction' see PARA 678 note 2. As to transactions at an undervalue see s 339; and PARAS 679, 680. As to preferences see s 340; and PARA 681 et seq.

28 For this purpose a debtor gives a preference to a person if: (1) that person is one of the debtor's creditors to whom a qualifying debt is owed or is a surety or guarantor for any such debt; and (2) the debtor does anything or suffers anything to be done which, in either case, has the effect of putting that person into a position which, in the event that a debt relief order is made in relation to the debtor, will be better than the position he would have been in if that thing had not been done: Insolvency Act 1986 Sch 4ZA Pt 2 para 10(2) (as added: see note 8). As to references to creditors to whom a qualifying debt is owed see PARA 102 note 7.

29 Insolvency Act 1986 Sch 4ZA Pt 2 paras 9(1), 10(1) (as added: see note 8).

107.   Presumptions applicable to the determination of an application.   In determining[1] an application for a debt relief order[2], the official receiver must presume[3]:

(1)   that the debtor[4] is an individual who is unable to pay his debts at the determination date[5] if that appears to the official receiver to be the case at the application date[6] from the information supplied in the application[7] and he has no reason to believe that the information supplied is incomplete or inaccurate, and he has no reason to believe that, by virtue of a change in the debtor's financial circumstances since the application date, the debtor may be able to pay his debts[8];

(2)   that a specified debt[9] of the amount specified in the application and owed to the creditor[10] as so specified is a qualifying debt[11] at the

application date if that appears to him to be the case from the information supplied in the application, and he has no reason to believe that the information supplied is incomplete or inaccurate[12];

(3)   that the condition that the debtor has a connection with England and Wales[13] is met if that appears to him to be the case from the information supplied in the application, any prescribed verification checks[14] relating to the condition have been made, and he has no reason to believe that the information supplied is incomplete or inaccurate[15];

(4)   that any other of the conditions to be met before the official receiver may make a debt relief order[16] is met if that appears to him to have been the case as at the application date from the information supplied in the application and he has no reason to believe that the information supplied is incomplete or inaccurate, any prescribed verification checks relating to the condition have been made, and he has no reason to believe that, by virtue of a change in circumstances since the application date, the condition may no longer be met[17].

1   As to the duty of the official receiver to consider and determine an application see PARA 105. As to the official receiver see PARA 35 et seq.
2   As to the meaning of 'debt relief order' see PARA 101 note 1.
3   Insolvency Act 1986 s 251D(1) (s 251D added by the Tribunals, Courts and Enforcement Act 2007 s 108(1), Sch 17).
4   As to the meaning of 'debtor' see PARA 102 note 4.
5   As to the meaning of 'determination date' see PARA 106 note 10.
6   As to the meaning of 'application date' see PARA 102 note 15.
7   As to the information to be supplied when making an application see PARA 102. References to information supplied in the application include information supplied to the official receiver in support of the application: Insolvency Act 1986 s 251D(6) (as added: see note 3).
8   Insolvency Act 1986 s 251D(2) (as added: see note 3).
9   'Specified debt' means a debt specified in the application: Insolvency Act 1986 s 251D(7) (as added: see note 3).
10   As to references to creditors to whom a qualifying debt is owed see PARA 102 note 7.
11   As to the meaning of 'qualifying debts' see PARA 101.
12   Insolvency Act 1986 s 251D(3) (as added: see note 3).
13   Ie the condition in the Insolvency Act 1986 Sch 4ZA Pt 1 para 1: see PARA 106.
14   As to the prescribed verification checks see the Insolvency Rules 1986, SI 1986/1925, r 5A.7(2) (added by SI 2009/642); and PARA 106.
15   Insolvency Act 1986 s 251D(4) (as added: see note 3).
16   Ie the conditions set out in the Insolvency Act 1986 Sch 4ZA: see PARA 106.
17   Insolvency Act 1986 s 251D(5) (as added: see note 3).

(2) MAKING AND EFFECT OF DEBT RELIEF ORDER

108.   Making of debt relief order.   When the official receiver[1] makes a debt relief order[2] on determining[3] an application for such an order[4]:

(1)   the order must be in writing and include the name and address of the debtor[5]; the date of, and the reference number allocated to, the debtor's application; a list of the debtor's qualifying debts[6] as at the application date[7], specifying the amount owed and the creditor's name, address and reference, if any; and the date on which the order was made[8];

(2)   the official receiver must give a copy of the order to the debtor[9]; make an entry for the order in the register of debt relief orders[10] containing the prescribed information about the order or the debtor[11]; notify the approved intermediary[12] through whom the debtor's application was made of the making and date of the order[13]; and cause an entry to be made in the individual insolvency register[14];

(3)   in any case in which there are other debt management arrangements[15]
       or attachment of earnings orders[16] in force in respect of the debtor, the
       official receiver must notify the court[17], or the body, as the case may be,
       responsible for making the debt management arrangements or orders, of
       the making of the debt relief order[18];

(4)   the official receiver must notify each creditor to whom a qualifying debt
       in respect of the order is owed[19], of the making, the date and the
       reference number of the order and its effect; the matters to which a
       creditor may object[20]; the name, address and telephone number of the
       official receiver sending the notice and the address to which any such
       objection may or must be sent[21].

1   As to the official receiver see PARA 35 et seq.
2   As to the meaning of 'debt relief order' see PARA 101 note 1.
3   As to the duty of the official receiver to consider and determine an application for a debt relief
     order see PARA 105.
4   Insolvency Act 1986 s 251E(1) (added by the Tribunals, Courts and Enforcement Act 2007
     s 108(1), Sch 17).
5   As to the meaning of 'debtor' see PARA 102 note 4.
6   As to the meaning of 'qualifying debts' see PARA 101.
7   As to the meaning of 'application date' see PARA 102 note 15.
8   Insolvency Act 1986 s 251E(2), (3) (as added: see note 4); Insolvency Rules 1986, SI 1986/1925,
     r 5A.11 (added by SI 2009/642).
9   Insolvency Act 1986 s 251E(4)(a) (as added: see note 4).
10   Ie the register maintained under the Insolvency Act 1986 s 251W: see PARA 105 note 6. For these
     purposes the date on which an entry relating to the making of a debt relief order is first made in
     the register is referred to as 'the effective date': Insolvency Act 1986 ss 251E(7), 251X(1)
     (s 251E as added (see note 4); s 251X added by the Tribunals, Courts and Enforcement
     Act 2007 Sch 17).
11   Insolvency Act 1986 s 251E(4)(b) (as added: see note 4).
12   As to the approved intermediary see PARA 103.
13   Insolvency Act 1986 s 251E(5) (as added: see note 4); Insolvency Rules 1986, SI 1986/1925,
     r 5A.12(1)(a) (r 5A.12 added by SI 2009/642).
14   Insolvency Act 1986 s 251E(5) (as added: see note 4); Insolvency Rules 1986, SI 1986/1925,
     r 5A.12(1)(b) (as added: see note 13). As to the individual insolvency register see PARA 28. The
     entry is to be made in the individual insolvency register in accordance with r 6A.5A: see PARA
     31.
15   'Other debt management arrangements' means an administration order under the County
     Courts Act 1984 Pt 6 (ss 112–112AI) (see PARA 887 et seq); an enforcement restriction order
     under Pt 6A (ss 117A–117X) (see PARA 916 et seq); a debt repayment plan arranged in
     accordance with a debt management scheme that is approved under the Tribunals, Courts and
     Enforcement Act 2007 Pt 5 Ch 4 (ss 109–133) (see PARA 931 et seq): Insolvency Act 1986
     s 251F(3) (added by the Tribunals, Courts and Enforcement Act 2007 Sch 17). If a debt relief
     order is made and immediately before the order is made, other debt management arrangements
     are in force in respect of the debtor, the other debt management arrangements cease to be in
     force when the debt relief order is made: Insolvency Act 1986 s 251F(1), (2) (as so added).
16   As to attachment of earnings orders see PARA 889.
17   As to the meaning of 'court' see PARA 6 note 8.
18   Insolvency Act 1986 s 251E(5) (as added: see note 4); Insolvency Rules 1986, SI 1986/1925,
     r 5A.12(2) (as added: see note 13).
19   As to references to creditors to whom a qualifying debt is owed see PARA 102 note 7.
20   Ie under the Insolvency Act 1986 s 251K: see PARA 113.
21   Insolvency Act 1986 s 251E(6) (as added: see note 4); Insolvency Rules 1986, SI 1986/1925,
     r 5A.13 (r 5A.13 added by SI 2009/642).

109. Moratorium from qualifying debts.   A moratorium commences on the
effective date[1] for a debt relief order[2] in relation to each qualifying debt[3]
specified in the order ('a specified qualifying debt')[4]. During the moratorium, the
creditor to whom a specified qualifying debt is owed[5] has no remedy in respect

of the debt[6], and may not commence a creditor's petition in respect of the debt or otherwise commence any action or other legal proceedings against the debtor[7] for the debt, except with the permission of the court[8] and on such terms as the court may impose[9].

If on the effective date a creditor to whom a specified qualifying debt is owed has any such petition, action or other proceeding pending in any court, the court may stay the proceedings on the petition, action or other proceedings, as the case may be, or allow them to continue on such terms as the court thinks fit[10].

The moratorium continues for a period of one year beginning with the effective date for the order, unless it terminates early[11] or is extended by the official receiver[12] or by the court[13]. The official receiver may only extend the moratorium period for the purpose of: (1) carrying out or completing an investigation relating to an objection[14], but if the extension is sought for this purpose the permission of the court is required[15]; (2) taking any action he considers necessary, whether as a result of an investigation or otherwise, in relation to the order; or (3) in a case where he has decided to revoke the order, providing the debtor with the opportunity to make arrangements for making payments towards his debts[16]. The official receiver may not extend the moratorium period beyond the end of the period of three months beginning after the end of the initial period of one year mentioned above[17]. The moratorium may be extended more than once, but any extension, whether by the official receiver or by the court, must be made before the moratorium would otherwise end[18].

Where the moratorium period is extended by the official receiver, notice of the extension and the period for which it is extended must be sent to the debtor subject to the debt relief order and to the creditors specified in it, and the official receiver must cause to be entered in the individual insolvency register[19]: (a) that such an extension has been made in relation to the debtor; (b) the date on which the extension was made; (c) its duration; and (d) the date of the anticipated end of the moratorium period[20].

Where a debtor dies at a time when a moratorium period under a debt relief order applies in relation to him or her[21] the official receiver must, as soon as reasonably practicable after receiving notice of the death of the debtor: (i) revoke the debt relief order[22]; (ii) cause a note of the fact and the date of the death to be entered on the individual insolvency register[23]; and (iii) send notice of the revocation to any creditor specified in the debt relief order as a creditor to whom a qualifying debt is owed, and to the personal representatives[24] of the deceased debtor[25]. In such notice the official receiver must identify the debtor, state the reason for the revocation and specify the date on which the revocation took effect[26].

1   As to the meaning of 'the effective date' see PARA 108 note 10.
2   As to the meaning of 'debt relief order' see PARA 101 note 1.
3   As to the meaning of 'qualifying debts' see PARA 101.
4   Insolvency Act 1986 s 251G(1) (s 251G added by the Tribunals, Courts and Enforcement Act 2007 s 108(1), Sch 17).
5   As to references to creditors to whom a qualifying debt is owed see PARA 102 note 7.
6   For these purposes references to the debt include a reference to any interest, penalty or other sum that becomes payable in relation to that debt after the application date: Insolvency Act 1986 s 251G(4) (as added: see note 4). As to the meaning of 'application date' see PARA 102 note 15. The Secretary of State's power to recover overpayment of benefits by deduction from current benefits is a 'remedy in respect of the debt' and thus not available to the Secretary of State during the moratorium: *Payne v Secretary of State for Work and Pensions* [2011] UKSC 60, [2012] 2 AC 1, [2012] 2 All ER 46.

7 As to the meaning of 'debtor' see PARA 102 note 4.

8 As to the meaning of 'court' see PARA 6 note 8.

9 Insolvency Act 1986 s 251G(2) (as added: see note 4). Section 251G(2) does not preclude the making of a possession order for rent arrears, or suspending that order, but the existence of a debt relief order would make it unreasonable for the court to suspend the order conditional on payment of rent arrears which were subject to the debt relief order: *Sharples v Places for People Homes Ltd* [2011] EWCA Civ 813, [2012] Ch 382, [2012] 1 All ER 582.

10 Insolvency Act 1986 s 251G(3) (as added: see note 4). Nothing in these provisions affects the right of a secured creditor of the debtor to enforce his security: s 251G(5) (as so added). As to secured creditors see PARA 574 et seq.

11 The moratorium terminates early if it terminates before the end of what would otherwise be the moratorium period, whether on the revocation of the order or by virtue of any other enactment: Insolvency Act 1986 s 251H(6) (s 251H added by the Tribunals, Courts and Enforcement Act 2007 Sch 17). As to the official receiver's power to revoke a debt relief order see PARA 115. As to the official receiver see PARA 35 et seq.

12 Ie under the Insolvency Act 1986 s 251H(2)–(5): see text to notes 14–18.

13 Insolvency Act 1986 s 251H(1) (as added: see note 11). The court may extend the moratorium period under s 251M: see PARA 116.

14 Ie under the Insolvency Act 1986 s 251K: see PARA 114.

15 Insolvency Act 1986 s 251H(3): (as added: see note 11).

16 Insolvency Act 1986 s 251H(2) (as added: see note 11).

17 Insolvency Act 1986 s 251H(4) (as added: see note 11).

18 Insolvency Act 1986 s 251H(5) (as added: see note 11).

19 As to the individual insolvency register see PARA 28.

20 Insolvency Rules 1986, SI 1986/1925, r 5A.20(a)(ii), (b) (r 5A.20 added by SI 2009/642). As to where the moratorium period is extended by the court see PARA 116.

21 Insolvency Rules 1986, SI 1986/1925, r 5A.27(1) (r 5A.27 added by SI 2009/642).

22 Insolvency Rules 1986, SI 1986/1925, r 5A.27(2)(a) (as added: see note 21).

23 Insolvency Rules 1986, SI 1986/1925, r 5A.27(2)(b) (as added: see note 21). As to the individual insolvency register see r 6A.8; and PARAS 28, 34.

24 As to personal representatives generally see WILLS AND INTESTACY vol 103 (2010) PARA 605 et seq.

25 Insolvency Rules 1986, SI 1986/1925, r 5A.27(2)(c) (as added: see note 21).

26 Insolvency Rules 1986, SI 1986/1925, r 5A.27(3) (as added: see note 21).

110. Prohibition from acting as a director: permission to act. It is an offence for a person to act as director of a company or directly or indirectly to take part in or be concerned in the promotion, formation or management of a company, without the leave of the court, at a time when: (1) he is an undischarged bankrupt; (2) a moratorium period[1] under a debt relief order[2] applies in relation to him; or (3) a bankruptcy restrictions order[3] or a debt relief restrictions order[4] is in force in respect of him[5].

An application by a person in relation to whom a moratorium period under a debt relief order applies, or in respect of whom a debt relief restrictions order or undertaking[6] is in force for permission[7] to act as a director of, or to take part or be concerned in the promotion, formation[8] or management of a company, must be supported by a witness statement[9]. The witness statement must identify the company and specify:

(a) the nature of its business[10] or intended business, and the place or places where that business is, or is to be, carried on[11];

(b) whether it is, or is to be, a private or a public company[12];

(c) the persons who are, or are to be, principally responsible for the conduct of its affairs, whether as directors[13], shadow directors[14], managers[15] or otherwise[16];

(d) the manner and capacity in which the applicant for permission proposes to take part or be concerned in the promotion or formation of the company or, as the case may be, its management[17];

(e)   the emoluments and other benefits to be obtained from the directorship[18]; and

(f)   if the company is already in existence, the date of its incorporation and the amount of its nominal and issued share[19] capital, and if not, the amount, or approximate amount of its proposed commencing share capital, and the sources from which that capital is to be obtained[20].

Where the applicant for permission intends to take part or be concerned in the promotion or formation of a company, the witness statement must contain an undertaking by the applicant that he or she will, within not less than five business days[21] of the company being incorporated, file in court[22] a copy of its memorandum of association[23] and certificate of incorporation[24].

The court must fix a venue[25] for the hearing of the application, and must give notice to the applicant accordingly[26]. The applicant must, not less than 28 days before the date fixed for the hearing, give notice of the venue to the official receiver[27], accompanied by copies of the application and the witness statement[28]. The official receiver may, not less than 14 days before the date fixed for the hearing, file in court a report of any matters which he considers ought to be drawn to the court's attention, and must send a copy of the report as soon as reasonably practicable after it is filed to the applicant[29]. The applicant may, no later than five business days before the date of the hearing, file in court a notice specifying any statements in the official receiver's report which he or she intends to deny or dispute[30] and send copies of such notice, not less than four business days before the date of the hearing, to the official receiver[31]. The official receiver may appear on the hearing of the application, and may make representations and put to the applicant such questions as the court may allow[32].

If the court grants the application for permission its order must specify that which by virtue of the order the applicant has permission to do[33]. The court may at the same time, having regard to any representations made by the official receiver on the hearing of the application, exercise in relation to the moratorium period or the debt relief order to which the applicant is subject, any power which it has[34]. Whether or not the application is granted, copies of the order must be sent by the court to the applicant and the official receiver[35].

1   As to moratorium periods see PARA 109.
2   As to the meaning of 'debt relief order' see PARA 101 note 1.
3   As to bankruptcy restrictions orders see PARA 657 et seq.
4   As to debt relief restrictions orders see PARA 125.
5   See the Company Directors Disqualification Act 1986 s 11(1); and PARA 729.
6   As to debt relief restrictions undertakings see PARA 127.
7   Ie permission under the Company Directors Disqualification Act 1986 s 11: see the text to notes 1–5; and PARA 729.
8   As to company formation see COMPANIES vol 14 (2009) PARA 102 et seq.
9   Insolvency Rules 1986, SI 1986/1925, r 5A.24(1) (r 5A.24 added by SI 2009/642; the Insolvency Rules 1986, SI 1986/1925, r 5A.24(1) amended by SI 2010/686). As to the meaning of 'witness statement' see PARA 161 note 7.
10   As to the meaning of 'business' see PARA 43 note 4.
11   Insolvency Rules 1986, SI 1986/1925, r 5A.24(2)(a) (r 5A.24 as added (see note 9); r 5A.24(2) amended by SI 2010/686).
12   Insolvency Rules 1986, SI 1986/1925, r 5A.24(2)(b) (as added and amended: see notes 9, 11). 'Private company' and 'public company' have the same meanings for these purposes as in the Companies Act 2006 s 4 (see COMPANIES vol 14 (2009) PARA 102): Insolvency Act 1986 s 436(2).
13   As to directors of a company see COMPANIES vol 14 (2009) PARA 478 et seq.
14   As to shadow directors see COMPANIES vol 14 (2009) PARA 479.
15   As to managers of companies see RECEIVERS vol 88 (2012) PARA 184.
16   Insolvency Rules 1986, SI 1986/1925, r 5A.24(2)(c) (as added and amended: see notes 9, 11).

17 Insolvency Rules 1986, SI 1986/1925, r 5A.24(2)(d) (as added and amended: see notes 9, 11).
18 Insolvency Rules 1986, SI 1986/1925, r 5A.24(2)(e) (as added and amended: see notes 9, 11).
19 'Share' has the same meaning for these purposes as in the Companies Act 2006 s 540 (see COMPANIES vol 15 (2009) PARA 1042): Insolvency Act 1986 s 436(2).
20 Insolvency Rules 1986, SI 1986/1925, r 5A.24(3) (r 5A.24 as added (see note 9); r 5A.24(3) amended by SI 2010/686).
21 As to the meaning of 'business day' see PARA 28 note 8.
22 As to the meaning of 'file in court' see PARA 57 note 13. As to the meaning of 'court' see PARA 6 note 8.
23 As to memoranda of association see COMPANIES vol 14 (2009) PARA 104.
24 Insolvency Rules 1986, SI 1986/1925, r 5A.24(4) (r 5A.24 as added (see note 9); r 5A.24(4) amended by SI 2009/2472; and SI 2010/686).
25 As to the meaning of 'venue' see PARA 46 note 22.
26 Insolvency Rules 1986, SI 1986/1925, r 5A.24(5) (r 5A.24 as added (see note 9); r 5A.24(5) amended by SI 2010/686).
27 As to the official receiver see PARA 35 et seq.
28 Insolvency Rules 1986, SI 1986/1925, r 5A.25(1) (r 5A.25 added by SI 2009/642; Insolvency Rules 1986, SI 1986/1925, r 5A.25(1) amended by SI 2010/686).
29 Insolvency Rules 1986, SI 1986/1925, r 5A.25(2) (r 5A.25 as added (see note 28); r 5A.25(2) amended by SI 2010/686).
30 Insolvency Rules 1986, SI 1986/1925, r 5A.25(3) (r 5A.25 as added (see note 28); r 5A.25(3) amended by SI 2010/686).
31 Insolvency Rules 1986, SI 1986/1925, r 5A.25(4) (r 5A.25 as added (see note 28); r 5A.25(4) amended by SI 2010/686).
32 Insolvency Rules 1986, SI 1986/1925, r 5A.25(5) (r 5A.25 as added (see note 28); r 5A.25(5) amended by SI 2010/686).
33 Insolvency Rules 1986, SI 1986/1925, r 5A.26(1) (r 5A.26 added by SI 2009/642; Insolvency Rules 1986, SI 1986/1925, r 5A.26(1) amended by SI 2010/686).
34 Insolvency Rules 1986, SI 1986/1925, r 5A.26(2) (r 5A.26 as added (see note 33); r 5A.26(2) amended by SI 2010/686). The power referred to is that under the Insolvency Act 1986 s 251M (see PARA 116).
35 Insolvency Rules 1986, SI 1986/1925, r 5A.26(3) (as added: see note 33).

111. Discharge from qualifying debts. At the end of the moratorium[1] applicable to a debt relief order[2] the debtor[3] is discharged from all the qualifying debts[4] specified in the order, including all interest, penalties and other sums which may have become payable in relation to those debts since the application date[5], unless the moratorium terminates early[6] and except any qualifying debt which the debtor incurred in respect of any fraud or fraudulent breach of trust[7] to which the debtor was a party[8].

The discharge of the debtor from qualifying debts does not release any person from any liability, whether as partner or co-trustee of the debtor or otherwise, from which the debtor is released by the discharge or any liability as surety[9] for the debtor or as a person in the nature of such a surety[10].

If the order is revoked by the court[11] after the end of the moratorium period, the qualifying debts specified in the order must, so far as practicable, be treated as though the above provision relating to the discharge from qualifying debts had never applied to them[12].

1 As to the moratorium see PARA 109.
2 As to the meaning of 'debt relief order' see PARA 101 note 1.
3 As to the meaning of 'debtor' see PARA 102 note 4.
4 As to the meaning of 'qualifying debts' see PARA 101. A liability to pay child support is not discharged: *Child Maintenance and Enforcement Commission v Beesley* [2010] EWCA Civ 1344, [2011] 3 All ER 233, [2011] 1 WLR 1704.
5 Insolvency Act 1986 s 251I(1) (s 251I added by the Tribunals, Courts and Enforcement Act 2007 s 108(1), Sch 17). As to the meaning of 'application date' see PARA 102 note 15.
6 Insolvency Act 1986 s 251I(2) (as added: see note 5). As to when a moratorium terminates early see PARA 109 note 11.

7   As to fraudulent breach of trust see *Woodland-Ferrari v UCL Group Retirement Benefits Scheme* [2002] EWHC 1354 (Ch), [2003] Ch 115, [2002] 3 All ER 670; and PARA 650.

8   Insolvency Act 1986 s 251I(3) (as added: see note 5).

9   As to sureties generally see FINANCIAL SERVICES AND INSTITUTIONS vol 49 (2008) PARA 1013 et seq.

10   Insolvency Act 1986 s 251I(4) (as added: see note 5).

11   Ie under the Insolvency Act 1986 s 251M: see PARA 116. As to the meaning of 'court' see PARA 6 note 8.

12   Insolvency Act 1986 s 251I(5) (as added: see note 5).

(3) DUTIES OF DEBTOR

112. Providing assistance to official receiver. At any time after the making of an application for a debt relief order[1], the debtor[2] must: (1) give to the official receiver[3] such information as to his affairs; (2) attend on the official receiver at such times; and (3) do all such other things, as the official receiver may reasonably require for the purpose of carrying out his functions in relation to the application or, as the case may be, the debt relief order made as a result of the application[4].

The debtor must notify the official receiver as soon as reasonably practicable if he becomes aware of any error in, or omission from, the information supplied to the official receiver in, or in support of, the application[5], or any change in his circumstances[6] between the application date[7] and the determination date[8] that would affect, or would have affected, the determination of the application[9].

These duties apply after, as well as before, the determination of the application for as long as the official receiver is able to exercise his functions in relation to the application[10].

If a debt relief order is made as a result of the application, the debtor must notify the official receiver as soon as reasonably practicable if: (a) there is an increase in his income during the moratorium period[11] applicable to the order[12]; (b) he acquires any property[13] or any property is devolved upon him during that period[14]; or (c) he becomes aware of any error in or omission from any information supplied by him to the official receiver after the determination date[15].

1   As to the making of an application for a debt relief order see PARA 102. As to the meaning of 'debt relief order' see PARA 101 note 1.

2   As to the meaning of 'debtor' see PARA 102 note 4.

3   As to the official receiver see PARA 35 et seq.

4   Insolvency Act 1986 s 251J(1), (2) (s 251J added by the Tribunals, Courts and Enforcement Act 2007 s 108(1), Sch 17).

5   Where the debtor is notifying the official receiver of such an error or omission the notification must include the nature of the error or omission and the reason for it: Insolvency Act 1986 s 251J(6) (as added: see note 4); Insolvency Rules 1986, SI 1986/1925, r 5A.17(1)(a) (r 5A.17 added by SI 2009/642).

6   Where the debtor is notifying the official receiver of such a change in his or her circumstances the notification must include the nature and date of the change: Insolvency Act 1986 s 251J(6) (as added: see note 4); Insolvency Rules 1986, SI 1986/1925, r 5A.17(1)(b) (as added: see note 5).

7   As to the meaning of 'application date' see PARA 102 note 15.

8   As to the meaning of 'determination date' see PARA 106 note 10.

9   Insolvency Act 1986 s 251J(3) (as added: see note 4). As to the duty of the official receiver to determine an application for a debt relief order see PARA 105.

10   Insolvency Act 1986 s 251J(4) (as added: see note 4).

11   As to the moratorium period see PARA 109.

12   Insolvency Act 1986 s 251J(5)(a) (as added: see note 4). Where the debtor is notifying the official receiver of such an increase the notification must include the amount and date of the

increase, the reason for it and its expected duration: s 251J(6) (as so added); Insolvency Rules 1986, SI 1986/1925, r 5A.17(2)(a) (as added: see note 5).

13 As to the meaning of 'property' see PARA 412.

14 Insolvency Act 1986 s 251J(5)(b) (as added: see note 4). Where the debtor is notifying the official receiver of such an acquisition or devolution the notification must include the nature and date of the acquisition or devolution, the reason for it and its value: s 251J(6) (as so added); Insolvency Rules 1986, SI 1986/1925, r 5A.17(2)(b) (as added: see note 5).

15 Insolvency Act 1986 s 251J(5)(c) (as added: see note 4). Where the debtor is notifying the official receiver of such an error or omission the notification must include the nature of the error or omission, the reason for it and the date at which the debtor became aware of it: s 251J(6) (as so added); Insolvency Rules 1986, SI 1986/1925, r 5A.17(2)(c) (as added: see note 5).

(4) OBJECTIONS, INVESTIGATIONS AND REVOCATION

113. Objections. Any person specified in a debt relief order[1] as a creditor to whom a specified qualifying debt[2] is owed[3] may object to the making of the order[4], the inclusion of the debt in the list of the debtor's[5] qualifying debts[6] or the details of the debt specified in the order[7]; and the official receiver[8] must consider every such objection[9].

Such an objection must be:

(1) made during the moratorium period[10] relating to the order and within 28 days of the date on which the creditor was notified[11] of the making of the order[12];

(2) made to the official receiver in writing[13], including: (a) the name and address of the creditor; (b) the name of the debtor and the reference number of the order; (c) what it is the creditor objects to[14]; (d) a statement indicating which ground[15] the creditor relies on; (e) a statement indicating the facts the creditor relies on; and (f) information and documents in support of the grounds and the facts the creditor relies on[16];

(3) based on one of the following grounds: (a) there is an error in, or an omission from, something specified in the debt relief order; (b) a bankruptcy order[17] has been made in respect of the debtor; (c) the debtor has made a proposal for an individual voluntary arrangement[18]; (d) the official receiver should not have been satisfied that: (i) the debts specified in the order were qualifying debts as at the application date[19]; (ii) the conditions that must be met before the official receiver may make a debt relief order[20] were met; (iii) the other conditions[21] were met, or that any failure to meet such condition did not prevent him or her from making the order; (iv) the condition that the debtor's monthly surplus income[22] on the determination date[23] does not exceed £50[24] was not met at any time after the order was made; or (v) the condition that the total value of the debtor's property[25] on the determination date[26] does not exceed £300[27] was not met at any time after the order was made[28].

1 As to the meaning of 'debt relief order' see PARA 101 note 1.

2 As to the meaning of 'specified qualifying debt' see PARA 109.

3 As to references to creditors to whom a qualifying debt is owed see PARA 102 note 7.

4 As to the making of a debt relief order see PARA 108.

5 As to the meaning of 'debtor' see PARA 102 note 4.

6 As to the meaning of 'qualifying debts' see PARA 101.

7 Insolvency Act 1986 s 251K(1) (s 251K added by the Tribunals, Courts and Enforcement Act 2007 s 108(1), Sch 17).

8 As to the official receiver see PARA 35 et seq.

9 Insolvency Act 1986 s 251K(3) (as added: see note 7).
10 As to the moratorium period see PARA 109.
11 As to the notification to be given to creditors see PARA 108.
12 Insolvency Act 1986 s 251K(2)(a) (as added: see note 7); Insolvency Rules 1986, SI 1986/1925, r 5A.14(1), (3) (r 5A.14 added by SI 2009/642).
13 Insolvency Act 1986 s 251K(2)(b) (as added: see note 7); Insolvency Rules 1986, SI 1986/1925, r 5A.14(2) (as added: see note 12).
14 Ie to which of the matters under the Insolvency Act 1986 s 251K the creditor objects: see text to notes 4–7.
15 Ie on which of the grounds listed in the Insolvency Rules 1986, SI 1986/1925, r 5A.14(4) the creditor relies: see text to notes 17–28.
16 Insolvency Act 1986 s 251K(2)(b), (d) (as added: see note 7); Insolvency Rules 1986, SI 1986/1925, r 5A.14(3) (as added: see note 12).
17 As to the meaning of 'bankruptcy order' see PARA 129.
18 Ie a proposal under the Insolvency Act 1986 Pt 8 (ss 252–263G): see PARA 43 et seq.
19 As to the meaning of 'application date' see PARA 102 note 15.
20 Ie the conditions set out in the Insolvency Act 1986 Sch 4ZA Pt 1: see PARA 106.
21 Ie the conditions set out in the Insolvency Act 1986 Sch 4ZA Pt 2: see PARA 106.
22 As to the debtor's monthly surplus income see PARA 106.
23 As to the meaning of 'determination date' see PARA 106 note 10. For these purposes references to the determination date are to be read as references to the time in question: Insolvency Rules 1986, SI 1986/1925, r 5A.14(5) (as added: see note 12).
24 Ie the condition set out in the Insolvency Act 1986 Sch 4ZA Pt 1 para 7: see PARA 106. See also the Insolvency Proceedings (Monetary Limits) Order 1986, SI 1986/1996, art 3, Schedule Pt II (art 3 amended by SI 2009/465; the Insolvency Proceedings (Monetary Limits) Order 1986, SI 1986/1996, Schedule Pt II substituted by SI 2004/547; and amended by SI 2009/465).
25 As to the meaning of 'property' see PARA 412. As to the value of the debtor's property see PARA 106.
26 See note 23.
27 Ie the condition set out in the Insolvency Act 1986 Sch 4ZA Pt 1 para 8: see PARA 106. See also the Insolvency Proceedings (Monetary Limits) Order 1986, SI 1986/1996, art 3, Schedule Pt II; and note 24.
28 Insolvency Act 1986 s 251K(2)(c) (as added: see note 7); Insolvency Rules 1986, SI 1986/1925, r 5A.14(4) (as added: see note 12).

114. Investigations. The official receiver[1] may, as part of his consideration of an objection[2] or on his own initiative and during or after the moratorium period[3], carry out an investigation of any matter that appears to the official receiver to be relevant to the making of any decision[4] in relation to a debt relief order of the debtor[5]. He may require any person to give him such information and assistance as he may reasonably require in connection with such an investigation[6].

The decisions to which an investigation may be directed are: (1) whether the order should be revoked or amended[7]; (2) whether an application should be made to the court[8]; or (3) whether any other steps should be taken in relation to the debtor[9]. If the official receiver decides to do none of those things he must notify the creditor of such decision[10].

If, after considering an objection, the official receiver is minded to revoke or amend the debt relief order, he must send to the debtor particulars of the objection, the ground and facts upon which the creditor relies and the address to which the debtor's comments must be sent, and invite the debtor to comment on them[11]. Provided they are made within 21 days of the particulars being sent to the debtor, the official receiver must consider any such comments before deciding whether to revoke or amend the debt relief order[12].

1 As to the official receiver see PARA 35 et seq.
2 Ie an objection by a person specified in a debt relief order as a creditor to whom a specified qualifying debt is owed under the Insolvency Act 1986 s 251K(1): see PARA 114. As to the

meaning of 'debt relief order' see PARA 101 note 1. As to the meaning of 'specified qualifying debt' see PARA 109. As to references to creditors to whom a qualifying debt is owed see PARA 102 note 7.

3   Insolvency Act 1986 s 251K(6) (s 251K added by the Tribunals, Courts and Enforcement Act 2007 s 108(1), Sch 17). As to the moratorium period see PARA 109.

4   Ie a decision under the Insolvency Act 1986 s 251K(5): see text to notes 8, 9.

5   Insolvency Act 1986 s 251K(4) (as added: see note 3). As to the meaning of 'debtor' see PARA 102 note 4.

6   Ie under the Insolvency Act 1986 s 251L: see PARA 115. If the official receiver decides to revoke or amend the order he must, within 14 days of making that decision, send notice to the creditor under the Insolvency Rules 1986, SI 1986/1925, r 5A.16 (see PARA 115) of the revocation or amendment: r 5A.15(4)(a)(i) (r 5A.15 added by SI 2009/642).

7   Insolvency Act 1986 s 251K(7) (as added: see note 3).

8   Ie under the Insolvency Act 1986 s 251M: see PARA 116. As to the meaning of 'court' see PARA 6 note 8. If the official receiver decides to apply to the court he must treat the creditor, if he or she would not otherwise be treated as such, as a person interested in any such application under the Insolvency Rules 1986, SI 1986/1925, r 5A.19(b) (see PARA 116) to whom notice of the application must be sent: r 5A.15(4)(a)(ii) (as added: see note 6).

9   Insolvency Act 1986 s 251K(5) (as added: see note 3). If the official receiver decides to take any other steps in relation to the debtor he must send notice to the creditor of the decision and of the steps he proposes to take: Insolvency Rules 1986, SI 1986/1925, r 5A.15(4)(a)(iii) (as added: see note 6).

10   Insolvency Rules 1986, SI 1986/1925, r 5A.15(4)(b) (as added: see note 6).

11   Insolvency Rules 1986, SI 1986/1925, r 5A.15(1), (2) (as added: see note 6).

12   Insolvency Rules 1986, SI 1986/1925, r 5A.15(3) (as added: see note 6).

115.   Power of official receiver to revoke or amend a debt relief order. The official receiver[1] may revoke or amend a debt relief order[2] during the applicable moratorium period[3] on the ground that:

(1)   any information supplied to the official receiver by the debtor[4] in, or in support of, the application[5], or after the determination date[6], was incomplete, incorrect, or otherwise misleading[7];

(2)   the debtor has failed to comply with the duty to provide assistance to the official receiver[8];

(3)   a bankruptcy order[9] has been made in relation to the debtor[10];

(4)   the debtor has made a proposal for an individual voluntary arrangement[11], or has notified the official receiver of his intention to do so[12];

(5)   the official receiver should not have been satisfied that: (a) the debts specified in the order were qualifying debts[13] of the debtor as at the application date[14]; (b) the conditions that must be met before the official receiver may make a debt relief order[15] were met[16]; (c) the other conditions[17] were met or that any failure to meet such a condition did not prevent his making the order[18]; or

(6)   either or both of the conditions that the debtor's monthly surplus income[19] on the determination date[20] does not exceed £50[21] and that the total value of the debtor's property[22] on the determination date does not exceed £300[23] are not met at any time after the order was made[24].

Where the official receiver decides to revoke the order he may revoke it either with immediate effect or with effect from such date, not more than three months after the date of the decision, as he may specify[25]. If the order has been revoked with effect from a specified date the official receiver may, if he thinks it appropriate to do so, revoke the order with immediate effect[26] and if he does so, any debtor or creditor to whom notice of the specified date has already been sent[27] must be notified by the official receiver of the earlier date on which the revocation has effect[28].

As soon as reasonably practicable after deciding to revoke a debt relief order, the official receiver must send notice of the decision to revoke to the debtor and any creditor specified in the debt relief order as a creditor to whom a qualifying debt is owed[29]. Such notice must identify the debtor and the date and reference number of the debt relief order, state the reasons for revocation and specify the date, whether immediate or specified[30], on or from which the revocation has effect[31]. Upon the revocation taking effect, provided that information concerning a debt relief order has not been deleted[32], the official receiver must cause the entry in the individual insolvency register[33] relating to the debt relief order[34] to be amended accordingly[35].

The official receiver may amend a debt relief order for the purpose of correcting an error in or omission from anything specified in the order[36] but may not add any debts that were not specified in the application for the debt relief order to the list of qualifying debts[37]. As soon as reasonably practicable after any such amendment the official receiver must: (i) send notice of the amendment to the debtor and any creditor specified in the debt relief order as a creditor to whom a qualifying debt is owed; (ii) identify the debtor and the date and reference number of the debt relief order, specify the amendment, specify the date on which the amendment was made, and state the reasons for it in the notice of .amendment; and (iii) cause the entry in the individual insolvency register relating to the amended debt relief order to be amended accordingly[38].

1   As to the official receiver see PARA 35 et seq.
2   As to the meaning of 'debt relief order' see PARA 101 note 1.
3   Insolvency Act 1986 s 251L(1) (s 251L added by the Tribunals, Courts and Enforcement Act 1986 s 108(1), Sch 17). As to the moratorium period see PARA 109.
4   As to the meaning of 'debtor' see PARA 102 note 4.
5   As to the information to be provided in, or in support of, an application see PARA 102.
6   As to the meaning of 'determination date' see PARA 106 note 10.
7   Insolvency Act 1986 s 251L(2)(a) (as added: see note 3).
8   Insolvency Act 1986 s 251L(2)(b) (as added: see note 3). The duty to provide assistance to the official receiver is provided for under s 251J: see PARA 112.
9   As to the meaning of 'bankruptcy order' see PARA 129.
10 Insolvency Act 1986 s 251L(2)(c) (as added: see note 3).
11 Ie a proposal under the Insolvency Act 1986 Pt 8 (ss 252–263G): see PARA 43 et seq.
12 Insolvency Act 1986 s 251L(2)(d) (as added: see note 3).
13 As to the meaning of 'qualifying debts' see PARA 101.
14 Insolvency Act 1986 s 251L(3)(a) (as added: see note 3). As to the meaning of 'application date' see PARA 102 note 15.
15 Ie the conditions set out in the Insolvency Act 1986 Sch 4ZA Pt 1: see PARA 106.
16 Insolvency Act 1986 s 251L(3)(b) (as added: see note 3).
17 Ie the conditions set out in the Insolvency Act 1986 Sch 4ZA Pt 2: see PARA 106.
18 Insolvency Act 1986 s 251L(3)(c) (as added: see note 3).
19 As to the debtor's monthly surplus income see PARA 106.
20 For this purpose references to the determination date are to be read as references to the time in question: Insolvency Act 1986 s 251L(4) (as added: see note 3).
21 Ie the condition set out in the Insolvency Act 1986 Sch 4ZA Pt 1 para 7: see PARA 106. See also the Insolvency Proceedings (Monetary Limits) Order 1986, SI 1986/1996, art 3, Schedule Pt II (art 3 amended by SI 2009/465; the Insolvency Proceedings (Monetary Limits) Order 1986, SI 1986/1996, Schedule Pt II substituted by SI 2004/547; and amended by SI 2009/465).
22 As to the meaning of 'property' see PARA 412. As to the value of the debtor's property see PARA 106.
23 Ie the condition set out in the Insolvency Act 1986 Sch 4ZA Pt 1 para 8: see PARA 106. See also the Insolvency Proceedings (Monetary Limits) Order 1986, SI 1986/1996, art 3, Schedule Pt II; and note 21.
24 Insolvency Act 1986 s 251L(4) (as added: see note 3). As to the making of a debt relief order see PARA 108. In deciding whether to revoke a debt relief order, the official receiver is exercising a

judicial function such that the decision is not subject to the public sector equality duty: *R (on the application of Howard) v Official Receiver* [2013] EWHC 1839 (Admin), [2013] NLJR 20, [2013] All ER (D) 73 (Jul).

25 Insolvency Act 1986 s 251L(5) (as added: see note 3). In considering when the revocation should take effect the official receiver must consider, in the light of the grounds on which the decision to revoke was made and all the other circumstances of the case, whether the debtor ought to be given the opportunity to make arrangements for making payments towards his debts: s 251L(6) (as so added).

26 Insolvency Act 1986 s 251L(7) (as added: see note 3).

27 Ie under the Insolvency Rules 1986, SI 1986/1925, r 5A.16(1): see text to notes 28–35.

28 Insolvency Act 1986 s 251L(10) (as added: see note 3); Insolvency Rules 1986, SI 1986/1925, r 5A.16(3) (r 5A.16 added by SI 2009/642).

29 Insolvency Act 1986 s 251L(10) (as added: see note 3); Insolvency Rules 1986, SI 1986/1925, r 5A.16(1)(a) (as added: see note 28). As to references to creditors to whom a qualifying debt is owed see PARA 102 note 7.

30 Ie whether specified under the Insolvency Act 1986 s 251L(5) or (7): see text to notes 25, 26.

31 Insolvency Act 1986 s 251L(10) (as added: see note 3); Insolvency Rules 1986, SI 1986/1925, r 5A.16(2) (as added: see note 28).

32 Ie under the Insolvency Rules 1986, SI 1986/1925, r 6A.5B: see PARA 31.

33 As to the individual insolvency register see PARA 28.

34 As to the duty to make an entry in the individual insolvency register see PARA 108.

35 Insolvency Act 1986 s 251L(10) (as added: see note 3); Insolvency Rules 1986, SI 1986/1925, r 5A.16(1)(b) (as added: see note 28).

36 Insolvency Act 1986 s 251L(8) (as added: see note 3).

37 Insolvency Act 1986 s 251L(9) (as added: see note 3).

38 Insolvency Act 1986 s 251L(10) (as added: see note 3); Insolvency Rules 1986, SI 1986/1925, r 5A.16(4) (as added: see note 28).

(5) ROLE OF THE COURT

116. Powers of the court in relation to debt relief orders. Any person may at any time make an application to the court[1] if he is dissatisfied by any act, omission or decision of the official receiver[2] in connection with a debt relief order[3] or an application[4] for such an order[5]. Where such an application to the court is made, if the person making the application is the debtor[6], notice of the application must be sent to the official receiver and to any creditor specified in the debt relief order or in the application for a debt relief order or, if the person making the application is a person other than the debtor, notice of the application must be sent to the official receiver and the debtor[7].

The official receiver may at any time make an application to the court for directions or an order in relation to any matter[8] arising in connection with a debt relief order or an application for such an order[9]. Where such an application to the court is made, notice of the application must be sent by the official receiver to the debtor and to any person appearing to the official receiver to have an interest in the application[10].

The court may extend the moratorium period[11] applicable to a debt relief order for the purposes of determining an application under these provisions[12], in which case notice of such extension and the period for which it is extended must be sent to the official receiver, who must send a copy to the debtor subject to the debt relief order and to the creditors specified in it[13]. The official receiver must cause to be entered in the individual insolvency register[14] that such an extension has been made in relation to the debtor, the date on which the extension was made, the duration of the extension and the date of the anticipated end of the moratorium period[15].

On an application under these provisions the court may dismiss the application or do one or more of the following:

(1)   quash the whole or part of any act or decision of the official receiver[16];

(2)   give the official receiver directions, including a direction that he reconsider any matter in relation to which his act or decision has been quashed under head (1) above[17];

(3)   make an order for the enforcement of any obligation on the debtor arising by virtue of the duty to assist the official receiver[18];

(4)   extend the moratorium period applicable to the debt relief order[19];

(5)   make an order revoking[20] or amending[21] the debt relief order[22];

(6)   make an order summoning a person to appear before the court[23]; or

(7)   make such other order as the court thinks fit[24].

1   As to the meaning of 'court' see PARA 6 note 8. As to the court to which an application under these provisions must be made see the Insolvency Rules 1986, SI 1986/1925, r 5A.21 (substituted by SI 2001/785).
2   As to the official receiver see PARA 35 et seq.
3   As to the meaning of 'debt relief order' see PARA 101 note 1.
4   As to the making of an application for a debt relief order see PARA 102.
5   Insolvency Act 1986 s 251M(1), (4) (s 251M added by the Tribunals, Courts and Enforcement Act 2007 s 108(1), Sch 17).
6   As to the meaning of 'debtor' see PARA 102 note 4.
7   Insolvency Rules 1986, SI 1986/1925, r 5A.19(a) (r 5A.19 added by SI 2009/642).
8   The matters the official receiver may make an application for directions or an order in relation to include, among other things, matters relating to the debtor's compliance with any duty arising under the Insolvency Act 1986 s 251J (see PARA 112): Insolvency Act 1986 s 251M(3) (as added: see note 5).
9   Insolvency Act 1986 s 251M(2), (4) (as added: see note 5).
10 Insolvency Rules 1986, SI 1986/1925, r 5A.19(b) (as added: see note 7).
11 As to the moratorium period see PARA 109.
12 Insolvency Act 1986 s 251M(5) (as added: see note 5).
13 Insolvency Rules 1986, SI 1986/1925, r 5A.20(a)(i) (r 5A.20 added by SI 2009/642).
14 As to the individual insolvency register see PARA 28.
15 Insolvency Rules 1986, SI 1986/1925, r 5A.20(b) (as added: see note 13).
16 Insolvency Act 1986 s 251M(6)(a) (as added: see note 5).
17 Insolvency Act 1986 s 251M(6)(b) (as added: see note 5).
18 Insolvency Act 1986 s 251M(6)(c) (as added: see note 5). As to the duty to assist the official receiver see s 251J; and PARA 112.
19 Insolvency Act 1986 s 251M(6)(d) (as added: see note 5). See also text to notes 11–15.
20 An order under this provision for the revocation of a debt relief order: (1) may be made during the moratorium period applicable to the debt relief order or at any time after that period has ended; (2) may be made on the court's own motion if the court has made a bankruptcy order in relation to the debtor during that period; (3) may provide for the revocation or the order to take effect on such terms and at such a time as the court may specify: Insolvency Act 1986 s 251M(7) (as added: see note 5). As to the meaning of 'bankruptcy order' see PARA 129.
21 An order under this provision for the amendment of a debt relief order may not add any debts that were not specified in the application for the debt relief order to the list of qualifying debts: Insolvency Act 1986 s 251M(8) (as added: see note 5). As to the meaning of 'qualifying debts' see PARA 101.
22 Insolvency Act 1986 s 251M(6)(e) (as added: see note 5).
23 Insolvency Act 1986 s 251M(6)(f) (as added: see note 5). An order summoning a person to appear before the court is made under the Insolvency Act 1986 s 251N: see PARA 118.
24 Insolvency Act 1986 s 251M(6)(g) (as added: see note 5).

117.   Persons at risk of violence.   In any case where disclosure or continuing disclosure to other persons, whether to the public generally or to specific persons, of the current address[1] or whereabouts of a debtor[2] might reasonably be expected to lead to violence against him or her or against a person who normally resides with him or her as a member of his or her family[3], the court[4] may:

(1)   on the application of a debtor subject to a debt relief order or the official receiver[5] in respect of such a debtor, order that the details in

respect of the debtor to be entered onto the individual insolvency register[6] must not include details of the debtor's current address or that the details of the debtor's current address kept on the individual insolvency register[7] must be removed from such register[8];

(2) on the application of a debtor subject to a debt relief restrictions order or the official receiver in respect of such a debtor, order that: (a) details of the debtor's current address are to be removed from any part of the court file of the proceedings in relation to the debtor which is open to inspection and be kept on a separate file not open to inspection; (b) the full title of the proceedings are to be amended by the removal of the details of the debtor's current address from the description of the debtor; (c) the details in respect of the debtor to be entered onto the debt relief restrictions register[9] are not to include details of the debtor's current address; or (d) the details of the debtor's current address kept on the debt relief restrictions register[10] are to be removed from such register[11];

(3) on the application of a debtor subject to a debt relief restrictions undertaking or the official receiver in respect of such a debtor, order that the details of the debtor's current address are to be excluded from the details in respect of the debtor to be entered onto the debt relief restrictions register[12], or that the details of the debtor's current address kept on the debt relief restrictions register[13] are to be removed from such register[14].

In any case where an application is made by a debtor under or by virtue of these provisions, the application must be accompanied by a witness statement[15] referring to these provisions[16] and containing sufficient evidence to satisfy the court to which the application was made that these provisions apply to or in respect of that debtor[17].

Where the court makes an order under the above provisions, it may further order that the full title of any proceedings, or the details in respect of the debtor kept on or to be entered onto the registers referred to above, are to instead include such other details of the debtor's addresses or whereabouts as the court thinks just, including details of any address at which the debtor has previously resided or carried on business[18].

Proceedings under these provisions may be ordered by the court to be transferred[19] on the application of the person in respect of whom the application is being made[20].

1 'Current address' means in relation to any debtor the address of his or her current place of residence and any address at which he or she currently carries on business: Insolvency Rules 1986, SI 1986/1925, r 5A.18(1) (r 5A.18 added by SI 2009/642). As to the meaning of 'debtor' for these purposes see note 2. As to the meaning of 'residence' see PARA 131 note 5.

2 'Debtor' means a person subject to a debt relief order, or a debt relief restrictions order or a debt relief restrictions undertaking: Insolvency Rules 1986, SI 1986/1925, r 5A.18(1) (as added: see note 1). As to the meaning of 'debt relief order' see PARA 101 note 1. As to debt relief restrictions orders see PARA 125. As to debt relief restrictions undertakings see PARA 127.

3 Insolvency Rules 1986, SI 1986/1925, r 5A.18(2) (as added: see note 1).

4 As to the meaning of 'court' see PARA 6 note 8.

5 As to the official receiver see PARA 35 et seq.

6 Ie entered under the Insolvency Rules 1986, SI 1986/1925, r 6A.5A: see PARA 31. As to the individual insolvency register see PARA 28.

7 Ie kept under the Insolvency Rules 1986, SI 1986/1925, Pt 6A (rr 6A.1–6A.8): see PARA 28 et seq.

8 Insolvency Rules 1986, SI 1986/1925, r 5A.18(3)(a) (as added: see note 1).

9 Ie entered under the Insolvency Rules 1986, SI 1986/1925, r 6A.7A: see PARA 33. As to the debt relief restrictions register see PARA 105 note 6.
10 Ie kept under the Insolvency Rules 1986, SI 1986/1925, Pt 6A (rr 6A.1–6A.8): see PARA 28 et seq.
11 Insolvency Rules 1986, SI 1986/1925, r 5A.18(3)(b) (as added: see note 1).
12 Ie entered under the Insolvency Rules 1986, SI 1986/1925, r 6A.7A: see PARA 33.
13 Ie kept under the Insolvency Rules 1986, SI 1986/1925, Pt 6A (rr 6A.1–6A.8): see PARA 28 et seq.
14 Insolvency Rules 1986, SI 1986/1925, r 5A.18(3)(c) (as added: see note 1).
15 As to the meaning of 'witness statement' see PARA 161 note 7.
16 Ie referring to the Insolvency Rules 1986, SI 1986/1925, r 5A.
17 Insolvency Rules 1986, SI 1986/1925, r 5A.18(6) (as added: see note 1).
18 Insolvency Rules 1986, SI 1986/1925, r 5A.18(4) (r 5A.18 as added (see note 1); r 5A.18(4) amended by SI 2010/686). As to the meaning of 'business' see PARA 43 note 4.
19 Ie transferred under the Insolvency Rules 1986, SI 1986/1925, r 7.11: see PARA 756.
20 Insolvency Rules 1986, SI 1986/1925, r 5A.18(5) (as added: see note 1).

118. Inquiry into debtor's dealings and property. The court[1], on the application of the official receiver[2], may make an order[3] summoning: (1) the debtor[4]; (2) the debtor's spouse or former spouse or the debtor's civil partner or former civil partner; or (3) any person appearing to the court to be able to give information or assistance concerning the debtor or his dealings, affairs and property[5], to appear before the court[6]. The court may require a person falling within head (3) to provide a written account of his dealings with the debtor or to produce any documents in his possession or under his control relating to the debtor or to the debtor's dealings, affairs or property[7].

Where a person fails without reasonable excuse to appear before the court when he is summoned to do so by an order under these provisions[8], the court may cause a warrant to be issued to a constable or prescribed officer of the court[9] for the arrest of that person, and for the seizure of any records[10] or other documents in that person's possession[11]. The court may authorise a person arrested under such a warrant to be kept in custody, and anything seized under such a warrant to be held, until that person is brought before the court under the warrant or until such time as the court may order[12].

1 As to the meaning of 'court' see PARA 6 note 8. As to the court to which an application under these provisions must be made see the Insolvency Rules 1986, SI 1986/1925, r 5A.21 (substituted by SI 2001/785).
2 As to the official receiver see PARA 35 et seq.
3 Insolvency Act 1986 s 251N(1) (s 251N added by the Tribunals, Courts and Enforcement Act 2007 s 108(1), Sch 17).
4 As to the meaning of 'debtor' see PARA 102 note 4.
5 As to the meaning of 'property' see PARA 412.
6 Insolvency Act 1986 s 251N(2) (as added: see note 3).
7 Insolvency Act 1986 s 251N(3) (as added: see note 3).
8 Insolvency Act 1986 s 251N(4) (as added: see note 3).
9 The prescribed officers of the court are, in the case of the High Court, the tipstaff and his assistants of the court, and, in the case of a county court, the district judge and the bailiffs: Insolvency Rules 1986, SI 1986/1925, r 7.21(2) (amended by SI 2009/642; and SI 2010/686).
10 As to the meaning of 'records' see PARA 20 note 6.
11 Insolvency Act 1986 s 251N(5) (as added: see note 3).
12 Insolvency Act 1986 s 251N(6) (as added: see note 3).

(6) OFFENCES

119. False representations and omissions. A person who makes an application for a debt relief order[1] is guilty of an offence[2], irrespective of whether or not a debt relief order is made[3] as a result of the application[4], if: (1) he knowingly or recklessly makes any false representation or omission in making the application or providing any information or documents to the official receiver in support of the application[5]; (2) he intentionally fails to comply with the duty to notify the official receiver as soon as reasonably practicable if he becomes aware of any error in, or omission from, the information supplied to the official receiver in, or in support of, the application or any change in his circumstances between the application date and the determination date that would affect, or would have affected, the determination of the application[6]; (3) he knowingly or recklessly makes any false representation or omission in providing any information to the official receiver in connection with such a duty or otherwise in connection with the application[7].

A person in respect of whom a debt relief order is made is guilty of an offence if: (a) he intentionally fails to comply with the duty to notify the official receiver as soon as reasonably practicable of an increase in his income, the acquisition of property[8], or an error in or omission from information supplied[9]; or (b) he knowingly or recklessly makes any false representation or omission in providing information to the official receiver in connection with such a duty or otherwise in connection with the performance by the official receiver of functions in relation to the order[10]. It is immaterial for the purposes of such an offence whether the offence is committed during or after the moratorium period[11] and whether or not the order is revoked[12] after the conduct constituting the offence takes place[13].

It is not a defence to an offence under these provisions that anything relied on, in whole or in part, as constituting the offence was done outside England and Wales[14].

1   As to the making of an application for a debt relief order see PARA 102. As to the meaning of 'debt relief order' see PARA 101 note 1.

2   Proceedings for an offence under these provisions may only be instituted by the Secretary of State or by or with the consent of the Director of Public Prosecutions: Insolvency Act 1986 s 251T(1) (s 251T added by the Tribunals, Courts and Enforcement Act 1986 s 108(1), Sch 17). As to the Secretary of State see PARA 19. As to the Director of Public Prosecutions see CRIMINAL PROCEDURE vol 27 (2010) PARAS 23, 33 et seq.

3   As to the making of a debt relief order see PARA 108.

4   Insolvency Act 1986 s 251O(3) (s 251O added by the Tribunals, Courts and Enforcement Act 2007 Sch 17).

5   Insolvency Act 1986 s 251O(1) (as added: see note 4). A person who commits such an offence is liable on conviction on indictment to imprisonment for a term not exceeding seven years or a fine, or to both, or on summary conviction to imprisonment for a term not exceeding 12 months or a fine not exceeding the statutory maximum, or to both: ss 251T(3), 430, Sch 10 (s 251T as added (see note 2); Sch 10 amended by the Tribunals, Courts and Enforcement Act 2007 Sch 20 Pt 1 paras 1, 15(1), (3)). As to the statutory maximum see SENTENCING AND DISPOSITION OF OFFENDERS vol 92 (2010) PARA 140.

6   Insolvency Act 1986 s 251O(2)(a) (as added: see note 4). Ie the duty under s 251J(3): see PARA 112. A person who commits such an offence is liable on conviction on indictment to imprisonment for a term not exceeding two years or a fine, or to both, or on summary conviction to imprisonment for a term not exceeding 12 months or a fine not exceeding the statutory maximum, or to both: ss 251T(3), 430, Sch 10 (s 251T as added (see note 2); Sch 10 as amended (see note 5)).

7   Insolvency Act 1986 s 251O(2)(b) (as added: see note 4). A person who commits such an offence is liable on conviction on indictment to imprisonment for a term not exceeding seven years or a fine, or to both, or on summary conviction to imprisonment for a term not exceeding 12 months or a fine not exceeding the statutory maximum, or to both: ss 251T(3), 430, Sch 10 (s 251T as added (see note 2); Sch 10 as amended (see note 5)).

8   As to the meaning of 'property' see PARA 412.

9   Insolvency Act 1986 s 251O(4)(a) (as added: see note 4). As to the duty to notify the official receiver see s 251J(5); and PARA 112. A person who commits such an offence is liable on

conviction on indictment to imprisonment for a term not exceeding two years or a fine, or to both, or on summary conviction to imprisonment for a term not exceeding 12 months or a fine not exceeding the statutory maximum, or to both: ss 251T(3), 430, Sch 10 (s 251T as added (see note 2); Sch 10 as amended (see note 5)).

10 Insolvency Act 1986 s 251O(4)(b) (as added: see note 4). A person who commits such an offence is liable on conviction on indictment to imprisonment for a term not exceeding seven years or a fine, or to both, or on summary conviction to imprisonment for a term not exceeding 12 months or a fine not exceeding the statutory maximum, or to both: ss 251T(3), 430, Sch 10 (s 251T as added (see note 2); Sch 10 as amended (see note 5)).

11 As to the moratorium period see PARA 109.

12 As to revocation of a debt relief order see PARA 115.

13 Insolvency Act 1986 s 251O(5) (as added: see note 4).

14 Insolvency Act 1986 s 251T(2) (as added: see note 2).

120.   Concealment or falsification of documents. A person in respect of whom a debt relief order[1] is made[2] is guilty of an offence[3] if, during the moratorium period[4] in relation to that order:

(1)   he does not provide, at the request of the official receiver[5], all his books, papers and other records[6] of which he has possession or control and which relate to his affairs[7];

(2)   he prevents the production to the official receiver of any books, papers or other records relating to his affairs[8];

(3)   he conceals, destroys, mutilates or falsifies, or causes or permits the concealment, destruction, mutilation or falsification of, any books, papers or other records relating to his affairs[9];

(4)   he makes, or causes or permits the making of, any false entries in any book, document or record relating to his affairs[10]; or

(5)   he disposes of, or alters or makes any omission in, or causes or permits the disposal, altering or making of any omission in, any book, document or record relating to his affairs[11].

A person in respect of whom a debt relief order is made is guilty of an offence if: (a) he did anything falling within heads (3)–(5) above during the period of 12 months ending with the application date[12]; or (b) he did anything falling within heads (2)–(5) above after that date but before the effective date[13].

A person is not guilty of an offence under these provisions if he proves that, in respect of the conduct constituting the offence, he had no intent to defraud or to conceal the state of his affairs[14]. It is immaterial for the purposes of an offence under these provisions whether or not the debt relief order in question is revoked[15] after the conduct constituting the offence takes place, but no offence is committed under these provisions by virtue of conduct occurring after the order is revoked[16].

A person who commits an offence under these provisions is liable on conviction on indictment to imprisonment for a term not exceeding seven years or a fine, or to both, or on summary conviction to imprisonment for a term not exceeding 12 months or a fine not exceeding the statutory maximum[17], or to both[18].

1   As to the meaning of 'debt relief order' see PARA 101 note 1.

2   As to the making of a debt relief order see PARA 108.

3   Proceedings for an offence under these provisions may only be instituted by the Secretary of State or by or with the consent of the Director of Public Prosecutions: Insolvency Act 1986 s 251T(1) (s 251T added by the Tribunals, Courts and Enforcement Act 1986 s 108(1), Sch 17). As to the Secretary of State see PARA 19. As to the Director of Public Prosecutions see CRIMINAL PROCEDURE vol 27 (2010) PARAS 23, 33 et seq.

4   As to the moratorium period see PARA 109.

5   As to the official receiver see PARA 35 et seq.

6   As to the meaning of 'records' see PARA 20 note 6.
7   Insolvency Act 1986 s 251P(1)(a) (s 251P added by the Tribunals, Courts and Enforcement Act 2007 s 108(1), Sch 17).
8   Insolvency Act 1986 s 251P(1)(b) (as added: see note 7).
9   Insolvency Act 1986 s 251P(1)(c) (as added: see note 7).
10 Insolvency Act 1986 s 251P(1)(d) (as added: see note 7).
11 Insolvency Act 1986 s 251P(1)(e) (as added: see note 7).
12 Insolvency Act 1986 s 251P(2)(a) (as added: see note 7). As to the meaning of 'application date' see PARA 102 note 15. In its application to a trading record this provision has effect as if the reference to 12 months were a reference to two years: s 251P(4) (as so added). 'Trading record' means a book, document or record which shows or explains the transactions or financial position of a person's business, including: (1) a periodic record of cash paid and received; (2) a statement of periodic stock-taking; and (3) except in the case of goods sold by way of retail trade, a record of goods sold and purchased which identifies the buyer and seller or enables them to be identified: s 251P(5) (as so added). As to the meaning of 'transaction' see PARA 678 note 2. As to the meaning of 'business' see PARA 43 note 4.
13 Insolvency Act 1986 s 251P(2)(b) (as added: see note 7). As to the meaning of 'the effective date' see PARA 108 note 10.
14 Insolvency Act 1986 s 251P(3) (as added: see note 7).
15 As to revocation of a debt relief order see PARA 115.
16 Insolvency Act 1986 s 251P(6) (as added: see note 7).
17 As to the statutory maximum see SENTENCING AND DISPOSITION OF OFFENDERS vol 92 (2010) PARA 140.
18 Insolvency Act 1986 ss 251T(3), 430, Sch 10 (s 251T as added (see note 3); Sch 10 amended by the Tribunals, Courts and Enforcement Act 2007 Sch 20 Pt 1 paras 1, 15(1), (3)).

121.   Fraudulent disposal of property. A person in respect of whom a debt relief order[1] is made[2] is guilty of an offence[3] if he made or caused to be made any gift or transfer of his property[4] during the period between the start of the period of two years ending with the application date[5] and the end of the moratorium period[6].

A person is not guilty of an offence under these provisions if he proves that, in respect of the conduct constituting the offence, he had no intent to defraud or to conceal the state of his affairs[7]. A person is taken to have proved that he had no such intent if sufficient evidence is adduced to raise an issue as to whether he had such intent, and the contrary is not proved beyond reasonable doubt[8].

It is immaterial for the purposes of an offence under these provisions whether or not the debt relief order in question is revoked[9] after the conduct constituting the offence takes place, but no offence is committed under these provisions by virtue of conduct occurring after the order is revoked[10].

A person who commits an offence under these provisions is liable on conviction on indictment to imprisonment for a term not exceeding two years or a fine, or to both, or on summary conviction to imprisonment for a term not exceeding 12 months or a fine not exceeding the statutory maximum[11], or to both[12].

1   As to the meaning of 'debt relief order' see PARA 101 note 1.
2   As to the making of a debt relief order see PARA 108.
3   Proceedings for an offence under these provisions may only be instituted by the Secretary of State or by or with the consent of the Director of Public Prosecutions: Insolvency Act 1986 s 251T(1) (s 251T added by the Tribunals, Courts and Enforcement Act 1986 s 108(1), Sch 17). As to the Secretary of State see PARA 19. As to the Director of Public Prosecutions see CRIMINAL PROCEDURE vol 27 (2010) PARAS 23, 33 et seq.
4   As to the meaning of 'property' see PARA 412. For this purpose 'transfer of property' includes causing or conniving at the levying of any execution against that property: Insolvency Act 1986 s 251Q(2) (s 251Q added by the Tribunals, Courts and Enforcement Act 2007 Sch 17).
5   As to the meaning of 'application date' see PARA 102 note 15.
6   Insolvency Act 1986 s 251Q(1) (as added: see note 4). As to the moratorium period see PARA 109.

7 Insolvency Act 1986 s 251Q(3) (as added: see note 4).
8 Insolvency Act 1986 s 251Q(4) (as added: see note 4).
9 As to revocation of a debt relief order see PARA 115.
10 Insolvency Act 1986 s 251Q(5) (as added: see note 4).
11 As to the statutory maximum see SENTENCING AND DISPOSITION OF OFFENDERS vol 92 (2010) PARA 140.
12 Insolvency Act 1986 ss 251T(3), 430, Sch 10 (s 251T as added (see note 3); Sch 10 amended by the Tribunals, Courts and Enforcement Act 2007 Sch 20 Pt 1 paras 1, 15(1), (3)).

122. Fraudulent dealing with property obtained on credit. A person in respect of whom a debt relief order[1] is made[2] is guilty of an offence[3] if during the relevant period[4] he disposed of any property[5] which he had obtained on credit and, at the time he disposed of it, had not paid for it[6]. A person is not guilty of such an offence if he proves that, in respect of the conduct constituting the offence, he had no intent to defraud or to conceal the state of his affairs[7].

Any other person is guilty of an offence if during the relevant period he acquired or received property[8] from a debtor[9] knowing or believing that the debtor owed money in respect of the property, and that the debtor did not intend, or was unlikely to be able, to pay the money he so owed[10].

A person is not guilty of an offence under these provisions if the disposal, acquisition or receipt of the property was in the ordinary course of a business[11] carried on by the debtor at the time of the disposal or receipt[12]. In determining whether that was the case, regard may be had in particular to the price paid for the property[13].

It is immaterial for the purposes of an offence under these provisions whether or not the debt relief order in question is revoked[14] after the conduct constituting the offence takes place, but no offence is committed under these provisions by virtue of conduct occurring after the order is revoked[15].

A person who commits an offence under these provisions is liable on conviction on indictment to imprisonment for a term not exceeding seven years or a fine, or to both, or on summary conviction to imprisonment for a term not exceeding 12 months or a fine not exceeding the statutory maximum[16], or to both[17].

1 As to the meaning of 'debt relief order' see PARA 101 note 1.
2 As to the making of a debt relief order see PARA 108.
3 Proceedings for an offence under these provisions may only be instituted by the Secretary of State or by or with the consent of the Director of Public Prosecutions: Insolvency Act 1986 s 251T(1) (s 251T added by the Tribunals, Courts and Enforcement Act 1986 s 108(1), Sch 17). As to the Secretary of State see PARA 19. As to the Director of Public Prosecutions see CRIMINAL PROCEDURE vol 27 (2010) PARAS 23, 33 et seq.
4 'Relevant period' means the period between the start of the period of two years ending with the application date, and the determination date: Insolvency Act 1986 s 251R(3) (s 251R added by the Tribunals, Courts and Enforcement Act 2007 Sch 17). As to the meaning of 'application date' see PARA 102 note 15. As to the meaning of 'determination date' see PARA 106 note 10.
5 As to the meaning of 'property' see PARA 412. For these purposes references to disposing of property include pawning or pledging it, and references to acquiring property must be read accordingly: Insolvency Act 1986 s 251R(7) (as added: see note 4).
6 Insolvency Act 1986 s 251R(1) (as added: see note 4).
7 Insolvency Act 1986 s 251R(6) (as added: see note 4).
8 See note 5.
9 'Debtor' means a person in respect of whom a debt relief order was made: Insolvency Act 1986 s 251R(2) (as added: see note 4).
10 Insolvency Act 1986 s 251R(2) (as added: see note 4).
11 As to the meaning of 'business' see PARA 43 note 4.
12 Insolvency Act 1986 s 251R(4) (as added: see note 4).
13 Insolvency Act 1986 s 251R(5) (as added: see note 4).

14 As to revocation of a debt relief order see PARA 115.
15 Insolvency Act 1986 s 251R(8) (as added: see note 4).
16 As to the statutory maximum see SENTENCING AND DISPOSITION OF OFFENDERS vol 92 (2010)
    PARA 140.
17 Insolvency Act 1986 ss 251T(3), 430, Sch 10 (s 251T as added (see note 3); Sch 10 amended by
    the Tribunals, Courts and Enforcement Act 2007 Sch 20 Pt 1 paras 1, 15(1), (3)).

123. Obtaining credit or engaging in business. A person in respect of whom a
debt relief order[1] is made[2] is guilty of an offence[3] if during the relevant period[4]:
(1) he obtains credit[5], either alone or jointly with any other person, without
giving the person from whom he obtains the credit the relevant information[6]
about his status[7], unless the amount of the credit is less than £500[8]; or (2) he
engages directly or indirectly in any business[9] under a name other than that in
which the order was made without disclosing to all persons with whom he enters
into any business transaction[10] the name in which the order was made[11].

A person who commits an offence under these provisions is liable on
conviction on indictment to imprisonment for a term not exceeding two years or
a fine, or to both, or on summary conviction to imprisonment for a term not
exceeding 12 months or a fine not exceeding the statutory maximum[12], or to
both[13].

1 As to the meaning of 'debt relief order' see PARA 101 note 1.
2 As to the making of a debt relief order see PARA 108.
3 Proceedings for an offence under these provisions may only be instituted by the Secretary of
   State or by or with the consent of the Director of Public Prosecutions: Insolvency Act 1986
   s 251T(1) (s 251T added by the Tribunals, Courts and Enforcement Act 1986 s 108(1), Sch 17).
   As to the Secretary of State see PARA 19. As to the Director of Public Prosecutions see CRIMINAL
   PROCEDURE vol 27 (2010) PARAS 23, 33 et seq.
4 'Relevant period' means the moratorium period relating to the debt relief order or the period for
   which a debt relief restrictions order is in force in respect of the person in respect of whom the
   debt relief order is made, as the case may be: Insolvency Act 1986 s 251S(3) (s 251S added by
   the Tribunals, Courts and Enforcement Act 2007 Sch 17). As to the moratorium period see PARA
   109. As to debt relief restrictions orders see PARA 125.
5 For this purpose the reference to a person obtaining credit includes: (1) where goods are bailed
   to him under a hire-purchase agreement, or agreed to be sold to him under a conditional sale
   agreement; and (2) where he is paid in advance, in money or otherwise, for the supply of goods
   or services: Insolvency Act 1986 s 251S(5) (as added: see note 4).
6 For this purpose the relevant information is the information that: (a) a moratorium is in force in
   relation to the debt relief order; (b) a debt relief restrictions order is in force in respect of him; or
   (c) both a moratorium and a debt relief restrictions order is in force: Insolvency Act 1986
   s 251S(2) (as added: see note 4). As to moratoriums see PARA 109.
7 Insolvency Act 1986 s 251S(1)(a) (as added: see note 4).
8 Insolvency Act 1986 s 251S(4) (as added: see note 4); Insolvency Proceedings (Monetary Limits)
   Order 1986, SI 1986/1996, art 3, Schedule Pt II (art 3 amended by SI 2009/465; the Insolvency
   Proceedings (Monetary Limits) Order 1986, SI 1986/1996, Schedule Pt II substituted by
   SI 2004/547; and amended by SI 2009/465).
9 As to the meaning of 'business' see PARA 43 note 4.
10 As to the meaning of 'transaction' see PARA 678 note 2.
11 Insolvency Act 1986 s 251S(1)(b) (as added: see note 4). As to the prohibition from acting as a
    director see PARA 110.
12 As to the statutory maximum see SENTENCING AND DISPOSITION OF OFFENDERS vol 92 (2010)
    PARA 140.
13 Insolvency Act 1986 ss 251T(3), 430, Sch 10 (s 251T as added (see note 3); Sch 10 amended by
    the Tribunals, Courts and Enforcement Act 2007 Sch 20 Pt 1 paras 1, 15(1), (3)).

124. Effect of debt relief orders. The restrictions imposed under debt relief
orders are the same as those that apply to an undischarged bankrupt, namely:
(1)   the person must disclose his status to a credit provider if he wishes to
       obtain credit of more than £500[1];

(2)   the person must not engage directly or indirectly in any business under a different name from that in which the order was made without disclosing to all persons with whom he enters into any business transaction the name in which the order was made[2];

(3)   the person must not act as the director of a company or take part in its promotion, formation or management unless he obtains permission from the court to do so[3];

(4)   the person may not act as an insolvency practitioner[4];

(5)   the person may not act as receiver or manager of the property of a company on behalf of debenture holders[5].

The other disqualifications of an undischarged bankrupt also apply to an individual in respect of whom a debt relief order has been made[6].

1   See the Insolvency Act 1986 s 251S(1)(a), (4), (5); and PARA 123.
2   See the Insolvency Act 1986 s 251S(1)(b); and PARA 123.
3   See the Company Directors Disqualification Act 1986 s 11(1); and PARA 729.
4   See the Insolvency Act 1986 s 390(4), (5); and PARA 727.
5   See the Insolvency Act 1986 s 31; and PARA 728.
6   See PARA 724.

(7) DEBT RELIEF RESTRICTIONS ORDERS AND UNDERTAKINGS

125. Debt relief restrictions order. A debt relief restrictions order[1] may be made by the court[2] in relation to a person in respect of whom a debt relief order[3] has been made[4]. Such an order may only be made on the application of the Secretary of State[5] or the official receiver[6] acting on a direction of the Secretary of State[7]. The application may be made at any time during the moratorium period[8] relating to the debt relief order in question, or after the end of that period if the court has given permission[9].

The court must grant an application for a debt relief restrictions order if it thinks it appropriate to do so having regard to the conduct of the debtor[10], whether before or after the making of the debt relief order[11], taking into account the following types of behaviour on the part of the debtor:

(1)   failing to keep records[12] which account for a loss of property[13] by the debtor, or by a business[14] carried on by him, where the loss occurred in the period beginning two years before the application date[15] for the debt relief order and ending with the date of the application for the debt relief restrictions order[16];

(2)   failing to produce records of that kind on demand by the official receiver[17];

(3)   entering into a transaction[18] at an undervalue[19] in the period beginning two years before the application date for the debt relief order and ending with the date of the determination of that application[20];

(4)   giving a preference[21] in the period beginning two years before the application date for the debt relief order and ending with the date of the determination of that application[22];

(5)   making an excessive pension contribution[23];

(6)   a failure to supply goods or services that were wholly or partly paid for[24];

(7)   trading at a time, before the date of the determination of the application

for the debt relief order, when the debtor knew or ought to have known that he was himself to be unable to pay his debts[25];

(8) incurring, before the date of the determination of the application for the debt relief order, a debt which the debtor had no reasonable expectation of being able to pay[26];

(9) failing to account satisfactorily to the court or the official receiver for a loss of property or for an insufficiency of property to meet his debts[27];

(10) carrying on any gambling, rash and hazardous speculation or unreasonable extravagance which may have materially contributed to or increased the extent of his inability to pay his debts before the application date for the debt relief order or which took place between that date and the date of the determination of the application for the debt relief order[28];

(11) neglect of business affairs of a kind which may have materially contributed to or increased the extent of his inability to pay his debts[29];

(12) fraud or fraudulent breach of trust[30]; or

(13) failing to co-operate with the official receiver[31].

The court must also, in particular, consider whether the debtor was an undischarged bankrupt[32] at some time during the period of six years ending with the date of the application for the debt relief order[33].

A debt relief restrictions order comes into force when it is made and ceases to have effect at the end of a date specified in the order[34], which must not be before the end of the period of two years beginning with the date on which the order is made, or after the end of the period of 15 years beginning with that date[35].

1 As to the meaning of 'debt relief restrictions order' see PARA 102 note 22.
2 As to the meaning of 'court' see PARA 6 note 8.
3 As to the meaning of 'debt relief order' see PARA 101 note 1.
4 Insolvency Act 1986 s 251V, Sch 4ZB para 1(1) (s 251V, Sch 4ZB added by the Tribunals, Courts and Enforcement Act 2007 s 108(1), (2), Schs 17, 19). As to the making of a debt relief order see PARA 108.
5 As to the Secretary of State see PARA 19.
6 As to the official receiver see PARA 35 et seq.
7 Insolvency Act 1986 Sch 4ZB para 1(2) (as added: see note 4). Where the Secretary of State applies to the court for a debt relief restrictions order to be made in relation to a person in respect of whom a debt relief order has been made under Sch 4ZB para 1, the application must be supported by a report by the Secretary of State: Insolvency Rules 1986, SI 1986/1925, r 6.253(1) (rr 6.252–6.256 added by SI 2009/642). 'Secretary of State' includes the official receiver acting in accordance with the Insolvency Act 1986 Sch 4ZB para 1(2): Insolvency Rules 1986, SI 1986/1925, r 6.252 (as so added). The report must include: (1) a statement of the conduct by reference to which it is alleged that it is appropriate for a debt relief restrictions order to be made; and (2) the evidence on which the Secretary of State relies in support of the application: Insolvency Rules 1986, SI 1986/1925, r 6.253(2) (as so added). Any evidence in support of an application for a debt relief restrictions order provided by persons other than the Secretary of State must be by way of a witness statement: r 6.253(3) (as so added; and amended by SI 2010/686). As to the meaning of 'witness statement' see PARA 161 note 7. The date for the hearing must be no earlier than eight weeks from the date when the court fixes the venue for the hearing: Insolvency Rules 1986, SI 1986/1925, r 6.253(4) (as so added). As to the meaning of 'venue' see PARA 46 note 22.
    The Secretary of State must serve notice of the application and the venue fixed by the court on the debtor not more than 14 days after the application is made at court: r 6.254(1) (as so added). Service must be accompanied by a copy of the application, together with copies of the report by the Secretary of State, any other evidence filed with the court in support of the application, and an acknowledgement of service: Insolvency Rules 1986, SI 1986/1925, r 6.254(2) (as so added). The defendant must file in court an acknowledgement of service of the application indicating whether or not he contests the application not more than 14 days after service on him of the application: r 6.254(3) (as so added). Where the defendant has failed to file

an acknowledgement of service and the time period for doing so has expired, the defendant may attend the hearing of the application but may not take part in the hearing unless the court gives permission: r 6.254(4) (as so added).

If the debtor wishes to oppose the application, he must within 28 days of the service of the application and evidence of the Secretary of State, file in court any evidence which he wishes the court to take into consideration, and must serve a copy of such evidence upon the Secretary of State within three business days of filing it at court: r 6.255(1) (as so added). As to the meaning of 'business day' see PARA 28 note 8. Within 14 days from receiving the copy of the debtor's evidence, the Secretary of State must file in court any further evidence in reply he wishes the court to take into consideration and must as soon as reasonably practicable serve a copy of that evidence upon the debtor: r 6.255(2) (as so added).

The court may make a debt relief restrictions order against the debtor, whether or not the latter appears and whether or not he has filed evidence in accordance with r 6.255: r 6.256(1) (as so added). Where the court makes a debt relief restrictions order, it must send two sealed copies to the Secretary of State: r 6.256(2) (as so added). As soon as reasonably practicable after receipt of the sealed copy of the order, the Secretary of State must send a sealed copy of the order to the debtor: r 6.256(3) (as so added).

8. As to the moratorium period see PARA 109.
9. Insolvency Act 1986 Sch 4ZB para 3 (as added: see note 4).
10. As to the meaning of 'debtor' see PARA 102 note 4.
11. Insolvency Act 1986 Sch 4ZB para 2(1) (as added: see note 4).
12. As to the meaning of 'records' see PARA 20 note 6.
13. As to the meaning of 'property' see PARA 412.
14. As to the meaning of 'business' see PARA 43 note 4.
15. As to the meaning of 'application date' see PARA 102 note 15.
16. Insolvency Act 1986 Sch 4ZB para 2(2)(a) (as added: see note 4).
17. Insolvency Act 1986 Sch 4ZB para 2(2)(b) (as added: see note 4).
18. As to the meaning of 'transaction' see PARA 678 note 2.
19. 'Undervalue' must be construed in accordance with the Insolvency Act 1986 Sch 4ZA Pt 2 para 9(2) (see PARA 106): Sch 4ZB para 2(4) (as added: see note 4).
20. Insolvency Act 1986 Sch 4ZB para 2(2)(c) (as added: see note 4). As to the determination of an application for a debt relief order see PARA 105.
21. 'Preference' must be construed in accordance with the Insolvency Act 1986 Sch 4ZA Pt 2 para 10(2) (see PARA 106): Sch 4ZB para 2(4) (as added: see note 4).
22. Insolvency Act 1986 Sch 4ZB para 2(2)(d) (as added: see note 4).
23. Insolvency Act 1986 Sch 4ZB para 2(2)(e) (as added: see note 4). 'Excessive pension contribution' must be construed in accordance with s 342A (see PARA 693): Sch 4ZB para 2(4) (as so added).
24. Insolvency Act 1986 Sch 4ZB para 2(2)(f) (as added: see note 4).
25. Insolvency Act 1986 Sch 4ZB para 2(2)(g) (as added: see note 4).
26. Insolvency Act 1986 Sch 4ZB para 2(2)(h) (as added: see note 4).
27. Insolvency Act 1986 Sch 4ZB para 2(2)(i) (as added: see note 4).
28. Insolvency Act 1986 Sch 4ZB para 2(2)(j) (as added: see note 4).
29. Insolvency Act 1986 Sch 4ZB para 2(2)(k) (as added: see note 4).
30. Insolvency Act 1986 Sch 4ZB para 2(2)(l) (as added: see note 4). As to fraudulent breach of trust see *Woodland-Ferrari v UCL Group Retirement Benefits Scheme* [2002] EWHC 1354 (Ch), [2003] Ch 115, [2002] 3 All ER 670; and PARA 650.
31. Insolvency Act 1986 Sch 4ZB para 2(2)(m) (as added: see note 4).
32. As to the meaning of 'bankrupt' see PARA 129. As to discharge from bankruptcy see PARA 638 et seq.
33. Insolvency Act 1986 Sch 4ZB para 2(3) (as added: see note 4).
34. Insolvency Act 1986 Sch 4ZB para 4(1) (as added: see note 4).
35. Insolvency Act 1986 Sch 4ZB para 4(2) (as added: see note 4). If both an interim debt relief restrictions order and a debt relief restrictions order are made, the date specified must not be before the end of the period of two years beginning with the date on which the interim order is made, or after the end of the period of 15 years beginning with that date: Sch 4ZB para 6 (as so added). As to interim debt relief restrictions orders see PARA 126.

126. Interim debt relief restrictions order. The court[1] may, at any time between the institution of an application for a debt relief restrictions order[2] and the determination of the application[3], make an interim debt relief restrictions order if it thinks that there are prima facie grounds to suggest that the application for the debt relief restrictions order will be successful and it is in the public interest to do so[4]. An interim debt relief restrictions order may only be made on the application of the Secretary of State[5] or the official receiver[6] acting on a direction of the Secretary of State[7].

Where the Secretary of State applies for such an order the court must fix a venue[8] for the hearing[9], and notice of the application must be given to the debtor[10] at least two business days[11] before the date set for the hearing unless the court directs otherwise[12]. The Secretary of State must file a report in court[13] as evidence[14] in support of any application for an interim debt relief restrictions order[15], which must include evidence of the debtor's conduct which is alleged to constitute the grounds for the making of an interim debt relief restrictions order and evidence of matters which relate to the public interest in making the order[16].

The debtor may file in court any evidence which he wishes the court to take into consideration and may appear at the hearing for an interim debt relief restrictions order[17]. The court may make an interim debt relief restrictions order against the debtor whether or not he appears, and whether or not he has filed evidence[18].

An interim debt relief restrictions order: (1) has the same effect as a debt relief restrictions order[19]; (2) comes into force when it is made[20]; and (3) ceases to have effect on the determination of the application for the debt relief restrictions order, on the acceptance of a debt relief restrictions undertaking[21] made by the debtor, or if the court discharges the interim debt relief restrictions order on the application of the person who applied for it or of the debtor[22].

Where the court makes an interim debt relief restrictions order, as soon as reasonably practicable, it must send two sealed copies of the order to the Secretary of State[23]. As soon as reasonably practicable after receipt of the sealed copies of the order, the Secretary of State must send a copy of the order to the debtor[24].

A person subject to an interim debt relief restrictions order may apply to the court to set the order aside[25]. Such an application must be supported by a witness statement[26] stating the grounds on which it is made[27], and the person making the application must send to the Secretary of State, not less than five business days before the hearing: (a) notice of his application; (b) notice of the venue; (c) a copy of his application; and (d) a copy of the supporting witness statement[28]. The Secretary of State may attend the hearing and call the attention of the court to any matters which seem to him to be relevant, and may himself give evidence or call witnesses[29]. Where the court sets aside an interim debt relief restrictions order two sealed copies of the order must be sent, as soon as reasonably practicable, to the Secretary of State by the court[30]. As soon as reasonably practicable after receipt of the sealed copies of the order, the Secretary of State must send a sealed copy of the order to the applicant[31].

1   As to the meaning of 'court' see PARA 6 note 8.
2   As to applications for debt relief restrictions orders see PARA 125.

3   Insolvency Act 1986 Sch 4ZB para 5(2) (Sch 4ZB added by the Tribunals, Courts and Enforcement Act 2007 s 108(2), Sch 19).

4   Insolvency Act 1986 Sch 4ZB para 5(1) (as added: see note 3).
5   As to the Secretary of State see PARA 19.
6   As to the official receiver see PARA 35 et seq.

7   Insolvency Act 1986 Sch 4ZB para 5(3) (as added: see note 3).
8   As to the meaning of 'venue' see PARA 46 note 22.

9   Insolvency Rules 1986, SI 1986/1925, r 6.257(1) (r 6.257 added by SI 2009/642; and amended by SI 2010/686). 'Secretary of State' includes the official receiver acting in accordance with the Insolvency Act 1986 Sch 4ZB para 1(2) (see PARA 125): Insolvency Rules 1986, SI 1986/1925, r 6.252 (added by SI 2009/642).
10   As to the meaning of 'debtor' see PARA 102 note 4.
11   As to the meaning of 'business day' see PARA 28 note 8.
12   Insolvency Rules 1986, SI 1986/1925, r 6.257(2) (as added and amended: see note 9).
13   As to the meaning of 'file in court' see PARA 57 note 13.
14   Any evidence by persons other than the Secretary of State in support of an application for an interim debt relief restrictions order must be by way of a witness statement: Insolvency Rules 1986, SI 1986/1925, r 6.258(3) (r 6.258 added by SI 2009/642; the Insolvency Rules 1986, SI 1986/1925, r 6.258(3) amended by SI 2010/686).
15   Insolvency Rules 1986, SI 1986/1925, r 6.258(1) (as added: see note 14).
16   Insolvency Rules 1986, SI 1986/1925, r 6.258(2) (as added: see note 14).
17   Insolvency Rules 1986, SI 1986/1925, r 6.259(1) (r 6.259 added by SI 2009/642).
18   Insolvency Rules 1986, SI 1986/1925, r 6.259(2) (as added: see note 17).
19   Insolvency Act 1986 Sch 4ZB para 5(4)(a) (as added: see note 3). As to debt relief restrictions orders see PARA 125.
20   Insolvency Act 1986 Sch 4ZB para 5(4)(b) (as added: see note 3).
21   As to debt relief restrictions undertakings see PARA 127.
22   Insolvency Act 1986 Sch 4ZB para 5(5) (as added: see note 3).
23   Insolvency Rules 1986, SI 1986/1925, r 6.259(3) (as added: see note 17).
24   Insolvency Rules 1986, SI 1986/1925, r 6.259(4) (as added: see note 17).
25   Insolvency Rules 1986, SI 1986/1925, r 6.260(1) (r 6.260 added by SI 2009/642).
26   As to the meaning of 'witness statement' see PARA 161 note 7.
27   Insolvency Rules 1986, SI 1986/1925, r 6.260(2) (r 6.260 as added (see note 25); r 6.260(2) amended by SI 2010/686).
28   Insolvency Rules 1986, SI 1986/1925, r 6.260(3) (r 6.260 as added (see note 25); r 6.260(3) amended by SI 2010/686).
29   Insolvency Rules 1986, SI 1986/1925, r 6.260(4) (as added: see note 25).
30   Insolvency Rules 1986, SI 1986/1925, r 6.260(5) (as added: see note 25).
31   Insolvency Rules 1986, SI 1986/1925, r 6.260(6) (as added: see note 25).

127.   Debt relief restrictions undertaking. A debtor[1] may offer a debt relief restrictions undertaking to the Secretary of State[2]. In determining whether to accept such an undertaking the Secretary of State must have regard to the same matters to which the court must have regard when deciding whether to grant an application for a debt relief restrictions order[3].

A reference in an enactment to a person in respect of whom a debt relief restrictions order has effect, or who is the subject of a debt relief restrictions order, includes a reference to a person in respect of whom a debt relief restrictions undertaking has effect[4].

A debt relief restrictions undertaking comes into force on being accepted[5] by the Secretary of State and ceases to have effect at the end of a date specified in the undertaking[6], such date not to be before the end of the period of two years beginning with the date on which the undertaking is accepted or after the period of 15 years beginning with that date[7].

As soon as reasonably practicable after a debt relief restrictions undertaking has been accepted by the Secretary of State, a copy must be sent to the person who offered the undertaking and to the official receiver[8].

On an application by the debtor the court[9] may annul a debt relief restrictions undertaking or provide for a debt relief restrictions undertaking to cease to have effect before the date specified in the undertaking as the date it ceases to have effect[10]. Such an application must be supported by a witness statement[11] stating the grounds on which it is made[12]. The applicant must give notice of the application and the venue[13], together with a copy of the witness statement supporting his application to the Secretary of State at least 28 days before the date fixed for the hearing[14].

1　As to the meaning of 'debtor' see PARA 102 note 4.
2　Insolvency Act 1986 Sch 4ZB para 7(1) (Sch 4ZB added by the Tribunals, Courts and Enforcement Act 2007 s 108(2), Sch 19). As to the Secretary of State see PARA 19.
3　Insolvency Act 1986 Sch 4ZB para 7(2) (as added: see note 2). As to the matters to which the Secretary of State must have regard see Sch 4ZB para 2(2), (3); and PARA 125.
4　Insolvency Act 1986 Sch 4ZB para 8 (as added: see note 2).
5　A debt relief restrictions undertaking authenticated by a person in relation to whom a debt relief order has been made is deemed to have been accepted by the Secretary of State for the purposes of the Insolvency Act 1986 Sch 4ZB para 9 when the undertaking is authenticated by the Secretary of State: Insolvency Rules 1986, SI 1986/1925, r 6.261 (added by SI 2009/642; and amended by SI 2010/686).
6　Insolvency Act 1986 Sch 4ZB para 9(1) (as added: see note 2).
7　Insolvency Act 1986 Sch 4ZB para 9(2) (as added: see note 2).
8　Insolvency Rules 1986, SI 1986/1925, r 6.262 (added by SI 2009/642).
9　As to the meaning of 'court' see PARA 6 note 8.
10　As to the meaning of 'witness statement' see PARA 161 note 7.
11　Insolvency Act 1986 Sch 4ZB para 9(3) (as added: see note 2).
12　Insolvency Rules 1986, SI 1986/1925, r 6.263(1) (r 6.263 added by SI 2009/642; the Insolvency Rules 1986, SI 1986/1925, r 6.263(1) amended by SI 2010/686).
13　As to the meaning of 'venue' see PARA 46 note 22.
14　Insolvency Rules 1986, SI 1986/1925, r 6.263(2) (r 6.263 as added (see note 12); r 6.263(2) amended by SI 2010/686).

128.　Effect of revocation of debt relief order.　Unless the court[1] directs otherwise, the revocation at any time of a debt relief order does not:

(1)　affect the validity of any debt relief restrictions order[2], interim debt relief restrictions order[3] or debt relief restrictions undertaking[4] which is in force in respect of the debtor[5];

(2)　prevent the determination of any application for a debt relief restrictions order, or an interim debt relief restrictions order, in relation to the debtor that was instituted before that time[6];

(3)　prevent the acceptance of a debt relief restrictions undertaking that was offered before that time[7]; or

(4)　prevent the institution or an application for a debt relief restrictions order or interim debt relief restrictions order in respect of the debtor, or the offer or acceptance of a debt relief restrictions undertaking by the debtor, after that time[8].

1　As to the meaning of 'court' see PARA 6 note 8.
2　As to debt relief restrictions orders see PARA 125.
3　As to interim debt relief restrictions orders see PARA 126.
4　As to debt relief restrictions undertakings see PARA 127.
5　Insolvency Act 1986 Sch 4ZB para 10(a) (Sch 4ZB added by the Tribunals, Courts and Enforcement Act 2007 s 108(2), Sch 19). As to the meaning of 'debtor' see PARA 102 note 4.
6　Insolvency Act 1986 Sch 4ZB para 10(b) (as added: see note 5).
7　Insolvency Act 1986 Sch 4ZB para 10(c) (as added: see note 5).
8　Insolvency Act 1986 Sch 4ZB para 10(d) (as added: see note 5).

6. BANKRUPTCY

(1) BANKRUPTCY PETITIONS

(i) In general

129. Meaning of 'bankrupt' and associated terminology. 'Bankrupt' means an individual who has been adjudged bankrupt and, in relation to a bankruptcy order, it means the individual adjudged bankrupt by that order[1]. 'Bankruptcy order' means an order adjudging an individual bankrupt[2]; and 'bankruptcy petition' means a petition to the court[3] for a bankruptcy order[4].

1 Insolvency Act 1986 s 381(1). As from a day to be appointed, s 381(1), (2) is amended by the Enterprise and Regulatory Reform Act 2013 s 71, Sch 19 paras 1, 52: see PARA 130 note 17.

    As to the application of the Insolvency Act 1986 s 381 in the case of the administration in bankruptcy of the insolvent estate of a deceased person dying before the presentation of a bankruptcy petition see PARA 46 note 4.

2 Insolvency Act 1986 s 381(2). See note 1. As to the making of bankruptcy orders see PARA 130 et seq.

3 As to the meaning of 'the court' see PARA 6 note 8.

4 Insolvency Act 1986 s 381(3). See note 1. As to bankruptcy petitions see PARA 130 et seq.

130. Who may present a bankruptcy petition. A petition[1] for a bankruptcy order to be made against an individual may be presented to the court in accordance with the provisions of the Insolvency Act 1986[2]:

(1)   by one of the individual's creditors or jointly by more than one of them[3];

(2)   by the individual himself[4];

(3)   by a temporary administrator appointed under the European Regulation on Insolvency Proceedings[5];

(4)   by a liquidator appointed under the European Regulation on Insolvency Proceedings[6];

(5)   by the supervisor[7] of, or any person, other than the individual, who is for the time being bound[8] by, a voluntary arrangement proposed by the individual and approved under Part 8 of the Insolvency Act 1986[9];

(6)   where a criminal bankruptcy order has been made against the individual[10].

Where a bankruptcy petition relating to an individual is presented by a person who is entitled to present a petition under two or more of heads (1) to (6) above, the petition is to be treated[11] as a petition under such one of those heads as may be specified in the petition[12].

If it appears to the court appropriate to do so on the grounds that there has been a contravention of the Insolvency Rules 1986[13] or for any other reason, the court has a general power to dismiss a bankruptcy petition or to stay proceedings on such a petition; and, where it stays proceedings on a petition, it may do so on such terms and conditions as it thinks fit[14].

Subject to the above provisions, the court may make a bankruptcy order on any such petition[15]; and a bankruptcy petition may not be withdrawn without the permission of the court[16].

As from a day to be appointed, debtors who wish to be made bankrupt must apply to an adjudicator for a bankruptcy order and a debtor will no longer be able to petition the court for such an order[17].

1   As to the meanings of 'bankruptcy petition' and 'bankruptcy order' see PARA 129. In
    bankruptcy, references in the Insolvency Rules 1986, SI 1986/1925, to 'the petitioner' or 'the
    petitioning creditor' include any person who has been substituted as such, or been given carriage
    of the petition: rr 13.1, 13.10.

2   Ie in accordance with the provisions of the Insolvency Act 1986 Pt 9 (ss 264–371). As to the
    amount of deposit as security for fees payable on presentation of a petition under s 264(1) see
    PARA 168.

3   Insolvency Act 1986 s 264(1)(a). As to creditors' petitions see PARA 164 et seq.

4   Insolvency Act 1986 s 264(1)(b). As to debtors' petitions see PARA 191 et seq. As from a day to
    be appointed, s 264(1)(b) is amended by the Enterprise and Regulatory Reform Act 2013 s 71,
    Sch 19 paras 1, 6: see the text and note 17.

5   Insolvency Act 1986 s 264(1)(ba) (added by SI 2002/1240). As to Council Regulation (EC)
    1346/2000 (OJ L160, 30.6.2000, p 1) ('European Regulation on Insolvency Proceedings') see
    PARAS 41, 42. A temporary administrator is one within the meaning of the European Regulation
    on Insolvency Proceedings art 38: see COMPANY AND PARTNERSHIP INSOLVENCY vol 16 (2011)
    PARAS 65, 399.

6   Insolvency Act 1986 s 264(1)(bb) (added by SI 2002/1240). A liquidator is one within the
    meaning of the European Regulation on Insolvency Proceedings art 2(b) appointed in
    proceedings by virtue of art 3(1): see PARA 41 note 7.

7   As to the supervisor of a voluntary arrangement see PARA 73 et seq.

8   As to the persons bound by a voluntary arrangement see PARA 69 head (2).

9   Insolvency Act 1986 s 264(1)(c). A voluntary arrangement is approved under the Insolvency
    Act 1986 Pt 8 (ss 252–263G): see PARA 43 et seq.

10 See the Insolvency Act 1986 s 264(1)(d) (repealed as from a day to be appointed by the Criminal
    Justice Act 1988 s 170(2), Sch 16). At the date at which this volume states the law no such day
    had been appointed. As to criminal bankruptcy orders see PARA 1. As to the making of petitions
    based on criminal bankruptcy orders see the Insolvency Act 1986 s 277 (amended by the
    Constitutional Reform Act 2005 s 40(4), Sch 9 Pt 1 para 44; repealed as from a day to be
    appointed by the Criminal Justice Act 1988 s 170(2), Sch 16). At the date at which this volume
    states the law no such day had been appointed.

11 Ie for the purposes of the Insolvency Act 1986 Pt 9 (ss 264–371).

12 Insolvency Act 1986 s 266(1). In the case of the administration in bankruptcy of the insolvent
    estate of a deceased person dying before the presentation of a bankruptcy petition, an insolvency
    administration petition must: (1) if a liquidator (within the meaning of the European Regulation
    on Insolvency Proceedings art 2(b) (see note 6)) has been appointed in proceedings by virtue of
    art 3(1) in relation to the deceased debtor, be served on him; (2) unless the court directs
    otherwise, be served on the personal representative; and (3) be served on such other persons as
    the court may direct: Insolvency Act 1986 s 266(1) (substituted by the Administration of
    Insolvent Estates of Deceased Persons Order 1986, SI 1986/1999, art 3(1), Sch 1 Pt II para 2(a)
    (substituted by SI 2002/1309)). As to the administration in bankruptcy of the insolvent estates
    of deceased persons see further PARA 830 et seq.
        As to the modification of the Insolvency Act 1986 ss 264, 266 by the Insolvent Partnerships
    Order 1994, SI 1994/2421, in relation to the bankruptcy of an individual member of an
    insolvent partnership see COMPANY AND PARTNERSHIP INSOLVENCY vol 17 (2011) PARAS 1282,
    1319, 1324, 1326.

13 Ie the Insolvency Rules 1986, SI 1986/1925.

14 Insolvency Act 1986 s 266(3). Pursuant to s 266(3), the court may dismiss a petition on the
    grounds of want of prosecution: *TSB Bank plc v Platts* [1997] BPIR 151. As to the exercise of
    the court's powers under the Insolvency Act 1986 s 266(3) in the context of a claim that a
    petition was presented for the ulterior purpose of preventing a debtor from proceeding with an
    action brought by him see *Re Ross (a bankrupt) (No 2)* [2000] BPIR 636, CA.
        Pursuant to the Insolvency Act 1986 s 266(3), the court may also dismiss the petition on the
    grounds that there is a prior foreign bankruptcy in respect of the debtor or on the ground that
    the debtor has no assets in the jurisdiction: *Re Thulin* [1995] 1 WLR 165. See also *Re
    McCulloch, ex p McCulloch* (1880) 14 ChD 716, CA; *Re Robinson, ex p Robinson* (1883) 22
    ChD 816, CA; *Re Artola Hermanos, ex p André Châle* (1890) 24 QBD 640, CA; *Re A Debtor
    (No 199 of 1922)* [1922] 2 Ch 470, CA.
        In the case of the administration in bankruptcy of the insolvent estate of a deceased person
    dying before the presentation of a bankruptcy petition, in the Insolvency Act 1986 s 266(3) for
    the words 'bankruptcy petition' there are to be substituted the words 'petition to the court for
    an insolvency administration order with or without costs': Administration of Insolvent Estates
    of Deceased Persons Order 1986, SI 1986/1999, Sch 1 Pt II para 2(b).

Without prejudice to the Insolvency Act 1986 s 266(3), where a petition under s 264(1)(a), (b) or (c) (see heads (1), (2), (5) in the text) in respect of an individual is pending at a time when a criminal bankruptcy order is made against him, or is presented after such an order has been so made, the court may, on the application of the Official Petitioner, dismiss the petition if it appears to it appropriate to do so: Insolvency Act 1986 s 266(4) (repealed, as from a day to be appointed, by the Criminal Justice Act 1988 Sch 16). At the date at which this volume states the law no such day had been appointed. See PARA 1. As from a day to be appointed, the Insolvency Act 1986 s 266(4) is amended by the Enterprise and Regulatory Reform Act 2013 s 71, Sch 19 paras 1, 8: see the text and note 17.

In the case of the administration in bankruptcy of the insolvent estate of a deceased person dying before the presentation of a bankruptcy petition, a petition for an insolvency administration order to be made may be presented to the court in accordance with the Insolvency Act 1986 Pt 9: (1) by one of the individual's creditors or jointly by more than one of them in the prescribed form; (2) by a temporary administrator appointed under the European Regulation on Insolvency Proceedings (see note 5) in the prescribed form with such variations as the case requires; (3) by a liquidator appointed under the European Regulation on Insolvency Proceedings (see note 6) in the prescribed form with such variations as the case requires; (4) by the supervisor of, or any person, other than the individual, who is for the time being bound by, a voluntary arrangement proposed by the individual and approved under the Insolvency Act 1986 Pt 8 in the prescribed form; or (5) where a criminal bankruptcy order has been made against the individual, by the Official Petitioner or by any person specified in the order in pursuance of the Powers of Criminal Courts Act 1973 s 39(3)(b) (repealed) in the prescribed form in any case where a creditor could present such a petition under head (1): Insolvency Act 1986 s 264(1) (amended by the Administration of Insolvent Estates of Deceased Persons Order 1986, SI 1986/1999, Sch 1 Pt II para 1(a)–(e) (amended by SI 2002/1309)). The prescribed forms are: (a) in a case falling within heads (1)–(3), the Administration of Insolvent Estates of Deceased Persons Order 1986, SI 1986/1999, Sch 3 Form 1; (b) in a case falling within head (4), Sch 3 Form 2; and (c) in a case falling within head (5), Sch 3 Form 3 (Sch 3 Forms 1, 2 substituted by SI 2002/1309).

15 Insolvency Act 1986 s 264(2). As to the procedure on presenting bankruptcy petitions see PARA 164 et seq; and as to bankruptcy orders see PARA 198 et seq. In the case of the administration in bankruptcy of the insolvent estate of a deceased person dying before the presentation of a bankruptcy petition, the court may make an insolvency administration order on any such petition as is mentioned in s 264(1) (see note 14) in the prescribed form: s 264(2) (amended by the Administration of Insolvent Estates of Deceased Persons Order 1986, SI 1986/1999, Sch 1 Pt II para 1(f)). For the prescribed form of insolvency administration order see the Administration of Insolvent Estates of Deceased Persons Order 1986, SI 1986/1999, Sch 3 Form 4 (substituted by SI 2002/1309).

16 See the Insolvency Act 1986 s 266(2); and PARA 187. In circumstances where the petition debt has been paid, secured or compounded for and there are supporting creditors, the court may order any such creditor to be substituted for the petitioner or on the hearing of the petition may make an order changing the carriage of the petition: see the Insolvency Rules 1986, SI 1986/1925, rr 6.30, 6.31; and PARAS 185, 186.

17 See the amendments made to the Insolvency Act 1986 by the Enterprise and Regulatory Reform Act 2013 s 71, Sch 19, which in the main replace references to 'the court' with references to 'the prescribed person', and replace references to 'bankruptcy petitions' with references to 'bankruptcy applications'. Amendments are made to the Insolvency Act 1986 ss 253, 255, 256A, 264–266, 272–274, 274A, 278, 279, 282–286, 288, 290, 293, 295, 297–299, 320, 321, 323, 334, 336, 337, 229–342, 342A, 343–348, 350, 351, 354–356, 358–360, 364, 376, 381, 383–385, 387, 389A, 390, 415, 421A, 424, 429, Sch 4ZA, Sch 4A, Sch 6. A provision which provides for the appointment of adjudicators and assistants (see s 398A) and provisions dealing with applications to adjudicators (ss 263H–263O) are prospectively added by the Enterprise and Regulatory Reform Act 2013 s 71, Sch 18. Provision is made by Sch 19 for the inclusion in Insolvency Rules of regulations dealing with practice and procedure of adjudicators (see the Insolvency Act 1986 Sch 9 paras 4A–4C) and as to appeals against determinations by adjudicators (see Sch 9 paras 24A–24D). The Department for Business, Innovation and Skills has indicated that these amendments are to come into force in 2015–16: see the Enterprise and Regulatory Reform Act 2013 Indicative Timetable, Table 4 (BIS, 6 June 2013).

131. Conditions to be satisfied in respect of debtor. A bankruptcy petition may not be presented to the court by one of the individual's creditors or jointly by more than one of them[1] or by the individual himself[2] unless the debtor[3]:

(1)   is domiciled[4] in England and Wales; or

(2)   is personally present in England and Wales on the day on which the petition is presented; or

(3)   at any time in the period of three years ending with that day:

       (a)   has been ordinarily resident[5] or has had a place of residence, in England and Wales; or

       (b)   has carried on business[6] in England and Wales[7].

The above provisions are subject to the European Regulation on Insolvency Proceedings[8]. In particular, under the European Regulation the courts of the member state within the territory of which the centre of the debtor's main interests is situated have jurisdiction to open insolvency proceedings and the courts of another member state only have jurisdiction to open insolvency proceedings with limited effects, if the debtor has an establishment within the territory of that member state[9].

1   Ie under the Insolvency Act 1986 s 264(1)(a): see PARA 130 head (1).

2   Ie under the Insolvency Act 1986 s 264(1)(b): see PARA 130 head (2).

3   'The debtor', in relation to a bankruptcy petition, means the individual to whom the petition relates: Insolvency Act 1986 s 385(1)(b). As from a day to be appointed, s 385(1)(b) is amended by the Enterprise and Regulatory Reform Act 2013 s 71, Sch 19 paras 1, 55: see PARA 130 note 17.

4   A person is domiciled in the country in which at the time of his birth the person on whom he was legally dependent was domiciled or in the country in which he has acquired a domicile by choice: see CONFLICT OF LAWS vol 19 (2011) PARA 339 et seq. The onus of proving the debtor's domicile is on the petitioning creditor, but prima facie evidence may be adduced so as to throw the burden on the debtor: *Re Mitchell, ex p Cunningham* (1884) 13 QBD 418, 53 LJ Ch 1067, CA. There is a presumption of continuing domicile so that, if the petitioning creditor establishes the debtor's domicile of origin, the onus is on the debtor to prove any change of domicile by choice: *Winans v A-G* [1904] AC 287, HL; *Re Lloyd Evans, National Provincial Bank v Evans* [1947] Ch 695. See also *Re Bird, ex p Debtor v IRC* [1962] 2 All ER 406, [1962] 1 WLR 686, CA. For the relevant principles of the law of domicile, including change of domicile by choice in the context of bankruptcy proceedings, see *Barlow Clowes International Ltd v Henwood* [2008] EWCA Civ 577, [2008] BPIR 778, [2008] All ER (D) 330 (May).

    A debtor's knowledge that the bankruptcy laws of another jurisdiction are more favourable to him cannot prevent him from acquiring domicile there: *Henwood v Barlow Clowes International Ltd (in liquidation)* [2007] EWHC 1579 (Ch), [2007] BPIR 1329 (rvsd on a different point [2008] EWCA Civ 577, [2008] BPIR 778, [2008] All ER (D) 330 (May)).

5   As to the meaning of 'ordinary residence' see CONFLICT OF LAWS 19 (2011) PARA 359. A person resides where in common parlance he lives, and a temporary absence is immaterial, provided that there is an intention to return and a house or lodging to which to return: see *R v St Leonard's Shoreditch (Inhabitants)* (1865) LR 1 QB 21; *R v Glossop Union* (1866) LR 1 QB 227. The word 'reside' implies a degree of permanence (*Levene v IRC* [1928] AC 217 at 222, 223, HL; *Fox v Stirk* [1970] 2 QB 463 at 477, [1970] 3 All ER 7 at 13, CA; *Brokelmann v Barr* [1971] 2 QB 602, [1971] 3 All ER 29), but a person may be resident in more than one place at the same time (*Levene v IRC*; *Langford Property Co Ltd v Tureman* [1949] 1 KB 29, sub nom *Langford Property Co Ltd v Athanassoglou* [1948] 2 All ER 722, CA; *Herbert v Byrne* [1964] 1 All ER 882, [1964] 1 WLR 519, CA; *Skjevesland v Geveren Trading* [2002] EWHC 2898 (Ch), [2003] BCC 391, [2003] BPIR 924; and contrast *Beck v Scholz* [1953] 1 QB 570, [1953] 1 All ER 814, CA).

6   For these purposes, the reference to an individual carrying on business includes: (1) the carrying on of business by a firm or partnership of which the individual is a member; and (2) the carrying on of business by an agent or manager for the individual or for such a firm or partnership: Insolvency Act 1986 s 265(2). See note 7. As to the meaning of 'business' see PARA 43 note 4. See also COMPETITION vol 18 (2009) PARA 370.

    Under the equivalent provision in the Bankruptcy Act 1914 (repealed) it was held that the words 'carry on business' denoted something of a permanent character, not merely an isolated transaction and that a business was carried on only where there was some degree of management or control: see *Brown v London and North Western Rly Co* (1863) 32 LJQB 318; *Graham v Lewis* (1888) 22 QBD 1, CA; *Cain v Butler* [1916] 1 KB 759 at 762; but contrast *Cornelius v Phillips* [1918] AC 199. See also *Kirkwood v Gadd* [1910] AC 422 at 423, HL;

Newman v Oughton [1911] 1 KB 792; *Transport and General Credit Corpn Ltd v Morgan* [1939] Ch 531, [1939] 2 All ER 17; *Re Brauch (a debtor), ex p Britannic Securities and Investments Ltd* [1978] Ch 316, [1978] 1 All ER 1004, CA; *Re Sarflax Ltd* [1979] Ch 592, [1979] 1 All ER 529.

Under the Bankruptcy Act 1914 (repealed) it was held that a business continued to be carried on until the trader had performed all the obligations that the fact of trading imposed on him: *Theophile v Solicitor-General* [1950] AC 186, [1950] 1 All ER 405, HL. Accordingly, under the 1914 Act (repealed) a debtor continued to carry on business until he had paid all his trade debts and satisfied all his tax and customs liabilities, notwithstanding the fact that he might have disposed of or otherwise ceased his business: *Theophile v Solicitor-General*; *Re Bird, ex p Debtor v IRC* [1962] 2 All ER 406, [1962] 1 WLR 686, CA.

The cases decided under the Bankruptcy Act 1914 (repealed) in these respects apply to the equivalent provisions in the Insolvency Act 1986: *Re A Debtor (No 784 of 1991)* [1992] Ch 554, sub nom *Re A Debtor (No 784 of 1991), ex p Debtor v IRC* [1992] 3 All ER 376.

The fact that there are unappealed tax assessments against a debtor based on his having carried on a business in England and Wales in the previous three years does not estop the debtor from challenging an assertion in a bankruptcy petition that he has carried on business in England and Wales in the previous three years: *Wilkinson v IRC* [1998] BPIR 418.

7   Insolvency Act 1986 s 265(1). As to the modification of the Insolvency Act 1986 s 265 by the Insolvent Partnerships Order 1994, SI 1994/2421, in relation to the bankruptcy of an individual member of an insolvent partnership see COMPANY AND PARTNERSHIP INSOLVENCY vol 17 (2011) PARAS 1276, 1318, 1325.

As from a day to be appointed, the Insolvency Act 1986 s 265 is substituted by the Enterprise and Regulatory Reform Act 2013 s 71, Sch 19 paras 1, 7: see PARA 130 note 17.

8   Ie Council Regulation (EC) 1346/2000 (OJ L160, 30.6.2000, p 1) on insolvency proceedings ('European Regulation on Insolvency Proceedings'): see PARAS 41, 42.

9   See the Insolvency Act 1986 s 265(3) (added by SI 2002/1240). See also PARA 42.

(ii) Creditor's Petition

A. IN GENERAL

132. Grounds of creditor's petition. A creditor's petition[1] must be in respect of one or more debts[2] owed by the debtor; and the petitioning creditor[3] or each of the petitioning creditors must be a person to whom the debt or, as the case may be, at least one of the debts, is owed[4].

A creditor's petition may, however, be presented to the court in respect of a debt only if, at the time the petition is presented:

(1)   the amount of the debt, or the aggregate amount of the debts, is equal to or exceeds the bankruptcy level[5];

(2)   the debt, or each of the debts, is for a liquidated sum[6] payable to the petitioning creditor, or one or more of the petitioning creditors, either immediately or at some certain, future time, and is unsecured[7];

(3)   the debt, or each of the debts, is a debt which the debtor appears either to be unable to pay or to have no reasonable prospect of being able to pay[8]; and

(4)   there is no outstanding application[9] to set aside a statutory demand served[10] in respect of the debt or any of the debts[11].

1   In the Insolvency Act 1986, 'creditor's petition' means a bankruptcy petition under s 264(1)(a) (see PARA 130 head (1)): s 385(1). As to the application of s 385 in the case of the administration in bankruptcy of the insolvent estate of a deceased person dying before the presentation of a bankruptcy petition see PARA 6 note 8.

2   As to identification of debts see the Insolvency Rules 1986, SI 1986/1925, r 6.8; and PARA 166.

3   As to the substitution of a petitioning creditor see the Insolvency Rules 1986, SI 1986/1925, r 6.30; and PARA 185.

4   Insolvency Act 1986 s 267(1). For guidance on completing the forms of petition under s 267 see *Practice Direction—Insolvency Proceedings* para 14; and PARA 165 note 7. Where a petition is

presented in respect of a debt which is not properly owed by the debtor to the petitioner or is disputed by the debtor, it may be an abuse of process: see PARAS 162, 188. A petition may be presented in respect of a debt which is not provable in the bankruptcy, although the court will exercise its discretion to make a bankruptcy order on such a petition only in special circumstances: *Levy v Legal Services Commission* [2001] 1 All ER 895, [2001] 1 FCR 178, CA; cf *Russell v Russell* [1999] 2 FCR 137, [1998] BPIR 259.

A single petition may be presented in respect of two or more debts owed by the debtor to separate creditors: *Re Allen, Re A Debtor (No 367 of 1992)* [1998] BPIR 319.

As to the modification of the Insolvency Act 1986 s 267(1) by the Insolvent Partnerships Order 1994, SI 1994/2421, in relation to the bankruptcy of an individual member of an insolvent partnership see COMPANY AND PARTNERSHIP INSOLVENCY vol 17 (2011) PARA 1280.

5 For these purposes, 'the bankruptcy level' is £750; but the Secretary of State may, by order in a statutory instrument, substitute any amount specified in the order for that amount or, as the case may be, for the amount which, by virtue of such an order, is for the time being the amount of the bankruptcy level: Insolvency Act 1986 s 267(4). An order may not, however, be made under s 267(4) unless a draft of it has been laid before, and approved by a resolution of, each House of Parliament: s 267(5). At the date at which this volume states the law no such order had been made.

6 As to liquidated sums see PARA 136. A debt is not to be regarded, for these purposes, as a debt for a liquidated sum by reason only that the amount of the debt is specified in a criminal bankruptcy order: Insolvency Act 1986 s 267(3) (repealed, as from a day to be appointed, by the Criminal Justice Act 1988 s 170(2), Sch 16). At the date at which this volume states the law no such day had been appointed. As to criminal bankruptcy orders see PARA 1.

A claim for solicitors' fees not as yet judicially assessed or determined is not a claim for a liquidated sum which could be the subject of a bankruptcy petition under the Insolvency Act 1986 s 267 unless it is converted into a debt capable of founding a petition by a binding agreement: *Truex v Toll* [2009] EWHC 396 (Ch), [2009] 4 All ER 419, [2009] 1 WLR 2121; see also *Wallace LLP v Yates* [2010] EWHC 1098 (Ch), [2010] BPIR 1041, [2010] All ER (D) 81 (Jun). A statutory demand based on an invoice for an unliquidated amount of solicitors' costs is inherently defective and cannot be transformed into one that can support a petition by a subsequent compromise agreement: *Orrick, Herrington & Sutcliffe (Europe) LLP v Frohlich* [2012] BPIR 169. As to when a liability under a guarantee constitutes a liquidated sum see *McGuinness v Norwich and Peterborough Building Society* [2011] EWCA Civ 1286, [2012] 2 All ER (Comm) 265, [2012] 2 BCLC 233.

7 As to secured creditors see PARAS 156, 574 et seq. A debt which is the debt, or one of the debts, in respect of which a creditor's petition is presented need not be unsecured if either: (1) the petition contains a statement by the person having the right to enforce the security that he is willing, in the event of the bankruptcy order being made, to give up his security for the benefit of all the bankrupt's creditors; or (2) the petition is expressed not to be made in respect of the secured part of the debt and contains a statement by that person of the estimated value at the date of the petition of the security for the secured part of the debt: Insolvency Act 1986 s 269(1). In a case falling within head (2), the secured and unsecured parts of the debt are to be treated for the purposes of ss 267–270 as separate debts: s 269(2).

In the case of the administration in bankruptcy of the insolvent estate of a deceased person dying before the presentation of a bankruptcy petition, s 269 applies with the modification that for the words 'ss 267–270' there are to be substituted the words 'ss 267, 269': Administration of Insolvent Estates of Deceased Persons Order 1986, SI 1986/1999, art 3(1), Sch 1 Pt II para 4. As to the administration in bankruptcy of the insolvent estates of deceased persons see further PARA 830 et seq.

As to the application of the Insolvency Act 1986 s 269 in the case of the bankruptcy of an individual member of an insolvent partnership see the Insolvent Partnerships Order 1994, SI 1994/2421; and COMPANY AND PARTNERSHIP INSOLVENCY vol 17 (2011) PARA 1273.

8 As to inability to pay see PARA 133.

9 Ie under the Insolvency Rules 1986, SI 1986/1925, r 6.4: see PARA 161. For these purposes, the application must be one which has been made within time and it is irrelevant that a grant of an extension of time may have been given: *Chohan v Times Newspapers Ltd* [2001] EWCA Civ 964, [2001] 1 WLR 1859, [2001] BPIR 943. A letter written to court to request the setting aside of the statutory demand does not constitute an application to set aside the statutory demand for these purposes: *Ariyo v Sovereign Leasing plc* [1998] BPIR 177, CA.

10 Ie under the Insolvency Act 1986 s 268: see PARA 133.

11 Insolvency Act 1986 s 267(2). A petition may be presented, notwithstanding that an application to set aside the statutory demand on which the petition is based is pending, where there are grounds for believing that the assets of the debtor are in jeopardy: *Re A Debtor (No 22 of 1993)*

[1994] 2 All ER 105, [1994] 1 WLR 46. Once the application to set aside the statutory demand has been dismissed, even if that order is appealed, a bankruptcy order may be made: *Ahmad v IRC* [2004] EWHC 2292 (Ch), [2005] BPIR 541, [2004] All ER (D) 435 (Jul).

In the case of the administration in bankruptcy of the insolvent estate of a deceased person dying before the presentation of a bankruptcy petition, a creditor's petition may, subject to the Insolvency Act 1986 s 267(3)–(5), be presented to the court in respect of a debt or debts only if, had the debtor been alive at the time the petition is presented: (1) the amount of the debt, or the aggregate amount of the debts, owed by the debtor would have been equal to or exceeded the bankruptcy level; or (2) the debt, or each of the debts, owed by the debtor would have been for a liquidated sum payable to the petitioning creditor, or one or more of the petitioning creditors, either immediately or at some certain future time, and would have been unsecured: s 267(2) (amended by the Administration of Insolvent Estates of Deceased Persons Order 1986, SI 1986/1999, Sch 1 Pt II para 3).

As to the modification of the Insolvency Act 1986 s 267(2) by the Insolvent Partnerships Order 1994, SI 1994/2421, in relation to the bankruptcy of an individual member of an insolvent partnership see COMPANY AND PARTNERSHIP INSOLVENCY vol 17 (2011) PARA 1280.

133. Inability to pay debts. For the above purposes[1], the debtor appears to be unable to pay a debt if, but only if, the debt is payable immediately and either:

(1) the petitioning creditor to whom the debt is owed has served on the debtor a demand ('the statutory demand')[2] in the prescribed form requiring him to pay the debt or to secure or compound for it to the satisfaction of the creditor, at least three weeks have elapsed since the demand was served and the demand has been neither complied with nor set aside; or

(2) execution or other process issued in respect of the debt on a judgment[3] or order of any court in favour of the petitioning creditor, or one or more of the petitioning creditors to whom the debt is owed, has been returned[4] unsatisfied in whole or in part[5].

For the above purposes[6], the debtor appears to have no reasonable prospect of being able to pay a debt if, but only if, the debt is not immediately payable; and:

(a) the petitioning creditor to whom it is owed has served on the debtor a demand (also known as 'the statutory demand')[7] in the prescribed form requiring him to establish to the satisfaction of the creditor that there is a reasonable prospect that the debtor will be able to pay the debt when it falls due;

(b) at least three weeks have elapsed since the demand was served; and

(c) the demand has been neither complied with nor set aside[8].

1 Ie for the purposes of the Insolvency Act 1986 s 267(2)(c): see PARA 132 head (3).
2 As to statutory demands see PARA 158 et seq.
3 A costs order made in favour of a party to proceedings creates a judgment debt in favour of the payee party, notwithstanding that the payee was in receipt of legal aid: *Re A Debtor (No 68/SD/97)* [1998] 4 All ER 779.
4 In order for a creditor to prove that execution has been returned unsatisfied he must show there has been a serious attempt to levy execution: *Re A Debtor (No 340 of 1992), ex p Debtor v First National Commercial Bank plc* [1996] 2 All ER 211, CA. There must be proof that the execution or other process has failed to satisfy the debt but the fact that the execution agent fails to indorse a statement on the writ will not be fatal to its validity as proof of an unsatisfied return: *Skarzynski v Chalford Property Co Ltd* [2001] BPIR 673, sub nom *Re a Debtor (No 78 of 2000)* [2000] All ER (D) 2117.
5 Insolvency Act 1986 s 268(1). As to expedited petitions see PARA 134.
   As to the modification of s 268 by the Insolvent Partnerships Order 1994, SI 1994/2421, in relation to the bankruptcy of an individual member of an insolvent partnership see COMPANY AND PARTNERSHIP INSOLVENCY vol 17 (2011) PARA 1281.
6 See note 1.
7 See note 2.
8 Insolvency Act 1986 s 268(2). As to the shortening of the three-week period see PARA 134.

134. Expedited petitions. In the case of a creditor's petition presented wholly or partly in respect of a debt which is the subject of a statutory demand[1], the petition may be presented before the end of the three-week period from the service of the demand[2] if there is a serious possibility that the debtor's property or the value of any of his property will be significantly diminished during that period and the petition contains a statement to that effect[3]. However, in such a case the court may not make a bankruptcy order until at least three weeks have elapsed since the service of any statutory demand[4].

1 Ie under the Insolvency Act 1986 s 268: see PARA 133. As to statutory demands see PARA 158 et seq.
2 Ie the period mentioned in the Insolvency Act 1986 s 268: see PARA 133.
3 Insolvency Act 1986 s 270. As to the application of s 270 in the case of the bankruptcy of an individual member of an insolvent partnership see the Insolvent Partnerships Order 1994, SI 1994/2421; and COMPANY AND PARTNERSHIP INSOLVENCY vol 17 (2011) PARA 1273.
4 See the Insolvency Act 1986 s 271; and PARA 198.

B. THE CREDITOR'S DEBT

135. In general. A creditor's petition may be presented to the court in respect of a debt or debts only if (inter alia) the debt, or each of the debts, is for a liquidated sum payable to the petitioning creditor, or one or more of the petitioning creditors, either immediately or at some certain, future time, and is unsecured[1]. Where the petitioning creditor serves a statutory demand, the demand must specify whether it is made in respect of a debt payable immediately or a debt not so payable[2]. If the amount claimed includes any charge by way of interest not previously notified to the debtor as a liability of his, or any other charge accruing from time to time, the amount or rate of the charge must be separately identified, and the grounds on which payment of it is claimed must be stated; and, in either case, the amount claimed must be limited to that which has accrued due at the date of the demand[3]. The amount of the debt, or the aggregate amount of the debts, must be equal to or exceed the bankruptcy level[4]. Statutory interest on a judgment debt becomes part of that debt[5] and may be relied on to make up the debt to the prescribed amount[6].

1 See PARA 132.
2 See PARA 158.
3 See PARA 158.
4 See PARA 132. The costs of an abortive execution cannot be added to a judgment debt for the purposes of making up the unsatisfied debt to the bankruptcy level; they do not form part of the judgment debt, or a debt in any sense, and may be recovered only out of the particular fund formed by the fruits of the particular execution, the debtor having no personal liability for them: *Re Long & Co, ex p Cuddeford* (1888) 20 QBD 316, CA. Similarly, the costs incurred in presenting a petition cannot be added to another debt for the purpose of making the debt up to the bankruptcy level: *Lilley v American Express Europe Ltd* [2000] BPIR 70.
5 *Re Clagett, ex p Lewis* (1887) 36 WR 653, CA.
6 Cf *Re Lehmann, ex p Hasluck* (1890) 7 Morr 181.

136. Liquidated sum. A covenant to pay the excess of debts due from a firm over debts due to it is not a covenant to pay a liquidated sum[1]. A claim arising from a failure to redeliver shares lent by one person to another has been held not to be a 'debt or sum of money due or claimed to be due'[2]; nor is there a debt due in respect of a liability under a bond of indemnity as to costs[3]. The amount of differences fixed under its rules by the default official, due to a stock exchange creditor by a defaulter, is a liquidated sum and, therefore, a good petitioning creditor's debt[4].

If the borrower under an equitable mortgage agrees to repay the principal on a stated day with interest at a fixed rate, and to execute a legal mortgage on the same terms as to interest, and, if the principal is not repaid on the stated day, there is a contract to pay interest at the rate fixed after that day, and, if the interest is not paid, there is a liquidated sum due[5].

A right to damages is not a right to a liquidated sum and cannot be made the basis for a petition until the damages have been liquidated[6]. Notwithstanding that a judgment is prima facie for a liquidated sum, the court may go behind the judgment to ascertain whether it is in fact liquidated[7]. Costs awarded to a litigant are not liquidated until assessed; and unassessed costs cannot in themselves constitute a debt on which a bankruptcy petition may be presented[8].

The amount owing under an unassessed bill in respect of professional services can constitute a liquidated sum[9]. A sum assessed by HM Revenue and Customs as owing in respect of unpaid tax can also constitute a liquidated sum in respect of which a petition may be presented[10], as can a liability for council tax[11].

1 *Re Broadhurst, ex p Broadhurst* (1852) 22 LJ Bcy 21, CA; *Walker v Broadhurst* (1853) 8 Exch 889.

2 *Owen v Routh* (1854) 14 CB 327 (decided under the Judgments Act 1838); cf *Utterson v Vernon* (1792) 4 Term Rep 570 (reconsidering the earlier determination of that case at (1790) 3 Term Rep 539).

3 *Johnson v Diamond* (1855) 11 Exch 73.

4 *Re Ward, ex p Ward* (1882) 22 ChD 132, CA. See also *Re Mendelssohn, ex p Mendelssohn* [1903] 1 KB 216, CA; on appeal sub nom *Mendelssohn v Ratcliff* [1904] AC 456, HL.

5 *Re King, ex p Furber* (1881) 17 ChD 191.

6 *Re Miller* [1901] 1 KB 51, CA. An award of damages by the verdict of a jury, without judgment or without an order giving effect to the verdict, has been held not to be a liquidation of the damages: *Re Muirhead, ex p Muirhead* (1876) 2 ChD 22 at 25, CA, distinguished in *Re A Debtor (No 975 of 1937)* [1938] 2 All ER 530, CA (final order to pay damages). Similarly, a right in equity to an account is not a right to a liquidated sum and cannot constitute the basis for a petition: *Hope v Premierpace (Europe) Ltd* [1999] BPIR 695; and see PARA 140 note 1. See also *Bennett v Filmer* [1998] BPIR 444.

7 *Re A Debtor, ex p Berkshire Finance Co Ltd v Debtor* (1962) 106 Sol Jo 468, DC (judgment for liquidated sum under a hire-purchase agreement, although the creditor had no more than a cause of action for unliquidated damages).

8 *Re A Debtor (No 20 of 1953), ex p Debtor v Scott* [1954] 3 All ER 74, [1954] 1 WLR 1190, CA. An order for an interim payment (see CPR r 25.6; and CIVIL PROCEDURE vol 11 (2009) PARA 324) is a liquidated sum in respect of which a bankruptcy petition may be presented: *Maxwell v Bishopsgate Investment Management Ltd (in liquidation)* (1993) Times, 11 February. As to claims for solicitors' fees see PARA 132 note 6.

9 *Re A Debtor (No 88 of 1991)* [1993] Ch 286, [1992] 4 All ER 301.

10 *Re A Debtor (No 960/SD/1992), ex p Debtor v IRC* [1993] STC 218n; *Arnold v Williams* [2008] EWHC 218 (Ch), [2008] BPIR 247; *Chamberlin v Revenue and Customs Comrs* [2011] EWCA Civ 271, [2011] STC 1237, [2011] BPIR 691; cf *R (on the application of Singh) v Revenue and Customs Comrs* [2010] UKUT 174 (TCC), [2010] STC 2020, [2010] BPIR 933. The same applies in respect of amounts assessed as owing in respect of value added tax by HM Revenue and Customs: *Cozens v Customs and Excise Comrs* [2000] BPIR 252, CA.

11 *Lonergan v Gedling BC* [2009] EWCA Civ 1569, [2010] RVR 100, [2010] BPIR 911.

137. Debt must be recoverable by legal process. Subject to the case of debts payable at some certain, future time, the debt must be one which is recoverable by legal process. Thus, a bankruptcy petition may not be presented in respect of a debt[1] which is barred by the Limitation Act 1980[2].

1 As to such debts see LIMITATION PERIODS vol 68 (2008) PARA 1010.

2 *Re Tynte, ex p Tynte* (1880) 15 ChD 125. A bankruptcy petition may be presented in respect of a judgment debt after the expiration of six years from the date on which the judgment became enforceable (see the Limitation Act 1980 s 24; and LIMITATION PERIODS vol 68 (2008) PARA

953): *Ridgeway Motors (Isleworth) Ltd v ALTS Ltd* [2005] EWCA Civ 92, [2005] 2 All ER 304, [2005] 1 WLR 2871 ('action upon a judgment' does not include insolvency proceedings brought by a judgment creditor).

138.   Sureties.   A surety cannot present a bankruptcy petition against his co-surety unless he has paid more than his proportion of the sum guaranteed[1].

1   *Re Snowdon, ex p Snowdon* (1881) 17 ChD 44, CA; *Wolmershausen v Gullick* [1893] 2 Ch 514 (where it was held that the liability of a bankrupt co-surety to contribution unascertained at the time of the bankruptcy was not a debt available for a petition); but see *Re Macdonald, ex p Grant* [1888] WN 130, CA (where it was held that a surety for a debt payable by instalments may, when one instalment has matured of which he has paid more than his share, petition against his co-surety); cf *Re A Debtor (No 66 of 1955), ex p Debtor v Trustee of Property of Waite (a bankrupt)* [1956] 3 All ER 225, [1956] 1 WLR 1226, CA.

139.   Merger of debts.   Under the Bankruptcy Act 1914, if a simple contract debt at the date of the act of bankruptcy became afterwards merged in a judgment or a security of a higher nature, the merger did not extinguish the debt for the purposes of bankruptcy proceedings, and the debt was still available as a petitioning creditor's debt[1]. It is apprehended that the same principle applies under the Insolvency Act 1986 where a contract debt at the date of the statutory demand[2] becomes merged in a judgment or security[3] before presentation of the bankruptcy petition.

1   *Re King and Beesley, ex p King and Beesley* [1895] 1 QB 189, DC.
2   As to statutory demands see PARA 158 et seq.
3   As to secured creditors see PARA 156.

140.   Equitable debt.   A petition may be founded on a High Court judgment for the payment of a liquidated sum in respect of an equitable liability[1], or on a debt to which a creditor is entitled in equity but not at law[2].

1   See CPR PD 70—*Enforcement of Judgments and Orders* para 1; *Re Faithfull, ex p Moore* (1885) 14 QBD 627, CA; and CIVIL PROCEDURE vol 12 (2009) PARA 1245. However, a right to damages arising out of an equitable liability or a right to an account in equity is not a right to a liquidated sum and, therefore, is not a debt in respect of which a creditor may present a bankruptcy petition: *Re Jones, ex p Jones* (1881) 18 ChD 109, CA (cited in *Re A Debtor (No 564 of 1949), ex p Customs and Excise Comrs v Debtor* [1950] Ch 282, [1950] 1 All ER 308, CA); *Hope v Premierpace (Europe) Ltd* [1999] BPIR 695.

2   As to the concurrent administration of law and equity see the Senior Courts Act 1981 s 49; and EQUITY vol 16(2) (Reissue) PARAS 499–500. The Bankruptcy Act 1869 s 6 (repealed) defined a debt as a liquidated sum due at law or in equity; but that definition does not appear in the Insolvency Act 1986. Judgments and orders are each enforced in the same manner: see CPR 70; and CIVIL PROCEDURE vol 12 (2009) PARA 1226 et seq.

C.   CREDITORS WHO MAY PETITION

141.   Which creditors may petition.   Any person who has a right to claim immediate payment of a sum of money due to him and is capable of giving a valid release to the debtor, or who will at a certain time in the future have such a right and be in a position to give a valid release, may in general present a bankruptcy petition against the debtor, subject to the statutory conditions being fulfilled[1]. It is possible, therefore, for a creditor to petition in bankruptcy, even though he has no immediate right of payment[2].

In the case of debts due to the Crown or to a government department, the petition is in general presented in the name of the government department concerned, but it may be presented by the Attorney General[3].

The sole creditor of a debtor may present a bankruptcy petition against the debtor[4]; and it appears that a creditor has a right to petition, however wealthy the debtor may appear to be and whatever prospect there may be of obtaining payment by other means, provided that a statutory demand has been served and not set aside[5].

1   As to the statutory conditions see PARAS 131–133.
2   See the Insolvency Act 1986 s 267(2)(b); and PARA 132 head (2).
3   See the Crown Proceedings Act 1947 s 17; and CROWN PROCEEDINGS AND CROWN PRACTICE vol 12(1) (Reissue) PARA 119. As to the court in which the petition must be presented see the Insolvency Rules 1986, SI 1986/1925, r 6.9A; and PARA 164.
4   'If the debtor has only one creditor, this is a point to be considered by the registrar on hearing the petition, but it cannot be laid down as a matter of principle that, if there is only one creditor, the registrar ought to dismiss the petition. The trustee in a bankruptcy may be able to set aside transactions and get in assets which could not be set aside or got in without an adjudication of bankruptcy. The mere fact that a man has only one creditor is not a sufficient ground for saying that bankruptcy proceedings cannot be maintained against him': *Re Hecquard, ex p Hecquard* (1889) 24 QBD 71 at 76, CA per Lindley LJ. See also *Re Painter, ex p Painter* [1895] 1 QB 85.
5   *Cornhill Insurance plc v Improvement Services Ltd* [1986] 1 WLR 114, [1986] BCLC 26. As to statutory demands see PARA 158 et seq.

142.   Companies.   A company may be a petitioning creditor[1]. It may act by any of its duly authorised officers[2], and may give a general authority to an officer to present bankruptcy petitions[3] in the future in respect of debts which may not have arisen at the date when the authority is given[4]. It is sufficient if the company's seal is affixed to the copy which constitutes the officer's authority[5], the sufficiency of which may be inquired into by the court, although the debtor has not taken objection to it[6]. Any person chosen bona fide by the company as its agent to present a bankruptcy petition becomes thereby an officer of the company for the purpose[7]. The petition must be in the company's name; if the company is in liquidation, the petition must be in the name of the company, and not of the liquidator[8].

1   *Re Collier, ex p Dan Rylands Ltd* (1891) 8 Morr 80; *Re Whitley, ex p Mirfield Commercial Co Ltd* (1891) 65 LT 351; *Re Sanders, ex p Sanders* (1894) 1 Mans 382.
2   Ie subject to the company's articles of association: see COMPANIES vol 14 (2009) PARA 227 et seq. A document is executed by a company by the affixing of its common seal or by signature by two authorised signatories or by the director of the company in the presence of a witness who attests the signature: see the Companies Act 2006 s 44; and COMPANIES vol 14 (2009) PARA 288.
3   An authority to an officer to sue on behalf of a company does not entitle him to present a bankruptcy petition: *Guthrie v Fisk* (1824) 3 B & C 178.
4   *Re A Debtor (No 28 of 1917), ex p Petitioning Creditors v Debtor* [1917] 2 KB 808, DC; cf *Re A Debtor, ex p Debtor (No 30 of 1914)* [1915] 1 KB 287 (where the authority given was held to be limited to acts of bankruptcy available at its date).
5   *Re Midgley* (1913) 108 LT 45.
6   *Re Sanders, ex p Sanders* (1894) 1 Mans 382.
7   *Re Tomkins & Co* [1901] 1 KB 476 (although the person nominated was only a clerk, the petition was held good).
8   *Re Winterbottom, ex p Winterbottom* (1886) 18 QBD 446; *Re Shirley, ex p Mackay* (1887) 58 LT 237; *Re Bassett, ex p Lewis* (1895) 2 Mans 177; *Re A Debtor (No 41 of 1951), ex p Debtor v Hunter (Liquidator of Marvel Paper Products Ltd)* [1952] Ch 192, [1952] 1 All ER 107, DC. The form of petition should be 'The AB Company Limited, In Liquidation, by CD its Liquidator'.

143.   Partners.   A petition by a partnership firm may be presented in the firm name, provided that the partnership is carrying on business within the jurisdiction[1]; and a firm consisting of two or more persons may present a petition, even though one of them is under a disability[2].

The fact that a partner has retired since judgment in the firm name was recovered against the debtor does not make it necessary that the court's permission should be obtained for a petition to be presented in the firm name[3]. If one of two partners who have filed a petition against a debtor becomes bankrupt before the petition is heard, the trustee of the bankrupt partner should be made a co-petitioner[4].

One partner may present a petition against a co-partner in respect of a distinct debt for which an action might have been brought notwithstanding the partnership, but not in a case where it would depend on taking partnership accounts whether the sum was due or not[5]. If a partner brings an action for an account and treats a debt due to him by his co-partner as mixed with the partnership accounts, he cannot afterwards present a petition in respect of that debt[6].

One of two joint obligees under a bond is not by himself a good petitioning creditor[7]; but, where one of several joint creditors has died, a petition may be presented by the survivors[8].

1 See CPR PD 7A—*How to Start Proceedings–the Claim Form* paras 5A, 5B; and CIVIL PROCEDURE vol 11 (2009) PARA 224.
2 *Harris v Beauchamp Bros* [1893] 2 QB 534.
3 *Re Hill, ex p Holt & Co* [1921] 2 KB 831.
4 *Re Owen, ex p Owen* (1884) 13 QBD 113, CA.
5 *Re Notley, ex p Notley* (1833) 1 Mont & A 46; *Windham v Paterson* (1815) 1 Stark 144; *Re Palmer, ex p Richardson & Son* (1833) 3 Deac & Ch 244.
6 *Re Gray, ex p Gray* (1835) 2 Mont & A 283.
7 *Brickland v Newsome* (1808) 1 Camp 474.
8 *Re Tucker, ex p Tucker* (1895) 2 Mans 358, CA.

144. Executors. One of several executors may present a petition in respect of a debt due to the executors[1]. An executor may present a petition against a debtor to the deceased before taking out a grant of probate[2]; but it is doubtful whether an executor may secure a bankruptcy order before probate has been obtained[3]. Where a petitioning creditor dies before a bankruptcy order is made, his executor may apply to carry on the proceedings[4].

1 *Treasure v Jones* (1785) cited 1 Selwyn's Nisi Prius (12th Edn) 253; *Ex p Brown* (1832) 1 Deac & Ch 118.
2 *Re Drakeley, ex p Paddy* (1818) 3 Madd 241; *Rogers v James* (1816) 7 Taunt 147.
3 See the cases cited in note 2; and *Re Masonic and General Life Assurance Co* (1885) 32 ChD 373. The court might stay proceedings until production of probate: *Tarn v Commercial Banking Co of Sydney* (1884) 12 QBD 294.
4 See CPR 19.8; and WILLS AND INTESTACY vol 103 (2010) PARAS 818, 1285.

145. Receivers. A receiver of an estate cannot as such present a bankruptcy petition in respect of a debt due to the estate which has not been assigned to him, even if the debtor has been ordered to pay the receiver; but, if the receiver is in a position to sue in his own name, he may present a petition[1]. If a receiver is the holder of a bill of exchange[2] or the assignee of a judgment debt[3], he may present a petition based on the debt.

Special rules apply to the enforcement of the payment of sums awarded in matrimonial causes in favour of the petitioner[4] or of the Queen's Proctor intervening[5].

1 *Re Sacker, ex p Sacker* (1888) 22 QBD 179, CA; *Re Macoun* [1904] 2 KB 700, CA.
2 *Re Lewis, ex p Harris* (1876) 2 ChD 423.
3 *Re Macoun* [1904] 2 KB 700, CA.

4 Where the co-respondent has been ordered to pay to the petitioner's solicitors the costs of the suit on their undertaking to lodge in court any sums recovered under the order, the solicitors cannot, it seems, present a bankruptcy petition in respect of those costs: *Re A Debtor (No 76 of 1929)* [1929] 2 Ch 146, CA.

5 The Queen's Proctor who has intervened in a divorce suit, and to whom a party has been ordered to pay costs, is not in the position of a receiver, and may present a bankruptcy petition against the party; and the Queen's Proctor for the time being may present the petition, although he did not hold the office when the costs payable by the party were incurred: *Re Rayner, ex p Rayner* (1877) 37 LT 38. As to intervention by the Queen's Proctor see MATRIMONIAL AND CIVIL PARTNERSHIP LAW vol 73 (2009) PARA 852.

146. Trustees. Where there are more trustees than one, as a general rule, they must all join as petitioning creditors. A person to whom a debt is due as a bare trustee may present a petition in certain cases, for example, when the beneficial owner of the debt is under disability[1]; but, when a debt is due to a person as a bare trustee for an absolute beneficial owner who is capable of dealing with the debt as he pleases, the trustee alone cannot present a petition on the debt, and the beneficial owner must join as co-petitioner[2]. If a person to whom a debt is due as trustee is also beneficially entitled to part of the debt, he may present a petition on the debt without joining the beneficiary[3].

A trustee in bankruptcy may present a petition in respect of a debt due to the bankrupt[4].

1 *Re Adams, ex p Culley* (1878) 9 ChD 307 at 311, CA per Cotton LJ.
2 *Re Adams, ex p Culley* (1878) 9 ChD 307, CA; *Re Hastings, ex p Dearle* (1884) 14 QBD 184, CA. Permission may be given to amend a petition presented by a bare trustee by joining the beneficiary: *Re Hastings, ex p Dearle*; *Re Ellis, ex p Hinshelwood* (1887) 4 Morr 283, CA. As to the time within which the petition must be amended see PARA 173.
3 *Re Gamgee, ex p Gamgee* (1891) 8 Morr 182, CA.
4 *Re Blakey, ex p Blakey* (1822) 1 Gl & J 197; *Re Bagley* [1911] 1 KB 317, CA; and see the Insolvency Act 1986 s 314(1)(a), Sch 5 para 2; and PARA 478 head (2).

147. Assignees of debts. The legal[1] or equitable assignee of a debt may present a bankruptcy petition without joining the assignor[2]; but a judgment creditor who has obtained a garnishee order against a person indebted to the judgment debtor cannot present a bankruptcy petition against that person[3].

1 See the Law of Property Act 1925 s 136(1); and CHOSES IN ACTION vol 13 (2009) PARA 72 et seq. Part of a debt cannot be legally assigned so as to enable the assignee to levy execution in respect of it: *Forster v Baker* [1910] 2 KB 636, CA; *Re Steel Wing Co Ltd* [1921] 1 Ch 349. It follows, therefore, that the assignee of part of a debt cannot issue a statutory demand or present a petition in respect of the debt.
2 A judgment debt arising out of an equitable liability is a legally enforceable debt, but the equitable liability itself is not a debt on which a bankruptcy petition may be founded: see *Re Jones, ex p Jones* (1881) 18 ChD 109, CA (cited in *Re A Debtor (No 564 of 1949), ex p Customs and Excise Comrs v Debtor* [1950] Ch 282, [1950] 1 All ER 308, CA); *Hope v Premierpace (Europe) Ltd* [1999] BPIR 695. A debt does not, however, cease to be a debt because the title to it is equitable, as where a legal debt is assigned in equity, and the assignee may present a petition in bankruptcy against the debtor without joining the assignor as co-petitioner: see *Re Baillie, ex p Cooper* (1875) LR 20 Eq 762.
3 *Re Combined Weighing and Advertising Machine Co* (1889) 43 ChD 99, CA.

148. Factors. A factor who sells goods in his own name, even though not on a del credere commission, may present a bankruptcy petition against the purchaser of the goods unless the principal has agreed with the factor to treat the purchaser as his own debtor, and has taken steps to recover the debt directly from the purchaser[1].

1 *Sadler v Leigh* (1815) 4 Camp 195.

149. Minors. A creditor who is a minor may present a bankruptcy petition by his litigation friend[1].

1 See CPR r 21.2(2); CHILDREN AND YOUNG PERSONS vol 9 (2012) PARA 10; CIVIL PROCEDURE vol 11 (2009) PARA 222; *Re Brocklebank, ex p Brocklebank* (1877) 6 ChD 358, CA (where an adjudication made on a petition presented by a minor by his next friend, based on non-compliance with a debtor's summons issued by the minor in person, was held valid).

150. Persons lacking capacity to conduct proceedings. A person lacking capacity to conduct proceedings may present a bankruptcy petition by his litigation friend[1].

1 See CPR r 21.2(1); and CIVIL PROCEDURE vol 11 (2009) PARA 222.

151. Married persons and civil partners. A married woman is in exactly the same position as regards the presentation of a bankruptcy petition as a man or a single woman[1].

If a spouse or civil partner owes debts in respect of credit provided by his or her spouse or civil partner, either may present a bankruptcy petition against the other[2].

1 See the Law Reform (Married Women and Tortfeasors) Act 1935 s 1(c); and MATRIMONIAL AND CIVIL PARTNERSHIP LAW vol 72 (2009) PARAS 204, 210. Cf PARA 10.
2 As to the ranking in priority of such debts see the Insolvency Act 1986 s 329; and PARA 597.

152. Bankrupts. An undischarged bankrupt may present a bankruptcy petition in respect of debts due to him which have not vested in his trustee, such as damages due to him in respect of his pain and suffering[1]. However, all causes of action relating to the recovery of the property of the bankrupt vest in the trustee in bankruptcy on the making of the bankruptcy order[2].

1 *Ord v Upton* [2000] Ch 352, [2000] 1 All ER 193, CA.
2 See the Insolvency Act 1986 s 306(1); PARA 398; and *Ord v Upton* [2000] Ch 352, [2000] 1 All ER 193, CA (where a cause of action consists partly of a personal claim for damages in respect of pain and suffering and partly of a claim for the recovery of property, it will vest in the trustee in bankruptcy and any damages received in respect of the personal claim will be held on trust for the bankrupt). As to the vesting of property in the trustee generally see PARA 397 et seq.

153. Landlord exercising concurrent remedies. A landlord who presents a bankruptcy petition against his tenant founded on an unsatisfied execution issued in respect of a judgment debt, and subsequently gives notice[1] to the tenant's subtenants requiring them to pay their rent direct to him as superior landlord, is not thereby prevented from continuing the bankruptcy proceedings and obtaining a bankruptcy order, provided that a debt equal to or exceeding the bankruptcy level[2] still remains after the receipt of any rent from the subtenants[3].

1 Ie under the Law of Distress Amendment Act 1908 s 6: see DISTRESS vol 13 (2007 Reissue) PARA 960. As from a day to be appointed, s 6 is repealed by the Tribunals, Courts and Enforcement Act 2007 ss 86, 146, Sch 14 para 20, Sch 23 Pt 4. At the date at which this volume states the law no such day had been appointed.
2 As to the meaning of 'the bankruptcy level' see PARA 132 note 5.
3 *Re A Debtor (No 549 of 1928)* [1929] 1 Ch 170, CA (decided under the Bankruptcy Act 1914 (repealed); landlord's petition founded on non-compliance with a bankruptcy notice based on the judgment; landlord able to continue proceedings to the making of a receiving order).

154. Foreigners. Provided that he is not an enemy alien[1], there is nothing to prevent a foreigner from presenting a bankruptcy petition if a debt is owing to him for which he could maintain an action[2], although he may be required to give security for costs[3].

1 As to the test of whether a person or a corporate body is an enemy alien see ARMED CONFLICT AND EMERGENCY vol 3 (2011) PARA 195. See further PARA 542.
2 *Re Myer, ex p Pascal* (1876) 1 ChD 509, CA.
3 See CPR r 25.12; and CIVIL PROCEDURE vol 11 (2009) PARA 745. See the Insolvency Rules 1986, SI 1986/1925, r 6.17; and PARA 172. See also Council Regulation (EC) 1346/2000 (OJ L160, 30.6.2000, p 1) on insolvency proceedings ('European Regulation on Insolvency Proceedings'); and PARAS 41, 42 et seq. As to cross-border insolvency proceedings see PARAS 826–829.

155. Stock Exchange. The proceedings in the liquidation of the contracts of a defaulting member by the default official[1] are not an accord and satisfaction of the member's debts and do not bar his creditors from suing him for the balance of their claims[2]; and any such creditor who has obtained judgment in such an action may maintain a petition in bankruptcy against the defaulter[3].

1 As to the default official see the Rules of the London Stock Exchange (2012) rr D050–D052. As to the rules of the London Stock Exchange see FINANCIAL SERVICES AND INSTITUTIONS vol 48 (2008) PARA 75.
2 *Mendelssohn v Ratcliff* [1904] AC 456, HL.
3 *Re Ward, ex p Ward* (1882) 22 ChD 132, CA; *Mendelssohn v Ratcliff* [1904] AC 456, HL.

156. Secured creditors. A creditor's petition may be presented to the court in respect of a debt or debts only if, at the time the petition is presented, the debt, or each of the debts, is or are unsecured[1]. However, a debt which is the debt, or one of the debts, in respect of which a creditor's petition is presented need not be unsecured if either:

(1) the petition contains a statement by the person having the right to enforce the security that he is willing, in the event of a bankruptcy order being made, to give up his security for the benefit of all the bankrupt's creditors[2]; or

(2) the petition is expressed not to be made in respect of the secured part of the debt and contains a statement by that person of the estimated value at the date of the petition of the security for the secured part of the debt[3].

1 See the Insolvency Act 1986 s 267(2)(b); and PARA 132 head (2). A debt is 'secured' to the extent that the person to whom the debt is owed holds security over any property of the person by whom it is owed: *Re A Debtor (No 310 of 1988), ex p Debtor v Arab Bank Ltd* [1989] 2 All ER 42, sub nom *Re A Debtor (No 310 of 1988)* [1989] 1 WLR 452.
2 See the Insolvency Act 1986 s 269(1)(a); and PARA 132. A statement made under s 269(1)(a) in circumstances where the creditor could not realise the security because of a challenge made by the debtor's wife will not be regarded as improper, even if the debtor has no other creditors: *Zandfarid v Bank of Credit and Commerce International SA (in liquidation)* [1996] 1 WLR 1420, [1996] BPIR 501. The rationale for the Insolvency Act 1986 s 269 is that a creditor who is fully secured over assets of the bankrupt has no interest in a bankruptcy: *White v Davenham Trust Ltd* [2011] EWCA Civ 747, [2011] Bus LR 1443, [2012] 1 BCLC 123.
3 See the Insolvency Act 1986 s 269(1)(b); and PARA 132. In a case falling within s 269(1)(b), the secured and unsecured parts of the debt are to be treated for the purposes of ss 267–270 as separate debts: see s 269(2); and PARA 132. Inadvertent failure to disclose in the petition security over the debtor's property which would still leave an unsecured debt of over £750 will be regarded as an irregularity which may be waived under the Insolvency Rules 1986, SI 1986/1925, r 7.55 (see PARA 783) provided it does not mislead or prejudice the debtor: *Barclays Bank plc v Mogg* [2003] EWHC 2645 (Ch), [2004] BPIR 259, [2003] All ER (D) 56 (Oct).

D. WHEN CREDITORS MAY NOT PETITION

157. When creditors may not petition. No bankruptcy petition relating to the debtor may be presented or proceeded with during the period for which an interim order is in force[1]. Where proceedings on a bankruptcy petition have been stayed by an interim order which ceases to have effect[2], that petition is deemed to have been dismissed unless the court otherwise orders[3]. Where the debtor is an undischarged bankrupt and the creditors' meeting approves the proposed voluntary arrangement, with or without modifications[4], the court may annul the bankruptcy order by which he was adjudged bankrupt[5].

A bankruptcy petition may be dismissed by the court where its presentation amounts to an abuse of the process of the court[6].

1 See the Insolvency Act 1986 s 252(2)(a); and PARA 45 head (1).
2 Ie under the Insolvency Act 1986 s 260(4): see PARA 69.
3 See Insolvency Act 1986 s 260(5); and PARA 69.
4 See PARA 62.
5 See the Insolvency Act 1986 s 261(1)(a); and PARA 70.
6 See PARA 188. 'Abuse of process' includes circumstances where, by presenting a petition or continuing bankruptcy proceedings or by threatening to do so, the creditor is attempting to obtain or has obtained an advantage to which he is not properly entitled: *Re Majory, A Debtor, ex p Debtor v FA Dumont Ltd* [1955] Ch 600, sub nom *Re A Debtor (No 757 of 1954), ex p Debtor v FA Dumont Ltd (Petitioning Creditor)* [1955] 2 All ER 65, CA; *Re Ross (a Bankrupt) (No 2)* [2000] BPIR 636, [2000] All ER (D) 583; cf *Hicks v Gulliver* [2002] BPIR 518. Such conduct on the part of the creditor is sometimes called 'extortion'. This includes circumstances where a petition is presented by a creditor in respect of a debt to which he is not properly entitled. Presentation of a petition may also amount to an abuse of process where the petition debt is genuinely disputed by the debtor.
  It is the court's duty to dismiss a petition which is made a means of extorting or attempting to extort money: *Re Atkinson, ex p Atkinson* (1892) 9 Morr 193, CA; *Re Otway, ex p Otway* [1895] 1 QB 812, CA; *Re Bebro* [1900] 2 QB 316, CA. Under the Insolvency Act 1986 the court may grant an application to set aside a statutory demand founded on a debt which is disputed by the debtor on grounds which appear to the court to be substantial: see the Insolvency Rules 1986, SI 1986/1925, r 6.5(4)(b); and PARA 162 head (b).

E. THE STATUTORY DEMAND

158. Form and content. A statutory demand[1] must be dated, and be authenticated[2] either by the creditor himself or by a person stating himself to be authorised to make the demand on the creditor's behalf[3]; and the demand must specify whether it is in respect of a debt[4] payable immediately or a debt[5] not so payable[6]. It must state the amount of the debt, and the consideration for it, or, if there is no consideration, the way in which it arises, and:

(1) if it relates to a debt payable immediately[7], and founded on a judgment or order of a court, it must give details of the judgment or order; and

(2) if it relates to a debt not so payable[8] it must state the grounds on which it is alleged that the debtor appears to have no reasonable prospect of paying the debt[9].

If the amount claimed in the demand includes:

(a) any charge by way of interest not previously notified to the debtor as a liability of his; or

(b) any other charge accruing from time to time,

the amount or rate of the charge must be separately identified, and the grounds on which payment of it is claimed must be stated[10]. In either case, the amount claimed must be limited to that which has accrued due at the date of the demand[11].

If the creditor holds any security[12] in respect of the debt, the full amount of the debt must be specified, but:

(i)   there must in the demand be specified the nature of the security, and the value which the creditor puts on it as at the date of the demand; and

(ii)   the amount of which payment is claimed by the demand must be the full amount of the debt, less the amount specified as the value of the security[13].

1   Ie under the Insolvency Act 1986 s 268: see PARA 133. For the prescribed forms of statutory demand see the Insolvency Rules 1986, SI 1986/1925, Sch 4 Form 6.1 (debt for liquidated sum payable immediately), Form 6.2 (debt for liquidated sum payable immediately following a judgment or order of the court), Form 6.3 (debt payable at future date) (all substituted by SI 2003/1730; and amended by SI 2010/686 and SI 2011/785). A document purporting to be a statutory demand which is served on a debtor is a statutory demand within the meaning of the Insolvency Rules 1986, SI 1986/1925, even if it is defective and liable to be set aside; it remains a statutory demand unless and until it is set aside by the court: *Re A Debtor (No 1 of 1987, Lancaster), ex p Debtor v Royal Bank of Scotland plc* [1989] 2 All ER 46, sub nom *Re A Debtor (No 1 of 1987)* [1989] 1 WLR 271, CA. See also *Agilo Ltd v Henry* [2010] EWHC 2717 (Ch), [2011] BPIR 297.
        The Insolvency Rules 1986, SI 1986/1925, r 6.1 does not apply to a demand made by the Financial Conduct Authority or the Prudential Regulation Authority under the Financial Services and Markets Act 2000 s 372(4)(a) (see FINANCIAL SERVICES AND INSTITUTIONS vol 48 (2008) PARA 501): see the Bankruptcy (Financial Services and Markets Act 2000) Rules 2001, SI 2001/3634, rr 2, 4(1) (r 2 amended by SI 2013/472). A demand must be dated and signed by a member of the relevant Authority's staff authorised by it for that purpose, and must specify that it is made under the Financial Services and Authorities Act 2000 s 372(4)(a): Bankruptcy (Financial Services and Markets Act 2000) Rules 2001, SI 2001/3634, r 4(2), (3). It must state the amount of the debt, to whom it is owed and the consideration for it or, if there is no consideration, the way in which it arises; but if the person to whom the debt is owed holds any security in respect of the debt of which the relevant Authority is aware: (1) the demand must specify the nature of the security and the value which the Authority puts on it as at the date of the demand; and (2) the amount of which payment is claimed by the demand must be the full amount of the debt less the amount specified as the value of the security: r 4(4). The demand must also state the grounds on which it is alleged that the individual appears to have no reasonable prospect of paying the debt: r 4(5). For these purposes, 'debt' means the sum referred to in the Financial Services and Authorities Act 2000 s 372(4)(a); 'person' excludes a body of persons corporate or unincorporate; and 'individual' has the meaning given by s 372(7) (see FINANCIAL SERVICES AND INSTITUTIONS vol 48 (2008) PARA 501): Bankruptcy (Financial Services and Markets Act 2000) Rules 2001, SI 2001/3634, r 2.

2   A document or information given, delivered or sent in hard copy form is sufficiently authenticated if it is signed by the person sending or supplying it: Insolvency Rules 1986, SI 1986/1925, r 12A.9(1) (r 12A added by SI 2010/686). A document or information given, delivered or sent in electronic form is sufficiently authenticated: (1) if the identity of the sender is confirmed in a manner specified by the recipient; or (2) where no such manner has been specified by the recipient, if the communication contains or is accompanied by a statement of the identity of the sender and the recipient has no reason to doubt the truth of that statement: Insolvency Rules 1986, SI 1986/1925, r 12A.9(2) (as so added).

3   Insolvency Rules 1986, SI 1986/1925, r 6.1(1) (amended by SI 2010/686). The Insolvency Rules 1986, SI 1986/1925, r 6.1 does not displace the general principle that a person may sign by the hand of another whom he has authorised to do so: *Re Horne (a bankrupt)* [2000] 4 All ER 550, sub nom *Horne v Dacorum Borough Council* [2000] BPIR 1047, CA. See *Coulter v Chief Constable of Dorset Police* [2004] EWCA Civ 1259, [2005] 1 WLR 130, [2005] BPIR 62.

4   Ie whether it is made under the Insolvency Act 1986 s 268(1): see PARA 133.

5   Ie whether it is made under the Insolvency Act 1986 s 268(2): see PARA 133.

6   Insolvency Rules 1986, SI 1986/1925, r 6.1(2).

7   See note 4.

8   See note 5.

9   Insolvency Rules 1986, SI 1986/1925, r 6.1(3).

10 Insolvency Rules 1986, SI 1986/1925, r 6.1(4).

11 Insolvency Rules 1986, SI 1986/1925, r 6.1(4).

12　As to the meaning of 'security' see PARA 574. As to secured creditors see PARA 574 et seq. For these purposes, 'security' refers only to security over property forming part of the debtor's estate: *Re A Debtor (No 310 of 1988), ex p Debtor v Arab Bank Ltd* [1989] 2 All ER 42, sub nom *Re A Debtor (No 310 of 1988)* [1989] 1 WLR 452.

13　Insolvency Rules 1986, SI 1986/1925, r 6.1(5). Disagreement as to the value of a security does not prevent a sum claimed in a statutory demand from being a liquidated sum, provided that the dispute does not bring into question whether the debtor is indebted to the creditor at all: *Re A Debtor (No 64 of 1992)* [1994] 2 All ER 177, [1994] 1 WLR 264. Failure to disclose that the debt is secured will invalidate the statutory demand if it leaves a balance of less than £750: *Platts v Western Trust & Savings Ltd* [1996] BPIR 339, [1993] 22 LS Gaz R 38; c f *Barclays Bank plc v Mogg* [2003] EWHC 2645 (Ch), [2004] BPIR 259, [2003] All ER (D) 56 (Oct) (inadvertent non-disclosure in petition waived as a curable irregularity).

159.　Information to be given. The statutory demand must include an explanation to the debtor of the following matters:

(1)　the purpose of the demand, and the fact that, if the debtor does not comply with the demand, bankruptcy proceedings may be commenced against him;

(2)　the time within which the demand must be complied with if that consequence is to be avoided;

(3)　the methods of compliance which are open to the debtor; and

(4)　his right to apply to the court[1] for the statutory demand to be set aside[2].

The demand must specify one or more named individuals with whom the debtor may, if he wishes, enter into communication with a view to securing or compounding for the debt to the satisfaction of the creditor or, as the case may be, establishing to the creditor's satisfaction that there is a reasonable prospect that the debt will be paid when it falls due; and, in the case of any individual so named in the demand, his address and telephone number, if any, must be given[3].

1　Ie under the Insolvency Rules 1986, SI 1986/1925, r 6.4: see PARA 161.

2　Insolvency Rules 1986, SI 1986/1925, r 6.2(1). The Insolvency Rules 1986, SI 1986/1925, r 6.2 does not apply to a demand made by the Financial Conduct Authority or the Prudential Regulation Authority under the Financial Services and Markets Act 2000 s 372(4)(a) (see FINANCIAL SERVICES AND INSTITUTIONS vol 48 (2008) PARA 501): Bankruptcy (Financial Services and Markets Act 2000) Rules 2001, SI 2001/3634, rr 2, 5(1) (r 2 amended by SI 2013/472). A demand must include an explanation to the individual of the following matters: (1) the purpose of the demand and the fact that, if the individual does not comply with the demand, bankruptcy proceedings may be commenced against him; (2) the time within which the demand must be complied with, if that consequence is to be avoided; (3) the methods of compliance which are open to the individual; and (4) the individual's right to apply to the court for the demand to be set aside: Bankruptcy (Financial Services and Markets Act 2000) Rules 2001, SI 2001/3634, r 5(2). The demand must specify the name and address (and telephone number, if any) of one or more persons with whom the individual may, if he wishes, enter into communication with a view to establishing to the relevant Authority's satisfaction that there is a reasonable prospect that the debt will be paid when it falls due or that the debt will be scoured or compounded: r 5(3). As to the meanings of 'individual' and 'debt' for these purposes see PARA 158 note 1.

3　Insolvency Rules 1986, SI 1986/1925, r 6.2(2).

160.　Requirements as to service. The creditor is[1] under an obligation to do all that is reasonable for the purpose of bringing the statutory demand to the debtor's attention and, if practicable in the particular circumstances, to cause personal service of the demand to be effected[2].

Where the statutory demand is for payment of a sum due under a judgment or order of any court and the creditor knows, or believes with reasonable cause:

(1)　that the debtor has absconded or is keeping out of the way with a view to avoiding service; and

(2)   there is no real prospect of the sum being recovered by execution or
          other process,

the creditor may advertise[3] the demand in such manner as the creditor thinks fit;
and the time limited for compliance with the demand runs from the date of the
advertisement's appearance or, as the case may be, its first appearance[4].

1   Ie by virtue of the Insolvency Rules 1986, SI 1986/1925. For the purposes of a demand made by
     the Financial Conduct Authority or the Prudential Regulation Authority under the Financial
     Services and Markets Act 2000 s 372(4)(a) (see FINANCIAL SERVICES AND INSTITUTIONS vol 48
     (2008) PARA 501), the Insolvency Rules 1986, SI 1986/1925, r 6.3 applies as if references to the
     debtor were references to an individual, and references to the creditor were references to the
     relevant Authority: Bankruptcy (Financial Services and Markets Act 2000) Rules 2001,
     SI 2001/3634, rr 2, 6(1) (r 2 amended by SI 2013/472). As to the meaning of 'individual' for
     these purposes see PARA 158 note 1.
2   Insolvency Rules 1986, SI 1986/1925, r 6.3(2). The creditor must take all reasonable steps to
     bring the statutory demand to the debtor's attention: *Re H (a debtor) (38-SD of 1997)* (2000)
     Times, 10 May, CA; and see *Regional Collection Services Ltd v Heald* [2000] BPIR 661, CA.
     The court may decline to file the petition if not satisfied that the creditor has discharged the
     obligation imposed on him by the Insolvency Rules 1986, SI 1986/1925, r 6.3(2): see r 6.11(9);
     and PARA 170.
        Rule 6.11 (see PARA 170) has effect as regards service of the statutory demand, and proof of
     that service by a certificate of service to be filed with a bankruptcy petition: r 6.3(1) (amended
     by SI 2010/686). As to the meaning of 'certificate of service' see PARA 176 note 1. As to the
     service   of   court   documents   in   insolvency   proceedings   generally   see   *Practice
     Direction—Insolvency Proceedings* para 6. Except where the Insolvency Rules 1986,
     SI 1986/1925, otherwise provide, CPR Pt 6 (see CIVIL PROCEDURE vol 11 (2009) PARA 138 et
     seq) applies to the service of court documents both within and out of the jurisdiction as modified
     by the *Practice Direction—Insolvency Proceedings* or as the court may otherwise direct:
     para 6.1.
        A statutory demand is deemed to be served on the date applicable to the method of service
     set out in CPR 6.26 (CIVIL PROCEDURE vol 11 (2009) PARA 151) unless the statutory demand is
     advertised in which case it is deemed served on the date of the appearance of the advertisement
     pursuant to the Insolvency Rules 1986, SI 1986/1925, r 6.3: *Practice Direction—Insolvency
     Proceedings* para 13.1.
        A statutory demand is not a document issued by the court; permission to serve out of the
     jurisdiction is not, therefore, required: *Practice Direction—Insolvency Proceedings* para 13.2.1.
     The Insolvency Rules 1986, SI 1986/1925, r 6.3(2) (requirements as to service) applies to service
     of   the   statutory   demand   whether   within   or   out   of   the   jurisdiction: *Practice
     Direction—Insolvency Proceedings* para 13.2.2. A creditor wishing to serve a statutory demand
     out of the jurisdiction in a foreign country with which a civil procedure convention has been
     made (including the Hague Convention) may and, if the assistance of a British Consul is desired,
     must adopt the procedure prescribed by CPR 6.42, 6.43 (see CIVIL PROCEDURE vol 11 (2009)
     PARAS 175–176): see *Practice Direction—Insolvency Proceedings* para 13.2.3. In all other cases,
     service of the demand must be effected by private arrangement in accordance with the
     Insolvency   Rules   1986,   SI   1986/1925,   r   6.3(2)   and   local   foreign   law: *Practice
     Direction—Insolvency Proceedings* para 13.2.4. When a statutory demand is to be served out of
     the jurisdiction, the time limits must be amended: see *Practice Direction—Insolvency
     Proceedings* paras 13.2.5–13.2.7.
        The creditor is under an obligation to do all that is reasonable to bring the statutory demand
     to the debtor's attention and, if practicable, to cause personal service to be effected (see the
     Insolvency Rules 1986, SI 1986/1925, r 6.3(2)): *Practice Direction—Insolvency Proceedings*
     para 13.3.1. In the circumstances set out in the Insolvency Rules 1986, SI 1986/1925, r 6.3(3)
     (see the text to notes 3, 4) the demand may instead be advertised: see *Practice
     Direction—Insolvency Proceedings* para 13.3.2.
3   Where personal service is not effected or the demand is not advertised in the limited
     circumstances permitted by the Insolvency Rules 1986, SI 1986/1925, r 6.3(3), substituted
     service is permitted, but the creditor must have taken all those steps which would justify the
     court making an order for substituted service of a petition: see *Practice Direction—Insolvency
     Proceedings* paras 13.3.3–13.3.4. Failure to comply with these requirements may result in the
     court declining to issue the petition (see the Insolvency Rules 1986, SI 1986/1925, r 6.11(9); and
     PARA 170) or dismissing it: *Practice Direction—Insolvency Proceedings* para 13.3.3.
4   Insolvency Rules 1986, SI 1986/1925, r 6.3(3) (amended by SI 2009/642).

161. Application to set aside statutory demand. Within the period of 18 days from the date of the service on him of the statutory demand or, where the demand is advertised[1], from the date of the advertisement's appearance or, as the case may be, its first appearance, the debtor may apply to the appropriate court[2] for an order setting the statutory demand aside[3].

As from, inclusive, the date on which the application is filed in court[4], the time limited for compliance with the statutory demand ceases to run, subject to any order of the court[5] where the application is dismissed[6].

The debtor's application must be supported by a witness statement[7] specifying the date on which the statutory demand came into his hands, and stating the grounds on which he claims that it should be set aside[8]. The witness statement must have attached to it a copy of the statutory demand[9].

1   Ie pursuant to the Insolvency Rules 1986, SI 1986/1925, r 6.3: see PARA 160.
2   An application to the court must be made to the court to which the debtor would in accordance with the Insolvency Rules 1986, SI 1986/1925, r 6.40A (see PARA 191) present the petition for the debtor's bankruptcy: r 6.4(2) (substituted by SI 2010/686). However, a debtor may make an application to the court to which in accordance with the Insolvency Rules 1986, SI 1986/1925, r 6.9A(1) (see PARA 164) a petition based on the debt in the statutory demand must be presented where that court is not the court to which the debtor would in accordance with r 6.40A (see PARA 191) present the petition for the debtor's bankruptcy if: (1) the creditor issuing the statutory demand is a minister of the Crown or a government department; (2) the debt in respect of which the statutory demand is made, or a part of it equal to or exceeding the bankruptcy level (see PARA 132 note 5), is the subject of a judgment or order of any court; and (3) the statutory demand specifies the date of the judgment or order and the court in which it was obtained and indicates the creditor's intention to present a bankruptcy petition against the debtor in the High Court or the Central London County Court: r 6.4(2A) (added by SI 2010/686; and amended by SI 2011/785).
     For the purposes of a demand made by the Financial Conduct Authority or the Prudential Regulation Authority under the Financial Services and Markets Act 2000 s 372(4)(a) (see FINANCIAL SERVICES AND INSTITUTIONS vol 48 (2008) PARA 501), the Insolvency Rules 1986, SI 1986/1925, r 6.4 applies with modifications: see the Bankruptcy (Financial Services and Markets Act 2000) Rules 2001, SI 2001/3634, rr 2, 7(a) (r 2 amended by SI 2013/472). As to the meaning of 'individual' for these purposes see PARA 158 note 1.
3   Insolvency Rules 1986, SI 1986/1925, r 6.4(1) (amended by SI 2009/642). As to the prescribed form of application see the Insolvency Rules 1986, SI 1986/1925, Sch 4 Form 6.4 (amended by SI 2010/686). Where, by any provision in the Insolvency Act 1986 Pts 7A-11 (ss 251A–385) or by the Insolvency Rules 1986, SI 1986/1925, the time for doing anything is limited, the court may extend the time, either before or after it has expired, on such terms, if any, as it thinks fit: Insolvency Act 1986 s 376. In the case of the administration in bankruptcy of the insolvent estate of a deceased person dying before the presentation of a bankruptcy petition, s 376 applies: Administration of Insolvent Estates of Deceased Persons Order 1986, SI 1986/1999, art 3(1), Sch 1 Pt II para 30. As to the administration in bankruptcy of the insolvent estates of deceased persons see further PARA 830 et seq.
     The application and witness statement in support, exhibiting a copy of the statutory demand, must be filed in court within 18 days of service of the statutory demand: *Practice Direction—Insolvency Proceedings* para 13.4.1 Where service is effected by advertisement, the period of 18 days is calculated from the date of the first appearance of the advertisement: para 13.4.1. Three copies of each document must be lodged with the application to enable the court to serve notice of the hearing date on the applicant, the creditor and the person named in Part B of the statutory demand: para 13.4.1. Where copies of the documents are not lodged with the application, any order of the registrar fixing a venue is conditional on copies of the documents being lodged on the next business day after the registrar's order otherwise the application will be deemed to have been dismissed: para 13.4.2.
     A debtor who wishes to apply to set aside a statutory demand after the expiration of 18 days from the date of service of the statutory demand must apply for an extension of time within which to apply: para 13.4.5. If the applicant wishes to apply for an injunction to restrain presentation of a petition, the application must be made to the judge together with the witness statement in the form prescribed in the Insolvency Rules 1986, SI 1986/1925, Sch 4 Form 6.5, as modified: see *Practice Direction—Insolvency Proceedings* para 13.4.5.

4   As to the meaning of 'file in court' see PARA 57 note 13.
5   Ie under the Insolvency Rules 1986, SI 1986/1925, r 6.5(6): see PARA 162.
6   Insolvency Rules 1986, SI 1986/1925, r 6.4(3).
7   A 'witness statement' means a witness statement verified by a statement of truth in accordance
     with CPR Pt 22 (see CIVIL PROCEDURE vol 11 (2009) PARAS 613, 982): Insolvency Rules 1986,
     SI 1986/1925, r 13.13(18) (added by SI 2010/686). A 'statement of truth' means a statement of
     truth in accordance with CPR Pt 22 (see CIVIL PROCEDURE vol 11 (2009) PARAS 613–616):
     Insolvency Rules 1986, SI 1986/1925, r 13.13(17) (added by SI 2010/686).
8   Insolvency Rules 1986, SI 1986/1925, r 6.4(4) (amended by SI 2010/686). For the prescribed
     form of witness statement in support of an application to set aside statutory demand see the
     Insolvency Rules 1986, SI 1986/1925, Sch 4 Form 6.5.
9   Insolvency Rules 1986, SI 1986/1925, r 6.4(5) (added by SI 2010/686).

162.   Hearing of application to set aside.   On receipt of an application to set
aside a statutory demand[1], the court may, if satisfied that no sufficient cause is
shown for it, dismiss it without giving notice to the creditor; and, as from and
including the date on which the application is dismissed, the time limited for
compliance with the statutory demand runs again[2]. If, however, the application is
not so dismissed, the court must fix a venue[3] for it to be heard, and must give at
least five business days'[4] notice of it to:

(1)   the debtor or, if the debtor's application was made by a solicitor[5] acting
       for him, to the solicitor;
(2)   the creditor; and
(3)   whoever is named in the statutory demand as the person with whom the
       debtor may enter into communication with reference to the demand, or,
       if more than one person is so named, the first of them[6].

On the hearing of the application, the court must consider the evidence then
available to it, and may either summarily determine the application or adjourn it,
giving such directions as it thinks appropriate[7].

The court may grant the application if:

(a)   the debtor appears to have a counterclaim, set-off or cross-demand
       which equals or exceeds the amount of the debt or debts specified in the
       statutory demand[8]; or
(b)   the debt is disputed on grounds which appear to the court to be
       substantial[9]; or
(c)   it appears that the creditor holds some security in respect of the debt
       claimed by the demand and either the statutory provisions relating to
       the disclosure of the nature and amount of the debt[10] are not complied
       with in respect of it, or the court is satisfied that the value of the security
       equals or exceeds the full amount of the debt[11]; or
(d)   the court is satisfied on other grounds that the demand ought to be set
       aside[12].

Where the creditor holds some security in respect of his debt, and the
statutory provisions relating to the disclosure of the nature and amount of the
debt[13] are complied with in respect of it but the court is satisfied that the security
is undervalued in the statutory demand, the creditor may be required to amend
the demand accordingly, but without prejudice to his right to present a
bankruptcy petition by reference to the original demand[14]. If the court dismisses
the application, it must make an order authorising the creditor to present a
bankruptcy petition either as soon as reasonably practicable, or on or after a
date specified in the order; and a copy of the order must be sent by the court as
soon as reasonably practicable to the creditor[15].

1   Ie under the Insolvency Rules 1986, SI 1986/1925, r 6.4: see PARA 161.

2   Insolvency Rules 1986, SI 1986/1925, r 6.5(1). For the purposes of a demand made by the
     Financial Conduct Authority or the Prudential Regulation Authority under the Financial
     Services and Markets Act 2000 s 372(4)(a) (see FINANCIAL SERVICES AND INSTITUTIONS vol 48
     (2008) PARA 501), the Insolvency Rules 1986, SI 1986/1925, r 6.5 applies as if references to the
     debtor were references to an individual, and, subject to the exceptions set out, as if references to
     the creditor were references to the relevant Authority: Bankruptcy (Financial Services and
     Markets Act 2000) Rules 2001, SI 2001/3634, rr 2, 6(1)(a), (b) (r 2 amended by SI 2013/472).
     References to the creditor in heads (2) and (c) of the text should be read as a reference to the
     person to whom the debt is owed and, in relation to head (2) of the text only, as if the reference
     to a creditor also included a reference to the relevant Authority: rr 2, 6(1)(c), (2) (r 2 as so
     amended). As to the meanings of 'individual', 'person' and 'debt' for these purposes see PARA
     158 note 1.
3   As to the meaning of 'venue' see PARA 46 note 22.
4   'Business day' means any day other than a Saturday, a Sunday, Christmas Day, Good Friday or
     a day which is a bank holiday in any part of England and Wales under or by virtue of the
     Banking and Financial Dealings Act 1971 (see TIME vol 97 (2010) PARA 321): Insolvency
     Rules 1986, SI 1986/1925, r 13.13(1) (substituted by SI 1999/1022; and amended by
     SI 2010/686).
5   For these purposes, the reference to a solicitor includes a reference to a body recognised by the
     Law Society under the Administration of Justice Act 1985 s 9 (see LEGAL PROFESSIONS vol 65
     (2008) PARA 515): Solicitors' Recognised Bodies Order 1991, SI 1991/2684, arts 2(1), 3, 4(a), 5,
     Sch 1 (amended by SI 2009/500).
6   Insolvency Rules 1986, SI 1986/1925, r 6.5(2) (amended by SI 2010/686).
7   Insolvency Rules 1986, SI 1986/1925, r 6.5(3).
8   Insolvency Rules 1986, SI 1986/1925, r 6.5(4)(a). This ground requires the court to go through
     a process of assessment in order to ascertain whether the counterclaim, set-off or cross-demand
     raised by the debtor equals or exceeds the sum claimed in the statutory demand: *Ruddock v
     Jeffrey Green Russell (a firm)* [2005] EWHC 3498 (Ch), [2005] All ER (D) 123 (Oct). Where
     the debtor claims to have a counterclaim, set-off or cross-demand, whether or not he could have
     raised it in the action in which the judgment or order was obtained, which equals or exceeds the
     amount of the debt or debts specified in the statutory demand, the court will normally set aside
     the statutory demand if, in its opinion, on the evidence there is a genuine triable issue: *Practice
     Direction—Insolvency Proceedings* para 13.4.4.
         The test of whether there is a genuine triable issue is for all practical purposes the same as
     the test under CPR 24.2(a) (see CIVIL PROCEDURE vol 11 (2009) PARA 524) of whether there is a
     real prospect of success in relation to the making of a summary judgment: *Ashworth v
     Newnote Ltd* [2007] EWCA Civ 793, [2007] All ER (D) 436 (Jul); *Abernethy v Hotbed Ltd*
     [2011] EWHC 1476 (Ch), [2011] BPIR 1547, [2011] All ER (D) 201 (May). The fact that a
     judge has previously held that the issue raised by the debtor is too insubstantial to be pleaded is
     an important consideration in deciding whether the debtor has a genuine triable issue, but it is
     not determinative: *Everards v Society of Lloyd's* [2003] EWHC 1890 (Ch), [2003] BPIR 1286,
     [2003] 36 LS Gaz R 40. The rule extends to a situation where the demand is based on a costs
     order made in the proceedings in which the counterclaim is being pursued: *Popely v Popely*
     [2004] EWCA Civ 463, [2004] BPIR 778, [2004] All ER (D) 346 (Apr). See also *Ahmed v
     Landstone Leisure Ltd* [2009] EWHC 125 (Ch), [2009] BPIR 227, [2009] All ER (D) 69 (Feb);
     Shaw v MFP Foundations & Piling Ltd [2010] EWHC 9 (Ch), [2010] 2 BCLC 85, [2010] BPIR
     397.
         Where the amount of the counterclaim, set-off or cross-demand does not equal or exceed the
     debt specified in the statutory demand, the court will not set the statutory demand aside: *Re A
     Debtor (No 10 of 1988, Aylesbury), ex p Lovell Construction (Southern) Ltd v Debtor* [1989]
     2 All ER 39, sub nom *Re A Debtor (No 10 of 1988)* [1989] 1 WLR 405; *AIB Finance Ltd v
     Debtors* [1997] 4 All ER 677, [1997] 2 BCLC 354 (affd on other grounds [1998] 2 All ER 929,
     [1998] 1 BCLC 665, CA). Where a right of equitable set-off is asserted but cannot be shown to
     exceed the amount claimed in the statutory demand, the statutory demand will not be set aside,
     since the court is entitled to make a bankruptcy order in respect of the net sum: *TSB Bank plc v
     Platts* [1998] 2 BCLC 1, sub nom *TSB Bank plc v Platts (No 2)* [1998] BPIR 284, CA. Where
     the counterclaim, set-off or cross-demand is unsustainable either in fact or in law, the statutory
     demand will not be set aside: *AIB Finance Ltd v Debtors* [1998] 2 All ER 929, [1998] 1 BCLC
     665, CA.
         It is not necessary that the counterclaim or cross-demand is available for set-off in law
     against the claimed debt: *Re Debtors (Nos 4449 and 4450 of 1998)* [1999] 1 All ER (Comm)
     149. A clause in a reconstruction contract requiring sums owed to be paid without any set-off or
     counterclaim does not preclude a debtor who has a counterclaim from having a statutory

demand set aside: *Re A Debtor (No 544/SD/98)* [2000] 1 BCLC 103 at 110, CA. A debtor can assert a counterclaim or cross-demand against a debt claimed in a statutory demand which arises from a dishonoured cheque: *Hofer v Strawson* [1999] 2 BCLC 336, [1999] BPIR 501. It is not necessary that a counterclaim or cross-demand arises in favour of the debtor in the same capacity as the debt demanded from him in the statutory demand: *Re A Debtor (No 87 of 1999)* [2000] BPIR 589. However, the legal character of the counterclaim or cross-demand relied on by a debtor has to be the same as the legal character of the debt claimed in the statutory demand: *Hurst v Bennett* [2001] EWCA Civ 182, [2001] 2 BCLC 290, [2001] BPIR 287. In relation to the winding up of companies see also *Re Bayoil SA, Seawind Tankers Corpn v Bayoil SA* [1999] 1 All ER 374, [1999] 1 WLR 147, CA.

9   Insolvency Rules 1986, SI 1986/1925, r 6.5(4)(b). Where the debtor disputes the debt, not being a debt subject to a judgment, order, liability order, costs certificate or tax assessment, the court will normally set aside the statutory demand if, in its opinion, on the evidence, there is a genuine triable issue: *Practice Direction—Insolvency Proceedings* para 13.4.4. The existence of an arguable point of law is not sufficient unless it can be shown that the point can only be resolved at trial: *Cale v Assiudoman KPS (Harrow) Ltd* [1996] BPIR 245.

Where a debt is genuinely disputed, the question whether or not the debtor is insolvent is irrelevant: see *Re A Company (No 00212 of 1995)* (1995) Times, 7 April, applying *Mann v Goldstein* [1968] 2 All ER 769, [1968] 1 WLR 1091 (company case). The fact that a debtor may be able to argue that he is not insolvent or that the creditor may be able to obtain payment by other means does not prevent a creditor from serving a demand followed, if there is no payment, by a petition: *Cornhill Insurance plc v Improvement Services Ltd* [1986] 1 WLR 114, [1986] BCLC 26 (company case). The court is not obliged to accept that there is a substantial dispute because unconditional permission to defend proceedings has been given under CPR Pt 24 (see CIVIL PROCEDURE vol 11 (2009) PARA 524 et seq), although this fact may be highly persuasive; the court may investigate the evidence and reach its own conclusion: *Re Welsh Brick Industries Ltd* [1946] 2 All ER 197, CA (company case).

It is not open to a creditor in response to an application to set aside a statutory demand to seek to rely on a debt other than the one claimed in the demand: *Re A Debtor (No 44 of 1997), Bennett v Filmer* [1998] BPIR 444. An overstatement of the debt is not of itself a ground for setting aside a statutory demand: *Re A Debtor (No 1 of 1987, Lancaster), ex p Debtor v Royal Bank of Scotland plc* [1989] 2 All ER 46, sub nom *Re A Debtor (No 1 of 1987)* [1989] 1 WLR 271, CA; *Re A Debtor (No 490/SD/1991), ex p Debtor v Printline (Offset) Ltd* [1992] 2 All ER 664, [1992] 1 WLR 507; *Re A Debtor (No 657/SD/91), ex p IRC v Debtor* [1992] STC 751, [1993] BCLC 180. Where a debt is partly disputed but the undisputed element is below the bankruptcy level, the court should generally exercise its discretion under the Insolvency Rules 1986, SI 1986/1925, r 6.5(4)(d) (see head (d) in the text) to dismiss the statutory demand: *Re A Debtor (Nos 49 and 50 of 1992)* [1995] Ch 66, [1994] 3 WLR 847, CA. Where there is a genuine dispute as to whether a demand has been served on behalf of the creditor, the demand will normally be set aside: *Agilo Ltd v Henry* [2010] EWHC 2717 (Ch), [2011] BPIR 297.

Where the debt claimed in the statutory demand is based on a judgment, order, liability order, costs certificate, tax assessment or decision of a tribunal, the court will not at this stage inquire into the validity of the debt nor, as a general rule, will it adjourn the application to await the result of an application to set aside the judgment, order decision, costs certificate or any appeal: *Practice Direction—Insolvency Proceedings* para 13.4.3. The court may, however, stand proceedings over where it is alleged that a judgment was obtained by fraud and impeachment proceedings are instituted: *Bowes v Directors of Hope Life Assurance and Guarantee Co* (1865) 11 HL Cas 389 (company case). As to the power of the court to go behind a judgment or order on the hearing of the petition see PARA 199 note 3.

Where a statutory demand is served in respect of a debt which is not properly owed by the debtor or which to the knowledge of the petitioner is genuinely disputed by the debtor, the presentation of the statutory demand may be an abuse of process and the demand may be set aside with an order for costs to be paid on an indemnity basis: see *Re A Company (No 0012209 of 1991)* [1992] 2 All ER 797, [1992] 1 WLR 351 (company case); and COMPANY AND PARTNERSHIP INSOLVENCY vol 16 (2011) PARA 431. See further PARA 188.

10 Ie the Insolvency Rules 1986, SI 1986/1925, r 6.1(5): see PARA 158.

11 Insolvency Rules 1986, SI 1986/1925, r 6.5(4)(c). A statutory demand which fails to state that security is held for the debt may be set aside except where it can be demonstrated that the debtor has suffered no prejudice by reason of the omission: *Re A Debtor (No 106 of 1992), Khan v Breezevale SARL* [1996] BPIR 190; and see PARA 158. Where there is a dispute as to the value of security held by the creditor, the court may determine the dispute either at the hearing of an application to set aside the statutory demand or at the hearing of the petition itself: *Platts v Western Trust & Savings Ltd* [1996] BPIR 339, CA. The debtor, when estimating the debt

against the value of the security, cannot include any potential cost of enforcing the debt: *Owo-Samson v Barclays Bank plc* [2003] EWCA Civ 714, [2003] BPIR 1373, [2003] All ER (D) 285 (May). See also *Fagg v Rushton* [2007] EWHC 657 (Ch), [2007] BPIR 1059.

12 Insolvency Rules 1986, SI 1986/1925, r 6.5(4)(d). It is not enough for a debtor seeking to invoke 'other grounds' to state that a statutory demand served on him was perplexing; even though the demand failed to give clear particulars as to how the amount claimed was ascertained, the debtor should show what he says is the true position as between himself and the creditor: *Re A Debtor (No 1 of 1987, Lancaster), ex p Debtor v Royal Bank of Scotland plc* [1989] 2 All ER 46, sub nom *Re a Debtor (No 1 of 1987)* [1989] 1 WLR 271, CA. The grounds under which a statutory demand might be set aside under the Insolvency Rules 1986, SI 1986/1925, r 6.5(4)(d) are of the same substance as those set out in r 6.5(4)(a)–(c) (see heads (a)–(c) in the text): *Re A Debtor (No 1 of 1987, Lancaster), ex p Debtor v Royal Bank of Scotland plc*. Such grounds include where the debtor has admitted that the debt is due and owing and is prepared to secure or compound it to the creditor's satisfaction: *Budge v AF Budge (Contractors) Ltd (in receivership and liquidation)* [1997] BPIR 366, CA. This may include the situation where a payment is to be made by the debtor to reduce the debt to below the bankruptcy level (*City Electrical Factors Ltd v Hardingham* [1996] BPIR 541) or where payment of a debt demanded in a foreign currency is to be paid in sterling at an appropriate rate (*Re A Debtor (No 51-SD-1991), ex p Ritchie Bros Auctioneers v Debtor* [1993] 2 All ER 40, [1992] 1 WLR 1294). However, it is not open to a debtor to argue that a statutory demand should be set aside on the basis that the creditor has unreasonably refused an offer to settle: *Re A Debtor (No 415-SD-1993), ex p Debtor v IRC* [1994] 2 All ER 168, [1994] 1 WLR 917. Cf the Insolvency Act 1986 s 271(3); and PARA 198. The fact that there is a risk of inconsistent verdicts in the ordinary and bankruptcy jurisdictions of the county court does not constitute a ground to set aside a statutory demand: *Re A Debtor (No 90 of 1997)* (1998) Times, 1 July. See also *Remblance v Octagon Assets Ltd* [2009] EWCA Civ 581, [2010] 2 All ER 688, [2010] 1 BCLC 10 (service of statutory demand on guarantor on basis that creditor could not claim against debtor by reason of cross-claim unjust); cf *White v Davenham Trust Ltd* [2011] EWCA Civ 747, [2011] Bus LR 1443, [2012] 1 BCLC 123 (existence of security which on a statutory demand against the debtor who gave security would bring the Insolvency Rules 1986, SI 1986/1925, r 6.5(4)(c) into operation is of itself irrelevant to a statutory demand served on a guarantor who has not himself given any security).

A formal defect in the statutory demand which does not mislead the debtor, as where the correct date of a guarantee is misstated, does not invalidate the demand: *Re A Debtor (No 190 of 1987)* (1988) Times, 21 May. Similarly, a formal defect in the statutory demand, such as the failure to state the consideration for the debt, will not ordinarily lead to a petition based on the demand being dismissed: *Oben v Blackman* [2000] BPIR 302, sub nom *Re Blackman (a debtor)* [1999] BCC 446.

13 See note 10.

14 The Insolvency Rules 1986, SI 1986/1925, r 6.5(5). The Insolvency Rules 1986, SI 1986/1925, r 6.5(5) does not apply to a demand made under the Financial Services and Markets Act 2000 s 372(4)(a) (see FINANCIAL SERVICES AND INSTITUTIONS vol 48 (2008) PARA 501): Bankruptcy (Financial Services and Markets Act 2000) Rules 2001, SI 2001/3634, r 6(3). In relation to such demands, where the person to whom the debt is owed holds some security in respect of his debt, and r 4(4) (see PARA 158) is complied with in respect of it but the court is satisfied that the security is undervalued in the demand, the Financial Conduct Authority or the Prudential Regulation Authority may be required to amend the demand accordingly, but without prejudice to its right to present a bankruptcy by reference to the original demand: rr 2, 6(3) (r 2 amended by SI 2013/472).

15 Insolvency Rules 1986, SI 1986/1925, r 6.5(6) (amended by SI 2009/642). For the prescribed form of order setting aside a statutory demand see the Insolvency Rules 1986, SI 1986/1925, Sch 4 Form 6.6. It is not open to a debtor to raise arguments which have been raised on an unsuccessful application to set aside a statutory demand on the hearing of the petition unless there has been some change of circumstances between the hearing of the application to set aside the demand and the hearing of the petition: *Turner v Royal Bank of Scotland* [2000] BPIR 683, CA; and see *Re a Debtor (No 27 of 1990), Brillouet v Hachette Magazines Ltd* [1996] BPIR 518 at 522, CA; cf *Eberhardt & Co Ltd v Mair* [1995] 3 All ER 963, [1995] 1 WLR 1180. If a debtor has not applied to set aside a statutory demand, he will not be precluded from raising a dispute at the hearing of the petition: *Barnes v Whitehead* [2004] BPIR 693.

In relation to an appeal from a decision on an application to set aside a statutory demand, the principles in *Ladd v Marshall* [1954] 3 All ER 745, [1954] 1 WLR 1489, CA, do not apply and fresh evidence may be admitted: *Royal Bank of Scotland v Binnell* [1996] BPIR 352; *Re a Debtor (No 223 SD of 1995), Norman Laurier v United Overseas Bank Ltd* [1996] BPIR 635;

Purvis v Customs and Excise Comrs [1999] BPIR 396; *Re A Debtor (No SD8/9 of 1998)* [2000] BCC 36, sub nom *Salvidge v Hussein* [1999] BPIR 410. However, such an appeal is in the nature of a true appeal; and, accordingly, events occurring after the decision under appeal are not relevant to the appeal: *Cozens v Customs and Excise Comrs* [2000] BPIR 252, CA. See also *Clifton v Barclays Bank plc* [1998] BPIR 565. See further PARA 761 et seq.

(iii) Debtor's Petition

163. Grounds of debtor's petition. A debtor's petition[1] may be presented to the court only on the grounds that the debtor is unable to pay his debts[2]; and the petition must be accompanied by a statement of the debtor's affairs[3], verified by a statement of truth[4], containing:

(1)   such particulars of the debtor's creditors and of his debts and other liabilities and of his assets as may be prescribed; and

(2)   such other information as may be prescribed[5].

1   In the Insolvency Act 1986, 'debtor's petition' means a bankruptcy petition presented by the debtor himself under s 264(1)(b) (see PARA 130 head (2)): s 385(1). As to the application of s 385 in the case of the administration in bankruptcy of the insolvent estate of a deceased person dying before the presentation of a bankruptcy petition see PARA 6 note 8.
    As from a day to be appointed, the definition of 'debtor's petition' and ss 272–274, 274A (debtors petitions) are repealed by the Enterprise and Regulatory Reform Act 2013 s 71, Sch 19 paras 1, 9, 55: see PARA 130 note 17.
2   Insolvency Act 1986 s 272(1). The test of whether a person is unable to pay his debts is not whether his assets exceed his liabilities but whether he is able to pay his debts as and when they fall due: *Re Coney (a bankrupt)* [1998] BPIR 333. See also *Paulin v Paulin* [2009] EWCA Civ 221, [2009] 3 All ER 88n, [2010] 1 WLR 1057; *Gittins v Serco Home Affairs* [2012] EWHC 651 (Ch), [2012] 4 All ER 1362, [2013] 1 WLR 1218.
    In the case of the administration in bankruptcy of the insolvent estate of a deceased person dying before the presentation of a bankruptcy petition, a debtor's petition in the prescribed form may be presented to the court only on the grounds that the estate of a deceased debtor is insolvent: Insolvency Act 1986 s 272(1) (amended by the Administration of Insolvent Estates of Deceased Persons Order 1986, SI 1986/1999, art 3(1), Sch 1 Pt II para 6). For the prescribed form of petition see the Administration of Insolvent Estates of Deceased Persons Order 1986, SI 1986/1999, Sch 3 Form 6 (substituted by SI 2002/1309). As to the administration in bankruptcy of the insolvent estates of deceased persons see further PARA 830 et seq.
    As to the modification of the Insolvency Act 1986 s 272 by the Insolvent Partnerships Order 1994, SI 1994/2421, in relation to the bankruptcy of an individual member of an insolvent partnership see COMPANY AND PARTNERSHIP INSOLVENCY vol 17 (2011) PARAS 1319, 1327.
3   The Insolvency Rules 1986, SI 1986/1925, rr 6.67–6.72 (see PARA 248 et seq) apply with respect to the statement of affairs: r 6.41(2). See also r 5.5; and PARA 55. For the prescribed form of statement of affairs see Sch 4 Form 6.28 (substituted by SI 2005/2114; and amended by SI 2010/686).
4   As to the meaning of 'statement of truth' see PARA 161 note 7.
5   Insolvency Act 1986 s 272(2); Insolvency Rules 1986, SI 1986/1925, r 6.41(1). As to material omissions in such a statement see the Insolvency Act 1986 s 356(1) and PARA 741; and as to the use of such a statement in evidence against the debtor see s 433 and PARA 802.

(2) PROCEDURE ON BANKRUPTCY PETITION

(i) Creditor's Petition

A. THE APPROPRIATE COURT

164. Court to which petition to be presented. Where the proceedings are allocated to the London insolvency district in relation to a debt relief order[1], or in relation to a petition presented by a minister of the Crown or a government department[2], the creditor must present the petition to the High Court where the petition debt is £50,000 or more or to the Central London County Court where the petition debt is less than £50,000[3]. In relation to other proceedings allocated to the London insolvency district[4], the creditor must present the petition to the High Court[5].

Where the debtor is resident[6] in England and Wales and the proceedings are not allocated to the London insolvency district, the creditor must present the petition to the debtor's own county court[7].

If the debtor is not resident in England and Wales but was resident or carried on business in England and Wales within the six months immediately preceding the presentation of the petition and the proceedings are not allocated to the London insolvency district, the petition may be presented either to the debtor's own county court or to the High Court[8].

Where there is in force for the debtor a voluntary arrangement[9], the petition must be presented to the court to which the nominee's report was submitted[10] or an application[11] has been made[12].

The petition must contain sufficient information to establish that it is presented in the appropriate court[13].

1 Ie under the Insolvency Rules 1986, SI 1986/1925, r 7.10ZA(a)(i)–(iv): see PARA 8.
2 Ie under the Insolvency Rules 1986, SI 1986/1925, r 7.10ZA(b): see PARA 8.

3 Insolvency Rules 1986, SI 1986/1925, r 6.9A(1) (r 6.9A added by SI 2011/785). As to bankruptcy courts see PARA 6. The Insolvency Rules 1986, SI 1986/1925, Pt 6 Ch 2 (rr 6.6–6.35) (see PARA 165 et seq) relate to a creditor's petition, and the making of a bankruptcy order thereon; and in Pt 6 Ch 2 'the debt' means, except where the context otherwise requires, the debt, or debts, in respect of which the petition is presented: r 6.6. Part 6 Ch 2 also applies to a petition presented under the Insolvency Act 1986 s 264(1)(c) (see PARA 130 head (5)) with any necessary modifications: Insolvency Rules 1986, SI 1986/1925, r 6.6. For the prescribed form of bankruptcy petition for default in connection with a voluntary arrangement see Sch 4 Form 6.10 (substituted by SI 2002/1307; and amended by SI 2010/686; and SI 2011/785).

4 Ie under the Insolvency Rules 1986, SI 1986/1925, r 7.10ZA(a)(v), (c), (d): see PARA 8.
5 Insolvency Rules 1986, SI 1986/1925, r 6.9A(2) (as added: see note 3).
6 As to the meaning of 'reside' see PARA 131 note 5.

7 Insolvency Rules 1986, SI 1986/1925, r 6.9A(3) (as added: see note 3). For this purpose, the debtor's own county court is: (1) where the debtor has carried on business in England and Wales within the six months immediately preceding the presentation of the petition, the county court for the insolvency district where for the longest period during those six months either the debtor carried on business, or the principal place of business was located, if business was carried on in more than one insolvency district; or (2) where the debtor has not carried on business in England and Wales within the six months immediately preceding the presentation of the petition, the county court for the insolvency district where the debtor resided for the longest period during those six months: r 6.9A(4) (as so added). As to the meaning of 'carry on business' see PARA 131 note 6. As from a day to be appointed, any reference however expressed that is or is deemed to be a reference to a county court held under the County Courts Act 1984 s 1 is to be read as a reference to the county court established by s A1 of that Act: see the Crime and Courts Act 2013 Sch 9 Pt 2 para 11(1)(a), (3)(c). At the date at which this volume states the law no such day had been appointed.

8 Insolvency Rules 1986, SI 1986/1925, r 6.9A(5) (as added: see note 3). See note 7.
9 Ie under the Insolvency Act 1986 Pt 8 (see PARA 43 et seq).
10 Ie under the Insolvency Act 1986 s 256 (see PARA 55).
11 Ie under the Insolvency Act 1986 s 256A(3) (see PARA 51).

12 Insolvency Rules 1986, SI 1986/1925, r 6.9A(6) (as added: see note 3), which is expressed to have effect notwithstanding any other provision of r 6.9A except r 6.9A(2) (see the text to note 5).

13 Insolvency Rules 1986, SI 1986/1925, r 6.9A(7) (as added: see note 3).

165. Identification of debtor. The petition must state the following matters with respect to the debtor, so far as they are within the petitioner's knowledge:

(1) his name, place of residence[1] and occupation, if any;

(2) the name or names in which he carries on business[2], if other than his true name, and whether, in the case of any business of a specified nature, he carries it on alone or with others;

(3) the nature of his business and the address or addresses at which he carries it on;

(4) any name or names, other than his true name, in which he has carried on business at or after the time when the debt[3] was incurred, and whether he has done so alone or with others;

(5) any address or addresses at which he has resided or carried on business at or after that time, and the nature of that business;

(6) whether the debtor has his centre of main interests or an establishment in another member state[4].

The particulars of the debtor so given determine the title of the proceedings[5]; and, if to the petitioner's personal knowledge the debtor has used any name other than the one specified under head (1) above, that fact must be stated in the petition[6].

Guidance as to the manner in which bankruptcy petitions should be completed has been given[7].

In any case where disclosure or continuing disclosure to other persons (whether to the public generally or to specific persons) of the current address[8] or whereabouts of a debtor might reasonably be expected to lead to violence against the debtor or against a person who normally resides with the debtor as a member of the debtor's family, the court may, on the application of the debtor, the official receiver[9], the trustee[10] or the Secretary of State[11], order that the debtor's details be kept confidential[12].

1 As to the meaning of 'residence' see PARA 131 note 5.
2 As to the meaning of 'carry on business' see PARA 131 note 6.
3 As to the meaning of 'the debt' see PARA 164 note 3.
4 Insolvency Rules 1986, SI 1986/1925, r 6.7(1) (amended by SI 2002/1307). As to the meanings of 'centre of main interests' and 'establishment' see Council Regulation (EC) 1346/2000 (OJ L160, 30.6.2000, p 1) on insolvency proceedings ('European Regulation on Insolvency Proceedings'); and PARA 42.
5 Insolvency Rules 1986, SI 1986/1925, r 6.7(2). As to amendment of the title of proceedings see PARA 202.
6 Insolvency Rules 1986, SI 1986/1925, r 6.7(3).
7 See *Practice Direction—Insolvency Proceedings* para 14. The attention of practitioners is drawn to the following points:
  (1) a creditor's petition does not require dating, signing or witnessing but must be verified in accordance with the Insolvency Rules 1986, SI 1986/1925, r 6.12 (see PARA 169);
  (2) in the heading it is only necessary to recite the debtor's name eg Re John William Smith or Re JW Smith (male); any alias or trading name will appear in the body of the petition;
  (3) where the petition is based solely on a statutory demand, only the debt claimed in the demand may be included in the petition;
  (4) attention is drawn to the Insolvency Rules 1986, SI 1986/1925, rr 6.7, 6.8, and in particular to r 6.8(1) where the 'aggregate sum' is made up of a number of debts (see PARA 166);
  (5) with regard to date of service of the statutory demand:
    (a) in the case of personal service, the date of service as set out in the certificate of service should be recited and whether service is effected before/after 17.00 hours

on Monday to Friday or at any time on a Saturday or a Sunday (see CPR 6.7(2), (3); and CIVIL PROCEDURE vol 11 (2009) PARA 151);

(b)   in the case of substituted service, otherwise than by advertisement, the date alleged (see PARA 175) in the certificate of service should be recited;

(c)   in the strictly limited case of service by advertisement under the Insolvency Rules 1986, SI 1986/1925, r 6.3 (see PARA 160), the date to be alleged is the date of the advertisement's appearance or, as the case may be, its first appearance (see r 6.3(3) and PARA 160; r 6.11(8) and PARA 170);

(6)   with regard to certificates at the end of the petition:

(a)   the petitioning creditor must, before presenting a petition, conduct a search for petitions presented against the debtor in the previous 18 months in the Royal Courts of Justice, in the Central London County Court and in any county court which he believes is or was within that period the debtor's own county court within the meaning of the Insolvency Rules 1986, SI 1986/1925, r 6.9A(3) (see PARA 164);

(b)   the following certificate must be included at the end of the petition:
'I/we certify that I/we have conducted a search for petitions presented against the debtor in the period of 18 months ending today and that [no prior petitions have been presented in the said period which are still pending] [a prior petition (No [])] has been presented and is pending in the [Court] and we are issuing this petition at risk as to costs]';

(7)   the deposit payable on presentation of the petition (see PARA 168) will be taken by the court and forwarded to the official receiver; in the Royal Courts of Justice the petition fee and deposit should be paid in the Fee Room, which will record the receipt and will impress two entries on the original petition, one in respect of the court fee and the other in respect of the deposit; in a District Registry or a county court the petition fee and deposit should be handed to the duly authorised officer of the court's staff who will record its receipt; in all cases cheque(s) for the whole amount should be made payable to 'HM Courts and Tribunals Service' or 'HMCTS': *Practice Direction—Insolvency Proceedings* paras 14.2–14.4.

As from a day to be appointed, any reference however expressed that is or is deemed to be a reference to a county court held under the County Courts Act 1984 s 1 is to be read as a reference to the county court established by s A1 of that Act: see the Crime and Courts Act 2013 Sch 9 Pt 2 para 11(1)(a), (3)(c). At the date at which this volume states the law no such day had been appointed.

8   'Current address' means, in relation to any debtor, the address of the debtor's current place of residence and any address at which the debtor currently carries on business; and 'debtor' means a person who is subject to a bankruptcy order, a bankruptcy restrictions order (see PARA 657 et seq) or a bankruptcy restrictions undertaking (see PARA 668 et seq): Insolvency Rules 1986, SI 1986/1925, r 6.235B(2) (r 6.235B added by SI 2010/686).

9   As to the official receiver see PARA 35 et seq.

10 As to the trustee see PARA 314 et seq.

11 As to the Secretary of State see PARA 19.

12 Insolvency Rules 1986, SI 1986/1925, r 6.235B(1) (as added: see note 8). The court may order that (see r 6.235B(3) (as so added)):

(1)   details of the debtor's current address be removed from any part of the court file of the proceedings in relation to the debtor which is open to inspection and be kept on a separate file not open to inspection;

(2)   the details in respect of the debtor to be entered in the bankruptcy order must not include details of the debtor's current address;

(3)   the full title of the proceedings must be amended by the removal of the details of the debtor's current address from the description of the debtor;

(4)   the details of the debtor to be included in any notice gazetted or otherwise advertised must not include details of the debtor's current address;

(5)   the details in respect of the debtor to be entered onto the individual insolvency register under r 6A.4 or the bankruptcy restrictions register under r 6A.6 (see PARA 32) must not include details of the debtor's current address; or

(6)   the details of the debtor's current address kept on the individual insolvency register or the bankruptcy restrictions register must be removed from such register.

'Gazetted' means advertised once in the Gazette: r 13.13(4A) (added by SI 2009/642; and amended by SI 2010/686). The 'Gazette' means the London Gazette: Insolvency Rules 1986, SI 1986/1925, r 13.13(4). As to the contents of notices to be gazetted see PARA 779.

Where the court makes an order under heads (2)–(6), it may further order that: (a) the description of the debtor to be inserted in the bankruptcy order; (b) the full title of the proceedings; (c) the details of the debtor required to be included in any notice to be gazetted or otherwise advertised; or (d) the details in respect of the debtor kept or to be entered on to the registers referred to in heads (4) and (5), as the case may be, must instead include such other details of the debtor's addresses or whereabouts as the court thinks just, including details of any address at which the debtor has previously resided or carried on business: r 6.235B(4) (as so added).

Where the court makes an order under head (3), the official receiver must as soon as reasonably practicable send notice of it to the Chief Land Registrar, for corresponding amendment of the register and, if the official receiver thinks fit, the official receiver may cause notice of the order to be gazetted, or both gazetted and given in such other manner as the official receiver thinks fit: r 6.235B(5) (as so added). Any such notice of the amendment of the title of the proceedings to be published must contain (i) the standard contents with the exception of the current address of the debtor; (ii) the amended title of the proceedings; and (iii) the date of the bankruptcy order, but must not include the description under which the proceedings were previously published: r 6.235B(6) (as so added).

'Standard contents' means: (A) in relation to a notice to be gazetted, the contents specified in rr 12A.33–12A.35 (see PARA 779); and (B) in relation to a notice to be advertised in any other way, the contents specified in rr 12A.38–12A.40 (see PARA 780): r 13.13(4B) (added by SI 2010/686).

In any case where an application is made in respect of a debtor under or by virtue of r 6.235B, the application must be accompanied by a witness statement referring to r 6.235B and containing sufficient evidence to satisfy the court that r 6.235B(1) applies to or in respect of that debtor: r 6.235B(7) (as so added).

166. Identification of the debt. There must be stated in the petition, with reference to every debt[1] in respect of which it is presented:

(1) the amount of the debt, the consideration for it[2], or, if there is no consideration, the way in which it arises, and the fact that it is owed to the petitioner;

(2) when the debt was incurred or became due;

(3) if the amount of the debt includes any charge by way of interest not previously notified to the debtor as a liability of his, or any other charge accruing from time to time, the amount or rate of the charge, separately identified, and the grounds on which it is claimed to form part of the debt, provided that such amount or rate must, in the case of a petition based on a statutory demand[3], be limited to that claimed in that demand;

(4) either that the debt is for a liquidated sum payable immediately, and the debtor appears to be unable to pay it, or that the debt is for a liquidated sum payable at some certain, future time, that time to be specified, and the debtor appears to have no reasonable prospect of being able to pay it, and, in either case[4], that the debt is unsecured[5].

Where the debt is one for which[6] a statutory demand must have been served on the debtor:

(a) there must be specified the date and manner of service of the statutory demand; and

(b) it must be stated that, to the best of the creditor's knowledge and belief, the demand has been neither complied with nor set aside[7], and no application to set it aside is outstanding[8].

If the case is one where the debt arises under a judgment or order of the court and execution has been returned unsatisfied[9], the court from which the execution or other process issued must be specified, and particulars must be given relating to the return[10].

1   As to the meaning of 'the debt' see PARA 164 note 3.

2   The failure to state the consideration for a debt in the petition will not by itself invalidate the petition: *Oben v Blackman* [2000] BPIR 302, sub nom *Re Blackman (a debtor)* [1999] BCC 446.

3   As to statutory demands see PARA 158 et seq.

4   Ie subject to the Insolvency Act 1986 s 269: see PARA 132.

5   Insolvency Rules 1986, SI 1986/1925, r 6.8(1) (amended by SI 1987/1919). See also PARA 165 note 7 head (4).

6   Ie under the Insolvency Act 1986 s 268: see PARA 133.

7   Ie in accordance with the Insolvency Rules 1986, SI 1986/1925: see PARAS 161, 162.

8   Insolvency Rules 1986, SI 1986/1925, r 6.8(2). A petition is not automatically or necessarily invalidated by a failure to state that no application to set aside the statutory demand is outstanding: *Re A Debtor (No 22 of 1993)* [1994] 2 All ER 105, [1994] 1 WLR 46. An application to set aside a statutory demand is not outstanding if the application has been dismissed and an appeal is pending: *Ahmad v IRC* [2004] EWHC 2292 (Ch), [2005] BPIR 541, [2004] All ER (D) 435 (Jul).

9   Ie under the Insolvency Act 1986 s 268(1)(b): see PARA 133 head (2).

10   Insolvency Rules 1986, SI 1986/1925, r 6.8(3).

C. PRESENTATION AND FILING

167. Presentation and filing. The petition, verified by a statement of truth[1], must be filed in court[2]; and no petition may be filed unless there is produced with it a receipt for the deposit payable on presentation[3] or the Secretary of State[4] has given written notice to the court that the petitioner has made suitable alternative arrangements for the payment of the deposit to the official receiver[5] and such notice has not been revoked[6] in relation to the petitioner[7].

The following copies of the petition must also be delivered to the court with the petition:

(1)   one for service on the debtor; and

(2)   if there is in force for the debtor a voluntary arrangement under Part 8 of the Insolvency Act 1986[8], and the petitioner is not the supervisor[9] of the arrangement, one copy for him[10].

Each of these copies must have applied to it the seal of the court, and must be issued to the petitioner[11]. The date and time of filing must be indorsed on the petition and on any copy so issued[12].

The court must fix a venue[13] for hearing the petition, and this also must be indorsed on the petition and on any copy so issued[14].

Where a petition contains a request for the appointment of a former supervisor as trustee[15], the person whose appointment is sought must, not less than two business days[16] before the day appointed for hearing the petition, file in court a report including particulars of:

(a)   a date on which he gave written notification to creditors bound by the arrangement of the intention to seek his appointment as trustee, such date to be at least seven business days before the day on which the report under this provision is filed; and

(b)   details of any response from creditors to that notice, including any objections to his appointment[17].

1   Ie in accordance with the Insolvency Rules 1986, SI 1986/1925, r 6.12(1): see PARA 169. For the prescribed form of statement of truth see Sch 4 Form 6.13A (added by SI 2010/686). As to the meaning of 'statement of truth' see PARA 161 note 7.

2   Insolvency Rules 1986, SI 1986/1925, r 6.10(1) (amended by SI 2010/686). As to the meaning of 'file in court' see PARA 57 note 13.

3   Insolvency Rules 1986, SI 1986/1925, r 6.10(2) (substituted by SI 2004/584). As to the deposit payable on presentation of the petition see PARA 168.

4   As to the Secretary of State see PARA 19.
5   As to the official receiver see PARA 35 et seq.
6   Such a notice may be revoked in relation to the petitioner in whose favour it is given by a further
     notice in writing to the court stating that the earlier notice is revoked in relation to the
     petitioner: Insolvency Rules 1986, SI 1986/1925, r 6.10(2B) (added by SI 2004/584).
7   Insolvency Rules 1986, SI 1986/1925, r 6.10(2), (2A) (r 6.10(2) substituted, and r 6.10(2A)
     added, by SI 2004/584).
8   Ie under the Insolvency Act 1986 Pt 8 (ss 252–263G): see PARA 43 et seq.
9   As to the supervisor of a voluntary arrangement see PARA 73 et seq.
10   Insolvency Rules 1986, SI 1986/1925, r 6.10(3) (amended by SI 1987/1919; and SI 2010/686).
11   Insolvency Rules 1986, SI 1986/1925, r 6.10(3).
12   Insolvency Rules 1986, SI 1986/1925, r 6.10(4).
13   As to the meaning of 'venue' see PARA 46 note 22.
14   Insolvency Rules 1986, SI 1986/1925, r 6.10(5).
15   Ie under the Insolvency Act 1986 s 297(5): see PARA 320.
16   As to the meaning of 'business day' see PARA 28 note 8.
17   Insolvency Rules 1986, SI 1986/1925, r 6.10(6) (added by SI 1987/1919; and amended by
     SI 2010/686).

168.   Deposit payable on presentation of petition. Where a bankruptcy
petition is presented the appropriate deposit[1] is payable by the petitioner and the
deposit is security for the payment of the relevant fees[2] and is to be used to
discharge those fees to the extent that the relevant assets[3] are insufficient for that
purpose[4].

Where a deposit is paid to the court, the court must[5] transmit the deposit paid
to the official receiver[6] attached to the court[7].

A deposit must be repaid to the person who made it in a case where a petition
is dismissed or withdrawn[8] except in the case of a bankruptcy petition where it is
required to pay any fees[9] to an insolvency practitioner[10].

In any case where a bankruptcy order[11] is made (including any case where the
order is subsequently annulled, rescinded or recalled), any deposit made must be
returned to the person who made it save to the extent that the relevant assets are
insufficient to discharge the fees for which the deposit is security[12].

1   The appropriate deposit is: (1) in relation to a bankruptcy petition presented under the
     Insolvency Act 1986 s 264(1)(b) (see PARA 130 head (2)), £525; and (2) in relation to a
     bankruptcy petition presented under s 264(1)(a), (ba), (bb), (c) or (d) (see PARA 130 heads
     (1), (3)–(6)), £700: Insolvency Proceedings (Fees) Order 2004, SI 2004/593, art 6(1) (amended
     by SI 2005/544; and SI 2011/1167). See also PARA 165 note 7 head (7).
2   'Relevant fees' means fee B1 together with any fees payable under the Insolvency Act 1986 s 273
     (see PARA 203): Insolvency Proceedings (Fees) Order 2004, SI 2004/593, art 6(1), Sch 2 para 2
     (amended by SI 2007/521). Where a court appoints an insolvency practitioner under the
     Insolvency Act 1986 s 273(2) to prepare and submit a report under s 274 the court must, on
     submission of the report, pay to the practitioner a fee of £450 (that sum being inclusive of value
     added tax): Insolvency Proceedings (Fees) Order 2004, SI 2004/593, art 5 (amended by
     SI 2010/732).
3   'Relevant assets' means the assets comprised in the estate of the bankrupt: Insolvency
     Proceedings (Fees) Order 2004, SI 2004/593, art 6(1).
4   Insolvency Proceedings (Fees) Order 2004, SI 2004/593, art 6(2) (amended by SI 2005/544).
5   Ie except to the extent that a fee is payable to an insolvency practitioner by virtue of the
     Insolvency Proceedings (Fees) Order 2004, SI 2004/593, art 5 (see note 2).
6   As to the official receiver see PARA 35 et seq.
7   Insolvency Proceedings (Fees) Order 2004, SI 2004/593, art 6(3).
8   As to the withdrawal of a bankruptcy petition see PARA 187.
9   Ie any fees arising under the Insolvency Proceedings (Fees) Order 2004, SI 2004/593, art 5 (see
     note 2).
10   Insolvency Proceedings (Fees) Order 2004, SI 2004/593, art 6(4).
11   As to bankruptcy orders see PARA 198 et seq.
12   Insolvency Proceedings (Fees) Order 2004, SI 2004/593, art 6(5). As to the prescribed order of
     priority of payment of costs etc of the bankruptcy, including the deposit, see PARA 590.

169.   Verification of petition. The petition must be verified by a statement of truth[1]; and, if the petition is in respect of debts[2] to different creditors, the debts to each creditor must be separately verified[3].

A statement of truth which is not contained in or endorsed upon the petition which it verifies must be sufficient to identify the petition and must specify the name of the debtor, the name of the petitioner and the court in which the petition is to be presented[4].

The statement of truth must be authenticated:

(1)   by the petitioner (or if there are two or more petitioners, any one of them);

(2)   by some person such as a director, company secretary or similar company officer, or a solicitor, who has been concerned in the matters giving rise to the presentation of the petition; or

(3)   by some responsible person who is duly authorised to authenticate the statement of truth and has the requisite knowledge of those matters[5].

Where the person authenticating the statement of truth is not the petitioner himself, or one of the petitioners, he must in the statement of truth identify himself and state the capacity in which, and the authority by which, he authenticates it, and the means of his knowledge of the matters verified in the statement of truth[6].

If the petition is based on a statutory demand[7], and more than four months have elapsed between the service of the demand and the presentation of the petition, the petition must include a statement explaining the reasons for the delay[8].

1   Insolvency Rules 1986, SI 1986/1925, r 6.12(1) (amended by SI 2010/686). As to the meaning of 'statement of truth' see PARA 161 note 7. For the prescribed form of statement of truth see the Insolvency Rules 1986, SI 1986/1925, Sch 4 Form 6.13A (added by SI 2010/686).
2   As to the meaning of 'the debt' see PARA 164 note 3.
3   Insolvency Rules 1986, SI 1986/1925, r 6.12(2).
4   Insolvency Rules 1986, SI 1986/1925, r 6.12(3A) (added by SI 2010/686).
5   Insolvency Rules 1986, SI 1986/1925, r 6.12(4) (amended by SI 2010/686).
6   Insolvency Rules 1986, SI 1986/1925, r 6.12(5) (amended by SI 2010/686).
7   As to statutory demands see PARA 158 et seq.
8   Insolvency Rules 1986, SI 1986/1925, r 6.12(7) (amended by SI 2010/686). As to the court's approach in dealing with unfairness caused by the late presentation of a petition see *Dunbar Assets plc v Fowler* [2013] BPIR 46, [2013] All ER (D) 02 (Jan).

170.   Proof of service of statutory demand. Where[1] the petition is required to be preceded by a statutory demand, there must be filed in court[2], with the petition, a certificate or certificates proving service of the demand[3]. Every certificate must be verified by a statement of truth[4] and have attached to it a copy of the demand as served[5].

If the demand has been served personally on the debtor, the certificate must be authenticated by the person who effected that service[6]. If service of the demand, however effected, has been acknowledged in writing either by the debtor himself, or by some person stating himself in the acknowledgment to be authorised to accept service on the debtor's behalf, the certificate must be authenticated either by the creditor or by a person acting on his behalf, and the acknowledgment of service must be exhibited to the certificate[7]. If neither of the above provisions applies, the certificate or certificates must be authenticated by a person or persons having direct personal knowledge of the means adopted for serving the statutory demand, and must:

(1) give particulars of the steps which have been taken[8] with a view to serving the demand personally; and

(2) state the means whereby, those steps having been ineffective, it was sought to bring the demand to the debtor's attention; and

(3) specify a date[9] by which, to the best of the knowledge, information and belief of the person authenticating the certificate, the demand will have come to the debtor's attention[10].

Where the creditor has taken advantage of the statutory provisions allowing advertisement of the demand[11], the certificate must be authenticated either by the creditor himself or by a person having direct personal knowledge of the circumstances; and there must be specified in the certificate the means of the creditor's knowledge or, as the case may be, belief so required, and the method by which, and the date or dates on which the statutory demand was advertised[12]. There must be exhibited to the certificate either a copy of any advertisement of the statutory demand or, where this is not reasonably practicable, the certificate must contain or attach a description of the contents of any such advertisement of the statutory demand[13].

The court may decline to file the petition if not satisfied that the creditor has discharged the obligation imposed on him by the statutory requirements[14] as to service[15].

1 Ie under the Insolvency Act 1986 s 268: see PARA 133.
2 As to the meaning of 'file in court' see PARA 57 note 13.
3 Insolvency Rules 1986, SI 1986/1925, r 6.11(1) (amended by SI 2010/686).
4 As to the meaning of 'statement of truth' see PARA 161 note 7.
5 Insolvency Rules 1986, SI 1986/1925, r 6.11(2) (amended by SI 1987/1919; and SI 2010/686).
6 Insolvency Rules 1986, SI 1986/1925, r 6.11(3) (amended by SI 2010/686). For the prescribed form of certificate of service of statutory demand see the Insolvency Rules 1986, SI 1986/1925, Sch 4 Form 6.11 (substituted by SI 1987/1919; and amended by SI 2010/686). See also *Practice Direction—Insolvency Proceedings* para 13.3.4; and PARA 160.
   For the purposes of a demand made by the Financial Conduct Authority or the Prudential Regulation Authority under the Financial Services and Markets Act 2000 s 372(4)(a) (see FINANCIAL SERVICES AND INSTITUTIONS vol 48 (2008) PARA 501), the Insolvency Rules 1986, SI 1986/1925, r 6.11 applies as if references to the debtor were references to an individual, and references to the creditor were references to the relevant Authority: Bankruptcy (Financial Services and Markets Act 2000) Rules 2001, SI 2001/3634, rr 2, 6(1) (r 2 amended by SI 2013/472). As to the meaning of 'individual' for these purposes see PARA 158 note 1.
7 Insolvency Rules 1986, SI 1986/1925, r 6.11(4) (amended by SI 2010/686).
8 The steps of which particulars are given for the purposes of the Insolvency Rules 1986, SI 1986/1925, r 6.11(5)(a) must be such as would have sufficed to justify an order for substituted service of a petition: r 6.11(6). As to substituted service see PARA 175.
9 If the certificate specifies a date for the purposes of compliance with the Insolvency Rules 1986, SI 1986/1925, r 6.11(5)(c), then, unless the court otherwise orders, that date is deemed for the purposes of the Insolvency Rules 1986, SI 1986/1925, to have been the date on which the statutory demand was served on the debtor: r 6.11(7) (amended by SI 2010/686).
10 Insolvency Rules 1986, SI 1986/1925, r 6.11(5) (amended by SI 1987/1919; and SI 2010/686). For the prescribed form of certificate of substituted service of statutory demand see the Insolvency Rules 1986, SI 1986/1925, Sch 4 Form 6.12 (amended by SI 2009/642; and SI 2010/686).
11 Ie under the Insolvency Rules 1986, SI 1986/1925, r 6.3(3): see PARA 160.
12 Insolvency Rules 1986, SI 1986/1925, r 6.11(8) (amended by SI 2009/642; and SI 2010/686). See also PARA 165 note 7 head (5).
13 Insolvency Rules 1986, SI 1986/1925, r 6.11(8) (as so amended).
14 Ie by the Insolvency Rules 1986, SI 1986/1925, r 6.3(2): see PARA 160.
15 Insolvency Rules 1986, SI 1986/1925, r 6.11(9). This a matter for the judge to decide on the facts of each case, although the test of the steps required to be taken by a petitioning creditor is a high one: *Regional Collection Services Ltd v Heald* [2000] BPIR 661, CA.

171. Notice to the Chief Land Registrar. When the petition is filed, the court must as soon as reasonably practicable send to the Chief Land Registrar notice of the petition together with a request that it may be registered in the register of pending actions[1].

1   Insolvency Rules 1986, SI 1986/1919, r 6.13 (amended by SI 2009/642). For the prescribed form of application for registration see the Insolvency Rules 1986, SI 1986/1925, Sch 4 Form 6.14 (substituted by SI 1987/1919; and amended by SI 2010/686). A failure to comply with the Insolvency Rules 1986, SI 1986/1925, r 6.13 is not actionable, whether as a breach of statutory duty or at common law: *Poulton's trustee in bankruptcy v Ministry of Justice* [2010] EWCA Civ 392, [2011] Ch 1, [2010] 4 All ER 600. On a sale of land by the bankrupt to a bona fide purchaser at a time when no bankruptcy restriction appears on the Register, even where the purchaser seeks to register his title after the bankruptcy restriction has been entered, the rights of the trustee in bankruptcy are avoided: *Pick v Chief Land Registrar* [2011] EWHC 206 (Ch), [2012] Ch 564, [2012] 3 WLR 3.

172. Security for costs. Where the debt[1] in respect of which the petition is presented is for a liquidated sum payable at some future time[2], it being claimed in the petition that the debtor appears to have no reasonable prospect of being able to pay it, the petitioning creditor may, on the debtor's application, be ordered to give security for the debtor's costs[3]. The nature and amount of the security to be ordered is in the court's discretion[4]; and, if an order is so made, there is to be no hearing of the petition until the whole amount of the security has been given[5].

1   As to the meaning of 'the debt' see PARA 164 note 3.
2   Ie under the Insolvency Act 1986 s 268(2): see PARA 133.
3   Insolvency Rules 1986, SI 1986/1925, r 6.17(1), (2). The general rules relating to costs (see CPR Pts 44, 47; and CIVIL PROCEDURE vol 12 (2009) PARA 1734 et seq) also apply: see the Insolvency Rules 1986, SI 1986/1925, r 7.51A(1) (added by SI 2010/686); and PARA 776.
4   Insolvency Rules 1986, SI 1986/1925, r 6.17(3). A solicitor's undertaking may be accepted by way of security for costs in lieu of a bond: *A Ltd v B Ltd* [1996] 1 WLR 665.
5   Insolvency Rules 1986, SI 1986/1925, r 6.17(4).

173. Amendment of petition. With the permission of the court, given on such terms, if any, as the court thinks just to impose, the petition may be amended at any time after presentation[1].

1   Insolvency Rules 1986, SI 1986/1925, r 6.22 (amended by SI 2010/686). As to the meaning of 'the debt' see PARA 164 note 3.

174. Consolidation of petitions. Where two or more bankruptcy petitions are presented against the same debtor, the court may order the consolidation of the proceedings, on such terms as it thinks just[1].

1   Insolvency Rules 1986, SI 1986/1925, r 6.236 (amended by SI 2010/686).

D. SERVICE OF THE PETITION

175. Service of the petition. The petition must be served personally on the debtor by an officer of the court, or by the petitioning creditor or his solicitor[1], or by a person instructed by the creditor or his solicitor for the purpose; and service must be effected by delivering to him a sealed copy of the petition[2]. If the court is satisfied by a witness statement[3] or other evidence on oath that prompt personal service cannot be effected because the debtor is keeping out of the way to avoid service of the petition or other legal process, or for any other cause, it may order substituted service to be effected in such manner as it thinks just[4].

Where an order for substituted service has been carried out, the petition is deemed duly served on the debtor[5]. If to the petitioner's knowledge there is in force for the debtor a voluntary arrangement under Part 8 of the Insolvency Act 1986[6], and the petitioner is not himself the supervisor of the arrangement, a copy of the petition must be sent by him to the supervisor[7].

If to the petitioner's knowledge, there is a member state liquidator[8] appointed in main proceedings[9] in relation to the bankrupt, a copy of the petition must be sent by him to the member state liquidator[10].

A bankruptcy petition may, with the permission of the court, be served outside England and Wales in such manner as the court may direct[11].

1 For these purposes, the reference to a solicitor includes a reference to a body recognised by the Law Society under the Administration of Justice Act 1985 s 9 (see LEGAL PROFESSIONS vol 65 (2008) PARA 515): Solicitors' Recognised Bodies Order 1991, SI 1991/2684, arts 2(1), 3, 4(a), 5, Sch 1 (amended by SI 2009/500).

2 Insolvency Rules 1986, SI 1986/1925, r 6.14(1).

3 As to the meaning of 'witness statement' see PARA 161 note 7.

4 Insolvency Rules 1986, SI 1986/1925, r 6.14(2) (amended by SI 2010/686). *Practice Direction—Insolvency Proceedings* para 13.3.4 states that in most cases, evidence of the following steps will suffice to justify making an order for substituted service:

   (1)   one personal call at the residence and place of business of the debtor where both are known or at either of such places as is known; where it is known that the debtor has more than one residential or business address, personal calls should be made at all the addresses;

   (2)   should the creditor fail to effect personal service, a first-class prepaid letter should be written to the debtor referring to the call(s), the purpose of the same and the failure to meet with the debtor, adding that a further call will be made for the same purpose at a specified time, date and place; at least two business days' notice should be given of the appointment and copies of the letter sent to all known addresses of the debtor; the appointment letter should also state that:

      (a)   in the event of the time and place not being convenient, the debtor should propose some other time and place reasonably convenient for the purpose;

      (b)   if the debtor fails to keep the appointment, application will be made to the court for an order for substituted service either by advertisement, or in such other manner as the court may think fit;

   (3)   when attending any appointment made by letter, inquiry should be made as to whether the debtor has received all letters left for him; if the debtor is away, inquiry should also be made as to whether or not letters are being forwarded to an address within the jurisdiction (England and Wales) or elsewhere;

   (4)   if the debtor is represented by a solicitor, an attempt should be made to arrange an appointment for personal service through such solicitor;

   (5)   the written evidence filed pursuant to the Insolvency Rules 1986, SI 1986/1925, r 6.11 (see PARA 170) should deal with all the above matters including all relevant facts as to the debtor's whereabouts and whether the appointment letter(s) have been returned.

5 Insolvency Rules 1986, SI 1986/1925, r 6.14(3). Where the court makes an order for service by first-class ordinary post, the order will normally provide that service be deemed to be effected on the seventh day after posting: *Practice Direction—Insolvency Proceedings* para 11.5. For the prescribed forms of order for substituted service and notice in the London Gazette see the Insolvency Rules 1986, SI 1986/1925, Sch 4 Forms 6.15A, 6.16 respectively (Form 6.15A added by SI 2010/686). As to the meaning of 'the Gazette' see PARA 165 note 12.

6 Ie under the Insolvency Act 1986 Pt 8 (ss 252–263G): see PARA 43 et seq.

7 Insolvency Rules 1986, SI 1986/1925, r 6.14(4) (added by SI 1987/1919).

8 'Member state liquidator' means a person falling within the definition of liquidator in Council Regulation (EC) 1346/2000 (OJ L160, 30.6.2000, p 1) ('European Regulation on Insolvency Proceedings'), art 2(b) (see PARA 41 note 7) appointed in proceedings to which it applies in a member state other than the United Kingdom: Insolvency Rules 1986, SI 1986/1925, r 13.13(11) (added by SI 2002/1307).

9 'Main proceedings' means proceedings opened in accordance with the European Regulation on Insolvency Proceedings art 3(1) and falling within the definition of insolvency proceedings in art 2(a) (see PARA 41 text to notes 8–12) and: (1) in relation to England and Wales set out in Annex A under the heading 'United Kingdom'; and (2) in relation to another member state, set

out in Annex A under the heading relating to that member state: Insolvency Rules 1986, SI 1986/1925, r 13.13(10) (added by SI 2002/1307).

10 Insolvency Rules 1986, SI 1986/1925, r 6.14(5) (added by SI 2002/1307). See further PARA 42.

11 Insolvency Rules 1986, SI 1986/1925, r 6.14(6) (added by SI 2010/686).

176.   Proof of service. Service of the petition must be proved by a certificate of service[1]. The certificate of service must be sufficient to identify the petition served and must specify:

(1)   the name of the debtor;

(2)   the name of the petitioner;

(3)   the court in which the petition was filed and the court reference number;

(4)   the date of the petition;

(5)   whether the copy served was a sealed copy;

(6)   the date on which service was effected; and

(7)   the manner in which service was effected[2].

Where substituted service has been ordered, the certificate of service must have attached to it a sealed copy of the order[3].

The certificate of service must be filed in court[4] as soon as reasonably practicable after service, and in any event not less than five business days[5] before the hearing of the petition[6].

1   Insolvency Rules 1986, SI 1986/1925, r 6.15A(1) (r 6.15A added by SI 2010/686). A 'certificate of service' means a certificate of service verified by a statement of truth: Insolvency Rules 1986, SI 1986/1925, r 13.13(16) (added by SI 2010/686). For the prescribed forms of certificate see Sch 4 Form 6.17A (certificate of personal service of bankruptcy petition), Sch 4 Form 6.18A (certificate of substituted service of bankruptcy petition) (both added by SI 2010/686). As to the importance of following the provisions as to service in view of the serious consequences of bankruptcy see *Re Awan* [2000] BPIR 241 (a decision under the former rules as to service).

2   Insolvency Rules 1986, SI 1986/1925, r 6.15A(2) (as added: see note 1).

3   Insolvency Rules 1986, SI 1986/1925, r 6.15A(3) (as added: see note 1).

4   As to the meaning of 'file in court' see PARA 57 note 13.

5   As to the meaning of 'business day' see PARA 28 note 8.

6   Insolvency Rules 1986, SI 1986/1925, r 6.15(4) (as added: see note 1).

177.   Death of debtor before service. If the debtor dies before service of the petition, the court may order service to be effected on his personal representatives, or on such other persons as it thinks just[1].

1   Insolvency Rules 1986, SI 1986/1925, r 6.16 (amended by SI 2010/686). As to the position where a debtor dies after service but before the hearing of the petition see *Berti v Steele Raymond (a firm)* [2001] EWCA Civ 2079, [2002] BPIR 683.

E. HEARING OF THE PETITION

178.   Date of hearing. The petition may not be heard until at least 14 days have elapsed since it was served on the debtor[1]. The court may, however, on such terms as it thinks just, hear the petition at an earlier date, if it appears that the debtor has absconded, or the court is satisfied that it is a proper case for an expedited hearing, or the debtor consents to a hearing within the 14 days[2].

Any of the following may appear and be heard, that is to say, the petitioning creditor, the debtor, the supervisor of any voluntary arrangement under Part 8 of the Insolvency Act 1986[3] in force for the debtor and any creditor who has given notice[4] of his intention to appear[5].

1   Insolvency Rules 1986, SI 1986/1925, r 6.18(1). As to service of the bankruptcy petition see PARAS 175–177.

2   Insolvency Rules 1986, SI 1986/1925, r 6.18(2) (amended by SI 2010/686).

3 Ie under the Insolvency Act 1986 Pt 8 (ss 252–263G): see PARA 43 et seq.
4 Ie under the Insolvency Rules 1986, SI 1986/1925, r 6.23: see PARA 180.
5 Insolvency Rules 1986, SI 1986/1925, r 6.18(3) (amended by SI 1987/1919).

179. Petition opposed by debtor. Where the debtor intends to oppose the petition, he must, not later than five business days[1] before the day fixed for the hearing, file in court[2] a notice specifying the grounds on which he will object to the making of a bankruptcy order and send a copy of the notice to the petitioning creditor or his solicitor[3].

1 As to the meaning of 'business day' see PARA 28 note 8.
2 As to the meaning of 'file in court' see PARA 57 note 13.
3 Insolvency Rules 1986, SI 1986/1925, r 6.21 (amended by SI 2010/686). For the prescribed form of notice of intention to oppose see the Insolvency Rules 1986, SI 1986/1925, Sch 4 Form 6.19. For these purposes, the reference to a solicitor includes a reference to a body recognised by the Law Society under the Administration of Justice Act 1985 s 9 (see LEGAL PROFESSIONS vol 65 (2008) PARA 515): Solicitors' Recognised Bodies Order 1991, SI 1991/2684, arts 2(1), 3, 4(a), 5, Sch 1 (amended by SI 2009/500).

180. Notice by persons intending to appear. Every creditor who intends to appear on the hearing of the petition must give to the petitioning creditor notice of his intention to do so[1]. The notice must specify:

(1) the name and address of the person giving it, and any telephone number and reference which may be required for communication with him or with any other person, to be also specified in the notice, authorised to speak or act on his behalf;

(2) whether his intention is to support or oppose the petition; and

(3) the amount and nature of his debt[2].

The notice must be sent so as to reach the addressee not later than 16.00 hours on the business day[3] before that which is appointed for the hearing, or, where the hearing has been adjourned, for the adjourned hearing[4].

A person failing to comply with the above provisions may appear on the hearing of the petition only with the permission of the court[5].

1 Insolvency Rules 1986, SI 1986/1925, r 6.23(1). For the prescribed form of notice of intention to appear see Sch 4 Form 6.20. As to the petitioning creditor's duty to prepare for the court a list of the creditors who have given notice under r 6.23 see PARA 181.
2 Insolvency Rules 1986, SI 1986/1925, r 6.23(2). As to the meaning of 'the debt' see PARA 164 note 3.
3 As to the meaning of 'business day' see PARA 28 note 8.
4 Insolvency Rules 1986, SI 1986/1925, r 6.23(3).
5 Insolvency Rules 1986, SI 1986/1925, r 6.23(4) (amended by SI 2010/686).

181. List of appearances. The petitioning creditor must prepare for the court a list of the creditors, if any, who have given notice of their intention to appear[1], specifying their names and addresses and, if known to him, their respective solicitors[2]. Against the name of each creditor in the list it must be stated whether his intention is to support the petition, or to oppose it[3]. On the day appointed for the hearing of the petition, a copy of the list must be handed to the court before the commencement of the hearing[4]; and, if any creditor is given permission to appear[5], the petitioner must add to the list the same particulars in respect of the person to whom permission has been given[6].

1 Ie under the Insolvency Rules 1986, SI 1986/1925, r 6.23: see PARA 180.
2 Insolvency Rules 1986, SI 1986/1925, r 6.24(1). For the prescribed form of list see Sch 4 Form 6.21. For these purposes, the reference to a solicitor includes a reference to a body recognised by

the Law Society under the Administration of Justice Act 1985 s 9 (see LEGAL PROFESSIONS vol 65 (2008) PARA 515): Solicitors' Recognised Bodies Order 1991, SI 1991/2684, arts 2(1), 3, 4(a), 5, Sch 1 (amended by SI 2009/500).

3   Insolvency Rules 1986, SI 1986/1925, r 6.24(2).

4   Insolvency Rules 1986, SI 1986/1925, r 6.24(3).

5   Ie under the Insolvency Rules 1986, SI 1986/1925, r 6.23(4): see PARA 180.

6   Insolvency Rules 1986, SI 1986/1925, r 6.24(4) (amended by SI 2010/686).

182.   Non-appearance of creditor.   If the petitioning creditor fails to appear on the hearing of the petition, no subsequent petition against the same debtor, either alone or jointly with any other person, may be presented by the same creditor in respect of the same debt, without the permission of the court to which the previous petition was presented[1].

1   Insolvency Rules 1986, SI 1986/1925, r 6.26 (amended by SI 2010/686). As to the principles to be applied in considering the exercise of the discretion given by the Insolvency Rules 1986, SI 1986/1925, r 6.26 see *Omgate Ltd v Gordon* [2001] BPIR 909, [2001] All ER (D) 83 (Apr) (permission may be granted retrospectively).

183.   Extension of time for hearing.   The petitioning creditor may, if the petition has not been served, apply to the court to appoint another venue[1] for the hearing; and the application must state the reasons why the petition has not been served[2]. No costs occasioned by the application may be allowed in the proceedings except by order of the court[3]. If the court appoints another day for the hearing, the petitioning creditor must as soon as reasonably practicable notify any creditor who has given notice[4] of his intention to appear[5].

1   As to the meaning of 'venue' see PARA 46 note 22.

2   Insolvency Rules 1986, SI 1986/1925, r 6.28(1), (2). All applications for an extension should include a statement of the date fixed for the hearing of the petition: *Practice Direction—Insolvency Proceedings* para 14.6.2. The petitioning creditor should attend, by solicitors or in person, on or before the hearing date to ascertain whether the application has reached the file and been dealt with; and it should not be assumed that an extension will be granted: para 14.6.3.

    Late applications for extension of hearing dates, and failure to attend on the listed hearing of a petition, will be dealt with as follows (para 14.6.1):

    (1)   if an application is submitted less than two clear working days before the hearing date (eg later than Monday for Thursday, or Wednesday for Monday), the costs of the application will not be allowed under the Insolvency Rules 1986, SI 1986/1925, r 6.28(3);

    (2)   if the petition has not been served and no extension has been granted by the time fixed for the hearing of the petition, and if no one attends for the hearing, the petition may be dismissed or relisted for hearing about 21 days later; the court will notify the petitioning creditor's solicitors (or the petitioning creditor in person) and any known supporting or opposing creditors or their solicitors of the new date and times; written evidence should be filed on behalf of the petitioning creditor explaining fully the reasons for the failure to apply for an extension or to appear at the hearing, and (if appropriate) giving reasons why the petition should not be dismissed;

    (3)   on the relisted hearing the court may dismiss the petition if not satisfied it should be adjourned or a further extension granted.

3   Insolvency Rules 1986, SI 1986/1925, r 6.28(3).

4   Ie under the Insolvency Rules 1986, SI 1986/1925, r 6.23: see PARA 180.

5   Insolvency Rules 1986, SI 1986/1925, r 6.28(4) (amended by SI 2009/642).

184.   Adjournment.   If the court adjourns[1] the hearing of the petition, then, unless the court otherwise directs, the petitioning creditor must as soon as reasonably practicable send to the debtor and, where any creditor has given notice of his intention to appear[2] but was not present at the hearing, to him, notice of the making of the order of adjournment; and the notice must state the venue[3] for the adjourned hearing[4].

1   The power to grant an adjournment is a matter for the discretion of the court and will be exercised if the making of an immediate bankruptcy order would cause injustice to the debtor: *IRC v Lee-Phipps* [2003] BPIR 803, [2003] All ER (D) 107 (Feb). However, the general principle is that a petitioning creditor is entitled to be paid his debt in full on the hearing of the petition unless there is a reasonable prospect of his being paid within a short period of time: *Re Gilmartin (a bankrupt), ex p Bankrupt v International Agency and Supply Ltd* [1989] 2 All ER 835, sub nom *Re Gilmartin (a bankrupt)* [1989] 1 WLR 513; *Dickins v Inland Revenue* [2004] EWHC 852 (Ch), [2004] BPIR 718, [2004] All ER (D) 122 (Apr); *Nottingham City Council v Pennant* [2009] EWHC 2437 (Ch), [2009] RVR 348, [2010] BPIR 430. Thus, on the hearing of a petition, the court should not grant repeated adjournments as a matter of course: *Re Heyl, ex p DP Morgan Ltd* [1918] 1 KB 452, CA. In particular, the practice of granting repeated adjournments of the petition to enable the debtor to repay his debts by instalments but where there is no prospect of payment in full within a reasonable time has been disapproved by the courts: *Re A Debtor (No 26 of 1983), Re A Debtor (No 72 of 1982)* [1984] 2 All ER 257, sub nom *Re A Debtor (No 72 of 1982), ex p Mumford Leasing Ltd v Debtor, Re A Debtor (No 26 of 1983), ex p Drygrass Ltd v Debtor* [1984] 1 WLR 1143, DC; *Judd v Williams* [1998] BPIR 88. As to adjournments in the light of medical evidence see *Levy v Ellis-Carr* [2012] EWHC 63 (Ch), [2012] BPIR 347, [2012] All ER (D) 196 (Jan). As to adjournments to enable the debtor to be legally registered see *Henry Butcher International Ltd v KG Engineering (a partnership)* [2004] EWCA Civ 1597, [2006] BPIR 60, 148 Sol Jo LB 1282. See also *De Louville De Toucy v Bonhams 1793 Ltd* [2011] EWHC 3809 (Ch), [2012] BPIR 793, [2011] All ER (D) 32 (Nov) (evidence that debtor suffering from mental incapacity).
2   Ie under the Insolvency Rules 1986, SI 1986/1925, r 6.23: see PARA 180.
3   As to the meaning of 'venue' see PARA 46 note 22.
4   Insolvency Rules 1986, SI 1986/1925, r 6.29 (amended by SI 2009/642). For the prescribed form of order see the Insolvency Rules 1986, SI 1986/1925, Sch 4 Form 6.23.

185. Substitution of petitioner. Where a creditor petitions and is subsequently found not entitled to do so, or where the petitioner:

(1)   consents to withdraw his petition or to allow it to be dismissed, or consents to an adjournment, or fails to appear in support of his petition when it is called on in court on the day originally fixed for the hearing, or on a day to which it is adjourned; or

(2)   appears, but does not apply for an order in the terms of the prayer of his petition,

the court may, on such terms as it thinks just, order that there be substituted as petitioner any creditor who:

(a)   has given notice[1] of his intention to appear at the hearing;

(b)   is desirous of prosecuting the petition; and

(c)   was, at the date on which the petition was presented, in such a position in relation to the debtor as would have enabled him, the creditor, on that date to present a bankruptcy petition in respect of a debt[2] or debts owed to him by the debtor (or in the case of the member state liquidator[3], owed to creditors in proceedings in relation to which he holds office), the statutory provisions[4] being satisfied in respect of that debt or those debts[5].

1   Ie under the Insolvency Rules 1986, SI 1986/1925, r 6.23: see PARA 180.
2   As to the meaning of 'the debt' see PARA 164 note 3.
3   As to the meaning of 'member state liquidator' see PARA 175 note 8.
4   Ie the Insolvency Act 1986 s 267(2)(a)–(d): see PARA 132 heads (1)–(4).
5   Insolvency Rules 1986, SI 1986/1925, r 6.30(1), (2) (amended by SI 2002/1307). For the prescribed form of order for the substitution of the petitioner on a creditor's petition see Sch 4 Form 6.24A (added by SI 1987/1919; and substituted by SI 2005/527). Substitution will be

ordered where the petitioner has assigned a judgment debt after presentation of a petition: *Re Strongmaster Ltd* [2002] EWHC 444 (Ch), [2002] BPIR 1259, [2002] All ER (D) 157 (Mar).

186. Change of carriage of petition. On the hearing of the petition, any person who claims to be a creditor of the debtor, and who has given notice[1] of his intention to appear at the hearing, may apply to the court for an order giving him carriage of the petition in place of the petitioning creditor, but without requiring any amendment of the petition[2].

The court may, on such terms as it thinks just, make a change of carriage order if satisfied that:

(1)   the applicant is an unpaid and unsecured creditor[3] of the debtor; and

(2)   the petitioning creditor either intends by any means to secure the postponement, adjournment or withdrawal of the petition, or does not intend to prosecute the petition, either diligently or at all[4].

The court must not make the order if satisfied that the petitioning creditor's debt[5] has been paid, secured or compounded for by means of:

(a)   a disposition of property made by some person other than the debtor; or

(b)   a disposition of the debtor's own property made with the approval of, or ratified by, the court[6].

A change of carriage order may be made whether or not the petitioning creditor appears at the hearing[7]; and, if the order is made, the person given the carriage of the petition is entitled to rely on all evidence previously adduced in the proceedings[8].

1   Ie under the Insolvency Rules 1986, SI 1986/1925, r 6.23: see PARA 180.

2   Insolvency Rules 1986, SI 1986/1925, r 6.31(1).

3   As to secured creditors see PARA 574 et seq.

4   Insolvency Rules 1986, SI 1986/1925, r 6.31(2). For the prescribed form of change of carriage order see Sch 4 Form 6.24B (added by SI 1987/1919).

5   As to the meaning of 'the debt' see PARA 164 note 3.

6   Insolvency Rules 1986, SI 1986/1925, r 6.31(3). Any such payment must be unconditional in the sense that it is not liable to be avoided under the provisions of the Insolvency Act 1986 in the event that a bankruptcy order is made: *Smith (a bankrupt) v Ian Simpson & Co (a firm)* [2001] Ch 239, [2000] 3 All ER 434, CA; and see PARA 198. As to the power of the court to approve or ratify a disposition of the debtor's own property see the Insolvency Act 1986 s 284; and PARA 213.

7   Insolvency Rules 1986, SI 1986/1925, r 6.31(4).

8   Insolvency Rules 1986, SI 1986/1925, r 6.31(5) (amended by SI 2010/686).

187. Petitioner seeking dismissal or permission to withdraw. Where the petitioner applies to the court for the petition to be dismissed, or for permission to withdraw it, he must, in any case where: (1) a creditor of the debtor has given notice[1] of intention to appear at the hearing of the petition; or (2) the court so orders, file with the court[2] a witness statement[3] specifying the grounds of the application and the circumstances in which it is made[4]. If, since the petition was filed, any payment has been made to the petitioner by way of settlement, in whole or in part, of the debt or debts in respect of which the petition was brought, or any arrangement has been entered into for securing or compounding it or them, the witness statement must also state:

(1)   what dispositions of property have been made for the purposes of the settlement or arrangement;

(2)   whether, in the case of any disposition, it was property of the debtor himself, or of some other person; and

(3)   whether, if it was property of the debtor, the disposition was made with the approval of, or has been ratified by, the court, and if so, specifying the relevant court order[5].

No order giving permission to withdraw a petition may be given before the petition is heard[6].

1   Ie under the Insolvency Rules 1986, SI 1986/1925, r 6.23: see PARA 180.
2   As to the meaning of 'file with the court' see PARA 57 note 13.
3   As to the meaning of 'witness statement' see PARA 161 note 7.
4   Insolvency Rules 1986, SI 1986/1925, r 6.32(1) (substituted by SI 2010/686). The court will then exercise its judgment on the same as to the propriety of permitting the withdrawal: *Re Bebro* [1900] 2 QB 316, CA.
5   Insolvency Rules 1986, SI 1986/1925, r 6.32(2) (amended by SI 2010/686). Where a petition is withdrawn or dismissed after payment of the petition debt, the petitioning creditor will be entitled to an order for the costs unless defects in his proceedings have unreasonably exposed the debtor to costs: *Re A Debtor (No 510 of 1997)* (1998) Times, 18 June.
6   Insolvency Rules 1986, SI 1986/1925, r 6.32(3) (amended by SI 2010/686). For the prescribed form of order see the Insolvency Rules 1986, SI 1986/1925, Sch 4 Form 6.22.

188.   Abuse of process.   A bankruptcy petition may be dismissed where its presentation is an abuse of the process of the court.

Where a petition is founded on a debt to which the petitioning creditor is not properly entitled, it may be dismissed as an abuse of process[1]. This includes the situation where the presentation of a petition amounts to an attempt by the petitioning creditor, through the commencement of bankruptcy proceedings, to obtain the payment of money or other advantages to which he is not properly entitled[2]. Such conduct on the part of the creditor is sometimes termed 'extortion'[3].

Where a petition debt is genuinely disputed by the debtor, the court may find that the presentation of the petition is an abuse of process[4].

If a petition is presented by a creditor, not bona fide with the view of obtaining an adjudication, but for some collateral purpose or with a view to putting pressure on the debtor, it may be dismissed as an abuse of the process of the court[5]. However, the mere fact that the petitioning creditor is actuated by a motive other than a desire to obtain a distribution of the debtor's assets in bankruptcy, for example, by a wish to put an end to a partnership with the debtor, does not constitute an abuse of the process of the court so as to disentitle the petitioning creditor to a bankruptcy order[6]. Where a petition is not presented solely for an ulterior motive and is at least partly for the purpose of seeking to obtain a dividend in the bankruptcy, it will not be treated as an abuse of process of the court[7].

The purchase of a debt in order to found a bankruptcy petition on it does not necessarily constitute an abuse of process[8].

1   In relation to the debts in respect of which a petition may be presented see also PARA 132. As to abuse of process by a debtor presenting his own petition see PARA 197.
2   *Re Majory, A Debtor, ex p Debtor v FA Dumont Ltd* [1955] Ch 600, sub nom *Re A Debtor (No 757 of 1954), ex p Debtor v FA Dumont Ltd (Petitioning Creditor)* [1955] 2 All ER 65, CA. This will include the situation where a creditor attempts to extort money as a condition of his assent to a transaction carried out by the debtor in order to avoid bankruptcy and afterwards presents a petition founded on the same transaction: *Re Shaw, ex p Gill* (1901) 83 LT 754, CA; *Re A Debtor (No 20 of 1904), ex p Debtor* (1904) 91 LT 664 (affd sub nom *Re Goldberg* (1904) 21 LTR 139, CA). See also *Re G, ex p B* (1900) 44 Sol Jo 345, CA; *Re Brindley, ex p Taylor, Sons & Co* [1906] 1 KB 377, CA; *Re A Debtor (No 883 of 1927)* [1928] Ch 199, CA. In the following cases the petitioner's conduct did not amount to extortion: *Re Bebro* [1900] 2 QB 316, CA; *Re Sunderland* [1911] 2 KB 658, CA; *Re Hay* (1913) 110 LT 47, DC; *Re Wilson, ex p Jones* (1916) 85 LJKB 1408, CA.

3   'Extortion', in relation to bankruptcy proceedings, has no special or artificial significance
     divorced from the ordinary implication of the word: *Re Majory, A Debtor, ex p Debtor v FA
     Dumont Ltd* [1955] Ch 600, sub nom *Re A Debtor (No 757 of 1954), ex p Debtor v FA
     Dumont Ltd (Petitioning Creditor)* [1955] 2 All ER 65, CA. However, because bankruptcy
     proceedings can be a potent instrument of oppression, the court will always look strictly at the
     conduct of a creditor who uses or threatens such proceedings, so as to ensure that he has not
     overstepped the recognised limits: *Re A Judgment Summons (No 25 of 1952), ex p Henlys Ltd*
     [1953] Ch 195 at 212, [1953] 1 All ER 424 at 432–433, CA; *Re Majory, A Debtor, ex p Debtor
     v FA Dumont Ltd* [1955] at 622 and 77. It is the court's duty to dismiss a petition which is made
     a means of extorting or attempting to extort money: *Re Atkinson, ex p Atkinson* (1892) 9 Morr
     193, CA; *Re Otway, ex p Otway* [1895] 1 QB 812, CA; *Re Bebro* [1900] 2 QB 316, CA.

4   *Re A Judgment Summons (No 25 of 1952), ex p Henlys Ltd* [1953] Ch 1 at 5, [1952] 2 All ER
     772 at 774; on appeal [1953] Ch 195 at 201–207, [1953] 1 All ER 424 at 426–430, CA per
     Jenkins LJ. The Court of Appeal, however, there held that extortion is not a bar to an order
     under the Debtors Act 1869 s 5 for the committal of the debtor. As to committal orders see PARA
     197 note 4.
          In relation to statutory demands see PARA 162; and in relation to proceedings on a creditor's
     petition see the Insolvency Act 1986 s 271(1) and PARA 198. In relation to the winding up of
     companies see COMPANY AND PARTNERSHIP INSOLVENCY vol 16 (2011) PARA 401.
          Other circumstances where the presentation of a petition may amount to an abuse of process
     include where, after dismissal of a petition presented by a creditor, he joins with another creditor
     in presenting a second petition founded, so far as the first creditor is concerned, on the same
     debt (*Re Leonard, ex p Yeomans and Heap* (1896) 3 Mans 317, CA); or where the petitioner
     has refused part of the debt tendered on his invitation so as to keep the debt above the minimum
     level required for the presentation of a petition (*Re A Debtor (No 883 of 1927)* [1928]
     Ch 199, CA).

5   *Re Davis, ex p King* (1876) 3 ChD 461, CA; *Re Adams, ex p Griffin* (1879) 12 ChD 480, CA;
     Re Baker, ex p Baker (1887) 5 Morr 5.

6   *King v Henderson* [1898] AC 720, PC.

7   *Re Ross (a bankrupt) (No 2)* [2000] BPIR 636, CA.

8   *Re Baker, ex p Baker* (1887) 5 Morr 5; but see *Re Adams, ex p Griffin* (1879) 12 ChD 480, CA.

189.   Malice in presenting petition.   Where a bankruptcy petition has been
presented maliciously and without reasonable and probable cause[1], an action
will, it seems, lie against the petitioning creditor, provided that the petition has
been dismissed or the adjudication annulled[2].

1   A petitioner is entitled to rely on advice from solicitor advising him to issue a formal petition:
     see *Jacob v Vockrodt* [2007] EWHC 2403 (QB), [2007] BPIR 1568.

2   *Farley v Danks* (1855) 4 E & B 493; *Johnson v Emerson and Sparrow* (1871) LR 6 Exch 329
     (cited with approval in *Roy v Prior* [1971] AC 470 at 479, [1970] 2 All ER 729 at 735, HL);
     Whitworth v Hall (1831) 2 B & Ad 695; *Metropolitan Bank Ltd v Pooley* (1885) 10 App Cas
     210, HL; *Jacob v Vockrodt* [2007] EWHC 2403 (QB), [2007] BPIR 1568, [2007] All ER (D)
     166 (Oct). In *Beechey v William Hill (Park Lane) Ltd* [1956] CLY 5442, the plaintiff's action
     failed on the ground that, since the bankruptcy had been annulled on payment of the debts in
     full, the proceedings had not terminated, vis-a-vis the defendants, in the plaintiff's favour. See
     further TORT vol 97 (2010) PARAS 662–663.

190.   Vacating registration on dismissal of petition.   If the petition is dismissed
or withdrawn by permission of the court, an order must be made at the same
time permitting vacation of the registration of the petition as a pending action;
and the court must send to the debtor two sealed copies of the order[1].

1   Insolvency Rules 1986, SI 1986/1925, r 6.27 (amended by SI 2010/686). For the prescribed
     form of order see the Insolvency Rules 1986, SI 1986/1925, Sch 4 Form 6.22. As to the giving of
     notice of the petition to the Chief Land Registrar see r 6.13; and PARA 171.

(ii) Debtor's Petition

191. Court to which petition to be presented. Where the proceedings are allocated to the London insolvency district in relation to a debt relief order[1], the debtor must present the petition to:

(1) the High Court where the unsecured liabilities set out in the statement of affairs attached to the petition total £100,000 or more;

(2) the Central London County Court where the unsecured liabilities set out in the statement of affairs attached to the petition total less than £100,000[2].

Where other proceedings are allocated to the London insolvency district[3], the debtor must present the petition to the High Court[4].

Where the debtor is resident[5] in England and Wales and the proceedings are not allocated to the London insolvency district, the debtor must in most cases present the petition to the debtor's own county court[6]. However, where, for whatever reason, it is not possible for the petition to be presented to the debtor's own county court and the debtor has carried on business[7] in England and Wales within the six months immediately preceding the presentation of the petition[8], the debtor may present the petition, with a view to expediting the presentation of the petition, to the court for the insolvency district in which the debtor resides, or to the nearest appropriate[9] full-time court[10]. Where the debtor has not carried on business in England and Wales within the six months immediately preceding the presentation of the petition, the debtor may present the petition to whichever court is specified as being the nearest full-time court to the county court for the insolvency district where the debtor resided for the longest period during those six months[11].

If the debtor is not resident in England and Wales but was resident or carried on business in England and Wales within the six months immediately preceding the presentation of the petition and the proceedings are not allocated to the London insolvency district, the debtor may present the petition either to the debtor's own county court or to the High Court[12].

Where there is in force for the debtor a voluntary arrangement[13], the petition must be presented to the court to which the nominee's report was submitted[14] or where a nominee has made a report[15], an application has been made[16].

The petition must contain sufficient information to establish that it is presented to the appropriate court[17].

1 Ie under the Insolvency Rules 1986, SI 1986/1925, r 7.10ZA(a)(i)–(iv): see PARA 8.

2 Insolvency Rules 1986, SI 1986/1925, r 6.40A(1) (r 6.40A added by SI 2010/686).

3 Ie under the Insolvency Rules 1986, SI 1986/1925, r 7.10ZA(a)(v) or (c)(ii): see PARA 8.

4 Insolvency Rules 1986, SI 1986/1925, r 6.40A(2) (as added: see note 2).

5 As to the meaning of 'reside' see PARA 131 note 5.

6 Insolvency Rules 1986, SI 1986/1925, r 6.40A(3) (as added: see note 2). For the purposes of r 6.40A, what constitutes the debtor's own county court is to be determined in accordance with r 6.9A(4) (see PARA 164): r 6.40A(5) (as so added). As from a day to be appointed, any reference however expressed that is or is deemed to be a reference to a county court held under the County Courts Act 1984 s 1 is to be read as a reference to the county court established by s A1 of that Act: see the Crime and Courts Act 2013 Sch 9 Pt 2 para 11(1)(a), (3)(c). At the date at which this volume states the law no such day had been appointed.

7 As to the meaning of 'carry on business' see PARA 131 note 6.

8 Ie where the Insolvency Rules 1986, SI 1986/1925, r 6.9A(4)(a) applies: see PARA 164.

9 Ie to whichever court is specified by the Insolvency Rules 1986, SI 1986/1925, Sch 2 as being the nearest full-time court in relation to the court in r 6.9A(4)(a) (see PARA 164), or the court for the insolvency district in which the debtor resides: r 6.40A(6)(a) (as added: see note 2).
10 Insolvency Rules 1986, SI 1986/1925, r 6.40A(6)(a) (as added: see note 2).
11 Insolvency Rules 1986, SI 1986/1925, r 6.40A(6)(b) (as added: see note 2).
12 Insolvency Rules 1986, SI 1986/1925, r 6.40A(4) (as added: see note 2).
13 Ie a voluntary arrangement under the Insolvency Act 1986 Pt 8 (ss 252–263G): see PARA 43 et seq.
14 Ie under the Insolvency Act 1986 s 256 (see PARA 55).
15 Ie under the Insolvency Act 1986 s 256A(3) (see PARA 51).
16 Insolvency Rules 1986, SI 1986/1925, r 6.40A(7) (as added: see note 2). Rule 6.40A(7) is expressed to apply notwithstanding any other provision of r 6.40A except r 6.40A(2).
17 Insolvency Rules 1986, SI 1986/1925, r 6.40A(8) (as added: see note 2). For the prescribed form of bankruptcy petition see Sch 4 Form 6.27 (substituted by SI 2002/1307; and amended by SI 2010/686; and SI 2011/785).

B. CONTENTS OF PETITION

192. Identification of debtor. The petition must state the following matters with respect to the debtor:

(1)   his name, place of residence[1] and occupation, if any;
(2)   the name or names in which he carries on business[2], if other than his true name, and whether, in the case of any business of a specified nature, he carries it on alone or with others;
(3)   the nature of his business and the address or addresses at which he carries it on;
(4)   any name or names, other than his true name, in which he has carried on business in the period in which any of his bankruptcy debts[3] were incurred and, in the case of any such business, whether he has carried it on alone or with others; and
(5)   any address or addresses at which he has resided or carried on business during that period, and the nature of that business[4].

If the debtor has at any time used a name other than one given under head (1) above, that fact must be stated in the petition[5]. The particulars of the debtor given under the above provisions determine the title of the proceedings[6].

1   As to the meaning of 'residence' see PARA 131 note 5.
2   As to the meaning of 'carry on business' see PARA 131 note 6.
3   As to the meaning of 'bankruptcy debt' see PARA 508.
4   Insolvency Rules 1986, SI 1986/1925, r 6.38(1).
5   Insolvency Rules 1986, SI 1986/1925, r 6.38(3).
6   Insolvency Rules 1986, SI 1986/1925, r 6.38(2).

193. Admission of insolvency. The petition must contain the statement that the petitioner is unable to pay his debts, and a request that a bankruptcy order be made against him[1].

If, within the period of five years ending with the date of the petition, the petitioner has been adjudged bankrupt[2], or has made a composition with his creditors in satisfaction of his debts or a scheme of arrangement of his affairs, or he has entered into any voluntary arrangement or been subject to an administration order under Part VI of the County Courts Act 1984[3], particulars of these matters must be given in the petition[4].

If there is at the date of the petition in force for the debtor a voluntary arrangement under Part 8 of the Insolvency Act 1986[5], the particulars required under the above provisions must contain a statement to that effect and the name and address of the supervisor of the arrangement[6].

1   Insolvency Rules 1986, SI 1986/1925, r 6.39(1).
2   As to bankruptcy orders on a debtor's petition see PARA 206 et seq.
3   Ie under the County Courts Act 1984 Pt VI (ss 112–117): see PARA 886 et seq.
4   Insolvency Rules 1986, SI 1986/1925, r 6.39(2).
5   Ie under the Insolvency Act 1986 Pt 8 (ss 252–263G): see PARA 43 et seq.
6   Insolvency Rules 1986, SI 1986/1925, r 6.39(3) (added by SI 1987/1919). As to the supervisor
    of a voluntary arrangement see PARA 73 et seq.

194.   Statement of affairs.   The petition must be accompanied by a statement
of the debtor's affairs, verified by a statement of truth[1].

1   Insolvency Rules 1986, SI 1986/1925, r 6.41(1) (amended by SI 2010/686). The Insolvency
    Rules 1986, SI 1986/1925, rr 6.67–6.72 (see PARAS 248–251) apply with respect to the
    statement of affairs: r 6.41(2). For the prescribed form of statement of affairs see Sch 4 Form
    6.28 (substituted by SI 2005/2114; and amended by SI 2010/686). As to the meaning of
    'statement of truth' see PARA 161 note 7.

C. PRESENTATION AND FILING

195.   Procedure for presentation and filing.   The petition and statement of
affairs must be filed in court[1], together with three copies of the petition, and one
copy of the statement; and no petition may be filed unless there is produced with
it the receipt for the deposit payable on presentation[2]. The court may hear the
petition as soon as reasonably practicable; but, if it does not do so, it must fix a
venue[3] for the hearing[4]. If, however, the petition contains particulars of a
voluntary arrangement under Part 8 of the Insolvency Act 1986[5] in force for the
debtor, the court must fix a venue for the hearing and give at least 14 days'
notice of it to the supervisor[6] of the arrangement; the supervisor may appear and
be heard on the petition[7].
   Of the three copies of the petition delivered:
   (1)   one must be returned to the petitioner, indorsed with any venue fixed;
   (2)   another so indorsed must be sent by the court to the official receiver;
         and
   (3)   the remaining copy must be retained by the court, to be sent to an
         insolvency practitioner, if appointed[8].
The copy of the statement of affairs must be sent by the court to the official
receiver[9].
   Where the court hears a petition as soon as reasonably practicable, or it will in
the opinion of the court otherwise expedite the delivery of any document to the
official receiver, the court may, instead of sending that document to the official
receiver, direct the bankrupt as soon as reasonably practicable to deliver it to
him[10].
   Where a petition contains a request for the appointment of a former
supervisor as trustee[11], the person whose appointment is sought must, not less
than two business days[12] before the day appointed for hearing the petition, file in
court a report including particulars of:
   (a)   a date on which he gave written notification to creditors bound by the
         arrangement[13] of the intention to seek his appointment as trustee, such
         date to be at least seven business days before the day on which the
         report under this provision is filed; and
   (b)   details of any response from creditors to that notice, including any
         objections to his appointment[14].

1   As to the meaning of 'file in court' see PARA 57 note 13.

2 Insolvency Rules 1986, SI 1986/1925, r 6.42(1) (amended by SI 2005/527). As to the fee payable on presentation of the petition see PARA 168.
3 As to the meaning of 'venue' see PARA 46 note 22.
4 Insolvency Rules 1986, SI 1986/1925, r 6.42(2) (amended by SI 1987/1919; and SI 2009/642).
5 Ie under the Insolvency Act 1986 Pt 8 (ss 252–263G): see PARA 43 et seq.
6 As to the supervisor of a voluntary arrangement see PARA 73 et seq.
7 Insolvency Rules 1986, SI 1986/1925, r 6.42(2A) (added by SI 1987/1919).
8 Insolvency Rules 1986, SI 1986/1925, r 6.42(3) (amended by SI 1987/1919). The appointment of the insolvency practitioner is under the Insolvency Act 1986 s 273(2): see PARA 203.
9 Insolvency Rules 1986, SI 1986/1925, r 6.42(4) (substituted by SI 2005/527).
10 Insolvency Rules 1986, SI 1986/1925, r 6.42(6) (added by SI 1987/1919; and amended by SI 2009/642).
11 Ie under the Insolvency Act 1986 s 297(5): see PARA 320.
12 As to the meaning of 'business day' see PARA 28 note 8.
13 As to the persons bound by the arrangement see PARA 69 head (2).
14 Insolvency Rules 1986, SI 1986/1925, r 6.42(7) (added by SI 1987/1919; and amended by SI 2010/686).

196. Notice to Chief Land Registrar. When the petition is filed, the court must as soon as reasonably practicable send to the Chief Land Registrar notice of the petition, for registration in the register of pending actions[1].

1 Insolvency Rules 1986, SI 1986/1925, r 6.43 (amended by SI 2009/642). For the prescribed form of application for registration see the Insolvency Rules 1986, SI 1986/1925, Sch 4 Form 6.14 (substituted by SI 1987/1919; and amended by SI 2010/686).

197. Abuse of process in presenting own petition. When the presentation of the petition by the debtor is an abuse of its process, the court may decline to make any order on it, or may rescind a bankruptcy order made on it[1]. Where, therefore, an undischarged bankrupt made a practice of incurring credit and then presenting his own petition to evade committal orders against him on judgment summonses, the presentation of such a petition was an abuse of the process of the court, and no bankruptcy order should be made on it, or, if made, it should be rescinded[2]; and the presentation of a bankruptcy petition against himself by a debtor who is already fully protected by an instalment order is an abuse of process[3]. However, the mere presentation by the debtor of a petition to evade a committal order under a judgment summons has been held not to constitute an abuse of the process of the court, it being the legislature's intention in a proper case to enable a debtor to relieve himself from the pressure of a committal order by obtaining an adjudication in bankruptcy against himself[4].

In order to deal with persistent abuses by foreign debtors seeking to take advantage of the court's bankruptcy jurisdiction, where the court has doubts about its jurisdiction a debtor may be required to file more detailed evidence[5] in order to establish that his centre of main interest[6] is in this country[7].

1 A joint petition presented by husband and wife, who are neither partners nor joint traders and have no joint assets or liabilities, in order to avoid paying two petition fees is an abuse of the process of the court; and in such a case the name of one of the joint petitioners will be struck out: *Re Bond* (1888) 21 QBD 17. Where a first petition has been dismissed for fraud, the court may dismiss any subsequent petition and order that no further petition be filed without permission: *Re Bachelor* (1855) 25 LTOS 248. See also *Re Sydney, ex p Sydney* (1875) 10 Ch App 208 (where a second petition was dismissed after sanction of a composition).
2 *Re Betts, ex p Official Receiver* [1901] 2 KB 39. A petition presented by a divorced husband or wife with the intention of frustrating the enforcement of his or her ex-spouse's financial or property rights will be an abuse of process: *Re Holliday (a bankrupt), ex p Trustee of Bankrupt v Bankrupt* [1981] Ch 405, [1980] 3 All ER 385, CA; *Woodley v Woodley (No 2)* [1993] 4 All ER 1010, [1994] 1 WLR 1167, CA.

3   *Re A Debtor (No 17 of 1966), ex p Debtor v Allen* [1967] Ch 590, [1967] 1 All ER 668, DC,
    distinguishing *Re Painter, ex p Painter* [1895] 1 QB 85, DC; *Re Hancock, ex p Hillearys* [1904]
    1 KB 585, CA.
4   *Re Painter, ex p Painter* [1895] 1 QB 85, DC; *Re Hancock, ex p Hillearys* [1904] 1 KB 585, CA;
    Re Archer, ex p Archer (1904) 20 TLR 390. As to committal orders (the jurisdiction to make
    which is now substantially restricted) see the Debtors Act 1869 s 5, the Administration of Justice
    Act 1970 s 11, Sch 4, the Attachment of Earnings Act 1971 s 3(4)–(7); and MAGISTRATES vol 71
    (2013) PARA 638 et seq.
5   Ie over and above that required by the Insolvency Rules 1986, SI 1986/1925, r 6.38 (see PARA
    192) and r 6.41 (see PARA 194).
6   As to the meaning of 'centre of main interest' see Council Regulation (EC) 1346/2000 (OJ L160,
    30.6.2000, p 1) on insolvency proceedings ('European Regulation on Insolvency Proceedings');
    and PARA 42.
7   *Re Eichler (a bankrupt) (No 2); Steinhardt v Eichler* [2011] BPIR 1293; *Official Receiver v
    Mitterfelner* [2009] BPIR 1075. See further the Insolvency Act 1986 s 282; and PARA 620.

(3) BANKRUPTCY ORDERS

(i) Creditor's Petition

198.   Proceedings on creditor's petition.   The court may not make a
bankruptcy order on a creditor's petition[1] unless it is satisfied that the debt, or
one of the debts, in respect of which the petition was presented is either:

(1)   a debt which, having been payable at the date of the petition or having
        since become payable, has neither been paid nor secured nor
        compounded for; or

(2)   a debt which the debtor has no reasonable prospect of being able to pay
        when it falls due[2].

In a case in which the petition contains a statement[3] that there is a serious
possibility that the debtor's property or the value of any of his property will be
significantly diminished during the three-week period from service of the
statutory demand, the court may not make a bankruptcy order until at least
three weeks have elapsed since the service of the statutory demand[4].

The court may dismiss the petition if it is satisfied that the debtor is able to
pay all his debts or is satisfied:

(a)   that the debtor has made an offer to secure or compound for a debt in
        respect of which the petition is presented;

(b)   that the acceptance of that offer would have required the dismissal of
        the petition; and

(c)   that the offer has been unreasonably refused;

and, in determining for the above purposes whether the debtor is able to pay all
his debts, the court must take into account his contingent and prospective
liabilities[5].

Nothing in the statutory provisions[6] prejudices the power of the court[7] to
authorise a creditor's petition to be amended by the omission of the creditor or
debt and to be proceeded with as if things done for the purposes of those
provisions had been done only by or in relation to the remaining creditors or
debts[8].

1   Ie under the Insolvency Act 1986 s 264(1)(a): see PARA 130 head (1).
2   Insolvency Act 1986 s 271(1). In determining, for these purposes, what constitutes a reasonable
    prospect that a debtor will be able to pay a debt when it falls due, it is to be assumed that the
    prospect given by the facts and other matters known to the creditor at the time he entered into
    the transaction resulting in the debt was a reasonable prospect: s 271(4).
        Where a payment in respect of the petition debt is made by a debtor out of his own property,
    the debt will only be paid within the meaning of s 271(1) where the payment is unconditional in

that it is not liable to be avoided in the event of the court making a bankruptcy order: *Smith v Ian Simpson & Co* [2001] Ch 239, [2000] 3 All ER 434, CA. The court may make a bankruptcy order notwithstanding that a payment has been made to reduce the petition debt to below the bankruptcy level: *Lilley v American Express Europe Ltd* [2000] BPIR 70; cf *Re Patel (a debtor)* [1986] 1 All ER 522, sub nom *Re Patel (a debtor), ex p Debtor v Dallamo* [1986] 1 WLR 221, DC (a decision under the Bankruptcy Act 1914).

The court will dismiss a petition if there is a genuine triable issue as to the existence of the petition debt, the test being the same as that applicable to statutory demands: *Markham v Karsten* [2007] EWHC 1509 (Ch), [2007] BPIR 1109, [2007] All ER (D) 377 (Jun). As to the test applicable to statutory demands see the Insolvency Rules 1986, SI 1986/1925, r 6.5(4); and PARA 162. Unless there is some change of circumstance, a debtor will not be allowed to reargue at the hearing of the petition the same grounds unsuccessfully raised in an application to set aside a statutory demand: *Turner v Royal Bank of Scotland* [2000] BPIR 683; cf *IRC v Lee-Phipps* [2003] BPIR 803, [2003] All ER (D) 107 (Feb); *Vaidya v Wijayawardhana* [2010] EWHC 716 (Ch), [2010] BPIR 1016, [2010] All ER (D) 14 (Apr). See also *Adams v Mason Bullock (a firm)* [2004] EWHC 2910 (Ch), [2005] BPIR 241, [2004] All ER (D) 292 (Dec). But where a debtor has made no application to set aside the statutory demand, he will not be precluded from raising matters in opposition to the petition which he could have raised in opposition to the statutory demand: *Barnes v Whitehead* [2004] BPIR 693.

In the case of the administration in bankruptcy of the insolvent estate of a deceased person dying before the presentation of a bankruptcy petition, the court may make an insolvency administration order on a petition for such an order under the Insolvency Act 1986 s 264(1) (see PARA 130 note 12) if it is satisfied: (1) that the debt, or one of the debts, in respect of which the petition was presented is a debt which: (a) having been payable at the date of the petition or having since become payable, has neither been paid nor secured or compounded for; or (b) has no reasonable prospect of being able to be paid when it falls due; and (2) that there is a reasonable probability that the estate will be insolvent: s 271(1) (substituted by the Administration of Insolvent Estates of Deceased Persons Order 1986, SI 1986/1999, art 3(1), Sch 1 Pt II para 5). A petition for an insolvency administration order may not, however, be presented to the court after proceedings have been commenced in any court of justice for the administration of the deceased debtor's estate: Insolvency Act 1986 s 271(2) (substituted by the Administration of Insolvent Estates of Deceased Persons Order 1986, SI 1986/1999, Sch 1 Pt II para 5). Where proceedings have been commenced in any such court for the administration of the deceased debtor's estate, that court may, if satisfied that the estate is insolvent, transfer the proceedings to the court exercising jurisdiction for the purposes of the Insolvency Act 1986 Pts 7A–11 (ss 251A–385): s 271(3) (substituted by the Administration of Insolvent Estates of Deceased Persons Order 1986, SI 1986/1999, Sch 1 Pt II para 5). Where proceedings have been transferred to the court so exercising jurisdiction, that court may make an insolvency administration order in the prescribed form as if a petition for such an order has been presented under the Insolvency Act 1986 s 264 (see PARA 130): s 271(4) (substituted by the Administration of Insolvent Estates of Deceased Persons Order 1986, SI 1986/1999, Sch 1 Pt II para 5). For the prescribed form of insolvency administration order see the Administration of Insolvent Estates of Deceased Persons Order 1986, SI 1986/1999, Sch 3 Form 5 (substituted by SI 2002/1309). Nothing in the Insolvency Act 1986 ss 264, 266, 269 or 271–273 invalidates any payment made or any act or thing done in good faith by the personal representative before the date of the insolvency administration order: s 271(5) (substituted by the Administration of Insolvent Estates of Deceased Persons Order 1986, SI 1986/1999, Sch 1 Pt II para 5). As to the administration in bankruptcy of the insolvent estates of deceased persons see further PARA 830 et seq.

As to the modification of the Insolvency Act 1986 s 271 by the Insolvent Partnerships Order 1994, SI 1994/2421, in relation to the bankruptcy of an individual member of an insolvent partnership see COMPANY AND PARTNERSHIP INSOLVENCY vol 17 (2011) PARAS 1283, 1320.

3   Ie such a statement as is required by the Insolvency Act 1986 s 270: see PARA 134.
4   Insolvency Act 1986 s 271(2). The statutory demand is served under s 268: see PARA 133.
5   Insolvency Act 1986 s 271(3). A voluntary arrangement proposed by a debtor pursuant to Pt 8 (ss 252–263G) is not an offer to each creditor which is capable of being accepted or refused by the petitioning creditor within the meaning of s 271(3): *Re a Debtor (No 2389 of 1989)* [1991] Ch 326, sub nom *Re a Debtor (No 2389 of 1989), ex p Travel and General Insurance Co plc v Debtor* [1990] 3 All ER 984.

The test of whether an offer has been unreasonably refused is whether the decision by the petitioning creditor falls outside the range of positions which could have been adopted by a hypothetical reasonable creditor in the circumstances: *Re a Debtor (No 32 of 1993)* [1994] 1 WLR 899, [1994] BCC 438; *Re a Debtor (No 6349 of 1994), IRC v Debtor* [1996] BPIR 271.

The test is an objective one and the court is not limited to taking into account only those considerations which were taken into account by the petitioning creditor himself: *Customs and Excise Comrs v Dougall* [2001] BPIR 269. The onus is on the debtor to be full, frank and open in making an offer to the petitioning creditor; accordingly, a creditor would not be acting unreasonably in rejecting an offer of property as security where the value of the property was unclear: *Maple Division Ltd v Wilson* [1999] BPIR 102. See *Ross v Revenue and Customs Comrs* [2010] EWHC 13 (Ch), [2010] 2 All ER 126, [2010] BPIR 652 (rejection of offer of legal charge over property well within range of reasonable responses open to Commissioners); *Revenue and Customs Comrs v Garwood* [2012] BPIR 575 (where the principles which emerge from the case law are summarised).

In addition to the grounds set out in the Insolvency Act 1986 s 271, the court will not make a bankruptcy order where to do so would not be fair and just: *Camden London Borough Council v Martin* [2009] EWHC 2040 (Ch), [2009] RVR 309, [2009] BPIR 1420.

6   Ie the Insolvency Act 1986 ss 267–271: see PARA 132 et seq.
7   Ie in accordance with the Insolvency Rules 1986, SI 1986/1925. As to the court's power to amend a creditor's petition see r 6.22; and PARA 173.
8   Insolvency Act 1986 s 271(5).

199.   Decision on hearing.   On the hearing of a creditor's petition[1], the court may make a bankruptcy order if satisfied that the statements in the petition are true, and the debt on which it is founded has not been paid, or secured or compounded for[2].

If the petition is brought in respect of a judgment debt, or a sum ordered by any court to be paid, the court may stay or dismiss the petition on the ground that an appeal is pending from the judgment or order, or that execution of the judgment has been stayed[3].

A petition preceded by a statutory demand[4] may not be dismissed on the ground only that the amount of the debt was overstated in the demand, unless the debtor, within the time allowed for complying with the demand, gave notice to the creditor disputing the validity of the demand on that ground; but, in the absence of such notice, the debtor is deemed to have complied with the demand if he has, within the time allowed, paid the correct amount[5].

1   As to creditors' petitions see PARAS 132 et seq, 164 et seq.
2   Insolvency Rules 1986, SI 1986/1925, r 6.25(1). As to the ability of a debtor to raise issues on the hearing of the petition which have already been raised on an unsuccessful application to set aside the statutory demand see PARA 162 note 12.
    On the hearing of a petition where a bankruptcy order is sought, in order to satisfy the court that the debt on which the petition is founded has not been paid or secured or compounded for, the court will normally accept as sufficient a certificate signed by the person representing the petitioning creditor in the following form:
'I certify that I have/my firm has made inquiries of the petitioning creditor(s) within the last business day prior to the hearing/adjourned hearing and to the best of my knowledge and belief the debt on which the petition is founded is still due and owing and has not been paid or secured or compounded for (save as to   )
Signed   Dated   '
    For convenience, in the Royal Courts of Justice this certificate is incorporated in the attendance sheet for the parties to complete when they come to court and which is filed after the hearing. It will be filed after the hearing. A fresh certificate will be required on each adjourned hearing: *Practice Direction—Insolvency Proceedings* para 14.5.
    The existence of a prior foreign bankruptcy or concurrent bankruptcy proceedings in respect of a debtor will not prevent the court from making a bankruptcy order against the debtor; but as to the court's power to dismiss a petition under the Insolvency Act 1986 s 266(3) on this ground see PARA 130.
    On appeal against a bankruptcy order, the court may require the bankrupt to give security for costs: *Hocking v Walker* [1997] BPIR 93, CA.
    For the purposes of a demand made by the Financial Conduct Authority or the Prudential Regulation Authority under the Financial Services and Markets Act 2000 s 372(4)(a) (see FINANCIAL SERVICES AND INSTITUTIONS vol 48 (2008) PARA 501), the Insolvency Rules 1986, SI 1986/1925, r 6.25 applies as if references to the debtor were references to an individual, and

references to the creditor were references to the relevant Authority: Bankruptcy (Financial Services and Markets Act 2000) Rules 2001, SI 2001/3634, rr 2, 6(1) (r 2 amended by SI 2013/472). As to the meaning of 'individual' for these purposes see PARA 158 note 1.

3   Insolvency Rules 1986, SI 1986/1925, r 6.25(2). As to the position where there is a pending appeal against the judgment on which the petition is based see *Heath v Tang, Stevens v Peacock* [1993] 4 All ER 694, [1993] 1 WLR 1421, CA; *Re A Debtor (No 799 of 1994), ex p Cobbs Property Services Ltd* [1995] 3 All ER 723, [1995] 1 WLR 467. For the prescribed form of dismissal of a bankruptcy petition see the Insolvency Rules 1986, SI 1986/1925, Sch 4 Form 6.22 (amended by SI 2010/686).

     Although a court will treat a judgment for a sum of money as prima facie evidence that the judgment creditor is indebted to the judgment debtor for that sum, the court may in appropriate circumstances go behind the judgment to inquire into the circumstances in which the judgment was obtained and, if so satisfied, treat it as not creating or evidencing any debt enforceable in bankruptcy proceedings: *McCourt and Siequien v Baron Meats Ltd and Official Receiver* [1997] BPIR 114, DC (a decision under the Bankruptcy Act 1914). See also *Re Yeatman, ex p Yeatman* (1880) 16 ChD 283, CA; *Eberhardt & Co Ltd v Mair* [1995] 3 All ER 963, [1995] 1 WLR 1180. The bankruptcy court has jurisdiction to go behind a default judgment and inquire as to the existence of a debt: *Royal Bank of Scotland v Farley* [1996] BPIR 638, CA.

4   As to statutory demands see PARA 158 et seq.

5   Insolvency Rules 1986, SI 1986/1925, r 6.25(3). As to the setting aside of statutory demands on the ground that the debt demanded is overstated see PARA 162 note 8.

200. Settlement and content of bankruptcy order. The bankruptcy order must be settled by the court; and the order must:

(1)   state the date of the presentation of the petition on which the order is made, and the date and time of the making of the order; and

(2)   contain a notice referring to the bankrupt's duties in relation to the official receiver[1], and in particular to the bankrupt's duty to give the official receiver such inventory of the bankrupt's estate and such other information, and to attend on the official receiver at such times, as the official receiver may reasonably require[2].

Subject to the statutory provisions relating to the effect of bankruptcy on enforcement procedures[3], the order may include provision staying any action or proceeding against the bankrupt[4]. Where the petitioning creditor is represented by a solicitor[5], the order must be indorsed with the latter's name, address, telephone number and reference, if any[6].

1   Ie under the Insolvency Act 1986 s 291: see PARA 239. As to the official receiver see PARA 35 et seq.

2   Insolvency Rules 1986, SI 1986/1925, r 6.33(1), (2) (r 6.33(2) amended by SI 2010/686). For the prescribed form of bankruptcy order see the Insolvency Rules 1986, SI 1986/1925, Sch 4 Form 6.25 (substituted by SI 2003/1730; and amended by SI 2010/686).

3   Ie the Insolvency Act 1986 s 346: see PARA 703 et seq.

4   Insolvency Rules 1986, SI 1986/1925, r 6.33(3).

5   For these purposes, the reference to a solicitor includes a reference to a body recognised by the Law Society under the Administration of Justice Act 1985 s 9 (see LEGAL PROFESSIONS vol 65 (2008) PARA 515): Solicitors' Recognised Bodies Order 1991, SI 1991/2684, arts 2(1), 3, 4(a), 5, Sch 1 (amended by SI 2009/500).

6   Insolvency Rules 1986, SI 1986/1925, r 6.33(4).

201. Action to follow making of order. At least two sealed copies of the bankruptcy order must be sent as soon as reasonably practicable by the court to the official receiver, who must as soon as reasonably practicable send one of them to the bankrupt[1]. On receipt of the sealed copies, the official receiver:

(1)   as soon as reasonably practicable must (a) send notice[2] of the making of the order to the Chief Land Registrar, for registration in the register of writs and orders affecting land; and (b) cause notice of the order to be gazetted[3]; and

(2)   may cause notice of the order to be advertised in such other manner as the official receiver thinks fit[4].

In addition to the standard contents[5], the notice to be gazetted and any notice to be advertised under head (2) above must state that a bankruptcy order has been made against the bankrupt, the date and time of making of the bankruptcy order, the name and address of the petitioning creditor and the date of presentation of the petition[6].

On the application of the bankrupt or a creditor, the court may order the official receiver to suspend action[7] pending a further order of the court[8]; and, where an order is so made, the applicant for the order must as soon as reasonably practicable deliver a copy of it to the official receiver[9].

1 Insolvency Rules 1986, SI 1986/1925, r 6.34(1) (amended by SI 2009/642).
2 For the prescribed form of notice see the Insolvency Rules 1986, SI 1986/1925, Sch 4 Form 6.26 (substituted by SI 1987/1919; and amended by SI 2010/686).
3 As to the meaning of 'gazetted' see PARA 165 note 12.
4 Insolvency Rules 1986, SI 1986/1925, r 6.34(2) (substituted by SI 2009/642). As to gazetting orders see PARA 778.
5 As to the meaning of 'standard contents' see PARA 165 note 12.
6 Insolvency Rules 1986, SI 1986/1925, r 6.34(2A) (added by SI 2010/686).
7 Ie under the Insolvency Rules 1986, SI 1986/1925, r 6.34(2) (see the text and notes 2–4) and r 6A.4(2) (see PARA 30).
8 Insolvency Rules 1986, SI 1986/1925, r 6.34(3) (amended by SI 1999/359; and SI 2005/527). An application under the Insolvency Rules 1986, SI 1986/1925, r 6.34(3) must be supported by a witness statement stating the grounds on which it is made: r 6.34(3) (amended by SI 2010/686). As to the meaning of 'witness statement' see PARA 161 note 7.
9 Insolvency Rules 1986, SI 1986/1925, r 6.34(4) (amended by SI 2009/642).

202.   Amendment of title of proceedings.   At any time after the making of a bankruptcy order, the official receiver or the trustee may apply to the court for an order amending the full title of the proceedings[1]. Where such an order is made, as soon as reasonably practicable the official receiver must send notice of it to the Chief Land Registrar, for corresponding amendment of the register[2]. If the official receiver thinks fit, notice of the order: (1) as soon as reasonably practicable, must be gazetted[3]; and (2) may be advertised in such other manner as the official receiver thinks fit[4].

In addition to the standard contents, the notice must state that an amendment to the full title of the proceedings has been made and specify the amendment[5].

1 Insolvency Rules 1986, SI 1986/1925, r 6.35(1). As to the title of the proceedings see PARA 165.
2 Insolvency Rules 1986, SI 1986/1925, r 6.35(2) (substituted by SI 2009/642).
3 As to gazetting notices see PARA 778.
4 Insolvency Rules 1986, SI 1986/1925, r 6.35(3) (added by SI 2009/642).
5 Insolvency Rules 1986, SI 1986/1925, r 6.35(4) (added by SI 2010/686). As to the meaning of 'standard contents' see PARA 165 note 12.

(ii)   Debtor's Petition

A.   APPOINTMENT OF INSOLVENCY PRACTITIONER

203.   Appointment of insolvency practitioner by the court.   On the hearing of a debtor's petition[1], the court may not make a bankruptcy order if it appears to the court:

(1)   that, if a bankruptcy order were made, the aggregate amount of the bankruptcy debts[2], so far as unsecured[3], would be less than the small bankruptcies level[4];

(2)   that, if a bankruptcy order were made, the value of the bankrupt's estate[5] would be equal to more than the minimum amount[6];

(3)   that, within the period of five years ending with the presentation of the petition, the debtor has neither been adjudged bankrupt nor made a composition with his creditors in satisfaction of his debts or a scheme of arrangement of his affairs; and

(4)   that it would be appropriate to appoint a person to prepare a report[7] stating whether the debtor is willing to make a proposal for a voluntary arrangement[8].

Where, on the hearing of the petition, it appears to the court as mentioned above, the court must appoint a person who is qualified to act as an insolvency practitioner in relation to the debtor[9] to prepare a report[10] and to act[11] in relation to any voluntary arrangement to which the report relates either as trustee or otherwise for the purpose of supervising its implementation[12].

Where the court does not appoint an insolvency practitioner under the provisions set out above, and it appears to the court that a debt relief order[13] would be made in relation to the debtor if, instead of presenting the petition, he had made an application for a debt relief order[14], if the court thinks it would be in the debtor's interests to apply for a debt relief order instead of proceeding on the petition, the court may refer the debtor to an approved intermediary for the purposes of making an application for a debt relief order[15].

1   As to debtors' petitions see PARAS 163, 191 et seq.
2   As to the meaning of 'bankruptcy debt' see PARA 508.
3   As to secured creditors see PARA 574 et seq.
4   For these purposes, 'the small bankruptcies level' means such amount as may for the time being be prescribed for the purposes of the Insolvency Act 1986 s 273: s 273(1). The amount so prescribed is £40,000: Insolvency Proceedings (Monetary Limits) Order 1986, SI 1986/1996, art 3, Schedule Pt II (art 3 amended by SI 2009/465; the Insolvency Proceedings (Monetary Limits) Order 1986, SI 1986/1996, Schedule Pt II substituted by SI 2004/547). As to the Secretary of State's power to prescribe monetary limits see PARA 19 note 9.
    In the Insolvency Act 1986, subject to s 384(2) and to s 342C(7) (see PARA 694) and s 342F(9) (see PARA 696 note 16), 'prescribed' means prescribed by the rules; and 'rules' means rules made under s 412 (see PARA 773): s 384(1) (amended by the Welfare Reform and Pensions Act 1999 s 84(1), Sch 12 paras 70, 72). However, references in the Insolvency Act 1986 Pts 7A–11 (ss 251A–385) to the amount prescribed for the purposes of any of s 251S(4) (see PARA 123), s 273, s 313A (see PARA 414), s 346(3) (see PARA 703 et seq), s 354(1), (2) (see PARAS 735, 736 respectively), s 358 (see PARA 744), s 360(1) (see PARA 747), s 364(2)(d) (see PARA 217 head (d)), Sch 4ZA paras 6–8 (see PARA 106), and references in those provisions to the prescribed amount, are to be read in accordance with s 418 (see PARA 19 note 9) and orders made under s 418: s 384(2) (amended by the Enterprise Act 2002 s 261(5); and the Tribunals, Courts and Enforcement Act 2007 s 108(3), Sch 20 paras 1, 4). As from a day to be appointed, the Insolvency Act 1986 s 384(1) is amended by the Enterprise and Regulatory Reform Act 2013 s 71, Sch 19 paras 1, 54: see PARA 130 note 17.
    In the case of the administration in bankruptcy of the insolvent estate of a deceased person dying before the presentation of a bankruptcy petition, the Insolvency Act 1986 s 384 applies: Administration of Insolvent Estates of Deceased Persons Order 1986, SI 1986/1999, art 3(1), Sch 1 Pt II para 32. As to the administration in bankruptcy of the insolvent estates of deceased persons see further PARA 830 et seq.
5   As to the meaning of 'the bankrupt's estate' see PARA 211.
6   For these purposes, 'the minimum amount' means such amount as may for the time being be prescribed for the purposes of the Insolvency Act 1986 s 273: s 273(1). The amount so prescribed is £4,000: Insolvency Proceedings (Monetary Limits) Order 1986, SI 1986/1996, art 3, Schedule Pt II (as amended: see note 4).
7   Ie under the Insolvency Act 1986 s 274: see PARA 205.
8   Insolvency Act 1986 s 273(1). Section 273 is subject to s 274: s 273(1). As from a day to be appointed, ss 272–274, 274A (debtors' petitions) are repealed by the Enterprise and Regulatory Reform Act 2013 s 71, Sch 19 paras 1, 9: see PARA 130 note 17.

In the case of the administration in bankruptcy of the insolvent estate of a deceased person dying before the presentation of a bankruptcy petition, the court must make an insolvency administration order in the prescribed form on the hearing of a petition presented under the Insolvency Act 1986 s 272 (see PARA 163) if it is satisfied that the deceased debtor's estate is insolvent: s 273 (substituted by the Administration of Insolvent Estates of Deceased Persons Order 1986, SI 1986/1999. Sch 1 Pt II para 7). For the prescribed form of insolvency administration order see the Administration of Insolvent Estates of Deceased Persons Order 1986, SI 1986/1999, Sch 3 Form 4 (substituted by SI 2002/1309).

As to the application of the Insolvency Act 1986 s 273 in the case of the bankruptcy of an individual member of an insolvent partnership see the Insolvent Partnerships Order 1994, SI 1994/2421; and COMPANY AND PARTNERSHIP INSOLVENCY vol 17 (2011) PARAS 1317, 1323.

9   As to insolvency practitioners and their qualification see PARA 40.

10   Ie under the Insolvency Act 1986 s 274: see PARA 205.

11   Ie subject to Insolvency Act 1986 s 258(3): see PARA 62.

12   Insolvency Act 1986 s 273(2). For the prescribed form of order of appointment of an insolvency practitioner to prepare a report under s 274(1) see the Insolvency Rules 1986, SI 1986/1925, Sch 4 Form 6.29.

13   As to debt relief orders see PARA 101 et seq.

14   Ie under the Insolvency Act 1986 Pt 7A (ss 251A–251X) (see PARA 101 et seq).

15   Insolvency Act 1986 s 274A(1), (2) (s 274A added by the Tribunals, Courts and Enforcement Act 2007 s 108(3), Sch 20 para 3). Where a reference is made to an approved intermediary, the court must stay proceedings on the petition on such terms and conditions as it thinks fit; but if following the reference a debt relief order is made in relation to the debtor the court must dismiss the petition: s 274A(3) (as so added).

     If, on the hearing of a debtor's bankruptcy petition, the court refers the debtor to an approved intermediary under s 274A for the purposes of making an application for a debt relief order, as soon as reasonably practicable after the making of the order of referral: (1) the court must send to the debtor a sealed copy of the order of referral; and (2) the debtor must send to the approved intermediary a copy of the order and copies of the debtor's petition and statement of affairs: Insolvency Rules 1986, SI 1986/1925, r 5A.22 (added by SI 2009/642).

204. Report of insolvency practitioner. If the court appoints an insolvency practitioner[1] to act in the debtor's case[2], it must as soon as reasonably practicable:

(1)   send to the person appointed a sealed copy of the order of appointment, and copies of the petition[3] and statement of affairs[4];

(2)   fix a venue[5] for the insolvency practitioner's report to be considered; and

(3)   send notice of the venue to the insolvency practitioner and the debtor[6].

The insolvency practitioner must file his report in court[7], and send one copy of it to the debtor, so as to be in his hands not less than three business days[8] before the date fixed for consideration of the report, and a further copy to the official receiver[9]. The debtor is entitled to attend when the report is considered, and must attend if so directed by the court; and, if he attends, the court must hear any representations which he makes with respect to any of the matters dealt with in the report[10].

1   As to insolvency practitioners and their qualification see PARA 40.

2   Ie under the Insolvency Act 1986 s 273(2): see PARA 203.

3   As to the debtor's petition see PARA 191 et seq.

4   As to the statement of affairs see PARA 194.

5   As to the meaning of 'venue' see PARA 46 note 22.

6   Insolvency Rules 1986, SI 1986/1925, r 6.44(1) (amended by SI 2009/642).

7   As to the meaning of 'file in court' see PARA 57 note 13.

8   As to the meaning of 'business day' see PARA 28 note 8.

9   Insolvency Rules 1986, SI 1986/1925, r 6.44(2) (amended by SI 1987/1919; and SI 2010/686).

10   Insolvency Rules 1986, SI 1986/1925, r 6.44(3).

205. Action on report of insolvency practitioner. A person appointed by the court[1] must inquire into the debtor's affairs[2] and, within such period as the court may direct, must submit a report to the court stating whether the debtor is willing, for the purposes of Part 8 of the Insolvency Act 1986[3], to make a proposal for a voluntary arrangement[4].

A report which states that the debtor is willing to make a proposal for a voluntary arrangement must also state:

(1) whether, in the opinion of the person making the report, a meeting of the debtor's creditors should be summoned to consider the proposal; and

(2) if in that person's opinion such a meeting should be summoned, the date on which, and time and place at which, he proposes the meeting should be held[5].

On considering a report under the above provisions, the court may:

(a) without any application, make an interim order[6], if it thinks that it is appropriate to do so for the purpose of facilitating the consideration and implementation of the debtor's proposal; or

(b) if it thinks it would be inappropriate to make such an order, make a bankruptcy order[7].

1 Ie under the Insolvency Act 1986 s 273: see PARA 203.
2 As to the meaning of references to a person's affairs see PARA 43 note 4.
3 Ie for the purposes of the Insolvency Act 1986 Pt 8 (ss 252–263G): see PARA 43 et seq.
4 Insolvency Act 1986 s 274(1). As to the application of s 274 in the case of the bankruptcy of an individual member of an insolvent partnership see the Insolvent Partnerships Order 1994, SI 1994/2421; and COMPANY AND PARTNERSHIP INSOLVENCY vol 17 (2011) PARAS 1317, 1323.

As from a day to be appointed, the Insolvency Act 1986 ss 272–274, 274A (debtors' petitions) are repealed by the Enterprise and Regulatory Reform Act 2013 s 71, Sch 19 paras 1, 9: see PARA 130 note 17.
5 Insolvency Act 1986 s 274(2). Where it has been reported to the court under s 274 that a meeting of the debtor's creditors should be summoned, the person making the report must, unless the court otherwise directs, summon that meeting for the time, date and place proposed in the report; and the meeting is then deemed to have been summoned under s 257 (see PARA 59), and ss 257(2), (3), 258–263 (see PARAS 59, 62 et seq) apply accordingly: s 274(5).
6 Ie under the Insolvency Act 1986 s 252: see PARA 45. An interim order made by virtue of s 274 ceases to have effect at the end of such period as the court may specify for the purpose of enabling the debtor's proposal to be considered by his creditors in accordance with the applicable provisions of Pt 8: s 274(4).
7 Insolvency Act 1986 s 274(3).

B. MAKING OF BANKRUPTCY ORDER

206. Settlement and content of bankruptcy order. The bankruptcy order must be settled by the court[1]; and the order must:

(1) state the date of the presentation of the petition on which the order is made, and the date and time of the making of the order; and

(2) contain a notice referring to the bankrupt's duties in relation to the official receiver[2], and in particular to the bankrupt's duty to give the official receiver such inventory of the bankrupt's estate and such other information, and attend on the official receiver at such times, as the official receiver may reasonably require[3].

Subject to the statutory provisions relating to the effect of bankruptcy on enforcement procedures[4], the order may include provision staying any action or proceeding against the bankrupt[5]. Where the bankrupt is represented by a solicitor[6], the order must be indorsed with the latter's name, address, telephone number and reference[7].

1 Insolvency Rules 1986, SI 1986/1925, r 6.45(1). For the prescribed form of bankruptcy order see Sch 4 Form 6.30 (substituted by SI 2003/1730; and amended by SI 2010/686).
2 Ie under the Insolvency Act 1986 s 291: see PARA 239.
3 Insolvency Rules 1986, SI 1986/1925, r 6.45(2) (amended by SI 2010/686).
4 Ie subject to the Insolvency Act 1986 s 346: see PARA 703 et seq.
5 Insolvency Rules 1986, SI 1986/1925, r 6.45(3).
6 For these purposes, the reference to a solicitor includes a reference to a body recognised by the Law Society under the Administration of Justice Act 1985 s 9 (see LEGAL PROFESSIONS vol 65 (2008) PARA 515): Solicitors' Recognised Bodies Order 1991, SI 1991/2684, arts 2(1), 3, 4(a), 5, Sch 1 (amended by SI 2009/500).
7 Insolvency Rules 1986, SI 1986/1925, r 6.45(4).

207. Action to follow making of order. At least two sealed copies of the bankruptcy order must be sent as soon as reasonably practicable by the court to the official receiver, who must (unless the official receiver is satisfied that the bankrupt has already received a copy of the order) as soon as reasonably practicable send one of them to the bankrupt[1]. On receipt of the sealed copies of the bankruptcy order, the official receiver:

(1) as soon as reasonably practicable must: (a) send notice[2] of the making of the order to the Chief Land Registrar, for registration in the register of writs and orders affecting land; and (b) cause notice of the order to be gazetted[3]; and

(2) may cause notice of the order to be advertised in such other manner as the official receiver thinks fit[4].

In addition to the standard contents[5], the notice to be gazetted and any notice to be advertised must state that a bankruptcy order has been made against the bankrupt, the date and time of making of the bankruptcy order, that the bankruptcy order was made on the debtor's own petition and the date of presentation of the petition[6].

On the application of the bankrupt or a creditor, the court may order the official receiver to suspend action[7], pending a further order of the court[8]. Any such application must be supported by a witness statement[9] stating the grounds on which it is made[10]. Where an order is made, the applicant must as soon as reasonably practicable deliver a copy of it to the official receiver[11].

1 Insolvency Rules 1986, SI 1986/1925, r 6.46(1) (amended by SI 2009/642; SI 2010/686). As to the official receiver see PARA 35 et seq.
2 For the prescribed form of notice see the Insolvency Rules 1986, SI 1986/1925, Sch 4 Form 6.26 (substituted by SI 1987/1919; and amended by SI 2010/686).
3 As to the meaning of 'gazetted' see PARA 165 note 12.
4 Insolvency Rules 1986, SI 1986/1925, r 6.46(2) (substituted by SI 2009/642). As to gazetting notices see PARA 778.
5 As to the meaning of 'standard contents' see PARA 165 note 12.
6 Insolvency Rules 1986, SI 1986/1925, r 6.46(2A) (added by SI 2010/686).
7 Ie under the Insolvency Rules 1986, SI 1986/1925, r 6.46(2) and r 6A.4(2) (see PARA 30).
8 Insolvency Rules 1986, SI 1986/1925, r 6.46(3) (amended by SI 1999/359; SI 2005/527; SI 2010/686).
9 As to the meaning of 'witness statement' see PARA 161 note 7.
10 Insolvency Rules 1986, SI 1986/1925, r 6.46(3A) (added by SI 2010/686).
11 Insolvency Rules 1986, SI 1986/1925, r 6.46(4) (amended by SI 2009/642).

208. Amendment of title of proceedings. At any time after the making of the bankruptcy order, the official receiver or the trustee may apply to the court for an order amending the full title of the proceedings[1]. Where such an order is made, the official receiver must as soon as reasonably practicable send notice of it to the Chief Land Registrar, for corresponding amendment of the register[2].

Where the official receiver thinks fit, notice of the order: (1) as soon as reasonably practicable must be gazetted[3]; and (2) may be advertised in such other manner as the official receiver thinks fit[4].

In addition to the standard contents[5], the notice must state that an amendment to the full title of the proceedings has been made and specify the amendment[6].

1 Insolvency Rules 1986, SI 1986/1925, r 6.47(1). As to the title of proceedings see PARA 192.
2 Insolvency Rules 1986, SI 1986/1925, r 6.47(2) (substituted by SI 2009/642).
3 As to the meaning of 'gazetted' see PARA 165 note 12.
4 Insolvency Rules 1986, SI 1986/1925, r 6.47(3) (added by SI 2009/642).
5 As to the meaning of 'standard contents' see PARA 165 note 12.
6 Insolvency Rules 1986, SI 1986/1925, r 6.47(4) (added by SI 2010/686).

(iii) Commencement and Duration of Bankruptcy Order

209. Commencement and duration of bankruptcy order. The bankruptcy of an individual against whom a bankruptcy order has been made:

(1) commences with the day on which the order is made; and

(2) continues until the individual is discharged under the statutory provisions[1].

1 Insolvency Act 1986 s 278. The statutory provisions referred to are ss 279–282 (see PARA 638 et seq): s 278. As from a day to be appointed, s 278 is amended by the Enterprise and Regulatory Reform Act 2013 s 71, Sch 19 paras 1, 11: see PARA 130 note 17.
   In the case of the administration in bankruptcy of the insolvent estate of a deceased person dying before the presentation of a bankruptcy petition, the bankruptcy of an individual commences with the day on which the insolvency administration order is made: Insolvency Act 1986 s 278 (amended by the Administration of Insolvent Estates of Deceased Persons Order 1986, SI 1986/1999, art 3(1), Sch 1 Pt II para 10). As to the administration in bankruptcy of the insolvent estates of deceased persons see further PARA 830 et seq.

(iv) Other Cases for Special Consideration

210. Default in connection with voluntary arrangement. The court may not make a bankruptcy order on a petition[1] by the supervisor of, or a person bound by, a voluntary arrangement proposed and approved under Part 8 of the Insolvency Act 1986[2] unless it is satisfied:

(1) that the debtor has failed to comply with his obligations under the voluntary arrangement[3]; or

(2) that information which was false or misleading in any material particular or which contained material omissions was contained in any statement of affairs[4] or other document supplied by the debtor, or was otherwise made available by the debtor to his creditors at or in connection with a meeting of creditors summoned under the statutory provisions[5]; or

(3) that the debtor has failed to do all such things as may for the purposes of the voluntary arrangement have been reasonably required of him by the supervisor of the arrangement[6].

Where a bankruptcy order is made on such a petition, any expenses properly incurred as expenses of the administration of the voluntary arrangement in question are a first charge on the bankrupt's estate[7].

The effect of bankruptcy on a voluntary arrangement will in general be as follows: (a) a trust will usually be created where the arrangement provides for monies and assets to be held for the benefit of creditors; (b) where the debtor is later made bankrupt, the effect of bankruptcy on the trusts created by the arrangement will depend on the terms of the arrangement, and where express provision is made as to what should happen in the event of bankruptcy effect will be given to that provision; (c) without such provision, the trust will continue according to its terms; and (d) creditors bound by the arrangement may prove in the bankruptcy for so much of their debt as has not been, or will not be, recovered under the trust[8].

1   Ie under the Insolvency Act 1986 s 264(1)(c): see PARA 130 head (5).
2   Ie under the Insolvency Act 1986 Pt 8 (ss 252–263G): see PARA 43 et seq.
3   See *Vadher v Weisgard* [1997] BCC 219, [1998] BPIR 295 (debtor's failure to co-operate); *Carter-Knight v Peat* [2000] BPIR 968 (bankruptcy order made where there were serious breaches of the debtor's obligations, even though these had been remedied by the date of the hearing).
4   As to the statement of affairs see PARA 55.
5   Ie summoned under the Insolvency Act 1986 Pt 8: see PARA 43 et seq. Information will be false or misleading in a material way if, had the true position been given, it would have been likely to make a material difference to the way in which creditors would have considered and assessed the proposals: *Re Tack* [2000] BPIR 164. Secret arrangements between creditors to which the debtor is privy may constitute a material omission if they are not disclosed: *Cadbury Schweppes plc v Somji* [2001] 1 WLR 615, sub nom *Somji v Cadbury Schweppes plc* [2001] BCLC 498, CA.
6   Insolvency Act 1986 s 276(1). The discretion whether to make a bankruptcy order will be exercised having regard to what is in the best interests of the creditors: *Re Bourne, Kaye v Bourne* [2004] EWHC 3236 (Ch), [2005] BPIR 590, [2004] All ER (D) 384 (Nov).
7   Insolvency Act 1986 s 276(2). As to the meaning of 'the bankrupt's estate' see PARA 211. In the case of the administration in bankruptcy of the insolvent estate of a deceased person dying before the presentation of a bankruptcy petition, s 276(2) applies: Administration of Insolvent Estates of Deceased Persons Order 1986, SI 1986/1999, art 3(1), Sch 1 Pt II para 8. As to the administration in bankruptcy of the insolvent estates of deceased persons see further PARA 830 et seq.
8   *Re NT Gallagher & Son Ltd (in liquidation)* [2002] EWCA Civ 404, [2002] 3 All ER 474, [2002] 1 WLR 2380.

(4) PROTECTION OF BANKRUPT'S ESTATE; INVESTIGATION OF HIS AFFAIRS

(i) In general

211.   Meaning of 'bankrupt's estate'.   A bankrupt's estate for the purposes of the Insolvency Act 1986[1] comprises:
(1)   all property[2] belonging to or vested in the bankrupt at the commencement of the bankruptcy[3]; and
(2)   any property which, by virtue of any of the provisions of the 1986 Act[4], is comprised in that estate or is treated as falling within head (1) above[5].
The above provisions do not, however, apply to:
(a)   such tools, books, vehicles and other items of equipment as are necessary to the bankrupt for use personally by him in his employment, business[6] or vocation[7];
(b)   such clothing, bedding, furniture, household equipment and provisions as are necessary for satisfying the basic domestic needs of the bankrupt and his family[8];
(c)   property held by the bankrupt on trust for any other person[9];

(d)   the right of nomination to a vacant ecclesiastical benefice[10];

(e)   a tenancy which is an assured tenancy[11] or assured agricultural occupancy[12] and the terms of which inhibit[13] an assignment[14];

(f)   a protected tenancy[15] in respect of which[16] no premium can lawfully be required as a condition of assignment[17];

(g)   a tenancy of a dwelling house by virtue of which the bankrupt is[18] a protected occupier of the dwelling house, and the terms of which inhibit[19] an assignment[20]; or

(h)   a secure tenancy[21] which is not capable[22] of being assigned[23].

References in the Insolvency Act 1986[24] to property, in relation to a bankrupt, include references to any power exercisable by him over or in respect of property, except in so far as the power is exercisable over or in respect of property not for the time being comprised in the bankrupt's estate and:

(i)   is so exercisable at a time after either the official receiver has had his release in respect of that estate[25] or a meeting summoned by the trustee of that estate[26] has been held; or

(ii)   cannot be so exercised for the benefit of the bankrupt;

and a power exercisable over or in respect of property is deemed[27] to vest in the person entitled to exercise it at the time of the transaction or event by virtue of which it is exercisable by that person, whether or not it becomes so exercisable at that time[28].

For these purposes[29], property comprised in a bankrupt's estate is so comprised subject to the rights of any person other than the bankrupt, whether as a secured creditor[30] of the bankrupt or otherwise, in relation thereto, but disregarding any rights in relation to which a statement[31] by a secured creditor was made in the petition on which the bankrupt was adjudged bankrupt, and any rights which have been otherwise given up in accordance with the Insolvency Rules 1986[32].

The above provisions have effect subject to the provisions of any enactment not contained in the Insolvency Act 1986 under which any property is to be excluded from a bankrupt's estate[33].

1   Ie for the purposes of any of the Insolvency Act 1986 Pts 7A-11 (ss 251A–385).

2   As to the types of property comprised in the bankrupt's estate which vest in a trustee see PARA 397 et seq. In specified circumstances, the bankrupt's home does not form part of the bankrupt's estate: see PARA 212.

3   As to the commencement of bankruptcy see PARA 209.

4   Ie for the purposes of any of the provisions of the Insolvency Act 1986 Pt 9 (ss 264–371).

5   Insolvency Act 1986 s 283(1). In the case of the administration in bankruptcy of the insolvent estate of a deceased person dying before the presentation of a bankruptcy petition, s 283 applies with the modifications: (1) that it has effect as if the petition had been presented and the insolvency administration order had been made on the date of death of the deceased debtor (Administration of Insolvent Estates of Deceased Persons Order 1986, SI 1986/1999, art 3(1), Sch 1 Pt II para 12); (2) that in the Insolvency Act 1986 s 283(2)(b) (see text head (b)) for the words 'bankrupt and his family' there are to be substituted the words 'family of the deceased debtor' (Administration of Insolvent Estates of Deceased Persons Order 1986, SI 1986/1999, Sch 1 Pt II para 12(a)); and (3) references in any of the Insolvency Act 1986 Pts VIII-XI (ss 252–385) to property, in relation to a deceased debtor, include the capacity to exercise and take proceedings for exercising all such powers over or in respect of property as might have been exercised by his personal representative for the benefit of the estate on the date of the insolvency administration order and as are specified in s 283(4) (see the text and notes 24–28) (s 283(4A) (added by the Administration of Insolvent Estates of Deceased Persons Order 1986, SI 1986/1999, Sch 1 Pt II para 12(b))). As to the administration in bankruptcy of the insolvent estates of deceased persons see further PARA 823 et seq.

As to the modification of the Insolvency Act 1986 s 283 by the Insolvent Partnerships Order 1994, SI 1994/2421, in relation to the bankruptcy of an individual member of an insolvent partnership see COMPANY AND PARTNERSHIP INSOLVENCY vol 17 (2011) PARAS 1305, 1328.

6   As to the meaning of 'business' see PARA 43 note 4.

7   Insolvency Act 1986 s 283(2)(a). Section 283(2) is subject to s 308 (see PARA 404): s 283(2). As to the modifications which apply in the case of the administration in bankruptcy of the insolvent estate of a deceased person dying before the presentation of a bankruptcy petition see note 5.

8   Insolvency Act 1986 s 283(2)(b). See also note 5. For these purposes, 'family', in relation to a bankrupt, means the persons, if any, who are living with him and are dependent on him: s 385(1).

9   Insolvency Act 1986 s 283(3)(a).

10 Insolvency Act 1986 s 283(3)(b). As to the right of nomination see ECCLESIASTICAL LAW vol 34 (2011) PARA 551.

11 Ie within the meaning of the Housing Act 1988 Pt 1 (ss 1–45): see LANDLORD AND TENANT vol 63 (2012) PARA 1098.

12 Ie within the meaning of the Housing Act 1988 Pt 1: see LANDLORD AND TENANT vol 64 (2012) PARA 1463.

13 Ie as mentioned in the Rent Act 1977 s 127(5): see LANDLORD AND TENANT vol 63 (2012) PARA 1028.

14 Insolvency Act 1986 s 283(3A)(a) (added by the Housing Act 1988 s 117(1)). The Insolvency Act 1986 s 283(3A) is subject to s 308A (see PARA 405): s 283(3A) (added by the Housing Act 1988 s 117(1)).

15 Ie within the meaning of the Rent Act 1977: see LANDLORD AND TENANT vol 63 (2012) PARA 931.

16 Ie by virtue of any provision of the Rent Act 1977 Pt IX (ss 119–128): see LANDLORD AND TENANT vol 63 (2012) PARA 1024 et seq.

17 Insolvency Act 1986 s 283(3A)(b) (added by the Housing Act 1988 s 117(1)). See also note 14.

18 Ie within the meaning of the Rent (Agriculture) Act 1976: see LANDLORD AND TENANT vol 64 (2012) PARAS 1424–1425.

19 See note 13.

20 Insolvency Act 1986 s 283(3A)(c) (added by the Housing Act 1988 s 117(1)). See also note 14.

21 Ie within the meaning of the Housing Act 1985 Pt IV (ss 79–117): see LANDLORD AND TENANT vol 64 (2012) PARA 1297 et seq.

22 Ie except in the cases mentioned in the Housing Act 1985 s 91(3): see LANDLORD AND TENANT vol 64 (2012) PARA 1324.

23 Insolvency Act 1986 s 283(3A)(d) (added by the Housing Act 1988 s 117(1)). See also note 14.

24 Ie in any of the Insolvency Act 1986 Pts 7A–11.

25 Ie under the Insolvency Act 1986 s 299(2): see PARA 380.

26 Ie under the Insolvency Act 1986 s 331: see PARA 616.

27 Ie for the purposes of the Insolvency Act 1986 Pts 7A-11.

28 Insolvency Act 1986 s 283(4). As to the modifications which apply in the case of the administration in bankruptcy of the insolvent estate of a deceased person dying before the presentation of a bankruptcy petition see note 5; and PARA 417.

29 Ie for the purposes of any provision in the Insolvency Act 1986 Pts 7A–11.

30 As to the meaning of 'secured creditor' see PARA 574.

31 Ie a statement such as is required by the Insolvency Act 1986 s 269(1)(a): see PARA 132 note 7 head (1).

32 Insolvency Act 1986 s 283(5). As from a day to be appointed, s 283(5) is amended by the Enterprise and Regulatory Reform Act 2013 s 71, Sch 19 paras 1, 14: see PARA 130 note 17.

33 Insolvency Act 1986 s 283(6). In general social security payments, certain pensions and analogous benefits are expressed to be inalienable, and not to pass to the trustee in bankruptcy or any other person acting on behalf of the recipient's creditors: see eg:

    (1)   the Local Government Superannuation Act 1937 s 23 and the Local Government Superannuation Act 1953 (both these last-named enactments were repealed by the Superannuation Act 1972 s 29(4), Sch 8, but, by virtue of s 29(2), Sch 7 para 5, Table, they have effect as provisions of regulations under s 7 or s 8(2); and see Sch 3 para 9) (see LOCAL GOVERNMENT vol 69 (2009) PARA 1 et seq);

    (2)   the Superannuation Act 1972 s 5 (amended by the Insolvency Act 1985 s 235(1), Sch 8 para 19(b); the Bankruptcy (Scotland) Act 1985 s 75(1), Sch 7 para 9; the Insolvency Act 1986 s 439(2), Sch 14) (see SOCIAL SECURITY AND PENSIONS vol 44(2) (Reissue) PARA 875);

(3)   the National Health Service (Compensation) Regulations 1974, SI 1974/1748, reg 40(1) (see HEALTH SERVICES vol 54 (2008) PARA 712);

(4)   the Police Pensions Act 1976 s 9 (see POLICE AND INVESTIGATORY POWERS vol 84 (2013) PARA 197);

(5)   the Firefighters' Pension Scheme (England) Order 2006, SI 2006/3432, art 2, Sch 1 r 6(3); and the Firefighters' Pension Scheme (Wales) Order 2007, SI 2007/1072, art 2, Sch 1 r 6(3) (see FIRE AND RESCUE SERVICES vol 51 (2013) PARA 48);

(6)   the Social Security Administration Act 1992 s 187(1) (see SOCIAL SECURITY AND PENSIONS);

(7)   the Merchant Shipping Act 1995 s 34 (see SHIPPING AND MARITIME LAW vol 93 (2008) PARA 471);

(8)   the Local Government Pension Scheme (Administration) Regulations 2008, SI 2008/239, reg 53(3) (see LOCAL GOVERNMENT vol 69 (2009) PARA 451);

(9)   the National Health Service Pension Scheme Regulations 1995, SI 1995/300, reg T3 (see HEALTH SERVICES vol 54 (2008) PARA 739);

(10) the Teachers' (Compensation for Redundancy and Premature Retirement) Regulations 1997, SI 1997/311, reg 27(2) (see EDUCATION vol 36 (2011) PARA 1008);

(11) the Teachers' Pensions Regulations 2010, SI 2010/990, reg 122 (see EDUCATION vol 36 (2011) PARA 1005); and

(12) the Welfare Reform and Pensions Act 1999 ss 11, 12 and the Occupational and Personal Pension Schemes (Bankruptcy) (No 2) Regulations 2002, SI 2002/836 (see PARA 395).

212.   Bankrupt's home ceasing to form part of estate. Where property comprised in the bankrupt's estate consists of an interest in a dwelling house[1] which at the date of the bankruptcy was the sole or principal residence of the bankrupt[2], the bankrupt's spouse or civil partner[3], or a former spouse or former civil partner of the bankrupt[4], at the end of the period of three years[5] beginning with the date of the bankruptcy that interest ceases to be comprised in the bankrupt's estate[6], and vests in the bankrupt, without conveyance, assignment or transfer[7].

The above provisions do not apply if during the period of three years beginning with the date of the bankruptcy: (1) the trustee realises the interest in the dwelling house[8]; (2) the trustee applies for an order for sale in respect of the dwelling house[9]; (3) the trustee applies for an order for possession of the dwelling house[10]; (4) the trustee applies for an order imposing a charge on the dwelling house for the benefit of the bankrupt's estate[11] in respect of that interest[12]; or (5) the trustee and the bankrupt agree that the bankrupt is to incur a specified liability to his estate, with or without the addition of interest from the date of the agreement, in consideration of which the interest in the dwelling house will cease to form part of the estate[13].

If the bankrupt does not inform the trustee or the official receiver of his interest in a property before the end of the period of three months beginning with the date of the bankruptcy, the three-year period does not begin with the date of the bankruptcy[14], but begins with the date on which the trustee or official receiver becomes aware of the bankrupt's interest[15].

The rules[16] may provide for the above provisions to have effect with the substitution of a shorter period for the period of three years beginning with the date of the bankruptcy in specified circumstances, which may be described by reference to action to be taken by a trustee in bankruptcy[17].

Transitional provisions apply in relation to an individual who is adjudged bankrupt on a petition presented before the above provisions come into force[18].

1   As to the meaning of 'dwelling house' see PARA 413 note 1.

2   Insolvency Act 1986 s 283A(1)(a) (s 283A added by the Enterprise Act 2002 s 261(1)). Where it appears to a trustee that the Insolvency Act 1986 s 283A(1) applies, the trustee must give notice

as soon as reasonably practicable to: (1) the bankrupt; (2) the bankrupt's spouse or civil partner (in a case falling within s 283A(1)(b) (see the text to note 3)); and (3) a former spouse or former civil partner of the bankrupt (in a case falling within s 283A(1)(c) (see the text to note 4)): Insolvency Rules 1986, SI 1986/1925, r 6.237(1) (substituted by SI 2003/1730; and amended by SI 2005/2114). Notice should be given in accordance with the Insolvency Rules 1986, SI 1986/1925, Sch 4 Form 6.83 (added by SI 2003/1730; and substituted by SI 2005/2114). The notice must contain: (a) the name of the bankrupt; (b) the address of the dwelling-house; and (c) if the dwelling-house is registered land, the title number: Insolvency Rules 1986, SI 1986/1925, r 6.237(2) (substituted by SI 2003/1730). A trustee must not give such notice any later than 14 days before the expiry of the three year period under the Insolvency Act 1986 s 283A(2) or (5): Insolvency Rules 1986, SI 1986/1925, r 6.237(3) (substituted by SI 2003/1730). 'Registered land' has the same meaning as in the Land Registration Act 2002 s 132(1) (see REAL PROPERTY AND REGISTRATION vol 87 (2012) PARA 459): Insolvency Rules 1986, SI 1986/1925, r 6.237E(1) (added by SI 2003/1730).

3 Insolvency Act 1986 s 283A(1)(b) (as added (see note 2); and amended by the Civil Partnership Act 2004 s 261(1), Sch 27 para 113(a)). See note 2.

4 Insolvency Act 1986 s 283A(1)(c) (as added (see note 2); and amended by the Civil Partnership Act 2004 s 261(1), Sch 27 para 113(b)). See note 2.

5 The court may substitute for this period a longer period in prescribed circumstances, and in such other circumstances as it thinks appropriate: Insolvency Act 1986 s 283A(6) (as added: see note 2). As to the meaning of 'prescribed' see PARA 203 note 4. The court may substitute for the period of three years such longer period as the court thinks just and reasonable in all the circumstances of the case: Insolvency Rules 1986, SI 1986/1925, r 6.237C (added by SI 2003/1730). Where the trustee in bankruptcy has sent notice to the bankrupt that he considers: (1) the continued vesting of the property in the bankrupt's estate to be of no benefit to creditors; or (2) the re-vesting to the bankrupt will facilitate a more efficient administration of the bankrupt's estate, then the period of three years is substituted with the period of one month from the date of that notice: Insolvency Rules 1986, SI 1986/1925, r 6.237CA (added by SI 2004/584).

6 Insolvency Act 1986 s 283A(2)(a) (as added: see note 2).

7 Insolvency Act 1986 s 283A(2)(b). Section 283A applies only to property belonging to or vested in the bankrupt at the commencement of the bankruptcy and not to property which by reason of other provisions of the Insolvency Act 1986 is treated as belonging to or vested in the bankrupt as at that date: *Stonham v Ramrattan* [2011] EWCA Civ 119, [2011] 4 All ER 392, [2011] 1 WLR 1617.

Where the dwelling-house is registered land (see note 2) and an entry has been made, or entries have been made, in the individual register or registers of the dwelling-house relating to the bankrupt's bankruptcy or the individual register or registers has or have been altered to reflect the vesting of the bankrupt's interest in a trustee in bankruptcy, the trustee must, within five business days of the vesting, make such application or applications to the Chief Land Registrar as are necessary to show in the individual register or registers of the dwelling-house that the interest has vested in the bankrupt: Insolvency Rules 1986, SI 1986/1925, r 6.237A(1), (2) (added by SI 2003/1730; and amended by SI 2005/2114; and SI 2010/686). 'Individual register' has the same meaning as in the Land Registration Rules 2003, SI 2003/1417, r 217 (see REAL PROPERTY AND REGISTRATION vol 87 (2012) PARA 330): Insolvency Rules 1986, SI 1986/1925, r 6.237E(2) (added by SI 2003/1730). The application must be made in accordance with the Land Registration Act 2002 and must be accompanied by: (1) evidence of the trustee's appointment (where not previously provided to the Chief Land Registrar); and (2) a certificate from the trustee stating that the interest has vested in the bankrupt under the Insolvency Act 1986 s 283A(2) or s 283A(4) (see note 13) or the Enterprise Act 2002 s 261(8) (see the text and note 18) (whichever is appropriate): Insolvency Rules 1986, SI 1986/1925, r 6.237A(3) (added by SI 2003/1730). As soon as reasonably practicable after making the application, the trustee must notify the bankrupt and if the dwelling-house was the sole or principal residence of his spouse or former spouse or civil partner or former civil partner, such person, that the application has been made: Insolvency Rules 1986, SI 1986/1925, r 6.237A(4) (added by SI 2003/1730; and amended by SI 2005/2114). The trustee must notify every person who (to his knowledge) either claims an interest in the dwelling-house, or is under any liability in respect of the dwelling-house that an application has been made: Insolvency Rules 1986, SI 1986/1925, r 6.237A(5) (added by SI 2003/1730).

Where the dwelling-house is unregistered land, the trustee must issue the bankrupt with a certificate as to the vesting in the form set out in the Insolvency Rules 1986, SI 1986/1925, Sch 4 Form 6.84 as soon as reasonably practicable; and the certificate is conclusive proof that the interest has vested in the bankrupt: r 6.237B(1), (2) (added by SI 2003/1730; and amended by

SI 2005/2114). As soon as reasonably practicable after issuing the certificate the trustee must, if the dwelling-house was the sole or principal residence of the bankrupt's spouse or former spouse or civil partner or former civil partner, notify such person, that the application has been made: Insolvency Rules 1986, SI 1986/1925, r 6.237B(3) (added by SI 2003/1730; and amended by SI 2005/2114). The trustee must notify every person who (to his knowledge) either claims an interest in the dwelling-house, or is under any liability in respect of the dwelling-house, that an application has been made: Insolvency Rules 1986, SI 1986/1925, r 6.237B(4) (added by SI 2003/1730).

8   Insolvency Act 1986 s 283A(3)(a) (as added: see note 2). 'Realise' does not include effecting a sale for future cash consideration at the stage before such cash is actually received: *Lewis v Metropolitan Properties Realisation Ltd* [2009] EWCA Civ 448, [2010] Ch 148, [2009] 4 All ER 141 (distinction to be made between concepts of sale and realisation and differing significance of trustee in bankruptcy's powers and limits placed on exercise thereof).

9   Insolvency Act 1986 s 283A(3)(b) (as added: see note 2).

10   Insolvency Act 1986 s 283A(3)(c) (as added: see note 2).

11   Ie an order under the Insolvency Act 1986 s 313: see PARA 413.

12   Insolvency Act 1986 s 283A(3)(d) (as added: see note 2).

13   Insolvency Act 1986 s 283A(3)(e) (as added: see note 2). Where an application of a kind described in heads (2)–(4) in the text is made during the period of three years beginning with the date of the bankruptcy and is dismissed, unless the court orders otherwise the interest to which the application relates will on the dismissal of the application cease to be comprised in the bankrupt's estate, and vest in the bankrupt, without conveyance, assignment or transfer: s 283A(4) (as so added).

14   Insolvency Act 1986 s 283A(5)(a) (as added: see note 2).

15   Insolvency Act 1986 s 283A(5)(b) (as added: see note 2).

16   Ie rules made under the Insolvency Act 1986 s 412.

17   Insolvency Act 1986 s 283A(7) (as added: see note 2). The rules may also, in particular, make provision: (1) requiring or enabling the trustee of a bankrupt's estate to give notice that s 283A applies or does not apply; (2) about the effect of a notice under head (1); (3) requiring the trustee of a bankrupt's estate to make an application to the Chief Land Registrar: s 283A(8) (as added: see note 2). Rules under head (2) may, in particular: (a) disapply s 283A; (b) enable a court to disapply s 283A; (c) make provision in consequence of a disapplication of s 283A; (d) enable a court to make provision in consequence of a disapplication of s 283A; (e) make provision, which may include provision conferring jurisdiction on a court or tribunal, about compensation: s 283A(9) (as added: see note 2).

18   See the Enterprise Act 2002 s 261(7)–(10). Section 261(7)–(10) only apply to bankruptcies made under the Insolvency Act 1986: *Pannell v Official Receiver* [2008] EWHC 736 (Ch), [2008] BPIR 629.

213.   Restrictions on disposition of property. Where a person is adjudged bankrupt, any disposition of property made by that person in the period to which the following provisions apply[1] is void except to the extent that it is or was made with the consent of the court, or is or was subsequently ratified by the court[2]. The above provisions apply to a payment, whether in cash or otherwise, as it applies to a disposition of property and, accordingly, where any payment is void by virtue of the above provisions, the person paid must hold the sum for the bankrupt as part of his estate[3].

The above provisions do not give a remedy against any person:

(1)   in respect of any property or payment which he received before the commencement of the bankruptcy in good faith[4], for value and without notice that the petition had been presented; or

(2)   in respect of any interest in property which derives from an interest in respect of which there is, by virtue of these provisions, no remedy[5].

Where, after commencement of his bankruptcy[6], the bankrupt has incurred a debt to a banker or other person by reason of the making of a payment which is void, that debt is deemed[7] to have been incurred before the commencement of the bankruptcy unless that banker or person had notice of the bankruptcy before the debt was incurred, or it is not reasonably practicable for the amount of the payment to be recovered from the person to whom it was made[8].

A disposition of property is void, notwithstanding that the property is not, or, as the case may be, would not be, comprised in the bankrupt's estate; but nothing in the above provisions affects any disposition made by a person of property held by him on trust for any other person[9].

1   The Insolvency Act 1986 s 284 applies to the period beginning with the day of the presentation of the petition for the bankruptcy order (see PARA 164 et seq) and ending with the vesting, under Pt 9 Ch 4 (ss 305–335: see PARA 397 et seq), of the bankrupt's estate in a trustee: s 284(3). As from a day to be appointed, s 284(3) is amended by the Enterprise and Regulatory Reform Act 2013 s 71, Sch 19 paras 1, 15: see PARA 130 note 17.
        A claim by a trustee in bankruptcy against a third party in relation to foreign property transferred by the widow of a deceased bankrupt to that party is a claim in rem as to ownership, to which the law of lex situs of the property applies: *Re Hayward* [1997] Ch 45, [1997] 1 All ER 32.

2   Insolvency Act 1986 s 284(1). As from a day to be appointed, s 284(1) is amended by the Enterprise and Regulatory Reform Act 2013 s 71, Sch 19 paras 1, 15: see PARA 130 note 17.
        In the case of the administration in bankruptcy of the insolvent estate of a deceased person dying before the presentation of a bankruptcy petition, the Insolvency Act 1986 s 284 applies with the modification that it has effect as if the petition had been presented and the insolvency administration order had been made on the date of death of the deceased debtor and with the relevant modifications to s 283 (see PARA 211 note 5): Administration of Insolvent Estates of Deceased Persons Order 1986, SI 1986/1999, art 3(1), Sch 1 Pt II para 12. As to the administration in bankruptcy of the insolvent estates of deceased persons see further PARA 830 et seq.
        As to the modification of the Insolvency Act 1986 s 284 by the Insolvent Partnerships Order 1994, SI 1994/2421, in relation to the bankruptcy of an individual member of an insolvent partnership see COMPANY AND PARTNERSHIP INSOLVENCY vol 17 (2011) PARAS 1307, 1330.
        As to a transfer of property order made in divorce proceedings in respect of property held by a person against whom a bankruptcy petition has been presented see *Re Flint (a bankrupt)* [1993] Ch 319, [1993] 2 WLR 537; *Re Mordant, Mordant v Halls* [1997] 2 FCR 378, [1995] BCC 209 (affd [1996] BPIR 302 at 315, CA); *Harper v O'Reilly* [1998] 3 FCR 475, [1997] BPIR 656; *Mountney v Treharne* [2002] EWCA Civ 1174, [2003] Ch 135, [2002] 3 WLR 1760; *Treharne & Sand v Forrester* [2003] EWHC 2784 (Ch), [2004] 1 FLR 1173, [2004] BPIR 338; *Bateman v Hyde* [2009] EWHC 81 (Ch), [2009] BPIR 737. Where assets of the bankrupt have been acquired by a third party for no consideration after commencement of the bankruptcy, the trustee is also entitled to the profits made from the use of those assets: see *Trustee of the Property of FC Jones & Sons (a firm) v Jones* [1997] Ch 159, [1996] 4 All ER 721, CA. As to the interpretation of the Insolvency Act 1986 s 284 generally see *Re Palmer (a debtor)* [1994] Ch 316, [1994] 3 All ER 835, CA; and see PARA 840. Cf the Insolvency Act 1986 s 127; and COMPANY AND PARTNERSHIP INSOLVENCY vol 17 (2011) PARAS 658–660.

3   Insolvency Act 1986 s 284(2). See *Pettit (trustee in bankruptcy of Thrussell) v Novakovic* [2007] BCC 462, [2007] BPIR 1643; cf *Hollicourt (Contracts) Ltd (in liquidation) v Bank of Ireland* [2001] Ch 555, [2001] 1 All ER 289, [2001] BPIR 47.

4   Knowledge that a statutory demand has not been complied with could be held to constitute a lack of good faith in a purchaser who proceeds with a transaction with a debtor: see *Re Dalton (a bankrupt), ex p Herrington & Carmichael (a firm) v Trustee* [1963] Ch 336, [1962] 2 All ER 499, DC. As to statutory demands see PARA 158 et seq.

5   Insolvency Act 1986 s 284(4). As from a day to be appointed, s 284(4) is amended by the Enterprise and Regulatory Reform Act 2013 s 71, Sch 19 paras 1, 15: see PARA 130 note 17.

6   As to the commencement of bankruptcy see PARA 209.

7   Ie for the purposes of any of the Insolvency Act 1986 Pts 7A–11 (ss 251A–385).

8   Insolvency Act 1986 s 284(5). As to the liability of a bank in relation to payments made from an account in credit after the presentation of a petition see *Hollicourt (Contracts) Ltd v Bank of Ireland* [2001] Ch 555, [2001] 1 All ER 289, [2001] BPIR 47, CA. See further FINANCIAL SERVICES AND INSTITUTIONS vol 49 (2008) PARAS 835, 847.

9   Insolvency Act 1986 s 284(6).

214. Restriction on proceedings and remedies. At any time when proceedings on a bankruptcy petition are pending or an individual has been adjudged bankrupt, the court may stay any action, execution or other legal process against the property or person of the debtor, or, as the case may be, of the bankrupt[1]. Any court in which proceedings are pending against any individual may, on proof that a bankruptcy petition has been presented in respect of that individual or that he is an undischarged bankrupt, either stay the proceedings or allow them to continue on such terms as it thinks fit[2].

After the making of a bankruptcy order, no person who is a creditor of the bankrupt in respect of a debt provable in the bankruptcy[3]:

(1) has any remedy against the property or person of the bankrupt in respect of that debt; or

(2) may, before the discharge of the bankrupt[4], commence any action or other legal proceedings against the bankrupt except with the permission of the court and on such terms as the court may impose[5].

Where any goods of an undischarged bankrupt are held by any person by way of pledge, pawn or other security, the official receiver may, after giving notice in writing of his intention to do so, inspect the goods[6]. Where such a notice has been given to any person, that person is not entitled, without the permission of the court, to realise his security unless he has given the trustee of the bankrupt's estate a reasonable opportunity of inspecting the goods and of exercising the bankrupt's right of redemption[7].

1 Insolvency Act 1986 s 285(1). As from a day to be appointed, s 285(1) is amended by the Enterprise and Regulatory Reform Act 2013 s 71, Sch 19 paras 1, 16: see PARA 130 note 17.

For these purposes, references to the property or goods of the bankrupt are to any of his property or goods, whether or not comprised in his estate: Insolvency Act 1986 s 285(6). As to the meaning of 'or other legal process' see *Smith (a bankrupt) v Braintree District Council* [1990] 2 AC 215, [1989] 3 All ER 897, HL; *Re A Debtor (No 1 of 1987, Lancaster), ex p Debtor v Royal Bank of Scotland plc* [1989] 2 All ER 46, sub nom *Re a Debtor (No 1 of 1987)* [1989] 1 WLR 271, CA.

In the case of the administration in bankruptcy of the insolvent estate of a deceased person dying before the presentation of a bankruptcy petition, the Insolvency Act 1986 s 285 applies with the modification that it has effect as if the petition had been presented and the insolvency administration order had been made on the date of death of the deceased debtor and with the relevant modifications to s 283 (see PARA 211 note 5): Administration of Insolvent Estates of Deceased Persons Order 1986, SI 1986/1999, art 3(1), Sch 1 Pt II para 12. As to the administration in bankruptcy of the insolvent estates of deceased persons see further PARA 830 et seq.

2 Insolvency Act 1986 s 285(2). As from a day to be appointed, s 285(2) is amended by the Enterprise and Regulatory Reform Act 2013 s 71, Sch 19 paras 1, 16: see PARA 130 note 17.

See *Re Smith (a bankrupt), ex p Braintree District Council* [1990] 2 AC 215, [1989] 3 All ER 897, HL (a case under the General Rate Act 1967 (repealed)); *Re A Debtor (No 1 of 1987, Lancaster), ex p Debtor v Royal Bank of Scotland plc* [1989] 2 All ER 46, sub nom *Re A Debtor (No 1 of 1987)* [1989] 1 WLR 271, CA; *Woodley v Woodley* [1993] 1 FCR 701, [1992] 2 FLR 417, CA; *Woodley v Woodley (No 2)* [1993] 4 All ER 1010, [1994] 1 WLR 1167, CA; *Re a Debtor (784 of 1991)* [1992] Ch 554, [1992] 3 All ER 376. Where civil proceedings were said to be prejudicial to subsequent criminal proceedings, the court ordered all interlocutory applications to be heard in private: see *Polly Peck International plc v Nadir* [1992] BCLC 746.

3 As to debts provable in the bankruptcy see PARA 507 et seq.

4 As to discharge from bankruptcy see PARA 638 et seq.

5 Insolvency Act 1986 s 285(3). Section 285(3) is subject to s 346 (see PARA 703 et seq) and s 347 (see PARA 711 et seq): s 285(3). Forfeiture for non-payment of rent is not a remedy or a security within the meaning of s 285, and the landlord is not a secured creditor: *Razzaq v Pala* [1997] 1 WLR 1336, [1997] BPIR 726; *Harlow District Council v Hall* [2006] EWCA Civ 156, [2006] 1 WLR 2116, [2006] 2 P & CR 296; see also *Sharples v Places for People Homes Ltd* [2011] EWCA Civ 813, [2012] Ch 38, [2012] 1 All ER 5822 (order for possession made in respect of assured tenancy). The entry of a judgment against a bankrupt in respect of a debt provable in

the bankruptcy is not a remedy within the meaning of the Insolvency Act 1986 s 285: *Heating Electrical Lighting and Piping Ltd (in liquidation) v Ross* [2012] EWHC 3764 (Civ), [2012] BPIR 122. Subject to the Insolvency Act 1986 s 285(5), s 285(3) does not affect the right of a secured creditor (see PARA 574) of the bankrupt to enforce his security: s 285(4). As to charging orders see *Wright v Nationwide Building Society* [2009] EWCA Civ 811, [2010] Ch 318, [2010] 2 WLR 1097; *Sandhu v Sidhu* [2011] EWHC 3675 (Ch), [2012] BPIR 456. The court has a discretion to allow a claimant to commence proceedings under s 285(3) when he has already served a claim form in the ordinary way against the bankrupt without realising that the latter was bankrupt: *Re Saunders (a bankrupt), Re Bearman (a bankrupt)* [1997] Ch 60, [1997] 3 All ER 992; *Bank of Scotland plc (t/a Birmingham Midshires) v Breytenbach* [2012] BPIR 1. Between the making of the bankruptcy order and the bankrupt's discharge, the Secretary of State is precluded from exercising his statutory rights to recover overpayment of benefits by deduction from other benefits payable: *Payne v Secretary of State for Work and Pensions* [2011] UKSC 60, [2012] 2 AC 1, [2012] 2 All ER 46. Retrospective permission can be given for the commencement of proceedings under the Insolvency Act 1986 s 285(3): *Governor and Co of the Bank of Ireland v Colliers International UK plc (in admin)* [2012] EWHC 2942 (Ch), [2013] 2 WLR 895, [2012] All ER (D) 255 (Oct) (affirming *Re Saunders (a bankrupt), Re Bearman (a bankrupt)*). As to the principles on which permission will be granted see *Bristol & West Building Society v Trustee of the property of Back (a bankrupt)* [1998] 1 BCLC 485, sub nom *Bristol & West Building Society v Trustee of the property of Back (a bankrupt) and Melinek (a bankrupt)* [1997] BCC 358 (application for permission after the commencement of proceedings); and see *Re Bank of Credit and Commerce International SA (No 4)* [1994] 1 BCLC 419; *National Bank of Kuwait v Menzies* [1994] 2 BCLC 306, [1995] BCC 453, sub nom *Menzies v National Bank of Kuwait SK* [1994] BCC 119, CA; *Re Taylor (A Bankrupt)* [2006] EWHC 3029 (Ch), [2007] Ch 150, [2001] 3 All ER 638. Cf the Insolvency Act 1986 s 130(2); and COMPANY AND PARTNERSHIP INSOLVENCY vol 17 (2011) PARA 851.

6   Insolvency Act 1986 s 285(5).
7   Insolvency Act 1986 s 285(5).

(ii) Powers of Court in Bankruptcy

215. General control of court. Every bankruptcy is under the general control of the court and the court has full power[1] to decide all questions of priorities and all other questions, whether of law or fact, arising in any bankruptcy[2].

An undischarged bankrupt or a discharged bankrupt whose estate is still being administered[3] must[4] do all such things as he may be directed to do by the court for the purposes of his bankruptcy or, as the case may be, the administration of that estate[5]; and the official receiver or the trustee of a bankrupt's estate may at any time apply to the court for a direction under this provision[6].

If any person without reasonable excuse fails to comply with any obligation so imposed on him[7], he is guilty of contempt of court and liable to be punished accordingly, in addition to any other punishment to which he may be subject[8].

1   Ie subject to the provisions of the Insolvency Act 1986 Pts 7A–11 (ss 251A–385).
2   Insolvency Act 1986 s 363(1). In the case of the administration in bankruptcy of the insolvent estate of a deceased person dying before the presentation of a bankruptcy petition, s 363 applies: Administration of Insolvent Estates of Deceased Persons Order 1986, SI 1986/1999, art 3(1), Sch 1 Pt II para 30. As to the administration in bankruptcy of the insolvent estates of deceased persons see further PARA 830 et seq. The powers conferred by the Insolvency Act 1986 s 363(1) are wide; for decisions under the similar provision in the Bankruptcy Act 1914 s 105 (repealed) see *Re Colgate (a bankrupt), ex p Trustee of Property of Bankrupt* [1986] Ch 439, [1986] 1 All ER 419, CA (where, in default of a creditors' meeting to fix the trustee's remuneration, the court fixed it itself); for decisions under the Insolvency Act 1986 s 363(1) see *Upton v Taylor and Colley* [1999] BPIR 168, DC; *Clements v Udal* [2002] 2 BCLC 606, [2001] BCC 658; *Law Society v Shah* [2007] EWHC 2841 (Ch), [2009] Ch 223, [2008] 3 WLR 1401; *Donaldson v O'Sullivan* [2008] EWCA Civ 879, [2009] 1 All ER 1087, [2009] 1 WLR 924.
3   Ie under the Insolvency Act 1986 Pt 9 Ch 4 (ss 305–335).
4   Ie without prejudice to any other provision of the Insolvency Act 1986 Pts 7A–11.
5   Insolvency Act 1986 s 363(2).

6   Insolvency Act 1986 s 363(3). As to the mode of application and the procedure see PARA 786 et
    seq.
7   Ie by the Insolvency Act 1986 s 363(2).
8   Insolvency Act 1986 s 363(4). As to contempt of court see CONTEMPT OF COURT vol 22 (2012)
    PARA 1 et seq; and as to offences see PARA 733 et seq.

216.   Seizure of bankrupt's property.   At any time after a bankruptcy order has
been made[1], the court may, on the application of the official receiver or the
trustee of the bankrupt's estate[2], issue a warrant authorising the person to whom
it is directed to seize any property comprised in the bankrupt's estate which is, or
any books, papers or records relating to the bankrupt's estate or affairs[3] which
are, in the possession or under the control of the bankrupt or any other person
who is required to deliver the property, books, papers or records to the official
receiver or trustee[4].

Any person executing such a warrant may, for the purpose of seizing any
property comprised in the bankrupt's estate or any books, papers or records
relating to the bankrupt's estate or affairs, break open any premises where the
bankrupt or anything that may be seized under the warrant is or is believed to be
and any receptacle of the bankrupt which contains or is believed to contain
anything that may be so seized[5].

If, after a bankruptcy order has been made, the court is satisfied that any
property comprised in the bankrupt's estate is, or any books, papers or records
relating to the bankrupt's estate or affairs are, concealed in any premises not
belonging to him, it may issue a warrant authorising any constable or prescribed
officer[6] of the court to search those premises for the property, books, papers or
records[7]. A warrant so issued to search premises not belonging to the bankrupt
authorises any person executing it to seize any property of the bankrupt found as
a result of the execution of the warrant[8].

Any property seized under a warrant issued under the above provisions[9] must
be:

(1)   lodged with, or otherwise dealt with as instructed by, whoever is
       specified in the warrant as authorised to receive it; or
(2)   kept by the officer seizing it pending the receipt of written orders from
       the court as to its disposal,
as may be directed by the warrant[10].

1   As to bankruptcy orders see PARA 198 et seq.
2   As to the meaning of 'the bankrupt's estate' see PARA 211.
3   As to the meaning of references to a person's affairs see PARA 43 note 4.
4   Insolvency Act 1986 s 365(1). In the case of the administration in bankruptcy of the insolvent
    estate of a deceased person dying before the presentation of a bankruptcy petition, s 365 applies:
    Administration of Insolvent Estates of Deceased Persons Order 1986, SI 1986/1999, art 3(1),
    Sch 1 Pt II para 30. As to the administration in bankruptcy of the insolvent estates of deceased
    persons see further PARA 830 et seq.
5   Insolvency Act 1986 s 365(2).
6   The person referred to in the Insolvency Act 1986 s 365(3) as the prescribed officer of the court
    is: (1) in the case of the High Court, the tipstaff and his assistants of the court; and (2) in the
    case of a county court, the district judge and the bailiffs: Insolvency Rules 1986, SI 1986/1925,
    r 7.21(2) (amended by SI 2010/686). As from a day to be appointed, any reference however
    expressed that is or is deemed to be a reference to a county court held under the County Courts
    Act 1984 s 1 is to be read as a reference to the county court established by s A1 of that Act: see
    the Crime and Courts Act 2013 Sch 9 Pt 2 para 11(1)(a), (3)(c). At the date at which this volume
    states the law no such day had been appointed.
7   Insolvency Act 1986 s 365(3). A warrant under s 365(3) may not be executed except in the
    prescribed manner and in accordance with its terms: s 365(4). As to execution of warrants
    generally see the Insolvency Rules 1986, SI 1986/1925, r 7.21; and PARA 750.

8   Insolvency Rules 1986, SI 1986/1925, r 7.25(1).
9   Ie issued under the Insolvency Act 1986 s 365(2) or (3).
10 Insolvency Rules 1986, SI 1986/1925, r 7.25(2).

217.   Power of arrest.   The court may cause a warrant to be issued to a constable or prescribed officer[1] of the court:

(1)   for the arrest of a debtor to whom a bankruptcy petition relates or of an undischarged bankrupt, or of a discharged bankrupt whose estate is still being administered[2]; and

(2)   for the seizure of any books, papers, records[3], money or goods in the possession of a person arrested under the warrant,

and may authorise a person arrested under such a warrant to be kept in custody, and anything seized under such a warrant to be held, in accordance with the Insolvency Rules 1986[4], until such time as the court may order[5].

The powers so conferred are exercisable in relation to a debtor or undischarged or discharged bankrupt if, at any time after the presentation of the bankruptcy petition relating to him or the making of the bankruptcy order against him, it appears to the court:

(a)   that there are reasonable grounds for believing that he has absconded, or is about to abscond, with a view to avoiding or delaying the payment of any of his debts or his appearance to a bankruptcy petition or to avoiding, delaying or disrupting any proceedings in bankruptcy against him or any examination of his affairs[6];

(b)   that he is about to remove his goods with a view to preventing or delaying possession being taken of them by the official receiver or the trustee of his estate;

(c)   that there are reasonable grounds for believing that he has concealed or destroyed, or is about to conceal or destroy, any of his goods or any books, papers or records which might be of use to his creditors in the course of his bankruptcy or in connection with the administration of his estate;

(d)   that he has, without the permission of the official receiver or the trustee of his estate, removed any goods in his possession which exceed in value the prescribed sum[7]; or

(e)   that he has failed, without reasonable excuse, to attend any examination ordered by the court[8].

When a person ('the arrested person') is arrested under a warrant issued under the above provisions:

(i)   the officer apprehending the arrested person must give him into the custody of the court in a case where the court is ready and able to deal with the arrested person, or where the court is not ready and able, the governor of the prison named in the warrant (or where that prison is not able to accommodate the arrested person, the governor of such other prison with appropriate facilities which is able to accommodate the arrested person), who must keep the arrested person in custody until such time as the court otherwise orders and must produce that person before the court at its next sitting; and

(ii)   any property in the arrested person's possession which may be seized must be lodged with, or otherwise dealt with as instructed by, whoever is specified in the warrant as authorised to receive it, or kept by the officer seizing it pending the receipt of written orders from the court as to its disposal, as may be directed by the court in the warrant[9].

1　The person referred to in the Insolvency Act 1986 s 364(1) as the prescribed officer of the court is: (1) in the case of the High Court, the tipstaff and his assistants of the court; and (2) in the case of a county court, the district judge and the bailiffs: Insolvency Rules 1986, SI 1986/1925, r 7.21(2) (amended by SI 2010/686). As from a day to be appointed, any reference however expressed that is or is deemed to be a reference to a county court held under the County Courts Act 1984 s 1 is to be read as a reference to the county court established by s A1 of that Act: see the Crime and Courts Act 2013 Sch 9 Pt 2 para 11(1)(a), (3)(c). At the date at which this volume states the law no such day had been appointed.

2　Ie under the Insolvency Act 1986 Pt 9 Ch 4 (ss 305–335).

3　As to the meaning of 'records' see PARA 20 note 6.

4　Ie the Insolvency Rules 1986, SI 1986/1925.

5　Insolvency Act 1986 s 364(1). As from a day to be appointed, s 364(1), (2) is amended by the Enterprise and Regulatory Reform Act 2013 s 71, Sch 19 paras 1, 50: see PARA 130 note 17.

　　The power of arrest does not conflict with the Convention for the Protection of Human Rights and Fundamental Freedoms ('the European Convention on Human Rights') (Rome, 4 November 1950; TS 71 (1953); Cmd 8969) art 5.1(b) (see RIGHTS AND FREEDOMS vol 88A (2013) PARAS 210, 222); however, if the arrest is made without notice, the evidence in support of the application must make it clear why the arrest is justified: *Hickling v Baker* [2007] EWCA Civ 287, [2007] 4 All ER 390, [2007] 1 WLR 2386.

　　As to the execution of warrants of arrest in other parts of the United Kingdom see the Insolvency Act 1986 s 426(7) and PARA 828; and as to the execution of warrants outside the court's district see the Insolvency Rules 1986, SI 1986/1925, r 7.24; and PARA 751. As to the execution of warrants generally see r 7.21; and PARA 750.

6　As to the meaning of references to a person's affairs see PARA 43 note 4.

7　For these purposes, the sum so prescribed is £1,000: Insolvency Proceedings (Monetary Limits) Order 1986, SI 1986/1996, art 3, Schedule Pt II (art 3 amended by SI 2009/465; the Insolvency Proceedings (Monetary Limits) Order 1986, SI 1986/1996, Schedule Pt II substituted by SI 2004/547). As to the Secretary of State's power to prescribe monetary limits see PARA 19 note 9.

8　Insolvency Act 1986 s 364(2). See note 5.

9　Insolvency Rules 1986, SI 1986/1925, r 7.22 (amended by SI 2010/686).

(iii) Interim Receiver

218. Interim receiver to be insolvency practitioner. A person who acts as interim receiver must be qualified to act as an insolvency practitioner in relation to the individual[1].

1　See the Insolvency Act 1986 s 388(2)(a). As to insolvency practitioners and their qualification see PARA 40; and COMPANY AND PARTNERSHIP INSOLVENCY vol 16 (2011) PARA 9 et seq. Nothing in s 388 applies to anything done by the official receiver: see s 388(5)(a) (substituted by the Bankruptcy (Scotland) Act 1993 s 11(1)). As to the application of the Insolvency Act 1986 s 388 in the case of the administration in bankruptcy of the insolvent estate of a deceased person dying before the presentation of a bankruptcy petition see PARA 40 note 9.

　　Nothing in s 388 applies to anything done (whether in the United Kingdom or elsewhere) in relation to insolvency proceedings under Council Regulation (EC) 1346/2000 (OJ L160, 30.6.2000, p 1) on insolvency proceedings ('European Regulation on Insolvency Proceedings') in a member state other than the United Kingdom: Insolvency Act 1986 s 388(6) (added by SI 2002/1240). See further PARAS 41, 42.

219. Power to appoint. If it is shown to be necessary for the protection of the debtor's property[1], the court may, at any time after the presentation of a bankruptcy petition[2] and before making a bankruptcy order[3], appoint the official receiver to be interim receiver of the debtor's property[4].

Where the court has, on a debtor's petition, appointed an insolvency practitioner to inquire into the debtor's affairs[5] and it is shown to the court to be necessary for the protection of the debtor's property as mentioned above[6], the court may, without making a bankruptcy order, appoint that practitioner, instead of the official receiver, to be interim receiver of the debtor's property[7].

1   For these purposes, references to the debtor's property are to all his property, whether or not it
     would be comprised in his estate if he were adjudged bankrupt: Insolvency Act 1986 s 286(8).
     As from a day to be appointed, s 286(8) is amended by the Enterprise and Regulatory Reform
     Act 2013 s 71, Sch 19 paras 1, 17: see PARA 130 note 17.
2   As to bankruptcy petitions see PARA 130 et seq.
3   As to bankruptcy orders see PARA 198 et seq.
4   Insolvency Act 1986 s 286(1). In the case of the administration in bankruptcy of the insolvent
     estate of a deceased person dying before the presentation of a bankruptcy petition,
     s 286(1), (3)–(8) (see note 1; and PARA 221 et seq) applies: Administration of Insolvent Estates of
     Deceased Persons Order 1986, SI 1986/1999, art 3(1), Sch 1 Pt II para 13. As to the
     administration in bankruptcy of the insolvent estates of deceased persons see further PARA 830
     et seq.
5   Ie under the Insolvency Act 1986 s 273: see PARA 203 et seq.
6   Ie as mentioned in the Insolvency Act 1986 s 286(1).
7   Insolvency Act 1986 s 286(2). See *Rio Properties Inc v Gibson Dunn & Crutcher* [2004] 1 WLR
     2702, [2004] BPIR 1203, CA (challenge to appointment of licensed insolvency practitioner
     dismissed).
        As from a day to be appointed, the Insolvency Act 1986 s 286(2) is repealed by the
     Enterprise and Regulatory Reform Act 2013 s 71, Sch 19 paras 1, 17: see PARA 130 note 17.

220.   Application for appointment. An application to the court for the
appointment of an interim receiver[1] may be made by a creditor, the debtor, an
insolvency practitioner appointed[2] to inquire into the debtor's affairs, a
temporary administrator or a member state liquidator appointed in main
proceedings[3].
     The application must be supported by an witness statement[4] stating:

(1)   the grounds on which it is proposed that the interim receiver should be
       appointed;
(2)   whether or not the official receiver has been informed of the application
       and, if so, has been furnished with a copy of it;
(3)   whether, to the applicant's knowledge, there has been proposed or is in
       force a voluntary arrangement under Part 8 of the Insolvency
       Act 1986[5]; and
(4)   the applicant's estimate of the value of the property or business in
       respect of which the interim receiver is to be appointed[6].

If an insolvency practitioner has been appointed to inquire into the debtor's
affairs, and it is proposed that he, and not the official receiver, should be
appointed interim receiver, and it is not the insolvency practitioner himself who
is the applicant for the order, the witness statement must state that he has
consented to act[7].
     The applicant must send copies of the application and the witness statement
to the person to be appointed interim receiver; and, if that person is the official
receiver and an insolvency practitioner has been appointed to inquire into the
debtor's affairs, and he is not himself the applicant, copies of the application and
witness statement must be sent by the applicant to the insolvency practitioner[8].
If, in any case where a copy of the application is to be so sent to a person, it is for
any reason not practicable to send a copy, that person must be informed of the
application in sufficient time to enable him to be present at the hearing[9].
     The official receiver and, if appointed, the insolvency practitioner may attend
the hearing of the application and make representations[10].

1   Ie under the Insolvency Act 1986 s 286: see PARA 219.
2   Ie under the Insolvency Act 1986 s 273(2): see PARA 203.
3   Insolvency Rules 1986, SI 1986/1925, r 6.51(1) (substituted by SI 2002/1307). As to the
     meanings of 'member state liquidator' and 'main proceedings' see PARA 175 notes 8, 9.
4   As to the meaning of 'witness statement' see PARA 161 note 7.

5 Ie under the Insolvency Act 1986 Pt 8 (ss 252–263G): see PARA 43 et seq.
6 Insolvency Rules 1986, SI 1986/1925, r 6.51(2) (amended by SI 2010/686).
7 Insolvency Rules 1986, SI 1986/1925, r 6.51(3) (amended by SI 2010/686).
8 Insolvency Rules 1986, SI 1986/1925, r 6.51(4) (amended by SI 2010/686).
9 Insolvency Rules 1986, SI 1986/1925, r 6.51(4) (amended by SI 2010/686).
10 Insolvency Rules 1986, SI 1986/1925, r 6.51(5).

221. Order of appointment. If satisfied that sufficient grounds are shown for the appointment of an interim receiver, the court may on the application make it on such terms as it thinks just[1]. The court may, however, by an order appointing any person to be an interim receiver direct that his powers are to be limited or restricted in any respect; but, save as so directed, an interim receiver has, in relation to the debtor's property[2], all the rights, powers, duties and immunities of a receiver and manager[3] pending the appointment of a trustee[4].

An order of the court appointing any person to be an interim receiver must require that person to take immediate possession of the debtor's property or, as the case may be, the part of it to which his powers as interim receiver are limited[5]; and it must state the nature and a short description of the property of which the person appointed is to take possession and the duties to be performed by him in relation to the debtor's affairs[6]. As soon as reasonably practicable after the order is made, the court must send two sealed copies of it to the person appointed interim receiver, one of which must be sent by him as soon as reasonably practicable to the debtor[7].

1 Insolvency Rules 1986, SI 1986/1925, r 6.51(6) (amended by SI 2010/686).
2 As to the meaning of references to the debtor's property see PARA 219 note 1.
3 Ie under the Insolvency Act 1986 s 287: see PARAS 229–231.
4 Insolvency Act 1986 s 286(3). As to the application of s 286 in a case of the administration in bankruptcy of the insolvent estate of a deceased person dying before the presentation of a bankruptcy petition see PARA 219 note 4.
5 Insolvency Act 1986 s 286(4).
6 Insolvency Rules 1986, SI 1986/1925, r 6.52(1). For the prescribed form of order see Sch 4 Form 6.32 (substituted by SI 2002/1307; and amended by SI 2010/686).
7 Insolvency Rules 1986, SI 1986/1925, r 6.52(2) (amended by SI 2009/642).

222. Deposit. Before an order appointing the official receiver as interim receiver is issued, the applicant for it must deposit with him, or otherwise secure to his satisfaction, such sum as the court directs to cover his remuneration and expenses[1]. If the sum deposited or secured subsequently proves to be insufficient, the court may, on application by the official receiver, order that an additional sum be deposited or secured; and, if the order is not complied with within two business days[2] after service on the person to whom the order is directed, the court may discharge the order appointing the interim receiver[3].

If a bankruptcy order is made after an interim receiver has been appointed, any money so deposited must, unless it is required by reason of insufficiency of assets for payment of remuneration and expenses of the interim receiver, or the deposit was made by the debtor out of his own property, be repaid to the person depositing it, or as the person may direct, out of the bankrupt's estate[4], in the prescribed order of priority[5].

1 Insolvency Rules 1986, SI 1986/1925, r 6.53(1).
2 As to the meaning of 'business day' see PARA 28 note 8.
3 Insolvency Rules 1986, SI 1986/1925, r 6.53(2) (amended by SI 2010/686). As to the order appointing an interim receiver see PARA 221.
4 As to the meaning of 'the bankrupt's estate' see PARA 211.

5 Insolvency Rules 1986, SI 1986/1925, r 6.53(3). For these purposes, 'prescribed order of priority' means the order of priority of payments laid down by Pt 6 Ch 23 (r 6.224: see PARA 590): r 13.13(7) (substituted by SI 1999/1022).

223. Security; failure to keep up security. Where an insolvency practitioner is appointed to be interim receiver[1], the cost of providing the security required[2] must be paid in the first instance by the interim receiver; but, if a bankruptcy order is not made, the person so appointed is entitled to be reimbursed out of the property of the debtor, and the court may make an order on the debtor accordingly; and, if a bankruptcy order is made, he is entitled to be reimbursed out of the estate[3] in the prescribed order of priority[4].

If the interim receiver fails to give or keep up his security, the court may remove him, and make such order as it thinks just as to costs[5]; and, if an order is so made removing the interim receiver, or discharging the order appointing him, the court must give directions as to whether any, and if so what, steps should be taken for the appointment of another person in his place[6].

1 Ie under the Insolvency Act 1986 s 286(2): see PARA 219 et seq.
2 Ie under the Insolvency Act 1986: see s 390(3); and PARA 40 note 3. As to the prescribed requirements for the existence of security see COMPANY AND PARTNERSHIP INSOLVENCY vol 16 (2011) PARAS 24, 25.
3 As to the meaning of 'the bankrupt's estate' see PARA 211.
4 Insolvency Rules 1986, SI 1986/1925, r 6.54(1), (2). As to the meaning of 'prescribed order of priority' see PARA 222 note 5.
5 Insolvency Rules 1986, SI 1986/1925, r 6.55(1) (amended by SI 2010/686).
6 Insolvency Rules 1986, SI 1986/1925, r 6.55(2).

224. Inquiry into debtor's dealings and property. Where an interim receiver has been appointed, the debtor must give him such inventory of his property[1] and such other information, and must attend on the interim receiver at such times, as the latter may for the purpose of carrying out his functions reasonably require[2].

The statutory provisions relating to inquiry into a bankrupt's dealings and property[3] and the court's enforcement powers thereunder[4] apply also where an interim receiver has been appointed as they apply where a bankruptcy order has been made as if references to the official receiver or the trustee were to the interim receiver, and references to the bankrupt and to his estate were, respectively, to the debtor and his property[5].

1 As to the meaning of references to the debtor's property see PARA 219 note 1.
2 Insolvency Act 1986 s 286(5). As to the application of s 286 in the case of the administration in bankruptcy of the insolvent estate of a deceased person dying before the presentation of a bankruptcy petition see PARA 219 note 4.
3 Ie the Insolvency Act 1986 s 366: see PARA 305 et seq.
4 Ie the Insolvency Act 1986 s 367: see PARA 312.
5 Insolvency Act 1986 s 368. In the case of the administration in bankruptcy of the insolvent estate of a deceased person dying before the presentation of a bankruptcy petition, s 368 applies: Administration of Insolvent Estates of Deceased Persons Order 1986, SI 1986/1999, art 3(1), Sch 1 Pt II para 30. As to the administration in bankruptcy of the insolvent estates of deceased persons see further PARA 830 et seq.

225. Restriction on proceedings and remedies. Where an interim receiver is appointed[1], the statutory restriction on proceedings and remedies[2] applies for the period between the appointment and the making of a bankruptcy order on the petition, or the dismissal of the petition, as if the appointment were the making of such an order[3].

1   Ie under the Insolvency Act 1986 s 286: see PARA 219 et seq.
2   Ie the Insolvency Act 1986 s 285(3): see PARA 214.
3   Insolvency Act 1986 s 286(6). As to the application of s 286 in the case of the administration in bankruptcy of the insolvent estate of a deceased person dying before the presentation of a bankruptcy petition see PARA 219 note 4.

226.   Power to ensure continuation of essential supplies by utilities.   An interim receiver has the like rights as the supervisor of a voluntary arrangement, the official receiver, a trustee in bankruptcy and a trustee under a deed of arrangement for ensuring continued supplies of gas, electricity, water and telecommunication services[1].

1   See the Insolvency Act 1986 s 372; and PARA 78.

227.   Remuneration.   The remuneration of the interim receiver, other than the official receiver, must be fixed by the court from time to time on his application[1]. In fixing the interim receiver's remuneration, the court must take into account:

(1)   the time properly given by him, as interim receiver, and his staff in attending to the debtor's affairs;

(2)   the complexity, or otherwise, of the case;

(3)   any respects in which, in connection with the debtor's affairs, there falls on the interim receiver any responsibility of an exceptional kind or degree;

(4)   the effectiveness with which the interim receiver appears to be carrying out, or to have carried out, his duties as such; and

(5)   the value and nature of the property with which he has to deal[2].

Without prejudice to any order the court may make as to costs, the interim receiver's remuneration, whether the official receiver or another, must be paid to him, and the amount of any expenses incurred by him, including the remuneration and expenses of any special manager[3], reimbursed:

(a)   if a bankruptcy order is not made, out of the property of the debtor; and

(b)   if a bankruptcy order is made, out of the estate[4] in the prescribed order of priority[5];

or, in either case, the relevant funds being insufficient, out of the deposit paid[6] by the applicant for the order appointing the interim receiver[7].

Unless the court otherwise directs, in a case falling within head (a) above, the interim receiver may retain out of the debtor's property such sums or property as are or may be required for meeting his remuneration and expenses[8].

1   Insolvency Rules 1986, SI 1986/1925, r 6.56(1). As to the official receiver's remuneration as interim receiver see PARA 39.
2   Insolvency Rules 1986, SI 1986/1925, r 6.56(2).
3   Ie any special manager appointed under the Insolvency Act 1986 s 370: see PARA 232 et seq.
4   As to the meaning of 'the bankrupt's estate' see PARA 211.
5   As to the meaning of 'prescribed order of priority' see PARA 222 note 5.
6   Ie under the Insolvency Rules 1986, SI 1986/1925, r 6.53: see PARA 222.
7   Insolvency Rules 1986, SI 1986/1925, r 6.56(3) (amended by SI 1987/1919).
8   Insolvency Rules 1986, SI 1986/1925, r 6.56(4) (added by SI 1987/1919).

228.   Termination of appointment.   A person ceases to be interim receiver of a debtor's property[1] if the bankruptcy petition relating to the debtor is dismissed, if a bankruptcy order is made on the petition or if the court by order or otherwise terminates the appointment[2].

The appointment of the interim receiver may be so terminated by the court on his application, or on that of the official receiver, the debtor or any creditor[3].

If the interim receiver's appointment terminates, in consequence of the dismissal of the bankruptcy petition or otherwise, the court may give such directions as it thinks just with respect to the accounts of his administration and any other matters which it thinks appropriate[4].

1   As to the meaning of references to the debtor's property see PARA 219 note 1.
2   Insolvency Act 1986 s 286(7). As to the application of s 286 in the case of the administration in bankruptcy of the insolvent estate of a deceased person dying before the presentation of a bankruptcy petition see PARA 219 note 4.
3   Insolvency Rules 1986, SI 1986/1925, r 6.57(1).
4   Insolvency Rules 1986, SI 1986/1925, r 6.57(2) (amended by SI 2010/686).

(iv) Receivership pending Appointment of Trustee

229. Receivership pending appointment of trustee. Between the making of a bankruptcy order[1] and the time at which the bankrupt's estate vests in the trustee[2], the official receiver is the receiver and the manager[3] of the bankrupt's estate[4] and is under a duty to act as such[5].

1   As to bankruptcy orders see PARA 198 et seq.
2   Ie under the Insolvency Act 1986 Pt 9 Ch 4 (ss 305–335): see PARA 397 et seq.
3   Ie subject to the Insolvency Act 1986 s 370: see PARA 232 et seq.
4   As to the meaning of 'the bankrupt's estate' see PARA 211.
5   Insolvency Act 1986 s 287(1). Section 287 does not apply where, by virtue of s 297 (see PARAS 320–321), the bankrupt's estate vests in a trustee immediately on the making of the bankruptcy order: s 287(5).
    In the case of the administration in bankruptcy of the insolvent estate of a deceased person dying before the presentation of a bankruptcy petition, s 287 applies: Administration of Insolvent Estates of Deceased Persons Order 1986, SI 1986/1999, art 3(1), Sch 1 Pt II para 14. As to the administration in bankruptcy of the insolvent estates of deceased persons see further PARA 830 et seq.
    As to the application of the Insolvency Act 1986 s 287 in the case of the bankruptcy of an individual member of an insolvent partnership see the Insolvent Partnerships Order 1994, SI 1994/2421; and COMPANY AND PARTNERSHIP INSOLVENCY vol 17 (2011) PARAS 1317, 1323.

230. Role of official receiver; duties and powers. The function of the official receiver while acting as receiver or manager of the bankrupt's estate[1] is to protect the estate; and, for this purpose, he has the same powers as if he were a receiver or manager appointed by the High Court[2], and he is entitled to sell or otherwise dispose of any perishable goods comprised in the estate and any other goods so comprised the value of which is likely to diminish if they are not disposed of[3].

While acting as receiver or manager of the estate, the official receiver:

(1)   must take all such steps as he thinks fit for protecting any property which may be claimed for the estate by the trustee of that estate;

(2)   is not, except in pursuance of directions given by the Secretary of State, required to do anything that involves his incurring expenditure;

(3)   may, if he thinks fit, and must, if so directed by the court, at any time summon a general meeting of the bankrupt's creditors[4].

1   As to the meaning of 'the bankrupt's estate' see PARA 211.
2   See RECEIVERS vol 88 (2012) PARA 1 et seq.
3   Insolvency Act 1986 s 287(2). Section 287 does not apply where, by virtue of s 297 (see PARAS 320–321), the bankrupt's estate vests in a trustee immediately on the making of the bankruptcy order: s 287(5).
    The provisions of s 287 apply in the case of the administration in bankruptcy of the insolvent estate of a deceased person dying before the presentation of a bankruptcy petition: see PARA 229 note 5.

The provisions of s 287 do not apply in the case of the bankruptcy of an individual member of an insolvent partnership: see PARA 229 note 5; and COMPANY AND PARTNERSHIP INSOLVENCY vol 17 (2011) PARAS 1317, 1323.

4   Insolvency Act 1986 s 287(3).

Under the Bankruptcy Act 1914 s 74(2) (repealed) the official receiver was required, as far as practicable, to consult the wishes of the creditors with respect to the management of the debtor's property. Such consultation is now discretionary only.

231. Liabilities of official receiver. Where:

(1)   the official receiver acting as receiver or manager of the bankrupt's estate[1] seizes or disposes of any property which is not comprised in the estate; and

(2)   at the time of the seizure or disposal the official receiver believes, and has reasonable grounds for believing, that he is entitled, whether in pursuance of an order of the court or otherwise, to seize or dispose of that property,

the official receiver is not to be liable to any person in respect of any loss or damage resulting from the seizure or disposal, except in so far as that loss or damage is caused by his negligence; and he has a lien on the property, or the proceeds of its sale, for such of the expenses of the bankruptcy as were incurred in connection with the seizure or disposal[2].

1   As to the meaning of 'the bankrupt's estate' see PARA 211.
2   Insolvency Act 1986 s 287(4). Section 287 does not apply where, by virtue of s 297 (see PARAS 320–321), the bankrupt's estate vests in a trustee immediately on the making of the bankruptcy order: s 287(5). As to the official receiver's immunity see *Mond v Hyde* [1999] QB 1097, [1998] 3 All ER 833, CA.

The provisions of the Insolvency Act 1986 s 287 apply in the case of the administration in bankruptcy of the insolvent estate of a deceased person dying before the presentation of a bankruptcy petition: see PARA 229 note 5.

The provisions of s 287 do not apply in the case of the bankruptcy of an individual member of an insolvent partnership: see PARA 229 note 5; and COMPANY AND PARTNERSHIP INSOLVENCY vol 17 (2011) PARAS 1317, 1323.

(v) Special Manager

232. Power to appoint special manager. On an application by the official receiver or the trustee of the bankrupt's estate[1] in any case where it appears to the official receiver or trustee that the nature of the estate, property or business, or the interests of the creditors generally, require the appointment of another person to manage the estate, property or business, the court may appoint any person to be the special manager:

(1)   of a bankrupt's estate;

(2)   of the business of an undischarged bankrupt; or

(3)   of the property or business of a debtor in whose case the official receiver has been appointed interim receiver[2].

1   As to the meaning of 'the bankrupt's estate' see PARA 216.
2   Insolvency Act 1986 s 370(1), (2). As to the appointment of the official receiver as interim receiver see s 286; and PARA 219 et seq.

In the case of the administration in bankruptcy of the insolvent estate of a deceased person dying before the presentation of a bankruptcy petition, s 370 applies: Administration of Insolvent Estates of Deceased Persons Order 1986, SI 1986/1999, art 3(1), Sch 1 Pt II para 30. As to the administration in bankruptcy of the insolvent estates of deceased persons see further PARA 830 et seq.

233. Application for appointment. An application[1] made by the official receiver or trustee for the appointment of a person to be special manager must be supported by a report setting out the reasons for the application; and the report must include the applicant's estimate of the value of the estate, property or business in respect of which the special manager is to be appointed[2].

1   Ie under the Insolvency Act 1986 s 370: see PARA 232.

2   Insolvency Rules 1986, SI 1986/1925, r 6.167(1).

234. Appointment and remuneration. The court's order appointing the special manager must specify the duration of his appointment, which may be for a period of time, or until the occurrence of a specified event; alternatively, the order may specify that the duration of the appointment is to be subject to a further order of the court[1].

The appointment of a special manager may be renewed by order of the court[2]; and the special manager's remuneration must be fixed from time to time by the court[3].

1   Insolvency Rules 1986, SI 1986/1925, r 6.167(2). For the prescribed form of order see Sch 4 Form 6.54 (amended by SI 2010/686).

2   Insolvency Rules 1986, SI 1986/1925, r 6.167(3).

3   Insolvency Rules 1986, SI 1986/1925, r 6.167(4).

235. Powers of special manager. A special manager appointed by the court[1] has such powers as may be entrusted to him by the court[2]; and this includes power to direct that any statutory provision[3] that has effect in relation to the official receiver, interim receiver or trustee is to have the like effect in relation to the special manager for the purposes of the carrying out by him of any of the functions of the official receiver, interim receiver or trustee[4]. A special manager may take part in the public examination of the bankrupt[5].

The acts of a person as a special manager are valid notwithstanding any defect in his appointment or qualifications[6].

1   Ie under the Insolvency Act 1986 s 370: see PARA 232.

2   Insolvency Act 1986 s 370(3). As to the application of s 370 in the case of the administration in bankruptcy of the insolvent estate of a deceased person dying before the presentation of a bankruptcy petition see PARA 232 note 2.

3   Ie any provisions in the Insolvency Act 1986 Pts 7A–11 (ss 251A–385).

4   Insolvency Act 1986 s 370(4).

5   See the Insolvency Act 1986 s 290(4)(c); and PARA 293 head (3).

6   Insolvency Act 1986 s 377. In the case of the administration in bankruptcy of the insolvent estate of a deceased person dying before the presentation of a bankruptcy petition, s 377 applies: Administration of Insolvent Estates of Deceased Persons Order 1986, SI 1986/1999, art 3(1), Sch 1 Pt II para 30. As to the administration in bankruptcy of the insolvent estates of deceased persons see further PARA 830 et seq.

236. Security; failure to keep up security. A special manager must give such security as may be prescribed[1]; and the appointment of the special manager[2] does not take effect until the person appointed has given, or, being allowed by the court to do so, undertaken to give, security to the person who applies for him to be appointed[3]. It is not, however, necessary that security should be given for each separate bankruptcy; but it may be given either specially for a particular bankruptcy, or generally for any bankruptcy in relation to which the special manager may be employed as such[4].

The amount of the security must be not less than the value of the estate, property or business in respect of which he is appointed, as estimated by the applicant in his report[5].

When the special manager has given security to the person applying for his appointment, that person's certificate as to the adequacy of the security must be filed in court[6]. The cost of providing the security must be paid in the first instance by the special manager but:

(1) where a bankruptcy order[7] is not made, he is entitled to be reimbursed out of the property of the debtor, and the court may make an order on the debtor accordingly; and

(2) where a bankruptcy order is made, he is entitled to be reimbursed out of the estate in the prescribed order of priority[8].

If the special manager fails to give the required security within the time stated for that purpose by the order appointing him, or any extension of that time that may be allowed, the official receiver or trustee, as the case may be, must report the failure to the court, which may thereupon discharge the order appointing the special manager[9].

If the special manager fails to keep up his security, the official receiver or trustee must report his failure to the court, which may thereupon remove the special manager, and make such order as it thinks just as to costs[10].

If an order is so made removing the special manager, or discharging the order appointing him, the court must give directions as to whether any, and if so what, steps should be taken for the appointment of another special manager in his place[11].

1 Insolvency Act 1986 s 370(5)(a). As to the application of s 370 in the case of the administration in bankruptcy of the insolvent estate of a deceased person dying before the presentation of a bankruptcy petition see PARA 232 note 2.

2 Ie under the Insolvency Act 1986 s 370: see PARA 232.

3 Insolvency Rules 1986, SI 1986/1925, r 6.168(1).

4 Insolvency Rules 1986, SI 1986/1925, r 6.168(2).

5 Insolvency Rules 1986, SI 1986/1925, r 6.168(3). The applicant's report is made under r 6.167(1) (see PARA 233): r 6.168(3).

6 Insolvency Rules 1986, SI 1986/1925, r 6.168(4). As to the meaning of 'file in court' see PARA 57 note 13.

7 As to bankruptcy orders see PARA 198 et seq.

8 Insolvency Rules 1986, SI 1986/1925, r 6.168(5). As to the meaning of 'prescribed order of priority' see PARA 222 note 5.

9 Insolvency Rules 1986, SI 1986/1925, r 6.169(1).

10 Insolvency Rules 1986, SI 1986/1925, r 6.169(2) (amended by SI 2010/686).

11 Insolvency Rules 1986, SI 1986/1925, r 6.169(3).

237. Accounting. The special manager must prepare and keep such accounts as may be prescribed[1]; and he must produce accounts, containing details of his receipts and payments, for the approval of the trustee[2]. The accounts must be in respect of three-month periods for the duration of the special manager's appointment, or for a lesser period, if his appointment terminates less than three months from its date, or from the date to which the last accounts were made up[3]. When the accounts have been approved, the special manager's receipts and payments must be added to those of the trustee[4].

1 Insolvency Act 1986 s 370(5)(b). A special manager must produce those accounts in accordance with the Insolvency Rules 1986, SI 1986/1925, to the Secretary of State or to such other persons as may be prescribed: Insolvency Act 1986 s 370(5)(c). The Insolvency Rules 1986, SI 1986/1925, r 6.170(1) requires production of the accounts to the trustee only: see the text and

note 2. As to the application of the Insolvency Act 1986 s 370 in the case of the administration in bankruptcy of the insolvent estate of a deceased person dying before the presentation of a bankruptcy petition see PARA 232 note 2.

2   Insolvency Rules 1986, SI 1986/1925, r 6.170(1).
3   Insolvency Rules 1986, SI 1986/1925, r 6.170(2).
4   Insolvency Rules 1986, SI 1986/1925, r 6.170(3).

238.   Termination of appointment. The special manager's appointment terminates if the bankruptcy petition is dismissed or if, an interim receiver having been appointed[1], the latter is discharged without a bankruptcy order having been made[2].

If the official receiver or the trustee is of opinion that the employment of the special manager is no longer necessary or profitable for the estate, he must apply to the court for directions, and the court may order the special manager's appointment to be terminated[3].

The official receiver or the trustee must make the same application if a resolution of the creditors is passed, requesting that the appointment be terminated[4].

1   Ie under the Insolvency Act 1986 s 286: see PARA 219 et seq.
2   Insolvency Rules 1986, SI 1986/1925, r 6.171(1). As to bankruptcy orders see PARA 198 et seq.
3   Insolvency Rules 1986, SI 1986/1925, r 6.171(2).
4   Insolvency Rules 1986, SI 1986/1925, r 6.171(3).

(vi) Investigation of Bankrupt's Affairs

A. BANKRUPT'S DUTIES IN RELATION TO OFFICIAL RECEIVER

239.   Duties of bankrupt in relation to official receiver. Where a bankruptcy order has been made[1], the bankrupt is under a duty:

(1)   to deliver possession of his estate[2] to the official receiver; and

(2)   to deliver up to the official receiver all books, papers and other records of which he has possession or control and which relate to his estate and affairs[3], including any which would be privileged from disclosure in any proceedings[4].

In the case of any part of the bankrupt's estate which consists of things possession of which cannot be delivered to the official receiver, and in the case of any property that may be claimed for the bankrupt's estate by the trustee, it is the bankrupt's duty to do all such things as may be required by the official receiver for the protection of those things or that property[5].

The bankrupt must give the official receiver such inventory of his estate and such other information, and must attend on the official receiver at such times, as the official receiver may[6] reasonably require[7].

If the bankrupt fails without reasonable excuse to comply with any of the above obligations, he is guilty of contempt of court and is liable to be punished accordingly, in addition to any other punishment to which he may be subject[8].

1   As to bankruptcy orders see PARA 198 et seq.
2   As to the meaning of 'the bankrupt's estate' see PARA 211.
3   As to the meaning of references to a person's affairs see PARA 43 note 4.
4   Insolvency Act 1986 s 291(1). Section 291(1) and s 291(2) (see the text to note 5) do not apply where, by virtue of s 297 (see PARAS 320–321), the bankrupt's estate vests in a trustee immediately on the making of the bankruptcy order: s 291(3). For a discussion of the law relating to privilege in bankruptcy see *Re Konigsberg (a bankrupt), ex p Trustee v Konigsberg* [1989] 3 All ER 289, sub nom *Re Konigsberg (a bankrupt), ex p Trustee of Property of Bankrupt v Konigsberg* [1989] 1 WLR 1257 (solicitor instructed jointly by bankrupt and wife).

In the case of the administration in bankruptcy of the insolvent estate of a deceased person dying before the presentation of a bankruptcy petition, the Insolvency Act 1986 s 291 applies: Administration of Insolvent Estates of Deceased Persons Order 1986, SI 1986/1999, art 3(1), Sch 1 Pt II para 17. As to the administration in bankruptcy of the insolvent estates of deceased persons see further PARA 830 et seq.

5   Insolvency Act 1986 s 291(2). See also note 4.

6   Ie for any of the purposes of the Insolvency Act 1986 Pt 9 Ch 2 (ss 283–291) or in connection with the making of a bankruptcy restrictions order: s 291(4)(a), (b) (s 291 substituted by the Enterprise Act 2002 s 269, Sch 23 paras 1, 5). As to bankruptcy restrictions orders see PARA 657 et seq.

7   Insolvency Act 1986 s 291(4) (as substituted: see note 6). Section 291(4) applies to a bankrupt after his discharge: s 291(5). See also *A-G's Reference (No 7 of 2000)* [2001] EWCA Crim 888, [2001] 1 WLR 1879 (privilege against self-incrimination is not absolute and is overridden by the bankrupt's duty under the Insolvency Act 1986 s 291 to deliver up documents). As to discharge from bankruptcy see PARA 638 et seq.

8   Insolvency Act 1986 s 291(6). As to contempt of court see CONTEMPT OF COURT vol 22 (2012) PARA 1 et seq; and as to offences see PARA 733 et seq.

B. BANKRUPT'S STATEMENT OF AFFAIRS; CREDITOR'S PETITION

240. Statement of affairs. Where a bankruptcy order has been made otherwise than on a debtor's petition[1], the bankrupt must submit a statement of his affairs to the official receiver before the end of the period of 21 days beginning with the commencement of the bankruptcy[2].

A bankrupt who:

(1)   without reasonable excuse fails to comply with the above obligation; or

(2)   without reasonable excuse submits a statement of affairs that does not comply with the prescribed requirements,

is guilty of a contempt of court and liable to be punished accordingly, in addition to any other punishment to which he may be subject[3].

1   As to the statement of affairs on a debtor's petition see PARA 248 et seq.

2   Insolvency Act 1986 s 288(1). As from a day to be appointed, s 288(1) is amended by the Enterprise and Regulatory Reform Act 2013 s 71, Sch 19 paras 1, 18: see PARA 130 note 17.

    If he thinks fit, the official receiver may release a bankrupt from his duty under the Insolvency Act 1986 s 288(1) or extend the period specified in s 288(1): s 288(3). See further PARA 244. As to the commencement of bankruptcy see PARA 209.

    In the case of the administration in bankruptcy of the insolvent estate of a deceased person dying before the presentation of a bankruptcy petition, s 288 applies; but, where an insolvency administration order has been made, the personal representative, or if there is no personal representative, such person as the court may on the application of the official receiver direct, must submit to the official receiver a statement of the deceased debtor's affairs containing particulars of the assets and liabilities of the estate as at the date of the insolvency administration order together with other particulars of the affairs of the deceased debtor in the prescribed form or as the official receiver may require; and the statement must be submitted before the end of the period of 56 days beginning with the date of a request by the official receiver for the statement or such longer period as he or the court may allow: s 288(1), (2) (substituted by the Administration of Insolvent Estates of Deceased Persons Order 1986, SI 1986/1999, art 3(1), Sch 1 Pt II para 15). For the prescribed form of statement of affairs see the Administration of Insolvent Estates of Deceased Persons Order 1986, SI 1986/1999, Sch 3 Form 7.

    In the case of the death of the debtor after the presentation of a bankruptcy petition, where a bankruptcy order has been made otherwise than on a debtor's petition and the debtor has subsequently died without submitting a statement of his affairs to the official receiver, the personal representative or such other person as the court, on the application of the official receiver, may direct must submit to the official receiver a statement of the deceased debtor's affairs containing particulars of the assets and liabilities of the estate as at the date of the order together with other particulars of the affairs of the deceased debtor in the prescribed form or as the official receiver may require; and the Insolvency Rules 1986, SI 1986/1925, apply to such a statement as they apply to an ordinary statement of affairs of a debtor: Insolvency Act 1986 s 288(1) (substituted by the Administration of Insolvent Estates of Deceased Persons Order 1986, SI 1986/1999, art 5, Sch 2 para 1). Such statement must be submitted before the end of the period of 56 days beginning with the date of a request by the official receiver for the statement or such longer period as he or the court may allow: Insolvency Act 1986 s 288(2) (substituted by the Administration of Insolvent Estates of Deceased Persons Order 1986, SI 1986/1999, Sch 2 para 1). As to the administration in bankruptcy of the insolvent estates of deceased persons see further PARA 830 et seq.

As to the modification of the Insolvency Act 1986 s 288 by the Insolvent Partnerships Order 1994, SI 1994/2421, in relation to the bankruptcy of an individual member of an insolvent partnership see COMPANY AND PARTNERSHIP INSOLVENCY vol 17 (2011) PARA 1284.

3   Insolvency Act 1986 s 288(4). As to contempt of court see CONTEMPT OF COURT vol 22 (2012) PARA 1 et seq; and as to offences see PARA 733 et seq.

241.   Form of statement of affairs.   The statement of affairs must contain such particulars of the bankrupt's creditors and of his debts and other liabilities and of his assets as may be prescribed, and such other information as may be prescribed[1]; and it must be in the prescribed form and contain all the particulars required by that form[2].

1   Insolvency Act 1986 s 288(2). The Insolvency Rules 1986, SI 1986/1925, rr 6.58–6.66 (see the text and note 2; and PARA 242 et seq) apply with respect to the statement of affairs required by the Insolvency Act 1986 s 288(1) (see PARA 240) to be submitted by the bankrupt, following a bankruptcy order made on a creditor's petition, and the further and other disclosure which is required of him in that case: Insolvency Rules 1986, SI 1986/1925, r 6.58.

As to the application of the Insolvency Act 1986 s 288 in the case of the administration in bankruptcy of the insolvent estate of a deceased person dying before the presentation of a bankruptcy petition see PARA 240 note 2; and as to the modification of s 288(1), (2) in the case of the death of a debtor after the presentation of a bankruptcy petition see PARA 240 note 2.

As to the modification of s 288 by the Insolvent Partnerships Order 1994, SI 1994/2421, in relation to the bankruptcy of an individual member of an insolvent partnership see COMPANY AND PARTNERSHIP INSOLVENCY vol 17 (2011) PARA 1284.

2   Insolvency Rules 1986, SI 1986/1925, r 6.59. For the prescribed form of statement of affairs see Sch 4 Form 6.33A (added by SI 2010/686).

242.   Verification and filing.   The bankrupt must be furnished by the official receiver with instructions for the preparation of his statement of affairs, and the forms required for that purpose[1].

The statement of affairs must be verified by a statement of truth[2] and delivered to the official receiver, together with one copy[3]; and the official receiver must file the verified statement in court[4].

1   Insolvency Rules 1986, SI 1986/1925, r 6.60(1). As to the prescribed form of the statement of affairs see PARA 241 note 2.
2   As to the meaning of 'statement of truth' see PARA 161 note 7.
3   Insolvency Rules 1986, SI 1986/1925, r 6.60(2) (amended by SI 2010/686).
4   Insolvency Rules 1986, SI 1986/1925, r 6.60(3). As to the meaning of 'file in court' see PARA 57 note 13.

243.   Limited disclosure.   Where the official receiver thinks that it would prejudice the conduct of the bankruptcy or might reasonably be expected to lead to violence against any person for the whole or part of the statement of affairs to be disclosed, he may apply to the court for an order of limited disclosure in respect of the statement, or any specified part of it[1]. The court may, on the application, order that the statement or, as the case may be, the specified part of it be not filed in court[2], or that it is to be filed separately and not be open to inspection otherwise than with the permission of the court[3].

1   Insolvency Rules 1986, SI 1986/1925, r 6.61(1) (amended by SI 2010/686).
2   As to the meaning of 'file in court' see PARA 57 note 13.
3   Insolvency Rules 1986, SI 1986/1925, r 6.61(2) (amended by SI 2010/686).

244. Release from duty to submit statement of affairs; extension of time. If he thinks fit, the official receiver may release the bankrupt from his duty to submit a statement of affairs[1], or extend the statutory period[2] for doing so; and, where the official receiver has refused to exercise his statutory power, the court may, if it thinks fit, exercise it[3].

The power of the official receiver to release the bankrupt from his duty to submit a statement of affairs, or to grant an extension of time, may be exercised at the official receiver's own discretion, or at the bankrupt's request[4]. If the bankrupt requests a release or extension of time and it is refused by the official receiver, he may apply to the court for it[5]. If the court thinks that no sufficient cause is shown for the application, it may dismiss it; but it may not do so unless the bankrupt has had an opportunity to attend for a hearing without notice being served on any other party, of which he has been given at least five business days' notice[6]; and, if the application is not so dismissed, the court must fix a venue[7] for it to be heard, and give notice to the bankrupt accordingly[8].

At least 14 days before the hearing, the bankrupt must send to the official receiver a notice stating the venue and accompanied by a copy of the application, and of any evidence which he, the bankrupt, intends to adduce in support of it[9].

The official receiver may appear and be heard on the application; and, whether or not he appears, he may file a written report of any matters which he considers ought to be drawn to the court's attention; and, if such a report is filed, it must be sent by the official receiver to the bankrupt, not later than five business days before the hearing[10].

Sealed copies of the order made on the application must be sent by the court to the bankrupt and the official receiver[11]. On any such application the bankrupt's costs must be paid in any event by him and, unless the court otherwise orders, no allowance towards them may be made out of the estate[12].

1 Ie under the Insolvency Act 1986 s 288(1): see PARA 240.
2 Ie the period specified in the Insolvency Act 1986 s 288(1): see PARA 240.

3 Insolvency Act 1986 s 288(3). As to the application of s 288 in the case of the administration in bankruptcy of the insolvent estate of a deceased person dying before the presentation of a bankruptcy petition see PARA 240 note 2.

4 Insolvency Rules 1986, SI 1986/1925, r 6.62(1).

5 Insolvency Rules 1986, SI 1986/1925, r 6.62(2).
6 As to the meaning of 'business day' see PARA 28 note 8.
7 As to the meaning of 'venue' see PARA 46 note 22.

8 Insolvency Rules 1986, SI 1986/1925, r 6.62(3) (amended by SI 2010/686).

9 Insolvency Rules 1986, SI 1986/1925, r 6.62(4).

10 Insolvency Rules 1986, SI 1986/1925, r 6.62(5) (amended by SI 2010/686).

11 Insolvency Rules 1986, SI 1986/1925, r 6.62(6).

12 Insolvency Rules 1986, SI 1986/1925, r 6.62(7).

245. Expenses of statement of affairs; assistance in preparation. If the bankrupt cannot himself prepare a proper statement of affairs, the official receiver may, at the expense of the estate, employ some person or persons to assist in the preparation of the statement[1].

At the request of the bankrupt, made on the grounds that he cannot himself prepare a proper statement, the official receiver may authorise an allowance payable out of the estate, in accordance with the prescribed order of priority[2], towards expenses to be incurred by the bankrupt in employing some person or persons to assist him in preparing it[3].

Any such request by the bankrupt must be accompanied by an estimate of the expenses involved; and the official receiver may only authorise the employment of a named person or a named firm, being in either case approved by him[4].

An authorisation so given by the official receiver must be subject to such conditions, if any, as he thinks fit to impose with respect to the manner in which any person may obtain access to relevant books and papers[5].

Nothing in the above provisions, however, relieves the bankrupt from any obligation with respect to the preparation, verification and submission of his statement of affairs, or to the provision of information to the official receiver or the trustee[6].

1 Insolvency Rules 1986, SI 1986/1925, r 6.63(1).
2 As to the meaning of 'prescribed order of priority' see PARA 222 note 5.
3 Insolvency Rules 1986, SI 1986/1925, r 6.63(2).
4 Insolvency Rules 1986, SI 1986/1925, r 6.63(3).
5 Insolvency Rules 1986, SI 1986/1925, r 6.63(4).
6 Insolvency Rules 1986, SI 1986/1925, r 6.63(5).

246. Submission and filing of accounts. At the request of the official receiver, the bankrupt must furnish him with accounts relating to his affairs of such nature, as at such date and for such period as he, the official receiver, may specify[1]. The period specified may begin from a date up to three years preceding the date of the presentation of the bankruptcy petition[2]; and, on the official receiver's application, the court may require accounts in respect of any earlier period[3].

The accounts to be so furnished must, if the official receiver so requires, be verified by a statement of truth[4], and, whether or not so verified, delivered to him within 21 days of the request, or such longer period as he may allow[5].

1 Insolvency Rules 1986, SI 1986/1925, r 6.64(1). Rule 6.63 (see PARA 245) applies, with the necessary modifications, in relation to accounts to be furnished under r 6.64 as it applies in relation to the statement of affairs: r 6.64(4). As to the statement of affairs see PARA 240 et seq.
2 Insolvency Rules 1986, SI 1986/1925, r 6.64(2). As to the presentation of the bankruptcy petition see PARA 195.
3 Insolvency Rules 1986, SI 1986/1925, r 6.64(3).
4 As to the meaning of 'statement of truth' see PARA 161 note 7.
5 Insolvency Rules 1986, SI 1986/1925, r 6.65(1) (amended by SI 2010/686).

247. Further disclosure. The official receiver may at any time require the bankrupt to submit, in writing, further information amplifying, modifying or explaining any matter contained in his statement of affairs[1], or in accounts submitted[2] by him[3]. The information must, if the official receiver so directs, be verified by a statement of truth[4], and, whether or not so verified, delivered to him within 21 days of the requirement, or such longer period as he may allow[5].

1 As to the statement of affairs see PARA 240 et seq.
2 Ie in pursuance of the Insolvency Act 1986 or the Insolvency Rules 1986, SI 1986/1925. As to the submission and filing of accounts see PARA 246.
3 Insolvency Rules 1986, SI 1986/1925, r 6.66(1).
4 As to the meaning of 'statement of truth' see PARA 161 note 7.
5 Insolvency Rules 1986, SI 1986/1925, r 6.66(2) (amended by SI 2010/686).

C. BANKRUPT'S STATEMENT OF AFFAIRS; DEBTOR'S PETITION

248. Statement of affairs; contents. The debtor's petition for his own bankruptcy must be accompanied by a statement of affairs, verified by a statement of truth[1]; and the statement of affairs required so to accompany the debtor's petition must be in the prescribed form, and must contain all the particulars required by that form[2].

1   See the Insolvency Rules 1986, SI 1986/1925, r 6.41(1) (amended by SI 2010/686); and PARA 163. As to the meaning of 'statement of truth' see PARA 161 note 7.
2   Insolvency Rules 1986, SI 1986/1925, r 6.68. For the prescribed form of statement of affairs see Sch 4 Form 6.28 (substituted by SI 2005/2114; and amended by SI 2010/686).
    The Insolvency Rules 1986, SI 1986/1925, rr 6.67–6.72 (see PARA 249 et seq) apply with respect to the statement of affairs required in the case of a person petitioning for a bankruptcy order to be made against him, and further disclosure which is required of him in that case: r 6.67.

249.   Submission and filing of accounts.   At the request of the official receiver, the bankrupt must furnish him with accounts relating to his, the debtor's, affairs of such nature, as at such date and for such period as he may specify[1]. The period may begin from a date up to three years preceding the date of the presentation of the bankruptcy petition[2]. On the official receiver's application, the court may require accounts in respect of any earlier period[3].

The accounts to be so furnished must, if the official receiver so requires, be verified by a statement of truth[4], and, whether or not so verified, delivered to him within 21 days of the request, or such longer period as he may allow[5].

1   Insolvency Rules 1986, SI 1986/1925, r 6.69(1).
2   Insolvency Rules 1986, SI 1986/1925, r 6.69(2). As to the presentation of the bankruptcy petition see PARA 195.
3   Insolvency Rules 1986, SI 1986/1925, r 6.69(3).
4   As to the meaning of 'statement of truth' see PARA 161 note 7.
5   Insolvency Rules 1986, SI 1986/1925, r 6.70(1) (amended by SI 2010/686).

250.   Expenses of preparing accounts; assistance in preparation.   If the bankrupt cannot himself prepare proper accounts[1], the official receiver may, at the expense of the estate, employ some person or persons to assist in their preparation[2].

At the request of the bankrupt, made on the grounds that he cannot himself prepare the accounts, the official receiver may authorise an allowance payable out of the estate, in accordance with the prescribed order of priority[3], towards expenses to be incurred by the bankrupt in employing some person or persons to assist him in their preparation[4].

Any such request by the bankrupt must be accompanied by an estimate of the expenses involved; and the official receiver may only authorise the employment of a named person or a named firm, being in either case approved by him[5].

An authorisation so given by the official receiver must be subject to such conditions, if any, as he thinks fit to impose with respect to the manner in which any person may obtain access to relevant books and papers[6].

Nothing in the above provisions, however, relieves the bankrupt from any obligation with respect to the preparation and submission of accounts, or to the provision of information to the official receiver or the trustee[7].

1   Ie under the Insolvency Rules 1986, SI 1986/1925, r 6.69: see PARA 249.
2   Insolvency Rules 1986, SI 1986/1925, r 6.71(1).
3   As to the meaning of 'prescribed order of priority' see PARA 222 note 5.
4   Insolvency Rules 1986, SI 1986/1925, r 6.71(2).
5   Insolvency Rules 1986, SI 1986/1925, r 6.71(3).
6   Insolvency Rules 1986, SI 1986/1925, r 6.71(4).
7   Insolvency Rules 1986, SI 1986/1925, r 6.71(5).

251. Further disclosure. The official receiver may at any time require the bankrupt to submit, in writing, further information amplifying, modifying or explaining any matter contained in his statement of affairs[1], or in accounts submitted[2] by him[3]. If the official receiver so directs, the information must be verified by a statement of truth[4], and, whether or not so verified, delivered to him within 21 days from the date of the requirement, or such longer period as he may allow[5].

1   As to the statement of affairs see PARA 248.
2   Ie in pursuance of the Insolvency Act 1986 or the Insolvency Rules 1986, SI 1986/1925. As to the submission and filing of accounts see PARA 249.
3   Insolvency Rules 1986, SI 1986/1925, r 6.72(1).
4   As to the meaning of 'statement of truth' see PARA 161 note 7.
5   Insolvency Rules 1986, SI 1986/1925, r 6.72(2) (amended by SI 2010/686).

(vii) Investigatory Duties of the Official Receiver

A. IN GENERAL

252. Duty to investigate. It is the duty of the official receiver to investigate the conduct and affairs of each bankrupt, including his conduct and affairs before the making of the bankruptcy order and to make such report, if any, to the court as he thinks fit[1]. However, where the official receiver thinks such an investigation is unnecessary, the duty does not apply[2].

1   Insolvency Act 1986 s 289(1) (s 289 substituted by the Enterprise Act 2002 s 258). A report by the official receiver under the Insolvency Act 1986 s 289 is, in any proceedings, prima facie evidence of the facts stated in it: s 289(4) (as so substituted). Where an application is made by the bankrupt under s 280 (see PARA 638 note 2) for his discharge from bankruptcy, it is the duty of the official receiver to make a report to the court about such matters as may be prescribed; and the court must consider that report before determining the application: s 289(3) (as so substituted).
      In the case of the administration in bankruptcy of the insolvent estate of a deceased person dying before the presentation of a bankruptcy petition, the official receiver is not under any duty to investigate the conduct and affairs of the deceased debtor unless he thinks fit but may make such report, if any, to the court as he thinks fit: s 289 (substituted by the Administration of Insolvent Estates of Deceased Persons Order 1986, SI 1986/1999, art 3(1), Sch 1 Pt II para 16). As to the administration in bankruptcy of the insolvent estates of deceased persons see PARA 830 et seq.
2   Insolvency Act 1986 s 289(2) (as substituted: see note 1).

B. INFORMATION TO CREDITORS

253. Report to creditors. At least once after the making of the bankruptcy order[1], the official receiver must send a report to creditors[2] with respect to the bankruptcy proceedings, and the state of the bankrupt's affairs[3].

1   As to bankruptcy orders see PARA 195 et seq.
2   Any reference in the Insolvency Rules 1986, SI 1986/1925, Pt 6 Ch 6 (rr 6.73–6.78D: see PARA 254 et seq) to creditors is to creditors of the bankrupt who are known to the official receiver: r 6.74 (amended by SI 2010/686).
3   Insolvency Rules 1986, SI 1986/1925, r 6.73(1) (renumbered by SI 1987/1919).

254. Report where statement of affairs lodged. Where the bankrupt has submitted a statement of affairs[1], the official receiver must send out to creditors[2] a report containing a summary of the statement (if he thinks fit, as amplified, modified or explained[3]), and such observations, if any, as he thinks fit to make with respect to it or to the bankrupt's affairs generally[4].

The official receiver need not, however, comply with the above obligation if he has previously reported to creditors with respect to the bankrupt's affairs, so far as known to him, and he is of opinion that there are no additional matters which ought to be brought to their attention[5].

1   As to the statement of affairs see PARA 240 et seq.
2   As to the meaning of references to creditors see PARA 253 note 2.
3   Ie by virtue of the Insolvency Rules 1986, SI 1986/1925, r 6.66 (see PARA 247) or r 6.72 (see PARA 251).
4   Insolvency Rules 1986, SI 1986/1925, r 6.75(1) (amended by SI 1987/1919; and SI 2010/686).
5   Insolvency Rules 1986, SI 1986/1925, r 6.75(2).

255. Statement of affairs dispensed with. Where the bankrupt has been released from the obligation to submit a statement of affairs[1], then, as soon as may be after the release has been granted, the official receiver must send to creditors[2] a report containing a summary of the bankrupt's affairs, so far as within his knowledge, and his observations, if any, with respect to it or the bankrupt's affairs generally[3].

The official receiver need not, however, comply with the above obligation if he has previously reported to creditors with respect to the bankrupt's affairs, so far as known to him, and he is of opinion that there are no additional matters which ought to be brought to their attention[4].

1   See PARA 244.
2   As to the meaning of references to creditors see PARA 253 note 2.
3   Insolvency Rules 1986, SI 1986/1925, r 6.76(1), (2).
4   Insolvency Rules 1986, SI 1986/1925, r 6.76(3).

256. General rule as to reporting. On the official receiver's application, the court may relieve him of any duty imposed on him to provide information to creditors[1], or authorise him to carry out the duty in a way other than is so required[2].

In considering whether to act as above, the court must have regard to the cost of carrying out the duty, to the amount of the funds available in the estate, and to the extent of the interest of creditors or any particular class of them[3].

1   Ie under the Insolvency Rules 1986, SI 1986/1925, Pt 6 Ch 6 (rr 6.73–6.78D): see PARAS 253–255, 257, 383–386. As to the meaning of references to creditors see PARA 253 note 2.
2   Insolvency Rules 1986, SI 1986/1925, r 6.77(1).
3   Insolvency Rules 1986, SI 1986/1925, r 6.77(2).

257. Bankruptcy order annulled. If the bankruptcy order is annulled[1], the duty of the official receiver to send reports[2] ceases[3].

1   See PARA 610 et seq.
2   Ie under the Insolvency Rules 1986, SI 1986/1925, Pt 6 Ch 6 (rr 6.73–6.77): see PARAS 253–256.
3   Insolvency Rules 1986, SI 1986/1925, r 6.78.

(viii) Official Receiver's Powers

A. IN GENERAL

258. Power to ensure continuation of essential supplies by utilities. The official receiver has the like rights as the supervisor of a voluntary arrangement, an interim receiver, a trustee in bankruptcy and a trustee under a deed of arrangement for ensuring continued supplies of gas, electricity, water and telecommunication services[1].

1   See the Insolvency Act 1986 s 372; and PARA 78.

259.   Power to call meetings.   The official receiver must summon a general meeting of the bankrupt's creditors for the purpose of appointing a trustee of the bankrupt's estate[1]; and he may at any time summon and conduct meetings of creditors for the purpose of ascertaining their wishes in all matters relating to the bankruptcy[2].

1   See PARA 261 et seq.
2   See PARA 266 et seq.

260.   Redirection of bankrupt's letters etc.   Where a bankruptcy order has been made[1], the court may from time to time, on the application of the official receiver, order a postal operator[2] to redirect and send or deliver to the official receiver or otherwise any postal packet[3] which would otherwise be sent or delivered by the postal operator concerned to the bankrupt at such place or places as may be specified in the order[4]. Any such order has effect for such period, not exceeding three months, as may be specified in the order[5].

1   See PARA 198 et seq.

2   For these purposes, 'postal operator' means a person who provides the service of conveying postal packets from one place to another by post or any of the incidental services of receiving, collecting, sorting and delivering postal packets: Postal Services Act 2011 s 27(3); applied by the Insolvency Act 1986 s 371(1) (amended by the Postal Services Act 2000 s 127(4), Sch 8 para 20; and the Postal Services Act 2011 s 91(1), Sch 12 paras 124, 125). As to the meaning of 'postal packet' see note 3.

3   For these purposes, 'postal packet' means a letter, parcel, packet or other article transmissible by post: Postal Services Act 2011 s 27(2); applied by the Insolvency Act 1986 s 371(1) (as amended: see note 2).

4   Insolvency Act 1986 s 371(1) (as amended: see note 2). For the prescribed form of order see the Insolvency Rules 1986, SI 1986/1925, Sch 4 Form 6.80 (substituted by SI 2005/527; and amended by SI 2009/642; and SI 2011/2085). The trustee of the bankrupt's estate has the like power to apply for such an order: see PARA 486. For a consideration of whether a redirection order pursuant to the Insolvency Act 1986 s 371(1) infringes the Convention for the Protection of Human Rights and Fundamental Freedoms ('the European Convention on Human Rights') (Rome, 4 November 1950; TS 71 (1953); Cmd 8969) art 8 see Application 33274/96 *Foxley v United Kingdom* (2000) 8 BHRC 571, [2000] BPIR 1009, ECtHR (opening of confidential communications with legal advisers violated the Convention for the Protection of Human Rights and Fundamental Freedoms art 8). See also *Singh v Official Receiver* [1997] BPIR 530 (where the court expressed reservations about the manner of obtaining such orders).
    An application for an order under the Insolvency Act 1986 s 371(1) by the official receiver or trustee in bankruptcy must be made without notice to the bankrupt or any other person, unless the court directs otherwise: Insolvency Rules 1986, SI 1986/1925, r 6.235A(1), (2) (r 6.235A added by SI 2005/527). Where the applicant is the official receiver, he must file a report with his application, and where the applicant is the trustee in bankruptcy, he must file a witness statement, setting out the reasons why such an order is sought, with his application: Insolvency Rules 1986, SI 1986/1925, r 6.235A(3) (as so added; and amended by SI 2010/686). The court must fix a venue for the hearing of the application if it thinks just and give notice to the applicant, and may make an order on such conditions as it thinks just: Insolvency Rules 1986, SI 1986/1925, r 6.235A(4), (5) (as so added; and amended by SI 2010/686). The order must identify the person on whom it is to be served, and need not be served on the bankrupt unless the court directs otherwise: Insolvency Rules 1986, SI 1986/1925, r 6.235A(6) (as so added). As to the meaning of 'venue' see PARA 46 note 22.
    In the case of the administration in bankruptcy of the insolvent estate of a deceased person dying before the presentation of a bankruptcy petition, the Insolvency Act 1986 s 371 applies:

Administration of Insolvent Estates of Deceased Persons Order 1986, SI 1986/1999, art 3(1), Sch 1 Pt II para 30. As to the administration in bankruptcy of the insolvent estates of deceased persons see further PARA 830 et seq.

5   Insolvency Act 1986 s 371(2).

B. FIRST MEETING OF CREDITORS

261.   First meeting of creditors.   Where a bankruptcy order has been made[1] it is the duty of the official receiver, as soon as practicable in the period of 12 weeks beginning with the day on which the order was made, to decide whether to summon a general meeting of the bankrupt's creditors for the purpose of appointing a trustee of the bankrupt's estate[2]. If the official receiver decides not to summon such a meeting, he must, before the end of the period of 12 weeks above mentioned, give notice of his decision to the court and to every creditor of the bankrupt who is known to the official receiver or is identified in the bankrupt's statement of affairs; and, as from the giving of such a notice, the official receiver is the trustee of the bankrupt's estate[3].

1   As to bankruptcy orders see PARA 198 et seq.
2   Insolvency Act 1986 s 293(1) (amended by the Enterprise Act 2002 ss 269, 278(2), Sch 23 paras 1, 7, Sch 26). The Insolvency Act 1986 s 293 does not apply where the bankruptcy order was made on a petition under s 264(1)(d) (criminal bankruptcy) (see PARA 130 head (6)); and it is subject to s 294(3) (see PARA 263) and s 297(6) (see PARA 320): s 293(1) (as so amended). As to the prospective repeal of s 264(1)(d), and as to the prospective amendment of s 293(1), see PARA 1 note 11. A meeting summoned under s 293 is known as the 'first meeting of creditors': see PARA 263 note 10.

In the case of the administration in bankruptcy of the insolvent estate of a deceased person dying before the presentation of a bankruptcy petition, ss 292–302 apply, except s 297(4), with the modification that, where a meeting of creditors is summoned for the purposes of any provision in ss 292–302, the rules regarding the trustee in bankruptcy and the creditors' committee apply accordingly: Administration of Insolvent Estates of Deceased Persons Order 1986, SI 1986/1999, art 3(1), Sch 1 Pt II para 18. As to the administration in bankruptcy of the insolvent estates of deceased persons see further PARA 830 et seq.

As to the modification of the Insolvency Act 1986 s 293 by the Insolvent Partnerships Order 1994, SI 1994/2421, in relation to the bankruptcy of an individual member of an insolvent partnership see COMPANY AND PARTNERSHIP INSOLVENCY vol 17 (2011) PARAS 1286, 1333.

3   Insolvency Act 1986 s 293(2), (3).

262.   Procedure.   If[1] the official receiver decides to summon a meeting of creditors, he must fix a venue[2] for the meeting, not more than four months from the date of the bankruptcy order[3]. When a venue has been fixed, notice of the meeting must be given to every creditor of the bankrupt who is known to the official receiver[4]. Notice must be given at least 14 days before the date fixed for the meeting[5]. The notice to creditors must state that proofs and, if applicable, proxies must be lodged at a specified place not later than 12.00 hours on the business day before the date fixed for the meeting in order for creditors to be entitled to vote at the meeting[6].

As soon as reasonably practicable, notice of the meeting must also be gazetted[7] and may be advertised in such other manner as the official receiver thinks fit[8]. In addition to the standard contents[9], the notice must state:

(1)   the purpose for which the meeting is summoned;

(2)   the venue fixed for the meeting; and

(3)   the time and date by which, and place at which, creditors must lodge proxies and hitherto unlodged proofs in order to be entitled to vote at the meeting[10].

1 Ie under the Insolvency Act 1986 s 293(1): see PARA 261.
2 As to the meaning of 'venue' see PARA 46 note 22.
3 Insolvency Rules 1986, SI 1986/1925, r 6.79(1). A person summoning a meeting may allow a meeting to be conducted and held in such a way that persons who are not present together at the same place may attend it: see the Insolvency Act 1986 s 379A; and PARA 267.
4 Insolvency Rules 1986, SI 1986/1925, r 6.79(2) (amended by SI 2010/686).
5 Insolvency Rules 1986, SI 1986/1925, r 6.79(3) (substituted by SI 2010/686).
6 Insolvency Rules 1986, SI 1986/1925, r 6.79(4) (substituted by SI 2010/686). As to proxies see PARA 276 et seq.
7 As to the meaning of 'gazetted' see PARA 165 note 12.
8 Insolvency Rules 1986, SI 1986/1925, r 6.79(5) (substituted by SI 2009/642).
9 As to the meaning of 'standard contents' see PARA 165 note 12.
10 Insolvency Rules 1986, SI 1986/1925, r 6.79(5A) (added by SI 2010/686).

263. Power of creditors to requisition meeting. Where, in the case of any bankruptcy the official receiver has not yet summoned, or has decided not to summon, a general meeting of the bankrupt's creditors for the purpose of appointing the trustee[1], any creditor of the bankrupt may request the official receiver to summon such a meeting for that purpose[2].

If such a request appears to the official receiver to be made with the concurrence of not less than one-quarter, in value, of the bankrupt's creditors, including the creditor making the request, it is the duty of the official receiver to summon the requested meeting[3].

Where the official receiver receives such a request by a creditor and it appears to him that the request is properly made, he must:

(1)   withdraw any notice already given by him[4] that he has decided not to summon such a meeting; and

(2)   fix the venue[5] of the meeting for not more than three months from his receipt of the creditor's request; and

(3)   act[6] as if he had decided[7] to summon the meeting[8].

A meeting summoned by the official receiver[9] is known as 'the first meeting of creditors'[10].

1 Ie under the Insolvency Act 1986 s 293: see PARA 261.
2 Insolvency Act 1986 s 294(1) (amended by the Enterprise Act 2002 ss 269, 278(2), Sch 23 paras 1, 8, Sch 26). As to the application of the Insolvency Act 1986 s 294 in the case of the administration in bankruptcy of the insolvent estate of a deceased person dying before the presentation of a bankruptcy petition see PARA 204 note 2.
   As to the modification of s 294 by the Insolvent Partnerships Order 1994, SI 1994/2421, in relation to the bankruptcy of an individual member of an insolvent partnership see COMPANY AND PARTNERSHIP INSOLVENCY vol 17 (2011) PARA 1333.
3 Insolvency Act 1986 s 294(2). Accordingly, where the duty imposed by s 294(2) has arisen, the official receiver is required neither to reach a decision for the purposes of s 293(1) (see PARA 261) nor, if he has reached one, to serve any notice under s 293(2) (see PARA 261): s 294(3).
4 Ie under the Insolvency Act 1986 s 293(2): see PARA 261.
5 As to the meaning of 'venue' see PARA 46 note 22.
6 Ie in accordance with the Insolvency Rules 1986, SI 1986/1925, r 6.79(2)–(5): see PARA 262.
7 Ie under the Insolvency Act 1986 s 293(1): see PARA 261.
8 Insolvency Rules 1986, SI 1986/1925, r 6.79(6).
9 Ie under the Insolvency Act 1986 s 293 (see PARA 261) or s 294.
10 Insolvency Rules 1986, SI 1986/1925, r 6.79(7).

264. Business at first meeting. At the first meeting of creditors[1], no resolutions may be taken other than the following:

(1)   a resolution to appoint a named insolvency practitioner[2] to be trustee in bankruptcy[3] or two or more named insolvency practitioners as joint trustees;

(2)   a resolution to establish a creditors' committee[4];

(3)   unless it has been resolved to establish a creditors' committee, a resolution specifying the terms on which the trustee is to be remunerated[5], or to defer consideration of that matter;

(4)   if, and only if, two or more persons are appointed to act jointly as trustee, a resolution specifying whether acts are to be done by both or all of them, or by only one;

(5)   where the meeting has been requisitioned by creditors[6], a resolution authorising payment out of the estate, as an expense of the bankruptcy, of the cost of summoning and holding the meeting;

(6)   a resolution to adjourn the meeting[7];

(7)   any other resolution which the chairman thinks it right to allow for special reasons[8].

1   As to the meaning of 'the first meeting of creditors' see PARA 263.
2   As to insolvency practitioners and their qualification see PARA 40.
3   As to the trustee in bankruptcy see PARA 314 et seq.
4   As to the creditors' committee see PARA 326 et seq.
5   As to the trustee's remuneration see PARA 348 et seq.
6   Ie under the Insolvency Act 1986 s 294: see PARA 263.
7   The meeting may be adjourned, either in accordance with a resolution under head (6) in the text or if the chairman thinks fit, but for not more than 14 days from the date on which it was fixed to commence, subject to any direction of the court: Insolvency Rules 1986, SI 1986/1925, r 6.80(2A) (r 6.80(2A)–(2C) added by SI 2010/686). If there are subsequently further adjournments, the final adjournment must not be to a day later than 14 days after the date on which the meeting was originally held, subject to any direction of the court: r 6.80(2B) (as so added). Where a meeting is adjourned under r 6.80, proofs and proxies may be used if lodged at any time up to 12.00 hours on the business day immediately before the adjourned meeting: r 6.80(2C) (as so added). As to proxies see PARA 276 et seq.
8   Insolvency Rules 1986, SI 1986/1925, r 6.80(1) (amended by SI 2010/686).

265. Failure of meeting to appoint trustee. If a meeting summoned by the official receiver[1] is held but no appointment of a person as trustee is made, it is the duty of the official receiver to decide whether to refer the need for an appointment to the Secretary of State[2]; and, on a reference made in pursuance of that decision, the Secretary of State must either make an appointment or decline to make one[3].

1   Ie under the Insolvency Act 1986 s 293 (see PARA 261) or s 294 (see PARA 263).
2   Insolvency Act 1986 s 295(1). As to the Secretary of State see PARA 19. As to the application of s 295 in the case of the administration in bankruptcy of the insolvent estate of a deceased person dying before the presentation of a bankruptcy petition see PARA 261 note 2.
    As to the modification of s 295 by the Insolvent Partnerships Order 1994, SI 1994/2421, in relation to the bankruptcy of an individual member of an insolvent partnership see COMPANY AND PARTNERSHIP INSOLVENCY vol 17 (2011) PARAS 1287, 1334.
3   Insolvency Act 1986 s 295(2). If the official receiver decides not to refer the need for an appointment to the Secretary of State or, on such a reference, the Secretary of State declines to make an appointment, the official receiver must give notice of his decision or, as the case may be, of the Secretary of State's decision to the court: s 295(3). As from the giving of notice under s 295(3) in a case in which no notice has been given under s 293(2) (see PARA 261), the official receiver is trustee of the bankrupt's estate: s 295(4).

C. MEETINGS OF CREDITORS

266. General power to call meetings. The official receiver may at any time summon and conduct meetings of creditors for the purpose of ascertaining their wishes in all matters relating to the bankruptcy[1].

When a venue[2] for the meeting has been fixed, notice of the meeting must be given by the convener to every creditor who is known to him; and the notice must be given at least 14 days before the date fixed for the meeting[3].

The notice must specify the purpose for which the meeting is summoned and state that proofs[4] and (if applicable) proxies[5] must be lodged at a specified place not later than 12.00 hours on the business day[6] before the date fixed for the meeting in order for creditors to be entitled to vote at the meeting[7].

As soon as reasonably practicable after sending notice of the meeting to the creditors, the convener must give additional notice of the meeting; and such notice must be gazetted[8] and may be advertised in such other manner as the convenor thinks fit[9]. In addition to the standard contents[10], the additional notice must specify:

(1) who summoned the meeting;

(2) if the meeting was summoned at the request of a creditor, the fact that it was so summoned and the provision of the Insolvency Act 1986 under which it was requested;

(3) the purpose for which the meeting is summoned;

(4) the venue fixed for the meeting; and

(5) the time and date by which, and place at which, creditors must lodge proxies and hitherto unlodged proofs in order to be entitled to vote at the meeting[11].

1 Insolvency Rules 1986, SI 1986/1925, r 6.81(1). In relation to any meeting of creditors, the person summoning it is known as 'the convener': r 6.81(1). The trustee has the like power to summon meetings of creditors: see PARA 481. A person summoning a meeting may allow a meeting to be conducted and held in such a way that persons who are not present together at the same place may attend it: see the Insolvency Act 1986 s 379A (added by SI 2010/18); and PARA 267.

2 As to the meaning of 'venue' see PARA 46 note 22.

3 Insolvency Rules 1986, SI 1986/1925, r 6.81(2) (amended by SI 2010/696). For the prescribed form of notice see the Insolvency Rules 1986, SI 1986/1925, Sch 4 Form 6.35 (amended by SI 2010/686).

4 As to proofs of debt see PARA 507 et seq.

5 As to proxies see PARA 276 et seq.

6 As to the meaning of 'business day' see PARA 28 note 8.

7 Insolvency Rules 1986, SI 1986/1925, r 6.81(3) (substituted by SI 2010/686).

8 As to the meaning of 'gazetted' see PARA 165 note 12.

9 Insolvency Rules 1986, SI 1986/1925, r 6.81(4) (substituted by SI 2009/642; and amended by SI 2010/686).

10 As to the meaning of 'standard contents' see PARA 165 note 12.

11 Insolvency Rules 1986, SI 1986/1925, r 6.81(5) (added by SI 2010/686).

267. Remote attendance at meetings. The following provisions apply to any meeting of the individual's creditors summoned under the Insolvency Act 1986 or the Insolvency Rules 1986[1] where: (1) a bankruptcy order is made against an individual or an interim receiver[2] of an individual's property is appointed; or (2) a voluntary arrangement in relation to an individual is proposed or is approved[3].

Where the person summoning a meeting ('the convener') considers it appropriate, the meeting may be conducted and held in such a way that persons who are not present together at the same place may attend it[4]. The convener of a meeting which is to be conducted and held in this manner may make whatever arrangements the convener considers appropriate to enable those attending the meeting to exercise their rights to speak or vote, and to ensure the identification of those attending the meeting and the security of any electronic means used to enable attendance[5].

Where in the reasonable opinion of the convener (a) a meeting will be attended by persons who will not be present together at the same place, and (b) it is unnecessary or inexpedient to specify a place for the meeting[6], any requirement[7] to specify a place for the meeting may be satisfied by specifying the arrangements the convener proposes to enable persons to exercise their rights to speak or vote[8].

If the notice of a meeting does not specify a place for the meeting, the convener is requested in accordance with the rules to specify a place for the meeting, and that request is made by not less than ten percent in value of the creditors, it is the duty of the convener to specify a place for the meeting[9].

1   Ie under the Insolvency Rules 1986, SI 1986/1925.
2   As to interim receivers see PARA 218 et seq.
3   Insolvency Act 1986 s 379A(1) (s 379A added by SI 2010/18). Voluntary arrangements are proposed or approved under the Insolvency Act 1986 Pt 8 (ss 252–263G) (see PARA 43 et seq). As to transitional provisions in relation to remote attendance see the Legislative Reform (Insolvency) (Miscellaneous Provisions) Order 2010, SI 2010/18, art 12.
4   Insolvency Act 1986 s 379A(2) (as added: see note 3). Where a meeting is conducted and held in the manner referred to in s 379A(2), a person attends the meeting if that person is able to exercise any rights which that person may have to speak and vote at the meeting: s 379A(3) (as so added). For these purposes: (1) a person exercises the right to speak at a meeting when that person is in a position to communicate to all those attending the meeting, during the meeting, any information or opinions which that person has on the business of the meeting; and (2) a person exercises the right to vote at a meeting when (a) that person is able to vote, during the meeting, on resolutions put to the vote at the meeting, and (b) that person's vote can be taken into account in determining whether or not such resolutions are passed at the same time as the votes of all the other persons attending the meeting: s 379A(4) (as so added). See also the Insolvency Rules 1986, SI 1986/1925, rr 12A.26, 12A.27 (added by SI 2010/686).
5   Insolvency Act 1986 s 379A(5) (as added: see note 3). In making the arrangements referred to in s 379A(5), the convener must have regard to the legitimate interests of the creditors and others attending the meeting in the efficient despatch of the business of the meeting: s 379A(7) (as so added).
6   In forming the opinion that it is unnecessary or inexpedient to specify a place for the meeting, the convener must have regard to the legitimate interests of the creditors and others attending the meeting in the efficient despatch of the business of the meeting: Insolvency Act 1986 s 379A(7) (as added: see note 3).
7   Ie any requirement under the Insolvency Act 1986 or the Insolvency Rules 1986, SI 1986/1925.
8   Insolvency Act 1986 s 379A(6) (as added: see note 3).
9   Insolvency Act 1986 s 379A(8) (as added: see note 3). Where the convener is requested to specify a place for the meeting, the request must be accompanied by:
    (1)   in the case of a request by creditors, a list of the creditors making or concurring with the request and the amounts of their respective debts in the insolvency proceedings in question (Insolvency Rules 1986, SI 1986/1925, r 12A.22(1), (2)(a) (r 12A.22 added by SI 2010/686));
    (2)   in the case of a request by contributories, a list of the contributories making or concurring with the request and their respective values (being the amounts for which they may vote at the meeting) (Insolvency Rules 1986, SI 1986/1925, r 12A.22(1), (2)(b) (as so added));
    (3)   in the case of a request by members, a list of the members making or concurring with the request and their voting rights (r 12A.22(1), (2)(c) (as so added)); and
    (4)   from each person concurring, written confirmation of that person's concurrence (r 12A.22(1), (2)(d) (as so added)).
    The request must be made within seven business days of the date on which the convener sent the notice of the meeting in question: r 12A.22(3) (as so added). As to the meaning of 'business day' see PARA 28 note 8.
    Where the convener considers that the request has been properly made in accordance with the Insolvency Act 1986 and the Insolvency Rules 1986, SI 1986/1925, r 12A, the convener must give notice to all those previously given notice of the meeting that it is to be held at a specified place, and as to whether the date and time are to remain the same or not: r 12A.22(4)(a) (as so added). The convener must set a venue (including specification of a place) for the meeting, the date of which must be not later than 28 days after the original date for the

meeting and must give at least 14 days' notice of that venue to all those previously given notice of the meeting: r 12A.22(4)(b), (c) (as so added). The notices may be given at the same or different times: r 12A.22(4).

Where (a) a request is made in respect of a final meeting under the Insolvency Act 1986 s 331 (see PARA 616); (b) an application is made under the Insolvency Rules 1986, SI 1986/1925, r 6.142 (see PARA 353) in respect of remuneration or expenses reported in the draft report for that meeting; and (c) the meeting cannot be held until the application (including any appeal) has been disposed of and any order of the court complied with, r 12A.22(4)(a) does not apply and the duty to set a venue (including specification of a place) for the meeting applies in relation to the meeting when it is finally held: r 12A.22(5) (as so added).

Where the convener has specified a place for the meeting in response to a request, the chairman of the meeting must attend the meeting by being present in person at that place: r 12A.22(6) (as so added).

The provisions of r 6.87 (expenses of summoning meetings: see PARA 273) do not apply to the summoning and holding of a meeting at a place specified in accordance with the Insolvency Act 1986 s 379A(8): Insolvency Rules 1986, SI 1986/1925, r 12A.22(7) (as so added).

As to the action to be taken where a person has been excluded from a meeting see rr 12A.23, 12A.24, 12A.25 (all added by SI 2010/686).

268. Chairman at a meeting. Where the convener[1] of a meeting is the official receiver, he, or a person nominated by him, must be chairman; and a nomination must be in writing, unless the nominee is another official receiver or a deputy official receiver[2]. Where the convener is other than the official receiver, the chairman must be he, or a person nominated by him in writing to act; and a person so nominated must be either one who is qualified to act as an insolvency practitioner in relation to the bankrupt[3], or an employee of the trustee or his firm who is experienced in insolvency matters[4].

1   As to the meaning of 'the convener' see PARA 266 note 1.
2   Insolvency Rules 1986, SI 1986/1925, r 6.82(1).
3   As to insolvency practitioners and their qualification see PARA 40.
4   Insolvency Rules 1986, SI 1986/1925, r 6.82(2).

269. Requisitioned meetings. A request by creditors to the official receiver for a meeting of creditors to be summoned must be accompanied by:

(1)   a list of the creditors concurring with the request and the amount of their respective claims in the bankruptcy;

(2)   from each creditor concurring, written confirmation of his concurrence; and

(3)   a statement of the purpose of the proposed meeting[1];

but the requirements of heads (1) and (2) above do not apply if the requisitioning creditor's debt is alone sufficient, without the concurrence of other creditors[2].

If the official receiver considers the request to be properly made, he must fix a venue[3] for the meeting, to take place not more than 28 days from the receipt of the request, and give 14 days' notice of the meeting, and of the venue for it, to creditors[4].

1   Insolvency Rules 1986, SI 1986/1925, r 6.83(1). For the prescribed form of request by creditors for a meeting see Sch 4 Form 6.34. Where a request for a creditors' meeting is made to the trustee, r 6.83 applies to him as it does to the official receiver: r 6.83(3). Rule 6.83 does not apply to voluntary arrangements under the Insolvency Act 1986 s 263A (see PARA 90): Insolvency Rules 1986, SI 1986/1925, r 6.83(4) (added by SI 2003/1730). As to remote attendance at meetings see PARA 267.
2   Insolvency Rules 1986, SI 1986/1925, r 6.83(1).
3   As to the meaning of 'venue' see PARA 46 note 22.
4   Insolvency Rules 1986, SI 1986/1925, r 6.83(2) (amended by SI 2010/686).

270. Attendance of bankrupt etc at meetings. Whenever a meeting of creditors is summoned, the convener[1] must give at least 14 days' notice of the meeting to the bankrupt[2]. If the meeting is adjourned, the chairman of the meeting must, unless for any reason it appears to him to be unnecessary or impracticable, give notice of the fact to the bankrupt, if the latter was not himself present at the meeting[3].

If the convener thinks fit, he may give notice to the bankrupt that he, the bankrupt, is required to be present, or in attendance[4].

In the case of any meeting, the bankrupt or any other person may, if he has given reasonable notice of his wish to be present, be admitted; but this is at the discretion of the chairman[5]. The chairman's decision is final as to what, if any, intervention may be made by the bankrupt, or by any other person admitted to the meeting under the above provisions[6].

If the bankrupt is not present, and it is desired to put questions to him, the chairman may adjourn the meeting with a view to obtaining his attendance[7]. Where the bankrupt is present at a creditors' meeting, only such questions may be put to him as the chairman may in his discretion allow[8].

1 As to the meaning of 'the convener' see PARA 266 note 1.
2 Insolvency Rules 1986, SI 1986/1925, r 6.84(1) (amended by SI 2010/686). For the prescribed form of notice see Sch 4 Form 6.36. As to remote attendance at meetings see PARA 267.
3 Insolvency Rules 1986, SI 1986/1925, r 6.84(2).
4 Insolvency Rules 1986, SI 1986/1925, r 6.84(3).
5 Insolvency Rules 1986, SI 1986/1925, r 6.84(4).
6 Insolvency Rules 1986, SI 1986/1925, r 6.84(4).
7 Insolvency Rules 1986, SI 1986/1925, r 6.84(5). As to adjournment see PARA 284.
8 Insolvency Rules 1986, SI 1986/1925, r 6.84(6).

271. Notice of meetings by advertisement only. In the case of any meeting to be held[1], the court may order that notice of it be given by advertisement, and not by individual notice to the persons concerned[2]. In considering whether to act under the above provisions, the court must have regard to the cost of advertisement, to the amount of the funds available in the estate, and to the extent of the interest of creditors or any particular class of them[3].

In addition to the standard contents[4], the advertisement must state:

(1) the venue[5] fixed for the meeting;
(2) that proofs and (if applicable) proxies[6] must be lodged at a specified place not later than 12.00 hours on the business day[7] before the date fixed for the meeting; and
(3) the date of the court order[8].

1 Ie under the Insolvency Act 1986 or the Insolvency Rules 1986, SI 1986/1925.
2 Insolvency Rules 1986, SI 1986/1925, r 6.85(1) (amended by SI 2010/686).
3 Insolvency Rules 1986, SI 1986/1925, r 6.85(2) (amended by SI 2010/686).
4 As to the meaning of 'standard contents' see PARA 165 note 12.
5 As to the meaning of 'venue' see PARA 46 note 22.
6 As to proxies see PARA 276 et seq.
7 As to the meaning of 'business day' see PARA 162 note 4.
8 Insolvency Rules 1986, SI 1986/1925, r 6.85(3) (added by SI 2010/686).

272. Venue of meetings. In fixing the venue[1] for a meeting of creditors, the person summoning the meeting must have regard to the convenience of the creditors[2]. Meetings must in all cases be summoned for commencement between the hours of 10.00 and 16.00 hours on a business day[3], unless the court otherwise directs[4]. With every notice summoning a creditors' meeting there must be sent out forms of proxy[5].

1   As to the meaning of 'venue' see PARA 46 note 22.
2   Insolvency Rules 1986, SI 1986/1925, r 6.86(1).
3   As to the meaning of 'business day' see PARA 28 note 8.
4   Insolvency Rules 1986, SI 1986/1925, r 6.86(2).
5   Insolvency Rules 1986, SI 1986/1925, r 6.86(3). For the prescribed form of proxy see Sch 4
    Form 8.4. As to proxies see PARA 276 et seq. As to remote attendance at meetings see PARA 267.

273.   Expenses of summoning meetings.   The expenses of summoning and
holding a meeting of creditors at the instance of any person other than the
official receiver or the trustee must be paid by that person, who must deposit
security for their payment with the trustee or, if no trustee has been appointed,
with the official receiver[1]. The sum to be deposited must be such as the trustee or,
as the case may be, the official receiver determines to be appropriate; and neither
may act without the deposit having been made[2].

Where a meeting is so summoned, it may vote that the expenses of
summoning and holding it are to be payable out of the estate, as an expense of
the bankruptcy[3]. To the extent that any deposit so made is not required for the
payment of expenses of summoning and holding the meeting, it must be repaid
to the person who made it[4].

1   Insolvency Rules 1986, SI 1986/1925, r 6.87(1).
2   Insolvency Rules 1986, SI 1986/1925, r 6.87(2).
3   Insolvency Rules 1986, SI 1986/1925, r 6.87(3).
4   Insolvency Rules 1986, SI 1986/1925, r 6.87(4).

274.   Resolutions.   At a meeting of creditors, a resolution is passed when a
majority, in value, of those present and voting, in person or by proxy[1], have
voted in favour of the resolution[2]. However, in the case of a resolution for the
appointment of a trustee:
(1)   if on any vote there are two nominees for appointment, the person who
       obtains the most support is appointed;
(2)   if there are three or more nominees, and one of them has a clear
       majority over both or all the others together, that one is appointed; and
(3)   in any other case, the chairman must continue to take votes,
       disregarding at each vote any nominee who has withdrawn and, if no
       nominee has withdrawn, the nominee who obtained the least support
       last time, until a clear majority is obtained for any one nominee[3].
The chairman may at any time put to the meeting a resolution for the joint
appointment of any two or more nominees[4].

Where a resolution is proposed which affects a person in respect of his
remuneration or conduct as trustee, or as proposed or former trustee, the vote of
that person, and of any partner or employee of his, may not be reckoned in the
majority required for passing the resolution; and this provision applies with
respect to a vote given by a person, whether personally or on his behalf by a
proxy-holder, either as creditor or as proxy-holder for a creditor[5].

1   As to proxies see PARA 276 et seq.
2   Insolvency Rules 1986, SI 1986/1925, r 6.88(1) (amended by SI 1987/1919).
3   Insolvency Rules 1986, SI 1986/1925, r 6.88(2) (amended by SI 2010/686).
4   Insolvency Rules 1986, SI 1986/1925, r 6.88(3).
5   Insolvency Rules 1986, SI 1986/1925, r 6.88(4) (amended by SI 1987/1919). The Insolvency
    Rules 1986, SI 1986/1925, r 6.88(4) is subject to r 8.6 (see PARA 280): r 6.88(4).

275.   Resolutions by correspondence.   In respect of any resolution which the
Insolvency Act 1986 does not require to be passed at a meeting[1], the trustee may

seek to obtain the passing of a resolution by creditors without holding a meeting by giving notice of the resolution to every creditor who is entitled to be notified of a meeting at which the resolution could be passed[2].

In order to be counted, votes must be received by the trustee in writing by 12.00 hours on the closing date[3] specified in the notice, and must be accompanied by a proof of debt[4] unless it has already been lodged[5]. If any vote cast by a creditor is received without a proof of debt, or the trustee decides that the creditor is not entitled to vote[6], then that creditor's vote must be disregarded[7].

For the resolution to be passed, the trustee must receive at least one valid vote by the closing date specified in the notice[8]. If no valid vote is received by the closing date specified, the trustee must call a meeting of creditors at which the resolution could be passed[9].

Creditors whose debts amount to at least 10 per cent of the bankrupt's total debts may, within five business days[10] from the giving of notice of the resolution[11], require the trustee to summon a meeting of creditors to consider the resolution[12].

1 Insolvency Rules 1986, SI 1986/1925, r 6.88A(9) (r 6.88A added by SI 2010/686).
2 Insolvency Rules 1986, SI 1986/1925, r 6.88A(1) (as added: see note 1). A reference in the Insolvency Rules 1986, SI 1986/1925, to a resolution passed at a creditors' meeting includes a reference to a resolution passed under r 6.88A: r 6.88A(8) (as so added).
3 The closing date is set at the discretion of the trustee, but in any event it must not be set less than 14 days from the giving of notice provided for in the Insolvency Rules 1986, SI 1986/1925, r 6.88A(1) (see the text to note 2): r 6.88A(4) (as so added).
4 Ie as required under the Insolvency Rules 1986, SI 1986/1925, r 6.93(1)(a) (see PARA 286 head (1)).
5 Insolvency Rules 1986, SI 1986/1925, r 6.88A(2) (as added: see note 1). The proof of debt is lodged under r 6.93 (see PARA 286).
6 Ie according to the Insolvency Rules 1986, SI 1986/1925, rr 6.93–6.94 (see PARAS 286–287).
7 Insolvency Rules 1986, SI 1986/1925, r 6.88A(3) (as added: see note 1).
8 Insolvency Rules 1986, SI 1986/1925, r 6.88A(5) (as added: see note 1).
9 Insolvency Rules 1986, SI 1986/1925, r 6.88A(6) (as added: see note 1).
10 As to the meaning of 'business day' see PARA 28 note 8.
11 Ie the giving of notice provided for in the Insolvency Rules 1986, SI 1986/1925, r 6.88A(1) (see the text to note 2).
12 Insolvency Rules 1986, SI 1986/1925, r 6.88A(7) (as added: see note 1).

276. Proxies and company representation. A proxy is an authority given by a person ('the principal') to another person ('the proxy-holder') to attend a meeting and speak and vote as his representative[1]. Proxies are for use at creditors' meetings[2].

Only one proxy may be given by a person for any one meeting at which he desires to be represented, and it may only be given to one person, being an individual aged 18 or over; but the principal may specify one or more other such individuals to be proxy-holder in the alternative, in the order in which they are named in the proxy[3]. A proxy for a particular meeting may[4] be given to whoever is to be the chairman of the meeting[5]; and for a meeting held as part of the proceedings in a bankruptcy it may be given to the official receiver[6]. Where the chairman or official receiver is given such a proxy, he cannot decline to be the proxy-holder in relation to that proxy[7].

A proxy requires the holder to give the principal's vote on matters arising for determination at the meeting, or to abstain, or to propose, in the principal's name, a resolution to be voted on by the meeting, either as directed or in accordance with the holder's own discretion[8].

Where a person is authorised to represent a corporation at a meeting of creditors or of the company or its contributories, he is required to produce to the chairman of the meeting a copy of the resolution from which he derives his authority[9].

1 Insolvency Rules 1986, SI 1986/1925, r 8.1(1). The authority conferred by a proxy is actual authority, not ostensible authority: *Horler v Rubin* [2012] EWCA Civ 4, [2013] 1 BCLC 1, [2012] BPIR 749.

2 Insolvency Rules 1986, SI 1986/1925, r 8.1(2) (amended by SI 1987/1919). The meetings referred to are those summoned or called under the Insolvency Act 1986 or the Insolvency Rules 1986, SI 1986/1925: r 8.1(2). For the prescribed form of proxy in a bankruptcy see Sch 4 Form 8.4. As to remote attendance at meetings see PARA 267.

3 Insolvency Rules 1986, SI 1986/1925, r 8.1(3).

4 Ie without prejudice to the generality of the Insolvency Rules 1986, SI 1986/1925, r 8.1(3).

5 As to the chairman at creditors' meetings in a bankruptcy see PARA 268; and as to the chairman as proxy-holder see PARA 282.

6 Insolvency Rules 1986, SI 1986/1925, r 8.1(4).

7 Insolvency Rules 1986, SI 1986/1925, r 8.1(5) (substituted by SI 1987/1919).

8 Insolvency Rules 1986, SI 1986/1925, r 8.1(6) (added by SI 1987/1919).

9 Insolvency Rules 1986, SI 1986/1925, r 8.7(1) (amended by SI 2010/686). The copy resolution must be under the seal of the corporation, or certified by the secretary or a director of the corporation to be a true copy: Insolvency Rules 1986, SI 1986/1925, r 8.7(2). This provision does not require the authority of a person to authenticate a proxy on behalf of a principal which is a corporation to be in the form of a resolution of that corporation: r 8.7(3) (added by SI 1987/1919; and amended by SI 2010/686).

277. Issue and use of forms. When notice is given of a meeting to be held in insolvency proceedings[1], and forms of proxy are sent out with the notice, no form so sent out may have inserted in it the name or description of any person[2]; and no form of proxy may be used at any meeting except that which is sent out with the notice summoning the meeting, or a substantially similar form[3]. A form of proxy must be authenticated by the principal[4], or by some person authorised by him, either generally or with reference to a particular meeting; and, if the form is authenticated by a person other than the principal, the nature of the person's authority must be stated[5].

1 As to the meaning of 'insolvency proceedings' see PARA 37 note 9.

2 Insolvency Rules 1986, SI 1986/1925, r 8.2(1). As to the sending of forms of proxies with the notice of a creditors' meeting in a bankruptcy see PARA 272.

3 Insolvency Rules 1986, SI 1986/1925, r 8.2(2).

4 As to the meaning of 'the principal' see PARA 276. As to authentication see PARA 158 note 2.

5 Insolvency Rules 1986, SI 1986/1925, r 8.2(3) (amended by SI 2010/686).

278. Use of proxies at meetings. A proxy given for a particular meeting may be used at any adjournment of that meeting[1]. Where the official receiver holds proxies for use at any meeting, his deputy, or any other official receiver, may act as proxy-holder[2] in his place; alternatively, the official receiver may in writing authorise another officer of the Department for Business, Innovation and Skills to act for him at the meeting and use the proxies as if that other officer were himself proxy-holder[3]. Where the responsible insolvency practitioner[4] holds proxies to be used by him as chairman of a meeting, and some other person acts as chairman, the other person may use the insolvency practitioner's proxies as if he were himself proxy-holder[5].

Where a proxy directs a proxy-holder to vote for or against a resolution for the nomination or appointment of a person as the responsible insolvency practitioner, the proxy-holder may, unless the proxy states otherwise, vote for or against, as he thinks fit, any resolution for the nomination or appointment of that person jointly with another or others[6].

A proxy-holder may propose any resolution which, if proposed by another, would be a resolution in favour of which, by virtue of the proxy, he would be entitled to vote[7]. Where a proxy gives specific directions as to voting, this does not, unless the proxy states otherwise, preclude the proxy-holder from voting at his discretion on resolutions put to the meeting which are not dealt with in the proxy[8].

1 Insolvency Rules 1986, SI 1986/1925, r 8.3(1).
2 As to the meaning of 'the proxy-holder' see PARA 276.
3 Insolvency Rules 1986, SI 1986/1925, rr 8.3(2), 13.13(2) (r 13.13(2) amended by SI 2009/2748).
4 'The responsible insolvency practitioner' means the person (other than the official receiver) acting in an individual insolvency, as the supervisor of a voluntary arrangement under the Insolvency Act 1986 Pt 8 (ss 252–263G) (see PARA 43 et seq), or as trustee (see PARA 314 et seq) or interim receiver (see PARA 218 et seq): Insolvency Rules 1986, SI 1986/1925, r 13.9(1)(b).
5 Insolvency Rules 1986, SI 1986/1925, r 8.3(3).
6 Insolvency Rules 1986, SI 1986/1925, r 8.3(4) (added by SI 1987/1919).
7 Insolvency Rules 1986, SI 1986/1925, r 8.3(5) (added by SI 1987/1919).
8 Insolvency Rules 1986, SI 1986/1925, r 8.3(6) (added by SI 1987/1919). See also *Horler v Rubin* [2012] EWCA Civ 4, [2013] 1 BCLC 1, [2012] BPIR 749.

279. Retention and inspection of proxies. Proxies used for voting at any meeting must be retained by the chairman of the meeting[1]. The chairman must, however, deliver the proxies, as soon as reasonably practicable after the meeting, to the responsible insolvency practitioner[2], where that is someone other than himself[3].

The office-holder[4] must, so long as proxies lodged with him are in his hands, allow them to be inspected, at all reasonable times on any business day[5], by the creditors[6]. Such right of inspection is also exercisable, in the case of an insolvent individual, by him[7].

Any person attending a meeting of creditors is entitled, immediately before or in the course of the meeting, to inspect proxies and associated documents, including proofs, sent or given, in accordance with directions contained in any notice convening the meeting, to the chairman of that meeting or to any other person by a creditor for the purpose of that meeting[8].

1 Insolvency Rules 1986, SI 1986/1925, r 8.4(1). As to the chairman at meetings see PARA 268.
2 As to the meaning of 'the responsible insolvency practitioner' see PARA 278 note 4.
3 Insolvency Rules 1986, SI 1986/1925, r 8.4(2) (amended by SI 2009/642).
4 As to the meaning of 'office-holder' see PARA 20 note 7.
5 As to the meaning of 'business day' see PARA 28 note 8.
6 Insolvency Rules 1986, SI 1986/1925, r 8.5(1)(a) (amended by SI 2010/686). For these purposes, 'creditors' means, in the case of an individual's bankruptcy, those creditors who have proved their debts, and, in any other case, persons who have submitted in writing a claim to be creditors of the individual concerned; but in neither case does it include a person whose proof has been wholly rejected for purposes of voting, dividend or otherwise: Insolvency Rules 1986, SI 1986/1925, r 8.5(2). As to proofs of debt see PARA 507 et seq. Where a member state liquidator (see PARA 175 note 8) has been appointed in relation to a person subject to insolvency proceedings, for the purposes of r 8.5(1), a member state liquidator appointed in main proceedings (see PARA 42) is deemed to be a creditor: r 8.8(1), (2) (added by SI 2002/1307). This provision is without prejudice to the generality of the right to participate referred to in Council Regulation (EC) 1346/2000 (OJ L160, 30.6.2000, p 1) on insolvency proceedings ('European Regulation on Insolvency Proceedings') art 32(3) (exercise of creditor's rights): Insolvency Rules 1986, SI 1986/1925, r 8.8(3) (added by SI 2002/1307).
   The Insolvency Rules 1986, SI 1986/1925, r 8.5 is subject to r 12A.51 (confidentiality of documents—grounds for refusing inspection) (see PARA 798): r 8.5(5) (added by SI 2010/686).

7   Insolvency Rules 1986, SI 1986/1925, r 8.5(3)(b). See note 6.
8   Insolvency Rules 1986, SI 1986/1925, r 8.5(4) (amended by SI 1987/1919). See note 6.

280.   Proxy-holder with financial interest.   A proxy-holder[1] may not vote in favour of any resolution which would directly or indirectly place him, or any associate[2] of his, in a position to receive any remuneration out of the bankrupt's estate, unless the proxy specifically directs him to vote in that way[3]. Where a proxy-holder has authenticated[4] the proxy as being authorised to do so by his principal[5] and the proxy specifically directs him to vote in that way, he may nevertheless not vote in that way unless he produces to the chairman of the meeting written authorisation from his principal sufficient to show that the proxy-holder was entitled so to authenticate the proxy[6].

The above provisions apply also to any person acting as chairman of a meeting and using proxies in that capacity[7]; and in their application to him, the proxy-holder is deemed an associate of his[8].

1   As to the meaning of 'the proxy-holder' see PARA 276.
2   As to the meaning of 'associate' see PARA 5.
3   Insolvency Rules 1986, SI 1986/1925, rr 8.6(1), 13.8(b) (amended by SI 2009/642).
4   As to authentication see PARA 158 note 2.
5   As to the meaning of 'the principal' see PARA 276.
6   Insolvency Rules 1986, SI 1986/1925, r 8.6(1A) (added by SI 1987/1919; and amended by SI 2010/686).
7   Ie under the Insolvency Rules 1986, SI 1986/1925, r 8.3: see PARA 278.
8   Insolvency Rules 1986, SI 1986/1925, r 8.6(2) (amended by SI 1987/1919).

281.   Rule against solicitation in obtaining proxies.   Where the court is satisfied that any improper solicitation has been used by or on behalf of the trustee in obtaining proxies, it may order that no remuneration out of the estate be allowed to any person by whom, or on whose behalf, the solicitation was exercised[1]. Such an order of the court overrides any resolution of the creditors' committee or the creditors, or any other provision[2] relating to the trustee's remuneration[3].

1   Insolvency Rules 1986, SI 1986/1925, r 6.148(1). As to improper solicitation in procuring the trustee's appointment see PARA 347. As to the meaning of 'trustee' see PARA 20 note 12.
2   Ie of the Insolvency Rules 1986, SI 1986/1925. As to the provisions relating to the trustee's remuneration see PARA 348 et seq.
3   Insolvency Rules 1986, SI 1986/1925, r 6.148(2).

282.   Chairman of meeting as proxy-holder.   Where the chairman at a meeting holds a proxy for a creditor, which requires him to vote for a particular resolution, and no other person proposes that resolution, he must himself propose it, unless he considers that there is good reason for not doing so; and, if he does not propose it, he must as soon as reasonably practicable after the meeting notify the principal of the reason why not[1].

1   Insolvency Rules 1986, SI 1986/1925, r 6.89 (amended by SI 2009/642).

283.   Suspension of meeting.   Once only in the course of any meeting, the chairman may, in his discretion and without an adjournment, declare the meeting suspended for any period of up to one hour[1].

1   Insolvency Rules 1986, SI 1986/1925, r 6.90.

284.   Adjournment.   The chairman at any meeting may, in his discretion, and must, if the meeting so resolves, adjourn it to such time and place as seems to him to be appropriate in the circumstances[1]. If, within 30 minutes from the time appointed for the commencement of a meeting, a quorum is not present, then the chairman may, at his discretion, adjourn the meeting to such time and place as he may appoint[2]; and any such adjournment may not be for a period of more than 14 days[3].

If within 30 minutes from the time appointed for commencement of a meeting there is no person present to act as chairman, the meeting stands adjourned to the same time and place in the following week or, if that is not a business day[4], to the business day immediately following[5]. This applies to further adjournments of a final meeting[6]. In the case of any other meeting, further adjournment must be to the same time and place in the following week or, if either: (1) that is not a business day, or (2) whether or not it is a business day, it is later than 14 days after the date on which the meeting in question was originally held, to the same time and place on the business day immediately preceding which is not later than 14 days after the date on which the meeting in question was originally held[7].

Where a meeting is adjourned, proofs[8] and proxies[9] may be used if lodged at any time up to midday on the business day immediately before the adjourned meeting[10].

1   Insolvency Rules 1986, SI 1986/1925, r 6.91(1). Rule 6.91(1) is subject to r 6.129(3) (see PARA 364) in a case where the trustee or his nominee is chairman and a resolution has been proposed for the trustee's removal: r 6.91(1).
2   Insolvency Rules 1986, SI 1986/1925, r 6.91(2) (amended by SI 1987/1919).
3   Insolvency Rules 1986, SI 1986/1925, r 6.91(3) (amended by SI 2010/686). The Insolvency Rules 1986, SI 1986/1925, r 6.86(1), (2) (see PARA 272) applies with regard to the venue of the adjourned meeting: r 6.91(3). As to the meaning of 'venue' see PARA 46 note 22.
4   As to the meaning of 'business day' see PARA 28 note 8.
5   Insolvency Rules 1986, SI 1986/1925, r 6.91(4A) (added by SI 2010/686).
6   Insolvency Rules 1986, SI 1986/1925, r 6.91(4B) (added by SI 2010/686).
7   Insolvency Rules 1986, SI 1986/1925, r 6.91(4C) (added by SI 2010/686).
8   As to proofs of debt see PARA 507 et seq.
9   As to proxies see PARA 276 et seq.
10 Insolvency Rules 1986, SI 1986/1925, r 6.91(5).

285.   Quorum. Any meeting of creditors is competent to act if a quorum is present[1]. A quorum is at least one creditor entitled to vote[2]. For these purposes, however, the reference to the creditor necessary to constitute a quorum is to those persons present or represented by proxy by any person including the chairman[3].

Where, at any meeting of creditors, the above provisions as to a quorum being present are satisfied by the attendance of the chairman alone, or one other person in addition to the chairman, and the chairman is aware, by virtue of proofs[4] and proxies[5] received or otherwise, that one or more additional persons would, if attending, be entitled to vote, the meeting may not commence until at least the expiry of 15 minutes after the time appointed for its commencement[6].

1   Insolvency Rules 1986, SI 1986/1925, r 12A.21(1) (added by SI 2010/686).
2   Insolvency Rules 1986, SI 1986/1925, r 12A.21(2)(a) (added by SI 2010/686).
3   Insolvency Rules 1986, SI 1986/1925, r 12A.21(3) (added by SI 2010/686).
4   As to proofs of debt see PARA 507 et seq.
5   As to proxies see PARA 276 et seq.
6   Insolvency Rules 1986, SI 1986/1925, r 12A.21(4) (added by SI 2010/686).

286.   Creditors' entitlement to vote; lodging of proofs. At a meeting of creditors a person is entitled to vote as a creditor only if:
    (1)   there has been duly lodged, by the time and date stated in the notice of

the meeting[1], a proof of the debt claimed to be due to him from the bankrupt[2], or in relation to a member state liquidator[3], is claimed to be due to creditors in proceedings in relation to which he holds office, and the claim has been admitted for the purpose of entitlement to vote[4]; and

(2)   there has been lodged, by the time and date stated in the notice of the meeting, any proxy[5] requisite for that entitlement[6].

The court may, in exceptional circumstances, by order declare the creditors, or any class of them, entitled to vote at creditors' meetings, without being required to prove their debts; and, where a creditor is so entitled, the court may, on the application of the trustee, make such consequential orders as it thinks just, as, for example, an order treating a creditor as having proved his debt for the purpose of permitting payment of dividend[7].

A creditor may not vote in respect of a debt for an unliquidated amount[8], or any debt whose value is not ascertained, except where the chairman agrees to put on the debt an estimated minimum value for the purpose of entitlement to vote and admits his proof for that purpose[9].

A secured creditor[10] is entitled to vote only in respect of the balance, if any, of his debt after deducting the value of his security as estimated by him[11].

A creditor may not vote in respect of a debt on, or secured by, a current bill of exchange or promissory note, unless he is willing:

(a)   to treat the liability to him on the bill or note of every person who is liable on it antecedently to the bankrupt, and against whom a bankruptcy order has not been made (or, in the case of a company, which has not gone into liquidation), as a security in his hands; and

(b)   to estimate the value of the security and (for the purpose of entitlement to vote, but not for dividend) to deduct it from his proof[12].

No vote may be cast by virtue of a debt more than once on any resolution put to the meeting[13].

Only the creditor's vote is counted where a creditor is entitled to vote[14], has lodged his claim in one or more sets of other proceedings[15], and votes (either in person or by proxy) on a resolution put to the meeting[16].

Where a creditor has lodged his claim in more than one set of other proceedings[17], and more than one member state liquidator seeks to vote by virtue of that claim, the entitlement to vote by virtue of that claim is exercisable by the member state liquidator in main proceedings, whether or not the creditor has lodged his claim in the main proceedings[18].

The chairman's decision in respect of any matter arising under the above provisions is subject to appeal to the court by any creditor, or by the bankrupt[19].

1   As to notice of the meeting see PARA 269. As to remote attendance at meetings see PARA 267.
2   As to proofs of debt see PARA 507 et seq.
3   As to the meaning of 'member state liquidator' see PARA 175 note 8.
4   Ie under the Insolvency Rules 1986, SI 1986/1925, r 6.94: see PARA 287. At a creditors' meeting, the chairman may allow a creditor to vote, notwithstanding that the creditor has failed to comply with r 6.93(1)(a) (see head (1) in the text), if satisfied that the failure was due to circumstances beyond the creditor's control: r 6.93A (added by SI 2010/686).
5   As to proxies see PARA 276 et seq.
6   Insolvency Rules 1986, SI 1986/1925, r 6.93(1) (amended by SI 2002/1307; and SI 2010/686).
7   Insolvency Rules 1986, SI 1986/1925, r 6.93(2) (amended by SI 2010/686). As to the meaning of references to the trustee see PARA 20 note 12.
8   'Unliquidated debt' includes not only all cases of damages to be ascertained, but also extends to any debt where the creditor fairly admits that he cannot state the amount: see *Re Canadian Pacific Colonization Corpn Ltd* (1891) 40 WR 40 at 41 (company case), distinguishing and explaining *Re Dummelow, ex p Ruffle* (1873) 8 Ch App 997. As to the meaning of 'bankruptcy debt' see PARA 508.

9	Insolvency Rules 1986, SI 1986/1925, r 6.93(3). As to the estimation of disputed debts for voting purposes see *Re a Debtor (No 222 of 1990), ex p Bank of Ireland* [1992] BCLC 137 (decided under the similar wording in the Insolvency Rules 1986, SI 1986/1925, r 5.17(3)); *Re A Company (No 004539 of 1993)* [1995] 1 BCLC 459, [1995] BCC 116; *Re A Debtor (No 574 of 1995)* [1998] 2 BCLC 124, sub nom *National Westminster Bank plc v Scher* [1998] BPIR 224. As to creditors' voting rights in relation to individual voluntary arrangements see PARA 63.

10	As to secured creditors see PARA 574.

11	Insolvency Rules 1986, SI 1986/1925, r 6.93(4). As to proprietary claims see *Re Prime Metal Trading Ltd* [1984] BCLC 543, 1 BCC 265.

12	Insolvency Rules 1986, SI 1986/1925, r 6.93(5).

13	Insolvency Rules 1986, SI 1986/1925, r 6.93(6) (added by SI 2002/1307).

14	Ie under the Insolvency Rules 1986, SI 1986/1925, r 6.93 and r 6.94 (admission of proof) (see PARA 287).

15	For the purposes of the Insolvency Rules 1986, SI 1986/1925, r 6.93(7), (8), 'other proceedings' means main proceedings, secondary proceedings or territorial proceedings in another member state: r 6.93(9) (added by SI 2002/1307). As to the meanings of 'main proceedings', 'secondary proceedings' and 'territorial proceedings' see PARA 42.

16	Insolvency Rules 1986, SI 1986/1925, r 6.93(7) (added by SI 2002/1307).

17	See note 15.

18	Insolvency Rules 1986, SI 1986/1925, r 6.93(8) (added by SI 2002/1307).

19	Insolvency Rules 1986, SI 1986/1925, r 6.94(2). As to appeals see PARA 761 et seq.

**287.	Admission and rejection of proof.**	At any creditors' meeting the chairman has power to admit or reject a creditor's proof for the purpose of his entitlement to vote; and the power is exercisable with respect to the whole or any part of the proof[1]. The chairman's decision under this provision is subject to appeal to the court by any creditor or by the bankrupt[2]. If the chairman is in doubt whether a proof should be admitted or rejected, he must mark it as objected to and allow the creditor to vote, subject to his vote being subsequently declared invalid if the objection to the proof is sustained[3].

If, on appeal, the chairman's decision is reversed or varied, or a creditor's vote is declared invalid, the court may order that another meeting be summoned, or make such other order as it thinks just[4]. An application to the court by way of appeal under these provisions against a decision of the chairman must be made not later than 21 days after the date of the meeting[5]. Neither the official receiver, nor any person nominated by him to be chairman, is personally liable for costs incurred by any person in respect of an application to the court under these provisions; and the chairman, if other than the official receiver or a person so nominated, is not so liable, unless the court makes an order to that effect[6].

1	Insolvency Rules 1986, SI 1986/1925, r 6.94(1). As to proofs of debt see PARA 507 et seq. As to remote attendance at meetings see PARA 267.

2	Insolvency Rules 1986, SI 1986/1925, r 6.94(2). As to appeals see PARA 761 et seq. As to the evidence admissible on appeal over a disputed debt see *Re A Debtor (No 574 of 1995)* [1998] 2 BCLC 124, sub nom *National Westminster Bank plc v Scher* [1998] BPIR 224; *Re A Company (No 004539 of 1993)* [1995] 1 BCLC 459, [1995] BCC 116.

3	Insolvency Rules 1986, SI 1986/1925, r 6.94(3). Cf, in relation to individual voluntary arrangements, r 5.22(4); and PARA 63.

4	Insolvency Rules 1986, SI 1986/1925, r 6.94(4).

5	Insolvency Rules 1986, SI 1986/1925, r 6.94(4A) (added by SI 2010/686).

6	Insolvency Rules 1986, SI 1986/1925, r 6.94(5).

**288.	Record of proceedings.**	The chairman at any creditors' meeting must cause minutes of the proceedings, authenticated[1] by him, to be retained by him as part of the records of the bankruptcy[2]. He must also cause to be made up and kept a list of all the creditors who attended the meeting[3]. The minutes of the meeting must include a record of every resolution passed; and if a creditors' committee has been established[4], the names and addresses of those elected to be members of the committee[5].

1 As to authentication see PARA 158 note 2.
2 Insolvency Rules 1986, SI 1986/1925, r 6.95(1) (amended by SI 2010/686).
3 Insolvency Rules 1986, SI 1986/1925, r 6.95(2). As to remote attendance at meetings see PARA 267.
4 As to the establishment of a creditors' committee see PARA 326.
5 Insolvency Rules 1986, SI 1986/1925, r 6.95(3) (amended by SI 2010/686).

(ix) Public Examination

289. Application for public examination. Where a bankruptcy order has been made[1], the official receiver may at any time before the discharge of the bankrupt[2] apply to the court for the public examination of the bankrupt[3].

1 As to bankruptcy orders see PARA 198 et seq.
2 As to discharge from bankruptcy see PARA 638 et seq.
3 Insolvency Act 1986 s 290(1).

290. Request by creditors for public examination. Unless the court otherwise orders, the official receiver must make an application for a public examination[1] if notice requiring him to do so is given to him[2] by one of the bankrupt's creditors with the concurrence of not less than one-half, in value, of those creditors, including the creditor giving notice[3].

Such a request[4] by a creditor to the official receiver must be made in writing and be accompanied by a list of the creditors concurring with the request and the amount of their respective claims in the bankruptcy, and from each creditor concurring, written confirmation of his concurrence and a statement of the reasons why the examination is requested; but, if the requisitioning creditor's debt is alone sufficient, the request may be made by that creditor without the concurrence of others[5]. Before an application to the court is made on the request, the requisitionist must deposit with the official receiver such sum as the latter may determine to be appropriate by way of security for the expenses of the hearing of a public examination, if ordered[6]. The official receiver must, within 28 days of receiving the request, make the application to the court[7], unless he is of opinion that the request is an unreasonable one in the circumstances, in which case he may apply to the court for an order relieving him from the obligation to make the application for a public examination[8]. If the court so orders, and the application for the order was made without notice to any other party, notice of the order must be given as soon as reasonably practicable by the official receiver to the requisitionist; and, if the application for such an order is dismissed, the official receiver's application for a public examination[9] must be made as soon as reasonably practicable on conclusion of the hearing of the application[10].

1 Ie under the Insolvency Act 1986 s 290(1): see PARA 289.
2 Ie in accordance with the Insolvency Rules 1986, SI 1986/1925.
3 Insolvency Act 1986 s 290(2).
4 For the prescribed form of request by creditors see the Insolvency Rules 1986, SI 1986/1925, Sch 4 Form 6.56.
5 Insolvency Rules 1986, SI 1986/1925, r 6.173(1).
6 Insolvency Rules 1986, SI 1986/1925, r 6.173(2).
7 Insolvency Rules 1986, SI 1986/1925, r 6.173(3).
8 Insolvency Rules 1986, SI 1986/1925, r 6.173(4). The official receiver would otherwise be required to make the application under the Insolvency Act 1986 s 290(2) (see the text to notes 1–3).

9 Ie under the Insolvency Act 1986 s 290(2).
10 Insolvency Rules 1986, SI 1986/1925, r 6.173(5) (amended by SI 2009/642; and SI 2010/686).

291. Order for public examination. On an application by the official receiver for a public examination[1], the court must direct that a public examination of the bankrupt be held on a day appointed by the court; and the bankrupt must attend on that day and be publicly examined as to his affairs[2], dealings and property[3].

If the official receiver applies to the court for the public examination of the bankrupt, a copy of the court's order[4] must, as soon as reasonably practicable after its making, be sent by the official receiver to the bankrupt[5].

1 See PARA 289.
2 As to the meaning of references to a person's affairs see PARA 43 note 4.
3 Insolvency Act 1986 s 290(3). As to the meaning of 'property' see PARA 412. As to the modification of s 290 by the Insolvent Partnerships Order 1994, SI 1994/2421, in relation to the bankruptcy of an individual member of an insolvent partnership see COMPANY AND PARTNERSHIP INSOLVENCY vol 17 (2011) PARA 1331.
4 For the prescribed form of order see the Insolvency Rules 1986, SI 1986/1925, Sch 4 Form 6.55 (substituted by SI 1987/1919; and amended by SI 2010/686).
5 Insolvency Rules 1986, SI 1986/1925, r 6.172(1) (amended by SI 2009/642).

292. Notice of hearing. The court's order for a public examination of the bankrupt[1] must appoint a venue[2] for the hearing and direct his attendance thereat[3]. The official receiver must give at least 14 days' notice[4] of the hearing:

(1)   if a trustee[5] has been nominated or appointed, to him;
(2)   if a special manager[6] has been appointed, to him; and
(3)   subject to any contrary direction of the court, to every creditor of the bankrupt who is known to the official receiver[7].

Where the official receiver thinks fit, a notice of the order must be gazetted[8] not less than 14 days before the day fixed for the hearing[9]. The official receiver may advertise the notice in such other manner as he thinks fit[10]. In addition to the standard contents[11], the notices must state the purpose of the hearing and the venue fixed for the hearing[12].

1 See PARA 291. For the prescribed form of order see the Insolvency Rules 1986, SI 1986/1925, Sch 4 Form 6.55 (substituted by SI 1987/1919; and amended by SI 2010/686).
2 As to the meaning of 'venue' see PARA 46 note 22.
3 Insolvency Rules 1986, SI 1986/1925, r 6.172(2). See also PARA 291.
4 As to the mode of giving notice see the Insolvency Rules 1986, SI 1986/1925, rr 13.3–13.5; and PARA 808.
5 See PARA 314 et seq.
6 See PARA 232 et seq.
7 Insolvency Rules 1986, SI 1986/1925, r 6.172(3) (amended by SI 2010/686).
8 As to the meaning of 'gazetted' see PARA 165 note 12.
9 Insolvency Rules 1986, SI 1986/1925, r 6.172(4) (substituted by SI 2009/642).
10 Insolvency Rules 1986, SI 1986/1925, r 6.172(5) (added by SI 2009/642).
11 As to the meaning of 'standard contents' see PARA 165 note 12.
12 Insolvency Rules 1986, SI 1986/1925, r 6.172(5A) (added by SI 2010/686).

293. Persons entitled to participate in public examination. The following may take part in the public examination of the bankrupt, and may question him concerning his affairs[1], dealings and property[2] and the causes of his failure, namely:

(1)   the official receiver and, where appropriate[3], the Official Petitioner;
(2)   the trustee of the bankrupt's estate[4], if his appointment has taken effect;
(3)   any person who has been appointed a special manager[5] of the bankrupt's estate or business;

(4)   any creditor of the bankrupt who has tendered a proof in the bankruptcy[6].

1   As to the meaning of references to a person's affairs see PARA 43 note 4.
2   As to the meaning of 'property' see PARA 412.
3   Ie on a petition under the Insolvency Act 1986 s 264(1)(d): see PARA 130 head (6). As to the prospective repeal of s 264(1)(d) see PARA 1 note 11.
4   See PARA 314 et seq.
5   See PARA 232 et seq.
6   Insolvency Act 1986 s 290(4). As from a day to be appointed, s 290(4) is amended by the Enterprise and Regulatory Reform Act 2013 s 71, Sch 19 paras 1, 19: see PARA 130 note 17. As to proofs of debt see PARA 507 et seq. As to the modification of the Insolvency Act 1986 s 290 by the Insolvent Partnerships Order 1994, SI 1994/2421, in relation to the bankruptcy of an individual member of an insolvent partnership see COMPANY AND PARTNERSHIP INSOLVENCY vol 17 (2011) PARA 1331.

294.   Failure to attend public examination.   If a bankrupt without reasonable excuse fails at any time to attend his public examination[1], he is guilty of a contempt of court and liable to be punished accordingly, in addition to any other punishment to which he may be subject[2].

1   Ie under the Insolvency Act 1986 s 290: see PARA 289 et seq.
2   Insolvency Act 1986 s 290(5). As to contempt of court see CONTEMPT OF COURT vol 22 (2012) PARA 1 et seq; and as to offences see PARA 733 et seq.
    As to the modification of the Insolvency Act 1986 s 290 by the Insolvent Partnerships Order 1994, SI 1994/2421, in relation to the bankruptcy of an individual member of an insolvent partnership see COMPANY AND PARTNERSHIP INSOLVENCY vol 17 (2011) PARA 1331.

295.   Bankrupt unfit for examination.   Where the bankrupt is a person who lacks capacity within the meaning of the Mental Capacity Act 2005[1] or is suffering from any physical affliction or disability rendering him unfit to undergo or attend for public examination, the court may, on an application being made to it[2], either stay the order for his public examination or direct that it is to be conducted in such manner and at such place as it thinks just[3].

Such an application must be made by a person who has been appointed by a court in the United Kingdom or elsewhere to manage the affairs of, or to represent, the bankrupt, or by a relative or friend of the bankrupt whom the court considers to be a proper person to make the application, or by the official receiver[4]. Where the application is made by a person other than the official receiver, then:

(1)   it must[5] be supported by a witness statement[6] of a registered medical practitioner as to the bankrupt's mental and physical condition;

(2)   at least five business days'[7] notice of the application must be given to the official receiver and the trustee, if any; and

(3)   before any order is made on the application, the applicant must deposit with the official receiver such sum as the latter certifies to be necessary for the additional expenses of any examination that may be ordered on the application[8].

An order made on the application may provide that the expenses of the examination are to be payable, as to a specified proportion, out of such a deposit, instead of out of the estate[9]. Where the application is made by the official receiver, it may be made without notice to any other party, and may be supported by evidence in the form of a report[10] by the official receiver to the court[11].

1   See MENTAL HEALTH AND CAPACITY vol 75 (2013) PARA 603.

2   Ie under the Insolvency Rules 1986, SI 1986/1925, r 6.174.
3   Insolvency Rules 1986, SI 1986/1925, r 6.174(1) (amended by SI 2007/1898; and SI 2010/686).
    For the prescribed form of order see the Insolvency Rules 1986, SI 1986/1925, Sch 4 Form 6.57
    (substituted by SI 2007/1898; and amended by SI 2010/686).
4   Insolvency Rules 1986, SI 1986/1925, r 6.174(2).
5   Ie unless the bankrupt is a person who lacks capacity within the meaning of the Mental Capacity
    Act 2005 (see MENTAL HEALTH AND CAPACITY vol 75 (2013) PARA 603).
6   As to the meaning of 'witness statement' see PARA 161 note 7.
7   As to the meaning of 'business day' see PARA 28 note 8.
8   Insolvency Rules 1986, SI 1986/1925, r 6.174(3) (amended by SI 2007/1898; and SI 2010/686).
9   Insolvency Rules 1986, SI 1986/1925, r 6.174(3) (as amended: see note 8).
10 As to the use of reports see the Insolvency Rules 1986, SI 1986/1925, r 7.9; and PARA 805.
11 Insolvency Rules 1986, SI 1986/1925, r 6.174(4) (amended by SI 2010/686).

296. Procedure at hearing. At the hearing the bankrupt must be examined on
oath; and he must answer all such questions as the court may put, or allow to be
put, to him[1]. Any of the persons allowed[2] to question the bankrupt may, with the
approval of the court (made known either at the hearing or in advance of it),
appear by solicitor or counsel; or he may in writing authorise another person to
question the bankrupt on his behalf[3]. The bankrupt may at his own expense
employ a solicitor with or without counsel, who may put to him such questions
as the court may allow for the purpose of enabling him to explain or qualify any
answers given by him, and may make representations on his behalf[4].

There must be made in writing such record of the examination as the court
thinks proper[5]; and the record must be read over either to or by the bankrupt,
authenticated[6] by him, and verified by a statement of truth[7] at a venue[8] fixed by
the court[9]. The written record may in any proceedings[10] be used as evidence
against the bankrupt of any statement made by him in the course of his public
examination[11]. If criminal proceedings have been instituted against the bankrupt,
and the court is of opinion that the continuance of the hearing would be
calculated to prejudice a fair trial of those proceedings, the hearing may be
adjourned[12].

1   Insolvency Rules 1986, SI 1986/1925, r 6.175(1). As to the enforcement of court orders
    generally see PARA 749.
2   Ie under the Insolvency Act 1986 s 290(4): see PARA 293.
3   Insolvency Rules 1986, SI 1986/1925, r 6.175(2).
4   Insolvency Rules 1986, SI 1986/1925, r 6.175(3).
5   As to shorthand writers see the Insolvency Rules 1986, SI 1986/1925, rr 7.16–7.18; and PARA
    304.
6   As to authentication see PARA 158 note 2.
7   As to the meaning of 'statement of truth' see PARA 161 note 7.
8   As to the meaning of 'venue' see PARA 46 note 22.
9   Insolvency Rules 1986, SI 1986/1925, r 6.175(4). For the prescribed form of affidavit see Sch 4
    Form 6.58 (amended by SI 2010/686).
10 Ie whether under the Insolvency Act 1986 or otherwise.
11 Insolvency Rules 1986, SI 1986/1925, r 6.175(5).
12 Insolvency Rules 1986, SI 1986/1925, r 6.175(6). As to adjournments see PARA 298. It would
    seem that the reference to criminal proceedings includes foreign criminal proceedings: *Re
    Rottmann (a bankrupt)* [2008] All ER (D) 266 (May) (order for private examination to avoid
    self-incrimination in foreign criminal proceedings) (affd [2009] EWCA Civ 473, [2010] 1 WLR
    67, [2009] Bus LR 1604).

297. Scope of public examination. On his public examination a bankrupt
cannot refuse to answer questions on the ground that his answers may tend to
incriminate him, and his answers are admissible as evidence against him in other
proceedings[1]. Before a question can be disallowed, the court must be satisfied
that the answer could not secure any further assets or rights to the creditors or

any protection to the public[2], and accordingly the bankrupt may be compelled to disclose a secret process or formula[3], or the source from which articles infringing a patent or trade mark have been bought[4].

Where the bankrupt is called as a witness as to any matter arising in the bankruptcy, he may be questioned by any person, including the party who called him, as to what account he gave of the matter at his public or private examination[5]. The bankrupt's answers on his public examination may be used against him on an application[6] to strike a solicitor's name off the roll[7], but not in proceedings brought against him in a representative capacity[8].

The statements made by a bankrupt at his public examination are not admissible in evidence in proceedings even in the same bankruptcy as against other parties[9], or the trustee in bankruptcy[10].

1 *R v Scott* (1856) 25 LJMC 128; *R v Robinson* (1867) LR 1 CCR 80; *R v Widdop* (1872) LR 2 CCR 3; *Re Firth, ex p Schofield* (1877) 6 ChD 230, CA; *Re Atherton* [1912] 2 KB 251; *R v Dawson* [1960] 1 All ER 558, [1960] 1 WLR 163, CCA; *R v Harris* [1970] 3 All ER 746, [1970] 1 WLR 1252 (applying *R v Scott*, and examining the relevant authorities, including *R v Widdop*, and *R v Erdheim* [1896] 2 QB 260). See also *Bishopsgate Investment Management Ltd (in provisional liquidation) v Maxwell* [1993] Ch 1, [1992] 2 All ER 856, CA (company case where the privilege against self-incrimination was stated obiter to have been abrogated by the Insolvency Act 1986 s 133 (public examination of officers)). As to the privilege against self-incrimination see further PARA 306.
2 *Re Paget, ex p Official Receiver* [1927] 2 Ch 85, CA.
3 *Re Stevenson* [1918–1919] B & CR 106; *Re Keene* [1922] 2 Ch 475, CA.
4 *Re Jawett* [1929] 1 Ch 108.
5 *Re Cunningham, ex p Official Receiver v Cunningham* (1898) 6 Mans 199, CA; *Re Osborne, ex p Lovell* (1899) 43 Sol Jo 480; *Re A Debtor, Jacobs v Lloyd* [1944] Ch 344, sub nom *Re Marsden, Jacobs v Lloyd* [1944] 1 All ER 597 (bankrupt may be cross-examined thereon by the party who calls him). However, this does not make the bankrupt's answers on his examination admissible against other parties: see the text and notes 9, 10. As to private examinations in bankruptcy see PARA 305 et seq.
6 Ie under the Solicitors Act 1974 s 47: see LEGAL PROFESSIONS vol 66 (2009) PARA 907.
7 *Re A Solicitor* (1890) 25 QBD 17 (decided under the Solicitors Act 1888 s 13 (repealed)).
8 *New Prance and Garrard's Trustee v Hunting* [1897] 2 QB 19, CA; affd on other grounds sub nom *Sharp v Jackson* [1899] AC 419, HL.
9 *Re Brunner* (1887) 19 QBD 572; *New Prance and Garrard's Trustee v Hunting* [1897] 2 QB 19, CA; affd on other grounds sub nom *Sharp v Jackson* [1899] AC 419, HL.
10 *Re Bottomley, ex p Brougham* (1915) 84 LJKB 1020.

298. Adjournment of public examination. The public examination may be adjourned by the court from time to time, either to a fixed date or generally[1].

Where the examination has been adjourned generally, the court may at any time on the application[2] of the official receiver or of the bankrupt fix a venue[3] for the resumption of the examination[4], and give directions as to the manner in which, and the time within which, notice of the resumed public examination is to be given to persons entitled to take part in it[5].

Where such an application is made by the bankrupt, the court may grant it on terms that the expenses of giving the required notices be paid by him and that, before a venue for the resumed public examination is fixed, he must deposit with the official receiver such sum as the latter considers necessary to cover those expenses[6]. Where the examination is adjourned, the official receiver may, there and then, make application[7] for suspension of the bankrupt's automatic discharge from bankruptcy[8]. If, on the hearing of such an application, the court makes an order suspending the bankrupt's discharge, copies of such order must be sent by the court to the official receiver, the trustee and the bankrupt[9].

1 Insolvency Rules 1986, SI 1986/1925, r 6.176(1). For the prescribed form of order see Sch 4 Form 6.59 (substituted by SI 1987/1919).

2   As to the mode of application and the procedure see PARA 786 et seq.
3   As to the meaning of 'venue' see PARA 46 note 22.
4   For the prescribed form of order see the Insolvency Rules 1986, SI 1986/1925, Sch 4 Form 6.60 (substituted by SI 1987/1919; and amended by SI 2010/686).
5   Insolvency Rules 1986, SI 1986/1925, r 6.176(2).
6   Insolvency Rules 1986, SI 1986/1925, r 6.176(3).
7   Ie under the Insolvency Act 1986 s 279(3): see PARA 640.
8   Insolvency Rules 1986, SI 1986/1925, r 6.176(4) (amended by SI 2010/686); and see *Re a Debtor (No 26 of 1991)* [1996] BCC 246, sub nom *Holmes v Official Receiver* [1996] BPIR 279 (where a public examination was adjourned and discharge suspended for a prescribed period).
9   Insolvency Rules 1986, SI 1986/1925, r 6.176(5) (added by SI 1999/359).

299.   Order for production of documents by inland revenue official.   On the application of the official receiver or the trustee of the bankrupt's estate, the court may[1] order an inland revenue official[2] to produce to the court:

(1)   any return, account or accounts submitted, whether before or after the commencement of the bankruptcy[3], by the bankrupt to any inland revenue official;

(2)   any assessment or determination made, whether before or after the commencement of the bankruptcy, in relation to the bankrupt by any inland revenue official; or

(3)   any correspondence, whether before or after the commencement of the bankruptcy, between the bankrupt and any inland revenue official[4].

1   Ie for the purposes of an examination under the Insolvency Act 1986 s 290 (see PARA 289 et seq) or proceedings under ss 366–368 (see PARAS 224, 305 et seq). Section 369 does not, however, apply for the purposes of an examination under ss 366, 367 (see PARA 305 et seq) which takes place by virtue of s 368 (see PARA 224): s 369(7).
2   For these purposes, 'inland revenue official' means any inspector or collector of taxes appointed by the Commissioners for Her Majesty's Revenue and Customs or any person appointed by the Commissioners to serve in any other capacity: Insolvency Act 1986 s 369(6) (amended by virtue of the Commissioners for Revenue and Customs Act 2005 s 50(1)). As to the Commissioners for Her Majesty's Revenue and Customs see CUSTOMS AND EXCISE vol 31 (2012) PARA 921.
3   As to the commencement of bankruptcy see PARA 209.
4   Insolvency Act 1986 s 369(1). The court may not address an order under s 369(1) to an inland revenue official unless it is satisfied that that official is dealing, or has dealt, with the affairs of the bankrupt: s 369(3). As to the application for such an order see PARA 300.
      In the case of the administration in bankruptcy of the insolvent estate of a deceased person dying before the presentation of a bankruptcy petition, s 369 applies: Administration of Insolvent Estates of Deceased Persons Order 1986, SI 1986/1999, art 3(1), Sch 1 Pt II para 30. As to the administration in bankruptcy of the insolvent estates of deceased persons see further PARA 830 et seq.
      As to the public interest immunity of tax documents see *Lonrho plc v Fayed (No 4)* [1994] QB 775, [1994] 1 All ER 870 at 882, CA.

300.   Application for order.   An application by the official receiver or the trustee for an order to the HM Revenue and Customs to produce documents[1] must specify, with such particularity as will enable the order, if made, to be most easily complied with, the documents whose production to the court is desired, naming the official to whom the order is to be addressed[2].

The court must fix a venue[3] for the hearing of the application[4]; and notice of the venue, accompanied by a copy of the application, must be sent by the applicant to the Commissioners for HM Revenue and Customs[5] at least 28 days before the hearing[6]. The notice must require the Commissioners, not later than five business days[7] before the date fixed for the hearing of the application, to inform the court whether they consent or object to the making of an order under these provisions[8]. If the Commissioners consent to the making of an order, they must inform the court of the name of the official to whom it should be addressed, if other than the one named in the application[9]; and, if the Commissioners object to the making of an order, they must secure that an officer of theirs attends the hearing of the application and, not less than five business days before it, deliver to the court a statement in writing of the grounds of their objection[10]. A copy of the statement must be sent as soon as reasonably practicable to the applicant[11].

1   Ie under the Insolvency Act 1986 s 369: see PARA 299.
2   Insolvency Rules 1986, SI 1986/1925, r 6.194(1) (amended by SI 2010/686).
3   As to the meaning of 'venue' see PARA 46 note 22.
4   Insolvency Rules 1986, SI 1986/1925, r 6.194(2).
5   As to the Commissioners for HM Revenue and Customs see CUSTOMS AND EXCISE vol 31 (2012) PARA 921.
6   Insolvency Rules 1986, SI 1986/1925, r 6.194(3) (amended by SI 2010/686).
7   As to the meaning of 'business day' see PARA 28 note 8.
8   Insolvency Rules 1986, SI 1986/1925, r 6.194(4) (amended by SI 2010/686).
9   Insolvency Rules 1986, SI 1986/1925, r 6.194(5).
10 Insolvency Rules 1986, SI 1986/1925, r 6.194(6) (amended by SI 2009/642; and SI 2010/686).
11 Insolvency Rules 1986, SI 1986/1925, r 6.194(6) (as amended: see note 10).

301. Making and service of order. If, on the hearing of the application[1], it appears to the court to be a proper case, the court may make the order applied for, with such modifications, if any, as appear appropriate having regard to any representations made on behalf of the Commissioners for HM Revenue and Customs[2].

The order:

(1)   may be addressed to an HM Revenue and Customs official other than the one named in the application;

(2)   must specify a time, not less than 28 days after service on the official to whom the order is addressed, within which compliance is required; and

(3)   may include requirements as to the manner in which documents to which the order relates are to be produced[3].

A sealed copy of the order must be served by the applicant on the official to whom it is addressed[4].

If the official is unable to comply with the order because he has not the relevant documents in his possession, and has been unable to obtain possession of them, he must deliver to the court a statement in writing as to the reasons for his non-compliance; and a copy of the statement must be sent as soon as reasonably practicable by the official to the applicant[5].

Where the court has made such an order for the purposes of any examination or proceedings, the court may, at any time after the document to which the order relates is produced to it, by order authorise the disclosure of the document, or of any part of its contents, to the official receiver, the trustee of the bankrupt's estate or the bankrupt's creditors[6].

1   Ie under the Insolvency Act 1986 s 369: see PARAS 299, 300.
2   Insolvency Rules 1986, SI 1986/1925, r 6.195(1). For the prescribed form of order see Sch 4 Form 6.69 (amended by SI 2010/686). As to the Commissioners for HM Revenue and Customs see CUSTOMS AND EXCISE vol 31 (2012) PARA 921.
3   Insolvency Rules 1986, SI 1986/1925, r 6.195(2) (amended by SI 2010/686).
4   Insolvency Rules 1986, SI 1986/1925, r 6.195(3).
5   Insolvency Rules 1986, SI 1986/1925, r 6.195(4) (amended by SI 2009/642).
6   Insolvency Act 1986 s 369(2). As to the application of s 369 in the case of the administration in bankruptcy of the insolvent estate of a deceased person dying before the presentation of a

bankruptcy petition see PARA 299 note 4. For the prescribed form of order see the Insolvency Rules 1986, SI 1986/1925, Sch 4 Form 6.70 (amended by SI 2010/686).

302. Disclosure and custody of documents. Where any document to which an order to HM Revenue and Customs to produce documents[1] relates is not in the possession of the HM Revenue and Customs official[2] to whom the order is addressed, it is the duty of that official to take all reasonable steps to secure possession of it, and, if he fails to do so, to report the reasons for his failure to the court[3]; and, where any document to which such an order relates is in the possession of an official other than the one to whom the order is addressed, it is the duty of the official in possession of the document, at the request of the official to whom the order is addressed, to deliver it to the official making the request[4]. Where, in compliance with an order to HM Revenue and Customs to produce documents[5], original documents are produced, and not copies, any person who, by order of the court[6], has them in his possession or custody is responsible to the court for their safe keeping and return as and when directed[7].

1 Ie an order under the Insolvency Act 1986 s 369(1): see PARA 299 et seq.
2 See PARA 299 note 2.
3 Insolvency Act 1986 s 369(4). As to the application of s 369 in the case of the administration in bankruptcy of the insolvent estate of a deceased person dying before the presentation of a bankruptcy petition see PARA 299 note 4.
4 Insolvency Act 1986 s 369(5).
5 Ie under the Insolvency Act 1986 s 369: see PARA 299 et seq.
6 Ie under the Insolvency Act 1986 s 369(2): see PARA 301.
7 Insolvency Rules 1986, SI 1986/1925, r 6.196.

303. Expenses of examination. Where a public examination of the bankrupt has been ordered by the court on a creditors' requisition[1], the court may order that the expenses of the examination are to be paid, as to a specified proportion, out of the deposit paid by the requisitionists[2], instead of out of the estate[3]. In no case do the costs and expenses of a public examination fall on the official receiver personally[4].

1 Ie under the Insolvency Rules 1986, SI 1986/1925, r 6.173: see PARA 290.
2 Ie under the Insolvency Rules 1986, SI 1986/1925, r 6.173(2): see PARA 290.
3 Insolvency Rules 1986, SI 1986/1925, r 6.177(1).
4 Insolvency Rules 1986, SI 1986/1925, r 6.177(2).

304. Nomination and appointment of shorthand writers. In the High Court the judge or registrar and, in a county court, a district judge, may in writing nominate one or more persons to be official shorthand writers to the court[1]. The court may, at any time in the course of insolvency proceedings[2], appoint a shorthand writer to take down the evidence of a person examined[3]. Where the official receiver applies to the court for an order appointing a shorthand writer, he must name the person he proposes for appointment[4].

The remuneration of a shorthand writer appointed in insolvency proceedings must be paid by the party at whose instance the appointment was made, or out of the bankrupt's estate, or otherwise, as the court may direct[5].

1 Insolvency Rules 1986, SI 1986/1925, r 7.16(1) (amended by SI 2010/686). As from a day to be appointed, any reference however expressed that is or is deemed to be a reference to a county court held under the County Courts Act 1984 s 1 is to be read as a reference to the county court established by s A1 of that Act: see the Crime and Courts Act 2013 Sch 9 Pt 2 para 11(1)(a), (3)(c). At the date at which this volume states the law no such day had been appointed.
2 As to the meaning of 'insolvency proceedings' see PARA 37 note 9.

3 Insolvency Rules 1986, SI 1986/1925, r 7.16(2). Such examination takes place under the Insolvency Act 1986 s 251N (see PARA 118), s 290 (see PARA 289 et seq) or s 366 (see PARA 305 et seq): Insolvency Rules 1986, SI 1986/1925, r 7.16(2).
4 Insolvency Rules 1986, SI 1986/1925, r 7.16(3) (amended by SI 2010/686).
5 Insolvency Rules 1986, SI 1986/1925, r 7.17(1). Any question arising as to the rates of remuneration payable must be determined by the court in its discretion: r 7.17(2) (substituted by SI 1993/602).

(x) Private Examination

305. Inquiry into bankrupt's dealings and property. At any time after a bankruptcy order has been made[1] the court may, on the application of the official receiver or the trustee of the bankrupt's estate[2], summon to appear before it:

(1)   the bankrupt or the bankrupt's spouse or former spouse or civil partner or former civil partner;

(2)   any person known or believed to have any property comprised in the bankrupt's estate in his possession or to be indebted to the bankrupt;

(3)   any person appearing to the court to be able to give information concerning the bankrupt or the bankrupt's dealings, affairs[3] or property[4].

The court may require any such person as is mentioned in heads (2) and (3) above to submit a witness statement verified by a statement of truth[5] to the court containing an account of his dealings with the bankrupt or to produce any documents in his possession or under his control relating to the bankrupt or the bankrupt's dealings, affairs or property[6]. Any person who appears or is brought before the court[7] may be examined on oath, either orally or by clarifying any matter or by giving further information, concerning the bankrupt or the bankrupt's dealings, affairs and property[8].

The purpose of a private examination is to assist the official receiver, the trustee or the interim receiver, as the case may be, who comes to the affairs of the bankrupt as a stranger, to investigate and to understand transactions done by, with or on behalf of the bankrupt or his business associates, many of which may be unrecorded or obscure[9]. The examination is not itself a litigious proceeding, but is to enable the trustee to inform himself, with as little expense and as much ease as possible[10], as to what course he should pursue in some matter or claim relating to the bankrupt's estate, which he is allowed to state privately[11] to the court, and to assess his chances of success in proceedings relating to it[12].

1   As to bankruptcy orders see PARA 198 et seq.
2   As to the meaning of 'the bankrupt's estate' see PARA 211.
3   As to the meaning of references to a person's affairs see PARA 43 note 4.
4   Insolvency Act 1986 s 366(1) (amended by the Civil Partnership Act 2004 s 261(1), Sch 27 para 120). As to the meaning of 'property' see PARA 412. The Insolvency Rules 1986, SI 1986/1925, Pt 9 (rr 9.1–9.6: see PARA 307 et seq) relates to applications to the court for an order under the Insolvency Act 1986 s 251N (see PARA 118) and s 366 (see PARA 305 et seq): Insolvency Rules 1986, SI 1986/1925, r 9.1(1)(b), (c) (r 9.1(1) substituted by SI 2010/686).

In the case of the administration in bankruptcy of the insolvent estate of a deceased person dying before the presentation of a bankruptcy petition, the Insolvency Act 1986 s 366 applies: Administration of Insolvent Estates of Deceased Persons Order 1986, SI 1986/1999, art 3(1), Sch 1 Pt II para 30. As to the administration in bankruptcy of the insolvent estates of deceased persons see further PARA 830 et seq.

The Insolvency Act 1986 s 366 applies where an interim receiver has been appointed under s 286 (see PARA 218 et seq) as it applies where a bankruptcy order has been made, as if: (1) references to the official receiver or the trustee were to the interim receiver; and (2) references to the bankrupt and to his estate were, respectively, to the debtor and his property: s 368. As to the application of s 368 in the case of the administration in bankruptcy of the insolvent estate of a deceased person dying before the presentation of a bankruptcy petition see PARA 224 note 5.

5 As to the meanings of 'witness statement' and 'statement of truth' see PARA 161 note 7.

6 Insolvency Act 1986 s 366(1) (amended by SI 2010/18).

7 Ie under the Insolvency Act 1986 s 366 or s 367.

8 See the Insolvency Act 1986 s 367(4). Section 367 applies where an interim receiver has been appointed under s 286 (see PARA 218 et seq) as it applies where a bankruptcy order has been made, as if: (1) references to the official receiver or trustee were to the interim receiver; and (2) references to the bankrupt and to his estate were, respectively, to the debtor and his property: s 368.

In the case of the administration in bankruptcy of the insolvent estate of a deceased person dying before the presentation of a bankruptcy petition, s 367 applies: Administration of Insolvent Estates of Deceased Persons Order 1986, SI 1986/1999, Sch 1 Pt II para 30.

9 Cf the Insolvency Act 1986 ss 236, 237 (inquiry into company's dealings etc; court's enforcement powers): see COMPANY AND PARTNERSHIP INSOLVENCY vol 17 (2011) PARA 637 et seq. See also *Re Overend, Gurney & Co, ex p Musgrave* (1867) 16 LT 378; *Re Gold Co* (1879) 12 ChD 77 at 84, CA; *Re Greys Brewery Co* (1883) 25 ChD 400; *Re North Australian Territory Co* (1890) 45 ChD 87 at 93, CA; *Re A Debtor (No 472 of 1950)* [1958] 1 All ER 581, [1958] 1 WLR 283, CA; *Re A Debtor (No 12 of 1958), ex p Trustee of Property of Debtor v Clegg* [1968] 2 All ER 425, [1968] 1 WLR 788, DC; *Re Rolls Razor Ltd (No 2)* [1970] Ch 576 at 591, 592, [1969] 2 All ER 1386 at 1396; *Cloverbay Ltd (Joint Administrators) v Bank of Credit and Commerce International SA* [1991] Ch 90, [1991] 1 All ER 894, CA; *British and Commonwealth Holdings plc (Joint Administrators) v Spicer and Oppenheim (a firm)* [1993] AC 426, [1992] 4 All ER 876, HL.

10 *Re Rolls Razor Ltd* [1968] 3 All ER 698 at 700.

11 See the Insolvency Rules 1986, SI 1986/1925, r 9.5(3); and PARA 310. See also *Re Murjani (a bankrupt)* [1996] 1 All ER 65, [1996] 1 WLR 1498.

12 *Learoyd v Halifax Joint Stock Banking Co* [1893] 1 Ch 686 at 692, 693.

306. Restrictions on exercise of power to order examination. Despite the considerations referred to above[1], the power to order a private examination is one which ought to be carefully exercised[2]; the court must be astute to prevent any oppressive, vexatious or unfair use of the power[3]. Factors which may be taken into account by the court in exercising its discretion include the following:

(1) whether the order is sought against those under a duty to co-operate with the office-holder;

(2) the views of the office-holder are to be given great weight;

(3) the office-holder is entitled not only to general information but to specific information concerning possible claims against specific persons;

(4) the mere fact that an office-holder has commenced or is about to commence proceedings against the respondent is not an absolute bar to the making of an order;

(5) the risk that a respondent might expose himself to liability is merely a factor to be taken into account, the risk of exposure to a fraud claim not being conclusive;

(6) the fact that a respondent may have to answer questions which expose him to criminal liability is not decisive;

(7) an oral examination is likely to be more oppressive than an order for production of documents[4].

1 See PARA 305.

2 See the leading cases decided under the similar provision relating to corporate insolvency in the Insolvency Act 1986 s 236: *Cloverbay Ltd (Joint Administrators) v Bank of Credit and Commerce International SA* [1991] Ch 90, [1991] 1 All ER 894, CA; *British & Commonwealth Holdings plc (Joint Administrators) v Spicer and Oppenheim (a firm)* [1993] AC 426, [1992] 4 All ER 876, HL; *Bishopsgate Investment Management Ltd (in provisional liquidation) v Maxwell* [1993] Ch 1, [1992] 2 All ER 856, CA; *Re RBG Resources Ltd, Shierson v Rastogi* [2002] EWCA Civ 1624, [2003] 1 WLR 586, [2002] BCC 1005. For older cases see *Re Wright,*

ex p Willey (1883) 23 ChD 118 at 128, CA; *Re Gregory, ex p Norton* [1935] Ch 65, CA; *Re A Debtor (No 472 of 1950)* [1958] 1 All ER 581, [1958] 1 WLR 283, CA; *Re Rolls Razor Ltd (No 2)* [1970] Ch 576 at 592, [1969] 3 All ER 1386 at 1397. Cf the Insolvency Act 1986 ss 236, 237 (inquiry into company's dealings etc; court's enforcement powers): see COMPANY AND PARTNERSHIP INSOLVENCY vol 17 (2011) PARA 637 et seq.

3 *Cloverbay Ltd (Joint Administrators) v Bank of Credit and Commerce International SA* [1991] Ch 90, [1991] 1 All ER 894, CA (the court must balance the liquidator's requirements against any risk of possible oppression to the proposed witness; ordering pre-trial depositions from parties suspected of fraud or dishonest behaviour may be oppressive); *British and Commonwealth Holdings plc (Joint Administrators) v Spicer and Oppenheim (a firm)* [1993] AC 426, [1992] 4 All ER 876, HL (court must bear in mind the public interest and the interests of those affected by the insolvency; oppression arising out of the expense to which a witness might be put can be compensated for by an order for costs).

There may be cases where the court may think it appropriate that no examination should be ordered until written questions have been submitted by the trustee to the person sought to be examined; but the unsworn answers to those questions may often prove no adequate substitute for an oral examination before the court: *Re Rolls Razor Ltd (No 2)* [1970] Ch 576 at 596, [1969] 3 All ER 1386 at 1400. There is no invariable requirement that a private examination should be preceded by written questions; it is a matter for the unfettered discretion of the court which has to determine how best the examination may be carried out balancing the views of the liquidator, which are entitled to be given great weight, against the requirement that the investigation should not be carried out in an oppressive or unfair manner to the persons being examined: *Re Norton Warburg Holdings Ltd* [1983] BCLC 235 (company case). There is an express power in the court to order examination on oath in order to clarify any matter or give further information: see the Insolvency Act 1986 s 367(4); and PARA 305.

As to the question of documents protected by legal professional privilege see *Re Murjani (a bankrupt)* [1996] 1 All ER 65, [1996] 1 WLR 1498; *Re Ouvaroff (a bankrupt)* [1997] BPIR 712; *Williams (trustee of the property of Nassim Mohammed) v Mohammed* [2011] EWHC 3293 (Ch), [2011] BPIR 1787. For company cases see also *Barclays Bank plc v Eustice* [1995] 4 All ER 511, [1995] 1 WLR 1238, CA; *Royscot Spa Leasing Ltd v Lovett* [1995] BCC 502, CA; *Dubai Bank Ltd v Galadari* [1990] Ch 98, [1989] 3 All ER 769, CA; and *Re Highgrade Traders Ltd* [1984] BCLC 151, CA.

As to the case of a solicitor witness see *Re A Debtor (No 472 of 1950)* [1958] 1 All ER 581, sub nom *Re A Debtor (No 472 of 1950), ex p Swirsky* [1958] 1 WLR 283, CA; *International Credit and Investment Co (Overseas) Ltd v Adham* [1997] 9 LS Gaz R 31 (power of the court to order a solicitor to disclose name and address of client should only be exercised in exceptional circumstances).

See also *Morris v Director of Serious Fraud Office* [1993] Ch 372, [1993] 1 All ER 788, CA (an order for the production of documents belonging to third parties and obtained by the Serious Fraud Office should not be made without hearing the third parties as owners of the documents); *Re Murjani (a bankrupt)* [1996] 1 All ER 65 at 78, [1996] 1 WLR 1498 at 1511–1512 (where exceptions to this practice are described).

The privilege against self-incrimination does not apply to bankruptcy examinations where the examinee is under a duty to co-operate with the office-holder: see *R v Kansal* [1993] QB 244, [1992] 3 All ER 844, CA. See also *Bishopsgate Investment Management Ltd (in provisional liquidation) v Maxwell* [1993] Ch 1, [1992] 2 All ER 856, CA; *Re London United Investments plc* [1992] Ch 578, [1992] 2 All ER 842, CA; *Bank of England v Riley* [1992] Ch 475, [1992] 1 All ER 769, CA; *Re Jeffrey S Levitt Ltd (in administrative receivership)* [1992] Ch 457, [1992] 2 All ER 509. As to the subsequent use in criminal proceedings of evidence obtained under compulsory powers see Case 43/1994/490/572 *Saunders v United Kingdom* (1997) 2 BHRC 358, [1998] 1 BCLC 362, ECtHR; *A-G's Reference (No 7 of 2000)* [2001] EWCA Crim 888, [2001] 1 WLR 1879, [2001] BPIR 953. Cf the Insolvency Act 1986 ss 133, 236 et seq; and COMPANY AND PARTNERSHIP INSOLVENCY vol 16 (2011) PARA 488 et seq; COMPANY AND PARTNERSHIP INSOLVENCY vol 17 (2011) PARAS 637, 643.

In general, orders for production of documents will not contravene the rights of correspondents under the Convention for the Protection of Human Rights and Fundamental Freedoms (Rome, 4 November 1950; TS 71 (1953); Cmd 8969) ('the European Convention on Human Rights') art 8 (see RIGHTS AND FREEDOMS vol 88A (2013) PARA 317): *Warner v Verfides* [2008] EWHC 2609 (Ch), [2009] Bus LR 500, [2009] BPIR 153.

As to confidential documents see *Pharaon v Bank of Credit and Commerce International SA (in liquidation) (Price Waterhouse (a firm) intervening), Price Waterhouse v Bank of Credit and Commerce International SA (in liquidation)* [1998] 4 All ER 455 (the need for disclosure will in general prevail over a claim to preserve confidentiality); *Joint Liquidators of Sasea Finance Ltd v KPMG* [1998] BCC 216; *Re Murjani (a bankrupt)* [1996] 1 All ER 65, [1996] 1 WLR 1498; *British & Commonwealth Holdings plc (Joint Administrators) v Spicer and Oppenheim (a firm)* [1993] AC 426, [1992] 4 All ER 876, HL (an order for the production of documents is not necessarily unreasonable on the grounds that it is inconvenient or causes extra work or expense); *Re Barlow Clowes Gilt Managers Ltd* [1992] Ch 208, [1991] 4 All ER 385. The court also has jurisdiction to order production of documents regardless of where they are located (*Re Mid-East Trading Ltd, Lehman Bros Inc v Phillips* [1998] 1 All ER 577, [1998] 1 BCLC 240, CA (a case under the Insolvency Act 1986 s 236)); but the court will take into account as a relevant factor the effect which an order may have on any obligations a foreign respondent may have under local laws (*Buchler v Al-Midani* [2005] EWHC 3183 (Ch), [2006] BPIR 867, [2005] All ER (D) 273 (Nov)).

4   *British and Commonwealth Holdings plc (Joint Administrators) v Spicer and Oppenheim (a firm)* [1993] AC 426, [1992] 4 All ER 876, HL.

307.   Obtaining order for examination.   The application[1] must be in writing and specify the grounds on which it is made[2]. The application must specify the name of the respondent[3]. There must be stated in the application whether it is an application for the respondent:

(1)   to be ordered to appear before the court; or

(2)   to be ordered to clarify any matter which is in dispute in the proceedings or to give additional information in relation to any such matter and, if so, the normal rules relating to further information[4] apply to any such order; or

(3)   to submit witness statements[5] (if so, particulars to be given of the matters to be included); or

(4)   to produce books, papers or other records (if so, the items in question to be specified),

or for any two or more of those purposes[6].

The application may be made without notice to any other party[7].

1   Ie an application for an order under the Insolvency Act 1986 s 366: see PARA 305. For the prescribed form of order see the Insolvency Rules 1986, SI 1986/1925, Sch 4 Form 9.1 (amended by SI 2009/2472).

2   Insolvency Rules 1986, SI 1986/1925, r 9.2(1) (amended by SI 2010/686). The statement is prima facie confidential by reason of r 9.5(3) (see PARA 310) and is not open to inspection by the respondent without the permission of the court. As to the position where inspection is sought by a respondent seeking to set aside an order made under the Insolvency Act 1986 s 366 see *Re British & Commonwealth Holdings plc (Nos 1 & 2)* [1992] Ch 342, [1992] 2 All ER 801, CA; affd sub nom *British & Commonwealth Holdings plc (Joint Administrators) v Spicer and Oppenheim (a firm)* [1993] AC 426, [1992] 4 All ER 876, HL (decided under the Insolvency Act 1986 s 236); *Re Murjani (a bankrupt)* [1996] 1 All ER 65, [1996] 1 WLR 1498. The proper course for an office-holder making an application is for him to put sensitive information in an annexure: *Re British & Commonwealth Holdings plc (Nos 1 & 2)*; *Re Murjani (a bankrupt)*.

3   Insolvency Rules 1986, SI 1986/1925, r 9.2(2) (substituted by SI 2010/686). For these purposes, 'the respondent' means the person in respect of whom an order is applied for: Insolvency Rules 1986, SI 1986/1925, r 9.1(2)(a). As to who may apply for an order see *Re Adlards Motor Group Holdings Ltd* [1990] BCLC 68 (the fact that the liquidator's application for examination is financed by a creditor will not in itself be a ground for refusing to make an order).

4   Ie CPR Pt 18: see CIVIL PROCEDURE vol 11 (2009) PARAS 611, 612.

5   As to the meaning of 'witness statement' see PARA 161 note 7.

6   Insolvency Rules 1986, SI 1986/1925, r 9.2(3) (amended by SI 1999/1022; and SI 2010/686).

7   Insolvency Rules 1986, SI 1986/1925, r 9.2(4) (amended by SI 2010/686). As to the mode of application and the procedure see PARA 786 et seq. In general, an application should be made with notice, but, where necessary, it may be made without notice being served on any other party: *Re Murjani (a bankrupt)* [1996] 1 All ER 65, [1996] 1 WLR 1498; *Re PFTZM (in liquidation), Jourdain v Paul* [1995] 2 BCLC 354, [1995] BCC 280; *Hill v Van Der Merwe* [2007] EWHC 1613 (Ch), [2007] BPIR 1562. If the application is made without notice being served on any other party, there is a duty to place all material facts before the court: *Re John T Rhodes Ltd (No 2)* (1987) 3 BCC 588 (company case).

308. Order for examination. The court may, whatever the purpose of the application, make any order which it has power[1] to make[2]. If the court orders the respondent[3] to appear before it, it must specify a venue[4] for his appearance, which must be not less than 14 days from the date of the order[5]. The court may, if it thinks fit, order that any person who, if within the jurisdiction of the court, would be liable to be summoned to appear before it[6] be examined in any part of the United Kingdom where he may be for the time being, or in any place outside the United Kingdom[7]. If the respondent is ordered to submit witness statements[8], the order must specify the matters which are to be dealt with in his witness statements, and the time within which they are to be submitted to the court[9]. If the order is to produce books, papers or other records, the time and manner of compliance must be specified[10].

The order must be served as soon as reasonably practicable on the respondent; and it must be served personally, unless the court otherwise orders[11].

1 Ie under the Insolvency Act 1986 s 366: see PARA 305. These provisions also apply to s 251N (see PARA 118).
2 Insolvency Rules 1986, SI 1986/1925, rr 9.1(2)(b), 9.3(1) (r 9.1(2)(b) substituted by SI 2009/642). For the prescribed form of order see PARA 307 note 1.
3 As to the meaning of 'the respondent' see PARA 307 note 3.
4 As to the meaning of 'venue' see PARA 46 note 22.
5 Insolvency Rules 1986, SI 1986/1925, r 9.3(2).
6 Ie under the Insolvency Act 1986 s 366: see PARA 305.
7 Insolvency Act 1986 s 367(3). As to the meaning of 'United Kingdom' see PARA 40 note 10. As to the application of s 367: (1) in the case of the administration in bankruptcy of the insolvent estate of a deceased person dying before the presentation of a bankruptcy petition; or (2) where an interim receiver has been appointed see PARA 305 note 8. An injunction may be obtained to restrain a person from leaving the jurisdiction pending the examination: *Morris v Murjani* [1996] 2 All ER 384, [1996] 1 WLR 848, CA, applying *Re Oriental Credit Ltd* [1988] Ch 204, [1988] 1 All ER 892.

The Insolvency Act 1986 s 367(3) re-enacts the power conferred by the Bankruptcy Act 1914 s 25(6) (repealed) which permitted an examination to take place outside the United Kingdom. In *Re Drucker, ex p Basden (No 2)* [1902] 2 KB 210, Wright J held that a similar power under the Bankruptcy Act 1883 s 27 (repealed) did not apply outside the jurisdiction of the Crown. 'It is impossible to suppose that the legislature intended to empower the court to order the examination of persons in foreign countries': *Re Drucker, ex p Basden (No 2)* at 211. Whether or not such a supposition may still be made, there remains the practical problem of enforcement.

In *Re Tucker (a bankrupt), ex p Tucker* [1990] Ch 148, [1988] 1 All ER 603, CA, a summons was issued under the Bankruptcy Act 1914 s 25(1) (repealed) requiring the bankrupt's brother to attend for examination in the High Court, the summons being served in Belgium where the bankrupt's brother was resident. The brother applied to have the order for service on him in Belgium set aside, although no application was made to have the summons itself set aside. The application was dismissed: see [1987] 2 All ER 23, [1987] 1 WLR 928. The brother appealed, and on the appeal the trustee sought an order for the brother's examination in Belgium. The Court of Appeal allowed the appeal and dismissed the trustee's application. Under the Bankruptcy Act 1914 s 25(1) (repealed) the court was empowered to issue summonses against persons resident in England only. However, under s 25(6) (repealed) the court had a discretion to make an order for the examination of a person before a court in a foreign country. Any person might be the subject of such an order which need not have been limited to persons who were British subjects. Before such an order could be made, however, the court had to be satisfied that there was proper machinery available to ensure compliance. Under the relevant United Kingdom/Belgian Convention an examination might be held in Belgium but not under any compulsion, and any summons served on the bankrupt's brother would have to state expressly that there was no compulsion for him to appear. The brother had shown himself unwilling to co-operate. In the circumstances the Court of Appeal considered that no useful purpose would be achieved by making an order for the examination of the brother before the Belgian court and, in the exercise of its discretion, refused the order sought.

As to the effect of the Insolvency Act 1986 s 426 on an examination directed to be conducted abroad see PARA 828.
8 As to the meaning of 'witness statement' see PARA 161 note 7.

9   Insolvency Rules 1986, SI 1986/1925, r 9.3(3) (amended by SI 2010/686).
10   Insolvency Rules 1986, SI 1986/1925, r 9.3(4).
11   Insolvency Rules 1986, SI 1986/1925, r 9.3(5) (amended by SI 2009/642).

309.   Procedure at examination.   At any examination of the respondent[1], the applicant may attend in person, or be represented by a solicitor with or without counsel, and may put such questions to the respondent as the court may allow[2]. Unless the applicant objects, the following persons may attend the examination with the permission of the court and may put questions to the respondent (but only through the applicant): (1) any person who could have applied for an order[3]; and (2) any creditor who has provided information on which the application[4] was made[5].

If the respondent is ordered to clarify any matter or to give additional information, the court must direct him as to the questions which he is required to answer, and as to whether his answers (if any) are to be made in a witness statement[6].

The respondent may at his own expense employ a solicitor with or without counsel, who may put to him such questions as the court may allow for the purposes of enabling him to explain or qualify any answers given by him, and may make representations on his behalf[7].

1   As to the meaning of 'the respondent' see PARA 307 note 3.
2   Insolvency Rules 1986, SI 1986/1925, r 9.4(1); and see *Re Richbell Strategic Holdings Ltd (in liquidation) (No 2)* [2000] 2 BCLC 794, [2001] BCC 409 (a person may not refuse to answer a question on the basis that the examiner already knows the answer; a person must answer questions to the best of his ability, even if he does not have access to relevant documents). As to the privilege against self-incrimination see PARA 306.
3   Ie under the Insolvency Act 1986 s 366: see PARA 305. These provisions also apply to s 251N (see PARA 118).
4   Ie under the Insolvency Act 1986 s 366: see PARA 305.
5   Insolvency Rules 1986, SI 1986/1925, r 9.4(2) (substituted by SI 2010/686).
6   Insolvency Rules 1986, SI 1986/1925, r 9.4(3) (substituted by SI 1999/1022; and amended by SI 2010/686). As to the meaning of 'witness statement' see PARA 161 note 7.
7   Insolvency Rules 1986, SI 1986/1925, r 9.4(5).

310.   Record of examination.   There must be made in writing such record of the examination as the court thinks proper; and the record must be read over either to or by the respondent[1] and authenticated[2] by him at a venue[3] fixed by the court[4]. The written record may in any proceedings[5] be used as evidence against the respondent of any statement made by him in the course of his examination[6].

Unless the court otherwise directs, the written record of questions put to the respondent and the respondent's answers, and any witness statements[7] submitted by the respondent in compliance with an order of the court[8], are not to be filed with the court[9].

The following documents are not open to inspection without an order of the court, by any person other than the applicant for an order, or any person who could have applied for such an order in respect of the affairs of the same bankrupt[10]:

(1)   the written record of the respondent's examination;
(2)   copies of questions put to the respondent or proposed to be put to the respondent and answers to questions given by the respondent;
(3)   any witness statement by the respondent; and
(4)   any document on the court file as shows the grounds for the application for an order[11].

The court may from time to time give directions as to the custody and inspection of any such documents and as to the furnishing of copies of, or extracts from, such documents[12].

1 As to the meaning of 'the respondent' see PARA 307 note 3.
2 As to authentication see PARA 158 note 2.
3 As to the meaning of 'venue' see PARA 46 note 22.

4 Insolvency Rules 1986, SI 1986/1925, r 9.4(6) (amended by SI 2010/686). As to the appointment of shorthand writers see PARA 304.

5 Ie whether under the Insolvency Act 1986 or otherwise.
6 Insolvency Rules 1986, SI 1986/1925, r 9.4(7). See further PARA 306 note 3.
7 As to the meaning of 'witness statement' see PARA 161 note 7.
8 Ie under the Insolvency Act 1986 s 366: see PARAS 305, 308. These provisions also apply to s 251N (see PARA 118).

9 Insolvency Rules 1986, SI 1986/1925, r 9.5(1) (substituted by SI 2010/686). As to the meaning of 'file with the court' see PARA 57 note 13.

10 Insolvency Rules 1986, SI 1986/1925, r 9.5(2) (substituted by SI 2010/686). As to the persons who may apply for such an order see PARA 305. The transcript of an examination may be protected by legal privilege and also by order of the court: *Hamilton v Naviede* [1995] 2 AC 75, sub nom *Re Arrows Ltd (No 4)*, *Hamilton v Naviede* [1994] 3 All ER 814, HL, applying *Rank Film Distributors Ltd v Video Information Centre (a firm)* [1982] AC 380, [1981] 2 All ER 76, HL; *AT & T Istel Ltd v Tully* [1993] AC 45, [1992] 3 All ER 523, HL.

11 Insolvency Rules 1986, SI 1986/1925, r 9.5(3) (substituted by SI 2010/686); and see *Re British and Commonwealth Holdings plc (Nos 1 & 2)* [1992] Ch 342, [1992] 2 All ER 801, CA; affd sub nom *British and Commonwealth Holdings plc (Joint Administrators) v Spicer and Oppenheim (a firm)* [1993] AC 426, [1992] 4 All ER 876, HL (court has a discretion whether or not to order disclosure to a third party of the statement of grounds). See also *Re Murjani (a bankrupt)* [1996] 1 All ER 65, [1996] 1 WLR 1498; *First Tokyo Index Trust v Gould* [1996] BPIR 406, Ct of Sess.

12 Insolvency Rules 1986, SI 1986/1925, r 9.5(4).

311.   Failure to appear. Where a person without reasonable excuse fails to appear before the court when he is summoned to do so[1] or there are reasonable grounds for believing that a person has absconded, or is about to abscond, with a view to avoiding his appearance before the court, the court may, for the purpose of bringing that person and anything in his possession before the court, cause a warrant to be issued to a constable or prescribed officer of the court[2] for the arrest of that person, and for the seizure of any books, papers, records[3], money or goods in that person's possession[4]. The court may authorise a person arrested under such a warrant to be kept in custody, and anything seized under such a warrant to be held[5] until that person is brought before the court under the warrant or until such other time as the court may order[6].

When a person is arrested under such a warrant, the officer arresting him must as soon as reasonably practicable bring him before the court issuing the warrant in order that he may be examined[7]. If he cannot immediately be brought up for examination, the officer must deliver him into the custody of the governor of the prison named in the warrant (or where that prison is not able to accommodate the arrested person, the governor of such other prison with appropriate facilities which is able to accommodate the arrested person), who must keep him in custody and produce him before the court as it may from time to time direct[8]. After arresting the person named in the warrant, the officer must as soon as reasonably practicable report to the court the arrest or delivery into custody, as the case may be, and apply to the court to fix a venue[9] for the person's examination[10]. The court must appoint the earliest practicable time for the examination, and must direct the governor of the prison to produce the person for examination at the time and place appointed, and as soon as reasonably practicable give notice of the venue to the person who applied for the warrant[11].

Any property in the arrested person's possession which may be seized must, as may be directed by the court, be lodged with, or otherwise dealt with as instructed by, whoever is specified in the warrant as authorised to receive it, or kept by the officer seizing it pending the receipt of written orders from the court as to its disposal[12].

1 Ie under the Insolvency Act 1986 s 366(1): see PARA 305.
2 The prescribed officers of the court are, in the case of the High Court, the tipstaff and his assistants of the court, and, in the case of a county court, the district judge and the bailiffs: Insolvency Rules 1986, SI 1986/1925, r 7.21(2) (amended by SI 2010/686). As from a day to be appointed, any reference however expressed that is or is deemed to be a reference to a county court held under the County Courts Act 1984 s 1 is to be read as a reference to the county court established by s A1 of that Act: see the Crime and Courts Act 2013 Sch 9 Pt 2 para 11(1)(a), (3)(c). At the date at which this volume states the law no such day had been appointed.
3 As to the meaning of 'records' see PARA 20 note 6.
4 Insolvency Act 1986 s 366(2), (3). As to the application of s 366 in the case of the administration in bankruptcy of the insolvent estate of a deceased person dying before the presentation of a bankruptcy petition see PARA 305 note 4.
5 Ie in accordance with the Insolvency Rules 1986, SI 1986/1925.
6 Insolvency Act 1986 s 366(4).
7 Insolvency Rules 1986, SI 1986/1925, r 7.23(1) (amended by SI 2009/642; and SI 2010/686). These provisions also apply to s 251N (see PARA 118).
8 Insolvency Rules 1986, SI 1986/1925, r 7.23(2) (amended by SI 2010/686).
9 As to the meaning of 'venue' see PARA 84 note 21.
10 Insolvency Rules 1986, SI 1986/1925, r 7.23(3) (amended by SI 2009/642.
11 Insolvency Rules 1986, SI 1986/1925, r 7.23(4).
12 Insolvency Rules 1986, SI 1986/1925, r 7.23(5).

312. Orders for delivery of property or payment. If it appears to the court, on consideration of any evidence obtained under examination[1], that any person has in his possession any property comprised in the bankrupt's estate[2], the court may, on the application of the official receiver or the trustee of the bankrupt's estate[3], order that person to deliver the whole or any part of the property to the official receiver or the trustee at such time, in such manner and on such terms as the court thinks fit[4].

If it appears to the court, on consideration of any evidence so obtained, that any person is indebted to the bankrupt, the court may, on the application of the official receiver or the trustee of the bankrupt's estate, order that person to pay him, at such time and in such manner as the court may direct, the whole or part of the amount due, whether in full discharge of the debt or otherwise, as the court thinks fit[5].

1 Ie under the Insolvency Act 1986 s 366 or s 367: see PARA 305 et seq.
2 As to the meaning of 'the bankrupt's estate' see PARA 211.
3 See PARA 305.
4 Insolvency Act 1986 s 367(1). As to the application of s 367: (1) in the case of the administration in bankruptcy of the insolvent estate of a deceased person dying before the presentation of a bankruptcy petition; or (2) where an interim receiver has been appointed, see PARA 305 note 8.
5 Insolvency Act 1986 s 367(2).

313. Costs of examination. Where the court has ordered an examination of any person[1] and it appears to it that the examination was made necessary because information had been unjustifiably refused by the respondent[2], it may order that the costs of the examination be paid by him[3].

Where the court makes an order against a person to deliver up property in his possession which belongs to the bankrupt[4], or to pay any amount in discharge of a debt due to the bankrupt[5], the costs of the application for the order may be ordered by the court to be paid by the respondent[6]. Otherwise the applicant's costs must be paid out of the bankrupt's estate, unless the court otherwise orders[7]. A person summoned to attend for examination must be tendered a reasonable sum in respect of travelling expenses incurred in connection with his attendance; but other costs falling on him are at the court's discretion[8]. Where the examination is on the application of the official receiver otherwise than in the capacity of trustee, no order may be made for the payment of costs by him[9].

1 Ie under the Insolvency Act 1986 s 366: see PARA 305 et seq. These provisions also apply to s 251N (see PARA 118).
2 As to the meaning of 'the respondent' see PARA 307 note 3.
3 Insolvency Rules 1986, SI 1986/1925, r 9.6(1). The costs of the examination include the costs of obtaining the order for the examination: *Hunt v Renzland* [2008] BPIR 1380; *Miller v Bain* [2002] BCC 899, [2003] BPIR 959, [2000] All ER (D) 2019.
4 Ie under the Insolvency Act 1986 s 367(1): see PARA 312.
5 Ie under the Insolvency Act 1986 s 367(2): see PARA 312.
6 Insolvency Rules 1986, SI 1986/1925, rr 9.1(2)(c), 9.6(2).
7 Insolvency Rules 1986, SI 1986/1925, rr 9.6(3), 13.8 (r 9.6(3) amended by SI 2008/737; the Insolvency Rules 1986, SI 1986/1925, rr 9.6(3), 13.8 amended by SI 2009/642). This does not apply in proceedings relating to debt relief orders or applications for debt relief orders (see PARA 101 et seq): see the Insolvency Rules 1986, SI 1986/1925, r 9.6(3) (as so amended).
8 Insolvency Rules 1986, SI 1986/1925, r 9.6(4). The discretion to award costs to the respondent extends not only to the costs of an oral examination but also to the costs of complying with other orders which may be made: *Re Aveling Barford Ltd* [1988] 3 All ER 1019, [1989] 1 WLR 360; *British and Commonwealth Holdings plc (Joint Administrators) v Spicer and Oppenheim (a firm)* [1993] AC 426, [1992] 4 All ER 876, HL. In the normal case the costs of complying with an order for the production of documents will fall on the respondent: *Morris v Director of Serious Fraud Office* [1993] Ch 372, [1993] 1 All ER 788; *Re Cloverbay Ltd* [1989] BCLC 724, 5 BCC 732.
9 Insolvency Rules 1986, SI 1986/1925, r 9.6(5).

(5) TRUSTEE IN BANKRUPTCY

(i) Appointment of Trustee

314. Trustee to be insolvency practitioner. No person may be appointed as trustee of a bankrupt's estate unless he is, at the time of the appointment, qualified to act as an insolvency practitioner in relation to the bankrupt[1].

1 Insolvency Act 1986 ss 292(2), 388(2)(a). As to insolvency practitioners and their qualification see PARA 40. Nothing in s 388 applies to anything done by the official receiver: see s 388(5)(a) (substituted by the Bankruptcy (Scotland) Act 1993 s 11(1)). As to the application of the Insolvency Act 1986 ss 292, 388 in the case of the administration in bankruptcy of the insolvent estate of a deceased person dying before the presentation of a bankruptcy petition see PARAS 40 note 9, 261 note 2.

Nothing in s 388 applies to anything done (whether in the United Kingdom or elsewhere) in relation to insolvency proceedings under Council Regulation (EC) 1346/2000 (OJ L160, 30.6.2000, p 1) on insolvency proceedings ('European Regulation on Insolvency Proceedings') in a member state other than the United Kingdom: Insolvency Act 1986 s 388(6) (added by SI 2002/1240). See further PARAS 41, 42.

315. Power to appoint trustee. The power to appoint a person as trustee of a bankrupt's estate, whether the first such trustee or a trustee appointed to fill any vacancy, is exercisable:

(1) by a general meeting of the bankrupt's creditors[1];

(2)　by the Secretary of State[2]; or

(3)　by the court[3].

Any power to appoint a person as trustee of a bankrupt's estate includes power to appoint two or more persons as joint trustees; but such an appointment must make provision as to the circumstances in which the trustees must act together and the circumstances in which one or more of them may act for the others[4].

The appointment of any person as trustee takes effect only if that person accepts the appointment in accordance with the Insolvency Rules 1986[5]; but, subject to that qualification, the appointment of any person as trustee takes effect at the time specified in his certificate of appointment[6].

1　As to creditors' meetings see PARA 266 et seq.
2　Ie under the Insolvency Act 1986 s 295(2) (see PARA 319), s 296(2) (see PARA 319) or s 300(6) (see PARA 370). As to the Secretary of State see PARA 19.
3　Insolvency Act 1986 s 292(1) (amended by the Enterprise Act 2002 ss 269, 278(2), Sch 23 para 6, Sch 26). The appointment by the court is under the Insolvency Act 1986 s 297 (see PARA 320): s 292(1) (as so amended). Section 292 is without prejudice to the provisions of Pt 9 Ch 3 (ss 292–304) under which the official receiver is, in certain circumstances, to be trustee of the estate: s 292(5). As to such circumstances see PARA 321.
　　As to the application of s 292 in the case of the administration in bankruptcy of the insolvent estate of a deceased person dying before the presentation of a bankruptcy petition see PARA 261 note 2.
　　As to the modification of s 292 by the Insolvent Partnerships Order 1994, SI 1994/2421, in relation to the bankruptcy of an individual member of an insolvent partnership see COMPANY AND PARTNERSHIP INSOLVENCY vol 17 (2011) PARAS 1302–1303, 1332.
4　Insolvency Act 1986 s 292(3).
5　Ie the Insolvency Rules 1986, SI 1986/1925.
6　Insolvency Act 1986 s 292(4).

316. Summoning of meeting to appoint first trustee. Where a bankruptcy order has been made[1] it is the duty of the official receiver, as soon as practicable in the period of 12 weeks beginning with the day on which the order was made, to decide whether to summon a general meeting of the bankrupt's creditors for the purpose of appointing a trustee of the bankrupt's estate[2]. If the official receiver decides not to summon such a meeting, he must, before the end of the period of 12 weeks mentioned above, give notice of his decision to the court and to every creditor of the bankrupt who is known to the official receiver or is identified in the bankrupt's statement of affairs[3].

1　As to bankruptcy orders see PARA 198 et seq.
2　Insolvency Act 1986 s 293(1) (amended by the Enterprise Act 2002 ss 269, 287(2), Sch 23 para 7, Sch 26). As to remote attendance at meetings see PARA 267. The Insolvency Act 1986 s 293 does not apply where the bankruptcy order was made on a petition under s 264(1)(d) (criminal bankruptcy) (see PARA 130 head (6)); and it is subject to the provision made in s 294(3) (see PARA 317) and s 297(6) (see PARA 320): s 293(1). As to the prospective repeal of s 264(1)(d), and as to the prospective amendment of s 293(1), see PARA 1 note 11.
　　As to the application of s 293 in the case of the administration in bankruptcy of the insolvent estate of a deceased person dying before the presentation of a bankruptcy petition see PARA 261 note 2.
　　As to the modification of s 293 by the Insolvent Partnerships Order 1994, SI 1994/2421, in relation to the bankruptcy of an individual member of an insolvent partnership see COMPANY AND PARTNERSHIP INSOLVENCY vol 17 (2011) PARAS 1286, 1333.
3　Insolvency Act 1986 s 293(2). As from the giving to the court of a notice under s 293(2), the official receiver is the trustee of the bankrupt's estate: s 293(3). As from a day to be appointed, s 293(2), (3) is amended by the Enterprise and Regulatory Reform Act 2013 s 71, Sch 19 paras 1, 20: see PARA 130 note 17.

317.　Power of creditors to requisition meeting.　Where, in the case of any bankruptcy the official receiver has not yet summoned, or has decided not to summon, a general meeting of the bankrupt's creditors for the purpose of appointing the trustee[1], any creditor of the bankrupt may request the official receiver to summon such a meeting for that purpose[2].

If such a request appears to the official receiver to be made with the concurrence of not less than one-quarter, in value, of the bankrupt's creditors, including the creditor making the request, it is the duty of the official receiver to summon the requested meeting[3].

1　Ie under the Insolvency Act 1986 s 293: see PARA 261.
2　Insolvency Act 1986 s 294(1) (amended by the Enterprise Act 2002 ss 269, 287(2), Sch 23 para 8, Sch 26). As to remote attendance at meetings see PARA 267. As to the application of the Insolvency Act 1986 s 294 in the case of the administration in bankruptcy of the insolvent estate of a deceased person dying before the presentation of a bankruptcy petition see PARA 261 note 2.
　　As to the modification of s 294 by the Insolvent Partnerships Order 1994, SI 1994/2421, in relation to the bankruptcy of an individual member of an insolvent partnership see COMPANY AND PARTNERSHIP INSOLVENCY vol 17 (2011) PARA 1286.
3　Insolvency Act 1986 s 294(2). Accordingly, where the duty imposed by s 294(2) has arisen, the official receiver is required neither to reach a decision for the purposes of s 293(1) (see PARA 316) nor, if he has reached one, to serve any notice under s 293(2) (see PARA 316): s 294(3).

318.　Appointment by creditors' meeting.　Where a person has been appointed trustee by resolution of a creditors' meeting[1], the chairman of the meeting must certify the appointment, but not unless and until the person to be appointed has provided him with a written statement to the effect that he is an insolvency practitioner duly qualified to act as trustee in relation to the bankrupt, and that he consents so to act[2].

The trustee's appointment is effective from the date on which the appointment is certified, that date to be indorsed on the certificate[3].

The chairman of the meeting, if not himself the official receiver, must send the certificate to the official receiver[4]; and the official receiver must in any case send the certificate to the trustee[5].

The official receiver may not be appointed as trustee by resolution of a creditors' meeting[6].

1　As to the creditors' meeting see PARA 317.
2　Insolvency Rules 1986, SI 1986/1925, r 6.120(1), (2). For the prescribed forms of appointment see Sch 4 Form 6.40 (certificate of appointment of trustee by creditors' meeting), Sch 4 Form 6.41 (certificate of appointment of two or more trustees by creditors' meeting). As to insolvency practitioners and their qualification see PARA 40.
3　Insolvency Rules 1986, SI 1986/1925, r 6.120(3) (substituted by SI 1987/1919).
4　Insolvency Rules 1986, SI 1986/1925, r 6.120(4) (substituted by SI 1987/1919).
5　Insolvency Rules 1986, SI 1986/1925, r 6.120(5) (added by SI 1987/1919; and amended by SI 2010/686).
6　Insolvency Rules 1986, SI 1986/1925, r.6.120A (added by SI 2010/686).

319.　Appointment by Secretary of State.　If a meeting summoned[1] by the official receiver is held but no appointment of a person as trustee is made, it is the duty of the official receiver to decide whether to refer the need for an appointment to the Secretary of State[2]. On a reference made in pursuance of that decision, the Secretary of State must either make an appointment or decline to make one[3].

If the official receiver decides not to refer the need for an appointment to the Secretary of State, or on such a reference the Secretary of State declines to make an appointment, the official receiver must give notice of his decision or, as the case may be, of the Secretary of State's decision to the court[4]. As from the giving of such notice in a case where no notice has been given by the official receiver of his decision not to summon a meeting of creditors[5], the official receiver is the trustee of the bankrupt's estate[6].

At any time when the official receiver is the trustee of a bankrupt's estate by virtue of any provision of the Insolvency Act 1986[7], he may apply to the Secretary of State for the appointment of a person as trustee instead of the official receiver[8]. On such an application the Secretary of State must either make an appointment or decline to make one[9].

Where the trustee of a bankrupt's estate has been appointed by the Secretary of State[10], the trustee must give notice to the bankrupt's creditors of his appointment or, if the court so allows, must advertise his appointment in accordance with the court's directions[11]. In that notice or advertisement the trustee must:

(1)   state whether he proposes to summon a general meeting of the bankrupt's creditors for the purpose of establishing a creditors' committee[12]; and

(2)   if he does not propose to summon such a meeting, set out the power of the creditors[13] to require him to summon one[14].

Where the official receiver refers[15] to the Secretary of State the need for an appointment of a trustee, or applies[16] to the Secretary of State to make the appointment, then, if the Secretary of State makes an appointment, he must send a copy of the certificate of appointment to the official receiver, who must transmit it to the person appointed[17]. The certificate must specify the date from which the trustee's appointment is effective[18].

1   Ie under the Insolvency Act 1986 s 293 (see PARA 316) or s 294 (see PARA 317).
2   Insolvency Act 1986 s 295(1). As to the Secretary of State see PARA 19. As to the application of s 295 in the case of the administration in bankruptcy of the insolvent estate of a deceased person dying before the presentation of a bankruptcy petition see PARA 261 note 2.
        As to the modification of s 295 by the Insolvent Partnerships Order 1994, SI 1994/2421, in relation to the bankruptcy of an individual member of an insolvent partnership see COMPANY AND PARTNERSHIP INSOLVENCY vol 17 (2011) PARAS 1287, 1334.
3   Insolvency Act 1986 s 295(2).
4   Insolvency Act 1986 s 295(3). As from a day to be appointed, s 295(3) is amended by the Enterprise and Regulatory Reform Act 2013 s 71, Sch 19 paras 1, 21: see PARA 130 note 17.
5   Ie under the Insolvency Act 1986 s 293(2): see PARA 316.
6   Insolvency Act 1986 s 295(4).
7   Ie by virtue of any provision in the Insolvency Act 1986 Pt 9 Ch 3 (ss 292–304), other than s 297(1) (see PARA 321 note 6). As to the prospective repeal of s 297(1) see PARA 1 note 11.
8   Insolvency Act 1986 s 296(1). As to the application of s 296 in the case of the administration in bankruptcy of the insolvent estate of a deceased person dying before the presentation of a bankruptcy petition see PARA 261 note 2.
        As to the modification of s 296 by the Insolvent Partnerships Order 1994, SI 1994/2421, in relation to the bankruptcy of an individual member of an insolvent partnership see COMPANY AND PARTNERSHIP INSOLVENCY vol 17 (2011) PARAS 1287, 1335.
9   Insolvency Act 1986 s 296(2). Such an application may be made notwithstanding that the Secretary of State has declined to make an appointment either on a previous application under s 296(1) or on a reference under s 295 or under s 300(4) (see PARA 370): s 296(3).
10 Ie whether under the Insolvency Act 1986 s 296 or otherwise.
11 Insolvency Act 1986 s 296(4).
12 Ie under the Insolvency Act 1986 s 301: see PARA 326 et seq.
13 Ie under the Insolvency Act 1986 Pt 9 (ss 264–371).
14 Insolvency Act 1986 s 296(5).
15 Ie under the Insolvency Act 1986 s 295 or s 300 (see PARA 370).
16 Ie under the Insolvency Act 1986 s 296.

17 Insolvency Rules 1986, SI 1986/1925, r 6.122(1), (2) (r 6.122(2) amended by SI 2010/686).

18 See the Insolvency Rules 1986, SI 1986/1925, r 6.122(2) (as amended: see note 17).

320. Appointment by the court. Where a bankruptcy order is made in a case in which an insolvency practitioner's report has been submitted to the court[1], the court, if it thinks fit, may, on making the order, appoint the person who made the report as trustee[2].

Where a bankruptcy order is made, whether or not on a petition[3] by the supervisor of, or any person, other than the individual, who is for the time being bound by, a voluntary arrangement proposed by the individual and approved under Part 8 of the Insolvency Act 1986[4], at a time when there is a supervisor[5] of a voluntary arrangement approved in relation to the bankrupt, the court, if it thinks fit, may, on making the order, appoint the supervisor of the arrangement as trustee[6].

Where the trustee of a bankrupt's estate has been appointed by the court, the trustee must give notice to the bankrupt's creditors of his appointment or, if the court so allows, must advertise his appointment in accordance with the directions of the court[7]. In that notice or advertisement he must:

(1) state whether he proposes to summon a general meeting of the bankrupt's creditors for the purpose of establishing a creditors' committee[8]; and

(2) if he does not propose to summon such a meeting, set out the power of the creditors[9] to require him to summon one[10].

Where the court appoints the trustee[11], the court's order may not issue unless and until the person appointed has filed in court[12] a statement to the effect that he is an insolvency practitioner duly qualified to be the trustee, and that he consents to act[13]. Thereafter, the court must send two copies of the order to the official receiver; and one of those copies must be sealed, and this must be sent by him to the person appointed as trustee[14]. The trustee's appointment takes effect from the date of the order[15].

1 Ie under the Insolvency Act 1986 s 274: see PARA 205.

2 Insolvency Act 1986 s 297(4) (amended by the Enterprise Act 2002 ss 269, 278(2), Sch 23 para 9(b), Sch 26). As from a day to be appointed, the Insolvency Act 1986 s 297(4) is repealed by the Enterprise and Regulatory Reform Act 2013 s 71, Sch 19 paras 1, 22: see PARA 130 note 17.

   Where an appointment is made under the Insolvency Act 1986 s 297(4) or s 297(5) (see the text and note 6), the official receiver is not under the duty imposed by s 293(1) (see PARA 316) to decide whether or not to summon a meeting of creditors: s 297(6). As from a day to be appointed, s 297(6) is amended by the Enterprise and Regulatory Reform Act 2013 s 71, Sch 19 paras 1, 22: see PARA 130 note 17.

   As to the application of the Insolvency Act 1986 s 297 in the case of the administration in bankruptcy of a deceased person dying before the presentation of a bankruptcy petition see PARA 261 note 2.

   As to the application of s 297 in the case of an individual member of an insolvent partnership itself being wound up as an unregistered company see the Insolvent Partnerships Order 1994, SI 1994/2421; and COMPANY AND PARTNERSHIP INSOLVENCY vol 17 (2011) PARA 1336. As to the modification in other circumstances of the Insolvency Act 1986 s 297 by the Insolvent Partnerships Order 1994, SI 1994/2421, in relation to the bankruptcy of an individual member of an insolvent partnership see COMPANY AND PARTNERSHIP INSOLVENCY vol 17 (2011) PARA 1336.

3 Ie under the Insolvency Act 1986 s 264(1)(c): see PARA 130 head (5).

4 Ie the Insolvency Act 1986 Pt 8 (ss 252–263G).

5 As to the supervisor of a voluntary arrangement see PARA 73 et seq.

6　Insolvency Act 1986 s 297(5). See also note 2. The supervisor will normally be appointed as trustee in the absence of any compelling complaint about his conduct of the voluntary arrangement: *Landsman v De Concilio* [2005] EWHC 267 (Ch), [2005] BPIR 829, [2005] All ER (D) 225 (Jan).

7　Insolvency Act 1986 s 297(7).

8　Ie under the Insolvency Act 1986 s 301: see PARA 326 et seq.

9　Ie under the Insolvency Act 1986 Pt 9 (ss 264–371).

10　Insolvency Act 1986 s 297(8).

11　Ie under the Insolvency Act 1986 s 297(4) or (5).

12　As to the meaning of 'file in court' see PARA 57 note 13.

13　Insolvency Rules 1986, SI 1986/1925, r 6.121(1), (2) (r 6.121(1) amended by SI 2003/1730). For the prescribed forms of orders of court see the Insolvency Rules 1986, SI 1986/1925, Sch 4 Form 6.42 (amended by SI 2010/686) (order of court appointing trustee), and the Insolvency Rules 1986, SI 1986/1925, Sch 4 Form 6.43 (amended by SI 2010/686) (order of court appointing two or more trustees). As to insolvency practitioners and their qualification see PARA 40.

14　Insolvency Rules 1986, SI 1986/1925, r 6.121(3).

15　Insolvency Rules 1986, SI 1986/1925, r 6.121(4).

321.　Official receiver as trustee.　If the official receiver decides not to summon a meeting of a bankrupt's creditors[1] and gives notice of such decision in accordance with the statutory provisions[2], he is, as from the giving of such notice to the court, the trustee of the bankrupt's estate[3].

If a meeting of a bankrupt's creditors is summoned[4] and held but no appointment of a person as trustee is made, then as from the giving of notice by the official receiver of his decision not to refer the need for an appointment to the Secretary of State, or on such a reference of the Secretary of State's decision to decline to make an appointment, the official receiver is[5] the trustee of the bankrupt's estate[6].

1　Ie under the Insolvency Act 1986 s 293: see PARA 316.

2　See PARA 316.

3　See the Insolvency Act 1986 s 293(2), (3); and PARA 316. As to the application of s 293 in the case of the administration in bankruptcy of the insolvent estate of a deceased person dying before the presentation of a bankruptcy petition see PARA 261 note 2.

4　Ie under the Insolvency Act 1986 s 293 (see PARA 316) or s 294 (see PARA 317).

5　Ie in a case in which no notice has been given under the Insolvency Act 1986 s 293(2).

6　Insolvency Act 1986 s 295(4). See further PARA 319. As to the application of s 295 in the case of the administration in bankruptcy of the insolvent estate of a deceased person dying before the presentation of a bankruptcy petition see PARA 261 note 2.

　　Where a bankruptcy order is made on a petition under s 264(1)(d) (see PARA 130 head (6)) in the case of a criminal bankruptcy order being made against an individual, the official receiver is the trustee of the bankrupt's estate: s 297(1). As to the prospective repeal of ss 264(1)(d), 297(1) see PARA 1 note 11. As to the application of s 297 in the case of the administration in bankruptcy of the insolvent estate of a deceased person dying before the presentation of a bankruptcy petition see PARA 261 note 2.

　　As to the application and modification of the Insolvency Act 1986 s 297 by the Insolvent Partnerships Order 1994, SI 1994/2421, see COMPANY AND PARTNERSHIP INSOLVENCY vol 17 (2011) PARA 1336.

322.　Authentication of appointment.　Where a trustee is appointed by a creditors' meeting[1], the court[2] or the Secretary of State[3], a sealed copy of the order of appointment or, as the case may be, a copy of the certificate of his appointment may in any proceedings be adduced as proof that he is duly authorised to exercise the powers and perform the duties of trustee of the bankrupt's estate[4].

1　Ie under the Insolvency Rules 1986, SI 1986/1925, r 6.120: see PARA 318.

2　Ie under the Insolvency Rules 1986, SI 1986/1925, r 6.121: see PARA 320.

3   Ie under the Insolvency Rules 1986, SI 1986/1925, r 6.122: see PARA 319.
4   Insolvency Rules 1986, SI 1986/1925, r 6.123 (amended by SI 2010/686).

323.   Advertisement of appointment.   A trustee who is appointed by a creditors' meeting[1], as soon as reasonably practicable after receiving the certificate of appointment, must give notice of that appointment[2]. Such notice must be gazetted[3] and may also be advertised in other such manner as the trustee thinks fit[4]. In addition to the standard contents[5], the notice must state that a trustee has been appointed by a creditors' meeting and the date of the appointment[6].

The expense of giving the notice must be borne in the first instance by the trustee; but he is entitled to be reimbursed by the estate, as an expense of the bankruptcy[7].

1   Ie under the Insolvency Rules 1986, SI 1986/1925, r 6.120: see PARA 318.
2   Insolvency Rules 1986, SI 1986/1925, r 6.124(1) (substituted by SI 2009/642).
3   As to the meaning of 'gazetted' see PARA 165 note 12.
4   Insolvency Rules 1986, SI 1986/1925, r 6.124(1) (as substituted: see note 2).
5   As to the meaning of 'standard contents' see PARA 165 note 12.
6   Insolvency Rules 1986, SI 1986/1925, r 6.124(1A) (added by SI 2010/686).
7   Insolvency Rules 1986, SI 1986/1925, r 6.124(2). Rule 6.124(2) applies also in the case of the
    notice or advertisement under the Insolvency Act 1986 s 296(4) (see PARA 319) and of the notice
    or advertisement under s 297(7) (see PARA 320): Insolvency Rules 1986, SI 1986/1925,
    r 6.124(2).

324.   Trustee's style.   The official name of the trustee is 'the trustee of the estate of ... a bankrupt' (inserting the name of the bankrupt); but he may be referred to as 'the trustee in bankruptcy' of the particular bankrupt[1].

1   Insolvency Act 1986 s 305(4). In the case of the administration in bankruptcy of the insolvent
    estate of a deceased person dying before the presentation of a bankruptcy petition, s 305 applies:
    Administration of Insolvent Estates of Deceased Persons Order 1986, SI 1986/1999, art 3(1),
    Sch 1 Pt II para 20. As to the administration in bankruptcy of the insolvent estates of deceased
    persons see further PARAS 473 note 4, 830 et seq.
        As to the modification of the Insolvency Act 1986 s 305 by the Insolvent Partnerships
    Order 1994, SI 1994/2421, in relation to the bankruptcy of an individual member of an
    insolvent partnership see COMPANY AND PARTNERSHIP INSOLVENCY vol 17 (2011) PARA 1291.

325.   Hand-over of assets to trustee.   Where the bankrupt's estate vests in the trustee[1] following a period in which the official receiver is the receiver and manager of the estate[2], or the trustee is appointed in succession to the official receiver acting as trustee, then, when the trustee's appointment takes effect, the official receiver must as soon as reasonably practicable do all that is required for putting him into possession of the estate[3].

On taking possession of the estate, the trustee must discharge any balance due to the official receiver on account of:

(1)   expenses properly incurred by him and payable under the Insolvency Act 1986 or the Insolvency Rules 1986; and

(2)   any advances made by him in respect of the estate, together with interest on such advances at the specified rate[4] on the date of the bankruptcy order[5].

Alternatively, the trustee may, before taking office, give to the official receiver a written undertaking to discharge any such balance out of the first realisation of assets[6].

The official receiver has a charge on the estate in respect of any sums due to him under the above provisions[7]; but, where the trustee has realised assets with a view to making those payments, the official receiver's charge does not extend in respect of sums deductible by the trustee from the proceeds of realisation, as being expenses properly incurred therein[8].

The trustee must from time to time out of the realisation of assets discharge all guarantees properly given by the official receiver for the benefit of the estate, and must pay all the official receiver's expenses[9].

The official receiver must give to the trustee all such information, relating to the affairs of the bankrupt and the course of the bankruptcy, as he, the official receiver, considers to be reasonably required for the effective discharge by the trustee of his duties in relation to the estate[10].

The trustee must also be furnished with any report of the official receiver[11] under the provisions of the Insolvency Rules 1986[12].

1 Ie under the Insolvency Act 1986 Pt 9 Ch 4 (ss 305–335): see PARA 397 et seq.
2 Ie according to the Insolvency Act 1986 s 287: see PARA 229.
3 Insolvency Rules 1986, SI 1986/1925, r 6.125(1), (2) (r 6.125 amended by SI 2009/642).
4 Ie at the rate specified in the Judgments Act 1838 s 17: see FINANCIAL SERVICES AND INSTITUTIONS vol 49 (2008) PARA 1307.
5 Insolvency Rules 1986, SI 1986/1925, r 6.125(3).
6 Insolvency Rules 1986, SI 1986/1925, r 6.125(4).
7 Ie under the Insolvency Rules 1986, SI 1986/1925, r 6.125(3) (see the text to notes 4, 5).
8 Insolvency Rules 1986, SI 1986/1925, r 6.125(5).
9 Insolvency Rules 1986, SI 1986/1925, r 6.125(6).
10 Insolvency Rules 1986, SI 1986/1925, r 6.125(7).
11 Ie under the Insolvency Rules 1986, SI 1986/1925, rr 6.73–6.78D: see PARAS 253–257, 383–386.
12 Insolvency Rules 1986, SI 1986/1925, r 6.125(8).

(ii) Control of Trustee

326. Creditors' committee. A general meeting of the bankrupt's creditors[1] may, in accordance with the Insolvency Rules 1986[2], establish a committee ('the creditors' committee') to exercise the functions conferred on it by or under the Insolvency Act 1986[3]. A general meeting of the bankrupt's creditors may not, however, establish such a committee, or confer any functions on such a committee, at any time when the official receiver is the trustee of the bankrupt's estate, except in connection with an appointment made by that meeting of a person to be trustee instead of the official receiver[4].

1 Ie whether summoned under the Insolvency Act 1986 ss 292–300 or otherwise.
2 Ie in accordance with the Insolvency Rules 1986, SI 1986/1925.
3 Insolvency Act 1986 s 301(1). As to the application of s 301 in the case of the administration in bankruptcy of the insolvent estate of a deceased person dying before the presentation of a bankruptcy petition see PARA 261 note 2.
   As to the modification of s 301 by the Insolvent Partnerships Order 1994, SI 1994/2421, in relation to the bankruptcy of an individual member of an insolvent partnership see COMPANY AND PARTNERSHIP INSOLVENCY vol 17 (2011) PARAS 1290, 1340.
4 Insolvency Act 1986 s 301(2).

327. Membership of the creditors' committee. The creditors' committee must consist of at least three, and not more than five, members[1]. A person claiming to be a creditor is entitled to be a member of the committee provided that: (1) that person has lodged a proof of debt[2]; (2) the proof of debt has neither been wholly disallowed for voting purposes, nor wholly rejected for the purpose of distribution or dividend; and (3) the debt is not fully secured[3].

A body corporate may be a member of the committee, but it cannot act as such otherwise than by a duly appointed representative[4].

1 Insolvency Rules 1986, SI 1986/1925, r 6.150(1).
2 As to proofs of debt see PARA 507 et seq.
3 Insolvency Rules 1986, SI 1986/1925, r 6.150(2) (substituted by SI 2010/686). As to secured creditors see PARA 574 et seq.
4 Insolvency Rules 1986, SI 1986/1925, r 6.150(3). The body corporate's representative is appointed under r 6.156 (see PARA 333): r 6.150(3).

328. Formalities of appointment. The creditors' committee does not come into being, and accordingly cannot act, until the trustee has issued a certificate of its due constitution[1]. If the chairman of the creditors' meeting which resolves to establish the committee is not the trustee, he must as soon as reasonably practicable give notice of the resolution to the trustee, or, as the case may be, the person appointed as trustee by that same meeting, and inform him of the names and addresses of the persons elected to be members of the committee[2].

No person may act as a member of the committee unless and until he has agreed to do so and, unless the relevant proxy or authorisation contains a statement to the contrary, such agreement may be given by his proxy-holder present at the meeting establishing the committee[3]; and the trustee's certificate of the committee's due constitution may not be issued before the minimum number of members[4] elected to be members of the committee have agreed to act and must be issued as soon as reasonably practicable thereafter[5]. As and when the others, if any, agree to act, the trustee must issue an amended certificate[6]. The certificate, and any amended certificate, must be filed in court[7] by the trustee as soon as reasonably practicable[8].

If after the first establishment of the committee there is any change in its membership, as soon as reasonably practicable the trustee must file with the court notice of the change[9].

The acts of the creditors' committee established for any bankruptcy are valid notwithstanding any defect in the appointment, election or qualifications of any member of the committee[10].

1 Insolvency Rules 1986, SI 1986/1925, r 6.151(1). For the prescribed form of certificate see Sch 4 Form 6.52.
2 Insolvency Rules 1986, SI 1986/1925, r 6.151(2) (amended by SI 2009/642).
3 Insolvency Rules 1986, SI 1986/1925, r 6.151(3) (substituted by SI 1987/1919; and amended by SI 2010/686). As to proxies see PARA 276 et seq.
4 Ie as set out in the Insolvency Rules 1986, SI 1986/1925, r 150 (see PARA 327).
5 Insolvency Rules 1986, SI 1986/1925, r 6.151(3A) (added by SI 1987/1919; and amended by SI 2010/686).
6 Insolvency Rules 1986, SI 1986/1925, r 6.151(4). For the prescribed form of amended certificate see Sch 4 Form 6.52.
7 As to the meaning of 'file in court' see PARA 57 note 13.
8 Insolvency Rules 1986, SI 1986/1925, r 6.151(5) (amended by SI 2010/686).
9 Insolvency Rules 1986, SI 1986/1925, r 6.151(6) (substituted by SI 2010/686).
10 Insolvency Act 1986 s 377. As to the application of s 377 in the case of the administration in bankruptcy of the insolvent estate of a deceased person dying before the presentation of a bankruptcy petition see PARA 235 note 6.

329. Obligations of trustee to committee. It is the duty of the trustee to report to the members of the creditors' committee all such matters as appear to him to be, or as they have indicated to him as being, of concern to them with respect to the bankruptcy[1]. However, in the case of matters so indicated to him by the committee, the trustee need not comply with any request for information where it appears to him that:

(1) the request is frivolous or unreasonable;

(2)   the cost of complying would be excessive, having regard to the relative importance of the information; or

(3)   the estate is without funds sufficient for enabling him to comply[2].

Where the committee has come into being more than 28 days after the appointment of the trustee, the latter must report to them, in summary form, what actions he has taken since his appointment, and must answer such questions as they may put to him regarding his conduct of the bankruptcy hitherto[3].

A person who becomes a member of the committee at any time after its first establishment is not entitled to require a report to him by the trustee, otherwise than in summary form, of any matters previously arising[4].

Nothing in the above provisions disentitles the committee, or any member of it, from having access to the trustee's records of the bankruptcy, or from seeking an explanation of any matter within the committee's responsibility[5].

1   Insolvency Rules 1986, SI 1986/1925, r 6.152(1).
2   Insolvency Rules 1986, SI 1986/1925, r 6.152(2).
3   Insolvency Rules 1986, SI 1986/1925, r 6.152(3).
4   Insolvency Rules 1986, SI 1986/1925, r 6.152(4).
5   Insolvency Rules 1986, SI 1986/1925, r 6.152(5).

330.   Meetings of creditors' committee.   Meetings of the creditors' committee must be held when and where determined by the trustee[1]. The trustee must, however, call a first meeting of the committee to take place within six weeks of the committee's establishment; and thereafter he must call a meeting:

(1)   if so requested by a member of the committee or his representative, the meeting then to be held within 21 days of the request being received by the trustee; and

(2)   for a specified date, if the committee has previously resolved that a meeting be held on that date[2].

The trustee must give five business days'[3] notice in writing of the venue[4] of any meeting to every member of the committee, or his representative, if designated for that purpose, unless in any case the requirement of the notice has been waived by or on behalf of any member; and waiver may be signified either at or before the meeting[5].

In addition to any functions conferred on a committee by any provision of the Insolvency Act 1986, a committee must assist the trustee in discharging the trustee's functions and act in relation to that trustee in such manner as may from time to time be agreed[6].

1   Insolvency Rules 1986, SI 1986/1925, r 6.153(1).
2   Insolvency Rules 1986, SI 1986/1925, r 6.153(2) (amended by SI 2010/686).
3   As to the meaning of 'business day' see PARA 28 note 8.
4   As to the meaning of 'venue' see PARA 46 note 22.
5   Insolvency Rules 1986, SI 1986/1925, r 6.153(3) (amended by SI 2010/686). Where the trustee has determined that a meeting should be conducted and held in the manner referred to in the Insolvency Rules 1986, SI 1986/1925, r 12A.26(2) (remote attendance), the notice period seven business days: r 6.153(4) (added by SI 2010/686).
6   Insolvency Rules 1986, SI 1986/1925, r 6.153(5) (added by SI 2010/686).

331.   Chairman at meetings.   The chairman at any meeting of the creditors' committee must be the trustee, or a person appointed by him in writing to act[1]. A person so appointed must be either:

(1)   one who is qualified to act as an insolvency practitioner in relation to the bankrupt[2]; or

(2) an employee of the trustee or his firm who is experienced in insolvency matters[3].

1 Insolvency Rules 1986, SI 1986/1925, r 6.154(1).
2 As to insolvency practitioners and their qualification see PARA 40.
3 Insolvency Rules 1986, SI 1986/1925, r 6.154(2) (amended by SI 2010/686).

332. Quorum. A meeting of the committee is duly constituted if due notice of it has been given to all the members and at least two of the members are present or represented[1].

1 Insolvency Rules 1986, SI 1986/1925, r 6.155.

333. Committee members' representatives. A member of the creditors' committee may, in relation to the business of the committee, be represented by another person duly authorised by him for that purpose[1].

A person acting as a committee member's representative must hold a letter of authority entitling him so to act, either generally or specially, and authenticated[2] by or on behalf of the committee member; and, for this purpose, any proxy in relation to any meeting of creditors of the bankrupt is, unless it contains a statement to the contrary, to be treated as such a letter of authority to act generally authenticated by or on behalf of the committee member[3]. The chairman at any meeting of the committee may call on a person claiming to act as a committee member's representative to produce his letter of authority, and may exclude him if it appears that his authority is deficient[4].

No member may be represented by:

(1) another member of the committee;
(2) a person who is at the same time representing another committee member;
(3) a body corporate;
(4) an undischarged bankrupt or a person in relation to whom a moratorium period under a debt relief order applies[5];
(5) a disqualified director; or
(6) a person who is subject to a bankruptcy restrictions order[6] (including an interim order), a bankruptcy restrictions undertaking[7], a debt relief restrictions order[8] (including an interim order) or a debt relief restrictions undertaking[9].

Where the representative of a committee member authenticates any document on the latter's behalf, the fact that he so authenticates must be stated below his authentication[10].

The acts of the committee are valid notwithstanding any defect in the appointment or qualifications of any committee member's representative[11].

1 Insolvency Rules 1986, SI 1986/1925, r 6.156(1).
2 As to authentication see PARA 158 note 2.
3 Insolvency Rules 1986, SI 1986/1925, r 6.156(2) (amended by SI 1987/1919; and SI 2010/686). As to proxies see PARA 276 et seq.
4 Insolvency Rules 1986, SI 1986/1925, r 6.156(3).
5 Ie under the Insolvency Act 1986 Pt 7A (ss 251A–251X) (see PARA 101 et seq).
6 As to bankruptcy restrictions orders see PARA 657 et seq.
7 As to bankruptcy restrictions undertakings see PARA 668 et seq.
8 As to debt relief restrictions orders see PARA 125 et seq.
9 Insolvency Rules 1986, SI 1986/1925, r 6.156(4) (substituted by SI 2010/686; and amended by SI 2012/2404). As to debt relief restrictions undertakings see PARA 127.
10 Insolvency Rules 1986, SI 1986/1925, r 6.156(6) (amended by SI 2010/686).
11 Insolvency Rules 1986, SI 1986/1925, r 6.156(7) (added by SI 1987/1919).

334. Voting rights and resolutions. At any meeting of the creditors' committee, each member, whether present himself or by his representative, has one vote; and a resolution is passed when a majority of the members present or represented have voted in favour of it[1].

Every resolution passed must be recorded in writing, either separately or as part of the minutes of the meeting; and the record must be authenticated by the chairman and kept with the records of the bankrutpcy[2].

1 Insolvency Rules 1986, SI 1986/1925, r 6.161(1).
2 Insolvency Rules 1986, SI 1986/1925, r 6.161(2) (amended by SI 2010/686).

335. Resolutions otherwise than at a meeting. The trustee may seek to obtain the agreement of members of the creditors' committee to a resolution by sending to every member, or his representative designated for the purpose, a copy of the proposed resolution[1]. Where the trustee makes use of this procedure, he must send out to members of the committee, or their representatives, as the case may be, a copy of any proposed resolution on which a decision is sought, which must be set out in such a way that agreement with or dissent from each separate resolution may be indicated by the recipient on the copy so sent[2]. Any member of the committee may, within seven business days[3] from the date of the trustee sending out a resolution, require the trustee to summon a meeting of the committee to consider the matters raised by the resolution[4]. In the absence of such a request, the resolution is deemed to have been carried in the committee if and when the trustee is notified in writing by a majority of the members that they concur with it[5].

A copy of every resolution passed under the above provisions, and a note that the concurrence of the committee was obtained, must be kept with the records of the bankruptcy[6].

1 Insolvency Rules 1986, SI 1986/1925, r 6.162(1).
2 Insolvency Rules 1986, SI 1986/1925, r 6.162(2) (amended by SI 1987/1919).
3 As to the meaning of 'business day' see PARA 28 note 8.
4 Insolvency Rules 1986, SI 1986/1925, r 6.162(3) (amended by SI 1987/1919).
5 Insolvency Rules 1986, SI 1986/1925, r 6.162(4).
6 Insolvency Rules 1986, SI 1986/1925, r 6.162(5).

336. Trustee's reports. As and when directed by the creditors' committee, but not more often than once in any period of two months, the trustee must send a written report to every member of the committee setting out the position generally as regards the progress of the bankruptcy and matters arising in connection with it, to which he, the trustee, considers the committee's attention should be drawn[1]. In the absence of any such directions by the committee, the trustee must send such a report not less often than once in every period of six months[2].

1 Insolvency Rules 1986, SI 1986/1925, r 6.163(1). The obligations imposed by r 6.163 are without prejudice to those imposed by r 6.152 (see PARA 329): r 6.163(3).
2 Insolvency Rules 1986, SI 1986/1925, r 6.163(2).

337. Expenses of members etc. The trustee must defray out of the estate, in the prescribed order of priority[1], any reasonable travelling expenses directly incurred by members of the creditors' committee or their representatives in respect of their attendance at the committee's meetings, or otherwise on the committee's business[2].

1   As to the meaning of 'prescribed order of priority' see PARA 222 note 5.
2   Insolvency Rules 1986, SI 1986/1925, r 6.164.

338.   Dealings by committee members and others.   No member of the creditors' committee, no committee member's representative, no person who is an associate[1] of a member of the committee or a committee member's representative, and no person who has been a member of the committee at any time in the last 12 months, may enter into any transaction whereby he:

(1)   receives out of the estate any payment for services given or goods supplied in connection with the estate's administration;

(2)   obtains any profit from the administration; or

(3)   acquires any asset forming part of the estate[2].

Such a transaction may, however, be entered into by such a person:

(a)   with the prior permission of the court; or

(b)   if he does so as a matter of urgency, or by way of performance of a contract in force before the commencement of the bankruptcy, and obtains the court's permission for the transaction, having applied for it without undue delay; or

(c)   with the prior sanction of the creditors' committee, where it is satisfied, after full disclosure of the circumstances, that the person will be giving full value in the transaction[3].

Where in the committee a resolution is proposed that sanction be accorded for a transaction to be entered into which, without that sanction or the permission of the court, would be in contravention of the above provisions, no member of the committee, and no representative of a member, may vote if he is to participate directly or indirectly in the transaction[4].

On the application of any person interested, the court may:

(i)   set aside a transaction on the ground that it has been entered into in contravention of the above provisions; and

(ii)   make with respect to it such other order as it thinks just, including an order requiring a person to whom the above provisions apply to account for any profit obtained from the transaction and compensate the estate for any resultant loss[5].

In the case of a person to whom these provisions apply as an associate of a member of the committee or of a committee member's representative, the court may not, however, make an order under heads (i) and (ii) above if satisfied that he entered into the relevant transaction without having any reason to suppose that, in doing so, he would contravene the above provisions[6].

The costs of an application to the court for permission under the above provisions do not fall on the estate, unless the court so orders[7].

1   As to the meaning of 'associate' see PARA 5.
2   Insolvency Rules 1986, SI 1986/1925, r 6.165(1), (2). As to the fiduciary duty of a committee member see *Re Bulmer, ex p Greaves* [1937] Ch 499, [1937] 1 All ER 323, CA. See also *Re FT Hawkins & Co Ltd* [1952] Ch 881, [1952] 2 All ER 467 (company case); *Taylor v Davies* [1920] AC 636 at 647, PC.
3   Insolvency Rules 1986, SI 1986/1925, r 6.165(3) (amended by SI 2010/686); and see eg *Re Spink (No 2), ex p Slater* (1913) 108 LT 811 (sanction given to trustee to pay member of committee of inspection for goods supplied to carry on bankrupt's business).
4   Insolvency Rules 1986, SI 1986/1925, r 6.165(4) (amended by SI 2010/686).
5   Insolvency Rules 1986, SI 1986/1925, r 6.165(5) (amended by SI 2010/686).
6   Insolvency Rules 1986, SI 1986/1925, r 6.165(6). In *Re Bulmer, ex p Greaves* [1937] Ch 499, [1937] 1 All ER 323, CA there was a purchase by the holder of a general proxy from a company which had been appointed a member of the committee of inspection. The purchaser was held to

be in a fiduciary position, even though he did not know that the property belonged to the bankrupt's estate and he was held liable to account for any profit made.

7   Insolvency Rules 1986, SI 1986/1925, r 6.165(7) (amended by SI 2010/686).

339.   Resignation; termination of membership; removal. A member of the creditors' committee may resign by notice in writing delivered to the trustee[1].

A person's membership of the creditors' committee is automatically terminated if:

(1)   he becomes bankrupt or has a debt relief order made in respect of him[2];

(2)   at three consecutive meetings of the committee he is neither present nor represented, unless at the third of those meetings it is resolved that these provisions are not to apply in his case; or

(3)   he ceases to be a creditor and a period of three months has elapsed from the date that that member ceased to be a creditor or is found never to have been a creditor[3].

If, however, the cause of termination is the member's bankruptcy, his trustee in bankruptcy replaces him as a member of the committee[4].

A member of the creditors' committee may be removed by resolution at a meeting of creditors, at least 14 days' notice having been given of the intention to move that resolution[5].

1   Insolvency Rules 1986, SI 1986/1925, r 6.157.
2   Ie under the Insolvency Act 1986 Pt 7A (ss 251A–251X) (see PARA 101 et seq).
3   Insolvency Rules 1986, SI 1986/1925, r 6.158(1) (amended by SI 2004/584; SI 2010/686; SI 2012/2404).
4   Insolvency Rules 1986, SI 1986/1925, r 6.158(2).
5   Insolvency Rules 1986, SI 1986/1925, r 6.159.

340.   Vacancies. If there is a vacancy in the membership of the creditors' committee, the vacancy need not be filled if the trustee and a majority of the remaining committee members so agree, provided that the number of members does not fall below three[1].

The trustee may appoint any creditor, being qualified to be a member of the committee, to fill the vacancy, if a majority of the other members of the committee agree to the appointment and the creditor concerned consents to act[2].

Alternatively, a meeting of creditors may resolve that a creditor be appointed, with his consent, to fill the vacancy; and, in this case, at least 14 days' notice must have been given of a resolution to make such an appointment, whether or not of a person named in the notice[3].

Where the vacancy is filled by an appointment made by a creditors' meeting at which the trustee is not present, the chairman of the meeting must report to the trustee the appointment which has been made[4].

1   Insolvency Rules 1986, SI 1986/1925, r 6.160(1), (2) (amended by SI 2010/686).
2   Insolvency Rules 1986, SI 1986/1925, r 6.160(3).
3   Insolvency Rules 1986, SI 1986/1925, r 6.160(4).
4   Insolvency Rules 1986, SI 1986/1925, r 6.160(5).

341.   Committee's functions vested in Secretary of State. The creditors' committee is not to be able or required to carry out its functions at any time when the official receiver is trustee of the bankrupt's estate[1]; but at any such time the functions of the committee under the Insolvency Act 1986 are vested in the Secretary of State, except to the extent that the Insolvency Rules 1986[2] otherwise provide[3]. Where, in the case of any bankruptcy, there is for the time being no creditors' committee and the trustee of the bankrupt's estate is a person other than the official receiver, the functions of such a committee are vested in the Secretary of State, except to the extent that the Insolvency Rules 1986 otherwise provide[4].

1   See PARA 321.
2   Ie the Insolvency Rules 1986, SI 1986/1925. At any time when the functions of the creditors' committee are vested in the Secretary of State under the Insolvency Act 1986 s 302(1) or (2), requirements of the Insolvency Act 1986 or the Insolvency Rules 1986, SI 1986/1925, about notices to be given, or reports to be made, to the committee by the trustee do not apply, otherwise than as enabling the committee to require a report as to any matter; and, where the committee's functions are so vested under the Insolvency Act 1986 s 302(2), they may be exercised by the official receiver: Insolvency Rules 1986, SI 1986/1925, r 6.166(1), (2). As to the Secretary of State see PARA 19.
3   Insolvency Act 1986 s 302(1). As to the application of s 302 in the case of the administration in bankruptcy of the insolvent estate of a deceased person dying before the presentation of a bankruptcy petition see PARA 261 note 2.
       As to the modification of s 302 by the Insolvent Partnerships Order 1994, SI 1994/2421, in relation to the bankruptcy of an individual member of an insolvent partnership see COMPANY AND PARTNERSHIP INSOLVENCY vol 17 (2011) PARA 1290.
4   Insolvency Act 1986 s 302(2).

342.   Control by the court.   If a bankrupt or any of his creditors or any other person is dissatisfied by any act, omission or decision of a trustee of the bankrupt's estate, he may apply to the court; and on such an application the court may confirm, reverse or modify any act or decision of the trustee, may give him directions or may make such other order as it thinks fit[1]. The trustee of a bankrupt's estate may apply to the court for directions in relation to any particular matter arising under the bankruptcy[2].

1   Insolvency Act 1986 s 303(1). In the case of the administration in bankruptcy of the insolvent estate of a deceased person dying before the presentation of a bankruptcy petition, s 303 applies: Administration of Insolvent Estates of Deceased Persons Order 1986, SI 1986/1999, art 3(1), Sch 1 Pt II para 19. As to the administration in bankruptcy of the insolvent estates of deceased persons see further PARA 830 et seq.
       As to the modification of the Insolvency Act 1986 s 303 by the Insolvent Partnerships Order 1994, SI 1994/2421, in relation to the bankruptcy of an individual member of an insolvent partnership see COMPANY AND PARTNERSHIP INSOLVENCY vol 17 (2011) PARA 1352.
       The Insolvency Act 1986 s 303(1) re-enacts the Bankruptcy Act 1914 s 80 (repealed) with three variations:
       (1)   the applicant under the Insolvency Act 1986 s 303(1) must be 'dissatisfied', whereas under the Bankruptcy Act 1914 s 80 (repealed) he had to be 'aggrieved'; but it is unlikely that this change of wording constitutes a material alteration. 'It may be that no change of substance was intended by the change in wording, but 'dissatisfied' is certainly no narrower than 'aggrieved', and is arguably wider. But in any event the words 'person aggrieved' were interpreted as words 'of wide import which should not be given a restrictive interpretation": *Re Cook* [1999] BPIR 881 at 883; *Miller (as trustee in bankruptcy of Bayliss) v Bayliss* [2009] EWHC 2063 (Ch), [2009] BPIR 1438, [2009] All ER (D) 83 (Aug); and see *Mahomed v Morris* [2000] 2 BCLC 536; *Re Edennote Ltd, Tottenham Hotspur plc v Ryman* [1995] 2 BCLC 248, [1995] BCC 389 (company cases). 'A person aggrieved must be a man who has suffered a legal grievance, a man against whom a decision has been pronounced which has wrongfully deprived him of something, or wrongfully refused him something or wrongfully affected his title to something': *Re Sidebotham, ex p Sidebotham* (1880) 14 ChD 458 at 465 per James LJ. 'But the definition of James LJ is not to be regarded as exhaustive. The words 'person aggrieved' are of wide import and should not be subjected to a restrictive interpretation. They do not include, of course, a mere busybody who is interfering in things which do not concern him; but they do include a person who has a genuine grievance because an order has been made which prejudicially affects his interests': *A-G of Gambia v N'Jie* [1961] AC 617 at 634, [1961] 2 All ER 504 at 511, PC per Lord Denning. See also *Re Whelan, ex p Sadler* (1878) 48 LJ Bcy 43; *Re Reed, Bowen & Co, ex p Official Receiver* (1887) 19 QBD 174; *Re Baron, ex p Debtor v*

Official Receiver [1943] Ch 177, [1943] 2 All ER 662. It would seem unlikely that the court will entertain an application by a person whose dissatisfaction did not arise through his being prejudicially affected by the trustee's act, decision or omission in question;

(2)   the word 'omission' has been added; thus the trustee's inactivity or neglect may found the requisite dissatisfaction;

(3)   the words 'may give him directions' have been added; under the Bankruptcy Act 1914 s 80 (repealed) the court was previously empowered to make 'such order in the premises as it thinks just'.

As to the circumstances in which the court would interfere under s 80 (repealed) see *Re Peters, ex p Lloyd* (1882) 47 LT 64, CA (the court will not interfere with the discretion of a trustee unless it is shown that the trustee is acting so very absurdly that no reasonable person would so act); *Re A Debtor (No 400 of 1940), ex p Debtor v Dodwell (Trustee)* [1949] Ch 236, [1949] 1 All ER 510 (the court will not on the application of the bankrupt interfere in the day to day administration of the estate, nor is the bankrupt entitled to question the exercise by the trustee in good faith of his discretion or to hold the trustee accountable for an error of judgment). In the latter case Harman J pointed out that, so far as the trustee's duties to supply accounts was concerned, the bankrupt was not concerned except as to any surplus. Harman J did not, however, attempt to define all the circumstances in which the court could interfere at the instance of the bankrupt.

The Insolvency Act 1986 s 303(1) provides a protective supervision of the insolvency administration so as to protect the bankrupt from any injustice caused by his inability to bring or defend proceedings after adjudication: see *Heath v Tang, Stevens v Peacock* [1993] 4 All ER 694, [1993] 1 WLR 1421, CA; *Green v Satsangi* [1998] 1 BCLC 458, [1998] BPIR 55. See further *Hamilton v Official Receiver* [1998] BPIR 602; *Re Hans Place Ltd (in liquidation)* [1993] BCLC 768, [1993] BCC 737; *Leon v York-o-Matic Ltd* [1966] 3 All ER 277, [1966] 1 WLR 1450; *Re Edennote Ltd, Tottenham Hotspur plc v Ryman* [1995] 2 BCLC 248, [1995] BCC 389 (company cases); the Insolvency Act 1986 s 168(1) and COMPANY AND PARTNERSHIP INSOLVENCY vol 16 (2011) PARA 522.

As to a bankrupt's standing to make an application under the Insolvency Act 1986 s 303 see *Engel v Peri* [2002] EWHC 799 (Ch), [2002] BPIR 961, [2002] All ER (D) 285 (Apr) (no universal requirement that the bankrupt must show there will be a surplus); *Canty v Boyden* [2006] EWCA Civ 194, [2006] BPIR 624, [2006] All ER (D) 96 (Feb). A bankrupt's wife may have standing to challenge the trustee's remuneration under the Insolvency Act 1986 s 303 in connection with an annulment application or as a person with an interest in the matrimonial home: *Woodbridge v Smith* [2004] BPIR 247.

2   Insolvency Act 1986 s 303(2). See *Craig v Humberclyde Industrial Finance Group Ltd* [1999] 1 WLR 129, sub nom *Re Hinckley Island Hotel Ltd, Craig v Humberclyde Industrial Finance Group Ltd* [1998] 2 BCLC 526, CA (company case); the Insolvency Act 1986 s 168(2); and COMPANY AND PARTNERSHIP INSOLVENCY vol 16 (2011) PARA 522. In relation to insolvent partnerships see also the Insolvency Act 1986 s 303(2A)–(2C) (added by SI 1994/2421); and COMPANY AND PARTNERSHIP INSOLVENCY vol 17 (2011) PARA 1352.

(iii) Bankrupt's Duties in relation to the Trustee

343.   Bankrupt's duties in relation to trustee.   The bankrupt must:

(1)   give to the trustee such information as to his affairs;

(2)   attend on the trustee at such times; and

(3)   do all such other things,

as the trustee may for the purposes of carrying out his functions reasonably require[1]; and this provision applies to a bankrupt after his discharge[2].

If the bankrupt without reasonable excuse fails to comply with any such obligation, he is guilty of contempt of court and liable to be punished accordingly, in addition to any other punishment to which he may be subject[3].

1   Insolvency Act 1986 s 333(1). As to circumstances where s 333 has been applied see *Fryer and Thompson v Brook* [1998] BPIR 687, CA (bankrupt not entitled to raise defences to possession proceedings which are inconsistent with his duty to assist realisation of property vested in the trustee); *Christofi v Barclays Bank plc* [1998] 2 All ER 484, [1998] 1 WLR 1245 (under the Bankruptcy Act 1914 a bankrupt was not entitled to insist that his bankers should not provide information required by trustee). As to discharge from bankruptcy see PARA 638 et seq.

In the case of the administration in bankruptcy of the insolvent estate of a deceased person dying before the presentation of a bankruptcy petition, the Insolvency Act 1986 s 333 applies: Administration of Insolvent Estates of Deceased Persons Order 1986, SI 1986/1999, art 3(1), Sch 1 Pt II para 26. As to the administration in bankruptcy of the insolvent estates of deceased persons see further PARA 830 et seq.

2 Insolvency Act 1986 s 333(3).
3 Insolvency Act 1986 s 333(4). As to contempt of court see CONTEMPT OF COURT vol 22 (2012) PARA 1 et seq; and as to offences see PARA 733 et seq. An injunction may be granted against the bankrupt if he fails to co-operate restraining him from leaving the jurisdiction: *Morris v Murjani* [1996] 2 All ER 384, [1996] 1 WLR 848. See also *Bagnall v Official Receiver* [2003] EWCA Civ 1925, [2004] 2 All ER 294, [2004] 1 WLR 2832 (failure of bankrupt to fulfil duties due to trustee may result in the suspension of an automatic discharge under the Insolvency Act 1986 s 279 (see PARA 638)).

(iv) Liability of the Trustee

344. Restoration of money etc. Where, on an application under the Insolvency Act 1986[1], the court is satisfied:

(1) that the trustee of a bankrupt's estate has misapplied or retained, or become accountable for, any money or other property comprised in the bankrupt's estate; or

(2) that a bankrupt's estate has suffered any loss in consequence of any misfeasance or breach of fiduciary or other duty by a trustee of the estate in the carrying out of his functions,

the court may order the trustee, for the benefit of the estate, to repay, restore or account for money or other property, together with interest at such rate as the court thinks just, or, as the case may be, to pay such sum by way of compensation in respect of the misfeasance or breach of fiduciary or other duty as the court thinks just[2].

The above provisions are, however, without prejudice to any liability arising apart therefrom[3].

Such an application may be made by the official receiver, the Secretary of State[4], a creditor of the bankrupt or, whether or not there is, or is likely to be, a surplus on final distribution[5], the bankrupt himself; but the permission of the court is required for the making of an application if it is to be made by the bankrupt or if it is to be made after the trustee has had his release[6].

1 Ie on an application under the Insolvency Act 1986 s 304. As to the mode of application and the procedure see PARA 786 et seq.
2 Insolvency Act 1986 s 304(1). In the case of the administration in bankruptcy of the insolvent estate of a deceased person dying before the presentation of a bankruptcy petition, s 304 applies: Administration of Insolvent Estates of Deceased Persons Order 1986, SI 1986/1999, art 3(1), Sch 1, Pt II para 19. As to the administration in bankruptcy of the insolvent estates of deceased persons see further PARA 830 et seq.
    Cf the Insolvency Act 1986 s 212 (summary remedy against delinquent directors, liquidators etc): see COMPANY AND PARTNERSHIP INSOLVENCY vol 17 (2011) PARA 646 et seq. It is submitted that the court will approach applications under s 304(1) in respect of trustees in bankruptcy in a like manner to applications under s 212 which has a long statutory history.
3 See the Insolvency Act 1986 s 304(1).
4 As to the Secretary of State see PARA 19.
5 Ie a surplus for the purposes of the Insolvency Act 1986 s 330(5): see PARA 615.
6 Insolvency Act 1986 s 304(2). The trustee has his release under s 299: see PARA 378 et seq.

345. Seizure of property not belonging to the estate. Where the trustee seizes or disposes of any property which is not comprised in the bankrupt's estate, and at the time of the seizure or disposal the trustee believes, and has reasonable grounds for believing, that he is entitled, whether in pursuance of an order of the court or otherwise, to seize or dispose of that property, the trustee is not liable to any person, whether under these provisions or otherwise, in respect of any loss or damage resulting from the seizure or disposal, except in so far as that loss or damage is caused by the negligence of the trustee; and he has a lien on the property, or the proceeds of its sale, for such of the expenses of the bankruptcy as were incurred in connection with the seizure or disposal[1].

1   Insolvency Act 1986 s 304(3). The existence of reasonable grounds is ultimately a question of fact. The grounds on which the trustee acted should be sufficient to induce in a reasonable person the required belief: see eg *McArdle v Egan* (1933) 150 LT 412; *Nakkuda Ali v Jayaratne* [1951] AC 66; *Registrar of Restrictive Trading Agreements v WH Smith & Son Ltd* [1969] 3 All ER 1065, [1969] 1 WLR 1460, CA; *R v IRC, ex p Rossminster Ltd* [1980] AC 952, [1980] 1 All ER 80, HL.
        As to the application of the Insolvency Act 1986 s 304 in the case of the administration in bankruptcy of the insolvent estate of a deceased person dying before the presentation of a bankruptcy petition see PARA 344 note 2.

346. Power of court to set aside certain transactions.   If in the administration of the estate the trustee enters into any transaction with a person who is an associate[1] of his, the court may, on the application of any person interested[2], set the transaction aside and order the trustee to compensate the estate for any loss suffered in consequence of it[3].

The above provisions do not, however, apply if either the transaction was entered into with the prior consent of the court, or it is shown to the court's satisfaction that the transaction was for value, and that it was entered into by the trustee without knowing, or having any reason to suppose, that the person concerned was an associate[4].

Nothing in the above provisions is to be taken as prejudicing the operation of any rule of law or equity with respect to a trustee's dealings with trust property, or the fiduciary obligations of any person[5].

1   As to the meaning of 'associate' see PARA 5.
2   'Person interested' was considered in *Re Beesley (Audrey), ex p Beesley (Terence Jack) v Official Receiver* [1975] 1 All ER 385, [1975] 1 WLR 568, DC for the purposes of the Bankruptcy Act 1914 s 29 (repealed) as meaning a person with a proprietary or pecuniary interest; but a mere spouse was not a 'person interested'. See also *Stevens v Hutchinson* [1953] Ch 299, sub nom *Re No 39 Carr Lane, Acomb; Stevens v Hutchinson* [1953] 1 All ER 699; *Re Roehampton Swimming Pool Ltd* [1968] 3 All ER 661, [1968] 1 WLR 1693.
3   Insolvency Rules 1986, SI 1986/1925, r 6.147(1).
4   Insolvency Rules 1986, SI 1986/1925, r 6.147(2).
5   Insolvency Rules 1986, SI 1986/1925, r 6.147(3). The trustee is not expressly precluded from purchasing property comprised in the bankrupt's estate; but he is subject to the general law applicable to the purchase of trust property by a trustee, that is to say that such a purchase is voidable at the instance of any beneficiary: see eg *Campbell v Walker* (1800) 5 Ves 678; and TRUSTS vol 48 (2007 Reissue) PARA 938 et seq.

347. Rule against solicitation.   Where the court is satisfied that any improper solicitation has been used by or on behalf of the trustee in obtaining proxies or procuring his appointment, it may order that no remuneration out of the estate is to be allowed to any person by whom, or on whose behalf, the solicitation was exercised[1].

An order of the court under the above provisions overrides any resolution of the creditors' committee or the creditors, or any other provision in the Insolvency Rules 1986 relating to the trustee's remuneration[2].

1   Insolvency Rules 1986, SI 1986/1925, r 6.148(1). As to proxies see PARA 276 et seq.
2   Insolvency Rules 1986, SI 1986/1925, r 6.148(2). As to the trustee's remuneration see PARA 348 et seq.

(v) Remuneration of the Trustee

348.   Fixing of remuneration.   The trustee is entitled to receive remuneration for his services as such[1]. The basis of remuneration is fixed:

(1)   as a percentage of the value of the assets in the bankrupt's estate which are realised or distributed[2], or of the one value and the other in combination;

(2)   by reference to the time properly given by the insolvency practitioner, as trustee, and his staff in attending to matters arising in the bankruptcy; or

(3)   as a set amount[3].

The basis of remuneration may be fixed as any one or more of the bases set out in heads (1) to (3), and different bases (or percentages in the case of head (1)) may be fixed in respect of different things done by the trustee[4]. Where the trustee is other than the official receiver, it is for the creditors' committee[5] (if there is one) to determine which of the bases set out in head (2) are to be fixed and in what combination, the percentages (if any) to be fixed under head (1) and the amount (if any) to be set under head (3)[6].

In arriving at that determination, the committee must have regard to the following matters:

(a)   the complexity, or otherwise, of the case;

(b)   any respects in which, in connection with the administration of the estate, there falls on the insolvency practitioner, as trustee, any responsibility of an exceptional kind or degree;

(c)   the effectiveness with which the insolvency practitioner appears to be carrying out, or to have carried out, his duties as trustee; and

(d)   the value and nature of the assets in the estate with which the trustee has to deal[7].

If there is no creditors' committee, or the committee does not make the requisite determination, the basis of the trustee's remuneration may be fixed, in accordance with heads (1) to (3) above, by a resolution of a meeting of creditors; and, in arriving at that determination, the creditors must have regard to the matters in heads (a) to (d) above[8].

Where the trustee is not the official receiver and the basis of his remuneration is not fixed as above within 18 months after the date of the trustee's appointment, the trustee is entitled to remuneration calculated in accordance with the statutory rules[9].

1   Insolvency Rules 1986, SI 1986/1925, r 6.138(1). As to the guiding principles to be applied to a remuneration application see *Brook v Reed (trustee in bankruptcy of estate of Helen Brook)* [2011] EWCA Civ 331, [2011] 3 All ER 743, [2012] 1 WLR 419; and the principles set out in *Practice Direction—Insolvency Proceedings* Pt 5.

2   As to the meaning of assets 'realised or distributed' see *Re a Debtor (No 29 of 1986)* [1997] BPIR 183, DC (a decision under the Bankruptcy Act 1914 s 82(1) (repealed)).

3   Insolvency Rules 1986, SI 1986/1925, r 6.138(2) (amended by SI 2010/686).

4   Insolvency Rules 1986, SI 1986/1925, r 6.138(3A), (3B) (added by SI 2010/686).

5   As to the creditors' committee see PARA 326 et seq.

6   Insolvency Rules 1986, SI 1986/1925, r 138(3C) (added by SI 2010/686).

7   Insolvency Rules 1986, SI 1986/1925, r 6.138(4).

8   Insolvency Rules 1986, SI 1986/1925, r 6.138(5) (amended by SI 2010/686).

9   Insolvency Rules 1986, SI 1986/1925, r 6.138(6) (substituted by SI 2004/584; and amended by SI 2010/686). Remuneration is calculated in such a case in accordance with the Insolvency Rules 1986, SI 1986/1925, r 6.138A (see PARA 349). As to the official receiver's remuneration see PARA 39.

349. Trustee's remuneration where it is not fixed. Where the trustee is not the official receiver and his remuneration is not fixed[1], the trustee is entitled by way of remuneration for his services as such, to such sum as is arrived at by:

(1) first applying the realisation scale[2] to the monies received by him from the realisation of the assets of the bankrupt (including any Value Added Tax thereon but after deducting any sums paid to secured creditors[3] in respect of their securities and any sums spent out of money received in carrying on the business of the bankrupt); and

(2) then adding to the sum arrived at under head (1) such sum as is arrived at by applying the distribution scale[4] to the value of assets distributed to creditors of the bankrupt (including sums paid in respect of preferential debts)[5].

However, that part of the trustee's remuneration calculated by reference to the realisation scale must not exceed such sum as is arrived at by applying the realisation scale to such part of the bankrupt's assets as are required to pay[6]:

(a) the bankruptcy debts (including any interest payable[7]) to the extent required to be paid[8] (ignoring those debts paid otherwise than out of the proceeds of the realisation of the bankrupt's assets or which have been secured to the satisfaction of the court);

(b) the expenses of the bankruptcy other than fees or the remuneration of the official receiver and any sums spent out of money received in carrying on the business of the bankrupt;

(c) fees payable by virtue of any order[9]; and

(d) the remuneration of the official receiver[10].

1 Insolvency Rules 1986, SI 1986/1925, r 6.138A(1) (r 6.138A added by SI 2004/584). Remuneration is fixed in accordance with the Insolvency Rules 1986, SI 1986/1925, r 6.138 (see PARA 348).
2 Ie the realisation scale set out in the Insolvency Rules 1986, SI 1986/1925, Sch 6 (added by SI 2004/584).
3 As to secured creditors see PARA 574 et seq.
4 Ie the distribution scale set out in the Insolvency Rules 1986, SI 1986/1925, Sch 6 (as added: see note 2).
5 Insolvency Rules 1986, SI 1986/1925, r 6.138A(2) (as added: see note 1).
6 Insolvency Rules 1986, SI 1986/1925, r 6.138A(3) (as added: see note 1).
7 Ie by virtue of the Insolvency Act 1986 s 328(4) (see PARA 596).
8 Ie required to be paid under the Insolvency Rules 1986, SI 1986/1925.
9 Ie any order made under the Insolvency Act 1986 s 415 (see PARA 825).
10 Insolvency Rules 1986, SI 1986/1925, r 6.138A(4) (as added: see note 1).

350. Other matters affecting remuneration. Where the trustee (not being the official receiver) sells assets on behalf of a secured creditor[1], he is entitled to such sum by way of remuneration as is arrived at by applying the realisation scale[2] to the monies received by him in respect of the assets realised (including any Value Added Tax thereon)[3].

Where there are joint trustees, it is for them to agree between themselves as to how the remuneration payable should be apportioned; and any dispute between them may be referred to the court for settlement by order, or to the creditors' committee or a meeting of creditors for settlement by resolution[4].

If the trustee is a solicitor[5] and employs his own firm, or any partner in it, to act on behalf of the estate, profit costs may not be paid unless this is authorised by the creditors' committee, the creditors or the court[6].

1 As to the meaning of 'secured creditor' see PARA 574.

2 Ie the realisation scale set out in the Insolvency Rules 1986, SI 1986/1925, Sch 6 (added by
   SI 2004/584).
3 Insolvency Rules 1986, SI 1986/1925, r 6.139(1) (substituted by SI 2004/584). As to the official
   receiver's remuneration see PARA 39.
4 Insolvency Rules 1986, SI 1986/1925, r 6.139(2).
5 For these purposes, the reference to a solicitor includes a reference to a body recognised by the
   Law Society under the Administration of Justice Act 1985 s 9 (see LEGAL PROFESSIONS vol 65
   (2008) PARA 515): Solicitors' Recognised Bodies Order 1991, SI 1991/2684, arts 2(1), 3, 4(a), 5,
   Sch 1 (amended by SI 2009/500).
6 Insolvency Rules 1986, SI 1986/1925, r 6.139(3).

351. Recourse of trustee to meeting of creditors. If the basis of the trustee's
remuneration has been fixed by the creditors' committee[1] and the trustee
considers the rate or amount to be insufficient or the basis to be inappropriate,
the trustee may request that the rate or amount be increased or the basis changed
by resolution of the creditors[2].

1 Ie under the Insolvency Rules 1986, SI 1986/1925, r 6.138 (see PARA 348). As to the creditors'
   committee see PARA 326 et seq.
2 Insolvency Rules 1986, SI 1986/1925, r 6.140A (added by SI 2010/686).

352. Recourse to the court. If the trustee considers that the basis of
remuneration fixed by the creditors' committee[1], or by resolution of the
creditors[2], or as under the statutory rules[3], is insufficient or inappropriate, the
trustee may apply to the court for an order changing it or increasing its amount
or rate[4].

The trustee must give at least 14 days' notice of his application to the
members of the creditors' committee, and the committee may nominate one or
more members to appear or be represented, and to be heard, on the application[5].

If there is no creditors' committee, the trustee's notice of his application must
be sent to such one or more of the bankrupt's creditors as the court may direct,
which creditors may nominate one or more of their number to appear or be
represented[6].

If it appears to be a proper case, the court may order the costs of the trustee's
application, including the costs of any member of the creditors' committee
appearing or being represented on it, or any creditor so appearing or being
represented, to be paid out of the estate[7].

1 Ie under the Insolvency Rules 1986, SI 1986/1925, r 6.138 (see PARA 348). As to the creditors'
   committee see PARA 326 et seq.
2 See PARA 348.
3 Ie under the Insolvency Rules 1986, SI 1986/1925, r 6.138(6): see PARA 348.
4 Insolvency Rules 1986, SI 1986/1925, r 6.141(1) (substituted by SI 2010/686).
5 Insolvency Rules 1986, SI 1986/1925, r 6.141(2).
6 Insolvency Rules 1986, SI 1986/1925, r 6.141(3).
7 Insolvency Rules 1986, SI 1986/1925, r 6.141(4) (amended by SI 1987/1919).

353. Creditors' claim that remuneration is, or other expenses are, excessive.
Any secured creditor[1], or any unsecured creditor with either the concurrence of
at least 10 per cent in value of the creditors (including that creditor) or the
permission of the court, or the bankrupt may apply to the court for one or more
of the orders set out in heads (1) to (5) below[2].

Application by a creditor may be made on the grounds that the remuneration
charged by the trustee, the basis fixed for the trustee's remuneration[3] or expenses
incurred by the trustee, is or are, in all the circumstances, excessive or
inappropriate[4]. Application by a creditor must[5] be made no later than eight

weeks[6] after receipt by the applicant of the progress report[7], or the draft report[8], which first reports the charging of the remuneration or the incurring of the expenses in question ('the relevant report')[9]. Application by the bankrupt may be made only on the grounds that the remuneration charged, or the expenses incurred, by the trustee are excessive and no later than eight weeks[10] after receipt by the bankrupt of the draft report[11].

When the application is made by a creditor, the court may dismiss it if it thinks that no sufficient cause is shown; but it must not do so unless the applicant has had an opportunity to attend the court for a hearing of which the applicant has been given at least five business days'[12] notice but which is without notice to any other party[13]. Application may be made by the bankrupt only with the permission of the court; and without prejudice to the generality of the matters which the court may take into account, permission must not be given unless the bankrupt shows that there is (or would be but for the remuneration or expenses in question), or that it is likely that there will be (or would be but for the remuneration or expenses in question), a surplus of assets to which the bankrupt would be entitled[14]. If, as the case may be, the application is not dismissed or the bankrupt is given permission, the court must fix a venue[15] for the application to be heard[16].

At least 14 days before the hearing, the applicant must send to the trustee a notice stating the venue so fixed; and the notice must be accompanied by a copy of the application, and of any evidence which the applicant intends to adduce in support of it[17]. If the court considers the application to be well-founded, it must make one or more of the following orders:

(1)   an order reducing the amount of remuneration which the trustee was entitled to charge;

(2)   an order fixing the basis of remuneration at a reduced rate or amount;

(3)   an order changing the basis of remuneration;

(4)   an order that some or all of the remuneration or expenses in question be treated as not being bankruptcy expenses;

(5)   an order that the trustee or the trustee's personal representative pay to such person as the court may specify as property comprised in the bankrupt's estate the amount of the excess of remuneration or expenses or such part of the excess as the court may specify;

and may make any other order that it thinks just; but an order under head (2) or head (3) may be made only in respect of periods after the period covered by the relevant report[18].

Unless the court orders otherwise, the costs of the application must be paid by the applicant, and do not fall on the estate[19].

1   As to the meaning of 'secured creditor' see PARA 574.
2   Insolvency Rules 1986, SI 1986/1925, r 6.142(1) (substituted by SI 2010/686).
3   Ie under the Insolvency Rules 1986, SI 1986/1925, r 6.138 (see PARA 348).
4   Insolvency Rules 1986, SI 1986/1925, r 6.142(1A) (added by SI 2010/686).
5   Ie subject to any order of the court under the Insolvency Rules 1986, SI 1986/1925, r 6.78C(5) (see PARA 385).
6   Or in a case falling within the Insolvency Rules 1986, SI 1986/1925, r 6.126 (trustee's resignation) (see PARA 358), four weeks.
7   As to the progress report see PARA 383.
8   Ie under the Insolvency Rules 1986, SI 1986/1925, r 6.78B (see PARA 384).
9   Insolvency Rules 1986, SI 1986/1925, r 6.142(1B) (added by SI 2010/686).
10   Or in a case falling within the Insolvency Rules 1986, SI 1986/1925, r 6.126 (trustee's resignation) (see PARA 358), four weeks after receipt by the bankrupt of notice under r 6.126(1C).

11 Insolvency Rules 1986, SI 1986/1925, r 6.142(1C) (added by SI 2010/686).
12 As to the meaning of 'business day' see PARA 28 note 8.
13 Insolvency Rules 1986, SI 1986/1925, r 6.142(2) (substituted by SI 2010/686).
14 Insolvency Rules 1986, SI 1986/1925, r 6.142(2A) (added by SI 2010/686).
15 As to the meaning of 'venue' see PARA 46 note 22.
16 Insolvency Rules 1986, SI 1986/1925, r 6.142(2B) (added by SI 2010/686).
17 Insolvency Rules 1986, SI 1986/1925, r 6.142(3).
18 Insolvency Rules 1986, SI 1986/1925, r 6.142(4) (substituted by SI 2010/686).
19 Insolvency Rules 1986, SI 1986/1925, r 6.142(5).

354. Review of remuneration. Where, after the basis of the trustee's remuneration has been fixed, there is a material and substantial change in the circumstances which were taken into account in fixing it, the trustee may request that it be changed[1]. The request must be made:

(1)   where the creditors' committee[2] fixed the basis, to the committee;
(2)   where the creditors fixed the basis, to the creditors;
(3)   where the court fixed the basis, by application to the court;
(4)   where the remuneration was fixed by application of the realisation scale[3], to the creditors' committee if there is one or otherwise to the creditors[4].

Any change in the basis for remuneration applies from the date of the request and not for any earlier period[5].

1   Insolvency Rules 1986, SI 1986/1925, r 6.142A(1) (r 6.142A added by SI 2010/686). The Insolvency Rules 1986, SI 1986/1925, r 6.142A does not apply where the trustee is the official receiver: r 6.142A(4) (as so added).
2   As to the creditors' committee see PARA 326 et seq.
3   Ie under the Insolvency Rules 1986, SI 1986/1925, r 6.138A (see PARA 349).
4   Insolvency Rules 1986, SI 1986/1925, r 6.142A(2) (as added: see note 1). Rules 6.138–6.142 (see PARAS 348–353) apply as appropriate: see r 6.142A(2) (as so added).
5   Insolvency Rules 1986, SI 1986/1925, r 6.142A(3) (as added: see note 1).

355. Remuneration of new trustee. If a new trustee is appointed in place of another, any determination, resolution or court order relating to remuneration[1] in effect immediately before the former trustee ceased to hold office continues to apply in respect of the remuneration of the new trustee until a further determination, resolution or court order is made in accordance with those provisions[2].

1   Ie the Insolvency Rules 1986, SI 1986/1925, rr 6.138–6.142A (see PARAS 348–354).
2   Insolvency Rules 1986, SI 1986/1925, r 6.142B(1) (r 6.142B added by SI 2010/686). The Insolvency Rules 1986, SI 1986/1925, r 6.142B does not apply where the new trustee is the official receiver: r 6.142B(2) (as so added).

356. Apportionment of set fee remuneration. In a case in which the basis of the trustee's remuneration is a set amount[1] and the trustee ('the former trustee') ceases, for whatever reason, to hold office before the time has elapsed or the work has been completed in respect of which the amount was set, application may be made for determination of what portion of the amount should be paid to the former trustee or the former trustee's personal representative in respect of the time which has actually elapsed or the work which has actually been done[2].

Application may be made by the former trustee or the former trustee's personal representative within the period of 28 days beginning with the date upon which the former trustee ceased to hold office, or by the trustee for the time being in office if the former trustee or the former trustee's personal representative has not applied by the end of that period[3].

Application must be made:

(1)   where the creditors' committee[4] fixed the basis, to the committee;

(2)   where the creditors fixed the basis, to the creditors for a resolution determining the portion;

(3)   where the court fixed the basis, to the court for an order determining the portion[5].

The applicant must give a copy of the application to the trustee for the time being in office or to the former trustee or the former trustee's personal representative, as the case may be ('the recipient')[6]. The recipient may within 21 days of receipt of the copy of the application give notice of intent to make representations to the creditors' committee or the creditors or to appear or be represented before the court, as the case may be[7]. No determination may be made upon the application until expiry of the 21-day period or, if the recipient does give notice of intent to make representations or appear, until the recipient has been afforded the opportunity to make representations or to appear or be represented, as the case may be[8].

If the former trustee or the former trustee's personal representative, whether or not the original applicant, considers that the portion determined upon application to the creditors' committee or the creditors is insufficient, that person may apply: (a) in the case of a determination by the creditors' committee, to the creditors for a resolution increasing the portion; (b) in the case of a resolution of the creditors[9], to the court for an order increasing the portion[10].

1   Ie under the Insolvency Rules 1986, SI 1986/1925, r 6.138(2)(c) (see PARA 348).
2   Insolvency Rules 1986, SI 1986/1925, r 6.142C(1) (r 6.142C added by SI 2010/686).
3   Insolvency Rules 1986, SI 1986/1925, r 6.142C(2) (as added: see note 2).
4   As to the creditors' committee see PARA 326 et seq.
5   Insolvency Rules 1986, SI 1986/1925, r 6.142C(3) (as added: see note 2).
6   Insolvency Rules 1986, SI 1986/1925, r 6.142C(4) (as added: see note 2).
7   Insolvency Rules 1986, SI 1986/1925, r 6.142C(5) (as added: see note 2).
8   Insolvency Rules 1986, SI 1986/1925, r 6.142C(6) (as added: see note 2).
9   Ie whether under the Insolvency Rules 1986, SI 1986/1925, r 6.142C(1) or under r 6.142C(7)(a) (see head (a) in the text).
10 Insolvency Rules 1986, SI 1986/1925, r 6.142C(7) (as added: see note 2). In such a case the provisions of r 6.142C(4)–(6) (see the text to notes 6–8) apply as appropriate: r 6.142C(7) (as so added).

(vi) Resignation, Removal or Vacancy in the Office of Trustee

357.   Resignation of trustee.   In the prescribed circumstances, the trustee may resign his office by giving notice of his resignation to the court[1].

1   Insolvency Act 1986 s 298(7). See further PARA 358 et seq. As from a day to be appointed, s 298(7) is amended by the Enterprise and Regulatory Reform Act 2013 s 71, Sch 19 paras 1, 23: see PARA 130 note 17.

As to the application of the Insolvency Act 1986 s 298 in the case of the administration in bankruptcy of the insolvent estate of a deceased person dying before the presentation of a bankruptcy petition see PARA 261 note 2.

As to the modification of s 298 by the Insolvent Partnerships Order 1994, SI 1994/2421, in relation to the bankruptcy of an individual member of an insolvent partnership see COMPANY AND PARTNERSHIP INSOLVENCY vol 17 (2011) PARA 1337.

As to the circumstances in which the court may make orders for the removal and replacement of trustees in multiple cases rather than following the resignation procedure see *Re Sankey Furniture Ltd, ex p Harding, Re Calorifique Ltd, ex p Betts* [1995] 2 BCLC 594; *Re Equity Nominees Ltd* [1999] 2 BCLC 19, [2000] BCC 84; and PARA 361.

358. Creditors' meeting to receive trustee's resignation. Before resigning his office, the trustee must call a meeting of creditors for the purpose of receiving his resignation[1]. The trustee must give at least 28 days' notice of the meeting[2]. The notice summoning the meeting must indicate that the purpose or one of the purposes of the meeting is to receive the trustee's resignation and draw the attention of the creditors to their right to claim[3] that the remuneration or other expenses of the trustee are excessive[4].

The notice to creditors and the bankrupt must be accompanied by an account of the trustee's administration of the bankrupt's estate, including: (1) a statement that the trustee has reconciled the account with that held by the Secretary of State[5] in respect of the bankruptcy; and (2) a progress report for the period commencing with the later of the date of the appointment of the trustee and the day immediately following the end of the period of the last progress report, and ending with the date of the meeting[6].

The trustee may only proceed under these provisions on grounds of ill health or because he intends ceasing to be in practice as an insolvency practitioner, or there is some conflict of interest or change of personal circumstances which precludes or makes impracticable the further discharge by him of the duties of trustee[7].

Where, however, two or more persons are acting as trustee jointly, any one of them may proceed under these provisions, without prejudice to the continuation in office of the other or others, on the ground that, in his opinion and that of the others, it is no longer expedient that there should continue to be the present number of joint trustees[8].

If there is no quorum present at the meeting summoned to receive the trustee's resignation, the meeting is deemed to have been held, a resolution is deemed passed that the trustee's resignation be accepted and the creditors are deemed not to have resolved against the trustee having his release[9].

1 Insolvency Rules 1986, SI 1986/1925, r 6.126(1) (amended by SI 2010/686).
2 Insolvency Rules 1986, SI 1986/1925, r 6.126(1A) (added by SI 2010/686). Notice of the meeting must be sent to the official receiver and to the bankrupt at the same time as it is sent to creditors: Insolvency Rules 1986, SI 1986/1925, r 6.126(1C) (added by SI 2010/686).
3 Ie under the Insolvency Rules 1986, SI 1986/1925, r 6.142 (see PARA 353).
4 Insolvency Rules 1986, SI 1986/1925, r 6.126(1B) (added by SI 2010/686).
5 As to the account held by the Secretary of State see PARA 22. As to the Secretary of State see PARA 19.
6 Insolvency Rules 1986, SI 1986/1925, r 6.126(2) (substituted by SI 2010/686). As to progress reports see PARA 383.
7 Insolvency Rules 1986, SI 1986/1925, r 6.126(3).
8 Insolvency Rules 1986, SI 1986/1925, r 6.126(4).
9 Insolvency Rules 1986, SI 1986/1925, r 6.126(5) (added by SI 1987/1919; and amended by SI 2010/686). The Insolvency Rules 1986, SI 1986/1925, r 6.126(5) does not apply where r 6.126A applies (see PARA 359): r 6.126(5) (as so added and amended). Where r 6.126(5) applies, any reference in the Insolvency Rules 1986, SI 1986/1925, to a resolution that the trustee's resignation be accepted is replaced by a reference to the making of a written statement, authenticated by the person who, had there been a quorum present, would have been chairman of the meeting, that no quorum was present and that the trustee may resign: r 6.126(6) (added by SI 1987/1919; and amended by SI 2010/686). As to the quorum at creditors' meetings see PARA 285. As to authentication see PARA 158 note 2.

359. Resignation where claim outstanding that trustee's remuneration is, or other expenses are, excessive. Where at the date of a meeting summoned for the purpose of receiving the trustee's resignation, an application made to the court that the trustee's remuneration is, or other expenses are, excessive[1], including any appeal, has not been disposed of[2], then at the meeting no resolution may be put regarding the trustee's release[3].

If at the meeting the trustee's resignation is accepted the meeting must be adjourned[4] to a day not less than 14 days after the day on which the application relating to excessive remuneration or expenses[5], including any appeal, has been disposed of[6]. The trustee must give at least 14 days' notice of the adjourned meeting to the creditors[7]. At the adjourned meeting: (1) a revised version of the account which accompanied the notice of the meeting must be laid showing any changes required as a result, or arising out of the application relating to excessive remuneration or expenses; and (2) a resolution for the release of the trustee whose resignation has been accepted must be put[8].

If there is no quorum present at the adjourned meeting, the meeting is deemed to have been held and the creditors are deemed to have resolved that the trustee be released[9]. Where the creditors have resolved at the adjourned meeting that the trustee be released (or are deemed to have so resolved), the chairman of the meeting (or the person who, had there been a quorum present would have been chairman of the meeting) must send as soon as reasonably practicable a certificate to that effect to the official receiver with a copy of the revised account and the official receiver must file a copy of the certificate in court[10].

If at the meeting the trustee's resignation is not accepted, the trustee must not summon any further meeting[11] until the application relating to excessive remuneration or expenses, including any appeal, has been disposed of[12].

1   Ie an application under the Insolvency Rules 1986, SI 1986/1925, r 6.142 (see PARA 353).
2   Insolvency Rules 1986, SI 1986/1925, r 6.126A(1) (r 6.126A added by SI 2010/686).
3   Insolvency Rules 1986, SI 1986/1925, r 6.126A(2) (as added: see note 2).
4   Ie notwithstanding anything in the Insolvency Rules 1986, SI 1986/1925, r 6.90 (suspension of meeting) (see PARA 283).
5   See note 1.
6   Insolvency Rules 1986, SI 1986/1925, r 6.126A(3) (as added: see note 2).
7   Insolvency Rules 1986, SI 1986/1925, r 6.126A(4) (as added: see note 2).
8   Insolvency Rules 1986, SI 1986/1925, r 6.126A(5) (as added: see note 2).
9   Insolvency Rules 1986, SI 1986/1925, r 6.126A(6) (as added: see note 2).
10 Insolvency Rules 1986, SI 1986/1925, r 6.126A(7) (as added: see note 2). As to the meaning of 'file in court' see PARA 57 note 13. Rule 6.126A(7) is subject to the powers of the court on an application being made to it by the trustee under r 6.128 (permission to resign granted by the court) (see PARA 361): r 6.126A(9) (as so added).
11 Ie under the Insolvency Rules 1986, SI 1986/1925, r 6.126 (see PARA 358).
12 Insolvency Rules 1986, SI 1986/1925, r 6.126A(8) (as added: see note 2). Rule 6.126 (see PARA 358) applies to any such further meeting with the modification that the account required to accompany the notice of the meeting must show any changes from the account which accompanied the notice of the earlier meeting called to receive the trustee's resignation, and in particular any changes required as a result of the application under r 6.142 (see PARA 353) and any further remuneration charged or expenses incurred: r 6.126A(10) (as so added). The creditors' rights to request further information under r 6.78C (see PARA 385) or to claim the trustee's remuneration or expenses to be excessive do not apply in respect of any matter included in that account which: (1) was included in the account which accompanied the notice of the earlier meeting called to receive the trustee's resignation; or (2) was the subject of the order of the court on the application made to it under r 6.142 (see PARA 353): Insolvency Rules 1986, SI 1986/1925, r 6.126A(11) (as added: see note 2).

360.   Action to follow acceptance of resignation. Where the chairman of the creditors' meeting summoned for the purpose of receiving the trustee's resignation[1] is other than the official receiver, and there is passed at the meeting any of the following resolutions:

(1)   that the trustee's resignation be accepted;

(2)   that a new trustee be appointed;

(3)   that the resigning trustee be not given his release,

the chairman must, within three business days[2] of the date of the resolution, send to the official receiver a copy of the resolution[3].

If it has been resolved to accept the trustee's resignation, the chairman must send to the official receiver a certificate to that effect[4].

If the creditors have resolved to appoint a new trustee, the certificate of his appointment must also be sent to the official receiver within that time; and the statutory provisions applicable where a trustee has been appointed trustee by a creditors' meeting[5] must be complied with in respect of it[6]. If the trustee's resignation is accepted, the notice of it[7] must be given by him as soon as reasonably practicable after the resolution has been passed; and he must send a copy of the notice to the official receiver[8]. The notice must be accompanied by a copy of the account sent to creditors[9]; and the official receiver must file a copy of the notice in court[10]. The trustee's resignation is effective as from the date on which the official receiver files the copy notice in court, that date to be indorsed on the copy notice[11].

1   See PARA 358.
2   As to the meaning of 'business day' see PARA 28 note 8.
3   Insolvency Rules 1986, SI 1986/1925, r 6.127(3) (amended by SI 2010/686).
4   Insolvency Rules 1986, SI 1986/1925, r 6.127(3) (as amended: see note 3). For the prescribed form of certificate see Sch 4 Form 6.44.
5   Ie the Insolvency Rules 1986, SI 1986/1925, r 6.120: see PARA 318.
6   Insolvency Rules 1986, SI 1986/1925, r 6.127(4).
7   Ie the notice required by the Insolvency Act 1986 s 298(7): see PARA 357.
8   Insolvency Rules 1986, SI 1986/1925, r 6.127(5) (amended by SI 2009/642; and SI 2010/686).
9   Ie the account sent to creditors under the Insolvency Rules 1986, SI 1986/1925, r 6.126(2): see PARA 358.
10 Insolvency Rules 1986, SI 1986/1925, r 6.127(6). As to the meaning of 'file in court' see PARA 57 note 13.
11 Insolvency Rules 1986, SI 1986/1925, r 6.127(7).

361.   Permission to resign granted by the court.   If at a creditors' meeting summoned to accept the trustee's resignation it is resolved that it be not accepted, the court may, on the trustee's application, make an order giving him permission to resign[1].

The court's order may include such provision as it thinks just with respect to matters arising in connection with the resignation, and must determine the date from which the trustee's release is effective[2].

The court must send two sealed copies of the order to the trustee, who must send one of the copies as soon as reasonably practicable to the official receiver[3]. On sending notice of his resignation to the court[4], the trustee must send a copy of it to the official receiver[5].

1   Insolvency Rules 1986, SI 1986/1925, r 6.128(1) (amended by SI 2010/686). For the prescribed form of order see the Insolvency Rules 1986, SI 1986/1925, Sch 4 Form 6.45 (amended by SI 2010/686).
2   Insolvency Rules 1986, SI 1986/1925, r 6.128(2) (amended by SI 2010/686).
3   Insolvency Rules 1986, SI 1986/1925, r 6.128(3) (amended by SI 2009/642).
4   Ie as required by the Insolvency Act 1986 s 298(7): see PARA 357. For the prescribed form of notice see the Insolvency Rules 1986, SI 1986/1925, Sch 4 Form 6.46 (amended by SI 2010/686).
5   Insolvency Rules 1986, SI 1986/1925, r 6.128(4).

362. Notice of resignation. Where a new trustee is appointed in place of one who has resigned, the new trustee must, in the notice of his appointment, state that his predecessor has resigned and, if it be the case, that he has been given his release[1].

1 Insolvency Rules 1986, SI 1986/1925, r 6.134 (amended by SI 2009/642).

363. Removal of trustee; in general. The trustee of a bankrupt's estate may be removed from office only by an order of the court or by a general meeting of the bankrupt's creditors summoned specially for that purpose in accordance with the Insolvency Rules 1986[1].

Where the official receiver is trustee[2], or a trustee is appointed by the Secretary of State[3] or[4] by the court, a general meeting of the bankrupt's creditors must be summoned for the purpose of replacing the trustee only if:

(1) the trustee thinks fit;

(2) the court so directs; or

(3) the meeting is requested by one of the bankrupt's creditors with the concurrence of not less than one-quarter, in value, of the creditors, including the creditor making the request[5].

1 Insolvency Act 1986 s 298(1). See further PARA 364 et seq. However, where by virtue of s 297(1) (see PARA 321 note 6) the official receiver is trustee on a criminal bankruptcy order being made against an individual, he may not be so removed from office: s 298(2). As to the prospective repeal of s 297(1) see PARA 1 note 11.

As to the application of s 298 in the case of the administration in bankruptcy of the insolvent estate of a deceased person dying before the presentation of a bankruptcy petition see PARA 261 note 2.

As to the modification of s 298 by the Insolvent Partnerships Order 1994, SI 1994/2421, in relation to the bankruptcy of an individual member of an insolvent partnership see COMPANY AND PARTNERSHIP INSOLVENCY vol 17 (2011) PARA 1337.

For an instance where the court exercised its power to remove see *Re Sankey Furniture Ltd, ex p Harding, Re Calorifique Ltd, ex p Betts* [1995] 2 BCLC 594 (retirement on grounds of ill health). See also *Re Keypak Homecare Ltd* [1987] BCLC 409, 3 BCC 558 (liquidator acted totally unreasonably in assigning a right of action by the company to a purchaser without attempting to realise the best price); *Re AJ Adams (Builders) Ltd, Re Autonational Extended Warranties Ltd* [1991] BCLC 359, [1991] BCC 62 (disqualification on loss of insolvency practitioner's licence); *Re Edennote Ltd, Tottenham Hotspur plc v Ryman* [1995] 2 BCLC 248, [1995] BCC 389 (court will not lightly remove its own officer and will have regard to the impact of removal on his professional standing and reputation) (all company cases decided under the Insolvency Act 1986 s 172). The court will scrutinise carefully an application by the debtor to remove a trustee: *Smedley v Brittain* [2008] BPIR 219. See also *Doffman v Wood* [2011] EWHC 4008 (Ch), [2012] BPIR 972.

As to the orders a court may make on removal see *Supperstone v Auger* [1999] BPIR 152 (court has jurisdiction to make block orders replacing an insolvency practitioner in all appointments regardless of whether the court is seised of all the insolvencies); *Clements v Udal* [2002] 2 BCLC 606, [2001] BPIR 454 (court has power to appoint additional or replacement office-holders on a temporary basis); *Re Equity Nominees Ltd* [1999] 2 BCLC 19, [2000] BCC 84 (replacements appointed where meetings of creditors and contributories would serve no useful purpose); *Darrell v Miller* [2003] EWHC 2811 (Ch), [2004] BPIR 470, [2003] All ER (D) 123 (Nov) (no power to backdate a block transfer order); *Saville v Gerrard* [2004] EWHC 1363 (Ch), [2005] BCC 433, [2004] BPIR 1332; *Donaldson v O'Sullivan (Official Receiver intervening)* [2008] EWCA Civ 879, [2009] 1 All ER 1087, [2009] 1 WLR 924. As to block transfer orders see now the Insolvency Rules 1986, SI 1986/1925, rr 10A–10D; and PARA 377.

2 Ie by virtue of the Insolvency Act 1986 s 293(3) (see PARA 321) or s 295(4) (see PARA 319).

3 As to the Secretary of State see PARA 19.

4 Ie otherwise than under the Insolvency Act 1986 s 297(5): see PARA 320.

5 Insolvency Act 1986 s 298(4).

364.   Meeting of creditors to remove trustee.   Where a meeting of creditors is summoned for the purpose of removing the trustee, the notice summoning it must indicate that this is the purpose, or one of the purposes, of the meeting, and the notice must draw the attention of creditors to the statutory provisions[1] with respect to the trustee's release[2]. A copy of the notice must at the same time also be sent to the official receiver[3].

At the meeting, a person other than the trustee or his nominee may be elected as chairman; but, if the trustee or his nominee is chairman and a resolution has been proposed for the trustee's removal, the chairman may not adjourn the meeting without the consent of at least one-half, in value, of the creditors present, in person or by proxy, and entitled to vote[4].

Where the chairman of the meeting is other than the official receiver, and there is passed at the meeting any of the following resolutions:

(1)   that the trustee be removed;

(2)   that a new trustee be appointed;

(3)   that the removed trustee be not given his release,

the chairman must, within three business days[5], send to the official receiver a copy of the resolution[6]. If it has been resolved to remove the trustee, the chairman must send to the official receiver a certificate to that effect[7].

If the creditors have resolved to appoint a new trustee, the certificate of his appointment must also be sent to the official receiver within that time; and the statutory provisions applicable where a trustee has been appointed by a creditors' meeting[8] must be complied with in respect of it[9].

1   Ie the Insolvency Act 1986 s 299(3): see PARA 379.
2   Insolvency Rules 1986, SI 1986/1925, r 6.129(1). For the prescribed form of notice see Sch 4 Form 6.35 (amended by SI 2010/686).
3   Insolvency Rules 1986, SI 1986/1925, r 6.129(2).
4   Insolvency Rules 1986, SI 1986/1925, r 6.129(3).
5   As to the meaning of 'business day' see PARA 28 note 8.
6   Insolvency Rules 1986, SI 1986/1925, r 6.129(4) (amended by SI 2010/686).
7   Insolvency Rules 1986, SI 1986/1925, r 6.129(4) (as amended: see note 6). For the prescribed form of certificate see Sch 4 Form 6.47.
8   Ie the Insolvency Rules 1986, SI 1986/1925, r 6.120: see PARA 318.
9   Insolvency Rules 1986, SI 1986/1925, r 6.129(5).

365.   Court's power to regulate meeting.   Where a meeting[1] of creditors to remove the trustee is to be held, or is proposed to be summoned, the court may, on the application of any creditor, give directions as to the mode of summoning it, the sending out and return of forms of proxy, the conduct of the meeting, and any other matter which appears to the court to require regulation or control[2].

1   Ie under the Insolvency Rules 1986, SI 1986/1925, r 6.129: see PARA 364.
2   Insolvency Rules 1986, SI 1986/1925, r 6.130.

366.   Procedure on removal.   Where the creditors have resolved that the trustee be removed, the official receiver must file the certificate of removal in court[1]. The resolution is effective as from the date on which the official receiver files the certificate of removal in court, and that date must be indorsed on the certificate[2]. A copy of the certificate, so indorsed, must be sent by the official receiver to the trustee who has been removed and, if a new trustee has been appointed, to him[3].

The official receiver may not file the certificate in court until the Secretary of State has certified to him that the removed trustee has reconciled his account with that held by the Secretary of State in respect of the bankruptcy[4].

1   Insolvency Rules 1986, SI 1986/1925, r 6.131(1). As to the meaning of 'file in court' see PARA 57 note 13.
2   Insolvency Rules 1986, SI 1986/1925, r 6.131(2).
3   Insolvency Rules 1986, SI 1986/1925, r 6.131(3).
4   Insolvency Rules 1986, SI 1986/1925, r 6.131(4). As to the Secretary of State see PARA 19; and as to the account held by the Secretary of State see PARA 22.

367.   Notice of removal.   Where a new trustee is appointed in place of one who has been removed, the new trustee must, in the notice of his appointment, state that his predecessor has been removed and, if it be the case, that he has been given his release[1].

1   Insolvency Rules 1986, SI 1986/1925, r 6.134 (amended by SI 2009/642).

368.   Removal of trustee by the court.   Where application is made to the court for the removal of the trustee, or for an order directing the trustee to summon a meeting of creditors for the purpose of removing him[1], the court may, if it thinks that no sufficient cause is shown for the application, dismiss it; but it may not do so unless the applicant has had an opportunity to attend the court for a hearing without notice being served on any other party, of which he has been given at least five business days' notice[2]. If the application is not so dismissed, the court must fix a venue[3] for it to be heard[4]. At least 14 days before the hearing, the applicant must send to the trustee and the official receiver notice stating the venue so fixed; and the notice must be accompanied by a copy of the application, and of any evidence which the applicant intends to adduce in support of it[5].

Subject to any contrary order of the court, the costs of the application do not fall on the estate[6].

Where the court removes the trustee:

(1)   it must send copies of the order of removal to him and to the official receiver;

(2)   the order may include such provision as the court thinks just with respect to the matters arising in connection with the removal; and

(3)   if the court appoints a new trustee, the statutory provisions relating to the appointment of a trustee by the court[7] apply[8].

1   Insolvency Rules 1986, SI 1986/1925, r 6.132(1).
2   Insolvency Rules 1986, SI 1986/1925, r 6.132(2) (amended by SI 2010/686). As to the meaning of 'business day' see PARA 28 note 8. For the prescribed form of order see the Insolvency Rules 1986, SI 1986/1925, Sch 4 Form 6.48 (amended by SI 2010/686).
3   As to the meaning of 'venue' see PARA 46 note 22.
4   Insolvency Rules 1986, SI 1986/1925, r 6.132(2) (as amended: see note 2).
5   Insolvency Rules 1986, SI 1986/1925, r 6.132(3).
6   Insolvency Rules 1986, SI 1986/1925, r 6.132(4).
7   Ie the Insolvency Rules 1986, SI 1986/1925, r 6.121: see PARA 320.
8   Insolvency Rules 1986, SI 1986/1925, r 6.132(5).

369.   Removal of trustee by Secretary of State.   If the trustee was appointed by the Secretary of State, he may be removed by a direction of the Secretary of State[1].

If the Secretary of State decides to remove the trustee, he must, before doing so, notify the trustee and the official receiver of his decision and the grounds of it, and specify a period within which the trustee may make representations against implementation of the decision[2].

If the Secretary of State directs the removal of the trustee, he must as soon as reasonably practicable file notice of his decision in court[3], and send notice to the trustee and the official receiver[4]. If the trustee is removed by direction of the Secretary of State, the court may make any such order in his case as it would have power to make if he had been removed by itself[5].

1   Insolvency Act 1986 s 298(5). As to the Secretary of State see PARA 19. As to the application of s 298 in the case of the administration in bankruptcy of the insolvent estate of a deceased person dying before the presentation of a bankruptcy petition see PARA 261 note 2.
2   Insolvency Rules 1986, SI 1986/1925, r 6.133(1).
3   As to the meaning of 'file in court' see PARA 57 note 13.
4   Insolvency Rules 1986, SI 1986/1925, r 6.133(2) (amended by SI 2009/642).
5   Insolvency Rules 1986, SI 1986/1925, r 6.133(3).

370.   Vacancy in office of trustee.   Where the appointment of a person as trustee of a bankrupt's estate fails to take effect or, such an appointment having taken effect, there is otherwise a vacancy[1] in the office of trustee, the official receiver is trustee until the vacancy is filled[2].

The official receiver may summon a general meeting of the bankrupt's creditors for the purpose of filling the vacancy and must summon such a meeting if required to do so[3] on a creditors' requisition[4].

If at the end of the period of 28 days beginning with the day on which the vacancy first came to the official receiver's attention he has not summoned, and is not proposing to summon, a general meeting of creditors for the purpose of filling the vacancy, he must refer the need for an appointment to the Secretary of State[5].

On such a reference the Secretary of State must either make an appointment or decline to make one[6]; and, if on a reference to the Secretary of State no appointment is made, the official receiver continues to be trustee of the bankrupt's estate, but without prejudice to his power to make a further reference[7].

1   For these purposes, references to a vacancy include a case where it is necessary, in relation to any property which is or may be comprised in a bankrupt's estate, to revive the trusteeship of that estate after the holding of a final meeting summoned under the Insolvency Act 1986 s 331 (see PARA 616) or the giving by the official receiver of notice under s 299(2) (see PARA 380): s 300(8).
    As to the application of s 300 in the case of the administration in bankruptcy of the insolvent estate of a deceased person dying before the presentation of a bankruptcy petition see PARA 261 note 2.
2   Insolvency Act 1986 s 300(1), (2). As to the modification of the Insolvency Act 1986 s 300 by the Insolvent Partnerships Order 1994, SI 1994/2421, in relation to the bankruptcy of an individual member of an insolvent partnership see COMPANY AND PARTNERSHIP INSOLVENCY vol 17 (2011) PARA 1339.
3   Ie in pursuance of the Insolvency Act 1986 s 314(7): see PARA 481.
4   Insolvency Act 1986 s 300(3).
5   Insolvency Act 1986 s 300(4). As to the Secretary of State see PARA 19.
6   Insolvency Act 1986 s 300(6) (amended by the Enterprise Act 2002 ss 269, 278(2), Sch 23 paras 1, 11, Sch 26).
7   Insolvency Act 1986 s 300(7).

371.   Loss of qualification as insolvency practitioner.   The trustee, not being the official receiver, must vacate office if he ceases to be a person who is for the time being qualified to act as an insolvency practitioner in relation to the bankrupt[1]. Where the trustee so vacates office, he must as soon as reasonably practicable give notice of his doing so to the official receiver, who must give notice to the Secretary of State[2]; and the official receiver must file in court[3] a copy of his notice[4].

1	Insolvency Act 1986 s 298(6). As to insolvency practitioners and their qualification see PARA 40. As to the application of s 298 in the case of the administration in bankruptcy of the insolvent estate of a deceased person dying before the presentation of a bankruptcy petition see PARA 261 note 2.
2	Insolvency Rules 1986, SI 1986/1925, r 6.144(1), (2) (amended by SI 2009/642). For the prescribed form of notice see the Insolvency Rules 1986, SI 1986/1925, Sch 4 Form 6.51. Rule 6.135 (see PARA 379) applies as regards the trustee obtaining his release, as if he had been removed by the court: r 6.144(3).
3	As to the meaning of 'file in court' see PARA 57 note 13.
4	Insolvency Rules 1986, SI 1986/1925, r 6.144(2) (as amended: see note 2).

372. Final meeting. The trustee must vacate office on giving notice to the court that a final meeting has been held[1] and of the decision, if any, of that meeting[2].

1	Ie under the Insolvency Act 1986 s 331: see PARA 616.
2	Insolvency Act 1986 s 298(8). As from a day to be appointed, s 298(8) is amended by the Enterprise and Regulatory Reform Act 2013 s 71, Sch 19 paras 1, 23: see PARA 130 note 17.

373. Annulment of bankruptcy order. The trustee must vacate office if the bankruptcy order is annulled[1].

1	Insolvency Act 1986 s 298(9). As to the annulment of bankruptcy orders see PARA 620 et seq.

374. Death of trustee. Where the trustee, other than the official receiver, has died, it is the duty of his personal representatives to give notice of the fact to the official receiver, specifying the date of the death[1]. This provision does not, however, apply if notice has been given under any of the following provisions[2].

If the deceased trustee was a partner in, or an employee of, a firm, notice may be given to the official receiver by a partner in the firm who is qualified to act as an insolvency practitioner[3], or is a member of any body recognised by the Secretary of State[4] for the authorisation of insolvency practitioners[5].

Notice of the death may be given by any person producing to the official receiver the relevant death certificate or a copy of it[6].

The official receiver must give notice to the court, for the purpose of fixing the date of the deceased trustee's release[7].

1	Insolvency Rules 1986, SI 1986/1925, r 6.143(1).
2	Insolvency Rules 1986, SI 1986/1925, r 6.143(1).
3	As to insolvency practitioners and their qualification see PARA 40.
4	As to the bodies recognised by the Secretary of State see COMPANY AND PARTNERSHIP INSOLVENCY vol 16 (2011) PARA 15. As to the Secretary of State see PARA 19.
5	Insolvency Rules 1986, SI 1986/1925, r 6.143(2).
6	Insolvency Rules 1986, SI 1986/1925, r 6.143(3).
7	Insolvency Rules 1986, SI 1986/1925, r 6.143(4). The date of the trustee's release is fixed in accordance with the Insolvency Act 1986 s 299(3)(a): see PARA 379 head (1).

375. Notice to official receiver of intention to vacate office. Where the trustee intends to vacate office, whether by resignation or otherwise, he must give notice of his intention to the official receiver together with notice of any creditors' meeting to be held in respect of his vacation of office, including any meeting to receive his resignation[1]; and the notice to the official receiver must be given at least 21 days before any such creditors' meeting[2].

Where there remains in the bankrupt's estate any property which has not been realised, applied, distributed or otherwise fully dealt with in the bankruptcy, the trustee must include in his notice to the official receiver details of the nature of that property, its value, or the fact that it has no value, its location, any action taken by the trustee to deal with that property or any reason for his not dealing with it, and the current position in relation to it[3].

1 Insolvency Rules 1986, SI 1986/1925, r 6.145(1) (substituted by SI 1987/1919).
2 Insolvency Rules 1986, SI 1986/1925, r 6.145(2) (substituted by SI 1987/1919).
3 Insolvency Rules 1986, SI 1986/1925, r 6.145(3) (added by SI 1987/1919).

376. Trustee's duties on vacating office. Where the trustee ceases to be in office as such, in consequence of removal[1], resignation[2] or cesser of qualification as an insolvency practitioner[3], he is under obligation as soon as reasonably practicable to deliver up to the person succeeding him as trustee the assets of the estate, after deduction of any expenses properly incurred, and distributions made, by him, and further to deliver up to that person:

(1) the records of the bankruptcy, including correspondence, proofs and other related papers appertaining to the bankruptcy while it was within his responsibility; and

(2) the bankrupt's books, papers and other records[4].

1 See PARA 363 et seq.
2 See PARA 357 et seq.
3 See PARA 371.
4 Insolvency Rules 1986, SI 1986/1925, r 6.146(1).

377. Block transfer of cases. Where an individual who is acting as an office-holder ('the outgoing office-holder') dies, retires from practice, or is otherwise unable or unwilling to continue in office, and it is expedient to transfer some or all of the cases in which the outgoing office-holder holds office to one or more office-holders ('the replacement office-holder') in a single transaction[1], the court has the power to make a block transfer order, appointing a replacement office-holder in the place of the outgoing office-holder to be trustee in a bankruptcy[2], or supervisor[3] of a voluntary arrangement[4].

The replacement office-holder must be qualified to act as an insolvency practitioner or, in the case of a voluntary arrangement, be a person authorised so to act[5].

An application for a block transfer order may be made to the registrar or district judge[6] for:

(1) the transfer to the High Court of the cases specified[7];

(2) the transfer of the cases back to the court from which they were transferred when a replacement office-holder has been appointed;

(3) the removal of the outgoing office-holder[8];

(4) the appointment of a replacement office-holder[9];

(5) such other order or direction as may be necessary or expedient in connection with any of the matters referred to above[10].

The application may be made by any of the following:

(a) the outgoing office-holder (if able and willing to do so);

(b) any person who holds office jointly with the outgoing office-holder;

(c) any person who is proposed to be appointed as the replacement office-holder;

(d) any creditor in a case subject to the application;

(e) the recognised professional body or recognised body by which the outgoing office-holder is or was authorised; or

(f) the Secretary of State[11].

An applicant (other than the Secretary of State) must give notice of the application to the Secretary of State at least five business days[12] before the hearing of the application[13].

The outgoing office-holder (if not the applicant or deceased), every person who holds office jointly with the outgoing office-holder and such person as the registrar or district judge directs must be made a respondent to the application and served with it[14].

The application must contain a schedule setting out: (i) the name of each case; (ii) the identity of the court having jurisdiction when the application is made; (iii) the case number (if any); and (iv) the capacity in which the outgoing office-holder was appointed[15].

The application must be supported by evidence setting out the circumstances which gave rise to it being expedient to appoint a replacement office-holder and exhibiting the written consent to act of each person who is proposed to be appointed as replacement office-holder[16].

The registrar or district judge may in the first instance consider the application without a hearing and make such order as the registrar or district judge thinks just[17]. In the first instance, the registrar or district judge may do any of the following:

(A)   make an order directing the transfer to the High Court of those cases not already within its jurisdiction for the purpose only of the substantive application;

(B)   if the documents are considered to be in order and that the matter is straightforward, make an order on the substantive application;

(C)   give any directions which are considered to be necessary including, if appropriate, directions for the joinder of any additional respondents or requiring the service of the application on any person or requiring additional evidence to be provided; or

(D)   if an order is not made on the substantive application, give directions for the further consideration of the substantive application by the registrar or district judge or a judge of the Chancery Division[18].

The applicant must ensure that a sealed copy of every order transferring any case to the High Court and of every order which is made on a substantive application is lodged with the court having jurisdiction over each case affected by such order for filing on the court file relating to that case[19].

In any case other than an application relating to the appointment of an administrator, in deciding to what extent, if any, the costs of making an application[20] should be paid as an expense of the insolvency proceedings to which the application relates, the factors to which the court must have regard include the reasons for the making of the application, the number of cases to which the application relates, the value of assets comprised in those cases and the nature and extent of the costs involved[21].

Any appointment[22] must be notified to the Secretary of State as soon as reasonably practicable and to the creditors, and such other persons as the court may direct, in such manner as the court may direct[23].

1   Insolvency Rules 1986, SI 1986/1925, rr 7.10A, 7.10B(1) (rr 7.10A–7.10D added by SI 2010/686).

2   Ie including a case where the official receiver is the trustee by virtue of the Insolvency Act 1986 s 300 (see PARA 370).

3   Ie under the Insolvency Act 1986 Pt 8 (ss 252–263G) (see PARA 43 et seq).

4   Insolvency Rules 1986, SI 1986/1925, r 7.10B(2) (as added: see note 1).

5   Insolvency Rules 1986, SI 1986/1925, r 7.10B(3) (as added: see note 1). As to insolvency
    practitioners and their qualification see PARA 40. As to persons authorised to act in voluntary
    arrangements see PARA 73 et seq.
6   Where all the cases in the schedule under the Insolvency Rules 1986, SI 1986/1925, r 7.10C(8)
    (see the text to note 15) are in a county court or more than one county court: (1) the application
    may be made to a district judge of a convenient county court having insolvency jurisdiction; and
    (2) rr 7.10C, 7.10D apply with appropriate modifications: rr 7.10C(10), 7.10D(7) (as added: see
    note 1). As from a day to be appointed, any reference however expressed that is or is deemed to
    be a reference to a county court held under the County Courts Act 1984 s 1 is to be read as a
    reference to the county court established by s A1 of that Act: see the Crime and Courts Act 2013
    Sch 9 Pt 2 para 11(1)(a), (3)(c). At the date at which this volume states the law no such day had
    been appointed.
7   Ie the cases specified in the schedule under the Insolvency Rules 1986, SI 1986/1925, r 7.10C(8)
    (see the text and note 15).
8   Ie by the exercise of any of the powers in the Insolvency Rules 1986, SI 1986/1925, r 7.10C(2).
    The powers are: (1) the Insolvency Act 1986 s 298 (see PARA 363 (where the case law in multiple
    appointment cases is considered)) and the Insolvency Rules 1986, SI 1986/1925, r 7.10B(2)
    (bankruptcy); and (2) the Insolvency Act 1986 s 263(5) (voluntary arrangement under Pt 8) (see
    PARA 76): Insolvency Rules 1986, SI 1986/1925, r 7.10C(2) (as added: see note 1).
9   Ie by the exercise of any of the powers in the Insolvency Rules 1986, SI 1986/1925, r 7.10C(3).
    The powers are: (1) the Insolvency Act 1986 s 298 (see PARA 363), s 303(2) (see PARA 342) and
    the Insolvency Rules 1986, SI 1986/1925, r 7.10B(2) (bankruptcy); and (2) the Insolvency
    Act 1986 s 263(5) (voluntary arrangement under Pt 8) (see PARA 76): Insolvency Rules 1986,
    SI 1986/1925, r 7.10C(3) (as added: see note 1)
10 Insolvency Rules 1986, SI 1986/1925, r 7.10C(1) (as added: see note 1).
11 Insolvency Rules 1986, SI 1986/1925, r 7.10C(4) (as added: see note 1).
12 As to the meaning of 'business day' see PARA 28 note 8.
13 Insolvency Rules 1986, SI 1986/1925, r 7.10C(6) (as added: see note 1).
14 Insolvency Rules 1986, SI 1986/1925, r 7.10C(7) (as added: see note 1).
15 Insolvency Rules 1986, SI 1986/1925, r 7.10C(8) (as added: see note 1).
16 Insolvency Rules 1986, SI 1986/1925, r 7.10C(9) (as added: see note 1).
17 Insolvency Rules 1986, SI 1986/1925, r 7.10D(1) (as added: see note 1).
18 Insolvency Rules 1986, SI 1986/1925, r 7.10D(2) (as added: see note 1).
19 Insolvency Rules 1986, SI 1986/1925, r 7.10D(3) (as added: see note 1).
20 Ie under the Insolvency Rules 1986, SI 1986/1925, r 7.10D.
21 Insolvency Rules 1986, SI 1986/1925, r 7.10D(4) (as added: see note 1).
22 Ie under the Insolvency Rules 1986, SI 1986/1925, r 7.10D.
23 Insolvency Rules 1986, SI 1986/1925, r 7.10D(6) (as added: see note 1).

(vii) Release of Trustee

A. IN THE COURSE OF ADMINISTRATION

378. Release of official receiver. Where the official receiver has ceased to be
the trustee of a bankrupt's estate and a person is appointed in his stead, the
official receiver has his release with effect from the following time, that is to say:

(1)   where that person is appointed by a general meeting of the bankrupt's
       creditors or by the Secretary of State[1], the time at which the official
       receiver gives notice to the court that he has been replaced; and

(2)   where that person is appointed by the court, such time as the court may
       determine[2].

1   As to the Secretary of State see PARA 19.
2   Insolvency Act 1986 s 299(1). As from a day to be appointed, s 299(1) is amended by the
    Enterprise and Regulatory Reform Act 2013 s 71, Sch 19 paras 1, 24: see PARA 130 note 17.
        Where the official receiver or the trustee has his release under the Insolvency Act 1986 s 299,
    he is, with effect from the time specified in s 299(1)–(4) (see PARAS 379, 380), discharged from
    all liability both in respect of acts or omissions of his in the administration of the estate and

otherwise in relation to his conduct as trustee; but nothing in s 299 prevents the exercise, in relation to a person who has had his release under s 299, of the court's powers under s 304 (see PARAS 344, 345): s 299(5).

As to the application of s 299 in the case of the administration in bankruptcy of the insolvent estate of a deceased person dying before the presentation of a bankruptcy petition see PARA 261 note 2.

379. Release of resigning or removed trustee. A person other than the official receiver who has ceased to be the trustee has his release with effect from the following time, that is to say:

(1)   in the case of a person who has been removed from office by a general meeting of the bankrupt's creditors that has not resolved against his release or who has died, the time at which notice is given to the court that that person has ceased to hold office[1];

(2)   in the case of a person who has been removed from office by a general meeting of the bankrupt's creditors that has resolved against his release, or by the court, or by the Secretary of State, or who has vacated office on ceasing to be qualified to act as an insolvency practitioner in relation to the bankrupt[2], such time as the Secretary of State may, on application by that person, determine[3];

(3)   in the case of a person who has resigned, from when his resignation is effective[4].

1   Insolvency Act 1986 s 299(3)(a); Insolvency Rules 1986, SI 1986/1925, r 6.135(1) (amended by SI 2010/686). As from a day to be appointed, the Insolvency Act 1986 s 299(3) is amended by the Enterprise and Regulatory Reform Act 2013 s 71, Sch 19 paras 1, 24: see PARA 130 note 17.

However, where the trustee's resignation is accepted under the Insolvency Rules 1986, SI 1986/1925, r 6.126A (see PARA 359), the trustee's release is effective as from the date on which the official receiver files the copy of the certificate under r 6.126A(7) in court, that date to be endorsed on the copy certificate: r 6.135(1A) (added by SI 2010/686). As to the meaning of 'file in court' see PARA 57 note 13. Where the trustee is removed by a meeting of creditors which has not resolved against his release, the fact of his release must be stated in the certificate of removal: Insolvency Rules 1986, SI 1986/1925, r 6.135(2). See also PARA 378. As to the application of the Insolvency Act 1986 s 299 in the case of the administration in bankruptcy of the insolvent estate of a deceased person dying before the presentation of a bankruptcy petition see PARA 261 note 2.

As to the modification of s 299 by the Insolvent Partnerships Order 1994, SI 1994/2421, in relation to the bankruptcy of an individual member of an insolvent partnership see COMPANY AND PARTNERSHIP INSOLVENCY vol 17 (2011) PARA 1339.

2   Ie under the Insolvency Act 1986 s 298(6): see PARA 371.

3   Insolvency Act 1986 s 299(3)(b). As to the Secretary of State see PARA 19. Where the trustee is removed by a creditors' meeting which has resolved against his release or is removed by the court, he must apply to the Secretary of State for his release: Insolvency Rules 1986, SI 1986/1925, r 6.135(3)(b). When the Secretary of State gives the release, he must certify it accordingly, and must send the certificate to the official receiver to be filed in court: r 6.135(4). A copy of the certificate must be sent by the Secretary of State to the former trustee, whose release is effective from the date of the certificate: r 6.135(5). For the prescribed form of application to the Secretary of State see Sch 4 Form 6.49.

4   Insolvency Act 1986 s 299(3)(c). Where the trustee resigns and the creditors' meeting called to receive his resignation has resolved against his release, he must apply to the Secretary of State for his release: Insolvency Rules 1986, SI 1986/1925, r 6.135(3)(a). When the Secretary of State gives the release, he must certify it accordingly, and must send the certificate to the official receiver to be filed in court: r 6.135(4). A copy of the certificate must be sent by the Secretary of State to the former trustee, whose release is effective from the date of the certificate: r 6.135(5).

B.   ON COMPLETION OF ADMINISTRATION

380. Release of official receiver. If the official receiver, while he is the trustee, gives notice to the Secretary of State that the administration of the bankrupt's estate[1] is for practical purposes complete, he has his release with effect from such time as the Secretary of State may determine[2]. However, before giving notice to the Secretary of State, the official receiver must send out notice of his intention to do so to all creditors of which he is aware, and to the bankrupt[3]. The notice in each case must be accompanied by a summary of the official receiver's receipts and payments as trustee[4].

When the Secretary of State has determined the date from which the official receiver is to have his release, he must give notice to the court that he has done so; and the notice must be accompanied by the summary of the official receiver's receipts and payments as trustee[5].

1 Ie in accordance with the Insolvency Act 1986 Pt 9 Ch 4 (ss 305–335).
2 Insolvency Act 1986 s 299(2). See also PARA 378 note 2. As to the application of s 299 in the case of the administration in bankruptcy of the insolvent estate of a deceased person dying before the presentation of a bankruptcy petition see PARA 261 note 2. As to the Secretary of State see PARA 19.
3 Insolvency Rules 1986, SI 1986/1925, r 6.136(1) (amended by SI 2004/584). The court may, on the official receiver's application, relieve him of any duty imposed on him by the Insolvency Rules 1986, SI 1986/1925, r 6.136, or authorise him to carry out the duty in a way other than there required: r 6.137A(1) (r 6.137A added by SI 2004/584). In considering whether to do so, the court must have regard to the cost of carrying out the duty, to the amount of the funds available in the estate, and to the extent of the interest of creditors or any particular class of them: Insolvency Rules 1986, SI 1986/1925, r 6.137A(2) (as so added).
4 Insolvency Rules 1986, SI 1986/1925, r 6.136(2).
5 Insolvency Rules 1986, SI 1986/1925, r 6.136(3).

381. Final meeting of creditors. Where the trustee is other than the official receiver, he must give at least 28 days' notice of the final meeting of creditors[1]; and the notice must be sent to all creditors of which he is aware, and to the bankrupt[2]. The trustee's report laid before the meeting must include a summary of his receipts and payments, including details of remuneration charged and expenses incurred by the trustee, details of the basis fixed for the trustee's remuneration, and a statement by him that he has reconciled his account with that which is held by the Secretary of State in respect of the bankruptcy[3].

At the final meeting, the creditors may question the trustee with respect to any matter contained in his report, and may resolve against him having his release[4].

The trustee must give notice to the court that the final meeting has been held; and the notice must state whether or not he has been given his release, and must be accompanied by a copy of the report laid before the final meeting; and a copy of the notice must be sent by the trustee to the Secretary of State[5].

If there is no quorum present at the final meeting, the trustee must report to the court that a final meeting was duly summoned[6], but there was no quorum present; and the final meeting is then deemed to have been held, and the creditors not to have resolved against the trustee having his release[7].

If the creditors at the final meeting have not so resolved, the trustee is released when the notice to the court that the final meeting has been held[8] is filed in court[9]; and, if they have so resolved, the trustee obtains his release from the Secretary of State[10].

1 Ie the meeting to be held under the Insolvency Act 1986 s 331: see PARA 616. As to remote attendance at meetings see PARA 267.
2 Insolvency Rules 1986, SI 1986/1925, r 6.137(1) (amended by SI 2004/584). The trustee, as soon as reasonably practicable after giving notice, must have gazetted a notice of the final meeting and may advertise notice of the meeting in such other manner as the trustee thinks fit: Insolvency Rules 1986, SI 1986/1925, r 6.137(1A) (r 6.137(1A)–(1C) added by SI 2010/686). As to the meaning of 'gazetted' see PARA 165 note 12. In addition to the standard contents, the

notice must state: (1) that the trustee has summoned the meeting; (2) if the meeting was summoned at the request of a creditor, the fact that it was so summoned and the provision of the Insolvency Act 1986 under which it was summoned; (3) the purpose for which the meeting was summoned; (4) the venue fixed for the meeting; and (5) the time and date by which, and place at which, creditors must lodge proxies and hitherto unlodged proofs in order to be entitled to vote at the meeting: Insolvency Rules 1986, SI 1986/1925, r 6.137(1B) (as so added). As to the meaning of 'standard contents' see PARA 165 note 12. As to proxies see PARA 276 et seq.

The final meeting must not be held unless r 6.78B (final report: see PARA 384) has been complied with; and if for that reason the meeting is not held: (a) the trustee must give notice of that fact as soon as reasonably practicable to all to whom notice of the meeting was given; and (b) fresh notice of the meeting complying with r 6.137 must be given when r 6.78B has been complied with: r 6.137(1C) (as so added).

The court may, on the trustee's application, relieve him of any duty imposed on him by r 6.137, or authorise him to carry out the duty in a way other than there required: r 6.137A(1) (r 6.137A added by SI 2004/584). In considering whether to do so, the court must have regard to the cost of carrying out the duty, to the amount of the funds available in the estate, and to the extent of the interest of creditors or any particular class of them: Insolvency Rules 1986, SI 1986/1925, r 6.137A(2) (as so added).

3   Insolvency Rules 1986, SI 1986/1925, r 6.137(2) (amended by SI 2010/686). As to the account held by the Secretary of State see PARA 22. As to the Secretary of State see PARA 19.

Where the trustee has sent a progress report to creditors in accordance with the Insolvency Rules 1986, SI 1986/1925, r 6.78A (see PARA 383), the report to be laid at the final meeting of creditors must also: (1) contain a receipts and payments account in the form of an abstract showing the receipts and payments during the period since the last progress report; and (2) include details of the remuneration charged and expenses incurred by the trustee during that period, and a description of the things done by the trustee during that period in respect of which that remuneration was charged and those expenses incurred: r 6.137(2A) (r 6.137(2A)–(2C) added by SI 2010/686).

In any case where the basis of the trustee's remuneration had not been fixed by the date to which the last progress report was made up, the receipts and payments account required by head (1) above must also include details of the remuneration charged in the period of any preceding progress report in which details of remuneration were not included: Insolvency Rules 1986, SI 1986/1925, r 6.137(2B) (as so added).

Where the basis of remuneration has been fixed as a set amount only, it is sufficient compliance with head (2) above for the trustee to state the amount which has been set and to supply details of the expenses charged within the period in question: r 6.137(2C) (as so added).

4   Insolvency Rules 1986, SI 1986/1925, r 6.137(3).

5   Insolvency Rules 1986, SI 1986/1925, r 6.137(4) (amended by SI 2005/527). For the prescribed form of notice to the court of the final meeting of creditors see the Insolvency Rules 1986, SI 1986/1925, Sch 4 Form 6.50.

6   Ie in accordance with the Insolvency Rules 1986, SI 1986/1925.

7   Insolvency Rules 1986, SI 1986/1925, r 6.137(5); Insolvency Act 1986 s 299(3)(d)(ii). As to the quorum at creditors' meetings see PARA 285.

8   Ie the notice under the Insolvency Rules 1986, SI 1986/1925, r 6.137(4): see the text and note 5.
9   As to the meaning of 'file in court' see PARA 57 note 13.

10   Insolvency Rules 1986, SI 1986/1925, r 6.137(6); Insolvency Act 1986 s 299(3)(d)(i). The release is obtained from the Secretary of State as provided by the Insolvency Rules 1986, SI 1986/1925, r 6.135 (see PARA 379): r 6.137(6).

C.   ON ANNULMENT OF BANKRUPTCY ORDER

382.   Release on annulment of bankruptcy order. Where a bankruptcy order is annulled[1], the trustee at the time of the annulment has his release with effect from such time as the court may determine[2].

1   As to annulment of bankruptcy orders see PARA 620 et seq.
2   Insolvency Act 1986 s 299(4). See also PARA 378 note 2. As to application of s 299 in the case of the administration in bankruptcy of the insolvent estate of a deceased person dying before the presentation of a bankruptcy petition see PARA 261 note 2.

(viii) Reports to Creditors

383. Trustee's accounts and reports. The trustee[1] must send a copy of a progress report containing the following information to the creditors[2] within two months of the end of the period covered by the report[3].

The progress report is a report which includes:

(1)   details of the court where the proceedings are and the relevant court reference number;

(2)   the bankrupt's name;

(3)   the title of the proceedings;

(4)   full details of the trustee's name and address and date of appointment, including any changes in office-holder;

(5)   details of the basis fixed for the remuneration of the trustee[4] (or if not fixed at the date of the report, the steps taken during the period of the report to fix it);

(6)   if the basis of remuneration has been fixed, a statement of (a) the remuneration charged by the trustee during the period of the report[5]; and (b) where the report is the first to be made after the basis has been fixed, the remuneration charged by the trustee during the periods covered by the previous reports[6], together with a description of the things done by the trustee during those periods in respect of which the remuneration was charged, irrespective in either case of whether payment was made in respect of that remuneration during that period;

(7)   a statement of the expenses incurred by the trustee during the period of the report, irrespective of whether payment was made in respect of them during that period;

(8)   details of progress during the period of the report, including a receipts and payments account in the form of an abstract showing receipts and payments during the period of the report;

(9)   details of any assets that remain to be realised;

(10)   a statement of the creditors' right to request information[7] and their right to challenge the trustee's remuneration and expenses[8]; and

(11)   any other relevant information for the creditors[9].

The progress report must cover the period of one year commencing on the date on which the trustee is appointed and every subsequent period of one year[10]. The period to be covered by a progress report ends on the date when a trustee ceases to act, and the period to be covered by each subsequent progress report is each successive period of one year beginning immediately after that date, subject to the further application of these provisions when another trustee ceases to act[11]. A progress report is not required for any period which ends after the trustee has sent a draft final report[12] to creditors[13].

1   The Insolvency Rules 1986, SI 1986/1925, r 6.78A does not apply where the trustee is the official receiver: r 6.78A(8) (r 6.78A added by SI 2010/686).

2   As to the meaning of references to creditors see PARA 253 note 2.

3   Insolvency Rules 1986, SI 1986/1925, r 6.78A(6) (as added: see note 1). The court may, on the trustee's application, extend the period of two months, or make such other order in respect of the content of the report as it thinks just: r 78A(7) (as so added).

4   Ie under the Insolvency Rules 1986, SI 1986/1925, r 6.138 (see PARA 348).

5   Where the basis for the remuneration is a set amount under the Insolvency Rules 1986, SI 1986/1925, r 6.138(2)(c) (see PARA 348), it may be shown as that amount without any apportionment to the period of the report: r 6.78A(2) (as added: see note 1).

6   See note 5.

7   Ie under the Insolvency Rules 1986, SI 1986/1925, r 6.78C (see PARA 385).

8   Ie under the Insolvency Rules 1986, SI 1986/1925, r 6.142 (see PARA 353).
9   Insolvency Rules 1986, SI 1986/1925, r 6.78A(1) (as added: see note 1).
10 Insolvency Rules 1986, SI 1986/1925, r 6.78A(3) (as added: see note 1).
11 Insolvency Rules 1986, SI 1986/1925, r 6.78A(4) (as added: see note 1).
12 Ie under the Insolvency Rules 1986, SI 1986/1925, r 6.78B (final report to creditors) (see PARA 384).
13 Insolvency Rules 1986, SI 1986/1925, r 6.78A(5) (as added: see note 1).

384.   Final report to creditors and bankrupt. The trustee[1] must, at least eight weeks before holding a final meeting[2], send to each creditor[3] known to the trustee and to the bankrupt a draft of the report which the trustee intends to lay before the meeting[4].

The draft report must:

(1)   contain such matters and be in such terms as would comply with the statutory rule[5] if the report were to be laid before a meeting as soon as reasonably practicable after the draft had been sent to creditors; and

(2)   be accompanied by a statement of the creditors' right to request information[6] and their right to challenge[7] the trustee's remuneration and expenses[8].

The trustee may not send a draft report to creditors under these provisions before giving notice of intention to declare a final dividend[9], or that no dividend or further dividend will be declared[10].

If any creditor has applied to the court to challenge the trustee's remuneration and expenses[11] and has given a copy of the application to the trustee, the final meeting may not be held until the application (including any appeal) has been disposed of and the trustee has complied with any order of the court[12].

1   The Insolvency Rules 1986, SI 1986/1925, r 6.78B does not apply where the trustee is the official receiver: r 6.78B(5) (r 6.78B added by SI 2010/686).
2   Ie in accordance with the Insolvency Act 1986 s 331 (see PARA 616).
3   As to the meaning of references to creditors see PARA 253 note 2.
4   Insolvency Rules 1986, SI 1986/1925, r 6.78B(1) (as added: see note 1). The report is laid before the meeting in accordance with r 6.137 (see PARA 381).
5   Ie in compliance with the Insolvency Rules 1986, SI 1986/1925, r 6.137 (see PARA 381).
6   Ie under the Insolvency Rules 1986, SI 1986/1925, r 6.78C (see PARA 385).
7   Ie under the Insolvency Rules 1986, SI 1986/1925, r 6.142 (see PARA 353).
8   Insolvency Rules 1986, SI 1986/1925, r 6.78B(2) (as added: see note 1).
9   Ie under the Insolvency Rules 1986, SI 1986/1925, r 11.2 (see PARA 603).
10 Insolvency Rules 1986, SI 1986/1925, r 6.78B(3) (as added: see note 1). Notice that no dividend or further dividend will be declared is given under r 11.7 (see PARA 608).
11 Ie under the Insolvency Rules 1986, SI 1986/1925, r 6.142 (see PARA 353).
12 Insolvency Rules 1986, SI 1986/1925, r 6.78B(4) (as added: see note 1).

385.   Creditors' request for further information. If within the required period[1] a secured creditor[2] or an unsecured creditor with the permission of the court, or at any time an unsecured creditor with the concurrence of at least 5 per cent in value of the unsecured creditors (including the creditor in question), makes a request in writing to the trustee[3] for further information about remuneration or expenses set out in a progress report[4] or in a draft report[5], the trustee must, within 14 days of receipt of the request, comply with the request except to the extent that the request is in respect of matter in a draft report or a progress report[6] which in either case was previously included in a separate progress report[7].

The trustee complies with the request by either:

(1)   providing all of the information asked for; or

(2)   so far as the trustee considers that (a) the time or cost of preparation of

the information would be excessive, or (b) disclosure of the information would be prejudicial to the conduct of the bankruptcy or might reasonably be expected to lead to violence against any person, or (c) the trustee is subject to an obligation of confidentiality in respect of the information, giving reasons for not providing all of the information[8].

Any creditor, who need not be the same as the creditor who asked for the information, may apply to the court within 21 days of the giving by the trustee of reasons for not providing all of the information asked for, or the expiry of the 14 days from receipt of the request, and the court may make such order as it thinks just[9].

1   Ie seven business days of receipt of the progress report where it is required by the Insolvency Rules 1986, SI 1986/1925, r 6.126 (see PARA 358), and 21 days of receipt of the report or draft report in any other case: r 6.78C(2) (r 6.78C added by SI 2010/686).
2   As to the meaning of references to creditors see PARA 253 note 2. As to secured creditors see PARAS 156, 574 et seq.
3   The Insolvency Rules 1986, SI 1986/1925, r 6.78C does not apply where the trustee is the official receiver: r 6.78C(6) (as added: see note 1).
4   Ie under the Insolvency Rules 1986, SI 1986/1925, r 6.78A(1)(f) or (g) (see PARA 383 heads (6), (7)).
5   Ie under the Insolvency Rules 1986, SI 1986/1925, r 6.78B (see PARA 384).
6   Ie a progress report required by the Insolvency Rules 1986, SI 1986/1925, r 6.126 (see PARA 358).
7   Insolvency Rules 1986, SI 1986/1925, r 6.78C(1) (as added: see note 1).
8   Insolvency Rules 1986, SI 1986/1925, r 6.78C(3) (as added: see note 1).
9   Insolvency Rules 1986, SI 1986/1925, r 6.78C(4) (as added: see note 1). Without prejudice to the generality of r 6.78C(4), the order of the court may extend the period of eight weeks or, as the case may be, four weeks provided for in r 6.142(1B) (see PARA 353) by such further period as the court thinks just: r 6.78C(5) (as so added).

386.   Distribution of property in specie.   Where there has been a distribution of property in specie to creditors[1], the trustee must comply with the following requirements in respect of any account or report which the trustee is required to prepare[2].

The trustee must:

(1)   in any account or summary of receipts and payments which is required to be included in the account or report, state the estimated value of the property distributed amongst the creditors during the period to which the account or report relates; and

(2)   as a note to the account or summary of receipts and payments, provide details of the basis of the valuation[3].

1   Ie under the Insolvency Act 1986 s 326 (see PARA 602). As to the meaning of references to creditors see PARA 253 note 2.
2   Insolvency Rules 1986, SI 1986/1925, r 6.78D(1) (r 6.78D added by SI 2010/686). This provision applies to accounts and reports prepared pursuant to any of the following: (1) the Insolvency Act 1986 s 331 (final meeting) (see PARA 616); (2) the Insolvency Rules 1986, SI 1986/1925, r 6.78A (reports to creditors) (see PARA 383); (3) r 6.78B (final report to creditors) (see PARA 384); (4) r 6.126 (creditors' meeting to receive trustee's resignation) (see PARA 358); (5) r 6.137 (final meeting of creditors) (see PARA 381).
3   Insolvency Rules 1986, SI 1986/1925, r 6.78D(2) (as added: see note 2).

(ix) Books, Accounts and Audit

387.   Duty to keep financial records; retention and delivery of records.   The trustee[1] must prepare and keep:

(1)   separate financial records in respect of each bankrupt; and

(2)   such other financial records as are required to explain the receipts and
       payments entered in the records described in head (1) above or in the
       records kept where the trustee carries on any business of the bankrupt[2],
       including an explanation of the source of any receipts and the
       destination of any payments;

and he must, subject to the provisions as to trading accounts[3], from day to day
enter in those records all the receipts and payments made by him[4].

The trustee must obtain and keep bank statements relating to any local bank
account[5] in the name of the bankrupt[6]. The trustee must submit financial records
to the creditors' committee when required for inspection[7]; and, if the committee
is not satisfied with the contents of the financial records so submitted, it may so
inform the Secretary of State, giving the reasons for its dissatisfaction, and the
Secretary of State may take such action as he thinks fit[8].

All records kept by the trustee[9] and any such records received by him from a
predecessor in that office must be retained by him for a period of six years
following his vacation of that office or, in the case of the official receiver, his
release as trustee[10], unless he delivers them to another trustee who succeeds him
in office[11]. Where the trustee is succeeded in office by another trustee, all such
records must be delivered to that successor forthwith, unless the bankruptcy is
for practical purposes complete and the successor is the official receiver, in which
case the records are only to be delivered to the official receiver if the latter so
requests[12].

1   As to the meaning of 'trustee' see PARA 24 note 2.
2   Ie under the Insolvency Regulations 1994, SI 1994/2507, reg 26: see PARA 388.
3   Ie subject to the Insolvency Rules 1986, SI 1986/1925, reg 26.
4   Insolvency Regulations 1994, SI 1994/2507, reg 24(1).
5   As to the meanings of 'local bank' and 'local bank account' see PARA 395 note 2.
6   Insolvency Regulations 1994, SI 1994/2507, reg 24(2).
7   Insolvency Regulations 1994, SI 1994/2507, reg 24(3).
8   Insolvency Regulations 1994, SI 1994/2507, reg 24(4). As to the creditors' committee see PARA
    326 et seq. As to the Secretary of State see PARA 19.
9   Ie under the Insolvency Regulations 1994, SI 1994/2507, regs 24, 26.
10 Ie under the Insolvency Act 1986 s 299: see PARAS 378–380.
11 Insolvency Regulations 1994, SI 1994/2507, reg 27(1).
12 Insolvency Regulations 1994, SI 1994/2507, reg 27(2).

388. Carrying on business. Where the trustee[1] carries on any business of the
bankrupt, he must:
(1)   keep a separate and distinct account of the trading, including, where
       appropriate, particulars of all local bank account[2] transactions; and
(2)   incorporate in the financial records required to be kept by him[3] the total
       weekly amounts of the receipts and payments made by him in relation
       to the account kept under head (1) above[4].

1   As to the meaning of 'trustee' see PARA 24 note 2.
2   As to the meanings of 'local bank' and 'local bank account' see PARA 395 note 2.
3   Ie under the Insolvency Regulations 1994, SI 1994/2507, reg 24: see PARA 387.
4   Insolvency Regulations 1994, SI 1994/2507, reg 26. As to retention and delivery of financial
    records see PARA 387; and as to production and inspection of such records see PARA 390.

389. Provision of accounts by trustee and audit of accounts. If required by
the Secretary of State at any time, the trustee[1] must send to the Secretary of State
an account of his receipts and payments as trustee of the bankrupt covering such
period as the Secretary of State may direct; and such account must, if so required
by the Secretary of State, be certified by the trustee[2].

Where the trustee vacates office prior to the holding of the final general meeting of creditors[3], he must, within 14 days of vacating office, send to the Secretary of State an account of his receipts and payments as trustee for any period not covered by an account previously so sent by him, or, if no such account has been sent, an account of his receipts and payments in respect of the whole period of his office[4].

Where a final general meeting of creditors:

(1) has been held[5]; or

(2) is deemed to have been held[6],

the trustee must send to the Secretary of State, in a case falling with head (1) above, within 14 days of the holding of that meeting and, in a case falling within head (2) above, within 14 days of his report to the court[7], an account of his receipts and payments as trustee which are not covered by any previous account so sent by him, or, if no such account has been sent, an account of his receipts and payments in respect of the whole period of his office[8].

Where a statement of affairs has been submitted under the Insolvency Act 1986, any account sent under these provisions must be accompanied by a summary of that statement of affairs and must show the amount of any assets realised and explain the reasons for any non-realisation of any assets not realised[9]. Where, however, a statement of affairs has not been submitted under the Insolvency Act 1986, any account sent under these provisions must be accompanied by a summary of all known assets and their estimated values and must show the amounts actually realised and explain the reasons for any non-realisation of any assets not realised[10].

Any account sent to the Secretary of State must, if he so requires, be audited; but, whether or not he requires the account to be audited, the trustee must send to him on demand any documents, including vouchers and bank statements, and any information relating to the account[11].

1 As to the meaning of 'trustee' see PARA 24 note 2.
2 Insolvency Regulations 1994, SI 1994/2507, reg 28(1). As to the Secretary of State see PARA 19.
3 Ie under the Insolvency Act 1986 s 331: see PARA 616.
4 Insolvency Regulations 1994, SI 1994/2507, reg 28(2).
5 See note 3.
6 Ie by virtue of the Insolvency Rules 1986, SI 1986/1925, r 6.137(5): see PARA 381.
7 Ie pursuant to Insolvency Rules 1986, SI 1986/1925, r 6.137(5).
8 Insolvency Regulations 1994, SI 1994/2507, reg 28(3).
9 Insolvency Regulations 1994, SI 1994/2507, reg 28(4).
10 Insolvency Regulations 1994, SI 1994/2507, reg 28(5).
11 Insolvency Regulations 1994, SI 1994/2507, reg 28(6).

390. Production and inspection of records. The trustee[1] must produce on demand to the Secretary of State, and allow him to inspect, any accounts, books and other records kept by the trustee, including any passed to him by a predecessor in office; and this duty to produce and inspect extends:

(1) to producing and allowing inspection at the premises of the trustee; and

(2) to producing and allowing inspection of any financial records[2] prepared by the trustee before 24 October 1994[3] and kept by him;

and any such demand may:

(a) require the trustee to produce any such accounts, books or other records to the Secretary of State, and allow him to inspect them at the same time as any account is sent to the Secretary of State[4] or at any time after such an account is sent to the Secretary of State, whether or not the Secretary of State requires the account to be audited; or

(b)   where it is made for the purpose of ascertaining whether the provisions[5] relating to the handling of money received by the trustee in the course of carrying out his functions have been, or are likely to be, complied with, be made at any time, whether or not an account has been sent, or should have been sent, to the Secretary of State[6] and whether or not the Secretary of State has required any account to be audited[7].

The trustee must allow the Secretary of State on demand to remove and take copies of any accounts, books and other records kept by the trustee, including any passed to him by a predecessor in office, whether or not they are kept at the premises of the trustee[8].

1   As to the meaning of 'trustee' see PARA 28 note 2.
2   Ie any financial records of the kind described in the Insolvency Regulations 1986, SI 1994/2507, reg 24(1)(b): see PARA 387 head (2).
3   Ie the date on which the Insolvency Regulations 1994, SI 1994/2507, came into force: see reg 1.
4   Ie under the Insolvency Regulations 1994, SI 1994/2507, reg 28: see PARA 389.
5   Ie any provisions of the Insolvency Regulations 1994, SI 1994/2507.
6   See note 4.
7   Insolvency Regulations 1994, SI 1994/2507, reg 29(1). As to the Secretary of State see PARA 19.
8   Insolvency Regulations 1994, SI 1994/2507, reg 29(2).

391.   Provision of information by trustee.   The trustee[1] must, within 14 days of the receipt of a request from the bankrupt or any creditor for a statement of his receipts and payments as trustee, supply free of charge to the person making the request, a statement of his receipts and payments as trustee during the period of one year ending on the most recent anniversary of his becoming trustee which preceded the request[2].

1   As to the meaning of 'trustee' see PARA 24 note 2.
2   Insolvency Regulations 1994, SI 1994/2507, reg 25.

392.   Disposal of insolvent's books, papers and other records.   The trustee[1], on the authorisation of the official receiver, during his tenure of office or on vacating office, or the official receiver while acting as trustee[2], may at any time sell, destroy or otherwise dispose of the books, papers and other records of the bankrupt[3].

1   As to the meaning of 'trustee' see PARA 24 note 2.
2   See PARA 321.
3   Insolvency Regulations 1994, SI 1994/2507, reg 30. As to the records to be kept by all insolvency practitioners see COMPANY AND PARTNERSHIP INSOLVENCY vol 16 (2011) PARA 50 et seq.

(x) Banking Accounts

393.   Payments into the Insolvency Services Account.   Subject to the provisions relating to local bank accounts where the trustee[1] exercises the power to carry on the business of the bankrupt[2], the trustee must pay all money received by him in the course of carrying out his functions as such without any deduction into the Insolvency Services Account[3] kept by the Secretary of State with the Bank of England to the credit of the bankrupt once every 14 days or forthwith if £5,000 or more has been received[4].

Every such payment of money into the Insolvency Services Account must be:
(1)   made through the Bank Giro System; or
(2)   sent direct to the Bank of England, Threadneedle Street, London EC2R

8AH, by cheque drawn in favour of the 'Insolvency Services Account' and crossed 'A/c payee only' 'Bank of England'; or

(3) made by electronic transfer;

and the trustee must on request be given by the Department for Business, Innovation and Skills a receipt for the money so paid[5].

Every payment of money made under heads (1) and (2) above must be accompanied by a form obtainable from that Department for that purpose or by a form that is substantially similar; and every payment of money made under head (3) above must specify the name of the trustee making the payment and the name of the bankrupt to whose credit such payment is made[6].

1 As to the meaning of 'trustee' see PARA 24 note 2.
2 Ie those contained in the Insolvency Regulations 1994, SI 1994/2507, reg 21: see PARA 395.
3 As to the Insolvency Services Account see PARA 22.
4 Insolvency Regulations 1994, SI 1994/2507, reg 20(1).
5 Insolvency Regulations 1994, SI 1994/2507, regs 3(3), 20(2) (reg 3(3) amended by SI 2009/2748; the Insolvency Regulations 1994, SI 1994/2507, reg 20(2) substituted by SI 2000/485).
6 Insolvency Regulations 1994, SI 1994/2507, reg 20(3) (amended by SI 2000/485).

394. Payment of disbursements etc out of the Insolvency Services Account.
The trustee[1] must[2], on application to the Department for Business, Innovation and Skills on a form obtainable from that Department or on a form which is substantially similar:

(1) be repaid all necessary disbursements made by him, and expenses properly incurred by him, in the course of his administration to the date of his vacation of office out of any money standing to the credit of the bankrupt in the Insolvency Services Account[3];

(2) obtain payment instruments to the order of the payee for sums which become payable on account of the bankrupt for delivery by the trustee to the persons to whom the payments are to be made[4].

In respect of an application made by the trustee under heads (1) or (2) above, the Secretary of State, if requested to do so by the trustee, may, however, at his discretion:

(a) make the payment which is the subject of the application to the trustee by electronic transfer; or

(b) as an alternative to the issue of payment instruments, make payment by electronic transfer to the persons to whom the trustee would otherwise deliver payment instruments[5].

On the trustee vacating office, he must be repaid by any succeeding trustee, out of any funds available for the purpose, any necessary disbursements made by him and any expenses properly incurred by him but not repaid before he vacates office[6].

1 As to the meaning of 'trustee' see PARA 24 note 2.
2 Ie subject to the Insolvency Regulations 1994, SI 1994/2507, reg 22(2A): reg 22(A1) (added by SI 2000/485).
3 Insolvency Regulations 1994, SI 1994/2507, reg 22(1), (3). As to the Insolvency Services Account see PARA 22. Any application to be made to the Secretary of State or to the Department or anything required to be sent to the Secretary of State or to the Department under the Insolvency Regulations 1994, SI 1994/2507, must be addressed to the Department for Business, Innovation and Skills, The Insolvency Service, PO Box 3690, Birmingham B2 4UY: reg 3(3) (amended by SI 2009/2748).
4 Insolvency Regulations 1994, SI 1994/2507, reg 22(2), (3).
5 Insolvency Regulations 1994, SI 1994/2507, reg 22(2A) (added by SI 2000/485).
6 Insolvency Regulations 1994, SI 1994/2507, reg 22(4).

395. Local bank account. Where the trustee[1] intends to exercise his power to carry on the business of the bankrupt, he may apply to the Secretary of State for authorisation to open a local bank account[2]; and the Secretary of State may authorise him to make his payments into and out of a specified bank, subject to a limit, instead of into and out of the Insolvency Services Account[3] if satisfied that an administrative advantage will be derived from having such an account[4]. Money received by a trustee relating to the purpose for which the account was opened may be paid into the local bank account to the credit of the bankrupt to whom the account relates[5]. Where a trustee opens a local bank account pursuant to an authorisation granted by the Secretary of State[6], he must open and maintain the account in the name of the bankrupt[7]. Where money which does not form part of the bankrupt's estate is provided to the trustee for a specific purpose, it must be clearly identifiable in a separate account[8].

Every trustee must keep proper records, including documentary evidence of all money paid into and out of every local bank account opened and maintained under these provisions[9]. The trustee must pay[10] without deduction any surplus over any authorised limit[11] into the Insolvency Services Account[12].

As soon as the trustee ceases to carry on the business of the bankrupt or vacates office or an authorisation given by the Secretary of State[13] is withdrawn, he must close the account and remit[14] any balance to the Insolvency Services Account[15].

1 As to the meaning of 'trustee' see PARA 24 note 2.
2 For these purposes, 'local bank account' means a current account opened with a local bank; and 'local bank' means any bank in, or in the neighbourhood of, the insolvency district in which the proceedings are taken or in the locality in which any business of the bankrupt is carried on: Insolvency Regulations 1994, SI 1994/2507, reg 3(1). 'Bank' means: (1) a person who has permission under the Financial Services and Markets Act 2000 to accept deposits; or (2) an EEA firm of the kind mentioned in s 31(1)(b), Sch 3 para 5(b) which has permission under Sch 3 para 15 as a result of qualifying for authorisation under Sch 3 para 12(1) to accept deposits: Insolvency Regulations 1994, SI 1994/2507, reg 3(1) (definition substituted by SI 2001/3649).
3 As to payments into and out of the Insolvency Services Account see PARAS 393, 394 respectively; and as to the Insolvency Services Account see PARA 22.
4 Insolvency Regulations 1994, SI 1994/2507, reg 21(1). As to the Secretary of State see PARA 19.
5 Insolvency Regulations 1994, SI 1994/2507, reg 21(2).
6 Ie pursuant to an authorisation granted under the Insolvency Regulations 1994, SI 1994/2507, reg 21(1).
7 Insolvency Regulations 1994, SI 1994/2507, reg 21(3).
8 Insolvency Regulations 1994, SI 1994/2507, reg 21(4).
9 Insolvency Regulations 1994, SI 1994/2507, reg 21(5). As to the financial records to be maintained by a responsible insolvency practitioner carrying on the business of the insolvent see PARA 387.
10 Ie in accordance with the Insolvency Regulations 1994, SI 1994/2507, reg 20(1): see PARA 393.
11 Ie any limit imposed by an authorisation granted under the Insolvency Regulations 1994, SI 1994/2507, reg 21(1).
12 Insolvency Regulations 1994, SI 1994/2507, reg 21(6).
13 See note 6.
14 See note 10.
15 Insolvency Regulations 1994, SI 1994/2507, reg 21(7).

396. Claiming money paid into the Insolvency Services Account. Any person claiming to be entitled to any money paid into the Insolvency Services Account[1] may apply to the Secretary of State for payment and must provide such evidence of the claim as the Secretary of State may require[2].

Any person dissatisfied with the decision of the Secretary of State in respect of his claim made under the above provisions may appeal to the court[3].

1   As to the Insolvency Services Account see PARA 26.
2   Insolvency Regulations 1994, SI 1994/2507, reg 32(1).
3   Insolvency Regulations 1994, SI 1994/2507, reg 32(2). As to the procedure on appeal see PARA 769.

(6) ADMINISTRATION OF BANKRUPT'S ESTATE; TRUSTEE'S POWERS; PROPERTY AVAILABLE FOR CREDITORS

(i) Vesting of Property in Trustee

397. In general. The object of bankruptcy law is that all the property comprised in the bankrupt's estate[1] should be realised by the trustee in bankruptcy and divided among the bankrupt's creditors[2]. Subject to certain statutory exceptions, the bankrupt's estate comprises:

(1)   all property belonging to or vested in the bankrupt at the commencement of the bankruptcy[3]; and

(2)   any property which is comprised in that estate or is treated as falling within head (1) above[4].

Property or other interests which the bankrupt acquires after the commencement of the bankruptcy do not form part of his estate unless, in certain circumstances, the trustee claims the property or other interest for the estate[5].

1   As to the meaning of 'the bankrupt's estate' see PARA 211.
2   See *Smith v Coffin* (1795) 2 Hy Bl 444 at 461; *Gibson v Carruthers* (1841) 8 M & W 321 at 333; *Re Thomas, ex p IRC v Falconer* [1984] 1 WLR 232, CA (rescission of an order dismissing a creditor's petition where the dismissal would have deprived the general body of creditors of the debtor's available assets). See also *Hollinshed v Hazleton* [1916] 1 AC 428 at 436, HL ('There is [a] principle of public policy ... that in bankruptcy the entire property of the bankrupt, of whatever kind or nature it be, whether alienable or inalienable, subject to be taken in execution, legal or equitable, or not so subject, shall, with the exception of some compassionate allowances for his maintenance, be appropriated and made available for the payment of his creditors'). Under the Insolvency Act 1986 after-acquired property does not automatically vest in the trustee (see PARA 458 et seq), but a trustee will in the proper discharge of his duties usually claim for the bankrupt's estate any after-acquired property of significant value.
3   As to the commencement of bankruptcy see PARA 209.
4   See the Insolvency Act 1986 s 283; and PARA 211.
5   See PARA 458 et seq.

398. Vesting of bankrupt's estate. The bankrupt's estate[1] vests in the trustee immediately on his appointment taking effect[2] or, in the case of the official receiver, on his becoming trustee[3]. Where any property which is, or is to be, comprised in the bankrupt's estate vests in the trustee[4], it so vests without any conveyance, assignment or transfer[5]. In the case of real estate situated outside the United Kingdom, the property may pass only according to the law of the place where it is situated[6]. Where the bankrupt is the proprietor of any registered land or charge, his trustee is entitled to be registered as proprietor in the place of the bankrupt on production of evidence that the land or charge is comprised in the bankrupt's estate[7].

1   As to the meaning of 'the bankrupt's estate' see PARA 211.
2   As to when the trustee's appointment takes effect see PARAS 318–320.
3   Insolvency Act 1986 s 306(1). In the case of the administration in bankruptcy of the insolvent estate of a deceased person dying before the presentation of a bankruptcy petition, s 306 applies:

Administration of Insolvent Estates of Deceased Persons Order 1986, SI 1986/1999, art 3(1), Sch 1 Pt II para 21. As to the administration in bankruptcy of the insolvent estates of deceased persons see further PARA 830 et seq.

4   Ie whether under the Insolvency Act 1986 s 306 or under any other provision of Pt 9 (ss 264–371).

5   Insolvency Act 1986 s 306(2). The bankrupt's entitlement to a residuary estate vests in the trustee who then becomes entitled to receive the assets representing the residuary estate as and when administration of estate is complete, in priority to the executor: *Re Hemming; Raymond Saul & Co (a' firm) v Holden* [2008] EWHC 2731 (Ch), [2009] Ch 313, [2009] 2 WLR 1257.

6   *Re Boustead, ex p Rogers* (1881) 16 ChD 665, CA; *Callender, Sykes & Co v Lagos Colonial Secretary and Davies* [1891] AC 460, PC; Case C-294/92 *Webb v Webb* [1994] QB 696, [1994] 3 All ER 911, ECJ; *Re Hayward* [1997] Ch 45, [1997] 1 All ER 32; *Ashurst v Pollard* [2001] Ch 595, [2001] 2 All ER 75, CA. By the rules of private international law, immovable property may be transferred only in accordance with the lex situs: see CONFLICT OF LAWS vol 19 (2011) PARA 695 et seq. See further PARA 412.

7   See the Land Registration Rules 2003, SI 2003/1417, r 168; and REAL PROPERTY AND REGISTRATION vol 87 (2012) PARA 235 et seq. As to when a trustee in bankruptcy vacates his office see r 169. As to the interests subject to which the trustee holds see PARA 406. As to the severance of a joint tenancy and the vesting of property in a trustee see *Re Dennis (a bankrupt)* [1996] Ch 80, [1995] 3 All ER 171, CA; *Re Palmer (a debtor)* [1994] Ch 316, [1994] 3 All ER 835, CA; and see PARA 840.

399.   Property subject to restraint order.   Where: (1) property is excluded from the bankrupt's estate by virtue of a restraint order[1]; (2) a receiver or administrator has not been appointed by order under the Proceeds of Crime Act 2002[2] in respect of the property; and (3) the restraint order is discharged[3], then on the discharge of the restraint order the property vests in the trustee as part of the bankrupt's estate[4]. However, this does not apply to the proceeds of property realised by a management receiver[5] to meet the receiver's remuneration and expenses[6].

1   Ie an order under the Proceeds of Crime Act 2002 s 417(2)(a) (see SENTENCING AND DISPOSITION OF OFFENDERS vol 92 (2010) PARA 424).

2   Ie an order under the Proceeds of Crime Act 2002 ss 50, 67A, 128, 131A, 198 or 215A (see SENTENCING AND DISPOSITION OF OFFENDERS vol 92 (2010) PARAS 439, 451).

3   Insolvency Act 1986 s 306A(1) (added by the Proceeds of Crime Act 2002 s 456, Sch 11 paras 1, 16; and amended by the Serious Crime Act 2007 s 74(2)(g), Sch 8 Pt 7 para 151, Sch 14). As from a day to be appointed, a further requirement is added that immediately after the discharge of the restraint order the property is not detained under or by virtue of the Proceeds of Crime Act 2002 ss 44A, 47J, 122A, 127J, 193A or 195J (not yet in force): see the Insolvency Act 1986 s 306A(1) (prospectively amended by the Policing and Crime Act 2009 s 112, Sch 7 Pt 6 paras 53, 54, Sch 8 Pt 4). At the date at which this volume states the law no such day had been appointed.

4   Insolvency Act 1986 s 306A(2) (as added: see note 3). As from a day to be appointed, s 306A(2) is substituted by the Policing and Crime Act 2009 Sch 7 Pt 6 paras 53, 54, to remove the wording 'on the discharge of the restraint order'. At the date at which this volume states the law no such day had been appointed.

5   Ie under the Proceeds of Crime Act 2002 s 49(2)(d) or s 197(2)(d) (see SENTENCING AND DISPOSITION OF OFFENDERS vol 92 (2010) PARA 438).

6   Insolvency Act 1986 s 306A(3) (as added: see note 3).

400.   Property released from detention.   As from a day to be appointed, where property is excluded from the bankrupt's estate by virtue of the Proceeds of Crime Act 2002[1], no order is in force in respect of the property[2], and the property is released, then the property vests in the trustee as part of the bankrupt's estate[3].

1   Ie under the Proceeds of Crime Act 2002 s 417(2)(b) (see SENTENCING AND DISPOSITION OF OFFENDERS vol 92 (2010) PARA 424).

2   Ie under the Proceeds of Crime Act 2002 ss 41, 50, 120, 128, 190 or 198 (see SENTENCING AND DISPOSITION OF OFFENDERS vol 92 (2010) PARA 424).

3   Insolvency Act 1986 s 306AA(1), (2) (added as from a day to be appointed by the Policing and Crime Act 2009 s 112(1), Sch 7 Pt 6 paras 53, 55). At the date at which this volume states the law no such day had been appointed.

401.   Property in respect of which a receivership or administration order has been made.   Where:

   (1)   property is excluded from the bankrupt's estate by virtue of the Proceeds of Crime Act 2002[1], being property in respect of which an order for the appointment of a receiver or administrator under certain provisions of that Act is in force;

   (2)   a confiscation order is made[2];

   (3)   the amount payable under the confiscation order is fully paid; and

   (4)   any of the property remains in the hands of the receiver or administrator, as the case may be,

the property vests in the trustee as part of the bankrupt's estate[3].

1   Ie by virtue of the Proceeds of Crime Act 2002 s 417(2)(b), (c) or (d) (see SENTENCING AND DISPOSITION OF OFFENDERS vol 92 (2010) PARA 424). As from a day to be appointed, this provision is amended to refer only to s 417(2)(c): see the Insolvency Act 1986 s 306B (prospectively amended by the Policing and Crime Act 2009 s 112(1), Sch 7 Pt 6 paras 53, 56). At the date at which this volume states the law no such day had been appointed.

2   Ie under the Proceeds of Crime Act 2002 ss 6, 92 or 156 (see SENTENCING AND DISPOSITION OF OFFENDERS vol 92 (2010) PARA 391).

3   Insolvency Act 1986 s 306B(1), (2) (added by the Proceeds of Crime Act 2002 s 456, Sch 11 paras 1, 16).

402.   Property in respect of which realisation order made.   As from a day to be appointed, where:

   (1)   property is excluded from the bankrupt's estate by virtue of the Proceeds of Crime Act 2002[1], being property in respect of which an order has been made authorising realisation of the property by an appropriate officer;

   (2)   a confiscation order is made[2];

   (3)   the amount payable under the confiscation order is fully paid; and

   (4)   any of the property remains in the hands of the appropriate officer,

the property vests in the trustee as part of the bankrupt's estate[3].

1   Ie by virtue of the Proceeds of Crime Act 2002 s 417(2)(d) (see SENTENCING AND DISPOSITION OF OFFENDERS vol 92 (2010) PARA 424).

2   Ie under the Proceeds of Crime Act 2002 ss 6, 92 or 156 (see SENTENCING AND DISPOSITION OF OFFENDERS vol 92 (2010) PARA 391).

3   Insolvency Act 1986 s 306BA(1), (2) (added as from a day to be appointed by the Policing and Crime Act 2009 s 112(1), Sch 7 Pt 6 paras 53, 57). At the date at which this volume states the law no such day had been appointed.

403.   Property subject to certain orders where confiscation order discharged or quashed.   Where:

   (1)   property is excluded from the bankrupt's estate by virtue of the Proceeds of Crime Act 2002[1];

   (2)   a confiscation order is made[2]; and

   (3)   the confiscation order is discharged[3] or quashed under that Act or in pursuance of any enactment relating to appeals against conviction or sentence,

any such property in the hands of a receiver[4] or an administrator[5] appointed under that Act vests in the trustee as part of the bankrupt's estate[6].

However, this does not apply to the proceeds of property realised by a management receiver[7] to meet the receiver's remuneration and expenses[8].

1 Ie by virtue of the Proceeds of Crime Act 2002 s 417(2)(a), (b), (c) or (d) (see SENTENCING AND DISPOSITION OF OFFENDERS vol 92 (2010) PARA 424).

2 Ie under the Proceeds of Crime Act 2002 ss 6, 92 or 156 (see SENTENCING AND DISPOSITION OF OFFENDERS vol 92 (2010) PARA 391).

3 Ie under the Proceeds of Crime Act 2002 ss 30, 114 or 180 (see SENTENCING AND DISPOSITION OF OFFENDERS vol 92 (2010) PARA 416).

4 Ie a receiver appointed under the Proceeds of Crime Act 2002 Pt 2 (ss 6–91) or Pt 4 (ss 156–239) (see SENTENCING AND DISPOSITION OF OFFENDERS vol 92 (2010) PARA 391 et seq).

5 Ie an administrator appointed under the Proceeds of Crime Act 2002 Pt 3 (ss 92–155).

6 Insolvency Act 1986 s 306C(1), (2) (added by the Proceeds of Crime Act 2002 s 456, Sch 11 paras 1, 16). As from a day to be appointed, the Insolvency Act 1986 s 306C(1)(a) (see head (1) in the text) is amended, and s 306C(2) is substituted to include mention of property in the hands of an appropriate officer: see s 306C(1), (2) (prospectively amended and substituted by the Policing and Crime Act 2009 s 112(1), Sch 7 Pt 6 paras 53, 58). At the date at which this volume states the law no such day had been appointed.

7 Ie under the Proceeds of Crime Act 2002 s 49(2)(d) or s 197(2)(d) (see SENTENCING AND DISPOSITION OF OFFENDERS vol 92 (2010) PARA 438).

8 Insolvency Act 1986 s 306C(3) (as added: see note 6).

404. Items of excess value. Where property is excluded from the bankrupt's estate[1], and it appears to the trustee that the realisable value of the whole or any part of that property exceeds the cost of a reasonable replacement[2] for that property or that part of it, the trustee may[3] by notice in writing claim that property or, as the case may be, that part of it for the bankrupt's estate[4]. However, except with the permission of the court, such a notice may not be served after the end of the period of 42 days beginning with the day on which the property in question first came to the knowledge of the trustee[5].

On the service on the bankrupt of such a notice, the property to which the notice relates vests in the trustee as part of the bankrupt's estate; and, except against a purchaser in good faith, for value and without notice of the bankruptcy, the trustee's title to that property has relation back to the commencement of the bankruptcy[6].

The trustee must apply the funds comprised in the estate to the purchase by or on behalf of the bankrupt of a reasonable replacement for any property vested in the trustee under the above provisions; and the duty imposed by the above provisions has priority over the obligation of the trustee to distribute the estate[7]. A purchase of replacement property may be made either before or after the realisation by the trustee of the value of the property vesting in him[8]. The trustee is, however, under no obligation to apply funds to the purchase of a replacement for property vested in him, unless and until he has sufficient funds in the estate for that purpose[9].

Where a third party proposes to the trustee that he, the third party, should provide the estate with a sum of money enabling the bankrupt to be left in possession of property which would otherwise be made to vest in the trustee, the trustee may accept that proposal, if satisfied that it is a reasonable one, and that the estate will benefit to the extent of the value of the property in question less the cost of a reasonable replacement[10].

1 Ie by virtue of the Insolvency Act 1986 s 283(2) (tools of trade, household effects etc): see PARA 211.

2 For the purposes of the Insolvency Act 1986 s 308, property is a reasonable replacement for other property if it is reasonably adequate for meeting the needs met by the other property: s 308(4).

3 Ie subject to the Insolvency Act 1986 s 309: see the text and note 5.

4 Insolvency Act 1986 s 308(1) (amended by the Housing Act 1988 s 140(1), Sch 17 para 73). In the case of the administration in bankruptcy of the insolvent estate of a deceased person dying before the presentation of a bankruptcy petition, the Insolvency Act 1986 s 308 applies: Administration of Insolvent Estates of Deceased Persons Order 1986, SI 1986/1999, art 3(1), Sch 1 Pt II para 23. As to the administration in bankruptcy of the insolvent estates of deceased persons see further PARA 823 et seq.

5 Insolvency Act 1986 s 309(1)(b). For these purposes: (1) anything which comes to the knowledge of the trustee is deemed in relation to any successor of his as trustee to have come to the knowledge of the successor at the same time; and (2) anything which comes, otherwise than under head (1), to the knowledge of a person before he is the trustee is deemed to come to his knowledge on his appointment taking effect or, in the case of the official receiver, on his becoming trustee: s 309(2).

   In the case of the administration in bankruptcy of the insolvent estate of a deceased person dying before the presentation of a bankruptcy petition, s 309 applies: Administration of Insolvent Estates of Deceased Persons Order 1986 Sch 1 Pt II para 23.

6 Insolvency Act 1986 s 308(2). As to the commencement of bankruptcy see PARA 209.

7 Insolvency Act 1986 s 308(3). See *Re Rayatt (a bankrupt)* [1998] 2 FLR 264, [1998] BPIR 495 (trustee not entitled to set off cost of reasonable replacement against bankrupt's arrears under an income payments order).

8 Insolvency Rules 1986, SI 1986/1925, r 6.187(1).

9 Insolvency Rules 1986, SI 1986/1925, r 6.187(2).

10 Insolvency Rules 1986, SI 1986/1925, r 6.188(1), (2).

405. Tenancies. On the service on the bankrupt by the trustee of a notice in writing[1], any tenancy:

(1) which is excluded[2] from the bankrupt's estate; and

(2) to which the notice relates,

vests in the trustee as part of the bankrupt's estate, and, except against a purchaser in good faith, for value and without notice of the bankruptcy, the trustee's title to that tenancy has relation back to the commencement of the bankruptcy[3].

However, except with the permission of the court, such a notice may not be served after the end of the period of 42 days beginning with the day on which the tenancy in question first came to the knowledge of the trustee[4].

1 Ie under the Insolvency Act 1986 s 308A.

2 Ie by virtue of the Insolvency Act 1986 s 283(3A): see PARA 211 heads (e)–(h).

3 Insolvency Act 1986 s 308A (added by the Housing Act 1988 s 117(2)). As to the commencement of the bankruptcy see PARA 209. In the case of the administration in bankruptcy of the insolvent estate of a deceased person dying before the presentation of a bankruptcy petition, s 308A applies: Administration of Insolvent Estates of Deceased Persons Order 1986, SI 1986/1999, art 3(1), Sch 1 Pt II para 23. As to the administration in bankruptcy of the insolvent estates of deceased persons see further PARA 830 et seq.

4 Insolvency Act 1986 s 309(1)(b) (amended by the Housing Act 1988 s 117(3)). For these purposes: (1) anything which comes to the knowledge of the trustee is deemed in relation to any successor of his as trustee to have come to the knowledge of the successor at the same time; and (2) anything which comes, otherwise than under head (1), to the knowledge of a person before he is the trustee is deemed to come to his knowledge on his appointment taking effect or, in the case of the official receiver, on his becoming trustee: Insolvency Act 1986 s 309(2). As to the extension of the time limit referred to in the text see s 376 (see PARA 498 note 2); and *Solomons v Williams* [2001] BPIR 1123, [2001] All ER (D) 299 (May); *Franses v Oomerjee* [2005] BPIR 1320.

   As to the application of s 309 in the case of the administration in bankruptcy of the insolvent estate of a deceased person dying before the presentation of a bankruptcy petition see PARA 404 note 5.

406. Title acquired by trustee. The general rule is that the trustee in bankruptcy takes no better title to property than the bankrupt himself had[1]. The bankrupt's property passes to the trustee in the same plight and condition in which it was in the bankrupt's hands, and is subject to all the equities[2] and liabilities[3] which affected it in the bankrupt's hands, to all dispositions which have been validly made by the bankrupt, and to all rights which have been validly acquired by third persons at the commencement of the bankruptcy[4].

If the bankrupt is possessed of an unincumbered estate in fee simple, that estate passes to the trustee; if he has an entailed interest or life interest[5], the trustee has that interest and no more. Where the trustee has been registered as the proprietor of any registered land or charge, he holds it on the trusts and subject to any minor interests under which the bankrupt held it[6].

1 *Bendall v McWhirter* [1952] 2 QB 466 at 487, [1952] 1 All ER 1307 at 1317, CA, per Romer LJ, who approved the proposition stated in the text to notes 2–4. Although the application to the facts of the case of the principle stated in the text, for the purposes of conferring on the deserted wife of a bankrupt a 'status of irremovability' with respect to the matrimonial home, which was binding on the husband's trustee in bankruptcy, was overruled in *National Provincial Bank Ltd v Ainsworth* [1965] AC 1175, [1965] 2 All ER 472, HL, the speeches in the House of Lords treat the principle as correctly stated and as unimpaired: see eg per Lord Wilberforce at 1256–1258 and at 499–501. See also note 3. As to the rights of a spouse or civil partner to occupy the matrimonial home see PARAS 672, 673.

2 *Re Scheibler, ex p Holthausen* (1874) 9 Ch App 722; *Re Garrud, ex p Newitt* (1881) 16 ChD 522 at 531, CA; *Re Wallis, ex p Jenks* [1902] 1 KB 719; *Re Clark, ex p Beardmore* [1894] 2 QB 393 at 410, CA; *Re Beeston, ex p Board of Trade* [1899] 1 QB 626 at 630, CA; *Re Wait* [1927] 1 Ch 606 at 629, CA. Thus, a statutory assignee, who first gives notice of his title to the trustees of a fund, obtains no priority by so doing over assignees for value, nor even over a prior statutory assignee, who may not have given notice: *Re Anderson, ex p New Zealand Official Assignee* [1911] 1 KB 896. The title of a trustee to goods which he finds in the bankrupt's possession is subject to the rights of third parties, including any right of the vendors of the goods to disaffirm the contract: *Re Eastgate, ex p Ward* [1905] 1 KB 465; *Tilley v Bowman Ltd* [1910] 1 KB 745. Property which the bankrupt before bankruptcy has affected to sell by a colourable transaction will be divisible among his creditors on bankruptcy: *Re Hirth, ex p Trustee* [1899] 1 QB 612, CA. Money paid into court before bankruptcy in an action brought against the bankrupt is specifically fixed with the claimant's equities, and the trustee has no rights over it except subject to such equities: *Hitchens v Congreve* (1831) Mont 225; *Murray v Arnold* (1862) 3 B & S 287; *Re Keyworth, ex p Banner* (1874) 9 Ch App 379.

   A trustee may be bound by, or rely upon, estoppels which have arisen against the bankrupt: *Shierson v Rastogi* [2007] EWHC 1266 (Ch), [2007] BPIR 891, [2007] All ER (D) 446 (May).

   As to property held by the bankrupt in trust see the Insolvency Act 1986 s 283(3)(a); and PARA 211 head (c). See also PARA 441 et seq.

3 As to liabilities incumbent on the trustee in bankruptcy see note 4. In *Bradley-Hole v Cusen* [1953] 1 QB 300, sub nom *Hole v Cuzen* [1953] 1 All ER 87, CA, a tenant was held entitled to deduct, from rent payable to his landlord's trustee in bankruptcy, rent previously overpaid by him to his landlord, pursuant to the Increase of Rent and Mortgage Interest (Restrictions) Act 1920 s 14(1) (repealed); that case, though following *Bendall v McWhirter* [1952] 2 QB 466, [1952] 1 All ER 1307, CA, which was overruled in *National Provincial Bank Ltd v Ainsworth* [1965] AC 1175, [1965] 2 All ER 472, HL, was itself treated by the House of Lords in *National Provincial Bank Ltd v Ainsworth* at 1222, 1258 and at 478, 500, 501 as correctly decided.

4 The trustee takes the bankrupt's property subject to all liens and contingent liabilities. Thus, where a person arrested was found in possession of money, and before conviction he was adjudged bankrupt, and on his conviction the money found on him was ordered to be applied towards the costs of the prosecution, the order was held to be valid, notwithstanding the intervening bankruptcy: *R v Roberts* (1873) LR 9 QB 77. In *Re Pascoe* [1944] Ch 219, [1944] 1 All ER 281, CA, however, where money, acquired by a bankrupt after his bankruptcy, was in the hands of the police and after his conviction the criminal court by order applied this money towards the costs of the prosecution, the Court of Appeal held that that order was ineffective to deprive the trustee of the money.

   A trustee is bound by the bankrupt's acknowledgments except in the exercise of his powers to admit or reject proofs: *London and Westminster Bank v Button* (1907) 51 Sol Jo 466; but cf *Re Van Laun, ex p Chatterton* [1907] 2 KB 23, CA; and see PARA 507 et seq.

Property, possession of which has been obtained by the bankrupt by fraud or mistake, does not pass to the bankrupt, and remains in the original owner: *Gladstone v Hadwen* (1813) 1 M & S 517; *Load v Green* (1846) 15 M & W 216 at 221; *Re Shackleton, ex p Whittaker* (1875) 10 Ch App 446; *Re Reed, ex p Barnett* (1876) 3 ChD 123; and see *Re Eastgate, ex p Ward* [1905] 1 KB 465; *Tilley v Bowman Ltd* [1910] 1 KB 745. However, the position is different where the bankrupt, having a voidable title to goods, has disposed of them to a bona fide purchaser without notice before the title has been avoided: see the Sale of Goods Act 1979 s 23; and SALE OF GOODS AND SUPPLY OF SERVICES vol 91 (2012) PARA 152 et seq. As to rights arising out of contracts made by the bankrupt see PARA 430.

5   As to the trustee's rights over the bankrupt's estate tail see PARA 479 head (7); as to the legal estate in settled land or property held on trust see PARA 442; and as to the rights of an assignee from the trustee in bankruptcy of an equitable life interest in real estate to be let into possession of the rents and profits see *Re Hunt, Pollard v Greake* [1900] WN 65; on appeal 36 LJNC 362, CA. Since 1 January 1997 it is no longer possible to create any new entailed interests: see REAL PROPERTY AND REGISTRATION vol 87 (2012) PARA 114.

6   See PARA 398.

407. Property exempt from vesting in trustee.

Certain allowances, pensions and other statutory benefits are expressly declared by the statutes creating them[1] to be inalienable and to be incapable of vesting in the trustee in bankruptcy or other representative of the creditors of the person to whom the payment is to be made[2].

Where a bankruptcy order is made against a person on a petition presented on or after 29 May 2000, any rights he has under an approved pension arrangement are excluded from his estate[3].

Where a person is adjudged bankrupt in England and Wales:

(1)   property for the time being subject to a freezing order[4], or an order having the like effect in Scotland, made before the order adjudging him bankrupt; and

(2)   any proceeds of property realised by a receiver appointed by the High Court for the time being in the hands of a receiver so appointed,

are excluded from the bankrupt's estate[5].

1   See PARA 211 note 33.

2   As to whether the trustee may make an application for an income payments order in respect of such payments see PARA 462 et seq.

3   See the Welfare Reform and Pensions Act 1999 s 11(1); the Occupational and Personal Pension Schemes (Bankruptcy) (No 2) Regulations 2002, SI 2002/836; and PERSONAL AND OCCUPATIONAL PENSIONS vol 80 (2013) PARA 285. As to the meaning of 'approved pension arrangement' see PERSONAL AND OCCUPATIONAL PENSIONS vol 80 (2013) PARA 285.
    The Secretary of State may by regulations make provision for or in connection with enabling rights of a person under an unapproved pension arrangement to be excluded from a bankrupt's estate: see the Welfare Reform and Pensions Act 1999 s 12(1); and PERSONAL AND OCCUPATIONAL PENSIONS vol 80 (2013) PARA 286. See the Occupational and Personal Pension Schemes (Bankruptcy) (No 2) Regulations 2002, SI 2002/836; and PERSONAL AND OCCUPATIONAL PENSIONS vol 80 (2013) PARA 286.
    As to the recovery of excessive pension contributions made by persons who have become bankrupt see PARA 693 et seq.
    As to the vesting in the trustee of pension rights not exempted by the foregoing provisions see *Krasner v Dennison, Lawrence v Lesser* [2001] Ch 76, [2000] 3 All ER 234, CA; *Patel v Jones* [2001] EWCA Civ 779, [2001] BPIR 919.

4   As to the making of freezing orders generally see the International Criminal Court Act 2001 s 38, Sch 6; and INTERNATIONAL RELATIONS LAW vol 61 (2010) PARA 449.

5   See the International Criminal Court Act 2001 Sch 6 para 9(1); and INTERNATIONAL RELATIONS LAW vol 61 (2010) PARA 449. Where an insolvency practitioner seizes or disposes of property which is subject to a freezing order and he reasonably believes that he is entitled to do so in the exercise of his functions and he would be so entitled if the property were not subject to a freezing order, the insolvency practitioner is not liable to any person in respect of any loss or

damage resulting from the seizure or disposal, except in so far as the loss or damage is caused by his negligence: see Sch 6 para 13(1), (2); and INTERNATIONAL RELATIONS LAW vol 61 (2010) PARA 449.

408. Bankrupt's documents and records. The trustee must take possession of all books, papers and other records which relate to the bankrupt's estate[1] or affairs[2] and which belong to him or are in his possession or under his control, including any which would be privileged from disclosure in any proceedings[3].

The bankrupt must deliver up to the trustee possession of any property, books, papers or other records of which he has possession or control and of which the trustee is required to take possession[4]. If any of the following is in possession of any property, books, papers or other records of which the trustee is required to take possession, namely:

(1) the official receiver;

(2) a person who has ceased to be trustee of the bankrupt's estate; or

(3) a person who has been the supervisor of a voluntary arrangement approved in relation to the bankrupt under Part 8 of the Insolvency Act 1986[5],

the official receiver or, as the case may be, that person must deliver up possession of the property, books, papers or records to the trustee[6].

If any person without reasonable excuse fails to comply with any such obligation[7], he is guilty of a contempt of court and liable to be punished accordingly, in addition to any other punishment to which he may be subject[8].

Any banker or agent of the bankrupt or any other person who holds any property to the account of, or for, the bankrupt must pay or deliver to the trustee all property in his possession or under his control which forms part of the bankrupt's estate and which he is not by law entitled to retain as against the bankrupt or trustee[9].

1 As to the meaning of 'the bankrupt's estate' see PARA 211.

2 As to the meaning of references to a person's affairs see PARA 43 note 4.

3 Insolvency Act 1986 s 311(1). This does not apply to personal items which do not form part of the bankrupt's estate: see *Haig v Aitken* [2001] Ch 110, [2000] 3 All ER 80 (personal correspondence even of a famous person which might be of value did not form part of the bankrupt's estate); Application 33274/96 *Foxley v United Kingdom* (2000) 8 BHRC 571, [2000] BPIR 1009, ECtHR (correspondence from legal advisers to bankrupt not part of the estate and should not even be opened by a trustee who had obtained a redirection order under the Insolvency Act 1986 s 371 (see PARA 260)).

In the case of the administration in bankruptcy of the insolvent estate of a deceased person dying before the presentation of a bankruptcy petition, the Insolvency Act 1986 s 311 applies: Administration of Insolvent Estates of Deceased Persons Order 1986, SI 1986/1999, art 3(1), Sch 1 Pt II para 23. As to the administration in bankruptcy of the insolvent estates of deceased persons see further PARA 830 et seq. As to the question of joint privilege see *Re Konigsberg (a bankrupt), ex p Trustee v Konigsberg* [1989] 3 All ER 289, sub nom *Re Konigsberg (a bankrupt), ex p Trustee of Property of Bankrupt v Konigsberg* [1989] 1 WLR 1257.

4 Insolvency Act 1986 s 312(1). Section 312(1) is without prejudice to the general duties of the bankrupt under s 333 (see PARA 343): s 312(1). See also PARA 239 note 7. In the case of the administration in bankruptcy of the insolvent estate of a deceased person dying before the presentation of a bankruptcy petition, s 312 applies: Administration of Insolvent Estates of Deceased Persons Order 1986, SI 1986/1999, Sch 1 Pt II para 23.

5 Ie under the Insolvency Act 1986 Pt 8 (ss 252–263G): see PARA 43 et seq.

6 Insolvency Act 1986 s 312(2).

7 Ie under the Insolvency Act 1986 s 312.

8 Insolvency Act 1986 s 312(4). As to contempt of court see CONTEMPT OF COURT vol 22 (2012) PARA 1 et seq; and as to offences see PARA 733 et seq.

9 Insolvency Act 1986 s 312(3).

409.   Property transferable on company books.   Where any part of the bankrupt's estate[1] consists of stock or shares in a company, shares in a ship, or any other property transferable in the books of a company, office or person, the trustee may exercise the right to transfer the property to the same extent as the bankrupt might have exercised it if he had not become bankrupt[2].

1   As to the meaning of 'the bankrupt's estate' see PARA 211.
2   Insolvency Act 1986 s 311(3). See *Re Bentham Mills Spinning Co* (1879) 11 ChD 900, CA; *Re Cannock and Rugeley Colliery Co, ex p Harrison* (1885) 28 ChD 363, CA; *Re Key & Son Ltd* [1902] 1 Ch 467; *Re London and Provincial Telegraph Co* (1870) LR 9 Eq 653.
     As to the application of the Insolvency Act 1986 s 311 in the case of the administration in bankruptcy of the insolvent estate of a deceased person dying before the presentation of a bankruptcy petition see PARA 408 note 3.

410.   Things in action.   Where any part of the bankrupt's estate[1] consists of things in action, they are deemed to have been assigned to the trustee; but notice of the deemed assignment need not be given except in so far as it is necessary, in a case where the deemed assignment is from the bankrupt himself, for protecting the priority of the trustee[2].

1   As to the meaning of 'the bankrupt's estate' see PARA 211.
2   Insolvency Act 1986 s 311(4). A trustee in bankruptcy is not in the position of an assignee or incumbrancer for value, but is only a statutory assignee; he cannot, therefore, by giving notice, gain priority over an assignee for value before the bankruptcy who has not given notice: *Re Wallis, ex p Jenks* [1902] 1 KB 719; and see *Re Anderson, ex p New Zealand Official Assignee* [1911] 1 KB 896; and PARAS 406, 420.
     As to the application of the Insolvency Act 1986 s 311 in the case of the administration in bankruptcy of the insolvent estate of a deceased person dying before the presentation of a bankruptcy petition see PARA 408 note 3.
     As to the vesting in the trustee of things in action see PARAS 412, 447 et seq.

411.   Goods held as security.   Where any goods comprised in the bankrupt's estate[1] are held by any person by way of pledge, pawn or other security and no notice has been served in respect of those goods by the official receiver[2], the trustee may serve such a notice in respect of the goods; and, whether or not a notice has been served[3], the trustee may, if he thinks fit, exercise the bankrupt's right of redemption in respect of any such goods[4].

1   As to the meaning of 'the bankrupt's estate' see PARA 211.
2   Ie under the Insolvency Act 1986 s 285(5): see PARA 214.
3   Ie under the Insolvency Act 1986 s 285(5) or s 311(5).
4   Insolvency Act 1986 s 311(5). A notice served by the trustee under s 311(5) has the same effect as a notice served by the official receiver under s 285(5): s 311(6).
     As to the application of s 311 in the case of the administration in bankruptcy of the insolvent estate of a deceased person dying before the presentation of a bankruptcy petition see PARA 408 note 3.

(ii)   Property Available to the Trustee

412.   Meaning of 'property'.   'Property' includes money, goods, things in action[1], land and every description of property wherever situated[2] and also obligations and every description of interest, whether present or future or vested or contingent, arising out of, or incidental to, property[3]. References in the Insolvency Act 1986[4] to property, in relation to a bankrupt, include references to any power exercisable by him over or in respect of property except in so far as the power is exercisable over or in respect of property not for the time being comprised in the bankrupt's estate[5] and:

(1)   is so exercisable at a time after either the official receiver has had his release[6] in respect of that estate or a meeting summoned by the trustee of that estate[7] has been held; or

(2)   cannot be so exercised for the benefit of the bankrupt;

and a power exercisable over or in respect of property is deemed[8] to vest in the person entitled to exercise it at the time of the transaction or event by virtue of which it is exercisable by that person, whether or not it becomes exercisable at that time[9].

1   As to 'things in action' see CHOSES IN ACTION; *Ord v Upton* [2000] Ch 352, [2000] 1 All ER 193, CA (all things in action relating to property are included in the bankrupt's estate and a bankrupt's action in negligence for damages for personal injury is a single cause of action for a hybrid claim, in part personal and in part relating to property, and, as such, vests in the trustee in bankruptcy though any damages received in respect of the personal claim will be held on trust for the bankrupt), following *Heath v Tang, Stevens v Peacock* [1993] 4 All ER 694, [1993] 1 WLR 1421; *Cork v Rawlins* [2001] EWCA Civ 197, [2001] Ch 792, sub nom *Cork v Rawlins* [2001] EWCA Civ 202, [2001] 4 All ER 50 (benefits payable under an insurance policy following a bankrupt's disablement, which are not calculated by reference to pain and suffering, are divisible among the creditors in the bankruptcy); *Dear v Reeves* [2001] EWCA Civ 277, [2002] Ch 1, [2001] 1 BCLC 643 (right of pre-emption is property within the meaning of the Insolvency Act 1986 s 436); and see *Ramsey v Hartley* [1977] 2 All ER 673, [1977] 1 WLR 686, CA (where it was held that the right to litigate a cause of action was a thing in action for the purposes of the Bankruptcy Act 1914 (repealed) which the trustee could assign to the bankrupt for a share of the net proceeds of the action, if any). See further PARA 447 et seq.

2   'Property wherever situated' means property anywhere in the world: *Singh v Official Receiver* [1997] BPIR 530. Under principles of private international law, personal property, wherever situated, will be held to have passed to the trustee: see *Re Osborn, ex p Trustee* [1931–32] B & CR 189; *Re Kooperman* [1928] B & CR 49. For the position as regards real property see PARA 398. Orders of a Lebanese court prohibiting the bankrupt from dealing with certain of his property were held to be of no effect on an English bankruptcy in *Buchler v Al-Midani and Al-Midani* [2006] BPIR 620.

As to the effect of the Convention on Jurisdiction and the Enforcement of Judgments in Civil and Commercial Matters (Brussels, 27 September 1968), enacted by the Civil Jurisdiction and Judgments Act 1982 (see CONFLICT OF LAWS vol 19 (2011) PARA 366 et seq), on a trustee's attempts to recover property situated abroad by proceedings in the English courts see *Re Hayward* [1997] Ch 45, [1997] 1 All ER 32; *Ashurst v Pollard* [2001] Ch 595, [2001] 2 All ER 75, CA.

As to cross-border insolvency see PARA 826 et seq.

3   Insolvency Act 1986 s 436(1) (numbered as such by SI 2009/1941). 'Property' in this context cannot refer to a mere hope or possibility of receiving property: *Re Campbell (a bankrupt)* [1997] Ch 14, [1996] 2 All ER 537 (prospect of compensation from the Criminal Injuries Compensation Board under the pending application did not vest in the trustee and there was no right to enforce an award); and see PARA 416.

As to the application of the Insolvency Act 1986 s 436 in the case of the administration in bankruptcy of the insolvent estate of a deceased person dying before the presentation of a bankruptcy petition see PARA 20 note 6.

The deposit paid by an underwriter on admission to Lloyd's does not constitute property which passes to his creditors on his bankruptcy (*Re Heathcote, ex p Trustee* (1912) Times, 17 July); nor is a British passport part of the bankrupt's property (*Re Suwalsky, Suwalsky v Trustee and Official Receiver* [1928] B & CR 142), although it may be impounded by the court in the exercise of its discretion pending fulfilment by the bankrupt of his duties (*Re Greystoke (a bankrupt) (No 2)* [1998] BPIR 77). Examples of property which have been held to fall within the Insolvency Act 1986 s 436 are milk quota (*Swift v Dairywise Farms Ltd* [2000] 1 All ER 320, [2000] 1 WLR 1177), a waste management licence (*Re Celtic Extraction Ltd (in liquidation), Re Bluestone Chemicals Ltd (in liquidation)* [2001] Ch 475, [1999] 4 All ER 684, CA), the rights of a songwriter to payments from the Performing Right Society (*Performing Right Society Ltd v Rowland, Rowland v Turp* [1997] 3 All ER 336, [1998] BPIR 128) and the entitlement of the holder of a fishing licence to be considered for the grant of a new licence (*Re Rae* [1995] BCC 102). The bankrupt's personal correspondence, even if of potential value, is of a peculiarly personal nature and does not constitute property which forms part of the bankrupt's estate available for creditors: *Haig v Aitken* [2001] Ch 110, [2000] 3 All ER 80.

As to the position of assets which are subject to an individual voluntary arrangement under the Insolvency Act 1986 Pt 8 (ss 252–263G) at the date of the bankruptcy order see PARA 89.

4   Ie in the Insolvency Act 1986 Pts 7A–11 (ss 251A–385).
5   As to the meaning of 'the bankrupt's estate' see PARA 211.
6   Ie under the Insolvency Act 1986 s 299(2): see PARA 380.
7   Ie under the Insolvency Act 1986 s 331: see PARA 616.
8   Ie for the purposes of any of the Insolvency Act 1986 Pts 7A–11.
9   Insolvency Act 1986 s 283(4). As to the modifications to s 283(4) which apply in the case of the administration in bankruptcy of the insolvent estate of a deceased person dying before the presentation of a bankruptcy petition see PARA 216 note 5.

413.   Charge on bankrupt's home. Where any property consisting of an interest in a dwelling house[1] which is occupied by the bankrupt or by his spouse or former spouse or by his civil partner or former civil partner is comprised in the bankrupt's estate[2] and the trustee is, for any reason, unable for the time being to realise that property, the trustee may apply to the court for an order imposing a charge on the property for the benefit of the bankrupt's estate[3]. If, on such an application, the court imposes a charge on any property, the benefit of that charge is comprised in the bankrupt's estate and is enforceable, up to the charged value[4] from time to time, for the payment of any amount which is payable otherwise than to the bankrupt out of the estate and of interest[5] on that amount at the prescribed rate[6].

Where the trustee applies to the court for such an order, the respondents to the application are any spouse or former spouse or civil partner or former civil partner of the bankrupt having or claiming to have an interest in the property, any other person appearing to have an interest in the property and such other persons as the court may direct[7]. The trustee must make a report to the court, containing the following particulars:

(1)   the extent of the bankrupt's interest in the property which is the subject of the application;
(2)   the amount which, at the date of the application, remains owing to unsecured creditors of the bankrupt; and
(3)   an estimate of the cost of realising the interest[8].

The terms of the charge to be imposed must be agreed between the trustee and the bankrupt or, failing agreement, must be settled by the court[9]. The court's order must also:

(a)   describe the property to be charged;
(b)   state whether the title to the property is registered and, if it is, specify the title number;
(c)   set out the extent of the bankrupt's interest in the property which has vested in the trustee[10];
(d)   indicate, by reference to any, or the total, amount which is payable otherwise than to the bankrupt out of the estate and of interest on that amount, how the amount of the charge to be imposed is to be ascertained;
(e)   set out the conditions, if any, imposed by the court under the Charging Orders Act 1979[11];
(f)   identify the date any property charged is to cease to be comprised in the bankrupt's estate and, subject to the charge (and any prior charge), is to vest in the bankrupt[12].

Where the court order is capable of giving rise to an application or applications under the Land Charges Act 1972 or the Land Registration Act 2002, the trustee must, as soon as reasonably practicable after the making of the court order or at the appropriate time, make the appropriate application[13] or applications to the Chief Land Registrar[14].

1 For these purposes, 'dwelling house' includes any building or part of a building which is occupied as a dwelling and any yard, garden, garage or outhouse belonging to the dwelling house and occupied with it: Insolvency Act 1986 s 385(1). As to the application of s 385 in the case of the administration in bankruptcy of the insolvent estate of a deceased person dying before the presentation of a bankruptcy petition see PARA 6 note 8.

2 As to the meaning of 'the bankrupt's estate' see PARA 211.

3 Insolvency Act 1986 s 313(1) (amended by the Civil Partnership Act 2004 s 261(1), Sch 27 para 114). See also *Gotham v Doodes* [2006] EWCA Civ 1080, [2007] 1 All ER 527, [2007] 1 WLR 86 (limitation period did not begin to run until the order for sale was made, not when the charge was created).

In the case of the administration in bankruptcy of the insolvent estate of a deceased person dying before the presentation of a bankruptcy petition, the Insolvency Act 1986 s 313 applies: Administration of Insolvent Estates of Deceased Persons Order 1986, SI 1986/1999, art 3(1), Sch 1 Pt II para 23. As to the administration in bankruptcy of the insolvent estates of deceased persons see further PARA 830 et seq.

4 For this purpose, the charged value means: (1) the amount specified in the charging order as the value of the bankrupt's interest in the property at the date of the order; plus (2) interest on that amount from the date of the charging order at the prescribed rate: Insolvency Act 1986 s 313(2A) (s 313(2A), (2B) added by the Enterprise Act 2002 s 216(2)(b)). In determining the value of an interest for these purposes the court must disregard any matter which it is required to disregard by the Insolvency Rules 1986, SI 1986/1925: Insolvency Act 1986 s 313(2B) (as so added).

5 The rate of interest applicable under the Insolvency Act 1986 s 313(2) is the rate specified in the Judgments Act 1838 s 17 (see FINANCIAL SERVICES AND INSTITUTIONS vol 49 (2008) PARA 1307) on the day on which the charge is imposed, and the rate so applicable must be stated in the court's order imposing the charge: Insolvency Rules 1986, SI 1986/1925, r 6.237D(5) (added by SI 2003/1730).

6 Insolvency Act 1986 s 313(2) (amended by the Enterprise Act 2002 s 216(2)(a)). An order under the Insolvency Act 1986 s 313 made in respect of property vested in the trustee must provide, in accordance with the Insolvency Rules 1986, SI 1986/1925, for the property to cease to be comprised in the bankrupt's estate and, subject to the charge, and any prior charge, to vest in the bankrupt: Insolvency Act 1986 s 313(3). The Charging Orders Act 1979 s 3(1), (2), (4), (5), (6) (see CIVIL PROCEDURE vol 12 (2009) PARA 1467 et seq) has effect in relation to orders under the Insolvency Act 1986 s 313 as in relation to charging orders under the Charging Orders Act 1979: Insolvency Act 1986 s 313(4) (amended by the Tribunals, Courts and Enforcement Act 2007 s 93(5), (6)). An order under the Charging Orders Act 1979 s 3(5) may not vary a charged value: Insolvency Act 1986 s 313(5) (added by the Enterprise Act 2002 s 261(2)(c)).

7 Insolvency Rules 1986, SI 1986/1925, r 6.237D(1), (2) (added by SI 2003/1730; and amended by SI 2005/2114).

8 Insolvency Rules 1986, SI 1986/1925, r 6.237D(3) (added by SI 2003/1730).

9 Insolvency Rules 1986, SI 1986/1925, r 6.237D(4) (added by SI 2003/1730).

10 In determining the value of the bankrupt's interest for these purposes, the court must disregard that part of the value of the property in which the bankrupt's interest subsists which is equal to the value of: (1) any loans secured by mortgage or other charge against the property; (2) any other third party interest; and (3) the reasonable costs of sale: Insolvency Rules 1986, SI 1986/1925, r 6.237D(10) (added by SI 2004/584).

11 Ie under the Charging Orders Act 1979 s 3(1): see CIVIL PROCEDURE vol 12 (2009) PARA 1467.

12 Insolvency Rules 1986, SI 1986/1925, r 6.237D(6) (added by SI 2003/1730). Unless the court is of the opinion that a different date is appropriate, the date under the Insolvency Rules 1986, SI 1986/1925, r 6.237D(6)(f) (see head (f) in the text) must be that of the registration of the charge in accordance with the Charging Orders Act 1979 s 3(2) (see CIVIL PROCEDURE vol 12 (2009) PARA 1481): Insolvency Rules 1986, SI 1986/1925, r 6.237D(7) (added by SI 2003/1730). For the prescribed form of order see the Insolvency Rules 1986, SI 1986/1925, Sch 4 Form 6.79A (added by SI 1987/1919; and amended by SI 2004/584).

13 An 'appropriate application' is: (1) an application under the Land Charges Act 1972 s 6(1)(a) (application for registration in the register of writs and orders affecting land); or (2) an application under the Land Registration Act 2002 for an entry in the register in respect of the charge imposed by the order; and such application under that Act as is necessary to show in the individual register or registers of the dwelling-house that the interest has vested in the bankrupt:

Insolvency Rules 1986, SI 1986/1925, r 6.237D(9) (added by SI 2003/1730). 'Individual register' has the same meaning as in the Land Registration Rules 2003, SI 2003/1417, r 217 (see REAL PROPERTY AND REGISTRATION vol 87 (2012) PARA 330): Insolvency Rules 1986, SI 1986/1925, r 6.237E(2) (added by SI 2003/1730).

14 Insolvency Rules 1986, SI 1986/1925, r 6.237D(8) (added by SI 2003/1730).

414. Low value home. Where property comprised in the bankrupt's estate[1] consists of an interest in a dwelling-house[2] which at the date of the bankruptcy was the sole or principal residence of the bankrupt, the bankrupt's spouse or civil partner, or a former spouse or former civil partner of the bankrupt, and the trustee applies for an order for the sale of the property, for an order for possession of the property or for an order imposing a charge on the property[3], the court must dismiss the application if the value of the interest is below the prescribed amount[4]. In determining the value of such an interest the court must disregard that part of the value of the property in which the bankrupt's interest subsists which is equal to the value of any loans secured by mortgage or other charge against the property, any other third party interest, and the reasonable costs of sale[5].

1   As to the meaning of 'the bankrupt's estate' see PARA 211.
2   As to the meaning of 'dwelling house' see PARA 413 note 1.
3   Insolvency Act 1986 s 313A(1) (s 313A added by the Enterprise Act 2002 s 261(3); and the Insolvency Act 1986 s 313A(1) amended by the Civil Partnership Act 2004 s 261(1), Sch 27 para 115). An application for an order imposing a charge on the property is made under the Insolvency Act 1986 s 313 (see PARA 413).
4   Insolvency Act 1986 s 313A(2) (as added: see note 3). For these purposes, the amount so prescribed is £1,000: Insolvency Proceedings (Monetary Limits) Order 1986, SI 1986/1996, art 3, Schedule Pt II (art 3 amended by SI 2009/465; the Insolvency Proceedings (Monetary Limits) Order 1986, SI 1986/1996, Schedule Pt II substituted by SI 2004/547). As to the meaning of 'prescribed' see PARA 203 note 4. As to the Secretary of State's power to prescribe monetary limits see PARA 19 note 10.
5   Insolvency Act 1986 s 313A(3) (as added: see note 3); Insolvency Proceedings (Monetary Limits) Order 1986, SI 1986/1996, art 5 (added by SI 2004/547).

415. Provisions for bankrupt's maintenance. Settlements providing for the determination of life estates on bankruptcy often contain provisions enabling the trustees in whom the trust estate is vested to apply the income to the maintenance of the bankrupt or of his wife and family. Where any interest at all remains in the bankrupt, it will pass to his creditors[1]; but, if the trustees have an absolute discretion as to the application of the income, no interest passes to the creditors[2] unless the trustees of the settlement, in the exercise of their discretion, pay to the bankrupt more than is necessary for his mere support; in that event, the trustee in bankruptcy will be able to claim the excess for the estate[3].

1   *Kearsley v Woodcock* (1843) 3 Hare 185. If property is so settled that the income cannot be paid to anyone but the bankrupt, and there is no direction to accumulate, the bankrupt's interest passes to his trustee in bankruptcy; in such a case a discretion to pay a larger or smaller amount to the bankrupt would, it seems, be determined by bankruptcy: *Green v Spicer* (1830) 1 Russ & M 395; *Piercy v Roberts* (1832) 1 My & K 4; *Snowdon v Dales* (1834) 6 Sim 524; *Younghusband v Gisborne* (1846) 15 LJ Ch 355.
2   *Holmes v Penney* (1856) 3 K & J 90; *Twopeny v Peyton* (1840) 10 Sim 487; *Godden v Crowhurst* (1842) 10 Sim 642; *Re Bullock, Good v Lickorish* (1891) 60 LJ Ch 341; and see *Re Coleman, Henry v Strong* (1888) 39 ChD 443, CA.
3   Where, at any time after the commencement of the bankruptcy, any property is acquired by, or devolves on, the bankrupt or there is an increase of the bankrupt's income, the bankrupt must, within the prescribed period, give the trustee notice of the property or, as the case may be, of the increase: Insolvency Act 1986 s 333(2). The trustee may by notice in writing claim for the bankrupt's estate any property which has been acquired by, or devolved on, the bankrupt since

the commencement of the bankruptcy (see s 307(1); and PARA 458 et seq) or may apply to the court for an income payments order (see s 310; and PARA 462 et seq).

416. Expectancies. A mere expectancy or possibility of an interest is not property[1], and, if it remains a possibility or expectancy while the bankruptcy lasts, it does not become divisible among the creditors; but, if it becomes an actual interest[2] during the bankruptcy, it is divisible among the creditors, if claimed by the trustee[3].

A possibility coupled with an interest passes on bankruptcy[4].

1　As to the meaning of 'property' see PARA 412.

2　*Johnson v Smiley* (1853) 17 Beav 223 at 230; *Re Inkson's Trusts* (1855) 21 Beav 310; *Re Duggan's Trusts* (1869) LR 8 Eq 697. A mere possibility, such as a presumptive title to an equitable estate tail or as next of kin, does not pass to the trustee: *Carleton v Leighton* (1805) 3 Mer 667; *Re Parsons, Stockley v Parsons* (1890) 45 ChD 51 (disapproving *Re Beaupré's Trusts* (1888) 21 LR Ir 397), applied in *Re Midleton's Will Trusts, Whitehead v Earl of Midleton* [1969] 1 Ch 600, [1967] 2 All ER 834. The possibility that a pecuniary benefit may accrue to the bankrupt by another person exercising in his favour an option which is only exercisable on a contingency does not pass on bankruptcy: *Re Suse and Sibeth, ex p Dever* (1887) 18 QBD 660, CA. An option which a bankrupt may exercise does pass: *Re Suse and Sibeth, ex p Dever* at 668; and see *Buckland v Papillon* (1866) 2 Ch App 67. If property is limited in trust for the members of a named class (e g the children of A and B) as another person shall appoint, and in default of appointment to all the members of the class, and one of the members of the class becomes bankrupt before any appointment is made, his interest is a mere possibility, and does not pass on bankruptcy: *Re Vizard's Trusts* (1866) 1 Ch App 588. If, in a limitation of this kind, an appointment is made by will, no member of the class has any property in the appointed share until the appointor's death; and, if one of the members of the class becomes bankrupt and obtains his discharge before the appointor's death, no interest passes to his creditors, except when the object of the appointment is only to fix the proportion which each member of the class should take: *Duke of Marlborough v Lord Godolphin* (1750) 2 Ves Sen 61; cf *Re Silber's Settlement, Public Trustee v Silber* [1920] WN 77. As to the nature of a mere expectancy or spes successionis see REAL PROPERTY AND REGISTRATION vol 87 (2012) PARA 178; and as to the extent to which such an expectancy is assignable see CHOSES IN ACTION vol 13 (2009) PARA 13 et seq.

　　Where there is a pending application to the Criminal Injuries Compensation Authority, the possibility of obtaining compensation does not vest in the trustee as there is no right to enforce an award: *Re Campbell (a bankrupt)* [1997] Ch 14, [1996] 2 All ER 537.

3　As to claiming after-acquired property see PARA 459.

4　Thus, where property is settled in trust for a tenant for life, and on his death to be divided among such of his children as should be living at his death, and one of the children becomes bankrupt before the death of the tenant for life, his interest in remainder passes on bankruptcy: *Higden v Williamson* (1732) 3 P Wms 132. If an income for life is given to a person then bankrupt to be paid to him on his obtaining his discharge, this is a contingent interest which vests in the trustee, and on the bankrupt obtaining his discharge vests in the trustee absolutely: *Davidson v Chalmers, Perry v Chalmers* (1864) 33 LJ Ch 622.

417. Property over which bankrupt has power of disposition. A general power of appointment over property is not, strictly speaking, property[1]; but, if it is exercisable by deed, it is within the extended meaning in which the term 'property' is used in the Insolvency Act 1986 in determining what property of the bankrupt is comprised in the bankrupt's estate[2]; such a power may be exercised by the trustee for the creditors' benefit so long as the bankrupt is living[3]. A general power of appointment which is exercisable by will only is not 'property' within the 1986 Act[4]; nor is a special power of appointment which is exercisable for the joint benefit of the bankrupt and another[5].

If a person who has an interest defeasible by virtue of an appointment by himself becomes bankrupt, he cannot thereafter exercise the power so as to deprive the trustee in bankruptcy of the interest which has already vested in the trustee[6]; but, if an interest is defeasible by virtue of an appointment by a third person, it seems that the trustee's interest may be defeated by such an appointment[7].

The capacity to release a special power of appointment does not, it seems, pass to the trustee in bankruptcy of the donee of the power[8].

A power of the beneficiary under a trust instrument to consent to a sale or lease of the trust property, or to the exercise of a power of advancement, is not extinguished by bankruptcy; but, as the exercise of the power may affect the interest of the trustee in bankruptcy, his sanction is necessary to the giving of consent[9]. If a power exercisable by the bankrupt is of such a nature that its exercise will not affect the trustee's interest, as, for example, where it is a power to appoint new trustees of the instrument, the trustee's consent is not necessary[10].

In the case of settled land, however, the statutory powers of the tenant for life are not assignable and remain exercisable by him despite bankruptcy[11] without his trustee in bankruptcy's consent to their exercise being required[12]; but the trustee is entitled to notice of any intended transaction[13]. Similarly, any additional or larger powers conferred on the tenant for life by the settlor appear to be exercisable without consent[14].

The protector of a settlement who becomes bankrupt remains protector after bankruptcy[15].

A right to a grant of administration to the estate of an intestate is not a right which passes to a trustee in bankruptcy[16]; but the court may in its discretion[17] make a grant to the trustee[18].

1   *Nichols to Nixey* (1885) 29 ChD 1005; *Re Armstrong, ex p Gilchrist* (1886) 17 QBD 521 at 527, 529, 531. As to the meaning of 'property' see PARA 412.
2   See the Insolvency Act 1986 s 283(4); and PARA 412.
3   *Nichols to Nixey* (1885) 29 ChD 1005.
4   *Re Guedalla, Lee v Guedalla's Trustee* [1905] 2 Ch 331; *Re Benzon, Bower v Chetwynd* [1914] 2 Ch 68, CA. In the earlier of these cases, it was further held that, although the bankrupt was undischarged at the date of his death, the creditors in the bankruptcy were precluded by what became the Bankruptcy Act 1914 s 7 (now in effect the Insolvency Act 1986 s 285(1): see PARA 214), from claiming against the appointed fund in the administration of his estate; but in the later case this point was left undecided. If the bankrupt dies after obtaining his discharge, the creditors in the bankruptcy cannot claim in the administration of his estate: *Jenney v Andrews* (1822) 6 Madd 264.
5   *Re Taylor's Settlement Trusts, Public Trustee v Taylor* [1929] 1 Ch 435. Such a power cannot be exercised by the bankrupt 'for his benefit' within the meaning of the Insolvency Act 1986 s 283(4)(b) (see PARA 412 head (2)): *Re Taylor's Settlement Trusts, Public Trustee v Taylor*. As to the effect of bankruptcy on the right to exercise a power of appointment see *Jones v Winwood* (1841) 10 Sim 150; *Haswell v Haswell* (1860) 2 De GF & J 456; *Wickham v Wing* (1865) 2 Hem & M 436; *Re Aylwin's Trusts* (1873) LR 16 Eq 585; and POWERS vol 36(2) (Reissue) PARA 380.
6   *Hole v Escott* (1838) 4 My & Cr 187; *Doe d Coleman v Britain* (1818) 2 B & Ald 93; *Badham v Mee* (1831) 7 Bing 695; *Badham v Mee* (1832) 1 My & K 32 at 34; *Re Cooper, Cooper v Slight* (1884) 27 ChD 565 at 569. See also *Dunlop v Johnston* (1867) LR 1 Sc & Div 109, HL (post-nuptial settlement, revocable by Scottish law, made in favour of wife by man who afterwards became bankrupt).
7   *Lee v Olding* (1856) 25 LJ Ch 580 (defeasible interest in half of fund; whole fund appointed to bankrupt after his discharge); and see *Re Vizard's Trusts* (1866) 1 Ch App 588.
8   It was so held in *Re Rose, Rose v Rose* [1904] 2 Ch 348, but the point was left undecided on appeal: see *Re Rose, Hasluck v Rose* [1905] 1 Ch 94, CA.
9   *Re Cooper, Cooper v Slight* (1884) 27 ChD 565 (power to consent to advancement); *Re Bedingfield and Herring's Contract* [1893] 2 Ch 332 (power to consent to sale); cf *Simpson v Bathurst, Shepherd v Bathurst* (1869) 5 Ch App 193 (power to renew leases).
10 *Hardaker v Moorhouse* (1884) 26 ChD 417.
11 See the Settled Land Act 1925 s 104(1); SETTLEMENTS vol 91 (2012) PARA 678; *Re Mansel's Settled Estates* [1884] WN 209; *Re Marquis of Ailesbury's Settled Estates* [1892] 1 Ch 506 at

535. The court may, however, under the Settled Land Act 1925 s 24 (see SETTLEMENTS vol 91 (2012) PARA 666), empower the trustees of the settlement to exercise the powers in the name and on behalf of the tenant for life: see *Re Thornhill's Settlement* [1941] Ch 24, [1940] 4 All ER 249, CA (where the trustee in bankruptcy obtained such an order).

The prohibition against assignment applies to a person having the powers of a tenant for life under the Settled Land Act 1925 s 20 (see SETTLEMENTS vol 91 (2012) PARA 663), but not to a mere statutory owner under s 23 (see SETTLEMENTS vol 91 (2012) PARA 667): *Re Craven Settled Estates* [1926] Ch 985. The legal estate in settled land does not vest in the trustee in bankruptcy of an estate owner until the estate owner becomes absolutely and beneficially entitled: see PARA 442.

Since 1 January 1997 it has not been possible to create settlements for the purposes of the Settled Land Act 1925, save in a very limited class of cases: see SETTLEMENTS vol 91 (2012) PARAS 506, 576 et seq.

12 See the Settled Land Act 1925 s 104(4), (10); and SETTLEMENTS vol 91 (2012) PARA 680.

13 See the Settled Land Act 1925 s 104(4) proviso (c); and SETTLEMENTS vol 91 (2012) PARA 680. The trustee has the same or a similar interest in land, money or securities for the time being representing the bankrupt's interest as he had by virtue of the bankruptcy in the land, money or securities then representing the bankrupt's interest: see s 104(4) proviso (a); and SETTLEMENTS vol 91 (2012) PARA 680. After notice of the bankruptcy to the trustees of the settlement, the consent of the assignee is required to an investment of capital money for the time being affected by the assignment in investments other than securities, and to any application of any such capital money: see s 104(4) proviso (b) (amended by the Trustee Act 2000 s 40(1), (3), Sch 2 para 16(1), Sch 4 Pt II); and SETTLEMENTS vol 91 (2012) PARA 680.

14 See the Settled Land Act 1925 s 109; and SETTLEMENTS vol 91 (2012) PARA 781.

15 See the Fines and Recoveries Act 1833 s 22; and REAL PROPERTY AND REGISTRATION vol 87 (2012) PARA 119.

16 *Re Turner's Goods* (1886) 12 PD 18.

17 Ie under the Senior Courts Act 1981 s 116: see WILLS AND INTESTACY vol 103 (2010) PARA 758.

18 *Re Turner's Goods* (1886) 12 PD 18; *Re Thacker's Goods* (1890) 54 JP 759; *Re Bowron's Goods* (1914) 84 LJP 92; and see WILLS AND INTESTACY vol 103 (2010) PARA 759; Tristram and Coote's Probate Practice (30th Edn, 2008) paras 5.252–5.257.

418.   Interests determinable on bankruptcy.   An interest in property, determinable and passing away to another person on the possessor's bankruptcy, does not become divisible among the bankrupt's creditors, if the settlor or person creating the interest is someone other than the bankrupt[1].

The rule is that the owner of property may, on alienation, qualify the interest of his alienee by a condition to take effect on the alienee's bankruptcy; but he cannot, by contract or otherwise, qualify his own interest by a similar condition, determining or controlling it in the event of his own bankruptcy to the disappointment or delay of his creditors[2]. Accordingly, by the use of apt words of limitation, where property is granted by one person to another in such a way that the interest granted determines on the grantee's bankruptcy and passes away to someone else, the property is not divisible among the grantee's creditors on his bankruptcy[3]. The instrument creating the interest must, however, use proper words of limitation to ensure that it does pass away from him in the event of his bankruptcy; otherwise his interest, whatever it may be, will be divisible among his creditors[4].

A person's rights under a personal pension scheme cannot be forfeited by reference to his bankruptcy[5].

1 *Re Ashby, ex p Wreford* [1892] 1 QB 872; *Roe d Hunter v Galliers* (1787) 2 Term Rep 133. As to the construction of clauses providing for determination of an interest on bankruptcy or insolvency see *Lear v Leggett* (1829) 2 Sim 479; *Re Muggeridge's Trusts* (1860) John 625; *Freeman v Bowen* (1865) 35 Beav 17; *Montefiore v Enthoven* (1867) LR 5 Eq 35; *Billson v Crofts* (1873) LR 15 Eq 314; *Re Walker, ex p Gould* (1884) 13 QBD 454; *Nixon v Verry* (1885) 29 ChD 196; *Re Harvey, ex p Pixley v Harvey* (1889) 6 Morr 95; *Re Carew, Carew v Carew* [1896] 2 Ch 311, CA; *Re Weibking, ex p Ward* [1902] 1 KB 713; *Re Cooper, Townend v Townend* (1917) 86 LJ Ch 507.

Under the Bankruptcy Act 1914 (repealed) the interest determined when the act of bankruptcy was committed, that being the date on which the bankruptcy was deemed to commence. Under the Insolvency Act 1986 the bankruptcy of an individual against whom a bankruptcy order has been made commences with the day on which the order is made: see s 278(a); and PARA 209 head (1).

2   *Mackintosh v Pogose* [1895] 1 Ch 505 at 511–514; *Wilson v Greenwood* (1818) 1 Swan 471; cf *Belmont Park Investments PTY Ltd v BNY Corporate Trustee Services Ltd* [2011] UKSC 38, [2012] 1 AC 383, [2012] 1 All ER 505; *Lomas v JFB Firth Rixson Inc* [2010] EWHC 3372 (Ch), [2011] 2 BCLC 120, [2011] BPIR 788. A forfeiture clause which is attached to an absolute vested gift may be void for repugnancy: see *Re Smith, Smith v Smith* [1916] 1 Ch 369 (where a forfeiture clause which applied both to vested and to contingent gifts was held not to be capable of being split up so as to be valid as to the contingent gifts, but to be wholly void). A forfeiture clause purporting to forfeit an absolute interest in possession in the event of alienation will be void as will be such a clause which purports similarly to forfeit a life or other limited interest in possession which is not, on the true construction of the instrument creating it, made determinable in the same events as those in which the forfeiture is expressed to operate, but there is nothing objectionable about such a forfeiture clause which purports to defeat a future interest in the event of purported alienation before it falls into possession or to create a gift over in the event in which an income interest in possession is, on the true construction of the trust instrument, expressed to be determinable; and, if a forfeiture clause purports to apply both to interests in possession and to future or determinable interests, it will be wholly void, even as to future or determinable interests, as to which it would have been valid if limited to interests within that class: *Re Scientific Investment Pension Plan Trusts* [1999] Ch 53, [1998] 3 All ER 154 (scheme trust deed did not vest an absolute interest in pension benefits in scheme members with the result that provision forfeiting members' entitlement in event of assignment or alienation terminated interests in possession under the scheme on bankruptcy and future interests (namely where the member had not reached retirement age) were subject to forfeiture on bankruptcy). Cf *Caboche v Ramsay, Bond v Ramsay* [1997] BPIR 377; *Malcolm v Benedict Mackenzie (a firm)* [2004] EWCA.Civ 1748, sub nom *Re Malcolm* [2005] 1 WLR 1238, [2005] ICR 611. See further the text and note 5. As to what interests may validly be made subject to forfeiture clauses see GIFTS vol 52 (2009) PARA 254.

3   *Rochford v Hackman* (1852) 9 Hare 475. Property cannot, however, be given to a person in such a way that it should go to him, when and as soon as he should be able to enjoy it for his own use and benefit, so as not to be subject to his debts: *Davidson v Chalmers, Perry v Chalmers* (1864) 33 LJ Ch 622.

4   *Brandon v Robinson* (1811) 1 Rose 197 (where a testator gave a fund to trustees on trust to pay the dividends into his son's hands, or to his order or receipt, to the intent that the same or any part of it should not be grantable or assignable by way of anticipation, but there was no gift over, and it was held that on the son's bankruptcy his interest passed to his creditors); *Graves v Dolphin* (1826) 1 Sim 66 (where an annuity, given to a person for his personal maintenance and support, which was not to be liable to his debts and was to be paid into his own hands and not to any other person, but in respect of which there was no gift over, was held not to be determinable on bankruptcy and passed to the annuitant's creditors). In *Bird v Johnson* (1854) 18 Jur 976, there was a proviso that, in the event of the grantee of an absolute interest becoming bankrupt before his interest became payable to him, so as to deprive him of the interest intended to be vested in or payable to him, it should cease and determine as if he were then dead; and it was held that, there being no sufficient limitation over and the condition being repugnant and void, there was no forfeiture on bankruptcy, though there would have been if the interest given had been for life alone.

5   See the Pension Schemes Act 1993 s 159A(1), (2) (s 159A added by the Welfare Reform and Pensions Act 1999 s 14(1); the Pensions Schemes Act 1993 s 159A(2) amended by SI 2005/2053); and see PERSONAL AND OCCUPATIONAL PENSIONS. As to forfeiture of rights under occupational pension schemes see the Pensions Act 1995 s 92(2) (amended by the Welfare Reform and Pensions Act 1999 ss 14(3), 88, Sch 13 Pt I); and PERSONAL AND OCCUPATIONAL PENSIONS vol 80 (2013) PARA 289. See also PARA 407. As to the recovery of excessive pension contributions see PARA 693.

419.   Interests determinable on alienation generally. Where the event of bankruptcy is not specifically referred to, a gift over of a life estate, in the event of the grantee alienating or charging his interest, may be so expressed as to effect a forfeiture of the life interest, or bring it to an end, on his bankruptcy[1], or as to take effect only if income is in the trustee's hands at the time[2], or as not to be effective on his bankruptcy[3]. However, a mere restriction against alienation in a gift or contract will not be effective to prevent the property from vesting, subject to the restriction, in the trustee[4].

1   *Re Cotgrave, Mynors v Cotgrave* [1903] 2 Ch 705 (gift over on 'alienating or incumbering or agreeing to alienate or incumber'); *Re Loftus-Otway, Otway v Otway* [1895] 2 Ch 235 ('liable to be deprived of beneficial enjoyment'); *Metcalfe v Metcalfe* [1891] 3 Ch 1, CA (forfeiture and gift over, if interest 'aliened, whereby the same would vest in any other person'); *Re Throckmorton, ex p Eyston* (1877) 7 ChD 145, CA (annuity to cease if donee did or permitted any act, deed, matter or thing, whereby the same should be aliened, charged or incumbered). See also *Re Parnham's Trusts* (1872) LR 13 Eq 413 (annulment of bankruptcy); *Re Amherst's Trusts* (1872) LR 13 Eq 464; *Rochford v Hackman* (1852) 9 Hare 475; *Cooper v Wyatt* (1821) 5 Madd 482; *Shee v Hale* (1807) 13 Ves 404; *Dommett v Bedford* (1796) 3 Ves 149.

2   *Re Laye, Turnbull v Laye* [1913] 1 Ch 298 (gift until grantee should do or suffer something, whereby the income or part of it, if belonging to him absolutely, 'becomes payable to some other person'), explaining *Re Sartoris's Estate, Sartoris v Sartoris* [1892] 1 Ch 11, CA. See also *Re Richardson's Will Trusts, Public Trustee v Llewellyn Evans' Trustee* [1958] Ch 504, [1958] 1 All ER 538 (order to secure divorce maintenance creating, or attempting to create, equitable charge on a protected interest effected a forfeiture).

3   *Re Laye, Turnbull v Laye* [1913] 1 Ch 298 ('have his affairs liquidated by arrangement or composition'; scheme for payment in full not such a liquidation). So, also, in *Re Parnham's Trust* (1876) 46 LJ Ch 80, a bankruptcy during a prior life interest, annulled during the continuance of that life interest, did not effect a forfeiture. In *Lear v Leggett* (1830) 1 Russ & M 690, where the proviso was that the life estate should not be subject to any alienation or disposition by sale, mortgage or otherwise, and if the tenant for life should charge or attempt to charge his interest, any such mortgage, sale or other disposition should be a forfeiture, it was held that the proviso did not apply to the case of alienation by an involuntary act such as bankruptcy then was, and that the life estate was not forfeited on bankruptcy.

    In *Re Moon, ex p Dawes* (1886) 17 QBD 275, CA, where a gift over was to take place if the grantee should assign, charge or otherwise dispose of the income or become bankrupt or do or suffer anything whereby the income, if payable to him absolutely, or any part of it would become vested in any other person, the mere act of the filing of a bankruptcy petition by the grantee did not operate as a forfeiture; in fact no bankruptcy followed, and the income would never have been 'vested' in any other person, if the income had been payable to the grantee absolutely; the limitations differ from those in *Re Sartoris's Estate, Sartoris v Sartoris* [1892] 1 Ch 11, CA, and *Re Loftus-Otway, Otway v Otway* [1895] 2 Ch 235 (cf *Re James, Clutterbuck v James* (1890) 62 LT 545).

    In *Re Harvey, ex p Pixley v Harvey* (1889) 6 Morr 95, a gift over of an annuity, in the event of the annuitant alienating, charging, incumbering or disposing of it, was held not to apply to his being adjudicated bankrupt on a creditor's petition; but contrast *Rochford v Hackman* (1852) 9 Hare 475, and *Re Amherst's Trusts* (1872) LR 13 Eq 464. In *Re Evans, Public Trustee v Evans* [1920] 2 Ch 304, CA, it was held that the words 'unless he attempts to become bankrupt' must be read in their strict grammatical sense, and as so read did not apply to a bankruptcy against his will or bankruptcy generally.

    In *Re Hamilton, FitzGeorge v FitzGeorge* (1921) 124 LT 737, CA, where the proviso was that the beneficiary should not do or suffer any act whereby his share of income would be assigned, an authority to the trustees of the will to pay the income over to a trustee under a scheme of composition, not communicated to the trustee of the scheme, was held not to be a good assignment, but merely a bare authority revocable by the beneficiary. In *Re Griffiths, Jones v Jenkins* [1926] Ch 1007, where there was a gift over in the event of the grantee anticipating, charging, assigning or otherwise disposing of the income, it was held that a bankruptcy petition presented by the grantee did not operate as a forfeiture; and *Re Cotgrave, Mynors v Cotgrave* [1903] 2 Ch 705 (cited in note 1) was doubted but distinguished.

4   *Krasner v Dennison, Lawrence v Lesser* [2001] Ch 76, [2000] 3 All ER 234, CA; and see PARA 418.

420.   Forfeiture in case of foreign bankruptcies.   The foreign bankruptcy of an individual domiciled in England may not work a forfeiture[1]; but personal estate in England[2], though not real estate[3], may pass to the assignee in his foreign bankruptcy.

1   *Re Hayward, Hayward v Hayward* [1897] 1 Ch 905 (life interest in English personalty determinable on bankruptcy; New Zealand bankruptcy of an individual domiciled in England; adjudication subsequently annulled; assignee not entitled); *Re James, Clutterbuck v James* (1890) 62 LT 545 (determinable life interest in personalty; sequestration of legatee's estate in Scotland, subsequently recalled; no forfeiture); c f *Re Aylwin's Trusts* (1873) LR 16 Eq 585 (determinable life interest in leaseholds; Australian bankruptcy of life tenant; forfeiture incurred); *Re Levy's Trusts* (1885) 30 ChD 119 (determinable life interest in rents and profits of real estate in England; adjudication in New South Wales; forfeiture incurred); *Bergerem v Marsh* (1921) 91 LJKB 80 (Belgian bankruptcy of an individual domiciled in England; personalty in England vested in Belgian trustee).

2   *Re Anderson, ex p New Zealand Official Assignee* [1911] 1 KB 896 (reversionary interest in personalty in income; individual domiciled in England made bankrupt in New Zealand and subsequently in England; New Zealand assignee entitled); *Re Craig, Catling v Esson* (1916) 86 LJ Ch 62 (reversionary interest; adjudication in Western Australia; assignees of trustee in bankruptcy entitled, without inquiry as to bankrupt's domicile); *Re Lawson's Trusts* [1896] 1 Ch 175 (fund in court paid to official assignee of deceased bankrupt in Bombay without administration in England); *Re Burke, King v Terry* (1919) 54 L Jo 430; and see *Re Davidson's Settlement Trusts* (1873) LR 15 Eq 383; *Re Blithman* (1866) LR 2 Eq 23.

3   *Waite v Bingley* (1882) 21 ChD 674 (bankruptcy in Australia; legal estate in land in England did not vest in assignee). As to the court's power to assist the courts of other jurisdictions in relation to insolvency proceedings see PARA 828. As to cross border insolvency see PARAS 826, 827.

421. Construction of forfeiture clauses.

In the construction of wills and settlements providing for the determination of a grantee's interest in the event of his bankruptcy, the court, for the sake of giving effect to the testator's or settlor's intention that property should not pass into hands other than those which the testator or settlor intended, has construed the clauses creating the limitation over in the event of bankruptcy in such a way as to apply them to a bankruptcy already existing, either at the date of the will or the settlement or at the time when the grantee's interest would, but for the bankruptcy, have fallen into his possession[1].

However, it appears to be well settled that, if a bankruptcy is annulled between the time when the title to a fund accrues to the bankrupt and the time when it would have become payable to him but for the bankruptcy, the bankrupt is in the same position as if he had never been bankrupt, and is entitled to receive the fund, if it has not been intercepted in the meantime[2].

1   *Manning v Chambers* (1847) 1 De G & Sm 282; *Seymour v Lucas* (1860) 1 Drew & Sm 177; *Trappes v Meredith* (1871) 7 Ch App 248; *Re Akeroyd's Settlement, Roberts v Akeroyd* [1893] 3 Ch 363, CA; *Re Evans, Public Trustee v Evans* [1920] 2 Ch 304, CA (applied in *Re Walker, Public Trustee v Walker* [1939] Ch 974, [1939] 3 All ER 902 (where the bankrupt obtained his discharge after the testator's death but before the annuity became first payable; and it was held that the forfeiture clause prevented the vesting of the annuity in the bankrupt)).

    Where there is a trust of a fund under the terms of which the trustees are bound to apply the income of the fund in a particular way on a given future contingency, the person who takes the income as a result of that trust on the happening of the contingency is a person who has an interest of a kind which, but for the forfeiture clause, is capable of vesting in his trustee in bankruptcy: *Re Clark, Clark v Clark* [1926] Ch 833 at 838. A conditional discharge on the bankrupt paying a sum of money does not terminate the operation of the forfeiture, if the money is not in fact paid: *Re Clark, Clark v Clark*.

2   Thus, in *White v Chitty* (1866) LR 1 Eq 372; *Lloyd v Lloyd* (1866) LR 2 Eq 722; *Robins v Rose* (1874) 43 LJ Ch 334; *Re Parnham's Trust* (1876) 46 LJ Ch 80; *Ancona v Waddell* (1878) 10 ChD 157, it was held that no forfeiture had taken place because the income had not been payable before the annulment of the bankruptcy. However, in *Sharp v Cosserat* (1855) 20 Beav 470; *Re Parnham's Trusts* (1872) LR 13 Eq 413; *Robertson v Richardson* (1885) 30 ChD 623; *Re Broughton, Peat v Broughton* (1887) 57 LT 8; *Metcalfe v Metcalfe* [1891] 3 Ch 1, CA; *Re Forder, Forder v Forder* [1927] 2 Ch 291, CA, it was held that a forfeiture had taken place because the income became payable before the annulment. See, however, *Samuel v Samuel* (1879) 12 ChD 152; *Re James, Clutterbuck v James* (1890) 62 LT 454.

422. Conditions for forfeiture on settlor's bankruptcy. No one may deal with his own property in such a way as to provide that, in the event of bankruptcy, it is to be distributed differently from the way the law prescribes[1]. This principle applies not only to a voluntary disposition which may be avoided if made with intent to defraud creditors[2], but also to a marriage settlement and any other contract for valuable consideration.

Thus, no one possessed of property may reserve that property to himself, until he should become bankrupt, and provide that on his bankruptcy it should pass to someone other than his creditors[3]. A provision in a marriage settlement or other disposition, by which a life interest determinable on bankruptcy is reserved to the owner, is ineffective as against the settlor's trustee in bankruptcy, so far as relates to the determination on bankruptcy; on the bankruptcy of the settlor his life interest will pass to his creditors[4]. If a settlor settles property on himself, until he shall assign, charge or incumber it, and assigns or charges the property before the bankruptcy, the limitation over will take effect, and will not be avoided by a subsequent bankruptcy; but, in the event of bankruptcy prior to an assignment or charge, the limitation over will not take effect[5].

Where a person who becomes bankrupt has been a party to a settlement which covers his own property and the property of another, and the settlement contains a provision terminating the life interest of the person who becomes bankrupt on his bankruptcy, that life interest will be realisable by the trustee in bankruptcy to the extent of the bankrupt's own property; but the limitation over on bankruptcy will be valid to the extent of the other person's property[6].

A court order varying a marriage settlement consequent on the dissolution of the marriage, whereby a settlor's interest is diminished, is not in itself an 'event' effecting a forfeiture of that interest[7].

1   *Re Jeavons, ex p Mackay, ex p Brown* (1873) 8 Ch App 643 at 647 (patentee sold the patent to manufacturers in return for royalties and was at the same time given a loan by the manufacturers on terms that they were entitled to retain one-half of the royalties towards repayment of a loan with a promise that, if he became bankrupt, they could retain the whole of the loan; the provision was held to be a fraud on the bankruptcy laws); and see *British Eagle International Airlines Ltd v Compagnie Nationale Air France* [1975] 2 All ER 390, [1975] 1 WLR 758, HL; *Belmont Park Investments PTY Ltd v BNY Corporate Trustee Services Ltd* [2011] UKSC 38, [2012] 1 AC 383, [2012] 1 All ER 505.

2   Ie under the Insolvency Act 1986 ss 423–425: see PARA 688 et seq. See *Freeman v Pope* (1870) 5 Ch App 538; *Re Wise, ex p Mercer* (1886) 17 QBD 290, CA; *Re Holland, Gregg v Holland* [1902] 2 Ch 360, CA (overruling *Re Pearson, ex p Stephens* (1876) 3 ChD 807); *Re Baker* [1936] Ch 61 (where a deed was held not to be impeachable either under the Law of Property Act 1925 s 172 (repealed) or under the Bankruptcy Act 1914 s 42 (repealed) (see now the Insolvency Act 1986 ss 423–425 and s 339 respectively)); *Re Eichholz, Eichholz's Trustee v Eichholz* [1959] Ch 708, [1959] 1 All ER 166. As to the avoidance of transactions at an undervalue see PARA 678 et seq; and as to the avoidance of voluntary dispositions made with the intent to defraud creditors see PARA 688 et seq.

3   *Whitmore v Mason* (1861) 2 John & H 204. See also *Casey's Trusts* (1855) 4 I Ch R 247. A resettlement by the bankrupt and another person, in exercise of a joint power of appointment, of property in which a bankrupt had an interest in default of appointment, is not a settlement of the bankrupt's own property for this purpose: *Re Ashby, ex p Wreford* [1892] 1 QB 872. A settlement of damages which a bankrupt recovered against a co-respondent for adultery (before the abolition of such damages by the Law Reform (Miscellaneous Provisions) Act 1970 s 7) was not a settlement of the bankrupt's own property: *Re Stephenson, ex p Brown* [1897] 1 QB 638.

4   *Higinbotham v Holme* (1812) 19 Ves 88; *Re Brewer's Settlement, Morton v Blackmore* [1896] 2 Ch 503. See also *Re Burroughs-Fowler, Burroughs-Fowler's Trustee v Burroughs-Fowler* [1916] 2 Ch 251 (where it was held that the bankrupt's life interest vested indefeasibly in his trustee in bankruptcy and was no longer capable of being affected by any subsequent act of forfeiture by the bankrupt, and that the trustee could make a good title to the income of the settled property during the remainder of the bankrupt's life); *Re Winwood's Settlement, Fisher v*

Winwood's Trustee (1916) 85 LJ Ch 799 (where the settlement conferred on the bankrupt a life interest in property settled by himself and a determinable interest in property settled by his father, and an annual sum directed to be held on the same trusts as the income of the settlement fund was apportioned); *Re Wombwell* (1921) 125 LT 437 (where the forfeiture clause in a settlement of property, belonging partly to the bankrupt and partly to a third party, was held void only to the extent of the bankrupt's property). If a settlement providing for the forfeiture of the settlor's life interest in the event of his bankruptcy is set aside as fraudulent under the Insolvency Act 1986 ss 423–425 (see PARA 678 et seq), the bankruptcy of the settlor may nonetheless, as against himself and those claiming under a second bankruptcy, operate as a forfeiture of his life interest: *Re Johnson Johnson, ex p Matthews and Wilkinson v Johnson Johnson and Dibb* [1904] 1 KB 134, DC.

5 *Brooke v Pearson* (1859) 27 Beav 181; *Knight v Browne* (1861) 30 LJ Ch 649; *Re Detmold, Detmold v Detmold* (1889) 40 ChD 585; *Re Brewer's Settlement, Morton v Blackmore* [1896] 2 Ch 503; and see *Re Carew's Trusts, Gellibrand v Carew* (1910) 103 LT 658 (overruled, in so far as it decided that an order varying a marriage settlement, brought about a forfeiture: see the text and note 7). A limitation over in the event of an alienation is valid, if there is an involuntary alienation by process of law in favour of a judgment creditor, but not where the involuntary alienation takes place by virtue of bankruptcy: see *Re Detmold, Detmold v Detmold*. Such a limitation over would not take effect on the assignment of the settlor's property for the benefit of his creditors generally: see *Re Detmold, Detmold v Detmold* at 588. See also *Re Balfour's Settlement, Public Trustee v Official Receiver* [1938] Ch 928, [1938] 3 All ER 259 (trustees having, before the bankruptcy, impounded to make good a breach of trust, nothing passed to the trustee in bankruptcy).

6 *Lester v Garland* (1832) 5 Sim 205; *Mackintosh v Pogose* [1895] 1 Ch 505; *Doherty v Power* [1916] 1 IR 337; *Re Wombwell* (1921) 125 LT 437.

7 *General Accident Fire and Life Assurance Corpn Ltd v IRC* [1963] 3 All ER 259, [1963] 1 WLR 1207, CA (a decision on the application of the Trustee Act 1925 s 33(1)), overruling *Re Carew's Trusts, Gellibrand v Carew* (1910) 103 LT 658.

423.   Condition impossible to perform because of bankruptcy. If, at the time of his bankruptcy, the bankrupt is entitled in possession or remainder, under a will or settlement, to an interest in premises which is subject to forfeiture on the breach of a condition, which would be broken if the interest were realised by the trustee in bankruptcy, for example, a condition that the person entitled to the use of the premises under the will or settlement should reside there, the interest nonetheless passes to the trustee, and it seems that on bankruptcy such a condition would cease to operate[1].

1 *Re Goldney, ex p Goldney* (1839) Mont & Ch 75; cf *Belmont Park Investments PTY Ltd v BNY Corporate Trustee Services Ltd* [2011] UKSC 38, [2012] 1 AC 383, [2012] 1 All ER 505.

424.   Leaseholds. Unless disclaimed by the trustee[1], the bankrupt's leasehold property passes to the trustee subject to the landlord's rights as to rent and to the enforcement of the covenants[2] which bind assigns, except those which are not enforceable against a tenant's trustee in bankruptcy, such as the covenant not to assign without the landlord's consent[3].

The bankrupt's property is also subject to rights of distress and to any rights of seizure which have been validly created in respect of it[4].

1 See PARA 499.

2 See *Re Solomon, ex p Dressler* (1878) 9 ChD 252, CA; *Wilson v Wallani* (1880) 5 ExD 155; *Titterton v Cooper* (1882) 9 QBD 473, CA; *Wilkins v Fry* (1816) 1 Mer 244 at 265. As to the landlord's right to distrain after bankruptcy see PARA 713; as to a mortgagee's right to stand in the landlord's place when distress has been levied on goods forming part of the mortgagee's security, and also on goods not forming part, see *Re Stephenson, ex p Stephenson* (1847) De G 586. As regards fixtures on demised premises, as between the landlord and the tenant's trustee in bankruptcy, the trustee is in the tenant's shoes, and is prima facie entitled to the tenant's or trade fixtures: *Stansfeld v Portsmouth Corpn* (1858) 27 LJCP 124; *Pugh v Arton* (1869) LR 8 Eq 626; *Re Walker, ex p Gould* (1884) 13 QBD 454; *Lambourn v McLellan* [1903] 2 Ch 268, CA. As regards farming leases see AGRICULTURAL LAND vol 1 (2008) PARA 301 et seq.

The right of a tenant to remain in occupation after the expiry of a lease by effluxion of time pursuant to the Landlord and Tenant Act 1954 Pt 1 (ss 1–22) (see LANDLORD AND TENANT vol 63 (2012) PARA 1227 et seq) constitutes property which vests in a trustee: *De Rothschild v Bell (a bankrupt)* [2000] QB 33, [1999] 2 All ER 722, CA.

A statutory tenant under the Rent Acts has a personal right only and, therefore, a statutory tenancy is not 'property' within the meaning of the Insolvency Act 1986 s 436 (see PARA 412), and does not pass to the trustee: *Sutton v Dorf* [1932] 2 KB 304, applied in *Smith v Odder* [1949] WN 249, CA. If a lease of a dwelling house has become vested in the tenant's trustee in bankruptcy, the tenant does not become a statutory tenant on the expiration of the lease (*Stafford v Levy* [1946] 2 All ER 256, CA), or on disclaimer by the trustee (see PARA 499). Where the trustee has disclaimed property under the Insolvency Act 1986 s 315 (see PARA 490) and the disclaimed property is property in a dwelling house, the court may, on the application of any person who at the time when the bankruptcy petition was presented was in occupation of or entitled to occupy the dwelling house, make an order on such terms as it thinks fit for the vesting of the disclaimed property in any such person: see s 320(1), (2)(c), (3)(c); and PARA 503 heads (3), (c) respectively. As from a day to be appointed, s 320(2)(c), (3)(c) is amended by the Enterprise and Regulatory Reform Act 2013 s 71, Sch 19 paras 1, 25: see PARA 130 note 17.

Where a lease creating a protected tenancy for the purposes of the Rent Act 1977 provided for re-entry on the tenant's bankruptcy and the tenant became bankrupt after becoming a statutory tenant, the bankruptcy was a breach or non-performance of an obligation of the previous protected tenancy which was applicable to the statutory tenancy: *Cadogan Estates Ltd v McMahon* [2001] 1 AC 378, [2001] BPIR 17, HL.

As to tenancies controlled by statute see the Insolvency Act 1986 s 283(3A); and PARA 211 heads (e)–(h).

3   See PARA 427.

4   *Krehl v Great Central Gas Co* (1870) LR 5 Exch 289; *Re Garrud, ex p Newitt* (1881) 16 ChD 522, CA; *Leman v Yorkshire Rly Waggon Co* (1881) 50 LJ Ch 293. As to a landlord's rights in respect of distress see PARA 711 et seq.

425.   Forfeiture of lease on bankruptcy. A proviso in a lease of land that the lease should be forfeited on the tenant's bankruptcy[1] is valid; and, where there is such a proviso and the tenant becomes bankrupt, no interest in the demised premises is divisible among the creditors[2]. However, a proviso of this kind applies only to the bankruptcy of the person in possession of the term created by the lease; if a tenant assigns his term and after the assignment becomes bankrupt, his bankruptcy does not operate to determine the lease[3].

1   Where a lease contains a condition as to forfeiture on the tenant's bankruptcy and on his assigning without licence, and, after the tenant's bankruptcy, the landlord accepts rent from the trustee and treats him as tenant, the condition is gone; it is not clear whether in such a case the landlord may insist on the condition as to forfeiture for assigning without licence: see *Dyke v Taylor* (1861) 30 LJ Ch 281.

2   *Roe d Hunter v Galliers* (1787) 2 Term Rep 133. If the landlord enters for forfeiture on a tenant's bankruptcy, any growing crops on the land belong to the landlord and not to the tenant's creditors: *Davis v Eyton* (1830) 7 Bing 154. A provision in a lease giving the tenant a right to compensation for certain crops 'at the expiration of the term' has no application when the landlord enters for a forfeiture on the tenant's bankruptcy: *Silcock v Farmer* (1882) 46 LT 404, CA; but see *Re Morrish, ex p Hart Dyke* (1882) 22 ChD 410, CA, applied in *Re ABC Coupler and Engineering Co Ltd (No 3)* [1970] 1 All ER 650, [1970] 1 WLR 702. As to the statutory rights to compensation for growing crops on the termination of the tenancy of an agricultural holding see AGRICULTURAL LAND vol 1 (2008) PARA 363 et seq.

If a landlord enters for a forfeiture on bankruptcy, and there is a special contract relating to fixtures which belong to the tenant, the trustee is entitled to a reasonable time to remove them: *Stansfield v Portsmouth Corpn* (1858) 27 LJCP 124. Apart from special contract or statute, the right to remove the fixtures is gone when the term is at an end: *Pugh v Arton* (1869) LR 8 Eq 626. As to the statutory rights of a tenant of an agricultural holding to remove fixtures see AGRICULTURAL LAND vol 1 (2008) PARAS 305, 336; and as to fixtures generally see LANDLORD AND TENANT vol 62 (2012) PARA 172 et seq.

Forfeiture has been held to take place on the presentation of a bankruptcy petition where the proviso in the lease provided for forfeiture on the filing of a petition in liquidation under former bankruptcy legislation: *Re Walker, ex p Gould* (1884) 13 QBD 454. If the landlord accepts rent from the trustee in bankruptcy, the right of forfeiture is gone: see note 1. The tenancy of an allotment garden may be terminated under a provision on re-entry on the tenant becoming bankrupt or compounding with his creditors: see the Allotments Act 1922 s 1(1)(e); and AGRICULTURAL LAND vol 1 (2008) PARA 564.

    Where the lease of a dwelling house contains a provision for forfeiture on bankruptcy, and the lessee is holding on as a tenant, the court may grant possession against him if he becomes bankrupt, on the ground that he has committed a breach of an obligation of his tenancy: *Re Drew* [1929] IR 504.

3   *Smith v Gronow* [1891] 2 QB 394. The proviso runs with the land: *Horsey Estate Ltd v Steiger* [1899] 2 QB 79.

426. Restrictions on, and relief against, forfeiture. If the term created by a lease is determinable on bankruptcy, then, except in certain specified cases[1], the landlord may exercise his right of forfeiture only subject to statutory conditions[2]. If the lessee's interest is sold[3] within one year from the bankruptcy, the landlord, even after the end of the year, may enforce his right only if he serves the notice required by the statutory conditions, and subject to the provisions as to relief against forfeiture contained in them[4].

    If, however, there has been no sale during the year, the restrictions on forfeiture cease at the end of the year, the landlord may enforce his right of re-entry without serving the statutory notice, and relief against forfeiture of the lease may no longer be claimed[5].

1   The Law of Property Act 1925 s 146 does not apply to a condition for forfeiture on the bankruptcy of the lessee if contained in a lease of: (1) agricultural or pastoral land; (2) mines or minerals; (3) a house used or intended to be used as a public house or beer shop; (4) a house let as a dwelling house, with the use of any furniture, books, works of art, or other chattels not being in the nature of fixtures; (5) any property with respect to which the tenant's personal qualifications are of importance for the preservation of the property's value or character, or on the ground of neighbourhood to the lessor, or to any person holding under him: s 146(9).

2   See generally the Law of Property Act 1925 s 146; and LANDLORD AND TENANT vol 63 (2012) PARA 758 et seq. Where any premises are let as a dwelling on a lease which is subject to a right of re-entry or forfeiture, it is not lawful to enforce that right otherwise than by proceedings in the court while any person is lawfully residing in the premises or part of them: see the Protection from Eviction Act 1977 s 2; and LANDLORD AND TENANT vol 63 (2012) PARA 801.

3   To come within this provision, a sale must be completed by conveyance, or the contract entered into must be an absolute contract for sale: *Re Henry Castle & Sons Ltd, Mitchell v Henry Castle & Sons Ltd* (1906) 94 LT 396.

4   See the Law of Property Act 1925 s 146(10)(a); and LANDLORD AND TENANT vol 63 (2012) PARA 774. See also *Civil Service Co-operative Society v McGrigor's Trustee* [1923] 2 Ch 347 at 355; *Pearson v Gee and Braceborough Spa Ltd* [1934] AC 272 at 277, 278, HL.

5   See the Law of Property Act 1925 s 146(10)(b); and LANDLORD AND TENANT vol 63 (2012) PARA 774. See also *Pearson v Gee and Braceborough Spa Ltd* [1934] AC 272 at 278, HL. The landlord's right of re-entry during the year is merely fettered and not abrogated: *Civil Service Co-operative Society v McGrigor's Trustee* [1923] 2 Ch 347. A re-entry within the year is void against the lessee's trustee in bankruptcy if the statutory notice has not been served: *Re Riggs, ex p Lovell* [1901] 2 KB 16. Although, in a case where the lessee's interest has not been sold, an application for relief against forfeiture of the lease may be made only within one year from the bankruptcy, the court's jurisdiction to entertain an application made during the year does not cease merely because the application is not dealt with before the year expires: *Pearson v Gee and Braceborough Spa Ltd* [1934] AC 272, HL. The right of any underlessee to claim relief under the Law of Property Act 1925 s 146(4) (see LANDLORD AND TENANT vol 63 (2012) PARA 775) is not affected by the expiry of the right to claim relief in respect of the lease which is forfeited: Law of Property (Amendment) Act 1929 s 1.

427. When covenant against assignment binds trustee. Whether a proviso for forfeiture of a term, in the event of the lessee assigning his interest without the lessor's assent, binds the lessee's trustee in bankruptcy depends on the wording of the proviso. If the covenant against assignment without consent includes the lessee's successors in title, then the trustee is bound by it[1]. If the covenant was made after 31 December 1925, it will include the successors in title to the lessee unless a contrary intention is expressed[2]. If, however, the covenant expressly relates only to executors, administrators or assigns, the trustee is not bound[3].

1   *Re Wright, ex p Landau v Trustee* [1949] Ch 729, [1949] 2 All ER 605 (a trustee in bankruptcy is a successor in title but is not an assign), distinguishing *Doe d Goodbehere v Bevan* (1815) 3 M & S 353. See also *Re Farrow's Bank Ltd* [1921] 2 Ch 164, CA; and see LANDLORD AND TENANT vol 62 (2012) PARA 630 et seq.

2   See the Law of Property Act 1925 s 79; and DEEDS AND OTHER INSTRUMENTS vol 32 (2012) PARA 457.

3   *Doe d Goodbehere v Bevan* (1815) 3 M & S 353; *Doe d Cheere v Smith* (1814) 5 Taunt 795; *Goring v Warner* (1724) 2 Eq Cas Abr 100; and see *Re Johnson, ex p Blackett* (1894) 70 LT 381.

428.   Mortgaged property. If any part of the property of the bankrupt has been mortgaged, the property passes to the trustee subject to the mortgagee's estate or interest[1], and subject to the mortgagee's rights to take possession even after the bankruptcy and to exercise all the other rights of a mortgagee. Thus, he will be entitled as against the trustee to the fixtures on the mortgaged property[2] and to growing crops there[3]. If a business is carried on there and the goodwill is not separable from the premises and would pass on a sale of the premises, the goodwill is comprised in the security[4].

A contract between a mortgagor and a mortgagee providing for a different distribution of the mortgagor's property in the event of his bankruptcy, or that the mortgagee should have an additional benefit on such an event, is void[5].

Any person claiming to be the legal or equitable mortgagee of land[6] belonging to the bankrupt may apply to the court for an order directing that the land be sold[7]. If satisfied as to the applicant's title, the court may direct accounts to be taken and inquiries to be made to ascertain:

(1)   the principal, interest and costs due under the mortgage; and

(2)   where the mortgagee has been in possession of the land or any part of it, the rents and profits, dividends, interest, or other proceeds received by him or on his behalf;

and directions may be given by the court with respect to any mortgage, whether prior or subsequent, on the same property, other than that of the applicant[8].

For the purpose of those accounts and inquiries, and of making title to the purchaser, any of the parties may be examined by the court, and must produce on oath before the court all such documents in their custody or under their control relating to the estate of the bankrupt as the court may direct; and the court may order any of the parties to clarify any matter which is in dispute in the proceedings or give additional information in relation to any such matter and the normal rules on further information[9] apply to any such order[10].

In any proceedings between a mortgagor and mortgagee, or the trustee of either of them, the court may order accounts to be taken and inquiries to be made in like manner as in the Chancery Division of the High Court[11].

The court may order that the land, or any specified part of it, be sold; and any party bound by the order and in possession of the land or part, or in receipt of the rents and profits from it, may be ordered to deliver up possession or receipt to the purchaser or to such other person as the court may direct[12]. The court may permit the person having conduct of the sale to sell the land in such manner as he thinks fit; alternatively, the court may direct that the land be sold as directed by the order[13].

The court's order may contain directions:

(a)   appointing the persons to have the conduct of the sale;

(b)   fixing the manner of sale, whether by contract conditional on the court's approval, private treaty, public auction or otherwise;

(c)   settling the particulars and conditions of sale;

(d)   obtaining evidence of the value of the property, and fixing a reserve or minimum price;

(e)   requiring particular persons to join in the sale and conveyance;

(f)   requiring the payment of the purchase money into court, or to trustees or others;

(g)   if the sale is to be by public auction, fixing the security, if any, to be given by the auctioneer, and his remuneration[14].

If the sale is to be by public auction, the court may direct that the mortgagee may appear and bid on his own behalf[15].

The proceeds of sale must be applied:

(i)   first, in payment of the expenses of the trustee, of and occasioned by the application to the court, of the sale and attendance thereat, and of any costs arising from the taking of accounts and making of inquiries[16]; and

(ii)   secondly, in payment of the amount found due to any mortgagee, for principal, interest and costs;

and the balance, if any, must be retained by or paid to the trustee[17].

Where the proceeds of sale are insufficient to pay in full the amount found due to any mortgagee, he is entitled to prove as a creditor for any deficiency, and to receive dividends rateably with other creditors, but not so as to disturb any dividend already declared[18].

1   *Re Caine's Mortgage Trusts* [1918] WN 370. As to the rights of a secured creditor, and as to the trustee's right to redeem, see PARA 574 et seq. Notwithstanding the trustee's failure to exercise his right to redeem, the mortgagee's rights as against the mortgaged property in the possession of the bankrupt may become statute-barred: *Cotterell v Price* [1960] 3 All ER 315, [1960] 1 WLR 1097.

2   *Re Allnut, ex p Spicer* (1837) 2 Deac 335; *Re Nutter, ex p Cotton* (1842) 2 Mont D & De G 725; *Re Stead, ex p Price* (1842) 2 Mont D & De G 518; *Re West, ex p Bentley* (1842) 2 Mont D & De G 591; *Re Mackie, ex p Tagart* (1847) De G 531; *Re Inwood, ex p Cowell* (1848) 17 LJ Bcy 16; *Mather v Fraser* (1856) 25 LJ Ch 361; *Waterfall v Penistone* (1856) 26 LJQB 100; *Boyd v Shorrock* (1867) LR 5 Eq 72; *Re Richards, ex p Astbury, ex p Lloyd's Banking Co* (1869) 4 Ch App 630; *Longbottom v Berry* (1869) 10 B & S 852; *Holland v Hodgson* (1872) LR 7 CP 328; *Re Kitchin, ex p Punnett* (1880) 16 ChD 226, CA; *Hobson v Gorringe* [1897] 1 Ch 182, CA; *Reynolds v Ashby & Son* [1904] AC 466, HL (distinguishing *Gough v Wood & Co* [1894] 1 QB 713, CA); *Monti v Barnes* [1901] 1 KB 205, CA; *Ellis v Glover and Hobson Ltd* [1908] 1 KB 388, CA.

3   The mortgagee may take possession of growing crops after the bankruptcy (*Bagnall v Villar* (1879) 12 ChD 812), but not when he claims under an unregistered bill of sale, and the growing crops have been severed and have become personal chattels and have not been taken by the grantee before the commencement of the bankruptcy; in such a case they will pass to the trustee (*Re Phillips, ex p National Mercantile Bank* (1880) 16 ChD 104, CA; and see FINANCIAL SERVICES AND INSTITUTIONS vol 50 (2008) PARA 1670).

4   *Re Kitchin, ex p Punnett* (1880) 16 ChD 226, CA (public house); *Chissum v Dewes* (1828) 5 Russ 29 (upholsterer's business); *King v Midland Rly Co* (1868) 17 WR 113 (baker's business). Stock-in-trade and other personal chattels on mortgaged premises, if not specifically included in the mortgage, will pass to the mortgagor's trustee in bankruptcy: *Re McManus, ex p Jardine* (1875) 10 Ch App 322; *Lyon & Co v London City and Midland Bank* [1903] 2 KB 135.

5   *Re Jeavons, ex p Mackay, ex p Brown* (1873) 8 Ch App 643; *Re Thompson, ex p Williams* (1877) 7 ChD 138, CA; *Re Johns, Worrell v Johns* [1928] 1 Ch 737; cf *Re Stockton Iron Furnace Co* (1879) 10 ChD 335. See also *Belmont Park Investments PTY Ltd v BNY Corporate Trustee Services Ltd* [2011] UKSC 38, [2012] 1 AC 383, [2012] 1 All ER 505.

6   For these purposes, 'land' includes any interest in, or right over, land: Insolvency Rules 1986, SI 1986/1925, r 6.197(1).

7   Insolvency Rules 1986, SI 1986/1925, r 6.197(1).

8   Insolvency Rules 1986, SI 1986/1925, r 6.197(2).

9　Ie CPR Pt 18: see CIVIL PROCEDURE vol 11 (2009) PARA 611 et seq.

10　Insolvency Rules 1986, SI 1986/1925, r 6.197(3) (amended by SI 1999/1022).

11　Insolvency Rules 1986, SI 1986/1925, r 6.197(4).

12　Insolvency Rules 1986, SI 1986/1925, r 6.198(1). Nothing in rr 6.198, 6.199 affects the rights in rem of creditors or third parties protected under Council Regulation (EC) 1346/2000 on insolvency proceedings (OJ L160, 30.06.00, p 1) ('European Regulation on Insolvency Proceedings') art 5 (third parties' rights in rem) (see PARAS 41, 42): Insolvency Rules 1986, SI 1986/1925, r 6.198(5) (added by SI 2002/1307).

13　Insolvency Rules 1986, SI 1986/1925, r 6.198(2). See note 12.

14　Insolvency Rules 1986, SI 1986/1925, r 6.198(3). See note 12.

15　Insolvency Rules 1986, SI 1986/1925, r 6.198(4). See note 12.

16　Ie as directed by the Insolvency Rules 1986, SI 1986/1925, r 6.197.

17　Insolvency Rules 1986, SI 1986/1925, r 6.199(1). See note 12.

18　Insolvency Rules 1986, SI 1986/1925, r 6.199(2). See note 12.

429.　Agricultural holdings and charges. The statutory requirements concerning the length of a notice to quit an agricultural holding and a tenant's right to serve a counter-notice are modified in the case of bankruptcy proceedings against the tenant[1].

Where a farmer who is adjudged bankrupt has created in favour of a bank an agricultural charge on any of the farming stock or other agricultural assets belonging to him, and the charge was created within three months of the date of the presentation of the bankruptcy petition and operated to secure any sum owing to the bank immediately prior to the giving of the charge, then, unless it is proved that the farmer immediately after the execution of the charge was solvent, the amount which but for this provision would have been secured by the charge is to be reduced by the amount of the sum so owing to the bank immediately prior to the giving of the charge, but without prejudice to the bank's right to enforce any other security for that sum or to claim payment thereof as an unsecured debt[2].

1　See AGRICULTURAL LAND vol 1 (2008) PARAS 376, 382.

2　Agricultural Credits Act 1928 s 8(5). As to registration of agricultural charges see s 9 (amended by the Land Charges Act 1972 s 18(1), Sch 3 para 7; and SI 2011/2436); and AGRICULTURAL PRODUCTION AND MARKETING vol 1 (2008) PARA 1331.

430.　Contracts. Rights arising out of contracts made by the bankrupt pass to the trustee, if not disclaimed[1] or discharged[2], subject to the rights of the persons with whom the bankrupt has contracted, and to the rights of third persons which have been created in respect of them[3]. Where a person is adjudged bankrupt, any disposition of property made by that person in the period beginning with the day of the presentation of the petition for the bankruptcy order[4] and ending with the vesting of the bankrupt's estate in a trustee[5] is void except to the extent that it is or was made with the consent of the court, or is or was subsequently ratified by the court[6]. The above provisions do not, however, give a remedy against any person:

(1)　in respect of any property or payment which he received before the commencement of the bankruptcy[7] in good faith, for value and without notice that the petition had been presented; or

(2)　in respect of any interest in property which derives from an interest in respect of which there is, by virtue of this provision, no remedy[8].

A disposition of property is void under the above provisions notwithstanding that the property is not or, as the case may be, would not be comprised in the bankrupt's estate; but nothing in the above provisions affects any disposition made by a person of property held by him on trust for any other person[9].

Although bankruptcy does not determine a contract if the trustee elects to go on with it, it does in some cases qualify the rights to which the trustee succeeds, which are not always the same as the bankrupt's rights would have been had he remained solvent.

Thus, on a sale of goods to the bankrupt, if both the property in the goods and the possession have passed to the bankrupt, the trustee takes the goods; and, if they have not been paid for, the vendor has no other remedy than to prove in the bankruptcy for the price[10]. Where the sale is without any stipulation as to credit, the seller has in all cases the unpaid seller's lien or right to retain possession until the price is paid; the bankrupt's trustee is not entitled to possession of the goods until he pays for them, and the seller may insist on being paid in full as a condition of parting with possession[11]. Moreover, on a sale of goods on credit, where the possession has not passed to the bankrupt, bankruptcy qualifies the buyer's rights; for, if the buyer becomes bankrupt before he has obtained possession of the goods, the seller may refuse to deliver the goods until they have been paid for[12]. Even though there has been part delivery of the goods, the seller's lien may be exercised over the remainder, except where the part delivery constitutes a waiver[13].

Where goods are to be delivered by instalments, to be paid for separately, the unpaid seller is not, after the bankruptcy, bound to deliver any more goods until the price is tendered to him; and, if a debt is due to the seller for goods already delivered, he may refuse to deliver any more goods until he is paid the debt already due, as well as the price of the goods which are still to be delivered[14]. Where the sale has been induced by the purchaser's fraud, the vendor is entitled, within a reasonable time after discovering the fraud, to repudiate the contract and retake possession of the goods[15].

If a bill of exchange has been given for the price of the goods and the buyer becomes insolvent, the seller's lien revives[16]. The lien may be exercised even though the seller is in possession of the goods as the buyer's agent or bailee[17].

1   Ie under the Insolvency Act 1986 s 315: see PARA 490 et seq.
2   Ie under the Insolvency Act 1986 s 345: see PARA 702.
3   *Re Garrud, ex p Newitt* (1881) 16 ChD 522 at 531, CA; and see PARA 406. Where an employer agreed with a retiring employee to make certain payments to his widow or daughter if he, the employee, died before a certain date, and the employee was subsequently adjudicated bankrupt and died before that date, his trustee in bankruptcy was held not entitled to intercept the payment: *Re Schebsman* [1944] Ch 83, [1943] 2 All ER 768, CA (approved in *Beswick v Beswick* [1968] AC 58, [1967] 2 All ER 1197, HL). As to contracts providing benefits for third parties generally see CONTRACT.
4   As to presentation of a petition for a bankruptcy order see PARA 130 et seq.
5   Ie under the Insolvency Act 1986 Pt 9 Ch 4 (ss 305–335): see PARA 397 et seq.
6   See the Insolvency Act 1986 s 284(1), (3); and PARA 213. Section 284(1) applies to a payment, whether in cash or otherwise, as it applies to a disposition of property and, accordingly, where any payment is void by virtue of s 284(1), the persons must hold the sum paid for the bankrupt as part of his estate: see s 284(2); and PARA 213.
7   As to the commencement of bankruptcy see PARA 209.
8   See the Insolvency Act 1986 s 284(4); and PARA 213.
9   See the Insolvency Act 1986 s 284(6); and PARA 213.
10 See *Re Shackleton, ex p Whittaker* (1875) 10 Ch App 446; but see *Re Dyton, Appleton v Hole* (1952) 102 L Jo 669 (agreement for assignment of lease of hotel and agreement for sale of furniture for a price payable by instalments; bankruptcy of purchaser before all instalments paid; vendor held to have equitable lien on furniture for unpaid instalments). As to vendor's lien generally see LIEN vol 68 (2008) PARA 859 et seq. Sub-purchasers of unappropriated goods will in general be unable to claim a beneficial interest in the chattels represented by their portions on the insolvency of the holder of the goods: see *Re Wait* [1927] 1 Ch 606, CA; *Re London Wine Co (Shippers) Ltd* [1986] PCC 121; *Re Goldcorp Exchange Ltd (in receivership)* [1995] 1 AC 74, [1994] 2 All ER 806, PC. However, unappropriated goods may be subject to a trust in

favour of the purchaser: *Hunter v Moss* [1994] 3 All ER 215, [1994] 1 WLR 452, CA; *Re Harvard Securities (in liquidation), Holland v Newbury* [1997] 2 BCLC 369, [1998] BCC 567; and see further PARA 444. As to when the property passes on a contract to sell goods see the Sale of Goods Act 1979 ss 16–19; and SALE OF GOODS AND SUPPLY OF SERVICES vol 91 (2012) PARA 107 et seq. As to when the property passes on a contract to build or to manufacture see *Reid v Macbeth and Gray* [1904] AC 223, HL; and see *Woods v Russell* (1822) 1 Dow & Ry KB 587; *Clarke v Spence* (1836) 4 Ad & El 448; *Laidler v Burlinson* (1837) 2 M & W 602; *Tripp v Armitage* (1839) 4 M & W 687; *Baker v Gray* (1856) 25 LJCP 161; *Wood v Bell* (1856) 25 LJQB 321: *Re Attwater, ex p Watts* (1862) 1 New Rep 170; *Seath v Moore* (1886) 11 App Cas 350, HL; *Bellamy v Davey* [1891] 3 Ch 540; BUILDING CONTRACTS; SALE OF GOODS AND SUPPLY OF SERVICES vol 91 (2012) PARAS 127–129.

11　See the Sale of Goods Act 1979 ss 39, 41(1)(a); and SALE OF GOODS AND SUPPLY OF SERVICES vol 91 (2012) PARA 234 et seq.

12　See the Sale of Goods Act 1979 ss 39, 41(1)(c); and SALE OF GOODS AND SUPPLY OF SERVICES vol 91 (2012) PARA 234 et seq.

13　See the Sale of Goods Act 1979 s 42; *Miles v Gorton* (1834) 2 Cr & M 504; and SALE OF GOODS AND SUPPLY OF SERVICES vol 91 (2012) PARA 241.

14　*Re Edwards, ex p Chalmers* (1873) 8 Ch App 289; and see SALE OF GOODS AND SUPPLY OF SERVICES vol 91 (2012) PARA 174 et seq.

15　*Re Eastgate, ex p Ward* [1905] 1 KB 465 (rescission after notice of act of bankruptcy); *Tilley v Bowman Ltd* [1910] 1 KB 745 (rescission after date of receiving order); *Gamage Ltd v Charlesworth* 1910 SC 257. Cf *Kin Tye Loong v Seth* (1920) 89 LJPC 113 (where it was held that the vendors had elected to affirm the sale); and see *Car and Universal Finance Co Ltd v Caldwell* [1965] 1 QB 525 at 558, [1964] 1 All ER 290 at 298, CA (where *Re Eastgate, ex p Ward* was referred to); *Newtons of Wembley Ltd v Williams* [1965] 1 QB 560, [1964] 3 All ER 532, CA.

16　*Gunn v Bolckow, Vaughan & Co* (1875) 10 Ch App 491; and see *New v Swain* (1828) Dan & Ll 193; *Dixon v Yates* (1833) 5 B & Ad 313; *Re Raatz, ex p Raatz* [1897] 2 QB 80, DC.

17　See the Sale of Goods Act 1979 s 41(2); *Grice v Richardson* (1877) 3 App Cas 319, PC; and SALE OF GOODS AND SUPPLY OF SERVICES vol 91 (2012) PARA 240. As to the seller's right of stoppage in transit see the Sale of Goods Act 1979 ss 39, 44; and SALE OF GOODS AND SUPPLY OF SERVICES vol 91 (2012) PARA 254 et seq.

431. Trustee's right to enforce contracts. Bankruptcy does not determine a contract[1], and included in the property which passes to the trustee on adjudication is the right of enforcing certain unexecuted or uncompleted contracts into which the bankrupt has entered, and from which benefits may accrue to the estate[2].

Thus, all rights under contracts which, if the bankrupt had died, would pass as part of his personal estate to his personal representatives pass to the trustee on his bankruptcy; but rights under contracts where the bankrupt's personal skill or conduct forms a material part of the consideration[3], which the trustee cannot perform on his behalf, such as a contract to render personal services, to paint a picture or to write a book, do not pass[4].

As regards unprofitable contracts, which the trustee could perform, he may elect either to adopt or to disclaim them[5]. Should he disclaim them, the persons who have contracted with the bankrupt may prove in the bankruptcy for damages for the value of the injury they have thereby sustained[6]; if the trustee insists on the contract being performed[7], he must perform the bankrupt's part of the contract, as and when the bankrupt should have done so himself[8].

1　*Brooke v Hewitt* (1796) 3 Ves 253 at 255; *Re Sneezum, ex p Davis* (1876) 3 ChD 463 at 473, CA; *Re Edwards, ex p Chalmers* (1873) 8 Ch App 289 at 293, 294; *Jennings' Trustee v King* [1952] Ch 899 at 908, [1952] 2 All ER 608 at 612. Bankruptcy of principal or agent usually determines the agent's authority to act as agent: *Re Douglas, ex p Snowball* (1872) 7 Ch App 534; *Markwick v Hardingham* (1880) 15 ChD 339, CA. As to powers of attorney see AGENCY vol 1 (2008) PARA 31 et seq; as to the general effect of the bankruptcy of principal or agent see AGENCY vol 1 (2008) PARAS 190–191 respectively; and as to the effect of bankruptcy in the case of partnership see PARA 436.

2 The simplest instance of such contracts would be a contract under which the bankrupt is entitled to a sum of money payable either before or after bankruptcy; the right to the debt passes to the trustee: *Morgan v Taylor* (1859) 28 LJCP 178; *Re Pooley, ex p Rabbidge* (1878) 8 ChD 367, CA; *McEntire v Potter & Co* (1889) 22 QBD 438. As to the position where the contract is unexecuted at the date of bankruptcy see *Bailey v Thurston & Co Ltd* [1903] 1 KB 137.

3 *Gibson v Carruthers* (1841) 8 M & W 321 at 333 per Parke B; and see *Knight v Burgess* (1864) 33 LJ Ch 727 (building contract); *Flood v Finlay* (1811) 2 Ball & B 9; *Bailey v Thurston & Co Ltd* [1903] 1 KB 137, CA; *Lucas v Moncrieff* (1905) 21 TLR 683 (contract to publish book); *Re Worthington, ex p Pathé Frères* [1914] 2 KB 299, CA (contract to procure subscriptions for shares).

4 An order with respect to salary or income under a contract for personal services may be made, as with any other income, under the Insolvency Act 1986 s 310: see PARA 462 et seq.

5 See the Insolvency Act 1986 s 315; and PARA 490 et seq.

6 Insolvency Act 1986 s 315(5). In the case of the administration in bankruptcy of the insolvent estate of a deceased person dying before the presentation of a bankruptcy petition, s 315 applies: Administration of Insolvent Estates of Deceased Persons Order 1986, SI 1986/1999, art 3(1), Sch 1 Pt II para 23. As to the administration in bankruptcy of the insolvent estates of deceased persons see further PARA 830 et seq.

7 As regards a contract to grant a lease to a bankrupt, the trustee may obtain an order for its specific performance on agreeing to be personally bound by the covenants into which the bankrupt could have been obliged to enter (*Powell v Lloyd* (1827) 1 Y & J 427; on appeal 2 Y & J 372, distinguishing the earlier cases to the contrary effect; and see *Buckland v Papillon* (1866) 2 Ch App 67); and as to the form of such a lease to the trustee see *Page v Broom* (1842) 6 Jur 308. A person to whom the benefit of an agreement for a lease has been assigned by a bankrupt, before he becomes bankrupt, is entitled to specific performance of the agreement, if solvent and willing to enter into the usual covenants, and if the consideration for it was not personal to the assignor: *Crosbie v Tooke* (1833) 1 My & K 431. However, the trustee is not entitled to specific performance of an agreement for a lease entered into for the bankrupt's personal accommodation: *Flood v Finlay* (1811) 2 Ball & B 9. The trustee in bankruptcy of the purchaser under a contract for the sale of land may recover damages for breach of contract if the vendor improperly repudiates the contract: *Jennings' Trustee v King* [1952] Ch 899, [1952] 2 All ER 608.

8 *Gibson v Carruthers* (1841) 8 M & W 321 at 333.

432. Uncompleted contracts relating to land. If, before his bankruptcy, the bankrupt has contracted to sell or mortgage property, the trustee takes the property subject to the obligation to fulfil the contract[1]. The legal estate in the property vests in the trustee subject to the equitable title of the purchaser to have the estate conveyed to him on payment of the purchase price[2]. If the purchaser, unaware of the bankruptcy, pays the balance of the purchase money to the bankrupt, he pays the wrong person and cannot compel the trustee to execute a conveyance without paying the purchase money again to him[3]. Specific performance of a contract by the bankrupt to purchase property will not normally be granted against the trustee[4].

Where a landowner who is subsequently adjudged bankrupt enters into a contract to sell his land, special protection is afforded to the purchaser under the conditions prescribed by the conveyancing statutes[5].

In the case of land, other than registered land, which the bankrupt has contracted to sell, the effectiveness, as against the trustee in bankruptcy, of a disposition in favour of a purchaser depends in the first instance on whether the bankruptcy petition has been registered against the vendor as a pending action[6], or a bankruptcy order has been registered as a writ or order affecting the land[7], such registration constituting actual notice to all persons and for all purposes connected with the land affected[8], and thus binding the purchaser.

If the land is registered land, the question whether the purchaser has express notice of a bankruptcy petition registered as a pending action becomes material, for, if he has, he will not be protected[9].

Whereas a pending land action does not bind a purchaser[10] without express notice of it unless it is registered as a pending action, as respects a petition in bankruptcy, the protection only applies in favour of a purchaser of a legal estate in good faith, for money or money's worth[11]. As respects bankruptcy orders, the protection afforded to a purchaser of the land against unregistered writs and orders[12] is restricted to a purchaser of a legal estate in good faith for money or money's worth[13]. The title of a trustee in bankruptcy is void as against a purchaser of a legal estate in good faith for money or money's worth, claiming under a conveyance made after the date of registration of the petition as a pending action, unless, at the date of the conveyance, either the registration of the petition as a pending action is in force[14], or the receiving order is registered in the register of writs and orders[15].

As soon as practicable after registration of a petition in bankruptcy as a pending action under the Land Charges Act 1972[16], the registrar must enter in the register, in relation to any registered estate or charge which appears to him to be affected, a notice in respect of the pending action[17]. As soon as practicable after registration of a bankruptcy order under the Land Charges Act 1972[18], the registrar must, in relation to any registered estate or charge which appears to him to be affected by the order, enter in the register a restriction reflecting the effect of the Insolvency Act 1986[19].

Where the proprietor of a registered estate or charge is adjudged bankrupt, the title of his trustee in bankruptcy is void as against a person to whom a registrable disposition of the estate or charge is made if: (1) the disposition is made for valuable consideration; (2) the person to whom the disposition is made acts in good faith; and (3) at the time of the disposition no notice or restriction is entered in relation to the registered estate or charge, and the person to whom the disposition is made has no notice of the bankruptcy petition or the adjudication[20].

1   *Pearce v Bastable's Trustee in Bankruptcy* [1901] 2 Ch 122; *Re Bastable, ex p Trustee* [1901] 2 KB 518, CA; *Re Taylor, ex p Norvell* [1910] 1 KB 562, CA; *Re Scheibler, ex p Holthausen* (1874) 9 Ch App 722.

2   *Re Pooley, ex p Rabbidge* (1878) 8 ChD 367 at 370, CA; *Re Scheibler, ex p Holthausen* (1874) 9 Ch App 722 at 726.

3   *Re Pooley, ex p Rabbidge* (1878) 8 ChD 367, CA; and see *Re Taylor, ex p Norvell* [1910] 1 KB 562, CA.

4   *Holloway v York* (1877) 25 WR 627. As to specific performance of a contract to grant a lease to a bankrupt, and as to a trustee's right to enforce contracts, see PARA 431.

5   The Land Charges Act 1972 provides for the registration of the several instruments and matters mentioned in it, some of which do not, or should not, appear in the abstract or epitome of title. The Land Charges Act 1972 must be considered in conjunction with the Law of Property Act 1925 s 198 and s 199. The registration of any instrument or matter in any register kept under the Land Charges Act 1972 or any local land charges register is deemed to constitute actual notice of the instrument or matter to all persons and for all purposes connected with the land affected: see the Law of Property Act 1925 s 198(1) (amended by the Local Land Charges Act 1975 s 17(2), Sch 1); and REAL PROPERTY AND REGISTRATION vol 87 (2012) PARA 785. A purchaser is not to be prejudicially affected by notice of any instrument or matter capable of such registration which is void or unenforceable against him under the 1972 Act: see the Law of Property 1925 s 199(1)(i); and REAL PROPERTY AND REGISTRATION vol 87 (2012) PARA 708. There is no positive obligation to register; the sanction lies in the effects and consequences of non-registration: see the Land Charges Act 1972 ss 4–7; and REAL PROPERTY AND REGISTRATION vol 87 (2012) PARA 693 et seq.

6   See the Land Charges Act 1972 ss 5, 8 (cited in note 14); PARAS 171, 196; and REAL PROPERTY AND REGISTRATION vol 87 (2012) PARA 740 et seq. As to the vacation of registration see s 1(6), (6A) (added by the County Courts Act 1984 s 148(1), Sch 2 Pt IV para 16; and substituted by SI 1991/784), the Land Charges Act 1972 s 5 (amended by the County Courts

Act 1984 Sch 2 Pt IV para 17; and the Insolvency Act 1985 s 235(1), (3), Sch 8 para 21(2), Sch 10 Pt III), the Land Charges Act 1972 s 8; and REAL PROPERTY AND REGISTRATION vol 87 (2012) PARA 693 et seq.

7   See the Land Charges Act 1972 s 6 (amended by the Insolvency Act 1985 Sch 8 para 21(3), Sch 10 Pt III); the Land Charges Act 1972 s 8 (cited in note 14); and REAL PROPERTY AND REGISTRATION vol 87 (2012) PARA 746 et seq.

8   See the Law of Property Act 1925 s 198(1) (cited in note 5).

9   See the Land Charges Act 1972 s 5(7); and REAL PROPERTY AND REGISTRATION vol 87 (2012) PARA 742. This is so notwithstanding the Law of Property Act 1925 s 199, whereby a purchaser is not normally prejudicially affected by express notice of an unregistered matter capable of registration under the Land Charges Act 1972.

10 Unless the context otherwise requires, 'purchaser' in the Land Charges Act 1972 means any person, including a mortgagee or lessee, who for valuable consideration takes any interest in land or in a charge on land: s 17(1).

11 See the Land Charges Act 1972 s 5(8) (amended by the Insolvency Act 1985 Sch 8 para 21(2)); and REAL PROPERTY AND REGISTRATION vol 87 (2012) PARA 742.

12 See the Land Charges Act 1972 s 6(4) (amended by the Senior Courts Act 1981 s 152(1), Sch 5; the County Courts Act 1984 s 148(1), Sch 2 Pt IV para 18; and the Constitutional Reform Act 2005 s 59(5), Sch 11 Pt 1 para 1(2)); and REAL PROPERTY AND REGISTRATION vol 87 (2012) PARA 750.

13 See the Land Charges Act 1972 s 6(5) (substituted by the Insolvency Act 1985 Sch 8 para 21(3)); and REAL PROPERTY AND REGISTRATION vol 87 (2012) PARA 750.

14 A registration ceases to have effect at the end of five years from the date on which it was made, but may be renewed from time to time and, if so renewed, has effect for five years from the date of renewal: see the Land Charges Act 1972 s 8; and REAL PROPERTY AND REGISTRATION vol 87 (2012) PARA 752. See also note 15.

15 See the Land Charges Act 1972 s 6(6) (amended by the Insolvency Act 1985 Sch 10 Pt III); and REAL PROPERTY AND REGISTRATION vol 87 (2012) PARA 742. The Land Charges Act 1972 s 6(6) refers to a 'receiving order'. It is apprehended that such reference was intended to be to a 'bankruptcy order' in line with the other amendments made to the 1972 Act by the Insolvency Act 1985 s 235(1), Sch 8 para 21(3) and that such amendment was omitted through an oversight on the part of the legislature.

    Any question arising whether the purchaser had knowledge, at the time of entering into the contract, of the registered bankruptcy petition, must be determined by reference to his actual knowledge: see the Law of Property Act 1969 s 24(1), (3); and REAL PROPERTY AND REGISTRATION vol 87 (2012) PARA 708.

16 See REAL PROPERTY AND REGISTRATION vol 87 (2012) PARA 739 et seq.

17 See the Land Registration Act 2002 s 86(2); and REAL PROPERTY AND REGISTRATION vol 87 (2012) PARA 532. Unless cancelled by the registrar in such manner as rules may provide, a notice entered under s 86(2) continues in force until a restriction is entered in the register under s 86(4) (see the text to note 19), or the trustee in bankruptcy is registered as proprietor: s 86(3).

18 See REAL PROPERTY AND REGISTRATION vol 87 (2012) PARA 746 et seq.

19 See the Land Registration Act 2002 s 86(4); and REAL PROPERTY AND REGISTRATION vol 87 (2012) PARA 743.

20 See the Land Registration Act 2002 s 86(5). Section 86(5) only applies if the relevant requirements are met in relation to the disposition, but, when they are met, has effect from the date of the disposition: s 86(6). Nothing in s 86 requires a person to whom a registrable disposition is made to make any search under the Land Charges Act 1972: Land Registration Act 2002 s 86(7). As to registrable dispositions see REAL PROPERTY AND REGISTRATION vol 87 (2012) PARA 427 et seq. As to registration requirements on the insolvency of a proprietor see REAL PROPERTY AND REGISTRATION vol 87 (2012) PARA 441.

433. Rights under insurance contract. Where the bankrupt is insured against liabilities to third parties and he incurs any such liability, either before or after the bankruptcy, his rights against the insurer under the contract of insurance in respect of the liability vest in the third party to whom the liability was incurred, and do not pass to the trustee in bankruptcy[1].

Where the Secretary of State has entered into an agreement for the reinsurance of a ship, aircraft or cargo against war risks, and the original insurer or any intermediate insurer becomes bankrupt, any sum payable by the Secretary of State or any intermediate insurer subsequent to the bankrupt insurer must be paid direct to the assured, and the assured's right to receive payment from the bankrupt insurer is, to the extent to which the risk has been so reinsured, extinguished[2].

1	See the Third Parties (Rights against Insurers) Act 1930 s 1 (amended by the Insolvency Act 1985 s 235(1), Sch 8 para 7(2); the Insolvency Act 1986 s 439(2), Sch 14; and SI 2003/2096); and INSURANCE vol 60 (2011) PARAS 651–656. The Third Parties (Rights against Insurers) Act 1930 s 1 applies only to liability for damage to a third party caused by the fault of the insured and not to legal liability insurance: *Tarbuck v Avon Insurance* [2002] QB 571, [2001] BPIR 1142. In the case of compulsory motor vehicle insurance, the transfer of rights against the insurer by virtue of the 1930 Act does not affect the bankrupt's liability to the third party: see the Road Traffic Act 1988 s 153; and ROAD TRAFFIC vol 90 (2011) PARA 710.

	The transfer of liability can only occur when that liability is fully established e g by judgment (see *Sea Voyager Maritime Inc v Bielecki (t/a Hughes Hooker & Co)* [1999] 1 All ER 628, [1999] 1 BCLC 133), agreement or admission of a proof (see *Law Society v Official Receiver* [2007] EWHC 2841 (Ch), [2007] BPIR 1595). The rights of the injured party against the insurer under the 1930 Act are subjected to and limited by the terms of the bankrupt's policy, and he may accordingly be met with the defence that he has not previously sued the bankrupt to judgment (*Post Office v Norwich Union Fire Insurance Society* [1967] 2 QB 363, [1967] 1 All ER 577, CA); or that notice of the proceedings taken against the bankrupt had not been given to the insurer with sufficient promptness (*Farrell v Federated Employers Insurance Association Ltd* [1970] 3 All ER 632, [1970] 1 WLR 1400, CA); but he cannot be met by the insurer with a plea of set-off of premiums unpaid by the bankrupt (*Murray v Legal and General Assurance Society Ltd* [1970] 2 QB 495, [1969] 3 All ER 794). The discharge of a person from bankruptcy does not affect the operation of the Third Parties (Rights against Insurers) Act 1930: see *Law Society v Official Receiver* [2007] EWHC 2841 (Ch), [2007] BPIR 1595. See further INSURANCE vol 60 (2011) PARA 653.

	As from a day to be appointed, the Third Parties (Rights against Insurers) Act 1930 is repealed by the Third Parties (Rights against Insurers) Act 2010 s 20(2), (3), Sch 3 para 3, Sch 4. At the date at which this volume states the law no such day had been appointed. The Third Parties (Rights against Insurers) Act 1930 s 1 will be replaced by the Third Parties (Rights against Insurers) Act 2010 ss 1, 4, under which similar provision is made: see INSURANCE vol 60 (2011) PARAS 657–665.

2	See the Marine and Aviation Insurance (War Risks) Act 1952 s 4; and INSURANCE vol 60 (2011) PARA 794.

434. Builder's bankruptcy. A stipulation in a building contract that on the bankruptcy of the builder the materials brought by him on the ground should be forfeited to the building owner is void, as being an attempt to control the use, after bankruptcy, of property vested in the bankrupt at the date of the bankruptcy; accordingly, the materials would, in the event of the builder's bankruptcy, pass to his trustee[1]. However, a stipulation is valid which provides that, on default of the builder in fulfilling his part of the agreement, the building owner might expel him, and forfeit the materials brought by the builder on the land. This right of forfeiture is not affected by the bankruptcy of the builder, and may be exercised after his bankruptcy[2].

1	*Re Harrison, ex p Jay* (1880) 14 ChD 19, CA; *Re Walker, ex p Barter, ex p Black* (1884) 26 ChD 510, CA; cf *Belmont Park Investments PTY Ltd v BNY Corporate Trustee Services Ltd* [2011] UKSC 38, [2012] 1 AC 383, [2012] 1 All ER 505.

2	*Brown v Bateman* (1867) LR 2 CP 272; *Re Waugh, ex p Dickin* (1876) 4 ChD 524; *Re Garrud, ex p Newitt* (1881) 16 ChD 522, CA; *Re Keen and Keen, ex p Collins* [1902] 1 KB 555. If a building agreement gives a power of forfeiture in the event of bankruptcy, and also in the event of the failure of the builder to complete, and the building owner seizes on bankruptcy, he cannot afterwards avail himself of the right to seize for the failure to complete: *Re Walker, ex p Barter, ex p Black* (1884) 26 ChD 510, CA. A clause in a building agreement, that materials brought on the ground are to be the property of the building owner, vests the materials in him, subject to a condition of defeasance, if the builder completes the work; such a clause is a security to the building owner for the performance of the work: *Hart v Porthgain Harbour Co Ltd* [1903] 1 Ch 690. See further BUILDING CONTRACTS vol 6 (2011) PARA 283 et seq.

435.   Shareholder's bankruptcy.   Where any part of the bankrupt's estate consists of stock or shares in a company, shares in a ship or any other property transferable in the books of a company, office or person, the trustee may exercise the right to transfer the property to the same extent as the bankrupt might have exercised it if he had not become bankrupt[1]. The trustee of a bankrupt shareholder may be refused the right to have a transfer of the bankrupt's shares registered which may preclude him from exercising the rights attached to the shareholding[2].

A proviso in a company's articles of association that a shareholder, in the event of his bankruptcy, should sell his shares to particular persons at a particular price is valid, if the price is fixed for all persons alike, and is not less than the fair price which might be obtained; but a provision that, in the event of bankruptcy, the shares should be sold at a lower price would be repugnant to the bankruptcy laws and, therefore, void[3].

1   See the Insolvency Act 1986 s 311(3); and PARA 409.
2   *Re HL Bolton Engineering Co Ltd* [1956] Ch 577, [1956] 1 All ER 799 (where the trustee, who had not been registered as the holder of the bankrupt's shares, was held to have no locus standi to present a winding-up petition); cf *Re K/9 Meat Supplies (Guildford) Ltd* [1966] 3 All ER 320, [1966] 1 WLR 1112 (where the bankrupt unsuccessfully petitioned for winding up at the instance of the trustee), considered by Lord Wilberforce and Lord Cross of Chelsea in *Ebrahimi v Westbourne Galleries Ltd* [1973] AC 360, [1972] 2 All ER 492, HL.
    The bankrupt may be required to exercise his vote in accordance with the trustee's or the official receiver's directions: *Morgan v Gray* [1953] Ch 83, [1953] 1 All ER 213; *Wise v Landsell* [1921] 1 Ch 420. The bankrupt shareholder retains, even after adjudication, the right to bring proceedings in his own name as a minority shareholder: see *Birch v Sullivan* [1958] 1 All ER 56, [1957] 1 WLR 1247.
3   *Borland's Trustee v Steel Bros & Co Ltd* [1901] 1 Ch 279; cf *Belmont Park Investments PTY Ltd v BNY Corporate Trustee Services Ltd* [2011] UKSC 38, [2012] 1 AC 383, [2012] 1 All ER 505.

436.   Share in partnership.   If the bankrupt has carried on business in partnership with other persons, then, subject to any agreement between the partners, the partnership is dissolved by bankruptcy[1]; but the trustee is entitled to the value of the bankrupt partner's share and to an account[2]. If, after the bankruptcy, the other partner continues to carry on the business with the capital as constituted at the time of the bankruptcy, the bankrupt partner's trustee is entitled to participate in the subsequent profits[3].

A proviso in a partnership agreement that, in the event of the bankruptcy of one of the partners, his share shall go over to his co-partners, is void as being in fraud of the bankruptcy laws[4]; so is a proviso that the bankrupt partner should, in the event of his bankruptcy, receive for his share a smaller sum than its real value[5]. Such arrangements between partners are valid only as between themselves, and do not bind creditors; and the trustee in bankruptcy of the bankrupt partner is entitled, in spite of such arrangements, to an account of the estate and profits of the partnership[6].

1   See the Partnership Act 1890 s 33(1); and PARTNERSHIP vol 79 (2008) PARA 177. A limited partnership is not dissolved by the bankruptcy of a limited partner: see the Limited Partnerships Act 1907 s 6(2); and PARTNERSHIP vol 79 (2008) PARA 227.
2   See *Wilson v Greenwood* (1818) 1 Swan 471; *Whitmore v Mason* (1861) 2 John & H 204; *Re Williams, ex p Warden* (1872) 21 WR 51.
3   *Crawshay v Collins* (1808) 15 Ves 218.
4   *Whitmore v Mason* (1861) 2 John & H 204; cf *Belmont Park Investments PTY Ltd v BNY Corporate Trustee Services Ltd* [2011] UKSC 38, [2012] 1 AC 383, [2012] 1 All ER 505.
5   *Wilson v Greenwood* (1818) 1 Swan 471; *Re Williams, ex p Warden* (1872) 21 WR 51. A provision in a partnership agreement that, on the bankruptcy of one partner, his share should be

taken by the solvent partners at a sum to be fixed by valuation and payable by instalments over a period may be void as repugnant to the bankruptcy laws: see *Wilson v Greenwood*.

6 *Re Williams, ex p Warden* (1872) 21 WR 51 at 52.

437. Goodwill of bankrupt's business. If the bankrupt has carried on a business, the goodwill of the business passes on adjudication to his trustee, except:

(1) where the business premises have been mortgaged and the goodwill is attached to the premises, in which case the goodwill is comprised in the security[1]; and

(2) where the goodwill is personal to the bankrupt, as in the case of a professional person, in which case, it seems, it would not pass[2].

Compensation which is given by statute to a bankrupt for the destruction of his business is analogous to goodwill and passes to the trustee[3].

On the sale by the trustee of the goodwill of the bankrupt's business, the bankrupt may, it seems, be compelled to join in the assignment of his business and goodwill for the benefit of his creditors[4]; but he cannot be compelled to enter into any covenant restricting him from carrying on the same business[5]. Whether the bankrupt has or has not joined in the assignment of the goodwill to the purchaser, he cannot be restrained from setting up a fresh business or from soliciting his former customers[6], except when he has agreed with the purchaser not to carry on a similar business[7]; although, even if he cannot be restrained, he cannot use the trade mark of the old business[8], or in any way represent himself as carrying on the business which has been sold[9].

1 See PARA 428 text and note 4.
2 See *Farr v Pearce* (1818) 3 Madd 74. The right to publish a newspaper which has been published by the bankrupt passes to his trustee: *Longman v Tripp* (1805) 2 Bos & PNR 67; *Re Baldwin, ex p Foss, ex p Baldwin* (1858) 2 De G & J 230. As to the rights of a trustee to the goodwill of a bankrupt's business see *Cruttwell v Lye* (1810) 17 Ves 335; *Re Thomas, ex p Thomas* (1841) 2 Mont D & De G 294 (revsd on another point 3 Mont D & De G 40); *Hudson v Osborne* (1869) 39 LJ Ch 79; *Walker v Mottram* (1881) 19 ChD 355, CA; *Buxton and High Peak Publishing and General Printing Co v Mitchell* (1885) Cab & El 527. As to the trustee's power to sell goodwill see the Insolvency Act 1986 s 314(1)(b), Sch 5 para 9; and PARA 479 head (1). Secret unwritten formulas used by the debtor in the manufacture of goods must be disclosed to the trustee as part of the goodwill of the business: *Re Keene* [1922] 2 Ch 475, CA; cf *Cotton v Gillard* (1874) 44 LJ Ch 90.
3 See *Chandler v Gardiner* (undated), cited in *Cruttwell v Lye* (1810) 17 Ves 335 at 338, 343 (where compensation to the proprietors of quays for the loss of their exclusive trade by the establishment of the West India Docks was held on bankruptcy to pass to their creditors).
4 *Walker v Mottram* (1881) 19 ChD 355 at 363, CA (decided under what became the Bankruptcy Act 1914 s 22(2), (3) (repealed) which prescribed the bankrupt's duties in more specific terms than does the Insolvency Act 1986 s 333(1) (see PARA 343)).
5 *Walker v Mottram* (1881) 19 ChD 355 at 363, CA. See *Cruttwell v Lye* (1810) 17 Ves 335. As to covenants in restraint of trade generally see COMPETITION vol 18 (2009) PARA 377 et seq.
6 *Walker v Mottram* (1881) 19 ChD 355, CA; and see *Trego v Hunt* [1896] AC 7 at 13, 14, 23, HL; *Jennings v Jennings* [1898] 1 Ch 378 at 383. This principle also applies where a debtor has executed a deed of assignment for the benefit of his creditors: see *Green & Sons (Northampton) Ltd v Morris* [1914] 1 Ch 562; *Farey v Cooper* [1927] 2 KB 384.
7 See *Clarkson v Edge* (1863) 33 Beav 227; *Buxton and High Peak Publishing and General Printing Co v Mitchell* (1885) Cab & El 527; and COMPETITION vol 18 (2009) PARA 1 et seq.
8 *Hudson v Osborne* (1869) 39 LJ Ch 79; *Hammond & Co v Malcolm Brunker & Co and Collyns* (1892) 9 RPC 301; but see *Cotton v Gillard* (1874) 44 LJ Ch 90.
9 *Hudson v Osborne* (1869) 39 LJ Ch 79.

438. Patents, trade marks and royalties. Patents, trade marks and royalties which belong to a bankrupt pass to his trustee[1]. If a patentee becomes bankrupt and his patent is sold by the trustee, the patentee is not afterwards estopped from alleging that the patent is invalid or otherwise impugning it[2].

A trustee in bankruptcy may register title to the patent[3]. The trustee may assign a registered trade mark with or without an assignment of the goodwill of the business, provided that the mark does not become deceptive in consequence[4].

1 *Hesse v Stevenson* (1803) 3 Bos & P 565 (patents); *Re Graydon, ex p Official Receiver* [1896] 1 QB 417 (royalties). See also *Performing Right Society Ltd v Rowland, Rowland v Turp* [1997] 3 All ER 336, [1998] BPIR 128 (distributions made by virtue of performing rights in works completed prior to a songwriter's bankruptcy are a transmissible property right and not a mere expectancy and as such vest in his trustee in bankruptcy). As to the vesting of copyright in the trustee in bankruptcy see the Copyright, Designs and Patents Act 1988 s 90(1); and COPYRIGHT vol 23 (2013) PARA 752.
2 *Smith v Cropper* (1885) 10 App Cas 249, HL.
3 As to registration of title to a patent see the Patents Act 1977 ss 32, 33; and PATENTS AND REGISTERED DESIGNS vol 79 (2008) PARA 585 et seq.
4 See the Trade Marks Act 1994 s 24(1); *RJ Reuter Co Ltd v Mulhens* [1954] Ch 50, [1953] 2 All ER 1160, CA; and TRADE MARKS AND TRADE NAMES vol 48 (2007 Reissue) PARA 129. As to applications for the correction of the trade marks register see the Trade Marks Act 1994 s 64; and TRADE MARKS AND TRADE NAMES vol 48 (2007 Reissue) PARA 121.

439. Right of action. A right of action which is vested in the bankrupt at the date of adjudication passes to the trustee, unless it is personal to the bankrupt[1]. Where a right of action is acquired by the bankrupt since the commencement of the bankruptcy and is not personal to him, it forms part of his after-acquired property[2] of which he must give notice to the trustee[3] and which the trustee may claim for the estate[4].

1 As to whether a right of action passes to the trustee see PARA 447 et seq. A trustee is entitled to reassign the right of action to the bankrupt for a share of the net proceeds of the proceedings: see *Ramsey v Hartley* [1977] 2 All ER 673, [1977] 1 WLR 686, CA; and PARA 478.
2 As to after-acquired property see PARA 458 et seq.
3 Ie under the Insolvency Act 1986 s 333(2): see PARA 460.
4 Ie under the Insolvency Act 1986 s 307: see PARA 458 et seq.

440. Rights of spouses and civil partners. Property which has been the subject of a gift to the bankrupt by the bankrupt's husband or wife or civil partner passes to the trustee in bankruptcy[1]. Property which has been the subject of a gift by the bankrupt to the bankrupt's husband or wife or civil partner will not pass to the trustee[2], unless the gift can be avoided as a transaction at an undervalue[3]. The rule that an effective gift inter vivos of personal chattels may be made only by deed or by delivery applies between husband and wife, as well as between strangers[4].

Neither a husband's nor a wife's right to administer the estate of a deceased spouse passes to the trustee of either of them who becomes bankrupt; but a grant of administration may in a proper case be made to the trustee in bankruptcy[5].

1 *Re Grainger, ex p Grainger* (1871) 24 LT 334.
2 *Re Whitehead, ex p Whitehead* (1885) 14 QBD 419, CA. In certain cases articles of jewellery have been treated as constituting paraphernalia, ie property belonging to a husband which his wife was permitted to wear for the decoration of her person and which were subject to the claims of the husband's creditors: see eg *Ridout v Earl of Plymouth* (1740) 2 Atk 104; *Graham v Londonderry* (1746) 3 Atk 393. Doubts exists how far the doctrine of paraphernalia is applicable at the present day (see MATRIMONIAL AND CIVIL PARTNERSHIP LAW vol 72 (2009) PARA 246); but as to the necessity for an unequivocal act for the transfer of chattels from a husband to his wife see note 4. In the absence of agreement to the contrary, a wife's savings from housekeeping money belong to her and her husband in equal shares: see the Married Women's Property Act 1964 s 1; and MATRIMONIAL AND CIVIL PARTNERSHIP LAW vol 72 (2009) PARA 245.
3 See PARA 678 et seq.

4   See *Re Cole (a bankrupt), ex p Trustee of Property of Bankrupt* [1964] Ch 175, [1963] 3 All ER
     433, CA; and see *Glaister-Carlisle v Glaister-Carlisle* (1968) 112 Sol Jo 215, CA. If a husband's
     act in itself is equivocal, ie if it is consistent equally with the husband's intention to transfer
     chattels to his wife or with an intention on his part to retain possession but to give the use and
     enjoyment of the chattels to his wife, the act does not constitute delivery: *Re Cole (a bankrupt)*,
     ex p Trustee of Property of Bankrupt at 192, 440. See further GIFTS vol 52 (2009) PARA 205.

5   See PARA 417. A lump sum order under the Matrimonial Causes Act 1973 s 23 (or the Civil
     Partnership Act 2004 Sch 5 para 2) can be made against a bankrupt but only where the court
     has a clear information as to the assets, liabilities and expenses in the bankruptcy and where
     there will be a surplus to which the bankrupt will become entitled in the foreseeable future, out
     of which a lump sum could be paid: *Hellyer v Hellyer* [1997] 1 FCR 340, [1997] BPIR 85, CA.
     Similarly, a periodical payments order under the Matrimonial Causes Act 1973 s 23 (or the Civil
     Partnership Act 2004 Sch 5 para 2) may be made against a bankrupt; but the available income
     will be subject to any income payments order made under the Insolvency Act 1986 s 310: *Albert
     v Albert (a bankrupt)* [1997] 2 FLR 791, [1996] BPIR 232, CA. A property adjustment order
     under the Matrimonial Causes Act 1973 s 24 (or the Civil Partnership Act 2004 Sch 5 para 7)
     cannot be made against a bankrupt in respect of property vested in his trustee: *Hellyer v Hellyer*
     [1997] 1 FCR 340, [1997] BPIR 85, CA; *McGladdery v McGladdery* [2000] 1 FCR 315, [2000]
     BPIR 1078, CA; *Ram v Ram* [2004] EWCA Civ 1684, [2004] 3 FCR 673, [2005] 2 FLR 75. As
     to lump sum orders see MATRIMONIAL AND CIVIL PARTNERSHIP LAW vol 72 (2009) PARA 476 et
     seq; as to periodical payments orders see MATRIMONIAL AND CIVIL PARTNERSHIP LAW vol 72
     (2009) PARA 458 et seq; and as to property adjustment orders see MATRIMONIAL AND CIVIL
     PARTNERSHIP LAW vol 72 (2009) PARA 498 et seq.

(iii) Trust Property

441. Property held on trust. The property comprised in the bankrupt's estate
does not include property held by him on trust for any other person[1]. The reason
for this exclusion is that property held by a bankrupt on trust for another person
is not the beneficial interest of the bankrupt, and is not, therefore, property
which, according to the general principles of bankruptcy law, could be divisible
among his creditors[2]. When a bankrupt holds property on trust for other persons
and has no beneficial interest in it himself, he has only a legal estate comprising
none of the qualities of property divisible among creditors[3]; if he holds property
on trust both for himself and for other persons, then the beneficial interest which
he has in that property is divisible among his creditors[4].

A bankrupt who is a trustee for sale remains such a trustee notwithstanding
his bankruptcy, unless and until he retires or is removed[5].

Property held by the bankrupt as executor or administrator or in any fiduciary
capacity is property held on trust within the meaning of the bankruptcy
legislation[6]. Money held by a person in a fiduciary position is considered to
belong to the person for whom he holds it[7].

1   See the Insolvency Act 1986 s 283(3)(a); and PARA 211 head (c). The client account of a
     bankrupt solicitor is property held by the bankrupt on trust for another, and so does not vest in
     the trustee in bankruptcy: *Re A Solicitor* [1952] Ch 328, [1952] 1 All ER 133. For a case where
     a lease was held in the joint names of the bankrupt and his wife, and the question was whether
     the presumption of advancement arose, see *Tew v Tew's Trustee* (1968) 207 Estates Gazette
     1111, DC. As from a day to be appointed the common law presumption of advancement is
     abolished: Equality Act 2010 s 199(1). The abolition does not affect any transfer made before
     s 199 comes into force: see s 199(2) (not yet in force).

2   See *Re Elford, ex p Gennys* (1829) Mont & M 258; *Boddington v Castelli* (1853) 1 E & B 879;
     Winch v Keeley (1787) 1 Term Rep 619; *Re Bell, ex p Debtor* (1908) 99 LT 939 (where it was
     held, in the case of an implied trust, that the trustee in bankruptcy could not take property
     which the debtor honestly considered he held on trust).

3   *Scott v Surman* (1742) Willes 400 at 402. As to property entrusted for a specific purpose see
     PARA 444.

4   It is doubtful whether, in cases where the bankrupt has a beneficial interest and is also a trustee,
     the legal estate does not pass. Where there is an express trust, it seems that the legal estate does

not pass; but, where the trust is an implied or constructive one, the legal estate may pass to the trustee in bankruptcy, who will hold it as trustee for the creditors and the other persons interested: see *Carvalho v Burn* (1833) 4 B & Ad 382 at 393; affd sub nom *Burn v Carvalho* 1 Ad & El 883 at 893. See also *Re McCarthy (a bankrupt), ex p Trustee of Bankrupt v McCarthy* [1975] 2 All ER 857, [1975] 1 WLR 807.

As to the position of a trustee of leaseholds on his bankruptcy, and as to the rights of his trustee in bankruptcy, see *Governors of St Thomas's Hospital v Richardson* [1910] 1 KB 271, CA. See also *Re Richardson, ex p Governors of St Thomas's Hospital* [1911] 2 KB 705, CA (money recovered under a right of indemnity which the bankrupt, as a trustee, had against the principal debtor, could not be treated as assets in the bankruptcy); considered in *Re Law Guarantee Trust and Accident Society Ltd, Liverpool Mortgage Insurance Co's Case* [1914] 2 Ch 617, CA; *British Union and National Insurance Co v Rawson* [1916] 2 Ch 476, CA; *Re Harrington Motor Car Co, ex p Chaplin* [1928] Ch 105, CA, and *Hood's Trustees v Southern Union General Insurance Co of Australasia* [1928] Ch 793, CA. The law as laid down in the last two cases, that an injured party was not subrogated to the rights under an insurance policy of the person responsible for the injury in the event of that person's insolvency, was altered by the Third Parties (Rights against Insurers) Act 1930: see PARA 433; and INSURANCE vol 60 (2011) PARA 651 et seq. *Re Richardson, ex p Governors of St Thomas's Hospital* was applied in *Selangor United Rubber Estates Ltd v Cradock* [1967] 2 All ER 1255, [1967] 1 WLR 1168. See also PARA 433.

Where a husband effected an insurance policy on his life 'for the benefit of his wife' in pursuance of the Married Women's Property Act 1870 (repealed), it was held that the interest in the policy money vested on the husband's bankruptcy in the trustee, subject only to the trust in favour of any wife who should, by surviving him, become his widow (*Re Collier* [1930] 2 Ch 37); but in *Cousins v Sun Life Assurance Society* [1933] Ch 126, CA (where a husband had effected an insurance policy on his life for the benefit of his named wife under the Married Women's Property Act 1882 s 11), *Re Collier* was doubted and the benefit of the policy was held not to pass to the trustee in the husband's bankruptcy.

5   *Re Solomon (a bankrupt), ex p Trustee of Property of Bankrupt v Solomon* [1967] Ch 573 at 579, sub nom *Re A Debtor, ex p Trustee v Solomon* [1966] 3 All ER 255 at 257.

6   An executor who carries on the trade of his testator under testamentary directions is personally liable for debts so incurred, but has a right to be indemnified out of the testator's assets (*Dowse v Gorton* [1891] AC 190, HL), and has a lien on the assets of the business, which lien passes to his trustee (*Jennings v Mather* [1902] 1 KB 1, CA (trustee under creditors' deed)). If the executor is in default, he is not entitled to an indemnity, except on the terms of making good his default, and his creditors will be in no better position: *Re Johnson, Shearman v Robinson* (1880) 15 ChD 548. If one of several executors is in default, the executors who are not in default are entitled to an indemnity: *Re Frith, Newton v Rolfe* [1902] 1 Ch 342. See further WILLS AND INTESTACY vol 103 (2010) PARA 1040.

7   *Pennell v Deffell* (1853) 4 De GM & G 372; *Re Hallett's Estate, Knatchbull v Hallett* (1880) 13 ChD 696, CA; *Re Mawson, ex p Hardcastle* (1881) 44 LT 523; *Taylor v Plumer* (1815) 3 M & S 562 at 574; *Frith v Cartland* (1865) 2 Hem & M 417; *Pinkett v Wright* (1842) 2 Hare 120; *Re Strachan, ex p Cooke* (1876) 4 ChD 123, CA; *Harris v Truman* (1882) 9 QBD 264, CA; *Gibert v Gonard* (1884) 52 LT 54. The same principle applies to property bought with stolen money: *Re Hulton, ex p Manchester and County Bank* (1891) 8 Morr 69, DC. In a case decided under Indian bankruptcy law, money invested in a firm for the benefit of a minor was held to have passed to the official assignee on members of the firm being adjudicated insolvent, but the beneficiary was held entitled to a charge on its assets for the money: *Madras Official Assignee v Krishnaji Bhat* (1933) 49 TLR 432, PC. As to the following of assets generally see EQUITY vol 16(2) (Reissue) PARA 861 et seq.

442. Legal estate in settled land.   For the purposes of determining, where the estate owner of any settled land[1] is bankrupt, whether the legal estate in the settled land is comprised in, or is capable of being claimed for, the bankrupt's estate, the legal estate in the settled land is deemed not to vest in the estate owner[2], unless and until the estate owner becomes absolutely and beneficially entitled to the settled land free from all limitations, powers and charges taking effect under the settlement[3].

1   As to the meaning of 'settled land' see the Settled Land Act 1925 ss 2, 117(1)(xxiv); and SETTLEMENTS vol 91 (2012) PARA 581.

2   As to the meaning of 'estate owner' see the Settled Land Act 1925 s 117(1)(xi); the Law of
    Property Act 1925 s 1(4); and SETTLEMENTS vol 91 (2012) PARA 598.

3   Settled Land Act 1925 s 103 (amended by the Insolvency Act 1985 s 235(1), Sch 8 para 3). As
    to the trustee's power to apply under the Settled Land Act 1925 s 24 (see SETTLEMENTS vol 91
    (2012) PARA 666) for the exercise of the powers under the 1925 Act see *Re Thornhill's
    Settlement* [1941] Ch 24, [1940] 4 All ER 249, CA; and PARA 417. Since 1 January 1997 it has
    not been possible to create settlements for the purposes of the Settled Land Act 1925, save in a
    very limited class of cases: see SETTLEMENTS vol 91 (2012) PARAS 506, 576 et seq.

443.   Property in factor's possession. A factor or mercantile agent entrusted
with the possession as well as the disposal of goods is a trustee of the goods, and
on his bankruptcy they will not pass to his trustee, but will belong to his
principal[1]. Nevertheless, the factor has a general lien on them for any debts due
to him from the principal on the general account between them, and this lien
passes to the factor's trustee in bankruptcy[2].

If goods are sold by a factor, the price belongs to the principal, subject to the
factor's lien; and, if the principal for whom the factor has sold goods becomes
bankrupt, the factor is entitled to his lien as against the principal's trustee in
bankruptcy[3]. If the factor receives the price of the goods and becomes bankrupt,
the purchase money or its proceeds, if they can be identified, will be the
principal's property, and will not pass to the factor's trustee[4], except where the
money has been mixed with the factor's money and is indistinguishable[5].

A person who receives goods from another and is entitled to sell them on any
terms he pleases, but is bound to pay the consignor a fixed price at a fixed time,
sells the goods on his own account, even though he describes himself as agent;
and the consignor cannot follow the purchase money, which passes to the seller's
trustee in bankruptcy[6].

1   *Godfrey v Furzo* (1733) 3 P Wms 185; *Re Jullian, ex p Dumas* (1754) 2 Ves Sen 582 at 585;
    Tooke v Hollingworth (1793) 5 Term Rep 215 at 227 (affd sub nom *Hollingworth v Tooke*
    (1795) 2 Hy Bl 501); *Barber & Sons v Rigley* (1922) 38 TLR 650 (transfer of shares bought by
    broker for client). Brokers (ie mercantile agents who are employed to sell goods without being
    put in possession of goods) may be in the position of trustees as regards money which they
    receive. A broker who is instructed to sell stock and invest the proceeds in a specified way is an
    agent into whose hands money is put to be applied in a particular way, and money so paid to
    him can be followed by a customer: *Re Strachan, ex p Cooke* (1876) 4 ChD 123, CA. Where the
    account is a speculative one, the relation may be merely that of creditor and debtor, and in such
    a case money in the hands of the broker would pass, on his bankruptcy, to his trustee: *King v
    Hutton* [1900] 2 QB 504, CA. See further AGENCY vol 1 (2008) PARA 141.

2   As to factor's lien see *Drinkwater v Goodwin* (1775) 1 Cowp 251; *Frith v Forbes* (1862) 4 De
    GF & J 409; *Brown, Shipley & Co v Kough* (1885) 29 ChD 848, CA; *Stevens v Biller* (1883) 25
    ChD 31, CA. See further AGENCY vol 1 (2008) PARA 114; BAILMENT AND PLEDGE vol 4 (2011)
    PARAS 154–155.

3   *Drinkwater v Goodwin* (1775) 1 Cowp 251.

4   *Taylor v Plumer* (1815) 3 M & S 562; *Harris v Truman* (1882) 9 QBD 264, CA.

5   *Taylor v Plumer* (1815) 3 M & S 562 at 575. For a consideration of the rights in equity to trace
    money into a banking account see FINANCIAL SERVICES AND INSTITUTIONS vol 49 (2008) PARA
    857; and as to following trust money generally see EQUITY vol 16(2) (Reissue) PARA 861 et seq.

6   *Re Neville, ex p White* (1871) 6 Ch App 397; affd sub nom *Towle & Co v White* 29 LT 78, HL.
    It is a question of fact whether a person sells as agent or as principal. There is nothing to prevent
    the principal from remunerating the agent by a commission varying according to the amount of
    the profit obtained by the sale, or to prevent his paying a commission depending on the surplus
    which the agent can obtain over and above the price which will satisfy the principal; the amount
    of the commission does not turn the agent into a purchaser: *Re Smith, ex p Bright* (1879) 10
    ChD 566 at 570, CA. See also *Re Cotton, ex p Cooke* (1913) 108 LT 310, CA (sale by
    auctioneer); and AGENCY vol 1 (2008) PARA 1.

444. Property entrusted for specific purpose. Property which is in the bankrupt's possession for a specific purpose does not, as a general rule, pass to the trustee, but is clothed with a species of trust and is subject to the same principles as trust property[1].

If bills of exchange and promissory notes, which are ordinarily delivered and remitted as cash, are specifically appropriated to a particular purpose, the owner will be entitled to have them restored to him if they remain in the bankrupt's hands at the time of bankruptcy, or will be entitled to the money received on them if the trustee in bankruptcy disposes of them[2].

1   *Re Brickwood, ex p Waring, Re Bracken, ex p Inglis* (1815) 19 Ves 345; *Re Manning, ex p Smith* (1834) 4 Deac & Ch 579; *Re Warwick and Clagett, ex p Brown* (1838) 3 Mont & A 471; *Steele v Stuart* (1866) LR 2 Eq 84; *Re Angerstein, ex p Angerstein* (1874) 9 Ch App 479; *Re Rogers, ex p Holland and Hannen* (1891) 8 Morr 243, CA; *Re Drucker, ex p Basden* [1902] 2 KB 237, CA; *Re Gothenburg Commercial Co* (1881) 44 LT 166, CA; *Re Watson, ex p Schipper* (1912) 107 LT 783, CA; *Bank of Scotland v Macleod* [1914] AC 311, HL (debenture, agreed to be assigned by company, held not clothed with a species of trust but to pass to the liquidator); *Re Hooley, ex p Trustee* (1915) 84 LJKB 1415.

    In *Barclays Bank Ltd v Quistclose Investments Ltd* [1970] AC 567, [1968] 3 All ER 651, HL, this principle was applied to a sum of money lent to a company (later wound up) for a specific purpose which was not implemented; the money, being still identifiable, was held to be impressed with a trust, and accordingly did not enure for the benefit of the general body of creditors, but was recoverable by the lender; see also *Re Margaretta Ltd, Freeman v Customs and Excise Comrs* [2005] STC 610, [2005] BCC 506, [2005] BPIR 834.

    Unappropriated parcels of shares agreed to be held by the vendor on trust for the buyer will not accrue to the benefit of the general body of creditors in the vendor's bankruptcy: *Hunter v Moss* [1994] 3 All ER 215, [1994] 1 WLR 452, CA; *Re Harvard Securities Ltd (in liquidation), Holland v Newbury* [1997] 2 BCLC 369, [1998] BCC 567.

    The trustee in bankruptcy will not be personally liable in respect of property received by the bankrupt for a specific purpose, unless it is shown that the property came into the trustee's possession with a knowledge of the purposes for which it was destined: *Kieran v Johnson* (1815) 1 Stark 109.

2   *Re Power and Warwick, ex p Smith* (1819) Buck 355; *Hollingworth v Tooke* (1795) 2 Hy Bl 501; *Re Foster, ex p Bond* (1840) 1 Mont D & De G 10; *Re Wise, ex p Atkins* (1842) 3 Mont D & De G 103; *Re Broad, ex p Neck* (1884) 13 QBD 740; *Re Suse, ex p Dever* (1884) 13 QBD 766, CA; *Phelps, Stokes & Co v Comber* (1885) 29 ChD 813, CA; *Re Yglesias, ex p Gomez* (1875) 10 Ch App 639; *Re Brown, ex p Plitt* (1889) 6 Morr 81.

445. Bills sent for collection. Bills which are remitted by a customer to a banker, and which are not carried by the banker to the customer's credit until the proceeds are received, will not, if undisposed of before bankruptcy, pass on the banker's bankruptcy to the trustee, but will belong to the customer subject to the banker's lien, being treated as sent to the banker merely for the purpose of obtaining payment when due[1].

If there is a contract express or implied between the banker and the customer that bills transmitted by the customer should be treated as cash, they will, on the banker's bankruptcy, belong to the trustee[2].

1   *Re Burrough, ex p Sollers* (1811) 1 Rose 155; *Re Boldero, ex p Pease* (1812) 1 Rose 232; *Thompson v Giles* (1824) 2 B & C 422; *Re Harrison, ex p Barkworth* (1858) 2 De G & J 194; *Re Mills, Bawtree & Co, ex p Stannard* (1893) 10 Morr 193. If the banker discounts a bill of this kind, or advances money on it, he will be entitled in the one case to the whole property in the bill, in the other to a lien on it for the advance: *Giles v Perkins* (1807) 9 East 12 at 14; *Carstairs v Bates* (1812) 3 Camp 301; *Re Boldero, ex p Pease*; *Re Wood, ex p M'Gae* (1816) 19 Ves 607; *Hornblower v Proud* (1819) 2 B & Ald 327; *Re Dilworth, ex p Benson* (1832) Mont & B 120. See generally FINANCIAL SERVICES AND INSTITUTIONS vol 49 (2008) PARAS 861, 862, 988.

2   *Re Brickwood, ex p Waring, Re Bracken, ex p Inglis* (1815) 19 Ves 345.

446. Rule in ex parte Waring. If both the customer and the banker are insolvent and the customer has deposited with the banker bills or goods to cover his acceptances, the holder of the acceptances will be entitled to have the bills or goods applied in the discharge of the acceptances[1], not because the holder of the bills has any lien on the bills or goods deposited with the banker or any equity to have them so applied, but in order to work out the equities between the two insolvent estates[2].

1 *Re Brickwood, ex p Waring, Re Bracken, ex p Inglis* (1815) 19 Ves 345. This is known as 'the rule in Waring's Case'. See also *Re Suse, ex p Dever* (1885) 14 QBD 611 at 620, CA per Brett MR ('Where as between the drawer and acceptor of a bill of exchange, a security has, by virtue of a contract between them, been specifically appropriated to meet that bill at maturity, and has been lodged for that purpose by the drawer with the acceptor, then, if both drawer and acceptor become insolvent and their estates are brought under a forced administration, the billholder, though neither party nor privy to the contract, is entitled to have the specifically appropriated security applied in or towards payment of the bill.').
   As to the application of the rule see *Powles v Hargreaves* (1853) 3 De GM & G 430; *Re New Zealand Banking Corpn, Hickie & Co's Case* (1867) LR 4 Eq 226; *Trimingham v Maud* (1868) LR 7 Eq 201; *Re Joint Stock Discount Co, Loder's Case* (1868) LR 6 Eq 491; *Re New Zealand Banking Corpn, Levi & Co's Case* (1869) LR 7 Eq 449; *Re General Rolling Stock Co, ex p Alliance Bank* (1869) 4 Ch App 423; *City Bank v Luckie* (1870) 5 Ch App 773; *Re Richardson, ex p Smart* (1872) 8 Ch App 220; *Re Leggatt, Re Gledstanes, ex p Dewhurst* (1873) 8 Ch App 965; *Vaughan v Halliday* (1874) 9 Ch App 561; *Re Barned's Banking Co, ex p Joint Stock Discount Co* (1875) 10 Ch App 198; *Re Lindsay, ex p Lambton* (1875) 10 Ch App 405; *Re Yglesias & Co, ex p General South American Co* (1875) 10 Ch App 635; *Re Yglesias, ex p Gomez* (1875) 10 Ch App 639; *Re Tappenbeck, ex p Banner* (1876) 2 ChD 278, CA; *Re Entwistle, ex p Arbuthnot* (1876) 3 ChD 477, CA; *Royal Bank of Scotland v Commercial Bank of Scotland* (1882) 7 App Cas 366, HL (where the rule was criticised).
2 *Re Burrough, ex p Sargeant* (1810) 1 Rose 153; and see *Ex p Twogood* (1812) 19 Ves 229; *Re Boldero, ex p Leeds Bank* (1812) 1 Rose 254; *Thompson v Giles* (1824) 2 B & C 422; *Re Dilworth, ex p Armitstead* (1828) 2 Gl & J 371; *Re Dilworth, ex p Thompson* (1828) Mont & M 102; *Re Dilworth, ex p Benson* (1832) Mont & B 120; *Re Forster, ex p Bond* (1840) 1 Mont D & De G 10; *Re Wise, ex p Edwards* (1842) 2 Mont D & De G 625; *Re Harrison, ex p Barkworth* (1858) 2 De G & J 194.

(iv) Proceedings by or against Trustee

447. Rights or causes of action. Certain rights or causes of action are included in the property of a bankrupt which vests in his trustee in bankruptcy[1]. These the trustee may enforce as a litigant, independently of any provisions in the bankruptcy legislation[2]. The trustee is also liable in certain cases to be made or joined as a defendant in actions by other parties[3].

Where an undischarged bankrupt is a contractor in respect of any contract liability with another person, that person may sue or be sued in respect of the contract without the joinder of the bankrupt[4].

1 *Re Byrne, ex p Henry* (1892) 9 Morr 213 (action for commission); *Re Perkins, Poyser v Beyfus* [1898] 2 Ch 182, CA (right to sue on covenant of indemnity given to bankrupt); *Wolff v Van Boolen* (1906) 94 LT 502 (right to set aside settlement); and see *British Union and National Insurance Co v Rawson* [1916] 2 Ch 476, CA. As to these categories of rights or causes of action which vest in the trustee see PARA 448 et seq; and as to other categories of rights or causes of action which remain vested in the bankrupt see PARA 448 note 13.
2 *Leeming v Lady Murray* (1879) 13 ChD 123.
3 *London School Board v Wall Bros* (1891) 8 Morr 202, CA; *Re Sykes, Jaram v Holmes* (1909) 100 LT 265; cf *Mulkerrins v PriceWaterhouseCoopers (a firm)* [2003] UKHL 41, [2003] 4 All ER 1, [2003] 1 WLR 1937.
4 Insolvency Act 1986 s 345(4). See also PARA 702. In the case of the administration in bankruptcy of the insolvent estate of a deceased person dying before the presentation of a bankruptcy petition, s 345 applies: Administration of Insolvent Estates of Deceased Persons

Order 1986, SI 1986/1999, art 3(1), Sch 1 Pt II para 28. As to the administration in bankruptcy of the insolvent estates of deceased persons see further PARA 830 et seq.

448. Causes of action vesting in trustee. All rights of action which relate directly to property comprised in the bankrupt's estate[1] pass to the trustee[2]. It is the function of the trustee to get in, realise and distribute the bankrupt's estate[3]; and, in carrying out that function and in the management of the bankrupt's estate, the trustee is entitled[4] to use his discretion[5]. Where a cause of action arises after the commencement of the bankruptcy[6], it constitutes after-acquired property[7] of which the bankrupt must give notice to the trustee[8] and which may be claimed for the estate by the trustee[9]. Where the right of action has passed to the trustee, if the bankrupt brings an action on it, it may be dismissed as frivolous or vexatious[10] or the trustee may intervene and be joined or substituted as claimant[11]. A bankrupt has no locus standi to bring an appeal against the judgment on which the petition debt is founded[12].

Where a cause of action arises in respect of the bankrupt's personal injury, personal inconvenience or damage to reputation, the right of action remains with the bankrupt[13].

1 As to the meaning of 'the bankrupt's estate' see PARA 211. See also PARA 412.
2 As to the general principles on which it is determined whether a right of action does or does not pass to the trustee see *Rose v Buckett* [1901] 2 KB 449 at 454, CA; *Drake v Beckham* (1843) 11 M & W 315 (affd sub nom *Beckham v Drake* (1849) 2 HL Cas 579 at 596, 627). As to what are sometimes known as 'mixed actions' or 'hybrid claims', including damage or loss both to the bankrupt's property and to the bankrupt personally, see PARA 449. If a trustee chooses not to adopt the right of action, the bankrupt may ask the trustee to assign it back to him: *Hamilton v Official Receiver* [1998] BPIR 602 (where the trustee refuses to assign, the bankrupt may apply for a direction under the Insolvency Act 1986 s 303(1) (see PARA 342) that the trustee do so); cf *Osborn v Cole* [1999] BPIR 251.

   Actions which pass to the trustee include the following: actions for breaches of contracts to deliver goods (*Wright v Fairfield* (1831) 2 B & Ad 727; *Stanton v Collier* (1854) 23 LJQB 116, CA), or to repair (*Gibbon v Dudgeon* (1881) 45 JP 748), or to indemnify (*Re Perkins, Poyser v Beyfus* [1898] 2 Ch 182, CA; *British Union and National Insurance Co v Rawson* [1916] 2 Ch 476, CA), or to provide funds to meet a bill of exchange (*Hill v Smith* (1844) 12 M & W 618), or to pay debts on the sale of a business (*Ashdown v Ingamells* (1880) 5 ExD 280, CA); for money earned by a bankrupt other than 'personal earnings' eg commission (*Re Byrne, ex p Henry* (1892) 9 Morr 213), or architect's remuneration (*Emden v Carte* (1881) 17 ChD 768, CA); for earnings in excess of what is necessary for the maintenance of the bankrupt and his family (*Mercer v Vans Colina* (1897) [1900] 1 QB 130n); for the return of premiums paid on an insurance policy (*Boddington v Castelli* (1853) 1 E & B 879); for wrongful dismissal (*Beckham v Drake* (1849) 2 HL Cas 579); for trespass or negligence causing injury to the bankrupt's property (*Wetherell v Julius* (1850) 10 CB 267; *Morgan v Steble* (1872) LR 7 QB 611; *Wilson v United Counties Bank Ltd* [1920] AC 102, HL), or involving the bankrupt in pecuniary liability (*Porter v Vorley* (1832) 9 Bing 93); for misrepresentation (*Hodgson v Sidney* (1866) LR 1 Exch 313); for fraud (*Motion v Moojen* (1872) LR 14 Eq 202); for conspiracy, resulting in mental and physical distress and loss of reputation (*Wenlock v Moloney* (1967) 111 Sol Jo 437, CA; but see PARA 449 note 2); for relief against a usurious bargain (*Payne v Dicker* (1871) 24 LT 492; on appeal 6 Ch App 578), or against forfeiture (*Howard v Fanshawe* [1895] 2 Ch 581); for a declaration that an absolute conveyance should stand only as a security (*Seear v Lawson* (1880) 15 ChD 426, CA); and for reopening accounts of the sale of goods and the recovery of sums found to be due on the accounts (*Guy v Churchill* (1888) 40 ChD 481).

   An action for unfair dismissal is a personal right since it reflects an aspect of a person's individuality and as a result it does not vest in the trustee in bankruptcy: *Grady v Prison Service* [2003] EWCA Civ 527, [2003] 3 All ER 745, [2003] BPIR 823. An action for racial discrimination will not vest in the trustee in bankruptcy provided it is limited to a claim for a declaration of discriminatory conduct under the Race Relations Act 1976 s 56(1)(a) (repealed) and/or a claim for injury to feelings under s 57(4) (repealed) (see now the Equality Act 2010; and DISCRIMINATION): *Khan v Trident Safeguards Ltd* [2004] EWCA Civ 624, [2004] ICR 1591, [2004] BPIR 881. See also *Miller v Bayliss* [2009] EWHC 2063 (Ch), [2009] BPIR 1438, [2009] All ER (D) 83 (Aug).

3   Ie in accordance with the Insolvency Act 1986 Pt 9 Ch 4 (ss 305–335).
4   Ie subject to the Insolvency Act 1986 Pt 9 Ch 4.
5   See the Insolvency Act 1986 s 305(2); and PARA 473.
6   As to the commencement of bankruptcy see PARA 209.
7   See PARA 458 et seq.
8   Ie under the Insolvency Act 1986 s 333(2): see PARA 460.
9   Ie under the Insolvency Act 1986 s 307: see PARA 458 et seq.
10 *Metropolitan Bank v Pooley* (1885) 10 App Cas 210, HL. As to summary judgment see
    CPR Pt 24; and CIVIL PROCEDURE vol 11 (2009) PARA 524 et seq. In *Kellaway v Bury* (1892) 66
    LT 599 at 602, CA, Lindley LJ said that the power to dismiss was a very strong power, and
    should only be exercised in cases which are clear and beyond all doubt; the court must see that
    the claimant has no case at all. See also *Boaler v Power* [1910] 2 KB 229, CA (where the trustee
    refused to continue an action begun by the bankrupt, which the master subsequently dismissed
    on the defendant's application; it was held that the bankrupt had no locus standi to appeal from
    the decision), applied in *Heath v Tang, Stevens v Peacock* [1993] 4 All ER 694, [1993] 1 WLR
    1421, CA. Where the trustee and bankrupt are co-defendants in proceedings related to property,
    the bankrupt has no locus standi to appeal against an adverse judgment: *James v
    Rutherford-Hodge* [2005] EWCA Civ 1580, [2006] BPIR 973, [2005] All ER (D) 333 (Oct).
11 Ie under CPR 19.2(4): see CIVIL PROCEDURE vol 11 (2009) PARA 213. See also *Affleck v
    Hammond* [1912] 3 KB 162; *Jameson & Co v Brick and Stone Co Ltd* (1879) 4 QBD 208;
    Bailey v Thurston & Co Ltd [1903] 1 KB 137, CA; *Re Wilson, ex p Vine* (1878) 8 ChD
    364, CA; *Trustee of Property of Lord v Great Eastern Rly Co* [1908] 1 KB 195; *Rose v Buckett*
    [1901] 2 KB 449, CA.
12 *Heath v Tang, Stevens v Peacock* [1993] 4 All ER 694, [1993] 1 WLR 1421, CA (the bankrupt
    may only pursue such an appeal through the trustee either by consent or by order of the court).
    See further *Royal Bank of Scotland v Farley* [1996] BPIR 638, CA. See *Dadourian Group
    International Inc v Simms* [2008] EWHC 723 (Ch), [2008] BPIR 508 (prior to appointment of
    trustee, court might have discretion to allow bankrupt to appeal); *R (on the application of
    Singh) v Revenue and Customs Comrs* [2010] UKUT 174 (TCC), [2010] STC 2020, [2010]
    BPIR 933 (bankrupt had no standing to bring application for judicial review).
13 Actions which remain with the bankrupt include the following: actions for wages or 'personal
    earnings' where these are no more than sufficient for the bankrupt's maintenance (see PARA
    450); negligence causing personal injury, or assault (see *Drake v Beckham* (1843) 11 M & W
    315 at 319; affd sub nom *Beckham v Drake* (1849) 2 HL Cas 579); for slander (*Benson v
    Flower* (1629) W Jo 215); for trespass, where the only grievance is personal annoyance to the
    bankrupt (*Clark v Calvert* (1819) 8 Taunt 742; *Brewer v Dew* (1843) 11 M & W 625; *Rogers
    v Spence* (1846) 12 Cl & Fin 700, HL; *Rose v Buckett* [1901] 2 KB 449, CA); for negligence or
    breach of duty on the part of a solicitor causing personal annoyance, such as restraint of the
    person (*Wetherell v Julius* (1850) 10 CB 267); for injury to credit (*Wilson v United Counties
    Bank Ltd* [1920] AC 102, HL; and see *Heath v Tang, Stevens v Peacock* [1993] 4 All ER 694,
    [1993] 1 WLR 1421, CA).
        If a bankrupt brings such an action and obtains damages, the trustee cannot intervene in the
    action and obtain an order for the payment of the amount of damages to him (*Re Wilson,
    ex p Vine* (1878) 8 ChD 364, CA; and see PARA 449); but it is possible that, if the sum awarded
    is more than is needed for the maintenance of the bankrupt and his family, the trustee could call
    on the bankrupt to account to him for the surplus (cf *Re Graydon, ex p Official Receiver* [1896]
    1 QB 417; *Re Ashby, ex p Wreford* [1892] 1 QB 872; *Re Roberts* [1900] 1 QB 122, CA).
        A bankrupt whose adjudication has not been set aside cannot bring an action against a
    person for maliciously procuring the adjudication: *Metropolitan Bank Ltd v Pooley* (1885) 10
    App Cas 210, HL; and see *Beechey v William Hill (Park Lane) Ltd* [1956] CLY 5442.
        A bankrupt has locus standi to resist possession proceedings taken by a mortgagee:
    Nationwide Building Society v Purvis [1998] BPIR 625, CA.

449. Transactions involving damage to person and property. Where two
separate and distinct causes of action arise from the same transaction, resulting
both in substantial damage to the bankrupt's property and in injury to the
bankrupt personally, the trustee is entitled to the right of action for damage to
the property, and the bankrupt retains his right to sue for the personal injury[1];
but, where there is but one cause of action resulting in direct loss to the property,
to which the bankrupt's personal injury is only incidental, the right of action may

not be split, but passes to the trustee[2], unless it gives rise to the possible award of aggravated damages[3] to the bankrupt, in which case the cause of action remains with him[4].

1   *Boddington v Castelli* (1853) 1 E & B 879; *Wilson v United Counties Bank Ltd* [1920] AC 102, HL. As to the apportionment of agreed damages paid in settlement of a bankrupt's claim arising out of both personal injury and injury to property see *Re Kavanagh, ex p Bankrupt v Jackson (Trustee)* [1950] 1 All ER 39n, DC. See also *Mulkerrins v PriceWaterhouseCoopers (a firm)* [2003] UKHL 41, [2003] 4 All ER 1, [2003] 1 WLR 1937.

2   *Ord v Upton* [2000] Ch 352, [2000] 1 All ER 193, CA (a claim for damages for injury to body and mind and for capacity to earn was in part personal and in part related to property and as such vested solely in the trustee, although he would hold any award for pain and suffering on constructive trust for the bankrupt). See also *Stanton v Collier* (1854) 23 LJQB 116, CA; *Hodgson v Sidney* (1866) LR 1 Exch 313 at 316; *Morgan v Steble* (1872) LR 7 QB 611; and see *Beckham v Drake* (1849) 2 HL Cas 579 at 629; *Rogers v Spence* (1846) 12 Cl & Fin 700 at 720, HL; *Rose v Buckett* [1901] 2 KB 449, CA; *Wilson v United Counties Bank Ltd* [1920] AC 102, HL (where the question of what happens when one and the same cause of action gives rise both to substantial damage to property and also to injury to the person was left undecided). See also *Wenlock v Moloney* (1967) 111 Sol Jo 437, CA (claim for damages for conspiracy to injure plaintiff in business and property; although consequences were mental distress and loss of reputation, those were not separate heads of damage (see PARA 448 note 2); claim passed to trustee). For earlier proceedings see *Wenlock v Moloney* [1965] 2 All ER 871, [1965] 1 WLR 1238, CA.

3   As to the nature of those damages see *Cassell & Co Ltd v Broome* [1972] AC 1027, [1972] 1 All ER 801, HL.

4   See *Brewer v Dew* (1843) 11 M & W 625; *Howard v Crowther* (1841) 8 M & W 601; *Rose v Buckett* [1901] 2 KB 449 at 456, CA; *Lord's Trustee v Great Eastern Rly Co* [1908] 1 KB 195 at 202; on appeal (without further expression of opinion on this point), [1908] 2 KB 54, CA; revsd sub nom *Great Eastern Rly Co v Lord's Trustee* [1909] AC 109, HL.

450. Contracts for personal services. Where the bankrupt's personal skill and labour are the basis of a contract, the right of action for breach of the contract passes to the trustee:

(1)   where the breach has occurred before the bankruptcy, and money is recoverable by the bankrupt as damages for the breach; or

(2)   where the bankrupt has completed the contract during the bankruptcy and money on the contract has become due[1], and the trustee has claimed the money on behalf of the bankrupt's estate[2], or has obtained an income payments order in respect of it, or which includes it[3].

Otherwise the right to sue for money recoverable as damages for a breach of the contract occurring after the commencement of the bankruptcy may be exercised by the bankrupt and he may retain the amount recovered, subject to his notifying the trustee as to its recovery and amount[4]. The trustee may then claim the damages for the bankrupt's estate, except in so far as such damages are required for meeting the reasonable domestic needs of the bankrupt and his family[5].

1   Ie has become due after the commencement of the bankruptcy. As to the commencement of bankruptcy see PARA 209.

2   Ie under the Insolvency Act 1986 s 307: see PARA 458 et seq. If the money or damages do not constitute income (see s 310(7); and PARA 462 note 3), such money or damages must be claimed by way of an income payments order: see the text and note 3.

3   Ie under the Insolvency Act 1986 s 310: see PARA 462 et seq.

4   As to the bankrupt's duty to notify the trustee of any property which he acquires or which devolves on him or of any increase in his income after the commencement of his bankruptcy see the Insolvency Act 1986 s 333(2); and PARAS 460, 468.

5   See the Insolvency Act 1986 s 310(2); and PARA 462. Section 310(2) relates only to income payments orders and not to property. The definition of income in s 310(7) is, however, probably sufficiently wide to cover all sums awarded by order of the court, whether damages or

otherwise, in respect of claims brought in respect of contracts for personal services. It is in any event a basic principle of bankruptcy law that the bankrupt should not be deprived of those fruits of his personal exertions which are necessary to enable him to live: see *Re Roberts* [1900] 1 QB 122 at 128, 129, CA; *King v Faraday & Partners Ltd* [1939] 2 KB 753, [1939] 2 All ER 478. Should the bankrupt invest or accumulate the proceeds of such an action, they may be claimed by the trustee: *Re Roberts*.

451.   Personal torts.   As a general rule[1], damages obtained by a bankrupt in an action in respect of a personal injury or personal inconvenience or damage to reputation after his adjudication are not property which the trustee may claim for the estate[2]. Where, however, the bankrupt uses his damages to invest or purchase property, that investment may be claimed by the trustee[3].

1   See, however, PARA 448 note 2.

2   The Insolvency Act 1986 does not contain any provision to that effect. The definition of 'property' for the purposes of s 307 (trustee's right to claim after-acquired property for the estate: see PARA 458 et seq) seems wide enough to cover such damages. However, the definition of 'property' in s 436 (see PARA 412) is substantially the same as that contained in the Bankruptcy Act 1914 s 167 (repealed) and for the purposes of the law prior to 29 December 1986 (see PARA 2) such damages were not treated as after-acquired property which passed automatically to the trustee: see *Re Job, ex p Graham* (1870) 21 LT 802; *Re Wilson, ex p Vine* (1878) 8 ChD 364, CA.

3   *Re Wilson, ex p Vine* (1878) 8 ChD 364, CA.

452.   Actions pending by or against bankrupt.   If the right of action which a bankrupt is enforcing is one which vests in his trustee, or is one which the trustee is entitled to enforce for the benefit of the creditors, the trustee may, on an application made by himself without notice being served on any other party, or by any party to the action, to the court in which the action is pending, alleging the devolution of the right of action, become a party to the action in place of the bankrupt or as co-claimant[1]; but the bankrupt cannot himself continue the action alone[2].

If the pending action is against the bankrupt, and it is not one which will be restrained or stayed on the ground that the claim on which it is founded is provable in the bankruptcy[3], the trustee may be made a party as defendant on an application made by the claimant or by one of the other parties to the action without notice being served on any other party[4]. Whether the bankrupt is claimant or defendant, if the trustee becomes a party, he adopts the whole action as from the beginning, and may be liable for the whole of the costs if he is unsuccessful[5]; but, if he is simply made a party to any proceedings on the application of another party to the proceedings, he will not, in general, be personally liable for costs unless the court otherwise directs[6].

Where a bankruptcy order has been made by the High Court or an interim receiver has been appointed or bankruptcy proceedings have been transferred to that Court from a county court, a judge of any Division of the High Court may, of his own motion, order the transfer to that Division of any proceedings brought by or against the bankrupt for the purpose of enforcing a claim against the bankrupt's estate, or brought by a person other than the bankrupt for the purpose of enforcing any such claim, including in either case proceedings of any description by a mortgagee, as are pending against the individual concerned either in another Division of the High Court or in a court in England and Wales other than the High Court[7]. Where proceedings are so transferred, the registrar may, subject to the directions of the judge, dispose of any matter arising in the proceedings which would, but for the transfer, have been disposed of in chambers or, in the case of proceedings transferred from a county court, by the district judge[8].

1 As to the substitution of the trustee see CPR 19.2(4); and CIVIL PROCEDURE vol 11 (2009) PARA 213. See also *Emden v Carte* (1881) 17 ChD 768, CA. A trustee who refuses to continue an action commenced by the bankrupt is not barred from beginning an action in his own name for the same relief: *Bennett v Gamgee* (1877) 46 LJQB 204, CA.

2 *Jackson v North Eastern Rly Co* (1877) 5 ChD 844, CA; *Eldridge v Burgess* (1878) 7 ChD 411; and see *Selig v Lion* [1891] 1 QB 513; *Pople v Evans* [1969] 2 Ch 255, [1968] 2 All ER 743. See also *Siroko v Murphy* [1955] IR 77. If one of two or more claimants is bankrupt, his trustee may be substituted as claimant: *Hoare & Co and Newton v Baker* (1887) 4 TLR 26, DC. As to whether the holding by the bankrupt of shares registered in his name confers rights, including rights of action, see PARA 435.

3 A pending action against the bankrupt for a provable debt will continue unless expressly stayed under the Insolvency Act 1986 s 285(1), (2) (see PARA 214) either by the bankruptcy court or by the court in which it is pending: *Réalisations Industrielles et Commerciales SA v Loescher & Partners* [1957] 3 All ER 241, [1957] 1 WLR 1026.

4 As to the procedure for adding and substituting parties see CPR 19.4; and CIVIL PROCEDURE vol 11 (2009) PARA 214.

5 *Watson v Holliday* (1882) 20 ChD 780 (affd (1883) 52 LJ Ch 543, CA); *Borneman v Wilson* (1884) 28 ChD 53, CA; *London School Board v Wall Bros* (1891) 7 TLR 566, CA; *Hill v Cooke-Hill* [1916] WN 61.

6 See the Insolvency Rules 1986, SI 1986/1925, r 7.39; and PARA 820.

7 See the Insolvency Rules 1986, SI 1986/1925, r 7.15(1)–(3); and PARA 760. The court has a discretion (see *Re Somes, ex p Deller v Somes* (1895) 2 Mans 396); and the transfer ought not to be made unless it is shown that it will be of advantage to the bankrupt's estate (*Re Ross, ex p Trustee* (1888) 5 Morr 281; and as to the considerations which guide the court in making a transfer see *Re White & Co, ex p Official Receiver* (1884) 1 Morr 77; *Re Champagné, ex p Kemp* (1893) 10 Morr 285). For an instance of a transfer see *Re Kay and Lovell* [1941] Ch 420, [1941] 2 All ER 67 (partnership action; both partners adjudicated bankrupt). As from a day to be appointed, any reference however expressed that is or is deemed to be a reference to a county court held under the County Courts Act 1984 s 1 is to be read as a reference to the county court established by s A1 of that Act: see the Crime and Courts Act 2013 Sch 9 Pt 2 para 11(1)(a), (3)(c). At the date at which this volume states the law no such day had been appointed.

8 See the Insolvency Rules 1986, SI 1986/1925, r 7.15(4); and PARA 760.

453. Trustee's powers as to proceedings. For the purpose of protecting the creditors of the bankrupt's estate[1] and the trustee himself, the trustee may, with the permission of the creditors' committee or the court, bring, institute or defend any action or legal proceedings relating to the property comprised in the bankrupt's estate[2], and compromise any actions brought by or against him[3]. The trustee may also, with the permission of the creditors' committee or the court, bring legal proceedings[4] under the Insolvency Act 1986[5].

These provisions apply only as between the trustee of the bankrupt's estate and the creditors; they do not preclude the trustee, as owner of a cause of action, from litigating it, or as defendant to an action from resisting it, without the consent of anyone[6], or from compromising an action to which he is a party. An opposing litigant cannot plead, in answer to the claim or defence of a trustee in bankruptcy as such, that the trustee has not obtained the permission of the creditors' committee or the court to the institution or defence of the action. The effect of the provisions is that the trustee may lose his right to be paid out of the bankrupt's estate the costs and expenses which he may have to pay or may incur in respect of such an action or proceeding, if he has not, before beginning, defending or compromising it, obtained such consent[7].

1 As to the meaning of 'the bankrupt's estate' see PARA 211.

2   See the Insolvency Act 1986 s 314(1)(a), Sch 5 para 2; and PARA 478 head (2). As to ratification of the trustee's acts see PARA 482.

3   See the Insolvency Act 1986 Sch 5 para 8; and PARA 478 head (8).

4   Ie under the Insolvency Act 1986 s 339 (see PARA 678 et seq), s 340 (see PARA 681 et seq) or s 423 (see PARA 689 et seq).

5   See the Insolvency Act 1986 Sch 5 para 2A; and PARA 478 head (3).

6   *Leeming v Lady Murray* (1879) 13 ChD 123; *Re Branson, ex p Trustee* [1914] 2 KB 701, approved in *Clark v Smith* [1940] 1 KB 126, [1939] 4 All ER 59, CA; and see *Re A Debtor (No 26A of 1975)* [1984] 3 All ER 995, [1985] 1 WLR 6.

7   *Re White, ex p Nichols* (1902) 46 Sol Jo 569; *Re Duncan, ex p Official Receiver* [1892] 1 QB 879, CA; and see *Re A Debtor (No 26A of 1975)* [1984] 3 All ER 995, [1985] 1 WLR 6 (trustee did not require permission under the Bankruptcy Act 1914 s 56 (repealed: see now the Insolvency Act 1986 Sch 5 Pt I (paras 1–8)) where the costs of litigation were going to be met either by the defendants or by the legal aid fund).

454.   Limit of expenditure.   When giving the trustee permission to bring, defend or compromise proceedings[1], the creditors' committee may limit the amount of money to be expended[2]. If this limit of expenditure is exceeded, or if the trustee has proceeded with an action or defence without first obtaining the required permission, he may in the first case lose his right to indemnity out of the estate for any expenses incurred by him in excess of the permitted limit, and in the second case lose his right to any indemnity at all[3].

1   See PARA 453.

2   *Re Duncan, ex p Official Receiver* [1892] 1 QB 879, CA.

3   *Re White, ex p Nichols* (1902) 46 Sol Jo 569; *Re Duncan, ex p Official Receiver* [1892] 1 QB 879, CA.

455.   Trustee as litigant.   Where a trustee brings or defends an action as a litigant, he is, as between himself and the other parties to the action, in the same position as any other litigant[1], that is to say, he must pay any debt, damages or costs which the other litigants recover against him out of his own pocket[2], and must obtain reimbursement, if he is entitled to it, out of the bankrupt's estate[3]. Consequently, a prudent trustee should, before embarking on litigation as claimant or defendant, see that he has sufficient assets in hand for his indemnity, or else obtain an indemnity from the creditors[4]. Where, however, an action is brought against the official receiver or the trustee as representing the debtor's estate, or where the official receiver or the trustee is made a party to proceedings on the application of any other party, he will not be made personally liable for costs unless the court otherwise directs[5]. The court may refuse to order the trustee to pay the costs of unsuccessful proceedings by him, if the matter was one proper to be brought before the court[6].

The trustee may sue or be sued in the official name of 'the trustee of the estate of ..., a bankrupt'[7]. In the High Court, he should bring any action in the division to which bankruptcy business is for the time being assigned, that is to say, the Chancery Division[8], unless it is one of a class specially assigned[9] to another division of the High Court[10].

1   The trustee in bankruptcy of a lessee under a lease which is subject to forfeiture on bankruptcy is liable for mesne profits in proceedings for possession by the lessor, if he identifies himself with the cause of a third party who wrongfully resists the lessor's claim: *Pelican v Moorhouse's Trustee* (1952) 159 Estates Gazette 266.

2   *Re Angerstein, ex p Angerstein* (1874) 9 Ch App 479; *Pitts v La Fontaine* (1880) 6 App Cas 482, PC; *Watson v Holliday* (1883) 52 LJ Ch 543, CA; *Re Mackenzie, ex p Sheriff of Hertfordshire* [1899] 2 QB 566 at 578, CA; *Borneman v Wilson* (1884) 28 ChD 53; *London School Board v Wall Bros* (1891) 7 TLR 566, CA (where the trustee adopted the action, although there was no order making him a party); *Trustee of the Property of Vickery (a*

bankrupt) v Modern Security Systems Ltd [1998] 1 BCLC 428, sub nom *Vickery v Modern Security Systems Ltd* [1998] BPIR 164, CA (trustee who adopts action likely to be held personally liable in event of failure for defendant's costs). As to a trustee's potential liability for costs where he has assigned a cause of action (see PARA 478 note 4) see *Hunt (as trustee in bankruptcy of Janan George Harb) v Harb* [2011] EWCA Civ 1239, [2012] 1 WLR 317, [2012] BPIR 117.

3   *Pitts v La Fontaine* (1880) 6 App Cas 482 at 486, PC. As to the effect of failure to obtain the consent of the creditors' committee or the court see PARA 453. A trustee must not appear on an appeal when his presence is unnecessary: *Re Arden, ex p Arden* (1884) 14 QBD 121, DC. He will not be entitled to indemnity in respect of the costs of a frivolous appeal: *Re Lock, ex p Poppleton* (1891) 8 Morr 51 at 57; *Re Vanderhaege, ex p Viney* [1888] WN 7, CA. Where a trustee shows carelessness in initiating litigation, he will not be entitled to an indemnity: *Re Bryant, ex p Gordon* (1889) 6 Morr 262.

4   *Re Angerstein, ex p Angerstein* (1874) 9 Ch App 479.

5   See the Insolvency Rules 1986, SI 1986/1925, r 7.39; and PARA 820. For instances where the official receiver or the trustee is expressly protected against an order for costs see r 6.105(6) (appeal against decision on proof: see PARA 551), r 6.142(5) (creditor's claim that remuneration is excessive: see PARA 353), r 6.177(2) (expenses of examination: see PARA 303), r 6.222 (costs on discharge from bankruptcy: see PARA 648).

   See also *Dansk Rekylriffel Syndikat Akt v Snell* [1908] 2 Ch 127 (where the trustee did not enter an appearance and costs were not given against him personally); *Hill v Cooke-Hill* [1916] WN 61 (where the trustee was ordered to pay the costs 'like any other unsuccessful litigant').

6   *Re Tetley, ex p Jeffrey* (1896) 3 Mans 226 at 236; affd 3 Mans 3121, CA (motion to set aside settlement).

7   See the Insolvency Act 1986 s 305(4); and PARA 324. On a transmission of office, the old trustee remains liable on the record until the new trustee is substituted in his place: see *Pooley's Trustee v Whetham* (1884) 28 ChD 38 at 52, CA. It seems that a trustee in bankruptcy could validly be a party in his own name (*Leeming v Lady Murray* (1879) 13 ChD 123 at 128), but any indorsement of claim should show any representative capacity (see CPR 16.2(3), (4); and CIVIL PROCEDURE vol 11 (2009) PARA 585).

8   See the Senior Courts Act 1981 s 61(1), Sch 1 para 1(e); and CIVIL PROCEDURE vol 11 (2009) PARA 44.

9   Ie by the Senior Courts Act 1981 s 61 or by the Civil Procedure Rules: see CIVIL PROCEDURE vol 11 (2009) PARA 43 et seq.

10 See note 9; the Insolvency Rules 1986, SI 1986/1925, r 7.15; and PARA 760.

456.   Trustee's power to compromise.   With the sanction of the creditors' committee[1] or the court[2], the trustee in bankruptcy may make such compromise or other arrangement as may be thought expedient with creditors, or persons claiming to be creditors, in respect of bankruptcy debts[3].

Without the need for permission, the trustee has power to:

(1)   refer to arbitration, or compromise on such terms as may be agreed, any debts, claims or liabilities subsisting or supposed to subsist between the bankrupt and any person who may have incurred any liability to the bankrupt[4]; and

(2)   make such compromise or other arrangement as may be thought expedient with respect to any claim arising out of or incidental to the bankrupt's estate made or capable of being made by the trustee on any person[5].

1   As to the creditors' committee see PARA 326 et seq.

2   The court will, in the absence of special circumstances, be unwilling to overrule the views of the creditors' committee or the creditors generally: *Re Ridgway, ex p Hurlbatt* (1889) 6 Morr 277; *Re Ridgway, ex p Clarke* (1891) 8 Morr 289; *Re Pilling, ex p Salaman* [1906] 2 KB 644; and see *Re Geiger* [1915] 1 KB 439 at 450, 451, 456, CA; *Re Salmon, ex p Official Receiver* [1916] 2 KB 510 at 516; cf *Re Bank of Credit and Commerce International SA (No 3)* [1993] BCLC 1490, sub nom *Re Bank of Credit and Commerce International SA (No 2)* [1992] BCC 715, CA.

3   Insolvency Act 1986 s 314(1)(a), Sch 5 para 7. In the case of the administration in bankruptcy of the insolvent estate of a deceased person dying before the presentation of a bankruptcy petition,

s 314 applies: Administration of Insolvent Estates of Deceased Persons Order 1986, SI 1986/1999, art 3(1), Sch 1 Pt II para 23. As to the administration in bankruptcy of the insolvent estates of deceased persons see further PARA 830 et seq.

4　Insolvency Act 1986 Sch 5 para 9A (added by SI 2010/18). See PARA 479.

5　Insolvency Act 1986 Sch 5 para 9B (added by SI 2010/18); and see *Re Ross (a bankrupt)* [1998] 1 BCLC 56, [1998] BCC 29, CA (the bankrupt will be bound by a compromise in the same way as the trustee unless expressly excluded). See PARA 479.

457.　Arbitration agreements to which bankrupt is party. Where a bankrupt becomes party to a contract containing an arbitration agreement[1] before the commencement of his bankruptcy, and the trustee in bankruptcy adopts the contract, the arbitration agreement is enforceable by or against the trustee in relation to matters arising from or connected with the contract[2]. If the trustee in bankruptcy does not adopt the contract and a matter to which the arbitration agreement applies needs to be determined in connection with, or for the purposes of, the bankruptcy proceedings, either the trustee with the consent of the creditors' committee, or any other party to the agreement, may apply to the court[3] which may, if it thinks fit, order that the matter be referred to arbitration in accordance with the arbitration agreement[4].

1　For these purposes, 'arbitration agreement' has the same meaning as in the Arbitration Act 1996 Pt I (ss 1–84) (see ARBITRATION vol 2 (2008) PARA 1213): Insolvency Act 1986 s 349A(4) (added by the Arbitration Act 1996 s 107(1), Sch 3 para 46).

2　Insolvency Act 1986 s 349A(1), (2) (added by the Arbitration Act 1996 Sch 3 para 46).

3　For these purposes, 'the court' means the court which has jurisdiction in the bankruptcy proceedings: Insolvency Act 1986 s 349A(4) (added by the Arbitration Act 1996 Sch 3 para 46). As to the appropriate courts see PARAS 6, 7.

4　Insolvency Act 1986 s 349A(3) (added by the Arbitration Act 1996 Sch 3 para 46).

(v)　After-acquired Property

458.　In general. The property[1] which vests in the trustee on his appointment taking effect or in the official receiver on his becoming trustee[2] is that property which belongs to the bankrupt at the commencement of the bankruptcy[3].

Property which is acquired by, or devolves on, the bankrupt after the commencement of the bankrupty[4] does not automatically vest in the trustee. The trustee may, however, by notice in writing[5] claim for the bankrupt's estate[6] any property which has been so acquired, or has so devolved on, the bankrupt since the commencement of the bankruptcy[7]. Such a notice may not be served in respect of:

(1)　any property[8] not forming part of the bankrupt's estate under the Insolvency Act 1986[9];

(2)　a dwelling house vesting in the bankrupt[10];

(3)　any property which by virtue of any other enactment[11] is excluded from the bankrupt's estate; or

(4)　without prejudice to an order of the court on an application for discharge[12], any property which is acquired by, or devolves on, the bankrupt after his discharge[13].

1　As to the meaning of 'property' see PARA 412; but see also note 8.

2　As to the vesting of the bankrupt's estate in the trustee or the official receiver see PARA 398.

3　As to the commencement of bankruptcy see PARA 209.

4　It is important to distinguish between property in respect of which the bankrupt has no interest at the date of the bankruptcy order but which he obtains later and property in respect of which the bankrupt has a future or contingent interest at the date of the bankruptcy order which passes with the estate to the trustee.

5 See PARA 459.
6 As to the meaning of 'the bankrupt's estate' see PARA 211.
7 Insolvency Act 1986 s 307(1). See *Hardy v Pallen* [1997] BCC 815, sub nom *Hardy (a bankrupt) v Buchler* [1997] BPIR 643 (the Insolvency Act 1986 s 307 extends to any commercial transaction carried on by or with the bankrupt and includes money borrowed by the bankrupt in circumstances where he had disclosed his bankruptcy to the lender). As to retrospective validation of after-acquired property seized by the trustee without prior notice to the bankrupt see *Pike (a bankrupt) v Cork Gully* [1997] BPIR 723, CA.

In the case of the administration in bankruptcy of the insolvent estate of a deceased person dying before the presentation of a bankruptcy petition, the Insolvency Act 1986 s 307 applies, with the modification that in s 307(1) for the words 'commencement of the bankruptcy' there are to be substituted the words 'date of death of the deceased debtor': Administration of Insolvent Estates of Deceased Persons Order 1986, SI 1986/1999, art 3(1), Sch 1 Pt II para 22. As to the administration in bankruptcy of the insolvent estates of deceased persons see further PARA 830 et seq.

The specific provisions of the Insolvency Act 1986 s 307 take priority over the general provisions of the Married Women's Property Act 1882 (see MATRIMONIAL AND CIVIL PARTNERSHIP LAW vol 72 (2009) PARA 224 et seq): *Rooney v Cardona* [1999] 1 WLR 1388, [1999] BPIR 291, CA. Any sum payable to an eligible student by way of a loan which he receives or is entitled to receive after the commencement of his bankruptcy, whether his entitlement arises before or after that date, is not to be treated as part of his estate or claimed for his estate under the Insolvency Act 1986 s 307, s 310 (see PARA 462) or s 310A (see PARA 469): see the Education (Student Loans) (Repayment) Regulations 2009, SI 2009/470, reg 80 (amended by SI 2010/661); and EDUCATION vol 36 (2011) PARA 1248.
8 References to property in the Insolvency Act 1986 s 307 do not include any property which, as part of the bankrupt's income, may be the subject of an income payments order under s 310 (see PARA 462): s 307(5). See also *Pike v Cork Gully* [1997] BPIR 723, CA; *Supperstone v Lloyd's Names Association Working Party* [1999] BPIR 832; *Krasner v Dennison, Lawrence v Lesser* [2001] Ch 76, [2000] 3 All ER 234, CA.
9 Ie property falling within the Insolvency Act 1986 s 283(2) or (3): see PARA 211 heads (a)–(d).
10 Ie property vesting in the bankrupt by virtue of the Insolvency Act 1986 s 283A (see PARA 212).
11 See PARA 211 note 33.
12 Ie under the Insolvency Act 1986 s 280(2)(c): see PARA 638 note 2.
13 Insolvency Act 1986 s 307(2) (amended by the Enterprise Act 2002 s 261(4)).

459. Trustee's notice of claim. Except with the permission of the court[1], a notice[2] by the trustee in bankruptcy claiming for the bankrupt's estate[3] any property which has been acquired by, or has devolved on, the bankrupt since the commencement of the bankruptcy[4] may not be served after the end of the period of 42 days beginning with the day on which it first came to the knowledge of the trustee that the property in question had been acquired by, or had devolved on, the bankrupt[5].

On service on the bankrupt of such a notice, the property[6] to which the notice relates vests in the trustee as part of the bankrupt's estate; and the trustee's title to that property has relation back to the time at which the property was acquired by, or devolved on, the bankrupt[7]. Where, whether before or after service of such a notice, a person acquires property in good faith, for value and without notice of the bankruptcy, or a banker enters into a transaction in good faith and without such notice, the trustee is not in respect of that property or transaction entitled by virtue of these provisions to any remedy against the person or banker, or any person whose title to any property derives from that person or banker[8].

1 As to the factors to which the court will have regard when considering an application for permission to give notice out of time see *Solomons v Williams* [2001] BPIR 1123; *Franses v Oomerjee* [2005] BPIR 1320.
2 Ie under the Insolvency Act 1986 s 307(1): see PARA 458.
3 As to the meaning of 'the bankrupt's estate' see PARA 211.
4 As to the commencement of bankruptcy see PARA 209.
5 Insolvency Act 1986 s 309(1)(a). For these purposes: (1) anything which comes to the knowledge of the trustee is deemed, in relation to any successor of his as trustee, to have come

to the knowledge of the successor at the same time; and (2) anything which comes, otherwise than under head (1), to the knowledge of a person before he is the trustee is deemed to come to his knowledge on his appointment taking effect or, in the case of the official receiver, on his becoming trustee: s 309(2).

As to the application of s 309 in the case of the administration in bankruptcy of the insolvent estate of a deceased person dying before the presentation of a bankruptcy petition see PARA 404 note 5.

6 As to the meaning of 'property' for these purposes see PARA 458 note 8.

7 Insolvency Act 1986 s 307(3). As to the application of s 307 in the case of the administration in bankruptcy of the insolvent estate of a deceased person dying before the presentation of a bankruptcy petition see PARA 458 note 7.

8 Insolvency Act 1986 s 307(4).

460. Bankrupt's duty to give notice to trustee. Where, at any time after the commencement of the bankruptcy[1], any property[2] is acquired by, or devolves on, the bankrupt, the bankrupt must give the trustee notice of the property[3]. Such notice must be given within 21 days of the bankrupt's becoming aware of the relevant facts[4].

If the bankrupt without reasonable excuse fails to comply with the above obligation, he is guilty of a contempt of court and liable to be punished accordingly, in addition to any other punishment to which he may be subject[5].

1 As to the commencement of bankruptcy see PARA 209.
2 Subject to the Insolvency Rules 1986, SI 1986/1925, r 6.200(5) (see PARA 461), r 6.200(1) does not apply to property acquired by the bankrupt in the ordinary course of a business carried on by him: r 6.200(4).

3 Insolvency Act 1986 s 333(2). As to the application of s 333 in the case of the administration in bankruptcy of the insolvent estate of a deceased person dying before the presentation of a bankruptcy petition see PARA 343 note 1.

4 Insolvency Rules 1986, SI 1986/1925, r 6.200(1).
5 Insolvency Act 1986 s 333(4). As to contempt of court see CONTEMPT OF COURT vol 22 (2012) PARA 1 et seq; and as to offences see PARA 733 et seq.

461. Disposal of property by bankrupt. Having served notice in respect of property acquired by or devolving on him[1], the bankrupt may not, without the trustee's consent in writing, dispose of it within the period of 42 days beginning with the date of the notice[2]. If, however, the bankrupt disposes of property before giving the notice or in contravention of the above provisions, it is his duty as soon as reasonably practicable to disclose to the trustee the name and address of the disponee, and to provide any other information which may be necessary to enable the trustee to trace the property and recover it for the estate[3].

If the bankrupt carries on a business, he must, when required by the trustee, furnish to the trustee information with respect to it, showing the total of goods bought and sold, or, as the case may be, services supplied, and the profit or loss arising from the business; and the trustee may require the bankrupt to furnish fuller details, including accounts, of the business carried on by him[4].

Where property has been disposed of by the bankrupt before giving notice or otherwise in contravention of the above provisions, the trustee may serve notice on the disponee, claiming the property as part of the estate[5]; and the trustee's notice must be served within 28 days of his becoming aware of the disponee's identity and an address at which he can be served[6].

Any expenses incurred by the trustee in acquiring title to after-acquired property are payable out of the estate, in the prescribed order of priority[7].

1 See PARA 460.

2 Insolvency Rules 1986, SI 1986/1925, r 6.200(2). Subject to r 6.200(5) (see the text and note 4), r 6.200(2), (3) does not apply to property acquired by the bankrupt in the ordinary course of a business carried on by him: r 6.200(4).
3 Insolvency Rules 1986, SI 1986/1925, r 6.200(3) (amended by SI 2009/642).
4 Insolvency Rules 1986, SI 1986/1925, r 6.200(5) (amended by SI 2010/686). See *Re a Debtor (No 26 of 1991)* [1996] BCC 246, sub nom *Holmes v Official Receiver* [1996] BPIR 279 (failure to produce accounts of a post-bankruptcy business was held to constitute grounds for suspension of the bankrupt's automatic discharge).
5 Ie by virtue of the Insolvency Act 1986 s 307(3): see PARA 459.
6 Insolvency Rules 1986, SI 1986/1925, r 6.201(1), (2).
7 Insolvency Rules 1986, SI 1986/1925, r 6.202. As to the meaning of 'prescribed order of priority' see PARA 222 note 5.

(vi) Income Payments Orders and Agreements

A. INCOME PAYMENTS ORDERS

462. In general. On the application of the trustee instituted before the discharge of the bankrupt[1], the court may make an order ('an income payments order') claiming for the bankrupt's estate[2] so much of the income of the bankrupt[3] during the period for which the order is in force as may be specified in the order[4]. The court may not, however, make an income payments order the effect of which would be to reduce the income of the bankrupt[5] below what appears to the court to be necessary for meeting the reasonable domestic needs[6] of the bankrupt and his family[7].

An income payments order must, in respect of any payment of income to which it is to apply, either:

(1)   require the bankrupt to pay to the trustee an amount equal to so much of that payment as is claimed by the order; or

(2)   require the person making the payment to pay so much of it as is so claimed to the trustee, instead of to the bankrupt[8].

An income payments order must specify the period during which it is to have effect; and that period may end after the discharge of the bankrupt, but may not end after the period of three years beginning with the date on which the order is made[9]. Subject to the three-year limit, an income payments order may be varied on the application of the trustee or the bankrupt, whether before or after discharge[10].

Sums received by the trustee under an income payments order form part of the bankrupt's estate[11].

1 Insolvency Act 1986 s 310(1A) (added by the Enterprise Act 2002 ss 259(1), (2), 278(2), Sch 26). As to discharge from bankruptcy see PARA 638 et seq. As to income payments agreements see PARA 469.
2 As to the meaning of 'the bankrupt's estate' see PARA 211.
3 For the purposes of the Insolvency Act 1986 s 310, the income of the bankrupt comprises every payment in the nature of income which is from time to time made to him or to which he from time to time becomes entitled, including any payment in respect of the carrying on of any business or in respect of any office or employment, despite anything in the Welfare Reform and Pensions Act 1999 s 11 or s 12 (see PARA 407; and PERSONAL AND OCCUPATIONAL PENSIONS vol 80 (2013) PARAS 285, 286), and any payment under a pension scheme but excluding: (1) any payment by way of guaranteed minimum pension; and (2) payments giving effect to the bankrupt's protected rights as a member of a pension scheme: Insolvency Act 1986 s 310(7) (amended by the Pensions Act 1995 s 122, Sch 3 para 15(b); the Welfare Reform and Pensions Act 1999 s 18, Sch 2 para 2); Insolvency Act 1986 s 310(8) (added by the Pensions Act 1995 Sch 3 para 15(b)). For these purposes, 'guaranteed minimum pension' and 'protected rights' have the same meanings as in the Pension Scheme Act 1993 ss 8(2), 10 (as it had effect before the commencement of the Pensions Act 2007 s 15(1)) (see PERSONAL AND OCCUPATIONAL

PENSIONS vol 80 (2013) PARAS 393, 398): Insolvency Act 1986 s 310(9) (added by the Pensions Act 1995 Sch 3 para 15(b); and substituted by SI 2011/1730). Where at the date of the bankruptcy the bankrupt is entitled to income by virtue of some right vested in him, that right together with income received by virtue of that right forms part of the estate and cannot be the subject of an income payments order: *Krasner v Dennison, Lawrence v Lesser* [2001] Ch 76, [2000] 3 All ER 234, CA (entire income accruing to bankrupt from pre-bankruptcy annuity contracts and personal pension schemes; but see now the subsequent legislative change effected by the Welfare Reform and Pensions Act 1999 s 11(2), referred to in PARA 407); cf *Patel v Jones* [2001] EWCA Civ 779, [2001] BPIR 919. It is not an obstacle to the granting of the order that the amount recoverable from the bankrupt is less than the fees payable to the receiver: *Official Receiver v Negus* [2011] EWHC 3719 (Ch), [2012] 1 WLR 1598, [2012] All ER (D) 124 (Jan). A bankrupt has an entitlement to a payment under a pension scheme not merely where the scheme is in payment of benefit but also where he would be entitled to payment merely by asking for payment: *Raithatha v Williamson* [2012] EWHC 909 (Ch), [2012] 3 All ER 1028, [2012] 1 WLR 3559.

A one-off payment is capable of constituting income for the purposes of the Insolvency Act 1986 s 310(7): *Supperstone v Lloyd's Names Association Working Party* [1999] BPIR 832; *Kilvert v Flackett* [1998] 2 FLR 806, [1998] BPIR 721.

4 Insolvency Act 1986 s 310(1). See also *Kilvert v Flackett* [1998] BPIR 721 (there must be some obvious justification as to why a payment which enhances the bankrupt's income should not be made the subject of an income payments order); *Green v Satsangi* [1998] 1 BCLC 458, [1998] BPIR 55 (income payments order did not impose tax liability on a trustee in bankruptcy). In the case of the administration in bankruptcy of the insolvent estate of a deceased person dying before the presentation of a bankruptcy petition, the Insolvency Act 1986 s 310 applies: Administration of Insolvent Estates of Deceased Persons Order 1986, SI 1986/1999, art 3(1), Sch 1 Pt II para 23. As to the administration in bankruptcy of the insolvent estates of deceased persons see further PARA 830 et seq.

5 Ie when taken together with any payments to which the Insolvency Act 1986 s 310(8) applies: see note 3.

6 Cf the Insolvency Act 1986 s 283(2)(b) (see PARA 211 head (b)) where a bankrupt's estate does not comprise (inter alia) such clothing, bedding, furniture, household equipment and provisions as are necessary for satisfying the *basic* domestic needs of the bankrupt and his family. See also *Re Rayatt (a bankrupt)* [1998] 2 FLR 264, [1998] BPIR 495 (private school fees held to constitute a reasonable domestic need); *Malcolm v Official Receiver* [1999] BPIR 97 (mortgage payments being made by the bankrupt were, in the circumstances, excessive).

7 Insolvency Act 1986 s 310(2) (amended by the Pensions Act 1995 Sch 3 para 15(a)). As to the meaning of 'family' see PARA 211 note 8. As to the needs of dependants not living with the bankrupt see *Re X (a bankrupt)* [1996] BPIR 494; and as to the needs of a former wife see *Albert v Albert (a bankrupt)* [1998] 1 FCR 331, [1996] BPIR 232, CA.

8 Insolvency Act 1986 s 310(3).

9 Insolvency Act 1986 s 310(6) (substituted by the Enterprise Act 2002 s 259(1), (4)).

10 Insolvency Act 1986 s 310(6A) (added by the Enterprise Act 2002 s 259(1), (4)).

11 Insolvency Act 1986 s 310(5).

463. Application for order. Where the trustee applies for an income payments order[1], the court must fix a venue[2] for the hearing of the application[3]. Notice of the application and of the venue must be sent to the bankrupt at least 28 days before the day fixed for the hearing, together with a copy of the trustee's application and a short statement of the grounds on which it is made[4].

The notice must inform the bankrupt that:

(1) unless at least five business days[5] before the date fixed for the hearing he sends to the court and to the trustee written consent[6] to an order being made in the terms of the application, he is required to attend the hearing; and

(2) if he attends, he will be given an opportunity to show cause why the order should not be made, or an order should be made otherwise than as applied for by the trustee[7].

1 Ie under the Insolvency Act 1986 s 310: see PARA 462. As to the mode of application and the procedure see PARA 786 et seq.

2 As to the meaning of 'venue' see PARA 46 note 22.
3 Insolvency Rules 1986, SI 1986/1925, r 6.189(1).
4 Insolvency Rules 1986, SI 1986/1925, r 6.189(2). For the prescribed form of notice of application see Sch 4 Form 6.64.
5 As to the meaning of 'business day' see PARA 28 note 8.
6 For the prescribed form of written consent see the Insolvency Rules 1986, SI 1986/1925, Sch 4 Form 6.64.
7 Insolvency Rules 1986, SI 1986/1925, r 6.189(3) (amended by SI 2010/686).

464. Action to follow making of order. Where the court makes an income payments order, a sealed copy of the order must, as soon as reasonably practicable after it is made, be sent by the trustee to the bankrupt[1]. If an order to the payer of the relevant income is made[2], a sealed copy of the order must also be sent by the trustee to the person to whom the order is directed[3].

Where the court makes an income payments order, it may, if it thinks fit, discharge or vary any attachment of earnings order that is for the time being in force to secure payments by the bankrupt[4].

1 Insolvency Rules 1986, SI 1986/1925, r 6.190(1) (amended by SI 2009/642). For the prescribed forms of order for income claimed under the Insolvency Act 1986 s 310(3)(a) (see PARA 462 head (1)) and s 310(3)(b) (see PARA 462 head (2)) see the Insolvency Rules 1986, SI 1986/1925, Sch 4 Forms 6.65, 6.66 (both amended by SI 2010/686).
2 Ie under the Insolvency Act 1986 s 310(3)(b): see PARA 462 head (2).
3 Insolvency Rules 1986, SI 1986/1925, r 6.190(2).
4 Insolvency Act 1986 s 310(4). As to attachment of earnings orders see PARA 889. As to the application of s 310 in the case of the administration in bankruptcy of the insolvent estate of a deceased person dying before the presentation of a bankruptcy petition see PARA 462 note 4.

465. Variation of order. If an income payments order is made requiring the bankrupt to pay the trustee an amount equal to so much of that payment as is claimed by the trustee[1], and the bankrupt does not comply with it, the trustee may apply to the court for the order to be varied so as to take effect as an order[2] to the payer of the relevant income[3]. The trustee's application may be made without notice to any other party[4].

Sealed copies of any order made on the application must, as soon as reasonably practicable after it is made, be sent by the court to the trustee and the bankrupt[5].

In the case of an order varying or discharging an income payments order being an order to the payer of the relevant income[6], an additional sealed copy must be sent to the trustee, for transmission as soon as reasonably practicable to the payor of the relevant income[7].

1 Ie under the Insolvency Act 1986 s 310(3)(a): see PARA 462 head (1).
2 Ie an order under the Insolvency Act 1986 s 310(3)(b): see PARA 462 head (2).
3 Insolvency Rules 1986, SI 1986/1925, r 6.191(1). For the prescribed form of order converting an income payments order made under the Insolvency Act 1986 s 310(3)(a) to an order under s 310(3)(b) see the Insolvency Rules 1986, SI 1986/1925, Sch 4 Form 6.67 (amended by SI 2010/686).
4 Insolvency Rules 1986, SI 1986/1925, r 6.191(2) (amended by SI 2010/686). There is an inherent jurisdiction in the court to set aside orders made on applications made without notice being served on any other party: see *Becker v Noel* [1971] 2 All ER 1248, [1971] 1 WLR 803, CA. Every court having jurisdiction for the purposes of the Insolvency Act 1986 Pts 7A–11 (ss 251A–385) may review, rescind or vary any order made by it in the exercise of that jurisdiction: s 375(1). See further PARA 761. As to setting aside orders made on applications made without notice being served on any other party generally see CIVIL PROCEDURE vol 12 (2009) PARA 1143. As to the possibility of appeal by the Crown as paymaster against an income payments order, despite there being no specific provision for such an appeal, see *Re Duckett, ex p Minister of Education v Trustee* [1964] Ch 398, sub nom *Re Duckett (a bankrupt), ex p Minister of Education v McLeod* [1964] 1 All ER 19, CA.

In the case of the administration in bankruptcy of the insolvent estate of a deceased person dying before the presentation of a bankruptcy petition, the Insolvency Act 1986 s 375 applies: Administration of Insolvent Estates of Deceased Persons Order 1986, SI 1986/1999, art 3(1), Sch 1 Pt II para 30. As to the administration in bankruptcy of the insolvent estates of deceased persons see further PARA 830 et seq.

5   Insolvency Rules 1986, SI 1986/1925, r 6.191(3) (amended by SI 2009/642).
6   See note 2.
7   Insolvency Rules 1986, SI 1986/1925, r 6.191(4) (amended by SI 2009/642).

466.   Order to payer of income; administration. Where a person receives notice of an income payments order being an order to the payer of the relevant income[1], with reference to income otherwise payable by him to the bankrupt, he must make the arrangements requisite for compliance with the order as soon as reasonably practicable[2]. When making any payment to the trustee, he may deduct the appropriate fee[3] towards the clerical and administrative costs of compliance with the income payments order; and he must give to the bankrupt a written statement of any amount so deducted by him[4].

Where a person receives notice of an income payments order imposing on him a requirement to pay so much of the payment as is so claimed to the trustee, instead of to the bankrupt[5], and either:

(1)   he is then no longer liable to make to the bankrupt any payment of income; or

(2)   having so made payments in compliance with the order, he ceases to be so liable,

he must as soon as reasonably practicable give notice of that fact to the trustee[6].

1   Ie an order under the Insolvency Act 1986 s 310(3)(b): see PARA 462 head (2).
2   Insolvency Rules 1986, SI 1986/1925, r 6.192(1) (amended by SI 2010/686). It is apprehended that a payer of income would be entitled to apply to the court to review, rescind or vary its order or to appeal against a decision on such an application under the Insolvency Act 1986 s 375: see further PARA 761.
3   For these purposes, 'the appropriate fee' means 50 pence: Insolvency Rules 1986, SI 1986/1925, r 13.11(a).
4   Insolvency Rules 1986, SI 1986/1925, r 6.192(2).
5   See note 1.
6   Insolvency Rules 1986, SI 1986/1925, r 6.192(3) (amended by SI 2009/642).

467.   Review of order. Where an income payments order is in force, either the trustee or the bankrupt may apply to the court for the order to be varied or discharged[1].

If the application is made by the trustee, the statutory provisions[2], with any necessary modifications, apply as in the case of an application for an income payments order[3]. If the application is made by the bankrupt, it must be accompanied by a short statement of the grounds on which it is made[4].

If the court thinks that no sufficient cause is shown for the application, it may dismiss the application; but it may not do so unless the applicant has had an opportunity to attend the court for a hearing without notice to any other party, of which he has been given at least five business days'[5] notice; and, if the application is not so dismissed, the court must fix a venue[6] for it to be heard[7].

At least 28 days before the date fixed for the hearing, the applicant must send to the trustee or the bankrupt, whichever of them is not himself the applicant, notice of the venue, accompanied by a copy of the application; and, where the applicant is the bankrupt, the notice must be accompanied by a copy of the statement of the grounds on which it is made[8].

If the trustee thinks fit, he may appear and be heard on the application; and, whether or not he intends to appear, he may, not less than five business days before the date fixed for the hearing, file a written report of any matters which he considers ought to be drawn to the court's attention; and if such a report is filed, a copy of it must be sent by the trustee to the bankrupt[9].

Sealed copies of any order made on the application must, as soon as reasonably practicable after the order is made, be sent by the court to the trustee, the bankrupt and the payer, if other than the bankrupt[10].

1   Insolvency Rules 1986, SI 1986/1925, r 6.193(1).
2   Ie the Insolvency Rules 1986, SI 1986/1925, r 6.189: see PARA 463.
3   Insolvency Rules 1986, SI 1986/1925, r 6.193(2).
4   Insolvency Rules 1986, SI 1986/1925, r 6.193(3).
5   As to the meaning of 'business day' see PARA 28 note 8.
6   As to the meaning of 'venue' see PARA 46 note 22.
7   Insolvency Rules 1986, SI 1986/1925, r 6.193(4) (amended by SI 2010/686).
8   Insolvency Rules 1986, SI 1986/1925, r 6.193(5).
9   Insolvency Rules 1986, SI 1986/1925, r 6.193(6) (amended by SI 2010/686).
10   Insolvency Rules 1986, SI 1986/1925, r 6.193(7) (amended by SI 2009/642). For the prescribed form of discharge or variation of order for income claimed under the Insolvency Act 1986 s 310 see the Insolvency Rules 1986, SI 1986/1925, Sch 4 Form 6.68.

468. Bankrupt's duty to give notice to trustee of increase in income. Where, at any time after the commencement of the bankruptcy[1], there is an increase in the bankrupt's income, the bankrupt must give the trustee notice of the increase[2]. Such notice must be given within 21 days of the bankrupt's becoming aware of the relevant facts[3].

If the bankrupt without reasonable excuse fails to comply with the above obligation, he is guilty of a contempt of court and liable to be punished accordingly, in addition to any other punishment to which he may be subject[4].

1   As to the commencement of bankruptcy see PARA 209.
2   Insolvency Act 1986 s 333(2). As to the application of s 333 in the case of the administration in bankruptcy of the insolvent estate of a deceased person dying before the presentation of a bankruptcy petition see PARA 343 note 1.
3   Insolvency Rules 1986, SI 1986/1925, r 6.200(1).
4   Insolvency Act 1986 s 333(4). As to contempt of court see CONTEMPT OF COURT vol 22 (2012) PARA 1 et seq; and as to offences see PARA 733 et seq.

B. INCOME PAYMENTS AGREEMENTS

469. In general. An 'income payments agreement' is a written agreement between a bankrupt and his trustee or between a bankrupt and the official receiver which provides: (1) that the bankrupt is to pay to the trustee or the official receiver an amount equal to a specified part or proportion of the bankrupt's income for a specified period; or (2) that a third person is to pay to the trustee or the official receiver a specified proportion of money due to the bankrupt by way of income for a specified period[1]. A provision of an income payments agreement of a kind specified in head (1) or head (2) above may be enforced as if it were a provision of an income payments order[2].

While an income payments agreement is in force the court may, on the application of the bankrupt, his trustee or the official receiver, discharge or vary an attachment of earnings order[3] that is for the time being in force to secure payments by the bankrupt[4].

An income payments agreement must specify the period during which it is to have effect; and that period may end after the discharge of the bankrupt[5] but may not end after the period of three years beginning with the date on which the agreement is made[6]. Subject to the three-year limit, an income payments agreement may be varied by written agreement between the parties or by the court on an application made by the bankrupt, the trustee or the official receiver[7].

The court: (a) may not vary an income payments agreement so as to include provision of a kind which could not be included in an income payments order; and (b) must grant an application to vary an income payments agreement if and to the extent that the court thinks variation necessary to avoid the reduction of the income of the bankrupt below what appears to the court to be necessary for meeting the reasonable domestic needs of the bankrupt and his family[8].

1   Insolvency Act 1986 s 310A(1) (s 310A added by the Enterprise Act 2002 s 305(1)). In the case of the administration in bankruptcy of the insolvent estate of a deceased person dying before the presentation of a bankruptcy petition, the Insolvency Act 1986 s 310A applies: Administration of Insolvent Estates of Deceased Persons Order 1986, SI 1986/1999, art 3(1), Sch 1 Pt II para 23. As to the administration in bankruptcy of the insolvent estates of deceased persons see further PARA 830 et seq.
2   Insolvency Act 1986 s 310A(2) (as added: see note 1). As to income payments orders see PARA 462. The provisions of s 310(5) (receipts to form part of estate) and s 310(7)–(9) (meaning of income) (see PARA 462) apply to an income payments agreement as they apply to an income payments order: s 310A(4) (as so added).
3   As to attachment of earnings orders see PARA 889.
4   Insolvency Act 1986 s 310A(3) (as added: see note 1).
5   As to discharge from bankruptcy see PARA 638 et seq.
6   Insolvency Act 1986 s 310A(5) (as added: see note 1).
7   Insolvency Act 1986 s 310A(6) (as added: see note 1).
8   Insolvency Act 1986 s 310A(7) (as added: see note 1). See s 310(2); and PARA 462 text and notes 5–7.

470. Approval of income payments agreements. An income payments agreement[1] can only be entered into prior to the discharge of the bankrupt[2]. Where an income payments agreement is to be entered into between the official receiver or trustee and the bankrupt[3], the official receiver or trustee must provide an income payments agreement to the bankrupt for his approval[4]. Within 14 days or such longer period as may be specified by the official receiver or trustee (whichever is appropriate) from the date on which the income payments agreement was sent, the bankrupt must: (1) if he decides to approve the draft income payments agreement, authenticate[5] the agreement and return it to the official receiver or trustee; or (2) if he decides not to approve the agreement, notify the official receiver or trustee in writing of his decision[6].

1   As to income payments agreements see PARA 469.
2   Insolvency Rules 1986, SI 1986/1925, r 6.193A(1) (added by SI 2003/1730). As to discharge from bankruptcy see PARA 638 et seq.
3   Ie under the Insolvency Act 1986 s 310A(1) (see PARA 469).
4   Insolvency Rules 1986, SI 1986/1925, r 6.193A(2) (added by SI 2003/1730).
5   As to authentication see PARA 158 note 2.
6   Insolvency Rules 1986, SI 1986/1925, r 6.193A(3) (added by SI 2003/1730; and amended by SI 2010/686).

471. Acceptance of income payments agreements. On receipt by the official receiver or trustee of the authenticated income payments agreement[1], the official receiver or trustee must authenticate and date it[2]. When the official receiver or the trustee authenticates and dates the income payments agreement, it comes into force and a copy must be sent to the bankrupt[3].

Where the agreement provides for payments by a third person to the official receiver or trustee who is not the official receiver[4], a notice of the agreement must be sent by the official receiver or trustee to that person[5]. The notice must contain:

(1) the full name and address of the bankrupt;

(2) a statement that an income payments agreement has been made, the date of it, and that it provides for the payment by the third person of sums owed to the bankrupt (or a part thereof) to be paid to the official receiver or trustee;

(3) the full name and address of the third person;

(4) a statement of the amount of money to be paid to the official receiver or trustee from the bankrupt's income, the period over which the payments are to be made, and the intervals at which the sums are to be paid; and

(5) the full name and address of the official receiver or trustee and the address or details of where the sums are to be paid[6].

When making any payment to the official receiver or the trustee, a person who has received notice of an income payments agreement with reference to income otherwise payable by him to the bankrupt may deduct the appropriate fee[7] towards the clerical and administrative costs of compliance with the income payments agreement[8].

1   As to income payments agreements see PARAS 469–470. As to authentication see PARA 158 note 2.

2   Insolvency Rules 1986, SI 1986/1925, r 6.193B(1) (added by SI 2003/1730; and amended by SI 2010/686).

3   Insolvency Rules 1986, SI 1986/1925, r 6.193B(2) (added by SI 2003/1730; and amended by SI 2010/686).

4   Ie in accordance with the Insolvency Act 1986 s 310A(1)(b) (see PARA 469 head (2)).

5   Insolvency Rules 1986, SI 1986/1925, r 6.193B(3) (added by SI 2003/1730).

6   Insolvency Rules 1986, SI 1986/1925, r 6.193B(4) (added by SI 2003/1730).

7   For this purpose, 'the appropriate fee' is 15 pence per A4 or A5 page, and 30 pence per A3 page: Insolvency Rules 1986, SI 1986/1925, r 13.11(b).

8   Insolvency Rules 1986, SI 1986/1925, r 6.193B(5) (added by SI 2003/1730). The person must give to the bankrupt a written statement of any amount deducted by him: Insolvency Rules 1986, SI 1986/1925, r 6.193B(5) (as so added).

472. Variation of agreement. Where an application is made to court for variation of an income payments agreement[1], the application must be accompanied by a copy of the agreement[2].

Where the bankrupt applies to the court for variation of an income payments agreement[3], he must send a copy of the application and notice of the venue to the official receiver or trustee (whichever is appropriate) at least 28 days before the date fixed for the hearing[4]. When the official receiver or trustee applies to the court for variation of an income payments agreement[5], he must send a copy of the application and notice of the venue[6] to the bankrupt at least 28 days before the date fixed for the hearing[7].

Where the court orders an income payments agreement that the bankrupt is to pay a proportion of his income[8] to be varied, so as to take the form of an agreement[9] providing that a third person is to make payments to the trustee or the official receiver, the official receiver or trustee must send a notice[10] to that third person[11].

When making any payment to the official receiver or the trustee a person who has received notice of an income payments agreement with reference to income otherwise payable by him to the bankrupt may deduct the appropriate fee[12] towards the clerical and administrative costs of compliance with the income payments agreement[13].

1   As to income payments agreements see PARAS 469–471.
2   Insolvency Rules 1986, SI 1986/1925, r 6.193C(1) (added by SI 2003/1730). For the prescribed form of variation of an income payments agreement under the Insolvency Act 1986 s 310A see the Insolvency Rules 1986, SI 1986/1925, r 6.193C(4), Sch 4 Form 6.81 (added by SI 2003/1730).
3   Ie under the Insolvency Act 1986 s 310A(6)(b) (see PARA 469).
4   Insolvency Rules 1986, SI 1986/1925, r 6.193C(2) (added by SI 2003/1730).
5   See note 3.
6   As to the meaning of 'venue' see PARA 46 note 22.
7   Insolvency Rules 1986, SI 1986/1925, r 6.193C(3) (added by SI 2003/1730).
8   Ie under the Insolvency Act 1986 s 310A(1)(a) (see PARA 469).
9   Ie an agreement under the Insolvency Act 1986 s 310A(1)(b) (see PARA 469).
10 Ie in accordance with the Insolvency Rules 1986, SI 1986/1925, r 6.193B(3) (see PARA 471).
11 Insolvency Rules 1986, SI 1986/1925, r 6.193C(5) (added by SI 2003/1730).
12 It appears that for these purposes, 'the appropriate fee' means 50 pence: see the Insolvency Rules 1986, SI 1986/1925, r 13.11(a) (amended by SI 2003/1730). The amending provision (see Sch 1 Pt 10 para 64) erroneously refers to the fee chargeable under the Insolvency Rules 1986, SI 1986/1925, r 6.193C(4).
13 Insolvency Rules 1986, SI 1986/1925, r 6.193C(6) (added by SI 2003/1730). The person must give to the bankrupt a written statement of any amount deducted by him: Insolvency Rules 1986, SI 1986/1925, r 6.193C(6) (as so added).

(vii) Trustee's Powers and Duties

473.   General functions of trustee.   The function of the trustee[1] is to get in, realise and distribute the bankrupt's estate[2]; and, in the carrying out of that function and in the management of the bankrupt's estate, the trustee is entitled[3] to use his own discretion[4].

1   Ie in relation to any bankruptcy where either: (1) the appointment of a person as trustee of a bankrupt's estates takes effect; or (2) the official receiver becomes trustee of a bankrupt's estate: see the Insolvency Act 1986 s 305(1).
2   Ie in accordance with the provisions of the Insolvency Act 1986 ss 305–335. As to the meaning of 'the bankrupt's estate' see PARA 211.
3   Ie subject to the Insolvency Act 1986 ss 305–335.
4   Insolvency Act 1986 s 305(1), (2). The discretion is that of the trustee and he will not be permitted simply to delegate his functions to another by, for example, a general power of attorney: *Segal v Pasram* [2008] 1 FLR 271, [2007] Fam Law 892, [2007] BPIR 881. In the case of the administration in bankruptcy of the insolvent estate of a deceased person dying before the presentation of a bankruptcy petition, the Insolvency Act 1986 s 305 applies: Administration of Insolvent Estates of Deceased Persons Order 1986, SI 1986/1999, art 3(1), Sch 1 Pt II para 20. However, in any such case, in the exercise of his functions under the Insolvency Act 1986 s 305 where an insolvency administration order has been made, the trustee must have regard to any claim by the personal representative to payment of reasonable funeral, testamentary and administration expenses incurred by him in respect of the deceased debtor's estate or, if there is no such personal representative, to any claim by any other person to payment of any such expenses incurred by him in respect of the estate provided that the trustee has sufficient funds in hand for the purpose, and such claims have priority over the preferential debts listed in s 386, Sch 6 (see PARA 591 et seq): s 305(5) (added by the Administration of Insolvent Estates of Deceased Persons Order 1986, SI 1986/1999, Sch 1 Pt II para 20). As to the administration in bankruptcy of the insolvent estates of deceased persons see further PARA 830 et seq.
    As to the modification of the Insolvency Act 1986 s 305 by the Insolvent Partnerships Order 1994, SI 1994/2421, in relation to the bankruptcy of an individual member of an insolvent partnership see COMPANY AND PARTNERSHIP INSOLVENCY vol 17 (2011) PARA 1341.

474.   Obligations of trustee to official receiver.   It is the duty of the trustee, if he is not the official receiver:

(1)   to furnish the official receiver with such information;

(2)   to produce to the official receiver, and permit inspection by the official receiver of, such books, papers and other records[1]; and

(3)   to give the official receiver such other assistance,

as the official receiver may reasonably require for the purpose of enabling him to carry out his functions[2] in relation to the bankruptcy[3].

On the application of the official receiver, the court may make such orders as it thinks necessary for enforcement of the trustee's statutory duty[4] to give information and assistance and to produce and allow inspection of books and records relating to the bankruptcy[5]. Such an order of the court may provide that all costs of and incidental to the official receiver's application are to be borne by the trustee[6].

1   As to the meaning of 'records' see PARA 20 note 6.
2   As to the official receiver's functions see PARA 37; and as to the power to contract out the official receiver's functions see PARA 38.
3   Insolvency Act 1986 s 305(3).
4   Ie under the Insolvency Act 1986 s 305(3).
5   Insolvency Rules 1986, SI 1986/1925, r 6.149(1).
6   Insolvency Rules 1986, SI 1986/1925, r 6.149(2).

475.   Acquisition by trustee of control. In relation to, and for the purpose of acquiring or retaining possession of, the bankrupt's estate[1], the trustee is in the same position as if he were a receiver of property appointed by the High Court[2]; and the court may, on his application, enforce such acquisition or retention accordingly[3].

The trustee must take possession of all books, papers and other records[4] which relate to the bankrupt's estate or affairs[5] and which belong to him or are in his possession or under his control, including any which would be privileged from disclosure in any proceedings[6]. The bankrupt must deliver up to the trustee possession of any property, books, papers or other records of which he has possession or control and of which the trustee is required to take possession[7].

If any of the following is in possession of any property, books, papers or other records of which the trustee is required to take possession, namely:

(1)   the official receiver;

(2)   a person who has ceased to be trustee of the bankrupt's estate; or

(3)   a person who has been the supervisor of a voluntary arrangement approved in relation to the bankrupt under Part 8 of the Insolvency Act 1986[8],

the official receiver or, as the case may be, that person must deliver up possession of the property, books, papers or records to the trustee[9].

Any banker or agent of the bankrupt or any other person who holds any property to the account of, or for, the bankrupt must pay or deliver to the trustee all property in his possession or under his control which forms part of the bankrupt's estate and which he is not by law entitled to retain as against the bankrupt or trustee[10].

If any person without reasonable excuse fails to comply with any of the above obligations, he is guilty of a contempt of court and liable to be punished accordingly, in addition to any other punishment to which he may be subject[11].

1   As to the meaning of 'the bankrupt's estate' see PARA 211.
2   See RECEIVERS vol 88 (2012) PARA 1 et seq.

3   Insolvency Act 1986 s 311(2). As to the application of s 311 in the case of the administration in bankruptcy of the insolvent estate of a deceased person dying before the presentation of a bankruptcy petition see PARA 408 note 3.

4   As to the meaning of 'records' see PARA 20 note 6.

5   As to the meaning of references to a person's affairs see PARA 43 note 4.

6   Insolvency Act 1986 s 311(1).

7   Insolvency Act 1986 s 312(1). Section 312(1) is without prejudice to the general duties of the bankrupt under s 333 (see PARA 343): s 312(1). As to the application of s 312 in the case of the administration in bankruptcy of the insolvent estate of a deceased person dying before the presentation of a bankruptcy petition see PARA 408 note 4; and as to the modification of s 312 by the Insolvent Partnerships Order 1994, SI 1994/2421, in relation to the bankruptcy of an individual member of an insolvent partnership see COMPANY AND PARTNERSHIP INSOLVENCY vol 17 (2011) PARA 1342.

8   Ie under the Insolvency Act 1986 Pt 8 (ss 252–263G): see PARA 43 et seq.

9   See the Insolvency Act 1986 s 312(2); and PARA 408.

10 Insolvency Act 1986 s 312(3).

11 Insolvency Act 1986 s 312(4). As to contempt of court see CONTEMPT OF COURT vol 22 (2012) PARA 1 et seq; and as to offences see PARA 733 et seq.

476.   Trustee's power of sale.   Without the consent of the creditors' committee or the court, the trustee may sell any part of the property for the time being comprised in the bankrupt's estate, including the goodwill and book debts of any business[1].

With the consent of the creditors' committee or the court, the trustee may accept as the consideration for the sale of any property comprised in the bankrupt's estate a sum of money payable at a future time subject to such stipulations as to security or otherwise as the creditors' committee or the court thinks fit[2]. The trustee should, however, realise the bankrupt's estate with all reasonable speed, primarily by selling the property comprised in the estate[3]. The trustee must exercise his own discretion as to the time and mode of sale, and, unless he does not exercise it bona fide, the court will not interfere[4].

It is not essential, however, that the trustee should realise all the bankrupt's property whatever its nature. With the permission of the creditors' committee, the trustee may divide in its existing form amongst the bankrupt's creditors, according to its estimated value, any property which from its peculiar nature or other special circumstances cannot be readily or advantageously sold[5].

The trustee may, by assignment, sell a right of action[6]; and the trustee may sell to the bankrupt himself[7].

Where the trustee, not being the official receiver, disposes of any property comprised in the bankrupt's estate to an associate[8] of the bankrupt, he must, if there is for the time being a creditors' committee, give notice to the committee of that exercise of his powers[9]. If in the administration of the estate the trustee enters into any transaction with a person who is an associate of his, the court may, on the application of any person interested, set the transaction aside and order the trustee to compensate the estate for any loss suffered in consequence of it[10]; but this does not apply if either the transaction was entered into with the prior consent of the court or it is shown to the court's satisfaction that the transaction was for value and that it was entered into by the trustee without knowing, or having reason to suppose, that the person concerned was an associate[11].

On a sale of real property the trustee is bound to make a good title as is any other vendor[12], although he may contract to sell only such title as the bankrupt has and may enforce the sale if the bankrupt had any title at all[13]. A trustee is under no liability under the covenants of the bankrupt's lease after he has parted with it and is not justified in stipulating that the predecessor should indemnify him against breaches of covenant as this might tend to reduce the value of the lease which is to be sold[14].

Where any part of the bankrupt's estate consists of stock or shares in a company, shares in a ship or any other property transferable in the books of a company, office or person, the trustee may exercise the right to transfer the property to the same extent as the bankrupt might have exercised it if he had not become bankrupt[15].

Where any property consisting of an interest in a dwelling house which is occupied by the bankrupt or by his spouse or former spouse or by his civil partner or former civil partner is comprised in the bankrupt's estate and the trustee is, for any reason, unable for the time being to realise that property, the trustee may apply to the court for an order imposing a charge on the property for the benefit of the bankrupt's estate[16].

1   See the Insolvency Act 1986 s 314(1)(b), Sch 5 para 9; and PARA 479 head (1).
2   See the Insolvency Act 1986 s 314(1)(a), Sch 5 para 3; and PARA 478 head (4).
3   *Ex p Goring* (1790) 1 Ves 168; *Re Miller, ex p Miller* (1840) 1 Mont D & De G 39; *Re Dumbell, ex p Hughes, ex p Lyons* (1802) 6 Ves 617; *Re Russell, ex p Montgomery* (1822) 1 Gl & J 338; *Re Atkinson* (1840) 1 Mont D & De G 238.
4   *Re Peters, ex p Lloyd* (1882) 47 LT 64, CA.
5   See the Insolvency Act 1986 s 326(1); and PARA 602. A permission given for the purposes of s 326(1) may not be a general permission but must relate to a particular proposed exercise of the power in question; and a person dealing with the trustee in good faith and for value is not to be concerned to inquire whether any permission so required has been given: see s 326(2); and PARA 602.

    In the case of the administration in bankruptcy of the insolvent estate of a deceased person dying before the presentation of a bankruptcy petition, s 326 applies: Administration of Insolvent Estates of Deceased Persons Order 1986, SI 1986/1999, art 3(1), Sch 1 Pt II para 23. As to the administration in bankruptcy of the insolvent estates of deceased persons see further PARA 830 et seq.
6   *Seear v Lawson* (1880) 15 ChD 426, CA; *Guy v Churchill* (1888) 40 ChD 481; *Ramsey v Hartley* [1977] 2 All ER 673, [1977] 1 WLR 686, CA. See further PARA 478. As to the assignment of a cause of action subject to the right of set-off see *Stein v Blake* [1996] AC 243, [1995] 2 All ER 961, HL.
7   *Kitson v Hardwick* (1872) LR 7 CP 473; *Re France, ex p Tinker* (1874) 9 Ch App 716; *Ramsey v Hartley* [1977] 2 All ER 673, [1977] 1 WLR 686, CA. See also PARA 478. Prior to 29 December 1986 (see PARA 2) there was some doubt whether the legal estate in real property could pass on a sale to the bankrupt before he had his discharge because, as after-acquired property, it would vest in his trustee: see *Re Pascoe* [1944] Ch 219, [1944] 1 All ER 281, CA. Such problems cannot now arise under the Insolvency Act 1986 as there is no automatic vesting of after-acquired property in the trustee: see PARA 458 et seq.
8   As to the meaning of 'associate' see PARA 5.
9   Insolvency Act 1986 s 314(6)(a).
10 See the Insolvency Rules 1986, SI 1986/1925, r 6.147(1); and PARA 346. It would seem that only a person who had a proprietary or pecuniary interest would be a 'person interested': see *Re Beesley (a bankrupt)* [1975] 1 All ER 385, [1975] 1 WLR 568, DC.
11 See the Insolvency Rules 1986, SI 1986/1925, r 6.147(2); and PARA 346.
12 *M'Donald v Hanson* (1806) 12 Ves 277.
13 *Freme v Wright* (1819) 4 Madd 364; but see *Edwards v Wickwar* (1865) LR 1 Eq 68 at 70. As to a condition that the trustee should not be required to show any further title than the vesting of the bankrupt's estate in the trustee see *Borell v Dann* (1843) 2 Hare 440 at 443, 455. If the trustee retains the title deeds or cannot deliver them to the purchaser (see the Law of Property Act 1925 s 45(9); and CONVEYANCING vol 23 (2013) PARA 80), he must give attested copies at the expense of the estate, and, unless he stipulates to the contrary, he must give an acknowledgment of the purchaser's right to the production of the title deeds, limited to the time of his continuance as trustee: *Re Leicester, ex p Stuart* (1815) 2 Rose 215.
14 *Wilkins v Fry* (1816) 1 Mer 244 at 265, 268.
15 See the Insolvency Act 1986 s 311(3); and PARA 409.
16 See the Insolvency Act 1986 s 313(1); and PARA 413.

477. Trustee as officer of the court; right to apply for directions. As an officer of the court, the trustee must act as is just and right, and the court will not allow him to take advantage of a mistake. This principle is commonly known as 'the rule in Ex parte James'[1], and the extent of its operation may be defined only by the case law[2]. However, the rule, which at best is exercised as a discretionary power of the court, appears to have been exercised only in cases where there has been some form of enrichment of the assets of a bankrupt or insolvent company at the expense of a person seeking recoupment[3].

The trustee of a bankrupt's estate may apply to the court for directions in relation to any particular matter arising under the bankruptcy[4]. The court is not, however, obliged to give him directions[5]; and, where he has obtained a decision, he should not as a rule appeal from it[6]. The trustee is under the general control of the court throughout the period of his administration of the bankrupt's estate[7].

1   See *Re Condon, ex p James* (1874) as reported in 9 Ch App 609 at 614 per James LJ, who said that the Court of Bankruptcy ought to be as honest as other people.

2   For cases where the rule was applied see *Re Carnac, ex p Simmonds* (1885) 16 QBD 308, CA; *Re Brown, Dixon v Brown* (1886) 32 ChD 597; *Re Tyler, ex p Official Receiver* [1907] 1 KB 865, CA; *Re Craig & Sons, ex p Hinchcliffe* [1916] 2 KB 497; *Re Thellusson, ex p Adby* [1919] 2 KB 735, CA; cf *Re Wilson, ex p Salaman* [1926] Ch 21. See, however, *Re Hall, ex p Official Receiver* [1907] 1 KB 875, CA (where the mistake arose through ignorance of the working of the bankruptcy laws); *Re Tricks, ex p Charles* (1885) 3 Morr 15 (where the trustee took advantage of a technicality); *Re Wigzell, ex p Hart* [1921] 2 KB 835, CA (which was to some extent met by the Bankruptcy (Amendment) Act 1926 s 4 (repealed)); *Scranton's Trustee v Pearse* [1922] 2 Ch 87, CA; cf *Tapster v Ward* (1909) 101 LT 503, CA; *Re Phillips* [1914] 2 KB 689; *Re Stokes, ex p Mellish* [1919] 2 KB 256. In *Re Gozzett* [1936] 1 All ER 79, CA, the court declined to extend the rule to a case where, there being no mistake, the creditors, who were builders, had failed to take the precaution of securing a charge on the property.

In *Re Clark, ex p Trustee v Texaco Ltd* [1975] 1 All ER 453 at 458, 459, [1975] 1 WLR 559 at 563, 564 Walton J formulated four conditions which should be present for the operation of the rule:

(1)   there must be some form of enrichment of the assets of the bankrupt by the person seeking to have the rule applied;

(2)   except in the most unusual cases, the claimant must not be in a position to submit an ordinary proof of debt;

(3)   the 'honest man' test should apply ie if such a man who would be personally affected by the result would be bound to admit that it would not be fair for him to keep the money, for his claim had no merits, then the rule applies so as to nullify the claim which he would otherwise have;

(4)   where the rule applies, it operates only to the extent necessary to nullify the enrichment of the estate; it does not necessarily restore the claimant to the status quo.

See also *Re Byfield, ex p Hill Samuel & Co Ltd v Trustee* [1982] Ch 267, [1982] 1 All ER 249 (where Goulding J held that the principle did not in general apply to cases where the point in question was not intimately linked with some voluntary conduct of the trustee in bankruptcy himself); *Green v Satsangi* [1998] 1 BCLC 458, [1998] BPIR 55. As to the application of the rule to the liquidator of a company see *Re Opera Ltd* [1891] 2 Ch 154 (revsd on other grounds [1891] 3 Ch 260, CA); *Re Regent Finance and Guarantee Corpn* [1930] WN 84; *Re TH Knitwear (Wholesale) Ltd* [1988] Ch 275, [1988] 1 All ER 860, CA; *Powdrill v Watson* [1994] 2 All ER 513, [1994] 2 BCLC 118, CA (affd [1995] 2 AC 394, [1995] 2 All ER 65, HL); and COMPANY AND PARTNERSHIP INSOLVENCY vol 16 (2011) PARA 521.

3   *Government of India, Ministry of Finance (Revenue Division) v Taylor* [1955] AC 491 at 512, 513, [1955] 1 All ER 292 at 300, HL per Lord Keith; and see *Re Cushla Ltd* [1979] 3 All ER 415 at 423, [1979] STC 615 at 623.

4   See the Insolvency Act 1986 s 303(2); and PARA 342. See also *Re Poole, ex p Cocks* (1882) 21 ChD 397, CA (where the trustee was directed to disregard the creditors' directions); *Re Oborne, ex p Marillier* (1896) 3 Mans 238.

5   See *Re Pilling, ex p Salaman* [1906] 2 KB 644; *Re Harrison and Ingram, ex p Whinney* (1905) 54 WR 203; *Re Webb & Sons, ex p Webb & Sons* (1887) 4 Morr 52.

6 If the appeal fails, the trustee may be made personally liable for the costs incurred; his proper course is to obtain the consent of the creditors and a guarantee from them: *Re Malden, Gibson & Co, ex p James* (1886) 3 Morr 185, PC.

7 See the Insolvency Act 1986 s 303; and PARA 342.

478. Trustee's powers exercisable with sanction. The trustee in bankruptcy with the sanction of the creditors' committee[1] or the court[2] has the following powers:

(1) power to carry on any business of the bankrupt so far as may be necessary for winding it up beneficially and so far as the trustee is able to do so without contravening any requirement imposed by or under any enactment[3];

(2) power to bring, institute or defend any action or legal proceedings relating to the property comprised in the bankrupt's estate[4];

(3) power to bring legal proceedings in relation to transactions at an undervalue[5], preferences[6] and transactions defrauding creditors[7];

(4) power to accept as the consideration for the sale of any property comprised in the bankrupt's estate a sum of money payable at a future time subject to such stipulations as to security or otherwise as the creditors' committee or the court thinks fit[8];

(5) power to mortgage or pledge any part of the property comprised in the bankrupt's estate for the purpose of raising money for the payment of his debts[9];

(6) power, where any right, option or other power forms part of the bankrupt's estate, to make payments or incur liabilities with a view to obtaining, for the benefit of the creditors, any property which is the subject of the right, option or power[10];

(7) power to make such compromise or other arrangement as may be thought expedient with creditors, or persons claiming to be creditors, in respect of any bankruptcy debts[11];

(8) power to make such compromise or other arrangement as may be thought expedient with respect to any claim arising out of or incidental to the bankrupt's estate made or capable of being made on the trustee by any person[12];

(9) power to appoint the bankrupt:

    (a) to superintend the management of his estate or any part of it;

    (b) to carry on his business, if any, for the benefit of his creditors; or

    (c) in any other respect to assist in administering the estate in such manner and on such terms as the trustee may direct[13].

A permission given for the above purposes may not be a general permission but must relate to a particular proposed exercise of the power in question; and a person dealing with the trustee in good faith and for value is not to be concerned to inquire whether any permission so required has been given[14]. Where, however, the trustee has done anything without the requisite permission, the court or the creditors' committee may, for the purpose of enabling him to meet his expenses out of the bankrupt's estate, ratify what the trustee has done; but the committee may not do so unless it is satisfied that the trustee has acted in a case of urgency and has sought its ratification without undue delay[15].

Where the trustee, not being the official receiver, in exercise of the powers conferred on him disposes of any property comprised in the bankrupt's estate to an associate[16] of the bankrupt, or employs a solicitor, he must, if there is for the time being a creditors' committee, give notice to the committee of that exercise of his powers[17].

With the permission of the creditors' committee the trustee may divide in its existing form amongst the bankrupt's creditors, according to its estimated value, any property which from its peculiar nature or other special circumstances cannot be readily or advantageously sold[18].

1　As to the creditors' committee see PARA 326 et seq.

2　The alternative of obtaining the court's consent was not available under the Bankruptcy Act 1914 s 56 (repealed). It is presumed that the trustee ought not to apply to the court where a creditors' committee is in place, except in exceptional circumstances.

3　Insolvency Act 1986 s 314(1)(a), Sch 5 para 1. As to the accounts to be kept and records to be maintained where the trustee so carries on business see PARA 387 et seq. The trustee may appoint the bankrupt to carry on the business: see head (9) in the text.
　　　As to the application of s 314 in the case of the administration in bankruptcy of the insolvent estate of a deceased person dying before the presentation of a bankruptcy petition see PARA 456 note 3.

4　Insolvency Act 1986 Sch 5 para 2. As to the trustee as litigant see PARA 455. The trustee may assign his rights to another person, including the bankrupt: *Guy v Churchill* (1888) 40 ChD 481; *Ramsey v Hartley* [1977] 2 All ER 673, [1977] 1 WLR 686, CA; *Weddell v JA Pearce and Major (a firm)* [1988] Ch 26, [1987] 3 All ER 624. See also *Seear v Lawson* (1880) 15 ChD 426, CA; *Re Arnold, ex p Official Receiver* (1891) 9 Morr 1. Provided that the terms of the assignment are proper and fair to the creditors, it is not champertous or otherwise objectionable but is a lawful means of realising an asset: *Norglen Ltd (in liquidation) v Reeds Rains Prudential Ltd* [1999] 2 AC 1, [1998] 1 All ER 218, HL. Trustees should exercise such power with circumspection: *Re Papaloizou* [1999] BPIR 106. For a case where a sale by a liquidator, under similar powers to those possessed by the trustee, was held to be champertous see *Grovewood Holdings plc v James Capel & Co Ltd* [1995] Ch 80, [1994] 4 All ER 417, but the correctness of this decision was doubted by Robert Walker J in *Re Oasis Merchandising Services Ltd, Ward v Aitken* [1995] 2 BCLC 493, [1995] BCC 911 (affd [1998] Ch 170, [1997] 1 All ER 1009, CA). As to a trustee's potential liability for costs where he has assigned a claim see *Hunt (as trustee in bankruptcy of Janan George Harb) v Harb* [2011] EWCA Civ 1239, [2012] 1 WLR 317, [2012] BPIR 117.
　　　It would appear that the statutory rights of recovery conferred on a trustee by the Insolvency Act 1986 do not form part of the property comprised in the bankrupt's estate for these purposes and are not assignable by him: *Re Ayala Holdings Ltd* [1993] BCLC 256; *Re Oasis Merchandising Services Ltd, Ward v Aitken*.
　　　The obtaining of the consent of the creditors' committee is for the estate's protection, not for the protection or benefit of third parties: see *Re A Debtor (No 26A of 1975)* [1984] 3 All ER 995, [1985] 1 WLR 6. A defendant to an action by a trustee may not avail himself as an answer to the proceedings of any failure by the trustee to obtain consent: *Re Branson, ex p Trustee* [1914] 2 KB 701.

5　Ie legal proceedings under the Insolvency Act 1986 s 339: see PARA 678.

6　Ie legal proceedings under the Insolvency Act 1986 s 340: see PARA 682.

7　Insolvency Act 1986 Sch 5 para 2A (added by the Enterprise Act 2002 s 262). Legal proceedings in relation to transactions defrauding creditors are brought under the Insolvency Act 1986 s 423: see PARA 689.

8　Insolvency Act 1986 Sch 5 para 3.

9　Insolvency Act 1986 Sch 5 para 4.

10　Insolvency Act 1986 Sch 5 para 5.

11　Insolvency Act 1986 Sch 5 para 7. As to the meaning of 'bankruptcy debt' see PARA 508. The bankrupt has no right to question the trustee's exercise of his judgment: *Re A Debtor, ex p Debtor v Dodwell (Trustee)* [1949] Ch 236, [1949] 1 All ER 510; and see PARA 456.

12　Insolvency Act 1986 Sch 5 para 8 (amended by SI 2010/18).

13　Insolvency Act 1986 s 314(2). It is submitted that 'on such terms as the trustee may direct' includes the payment of remuneration to the bankrupt for his costs. Cf the Bankruptcy Act 1914 s 58 (repealed) under which there was express power to make an allowance to the bankrupt.

14　Insolvency Act 1986 s 314(3).

15　Insolvency Act 1986 s 314(4); and see PARA 482.

16　As to the meaning of 'associate' see PARA 5.

17 Insolvency Act 1986 s 314(6); and see PARA 480. For these purposes, the reference to a solicitor includes a reference to a body recognised by the Law Society under the Administration of Justice Act 1985 s 9 (see LEGAL PROFESSIONS vol 65 (2008) PARA 515): Solicitors' Recognised Bodies Order 1991, SI 1991/2684, arts 2(1), 3, 4(a), 5, Sch 1 (amended by SI 2009/500).

As to the employment by the trustee of the petitioning creditor's solicitor and the potential conflict of interest which might arise see *Re Schuppan (a bankrupt)* [1997] 1 BCLC 211, sub nom *Re Schuppan, Trustee of Estate of Schuppan v Schuppan* [1997] BPIR 271; *Re Baron Investments (Holdings) Ltd (in liquidation), Halstuk v Venvil* [2000] 1 BCLC 272.

18 Insolvency Act 1986 s 326(1). See further PARAS 476, 602. As to the application of s 326 in the case of the administration in bankruptcy of the insolvent estate of a deceased person dying before the presentation of a bankruptcy petition see PARA 476 note 5.

479. Trustee's powers exercisable without sanction. The trustee has, without the sanction of either the court or the creditors' committee, the following powers:

(1)   power to sell any part of the property[1] for the time being comprised in the bankrupt's estate[2], including the goodwill[3] and book debts of any business[4];

(2)   power to refer to arbitration[5], or compromise on such terms as may be agreed on, any debts, claims or liabilities subsisting or supposed to subsist between the bankrupt and any person who may have incurred any liability to the bankrupt[6];

(3)   power to make such compromise or other arrangement as may be thought expedient with respect to any claim arising out of or incidental to the bankrupt's estate made or capable of being made by the trustee on any person[7];

(4)   power to give receipts for any money received by him, being receipts which effectually discharge the person paying the money from all responsibility in respect of its application[8];

(5)   power to prove, rank, claim and draw a dividend in respect of such debts due to the bankrupt as are comprised in his estate[9];

(6)   power to exercise in relation to any property comprised in the bankrupt's estate any powers the capacity to exercise which is vested in him[10] under the Insolvency Act 1986[11];

(7)   power to deal with any property comprised in the estate to which the bankrupt is beneficially entitled as tenant in tail in the same manner as the bankrupt might have dealt with it[12];

(8)   power, by the giving of the prescribed notice, to disclaim any onerous property notwithstanding that he has taken possession of it, endeavoured to sell it or otherwise exercised his rights of ownership in relation to it[13];

(9)   power, by notice in writing, to claim for the bankrupt's estate any property which has been acquired by, or has devolved on, the bankrupt since the commencement of the bankruptcy[14];

(10)   power, on application to the court, to claim for the bankrupt's estate so much of the income of the bankrupt during the period for which the order is in force as may be specified in the order[15];

(11)   power, by notice in writing, to claim for the bankrupt's estate property or part of property excluded from the bankrupt's estate where it appears to the trustee that the realisable value of the whole or any part of such property exceeds the cost of a reasonable replacement for that property or that part of it[16];

(12) power, by notice in writing, to redeem the security of a creditor whose debt is secured[17].

1 As to the meaning of 'property' see PARA 412.
2 As to the meaning of 'the bankrupt's estate' see PARA 211.
3 See PARA 437.
4 Insolvency Act 1986 s 314(1)(b), Sch 5 para 9. As to the trustee's power of sale see further PARA 476.
   As to the application of s 314 in the case of the administration in bankruptcy of the insolvent estate of a deceased person dying before the presentation of a bankruptcy petition see PARA 456 note 3.
5 As to arbitration agreements to which a bankrupt is a party see the Insolvency Act 1986 s 349A; and PARA 457.
6 Insolvency Act 1986 Sch 5 para 9A (added by SI 2010/18).
7 Insolvency Act 1986 Sch 5 para 9B (added by SI 2010/18).
8 Insolvency Act 1986 Sch 5 para 10.
9 Insolvency Act 1986 Sch 5 para 11.
10 Ie under the Insolvency Act 1986 Pts 8–11 (ss 252–385).
11 Insolvency Act 1986 Sch 5 para 12.
12 Insolvency Act 1986 Sch 5 para 13. Since 1 January 1997 it is no longer possible to create any new entailed interests: see REAL PROPERTY AND REGISTRATION vol 87 (2012) PARA 114.
13 See PARA 490 et seq.
14 See PARA 458 et seq.
15 See PARA 462 et seq.
16 See PARA 404.
17 See PARA 574 et seq.

480. Trustee's ancillary powers. For the purpose of, or in connection with, the exercise of any of his powers under the Insolvency Act 1986[1], the trustee may, by his official name[2]:

(1) hold property of every description;
(2) make contracts;
(3) sue and be sued;
(4) enter into engagements binding on himself and, in respect of the bankrupt's estate, on his successor in office;
(5) employ an agent[3];
(6) execute any power of attorney, deed or other instrument;

and he may do any other act which is necessary or expedient for the purposes of or in connection with the exercise of those powers[4].

1 Ie under the Insolvency Act 1986 Pts 8–11 (ss 252–385).
2 See PARA 324.
3 Where the trustee employs a solicitor, he must, if there is for the time being a creditors' committee, give notice to the committee of that exercise of his powers: Insolvency Act 1986 s 314(6)(b). See further PARA 478.
   As to the application of s 314 in the case of the administration in bankruptcy of the insolvent estate of a deceased person dying before the presentation of a bankruptcy petition see PARA 456 note 3.
4 Insolvency Act 1986 s 314(5), Sch 5 para 14.

481. Power to summon meetings of creditors. If the trustee thinks fit, he may[1] at any time summon a general meeting of the bankrupt's creditors[2]; and he must summon such a meeting if he is requested to do so by a creditor of the bankrupt and the request is made with the concurrence of not less than one-tenth, in value, of the bankrupt's creditors, including the creditor making the request[3].

1 Ie without prejudice to the generality of the Insolvency Act 1986 s 314(5), Sch 5 para 14: see PARA 480.

2   As to creditors' meetings see PARA 266 et seq.
3   Insolvency Act 1986 s 314(7). Cf s 294(2); and PARA 263.
    As to the application of s 314 in the case of the administration in bankruptcy of the insolvent
    estate of a deceased person dying before the presentation of a bankruptcy petition see PARA 456
    note 3; and as to the modification of s 314(7) by the Insolvent Partnerships Order 1994,
    SI 1994/2421, in relation to the bankruptcy of an individual member of an insolvent partnership
    see COMPANY AND PARTNERSHIP INSOLVENCY vol 17 (2011) PARA 1294.

482.   Extent of consent; ratification of trustee's acts.   Where the trustee
requires the permission of the creditors' committee or the court[1], a permission so
given may not be a general permission but must relate to a particular proposed
exercise of the power in question; and a person dealing with the trustee in good
faith and for value is not to be concerned to inquire whether any permission
required has been given[2]. Strangers to the bankruptcy cannot raise as a defence
the absence of permission[3]. Where the trustee has done anything without the
requisite permission, the court or the creditors' committee may, for the purpose
of enabling him to meet his expenses out of the bankrupt's estate[4], ratify what
the trustee has done; but the committee may not do so unless it is satisfied that
the trustee has acted in a case of urgency and has sought its ratification without
undue delay[5].

1   See PARA 478.
2   See the Insolvency Act 1986 s 314(3); and PARA 478.
3   *Weddell v Pearce and Major* [1988] Ch 26 at 37 per Scott J; *Lee v Sangster* (1857) 2 CBNS 1;
    Re Branson, ex p Trustee [1914] 2 KB 701; *Clark v Smith* [1940] 1 KB 126; *Re A Debtor
    (No 26A of 1975)* [1984] 3 All ER 995, [1985] 1 WLR 6.
4   A third party dealing in good faith and for value need not be concerned as to the granting of a
    permission to the trustee with which he is involved. However, there remains the case where a
    trustee acts without permission in a transaction with a third party who is not acting bona fide.
    The transaction would be liable to be set aside under the general law. The creditors would be
    unlikely to want to ratify such acts but would presumably have the power to do so.
5   Insolvency Act 1986 s 314(4); and see PARA 478. As to the application of s 314 in the case of the
    administration in bankruptcy of the insolvent estate of a deceased person dying before the
    presentation of a bankruptcy petition see PARA 456 note 3.

483.   Adjustment of prior and other transactions.   Where an individual is
adjudged bankrupt, the trustee in bankruptcy may apply to the court under the
statutory provisions relating to transactions at an undervalue[1], preferences[2] and
extortionate credit transactions[3].

1   See the Insolvency Act 1986 s 339; and PARA 678 et seq.
2   See the Insolvency Act 1986 s 340; and PARA 681 et seq.
3   See the Insolvency Act 1986 s 343; and PARA 697 et seq.

484.   Exercise of powers outside jurisdiction.   Nothing in the Insolvency
Act 1986 is to be construed as restricting the capacity of the trustee to exercise
any of his powers outside England and Wales[1].

1   Insolvency Act 1986 s 314(8). As to the application of s 314 in the case of the administration in
    bankruptcy of the insolvent estate of a deceased person dying before the presentation of a
    bankruptcy petition see PARA 456 note 3.

485.   Power to ensure continuation of essential supplies by utilities.   A trustee
has the like rights as the supervisor of a voluntary arrangement, the official
receiver, an interim receiver and a trustee under a deed of arrangement for
ensuring continued supplies of gas, electricity, water and telecommunication
services[1].

1   See the Insolvency Act 1986 s 372; and PARA 78.

486. Redirection of bankrupt's letters etc. Where a bankruptcy order has been made, a trustee in bankruptcy has the like power as the official receiver to apply to the court for the redirection of the bankrupt's letters etc[1].

1 See the Insolvency Act 1986 s 371; and PARA 260.

487. Seizure of bankrupt's property. The trustee in bankruptcy has the like power as the official receiver to apply to the court for an order for the seizure of the property comprised in the bankrupt's estate[1].

1 See the Insolvency Act 1986 s 365; and PARA 216.

488. Inquiry into bankrupt's dealings and property. The trustee in bankruptcy has the like power as the official receiver to apply to the court for an order requiring the bankrupt and certain specified persons to appear before it in connection with any inquiry into the bankrupt's dealings and property[1] and to apply for an order for the production of documents by the inland revenue[2].

1 See PARA 305 et seq.
2 See PARA 299 et seq.

489. Second bankruptcy. Where a bankruptcy order is made against an undischarged bankrupt, the existing trustee[1] must take into his custody or under his control all property and money to which the statutory provisions relating to stay of distribution apply[2], in so far as he has not already done so as part of his duties as trustee in the earlier bankruptcy[3]. Where any of that property consists of perishable goods, or goods the value of which is likely to diminish if they are not disposed of, the existing trustee has power to sell or otherwise dispose of the goods[4]. The proceeds of any such sale or disposal must be held, under the existing trustee's control, with the other property and money comprised in the bankrupt's estate[5]. The existing trustee must, as and when requested by the trustee for the purposes of the later bankruptcy, deliver up to the latter all such property and money as is in his custody or under his control[6]. Any expenses incurred by the existing trustee in complying with his obligations[7] must be defrayed out of, and are a charge on, all such property and money[8], whether in the hands of the existing trustee or of the trustee for the purposes of the later bankruptcy[9].

Where the existing trustee has been given the prescribed notice[10] of the presentation of the petition for the later bankruptcy, any distribution or other disposition by him of any after-acquired property[11], any money paid to the existing trustee in pursuance of an income payments order[12] and any property or money which is, or in the hands of the existing trustee represents, the proceeds of sale or application of such property or money, if made after the giving of the notice, is void except to the extent that it was made with the consent of the court or is or was subsequently ratified by the court[13].

1 For these purposes, 'the existing trustee' means the trustee, if any, of the bankrupt's estate for the purposes of the earlier bankruptcy: Insolvency Act 1986 s 334(1)(c) (applied by the Insolvency Rules 1986, SI 1986/1925, r 6.225(2)). 'The earlier bankruptcy' means the bankruptcy (or, as the case may be, most recent bankruptcy) from which the bankrupt has not been discharged at the commencement of the later bankruptcy: Insolvency Act 1986 s 334(1)(b) (applied by the Insolvency Rules 1986, SI 1986/1925, r 6.225(2)). 'The later bankruptcy' means the bankruptcy arising from the order made against an undischarged bankrupt: Insolvency Act 1986 s 334(1)(a) (applied by the Insolvency Rules 1986, SI 1986/1925, r 6.225(2)).
2 Ie such property and money as is referred to in the Insolvency Act 1986 s 334(3): see PARA 617.
3 Insolvency Rules 1986, SI 1986/1925, rr 6.225(1), 6.226(1).

4   Insolvency Rules 1986, SI 1986/1925, r 6.226(2).
5   Insolvency Rules 1986, SI 1986/1925, r 6.226(3).
6   Insolvency Rules 1986, SI 1986/1925, r 6.227.
7   Ie in compliance with the Insolvency Act 1986 s 335(1) (see PARA 618) and the Insolvency Rules 1986, SI 1986/1925, rr 6.225–6.228.
8   See note 2.
9   Insolvency Rules 1986, SI 1986/1925, r 6.228.
10 For the prescribed form of notice to the existing trustee of the presentation of a petition for a later bankruptcy see the Insolvency Rules 1986, SI 1986/1925, Sch 4 Form 6.78 (substituted by SI 1987/1919).
11 Ie under the Insolvency Act 1986 s 307(3): see PARA 459.
12 Ie under the Insolvency Act 1986 s 310: see PARA 462.
13 See the Insolvency Act 1986 s 334(2); and PARA 617. Section 334(2) is without prejudice to s 284 (restrictions on dispositions of property following bankruptcy order: see PARA 213): s 334(2). As to the adjustment between earlier and later bankrupt estates see s 335; and PARAS 618, 619.

In the case of the administration in bankruptcy of the insolvent estate of a deceased person dying before the presentation of a bankruptcy petition, s 334 applies: Administration of Insolvent Estates of Deceased Persons Order 1986, SI 1986/1999, art 3(1), Sch 1 Pt II para 26. As to the administration in bankruptcy of the insolvent estates of deceased persons see further PARA 830 et seq.

(viii) Disclaimer of Onerous Property

490.   Power to disclaim onerous property.   By the giving of the prescribed notice[1], the trustee may disclaim any onerous property[2] and may do so notwithstanding that he has taken possession of it, endeavoured to sell it or otherwise exercised his rights of ownership in relation to it[3]. Such power is exercisable at any time during the trustee's administration of the bankrupt's estate[4].

1   As to the prescribed notice see PARA 493.
2   As to the meaning of 'onerous property' see PARA 491.
3   Insolvency Act 1986 s 315(1). As to the application of s 315 in the case of the administration in bankruptcy of the insolvent estate of a deceased person dying before the presentation of a bankruptcy petition see PARA 431 note 6.
4   Under the Bankruptcy Act 1914 s 54(1) (repealed) the trustee's power of disclaimer was exercisable within 12 months after the first appointment of a trustee or such extended period as might be allowed by the court, provided that, where any such property had not come to the knowledge of the trustee within one month after such appointment, he might disclaim such property at any time within 12 months after he had become aware thereof or such extended period as might be allowed by the court. No time limit is, however, specified by the Insolvency Act 1986 for the exercise of the trustee's power of disclaimer.

491.   Meaning of 'onerous property'.   For the purposes of disclaimer, onerous property comprises any unprofitable contract and any other property comprised in the bankrupt's estate[1] which is unsaleable or not readily saleable, or is such that it may give rise to a liability to pay money or perform any other onerous act[2]. A notice of disclaimer may not, however, be given[3] in respect of any property that has been claimed as after-acquired property[4] or personal property of the bankrupt exceeding a reasonable replacement value[5], or certain tenancies[6], except with the permission of the court[7].

1   As to the meaning of 'the bankrupt's estate' see PARA 211.
2   Insolvency Act 1986 s 315(2). For cases decided under the equivalent provision relating to corporate insolvency in the Insolvency Act 1986 s 178 on the meaning of onerous property see *Re Mineral Resources Ltd (in liquidation), Environment Agency v Stout* [1999] 1 All ER 746, [1999] 2 BCLC 516; *Re Celtic Extraction Ltd (in liquidation), Re Bluestone Chemicals Ltd (in liquidation)* [2001] Ch 475, [1999] 4 All ER 684 (waste management licences); *Re SSSL Realisations (2002) Ltd (in liquidation)* [2006] EWCA Civ 7, [2006] Ch 610, [2006] 2 WLR

1369; and COMPANY AND PARTNERSHIP INSOLVENCY vol 17 (2011) PARA 824 et seq. As to the application of the Insolvency Act 1986 s 315 in the case of the administration in bankruptcy of the insolvent estate of a deceased person dying before the presentation of a bankruptcy petition see PARA 431 note 6.

The wording of s 315 differs markedly from its statutory predecessor, the Bankruptcy Act 1914 s 54 (repealed). Nevertheless, while the procedure to be adopted under the Insolvency Act 1986 and the Insolvency Rules 1986, SI 1986/1925 (see PARA 493 et seq) has been altered, much of the substantive effect of the Bankruptcy Act 1914 (repealed) has been reproduced in the Insolvency Act 1986. Earlier decisions may still be referred to for assistance. An agreement for a lease may be disclaimed: *Re Maughan, ex p Monkhouse* (1885) 14 QBD 956. As to disclaiming the residual liabilities under a lease which has been determined see *Re Throckmorton, ex p Paterson* (1879) 11 ChD 908, CA; *Re Morrish, ex p Hart Dyke* (1882) 22 ChD 410, CA (both decided under the Bankruptcy Act 1869 (repealed), the effect of which, as regards the date when the disclaimer operated, was different from that of the Bankruptcy Act 1914 (repealed) and the Insolvency Act 1986); and *Re ABC Coupler and Engineering Co Ltd (No 3)* [1970] 1 All ER 650, [1970] 1 WLR 702 (company case).

As to Rent Act tenancies see PARA 503 note 5.

Freehold property may be onerous property where it is burdened with onerous covenants: see *Re Mercer and Moore* (1880) 14 ChD 287; *Re Thomas, ex p Woods and Forest Comrs* (1888) 21 QBD 380 at 383, DC. If the trustee disclaims any property, he must disclaim the whole of it, and may not keep part and disclaim part: *Re Fussell, ex p Allen* (1882) 20 ChD 341, CA. He cannot disclaim a contract for the sale of leasehold property unless he disclaims the lease itself: *Re Kerkham, ex p Trustee and Martelli* (1886) 80 LT Jo 322; *Re Bastable, ex p Trustee* [1901] 2 KB 518, CA; *Pearce v Bastable's Trustee in Bankruptcy* [1901] 2 Ch 122 at 125. Where the bankrupt has made a contract to purchase land and also a sub-contract to sell the same land after having erected a building on it, the trustee may disclaim the sub-contract without being obliged to disclaim the contract: *Re Gough, Hanning v Lowe* (1927) 96 LJ Ch 239, DC.

3	Ie under the Insolvency Act 1986 s 315: see PARA 493.
4	Ie under the Insolvency Act 1986 s 307: see PARA 459.
5	Ie under the Insolvency Act 1986 s 308: see PARA 404.
6	Ie under the Insolvency Act 1986 s 308A: see PARA 405.
7	Insolvency Act 1986 s 315(4) (amended by the Housing Act 1988 s 117(4)).

**492.	Effect of disclaimer.** A disclaimer of onerous property[1] operates so as to determine, as from the date of the disclaimer, the rights, interests and liabilities of the bankrupt and his estate[2] in or in respect of the property disclaimed, and discharges the trustee from all personal liability in respect of that property as from the commencement of his trusteeship, but does not, except so far as is necessary for the purpose of releasing the bankrupt, the bankrupt's estate and the trustee from any liability, affect the rights or liabilities of any other person[3]. Thus, a disclaimer by a trustee of a lease which the bankrupt holds by assignment does not affect the liability of the assignor under his covenants to the landlord[4]. The guarantor of the bankrupt's obligations under the lease will, similarly, not be released from further liability to the landlord but he may be entitled to prove in the bankrupt's estate for an indemnity[5].

1	As to the meaning of 'onerous property' see PARA 491.
2	As to the meaning of 'the bankrupt's estate' see PARA 211.
3	Insolvency Act 1986 s 315(3). As to the application of s 315 in the case of the administration in bankruptcy of the insolvent estate of a deceased person dying before the presentation of a bankruptcy petition see PARA 431 note 6.
4	*Warnford Investments Ltd v Duckworth* [1979] Ch 127, [1978] 2 All ER 517. Where the assignor becomes bankrupt after the bankruptcy of the assignee, his trustee may disclaim the assignor's obligations under the lease, even though the lease may not have become revested in the assignor on the assignee's bankruptcy, the meaning of 'property' in the Insolvency Act 1986 s 436 (see PARA 412) being sufficiently wide to cover such obligation to the landlord and, further, such obligations arising under an unprofitable contract. As to the surplus realised after payment of a mortgage debt on a disclaimed lease see *Lee v Lee* [1998] 2 BCLC 219, [1999] BCC 268.

5   *Hindcastle Ltd v Barbara Attenborough Associates Ltd* [1997] AC 70, [1996] 1 All ER
     737, HL, overruling *Stacey v Hill* [1901] 1 KB 660; cf *Warnford Investments Ltd v Duckworth*
     [1979] Ch 127, [1978] 2 All ER 517; *Murphy v Sawyer-Hoare (Stacey and Bowie, third parties)*
     [1994] 2 BCLC 59 (company cases). See further COMPANY AND PARTNERSHIP INSOLVENCY
     vol 17 (2011) PARA 826.

493.   Trustee's notice of disclaimer.   Where the trustee disclaims property[1], the
notice of disclaimer must contain such particulars of the property disclaimed as
enable it to be easily identified[2]. The notice of disclaimer must be authenticated
and dated by the trustee[3]. As soon as reasonably practicable after authenticating
the notice of disclaimer, the trustee must:

(1)   file a copy of the notice with the court[4]; and

(2)   in any case where the disclaimer is of registered land[5], send a copy of
       the notice to the Chief Land Registrar[6].

The date of the prescribed notice[7] is that on which the trustee authenticates
it[8].

1   Ie under the Insolvency Act 1986 s 315: see PARA 490 et seq.
2   Insolvency Rules 1986, SI 1986/1925, r 6.178(1). For the prescribed form of notice of disclaimer
     under the Insolvency Act 1986 s 315 see the Insolvency Rules 1986, SI 1986/1925, Sch 4 Form
     6.61A (added by SI 2010/686).
3   Insolvency Rules 1986, SI 1986/1925, r 6.178(2) (substituted by SI 2010/686). As to
     authentication see PARA 158 note 2.
4   As to the meaning of 'file with the court' see PARA 57 note 13.
5   Ie as defined in the Land Registration Act 2002 s 132(1) (see REAL PROPERTY AND
     REGISTRATION vol 87 (2012) PARA 459).
6   Insolvency Rules 1986, SI 1986/1925, r 6.178(3) (substituted by SI 2010/686).
7   Ie for the purposes of the Insolvency Act 1986 s 315(3): see PARA 492.
8   Insolvency Rules 1986, SI 1986/1925, r 6.178(4) (amended by SI 2010/686).

494.   Communication of disclaimer to persons interested.   Within seven
business days[1] after the date of the notice of disclaimer[2], the trustee must send or
give copies of the notice to the following persons[3]:

(1)   where the property disclaimed is of a leasehold nature, he must send or
       give a copy of the notice to every person who, to his knowledge, claims
       under the bankrupt as underlessee or mortgagee[4];

(2)   where the disclaimer is of property in a dwelling house[5], he must send
       or give a copy to every person who, to his knowledge, is in occupation
       of, or claims a right to occupy, the house[6];

(3)   he must in any case send or give a copy of the notice to every person
       who, to his knowledge, claims an interest in the disclaimed property, or
       is under any liability in respect of the property, not being a liability
       discharged by the disclaimer[7];

(4)   if the disclaimer is of an unprofitable contract, he must send or give
       copies of the notice to all such persons as, to his knowledge, are parties
       to the contract or have interests under it[8].

If subsequently it comes to the trustee's knowledge, in the case of any person,
that he has such an interest in the disclaimed property as would have entitled
him to receive a copy of the notice of disclaimer in pursuance of heads (1) to (4)
above, the trustee must then as soon as reasonably practicable send or give to
that person a copy of the notice; but compliance with this provision is not
required if the trustee is satisfied that the person has already been made aware of
the disclaimer and its date, or the court, on the trustee's application, orders that
compliance is not required in that particular case[9].

The trustee disclaiming property may[10], at any time, send or give copies of the notice of the disclaimer to any persons who in his opinion ought, in the public interest or otherwise, to be informed of the disclaimer[11].

1 As to the meaning of 'business day' see PARA 28 note 8.
2 Ie under the Insolvency Rules 1986, SI 1986/1925, r 6.178: see PARA 493.
3 Insolvency Rules 1986, SI 1986/1925, r 6.179(1) (substituted by SI 2010/686). For the prescribed form of notice of disclaimer and the relevant indorsements by the court and the trustee see the Insolvency Rules 1986, SI 1986/1925, Sch 4 Form 6.61 (substituted by SI 1987/1919).
4 Insolvency Rules 1986, SI 1986/1925, r 6.179(2).
5 As to the meaning of 'dwelling house' see PARA 413 note 1.
6 Insolvency Rules 1986, SI 1986/1925, r 6.179(3). A notice or copy notice to be served on any person under the age of 18 in relation to the disclaimer of property in a dwelling house is sufficiently served if sent or given to the parent or guardian of that person: r 6.179(7) (added by SI 1987/1919). A child living with his parent is not a person in actual occupation of the property: *Hypo-Mortgage Services Ltd v Robinson* [1997] 2 FCR 422, [1997] 2 FLR 71n, CA.
7 Insolvency Rules 1986, SI 1986/1925, r 6.179(4).
8 Insolvency Rules 1986, SI 1986/1925, r 6.179(5).
9 Insolvency Rules 1986, SI 1986/1925, r 6.179(6) (amended by SI 2009/642). As to the mode of application and the procedure see PARA 786 et seq.
10 Ie without prejudice to his obligations under the Insolvency Act 1986 ss 315–319 (see PARAS 490–492, 496 et seq) and under the Insolvency Rules 1986, SI 1986/1925, rr 6.178, 6.179 (see PARA 493).
11 Insolvency Rules 1986, SI 1986/1925, r 6.180 (amended by SI 2010/686).

495. Duty to keep court informed. The trustee must include in that trustee's records of the insolvency a record of:
(1) the persons to whom that trustee has sent or given copies of the notice of disclaimer[1], showing their names and addresses, and the nature of their respective interests;
(2) the dates on which the copies of the notice of disclaimer were sent or given to those persons;
(3) the date on which a copy of the notice of disclaimer was filed with the court[2]; and
(4) where applicable, the date on which a copy of the notice was sent[3] to the Chief Land Registrar[4].

1 Ie under the Insolvency Rules 1986, SI 1986/1925, r 6.179 and r 6.180: see PARA 494.
2 Ie as required by the Insolvency Rules 1986, SI 1986/1925, r 6.178(3)(a): see PARA 493 head (1).
3 Ie as required by the Insolvency Rules 1986, SI 1986/1925, r 6.178(3)(b): see PARA 493 head (2).
4 Insolvency Rules 1986, SI 1986/1925, r 6.181A (added by SI 2010/686).

496. Application by trustee for permission to disclaim. A notice of disclaimer of onerous property[1] may not be given in respect of any property that has been claimed for the estate as after-acquired property[2] or personal property of the bankrupt exceeding a reasonable replacement value[3], or certain tenancies[4], except with the permission of the court[5]. Where the trustee requires the permission of the court to disclaim property claimed for the bankrupt's estate, he may apply for that permission without notice to any other party[6]. The application must be accompanied by a report:
(1) giving such particulars of the property proposed to be disclaimed as enable it to be easily identified;
(2) setting out the reasons why, the property having been claimed for the estate, the court's permission to disclaim is now applied for; and
(3) specifying the persons, if any, who have been informed of the trustee's intention to make the application[7].

If it is stated in the report that any person has consented to the disclaimer, a copy of that consent must be annexed to the report[8].

On consideration of the application, the court may grant the permission applied for; and it may, before granting permission, order that notice of the application be given to all such persons who, if the property is disclaimed, will be entitled to apply for a vesting or other order[9] and fix a venue[10] for the hearing of the application[11].

1   As to the meaning of 'onerous property' see PARA 491.
2   Ie under the Insolvency Act 1986 s 307: see PARA 459.
3   Ie under the Insolvency Act 1986 s 308: see PARA 404.
4   Ie under the Insolvency Act 1986 s 308A: see PARA 405.
5   Insolvency Act 1986 s 315(4) (amended by the Housing Act 1988 s 117(4)). See further PARA 491. As to the application of the Insolvency Act 1986 s 315(4) in the case of the administration in bankruptcy of the insolvent estate of a deceased person dying before the presentation of a bankruptcy petition see PARA 431 note 6.
6   Insolvency Rules 1986, SI 1986/1925, r 6.182(1) (amended by SI 2010/686).
7   Insolvency Rules 1986, SI 1986/1925, r 6.182(2) (amended by SI 2010/686).
8   Insolvency Rules 1986, SI 1986/1925, r 6.182(3) (amended by SI 2010/686).
9   Ie under the Insolvency Act 1986 s 320: see PARA 503 et seq.
10 As to the meaning of 'venue' see PARA 46 note 22.
11 Insolvency Rules 1986, SI 1986/1925, r 6.182(4) (amended by SI 2010/686).

497.   Interest in property to be declared on request.   If, in the case of property which the trustee has the right to disclaim, it appears to him that there is some person who claims, or may claim, to have an interest in the property, he may give notice to that person calling on him to declare within 14 days whether he claims any such interest and, if so, the nature and extent of it[1]. Failing compliance with the notice, the trustee is entitled to assume that the person concerned has no such interest in the property as will prevent or impede its disclaimer[2].

1   Insolvency Rules 1986, SI 1986/1925, r 6.184(1). For the prescribed form of notice of intended disclaimer to an interested party see Sch 4 Form 6.63.
2   Insolvency Rules 1986, SI 1986/1925, r 6.184(2).

498.   Application requiring the trustee to decide whether or not to disclaim.   A notice of disclaimer may not be given[1] in respect of any property if a person interested in the property has applied in writing to the trustee or one of his predecessors as trustee requiring the trustee or that predecessor to decide whether he will disclaim or not, and the period of 28 days[2] beginning with the day on which that application was made has expired without a notice of disclaimer having been given in respect of that property[3]. Such application must be delivered to the trustee personally, by electronic means[4] or by any other means of delivery which enables proof of receipt of the application by the trustee to be provided, if requested, and must be made in the form known as 'notice to elect', or a substantially similar form[5].

In a case where the property concerned cannot be disclaimed by the trustee without the permission of the court[6], if, within the period of 28 days mentioned above, the trustee applies to the court for permission to disclaim, the court must extend the time allowed for giving notice of disclaimer to a date not earlier than the date fixed for the hearing of the application[7].

The trustee is deemed to have adopted any contract[8] which, by virtue of the above provisions[9], he is not entitled to disclaim[10].

1   See PARA 490 et seq.
2   Cf the Insolvency Act 1986 s 178(5) (cited in COMPANY AND PARTNERSHIP INSOLVENCY vol 17 (2011) PARA 830) where the period referred to in corporate insolvency is '28 days or such longer

period as the court may allow'. Whether the omission of a corresponding provision in relation to individual insolvency was intended to prevent an extension of time seems unlikely, however. Where, by any provision in Pts 7A–11 (ss 251A–385) or by the Insolvency Rules 1986, SI 1986/1925, the time for doing anything is limited, the court may extend the time, either before or after it has expired, on such terms, if any, as it thinks fit: Insolvency Act 1986 s 376. As from a day to be appointed, s 376 is amended by the Enterprise and Regulatory Reform Act 2013 s 71, Sch 19 paras 1, 51: see PARA 130 note 17.

It is submitted that the trustee may apply for an extension of time but, as was the case before 29 December 1986 (see PARA 2), he will have to show special circumstances, particularly where he applies retrospectively when he must excuse the delay: see *Re Jones, ex p Lovering* (1874) 9 Ch App 586; *Re Richardson, ex p Harris* (1880) 16 ChD 613.

As to the application of the Insolvency Act 1986 s 376 in the case of the administration in bankruptcy of the insolvent estate of a deceased person dying before the presentation of a bankruptcy petition see PARA 161 note 3.

3 Insolvency Act 1986 s 316(1). In the case of the administration in bankruptcy of the insolvent estate of a deceased person dying before the presentation of a bankruptcy petition, s 316 applies: Administration of Insolvent Estates of Deceased Persons Order 1986, SI 1986/1999, Sch 1 Pt II para 23. As to the administration in bankruptcy of the insolvent estates of deceased persons see further PARA 830 et seq.

4 Ie in accordance with the Insolvency Rules 1986, SI 1986/1925, Pt 12A (rr 12A.1–12A.57): see PARA 810.

5 Insolvency Rules 1986, SI 1986/1925, r 6.183(1), (2) (substituted by SI 2010/686). For the prescribed form of notice to elect see the Insolvency Rules 1986, SI 1986/1925, Sch 4 Form 6.62.

6 See PARA 496.

7 Insolvency Rules 1986, SI 1986/1925, r 6.183(3) (amended by SI 2010/686).

8 In this context it is possible that 'contract' does not include a lease: see *Re ABC Coupler and Engineering Co Ltd (No 3)* [1970] 1 All ER 650 at 669, [1970] 1 WLR 702 at 722 per Plowman J (a company case interpreting the Companies Act 1948 s 323(4) (repealed), a provision not incorporated in the Insolvency Act 1986). However, the bankrupt's estate in the lease passes to the trustee and, unless the lease is disclaimed by him, the trustee is liable to pay the rent reserved by, and to observe and perform the tenant's covenants contained in, the lease: see PARA 424.

9 Ie the Insolvency Act 1986 s 316(1): see the text and notes 1–3.

10 Insolvency Act 1986 s 316(2).

499. Disclaimer of leaseholds. The disclaimer[1] of any property of a leasehold nature does not take effect unless a copy of the disclaimer has been served, so far as the trustee is aware of their addresses, on every person claiming under the bankrupt as underlessee or mortgagee[2] and either:

(1) no application is made for a vesting order[3] with respect to that property before the end of the period of 14 days beginning with the day on which the last notice of disclaimer was served; or

(2) where such an application has been made, the court directs that the disclaimer is to take effect[4].

Where the court gives a direction under head (2) above, it may also, instead of or in addition to any order it makes[5], make such orders with respect to fixtures, tenant's improvements and other matters arising out of the lease as it thinks fit[6].

1 Ie under the Insolvency Act 1986 s 315: see PARA 490 et seq.

2 See PARA 494.

3 Ie under the Insolvency Act 1986 s 320: see PARA 503.

4 Insolvency Act 1986 s 317(1). In the case of the administration in bankruptcy of the insolvent estate of a deceased person dying before the presentation of a bankruptcy petition, s 317 applies: Administration of Insolvent Estates of Deceased Persons Order 1986, SI 1986/1999, art 3(1), Sch 1 Pt II para 23. As to the administration in bankruptcy of the insolvent estates of deceased persons see further PARA 830 et seq.

5 See note 3.

6 Insolvency Act 1986 s 317(2). See further PARA 502.

500. Disclaimer of dwelling house. Without prejudice to the statutory provisions as to disclaimer of leaseholds[1], the disclaimer of a dwelling house[2] does not take effect unless a copy of the disclaimer has been served, so far as the trustee is aware of their addresses, on every person in occupation of or claiming a right to occupy the dwelling house[3] and either:

(1) no application for a vesting order[4] is made with respect to the property before the end of the period of 14 days beginning with the day on which the last notice served under the above provisions was served; or

(2) where such an application has been made, the court directs that the disclaimer is to take effect[5].

1 Ie the Insolvency Act 1986 s 317: see PARA 499.
2 As to the meaning of 'dwelling house' see PARA 413 note 1.
3 See PARA 494.
4 Ie under the Insolvency Act 1986 s 320: see PARA 503.
5 Insolvency Act 1986 s 318. In the case of the administration in bankruptcy of the insolvent estate of a deceased person dying before the presentation of a bankruptcy petition, s 318 applies: Administration of Insolvent Estates of Deceased Persons Order 1986, SI 1986/1999, art 3(1), Sch 1 Pt II para 23. As to the administration in bankruptcy of the insolvent estates of deceased persons see further PARA 830 et seq.

501. Disclaimer of land subject to a rentcharge. Where, in consequence of the disclaimer[1] of any land subject to a rentcharge[2], that land vests by operation of law in the Crown or any other person ('the proprietor'), the proprietor and the proprietor's successors in title are not subject to any personal liability in respect of any sums becoming due under the rentcharge except sums becoming due after the proprietor, or some person claiming under or through the proprietor, has taken possession or control of the land or has entered into occupation of it[3].

1 Ie under the Insolvency Act 1986 s 315: see PARA 490 et seq.
2 As to rentcharges see REAL PROPERTY AND REGISTRATION vol 87 (2012) PARA 1104 et seq.
3 Insolvency Act 1986 s 319(1), (2). Section 319 debars the owner of the rentcharge, except as mentioned in the text, from suing the Crown or other mesne landlord personally in respect of the rentcharge, but does not affect his rights against the land.
   In the case of the administration in bankruptcy of the insolvent estate of a deceased person dying before the presentation of a bankruptcy petition, s 319 applies: Administration of Insolvent Estates of Deceased Persons Order 1986, SI 1986/1999, art 3(1), Sch 1 Pt II para 23. As to the administration in bankruptcy of the insolvent estates of deceased persons see further PARA 830 et seq.

502. Application for vesting order. An application by any person for an order of the court to vest or deliver disclaimed property[1] must be made within three months of the applicant becoming aware of the disclaimer, or of his receiving a copy of the trustee's notice of disclaimer[2], whichever is the earlier[3].

With his application the applicant must file in court[4] a witness statement[5]:

(1) stating whether he applies as a person who claims an interest in the disclaimed property[6] or a person who is under a liability in respect of the disclaimed property, not being a liability discharged by the disclaimer[7], or as a person who, at the time when the bankruptcy petition was presented, was in occupation of or entitled to occupy the dwelling house[8];

(2) specifying the date on which he received a copy of the trustee's notice of disclaimer, or otherwise became aware of the disclaimer; and

(3) specifying the grounds of his application and the order which he desires the court to make[9].

The court must fix a venue[10] for the hearing of the application; and the applicant must, not later than five business days[11] before the date fixed, give to the trustee notice of the venue, accompanied by copies of the application and the witness statement[12].

On the hearing of the application, the court may give directions as to the other persons, if any, who should be sent or given notice of the application and the grounds on which it is made[13]; and sealed copies of any order made on the application must be sent by the court to the applicant and the trustee[14].

In a case where the property disclaimed is of a leasehold nature or is property in a dwelling house, and the effect of the disclaimer is suspended[15], a direction must be included in the court's order giving effect to the disclaimer, unless at the time when the order is issued, other applications for vesting orders are pending in respect of the same property[16].

1 Ie under the Insolvency Act 1986 s 320: see PARA 503.
2 Ie a notice sent under the Insolvency Rules 1986, SI 1986/1925, r 6.179: see PARA 494.
3 Insolvency Rules 1986, SI 1986/1925, r 6.186(1), (2).
4 As to the meaning of 'file in court' see PARA 57 note 13.
5 As to the meaning of 'witness statement' see PARA 161 note 7.
6 Ie under the Insolvency Act 1986 s 320(2)(a): see PARA 503 head (1).
7 Ie under the Insolvency Act 1986 s 320(2)(b): see PARA 503 head (2).
8 Ie under the Insolvency Act 1986 s 320(2)(c): see PARA 503 head (3). As to the meaning of 'dwelling house' see PARA 413 note 1.
9 Insolvency Rules 1986, SI 1986/1925, r 6.186(3) (amended by SI 2010/686).
10 As to the meaning of 'venue' see PARA 46 note 22.
11 As to the meaning of 'business day' see PARA 28 note 8.
12 Insolvency Rules 1986, SI 1986/1925, r 6.186(4) (amended by SI 2010/686).
13 Insolvency Rules 1986, SI 1986/1925, r 6.186(5).
14 Insolvency Rules 1986, SI 1986/1925, r 6.186(6).
15 Ie under the Insolvency Act 1986 s 317 (see PARA 499) or s 318 (see PARA 500).
16 Insolvency Rules 1986, SI 1986/1925, r 6.186(7).

503. Orders vesting disclaimed property; in general. Where the trustee has disclaimed property[1], then, on application by:

(1)	any person who claims an interest in the disclaimed property[2];
(2)	any person who is under any liability in respect of the disclaimed property, not being a liability discharged by the disclaimer; or
(3)	where the disclaimed property is property in a dwelling house, any person who at the time when the bankruptcy petition was presented was in occupation of or entitled to occupy the dwelling house[3],

the court may make an order on such terms as it thinks fit for the vesting of the disclaimed property in, or for its delivery to:

(a)	a person entitled to it or a trustee[4] for such a person;
(b)	a person subject to such a liability as is mentioned in head (2) above or a trustee for such a person; or
(c)	where the disclaimed property is property in a dwelling house, any person who at the time when the bankruptcy petition was presented was in occupation of or entitled to occupy the dwelling house[5].

The court may not, however, make an order in favour of the persons referred to in head (b) above except where it appears to the court that it would be just to do so for the purpose of compensating the person subject to the liability in respect of the disclaimer[6].

Such an order vesting property in any person need not be completed by any conveyance, assignment or transfer[7].

1   It is not open to an applicant to seek a vesting order unless and until the trustee has disclaimed the property: *Khan-Ghauri v Dunbar Bank plc* [2001] BPIR 618.

2   Any person interested may apply eg parties claiming under the bankrupt or the lessor (*Re Cock, ex p Shilson* (1887) 20 QBD 343; *Re Finley, ex p Clothworkers' Co* (1888) 21 QBD 475; *Re Britton* (1889) 6 Morr 130; *Re Baker, ex p Lupton* [1901] 2 KB 628, CA), or the lessee who, owing to the bankruptcy of an assignee of the lease, is compelled to pay the rent (*Re Morgan, ex p Morgan* (1889) 22 QBD 592). If there is nothing more than a lease, the disclaimer of the lease determines the lessee's interest in it under the Insolvency Act 1986 s 315(3). He avoids all his liabilities and loses all his rights by virtue of the disclaimer. There is no need of any provision vesting the property in the landlord, for the natural and legal effect of s 315(3) is that the reversion will be accelerated; but, although there is nothing to be vested in the landlord, he may require delivery of possession, and, if so, he can obtain it under s 320(3) (*Re Hyams, ex p Lindsay v Hyams* (1923) 93 LJ Ch 184 at 186, CA); per contra, if any other interest has been created, the lease may be revived (*Re Thompson and Cottrell's Contract* [1943] Ch 97, [1943] 1 All ER 169). See also *Hackney London Borough v Crown Estates Comrs* [1996] BPIR 428; *Lloyds Bank SF Nominees v Aladdin Ltd (in liquidation)* [1996] 1 BCLC 720, CA; *Re Spirit Motorsport Ltd (in liquidation)* [1996] 1 BCLC 684; cf *Re Vedmay Ltd* [1994] 1 BCLC 676. See also *Fenland District Council v Sheppard* [2011] EWHC 2829 (Ch), [2012] 1 EGLR 49, [2012] BPIR 289 (vesting order in favour of first chargee did not effect a merger of the charge with the freehold); *Re Ballast plc, St Paul Travellers Insurance Co Ltd v Dargan* [2006] EWHC 3189 (Ch), [2007] BCC 620, [2007] BPIR 117 (right of insurer to be subrogated to a cause of action was not a proprietory interest and therefore insurer had no standing to apply for a vesting order).

3   As to the meaning of 'dwelling house' see PARA 413 note 1.

4   See *Re Holmes, ex p Ashworth* [1908] 2 KB 812, DC (where a lessee mortgaged by sub-demise four portions of a plot of land, and an order was made vesting the whole plot, including a portion not mortgaged, in a trustee for the mortgages). See also *Lee v Lee* [1998] 2 BCLC 219, [1999] BCC 268, CA (court's discretion to return surplus proceeds of sale of disclaimed lease vested in a mortgagee to trustee in bankruptcy).

5   Insolvency Act 1986 s 320(1)–(3). As to the position where the property is of a leasehold nature see PARA 504. In the case of the administration in bankruptcy of the insolvent estate of a deceased person dying before the presentation of a bankruptcy petition, s 320 applies: Administration of Insolvent Estates of Deceased Persons Order 1986, SI 1986/1999, art 3(1), Sch 1 Pt II para 23. As to the administration in bankruptcy of the insolvent estates of deceased persons see further PARA 830 et seq.
     The Insolvency Act 1986 s 320(3)(c) (see head (c) in the text) will include the bankrupt's spouse or civil partner in occupation or with a right to occupy under the Family Law Act 1996: see MATRIMONIAL AND CIVIL PARTNERSHIP LAW vol 72 (2009) PARA 285 et seq. It will also include a tenant under a Rent Act protected tenancy. On the bankruptcy of a protected tenant, his contractual interest passes to the trustee in bankruptcy with the rest of his property: see PARA 424. Where the trustee disclaims, the contractual interest determines and the bankrupt tenant cannot become a statutory tenant of the dwelling house because he was not the protected tenant immediately before the termination of the protected tenancy: see the Rent Act 1977 s 2(1); *Reeves v Davies* [1921] 2 KB 486; *Smalley v Quarrier* [1975] 2 All ER 688, [1975] 1 WLR 938; and LANDLORD AND TENANT vol 63 (2012) PARA 945. The landlord may, therefore, recover possession of the dwelling house. Where the bankrupt is a statutory tenant, however, his statutory tenancy is personal to him and does not pass to his trustee: see *Sutton v Dorf* [1932] 2 KB 304; and PARA 424. The bankrupt statutory tenant is entitled to continue to enjoy his personal right to occupy the dwelling house. The bankrupt former protected tenant may apply for a vesting order, possibly in competition with the landlord where the court ought to have regard to general Rent Act principles: see LANDLORD AND TENANT. A further potential applicant under the Insolvency Act 1986 s 320(3)(c) (see head (c) in the text) is the bankrupt himself, particularly where he is entitled to occupy the dwelling house under s 337: see PARA 675.

6   Insolvency Act 1986 s 320(4). As to the exercise of the court's discretion to make a vesting order under the analogous provisions of the Companies Act 1985 s 619(5) (repealed) see *Re AE Realisations (1985) Ltd* [1987] 3 All ER 83, [1988] 1 WLR 200.

7   Insolvency Act 1986 s 320(6). The effect of any order under s 320 must be taken into account in assessing for the purposes of s 315(5) (see PARA 505) the extent of any loss or damage sustained by any person in consequence of the disclaimer: s 320(5).

504.   Vesting of disclaimed property; leases.   The court may not make an order[1] vesting property of a leasehold nature in any person, except on terms making that person:

(1)   subject to the same liabilities and obligations as the bankrupt was subject to under the lease on the day the bankruptcy petition was presented; or

(2)   if the court thinks fit, subject to the same liabilities and obligations as that person would be subject to if the lease had been assigned to him on that day[2].

For the purposes of an order relating to only part of any property comprised in a lease, the above conditions apply as if the lease comprised only the property to which the order relates[3].

Where the above conditions apply and no person is willing to accept a vesting order on the terms required which satisfy those conditions, the court may, by order, vest the bankrupt's estate or interest in the property in any person who is liable, whether personally or in a representative capacity, and whether alone or jointly with the bankrupt, to perform the lessee's covenants in the lease; and the court may vest that estate and interest in such a person freed and discharged from all estates, incumbrances and interests created by the bankrupt[4]. Where the above conditions apply and a person declines to accept any vesting order, that person is excluded from all interest in the property[5].

1   Ie under the Insolvency Act 1986 s 320: see PARA 503.
2   Insolvency Act 1986 s 321(1). As from a day to be appointed, s 321(1) is amended by the Enterprise and Regulatory Reform Act 2013 s 71, Sch 19 paras 1, 26: see PARA 130 note 17.
        The Insolvency Act 1986 s 321(1) follows the Bankruptcy Act 1914 s 54(6) proviso (b) (repealed): see *Re Walker, ex p Mills* (1895) 64 LJQB 783; *Re Carter and Ellis, ex p Savill Bros* [1905] 1 KB 735 at 742, 755, CA (where an order was made vesting certain leases in mortgagees by sub-demise, subject only to the same liabilities and obligations as if the leases had been assigned to them at the date when the bankruptcy petition was filed; this enabled the mortgagees to rid themselves of their liability by assignment, as well as to limit their liability to breaches of covenant that occurred after the filing of the petition). The court has a discretion, and is not obliged to make the modifications referred to; but, if the exercise of the discretion in favour of the mortgagee will place him in no better position, and the lessor in no worse position, than if there had been no disclaimer, the discretion ought to be exercised in favour of the mortgagee: *Re Carter and Ellis, ex p Savill Bros*.
        In the case of the administration in bankruptcy of the insolvent estate of a deceased person dying before the presentation of a bankruptcy petition, the Insolvency Act 1986 s 321 applies: Administration of Insolvent Estates of Deceased Persons Order 1986, SI 1986/1999, art 3(1), Sch 1 Pt II para 23. As to the administration in bankruptcy of the insolvent estates of deceased persons see further PARA 830 et seq.
3   Insolvency Act 1986 s 321(2).
4   Insolvency Act 1986 s 321(3).
5   Insolvency Act 1986 s 321(4).

505.   Rights of persons injured by disclaimer.   Any person sustaining loss or damage in consequence of the operation of a disclaimer[1] is deemed to be a creditor of the bankrupt to the extent of the loss or damage and accordingly may prove for the loss or damage as a bankruptcy debt[2].

1   Ie under the Insolvency Act 1986 s 315: see PARA 490 et seq.
2   Insolvency Act 1986 s 315(5). The effect of any vesting order must be taken into account in assessing the extent of any loss or damage sustained by a person in consequence of the disclaimer: see s 320(5); and PARA 503 note 7. In *Re Hide, ex p Llynvi Coal and Iron Co* (1871) 7 Ch App 28, the measure of damages for the disclaimer of the bankrupt's agreement to take a lease for ten years was held to be the difference between the rent paid under the agreement and the rent obtainable at the time of the disclaimer. On the disclaimer of a lease with a covenant to repair, the measure of the landlord's damages for breach of covenant is limited to the amount, if

any, by which the value of the reversion, whether immediate or not, is diminished owing to breach of the covenant: see the Landlord and Tenant Act 1927 s 18(1); and LANDLORD AND TENANT vol 62 (2012) PARA 605.

On a disclaimer of shares, the measure of damages is the amount unpaid on the shares, less the value of any advantages which may accrue from them: *Re Hallett, ex p National Insurance Co* (1894) 1 Mans 380. As to damages on disclaimer of a contract to take up shares see *Re Hooley, ex p United Ordnance and Engineering Co Ltd* [1899] 2 QB 579. See further PARA 534. If a trustee disclaims a contract to purchase land, the vendor is entitled to retain the deposit, even if there is no stipulation as to forfeiture of the deposit: *Re Parnell, ex p Barrell* (1875) 10 Ch App 512.

On a disclaimer of a lease, the normal measure of compensation is for the loss of the right to future rent to be measured by the difference between the rent and other payments which the landlord would have received in future but for the disclaimer and the rent and other sums which the disclaimer will enable him to receive by reletting, such amount to be discounted at an appropriate rate to reflect accelerated receipt of sums which would otherwise only fall due in the future: *Christopher Moran Holdings Ltd v Bairstow* [2000] 2 AC 172, sub nom *Re Park Air Services plc, Christopher Moran Holdings Ltd v Bairstow* [1999] 1 All ER 673, HL.

As to the application of the Insolvency Act 1986 s 315 in the case of the administration in bankruptcy of the insolvent estate of a deceased person dying before the presentation of a bankruptcy petition see PARA 431 note 6.

506. Disclaimer presumed valid and effective. Any disclaimer of property by the trustee is presumed valid and effective, unless it is proved that he has been in breach of his duty with respect to the giving of notice of disclaimer, or otherwise under the above provisions[1] relating to disclaimer[2].

1 Ie under the Insolvency Act 1986 ss 315–319 and the Insolvency Rules 1986, SI 1986/1925, rr 6.178–6.186: see PARA 490 et seq.
2 Insolvency Rules 1986, SI 1986/1925, r 6.185.

(7) PROOF OF DEBTS

(i) Debts Provable in Bankruptcy

507. Effect of bankruptcy on creditors' rights. After the making of a bankruptcy order[1] no person who is a creditor of the bankrupt in respect of a debt provable in the bankruptcy[2]:

(1) has any remedy against the property or person of the bankrupt in respect of that debt; or

(2) may, before the discharge of the bankrupt, commence any action or other legal proceedings against the bankrupt except with the permission of the court and on such terms as the court may impose[3].

In place of their rights to enforce their claims against the bankrupt and his property, the creditors acquire a right to share proportionally in the distribution[4] by the trustee of the bankrupt's estate of the bankrupt's assets which become vested in the trustee[5].

All claims which may be proved in the bankruptcy against the bankrupt are called 'provable debts'[6]; a person claiming to be a creditor of the bankrupt who wishes to recover his debt in whole or in part and who submits his claim in writing to the official receiver, where acting as receiver and manager, or to the trustee, is referred to as 'proving for his debt'; and the document by which he seeks to establish his claim is his 'proof '[7].

1 As to where there has been a previous bankruptcy see PARAS 489, 617 et seq.
2 As to provable debts see the Insolvency Rules 1986, SI 1986/1925, r 12.3; and PARA 508.
3 See the Insolvency Act 1986 s 285(3); and PARA 214. Section 285(3) is subject to s 346 (enforcement procedures: see PARA 703 et seq) and s 347 (limited right to distress: see PARA 711

et seq) (s 285(3)); and s 285(3) does not affect the right of a secured creditor of the bankrupt to enforce his security (s 285(4)). As to secured creditors see PARA 574 et seq.
4   As to the distribution of a bankrupt's estate see PARA 587 et seq.
5   See PARA 397 et seq; and *Re Higginson and Dean, ex p A-G* [1899] 1 QB 325 at 333, DC.
6   See note 2.
7   See the Insolvency Rules 1986, SI 1986/1925, r 6.96; and PARA 544. The form of proof is known as 'proof of debt': see r 6.96(3); and PARA 544.

508.   Provable debts.   The proof of any bankruptcy debt by a secured or unsecured creditor of the bankrupt and the admission or rejection of any proof must take place in accordance with the Insolvency Rules 1986[1]. A bankruptcy debt, in relation to a bankrupt, means any of the following:

(1)   any debt or liability[2] to which he is subject at the commencement of the bankruptcy[3];

(2)   any debt or liability to which he may become subject after the commencement of the bankruptcy, including after his discharge from bankruptcy[4], by reason of any obligation incurred[5] before the commencement of the bankruptcy; and

(3)   any interest provable[6] under the Insolvency Act 1986[7].

In determining, for these purposes, whether any liability in tort is a bankruptcy debt, the bankrupt is deemed to become subject to that liability by reason of an obligation incurred at the time when the cause of action accrued[8].

In bankruptcy, all claims by creditors are provable as debts against the bankrupt, whether they are present or future, certain or contingent, ascertained or sounding only in damages[9].

However, the following are not provable:

(a)   any fine[10] imposed for an offence, and any obligation (other than an obligation to pay a lump sum or to pay costs) arising under an order made in family proceedings[11] or any obligation arising under a maintenance calculation made under the Child Support Act 1991[12];

(b)   any obligation arising under a confiscation order made under the Drug Trafficking Act 1994[13], under the Proceeds of Crime (Scotland) Act 1995[14], under the Criminal Justice Act 1988[15] or under Parts 2, 3 or 4[16] of the Proceeds of Crime Act 2002[17].

Any claim arising under a restitution order[18] is not provable except at a time when all other claims of creditors in the bankruptcy, other than under a restitution order, have been paid[19] in full with interest[20].

Nothing in the above provisions prejudices any enactment or rule of law under which a particular kind of debt is not provable, whether on grounds of public policy or otherwise[21].

1   Insolvency Act 1986 s 322(1). As to secured creditors see PARA 574 et seq.
    In the case of the administration in bankruptcy of the insolvent estate of a deceased person dying before the presentation of a bankruptcy petition, s 322 applies: Administration of Insolvent Estates of Deceased Persons Order 1986, SI 1986/1999, art 3(1), Sch 1 Pt II para 23. As to the administration in bankruptcy of the insolvent estates of deceased persons see further PARA 830 et seq.
2   For the purposes of references in the Insolvency Act 1986 Pts 7A–11 (ss 251A–385) to a debt or liability, it is immaterial whether the debt or liability is present or future, whether it is certain or contingent or whether its amount is fixed or liquidated, or is capable of being ascertained by fixed rules or as a matter of opinion; and references in Pts 7A–11 to owing a debt are to be read accordingly: ss 382(3), 385(1). In Pts 7A–11, except in so far as the context otherwise requires, 'liability' means, subject to s 382(3), a liability to pay money or money's worth, including any liability under an enactment, any liability for breach of trust, any liability in contract, tort or bailment and any liability arising out of an obligation to make restitution: s 382(4). Liability under the Child Support Act 1991 to pay child support maintenance to any person is not a debt

or liability for the purposes of the Insolvency Act 1986 Pt 8 (ss 252–263G): s 382(5) (added by the Welfare Reform Act 2012 s 142(1)). The Insolvency Act 1986 s 382(1) only deals with the debts and liabilities of the debtor, and not those of his personal representatives: *Wicks v Russell* [2008] EWHC 2713 (Ch), [2009] BIPR 194, [2008] All ER (D) 53 (Dec).

3　As to the commencement of bankruptcy see PARA 209.

4　As to discharge from bankruptcy see PARA 638 et seq.

5　As to the meaning of 'obligation incurred' see *Re Nortel GMBH (in admin); Re Lehman Brothers International (Europe) (in admin)* [2013] UKSC 52, [2013] 3 WLR 504, [2013] 2 BCLC 135 (where it was held that the type of debt of liability referred to in the corporate insolvency provision equivalent to head (2) in the text was directed at contingent debts and liabilities); and see further PARA 510.

6　Ie provable as mentioned in the Insolvency Act 1986 s 322(2): see PARA 559.

7　Insolvency Act 1986 s 382(1). Until a day to be appointed, a bankruptcy debt also means any amount specified in pursuance of the Powers of Criminal Courts Act 1973 s 39(3)(c) (repealed) in any criminal bankruptcy order made against a bankrupt before the commencement of the bankruptcy: see the Insolvency Act 1986 s 382(1)(c) (prospectively repealed by the Criminal Justice Act 1988 s 170(2), Sch 16). As to the prospective repeal of the Insolvency Act 1986 s 382(1)(c) see PARA 1 note 11.

　　In the case of the administration in bankruptcy of the insolvent estate of a deceased person dying before the presentation of a bankruptcy petition, the Insolvency Act 1986 s 382 applies with the modification that in the definition of 'bankruptcy debt' for the words 'commencement of the bankruptcy' wherever they occur there are to be substituted the words 'date of death of the deceased debtor': Administration of Insolvent Estates of Deceased Persons Order 1986, SI 1986/1999, Sch 1 Pt II para 31.

8　Insolvency Act 1986 s 382(2). Under the Bankruptcy Act 1914 s 30(1) (repealed) demands in the nature of unliquidated damages arising otherwise than by reason of a contract, promise or breach of trust were not provable in bankruptcy. However, by virtue of the Insolvency Act 1986 s 382(2), where the cause of action accrued before the commencement of the bankruptcy, the unliquidated claim in tort becomes a bankruptcy debt and the person claiming that he has suffered loss and damage becomes a creditor of the bankrupt. See further *Re T & N Ltd* [2005] EWHC 2870 (Ch), [2006] 3 All ER 697, [2006] 1 WLR 1728 (a decision whose effect has now been reversed in the corporate insolvency context by changes to the rules). Discharge from bankruptcy does not, however, except to such extent and on such conditions as the court may direct, release the bankrupt from any bankruptcy debt which consists in a liability to pay damages for negligence, nuisance or breach of a statutory, contractual or other duty, or to pay damages by virtue of the Consumer Protection Act 1987 Pt I (ss 1–9) (see CONSUMER PROTECTION vol 21 (2011) PARA 642 et seq) being in either case damages in respect of personal injuries to any person: Insolvency Act 1986 s 281(5)(a) (amended by the Consumer Protection Act 1987 s 48(1), Sch 4 para 12). For these purposes, 'personal injuries' includes death and any disease or other impairment of a person's physical or mental condition: Insolvency Act 1986 s 281(8). See further PARA 650.

　　As to accrual of causes of action see LIMITATION PERIODS. The power of the court to award interest on damages in respect of claims in tort, whether under the Senior Courts Act 1981 s 35A (added by the Administration of Justice Act 1982 s 15(1), Sch 1 Pt I) or the County Courts Act 1984 s 69 (amended by the Courts and Legal Services Act 1990 s 125(3), Sch 18 para 46; the Civil Procedure Act 1997 s 10, Sch 2 para 2(1), (2)), arises only on judgment. The claimant will presumably be able to rely on the Insolvency Rules 1986, SI 1986/1925, r 6.113 to claim interest: see PARA 559.

9　Insolvency Rules 1986, SI 1986/1925, r 12.3(1) (amended by SI 2003/1730).

10　For these purposes, 'fine' has the meaning given by the Insolvency Act 1986 s 281(8) (see PARA 650 note 5): Insolvency Rules 1986, SI 1986/1925, r 12.3(2) (amended by SI 1993/602). See also *Marcus v Institute of Chartered Accountants* [2004] EWHC 3010 (Ch), [2005] BPIR 413, [2004] All ER (D) 27 (Dec) (for the purposes of these provisions 'fine' means a fine imposed by a criminal court and does not include a penalty imposed by a regulatory body which is accordingly a provable debt).

11　For these purposes, 'family proceedings' has the meaning given by the Insolvency Act 1986 s 281(8) (see PARA 650 note 9): Insolvency Rules 1986, SI 1986/1925, r 12.3(2) (amended by SI 1993/602). Discharge from bankruptcy does not, however, except to such extent and on such condition as the court may direct, release the bankrupt from any bankruptcy debt which arises under any order made in family proceedings or under a maintenance calculation made under the Child Support Act 1991: see the Insolvency Act 1986 s 281(5)(b); and PARA 650 head (4)(b).

12　Ie under the Child Support Act 1991: see CHILDREN AND YOUNG PERSONS vol 9 (2012) PARA 573 et seq.

13　Ie under the Drug Trafficking Act 1994 s 2.

14　Ie under the Proceeds of Crime (Scotland) Act 1995 ss 1, 8.

15　Ie under the Criminal Justice Act 1988 s 71.

16　Ie under the Proceeds of Crime Act 2002 Pt 2 (ss 6–91), Pt 3 (ss 92–155), Pt 4 (ss 93–239).

17　Insolvency Rules 1986, SI 1986/1925, r 12.3(2) (amended by SI 1987/1919; SI 1989/397; SI 1993/602; SI 2003/1730; SI 2005/527); Interpretation Act 1978 s 17(2)(b). Any obligation arising from a payment out of the social fund under the Social Security Contributions and Benefits Act 1992 s 138(1)(b) (repealed) by way of crisis loan or budgeting loan is also not provable: see the Insolvency Rules 1986, SI 1986/1925, r 12.3(2) (amended by SI 2012/469). As to the social fund see SOCIAL SECURITY AND PENSIONS vol 44(2) (Reissue) PARAS 228–236.

18　Ie any claim arising by virtue of the Financial Services and Markets Act 2000 s 382(1)(a), not being a claim also arising by virtue of s 382(1)(b) (see FINANCIAL SERVICES AND INSTITUTIONS vol 48 (2008) PARA 472).

19　Ie under the Insolvency Act 1986 s 328(4): see PARA 596.

20　Insolvency Rules 1986, SI 1986/1925, r 12.3(2A) (added by SI 1987/1919; and amended by SI 2001/3649; and SI 2003/1730).

21　Insolvency Rules 1986, SI 1986/1925, r 12.3(3). Since it may be assumed that a foreign maintenance order providing for periodic payments is variable by the court making the order, it is not a final and conclusive order and so cannot be enforced in England at common law and is not provable by virtue of a rule of law for the purposes of r 12.3(3): *Cartwright v Cartwright* [2002] EWCA Civ 931, [2002] 2 FCR 760, [2002] 2 FLR 610.

509.　Unliquidated damages. A claim for unliquidated damages is a provable debt[1], whether the liability is one to which the bankrupt is subject at the commencement of the bankruptcy[2] or one to which he may become subject after the commencement of the bankruptcy by reason of any obligation incurred before the commencement of the bankruptcy[3].

In determining whether any liability in tort is a bankruptcy debt, the bankrupt is deemed to become subject to that liability by reason of an obligation incurred at the time when the cause of action accrued[4].

1　See the Insolvency Rules 1986, SI 1986/1925, r 12.3(1); and PARA 508.

2　As to the commencement of bankruptcy see PARA 209.

3　See the Insolvency Act 1986 s 382(1)(a), (b); and PARA 508 heads (1), (2).

4　See the Insolvency Act 1986 s 382(2); and PARA 508.

510.　Contingent debts. The trustee must estimate the value of any bankruptcy debt which, by reason of its being subject to any contingency or contingencies or for any other reason, does not bear a certain value[1].

Where the value of a bankruptcy debt is estimated by the trustee[2] or by the court[3], the amount provable in the bankruptcy in respect of the debt is the amount of the estimate[4].

Generally, all contingent liabilities which may end in the payment of money, and which have not been declared incapable of being fairly estimated, are provable[5]. Thus, where the assignee of a lease becomes bankrupt, the lessee or assignor who is liable in respect of the rent and covenants, and whom the bankrupt has covenanted, or is liable, to indemnify, may prove[6].

1　Insolvency Act 1986 s 322(3); and see PARA 554. A contingent liability is one which, by reason of something done by the person bound, will necessarily arise or come into being, if one or more of certain events occur, or do not occur: *Winter v IRC* [1963] AC 235 at 249, [1961] 3 All ER 855 at 859, HL; applied in *Re Nortel GMBH (in admin); Re Lehman Brothers International (Europe) (in admin)* [2013] UKSC 52, [2013] 3 WLR 504, [2013] All ER (D) 283 (Jul). In valuing contingent claims account can be taken of matters occurring after the date of the bankruptcy order under the 'hindsight principle': *Wight v Eckhardt Marine GmbH* [2003] UKPC 37, [2004] 1 AC 147, [2003] 3 WLR 414. As to the application of the Insolvency Act 1986 s 322 in the case of the administration in bankruptcy of the insolvent estate of a deceased person dying before the presentation of a bankruptcy petition see PARA 508 note 1.

2　Ie under the Insolvency Act 1986 s 322(3).

3 Ie under the Insolvency Act 1986 s 303: see PARA 342.
4 Insolvency Act 1986 s 322(4).
5 *Hardy v Fothergill* (1888) 13 App Cas 351 at 360, 361, HL. For other instances see *Re Allen & Co, ex p Strong and Hanbury* (1893) 10 Morr 84 (breach of covenant to purchase goods for a certain number of years); *Re Gieve, ex p Shaw* (1899) 80 LT 737, CA (value of annuity); *Barnett v King* [1891] 1 Ch 4, CA (liability to pay a sum out of estate after death). A costs order made against a bankrupt after his discharge in proceedings commenced before his bankruptcy is a contingent debt: *Re Nortel GMBH (in admin); Re Lehman Brothers International (Europe) (in admin)* [2013] UKSC 52, [2013] 3 WLR 504, [2013] All ER (D) 283 (Jul), overruling *Glenister v Rowe* [2000] Ch 76, [1999] 3 All ER 452, CA. As to annuities see PARA 519; and as to claims by alien enemies see PARA 542.
6 *Hardy v Fothergill* (1888) 13 App Cas 351, HL; *Re Hinks, ex p Verdi* (1886) 3 Morr 218; *Re Carruthers, ex p Tobit* (1895) 2 Mans 172; *Re Perkins, Poyser v Beyfus* [1898] 2 Ch 182, CA. As to the contingent liability of an assignor of a lease to his landlord see *James Smith & Sons (Norwood) Ltd v Goodman* [1936] Ch 216, CA.

511. Court's power to examine debt. A proof may be admitted for dividend either for the whole amount claimed by the creditor, or for part of that amount; but, if the trustee rejects a proof in whole or in part, he must prepare a written statement of his reasons for doing so, and send it as soon as reasonably practicable to the creditor[1].

Every bankruptcy is under the general control of the court and the court has full power[2] to decide all questions of priorities and all other questions, whether of law or fact, arising in any bankruptcy[3]. The court has the right to inquire into the consideration for a debt, including a judgment debt; its power to do so is not confined to examination of the petitioning creditor's debt on which a bankruptcy order is sought to be obtained[4].

1 See the Insolvency Rules 1986, SI 1986/1925, r 6.104(1), (2); and PARA 550.
2 Ie subject to the provisions in the Insolvency Act 1986 Pts 7A–11 (ss 251A–385).
3 See the Insolvency Act 1986 s 363(1); and PARA 215.
4 *Re Onslow, ex p Kibble* (1875) 10 Ch App 373; *Re Tollemache, ex p Revell* (1884) 13 QBD 720, CA; *Re Tollemache, ex p Edwards* (1884) 14 QBD 415, CA; *Re Tollemache, ex p Bonham* (1885) 14 QBD 604, CA; *Re Tollemache, ex p Anderson* (1885) 14 QBD 606, CA; *Re Lennox, ex p Lennox* (1885) 16 QBD 315, CA; *Re Flatau, ex p Scotch Whisky Distillers Ltd* (1888) 22 QBD 83, CA; *Re Beauchamp, ex p Beauchamp* [1904] 1 KB 572, CA; *Re Van Laun, ex p Pattullo* [1907] 1 KB 155 (affd sub nom *Re Van Laun, ex p Chatterton* [1907] 2 KB 23, CA).

A debt which would have been postponed for purposes of proof under the Insolvency Act 1986 s 329 continues to be so postponed, even after it has been converted into a judgment: *Re Lupkovics, ex p Trustee v Freville* [1954] 2 All ER 125, [1954] 1 WLR 1234.

As to going behind a judgment obtained by a compromise see *Re Blythe, ex p Banner* (1881) 17 ChD 480, CA; *Miles v New Zealand Alford Estate Co* (1886) 32 ChD 266, CA; *Re Hawkins, ex p Troup* [1895] 1 QB 404, CA; *Re Mead* [1916] 2 IR 285, CA. As to moneylending cases see PARA 543.

The court will not go behind an assessment for taxes made against the bankrupt: see *Re Calvert, ex p Calvert* [1899] 2 QB 145; applied in *Re B Moschi, ex p R Moschi v IRC* (1953) 35 TC 92. See further INCOME TAXATION.

512. Double proof not allowed. It does not follow that, if there is a provable debt, the right of proof may be insisted on in every case; for it is a well-established principle that there cannot be two proofs in respect of one debt; and this is so, even where there are separate contracts in respect of the same debt[1].

1 *Re Oriental Commercial Bank, ex p European Bank* (1871) 7 Ch App 99; *Re Hoey, ex p Hoey* (1918) 88 LJKB 273, DC; *Deering v Bank of Ireland* (1886) 12 App Cas 20, HL. The first two cases were cited and applied in *The Liverpool (No 2)* [1963] P 64 at 80, [1960] 3 All ER 307, CA (a salvage case). See also *Barclays Bank Ltd v TOSG Trust Fund Ltd* [1984] AC 626, [1984] 1 All ER 628, CA; affd [1984] AC 626, [1984] 1 All ER 1060, HL (the court will

examine the substance of the transactions which have given rise to the potential application of the rule to determine who has the better right). As to the application of this rule to proofs by sureties see PARA 521 et seq. See also PARAS 565 note 5, 573 note 6.

Under the Bankruptcy Act 1914 s 32, Sch 2 r 19 (repealed), if a debtor was, at the date of the receiving order, liable in respect of distinct contracts (see e g *Re Jeffery, ex p Honey* (1871) 7 Ch App 178 (where there was a joint and several promissory note)) as a member of two or more distinct firms, or as a sole contractor, and also as a member of a firm, proof might be made in respect of the contracts against the properties respectively liable on them, if there were in fact distinct properties (*Re Hooper, Banco de Portugal v Waddell* (1880) 5 App Cas 161, HL; and see *Re Somes, ex p De Lemos* (1896) 3 Mans 131), even though the firms were in whole or in part comprised of the same individuals, or the sole contractor was also one of the joint contractors. The provisions of the Bankruptcy Act 1914 Sch 2 r 19 (repealed), which abolished the former requirement that the creditor had to elect against which estate he would prove, is not re-enacted in the Insolvency Act 1986 or the Insolvency Rules 1986, SI 1986/1925. The creditor's election (see *Re Kent County Gas Light & Coke Co Ltd* [1913] 1 Ch 92) was not lost merely because he had proved and received dividend; he could change his election on refunding any dividend received with interest at 4%, but, on changing his election, he could not disturb any dividend already paid (*Re Collie, ex p Adamson* (1878) 8 ChD 807, CA).

The estate of a firm may be liable where all the partners have contracted, although not in the partnership name, and even though the liability contracted is not for partnership purposes: *Re Welch, ex p Stone* (1873) 8 Ch App 914; *Re Laine and Longman, ex p Berner and Neilson* (1886) 56 LJQB 153. Where trust money entrusted to a firm for investment has been converted by it, proof may be allowed against the firm's estate on its contract to invest or restore, and against that of one partner, who was trustee, on his contract to perform his trust: *Re Parkers, ex p Sheppard* (1887) 19 QBD 84; *Re Lake, ex p Howe Trustees* [1903] 1 KB 439.

513.   Foreign creditors. Ordinarily, a foreign creditor has a right of proof[1]; but, if, in proceedings for the administration of the bankrupt's property abroad, he has received any sum which would be divisible amongst the bankrupt's creditors generally, the sum must be brought into account before he may be allowed to prove in England[2].

1   Foreign revenue claims are in general not enforceable in an English bankruptcy: see PARA 515. As to cross-border insolvency see PARA 826 et seq.

2   *Re Douglas, ex p Wilson* (1872) 7 Ch App 490; *Re Hooper, Banco de Portugal v Waddell* (1880) 5 App Cas 161, HL. This only applies, however, to what he has obtained by process abroad; if, apart from such process, he is by foreign law a secured creditor, he may value his security and prove for the balance of his debt: *Re Somes, ex p De Lemos* (1896) 3 Mans 131; and see *Re Suidair International Airways Ltd* [1951] Ch 165, [1950] 2 All ER 920; *Cleaver v Delta American Reinsurance Co (in liquidation)* [2001] UKPC 6, [2001] 2 AC 328, [2001] 2 WLR 1202.

As to proof on a contract made abroad, when the remedy is there barred by non-registration, see PARA 514 text to note 4.

514.   Illegality or absence of consideration. Debts founded on an illegal consideration are not provable[1]; but, where the consideration was in part legal, proof in part has been allowed[2], and proof was allowed where a genuine debt existed, founded on an independent contract antecedent to such an illegal arrangement[3].

Proof may be allowed on a contract made abroad, even though, because of some defect, such as want of registration of the contract, no remedy lies on it abroad[4]; and a contract made with one of its members by an unregistered society requiring registration as a company[5] may give a right to prove where the member has recognised, acquiesced in and ratified the subsequent registration of the company[6].

1   *Ex p Thompson* (1746) 1 Atk 125; *Re Scott, ex p Bell* (1813) 1 M & S 751; *Re Aldebert & Co, ex p Schmaling* (1817) Buck 93; *Re Grazebrook, ex p Chavasse* (1865) 4 De GJ & Sm 655; and see the cases cited in note 2. As to the effect of the illegality on a contract see further CONTRACT vol 22 (2012) PARA 427 et seq.

2 _Ex p Mather_ (1797) 3 Ves 373; _Ex p Bulmer, Ex p Ellis_ (1807) 13 Ves 313. However, as to the effect of the consideration being partly illegal see _Kearney v Whitehaven Colliery Co_ [1893] 1 QB 700, CA; and CONTRACT vol 22 (2012) PARA 459.

3 _Re Guerrier, ex p Leslie_ (1882) 20 ChD 131, CA (debt founded on original transaction with a bank for an overdraft, not on the felony of forging bills deposited to secure it; proof allowed).

4 _Re Melbourn, ex p Melbourn_ (1870) 6 Ch App 64. See also _Thurburn v Steward_ (1871) LR 3 PC 478.

5 See COMPANIES vol 14 (2009) PARA 24 et seq.

6 _Re Thomas, ex p Poppleton_ (1884) 14 QBD 379.

515. Foreign revenue claims. Claims to prove in an English bankruptcy for debts due to a foreign State, or an agency of a foreign State, for tax or for debts analogous to taxes, such as social security contributions, are not admissible[1].

1 _Government of India, Ministry of Finance (Revenue Division) v Taylor_ [1955] AC 491, [1955] 1 All ER 292, HL; cf _Peter Buchanan Ltd and Macharg v McVey_ (1951) a decision of the Supreme Court of the Republic of Ireland, reported only at [1955] AC 516n at 530n; _Metal Industries (Salvage) Ltd v ST Harle (Owners)_ 1962 SLT 114, Ct of Sess; _Re Gibbons, ex p Walter_ [1960] Ir Jur Rep 60; and see _Brokaw v Seatrain UK Ltd_ [1971] 2 QB 476, [1971] 2 All ER 98, CA. See, however, _Re Islington Metal & Plating Works Ltd_ [1983] 3 All ER 218, [1984] 1 WLR 14; _Williams and Humbert Ltd v W & H Trade Marks (Jersey) Ltd_ [1986] AC 368, [1985] 2 All ER 208, HL; _Re State of Norway's Application_ [1987] QB 433, [1989] 1 All ER 661, CA. See also _Re Tucker_ [1988] Fin LR 323, IoM HC.

516. Agreement in fraud of other creditors. A right of proof may be affected or lost where the agreement is in effect a fraud on the other creditors[1]. Voluntary bonds entered into in good faith and in such circumstances as not to be a fraud on the creditors generally, are, however, provable equally with the other debts[2].

1 _Re Gomersall_ (1875) 1 ChD 137, CA; affd sub nom _Jones v Gordon_ (1877) 2 App Cas 616, HL (where bills for £1,727 drawn on the bankrupts by their agent were bought by A, who knew of the bankrupt's embarrassments, from a third party for £200, and A was not allowed to prove for more than £200). See also _Re Bentley, ex p Vere_ (1835) 2 Mont & A 123; _Hall v Dyson_ (1852) 17 QB 785; _Nerot v Wallace_ (1789) 3 Term Rep 17; _Murray v Reeves_ (1828) 8 B & C 421; _Kearley v Thomson_ (1890) 24 QBD 742, CA; _Re McHenry, McDermott v Boyd, Levita's Claim_ [1894] 3 Ch 365, CA (a case relating to annulment by consent under the Bankruptcy Act 1869 (repealed)); _Re Stewart, ex p Pottinger_ (1878) 8 ChD 621, CA; _Re Myers, ex p Myers_ [1908] 1 KB 941. See further PARA 528 note 1.

2 _Re Stewart, ex p Pottinger_ (1878) 8 ChD 621, CA; _Re Coates, ex p Scott_ (1892) 9 Morr 87.

517. Costs of legal proceedings. Costs awards in proceedings commenced before the bankruptcy order are provable debts whether the award of costs is made before or after the bankruptcy order, in the latter case being provable as contingent debts[1].

On a reference by consent to arbitration, the costs of the reference are provable, even though not awarded until after the bankruptcy order[2].

1 _Re Nortel GMBH (in admin); Re Lehman Brothers International (Europe) (in admin)_ [2013] UKSC 52, [2013] 3 WLR 504, [2013] All ER (D) 283 (Jul), overruling _Glenister v Rowe_ [2000] Ch 76, [1999] 3 All ER 452, CA, and earlier cases to contrary effect. As to contingent debts see PARA 510.

2 _Re Smith, ex p Edwards_ (1886) 3 Morr 179. See also _Re Pickering, ex p Harding_ (1854) 5 De GM & G 367.

518. Statute-barred debts. A debt barred by the Limitation Acts[1] is not provable[2]; but a creditor's rights in respect of any lien held by him may be enforceable, even though his debt is barred[3].

After the bankruptcy order, and during and for the purposes of the bankruptcy proceedings, time ceases to run in respect of provable debts[4]; but, where it has begun to run before the bankruptcy, it continues to run in respect of any rights to pursue any other remedies[5]. It appears that neither the insertion by the bankrupt of a debt in his statement of affairs[6], nor his answers at his examination[7], amounts to an acknowledgment sufficient to postpone the running of time for the purpose of proceedings apart from the bankruptcy. Nor can an acknowledgment of liability and a promise to pay the balance be inferred from a payment under a foreign sequestration[8]. A payment of a dividend in bankruptcy will not, it seems, amount to a part payment, so as to prevent the running of time in favour of the debtor[9].

1   See LIMITATION PERIODS vol 68 (2008) PARA 901 et seq.

2   *Ex p Dewdney, ex p Seaman* (1809) 15 Ves 479; *Re Dewdney, ex p Roffey* (1815) 2 Rose 245; *Re Coles, ex p Ross* (1827) 2 Gl & J 330; *Cotterell v Price* [1960] 3 All ER 315, [1960] 1 WLR 1097.

3   *Re Hepburn, ex p Smith* (1884) 14 QBD 394 at 400. See further LIMITATION PERIODS vol 68 (2008) PARA 942.

4   *Re Coles, ex p Ross* (1825) 2 Gl & J 46 (on appeal 2 Gl & J 330); *Re Westby, ex p Lancaster Banking Corpn* (1879) 10 ChD 776 at 784; *Re Crosley, Munns v Burn* (1887) 35 ChD 266, CA. See also *Re Stock, ex p Amos* (1896) 3 Mans 324 (where after the termination, by reason of the debtor's default, of a composition which had extended over several years, the creditors were held remitted to their rights); *Re Cullwick, ex p London Senior Official Receiver* [1918] 1 KB 646 (right of trustee in prior bankruptcy to prove in subsequent bankruptcy). The court may, however, refuse to admit proof of a debt, if the creditor's delay before proving inhibits a proper inquiry: *Re Tollemache, ex p Revell* (1884) 13 QBD 720, CA, applied in *Re Browne (a bankrupt) ex p Official Receiver v Thompson* [1960] 2 All ER 625, [1960] 1 WLR 692; *Re Tollemache, ex p Edwards* (1884) 14 QBD 415, CA.

5   *Re Benzon, Bower v Chetwynd* [1914] 2 Ch 68 at 75, 76, CA; *Cotterell v Price* [1960] 3 All ER 315, [1960] 1 WLR 1097; *Anglo Manx Bank Ltd v Aitkin* [2002] BPIR 215, [2001] All ER (D) 31 (Oct); cf *Financial Services Compensation Scheme Ltd v Larnell (Insurances) Ltd* [2005] EWCA Civ 1408, [2006] QB 808, [2006] 2 WLR 751 (a claim under the Third Parties (Rights Against Insurers) Act 1930). See further LIMITATION PERIODS vol 68 (2008) PARA 936.

6   *Everett v Robertson* (1858) 1 E & E 16; *Pott v Clegg* (1847) 16 M & W 321; *Courtenay v Williams* (1844) 3 Hare 539; affd 15 LJ Ch 204; approved in *McDonnell v Broderick* [1896] 2 IR 136 at 167; *Re Levey, ex p Topping* (1865) 4 De GJ & Sm 551 (scheduling of debt to deed of arrangement not sufficient to entitle creditor to prove in subsequent bankruptcy).

The decisions in *Everett v Robertson, Courtenay v Williams* and *Re Levey, ex p Topping* were on the ground that an acknowledgment in respect of a simple contract debt must import a promise to pay. Under the Limitation Act 1980 ss 29(5), 30, 31(6) an acknowledgment need no longer import a promise to pay. It seems, however, that *Everett v Robertson*, and cases decided on similar grounds, will still be good law, since a barred debt is not extinguished and a debtor's statement of affairs is a compulsory document which must contain a list of all his creditors and be submitted to the official receiver: see the Insolvency Act 1986 s 272 (debtor's petition: see PARA 163) and s 288 (creditor's petition: see PARA 240). The official receiver is not the agent of the creditor, and it would seem that, apart from any other considerations, the provisions of the Limitation Act 1980 s 30 as to 'acknowledgment' are not satisfied merely by the inclusion of a debt in a statement of affairs.

An admission of a debt in a deceased bankrupt's statement of affairs has been held not to be conclusive evidence of its existence for purposes of proof: *Re Tollemache, ex p Revell* (1884) 13 QBD 720, CA; *Re Tollemache, ex p Edwards* (1884) 14 QBD 415, CA; *Re Browne (a bankrupt), ex p Official Receiver v Thompson* [1960] 2 All ER 625, [1960] 1 WLR 692; cf *Smallcombe v Bruges* (1824) M'Cle 45. See further LIMITATION PERIODS.

7   *Taylor v Hollard* [1902] 1 KB 676; *Re Lee, ex p Grunwaldt* [1920] 2 KB 200.

8   *Courtenay v Williams* (1844) 3 Hare 539; affd 15 LJ Ch 204.

9   See *Davies v Edwards* (1851) 7 Exch 22 (dividend in insolvency paid to holder of promissory note held not to have preserved right of action on note); *Re Levey, ex p Topping* (1865) 4 De GJ & Sm 551 (payment of dividend under deed of arrangement held not to have preserved right of proof in subsequent bankruptcy); *Taylor v Hollard* [1902] 1 KB 676 (action on English judgment; right of action held not to have been preserved by payment to plaintiff by foreign sequestrators of defendant's estate in respect of foreign judgment on same matter). These cases were, however, decided on the principle that a promise to pay the remainder must be imported if

the part payment were to be effective; under the present statute such a promise need not be imported: see the Limitation Act 1980 ss 29(5), 30, 31(6); and the cases cited in note 6.

519. Annuities. An annuity is a contingent liability[1], the value of which may be estimated for proof. Thus, an estimate may be made of the value of an annuity defeasible on a woman's marrying again[2], or on a resumption of cohabitation by husband and wife, or on dissolution of marriage by any future act of either, or on the wife leading an unchaste life[3]. The following annuities have also been held to be capable of valuation and provable: an annuity to a wife in lieu of repayment by her husband of money lent by her for his business[4]; an annuity to a retiring partner, determinable on breach of covenant not to trade within a limited area[5]; an annuity payable during the continuance of certain works which might cease at any time[6]; and an annuity payable until the annuitant should do some act whereby the annuity, if belonging to him absolutely, would have become vested in another[7].

In estimating the value, all proper contingencies should be taken into account. Thus, a valuation which did not take into account a clause in a separation deed between husband and wife whereby the annuity should cease if cohabitation should be resumed, and a covenant indemnifying the husband against the wife's debts, would be incorrect[8]. However, a clause making an annuity cease on the resumption of cohabitation between two persons not husband and wife would be void, and could be disregarded in making the estimate[9].

If the annuitant should die after the receipt of a dividend, and the dividend is greater than the amount which the bankrupt would have had to pay had he remained solvent, the proof or dividend cannot be disturbed[10].

Where the annuitant dies before the proof has been dealt with, the value of the annuity will be taken to be the amount of the payments falling due up to the date of the death[11].

If arrears of the annuity are included in the assessment, and others besides the existing annuitant may become interested under the trusts of the annuity, the dividend must be apportioned by the trustees of the annuity, the portion representing arrears paid to the annuitant, and the balance invested in the purchase of a new annuity[12].

1   As to liability see *Greeves v Tofield* (1880) 14 ChD 563, CA (unregistered annuity charged on land valid against trustee in bankruptcy). See also the Insolvency Act 1986 s 382(3); and PARA 508.

2   *Re Blakemore, ex p Blakemore* (1877) 5 ChD 372, CA. As to the valuation of a tax-free annuity secured by the covenant of a deceased person see *Re Viscount Rothermere, Mellors, Basden & Co v Coutts & Co* [1945] Ch 72, [1944] 2 All ER 593 (value equal to sum required to purchase consols sufficient, by dividend and capital, to provide the gross annuity for normal expectation of life). As to annuities generally see REAL PROPERTY AND REGISTRATION vol 87 (2012) PARA 1104 et seq.

3   *Re Batey, ex p Neal* (1880) 14 ChD 579, CA; *Victor v Victor* [1912] 1 KB 247, CA; *McQuiban v McQuiban* [1913] P 208. Although after bankruptcy a wife cannot in these circumstances maintain an action on the covenant for the annuity (*Victor v Victor*; *McQuiban v McQuiban*), she was held not to be disabled from obtaining an order for maintenance under the Summary Jurisdiction (Separation and Maintenance) Acts 1895 to 1949 (repealed) (*Dewe v Dewe, Snowdon v Snowdon* [1928] P 113). See now the Domestic Proceedings and Magistrates' Courts Act 1978; and MATRIMONIAL AND CIVIL PARTNERSHIP LAW vol 73 (2009) PARA 553 et seq.

4   *Re Slade, Crewkerne United Breweries Ltd v Slade* [1921] 1 Ch 160.

5   *Re Jackson, ex p Jackson* (1872) 27 LT 696.

6   *Re Borron, ex p Parratt* (1836) 1 Deac 696.

7   *Re Sinclair, Allen v Sinclair, Hodgkins v Sinclair* [1897] 1 Ch 921.

8   *Re Grieves, ex p Pearce* (1879) 13 ChD 262 at 265, CA.

9	*Re Wood, ex p Naden* (1874) 9 Ch App 670; and see *Re Abdy, Rabbeth v Donaldson* [1895] 1 Ch 455, CA.

10	*Re Pannell, ex p Bates* (1879) 11 ChD 914, CA. Cf *Re Miller, ex p Wardley* (1877) 6 ChD 790 (where the bankrupt died before any dividend was paid).

11	*Re Dodds, ex p Vaughan's Executors* (1890) 25 QBD 529. See also *Re Bridges, Hill v Bridges* (1881) 17 ChD 342; *Re Northern Counties of England Fire Insurance Co, MacFarlane's Claim* (1880) 17 ChD 337.

12	*Re Beecham's Settlement, Johnson v Beecham* [1934] Ch 183.

**520.	Guarantees.**	When a guarantee limits a surety's liability to a fixed sum, the surety may be liable either to pay a limited sum towards the ultimate balance remaining due after all money obtainable from other sources has been applied in reducing the debt of the principal debtor or as surety for a part of the debt only[1]. In the former case the creditor has the right to prove against the debtor's estate for the whole of his debt until he has received 100 pence in the pound, notwithstanding that he has received some payment from the surety; and the surety has not, by reason of that payment, any right of proof in preference or priority to the creditor[2]. If, however, in such a case, the surety pays the whole debt, or if, being surety for a part of it only, he pays that part, then, as regards the amount so paid, he is subrogated to the rights of the creditor[3].

The creditor is not entitled to the benefit of a security obtained by the surety from the debtor, and so need have no regard to it in his proof[4].

1	*Gray v Seckham* (1872) 7 Ch App 680; *Hobson v Bass* (1871) 6 Ch App 792; *Ellis v Emmanuel* (1876) 1 ExD 157, CA; *Re Sass, ex p National Provincial Bank of England* [1896] 2 QB 12; *Re Butlers Wharf Ltd* [1995] 2 BCLC 43, [1995] BCC 717. As to the liabilities of a surety see FINANCIAL SERVICES AND INSTITUTIONS vol 49 (2008) PARA 1090 et seq.

2	*Re Sass, ex p National Provincial Bank of England* [1896] 2 QB 12, applied in *Ulster Bank Ltd v Lambe* [1966] NI 161; *Re Amalgamated Investment and Property Co Ltd* [1985] Ch 349, [1984] 3 All ER 272; *Re Polly Peck International plc (in administration)* [1996] 2 All ER 433, sub nom *Re Polly Peck International plc (in administration) (No 3)* [1996] 1 BCLC 428. It seems that this rule applies even where the surety's contract does not expressly provide that, as between him and the creditor, the creditor is to have the benefit of all dividends: *Re Sass, ex p National Provincial Bank of England.* As to waiver of a surety's rights in favour of the creditor see further FINANCIAL SERVICES AND INSTITUTIONS vol 49 (2008) PARA 1146. The position is the same even though the payment by the surety may have been made not out of his own money but out of the proceeds of a security given to him by the debtor: *Midland Banking Co v Chambers* (1869) 4 Ch App 398. See also *Re Fernandes, ex p Hope* (1844) 3 Mont D & De G 720; *Re Sellers, ex p Midland Banking Co* (1878) 38 LT 395; *Re Rees, ex p National Provincial Bank of England* (1881) 17 ChD 98, CA; and FINANCIAL SERVICES AND INSTITUTIONS vol 49 (2008) PARA 1148.

3	*Re Sass, ex p National Provincial Bank of England* [1896] 2 QB 12 (if the creditor has received the dividend on the amount so paid by the surety, he will hold it for the surety). See also *Mackinnon's Trustee v Bank of Scotland* 1915 SC 411, Ct of Sess (where a surety under a guarantee for payment of all sums up to a stated amount for which the debtor might become liable to the creditor paid the sum for which he was liable before the debtor's bankruptcy, and it was held that this payment went to reduce the debt for which the creditor could prove). Where, at the time of the guarantee of a current account with the bank, the debtor had already, to the bank's knowledge, but not to the surety's knowledge, committed an act of bankruptcy under the law in force prior to the Insolvency Act 1986 (the equivalent under the 1986 Act being knowledge of the presentation of a bankruptcy petition), the surety's payments were appropriated to such part of the creditor's debt as had been secured before the act of bankruptcy and was provable: *Re Mason, ex p Sharp* (1844) 3 Mont D & De G 490.

4	*Re Walker, Sheffield Banking Co v Clayton* [1892] 1 Ch 621; *Re Yewdall, ex p Barnfather* (1877) 46 LJ Bcy 87 (affd 46 LJ Bcy 109, CA).

**521.	Creditor's right of proof against surety.**	A creditor may prove against the estate of a bankrupt surety on his guarantee. He must, however, establish the surety's liability, and, in the absence of agreement, this cannot be done merely by showing that the debtor has admitted the debt, or that judgment for it has been signed against him[1]. The creditor must give credit for any amount which he has realised before proving, or for dividends which have been declared in the principal debtor's bankruptcy, even if not actually received[2]; but, where there are several sureties jointly and severally liable, the creditor is entitled to prove against the bankrupt surety's estate for the whole of the debt, without giving credit for any sums received from the other co-sureties since the date of the bankruptcy order, provided that he does not recover more than 100 pence in the pound in all[3].

Money deposited with the creditor by a co-surety, to be appropriated by the creditor when he thinks fit towards payment, so far as it will go, of the debt, need not be deducted when the creditor proves against the surety's estate before the appropriation[4].

1   *Re Kitchin, ex p Young* (1881) 17 ChD 668, CA. See also PARA 511.

2   *Re Blakeley, ex p Aachener Disconto Gesellschaft* (1892) 9 Morr 173. Cf *Re Bunyard, ex p Newton, ex p Griffin* (1880) 16 ChD 330, CA; *Re Firth, ex p Schofield* (1879) 12 ChD 337, CA; *Re Blackburne, ex p Strouts* (1892) 9 Morr 249.

3   *Re Houlder* [1929] 1 Ch 205.

4   *Commercial Bank of Australia Ltd v Wilson & Co's Estate Official Assignee* [1893] AC 181, PC.

522.   Surety's right of proof against principal debtor.   A surety cannot exercise a right of proof in the debtor's bankruptcy, so long as the principal creditor has not been paid in full in respect of the debt guaranteed and has himself proved or is entitled to prove[1]. He is, however, a person to whom an individual may give a preference which may be set aside or adjusted by the court on an application by the trustee of that individual when subsequently adjudged bankrupt[2]. Where a surety, party to a promissory note, pays the note at maturity, he is allowed to prove not only for the principal but also for interest from the date of payment to the date of the bankruptcy order[3].

No proof may be made by a surety for the cost of maintaining a security, where the principal debt has been extinguished[4].

1   *Re Fenton, ex p Fenton Textile Association Ltd* [1931] 1 Ch 85, CA (where the earlier decisions in *Re Parrott, ex p Whittaker* (1891) 8 Morr 49; *Re Paine, ex p Read* [1897] 1 QB 122; *Re Herepath and Delmar, ex p Delmar* (1890) 7 Morr 129 at 190; *Wolmershausen v Gullick* [1893] 2 Ch 514; *Re Blackpool Motor Car Co Ltd, Hamilton v Blackpool Motor Car Co Ltd* [1901] 1 Ch 77 were reviewed). See also *Re Fothergill, ex p Turquand* (1876) 3 ChD 445, CA; *Ex p Wildman* (1750) 1 Atk 109; *Ex p Marshal* (1752) 1 Atk 129; *Ex p Rushforth* (1805) 10 Ves 409 at 416. The difficulty is that there cannot be double proof in respect of the same debt (*Re Oriental Commercial Bank, ex p European Bank* (1871) 7 Ch App 99; *Re Fenton, ex p Fenton Textile Association* at 109; and see PARA 512), so that, if the principal creditor has not been paid off and proves, the surety's proof would not be effective: *Re A Debtor (No 66 of 1955), ex p Debtor v Trustee of Property of Waite (a bankrupt)* [1956] 3 All ER 225, [1956] 1 WLR 1226, CA. The rule against double proof takes priority and excludes the rule in *Cherry v Boultbee* (see PARA 573) whereby a person cannot share in a fund in relation to which he is a debtor without first paying his debt: *Re Kaupthing Singer and Friedlander Ltd (in admin)* [2011] UKSC 48, [2012] 1 AC 804, [2012] 1 All ER 883.

2   See the Insolvency Act 1986 s 340(3); and PARA 681.

3   *Re Evans, ex p Davies* (1897) 4 Mans 114; cf *Re Fox, Walker & Co, ex p Bishop* (1880) 15 ChD 400 at 415, CA.

4   *Re Moss, ex p Hallett* [1905] 2 KB 307. Proof has, however, been allowed against the estate of a person who guaranteed payment of interest on a company's debenture until the principal sum should be repaid, even though the company had gone into liquidation and had been dissolved: *Re Fitzgeorge, ex p Robson* [1905] 1 KB 462.

523. Surety's right of proof against co-sureties. A surety has a right of proof against a co-surety for a just proportion of the debt when he has paid the creditor's debt and taken an assignment of his securities[1]; and, even if he has not paid the creditor, and his liability has not been ascertained, he will have a right to a declaration that, when he has paid more than his due proportion, the co-surety must contribute, and in respect of that right he will be entitled to prove against the co-surety's estate[2].

1 *Re Clark, ex p Stokes and Goodman* (1848) De G 618; *Re Parker, Morgan v Hill* [1894] 3 Ch 400, CA. See also *Re Snowdon, ex p Snowdon* (1881) 17 ChD 44, CA.
2 *Wolmershausen v Gullick* [1893] 2 Ch 514. The Limitation Act 1980 will not run against the surety until his liability has been ascertained: *Wolmershausen v Gullick*. As to the effect of a compromise with the trustee in bankruptcy of one of several co-sureties see *Re Wolmershausen, Wolmershausen v Wolmershausen* (1890) 62 LT 541; cf *Re Armitage, ex p Good* (1877) 5 ChD 46, CA; *Re EWA* [1901] 2 KB 642, CA. See also *Re Tuchmann* [1960] CA Transcript 9A; and see FINANCIAL SERVICES AND INSTITUTIONS vol 49 (2008) PARA 1175.

524. Negotiable instruments. The 'bankruptcy rules' relating to cheques, bills of exchange and promissory notes apply, notwithstanding anything in the Bills of Exchange Act 1882[1]. Under those 'rules' a holder of a bill or note may proceed against the different parties liable until he has received 100 pence in the pound on it. Thus, if A discounts bills drawn by one firm on another, and both firms become bankrupt, A, holding the bill, is entitled to prove against both estates, and to receive all dividends he can until he receives 100 pence in the pound and interest, whether the drawer is surety for the acceptor or vice versa; for the surety cannot receive anything until the bill-holder is fully paid[2]. If, however, before proof, A has received any payment from any party or any estate liable on the bill, or if any dividend has been declared[3], he must, when proving, give credit for the amount of that payment or dividend[4].

If the drawer or indorsee of a bill is bankrupt, notice of dishonour may be given either to the party himself or to his trustee[5].

Proof may be made in the bankruptcy of the maker of a promissory note payable on demand, even though no demand has been made before the bankruptcy[6]. Proof may be made on a promissory note payable with interest at a fixed period after notice, even though no notice was given[7].

Unless the trustee allows, a proof in respect of money owed on a bill of exchange, promissory note, cheque or other negotiable instrument or security cannot be admitted unless there is produced the instrument or security itself or a copy of it, certified by the creditor or his authorised representative to be a true copy[8].

1 See the Bills of Exchange Act 1882 s 97(1); and FINANCIAL SERVICES AND INSTITUTIONS vol 49 (2008) PARA 847. In *Re Keever (a bankrupt), ex p Trustee of Property of Bankrupt v Midland Bank Ltd* [1967] Ch 182, [1966] 3 All ER 631, it was held that the Bills of Exchange Act 1882 s 97(1) refers not to the bankruptcy rules as such, but to bankruptcy law generally.
2 *Re Fothergill, ex p Turquand* (1876) 3 ChD 445, CA; and see PARA 522. See also *Ex p Wildman* (1750) 1 Atk 109; *Ex p Marshal* (1752) 1 Atk 129; *Ex p Rushforth* (1805) 10 Ves 409 at 416.
3 *Ex p Leers* (1802) 6 Ves 644; *Re Stein, ex p Royal Bank of Scotland* (1815) 2 Rose 197; *Re Watson, ex p Todd* (1815) 2 Rose 202n.
4 *Cooper v Pepys* (1741) 1 Atk 107; *Ex p Rushforth* (1805) 10 Ves 409; *Re Houghton, ex p Tayler* (1857) 1 De G & J 302.
5 See the Bills of Exchange Act 1882 s 49(10); and FINANCIAL SERVICES AND INSTITUTIONS vol 49 (2008) PARA 1530; cf *Re Bellman, ex p Baker* (1877) 4 ChD 795, CA. As to notice of dishonour generally see FINANCIAL SERVICES AND INSTITUTIONS vol 49 (2008) PARA 1524 et seq.
6 *Ex p Beaufoy* (1787) 1 Cooke's Bankrupt Laws (8th Edn) 180; *Re Mayor, ex p Whitworth* (1841) 2 Mont D & De G 158. Cf the Bills of Exchange Act 1882 s 87(1); and FINANCIAL SERVICES AND INSTITUTIONS vol 49 (2008) PARA 1520.

7   *Re Mantle, ex p Elgar* (1826) 2 Gl & J 1; *Re Dowman, ex p Dowman* (1827) 2 Gl & J 241;
    Clayton v Gosling (1826) 5 B & C 360, explained in *Re Browne and Wingrove, ex p Ador*
    [1891] 2 QB 574 at 579, CA. As to the amount payable on a future debt see PARA 613.
8   See the Insolvency Rules 1986, SI 1986/1925, r 6.108; and PARA 585.

525.   Debts secured by bills of larger amount.   Where bills have been given by
the bankrupt to a creditor for a debt, and the creditor still holds them at the date
of the bankruptcy order, he may prove only for the actual amount of the debt
remaining due, even though the amount of the bills is greater[1]; and the same is
true where the bills have been received by the creditor in pursuance of a
guarantee given to him by the bankrupt as surety for a debtor[2].

Where, however, there is no immediate contract between the creditor and the
surety, as where the debtor hands the creditor bills bearing the names of third
parties as collateral security for a debt less than the amount of the bills, the
creditor may prove in their bankruptcies for the full amount of the bills[3], though
he may not receive more than the amount actually due to him in respect of
principal[4] and interest accrued on it, whether before or after the bankruptcy
order[5].

1   *Ex p Bloxham* (1802) 6 Ves 600; *Re Willats, ex p Reader* (1819) Buck 381.
2   *Re Willats, ex p Reader* (1819) Buck 381.
3   *Ex p Bloxham* (1802) 6 Ves 600; *Re Willats, ex p Reader* (1819) Buck 381; *Re Corson, ex p De
    Tastet* (1810) 1 Rose 10. It is immaterial that the bills were accepted for the debtor's
    accommodation: *Re Bunyard, ex p Newton, ex p Griffin* (1880) 16 ChD 330, CA.
4   *Re Corson, ex p De Tastet* (1810) 1 Rose 10; *Re Firth, ex p Schofield* (1879) 12 ChD 337, CA.
5   *Re Fowler, ex p Martin* (1814) 2 Rose 87; *Re Peirson and Sammon, ex p Sammon* (1832) 1
    Deac & Ch 564; *Re Wood, ex p Fairlie, Bonham & Co* (1833) 3 Deac & Ch 285; *Re Caldwell,
    ex p Reed* (1833) 3 Deac & Ch 481; *Re Joint Stock Discount Co, Warrant Finance Co's Case*
    (1869) 5 Ch App 86.

526.   Payment of part of debt proved for.   A creditor with several separate
debts cannot, by means of his form of proof, obtain more than 100 pence in the
pound and interest[1], if any, on each of them. Thus, a creditor who has
discounted for the bankrupt several bills drawn by the bankrupt may not prove
for a bill that has been paid by the acceptor, though others remain unpaid, and a
proof made before payment will, after payment, be expunged, so far as it will
go[2]. Thus, where the bankrupt has indorsed bills to the creditor by way of
collateral security, and any of them has been paid in full by another party, the
creditor must deduct the amount so paid from his proof or refund the proper
amount from any dividend paid[3].

1   As to interest see the Insolvency Act 1986 s 322(2); and PARA 559.
2   *Re Cowell, ex p Barratt* (1823) 1 Gl & J 327, followed in *Re Morris, James v London and
    County Banking Co* [1899] 1 Ch 485, CA (where a bank, holder of four bills, two of which
    were drawn by A and accepted by B, and two drawn by C and accepted by D, and all indorsed
    by the debtor, was not entitled to apply the surplus over 100 pence in the pound received from
    various sources on the first two bills to meet a deficiency on the other two; this the bank
    attempted to do by consolidating its debts and securities).
3   *Re Moulson, ex p Burn* (1814) 2 Rose 55; *Re Bentley, ex p Brunskill* (1835) 4 Deac & Ch 442.
    See also *Re Cowell, ex p Barratt* (1823) 1 Gl & J 327; *Re Pritchard, ex p Hornby* (1844) De G
    69.

527.   Proof by pledgee of bill.   If a bill handed by the bankrupt to his creditor,
even though indorsed[1], was intended to be merely by way of deposit or pledge, it
appears that the creditor should, before proof, sell or value the bill[2]. Where a bill
is deposited by the acceptor with A, and A pledges it with B, the proof of B, who

has no general property in the bill against the acceptor's estate in bankruptcy, would depend on the state of the accounts between the acceptor and A[3].

1   The indorsement would prima facie indicate that it was intended to pass the property in the bill with full remedies against all parties: *Ex p Twogood* (1812) 19 Ves 229.
2   *Ex p Baldwin* (1799) cited in 19 Ves at 230; Insolvency Rules 1986, SI 1986/1925, r 6.109 (see PARA 575), r 6.115 (see PARA 576); and as to the redemption of security by the trustee see PARA 578. See also *Re Early and Smith, ex p Early's Executors* (1866) 14 LT 296.
3   *Re Claughton, ex p Britten* (1833) 3 Deac & Ch 35; *Re Barker, ex p Philipps* (1840) 1 Mont D & De G 232.

528. Purchase of bills of exchange. Where, in good faith, a person purchases bills, to which the debtor is a party, for less than their face value, proof may be made for the whole amount[1]. Proof is also allowed by a creditor who has made a fresh advance against bills given for that advance and for a debt provable in a former bankruptcy[2]. Discount need not be deducted in proving on a bill discounted[3].

1   *Ex p Lee* (1721) 1 P Wms 782; *Jones v Gordon* (1877) 2 App Cas 616 at 622, 631, 632, HL. It is otherwise where the purchaser knows that the bills were issued with the intention of defeating creditors in bankruptcy: *Jones v Gordon*; cf PARA 516 note 1; and see FINANCIAL SERVICES AND INSTITUTIONS.
2   *Re Aylmer, ex p Aylmer* (1894) 1 Mans 391; cf *Re Bonacina, Le Brasseur v Bonacina* [1912] 2 Ch 394, CA.
3   *Ex p Marlar* (1746) 1 Atk 150.

529. Accommodation bills. A person who puts his name on a bill for the accommodation of another stands in the position of a surety, and, if he takes up the bill, he may prove in the other's bankruptcy[1]. Where there is mutual accommodation paper and a bankruptcy of one party, the solvent party must, before proof, take up his own paper and so relieve the bankrupt's estate[2]. If both parties become bankrupt, there can be no proof on either side in respect of the accommodation paper, but, if there is a cash balance on either side, proof may be made for that[3]. If, however, after satisfying the holders of the bills, the estate ultimately indebted in the accommodation transactions has any surplus, proof may be made against it in respect of those transactions[4].

1   *Haigh v Jackson* (1838) 3 M & W 598. See also PARA 522; and *Re Oriental Commercial Bank, ex p European Bank* (1871) 7 Ch App 99; *Re Fothergill, ex p Turquand* (1876) 3 ChD 445, CA.
2   *Re Bowness and Padmore* (1789) 1 Cooke's Bankrupt Laws (8th Edn) 183; and see *Re Lynn, ex p Read* (1822) 1 Gl & J 224.
3   *Ex p Walker* (1798) 4 Ves 373; *Ex p Earle* (1800) 5 Ves 833.
4   *Ex p Rawson, ex p Lloyd* (1821) Jac 274; *Re Living, ex p Laforest, ex p Wetherell* (1833) 2 Deac & Ch 199. See also *Ex p Metcalfe* (1805) 11 Ves 404 (where, on a proof for cash balance, dividends were retained). Where, however, A, at the time of his bankruptcy, owed B a cash balance but had given him bills negotiated by B in respect of part of it, and the bills had been proved against A's estate, the proof of the trustee of B's estate was confined to the difference between the cash balance and the acceptances given in respect of it, although B had accepted bills for A on a consideration which failed, and these had also been negotiated and proved against B's estate: *Re Charles, ex p Macredie* (1873) 8 Ch App 535. See also *Re London, Bombay and Mediterranean Bank, ex p Cama* (1874) 9 Ch App 686.

530. Proof by bona fide holder of bill. Whether a bill is accepted for value or for the accommodation of the drawer, a bona fide holder for valuable consideration, to whom the bill has been transferred by the drawer as security for a debt less than the amount of the bill, may prove against the acceptor's estate for the whole amount of the bill, and receive dividends until he has received the whole debt[1].

If the bankrupt has accepted bills against a loan and given security, and the creditor discounts the bills, the security should be applied in taking up the bill so as to relieve the estate from proof by the holder[2].

1 *Re Bunyard, ex p Newton, ex p Griffin* (1880) 16 ChD 330, CA.
2 *Re Kattengell, ex p Mann* (1877) 5 ChD 367, CA. The creditor cannot so deal with his debt as to divide it into two debts, and, by so doing, evade the bankruptcy law as to security: *Baines v Wright* (1885) 16 QBD 330, CA.

531. Unindorsed bills. Where the creditor takes a bill for an existing debt without obtaining the debtor's indorsement, and the bill turns out to be worthless, the creditor may prove in the debtor's bankruptcy in respect of the debt; but, if there is no existing debt, and the bill is discounted without indorsement, this is a mere purchase of the bill, and there is no right of proof[1].

1 *Ex p Blackburne* (1804) 10 Ves 204 at 206. See also *Re Goodchild, ex p Hustler* (1821) 1 Gl & J 9.

532. Foreign bills. The drawer of a foreign bill of exchange accepted in England and dishonoured and protested may prove for damages in the nature of re-exchange against the acceptor's estate, whether he has paid these damages before the date of the bankruptcy order[1], or remains liable to pay them[2].

1 *Francis v Rucker* (1768) Amb 672; *Walker v Hamilton* (1860) 1 De GF & J 602; *Re General South American Co* (1877) 7 ChD 637.
2 *Re Gillespie, ex p Robarts* (1886) 18 QBD 286; and see *Re Commercial Bank of South Australia* (1887) 36 ChD 522. As to a bill dishonoured abroad see FINANCIAL SERVICES AND INSTITUTIONS.

533. Bill brokers. A bill broker who discounts bills for an acceptor and then rediscounts them with his bank may prove in the acceptor's bankruptcy for the amount paid to the bank, even though the broker has not indorsed the bills, but is liable to the bank by virtue of a general guarantee given to the bank in respect of all bills discounted with it[1].

1 *Re Fox, Walker & Co, ex p Bishop* (1880) 15 ChD 400, CA; and see FINANCIAL SERVICES AND INSTITUTIONS vol 49 (2008) PARA 1491.

534. Calls on shares. A company[1], or its liquidator in its name and on its behalf[2], may prove against a bankrupt's estate for the estimated value of the bankrupt's liability to future calls, as well as for calls already made[3].

If a contributory becomes bankrupt, either before or after he has been placed on the list of contributories, his trustee in bankruptcy represents him for all purposes of the winding up, and is a contributory accordingly[4]. The trustee may be called on to admit to proof against the bankrupt's estate, or otherwise allow to be paid out of the bankrupt's assets in due course of law, any money due from the bankrupt in respect of his liability to contribute to the company's assets[5].

Where a company under its articles of association has forfeited shares for non-payment of money due on allotment and for calls, and the articles provide that, notwithstanding forfeiture, the ex-shareholder is to be liable to pay all calls or other money owing on the shares at the time of the forfeiture, then, if the shares are subsequently sold and re-allotted to other persons at a loss, the company, on the subsequent bankruptcy of the ex-shareholder, is entitled to prove only for the actual loss suffered, that is, the difference between the amount received on the re-allotment of the forfeited shares and the amount due at the date of the forfeiture[6].

1 *Re Mercantile Mutual Marine Insurance Association* (1883) 25 ChD 415; *Re McMahon, Fuller v McMahon* [1900] 1 Ch 173.

2 See the Insolvency Act 1986 s 167(1)(b), Sch 4 para 8; and COMPANY AND PARTNERSHIP INSOLVENCY vol 16 (2011) PARA 527; COMPANY AND PARTNERSHIP INSOLVENCY vol 17 (2011) PARA 667.

3 See the Insolvency Act 1986 s 82(4); and COMPANY AND PARTNERSHIP INSOLVENCY vol 17 (2011) PARA 667. Where shares are disclaimed, proof may be allowed for the whole balance unpaid on them, deducting the value of anything accruing to the company by reason of the disclaimer: *Re Hallet, ex p National Insurance Co* (1894) 1 Mans 380. Where, however, the bankrupt is only under contract to take up shares, and this contract is disclaimed, proof is allowed only in respect of damages for this breach of contract: *Re Hooley, ex p United Ordnance and Engineering Co Ltd* [1899] 2 QB 579; and see PARA 505. As to proof in respect of non-delivery of goods see *Re Voss, ex p Llansamlet Tin Plate Co* (1873) LR 16 Eq 155.

    If the dividend is less than 100 pence in the pound, payment of it does not entitle the bankrupt's estate to rank as a fully-paid shareholder in the company's liquidation: *Re West Coast Gold Fields Ltd, Rowe's Trustee's Claim* [1906] 1 Ch 1, CA.

4 See the Insolvency Act 1986 s 82(1), (2); and COMPANY AND PARTNERSHIP INSOLVENCY vol 17 (2011) PARA 667.

5 See the Insolvency Act 1986 s 82(3); and COMPANY AND PARTNERSHIP INSOLVENCY vol 17 (2011) PARA 667.

6 *Re Bolton, ex p North British Artificial Silk Ltd* [1930] 2 Ch 48.

535. Rent. After the disclaimer of a lease[1], a landlord may prove for the loss or damage which he has sustained in consequence of the operation of the disclaimer, which is normally measured by reference to the difference between the rent and other payments which the landlord would have received in future but for the disclaimer and the rents and other payments which the disclaimer will enable him to receive by reletting[2].

The assignor of a lease holding a covenant of indemnity from the assignee may, on the assignee's bankruptcy, prove for a portion of the rent until the premises can be relet, for the loss, if any, in the letting value, and also for a sum in respect of dilapidations against which he has been indemnified[3].

In the case of rent and other payments of a periodical nature, the creditor may prove for any amounts due and unpaid up to the date of the bankruptcy order[4]. Where at that date any payment was accruing due, the creditor may prove for so much as would have fallen due at that date, if accruing from day to day[5].

Where a lease is existing and has not been disclaimed, the landlord cannot prove in the tenant's bankruptcy for rent which has not become due and payable[6].

1 As to disclaimer of leases by the trustee see PARA 490 et seq.

2 *Christopher Moran Holdings Ltd v Bairstow* [2000] 2 AC 172, sub nom *Re Park Air Services plc, Christopher Moran Holdings Ltd v Bairstow* [1999] 1 All ER 673, HL (as in the case of an award for wrongful termination of contract, allowance will be made for accelerated receipt of any sums which had not fallen due at the date of breach, and which the contract did not make immediately due and payable in the event of breach). As to the limitation of the amount recoverable for dilapidations see the Landlord and Tenant Act 1927 s 18(1); and PARA 505 note 2.

3 *Re Carruthers, ex p Tobit* (1895) 2 Mans 172.

4 See the Insolvency Rules 1986, SI 1986/1925, r 6.112(1); and PARA 558.

5 See the Insolvency Rules 1986, SI 1986/1925, r 6.112(2); and PARA 558.

6 *Christopher Moran Holdings Ltd v Bairstow* [2000] 2 AC 172, sub nom *Re Park Air Services plc, Christopher Moran Holdings Ltd v Bairstow* [1999] 1 All ER 673, HL. As to proof in the liquidation of a company see further COMPANY AND PARTNERSHIP INSOLVENCY vol 17 (2011) PARA 707 et seq.

536. Insurance money. Where premises are burned down and the tenant who is bound to reinstate them becomes bankrupt, proof may be allowed for the sum required to reinstate them, without deducting anything which the landlord has already received from an insurance company[1].

1   *Re Blackburne, ex p Strouts* (1892) 9 Morr 249. The creditor would presumably be a trustee for the insurance company of the dividends received on his proof, in circumstances where the insurance company would have had a subrogated claim against the tenant, now bankrupt: see INSURANCE vol 60 (2011) PARA 220.

537. Counsel's fees. A solicitor cannot pledge his client's credit to counsel, instructed on the client's behalf; counsel has, therefore, no right of proof for his fees, whether for litigious or non-litigious work, against the client's estate, even if the client has not paid them to the solicitor[1]. If the solicitor has received the fees and, not having paid them, becomes bankrupt, counsel would not, it seems, be entitled to prove for them[2]; but, if the fees are received by the trustee after bankruptcy, they should be paid to counsel[3]. If the trustee receives a lump sum from the client in settlement of the solicitor's whole bill of costs, it may be that a proportionate amount of it should be paid to counsel for his fees[4].

1   *Mostyn v Mostyn* (1870) 5 Ch App 457; *Rondel v Worsley* [1969] 1 AC 191, [1967] 3 All ER 993, HL.
2   *Wells v Wells* [1914] P 157 at 166, CA; *Re Sandiford (No 2), Italo-Canadian Corpn Ltd v Sandiford* [1935] Ch 681; both those decisions having been approved in *Rondel v Worsley* [1969] 1 AC 191, [1967] 3 All ER 993, HL: see eg at 279 and at 1031 per Lord Upjohn. It would seem, however, that, if counsel has entered into a contract with the solicitor concerning his fees, counsel should be entitled to prove for them.
3   *Re Hall* (1856) 2 Jur NS 1076; but this decision was doubted in *Wells v Wells* [1914] P 157, CA.
4   *Re Clift, ex p Colquhoun* (1890) 38 WR 688. It is not clear whether the trustee could agree to accept a lump sum from the client, excluding counsel's fees.

538. Proof by secured creditors. If a secured creditor[1] realises his security, he may prove for the balance of his debt, after deducting the amount realised[2]. If a secured creditor voluntarily surrenders his security for the general benefit of creditors, he may prove for his whole debt, as if it were unsecured[3].

If a secured creditor omits to disclose his security in his proof of debt, he must surrender his security for the general benefit of creditors, unless the court, on application by him, relieves him from the effect of this provision on the ground that the omission was inadvertent or the result of honest mistake[4]. If the court grants that relief, it may require or allow the creditor's proof of debt to be amended, on such terms as may be just[5].

1   As to the meaning of 'secured creditor' see PARA 574.
2   See the Insolvency Rules 1986, SI 1986/1925, r 6.109(1); and PARA 575.
3   See the Insolvency Rules 1986, SI 1986/1925, r 6.109(2); and PARA 575.
4   See the Insolvency Rules 1986, SI 1986/1925, r 6.116(1); and PARA 577.
5   See the Insolvency Rules 1986, SI 1986/1925, r 6.116(2); and PARA 577.

539. Executors. In general, one of several executors may prove on behalf of himself and the others[1]. If an executor refuses to make a proof, a residuary legatee or other person interested may be given permission to prove[2].

Where a sole executor becomes bankrupt, it seems that he cannot prove in his representative capacity against himself without a court order[3]. In such a case, a legatee may apply for permission to prove[4].

1   *Re Manning, ex p Smith and Anderdon* (1836) 1 Deac 385; *Re Wright, ex p Phillips* (1837) 2 Deac 334. See also *Re Davis, ex p Courtney* (1835) 2 Mont & A 227 (where one of two executors became bankrupt).
2   *Re Strahan, Paul and Bates, ex p Caldwell* (1865) 13 WR 952.

3 *Re Howard and Gibbs, ex p Shaw* (1822) 1 Gl & J 127; *Re Colman, ex p Colman* (1833) 2 Deac & Ch 584.

4 *Re Warne, ex p Moody* (1816) 2 Rose 413; *Re Boyes, ex p Beilby, Re Boyes, ex p Hall and Boyes* (1821) 1 Gl & J 167. Proof may be made in respect of a legacy against an executor who has received assets: *Walcott v Hall* (1788) 2 Bro CC 305; *Re Warne, ex p Moody* (1816) 2 Rose 413.

540.   Trustees and beneficiaries.   All trustees should, if possible, join in a proof[1].

Where one of two trustees who have committed a breach of trust becomes bankrupt, proof for the full amount of the trust money lost may be made against the bankrupt's estate, even though a sum by way of compromise has been received from the other trustee[2].

Where trustees have become bankrupt, the beneficiaries may themselves prove against the bankrupt estate with the permission of the court[3].

1 *Re Manning, ex p Smith and Anderdon* (1836) 2 Mont & A 536; *Re Wright, ex p Phillips* (1837) 2 Deac 334.

2 *Edwards v Hood-Barrs* [1905] 1 Ch 20. See also *Re Lake, ex p Howe Trustees* [1903] 1 KB 439 (where the beneficiaries' right of proof was affected by the compromise of an action without the permission of the trustee in bankruptcy of their trustee); *Re Macfadyen, ex p Vizianagaram Mining Co Ltd* [1908] 2 KB 817, CA (where a proof was allowed both against the joint estate of a firm and the separate estate of a defaulting trustee). As to remedies against trustees see *Re Ridgway, ex p Mein* (1886) 3 Morr 212; *Smith v Patrick* [1901] AC 282 at 295, HL. As to the trustee's liability for a breach of trust generally see TRUSTS vol 48 (2007 Reissue) PARA 1084 et seq.

3 *Re Bradley, ex p Walton* (1910) 54 Sol Jo 377.

541.   Other provable debts.   A release given to a debtor in a deed of arrangement which is afterwards superseded by a bankruptcy will not prevent proof in the bankruptcy, unless it is clear that it was intended that it should do so[1].

A creditor who has accounted to the trustee for money or goods received from the bankrupt by way of preference[2] may prove for his debt with the other creditors[3].

Where, on the true construction of a contract, a sum named to be paid for breach of contract is to be regarded as a penalty[4], proof will be allowed only for the actual damage sustained[5].

Proof may be made on an implied promise to indemnify[6].

In the absence of novation, a mortgagee cannot prove against the estate of the assignee of the equity of redemption for arrears of interest, even though the latter has paid some interest[7].

Commission for finding a purchaser is provable, even though the actual sale is not carried out until after bankruptcy[8]. If, however, according to the terms of the contract of agency, no commission is payable unless the property is sold[9], and the sale is completed by the trustee after the bankruptcy order, then it would seem that the trustee might be held to have adopted the contract with the agent, and the agent might be entitled to his commission in full from the trustee.

1 *Re Stephenson, ex p Official Receiver* (1888) 20 QBD 540, DC; and see *Re Clement, ex p Goas* (1886) 3 Morr 153, CA; *Re Stock, ex p Amos* (1896) 3 Mans 324. As to the effect of bankruptcy on an individual voluntary arrangement see PARA 89.

2 As to the avoidance of transactions on grounds of preference see PARA 678 et seq.

3 *Re Stephenson, ex p Official Receiver* (1888) 20 QBD 540. As to proof under a bankrupt's marriage settlement see *Re Tonnies, ex p Bishop* (1873) 8 Ch App 718; *Re Knight, ex p Cooper* (1885) 2 Morr 223. Cf *Re Cawley, Clancy v Munster and Leinster Bank Ltd* [1959] IR 330.

4 As to the criteria applicable in determining what is a penalty see *Bridge v Campbell Discount Co Ltd* [1962] AC 600, [1962] 1 All ER 385, HL; and DAMAGES vol 12(1) (Reissue) PARA 1065 et seq.

5 *Re Newman, ex p Capper* (1876) 4 ChD 724, CA. See the observations on that case in *Wallis v Smith* (1882) 21 ChD 243, CA, and on this latter case in *Willson v Love* [1896] 1 QB 626, CA; and see DAMAGES.

6 *Re Chappell, ex p Ford* (1885) 16 QBD 305, CA (mortgagee postponing his security at mortgagor's request).

7 *Re Errington, ex p Mason* [1894] 1 QB 11.

8 *Re Beale, ex p Durrant* (1888) 5 Morr 37.

9 As to the construction of provisions as to remuneration in contracts of agency see AGENCY vol 1 (2008) PARA 101 et seq.

542. Alien enemies. At common law[1], the alien enemy's right to recover a debt which would, but for the existence of a state of war, be provable in bankruptcy, is only suspended, and a claim, therefore, would be a future liability which the trustee would be bound to assess[2], retaining the money until the end of the war[3].

1 The provisions of the Trading with the Enemy (Insolvency) Order 1940, SR & O 1940/1419, art 1, which provided that enemy assets were to be transferred to a custodian appointed by the Board of Trade, were repealed by the Trading with the Enemy (Revocation) Order 2011, SI 2011/2923. See ARMED CONFLICT AND EMERGENCY vol 3 (2011) PARA 207.

2 See PARA 510.

3 *Ex p Boussmaker* (1806) 13 Ves 71 (where the court ordered that the claim be entered and the dividend be reserved); *Porter v Freudenberg* [1915] 1 KB 857 at 873, 874, CA; *Re Hilckes, ex p Muhesa Rubber Plantations Ltd* [1917] 1 KB 48 at 60, CA per Scrutton LJ. As to the test of whether a person or a corporate body is an enemy alien see ARMED CONFLICT AND EMERGENCY vol 3 (2011) PARA 195. An alien enemy cannot appeal, during hostilities, against the trustee's decision as to his proof: *Re Wilson and Wilson, ex p Marum* (1915) 84 LJKB 1893.

543. Consumer credit; extortionate credit transactions. Where a person is adjudged bankrupt who is or has been a party to a transaction for, or involving, the provision to him of credit, the court may, on the application of the trustee of the bankrupt's estate, make an order with respect to the transaction if the transaction is or was extortionate and was not entered into more than three years before the commencement of the bankruptcy[1].

1 See the Insolvency Act 1986 s 343(1), (2); and PARA 697 et seq.

(ii) Procedure for Proving

544. Meaning of 'prove'. A person claiming to be a creditor of the bankrupt and wishing to recover his debt in whole or in part must[1] submit his claim in writing to the official receiver, where acting as receiver and manager, or to the trustee[2]. The creditor is referred to as 'proving' for his debt; and the document by which he seeks to establish his claim is his 'proof'[3].

A proof must be in the form known as 'proof of debt', whether the form prescribed or a substantially similar form, which must be made out by or under the directions of the creditor, and authenticated by him or a person authorised in that behalf[4]. Where a debt is due to a minister of the Crown or a government department, the proof need not be in that form, provided that there are shown all such particulars of the debt as are required in the form used by other creditors, and as are relevant in the circumstances[5].

1 Ie subject to any order of the court under the Insolvency Rules 1986, SI 1986/1925, r 6.93(2): see PARA 286. For a case where proof was dispensed with in corporate insolvency see *Re Theo Garvin Ltd* [1969] 1 Ch 624, [1967] 3 All ER 497 (claims for interest on money accepted as deposit).

2 Insolvency Rules 1986, SI 1986/1925, r 6.96(1).
3 Insolvency Rules 1986, SI 1986/1925, r 6.96(2). As to the supply of forms see PARA 545; and as to the contents of a proof see PARA 546.
4 Insolvency Rules 1986, SI 1986/1925, r 6.96(3) (amended by SI 2010/686). For the prescribed form of proof of debt see the Insolvency Rules 1986, SI 1986/1925, Sch 4 Form 6.37 (substituted by SI 2004/584). As to authentication see PARA 158 note 2.
  Where an existing trustee proves in a later bankruptcy under the Insolvency Act 1986 s 335(5) (see PARA 618), the proof must be in the prescribed form: Insolvency Rules 1986, SI 1986/1925, r 6.96(5). For the prescribed form of proof by an existing trustee as a claim in a later bankruptcy see Sch 4 Form 6.38.
5 Insolvency Rules 1986, SI 1986/1925, r 6.96(4).

545. Supply of forms. A form of proof[1] must be sent to any creditor of the bankrupt by the official receiver or trustee where the creditor so requests[2].

1 See PARA 544.
2 Insolvency Rules 1986, SI 1986/1925, r 6.97 (substituted by SI 2004/584).

546. Contents of proof. The following matters must be stated in a creditor's proof of debt[1]:

(1) the creditor's name and address, and, if a company, its company registration number;

(2) the total amount of his claim (including any value added tax) as at the date of the bankruptcy order[2], less any deduction[3];

(3) whether or not that amount includes outstanding uncapitalised interest[4];

(4) particulars of how and when the debt was incurred by the debtor;

(5) particulars of any security held, the date when it was given and the value which the creditor puts upon it[5];

(6) details of any reservation of title in respect of goods to which the debt refers; and

(7) the name, and address and authority of the person authenticating the proof, if other than the creditor himself[6].

There must be specified in the proof any documents by reference to which the debt can be substantiated; but, subject to the following provision, it is not essential that such documents be attached to the proof or submitted with it[7].

The trustee, the official receiver, acting as receiver and manager or the chairman or convener of any meeting, may call for any document or other evidence to be produced to him, where he thinks it necessary for the purpose of substantiating the whole or any part of the claim made in the proof[8].

1 Ie subject to the Insolvency Rules 1986, SI 1986/1925, r 6.96(4) (debt due to a minister of the Crown or government department): see PARA 544.
2 As to bankruptcy orders see PARA 198 et seq.
3 Ie any deduction under the Insolvency Rules 1986, SI 1986/1925, r 6.110: see PARA 556.
4 As to the provisions relating to interest on debts see PARA 596.
5 As to secured creditors see PARA 574 et seq.
6 Insolvency Rules 1986, SI 1986/1925, r 6.98(1) (substituted by SI 2004/1070; and amended by SI 2010/686). For the prescribed form of proof of debt see the Insolvency Rules 1986, SI 1986/1925, Sch 4 Form 6.37 (substituted by SI 2004/584). As to authentication see PARA 158 note 2.
7 Insolvency Rules 1986, SI 1986/1925, r 6.98(2). If the claim is made under a negotiable instrument, a certified copy of the negotiable instrument must be produced, unless the trustee otherwise allows: see r 6.108; and PARA 585.
8 Insolvency Rules 1986, SI 1986/1925, r 6.98(3) (amended by SI 2004/584).

547. Cost of proving. Every creditor bears the cost of proving his own debt, including such as may be incurred in providing documents or evidence substantiating the claim made in the proof[1]; and costs incurred by the trustee in estimating the value of a bankruptcy debt not bearing a certain value[2] fall on the estate, as an expense of the bankruptcy[3].

The above provisions apply unless the court otherwise orders[4].

1 Insolvency Rules 1986, SI 1986/1925, r 6.100(1). As to providing such documents as evidence see r 6.98(3); and PARA 546.
2 Ie under the Insolvency Act 1986 s 322(3): see PARA 510.
3 Insolvency Rules 1986, SI 1986/1925, r 6.100(2).
4 Insolvency Rules 1986, SI 1986/1925, r 6.100(3).

548. Trustee to allow inspection of proofs. The trustee must, so long as proofs lodged with him are in his hands, allow them to be inspected, at all reasonable times on any business day[1], by any of the following persons:

(1) any creditor who has submitted his proof of debt, unless his proof has been wholly rejected for purposes of dividend or otherwise[2];

(2) the bankrupt; and

(3) any person acting on behalf of either of the above[3].

1 As to the meaning of 'business day' see PARA 28 note 8.
2 As to rejection of proofs for purposes of dividend see PARA 550.
3 Insolvency Rules 1986, SI 1986/1925, r 6.101.

549. Transmission of proofs to trustee. Where a trustee is appointed, the official receiver must as soon as reasonably practicable transmit to him all the proofs which he has so far received, together with an itemised list of them[1]. The trustee must authenticate the list by way of receipt for the proofs, and return it to the official receiver[2]. From then on, all proofs of debt must be sent to the trustee and retained by him[3].

If a new trustee is appointed in place of another, the former trustee must as soon as reasonably practicable transmit to the new one all proofs which the former trustee has received, together with an itemised list of them[4]. The new trustee must authenticate the list by way of receipt for the proofs, and return it to the former trustee[5]. From then on, all proofs of debt must be sent to and retained by the new trustee[6].

Where the trustee ceases to be in office as such, in consequence of removal, resignation or cesser of qualification as an insolvency practitioner, he is under obligation as soon as reasonably practicable to deliver up to the person succeeding him as trustee (inter alia) proofs of debt[7].

1 Insolvency Rules 1986, SI 1986/1925, r 6.103(1) (amended by SI 2009/942).
2 Insolvency Rules 1986, SI 1986/1925, r 6.103(2) (amended by SI 2010/686). As to authentication see PARA 158 note 2.
3 Insolvency Rules 1986, SI 1986/1925, r 6.103(3).
4 Insolvency Rules 1986, SI 1986/1925, r 6.103A(1) (added by SI 2010/686).
5 Insolvency Rules 1986, SI 1986/1925, r 6.103A(2) (added by SI 2010/686).
6 Insolvency Rules 1986, SI 1986/1925, r 6.103A(3) (added by SI 2010/686).
7 See the Insolvency Rules 1986, SI 1986/1925, r 6.146; and PARA 376.

550. Admission and rejection of proofs for dividend. A proof may be admitted for dividend either for the whole amount claimed by the creditor, or for part of that amount[1]. If the trustee rejects a proof in whole or in part, he must prepare a written statement of his reasons for doing so, and send it as soon as reasonably practicable to the creditor[2].

1 Insolvency Rules 1986, SI 1986/1925, r 6.104(1).

2   Insolvency Rules 1986, SI 1986/1925, r 6.104(2) (amended by SI 2009/642). Under the provisions of the Bankruptcy Act 1914 s 32, Sch 2 r 23 (repealed) the trustee had to examine every proof lodged with him and the grounds of the debt, even though the proof was based on a judgment, a covenant or an account stated: *Re Van Laun, ex p Chatterton* [1907] 2 KB 23, CA; *Re Lupkovics, ex p Trustee v Freville* [1954] 2 All ER 125, [1954] 1 WLR 1234; and see PARA 511 note 4. As to appeals against the trustee's decision on proof see PARA 551.

551. Appeal against decision on proof. If a creditor is dissatisfied with the trustee's decision with respect to his proof, including any decision on the question of preference[1], he may apply to the court for the decision to be reversed or varied; and the application[2] must be made within 21 days of his receiving the statement of reasons for rejecting the proof[3]. The bankrupt or any other creditor may, if dissatisfied with the trustee's decision admitting or rejecting the whole or any part of a proof, make such an application within 21 days of becoming aware of the trustee's decision[4].

Where any such application is made to the court, the court must fix a venue[5] for the application to be heard, notice of which must be sent by the applicant to the creditor who lodged the proof in question, if it is not himself, and to the trustee[6]. The trustee must, on receipt of the notice, file in court[7] the relevant proof, together, if appropriate, with a copy of the statement of reasons rejecting the proof[8]. After the application has been heard and determined, the proof must, unless it has been wholly disallowed, be returned by the court to the trustee[9]. The official receiver is not personally liable for costs incurred by any person in respect of any such application; and the trustee, if other than the official receiver, is not so liable, unless the court makes an order to that effect[10].

1   As to preferential creditors see PARA 591 et seq.
2   As to the mode of application and the procedure see PARA 786 et seq.
3   Insolvency Rules 1986, SI 1986/1925, r 6.105(1). As to the requirement that the trustee send a statement of reasons for rejecting the proof see r 6.104(2); and PARA 550.
4   Insolvency Rules 1986, SI 1986/1925, r 6.105(2).
5   As to the meaning of 'venue' see PARA 46 note 22.
6   Insolvency Rules 1986, SI 1986/1925, r 6.105(3).
7   As to the meaning of 'file in court' see PARA 57 note 13.
8   Insolvency Rules 1986, SI 1986/1925, r 6.105(4). The court will decide on the merits on the evidence before it; its function is not that of deciding merely whether the rejection was right or wrong on the evidence available to the trustee: *Re Kentwood Construction Ltd* [1960] 2 All ER 655n, [1960] 1 WLR 646; *Re Trepca Mines Ltd* [1960] 3 All ER 304n, [1960] 1 WLR 1273, CA (company cases).
9   Insolvency Rules 1986, SI 1986/1925, r 6.105(5).
10 Insolvency Rules 1986, SI 1986/1925, r 6.105(6).

552. Withdrawal or variation of proof. A creditor's proof may at any time, by agreement between himself and the trustee, be withdrawn or varied as to the amount claimed[1].

1   Insolvency Rules 1986, SI 1986/1925, r 6.106. As to appeals against the trustee's decision on proof see PARA 551. See also the Insolvency Act 1986 s 303(1); and PARA 342.

553. Expunging of proof by the court. The court may expunge a proof or reduce the amount claimed:

    (1)   on the trustee's application[1], where he thinks that the proof has been improperly admitted, or ought to be reduced; or

    (2)   on the application[2] of a creditor, if the trustee declines to interfere in the matter[3].

Where any such application is made to the court, the court must fix a venue[4] for the application to be heard, notice of which must be sent by the applicant:

    (a)   in the case of an application by the trustee, to the creditor who made the proof; and

    (b)   in the case of an application by a creditor, to the trustee and to the creditor who made the proof, if not himself[5].

Mere lapse of time does not bar the court's right to expunge or reduce a proof[6]. If a proof is expunged or reduced, a creditor may retain any dividend previously received[7]; but he is not entitled to receive any further dividend without giving credit for the overpayment in respect of his original proof[8].

The proof of a limited company, which is dissolved after the company has proved, should not be expunged; but the dividends after dissolution devolve on the Crown as bona vacantia[9], unless, it would seem, at the time of the dissolution there were unsatisfied debenture holders[10].

1   As to the mode of application and the procedure see PARA 786 et seq.
2   See note 1.
3   Insolvency Rules 1986, SI 1986/1925, r 6.107(1).
4   As to the meaning of 'venue' see PARA 46 note 22.
5   Insolvency Rules 1986, SI 1986/1925, r 6.107(2).
6   *Re Tait, ex p Harper* (1882) 21 ChD 537, CA. No time limit is prescribed by the Insolvency Rules 1986, SI 1986/1925.
7   See *Re Tait, ex p Harper* (1882) 21 ChD 537, CA.
8   *Re Searle, Hoare & Co* [1924] 2 Ch 325; and see *Re Pilling, ex p Ogle, ex p Smith* (1873) 8 Ch App 711; *Re Browne (a bankrupt), ex p Official Receiver v Thompson* [1960] 2 All ER 625, [1960] 1 WLR 692.
9   *Re Higginson and Dean, ex p A-G* [1899] 1 QB 325. The opinion expressed in the judgment given in this case at 332, relating to the necessity for a trust in order to enable the Crown to recover property as bona vacantia, was disapproved in *Re Wells, Swinburne-Hanham v Howard* [1933] Ch 29, CA.
10   *Gough's Garages Ltd v Pugsley* [1930] 1 KB 615.

(iii) Quantification of Claim

554. Estimate of quantum. The function of the trustee is to get in, realise and distribute the bankrupt's estate[1]; and, for this purpose, he must consider the proofs submitted and either admit or reject each proof in whole or in part[2]. The trustee must estimate the value of any bankruptcy debt which, by reason of its being subject to any contingency or contingencies or for any other reason, does not bear a certain value[3]. Where the value of a bankruptcy debt is so estimated by the trustee, or by the court[4], the amount provable in the bankruptcy in respect of the debt is the amount of the estimate[5].

1   See the Insolvency Act 1986 s 305(2); and PARA 473.
2   See the Insolvency Rules 1986, SI 1986/1925, r 6.104; and PARA 550.
3   Insolvency Act 1986 s 322(3); and see PARA 510. In quantifying a claim which is contingent as at the date of the bankruptcy order, events which have occurred between that date and the date it becomes necessary to value the claim will be taken into account: *Stein v Blake* [1996] AC 243 at 252, [1995] 2 All ER 961 at 964, 965, HL. As to the application of the Insolvency Act 1986 s 322 in the case of the administration in bankruptcy of the insolvent estate of a deceased person dying before the presentation of a bankruptcy petition see PARA 508 note 1.
4   Ie under the Insolvency Act 1986 s 303: see PARA 342.
5   Insolvency Act 1986 s 322(4).

555. Secured creditors. Particulars of any security held, the date when it was given and the value which the creditor puts on it must be stated in a creditor's proof of debt[1].

A secured creditor[2] may, with the agreement of the trustee or the permission of the court, at any time alter the value which he has, in his proof of debt, put on his security[3]. If, however, a secured creditor, being the petitioner, has in the petition put a value on his security, or has voted in respect of the unsecured balance of his debt, he may revalue his security only with the permission of the court[4]. If the trustee is dissatisfied with the value which a secured creditor puts on his security, he may require any property comprised in the security to be offered for sale[5]. The trustee may at any time give notice to a creditor whose debt is secured that he proposes, at the expiration of 28 days from the date of the notice, to redeem the security at the value put on it in the creditor's proof[6]. The creditor then has 21 days, or such longer period as the trustee may allow, in which, if he so wishes, to exercise his right to revalue his security; and, if the creditor so revalues his security, the trustee may only redeem at the new value[7]. If the trustee redeems the security, the cost of transferring it is borne by the estate[8]. If a creditor who has valued his security subsequently realises it, whether or not at the instance of the trustee, the net amount realised is to be substituted for the value previously put by the creditor on the security, and that amount is to be treated in all respects as an amended valuation made by him[9].

1 See the Insolvency Rules 1986, SI 1986/1925, r 6.98(1)(e); and PARA 546 head (5).
2 As to the meaning of 'secured creditor' see PARA 574.
3 Insolvency Rules 1986, SI 1986/1925, r 6.115(1) (amended by SI 2010/686).
4 Insolvency Rules 1986, SI 1986/1925, r 6.115(2) (amended by SI 2010/686).
5 See the Insolvency Rules 1986, SI 1986/1925, r 6.118; and PARA 579.
6 See the Insolvency Rules 1986, SI 1986/1925, r 6.117(1); and PARA 578.
7 See the Insolvency Rules 1986, SI 1986/1925, r 6.117(2); and PARA 578.
8 See the Insolvency Rules 1986, SI 1986/1925, r 6.117(3); and PARA 578.
9 See the Insolvency Rules 1986, SI 1986/1925, r 6.119; and PARA 580.

556. Trade and other discounts. There must in every case be deducted from the claim all trade and other discounts which would have been available to the bankrupt but for his bankruptcy, except any discount for immediate, early or cash settlement[1].

1 Insolvency Rules 1986, SI 1986/1925, r 6.110.

557. Debt in foreign currency. For the purpose of proving a debt incurred or payable in a currency other than sterling, the amount of the debt must be converted into sterling at the official exchange rate[1] prevailing on the date of the bankruptcy order[2].

1 For these purposes, 'the official exchange rate' is the middle exchange rate on the London Foreign Exchange Market at the close of business, as published for the date in question; and, in the absence of any such published rate, it is such rate as the court determines: Insolvency Rules 1986, SI 1986/1925, r 6.111(2) (amended by SI 2003/1730).
2 Insolvency Rules 1986, SI 1986/1925, r 6.111(1). Where the creditor is proving in respect of a claim for damages in tort in a foreign currency (see *Eleftherotria (Owners) v Despina R (Owners),The Despina R* [1979] AC 685, [1979] 1 All ER 421, HL), the bankrupt is deemed to become subject to such liability by reason of an obligation incurred at the time the cause of action accrued: see the Insolvency Act 1986 s 382(2); and PARA 508.

558. Payments of a periodical nature. In the case of rent and other payments of a periodical nature, the creditor may prove for any amounts due and unpaid up to the date of the bankruptcy order[1]. Where at that date any payment was accruing due, the creditor may prove for so much as would have fallen due at that date, if accruing from day to day[2].

1 Insolvency Rules 1986, SI 1986/1925, r 6.112(1). As to the position with regard to future rent or other payments of a periodical nature not presently due see PARA 535; cf PARA 560.

2 Insolvency Rules 1986, SI 1986/1925, r 6.112(2). As to liability for rent of a trustee who does not disclaim a lease see PARAS 424, 498; and as to distress for rent see PARA 711 et seq.

559. Proof for interest. Where a bankruptcy debt bears interest, that interest is provable as part of the debt, except in so far as it is payable in respect of any period after the commencement of the bankruptcy[1].

In the following circumstances the creditor's claim may include interest on the debt at the prescribed rate[2] for periods before the bankruptcy order, although not previously reserved or agreed[3]. If the debt is due by virtue of a written instrument, and payable at a certain time, interest may be claimed for the period from that time to the date of the bankruptcy order[4]. If the debt is due otherwise, interest may only be claimed if, before the presentation of the bankruptcy petition, a demand for payment was made in writing by or on behalf of the creditor, and notice given that interest would be payable from the date of the demand to the date of payment[5]. In that case, interest may only be claimed for the period from the date of the demand to that of the bankruptcy order[6]; and, for all the purposes of the Insolvency Act 1986 and the Insolvency Rules 1986, interest is chargeable at a rate not exceeding the prescribed rate[7].

1 Insolvency Act 1986 s 322(2). As to the payment of interest on debts proved in the bankruptcy see PARA 596; and as to the commencement of bankruptcy see PARA 209.
2 The rate of interest to be claimed is the rate specified in the Judgments Act 1838 s 17 (see FINANCIAL SERVICES AND INSTITUTIONS vol 49 (2008) PARA 1307) on the date of the bankruptcy order: Insolvency Rules 1986, SI 1986/1925, r 6.113(5) (added by SI 1987/1919).
3 Insolvency Rules 1986, SI 1986/1925, r 6.113(1).
4 Insolvency Rules 1986, SI 1986/1925, r 6.113(2).
5 Insolvency Rules 1986, SI 1986/1925, r 6.113(3) (amended by SI 1987/1919).
6 Insolvency Rules 1986, SI 1986/1925, r 6.113(4) (substituted by SI 1987/1919).
7 Insolvency Rules 1986, SI 1986/1925, r 6.113(3) (amended by SI 1987/1919).

560. Debt payable at future time. A creditor may prove for a debt of which payment was not yet due at the date of the bankruptcy order, but subject to the provisions[1] for the adjustment of dividends where payment is made before time[2].

1 Ie subject to the Insolvency Rules 1986, SI 1986/1925, r 11.13: see PARA 613.
2 Insolvency Rules 1986, SI 1986/1925, r 6.114.

(iv) Mutual Credit and Set-off

561. Right of set-off. Where before the commencement of the bankruptcy[1] there have been mutual credits[2], mutual debts[3] or other mutual dealings[4] between the bankrupt and any creditor of the bankrupt proving or claiming to prove for a bankruptcy debt[5], an account must be taken of what is due from each party to the other in respect of mutual dealings and the sums due from one party must be set off against the sums due from the other[6]. Only the balance, if any, of the account so taken is provable as a bankruptcy debt or, as the case may be, is to be paid to the trustee as part of the bankrupt's estate[7]. The claims on each side must be such as to result in pecuniary liabilities in respect of which the account may be taken[8]. The right is subject to the rule against double proof, and is not available in favour of a surety when the principal creditor's right of proof in respect of the debt guaranteed is still subsisting[9].

As a result of the operation of set-off, which is automatic and self-executing, mutual claims only remain in existence for the purpose of ascertaining a balance of account between them and the trustee in bankruptcy may, therefore, only validly assign any net balance owing to the insolvent estate on the taking of the account[10].

1   As to the commencement of bankruptcy see PARA 209.

2   'Mutual credits' arise when one or both parties to the transaction allow the other to pay the sums he owes at a future date or on the happening of an agreed event or contingency: *Re Prescot, ex p Prescot* (1753) 1 Atk 230; *Young v Bank of Bengal* (1836) 1 Moo PCC 150. Each credit must, however, be of such a nature that it will eventually become a debt, not eg a mere deposit of property: *Rose v Hart* (1818) 8 Taunt 499; *Rose v Sims* (1830) 1 B & Ad 521.

3   'Mutual debts' include debts which are contingent as at the date of the bankruptcy order: *Re West End Networks Ltd (in liquidation); Secretary of State for Trade and Industry v Frid* [2004] UKHL 24, [2004] 2 AC 506, [2004] 2 All ER 1042. As to contingent debts see PARA 510.

4   'Mutual dealings' is capable of wide interpretation and covers most transactions between the bankrupt and the other party which may give rise to rights or liabilities between them: see *Re Charge Card Services Ltd* [1987] Ch 150, [1986] 3 All ER 289 (affd [1989] Ch 497, [1988] 3 All ER 702, CA); and PARA 562 et seq.

5   As to the meaning of 'bankruptcy debt' see PARA 508. The right may be claimed by a person who is sued by the trustee in respect of a debt due to the estate: see *Peat v Jones & Co* (1881) 8 QBD 147, CA; *Jack v Kipping* (1882) 9 QBD 113, DC; *Re City Equitable Fire Insurance Co (No 2)* [1930] 2 Ch 293, CA.

6   Insolvency Act 1986 s 323(1), (2). Sums due from the bankrupt to another party may not be included in the account taken under s 323(2) if that other party had notice at the time they became due that a bankruptcy petition relating to the bankrupt was pending: s 323(3). The words 'at the time they became due' in s 323(3) refer to the time at which the obligation was created and not the time when payment should be made under that obligation: *Coe v Ashurst* [1999] BPIR 662. As from a day to be appointed, the Insolvency Act 1986 s 323(3) is amended by the Enterprise and Regulatory Reform Act 2013 s 71, Sch 19 paras 1, 27: see PARA 130 note 17.

     In the case of the administration in bankruptcy of the insolvent estate of a deceased person dying before the presentation of a bankruptcy petition, the Insolvency Act 1986 s 323 applies: Administration of Insolvent Estates of Deceased Persons Order 1986, SI 1986/1999, art 3(1), Sch 1 Pt II para 23. As to the administration in bankruptcy of the insolvent estates of deceased persons see further PARA 830 et seq.

7   Insolvency Act 1986 s 323(4).

8   *Rose v Hart* (1818) 8 Taunt 499; *Naoroji v Chartered Bank of India* (1868) LR 3 CP 444; *Eberle's Hotels and Restaurant Co Ltd v Jonas* (1887) 18 QBD 459, CA (claim in detinue for the return of specific goods deposited to secure a debt not mutual dealings); *Palmer v Day & Sons* [1895] 2 QB 618. It is not necessary that the pecuniary claims in question arise out of contract: *Re DH Curtis (Builders) Ltd* [1978] Ch 162, [1978] 2 All ER 183; *Re Cushla Ltd* [1979] 3 All ER 415, [1979] STC 615.

9   See PARA 522; *Re Fenton, ex p Fenton Textile Association* [1931] 1 Ch 85 at 112, CA; *Re A Debtor (No 66 of 1955), ex p Debtor v Trustee of Property of Waite (a bankrupt)* [1956] 2 All ER 94, [1956] 1 WLR 480 (affd [1956] 3 All ER 225, [1956] 1 WLR 1226, CA); *Re Glen Express Ltd* [2000] BPIR 456; *Re Kaupthing Singer and Friedlander Ltd (in admin)* [2011] UKSC 48, [2012] 1 AC 804, [2012] 1 All ER 883; and see PARA 565.

10   *Stein v Blake* [1996] AC 243, [1995] 2 All ER 961, HL (set-off estimated without the need for a proof to be lodged).

562. Application of set-off provisions mandatory. The right of set-off, and the obligation to set off[1], being prescribed by the Insolvency Act 1986 for the purposes of the administration of the bankrupt's property[2], cannot be excluded by the terms of any contract between the bankrupt and the other party, in their application to any transaction falling within the ambit of the 1986 Act[3]. A creditor and debtor may, however, agree to the contractual subordination of indebtedness between them, to take effect on the debtor's insolvency[4]. The set-off provisions in insolvency prevail over those of foreign jurisdictions[5].

1   See PARA 561.

2   The object of the mutual credit and set-off provisions is to do substantial justice between the parties where a debt is really due from the bankrupt to the debtor to his estate: *Forster v Wilson*

(1843) 12 M & W 191 at 203, 204 per Parke B. The effect of the provisions is to enable the creditor of the bankrupt who is also the bankrupt's debtor to recover his claim in full to the extent of the debt he owes to the bankrupt.

3   *National Westminster Bank Ltd v Halesowen Presswork and Assemblies Ltd* [1972] AC 785, [1972] 1 All ER 641, HL (set-off as between separate bank accounts), applying *Rolls Razor Ltd v Cox* [1967] 1 QB 552, [1967] 1 All ER 397, CA; in the first-cited case, earlier dicta on the point, such as in *Re Vaughan, ex p Fletcher* (1877) 6 ChD 350 at 356, CA; *British Guiana Bank v Official Receiver* (1911) 104 LT 754 at 755, PC; *Victoria Products Ltd v Tosh & Co Ltd* (1940) 165 LT 78, and *Re EJ Morel (1934) Ltd* [1962] Ch 21, [1962] 1 All ER 796, were discussed. See also *British Eagle International Airlines Ltd v Compagnie Nationale Air France* [1975] 2 All ER 390, [1975] 1 WLR 758, HL.

4   *Re Maxwell Communications Corpn plc (No 2)* [1994] 1 All ER 737, sub nom *Re Maxwell Communications Corpn plc* [1993] 1 WLR 1402.

5   *Re Bank of Credit and Commerce International SA (No 10)* [1997] Ch 213, [1996] 4 All ER 796. As to cross border insolvency see further PARA 826 et seq.

563.   Where right of set-off available.   Sums due from the bankrupt to another party may not be included in the account taken[1] if that other party had notice at the time they became due that a bankruptcy petition relating to the bankrupt was pending[2]. The benefit[3] of the statutory right of set-off[4] is, therefore, not allowed to any person to the extent that he gave credit to the debtor with knowledge that a bankruptcy petition had been presented, nor is the right available to a creditor who has given an undertaking not to prove[5].

Where the creditor enters into a transaction with the debtor without notice of the petition and there is a liability of the bankrupt at the date of his being made bankrupt, it is immaterial that the actual amount of the debt is not ascertained until afterwards[6].

This right of set-off takes its origin from the fact that bankruptcy jurisdiction is an equitable jurisdiction[7], and, therefore, as the court proceeds on equitable principles, an equitable debt may be set off against a legal debt[8].

A right of set-off may exist not only where two debts are due, but also where debts will not become due until a future date or are contingent, and where the claim on one side is for unliquidated damages, provided, in cases where the claim for unliquidated damages is in the hands of the creditor not the bankrupt, that it is provable in the bankruptcy[9]. It is not essential for the right of set-off to apply that the mutual debts, mutual credits or mutual dealings involved arise out of contract[10]. They must, however, be capable of forming the subject matter of an account[11]. There can, therefore, be no right of set-off where the claim on the one side is for the specific return of goods[12] or in respect of money or goods deposited for a specific purpose which has not been carried out[13], or of a balance of such money remaining when it has been carried out[14]. However, the right exists where there is a debt on one side and a delivery of property with directions to turn it into money on the other[15].

A right of set-off may not be introduced by contract between the parties where there is no mutuality[16].

1   Ie under the Insolvency Act 1986 s 323(2): see PARA 561.

2   Insolvency Act 1986 s 323(3). The exception in s 323(3) does not extend to a debt arising under a contract entered into before the presentation of a bankruptcy petition: *Coe v Ashurst* [1999] BPIR 662. As to the application of the Insolvency Act 1986 s 323 in the case of the administration in bankruptcy of the insolvent estate of a deceased person dying before the presentation of a bankruptcy petition see PARA 561 note 6.

3   See PARA 562 note 2.

4   See PARA 561.

5   *Kitchen's Trustee v Madders and Madders* [1950] Ch 134, [1949] 2 All ER 1079, CA; explained
     in *Bradley-Hole v Cusen* [1953] 1 QB 300, [1953] 2 WLR 193, sub nom *Hole v Cuzen* [1953]
     1 All ER 87, CA.

6   *Re Asphaltic Wood Pavement Co, Lee and Chapman's Case* (1885) 30 ChD 216, CA; *Re
     Daintrey, ex p Mant* [1900] 1 QB 546, CA; *Sovereign Life Assurance Co v Dodd* [1892] 1 QB
     405 (affd [1892] 2 QB 573, CA); *Re City Life Assurance Co Ltd, Grandfield's Case,
     Stephenson's Case* [1926] Ch 191, CA. In the last-cited case, it was stated that *Re Lankester,
     ex p Price* (1875) 10 Ch App 648 was inconsistent with the first-cited case, and, having regard
     also to subsequent changes in the statute law, was not to be treated as binding. See also *National
     Westminster Bank Ltd v Halesowen Presswork and Assemblies Ltd* [1972] AC 785, [1972]
     1 All ER 641, HL; *Re West End Networks Ltd (in liquidation), Secretary of State for Trade and
     Industry v Frid* [2004] UKHL 24, [2004] 2 AC 506, [2004] 2 All ER 1042. The result of the
     authorities is that it is not necessary that there should be mutual debts existing at the date of the
     bankruptcy order; it is sufficient if there are obligations the breach of which may give rise to a
     claim for damages provable in the bankruptcy. These principles are applicable to the claim of a
     mortgagor policy-holder, and the actuarial value of his policy may be set off against the
     mortgage debt (*Re National Benefit Assurance Co Ltd* [1924] 2 Ch 339; *Re City Life
     Assurance Co Ltd, Grandfield's Case, Stephenson's Case*), unless the insurance company, though
     without notice to the mortgagor, has equitably assigned the mortgage, in which case there is no
     longer a mutual debt: *Re City Life Assurance Co Ltd, Grandfield's Case, Stephenson's Case*. See
     also *Elgood v Harris* [1896] 2 QB 491; *Re Rushforth, ex p Holmes & Sons* (1906) 95 LT 807;
     Re HE Thorne & Son Ltd [1914] 2 Ch 438; and COMPANIES.

7   *Lister v Hooson* [1908] 1 KB 174 at 178, CA. For cases where equitable rights have been
     recognised in set-off see PARA 567 note 1.

8   *Mathieson's Trustee v Burrup, Mathieson & Co* [1927] 1 Ch 562. There is no right of set-off
     against the equity of exoneration: *Bateman v Williams* [2009] EWHC 1760 (Ch), [2009] BPIR
     973, [2009] All ER (D) 317 (Jul).

9   See *Re Prescot, ex p Prescot* (1753) 1 Atk 230; *Booth v Hutchinson* (1872) LR 15 Eq 30; *Peat
     v Jones & Co* (1881) 8 QBD 147, CA; *Jack v Kipping* (1882) 9 QBD 113, DC; *Re Mid-Kent
     Fruit Factory* [1896] 1 Ch 567; *Re Daintrey, ex p Mant* [1900] 1 QB 546, CA; *Re Rushforth,
     ex p Holmes & Sons* (1906) 95 LT 807; *Tilley v Bowman Ltd* [1910] 1 KB 745 (where a vendor
     was held entitled to set off damages caused by the bankrupt (ie a sum paid to a pawnbroker to
     redeem certain goods) against an amount paid on account of the purchase price); and see *Rolls
     Razor Ltd v Cox* [1967] 1 QB 552, [1967] 1 All ER 397, CA; *Re West End Networks Ltd (in
     liquidation), Secretary of State for Trade and Industry v Frid* [2004] UKHL 24, [2004] 2 AC
     506, [2004] 2 All ER 1042. As to debts provable in the bankruptcy see PARA 508.

10   *Re West End Networks Ltd (in liquidation), Secretary of State for Trade and Industry v Frid*
     [2004] UKHL 24, [2004] 2 AC 506, [2004] 2 All ER 1042; *Re DH Curtis (Builders) Ltd* [1978]
     Ch 162 at 170, [1978] 2 All ER 183 at 188 (where, after an extensive analysis of the authorities,
     Brightman J expressed the conviction that the dictum of Vaughan Williams J in *Re Mid-Kent
     Fruit Factory Ltd* [1896] 1 Ch 567 at 570 that the set-off provisions encompassed 'claims as
     well in respect of debts as of damages liquidated or unliquidated *provided they arise out of
     contract*' was wrong). *Re DH Curtis (Builders) Ltd* was followed in *Re Cushla Ltd* [1979]
     3 All ER 415, [1979] STC 615.

11   Ie for the purposes of the Insolvency Act 1986 s 323(2); and see PARA 561 text and note 8; and
     the cases cited.

12   *Re Robinson, ex p Flint* (1818) 1 Swan 30; *Key v Flint* (1817) 8 Taunt 21; *Rose v Hart* (1818)
     8 Taunt 499; *Re Winter, ex p Bolland* (1878) 8 ChD 225; *Eberle's Hotels and
     Restaurant Co Ltd v Jonas* (1887) 18 QBD 459, CA; *Lord's Trustee v Great Eastern Rly Co*
     [1908] 2 KB 54, CA (on appeal on another point sub nom *Great Eastern Rly Co v Lord's
     Trustee* [1909] AC 109, HL); *Ellis & Co's Trustee v Dixon-Johnson* [1925] AC 489, HL; *Rolls
     Razor Ltd v Cox* [1967] 1 QB 552, [1967] 1 All ER 397, CA; and see *Handley Page Ltd v
     Customs and Excise Comrs and Rockwell Machine Tool Co Ltd* [1970] 2 Lloyd's Rep 459; affd
     [1971] 2 Lloyd's Rep 298, CA.

13   *Buchanan v Findlay* (1829) 9 B & C 738; *Re Pollitt, ex p Minor* [1893] 1 QB 455, CA; *National
     Westminster Bank Ltd v Halesowen Presswork and Assemblies Ltd* [1972] AC 785, [1972]
     1 All ER 641, HL (where, at 808, 812 and at 651, 663, the cases on 'special purpose' are
     discussed; money is paid for a special or specific purpose so as to exclude mutuality of dealing
     within the Insolvency Act 1986 s 323 if the money is paid in such circumstances that it would be
     a misappropriation to use it for any other purpose than that for which it is paid).

14   *Re Mid-Kent Fruit Factory Ltd* [1896] 1 Ch 567; *Re City Equitable Fire Insurance Co (No 2)*
     [1930] 2 Ch 293, CA.

15 *Naoroji v Chartered Bank of India* (1868) LR 3 CP 444; *Astley v Gurney* (1869) LR 4 CP 714; *Palmer v Day & Sons* [1895] 2 QB 618, CA; *Rolls Razor Ltd v Cox* [1967] 1 QB 552, [1967] 1 All ER 397, CA.

16 *Re Bank of Credit and Commerce International SA (No 8)* [1998] AC 214, [1997] 4 All ER 568, HL.

564. Secured debts. A right of set-off may exist, even though one of the debts is secured[1], and even though the parties did not originally intend to have mutual dealings, as where a person has received, before the date of the bankruptcy order, and without notice of a bankruptcy petition presented against the bankrupt, a bill of exchange on which the bankrupt is liable[2], and, it would seem, even though proof of a debt is postponed by law[3]. Where, however, a creditor is secured for his debt and does not prove in the bankruptcy, a debt due from him to the insolvent estate cannot be set-off against that secured debt[4].

1 *Re Deveze, ex p Barnett* (1874) 9 Ch App 293; and see *McKinnon v Armstrong Bros & Co* (1877) 2 App Cas 531, HL.
2 *Alsager v Currie* (1844) 12 M & W 571. See also *Hankey v Smith* (1789) 3 Term Rep 507n; *Collins v Jones* (1830) 10 B & C 777; *Baker v Lloyds Bank Ltd* [1920] 2 KB 322.
3 *Re Lonergan, ex p Sheil* (1877) 4 ChD 789, CA.
4 *Re Norman Holding Co Ltd* [1990] 3 All ER 757, [1991] 1 WLR 10.

565. Rights determined at date of bankruptcy order. The mutual credits, mutual debts or other mutual dealings between the bankrupt and any creditor of the bankrupt proving or claiming to prove for a bankruptcy debt must have arisen before the commencement of the bankruptcy[1], even though by their nature they give rise to a future debt or obligation which may be so proved. A right of set-off not existing at the date of the bankruptcy order cannot generally be acquired afterwards[2].

A surety who, after the bankruptcy order, pays off the debt and takes over from the principal creditor his securities, including a bill of exchange on which the bankrupt is liable, may set off the amount of the bill against a debt due by himself to the estate[3]; and so, it seems, may a person who, since the date of the bankruptcy order, has been compelled to take up an acceptance of the bankrupt[4]. A surety who has not paid off the debt can set off his contingent liability as surety against sums due by him to the bankrupt[5].

1 See the Insolvency Act 1986 s 323(1); and PARA 561. As to the commencement of bankruptcy see PARA 209.
2 *Dickson v Evans* (1794) 6 Term Rep 57; *Re Milan Tramways Co, ex p Theys* (1884) 25 ChD 587, CA.
3 *Re Moseley Green Coal and Coke Co, Barrett's Case* (1865) 5 New Rep 496, distinguished in *Re A Debtor (No 66 of 1955), ex p Debtor v Trustee of the Property of Waite (a bankrupt)* [1956] 3 All ER 225, [1956] 1 WLR 1226, CA (cited in note 5).
4 Cf *Bolland v Nash* (1828) 8 B & C 105; *Collins v Jones* (1830) 10 B & C 777; *McKinnon v Armstrong Bros & Co* (1877) 2 App Cas 531, HL; and see *Handley Page Ltd v Customs and Excise Comrs and Rockwell Machine Tool Co Ltd* [1970] 2 Lloyd's Rep 459 (affd [1971] 2 Lloyd's Rep 298, CA).
5 *Re West End Networks Ltd (in liquidation), Secretary of State for Trade and Industry v Frid* [2004] UKHL 24, [2004] 2 AC 506, [2004] 2 All ER 1042, overruling *Re A Debtor (No 66 of 1955), ex p Debtor v Trustee of the Property of Waite (a bankrupt)* [1956] 3 All ER 225, [1956] 1 WLR 1226, CA.
      As to the rights of a person induced by fraud to become a surety see PARA 568; and as to the right to indemnity out of the debtor's share in the surety's estate see PARA 573.

566. Cases where set-off allowed. Set-off will be allowed between a debt due to one party and the amount of acceptances given to him by the other which are outstanding in the hands of third parties[1].

There may be set-off between factors and those who deal with them without any knowledge of principals[2].

A salesman in possession of money, the proceeds of sale of his employer's goods, or those goods still unsold, is in principle entitled to set off his unpaid commission against that money or those goods[3].

If a contributory of a company is bankrupt, debts due to him or to an assignee from him before his bankruptcy[4] may be set off against calls[5]; but there is no similar right of set-off in a contributory who is not bankrupt[6].

A residuary legatee may claim a set-off against the amount misappropriated by him as executor[7].

It is within the court's discretion to allow a debt due to a creditor to be set off against costs which the creditor has been ordered to pay in respect of a bankruptcy petition against the debtor[8].

The set-off rules are equally applicable to the administration of a deceased's estate in bankruptcy[9]; and this applies even where the amount due from the insolvent only ripened into a debt after the insolvent's death[10].

1 *Re Charles, ex p Macredie* (1873) 8 Ch App 535; *Re London, Bombay and Mediterranean Bank, ex p Cama* (1874) 9 Ch App 686. As to cross-accommodation acceptances where both parties are bankrupt see *Ex p Walker* (1798) 4 Ves 373; *Ex p Rawson, ex p Lloyd* (1821) Jac 274; *Re Living, ex p Laforest, ex p Wetherell* (1833) 2 Deac & Ch 199.

2 *Re Henley, ex p Dixon* (1876) 4 ChD 133, CA; cf *Cooke & Sons v Eshelby* (1887) 12 App Cas 271, HL; *Montagu v Forwood* [1893] 2 QB 350, CA.

3 *Rolls Razor Ltd v Cox* [1967] 1 QB 552, [1967] 1 All ER 397, CA.

4 *Re Universal Banking Corpn, ex p Strang* (1870) 5 Ch App 492.

5 *Re Duckworth* (1867) 2 Ch App 578; *Re Anglo-Greek Steam Navigation and Trading Co, Carralli and Haggard's Claim* (1869) 4 Ch App 174. Cf *Re GEB (a debtor)* [1903] 2 KB 340, CA. The grounds on which a bankrupt contributory's debts may be set off against calls for which he is liable do not apply where the contributory is a company in liquidation; eg, if two companies are in liquidation, one indebted to the other for money lent and the other indebted to the first company for calls, there can be no set-off (*Re Auriferous Properties Ltd* [1898] 1 Ch 691), and no dividend can be received on the debts until all calls have been paid up (*Re Auriferous Properties Ltd (No 2)* [1898] 2 Ch 428); and see COMPANY AND PARTNERSHIP INSOLVENCY vol 17 (2011) PARA 696. Cf *Re Peruvian Railway Construction Co Ltd* [1915] 2 Ch 144; affd [1915] 2 Ch 442, CA (claim by executors of insolvent shareholder indebted to company to share in surplus assets on winding up of company).

6 *Re Overend, Gurney & Co, Grissell's Case* (1864) 1 Ch App 528; *Re Hiram Maxim Lamp Co* [1903] 1 Ch 70.

7 *Re Chapman, ex p Parker* (1887) 4 Morr 109, DC. See also *Re Crosthwaite, ex p Turner* (1852) 2 De GM & G 927. Cf *Re Welch, ex p Stone* (1873) 8 Ch App 914.

8 *Re A Debtor (No 21 of 1950) (No 2), ex p Petitioning Creditors v Debtor* [1951] Ch 612, [1951] 1 All ER 600, DC. The decision in this case, applying *Reid v Cupper* [1915] 2 KB 147, CA and *Knight v Knight* [1925] Ch 835, CA, was based on the conclusion that earlier decisions, such as *Re Adams, ex p Griffin* (1880) 14 ChD 37, CA, *Re Bassett, ex p Lewis* [1896] 1 QB 219 and *Re Drummond, ex p Ashmore* [1909] 2 KB 622, are no longer authoritative as regards set-off against costs in bankruptcy proceedings, both by reason of the repeal of the earlier rules, and because the jurisdiction to allow or disallow such a set-off was essentially discretionary, and might be exercised, even where it adversely affected a solicitor's lien. See also *Young v Mead* [1917] 2 IR 258 (cited in *Re A Debtor (No 21 of 1950) (No 2), ex p Petitioning Creditors v Debtor* [1951] Ch 612, [1951] 1 All ER 600, DC).

9 See PARA 561 note 6.

10 *Watkins v Lindsay & Co* (1898) 5 Mans 25. As to the right of set-off in an administration in Chancery see *Re Smith, Green v Smith* (1883) 22 ChD 586; *Re Gedney, Smith v Grummitt* [1908] 1 Ch 804.

567. No set-off where debt assigned. The provision as to mutual credit applies only as between the bankrupt and a creditor[1], and, therefore, in general does not apply where the debt due to the bankrupt has been assigned by him before the bankruptcy order[2].

1   *Turner v Thomas* (1871) LR 6 CP 610. Equitable rights are recognised in set-off: *Forster v Wilson* (1843) 12 M & W 191; *Bailey v Finch* (1871) LR 7 QB 34; *Bailey v Johnson* (1872) LR 7 Exch 263; *Middleton v Pollock, ex p Nugee* (1875) LR 20 Eq 29; *Bankes v Jarvis* [1903] 1 KB 549; and see PARAS 561, 563. However, an allegation that the party claiming set-off has a beneficial interest in the debt is not enough. Set-off will not be permitted if that party cannot demonstrate his entitlement to a beneficial interest without further inquiry: *Bank of Credit and Commerce International SA (in liquidation) v Al Saud* [1997] 1 BCLC 457, [1997] BCC 63.

2   *De Mattos v Saunders* (1872) LR 7 CP 570; *Re Asphaltic Wood Pavement Co, Lee and Chapman's Case* (1885) 30 ChD 216, CA; *Re City Life Assurance Co Ltd, Grandfield's Case, Stephenson's Case* [1926] Ch 191, CA; cf *Re Pinto Leite & Nephews, ex p Visconde Des Olivaes* [1929] 1 Ch 221. For a case where, in a winding up, a debt acquired by assignment was held not to be available to be set off see *Re Eros Films Ltd* [1963] Ch 565, [1963] 1 All ER 383.

568.   Joint and separate debts.   In the absence of agreement, express or implied[1], there is no set-off between joint and separate debts[2]; but, if one joint debtor is a surety for the other, the principal debtor may set off against the joint debt a debt due to himself[3]; and a person induced to become surety by the creditor's fraud may set off his claim in respect of the fraud against the debt due by the principal debtor[4].

1   *Kinnerley v Hossack* (1809) 2 Taunt 170; *Tyso v Pettit* (1879) 40 LT 132.

2   *Ex p Twogood* (1805) 11 Ves 517; *New Quebrada Co v Carr* (1869) LR 4 CP 651. Cf *Slipper v Stidstone* (1794) 5 Term Rep 493; *French v Andrade* (1796) 6 Term Rep 582 (surviving partner).

3   *Ex p Hanson* (1806) 12 Ves 346; *Ex p Hanson* (1811) 18 Ves 232.

4   *Ex p Stephens* (1805) 11 Ves 24; and see *Ex p Hanson* (1806) 12 Ves 346 at 348; *Vulliamy v Noble* (1817) 3 Mer 593 at 621; *Middleton v Pollock, ex p Knight and Raymond* (1875) LR 20 Eq 515 at 519, 521.

569.   Debts due in different rights.   In order that debts may be set off, they must be due respectively in the same right[1]; and, therefore, debts due to or from executors personally cannot be set off against debts due from or to them in their capacity as executors[2], nor may debts due to or from a trustee in bankruptcy personally be set off against debts due from or to the bankrupt[3]. Where a creditor has received money since the bankruptcy which, on its receipt, belongs in equity to the trustee in bankruptcy, he cannot set off against it a debt due to him by the bankrupt[4].

Where the bankrupt gave funds to his solicitor for the costs of a specific purpose which was not carried out because of his bankruptcy, such funds could not be set off by the solicitor against a debt for costs incurred in other matters[5]. A creditor with a judgment debt against the bankrupt may set off his liability to repay money which he received as a preference[6] and which he has been ordered to repay[7].

1   See *National Westminster Bank Ltd v Halesowen Presswork and Assemblies Ltd* [1972] AC 785 at 821, 822, [1972] 1 All ER 641 at 663, 664, HL, per Lord Kilbrandon; *Lister v Hooson* [1908] 1 KB 174, CA. See also *Re A Debtor, ex p Peak Hill Goldfield Ltd* [1909] 1 KB 430, CA (where the bankrupt held debenture stock in the petitioning creditor company, and it was held that an essential change had been effected by the appointment of a receiver, so that thenceforward there were no mutual credits between the petitioning creditor and the debtor); *Re Jane, ex p Trustee* (1914) 110 LT 556, CA (where the relation between the bankrupt and joint debtors was severed).

2   *Bishop v Church* (1748) 3 Atk 691. See also *Re Willis Percival & Co, ex p Morier* (1879) 12 ChD 491, CA; *Middleton v Pollock, ex p Nugee* (1875) LR 20 Eq 29; and cf *Bailey v Finch* (1871) LR 7 QB 34.

3   *Lister v Hooson* [1908] 1 KB 174, CA; *Re Kirk, ex p Whitehead* (1821) 1 Gl & J 39; *West v Pryce* (1825) 2 Bing 455; *Groom v Mealey* (1835) 2 Bing NC 138; *Alloway v Steere* (1882) 10 QBD 22 (rent due before bankruptcy and value of tillages payable to trustee who carried on farm); *Kitchen's Trustee v Madders* [1950] Ch 134, [1949] 2 All ER 1079, CA (rent due to

trustee, and damages awarded against bankrupt), explained in *Bradley-Hole v Cusen* [1953] 1 QB 300, [1953] 1 All ER 87, CA, and applied in *Re A Debtor (No 66 of 1955), ex p Debtor v Trustee of the Property of Waite (a bankrupt)* [1956] 3 All ER 225, [1956] 1 WLR 1226, CA. Cf *Re Wilson, ex p Lord Hastings* (1893) 10 Morr 219 (custom of the country). See also *Re Morrish, ex p Hart Dyke* (1882) 22 ChD 410, CA.

4   *Elgood v Harris* [1896] 2 QB 491 (salvage received by insurance broker in respect of a loss paid by bankrupt underwriter).

5   *Re Pollitt, ex p Minor* [1893] 1 QB 455, CA; and see *Re British Folding Bed Co, ex p Trustee v NA Woodiwiss & Co* [1948] Ch 635, [1948] 2 All ER 216.

6   As to preferences see PARA 681 et seq.

7   *Re A Debtor (No 82 of 1926)* [1927] 1 Ch 410.

570.   Set-off by or against the Crown.   There is mutuality between the bankrupt and all departments of the Crown; accordingly one Crown department may set off against a debt owed by it to the bankrupt a debt owed by him to another Crown department[1].

1   *Re DH Curtis (Builders) Ltd* [1978] Ch 162, [1978] 2 All ER 183; *Re Cushla Ltd* [1979] 3 All ER 415, [1979] STC 615; *Re Unit 2 Windows Ltd* [1985] 3 All ER 415, [1985] 1 WLR 1383 (company cases); *R v Secretary of State for Social Security, ex p Taylor and Chapman* [1997] BPIR 505; *Mulvey v Secretary of State for Social Security* [1997] BPIR 696, HL. However, a fine imposed on the bankrupt for an offence is not a debt provable in bankruptcy (see PARA 508) and will not come within the set-off provisions of the Insolvency Act 1986 s 323.

571.   Set-off of contingent debts.   Debts which are wholly contingent at the date of the bankruptcy order, being debts provable in bankruptcy, are capable of set-off where they have resulted from mutual dealings[1].

1   *Re West End Networks Ltd (in liquidation), Secretary of State for Trade and Industry v Frid* [2004] UKHL 24, [2004] 2 AC 506, [2004] 2 All ER 1042. See also *Re Bank of Credit and Commerce International (No 8)* [1998] AC 214, [1997] 4 All ER 568, HL. As to contingent debts see PARA 510.

572.   Set-off where preferential and non-preferential debts.   Where a creditor has both a preferential claim and a non-preferential claim against the bankrupt's estate, and is owed a debt by the bankrupt at the commencement of the bankruptcy[1], the amount due to the creditor must be set off rateably against the non-preferential debt and the preferential debt, in proportion to the respective amounts of those debts[2].

1   As to the commencement of bankruptcy see PARA 209.

2   *Re Unit 2 Windows Ltd* [1985] 3 All ER 647, [1985] 1 WLR 1383 (company case). As to preferential debts see PARA 591 et seq.

573.   Rule in Cherry v Boultbee.   If a legatee becomes bankrupt after the testator's death and owes money to his estate, the trustee in bankruptcy is in no better position than the legatee[1]. This is not a case of set-off, as there are no mutual debts[2], nor of retainer[3]; the principle is that a person who owes money which would swell the mass of the deceased's estate is bound to make his contribution to the estate before taking a part share out of it, such as a share of the residuary estate[4]. The principle does not, therefore, prevent a legatee from taking a specific legacy before contributing to the general residuary estate[5]. It extends to the right of a deceased's estate to indemnity in respect of payments made as surety for the legatee[6].

If, however, the legatee becomes bankrupt before the testator's death, there is no right to withhold the bankrupt's share as beneficiary[7], except to the extent of any dividend declared or composition payable in the bankruptcy[8]. Where the testator has expressly directed that debts from the legatee should be deducted from his share in the estate, the personal representative should make the deduction, giving credit for any dividend received by the testator in his lifetime[9].

1　*Bousfield v Lawford* (1863) 1 De GJ & Sm 459; *Re Batchelor, Sloper v Oliver* (1873) LR 16 Eq 481; *Re Watson, Turner v Watson* [1896] 1 Ch 925.

2　*Courtenay v Williams* (1846) 15 LJ Ch 204.

3　*Re Akerman, Akerman v Akerman* [1891] 3 Ch 212 at 219.

4　*Cherry v Boultbee* (1839) 4 My & Cr 442 at 448; *Courtenay v Williams* (1846) 15 LJ Ch 204; *Re Akerman, Akerman v Akerman* [1891] 3 Ch 212. See also WILLS AND INTESTACY vol 103 (2010) PARAS 1066, 1067.

5　*Re Akerman, Akerman v Akerman* [1891] 3 Ch 212. For a case where a legacy was held not to be specific see *Re Richardson, ex p Thompson v Hutton* (1902) 86 LT 25.

6　*Re Watson, Turner v Watson* [1896] 1 Ch 925; *Re Melton, Milk v Towers* [1918] 1 Ch 37, CA (overruling *Re Binns, Lee v Binns* [1896] 2 Ch 584). The application of the principle is subject to and excluded by the rule against double proof (see PARA 512): *Re Kaupthing Singer and Friedlander Ltd (in admin)* [2011] UKSC 48, [2012] 1 AC 804, [2012] 1 All ER 883. Where an annuitant creditor proved in the bankruptcy of the legatee who was the principal debtor, and the liability in respect of the annuity was thereby quantified, the surety's personal representatives were entitled to obtain indemnity out of the legatee's interest in the deceased surety's estate to the extent of the creditor's proof, less the dividends paid to the creditor: *Re Lennard, Lennard's Trustee v Lennard* [1934] Ch 235.

7　*Cherry v Boultbee* (1839) 4 My & Cr 442; *Re Hodgson, Hodgson v Fox* (1878) 9 ChD 673; *Re Rees, Rees v Rees* (1889) 60 LT 260. See also *Re Pink, Pink v Pink* [1912] 1 Ch 498; affd [1912] 2 Ch 528, CA.

8　*Cherry v Boultbee* (1839) 4 My & Cr 442 at 448; *Re Orpen, Beswick v Orpen* (1880) 16 ChD 202; cf *Re Peruvian Railway Construction Co Ltd* [1915] 2 Ch 442, CA.

9　*Re Ainsworth, Millington v Ainsworth* [1922] 1 Ch 22.

(v)　Secured Creditors

574.　Meaning of 'secured creditor'. 'Creditor':

(1)　in relation to a bankrupt, means a person to whom any of the bankruptcy debts[1] is owed; and

(2)　in relation to an individual to whom a bankruptcy petition relates, means a person who would be a creditor in the bankruptcy if a bankruptcy order were made on that petition[2].

A debt is secured[3] for the purposes of the Insolvency Act 1986[4] to the extent that the person to whom the debt is owed holds any security[5] for the debt, whether a mortgage, charge, lien or other security, over any property of the person by whom the debt is owed[6].

1　As to the meaning of 'bankruptcy debt' see PARA 508.

2　Insolvency Act 1986 s 383(1)(a), (b). In the case of an amount falling within s 382(1)(c) (see PARA 508 note 7), 'person to whom any of the bankruptcy debts is owed' means the person in respect of whom that amount is specified in the criminal bankruptcy order in question: s 383(1)(a). As to the prospective repeal of s 383(1)(a) (in part) see PARA 1 note 11. As from a day to be appointed, s 383(1)(b) is amended by the Enterprise and Regulatory Reform Act 2013 s 71, Sch 19 paras 1, 53: see PARA 130 note 17.

　　In the case of the administration in bankruptcy of the insolvent estate of a deceased person dying before the presentation of a bankruptcy petition, the Insolvency Act 1986 s 383 applies: Administration of Insolvent Estates of Deceased Persons Order 1986, SI 1986/1999, art 3(1), Sch 1 Pt II para 32. As to the administration in bankruptcy of the insolvent estates of deceased persons see further PARA 830 et seq.

3　Ie subject to the Insolvency Act 1986 s 383(3), (4) and any provision of the Insolvency Rules 1986, SI 1986/1925, requiring a creditor to give up his security for the purposes of proving a debt (see rr 6.116, 6.117; and PARAS 577, 578 respectively). Where a statement such as is mentioned in the Insolvency Act 1986 s 269(1)(a) (see PARA 156 head (1)) has been made by a secured creditor for the purposes of any bankruptcy petition and a bankruptcy order is subsequently made on that petition, the creditor is deemed for the purposes of Pts 7A–11 (ss 251A–385) to have given up the security specified in the statement: s 383(3).

'Secured' and related expressions are to be construed in accordance with s 383: s 385(1). As to the application of s 385 in the case of the administration in bankruptcy of the insolvent estate of a deceased person dying before the presentation of a bankruptcy petition see PARA 6 note 8.

4   Ie for the purposes of the Insolvency Act 1986 Pts 7A–11.

5   For these purposes, the reference to a security does not include a lien on books, papers or other records, except to the extent that they consist of documents which give a title to property and are held as such: Insolvency Act 1986 s 383(4). As to a banker's lien see *Re Keever (a bankrupt), ex p Trustee of the Property of the Bankrupt v Midland Bank Ltd* [1967] Ch 182, [1966] 3 All ER 631.

6   Insolvency Act 1986 s 383(2).

575.   Proof by secured creditors.   If a secured creditor[1] realises his security, he may prove for the balance of his debt, after deducting the amount realised[2]. He may appropriate the proceeds of realisation as he thinks fit between the claims which are provable and not provable, or between preferential and non-preferential claims in the bankruptcy[3]. The net profit of the realisation may not be applied to interest accrued after the date of the bankruptcy order[4]; but profits made from an unrealised security may be so applied[5]. A creditor who holds several securities in respect of different debts must apply the proceeds of each security to its particular debt, and the surplus funds of one security may not be applied to make good the deficiency of another[6].

If a secured creditor voluntarily surrenders his security for the general benefit of creditors, he may prove for the whole debt, as if it were unsecured[7].

1   As to the meaning of 'secured creditor' see PARA 574.

2   Insolvency Rules 1986, SI 1986/1925, r 6.109(1). As to the position where a creditor values his security for the purposes of proof and subsequently realises his security see PARA 580.

3   *Ex p Hunter* (1801) 6 Ves 94; *Re Fox and Jacobs, ex p Discount Banking Co of England and Wales* [1894] 1 QB 438. See also *Re Foster, ex p Dickin* (1875) LR 20 Eq 767 (where a creditor held security on the property of A for debts owed by both A and the joint estate of A and B; in the subsequent insolvencies the creditor was entitled to apply the proceeds of the realisation of the security between his joint and separate debts in whatever way was most for his advantage and, to enable him to secure this option, he was entitled to apply to the court to have a dividend on the joint estate declared before the declaration of a dividend on the separate estates).

4   *Re Bulmer, ex p Johnson* (1853) 3 De GM & G 218; *Re William Hall (Contractors) Ltd* [1967] 2 All ER 1150, [1967] 1 WLR 948.

5   *Quartermaine's Case* [1892] 1 Ch 639; *Re Savin* (1872) 7 Ch App 760.

6   *Re Newton, ex p Bignold* (1836) 2 Deac 66.

7   Insolvency Rules 1986, SI 1986/1925, r 6.109(2). As to the position of a secured creditor who issues a bankruptcy petition containing a statement that he is willing to give up his security for the benefit of all the bankrupt's creditors see the Insolvency Act 1986 s 269(1)(a); and PARA 156 head (1). The surrender of the security does not discharge a surety: *Rainbow v Juggins* (1880) 5 QBD 422, CA. The surrender by a first mortgagee of his security puts the trustee in his place, and does not accelerate the rights of subsequent mortgagees: *Cracknall v Janson* (1877) 6 ChD 735. Cf, however, *Moor v Anglo-Italian Bank* (1879) 10 ChD 681 at 690. See also *Bell v Sunderland Building Society* (1883) 24 ChD 618; *Re Pidcock, Penny v Pidcock* (1907) 51 Sol Jo 514; *C & W Berry Ltd v Armstrong-Moakes* [2007] EWHC 2101 (QB), [2008] 1 P & CR D2, [2007] All ER (D) 82 (Sep).

576.   Value of security.   A secured creditor[1] may, with the agreement of the trustee or the permission of the court, at any time alter the value which he has, in his proof of debt, put on his security[2]. If, however, a secured creditor, being the petitioner, has in the petition put a value on his security, or has voted[3] in respect of the unsecured balance of his debt, he may revalue his security only with permission of the court[4].

1   As to the meaning of 'secured creditor' see PARA 574.

2   Insolvency Rules 1986, SI 1986/1925, r 6.115(1) (amended by SI 2010/686). Particulars of any security held, the date when it was given and the value which the creditor puts on it must be stated in a creditor's proof of debt: see r 6.98(1)(e); and PARA 546 head (5).
3   As to voting by a secured creditor see PARA 286.
4   Insolvency Rules 1986, SI 1986/1925, r 6.115(2) (amended by SI 2010/686). As to the mode of application and the procedure see PARA 786 et seq; and as to dividends payable to a secured creditor who revalues his security see PARA 610.

577.   Surrender for non-disclosure. If a secured creditor[1] omits to disclose his security in his proof of debt, he must surrender his security for the general benefit of creditors, unless the court, on application[2] by him, relieves him from the effect of this provision, on the ground that the omission was inadvertent or the result of honest mistake[3]. If the court grants that relief, it may require or allow the creditor's proof of debt to be amended, on such terms as may be just[4].

1   As to the meaning of 'secured creditor' see PARA 574.
2   As to the mode of application and the procedure see PARA 786 et seq.
3   Insolvency Rules 1986, SI 1986/1925, r 6.116(1); and see *Re Henry Lister & Co Ltd* [1892] 2 Ch 417. Inadvertence covers a case where the omission is accidental, but not where the omission was made deliberately and on purpose: *Re Burr, ex p Clarke* (1892) 67 LT 232; *Re Safety Explosives Ltd* [1904] 1 Ch 226, CA; *Re Rowe, ex p West Coast Gold Fields Ltd* [1904] 2 KB 489.
4   Insolvency Rules 1986, SI 1986/1925, r 6.116(2). Nothing in r 6.116 affects the rights in rem of creditors or third parties protected under Council Regulation (EC) 1346/2000 on insolvency proceedings (OJ L160, 30.06.00, p 1) ('European Regulation on Insolvency Proceedings') art 5 (third parties' rights in rem) (see PARAS 41, 42): Insolvency Rules 1986, SI 1986/1925, r 6.116(3) (added by SI 2002/1307).

578.   Redemption by trustee. The trustee may at any time give notice to a creditor whose debt is secured[1] that he proposes, at the expiration of 28 days from the date of the notice, to redeem the security at the value put on it in the creditor's proof[2]. The creditor then has 21 days, or such longer period as the trustee may allow, in which, if he so wishes, to exercise his right to revalue his security, with the permission of the court where this is required[3]; and, if the creditor revalues his security, the trustee may only redeem at the new value[4]. If the trustee redeems the security, the cost of transferring it is borne by the estate[5].

A secured creditor may at any time, by a notice in writing, call on the trustee to elect whether he will or will not exercise his power to redeem the security at the value then placed on it; and the trustee then has three months in which to exercise the power or determine not to exercise it[6].

1   As to the meaning of 'secured creditor' see PARA 574.
2   Insolvency Rules 1986, SI 1986/1925, r 6.117(1). Nothing in r 6.117 affects the rights in rem of creditors or third parties protected under Council Regulation (EC) 1346/2000 on insolvency proceedings (OJ L160, 30.06.00, p 1) ('European Regulation on Insolvency Proceedings') art 5 (third parties' rights in rem) (see PARAS 41, 42): Insolvency Rules 1986, SI 1986/1925, r 6.116(3) (added by SI 2002/1307).
3   Ie where the Insolvency Rules 1986, SI 1986/1925, r 6.115(2) applies: see PARA 576.
4   Insolvency Rules 1986, SI 1986/1925, r 6.117(2) (amended by SI 2010/686).
5   Insolvency Rules 1986, SI 1986/1925, r 6.117(3).
6   Insolvency Rules 1986, SI 1986/1925, r 6.117(4) (amended by SI 2010/686).

579.   Test of security's value. If he is dissatisfied with the value which a secured creditor[1] puts on his security, whether in his proof or by way of revaluation[2], the trustee may require any property comprised in the security to be offered for sale[3]. The terms of sale must be such as may be agreed, or as the court may direct; and, if the sale is by auction, the trustee on behalf of the estate, and the creditor on his own behalf, may appear and bid[4].

The above provisions do not, however, apply if the security has been revalued and the revaluation has been approved by the court[5].

1   As to the meaning of 'secured creditor' see PARA 574.
2   Ie under the Insolvency Rules 1986, SI 1986/1925, r 6.117: see PARA 578.
3   Insolvency Rules 1986, SI 1986/1925, r 6.118(1). Nothing in r 6.118 affects the rights in rem of creditors or third parties protected under Council Regulation (EC) 1346/2000 on insolvency proceedings (OJ L160, 30.06.00, p 1) ('European Regulation on Insolvency Proceedings') art 5 (third parties' rights in rem) (see PARAS 41, 42): Insolvency Rules 1986, SI 1986/1925, r 6.116(3) (added by SI 2002/1307).
4   Insolvency Rules 1986, SI 1986/1925, r 6.118(2).
5   Insolvency Rules 1986, SI 1986/1925, r 6.118(3).

580.   Realisation of security by creditor. If a creditor who has valued his security[1] subsequently realises it, whether or not at the instance of the trustee[2], the net amount realised must be substituted for the value previously put by the creditor on the security, and that amount is to be treated in all respects as an amended valuation made by him[3].

1   See PARA 576 et seq.
2   See PARA 579.
3   Insolvency Rules 1986, SI 1986/1925, r 6.119.

581.   Partners. For the purposes of the rules as to proof by secured creditors[1], the joint estate of partners is to be considered as different from the separate estate of any partner. Therefore, a partnership creditor having a security for his debt on the separate estate of one partner need not value or give up his security[2], and conversely a creditor of one partner is not obliged to give up or value a security which he holds on the joint estate[3].

Where, however, A and B deposit a lease, granted to them as tenants in common beneficially, with a bank to secure a loan to A, and A becomes bankrupt, the bank must deduct half the value of the lease, for in this case the security is on A's separate estate, not on the joint estate[4].

A creditor having a lien on shares standing in the name of one debtor must, in proving against the joint estate of the debtor and his partner, treat the shares as security if in fact they are partnership property[5].

1   See PARAS 575–580.
2   *Re Bell, ex p Peacock* (1825) 2 Gl & J 27; *Re Brettell, ex p Bowden* (1832) 1 Deac & Ch 135; *Re Turner, ex p West Riding Union Banking Co* (1881) 19 ChD 105, CA; *Re Hart, ex p Caldicott* (1884) 25 ChD 716, CA; *Re Dutton, Massey & Co, ex p Manchester and Liverpool District Banking Co* [1924] 2 Ch 199, CA. See also the cases cited in note 3.
3   See the cases cited in note 2; and *Re Fraser, Trenholm & Co, ex p English and American Bank* (1868) 4 Ch App 49; *Rolfe and Bank of Australasia v Flower, Salting & Co* (1865) LR 1 PC 27.
4   *Re Turner, ex p West Riding Union Banking Co* (1881) 19 ChD 105, CA, considered in *Re Rushton (a bankrupt), ex p National Westminster Bank Ltd v Official Receiver (Trustee of Bankrupt)* [1972] Ch 197, [1971] 2 All ER 937.
5   *Re Clarke, ex p Connell* (1838) 3 Deac 201; *Re Collie, ex p Manchester and County Bank* (1876) 3 ChD 481, CA; and see *Re Cooksey, ex p Portal & Co* (1900) 83 LT 435.

582.   Appropriation of securities. Where property of one partner is held as a security both for his debt and for a debt of his firm, the creditor may realise it and pay himself the partner's debt in full, and then, placing the balance of the security to a suspense account, prove for the whole amount of the joint debt[1]. In such a case he may appropriate his security to the best advantage, and the court would, if necessary, in a proper case order a dividend on the joint estate to be declared before one on the separate estate[2]. On the bankruptcy of a debtor whose debt is guaranteed, the creditor may place the proceeds of any securities given by the guarantor which have been realised, together with any other payments made by the guarantor, on a suspense, or securities realised, account and prove in the debtor's bankruptcy to the full extent of the debt[3].

1 *Re Walker & Co, ex p Watson* (1880) 42 LT 516.
2 *Re Foster, ex p Dickin* (1875) LR 20 Eq 767.
3 *Re Sass, ex p National Provincial Bank of England Ltd* [1896] 2 QB 12.

583. Property in which third party is interested. Where a security is granted over a property which belongs to the bankrupt and a third party jointly, then, in so far as the bankrupt's interest is a beneficial one, the creditor is secured to that extent, and he may not prove in the bankruptcy without acknowledging the security[1]. There is no difference between property owned by the bankrupt as tenant in common and property owned by the bankrupt as joint tenant with the third party. Where the property, if given up, would augment the bankrupt's estate, credit must be given for its value as security[2].

Where a creditor has realised a security granted by a third party on property which was in fact the property of the bankrupt, he must deduct the amount realised before proving[3]. However, where shares, on which a company has a lien for debts of a shareholder, are registered in A's name, but belong in equity to B, the company is not a secured creditor of B for the purpose of either petition or proof in bankruptcy[4]. A creditor who obtains judgment for the purchase price of specific shares is a secured creditor in respect of the judgment debt, because he is entitled to keep the shares until the purchaser, having become the equitable owner, pays the price[5]. Again, where consignors send goods to the debtor for sale, drawing bills on him which they indorse to bankers to whom they send the bills of lading, and the bills are accepted 'payable on the delivery up of the bills of lading', this form of acceptance makes the goods the property of the debtor; the bank must, therefore, in proving against the debtor's estate, treat them as such and prove as secured creditors[6]. If, however, the debtor has absolutely parted with the property before the bankruptcy order, no question of security arises[7]. No credit need be given by a creditor in his proof for a voluntary payment made by a stranger in respect of a loss caused by the bankrupt[8].

1 *Re Rushton (a bankrupt), ex p National Westminster Bank Ltd v Official Receiver (Trustee of Bankrupt)* [1972] Ch 197, [1971] 2 All ER 937.
2 *Re Turner, ex p West Riding Union Banking Co* (1881) 19 ChD 105, CA; *Re Rushton (a bankrupt), ex p National Westminster Bank Ltd v Official Receiver (Trustee of Bankrupt)* [1972] Ch 197, [1971] 2 All ER 937.
3 *Re Cooksey, ex p Portal & Co* (1900) 83 LT 435 (where the property was the bankrupt's, although represented by him to be his wife's); cf the cases cited in PARA 581 note 5.
4 *Re Perkins, ex p Mexican Santa Barbara Mining Co* (1890) 24 QBD 613, CA; cf *Bradford Banking Co Ltd v Briggs* (1886) 12 App Cas 29, HL.
5 *Re A Debtor (No 6 of 1941)* [1943] Ch 213, [1943] 1 All ER 553, CA.
6 *Re Howe, ex p Brett* (1871) 6 Ch App 838.
7 *Re Hallett & Co, ex p Cocks, Biddulph & Co* [1894] 2 QB 256, CA (where a promissory note in favour of the debtors, and the guarantee of a third party for its payment, had been handed to the creditors with the intention that they should become their property).
8 *Re Rowe, ex p Derenburg & Co* [1904] 2 KB 483, CA.

584. Unauthorised investment of trust fund. A beneficiary may, if he can, follow trust money into an unauthorised investment, and may also prove for the whole of the missing fund[1]; but it is otherwise if by his conduct he adopts the investment[2].

1   *Re Biddulph, ex p Biddulph, ex p Barnewall* (1849) 3 De G & Sm 587; *Re Oatway, Hertslet v Oatway* [1903] 2 Ch 356. As to the following of trust money see EQUITY vol 16(2) (Reissue) PARA 861 et seq.

2   *Re Lake, ex p Howe Trustees* [1903] 1 KB 439.

585.   Negotiable instruments etc.   Unless the trustee allows, a proof in respect of money owed on a bill of exchange, promissory note, cheque or other negotiable instrument or security cannot be admitted unless there is produced the instrument or security itself or a copy of it, certified by the creditor or his authorised representative to be a true copy[1].

Where bills bearing the debtor's and other names are indorsed by the debtor to a creditor, the test whether they should be valued as securities or not is whether the indorsement was intended to make the debtor liable as indorser of the bills[2]. Thus, proof was allowed to the full amount of bills indorsed to a banker to be discounted[3], or accepted by the bankrupt although subsequently indorsed and deposited by the party accommodated[4]; but an indorsement to a banker for the purpose of collection does not make the debtor liable as indorser, and, if the banker has a lien, that right is a security[5].

Generally, where a bill bearing the names of third parties is indorsed and handed to a creditor, he may proceed against all parties to the bill until he receives 100 pence in the pound and interest[6].

1   Insolvency Rules 1986, SI 1986/1925, r 6.108. Particulars of any security held, the date when it was given and the value which the creditor puts on it must be stated in a creditor's proof of debt: see r 6.98(1)(e); and PARA 546 head (5).

2   *Re Firth, ex p Schofield* (1879) 12 ChD 337 at 347.

3   *Re Firth, ex p Schofield* (1879) 12 ChD 337 at 345. See also *Ex p Twogood* (1812) 19 Ves 229; *Re Claughton, ex p Britten* (1833) 3 Deac & Ch 35; *Re Bentley, ex p Brunskill* (1835) 2 Mont & A 220; *Dawson v Isle* [1906] 1 Ch 633.

4   *Re Barker, ex p Phillips* (1840) 1 Mont D & De G 232 (amount receivable in dividend limited).

5   *Clydesdale Bank Ltd v James Allan, Senior & Sons (Liquidators)* 1926 SC 235, Ct of Sess; *Re Keever (a bankrupt), ex p Trustee of Property of Bankrupt v Midland Bank Ltd* [1967] Ch 182, [1966] 3 All ER 631.

6   *Re Fowler, ex p Martin* (1814) 2 Rose 87; *Re Peirson and Sammon, ex p Sammon* (1832) 1 Deac & Ch 564; *Re Caldwell, ex p Reed* (1833) 3 Deac & Ch 481; *Re Bunyard, ex p Newton, ex p Griffin* (1880) 16 ChD 330, CA. Any surplus received by the creditor would belong to the debtor or his trustee: *Re Morris, James v London and County Banking Co* [1899] 1 Ch 485, CA. As to bills of exchange see further PARA 524.

586.   Guarantor's equity of exoneration.   Where a debtor and a guarantor both charge their properties to secure the debt, the guarantor's equity of exoneration is to have the debt paid out of the debtor's property before the guarantor's property is appropriated for the debt[1]. Where a father conveyed his property into the joint names of himself and his son to enable the son to obtain a loan and a charge was executed on the property by both father and son as security, on the bankruptcy of the son the father was entitled to insist that the bankrupt's share was used to pay the loan in priority to his share[2].

1   See *Gee v Liddell* [1913] 2 Ch 62 at 72.

2   *Re A Debtor (No 24 of 1971), ex p Marley v Trustee of Property of Debtor* [1976] 2 All ER 1010, [1976] 1 WLR 952, DC. As to a spouse's equity of exoneration see *Re Pittortou (a Bankrupt), ex p Trustee of Property of Bankrupt v Bankrupt* [1985] 1 All ER 285, [1985] 1 WLR 58; and PARA 674.

(8) DISTRIBUTION OF BANKRUPT'S ESTATE

(i) Priority of Debts

587. General order of payment. The trustee must distribute the assets available for distribution[1] in accordance with the prescribed order of payment[2]. Subject to the statutory provisions[3], the Crown has no priority in bankruptcy over other unsecured creditors in respect of debts due to the Crown[4]. To be entitled to share in the distribution, the creditor must have proved his debt[5]; and, if he is a secured creditor, he must have complied with the provisions relating to secured creditors[6]. All debts proved in the bankruptcy in the same category of priority rank equally between themselves[7]; and the order of priority for payment is:

(1) the expenses of the bankruptcy[8];
(2) the debts of preferential creditors[9];
(3) the debts of ordinary creditors[10];
(4) interest arising on the debts[11] of both preferential and ordinary creditors since the commencement of the bankruptcy[12];
(5) the debts due to the bankrupt's spouse or civil partner, and any interest payable in respect of such debts[13];
(6) any balance to be returned to the bankrupt[14].

The statutory provisions[15] relating to priority of debts and debts due to a spouse or civil partner are without prejudice to any provision of the Insolvency Act 1986[16] or any other Act[17] under which the payment of any debt or the making of any other payment is, in the event of bankruptcy, to have a particular priority or to be postponed[18].

1 The assets available for distribution in the bankruptcy are those which remain after satisfying the claims of secured creditors, so far as their rights remain unaffected: see PARA 560 et seq.
2 See the Insolvency Act 1986 ss 328, 329; the Insolvency Rules 1986, SI 1986/1925, rr 6.46A, 6.224, 10.4, 12.2; and PARA 588 et seq.
3 See PARA 591 et seq.
4 *Food Controller v Cork* [1923] AC 647, HL.
5 See PARA 507 et seq.
6 See PARA 574 et seq.
7 See the Insolvency Act 1986 s 328(2), (3); and *Farmers' Mart Ltd v Milne* [1915] AC 106, HL (where an agreement by a trustee that, in consideration that certain creditors would consent to his acting as trustee, he would allow part of his remuneration to be applied in securing to those creditors a larger dividend than the other creditors would receive was stated to be a fraud on the bankruptcy laws, the object of which was to secure equal distribution of the bankrupt's assets). See also *Pritchard v Westminster Bank Ltd* [1969] 1 All ER 999, [1969] 1 WLR 547, CA (where the court held that a garnishee order which had the effect of giving the plaintiff preference over all other creditors should not have been made absolute).
8 See PARA 588.
9 See PARA 591.
10 See PARA 595.
11 A distinction is to be drawn between interest arising on a debt prior to the commencement of bankruptcy which, subject to the Insolvency Rules 1986, SI 1986/1925, is itself a bankruptcy debt and provable in the bankruptcy (see PARA 507 et seq), and interest on a bankruptcy debt from the commencement of the bankruptcy which is payable at the prescribed rate (see PARA 596), but is postponed to the payment of ordinary debts, whether it is interest payable on preferential or ordinary debts.
12 See PARA 596. As to the commencement of bankruptcy see PARA 209.
13 See PARA 597. Certain claims under the Financial Services and Markets Act 2000 are also not provable until prior claims have been paid in full with interest: see the Insolvency Rules 1986, SI 1986/1925, r 12.3(2A)(a); and PARA 508.
14 See the Insolvency Act 1986 s 330(5); and PARA 615.

15 Ie the Insolvency Act 1986 ss 328, 329: see PARA 591 et seq.

16 See eg the Insolvency Act 1986 s 335(6); and PARA 618.

17 See eg the Partnership Act 1890 s 3 (see PARA 598); the Friendly Societies Act 1974 s 59 (see PARA 599); and the Employment Rights Act 1996 Pt XII (ss 182–190) (see EMPLOYMENT vol 39 (2009) PARA 556 et seq).

18 Insolvency Act 1986 s 328(6). As to the application of s 328 in the case of the administration in bankruptcy of the insolvent estate of a deceased person dying before the presentation of a bankruptcy petition see PARA 591 note 3.

588.   Bankruptcy expenses.   The expenses of the bankruptcy rank in priority before preferential and other debts[1]. All fees, costs, charges and other expenses incurred in the course of bankruptcy proceedings are to be regarded as expenses of the bankruptcy[2]. Any expenses[3] incurred by the official receiver, in whatever capacity he may be acting, in connection with proceedings taken against him in insolvency proceedings[4] are to be treated as expenses of the insolvency proceedings[5].

1   See the Insolvency Act 1986 s 328(2); and PARA 591.

2   Insolvency Rules 1986, SI 1986/1925, r 12.2(1) (amended by SI 2003/1730).

3   For these purposes, 'expenses' includes damages: Insolvency Rules 1986, SI 1986/1925, r 10.4(1).

4   As to the meaning of 'insolvency proceedings' see PARA 37 note 9.

5   Insolvency Rules 1986, SI 1986/1925, r 10.4(1). In respect of any sums due to him under r 10.4(1) in connection with insolvency proceedings, other than proceedings relating to debt relief orders or applications for debt relief orders (see PARA 101 et seq), the official receiver has a charge on the insolvent estate: r 10.4(2) (amended by SI 2009/642). As to the meaning of 'the insolvent estate' see PARA 53 note 17.

589.   Expenses of voluntary arrangements.   Where a bankruptcy order is made on a petition[1] by the supervisor of, or any person, other than the individual, who is for the time being bound by, a voluntary arrangement proposed by the individual and approved under Part 8 of the Insolvency Act 1986[2], any expenses properly incurred as expenses of the administration of the voluntary arrangement in question are a first charge on the bankrupt's estate[3].

Where a bankruptcy order is made on a debtor's petition[4] and there is at the time of the petition in force a voluntary arrangement under Part 8 of the Insolvency Act 1986, any expenses properly incurred as expenses of the administration of the arrangement in question are a first charge on the bankrupt's estate[5].

1   Ie under the Insolvency Act 1986 s 264(1)(c): see PARA 124 head (3).

2   Ie under the Insolvency Act 1986 Pt 8 (ss 252–263G): see PARA 43 et seq.

3   Insolvency Act 1986 s 276(2). As to the meaning of 'the bankrupt's estate' see PARA 211.

4   As to debtor's petitions see PARAS 163, 191 et seq.

5   Insolvency Rules 1986, SI 1986/1925, r 6.46A (added by SI 1987/1919).

590.   General rule as to priority of bankruptcy expenses.   The expenses of the bankruptcy are payable out of the estate in the following order of priority:

(1)   expenses or costs which: (a) are properly chargeable or incurred by the official receiver or the trustee in preserving, realising or getting in any of the assets of the bankrupt or otherwise relating to the conduct of any legal proceedings which he has power to bring (whether the claim on which the proceedings are based forms part of the estate or otherwise) or defend; (b) relate to the employment of a shorthand writer, if appointed by an order of the court made at the instance of the official

receiver in connection with an examination; or (c) are incurred in holding an examination[1] where the application was made by the official receiver[2];

(2) any other expenses incurred or disbursements made by the official receiver or under his authority, including those incurred or made in carrying on the business of a debtor or bankrupt[3];

(3) the fees payable under any fees order made[4], including those payable to the official receiver, other than the fee referred to in head (4) below, and any remuneration payable to him under general regulations[5];

(4) the fee payable under any fees order made[6] for the performance by the official receiver of his general duties as official receiver[7], and any repayable deposit lodged by the petitioner under any such order as security for such fee, except where the deposit is applied to the payment of the remuneration of an insolvency practitioner appointed[8] by the court on a debtor's petition[9];

(5) the cost of any security provided[10] by an interim receiver, trustee or special manager[11];

(6) the remuneration of the interim receiver, if any[12];

(7) any deposit lodged on an application for the appointment of an interim receiver[13];

(8) the costs of the petitioner, and of any person appearing on the petition whose costs are allowed by the court[14];

(9) the remuneration of the special manager, if any[15];

(10) any amount payable to a person employed or authorised[16] to assist in the preparation of a statement of affairs or of accounts[17];

(11) any allowance made, by order of the court, towards costs on an application for release from the obligation to submit a statement of affairs, or for an extension of time for submitting such a statement[18];

(12) the costs of employing a shorthand writer in any case other than one appointed by an order of the court at the instance of the official receiver in connection with an examination[19];

(13) any necessary disbursements by the trustee in the course of his administration, including expenses incurred by members of the creditors' committee or their representatives and allowed[20] by the trustee, but not including any payment of capital gains tax in circumstances referred to in head (16) below[21];

(14) the remuneration or emoluments of any person, including the bankrupt, who has been employed by the trustee to perform[22] any services for the estate[23];

(15) the remuneration of the trustee, up to any amount not exceeding that which is payable to the official receiver[24];

(16) the amount of any capital gains tax on chargeable gains accruing on the realisation of any asset of the bankrupt, without regard to whether the realisation is effected by the trustee, a secured creditor or a receiver or manager appointed to deal with a security[25];

(17) the balance, after payment of any sums due under head (15) above, of any remuneration due to the trustee[26];

(18) any other expenses properly chargeable by the trustee in carrying out his functions in the bankruptcy[27].

1   Ie an examination under the Insolvency Rules 1986, SI 1986/1925, r 6.174 (examinee unfit): see PARA 295.

2 Insolvency Rules 1986, SI 1986/1925, r 6.224(1)(a) (substituted by SI 2002/2712). As to after-acquired property see PARA 458 et seq. For the interpretation of the equivalent provision in relation to companies, ie the Insolvency Rules 1986, SI 1986/1925, r 4.218(1), see *Re MC Bacon Ltd* [1991] Ch 127, [1990] 3 WLR 646; *Re Exchange Travel (Holdings) Ltd (in liquidation) (No 3), Katz v McNally* [1997] 2 BCLC 579, sub nom *Katz v McNally* [1998] BCC 784, CA; *Mond v Hammond Suddards (a firm)* [2000] Ch 40, [1999] 3 WLR 697, CA; *Re Toshoku Finance UK plc* [2002] UKHL 6, [2002] 3 All ER 961, [2002] 1 WLR 671; *Lewis v IRC* [2001] 3 All ER 499, sub nom *Re Floor Fourteen Ltd, Lewis v IRC* [2001] 2 BCLC 392, CA; *Re Nortel GMBH (in admin); Re Lehman Brothers International (Europe) (in admin)* [2013] UKSC 52, [2013] 3 WLR 504, [2013] 2 BCLC 135.
3 Insolvency Rules 1986, SI 1986/1925, r 6.224(1)(b).
4 Ie any order made under the Insolvency Act 1986 s 415 or s 415A: see PARA 825.
5 Insolvency Rules 1986, SI 1986/1925, r 6.224(1)(c) (substituted by SI 1995/586; and amended by SI 2004/584).
6 Ie any order made under the Insolvency Act 1986 s 415: see PARA 825.
7 Insolvency Rules 1986, SI 1986/1925, r 6.224(1)(d)(i) (substituted by SI 1995/586).
8 Ie under the Insolvency Act 1986 s 273: see PARA 200.
9 Insolvency Rules 1986, SI 1986/1925, r 6.224(1)(d)(ii) (substituted by SI 1995/586).
10 Ie in accordance with the Insolvency Act 1986 or the Insolvency Rules 1986, SI 1986/1925.
11 Insolvency Rules 1986, SI 1986/1925, r 6.224(1)(e).
12 Insolvency Rules 1986, SI 1986/1925, r 6.224(1)(f). As to the interim receiver see PARA 218 et seq.
13 Insolvency Rules 1986, SI 1986/1925, r 6.224(1)(g).
14 Insolvency Rules 1986, SI 1986/1925, r 6.224(1)(h).
15 Insolvency Rules 1986, SI 1986/1925, r 6.224(1)(j). As to the special manager see PARA 232 et seq.
16 Ie under the Insolvency Rules 1986, SI 1986/1925, Pt 6 Ch 5 (rr 6.58–6.72): see PARA 241 et seq.
17 Insolvency Rules 1986, SI 1986/1925, r 6.224(1)(k).
18 Insolvency Rules 1986, SI 1986/1925, r 6.224(1)(l). As to the release from the obligation to submit a statement of affairs and the extension of time for submitting such a statement see PARA 244.
19 Insolvency Rules 1986, SI 1986/1925, r 6.224(1)(la) (added by SI 2002/2712).
20 Ie under the Insolvency Rules 1986, SI 1986/1925, r 6.164: see PARA 337.
21 Insolvency Rules 1986, SI 1986/1925, r 6.224(1)(m). For the interpretation of the corresponding provision in relation to companies see *Re Toshoku Finance UK plc* [2002] UKHL 6, [2002] 3 All ER 961, [2002] 1 WLR 671; *Re Nortel GMBH (in admin); Re Lehman Brothers International (Europe) (in admin)* [2013] UKSC 52, [2013] 3 WLR 504, [2013] 2 BCLC 135.
22 Ie as required or authorised by or under the Insolvency Act 1986 or the Insolvency Rules 1986, SI 1986/1925.
23 Insolvency Rules 1986, SI 1986/1925, r 6.224(1)(n).
24 Insolvency Rules 1986, SI 1986/1925, r 6.224(1)(o). As to the trustee's remuneration generally see PARA 348 et seq. As to the amount payable to the official receiver see Sch 6; and PARA 349.
25 Insolvency Rules 1986, SI 1986/1925, r 6.224(1)(p).
26 Insolvency Rules 1986, SI 1986/1925, r 6.224(1)(q).
27 Insolvency Rules 1986, SI 1986/1925, r 6.224(1)(r) (added by SI 2002/2712).

591. Preferential debts generally. In the distribution of the bankrupt's estate[1], his preferential debts[2] must be paid in priority to other debts[3]. Preferential debts rank equally between themselves after the expenses of the bankruptcy and must be paid in full unless the bankrupt's estate is insufficient for meeting them in which case they abate in equal proportions between themselves[4]. Preferential debts are considered subsequently[5]. Where a preferential debt is expressed to be referable to debts of the bankrupt which have accrued during a specified period next before 'the relevant date', that date is:

(1) where at the time the bankruptcy order was made there was an interim receiver appointed[6], the date on which the interim receiver was first appointed after the presentation of the bankruptcy petition; or

(2) otherwise, the date of the making of the bankruptcy order[7].

1 As to the meaning of 'the bankrupt's estate' see PARA 211.
2 A reference in the Insolvency Act 1986 to the preferential debts of an individual is to the debts listed in s 386(1), Sch 6 (see PARA 592 et seq); and references to preferential creditors are to be read accordingly: s 386(1) (amended by the Enterprise Act 2002 s 251(3)). The Insolvency Act 1986 Sch 6 is to be read with the Pension Schemes Act 1993 s 128, Sch 4 (see SOCIAL SECURITY AND PENSIONS vol 44(2) (Reissue) PARA 859): Insolvency Act 1986 s 386(3) (amended by the Pension Schemes Act 1993 s 190, Sch 8 para 18). In the Insolvency Act 1986 Sch 6, 'the debtor' means the individual concerned: s 386(2).

In the case of the administration in bankruptcy of the insolvent estate of a deceased person dying before the presentation of a bankruptcy petition, s 386 applies: Administration of Insolvent Estates of Deceased Persons Order 1986, SI 1986/1999, art 3(1), Sch 1 Pt II para 34. As to the administration in bankruptcy of the insolvent estates of deceased debtors see further PARA 830 et seq.
3 Insolvency Act 1986 s 328(1). Section 328 is without prejudice to any provision of the Insolvency Act 1986 or any other Act under which the payment of any debt or the making of any other payment is, in the event of bankruptcy, to have a particular priority or to be postponed: s 328(6).

In the case of the administration in bankruptcy of the insolvent estate of a deceased person dying before the presentation of a bankruptcy petition, s 328 applies with the modification that for the words 'commencement of the bankruptcy' there are to be substituted the words 'date of death of the deceased debtor': Administration of Insolvent Estates of Deceased Persons Order 1986, SI 1986/1999, Sch 1 Pt II para 24.

As to the modification of the Insolvency Act 1986 s 328 by the Insolvent Partnerships Order, SI 1994/2421, in relation to the bankruptcy of an individual member of an insolvent partnership see COMPANY AND PARTNERSHIP INSOLVENCY vol 17 (2011) PARAS 1297–1300, 1344.
4 Insolvency Act 1986 s 328(2). By virtue of the Mercantile Law Amendment Act 1856 s 5, a surety who discharges a preferred debt will be entitled to the creditor's priority: *Re Lamplugh Iron Ore Co Ltd* [1927] 1 Ch 308; *Re Lord Churchill, Manisty v Churchill* (1888) 39 ChD 174. Secured creditors in bankruptcy are not affected: *Richards v Kidderminster Overseers, Richards v Kidderminster Corpn* [1896] 2 Ch 212.

As to preferential payments by a trustee under a deed of arrangement see the Deeds of Arrangement Act 1914 s 17 (see PARA 866); and as to payment of expenses of a trustee who acts under a void deed see s 21 (see PARA 876).
5 See PARA 592 et seq.
6 Ie under the Insolvency Act 1986 s 286: see PARA 219 et seq.
7 Insolvency Act 1986 s 387(1), (6). For the purposes of s 258 (individual voluntary arrangements: see PARA 62), 'the relevant date' is, in relation to a debtor who is not an undischarged bankrupt: (1) where an interim order has been made under s 252 with respect to his proposal, the date of that order; and (2) in any other case, the date on which the voluntary arrangement takes effect: s 387(1), (5) (amended by the Insolvency Act 2000 ss 3, 16(1), (3), Sch 3 paras 1, 15). As from a day to be appointed, s 387(6)(a) (see head (1) in the text) is amended by the Enterprise and Regulatory Reform Act 2013 s 71, Sch 19 paras 1, 56: see PARA 130 note 17.

In the case of the administration in bankruptcy of the insolvent estate of a deceased person dying before the presentation of a bankruptcy petition, the Insolvency Act 1986 s 387(1), (5), (6) applies with the modification that in s 387(6)(a), (b) (see heads (1), (2) in the text) for the reference to the making of the bankruptcy order there is to be substituted a reference to the date of death of the deceased debtor: Administration of Insolvent Estates of Deceased Persons Order 1986, SI 1986/1999, Sch 1 Pt II para 35.

As to the modification of the Insolvency Act 1986 s 387 by the Insolvent Partnerships Order 1994, SI 1994/2421, in relation to the bankruptcy of an individual member of an insolvent partnership see COMPANY AND PARTNERSHIP INSOLVENCY vol 17 (2011) PARA 1349.

592. Contributions to occupational pension schemes. Any sum which is owed by the bankrupt and is a sum to which the statutory provisions relating to contributions to occupational pension schemes and state scheme premiums[1] apply constitutes a preferential debt[2].

1 Ie to which the Pension Schemes Act 1993 s 128, Sch 4 applies: see SOCIAL SECURITY AND PENSIONS vol 44(2) (Reissue) PARA 859.
2 Insolvency Act 1986 s 386, Sch 6 para 8 (amended by the Pension Schemes Act 1993 s 190, Sch 8 para 18). As to the application of the Insolvency Act 1986 s 386 in the case of the

administration in bankruptcy of the insolvent estate of a deceased person dying before the presentation of a bankruptcy petition see PARA 591 note 2.

593. Remuneration etc of employees. The following sums due to employees constitute preferential debts:

(1)   so much of any amount as does not exceed so much as may be prescribed by order made by the Secretary of State[1] which is owed by the bankrupt to a person who is or has been an employee of the bankrupt, and which is payable by way of remuneration in respect of the whole or any part of the period of four months next before the relevant date[2];

(2)   an amount owed by way of accrued holiday remuneration, in respect of any period of employment before the relevant date, to a person whose employment by the bankrupt has been terminated, whether before, on or after that date[3];

(3)   so much of any sum owed in respect of money advanced for the purpose as has been applied for the payment of a debt which, if it had not been paid, would have been a debt falling within either head (1) or head (2) above[4];

(4)   so much of any amount as does not exceed such amount as may be prescribed by order made by the Secretary of State which is ordered, whether before or after the relevant date, to be paid by the bankrupt under the Reserve Forces (Safeguard of Employment) Act 1985, and is so ordered in respect of a default made by the bankrupt before that date in the discharge of his obligations under that Act[5].

For these purposes, a sum is payable by the bankrupt to a person by way of remuneration in respect of any period if:

(a)   it is paid as wages or salary, whether payable for time or for piece work or earned wholly or partly by way of commission, in respect of services rendered to the bankrupt in that period[6]; or

(b)   it is an amount payable by the bankrupt in respect of that period and constitutes a guarantee payment[7] or any payment for time off[8] or remuneration on suspension on medical grounds or on maternity grounds[9] or remuneration under a protective award[10] made by an employment tribunal[11].

In a case in which a person's employment has been terminated by or in consequence of his employer being adjudged bankrupt, holiday remuneration is deemed to have accrued to that person in respect of any period of employment if, by virtue of that person's contract of employment or of any enactment or of an order or direction made under an enactment[12], that remuneration would have accrued in respect of that period if that person's employment had continued until he became entitled to be allowed the holiday[13].

Without prejudice to these provisions, any remuneration payable by the bankrupt to a person in respect of a period of holiday or of absence from work through sickness or other good cause is deemed to be wages or, as the case may be, salary in respect of services rendered to the bankrupt in that period; and, for these purposes, references to remuneration in respect of a period of holiday include any sums which, if they had been paid, would have been treated for the purposes of the enactments relating to social security[14] as earnings in respect of that period[15].

1   Orders made under the Insolvency Act 1986 s 386, Sch 6 para 9 or Sch 6 para 12 (see the text and note 5) may contain such transitional provisions as may appear to the Secretary of State

necessary or expedient and must be made by statutory instrument subject to annulment in pursuance of a resolution of either House of Parliament: Sch 6 para 16(a), (b). The amount prescribed for the purposes of Sch 6 para 9 (see the text and note 2) and Sch 6 para 12 (see the text and note 5) is £800: Insolvency Proceedings (Monetary Limits) Order 1986, SI 1986/1996, art 4.

As to the application of the Insolvency Act 1986 s 386 in the case of the administration in bankruptcy of the insolvent estate of a deceased person dying before the presentation of a bankruptcy petition see PARA 591 note 2.

2   Insolvency Act 1986 Sch 6 para 9. As to the meaning of 'the relevant date' see PARA 591. As to the amount prescribed for the purposes of Sch 6 para 9 see note 1.

3   Insolvency Act 1986 Sch 6 para 10.

4   Insolvency Act 1986 Sch 6 para 11. Whether a wages cheque drawn by a bankrupt on an overdrawn account is regarded as paid out of money advanced for the purpose depends on the way in which the account is kept: see *Re Primrose (Builders) Ltd* [1950] Ch 561, [1950] 2 All ER 334 (where payments credited to an account were not regarded as appropriated to sums advanced by a bank for wages); *Re EJ Morel (1934) Ltd* [1962] Ch 21, [1961] 1 All ER 796 (current account and wages account interdependent: contrary result). See also *Re Rampgill Mill Ltd* [1967] Ch 1138, [1967] 1 All ER 56 (no wages account; lending bank arranged for another bank to cash company's cheques, principally for wages; money held to have been advanced for wages).

5   Insolvency Act 1986 Sch 6 para 12. As to the amount prescribed for the purposes of Sch 6 para 12 see note 1. As to the Reserve Forces (Safeguard of Employment) Act 1985 see ARMED FORCES vol 3 (2011) PARA 370.

6   Insolvency Act 1986 Sch 6 para 13(1)(a).

7   Ie under the Employment Rights Act 1996 Pt III (ss 28–35): see EMPLOYMENT vol 39 (2009) PARA 237 et seq.

8   Ie under the Employment Rights Act 1996 s 53 (looking for work etc: see EMPLOYMENT vol 39 (2009) PARA 303) or s 56 (ante-natal care: see EMPLOYMENT vol 39 (2009) PARA 307) or the Trade Union and Labour Relations (Consolidation) Act 1992 s 169 (trade union duties: see EMPLOYMENT vol 40 (2009) PARA 1014).

9   Ie under the Employment Rights Act 1986 Pt VII (ss 64–70A): see EMPLOYMENT vol 39 (2009) PARA 316 et seq.

10   Ie under the Trade Union and Labour Relations (Consolidation) Act 1992 s 189 (trade union duties): see EMPLOYMENT vol 41 (2009) PARA 1155.

11   Insolvency Act 1986 Sch 6 para 13(1)(b), (2) (substituted by the Employment Rights Act 1996 s 240, Sch 1 para 29). As to the rights of an employee on the insolvency of his employer to obtain payments from the Secretary of State see the Pension Schemes Act 1993 Pt VII Ch II (ss 123–127); the Employment Rights Act 1996 Pt XII (ss 182–190); and EMPLOYMENT vol 39 (2009) PARA 556 et seq; SOCIAL SECURITY AND PENSIONS vol 44(2) (Reissue) PARA 853 et seq.

12   For these purposes, the reference to any enactment includes an order or direction made under an enactment: Insolvency Act 1986 Sch 6 para 14(3).

13   Insolvency Act 1986 Sch 6 para 14(1)(a), (2). As from a day to be appointed, Sch 6 para 14(1) is amended by the Enterprise and Regulatory Reform Act 2013 s 71, Sch 19 paras 1, 64: see PARA 130 note 17.

14   See SOCIAL SECURITY AND PENSIONS.

15   Insolvency Act 1986 Sch 6 para 15.

594. Levies on coal and steel production.

Any sums due at the relevant date[1] from the bankrupt in respect of the levies on the production of coal and steel[2] or any surcharge for delay[3] constitute preferential debts[4].

1   As to the meaning of 'the relevant date' see PARA 591.

2   Ie the levies referred to in the Treaty establishing the European Coal and Steel Treaty (Paris, 18 April 1951; TS 16 (1979); Cmnd 7461) ('the ECSC Treaty') arts 49, 50. By virtue of art 97, the ECSC Treaty expired in 2002. The sectors previously covered by the ECSC Treaty are now subject to the rules of the Treaty on the Functioning of the European Union (Rome, 25 March 1957; TS 1 (1973); Cmnd 5179) (previously the EC Treaty: see CONSTITUTIONAL LAW AND HUMAN RIGHTS).

3   Ie any surcharge for delay provided for in the ECSC Treaty, art 50(3); ECSC High Authority Decision 3–52, art 6.

4   Insolvency Act 1986 s 386, Sch 6 para 15A (added by SI 1987/2093). As to the application of the Insolvency Act 1986 s 386 in the case of the administration in bankruptcy of the insolvent estate of a deceased person dying before the presentation of a bankruptcy petition see PARA 591 note 2.

595.   Ordinary debts. Debts which are neither preferential debts[1] nor debts owed in respect of credit provided by the bankrupt's spouse or civil partner[2] rank equally between themselves, and, after the preferential debts, must be paid in full unless the bankrupt's estate is insufficient for meeting them, in which case they abate in equal proportions between themselves[3].

1   As to preferential debts see PARA 591 et seq.
2   Ie under the Insolvency Act 1986 s 329: see PARA 597.
3   Insolvency Act 1986 s 328(3). Section 328 is without prejudice to any provision of the Insolvency Act 1986 or any other Act under which the payment of any debt or the making of any other payment is, in the event of bankruptcy, to have a particular priority or to be postponed: s 328(6).
    As to the application of s 328 in the case of the administration in bankruptcy of the insolvent estate of a deceased person dying before the presentation of a bankruptcy petition, and as to the modification of s 328 in relation to the bankruptcy of an individual member of an insolvent partnership, see PARA 591 note 3.

596.   Interest on debts. Any surplus remaining after the payment of preferential debts[1] or debts which are ordinary debts and rank equally[2] is to be applied in paying interest on those debts in respect of the periods during which they have been outstanding since the commencement of the bankruptcy[3]; and interest on preferential debts ranks equally with interest on debts other than preferential debts[4]. The rate of interest so payable in respect of any debt is whichever is the greater of the rate specified in the Judgments Act 1838[5] at the commencement of the bankruptcy and the rate applicable to that debt apart from the bankruptcy[6].

1   As to preferential debts see PARA 591 et seq.
2   Ie under the Insolvency Act 1986 s 328(3): see PARA 595.
3   As to the commencement of bankruptcy see PARA 209.
4   Insolvency Act 1986 s 328(4). Section 328 is without prejudice to any provision of the Insolvency Act 1986 or any other Act under which the payment of any debt or the making of any other payment is, in the event of bankruptcy, to have a particular priority or to be postponed: s 328(6).
    As to the application of s 328 in the case of the administration in bankruptcy of the insolvent estate of a deceased person dying before the presentation of a bankruptcy petition, and as to the modification of s 328 in relation to the bankruptcy of an individual member of an insolvent partnership, see PARA 591 note 3.
5   Ie the Judgments Act 1838 s 17: see FINANCIAL SERVICES AND INSTITUTIONS vol 49 (2008) PARA 1307.
6   Insolvency Act 1986 s 328(5).

597.   Debts to bankrupt's spouse or civil partner. Bankruptcy debts[1] owed in respect of credit provided by a person who, whether or not the bankrupt's spouse or civil partner at the time the credit was provided, was the bankrupt's spouse or civil partner at the commencement of the bankruptcy[2] rank in priority after the debts which are not preferential debts and interest on ordinary and preferential debts[3] and are payable with interest[4] in respect of the period during which they have been outstanding since the commencement of the bankruptcy, such interest having the same priority as the debts on which it is payable[5].

The above provisions are without prejudice to any provision of the Insolvency Act 1986 or any other Act under which the payment of any debt or the making of any other payment is, in the event of bankruptcy, to have a particular priority or to be postponed[6].

1   As to the meaning of 'bankruptcy debt' see PARA 508.

2   As to the commencement of bankruptcy see PARA 209.

3   Ie the debts and interest required to be paid in pursuance of the Insolvency Act 1986 s 328(3), (4): see PARAS 595, 596.

4   Ie at the rate specified in Insolvency Act 1986 s 328(5): see PARA 596.

5   Insolvency Act 1986 s 329(1), (2) (s 329(1) amended by the Civil Partnership Act 2004 s 261(1), Sch 27 para 116). In the case of the administration in bankruptcy of the insolvent estate of a deceased person dying before the presentation of a bankruptcy petition, the Insolvency Act 1986 s 329 applies with the modification that for the words 'commencement of the bankruptcy' there are to be substituted the words 'date of death of the deceased debtor': Administration of Insolvent Estates of Deceased Persons Order 1986, SI 1986/1919, art 3(1), Sch 1 Pt II para 24. As to the administration in bankruptcy of the insolvent estates of deceased persons see further PARA 830 et seq.

6   Insolvency Act 1986 s 328(6). As to the application of s 328 in the case of the administration in bankruptcy of the insolvent estate of a deceased person dying before the presentation of a bankruptcy petition, and as to the modification of s 328 in relation to the bankruptcy of an individual member of an insolvent partnership, see PARA 591 note 3.

598.   Loans for business purposes.   Where a loan is made to a person engaged or about to engage in any business[1], on a contract with that person, whether oral or written[2], that the lender is to receive either a rate of interest varying with the profits[3], or a share of the profits arising from carrying on the business[4], then, if the borrower is adjudged bankrupt, or enters into an arrangement to pay his creditors less than 100 pence in the pound, or dies insolvent, the lender will not be entitled to recover anything in respect of his loan[5], until the claims of the borrower's other creditors for valuable consideration in money or money's worth have been satisfied[6].

The creditor who is party to such a contract will be so postponed, even if the contract is for payment of a fixed sum out of the profits[7], or, where that is the real contract, even if the fixed sum is described as a salary[8], or where a certain sum is to be paid for interest from which, if the borrower should be unable to pay it, a certain defined allowance would be made[9]. Where money is lent to a person engaged in business at interest varying with the profits, and security is given for the loan, the lender's rights in the security will not be affected by the borrower's bankruptcy[10].

In the same way, where a person sells the goodwill of his business and receives in consideration for it, by way of annuity or otherwise, a portion of the profits of the business, that receipt will not of itself make him a partner in the business or liable as such[11]; but, if the buyer is adjudged bankrupt, enters into an arrangement to pay his creditors less than 100 pence in the pound, or dies insolvent, the seller of the goodwill cannot prove[12] or recover anything in respect of the profits, until the claims of all the other creditors for valuable consideration in money or money's worth have been satisfied[13].

If a person advances money to another, not by way of loan but as a contribution to the capital of a business carried on for their joint benefit, the person who has made the advance, even though he is not a partner in the business and has received no share of the profits as such, is debarred from proving in the bankruptcy of the recipient of the money in competition with the creditors of the business[14].

1   The term 'business' applies not only to a lifelong or universal business, but also to any separate commercial venture on which a trader or firm of traders embarks: *Re Abenheim, ex p Abenheim* (1913) 109 LT 219; and see PARTNERSHIP vol 79 (2008) PARA 6.

2   *Re Fort, ex p Schofield* [1897] 2 QB 495, CA.

3   As to the meaning of 'profits' see *Re Spanish Prospecting Co Ltd* [1911] 1 Ch 92 at 98, CA; and see PARTNERSHIP vol 79 (2008) PARA 129.

4   Such a contract was held not to be established where a debt, left on deposit in a firm on terms that a third party should be credited with a share of profits, was subsequently transferred in equity to the third party: *Re Pinto Leite and Nephews, ex p Visconde Des Olivaes* [1929] 1 Ch 221. Such a contract will not of itself, provided that it is in writing and signed by or on behalf of all the parties to it, make the lender a partner: see the Partnership Act 1890 s 2(3)(d); and PARTNERSHIP vol 79 (2008) PARA 20.

   As to when there will be a partnership see PARTNERSHIP vol 79 (2008) PARA 10 et seq; *Re Megevand, ex p Delhasse* (1878) 7 ChD 511, CA; *Re Howard, ex p Tennant* (1877) 6 ChD 303, CA; *Walker v Hirsch* (1884) 27 ChD 460, CA; *Badeley v Consolidated Bank* (1888) 38 ChD 238, CA; *Davis v Davis* [1894] 1 Ch 393; *Re Young, ex p Jones* [1896] 2 QB 484; *Re Beard & Co, ex p Trustee* [1915] HBR 191, CA; *Re Pinto Leite and Nephews, ex p Visconde Des Olivaes* [1929] 1 Ch 221.

5   He may not even prove his debt in competition with other creditors: *Re Grason, ex p Taylor* (1879) 12 ChD 366, CA; and see *Re Tew, ex p Mills* (1873) 8 Ch App 569.

6   See the Partnership Act 1890 ss 2(3)(d), 3; and PARTNERSHIP vol 79 (2008) PARAS 20, 22, 23. These provisions are not affected by the Insolvency Act 1986: see s 328(6); and PARA 591 note 3.

7   *Re Young, ex p Jones* [1896] 2 QB 484.

8   *Re Stone* (1886) 33 ChD 541. The time when the loan was made is the important one: *Re Stone*; *Re Tew, ex p Mills* (1873) 8 Ch App 569. If, by the terms of the original contract, the case falls within the Partnership Act 1890 s 2 (see PARTNERSHIP vol 79 (2008) PARA 10 et seq), no alteration will take the case out of s 2 which does not amount to a repayment of the loan and the making of a fresh one: *Re Tew, ex p Mills*; *Re Grason, ex p Taylor* (1879) 12 ChD 366, CA; *Re Hildesheim, ex p Trustee* [1893] 2 QB 357. See also *Re Mason, ex p Bing* [1899] 1 QB 810 (where the original loan was to two partners, and, the partnership having been dissolved, the remaining partner took over the firm's liabilities).

9   *Re Vince, ex p Trustee in Bankruptcy* [1892] 1 QB 587; revsd sub nom *Re Vince, ex p Baxter* [1892] 2 QB 478, CA, but only on the ground that the 'due allowance' mentioned in the contract was unintelligible, and that the contract was, therefore, inoperative.

10 *Re Lonergan, ex p Sheil* (1877) 4 ChD 789, CA; *Badeley v Consolidated Bank* (1888) 38 ChD 238, CA.

11 See the Partnership Act 1890 s 2(3)(e); and PARTNERSHIP vol 79 (2008) PARA 17.

12 See the cases cited in note 5.

13 See the Partnership Act 1890 s 3; and PARTNERSHIP vol 79 (2008) PARAS 22, 23. Nevertheless, where a person sells a business in consideration of an annuity which is not stated to be payable out of the profits, the seller's right of proof against the buyer's estate will not be postponed: *Re Gieve, ex p Shaw* (1809) 80 LT 737, CA. As to the meaning of 'profits' see note 3. A creditor is not 'satisfied' until he has received 100 pence in the pound on his admitted claim, interest, if any, payable on the claim to the date of the bankruptcy order (see PARA 209) and interest from the date of the bankruptcy order: see the Insolvency Act 1986 s 328; and PARA 591 et seq.

14 *Re Meade, ex p Humber v Palmer* [1951] Ch 774, [1951] 2 All ER 168, DC.

599.   Friendly societies.

In the bankruptcy[1] of an officer of a friendly society[2] who, by virtue of his office, has in his possession money or property of the society, the trustees of the society have a right to receive that money or property in preference to any other debt or claim against the officer's estate[3]. If the officer has received the money or property by virtue of his office[4], it is immaterial that it cannot be traced[5], or that he wrongfully omitted to pay it over after receipt[6], or that there was a want of due diligence on the society's part[7], or that at the date of the bankruptcy he has ceased to be an officer of the society[8].

This preferential right in the trustees of the society applies only in the case of properly constituted officers[9], and does not apply in the case of a society's bankers[10], even though appointed under the rules[11].

1   For these purposes, 'bankruptcy' includes the liquidation of a debtor's affairs by arrangement: Friendly Societies Act 1974 s 59(3). It is doubtful, however, whether this will apply to a

voluntary arrangement approved under the Insolvency Act 1986 Pt 8 (ss 252–263G) (see PARA 43 et seq). 'Preferential debt' (the priority of which may not be affected by any such approved arrangement: see s 258(5)) means any debt listed in s 386(1), Sch 6 (see PARA 592 et seq): s 386(1). Schedule 6 does not include debts owed to the trustees of friendly societies.

2   For these purposes, 'officer of a friendly society' includes any trustee, treasurer, secretary or member of the committee of management of a society or branch, or any person appointed by the society or branch, to sue and be sued on its behalf: Friendly Societies Act 1974 s 111(1). As to who is an officer see *Re Ashley, ex p Appach* (1840) 1 Mont D & De G 83; *Re Baston, ex p Riddell* (1842) 3 Mont D & De G 80 (savings bank); *Re Wise, ex p Whipham* (1844) 3 Mont D & De G 564; *Re Rufford and Wragge, ex p Orford* (1852) 1 De GM & G 483.

3   Friendly Societies Act 1974 s 59(2). Nothing in the Insolvency Act 1986 s 328 (see PARA 587) prejudices this provision: s 328(6). If the transaction amounted in substance to a loan to the bankrupt, there will be no priority (*Ex p Amicable Society of Lancaster* (1801) 6 Ves 98; *Ex p Ross* (1802) 6 Ves 802; *Ex p Stamford Friendly Society* (1808) 15 Ves 280; *Re Shattock, ex p Long Ashton Junior Friendly Society* (1861) 5 LT 370), even though an agreement to pay interest on money to come into an officer's hands will not defeat a claim to priority (*Re Woodlife, ex p Ray* (1839) 3 Deac 537).

4   The officer must have obtained the money or property by virtue of his office: *Re Aberdein, Hagon v Aberdein* [1896] WN 154; and see *Re Thick, ex p Buckland* (1818) Buck 214; *Re Jardine, ex p Fleet* (1850) 4 De G & Sm 52 (savings bank). To determine if he has, the Friendly Societies Act 1974 s 59 is construed strictly: *Ex p Ross* (1802) 6 Ves 802; *Re West of England and South Wales District Bank, ex p Swansea Friendly Society* (1879) 11 ChD 768 (where it was held that an incorporated company cannot be an officer).

5   *Re Miller, ex p Official Receiver* [1893] 1 QB 327, CA.

6   *Re Welch, ex p Trustees of the Oddfellows Society* (1894) 63 LJQB 524.

7   *Moors v Marriott* (1878) 7 ChD 543; cf *Re Welch, ex p Trustees of the Oddfellows Society* (1894) 63 LJQB 524. See also *Re Baker, ex p Burge* (1841) 1 Mont D & De G 540; *Absolom v Gething* (1863) 32 LJ Ch 786.

8   *Re Eilbeck, ex p Trustees of the Good Intent Lodge No 987 of the Grand United Order of Oddfellows* [1910] 1 KB 136.

9   *Re Thick, ex p Buckland* (1818) Buck 214; *Re Aberdein, Hagon v Aberdein* [1896] WN 154.

10 *Re Rufford and Wragge, ex p Orford* (1852) 1 De GM & G 483; *Re West of England and South Wales District Bank, ex p Swansea Friendly Society* (1879) 11 ChD 768.

11 *Re Clarke, ex p Harris* (1845) De G 162.

(ii) Means of Distribution

600. Payment by dividend. Whenever the trustee has sufficient funds in hand for the purpose, he must, subject to the retention of such sums as may be necessary for the expenses of the bankruptcy, declare and distribute dividends among the creditors in respect of the bankruptcy debts which they have respectively proved[1].

The trustee[2] must pay every dividend by payment instruments[3] which must be prepared by the Department for Business, Innovation and Skills[4] on the application of the trustee and transmitted to him for distribution amongst the creditors[5]. However, in respect of such an application made by the trustee, the Secretary of State, if requested to do so by the trustee, may, at his discretion, as an alternative to the issue of payment instruments, make payment by electronic transfer to the persons to whom the trustee would otherwise deliver payment instruments[6].

Any application for such a payment instrument or payment by electronic transfer must be made by the trustee on a form obtainable from the Department for the purpose or on a form which is substantially similar[7]. The trustee must enter the total amount of every dividend that he desires to pay in the records to be kept[8] in one sum[9].

On the trustee's vacating office, he must send to the Department any valid unclaimed or undelivered payment instruments for dividends after indorsing them with the word 'cancelled'[10].

1 Insolvency Act 1986 s 324(1). In the case of the administration in bankruptcy of the insolvent estate of a deceased person dying before the presentation of a bankruptcy petition, s 324 applies: Administration of Insolvent Estates of Deceased Persons Order 1986, SI 1986/1999, art 3(1), Sch 1 Pt II para 23. As to the administration in bankruptcy of the insolvent estates of deceased persons see further PARA 830 et seq. As to distribution in the case of criminal bankruptcy see the Insolvency Act 1986 s 327. As to the prospective repeal of s 327 see PARA 1 note 11.
2 As to the meaning of 'trustee' see PARA 24 note 2.
3 For these purposes, 'payment instrument' means a cheque or payable order: Insolvency Regulations 1994, SI 1994/2507, reg 3(1).
4 See the Insolvency Regulations 1994, SI 1994/2507, reg 3(3) (amended by SI 2009/2748).
5 Insolvency Regulations 1994, SI 1994/2507, reg 23(1) (amended by SI 2000/485).
6 Insolvency Regulations 1994, SI 1994/2507, reg 23(1A) (added by SI 2000/485).
7 Insolvency Regulations 1994, SI 1994/2507, reg 23(2) (amended by SI 2000/485).
8 Ie under the Insolvency Regulations 1994, SI 1994/2507, reg 24: see PARA 387.
9 Insolvency Regulations 1994, SI 1994/2507, reg 23(3).
10 Insolvency Regulations 1994, SI 1994/2507, reg 23(4).

601. Unclaimed funds and dividends. Any money in the hands of the trustee[1] at the date of his vacation of office, or which comes into the hands of any former trustee at any time after his vacation of office, representing, in either case, unclaimed or undistributed assets of the bankrupt or dividends, must forthwith be paid by him into the Insolvency Services Account[2]. The Secretary of State must from time to time pay into the Consolidated Fund[3] out of the Insolvency Services Account so much of the sums standing to the credit of that Account as represents dividends which were declared before such date as the Treasury may from time to time determine and have not been claimed, and balances ascertained before that date which are too small to be divided among the persons entitled to them[4].

1 As to the meaning of 'trustee' see PARA 24 note 2.
2 Insolvency Regulations 1994, SI 1994/2507, reg 31. As to the Insolvency Services Account see PARA 22.
3 As to the Consolidated Fund see CONSTITUTIONAL LAW AND HUMAN RIGHTS vol 8(2) (Reissue) PARA 711.
4 See the Insolvency Act 1986 s 407(1); and PARA 25.

602. Distribution of property in specie. With the permission of the creditors' committee[1], the trustee may divide in its existing form amongst the bankrupt's creditors, according to its estimated value, any property which from its peculiar nature or other special circumstances cannot be readily or advantageously sold[2]. A permission so given may not be a general permission but must relate to a particular proposed exercise of the power in question; and a person dealing with the trustee in good faith and for value is not to be concerned to inquire whether any requisite permission has been given[3].

Where the trustee has done anything without the requisite permission, the court or the creditors' committee may, for the purpose of enabling him to meet his expenses out of the bankrupt's estate, ratify what the trustee has done; but the committee may not do so unless it is satisfied that the trustee acted in a case of urgency and has sought its ratification without undue delay[4].

1 As to the creditors' committee see PARA 326 et seq.
2 Insolvency Act 1986 s 326(1). The power conferred by s 326(1) is without prejudice to ss 315–319 (disclaimer: see PARA 490 et seq): s 326(1). As to the application of s 326 in the case of the administration in bankruptcy of the insolvent estate of a deceased person dying before the presentation of a bankruptcy petition see PARA 476 note 5.
3 Insolvency Act 1986 s 326(2).
4 Insolvency Act 1986 s 326(3).

(iii) Declaration and Payment of Dividend

603. Notice of intended dividend. Before declaring a dividend, the trustee must give notice of his intention to do so to all creditors whose addresses are known to him and who have not proved their debts and where a member state liquidator[1] has been appointed in relation to the insolvent, to that person[2]. Before declaring a first dividend the trustee must give notice[3] of the intended dividend; and, as soon as reasonably practicable, such notice must be gazetted[4] and may be advertised in such manner as the trustee thinks fit[5].

Any such notice and any notice of a first dividend must specify a date ('the last date for proving') up to which proofs may be lodged; and the date must be the same for all creditors, and be not less than 21 days from the date of the notice[6]. The trustee must in his notice state the intention to declare a dividend, specified as interim or final, as the case may be, within the period of two months from the last date for proving[7].

1 As to the meaning of 'member state liquidator' see PARA 175 note 8.
2 Insolvency Act 1986 s 324(2); Insolvency Rules 1986, SI 1986/1925, rr 11.2(1), 13.9A (r 11.2(1) amended by SI 2002/1307; and the Insolvency Rules 1986, SI 1986/1925, rr 11.2(1) amended, and r 13.9A added, by SI 2010/686). As to the application of the Insolvency Act 1986 s 324 in the case of the administration in bankruptcy of the insolvent estate of a deceased person dying before the presentation of a bankruptcy petition see PARA 600 note 1.
3 In addition to the standard contents, the notice must: (1) state that the office-holder intends to declare a first dividend; and (2) specify the date by which and place at which proofs must be lodged: Insolvency Rules 1986, SI 1986/1925, r 11.2(1C) (added by SI 2010/686).
4 As to the meaning of 'gazetted' see PARA 165 note 12.
5 Insolvency Rules 1986, SI 1986/1925, r 11.2(1A) (added by SI 1987/1919; substituted by SI 2009/642; and amended by SI 2010/686). This requirement does not apply where the trustee has previously, by notice which has been gazetted, invited creditors to prove their debts: Insolvency Rules 1986, SI 1986/1925, r 11.2(1B) (added by SI 2009/642; and amended by SI 2010/686). As to proofs of debt see PARA 507 et seq.
6 Insolvency Rules 1986, SI 1986/1925, r 11.2(2) (amended by SI 1987/1919).
7 Insolvency Rules 1986, SI 1986/1925, r 11.2(3) (amended by SI 2010/686).

604. Final admission and rejection of proofs. Within five business days[1] from the last date for proving[2], the trustee must deal with every creditor's proof, in so far as not already dealt with, by admitting or rejecting it in whole or in part[3], or by making such provision as he thinks fit in respect of it[4]. The trustee is not obliged to deal with proofs lodged after the last date for proving; but he may do so, if he thinks fit[5].

In the declaration of a dividend no payment is to be made more than once by virtue of the same debt[6]. Subject to the provision relating to the assignment of the right to a dividend[7], where a creditor has proved, and a member state liquidator[8] has proved in relation to the same debt, payment must only be made to the creditor[9].

1 As to the meaning of 'business day' see PARA 28 note 8.
2 As to the meaning of 'the last date for proving' see PARA 603.
3 As to admission and rejection of proofs see PARA 550.
4 Insolvency Rules 1986, SI 1986/1925, rr 11.3(1), 13.9A (r 11.3(1) amended, and r 13.9A added, by SI 2010/686).
5 Insolvency Rules 1986, SI 1986/1925, r 11.3(2) (amended by SI 2010/686).
6 Insolvency Rules 1986, SI 1986/1925, r 11.3(3) (added by SI 2002/1307).
7 Ie subject to the Insolvency Rules 1986, SI 1986/1925, r 11.11: see PARA 611.
8 As to the meaning of 'member state liquidator' see PARA 175 note 8.
9 Insolvency Rules 1986, SI 1986/1925, r 11.3(4) (added by SI 2002/1307).

605. Postponement or cancellation of dividend. If in the period of two months stated in the trustee's notice of dividend[1]:

(1)   the trustee has rejected a proof in whole or in part and application is made to the court for his decision to be reversed or varied[2]; or

(2)   application is made to the court for the trustee's decision on a proof to be reversed or varied, or for a proof to be expunged, or for a reduction of the amount claimed[3],

the trustee may postpone or cancel the dividend[4].

1   Ie the period referred to in the Insolvency Rules 1986, SI 1986/1925, r 11.2(3): see PARA 603.
2   See PARAS 550, 551.
3   See PARAS 552, 553.
4   Insolvency Rules 1986, SI 1986/1925, rr 11.4, 13.9A (r 11.4 amended, and r 13.9A added, by SI 2010/686).

606. Decision to declare dividend; provisions. If the trustee has not, in the period of two months stated in his notice of intended dividend[1], had cause to postpone or cancel the dividend, he must within that period proceed to declare the dividend of which he gave notice[2]. Except with the permission of the court, the trustee may not declare the dividend so long as there is pending any application to the court to reverse or vary a decision of his on a proof[3], or to expunge a proof or to reduce the amount claimed[4]; and, if the court so gives permission, the trustee must make such provision in respect of the proof in question as the court directs[5]. In the calculation and distribution of a dividend the trustee must make provision for:

(1)   any bankruptcy debts[6] which appear to him to be due to persons who, by reason of the distance of their place of residence, may not have had sufficient time to tender and establish their proofs;

(2)   any bankruptcy debts which are the subject of claims which have not yet been determined; and

(3)   disputed proofs and claims[7].

1   Ie the period referred to in the Insolvency Rules 1986, SI 1986/1925, r 11.2(3): see PARA 603.
2   Insolvency Rules 1986, SI 1986/1925, rr 11.5(1), 13.9A (r 11.5(1) amended, and r 13.9A added, by SI 2010/686).
3   See PARA 551.
4   See PARAS 552, 553.
5   Insolvency Rules 1986, SI 1986/1925, r 11.5(2) (amended by SI 2010/686).
6   See PARA 508.
7   Insolvency Act 1986 s 324(4). As to the application of s 324 in the case of the administration in bankruptcy of the insolvent estate of a deceased person dying before the presentation of a bankruptcy petition see PARA 600 note 1.

607. Notice of declaration. The trustee must give notice[1] of the dividend to all creditors who have proved their debts and, where a member state liquidator[2] has been appointed in relation to the insolvent, to that person[3]. The notice must include the following particulars relating to the insolvency and the administration of the bankrupt's estate:

(1)   amounts realised from the sale of assets, indicating, so far as practicable, amounts raised by the sale of particular assets;

(2)   payments made by the trustee in the administration of the bankrupt's estate;

(3)   provision, if any, made for unsettled claims, and funds, if any, retained for particular purposes;

(4)   the total amount to be distributed, and the rate of dividend;

(5) whether, and if so when, any further dividend is expected to be declared[4].

The dividend may be distributed simultaneously with the notice declaring it[5].

Payment of dividend may be made by post, or arrangements may be made with any creditor for it to be paid to him in another way, or held for his collection[6]; and, where a dividend is paid on a bill of exchange or other negotiable instrument[7], the amount of the dividend must be indorsed on the instrument, or on a certified copy of it, if required to be produced by the holder for that purpose[8].

1 As to the mode of giving notice see PARA 808.
2 As to the meaning of 'member state liquidator' see PARA 175 note 8.
3 Insolvency Act 1986 s 324(3); Insolvency Rules 1986, SI 1986/1925, rr 11.6(1), 13.9A (r 11.6(1) amended by SI 2002/1307 and SI 2010/686; the Insolvency Rules 1986, SI 1986/1925, r 13.9A added by SI 2010/686). As to the application of the Insolvency Act 1986 s 324 in the case of the administration in bankruptcy of the insolvent estate of a deceased person dying before the presentation of a bankruptcy petition see PARA 600 note 1.
4 Insolvency Rules 1986, SI 1986/1925, r 11.6(2) (amended by SI 2010/686).
5 Insolvency Rules 1986, SI 1986/1925, r 11.6(3).
6 Insolvency Rules 1986, SI 1986/1925, r 11.6(4).
7 As to proof in respect of negotiable instruments see PARA 585.
8 Insolvency Rules 1986, SI 1986/1925, r 11.6(5).

608. Notice of no, or no further, dividend. If the trustee gives notice[1] to creditors that he is unable to declare any dividend or, as the case may be, any further dividend[2], the notice must contain a statement to the effect either that no funds have been realised or that the funds realised have already been distributed or used or allocated for defraying the expenses of administration[3].

1 As to the mode of giving notice see PARA 808.
2 See PARA 607 text to note 3.
3 Insolvency Rules 1986, SI 1986/1925, rr 11.7, 13.9A (r 11.7 amended, and r 13.9A added, by SI 2010/686). As to the expenses of the bankruptcy see PARAS 588–590.

609. Proof made or altered after payment of dividend. Neither a creditor who has not proved his debt before the declaration of any dividend[1] nor a creditor who increases the amount claimed in his proof after a payment of dividend[2] is entitled to disturb[3] the distribution of the dividend[4]; but, when he has proved his debt or increased his proof, as the case may be, he is entitled to be paid, out of any money for the time being available for the payment of any further dividend, any dividend or dividends which he has failed to receive[5]. Any dividend or dividends so payable must be paid before such money is applied to the payment of any such further dividend[6].

If, after a creditor's proof has been admitted, the proof is withdrawn or expunged, or the amount of it is reduced, the creditor is liable to repay to the trustee, for the credit of the bankrupt's estate, any amount overpaid by way of dividend[7].

1 Insolvency Act 1986 s 325(1). In the case of the administration in bankruptcy of the insolvent estate of a deceased person dying before the presentation of a bankruptcy petition, s 325 applies: Administration of Insolvent Estates of Deceased Persons Order 1986, SI 1986/1999, art 3(1), Sch 1 Pt II para 23. As to the administration in bankruptcy of the insolvent estates of deceased persons see further PARA 830 et seq.
2 Insolvency Rules 1986, SI 1986/1925, r 11.8(1).
3 Ie whether by reason that he has not participated in it, or participated to the right extent or otherwise.

4   Or, in the case of a creditor who proves late, any other dividend declared before his debt was
     proved: Insolvency Act 1986 s 325(1).
5   Insolvency Act 1986 s 325(1)(a); Insolvency Rules 1986, SI 1986/1925, r 11.8(1).
6   Insolvency Act 1986 s 325(1)(b); Insolvency Rules 1986, SI 1986/1925, r 11.8(2).
7   Insolvency Rules 1986, SI 1986/1925, rr 11.8(3), 13.9A (r 11.8 amended, and r 13.9A added,
     by SI 2010/686).

610.   Secured creditors. Where a creditor revalues his security at a time when
a dividend has been declared, the following provisions apply[1].

If the revaluation results in a reduction of his unsecured claim ranking for
dividend, the creditor must as soon as reasonably practicable repay to the
trustee, for the credit of the bankrupt's estate, any amount received by him as
dividend in excess of that to which he would be entitled having regard to the
revaluation of the security[2].

If the revaluation results in an increase of his unsecured claim, the creditor is
entitled to receive from the trustee, out of any money for the time being available
for the payment of a further dividend, before any such further dividend is paid,
any dividend or dividends which he has failed to receive, having regard to the
revaluation of the security; but the creditor is not entitled to disturb any dividend
declared, whether or not distributed, before the date of the revaluation[3].

If a creditor contravenes any provision[4] relating to the valuation of securities,
the court may, on the application[5] of the trustee, order that the creditor be
wholly or partly disqualified from participation in any dividend[6].

1   Insolvency Rules 1986, SI 1986/1925, r 11.9(1). As to revaluation by a creditor of his security
     see PARA 576.
2   Insolvency Rules 1986, SI 1986/1925, rr 11.9(2), 13.8(b), 13.9A (rr 11.9(2), 13.8(b) amended
     by SI 2009/642; the Insolvency Rules 1986, SI 1986/1925, rr 11.9(2), 13.9A amended by
     SI 2010/686).
3   Insolvency Rules 1986, SI 1986/1925, rr 11.9(3), 13.9A (r 11.9(3) amended, and r 13.9A added,
     by SI 2010/686).
4   Ie any provision of the Insolvency Act 1986 or the Insolvency Rules 1986, SI 1986/1925: see
     PARA 575 et seq.
5   As to the mode of application and the procedure see PARA 786 et seq.
6   Insolvency Rules 1986, SI 1986/1925, rr 11.10, 13.9A (r 11.10 amended, and r 13.9A added, by
     SI 2010/686).

611.   Assignment of right to dividend. If a person entitled to a dividend gives
notice[1] to the trustee that he wishes the dividend to be paid to another person, or
that he has assigned his entitlement to another person, the trustee must pay the
dividend to that other accordingly[2]. A notice so given must specify the name and
address of the person to whom payment is to be made[3].

1   As to the mode of giving notice see PARA 808.
2   Insolvency Rules 1986, SI 1986/1925, rr 11.11(1), 13.9A (r 11.11 amended, and r 13.9A added,
     by SI 2010/686).
3   Insolvency Rules 1986, SI 1986/1925, r 11.11(2).

612.   Preferential creditors. The provisions relating to declaration and
payment of dividends[1] apply with respect to any distribution made in the
bankruptcy to preferential creditors[2], with such adaptations as are appropriate
considering that such creditors are of a limited class[3], save that the notice of the
intended dividend by the trustee[4], where a dividend is to be declared for
preferential creditors, need only be given to those creditors in whose case he has
reason to believe that their debts are preferential; and notice of the intended
dividend need only be gazetted[5] if the trustee thinks fit[6].

1   Ie the Insolvency Rules 1986, SI 1986/1925, rr 11.1–11.13: see PARAS 603 et seq, 613.
2   See PARA 591.
3   Insolvency Rules 1986, SI 1986/1925, r 11.12(1).
4   Ie the notice under the Insolvency Rules 1986, SI 1986/1925, r 11.12.
5   As to the meaning of 'gazetted' see PARA 165 note 12.
6   Insolvency Rules 1986, SI 1986/1925, rr 11.12(2), 13.9A (r 11.12(2) amended by SI 1987/1919;
    and SI 2010/686; the Insolvency Rules 1986, SI 1986/1925, r 13.9A added by SI 2010/686).

613.   Debts payable at future time.   Where a creditor has proved for a debt of
which payment is not due at the date of the declaration of dividend[1], he is
entitled to dividend equally with other creditors, but subject to a reduction in
respect of his admitted proof[2].

1   As to proof of debts payable at a future time see PARA 560.
2   Insolvency Rules 1986, SI 1986/1925, r 11.13(1). For the purpose of dividend, and for no other
    purpose, the amount of the creditor's admitted proof, or, if a distribution has previously been
    made to him, the amount remaining outstanding in respect of his admitted proof, must be
    reduced by applying the following formula: $X/1.05n$ where 'X' is the value of the admitted
    proof, and 'n' is the period beginning with the date of the bankruptcy order and ending with the
    date on which the payment of the creditor's debt would otherwise be due expressed in years and
    months in a decimalised form: r 11.13(2), (3)(c) (substituted by SI 2005/527).
        This rule does not apply in calculating the compensation due to a landlord following
    disclaimer of a lease: *Christopher Moran Holdings Ltd v Bairstow* [2000] 2 AC 172, sub nom
    Re Park Air Services plc, Christopher Moran Holdings Ltd v Bairstow [1999] 1 All ER 673, HL.

614.   Refusal by trustee to pay dividend.   No action lies against the trustee for
a dividend; but, if the trustee refuses to pay a dividend, the court may, if it thinks
fit, order[1] him to pay it and also to pay, out of his own money, interest[2] on the
dividend from the time it was withheld, and the costs of the proceedings in which
the order to pay is made[3].

1   As to the mode of application and the procedure see PARA 786 et seq.
2   Ie at the rate for the time being specified in the Judgments Act 1838 s 17: see FINANCIAL
    SERVICES AND INSTITUTIONS vol 49 (2008) PARA 1307.
3   Insolvency Act 1986 s 325(2). As to the application of s 325 in the case of the administration in
    bankruptcy of the insolvent estate of a deceased person dying before the presentation of a
    bankruptcy petition see PARA 609 note 1.

615.   Final distribution.   When the trustee has realised all the bankrupt's
estate[1] or so much of it as can, in the trustee's opinion, be realised without
needlessly protracting the trusteeship, he must give notice in the prescribed
manner[2] either of his intention to declare a final dividend or that no dividend, or
further dividend, will be declared[3]. Such notice must contain the prescribed
particulars[4] and must require claims against the bankrupt's estate to be
established by a date ('the final date') specified in the notice[5]. On the application
of any person, the court may postpone the final date[6].
    After the final date, the trustee must:

(1)   defray any outstanding expenses of the bankruptcy out of the
      bankrupt's estate; and

(2)   if he intends to declare a final dividend, declare and distribute that
      dividend without regard to the claim of any person in respect of a debt
      not already proved in the bankruptcy[7].

If a surplus remains after payment in full and with interest of all the
bankrupt's creditors and the payment of the expenses of the bankruptcy, the
bankrupt is entitled to the surplus[8].

1   As to the meaning of 'the bankrupt's estate' see PARA 211.

2 Ie under the Insolvency Rules 1986, SI 1986/1925, r 11.2 (notice of intended dividend: see PARA 603) or r 11.7 (notice of no, or no further, dividend: see PARA 608). As to the mode of giving notice see PARA 808.

3 Insolvency Act 1986 s 330(1). In the case of the administration in bankruptcy of the insolvent estate of a deceased person dying before the presentation of a bankruptcy petition, s 330 applies with the modification that in s 330(5) (see the text to note 8) for the words 'the bankrupt is entitled to the surplus' there are to be substituted the words 'the surplus must be paid to the personal representative unless the court otherwise orders'; and there is to be added s 330(6) which provides that s 330(5) is subject to Council Regulation (EC) 1346/2000 (OJ L160, 30.6.2000, p 1) on insolvency proceedings ('European Regulation on Insolvency Proceedings') art 35 (surplus in secondary proceedings to be transferred to main proceedings) (see PARAS 41, 42): Administration of Insolvent Estates of Deceased Persons Order 1986, SI 1986/1999, art 3(1), Sch 1 Pt II para 25 (substituted by SI 2002/1309). As to the administration in bankruptcy of the insolvent estates of deceased persons see further PARA 830 et seq.

4 Ie under the Insolvency Rules 1986, SI 1986/1925, rr 11.1–11.13: see PARA 603 et seq.

5 Insolvency Act 1986 s 330(2).

6 Insolvency Act 1986 s 330(3). As to the mode of application and the procedure see PARA 786 et seq.

7 Insolvency Act 1986 s 330(4). In the case of the death of a debtor after the presentation of a bankruptcy petition, at the end of s 330(4)(b) (see text head (2)) there are to be added the words 'and of the personal representative of a debtor dying after the presentation of a bankruptcy petition in respect of reasonable funeral and testamentary expenses of which notice has not already been given to the trustee': Administration of Insolvent Estates of Deceased Persons Order 1986, SI 1986/1999, art 5(1), Sch 2 para 2.

8 Insolvency Act 1986 s 330(5). See also note 3. The provisions of s 330(5) are subject to the European Regulation on Insolvency Proceedings art 35 (surplus in secondary proceedings to be transferred to main proceedings) (see PARA 42): Insolvency Act 1986 s 330(6) (added by SI 2002/1240).

616.   Final meeting of creditors.   Where it appears to the trustee that the administration of the bankrupt's estate[1] is for practical purposes complete and the trustee is not the official receiver, the trustee must summon a final general meeting[2] of the bankrupt's creditors which must receive the trustee's report of his administration of the bankrupt's estate and must determine whether the trustee should[3] have his release[4].

If the trustee thinks fit, he may give the notice summoning the final general meeting at the same time as giving notice[5] of final distribution; but, if summoned for an earlier date, that meeting must be adjourned (and, if necessary, further adjourned) until a date on which the trustee is able to report to the meeting that the administration of the bankrupt's estate is for practical purposes complete[6].

Where there is comprised in the bankrupt's estate property consisting of an interest in a dwelling house[7] which is occupied by the bankrupt or by his spouse or former spouse or by his civil partner or former civil partner, and the trustee has been unable for any reason to realise that property, the trustee may not so summon a final meeting unless either:

(1)   the court has made an order[8] imposing a charge on that property for the benefit of the bankrupt's estate;

(2)   the court has declined to make such an order; or

(3)   the Secretary of State has issued a certificate to the trustee stating that it would be inappropriate or inexpedient for such an application to be made in the case in question[9].

In the administration of the bankrupt's estate it is the trustee's duty to retain sufficient sums from the estate to cover the expenses of summoning and holding the meeting required by the above provisions[10].

1 Ie in accordance with the Insolvency Act 1986 Pt 9 Ch 5 (ss 305–335). As to the meaning of 'the bankrupt's estate' see PARA 211.

2   As to the procedure for the holding of the final meeting see PARA 381.

3   Ie under the Insolvency Act 1986 s 299: see PARA 381.

4   Insolvency Act 1986 s 331(1), (2). In the case of the administration in bankruptcy of the insolvent estate of a deceased person dying before the presentation of a bankruptcy petition, s 331 applies: Administration of Insolvent Estates of Deceased Persons Order 1986, SI 1986/1999, art 3(1), Sch 1 Pt II para 26. As to the administration in bankruptcy of the insolvent estates of deceased persons see further PARA 830 et seq.

   As to the modification of the Insolvency Act 1986 s 331 by the Insolvent Partnerships Order 1994, SI 1994/2421, in relation to the bankruptcy of an individual member of an insolvent partnership see COMPANY AND PARTNERSHIP INSOLVENCY vol 17 (2011) PARA 1348.

5   Ie under the Insolvency Act 1986 s 330(1): see PARA 615.

6   Insolvency Act 1986 s 331(3).

7   As to the meaning of 'dwelling house' see PARA 413 note 1. As to the rights of occupation of a dwelling house forming part of the estate held by the bankrupt, his spouse or civil partner or former spouse or civil partner, and as to the right of the trustee to realise the dwelling house, see PARA 672 et seq.

8   Ie under the Insolvency Act 1986 s 313: see PARA 413.

9   Insolvency Act 1986 s 332(1), (2) (s 332(1) amended by the Civil Partnership Act 2004 s 261(1), Sch 17 para 117). In the case of the administration in bankruptcy of the insolvent estate of a deceased person dying before the presentation of a bankruptcy petition, the Insolvency Act 1986 s 332 applies: Administration of Insolvent Estates of Deceased Persons Order 1986, SI 1986/1999, Sch 1 Pt II para 26.

10 Insolvency Act 1986 s 331(4).

(iv) Second Bankruptcy

617. Stay of distribution in case of second bankruptcy. Where a bankruptcy order is made against an undischarged bankrupt and the existing trustee[1] has been given the prescribed notice[2] of the presentation of the petition for the later bankruptcy[3], any distribution or other disposition by him of:

(1)   any property which is vested in the existing trustee as after-acquired property[4];

(2)   any money paid to the trustee in pursuance of an income payments order[5]; and

(3)   any property or money which is, or in the hands of the existing trustee represents, the proceeds of sale or application of property or money falling within head (1) or head (2) above,

if made after the giving of the notice, is void except to the extent that it was made with the consent of the court or is or was subsequently ratified by the court[6].

The above provisions are without prejudice to the statutory restrictions[7] on dispositions of property following the making of a bankruptcy order[8].

1   For these purposes, 'the existing trustee' means the trustee, if any, of the bankrupt's estate for the purposes of the earlier bankruptcy: Insolvency Act 1986 s 334(1)(c). 'The earlier bankruptcy' means the bankruptcy (or, as the case may be, most recent bankruptcy) from which the bankrupt has not been discharged at the commencement of the later bankruptcy: s 334(1)(b). As to the meaning of 'the later bankruptcy' see note 3.

2   For the prescribed form of notice to the existing trustee of the presentation of a petition for a later bankruptcy see the Insolvency Rules 1986, SI 1986/1925, Sch 4 Form 6.78 (substituted by SI 1987/1919).

3   For these purposes, 'the later bankruptcy' means the bankruptcy arising from a bankruptcy order made against an undischarged bankrupt: Insolvency Act 1986 s 334(1)(a).

4   Ie under the Insolvency Act 1986 s 307(3): see PARA 459.

5   Ie under the Insolvency Act 1986 s 310: see PARA 462.

6   Insolvency Act 1986 s 334(1)–(3).

   In the case of the administration in bankruptcy of the insolvent estate of a deceased person dying before the presentation of a bankruptcy petition, ss 334, 335 apply: Administration of

Insolvent Estates of Deceased Persons Order 1986, SI 1986/1999, art 3(1), Sch 1 Pt II para 26. As to the administration in bankruptcy of the insolvent estates of deceased persons see further PARA 830 et seq.

7 Ie the Insolvency Act 1986 s 284: see PARA 213.

8 Insolvency Act 1986 s 334(2). As from a day to be appointed, s 334(2) is amended by the Enterprise and Regulatory Reform Act 2013 s 71, Sch 19 paras 1, 28: see PARA 130 note 17.

618. Adjustment between earlier and later bankrupt estates. Where a bankruptcy order is made against an undischarged bankrupt, then, with effect from the commencement of the later bankruptcy[1]:

(1) any property which is vested in the existing trustee[2] as after-acquired property[3];

(2) any money paid to the existing trustee in pursuance of an income payments order[4]; and

(3) any property or money which is, or in the hands of the existing trustee represents, the proceeds of sale or application of property or money falling within head (1) or head (2) above,

which, immediately before the commencement of that bankruptcy, is comprised in the bankrupt's estate[5] for the purposes of the earlier bankruptcy[6], is to be treated as comprised in the bankrupt's estate for the purposes of the later bankruptcy and, until there is a trustee of that estate, is to be dealt with by the existing trustee[7].

Any sums which in pursuance of an income payments order[8] are payable after the commencement of the later bankruptcy to the existing trustee form part of the bankrupt's estate for the purposes of the later bankruptcy; and the court may give such consequential directions for the modification of the order as it thinks fit[9].

Except as provided above[10], property which is, or is capable of being[11], comprised in the bankrupt's estate for the purposes of the earlier bankruptcy, or of any bankruptcy prior to it, is not comprised in his estate for the purposes of the later bankruptcy[12].

The creditors of the bankrupt in the earlier bankruptcy and the creditors of the bankrupt in any bankruptcy prior to the earlier one, are not to be creditors of his in the later bankruptcy in respect of the same debts; but the existing trustee may prove in the later bankruptcy for:

(a) the unsatisfied balance of the debts provable against the bankrupt's estate in the earlier bankruptcy;

(b) any interest payable on that balance; and

(c) any unpaid expenses of the earlier bankruptcy[13].

Any amount so provable[14] ranks in priority after all the other debts provable in the later bankruptcy and after interest on those debts and, accordingly, may not be paid unless those debts and that interest have first been paid in full[15].

1 As to the meaning of 'the later bankruptcy' see PARA 617 note 3. As to the commencement of bankruptcy see PARA 209.

2 As to the meaning of 'the existing trustee' see PARA 617 note 1.

3 Ie under the Insolvency Act 1986 s 307(3): see PARA 459.

4 Ie under the Insolvency Act 1986 s 310: see PARA 462.

5 As to the meaning of 'the bankrupt's estate' see PARA 211.

6 As to the meaning of 'the earlier bankruptcy' see PARA 617 note 1.

7 Insolvency Act 1986 ss 334(1), (3), 335(1). As to the application of ss 334, 335 in the case of the administration in bankruptcy of the insolvent estate of a deceased person dying before the presentation of a bankruptcy petition see PARA 617 note 6.

8 See note 4.

9 Insolvency Act 1986 s 335(2).

10 Ie in the Insolvency Act 1986 s 335(1)–(3) (see the text and notes 1–9; and PARA 619) and in s 334 (see PARA 617).

11 Ie by virtue of the Insolvency Act 1986 s 308 (personal property of the bankrupt exceeding a reasonable replacement value: see PARA 404) or s 308A (vesting in trustee of certain tenancies: see PARA 405).

12 Insolvency Act 1986 s 335(4) (amended by the Housing Act 1988 s 140(1), Sch 17 para 74).

13 Insolvency Act 1986 s 335(5).

14 Ie under the Insolvency Act 1986 s 335(5).

15 Insolvency Act 1986 s 335(6).

619. Expenses of trustees of earlier estate. Anything comprised in a bankrupt's estate by virtue of the above provisions[1] is so comprised subject to a first charge in favour of the existing trustee[2] for any bankruptcy expenses incurred by him in relation thereto[3]. Any expenses so incurred by the existing trustee[4] must be defrayed out of, and are a charge on:

(1) any property which is vested in the existing trustee as after-acquired property[5];

(2) any money paid to the existing trustee in pursuance of an income payments order[6]; and

(3) any property or money which is, or in the hands of the existing trustee represents, the proceeds of sale or application of property or money falling within head (1) or head (2) above,

whether in the hands of the existing trustee or of the trustee for the purposes of the later bankruptcy[7].

1 Ie by virtue of the Insolvency Act 1986 s 335(1) or (2): see PARA 618.

2 As to the meaning of 'the existing trustee' see PARA 607 note 1.

3 Insolvency Act 1986 s 335(3). As to the application of s 335 in the case of the administration in bankruptcy of the insolvent estate of a deceased person dying before the presentation of a bankruptcy petition see PARA 617 note 6.

4 Ie in compliance with the Insolvency Act 1986 s 335(1) (see PARA 618) or the Insolvency Rules 1986, SI 1986/1925, rr 6.225–6.228 (see the text and notes 5–7; and PARA 489).

5 Ie under the Insolvency Act 1986 s 307(3): see PARA 459.

6 Ie under the Insolvency Act 1986 s 310: see PARA 462.

7 Insolvency Rules 1986, SI 1986/1925, r 6.228.

(9) ANNULMENT OF BANKRUPTCY ORDER; DISCHARGE

(i) Annulment of Bankruptcy Order

A. IN GENERAL

620. Grounds for annulment. The court may annul a bankruptcy order if it at any time appears to the court:

(1) that, on any grounds existing at the time the order was made, the order ought not to have been made[1]; or

(2) that, to the extent required by the Insolvency Rules 1986[2], the bankruptcy debts[3] and the expenses of the bankruptcy[4] have all, since the making of the order, been either paid or secured for to the satisfaction of the court[5].

The court may annul a bankruptcy order whether or not the bankrupt has been discharged from the bankruptcy[6]. Where the court annuls a bankruptcy order it has to consider who should pay the trustee's remuneration and costs[7].

Where the creditors' meeting summoned to consider a proposal for a voluntary arrangement[8] approves the arrangement, with or without modifications, and the debtor is an undischarged bankrupt, the court must annul the bankruptcy order by which he was adjudged bankrupt and may give such directions with respect to the conduct of the bankruptcy and the administration of the bankrupt's estate as it thinks appropriate for facilitating the implementation of the approved voluntary arrangement[9].

1 See PARA 621.
2 Ie by the Insolvency Rules 1986, SI 1986/1925.
3 As to the meaning of 'bankruptcy debt' see PARA 508.
4 See PARA 588.
5 Insolvency Act 1986 s 282(1). See PARA 622. In the case of the administration in bankruptcy of the insolvent estate of a deceased person dying before the presentation of a bankruptcy petition, s 282(1) applies: Administration of Insolvent Estates of Deceased Persons Order 1986, SI 1986/1999, art 3(1), Sch 1 Pt II para 11. As to the administration in bankruptcy of the insolvent estates of deceased persons see further PARA 830 et seq.
   Until a day to be appointed, a bankruptcy order against an individual on a petition under the Insolvency Act 1986 s 264(1)(a), (b) or (c) may be annulled by the court if at any time it appears to the court that the petition was pending at a time when a criminal bankruptcy order was made against the individual or was presented after such an order was made and no appeal is pending against the individual's conviction of any offence by virtue of which the criminal bankruptcy order was made: see the Insolvency Act 1986 s 282(2) (prospectively repealed by the Criminal Justice Act 1988 s 170(2), Sch 16). At the date at which this volume states the law no such day had been appointed. As to criminal bankruptcy orders see PARA 1.
   As from a day to be appointed, the Insolvency Act 1986 s 282(2) is amended by the Enterprise and Regulatory Reform Act 2013 s 71, Sch 19 paras 1, 13. At the date at which this volume states the law no such day had been appointed. As to the changes proposed by the Enterprise and Regulatory Reform Act 2013 see PARA 130.
6 Insolvency Act 1986 s 282(3).
7 In general if the grounds for annulment are as in head (2) of the text it will be for the debtor to pay or procure payment of such remuneration costs but if the grounds of annulment are as in head (1) of the text, it will not necessarily be the case that the petitioning creditor should be responsible: *Butterworth v Soutter* [2000] BPIR 582; *London Borough of Redbridge v Mustafa* [2010] EWHC 1105 (Ch), [2011] RVR 45, [2010] BPIR 893; and see *Thornhill v Atherton* [2004] EWCA Civ 1858, [2005] BPIR 437, [2004] All ER (D) 316 (Dec); *Tetteh v Lambeth London Borough Council* [2008] BPIR 241. As to applications on the ground that the trustee's remuneration and charges are excessive see PARA 625.
8 Ie under the Insolvency Act 1986 s 257: see PARA 59.
9 See the Insolvency Act 1986 s 261; and PARA 70.

621. Orders which ought not to have been made. A bankruptcy order made in respect of a debt on which the petition was founded and which did not exist at the date of the order or was otherwise unenforceable against the debtor may be annulled[1]. A bankruptcy order made in proceedings which are an abuse of the process of the court may also be annulled[2], as may an order made on evidence relating to the debtor which was untrue[3], or where the debtor was dead at the time when bankruptcy proceedings were taken against him[4], or where the debtor was a minor and the debt was not enforceable against the debtor[5], or where the debtor lacked mental capacity to engage in the bankruptcy process[6]. The grounds on which the order ought not to have been made must have been existing at the time the bankruptcy order was made[7]. Bankruptcy being a class remedy, a court should not annul a bankruptcy order by consent without investigation[8].

1 *Royal Bank of Scotland v Farley* [1996] BPIR 638, CA. Where, on an application to annul, the petition debt is genuinely disputed the court will grant the annulment where there are special circumstances such as other creditors who have undoubted debts or other clear evidence of insolvency: *Guinan v Caldwell Associates Ltd* [2003] EWHC 3348 (Ch), [2004] BPIR 531, [2004] All ER (D) 123 (Mar).
2 *Re Painter, ex p Painter* [1895] 1 QB 85; *Re A Debtor (No 17 of 1966), ex p Debtor v Allen* [1967] Ch 590, [1967] 1 All ER 668, DC. As to when a petition is an abuse of the process of the

court see PARAS 188, 197. In the case of a bankruptcy order made on a debtor's petition, the order may be annulled if it was obtained as a device to defeat a claim against the debtor: *Woodley v Woodley (No 2)* [1993] 4 All ER 1010, [1994] 1 WLR 1167, CA; *Paulin v Paulin* [2009] EWCA Civ 221, [2009] 3 All ER 88n, [2010] 1 WLR 1057; cf *F v F (Divorce: Annulment of Bankruptcy Order)* [1994] 2 FCR 689, sub nom *F v F (Divorce: Insolvency: Annulment of Bankruptcy Order)* [1994] 1 FLR 359. See also *Ella v Ella* [2008] EWHC 3258 (Ch), [2009] BPIR 441; *Arif v Zar* [2012] EWCA Civ 986, [2012] BPIR 948, [2012] All ER (D) 243 (Jul). Where the debtor has been misled into not attending the hearing of the petition at which a bankruptcy order is made, the court may annul the order regardless of the strength of the debtor's opposition to the petition: see *Hope v Premierpace (Europe) Ltd* [1999] BPIR 695.

3   See *Re Bright, ex p Wingfield and Blew* [1903] 1 KB 735. See also *Paulin v Paulin* [2009] EWCA Civ 221, [2010] 1 WLR 1057, [2009] 2 FCR 477 (motives in procuring order, based on substantially dishonest statement of affairs, militated in favour of exercising discretion to annul it); distinguished in *Mekarska v Ruiz* [2011] EWHC 913 (Fam), [2011] 2 FCR 608, [2011] 2 FLR 608. See also *Gittins v Serco Home Affairs* [2012] EWHC 651 (Ch), [2012] 4 All ER 1362, [2013] 1 WLR 1218 (prisoner's appeal against annulment of bankruptcy order allowed).

4   *Re Stanger, ex p Geisel* (1882) 22 ChD 436, CA (decided under the Bankruptcy Act 1869 (repealed)). As to the administration in bankruptcy of the insolvent estates of deceased persons see PARA 830 et seq. If a debtor dies before service of the petition, the court may order service to be effected on his personal representatives, or on such other persons as it thinks just: see the Insolvency Rules 1986, SI 1986/1925, r 6.16; and PARA 177.

5   *Re Davenport, ex p Bankrupt v Eric Street Properties Ltd* [1963] 2 All ER 850, [1963] 1 WLR 817, CA, as explained in *Re Noble (a bankrupt), ex p Bankrupt v Official Receiver* [1965] Ch 129, [1964] 2 All ER 522, CA.

6   *Haworth v Cartmel* [2011] EWHC 36 (Ch), [2011] BPIR 428, [2011] All ER (D) 23 (Mar).

7   See the Insolvency Act 1986 s 282(1)(a); and PARA 620 head (1). The court may, however, take into account evidence subsequently filed relating to the state of affairs existing at the date of the bankruptcy order: see *Re Dunn, ex p Official Receiver v Dunn* [1949] Ch 640, [1949] 2 All ER 388, CA. The court may also inquire behind a judgment, even though there was no application to set aside the judgment effective at the time when the bankruptcy order was made: *Royal Bank of Scotland v Farley* [1996] BPIR 638, CA. See also *Flett v Revenue and Customs Comrs* [2010] EWHC 2662 (Ch), [2010] BPIR 1075.

    The court also has a parallel jurisdiction to rescind a bankruptcy order on evidence of a significant change of circumstances following the making of the order: see the Insolvency Act 1986 s 375(1) (cited in PARA 761); and *Fitch v Official Receiver* [1996] 1 WLR 242, [1996] BPIR 152, CA; *Housiaux (t/a Harpers of Weybridge) v Customs and Excise Comrs* [2003] EWCA Civ 257, [2003] BPIR 858, [2003] All ER (D) 295 (Jan); cf *Johnson v Tandridge District Council* [2007] EWHC 3325 (Ch), [2008] BPIR 405, [2007] All ER (D) 350 (Oct) (where the bankrupt alleges he was unaware of the petition he should apply for annulment rather than rescission); *Revenue and Customs Comrs v Cassells* [2008] EWHC 3180 (Ch), [2009] STC 1047, [2009] BPIR 284 (proper course is rescission rather than annulment where tax assessments shown after the making of the bankruptcy order to have been incorrect).

8   *Housiaux (t/a Harpers of Weybridge) v Customs and Excise Comrs* [2003] EWCA Civ 257, [2003] BPIR 858, [2003] All ER (D) 295 (Jan); *Leicester v Plumtree Farms Ltd* [2003] EWHC 206 (Ch), [2004] BPIR 296.

622. Debts and expenses paid in full. 'Payment in full' means payment in cash to the amount of 100 pence in the pound on all bankruptcy debts[1] proved[2] in the bankruptcy[3]. In exercising its discretion whether or not to annul a bankruptcy order, the court may take into account whether interest on debts from the date of the bankruptcy order has been paid or secured[4].

The court may decline to annul a bankruptcy order where the bankrupt has paid off all proved debts but there are known to be creditors who have not proved and are unpaid[5].

The assent of the creditors to an annulment of the bankruptcy by having given to the bankrupt absolute release will not of itself be sufficient to entitle the bankrupt to have the bankruptcy annulled[6].

If a debt is disputed, or a creditor who has proved can no longer be traced, the bankrupt must have given such security, in the form of money paid into court, or a bond entered into with approved sureties, as the court considers adequate to satisfy any sum that may subsequently be proved to be due to the creditor concerned and, if the court thinks just, costs[7]. Where security has been so given in the case of an untraced creditor, the court may direct that particulars of the alleged debt, and the security, be advertised in such manner as it thinks just[8]. If advertisement is so ordered, and no claim on the security is made within 12 months from the date of the advertisement, or the first advertisement, if more than one, the court must, on application in that behalf, order the security to be released[9].

The annulment of the bankruptcy order on the ground that the bankruptcy debts and expenses have been paid in full or secured to the satisfaction of the court is in the court's discretion[10]; and, even where the debts are paid in full, an order of annulment may be refused where the bankrupt has been guilty of misconduct in relation to his affairs[11]. An applicant for annulment under the above grounds may apply to the court if the trustee's remuneration and costs are considered to be excessive[12].

1   As to the meaning of 'bankruptcy debt' see PARA 508. Interest provable under the Insolvency Act 1986 s 322(2) (see PARA 559) is a bankruptcy debt: see s 382(1)(d); and PARA 508 head (3).
2   As to proofs of debt see PARA 507 et seq.
3   An unconditional release of a debt is not equivalent to payment in full for these purposes: *Re Keet* [1905] 2 KB 666, CA; *Re Burnett, ex p Official Receiver* (1894) 1 Mans 89 (where W, a friend of the bankrupt, on his behalf took an assignment of the debts amounting to £1,600 for £140, and another friend on the like behalf paid W the full amount of the debts, which were then reassigned to the bankrupt; this was held not to be payment in full by the bankrupt). Where, however, a bankrupt has entered into a binding voluntary arrangement under the Insolvency Act 1986 Pt 8 (ss 252–263G) (see PARA 43 et seq) and is subsequently made bankrupt on the petition of a creditor not bound by the arrangement, the debts comprised in the arrangement are to be treated as paid in full for the purposes of s 282(1)(b) (see PARA 620 head (2)): *Re McKeen (a debtor)* [1995] BCC 412. Where a creditor, prior to the hearing of an application for annulment, has with the consent of the trustee withdrawn his proof, the Insolvency Act 1986 s 282(1)(b) does not require payment of that debt: *Official Receiver v McKay* [2009] EWCA Civ 467, [2010] Ch 303, [2010] 2 WLR 891 (which also warns against reliance on pre-1986 cases).
4   See the Insolvency Rules 1986, SI 1986/1925, r 6.211(5); and PARA 629.
5   *Re Robertson (a bankrupt)* [1989] 1 WLR 1139. Creditors who have not proved their debts at the date of the filing of an application to annul must be given notice of the hearing and afforded an opportunity to prove: *Re Robertson (a bankrupt)*. As to the giving of notice to creditors who have not proved see PARA 627. See also *Gill v Quinn* [2004] EWHC 883 (Ch), [2005] BPIR 129, [2004] All ER (D) 21 (Apr) (annulment refused when application made late and creditors could not be traced); cf *Savage v Howard* [2006] EWHC 3693 (Ch), [2007] BPIR 1097, [2006] All ER (D) 13 (Feb).
6   *Re Gyll, ex p Board of Trade* (1888) 5 Morr 272; *Re Hester, ex p Hester* (1889) 22 QBD 632, CA; *Re Dixon and Cardus, ex p Dixon and Cardus* (1888) 5 Morr 291; and see *Re A Debtor (No 12 of 1970), ex p Official Receiver v Debtor* [1971] 1 All ER 504, [1971] 1 WLR 261, DC; affd [1971] 2 All ER 1494, [1971] 1 WLR 1212, CA; *Housiaux (t/a Harpers of Weybridge) v Customs and Excise Comrs* [2003] EWCA Civ 257, [2003] BPIR 858, [2003] All ER (D) 295 (Jan).
7   See the Insolvency Rules 1986, SI 1986/1925, r 6.211(3); and PARA 629; and see *Hirani v Rendle* [2003] EWHC 2538 (Ch), [2004] BPIR 274, [2003] All ER (D) 27 (Nov). An order for annulment may be suspended until specified conditions are met: *Halabi v Camden London Borough Council* [2008] EWHC 322 (Ch), [2008] BPIR 370, [2008] All ER (D) 213 (Feb); cf PARA 629. In the case of a disputed bankruptcy debt, time begins to run for the purposes of the Limitation Act 1980 from the date of the annulment; and time ceases to run for limitation purposes on the making of a bankruptcy order (see PARA 518), but only in respect of debts provable in the bankruptcy, and not in respect of the creditor's right to pursue other remedies: *Re Benzon, Bower v Chetwynd* [1914] 2 Ch 68 at 75, 76, CA; *Cotterell v Price* [1960] 3 All ER 315, [1960] 1 WLR 1097. It will be in exceptional cases only that there are other remedies in respect of which time will continue to run for limitation purposes.

8   See the Insolvency Rules 1986, SI 1986/1925, r 6.211(4); and PARA 629. It would seem that time
    does not run for limitation purposes while the debt is secured, by payment into court or
    otherwise: see *Re Dennis, ex p Dennis* [1895] 2 QB 630.
9   See the Insolvency Rules 1986, SI 1986/1925, r 6.211(4).
10 See the Insolvency Act 1986 s 282(1); and PARA 620.
11 *Re Taylor, ex p Taylor* [1901] 1 KB 744, DC; *Re Keet* [1905] 2 KB 666, CA; and see *Re A
    Debtor (No 37 of 1976), ex p Taylor v Debtor* [1980] Ch 565, [1980] 1 All ER 129, DC.
        Where the bankrupt has concealed assets from his trustee and is in any event likely to be
    soon made bankrupt a second time, an annulment will be refused: *Re a Bankrupt (No 622 of
    1995), Artman v Artman* [1996] BPIR 511.
12 See the Insolvency Rules 1986, SI 1986/1925, r 6.207A; and PARA 625.

B. PROCEDURE

623.   Application for annulment.   An application to the court for the
annulment of a bankruptcy order[1] must specify whether it is made on the
grounds that:

(1)   the order ought not to have been made[2]; or
(2)   the debts and expenses of the bankrupt have all been paid or secured[3].

In either case, the application must be supported by a witness statement[4]
stating the grounds on which it is made; and, where it is made under head (2)
above, there must be set out in the witness statement all the facts by reference to
which the court is required to be satisfied before annulling the bankruptcy
order[5].

A copy of the application and the witness statement in support must be filed
in court[6]; and the court must give to the applicant notice of the venue[7] fixed for
the hearing[8].

The applicant must give to the official receiver and, if other, the trustee notice
of the venue, accompanied by copies of the application and the witness
statement:

(a)   where the application is made on the grounds specified in head (1)
      above, in sufficient time to enable them to be present at the hearing; and
(b)   where the application is made on the grounds specified in head (2)
      above, not less than 28 days before the hearing[9].

Where the application is made on the grounds specified in head (1) above,
such provisions must additionally be complied with in relation to the person on
whose petition the bankruptcy order was made[10]. Where the applicant is not the
bankrupt all notices, documents and evidence required to be given, sent or
delivered to another party by the applicant must also be given, sent or delivered
to the bankrupt[11].

1   Ie under the Insolvency Act 1986 s 282(1): see PARA 620.
2   Ie under the Insolvency Act 1986 s 282(1)(a): see PARA 620 head (1).
3   Insolvency Rules 1986, SI 1986/1925, r 6.206(1). The application for annulment under head (2)
    in the text is on the grounds specified in the Insolvency Act 1986 s 282(1)(b) (see PARA 620
    head (2)): Insolvency Rules 1986, SI 1986/1925, r 6.206(1). Part 6 Ch 21 (rr 6.206–6.214: see
    PARA 623 et seq) applies to an application to the court under the Insolvency Act 1986 s 282(2)
    (annulment of bankruptcy order on criminal bankruptcy petition: see PARA 620 note 5) as it
    applies to an application under s 282(1), with any necessary modifications: Insolvency
    Rules 1986, SI 1986/1925, r 6.234(3). See, however, PARA 1 note 11.
4   As to the meaning of 'witness statement' see PARA 161 note 7.
5   Insolvency Rules 1986, SI 1986/1925, r 6.206(2) (amended by SI 2010/686). As to the facts in
    respect of which the court is required to be satisfied see the Insolvency Rules 1986,
    SI 1986/1925, r 6.211; and PARA 629.
6   As to the meaning of 'file in court' see PARA 57 note 13.
7   As to the meaning of 'venue' see PARA 84 note 21.
8   Insolvency Rules 1986, SI 1986/1925, r 6.206(3) (amended by SI 2010/686).

9 Insolvency Rules 1986, SI 1986/1925, r 6.206(4) (amended by SI 1987/1919; and SI 2010/686).
10 Insolvency Rules 1986, SI 1986/1925, r 6.206(5) (added by SI 1987/1919).
11 Insolvency Rules 1986, SI 1986/1925, r 6.206(6) (added by SI 2003/1730; and amended by SI 2010/686). This requirement applies in relation to all the provisions of the Insolvency Rules 1986, SI 1986/1925, Pt 6 Ch 21 (rr 6.206–6.214: see PARA 624 et seq).

624. Report by trustee. Where the application for the annulment of a bankruptcy order is made on the grounds that the debts and expenses of the bankruptcy have all been paid or secured[1], then, not less than 21 days before the date fixed for the hearing, the trustee, or, if no trustee has been appointed, the official receiver, must file in court[2] a report with respect to the following matters:

(1) the circumstances leading to the bankruptcy;
(2) in summarised form, the extent of the bankrupt's assets and liabilities at the date of the bankruptcy order and at the date of the present application;
(3) details of creditors, if any, who are known to have claims, but have not proved; and
(4) such other matters as the person making the report considers to be, in the circumstances, necessary for the information of the court[3].

Where the trustee is other than the official receiver, the report must also include a statement of: (a) the trustee's remuneration; (b) the basis fixed for the trustee's remuneration[4]; (c) the expenses incurred by the trustee[5].

The report must include particulars of the extent, if any, to which, and the manner in which, the debts and expenses of the bankruptcy have been paid or secured; and, in so far as debts and expenses are unpaid but secured, the person making the report must state in it whether, and to what extent, he considers the security to be satisfactory[6].

A copy of the report must be sent to the applicant at the same time that it is filed in court; and he may, if he wishes, file further witness statements[7] in answer to statements made in the report[8]. Copies of any such affidavits must be sent by the applicant to the official receiver and, if other, the trustee[9]. If the trustee is other than the official receiver, a copy of his report must be sent to the official receiver at least 21 days before the hearing; and the official receiver may then file an additional report, a copy of which must be sent to the applicant at least five business days before the hearing[10].

1 Ie under the Insolvency Act 1986 s 282(1)(b): see PARA 620 head (2).
2 As to the meaning of 'file in court' see PARA 57 note 13.
3 Insolvency Rules 1986, SI 1986/1925, r 6.207(1), (2). 'Such other matters' presumably includes the conduct of the bankrupt during the proceedings: cf the Bankruptcy Rules 1952, SI 1952/2113, r 184(1) (revoked).
4 Ie under the Insolvency Rules 1986, SI 1986/1925, r 6.138: see PARA 348.
5 Insolvency Rules 1986, SI 1986/1925, r 6.207(2A) (added by SI 2010/686).
6 Insolvency Rules 1986, SI 1986/1925, r 6.207(3).
7 As to the meaning of 'witness statement' see PARA 161 note 7.
8 Insolvency Rules 1986, SI 1986/1925, r 6.207(4).
9 Insolvency Rules 1986, SI 1986/1925, r 6.207(4). A copy must be sent to the bankrupt if he is not the applicant: see r 6.206(6); and PARA 623.
10 Insolvency Rules 1986, SI 1986/1925, r 6.207(5). As to the hearing see PARA 628. As to the meaning of 'business day' see PARA 28 note 8.

625. Applicant's claim that remuneration is, or expenses are, excessive. Where the trustee is other than the official receiver and application for annulment is made on the grounds that the debts and expenses of the bankruptcy have all been paid or secured[1], the applicant may also apply to the court for one or more of the orders in heads (1) to (3) below on the ground that the remuneration charged or expenses incurred by the trustee is or are, in all the circumstances, excessive[2]. The application must be made no later than five business days[3] before the date fixed for the hearing[4] of the application for annulment and be accompanied by a copy of any evidence which the applicant intends to adduce in support[5]. The applicant must send a copy of the application and of any evidence accompanying it to the trustee at the same time that the application is made[6].

If the court annuls the bankruptcy order[7] and considers the application for an order[8] to be well-founded, it must also make one or more of the following orders:

(1)   an order reducing the amount of remuneration which the trustee was entitled to charge;

(2)   an order that some or all of the remuneration or expenses in question be treated as not being bankruptcy expenses;

(3)   an order that the trustee or the trustee's personal representative pay to the applicant the amount of the excess of remuneration or expenses or such part of the excess as the court may specify;

and may make any other order that it thinks just[9].

1   Ie under the Insolvency Act 1986 s 282(1)(b): see PARA 620 head (2).
2   Insolvency Rules 1986, SI 1986/1925, r 6.207A(1) (added by SI 2010/686).
3   As to the meaning of 'business day' see PARA 28 note 8.
4   As to the hearing see PARA 628.
5   Insolvency Rules 1986, SI 1986/1925, r 6.207A(2) (added by SI 2010/686).
6   Insolvency Rules 1986, SI 1986/1925, r 6.207A(3) (added by SI 2010/686). A copy must be sent to the bankrupt if he is not the applicant: see r 6.206(6); and PARA 623.
7   See note 1.
8   Ie under the Insolvency Rules 1986, SI 1986/1925, r 6.207A(1): see the text to notes 1–2.
9   Insolvency Rules 1986, SI 1986/1925, r 6.207A(4) (added by SI 2010/686).

626.   Power of court to stay proceedings.   In advance of the hearing, the court may make an interim order staying any proceedings which it thinks ought, in the circumstances of the application, to be stayed[1].

Except in relation to an application for an order staying all or any part of the proceedings in the bankruptcy, application for such an order may be made without notice to any other party[2].

Where application is made for such an order staying all or any part of the proceedings in the bankruptcy, the applicant must send copies of the application to the official receiver and, if other, the trustee in sufficient time to enable them to be present at the hearing and, if they wish to do so, make representations[3].

Where the court makes an order staying all or any part of the proceedings in the bankruptcy, the statutory provisions[4] nevertheless continue to apply to any application for, or other matters in connection with, the annulment of the bankruptcy order[5].

If the court makes an order under the above provisions, it must send copies of the order to the applicant, the official receiver and, if other, the trustee[6].

1   Insolvency Rules 1986, SI 1986/1925, r 6.208(1).
2   Insolvency Rules 1986, SI 1986/1925, r 6.208(2) (substituted by SI 1987/1919; and amended by SI 2010/686).
3   Insolvency Rules 1986, SI 1986/1925, r 6.208(3) (added by SI 1987/1919). A copy must be sent to the bankrupt if he is not the applicant: see r 6.206(6); and PARA 623.
4   Ie the Insolvency Rules 1986, SI 1986/1925, rr 6.206–6.214.

5   Insolvency Rules 1986, SI 1986/1925, r 6.208(4) (added by SI 1987/1919).
6   Insolvency Rules 1986, SI 1986/1925, r 6.208(5) (added by SI 1987/1919).

627.   Notice to creditors who have not proved.   Where the application for annulment is made on the grounds that the debts and expenses of the bankruptcy have all been paid or secured[1], and it has been reported to the court[2] that there are known creditors of the bankrupt who have not proved, the court may:

(1)   direct the trustee or, if no trustee has been appointed, the official receiver, to send notice of the application to such of those creditors as the court thinks ought to be informed of it, with a view to their proving their debts[3], if they so wish, within 21 days; and

(2)   direct the trustee or, if no trustee has been appointed, the official receiver, to advertise the fact that the application has been made, so that creditors who have not proved may do so within a specified time; and

(3)   adjourn the application meanwhile, for any period not less than 35 days[4].

1   Ie under the Insolvency Act 1986 s 282(1)(b): see PARA 620 head (2).
2   Ie under the Insolvency Rules 1986, SI 1986/1925, r 6.207: see PARA 624.
3   As to proofs of debt see PARA 507 et seq.
4   Insolvency Rules 1986, SI 1986/1925, r 6.209 (amended by SI 1987/1919). See also *Re Robertson (a bankrupt)* [1989] 1 WLR 1139; and PARA 622 text and note 11.

628.   The hearing.   The trustee must attend the hearing of the application[1]; and the official receiver, if he is not the trustee, may attend, but is not required to do so unless he has filed[2] a report[3]. If the court makes an order on the application or on an application that remuneration or expenses are excessive[4], it must send copies of the order to the applicant, the official receiver and, if other, the trustee[5].

1   Insolvency Rules 1986, SI 1986/1925, r 6.210(1).
2   Ie under the Insolvency Rules 1986, SI 1986/1925, r 6.207: see PARA 624.
3   Insolvency Rules 1986, SI 1986/1925, r 6.210(2).
4   Ie an application under the Insolvency Rules 1986, SI 1986/1925, r 6.207A: see PARA 625.
5   Insolvency Rules 1986, SI 1986/1925, r 6.210(3) (amended by SI 2010/686). For the prescribed form of order of annulment under the Insolvency Act 1986 s 282 see the Insolvency Rules 1986, SI 1986/1925, Sch 4 Form 6.71 (substituted by SI 2004/584; and amended by SI 2009/642; and SI 2010/686).

629.   Matters to be proved where debts and expenses paid or secured.   The following provisions apply with regard to the matters which must be proved to the satisfaction of the court in an application for the annulment of a bankruptcy order[1] on the grounds that the debts and expenses of the bankruptcy have all been paid or secured and may be taken into account by the court on hearing such an application[2].

All bankruptcy debts[3] which have been proved must have been paid in full or secured in full to the satisfaction of the court[4]. If, however, a debt is disputed, or a creditor who has proved can no longer be traced, the bankrupt must have given such security, in the form of money paid into court, or a bond entered into with approved sureties, as the court considers adequate to satisfy any sum that may subsequently be proved to be due to the creditor concerned and, if the court thinks just, costs[5]. Where security has been so given in the case of an untraced creditor, the court may direct that particulars of the alleged debt, and the security, be advertised in such manner as it thinks just; and, if advertisement is so ordered, and no claim on the security is made within 12 months from the date of the advertisement, or the first advertisement, if more than one, the court must, on application in that behalf, order the security to be released[6].

In determining whether to annul a bankruptcy order[7], the court may, if it thinks just and without prejudice to the generality of its discretion[8], take into account whether any sums have been paid or payment of any sums has been secured in respect of post-commencement interest[9] on the bankruptcy debts which have been proved[10].

1   Ie under the Insolvency Act 1986 s 282(1)(b): see PARA 620 head (2).
2   Insolvency Rules 1986, SI 1986/1925, r 6.211(1) (amended by SI 2010/686).
3   As to the meaning of 'bankruptcy debt' see PARA 508.
4   Insolvency Rules 1986, SI 1986/1925, r 6.211(2) (amended by SI 2010/686). As to the meaning of 'payment in full' see PARA 622. As to proofs of debt see PARA 507 et seq. For the purposes of the Insolvency Rules 1986, SI 1986/1925, r 6.211(2), (5), security includes an undertaking given by a solicitor and accepted by the court: r 6.211(6) (added by SI 2010/686).
5   Insolvency Rules 1986, SI 1986/1925, r 6.211(3) (amended by SI 2010/686).
6   Insolvency Rules 1986, SI 1986/1925, r 6.211(4) (amended by SI 2010/686).
7   Ie under the Insolvency Act 1986 s 282(1)(b): see PARA 620 head (2).
8   Ie under the Insolvency Act 1986 s 282(1): see PARA 620.
9   'Post-commencement interest' means interest on the bankruptcy debts at the rate specified in the Insolvency Act 1986 s 328(5) (see PARA 596) in respect of periods during which those debts have been outstanding since the commencement of the bankruptcy: Insolvency Rules 1986, SI 1986/1925, r 6.211(7) (added by SI 2010/686).
10 Insolvency Rules 1986, SI 1986/1925, r 6.211(5) (added by SI 2010/686). See note 4. As to the exercise of discretion see *Harper v Buchler* [2004] BPIR 724; *Wilcock v Duckworth* [2005] BPIR 682.

630. Notice to creditors. Where the official receiver has notified creditors of the debtor's bankruptcy, and the bankruptcy order is annulled, he must as soon as reasonably practicable notify them of the annulment[1].

Expenses incurred by the official receiver in giving such notice are a charge in his favour on the property of the former bankrupt, whether or not actually in his hands[2].

Where any property is in the hands of a trustee or any person other than the former bankrupt himself, the official receiver's charge is valid subject only to any costs that may be incurred by the trustee or that other person in effecting realisation of the property for the purpose of satisfying the charge[3].

1   Insolvency Rules 1986, SI 1986/1925, r 6.212(1) (amended by SI 2009/642).
2   Insolvency Rules 1986, SI 1986/1925, r 6.212(2).
3   Insolvency Rules 1986, SI 1986/1925, r 6.212(3).

631. Other matters arising on annulment. In an order annulling a bankruptcy order[1], the court must include provision permitting vacation of the registration of the bankruptcy petition as a pending action[2], and of the bankruptcy order[3], in the register of writs and orders affecting land[4].

The court must as soon as reasonably practicable give notice of the making of the order to the Secretary of State[5].

Within 28 days of the making of the order, the former bankrupt may require the Secretary of State to give notice of the making of the order; and as soon as reasonably practicable, such notice must be gazetted[6] and advertised in the same manner as the bankruptcy order to which it relates was advertised[7]. Any such requirement by the former bankrupt must be addressed to the Secretary of State in writing[8].

1   Ie under the Insolvency Act 1986 s 282 (see PARA 620).

2   Ie under the Insolvency Rules 1986, SI 1986/1925, r 6.13 (see PARA 171) and r 6.43 (see PARA 196).
3   Ie under the Insolvency Rules 1986, SI 1986/1925, r 6.34(2)(a) (see PARA 201 head (1)) and r 6.46(2)(a) (see PARA 207 head (1)).
4   Insolvency Rules 1986, SI 1986/1925, r 6.213(1) (amended by SI 1987/1919; and SI 2003/1730).
5   Insolvency Rules 1986, SI 1986/1925, r 6.213(2) (amended by SI 2009/642).
6   As to the meaning of 'gazetted' see PARA 165 note 12.
7   Insolvency Rules 1986, SI 1986/1925, r 6.213(3) (substituted by SI 2009/642). In addition to the standard contents, the notice must state: (1) the name of the former bankrupt; (2) the date on which the bankruptcy order was made; (3) that the bankruptcy order against the former bankrupt has been annulled under the Insolvency Act 1986 s 282(1) (see PARA 620); and (4) the date of the annulment: Insolvency Rules 1986, SI 1986/1925, r 6.213(3A) (added by SI 2010/686). As to the meaning of 'standard contents' see PARA 165 note 12.
    Where the former bankrupt has died, or is a person incapable of managing his affairs, within the meaning of the Insolvency Rules 1986, SI 1986/1925, rr 7.43–7.46 (see PARA 824), the references to him in r 6.213(3), (4) are to be read as referring to his personal representative, or, as the case may be, a person appointed by the court to represent or act for him: r 6.213(5).
8   Insolvency Rules 1986, SI 1986/1925, r 6.213(4) (amended by SI 2004/584).

C.   EFFECT OF ANNULMENT OF BANKRUPTCY ORDER

632.   Effect of annulment on petition and bankruptcy order.   The order of annulment[1] orders that the bankruptcy order be annulled and that the petition on which it is made be dismissed[2]. The court must include in such an order provision permitting vacation of the registration of the bankruptcy petition as a pending action[3], and of the bankruptcy order[4], in the register of writs and orders affecting land[5].

1   Ie under the Insolvency Act 1986 s 282 (see PARA 620).
2   For the prescribed form of order of annulment see the Insolvency Rules 1986, SI 1986/1925, Sch 4 Form 6.71 (substituted by SI 2004/584; and amended by SI 2009/642; and SI 2010/686).
3   Ie under the Insolvency Rules 1986, SI 1986/1925, r 6.13 (see PARA 171) and r 6.43 (see PARA 196).
4   Ie under the Insolvency Rules 1986, SI 1986/1925, r 6.34(2)(a) (see PARA 201 head (1)) and r 6.46(2)(a) (see PARA 207 head (1)).
5   Insolvency Rules 1986, SI 1986/1925, r 6.213(1) (amended by SI 1987/1919; and SI 2003/1730).

633.   Effect of annulment on property and rights.   Where the court annuls a bankruptcy order[1]:

(1)   any sale or other disposition of property, payment made or other thing duly done under any provision in the Insolvency Act 1986[2], by or under the authority of the official receiver or a trustee of the bankrupt's estate or by the court is valid[3]; but

(2)   if any of the bankrupt's estate is then vested in such a trustee[4], it vests in such person as the court may appoint or, in default of any such appointment, reverts to the bankrupt on such terms, if any, as the court may direct;

and the court may include in its order such supplemental provisions as may be authorised[5] by the Insolvency Rules 1986[6]. In the absence of such provisions by the court, the debtor would appear to be remitted to his original rights in respect of his property[7].

An annulment order made on the ground that all the debts have been paid in full creates an estoppel by record, so that a creditor cannot recover a debt for which he agreed not to prove[8]; but it does not debar a creditor, who has merely abstained from proving, from suing the debtor after the annulment, his right to sue no longer being suspended by the bankruptcy[9].

Annulment will remove the various disqualifications to which a bankrupt is subject[10].

1 Ie whether under the Insolvency Act 1986 s 261 (see PARA 70), s 263D (see PARA 95) or s 282 (see PARA 620).
2 Ie under any provision in the Insolvency Act 1986 Pts 7A-11 (ss 251A–385).
3 This would appear to cover such acts as the rejection of a proof by the trustee, so that the claim for the debt which was the subject of the proof may not be enforceable after annulment: *Brandon v McHenry* [1891] 1 QB 538, CA; and see *Seaton v Deerhurst* [1895] 1 QB 853, CA.
4 See note 2.
5 Ie under the Insolvency Rules 1986, SI 1986/1925.
6 Insolvency Act 1986 s 282(4) (amended by the Enterprise Act 2002 s 269, Sch 23 paras 1, 4). In the case of the administration in bankruptcy of the insolvent estate of a deceased person dying before the presentation of a bankruptcy petition, the Insolvency Act 1986 s 282(4) applies: Administration of Insolvent Estates of Deceased Persons Order 1986, SI 1986/1999, art 3(1), Sch 1 Pt II para 11. As to the administration in bankruptcy of the insolvent estates of deceased persons see further PARA 830 et seq.
7 See *Bailey v Johnson* (1872) LR 7 Exch 263 (decided under the Bankruptcy Act 1869 s 81 (repealed), where the debtor after annulment was allowed to set off against the claim of the petitioning creditors' trustee (bankers who had themselves become bankrupt) the amount of the proceeds of the sale of the debtor's estate paid into their bank). See also *Re Chidley, Re Lennard* (1875) 1 ChD 177, CA; *West v Baker* (1875) 1 ExD 44 (both decided under the Bankruptcy Act 1869 (repealed), where, after annulment for the purposes of composition proceedings, the debtor's property became vested in a person other than the debtor). In the former case, that person held it discharged from an execution which would have been invalid in bankruptcy; in the latter a debt provable in bankruptcy was allowed to be set off against a demand for a debt due to the debtor. See also *Re Simons, ex p Allard* (1881) 16 ChD 505, CA and *Re Croom, England v Provincial Assets Co* [1891] 1 Ch 695 (where the annulment was followed by a scheme); *Re Newman, ex p Official Receiver* [1899] 2 QB 587 (where the receiving order against the trustee in bankruptcy was rescinded).
8 *John v Mendoza* [1939] 1 KB 141, [1938] 4 All ER 472.
9 *More v More* [1962] Ch 424, [1962] 1 All ER 125, applying *Brandon v McHenry* [1891] 1 QB 538, CA, and declining to follow *John v Mendoza* [1939] 1 KB 141, [1938] 4 All ER 472. See also *IRC v McEntaggart* [2004] EWHC 3431 (Ch), [2006] 1 BCLC 476, [2006] BPIR 750; *Lambeth London Borough Council v Simon* [2007] BPIR 1629. As to the suspension of the creditors' remedies in bankruptcy see the Insolvency Act 1986 s 285; and PARA 214.
10 See PARA 722 et seq.

634. Effect of annulment on forfeitures. In the case of a gift by will or settlement of rent or other income to a donee defeasible on its becoming payable to some other person, the forfeiture takes effect, notwithstanding annulment of a bankruptcy order, if before the annulment it becomes the duty of the trustees of the will or settlement to make a payment which, but for the forfeiture clause, the trustee in bankruptcy of the donee would be entitled to receive[1]. In such a case the trustee need not have actually claimed the income[2]. If, however, the annulment order is made, or if, though the order is not actually made, there are circumstances which entitle the donee to claim it as a matter of right[3] before any income becomes payable, there will be no forfeiture[4]. The principle is that the annulment will be in time to save forfeiture if it takes place before any income becomes payable to the beneficiary, but not if it takes place after the trustees have received income which may properly be treated as payable to or as retained or appropriated for the beneficiary[5].

Where, by a lease, there is a right of re-entry on bankruptcy, it is doubtful whether an action to enforce that right could be defeated by an annulment of the bankruptcy order after the action has begun[6]; but it is submitted that the right to enforce the forfeiture which has already arisen would not be defeated[7].

1 *Re Parnham's Trusts* (1872) LR 13 Eq 413; *Robertson v Richardson* (1885) 30 ChD 623;
   Metcalfe v Metcalfe (1889) 43 ChD 633 (affd [1891] 3 Ch 1, CA); *Re Loftus-Otway, Otway v
   Otway* [1895] 2 Ch 235; *Re Forder, Forder v Forder* [1927] 2 Ch 291.
2 *Robertson v Richardson* (1885) 30 ChD 623.
3 *Metcalfe v Metcalfe* (1889) 43 ChD 633 at 642 (affd [1893] 3 Ch 1, CA); *Re Forder, Forder v
   Forder* [1927] 2 Ch 291, CA.
4 *White v Chitty* (1866) LR 1 Eq 372; *Lloyd v Lloyd* (1866) LR 2 Eq 722; *Trappes v Meredith*
   (1869) LR 9 Eq 299 (further proceedings (1870) LR 10 Eq 604; revsd 7 Ch App 248); *Re
   Parnham's Trust* (1876) 46 LJ Ch 80; *Samuel v Samuel* (1879) 12 ChD 152.
5 *Re Forder, Forder v Forder* [1927] 2 Ch 291 at 321, CA.
6 *Smith v Gronow* [1891] 2 QB 394.
7 Cf *Metcalfe v Metcalfe* (1889) 43 ChD 633 (affd [1893] 3 Ch 1, CA); *Re Loftus-Otway, Otway
   v Otway* [1895] 2 Ch 235.

635. Effect of annulment on statute-barred rights. Since on annulment
nothing reverts to the debtor which was not vested in the trustee, the debtor's
rights to property will be barred by the Limitation Act 1980, if the trustee's
rights had become so barred[1].

1 *Markwick v Hardingham* (1880) 15 ChD 339, CA.

636. Effect of annulment on prosecutions. The provisions of the Insolvency
Act 1986 relating to bankruptcy offences[1] apply whether or not the bankruptcy
order is annulled, but proceedings for such an offence may not be instituted after
the annulment[2].

1 Ie the Insolvency Act 1986 Pt 9 Ch 6 (ss 350–362): see PARA 733 et seq.
2 Insolvency Act 1986 s 350(2); and see PARA 733. Section 350(2) only applies to proceedings
   under offences under the Insolvency Act 1986; it provides no defence to a prosecution under the
   Company Directors Disqualification Act 1986 s 11 (see PARA 729) for acting as a director while
   an undischarged bankrupt: *IRC v McEntaggart* [2004] EWHC 3431 (Ch), [2006] 1 BCLC 476,
   [2006] BPIR 750.

637. Trustee's final account. Where a bankruptcy order is annulled[1], this does
not of itself release the trustee from any duty or obligation imposed on him[2] to
account for all his transactions in connection with the former bankrupt's estate[3].
The trustee must submit a copy of his final account to the Secretary of State, as
soon as practicable after the court's order annulling the bankruptcy order, and he
must file a copy of the final account in court[4].

The final account must include a summary of the trustee's receipts and
payments in the administration, and contain a statement to the effect that he has
reconciled his account with that which is held by the Secretary of State in respect
of the bankruptcy[5].

The trustee is released from such time as the court may determine, having
regard to whether the trustee has submitted his final account to the Secretary of
State and filed a copy of it in court[6], and any security given[7] has been, or will be,
released[8].

1 Ie under the Insolvency Act 1986 s 282 (see PARA 620).
2 Ie by or under the Insolvency Act 1986 or the Insolvency Rules 1986, SI 1986/1925.
3 Insolvency Rules 1986, SI 1986/1925, r 6.214(1) (amended by SI 1987/1919; and
   SI 2003/1730). The court has inherent jurisdiction to deal with a trustee's expenses where the
   bankruptcy order has been set aside on appeal and the trustee has not been notified; jurisdiction
   to deal with the trustee's costs upon annulment should extend equally to the case of an appeal:
   see *Appleyard v Wewelwala* [2012] EWHC 3302 (Ch), [2013] 1 All ER 1383, [2013] 1 WLR
   752. Where unpaid costs and expenses of the trustee are secured as a condition of obtaining an
   annulment, they can still be challenged under the Insolvency Rules 1986, SI 1986/1925, r 6.214:
   Hirani v Rendle [2003] EWHC 2538 (Ch), [2004] BPIR 274, [2003] All ER (D) 27 (Nov)

4 Insolvency Rules 1986, SI 1986/1925, r 6.214(2). As to the meaning of 'file in court' see PARA 57 note 13.
5 Insolvency Rules 1986, SI 1986/1925, r 6.214(3). As to the account held by the Secretary of State see PARA 22.
6 Ie under the Insolvency Rules 1986, SI 1986/1925, r 6.214(2).
7 Ie under the Insolvency Rules 1986, SI 1986/1925, r 6.211(3): see PARA 629.
8 Insolvency Rules 1986, SI 1986/1925, r 6.214(4).

(ii) Discharge of Bankruptcy Order

A. IN GENERAL

638. Discharge of bankruptcy order. The bankruptcy of an individual against whom a bankruptcy order has been made commences with the day on which the order is made, and continues until the individual is discharged[1]. A bankrupt is discharged from bankruptcy at the end of the period of one year beginning with the date on which the bankruptcy commences[2].

If before the end of that period the official receiver files with the court[3] a notice stating that investigation of the conduct and affairs of the bankrupt[4] is unnecessary or concluded, the bankrupt is discharged when the notice is filed[5].

The provisions set out above are without prejudice to any power of the court to annul a bankruptcy order[6].

1 See the Insolvency Act 1986 s 278; and PARA 209.
2 Insolvency Act 1986 s 279(1) (s 279 substituted by the Enterprise Act 2002 s 256(1)). As to the commencement of bankruptcy see PARA 209. As to the court's power to suspend discharge see the Insolvency Act 1986 s 279(3); and PARA 640. The Insolvency Act 1986 s 279(1)–(5) does not apply in the case of an individual who is adjudged bankrupt on a petition under s 264(1)(d) (criminal bankruptcy), and the bankrupt is discharged from bankruptcy by an order of the court under s 280: s 279(6) (as so substituted). As to the prospective repeal of s 264(1)(d) see PARA 1 note 11. As from a day to be appointed, the word 'adjudged' in s 279(6) is replaced by 'made' by the Enterprise and Regulatory Reform Act 2013 s 71, Sch 19 paras 1, 12. At the date at which this volume states the law no such day had been appointed. As to the changes proposed by the Enterprise and Regulatory Reform Act 2013 see PARA 130.
    An application for an order of the court discharging an individual from criminal bankruptcy in a case falling within s 279(6) may be made by the bankrupt at any time after the end of the period of five years beginning with the date on which the bankruptcy commences: s 280(1) (amended by the Enterprise Act 2002 s 269, Sch 23 paras 1, 3). On such an application the court may: (1) refuse to discharge the bankrupt from the bankruptcy; (2) make an order discharging him absolutely; or (3) make an order discharging him subject to such conditions with respect to any income which may subsequently become due to him, or with respect to property devolving on him, or acquired by him, after his discharge, as may be specified in the order: Insolvency Act 1986 s 280(2). The court may provide for an order falling within head (2) or head (3) above to have immediate effect or to have its effect suspended for such period, or until the fulfilment of such conditions, including a condition requiring the court to be satisfied as to any matter, as may be specified in the order: s 280(3).
3 As to the meaning of 'file with the court' see PARA 57 note 13.
4 Ie under the Insolvency Act 1986 s 289: see PARA 252.
5 Insolvency Act 1986 s 279(2) (as substituted: see note 2). In relation to bankruptcy orders made before 1 October 2013, where the official receiver intends to file a notice that an investigation of the conduct and affairs of a bankrupt is unnecessary or concluded under s 279(2), he must give notice in writing to all creditors of which he is aware and any trustee of his intention to file such a notice: Insolvency Rules 1986, SI 1986/1925, r 6.214A(1) (r 6.214A added by SI 2003/1730; and revoked, in relation to bankruptcy orders made on or after 1 October 2013, by SI 2013/2135). Where a creditor or a trustee receives written notice of the official receiver's intention to file such a notice and he has any objection to the official receiver filing the notice, he may, within 28 days of the date of such written notice, inform the official receiver in writing of his objection and give reasons for that objection: Insolvency Rules 1986, SI 1986/1925, r 6.214A(2) (as so added). The official receiver must not file the notice until the period allowed for creditors or a trustee to object has expired: r 6.214A(3) (as so added). Where the official

receiver receives no objection from either a creditor or a trustee he may file a notice by sending to the court two copies of the prescribed form; the court must indorse each copy with the date of filing and return one copy to the official receiver who must then send a copy of the indorsed form to the bankrupt: r 6.214A(4) (as so added; and substituted by SI 2004/584). As to the prescribed form see the Insolvency Rules 1986, SI 1986/1925, Sch 4 Form 6.82 (substituted by SI 2004/584). Where the official receiver receives an objection under the Insolvency Rules 1986, SI 1986/1925, r 6.214A and he rejects that objection, he must not file the notice until he has: (1) given notice of the rejection (and his reasons) to the complainant; and (2) the period of time for an appeal by the complainant under r 7.50(2) (see PARA 767) has expired, or an appeal under that rule has been determined by the court: r 6.214A(5) (as so substituted).

6   Insolvency Act 1986 s 279(7) (as substituted: see note 2). As to the power to annul a bankruptcy order see s 282; and PARA 620.

639. Certificate of discharge. Where it appears to the court that a bankrupt is discharged, whether by expiration of time or otherwise, the court must, on his application, issue to him a certificate of his discharge, and the date from which it is effective[1].

The discharged bankrupt may within 28 days of the order require the Secretary of State to give notice of the discharge and as soon as reasonably practicable such notice must be gazetted[2] and advertised in such manner as the bankruptcy order to which it relates was advertised[3]. Any such requirement by the former bankrupt must be addressed to the Secretary of State in writing[4].

1   Insolvency Rules 1986, SI 1986/1925, r 6.220(1). For the prescribed form of certificate of discharge see Sch 4 Form 6.77 (amended by SI 1991/495; SI 2009/642; and SI 2010/686). A fee of £70 is payable on issue of a certificate of discharge: Civil Proceedings Fees Order 2008, SI 2008/1053, art 2, Sch 1 Fee 3.4(a) (Sch 1 substituted by SI 2011/586).
2   As to the meaning of 'gazetted' see PARA 165 note 12.
3   Insolvency Rules 1986, SI 1986/1925, r 6.220(2) (substituted by SI 2009/642; and amended by SI 2010/686). In addition to the standard contents, the notice must state: (1) the name of the former bankrupt; (2) the date of the bankruptcy order; (3) that a certificate of discharge has been issued; (4) the date of the certificate; and (5) the date from which the discharge is effective: Insolvency Rules 1986, SI 1986/1925, r 6.220(2A) (added by SI 2010/686). As to the meaning of 'standard contents' see PARA 165 note 12.
     Where the former bankrupt has died, or is a person incapable of managing his affairs, within the meaning of Pt 7 Ch 7 (rr 7.43–7.46) (see PARA 824), the references to him in r 6.220(2) and r 6.220(3) are to be read as referring to his personal representative or, as the case may be, a person appointed by the court to represent or act for him: r 6.220(4).
4   Insolvency Rules 1986, SI 1986/1925, r 6.220(3) (amended by SI 2010/686). See also note 3.

B. SUSPENSION OF DISCHARGE

640. Court's power to suspend discharge. Where the court is satisfied on the application of the official receiver or the trustee of the bankrupt's estate that an undischarged bankrupt has failed or is failing to comply with an obligation under Part 9 of the Insolvency Act 1986[1], the court may order that the one-year period for discharge of bankruptcy[2] is to cease to run until the end of a specified period or the fulfilment of a specified condition[3]. Where the bankrupt's public examination is adjourned, the official receiver may there and then make application for the suspension of the bankrupt's automatic discharge[4].

1   Ie the Insolvency Act 1986 Pt 9 (ss 264–371).
2   See the Insolvency Act 1986 s 279(1); and PARA 638.
3   Insolvency Act 1986 s 279(3) (s 279 substituted by the Enterprise Act 2002 s 256(1)). 'Condition' includes a condition requiring that the court be satisfied of something: Insolvency Act 1986 s 279(5) (as so substituted). Section 279 is without prejudice to any power of the court to annul a bankruptcy order: s 279(4).

The court does not have jurisdiction to give directions to the official receiver as to the exercise of his function in deciding whether or not to make such an application: *Hardy v Focus Insurance Co Ltd* [1997] BPIR 77.

For an example of the exercise by the court of its discretion to suspend automatic discharge see *Re A Debtor (No 26 of 1991)* [1996] BCC 246, sub nom *Holmes v Official Receiver* [1996] BPIR 279 (bankrupt failing to comply with obligation to file with the trustee accounts of his bankruptcy business). See also *Shierson v Rastogi* [2007] EWHC 1266 (Ch), [2007] BPIR 891, [2007] All ER (D) 446 (May); *Bramston v Haut* [2012] EWHC 1279 (Ch), [2012] All ER (D) 263 (May); *Chadwick (trustee in bankruptcy of Nash) v Nash* [2012] BPIR 70.

Where the return date for the official receiver's application is listed after the date on which the automatic discharge is due to take effect, the court may make an interim order suspending the bankrupt's discharge until the earliest date when the matter can be fully heard: *Jacobs v Official Receiver* [1998] 3 All ER 250, sub nom *Re Jacobs (a bankrupt)* [1999] 1 WLR 619; approved in *Bagnall v Official Receiver* [2003] EWCA Civ 1925, [2004] 2 All ER 294, [2004] 1 WLR 2832.

4   Insolvency Rules 1986, SI 1986/1925, r 6.176(4) (amended by SI 2010/686). As to the adjournment of a bankrupt's public examination see PARA 298 et seq.

641. Application for suspension of discharge. Where the official receiver, or any trustee who is not the official receiver, applies to the court for an order[1] suspending the automatic discharge of the bankrupt, but not where the official receiver makes that application[2] on the adjournment of the bankrupt's public examination, the official receiver, or any trustee who is not the official receiver, must with his application file evidence in support setting out the reasons why it appears to him that such an order should be made[3]. The court must fix a venue[4] for the hearing of the application, and give notice of it to the official receiver, the trustee who is not the official receiver and the bankrupt[5].

Copies of the official receiver's report must be sent by him to the bankrupt and any trustee who is not the official receiver, so as to reach them at least 21 days before the date fixed for the hearing[6]. Copies of the trustee's evidence in support must be sent by him to the official receiver and the bankrupt, so as to reach them at least 21 days before the date fixed for the hearing[7].

Not later than five business days[8] before the date of the hearing, the bankrupt may file in court[9] a notice specifying any statements in the official receiver's or trustee's evidence in support which he intends to deny or dispute[10]; and, if he so gives notice, he must send copies of it, not less than four business days before the date of the hearing, to the official receiver and the trustee[11].

If the court makes an order suspending the bankrupt's discharge, copies of the order must be sent by the court to the official receiver, any trustee who is not the official receiver and the bankrupt[12]. No costs or expenses in respect of the application fall on the official receiver personally[13].

1   Ie under the Insolvency Act 1986 s 279(3): see PARA 640.
2   Ie pursuant to the Insolvency Rules 1986, SI 1986/1925, r 6.176(4): see PARA 640.
3   Insolvency Rules 1986, SI 1986/1925, r 6.215(1), (2) (substituted by SI 2003/1730).
4   As to the meaning of 'venue' see PARA 46 note 22. As to the hearing of such applications see PARA 786 note 2.
5   Insolvency Rules 1986, SI 1986/1925, r 6.215(3) (substituted by SI 2003/1730).
6   Insolvency Rules 1986, SI 1986/1925, r 6.215(4) (substituted by SI 2003/1730).
7   Insolvency Rules 1986, SI 1986/1925, r 6.215(5) (substituted by SI 2003/1730).
8   As to the meaning of 'business day' see PARA 28 note 8.
9   As to the meaning of 'file in court' see PARA 57 note 13.
10   Insolvency Rules 1986, SI 1986/1925, r 6.215(6) (substituted by SI 2003/1730; and amended by SI 2010/686). For the prescribed form of order of suspension of discharge see the Insolvency Rules 1986, SI 1986/1925, Sch 4 Form 6.72 (substituted by SI 2003/1730; and amended by SI 2010/686).
11   Insolvency Rules 1986, SI 1986/1925, r 6.215(7) (substituted by SI 2003/1730).

12 Insolvency Rules 1986, SI 1986/1925, r 6.215(8) (substituted by SI 2003/1730).
13 See the Insolvency Rules 1986, SI 1986/1925, r 6.222; and PARA 648.

642. Lifting of suspension of discharge. Where the court makes an order[1] that the one-year period after which the bankrupt may have his discharge, is to cease to run, the bankrupt may apply to it for the order to be discharged[2].

The court must fix a venue[3] for the hearing of the application; and the bankrupt must, not less than 28 days before the date fixed for the hearing, give notice of the venue to the official receiver and any trustee who is not the official receiver, accompanied in each case by a copy of the application[4]. The official receiver and the trustee may appear and be heard on the bankrupt's application; and, whether or not they appear, the official receiver and trustee may file in court[5] evidence in support of any matters which either of them considers ought to be drawn to the court's attention[6].

If the court's order was for the relevant period to cease to run until the fulfilment of a specified condition[7], the court may request a report from the official receiver or the trustee as to whether those conditions have or have not been fulfilled[8].

If a report is so filed[9], copies of it must be sent by the official receiver or trustee to the bankrupt and to either the official receiver or trustee, depending on which has filed the report, not later than 14 days before the hearing[10].

Not later than five business days[11] before the date of the hearing, the bankrupt may file in court a notice specifying any statements in the official receiver's or trustee's report which he intends to deny or dispute; and, if he so gives notice, he must send copies of it, not less than four business days before the date of the hearing, to the official receiver and the trustee[12].

If, on the bankrupt's application, the court, being satisfied that the on-year period should begin to run again, discharges the order, it must issue to the bankrupt a certificate that it has done so, with effect from a specified date and it must send copies of the certificate to the official receiver and the trustee[13].

1 Ie under the Insolvency Act 1986 s 279(3): see PARA 640.
2 Insolvency Rules 1986, SI 1986/1925, r 6.216(1) (substituted by SI 2003/1730).
3 As to the meaning of 'venue' see PARA 46 note 22. As to the hearing of such applications see PARA 786 note 2.
4 Insolvency Rules 1986, SI 1986/1925, r 6.216(2) (substituted by SI 2003/1730).
5 As to the meaning of 'file in court' see PARA 57 note 13.
6 Insolvency Rules 1986, SI 1986/1925, r 6.216(3) (substituted by SI 2003/1730).
7 Ie under the Insolvency Act 1986 s 279(3)(b): see PARA 640.
8 Insolvency Rules 1986, SI 1986/1925, r 6.216(4) (substituted by SI 2003/1730).
9 Ie under the Insolvency Rules 1986, SI 1986/1925, r 6.216(3) or (4): see the text to notes 5–8.
10 Insolvency Rules 1986, SI 1986/1925, r 6.216(5) (substituted by SI 2003/1730).
11 As to the meaning of 'business day' see PARA 28 note 8.
12 Insolvency Rules 1986, SI 1986/1925, r 6.216(6) (substituted by SI 2003/1730; and amended by SI 2010/686).
13 Insolvency Rules 1986, SI 1986/1925, r 6.216(7) (substituted by SI 2003/1730). For the prescribed form of order lifting suspension of discharge see the Insolvency Rules 1986, SI 1986/1925, Sch 4 Form 6.73 (substituted by SI 2003/1730; and amended by SI 2010/686). For the prescribed form of certificate that the order suspending discharge has been lifted see the Insolvency Rules 1986, SI 1986/1925, Sch 4 Form 6.74.

C. PROCEDURE ON APPLICATION FOR DISCHARGE

643. Application by bankrupt for discharge. If the bankrupt applies for an order discharging him from bankruptcy[1], he must give to the official receiver notice of the application, and deposit with him such sum as the latter may require to cover his costs of the application[2].

If satisfied that the above provisions have been complied with, the court must fix a venue[3] for the hearing of the application and give at least 42 days' notice of it to the official receiver and the bankrupt[4]. The official receiver must give notice accordingly to the trustee, and to every creditor who, to the official receiver's knowledge, has a claim outstanding against the estate which has not been satisfied[5]; and such notices must be given not later than 14 days before the date fixed for the hearing of the bankrupt's application[6].

1   Ie under the Insolvency Act 1986 s 280: see PARA 638 note 2. Where an application is made by the bankrupt under s 280 for his discharge from bankruptcy, it is the duty of the official receiver to make a report to the court with respect to the prescribed matters; and the court must consider that report before determining what order, if any, to make under s 280: see s 289(3); and PARA 252. As to the official receiver's report see PARA 644.
2   Insolvency Rules 1986, SI 1986/1925, r 6.217(1).
3   As to the meaning of 'venue' see PARA 46 note 22.
4   Insolvency Rules 1986, SI 1986/1925, r 6.217(2).
5   Insolvency Rules 1986, SI 1986/1925, r 6.217(3).
6   Insolvency Rules 1986, SI 1986/1925, r 6.217(4).

644.   Report of the official receiver.   Where the bankrupt makes application for an order discharging him from bankruptcy[1], the official receiver must, at least 21 days before the date fixed for the hearing of the application, file in court[2] a report containing the following information with respect to the bankrupt:

(1)   any failure by him to comply with his obligations under the Insolvency Act 1986[3];

(2)   the circumstances surrounding the present bankruptcy, and those surrounding any previous bankruptcy of his;

(3)   the extent to which, in the present and in any previous bankruptcy, his liabilities have exceeded his assets; and

(4)   particulars of any distribution[4] which has been, or is expected to be, made to creditors in the present bankruptcy or, if such is the case, that there has been and is to be no distribution;

and the official receiver must include in his report any other matters which, in his opinion, ought to be brought to the court's attention[5].

The official receiver must send a copy of his report to the bankrupt and the trustee, so as to reach them at least 14 days before the date of the hearing of the application[6].

Not later than five business[7] days before the date of the hearing, the bankrupt may file in court a notice specifying any statements in the official receiver's report which he intends to deny or dispute; and, if he so gives notice, he must send copies of it, not less than four days before the date of the hearing, to the official receiver and the trustee[8].

The official receiver, the trustee and any creditor may appear on the hearing of the bankrupt's application, and may make representations and put to the bankrupt such questions as the court may allow[9].

1   Ie under the Insolvency Act 1986 s 280: see PARA 638 note 2.
2   As to the meaning of 'file in court' see PARA 57 note 13.
3   Ie under the Insolvency Act 1986 Pts 8–11 (ss 252–385).
4   As to distributions see PARA 587 et seq.
5   Insolvency Rules 1986, SI 1986/1925, r 6.218(1). For the prescribed fee see the Insolvency Proceedings (Fees) Order 2004, SI 2004/593, Sch 2 para 2 (amended by SI 2007/521).

6　Insolvency Rules 1986, SI 1986/1925, r 6.218(2).

7　As to the meaning of 'business day' see PARA 28 note 8.

8　Insolvency Rules 1986, SI 1986/1925, r 6.218(3) (amended by SI 2010/686). For the prescribed form of notice see the Insolvency Rules 1986, SI 1986/1925, Sch 4 Form 6.75 (amended by SI 2010/686).

9　Insolvency Rules 1986, SI 1986/1925, r 6.218(4). As to the appearance of creditors see PARA 645.

645.　Appearance and conduct of creditors.　Any creditor may appear on the hearing of the bankrupt's application for discharge and may make representations and put to the bankrupt such questions as the court may allow[1].

Although creditors are under no obligation to appear on the hearing of an application for discharge, they must not contract themselves out of the opportunity of appearing[2]. Such contracts are illegal[3]; and an agreement by a trustee binding himself, at the instance of the bankrupt, to prevent any objection by the creditors to an order of discharge is most improper[4]. Suspicion of a fraudulent bargain to buy off opposition by creditors is insufficient ground for an application to rescind an order of discharge, but it may justify the court in allowing an application to stand over to allow investigation[5].

1　Insolvency Rules 1986, SI 1986/1925, r 6.218(4).

2　*Kearley v Thomson* (1890) 24 QBD 742 at 745, CA.

3　*Hall v Dyson* (1852) 17 QB 785.

4　*Re Shaw* [1917] 2 KB 734, CA (where it was also held that the purchase of debts from individual creditors at different prices, without the fullest possible disclosure to them of every material fact, was a most dangerous proceeding, and was rightly taken into consideration by the registrar in making an order suspending the bankrupt's discharge).

5　The bribery of a creditor is contrary to the policy of bankruptcy law and is misconduct during the bankruptcy, which may amount to a bankruptcy offence contrary to the Insolvency Act 1986 s 356(2)(d) (see PARA 742 head (4)) which the court would take into consideration in exercising its discretion under s 280(2) (see PARA 638 note 2). Cf *Re Andrews, ex p Barrow* (1881) 18 ChD 464, CA (where it was held that a contract between a compounding debtor and a creditor, made after the composition by the debtor with his creditors had been entered into but before it had been completely carried out, to pay to the creditor his debt in full, was inconsistent with good faith to the creditors generally and was void).

646.　Order of discharge on application.　An order of the court discharging the bankrupt from bankruptcy either absolutely[1] or subject to conditions with respect to income or property[2] must bear the date on which it is made, but does not take effect until such time as it is drawn up by the court[3]. The order then has effect retrospectively to the date on which it was made[4].

Copies of any order made by the court on an application by the bankrupt for discharge[5] must be sent by the court to the bankrupt, the trustee and the official receiver[6].

Where it appears to the court that a bankrupt is discharged, whether by expiration of time or otherwise, the court must, on his application, issue to him a certificate of his discharge, and the date from which it is effective[7].

1　Ie under the Insolvency Act 1986 s 280(2)(b): see PARA 638 note 2 head (2).

2　Ie under the Insolvency Act 1986 s 280(2)(c): see PARA 638 note 2 head (3).

3　Insolvency Rules 1986, SI 1986/1925, r 6.219(1). For the prescribed form of order see Sch 4 Form 6.76 (amended by SI 1991/495; and SI 2009/642).

4　Insolvency Rules 1986, SI 1986/1925, r 6.219(2).

5　Ie under the Insolvency Act 1986 s 280: see PARA 638 note 2.

6　Insolvency Rules 1986, SI 1986/1925, r 6.219(3).

7　See the Insolvency Rules 1986, SI 1986/1925, r 6.220; and PARA 639.

647. Review or appeal of order. Every court having jurisdiction for the purposes of the Insolvency Act 1986[1] may review, rescind or vary any order made by it in the exercise of that jurisdiction[2]. The order may also be appealed[3]; and an order made by the court on an application by the bankrupt for discharge[4] may not be issued or gazetted[5] until the time allowed for appealing has expired or, if an appeal is entered, until the appeal has been determined[6].

1 Ie under the Insolvency Act 1986 Pts 7A–11 (ss 251A–385). As to the courts having jurisdiction see PARAS 6, 7.
2 See the Insolvency Act 1986 s 375(1); and PARA 761. As to the application of s 375 in the case of the administration in bankruptcy of the insolvent estate of a deceased person dying before the presentation of a bankruptcy petition see PARA 465 note 4.
3 See the Insolvency Act 1986 s 375(2); and PARA 761.
4 Ie under the Insolvency Act 1986 s 280: see PARA 638 note 2.
5 As to the meaning of 'gazetted' see PARA 165 note 12.
6 Insolvency Rules 1986, SI 1986/1925, r 6.221.

648. Official receiver's costs. In no case do any costs or expenses arising under the above provisions[1] fall on the official receiver personally[2].

1 Ie the Insolvency Rules 1986, SI 1986/1925, Pt 6 Ch 22 (rr 6.215–6.222): see PARA 641 et seq.
2 Insolvency Rules 1986, SI 1986/1925, r 6.222.

D. EFFECT OF DISCHARGE

649. Effect of discharge. Where a bankrupt is discharged, the discharge releases him from all the bankruptcy debts[1], but has no effect:

(1) on the functions, so far as they remain to be carried out, of the trustee of his estate[2]; or

(2) on the operation, for the purposes of the carrying out of those functions, of the provisions of Part 9 of the Insolvency Act 1986[3];

and, in particular, discharge does not affect the right of any creditor of the bankrupt to prove in the bankruptcy[4] for any debt from which the bankrupt is released[5].

On obtaining his order of discharge, the bankrupt will cease to be subject to the various disqualifications which he is under as an undischarged bankrupt[6].

1 As to the meaning of 'bankruptcy debt' see PARA 508.
2 As to the trustee's functions see PARA 473 et seq.
3 Ie the Insolvency Act 1986 Pt 9 (ss 264–371).
4 As to proofs of debt see PARA 507 et seq.
5 Insolvency Act 1986 s 281(1). Section 281(1) is subject to s 281(2)–(8): see PARAS 650, 651. The effect of discharge on debts is to bar remedies, other than by way of proof, but not to extinguish the underlying cause of action: *Law Society v Shah* [2007] EWHC 2841 (Ch), [2009] Ch 223, [2008] 3 WLR 1401.
6 See PARA 722 et seq.

650. Debts and liabilities from which discharge is no release. With respect to the bankrupt, discharge does not:

(1) affect the right of any secured creditor[1] of the bankrupt to enforce his security for the payment of a debt from which the bankrupt is released[2];

(2) release the bankrupt from any bankruptcy debt which he incurred in respect of, or forbearance in respect of which was secured by means of, any fraud[3] or fraudulent breach of trust to which he was a party[4];

(3) release the bankrupt from any liability in respect of a fine[5] imposed for an offence or from any liability under a recognisance except, in the case

of a penalty imposed for an offence under an enactment relating to the
public revenue or of a recognisance, with the consent of the Treasury[6];

(4)   except to such extent and on such conditions as the court may direct,
release the bankrupt from any bankruptcy debt which:

(a)   consists in a liability to pay damages for negligence, nuisance or
breach of a statutory, contractual or other duty, or to pay
damages by virtue of Part I of the Consumer Protection
Act 1987[7], being in either case damages in respect of personal
injuries[8] to any person; or

(b)   arises under any order made in family proceedings[9] or under a
maintenance calculation[10] made under the Child Support
Act 1991[11];

(5)   release the bankrupt from such other bankruptcy debts, not being debts
provable in his bankruptcy, as are prescribed[12];

(6)   release the bankrupt from any obligation arising under a confiscation
order made under the Drug Trafficking Offences Act 1986[13], the
Criminal Justice (Scotland) Act 1987[14], the Criminal Justice Act 1988[15]
or under the Proceeds of Crime Act 2002[16] or any obligation arising
from a payment out of the social fund[17] by way of crisis loan or
budgeting loan[18].

1   As to the meaning of 'secured creditor' see PARA 574.
2   Insolvency Act 1986 s 281(2).
3   For these purposes, 'fraud' means actual fraud and does not include constructive fraud, such as
undue influence: *Mander v Evans* [2001] 3 All ER 811, [2001] 1 WLR 2378.
4   Insolvency Act 1986 s 281(3). Dishonesty is an essential ingredient of a fraudulent breach of
trust: *Woodland-Ferrari v UCL Group Retirement Benefits Scheme* [2002] EWHC 1354 (Ch),
[2003] Ch 115, [2002] 3 All ER 670.
5   For these purposes, 'fine' means the same as in the Magistrates' Courts Act 1980 (see
SENTENCING AND DISPOSITION OF OFFENDERS vol 92 (2010) PARA 139): Insolvency Act 1986
s 281(8). The reference to a fine includes a reference to a confiscation order under the Proceeds
of Crime Act 2002 Pt 2, 3 or 4 (see SENTENCING AND DISPOSITION OF OFFENDERS vol 92 (2010)
PARA 390 et seq): Insolvency Act 1986 s 281(4A) (added by the Proceeds of Crime Act 2002
s 456, Sch 11 paras 1, 16).
6   Insolvency Act 1986 s 281(4).
7   Ie the Consumer Protection Act 1987 Pt I (ss 1–9): see CONSUMER PROTECTION vol 21 (2011)
PARA 642 et seq.
8   For these purposes, 'personal injuries' includes death and any disease or other impairment of a
person's physical or mental condition: Insolvency Act 1986 s 281(8).
9   For these purposes, 'family proceedings' means: (1) family proceedings within the meaning of
the Magistrates' Courts Act 1980 (see MAGISTRATES vol 71 (2013) PARA 578) and any
proceedings which would be such proceedings but for s 65(1)(ii) (proceedings for the variation
of an order for periodical payments: see MAGISTRATES vol 71 (2013) PARA 578); and (2) family
proceedings within the meaning of the Matrimonial and Family Proceedings Act 1984 Pt V
(ss 32–42) (see MATRIMONIAL AND CIVIL PARTNERSHIP LAW vol 73 (2009) PARA 737): Insolvency
Act 1986 s 281(8) (amended by the Children Act 1989 s 92(11), Sch 11 para 11(2)).
10   Ie a maintenance calculation under the Child Support Act 1991: see CHILDREN AND YOUNG
PERSONS vol 9 (2012) PARA 573 et seq.
11   Insolvency Act 1986 s 281(5) (amended by the Consumer Protection Act 1987 s 48(1), Sch 4
para 12; the Children Act 1989 s 108(7), Sch 11 para 11(1), Sch 15; the Child Support Act 1991
s 58(13), Sch 5 para 7; the Child Support, Pensions and Social Security Act 2000 s 26, Sch 3
para 6). See *McRoberts v McRoberts* [2012] EWHC 2966 (Ch), [2013] 1 WLR 1601, [2012] All
ER (D) 12 (Nov) (application for release of discharged bankrupt from an obligation under an
order in family proceedings to pay the respondent a lump sum, on the basis that the obligation
could be varied by the matrimonial courts and release would not cause prejudice to the
respondent, refused).
12   Insolvency Act 1986 s 281(6).
13   Ie under the Drug Trafficking Offences Act 1986 s 1.

14 Ie under the Criminal Justice (Scotland) Act 1987 s 1.
15 Ie under the Criminal Justice Act 1988 s 71.
16 Ie under Proceeds of Crime Act 2002 Pt 2, 3 or 4 (see SENTENCING AND DISPOSITION OF
    OFFENDERS vol 92 (2010) PARA 390 et seq).
17 Ie under the Social Security Contributions and Benefits Act 1992 s 138(1)(b) (repealed). As to
    the social fund see SOCIAL SECURITY AND PENSIONS vol 44(2) (Reissue) PARAS 228–236.
18 Insolvency Rules 1986, SI 1986/1925, r 6.223 (amended by SI 1987/1919; SI 1989/397;
    SI 2003/1730; SI 2012/469).

651.   Effect of discharge on third parties.   Where a bankrupt is discharged, the discharge releases him from all the bankruptcy debts[1], but does not affect the right of any creditor of the bankrupt to prove in the bankruptcy for a debt from which the bankrupt is released[2]; nor does discharge affect the right of any secured creditor[3] of the bankrupt to enforce his security for the payment of a debt from which the bankrupt is released[4]. Discharge does not release any person other than the bankrupt from any liability, whether as partner or co-trustee of the bankrupt or otherwise, from which the bankrupt is released by the discharge, or from any liability as surety for the bankrupt or as a person in the nature of such a surety[5].

1 As to the meaning of 'bankruptcy debt' see PARA 508.
2 Insolvency Act 1986 s 281(1). As to the priority of creditors who prove their debts after
   payment of a dividend see PARA 609.
3 As to the meaning of 'secured creditor' see PARA 574.
4 Insolvency Act 1986 s 281(2).
5 Insolvency Act 1986 s 281(7).

652.   Effect of discharge on prosecutions.   Without prejudice to his liability in respect of a subsequent bankruptcy, the bankrupt is not guilty of an offence[1] in respect of anything done after his discharge; but nothing[2] prevents the institution of proceedings against a discharged bankrupt for an offence committed before his discharge[3].

1 Ie under the Insolvency Act 1986 Pt 9 Ch 6 (ss 350–362): see PARA 733 et seq.
2 Ie in the Insolvency Act 1986 Pts 7A–11 (ss 251A–362).
3 Insolvency Act 1986 s 350(3); and see PARA 733. This is without prejudice to any provision of
   Pt 9 Ch 6 which applies to a person in respect of whom a bankruptcy restrictions order is in
   force: see s 350(3A) (added by the Enterprise Act 2002 s 257(3), Sch 21 para 2). As to
   bankruptcy restrictions orders see PARA 657 et seq.

653.   Duties of discharged bankrupt.   After his discharge, the bankrupt must give to the trustee such information as to his affairs, attend on the trustee at such times, and do all such other things, as the trustee may[1] reasonably require[2].

1 Ie for the purposes of carrying out his functions under any of the Insolvency Act 1986 Pts 7A–11
   (ss 251A–385).
2 Insolvency Act 1986 s 333(1), (3). As to the application of s 333 in the case of the
   administration in bankruptcy of the insolvent estate of a deceased person dying before the
   presentation of a bankruptcy petition see PARA 343 note 1.

(10) POST-DISCHARGE RESTRICTIONS

(i) In general

654.   Bankruptcy restrictions orders and undertakings.   On the application of the Secretary of State, or the official receiver acting on the direction of the Secretary of State, the court must make a bankruptcy restrictions order if it thinks it appropriate having regard to the conduct of the bankrupt whether before or after the making of the bankruptcy order[1]. A bankruptcy restrictions order imposes certain restrictions on a bankrupt for a set period of between 2 and 15 years[2]. A bankruptcy restrictions undertaking has the same effect as a bankruptcy restrictions order but does not require an application to court[3].

A breach of a bankruptcy restrictions order or a bankruptcy restrictions undertaking is a criminal offence and may lead to a criminal penalty such as imprisonment or a fine[4].

1 As to bankruptcy restrictions orders see PARA 657 et seq.
2 See PARA 655.
3 As to bankruptcy restrictions undertakings see PARA 668 et seq.
4 See the Insolvency Act 1986 s 350(3A), (6) (s 350(3A) added by the Enterprise Act 2002 s 257(3), Sch 21 para 2).

655. Effect of bankruptcy restrictions orders and undertakings. The restrictions imposed under bankruptcy restrictions orders and undertakings are the same as those that apply to an undischarged bankrupt, namely:

(1) the person must disclose his status to a credit provider if he wishes to obtain credit of more than £500[1];

(2) the person must not carry on business in a different name from that under which he was made bankrupt without disclosing that he wishes to carry on business with the name or trading style he used when he was made bankrupt[2];

(3) the person must not act as the director of a company or take part in its promotion, formation or management unless he obtains permission from the court to do so[3];

(4) the person may not act as an insolvency practitioner[4];

(5) the person may not act as receiver or manager of the property of a company on behalf of debenture holders[5].

The other disqualifications of an undischarged bankrupt also apply during the period of a bankruptcy restrictions order or undertaking[6]. A person the subject of a bankruptcy restrictions order or undertaking is disqualified from being a member of Parliament or of a local authority[7].

1 See the Insolvency Act 1986 s 360(1)(a), (5), (6); and PARA 747.
2 See the Insolvency Act 1986 s 360(1)(b), (5), (6); and PARA 747.
3 See the Company Directors Disqualification Act 1986 s 11(1); and PARA 729.
4 See the Insolvency Act 1986 s 390(5); and PARA 727.
5 See the Insolvency Act 1986 s 31; and PARA 728.
6 See PARA 724.
7 See PARAS 722, 723.

656. Registration. The Secretary of State must maintain a register of bankruptcy restrictions orders[1], interim bankruptcy restrictions orders[2], and bankruptcy restrictions undertakings[3] ('the bankruptcy restrictions register'), which must be open to public inspection[4].

1 As to bankruptcy restrictions orders see PARA 657 et seq.
2 As to interim bankruptcy restrictions orders see PARA 663 et seq.
3 Insolvency Act 1986 Sch 4A para 12 (added by the Enterprise Act 2002 s 257(2), Sch 20). As to bankruptcy restrictions undertakings see PARA 668 et seq.
4 See the Insolvency Rules 1986, SI 1986/1925, r 6A.1; and PARA 28.

(ii) Bankruptcy Restrictions Order

657. Making of bankruptcy restrictions order. A bankruptcy restrictions order may be made by the court[1] on the application of the Secretary of State or the official receiver acting on a direction of the Secretary of State[2].

1 Insolvency Act 1986 s 281A, Sch 4A para 1(1) (s 281A, Sch 4A added by the Enterprise Act 2002 s 257(1), (2), Sch 20).
2 Insolvency Act 1986 Sch 4A para 1(2). For the purposes of the Insolvency Rules 1986, SI 1986/1925, Pt 6 Chs 28–30 (rr 6.240–6.251), 'Secretary of State' includes the official receiver acting in accordance with the Insolvency Act 1986 Sch 4A para 1(2): Insolvency Rules 1986, SI 1986/1925, r 6.240 (added by SI 2003/1730).

658. Application for bankruptcy restrictions order. An application for a bankruptcy restrictions order in respect of a bankrupt must be made before the end of the period of one year beginning with the date on which the bankruptcy commences[1], or with the permission of the court[2].

Where the Secretary of State[3] applies to the court for a bankruptcy restrictions order[4], the application must be supported by a report by the Secretary of State[5] which must include: (1) a statement of the conduct by reference to which it is alleged that it is appropriate for a bankruptcy restrictions order to be made; and (2) the evidence on which the Secretary of State relies in support of the application[6]. Any evidence in support of an application for a bankruptcy restrictions order provided by persons other than the Secretary of State must be by way of a witness statement[7].

The date for the hearing must be no earlier than eight weeks from the date when the court fixes the venue[8] for the hearing[9].

1 Insolvency Act 1986 Sch 4A para 3(1)(a) (Sch 4A added by the Enterprise Act 2002 s 257(2), Sch 20). This period ceases to run in respect of a bankrupt while the period set for his discharge is suspended under the Insolvency Act 1986 s 279(3) (see PARA 640): Sch 4A para 3(2) (as so added).
2 Insolvency Act 1986 Sch 4A para 3(1)(b) (as added: see note 1). As to the grant of permission see *Official Receiver v Baars* [2009] BPIR 524.
3 See PARA 657 note 2.
4 Ie under the Insolvency Act 1986 Sch 4A para 1: see PARA 657.
5 Insolvency Rules 1986, SI 1986/1925, r 6.241(1) (added by SI 2003/1730).
6 Insolvency Rules 1986, SI 1986/1925, r 6.241(2) (added by SI 2003/1730).
7 Insolvency Rules 1986, SI 1986/1925, r 6.241(3) (added by SI 2003/1730; and amended by SI 2010/686). As to the meaning of 'witness statement' see PARA 161 note 7.
8 As to the meaning of 'venue' see PARA 46 note 22.
9 Insolvency Rules 1986, SI 1986/1925, r 6.241(4) (added by SI 2003/1730).

659. Service on the defendant. The Secretary of State[1] must serve notice of the application and the venue[2] fixed by the court on the bankrupt not more than 14 days after the application is made at court[3]. Service must be accompanied by a copy of the application, together with copies of the report by the Secretary of State[4], any other evidence filed with the court[5] in support of the application, and an acknowledgement of service[6].

The defendant must file in court an acknowledgement of service of the application indicating whether or not he contests the application not more than 14 days after service on him of the application[7]. Where the defendant has failed to file an acknowledgement of service and the time period for doing so has expired, the defendant may attend the hearing of the application but may not take part in the hearing unless the court gives permission[8].

1 See PARA 657 note 2.

2   As to the meaning of 'venue' see PARA 46 note 22.
3   Insolvency Rules 1986, SI 1986/1925, r 6.242(1) (added by SI 2003/1730).
4   See PARA 658.
5   As to the meaning of 'file with the court' see PARA 57 note 13.
6   Insolvency Rules 1986, SI 1986/1925, r 6.242(2) (added by SI 2003/1730).
7   Insolvency Rules 1986, SI 1986/1925, r 6.242(3) (added by SI 2003/1730).
8   Insolvency Rules 1986, SI 1986/1925, r 6.242(4) (added by SI 2003/1730).

660.   The bankrupt's evidence.   If the bankrupt wishes to oppose the application for a bankruptcy restrictions order[1], within 28 days of the service of the application and evidence of the Secretary of State[2], he must file in court[3] any evidence which he wishes the court to take into consideration, and must serve a copy of such evidence upon the Secretary of State within three business days[4] of filing it at court[5].

Within 14 days from receiving the copy of the bankrupt's evidence, the Secretary of State must file in court any further evidence in reply he wishes the court to take into consideration and must as soon as reasonably practicable serve a copy of that evidence upon the bankrupt[6].

The court may make a bankruptcy restrictions order against the bankrupt, whether or not the latter appears, and whether or not he has filed evidence[7].

1   See PARA 658.
2   See PARA 657 note 2.
3   As to the meaning of 'file in court' see PARA 57 note 13.
4   As to the meaning of 'business day' see PARA 28 note 8.
5   Insolvency Rules 1986, SI 1986/1925, r 6.243(1) (added by SI 2003/1730; and amended by SI 2010/686).
6   Insolvency Rules 1986, SI 1986/1925, r 6.243(2) (added by SI 2003/1730).
7   Insolvency Rules 1986, SI 1986/1925, r 6.244(1) (added by SI 2003/1730).

661.   Grounds for making a bankruptcy restrictions order.   The court must grant an application for a bankruptcy restrictions order[1] if it thinks it appropriate having regard to the conduct of the bankrupt, whether before or after the making of the bankruptcy order[2]. The court must, in particular, take into account any of the following kinds of behaviour on the part of the bankrupt:

(1)   failing to keep records which account for a loss of property by the bankrupt, or by a business carried on by him, where the loss occurred in the period beginning two years before petition[3] and ending with the date of the application[4];

(2)   failing to produce records of that kind on demand by the official receiver or the trustee[5];

(3)   entering into a transaction at an undervalue[6];

(4)   giving a preference[7];

(5)   making an excessive pension contribution[8];

(6)   a failure to supply goods or services which were wholly or partly paid for which gave rise to a claim provable in the bankruptcy[9];

(7)   trading at a time before commencement of the bankruptcy when the bankrupt knew or ought to have known that he was himself to be unable to pay his debts[10];

(8)   incurring, before commencement of the bankruptcy, a debt which the bankrupt had no reasonable expectation of being able to pay[11];

(9)   failing to account satisfactorily to the court, the official receiver or the trustee for a loss of property or for an insufficiency of property to meet bankruptcy debts[12];

(10) carrying on any gambling, rash and hazardous speculation or unreasonable extravagance which may have materially contributed to or increased the extent of the bankruptcy or which took place between presentation of the petition and commencement of the bankruptcy[13];

(11) neglect of business affairs of a kind which may have materially contributed to or increased the extent of the bankruptcy[14];

(12) fraud or fraudulent breach of trust[15];

(13) failing to cooperate with the official receiver or the trustee[16].

The court must also, in particular, consider whether the bankrupt was an undischarged bankrupt at some time during the period of six years ending with the date of the bankruptcy to which the application relates[17].

1   See PARA 658.

2   Insolvency Act 1986 Sch 4A para 2(1) (Sch 4A added by the Enterprise Act 2002 s 257(2), Sch 20). For the court's general approach to the hearing of applications for a bankruptcy restrictions order see *Official Receiver v Merchant* [2006] BPIR 1525. The court is required to examine and evaluate the bankrupt's conduct and to form a view whether a bankruptcy restrictions order should be made in the interests of the public and if so impose at least the minimum period: *Randhawa v Official Receiver* [2006] EWHC 2946 (Ch), [2007] 1 All ER 755, [2007] 1 WLR 1700; applied in *Official Receiver v Pyman* [2007] EWHC 2002 (Ch), [2007] BPIR 1150, [2007] All ER (D) 25 (Mar). The fact that a charge is void as opposed to voidable is immaterial when the bankrupt knows of his insolvency and intended to make an asset unavailable to his creditors: *Official Receiver v Bathurst* [2008] EWHC 1724 (Ch), [2008] BPIR 1548, [2008] All ER (D) 18 (Jun).

3   'Before petition' is to be construed in accordance with the Insolvency Act 1986 s 351(c) (see PARA 735 note 5): Sch 4A para 2(4) (as added: see note 2). As from a day to be appointed, Sch 4A para 2(4) is amended by the Enterprise and Regulatory Reform Act 2013 s 71, Sch 19 paras 1, 63: see PARA 130 note 17.

4   Insolvency Act 1986 Sch 4A para 2(2)(a) (as added: see note 2). As from a day to be appointed, Sch 4A para 2(2)(a) is amended by the Enterprise and Regulatory Reform Act 2013 s 71, Sch 19 paras 1, 63: see PARA 130 note 17. For this purpose 'property' is not necessarily limited to property of the bankrupt: *Official Receiver v Doganci* [2007] BPIR 87.

5   Insolvency Act 1986 Sch 4A para 2(2)(b) (as added: see note 2).

6   Insolvency Act 1986 Sch 4A para 2(2)(c) (as added: see note 2). 'Undervalue' is to be construed in accordance with s 339 (see PARA 678 et seq): Sch 4A para 2(4) (as so added).

7   Insolvency Act 1986 Sch 4A para 2(2)(d) (as added: see note 2). 'Preference' is to be construed in accordance with s 340 (see PARA 681 et seq): Sch 4A para 2(4) (as so added).

8   Insolvency Act 1986 Sch 4A para 2(2)(e) (as added: see note 2). 'Excessive pension contribution' is to be construed in accordance with s 342A (see PARA 693): Sch 4A para 2(4) (as so added).

9   Insolvency Act 1986 Sch 4A para 2(2)(f) (as added: see note 2). As to proofs of debt see PARA 507 et seq.

10 Insolvency Act 1986 Sch 4A para 2(2)(g) (as added: see note 2).

11 Insolvency Act 1986 Sch 4A para 2(2)(h) (as added: see note 2). As to the commencement of bankruptcy see PARA 209.

12 Insolvency Act 1986 Sch 4A para 2(2)(i) (as added: see note 2). As to the meaning of 'bankruptcy debt' see PARA 508.

13 Insolvency Act 1986 Sch 4A para 2(2)(j) (as added: see note 2). As from a day to be appointed, Sch 4A para 2(2)(j) is amended by the Enterprise and Regulatory Reform Act 2013 s 71, Sch 19 paras 1, 63: see PARA 130 note 17.

14 Insolvency Act 1986 Sch 4A para 2(2)(k) (as added: see note 2).

15 Insolvency Act 1986 Sch 4A para 2(2)(l) (as added: see note 2).

16 Insolvency Act 1986 Sch 4A para 2(2)(m) (as added: see note 2).

17 Insolvency Act 1986 Sch 4A para 2(3) (as added: see note 2). The court should take into account such an earlier bankruptcy: *Official Receiver v Pyman* [2007] BPIR 1150, [2007] All ER (D) 25 (Mar).

662.   Making and duration of bankruptcy restrictions order. A bankruptcy restrictions order comes into force when it is made[1], and ceases to have effect at the end of a date specified in the order[2]. The date specified must not be before the end of the period of two years beginning with the date on which the order is made, or after the end of the period of 15 years beginning with that date[3].

Where the court makes a bankruptcy restrictions order, it must send two sealed copies to the Secretary of State[4]. As soon as reasonably practicable after receipt of the sealed copy of the order, the Secretary of State must send a sealed copy of the order to the bankrupt[5].

1 Insolvency Act 1986 Sch 4A para 4(1)(a) (Sch 4A added by the Enterprise Act 2002 s 257(2), Sch 20).
2 Insolvency Act 1986 Sch 4A para 4(1)(b) (as added: see note 1). The guidelines to be applied in considering the duration of a bankruptcy restrictions order will be analogous to those which apply in the case of a disqualification order against an unfit director of an insolvent company (see COMPANY AND PARTNERSHIP INSOLVENCY vol 17 (2011) PARA 1072 et seq): *Randhawa v Official Receiver* [2006] EWHC 2946 (Ch), [2007] 1 All ER 755, [2007] 1 WLR 1700; *Official Receiver v Bathurst* [2008] EWHC 1724 (Ch), [2008] BPIR 1548, [2008] All ER (D) 286 (May). See also *Official Receiver v Pyman* [2007] BPIR 1150, [2007] All ER (D) 25 (Mar)
3 Insolvency Act 1986 Sch 4A para 4(2) (as added: see note 1). In a case in which both an interim bankruptcy restrictions order (see PARA 663 et seq) and a bankruptcy restrictions order are made, Sch 4A para 4(2) has effect in relation to the bankruptcy restrictions order as if a reference to the date of that order were a reference to the date of the interim order: Sch 4A para 6 (as added: see note 1).
4 Insolvency Rules 1986, SI 1986/1925, r 6.244(2) (added by SI 2003/1730).
5 Insolvency Rules 1986, SI 1986/1925, r 6.244(3) (added by SI 2003/1730).

(iii) Interim Bankruptcy Restrictions Order

663. Application for interim bankruptcy restrictions order. At any time between the institution of an application for a bankruptcy restrictions order[1], and the determination of the application[2], the court may make an interim bankruptcy restrictions order if it thinks that there are prima facie grounds to suggest that the application for the bankruptcy restrictions order will be successful[3], and it is in the public interest to make an interim order[4].

An interim bankruptcy restrictions order may be made only on the application of: (1) the Secretary of State; or (2) the official receiver acting on a direction of the Secretary of State[5]. Where the Secretary of State applies for an interim bankruptcy restrictions order, the court must fix a venue[6] for the hearing[7]. Notice of an application for an interim bankruptcy restrictions order must be given to the bankrupt at least two business days[8] before the date set for the hearing unless the court directs otherwise[9].

1 As to bankruptcy restrictions orders see PARA 657 et seq.
2 Insolvency Act 1986 Sch 4A para 5(1) (Sch 4A added by the Enterprise Act 2002 s 257(2), Sch 20).
3 As to the grounds for making a bankruptcy restrictions order see PARA 661.
4 Insolvency Act 1986 Sch 4A para 5(2) (as added: see note 2). See also *Official Receiver v Merchant* [2006] BPIR 1525.
5 Insolvency Act 1986 Sch 4A para 5(3) (as added: see note 2). As to the meaning of 'Secretary of State' see PARA 657 note 2.
6 As to the meaning of 'venue' see PARA 46 note 22.
7 Insolvency Rules 1986, SI 1986/1925, r 6.245(1) (added by SI 2003/1730).
8 As to the meaning of 'business day' see PARA 28 note 8.
9 Insolvency Rules 1986, SI 1986/1925, r 6.245(2) (added by SI 2003/1730).

664. The case against the defendant. The Secretary of State[1] must file a report in court[2] as evidence in support of any application for an interim bankruptcy restrictions order[3]. The report must include evidence of the bankrupt's conduct which is alleged to constitute the grounds for the making of an interim bankruptcy restrictions order and evidence of matters which relate to the public interest in making the order[4]. Any evidence by persons other than the Secretary of State in support of an application for an interim bankruptcy restrictions order must be by way of a witness statement[5].

1 See PARA 657 note 2.
2 As to the meaning of 'file in court' see PARA 57 note 13.
3 Insolvency Rules 1986, SI 1986/1925, r 6.246(1) (added by SI 2003/1730).
4 Insolvency Rules 1986, SI 1986/1925, r 6.246(2) (added by SI 2003/1730).
5 Insolvency Rules 1986, SI 1986/1925, r 6.246(3) (added by SI 2003/1730; and amended by SI 2010/686). As to the meaning of 'witness statement' see PARA 161 note 7.

665. Making an interim bankruptcy restrictions order. The bankrupt may file in court[1] any evidence which he wishes the court to take into consideration and may appear at the hearing for an interim bankruptcy restrictions order[2]. The court may make an interim bankruptcy restrictions order against the bankrupt, whether or not the latter appears, and whether or not he has filed evidence[3].

Where the court makes an interim bankruptcy restrictions order, two sealed copies of the order must be sent, as soon as reasonably practicable, to the Secretary of State[4]. As soon as reasonably practicable after receipt of the sealed copies of the order, the Secretary of State must send a copy of the order to the bankrupt[5].

1 As to the meaning of 'file in court' see PARA 57 note 13.
2 Insolvency Rules 1986, SI 1986/1925, r 6.247(1) (added by SI 2003/1730).
3 Insolvency Rules 1986, SI 1986/1925, r 6.247(2) (added by SI 2003/1730).
4 Insolvency Rules 1986, SI 1986/1925, r 6.247(3) (added by SI 2003/1730). See PARA 657 note 2.
5 Insolvency Rules 1986, SI 1986/1925, r 6.247(4) (added by SI 2003/1730).

666. Effect and duration of interim bankruptcy restrictions order. An interim bankruptcy restrictions order has the same effect as a bankruptcy restrictions order[1], and comes into force when it is made[2]. An interim order ceases to have effect on the determination of the application for the bankruptcy restrictions order[3], on the acceptance of a bankruptcy restrictions undertaking made by the bankrupt[4], or if the court discharges the interim order on the application of the person who applied for it or of the bankrupt[5].

1 As to the effect of bankruptcy restrictions orders and undertakings see PARA 655.
2 Insolvency Act 1986 Sch 4A para 5(4) (Sch 4A added by the Enterprise Act 2002 s 257(2), Sch 20).
3 See PARA 658.
4 See PARA 668.
5 Insolvency Act 1986 Sch 4A para 5(5) (as added: see note 2).

667. Application to set aside an interim bankruptcy restrictions order. A bankrupt may apply to the court to set aside an interim bankruptcy restrictions order[1]. The application must be supported by a witness statement stating the grounds on which the application is made[2].

Where a bankrupt applies to set aside an interim bankruptcy restrictions order, he must send to the Secretary of State[3], not less than five business days[4] before the hearing: (1) notice of his application; (2) notice of the venue[5]; (3) a copy of his application; and (4) a copy of the supporting witness statement[6].

The Secretary of State may attend the hearing and call the attention of the court to any matters which seem to him to be relevant, and may himself give evidence or call witnesses[7].

Where the court sets aside an interim bankruptcy restrictions order, two sealed copies of the order must be sent, as soon as reasonably practicable, to the Secretary of State by the court[8]. As soon as reasonably practicable after receipt of the sealed copies of the order, the Secretary of State must send a sealed copy of the order to the bankrupt[9].

1   Insolvency Rules 1986, SI 1986/1925, r 6.248(1) (added by SI 2003/1730).
2   Insolvency Rules 1986, SI 1986/1925, r 6.248(2) (added by SI 2003/1730; and amended by SI 2010/686). As to the meaning of 'witness statement' see PARA 161 note 7.
3   See PARA 657 note 2.
4   As to the meaning of 'business day' see PARA 28 note 8.
5   As to the meaning of 'venue' see PARA 46 note 22.
6   Insolvency Rules 1986, SI 1986/1925, r 6.248(3) (added by SI 2003/1730; and amended by SI 2010/686).
7   Insolvency Rules 1986, SI 1986/1925, r 6.248(4) (added by SI 2003/1730).
8   Insolvency Rules 1986, SI 1986/1925, r 6.248(5) (added by SI 2003/1730).
9   Insolvency Rules 1986, SI 1986/1925, r 6.248(6) (added by SI 2003/1730).

(iv) Bankruptcy Restrictions Undertaking

668.   Offer of bankruptcy restrictions undertaking.   A bankrupt may offer a bankruptcy restrictions undertaking to the Secretary of State[1]. In determining whether to accept a bankruptcy restrictions undertaking the Secretary of State must have regard to the same matters relating to the behaviour of the bankrupt[2] which the court must take into account in deciding whether to make a bankruptcy restrictions order[3]. He must also consider whether the bankrupt was an undischarged bankrupt at some time during the period of six years ending with the date of the bankruptcy to which the application relates[4].

1   Insolvency Act 1986 Sch 4A para 7(1) (Sch 4A added by Enterprise Act 2002 s 257(2), Sch 20). See PARA 657 note 2.
2   As to those matters see the Insolvency Act 1986 Sch 4A para 2(2); and PARA 661.
3   Insolvency Act 1986 Sch 4A para 7(2) (as added: see note 1). A reference in an enactment to a person in respect of whom a bankruptcy restrictions order has effect, or who is 'the subject of' a bankruptcy restrictions order, includes a reference to a person in respect of whom a bankruptcy restrictions undertaking has effect: Sch 4A para 8 (as so added).
4   See the Insolvency Act 1986 Sch 4A paras 2(2), 7(2) (as added: see note 1); and PARA 661.

669.   Acceptance and duration of bankruptcy restrictions undertaking.   A bankruptcy restrictions undertaking comes into force on being accepted by the Secretary of State[1], and ceases to have effect at the end of a date specified in the undertaking[2]. The date specified must not be before the end of the period of two years beginning with the date on which the undertaking is accepted, or after the end of the period of 15 years beginning with that date[3].

As soon as reasonably practicable after a bankruptcy restrictions undertaking has been accepted by the Secretary of State, a copy must be sent to the bankrupt and filed in court[4] and sent to the official receiver if he is not the applicant[5].

1   A bankruptcy restrictions undertaking authenticated by the bankrupt is deemed to have been accepted by the Secretary of State for the purposes of the Insolvency Act 1986 Sch 4A para 9 when the undertaking is authenticated by the Secretary of State: Insolvency Rules 1986, SI 1986/1925, r 6.249 (added by SI 2003/1730; and amended by SI 2010/686). As to the Secretary of State see PARA 657 note 2. As to authentication see PARA 158 note 2.
2   Insolvency Act 1986 Sch 4A para 9(1) (Sch 4A added by Enterprise Act 2002 s 257(2), Sch 20).
3   Insolvency Act 1986 Sch 4A para 9(2) (as added: see note 2).
4   As to the meaning of 'file in court' see PARA 57 note 13.
5   Insolvency Rules 1986, SI 1986/1925, r 6.250 (added by SI 2003/1730).

670. Application to annul bankruptcy restrictions undertaking. On an application by the bankrupt the court may: (1) annul a bankruptcy restrictions undertaking[1]; or (2) provide for a bankruptcy restrictions undertaking to cease to have effect before the date specified in the undertaking[2].

The application by the bankrupt must be supported by a witness statement[3] stating the grounds on which it is made[4].

The bankrupt must give notice of the application and the venue[5], together with a copy of the witness statement supporting his application to the Secretary of State[6] at least 28 days before the date fixed for the hearing[7].

The Secretary of State may attend the hearing and call the attention of the court to any matters which seem to him to be relevant, and may himself give evidence or call witnesses[8].

The court must send a sealed copy of any order annulling or varying the bankruptcy restrictions undertaking to the Secretary of State and the bankrupt[9].

1   Insolvency Act 1986 Sch 4A para 9(3)(a) (Sch 4A added by Enterprise Act 2002 s 257(2), Sch 20).
2   Insolvency Act 1986 Sch 4A para 9(3)(b) (as added: see note 1).
3   As to the meaning of 'witness statement' see PARA 161 note 7.
4   Insolvency Rules 1986, SI 1986/1925, r 6.251(1) (added by SI 2003/1730; and amended by SI 2010/686).
5   As to the meaning of 'venue' see PARA 46 note 22.
6   See PARA 657 note 2.
7   Insolvency Rules 1986, SI 1986/1925, r 6.251(2) (added by SI 2003/1730; and amended by SI 2010/686).
8   Insolvency Rules 1986, SI 1986/1925, r 6.251(3) (added by SI 2003/1730).
9   Insolvency Rules 1986, SI 1986/1925, r 6.251(4) (added by SI 2003/1730).

(v) Annulment of Bankruptcy Order

671. Effect of annulment of bankruptcy order. Where a bankruptcy order is annulled on the grounds that the order ought not to have been made[1], or in relation to a criminal bankruptcy order[2], any bankruptcy restrictions order[3], interim order[4] or undertaking[5] which is in force in respect of the bankrupt is annulled[6], no new bankruptcy restrictions order or interim order may be made in respect of the bankrupt[7], and no new bankruptcy restrictions undertaking by the bankrupt may be accepted[8].

Where a bankruptcy order is annulled following the approval of a voluntary arrangement[9] or on the grounds that the debts and expenses of the bankruptcy have all been paid or secured[10]:

(1)   the annulment does not affect any bankruptcy restrictions order, interim order or undertaking in respect of the bankrupt[11];

(2)   the court may make a bankruptcy restrictions order in relation to the bankrupt on an application instituted before the annulment[12];

(3)   the Secretary of State may accept a bankruptcy restrictions undertaking offered before the annulment[13]; and

(4)   an application for a bankruptcy restrictions order or interim order in respect of the bankrupt may not be instituted after the annulment[14].

1   Ie under the Insolvency Act 1986 s 282(1)(a): see PARA 620 head (1).
2   Ie under the Insolvency Act 1986 s 282(2) (see PARA 620).
3   As to bankruptcy restrictions orders see PARA 657 et seq.
4   As to interim bankruptcy restrictions orders see PARA 663 et seq.
5   As to bankruptcy restrictions undertakings see PARA 668 et seq.
6   Insolvency Act 1986 Sch 4A para 10(a) (Sch 4A added by Enterprise Act 2002 s 257(2), Sch 20).
7   Insolvency Act 1986 Sch 4A para 10(b) (as added: see note 6).

8 Insolvency Act 1986 Sch 4A para 10(c) (as added: see note 6).
9 Ie under the Insolvency Act 1986 s 261 (see PARA 70), s 263D (see PARA 95) or s 282(1)(b) (see PARA 620 head (2)).
10 Ie under the Insolvency Act 1986 s 282(1)(b): see PARA 620 head (2).
11 Insolvency Act 1986 Sch 4A para 11(a) (as added: see note 6).
12 Insolvency Act 1986 Sch 4A para 11(b) (as added: see note 6). See *Jenkins v Official Receiver* [2007] EWHC 1402 (Ch), [2007] BPIR 740, [2007] All ER (D) 139 (Apr) (bankruptcy annulled on bankrupt's application but bankruptcy restrictions order thereupon made).
13 Insolvency Act 1986 Sch 4A para 11(c) (as added: see note 6).
14 Insolvency Act 1986 Sch 4A para 11(d) (as added: see note 6).

(11) EFFECT OF BANKRUPTCY ON CERTAIN RIGHTS, TRANSACTIONS ETC

(i) Rights of Occupation

672. Rights under trusts of land. Where a person who is subsequently adjudged bankrupt and another person holds a beneficial interest in land, and are together trustees of land or have an interest in a property which is subject to a trust of land, then, on the vesting of the bankrupt's estate in his trustee in bankruptcy[1], the trustee will acquire all the rights previously vested in the bankrupt as a trustee of land, including, as the holder of a beneficial interest in the land or property, the right to apply to the court for an order in the event that the trustees of land refuse to sell or to exercise any of their other powers[2].

Any application by the trustee of the bankrupt's estate for an order under the Trusts of Land and Appointment of Trustees Act 1996[3] for an order for the sale of land must be made to the court having jurisdiction in relation to the bankruptcy[4].

On such an application the court must make such order as it thinks just and reasonable having regard to:

(1) the interests of the bankrupt's creditors;
(2) where the application is made in respect of land which includes a dwelling house[5] which is or has been the home of the bankrupt or the bankrupt's spouse or civil partner or former spouse or former civil partner:
    (a) the conduct of the spouse, civil partner, former spouse or former civil partner, so far as contributing to the bankruptcy;
    (b) the needs and financial resources of the spouse, civil partner, former spouse or former civil partner; and
    (c) the needs of any children; and
(3) all the circumstances of the case other than the needs of the bankrupt[6].

Where such an application is made after the end of the period of one year beginning with the first vesting[7] of the bankrupt's estate in the trustee in bankruptcy, the court must assume, unless the circumstances of the case are exceptional, that the interest of the bankrupt's creditors outweigh all other considerations[8].

1 As to the vesting of the bankrupt's estate in the trustee see PARA 397 et seq.
2 As to the powers of the court in relation to trusts of land see the Trusts of Land and Appointment of Trustees Act 1996 s 14; REAL PROPERTY AND REGISTRATION vol 87 (2012) PARA 106; and TRUSTS vol 48 (2007 Reissue) PARA 1038. See *Avis v Turner* [2007] EWCA Civ 748, [2008] Ch 218, sub nom *Turner v Avis* [2007] 4 All ER 1103. Where the bankrupt's co-owner is in occupation, a trustee may be entitled to occupation rent or equitable compensation: see *Re Barcham* [2008] EWHC 1505 (Ch), [2009] 1 All ER 145, sub nom *French v Barcham* [2009] 1 WLR 1124.

3 Ie under the Trusts of Land and Appointment of Trustees Act 1996 s 14.
4 Insolvency Act 1986 s 335A(1) (s 335A added by the Trusts of Land and Appointment of
   Trustees Act 1996 s 25(1), Sch 3 para 23). The jurisdiction conferred by the Insolvency Act 1986
   s 335A is exclusive to the bankruptcy. As to the courts having jurisdiction in bankruptcy see
   PARAS 6, 7; as to the allocation of bankruptcy proceedings see PARA 786; and as to the transfer
   of proceedings between bankruptcy courts see PARA 756.
      Section 335A came into force on 1 January 1997: see the Trusts of Land and Appointment of
   Trustees Act 1996 (Commencement) Order 1996, SI 1996/2974, art 2. However, the powers
   conferred on the court by the Insolvency Act 1986 s 335A are exercisable on an application
   whether it is made before or after the commencement of s 335A: s 335A(4) (as so added).
      In the case of the administration in bankruptcy of the insolvent estate of a deceased person
   dying before the presentation of a bankruptcy petition, s 335A applies: Administration of
   Insolvent Estates of Deceased Persons Order 1986, SI 1986/1999, art 3(1), Sch 1 Pt II para 26.
   As to the administration in bankruptcy of the insolvent estates of deceased persons see further
   PARA 830 et seq.
5 As to the meaning of 'dwelling house' see PARA 413 note 1.
6 Insolvency Act 1986 s 335A(2) (as added (see note 4); and amended by the Civil Partnership
   Act 2004 s 261(1), Sch 27 para 118). It is an abuse of process for a trustee in bankruptcy to
   make an application for possession and sale of a bankrupt's former matrimonial home on behalf
   of a secured creditor: *Re Ng (a bankrupt)* [1997] BCC 507, sub nom *Re Ng (a bankrupt)*,
   Trustee of the Estate of Ng v Ng [1997] BPIR 267. See also *Byford v Butler* [2003] EWHC 1267
   (Ch), [2004] 1 P & CR 159 (co-owner remained in sole occupation of matrimonial home; as
   co-owner's occupation prevented trustee in bankruptcy from obtaining any benefit from
   property, payment of occupation rent was reasonable). It is axiomatic that what creditors want
   is to be paid their money as soon as possible and, therefore, it is not necessary for the trustee in
   bankruptcy to do very much by way of positive evidence to ascertain their identity or their
   concerns: *Nicholls v Lan* [2006] EWHC 1255 (Ch), [2007] 1 FLR 744, [2006] BPIR 1243. Any
   agreement between co-owners of property to postpone sale can be varied or discharged by the
   court on an application by the trustee under these provisions: *Avis v Turner* [2007] EWCA Civ
   748, [2008] Ch 218, sub nom *Turner v Avis* [2007] 4 All ER 1103.
7 Ie under the Insolvency Act 1986 Pt 9 Ch 4 (ss 305–335): see PARA 397 et seq. Section 335A(2)
   effectively re-enacts the law in force prior to 29 December 1986 (see PARA 2) in respect of an
   application by a trustee for possession of the matrimonial home under the Law of Property
   Act 1925 s 30 (repealed: see now the Trusts of Land and Appointment of Trustees Act 1996
   s 14). In *Re Turner (a bankrupt), ex p Trustee of Property of Bankrupt v Turner (a bankrupt)*
   [1975] 1 All ER 5, [1974] 1 WLR 1556, it was held that, in exercising its discretion as to
   whether or not to order a sale, the question for the court was whose voice in equity ought to
   prevail and that, in the absence of special considerations, the trustee's statutory duty to realise
   the husband's interest in the property gave him the stronger claim. See also *Re Solomon (a
   bankrupt), ex p Trustee of Property of Bankrupt v Solomon* [1967] Ch 573, [1966] 3 All ER
   255; *Re Densham (a bankrupt), ex p Trustee of Property of Bankrupt v Bankrupt* [1975]
   3 All ER 726, [1975] 1 WLR 1519; *Re Bailey (a bankrupt) (No 25 of 1975)* [1977] 2 All ER 26,
   [1977] 1 WLR 278, DC; *Re Lowrie (a bankrupt), ex p Trustee of Bankrupt v Bankrupt* [1981]
   3 All ER 353, DC; *Re Citro (a bankrupt)* [1991] Ch 142, [1990] 3 All ER 952, CA; *Lloyds
   Bank plc v Byrne* [1993] 2 FCR 41, [1993] 1 FLR 369, CA; *Abbey National plc v Moss* [1994]
   2 FCR 587, [1994] 1 FLR 307, CA (mother and daughter were joint owners); *Zandfarid v Bank
   of Credit and Commerce International SA (in liquidation)* [1996] 1 WLR 1420, [1997] 1 FCR
   78; *Trustee of the Estate of Eric Bowe (a bankrupt) v Bowe* [1998] 2 FLR 439, [1997] BPIR 747
   (probability that the whole of the net proceeds of sale of the home will be absorbed in defraying
   the expenses of the bankruptcy not exceptional); *Harrington v Bennett* [2000] BPIR 630 (a case
   decided under the new, amended provisions; 'exceptional' means outside the usual melancholy
   consequences of debt or improvidence); *Dean v Stout* [2005] EWHC 3315 (Ch), [2006] 1 FLR
   725, [2005] BPIR 1113 (fact that bankrupt's wife had reduced the petitioning creditor's debt,
   other creditors had been paid in full and the mortgage on the property had been fully paid were
   held not to be 'exceptional circumstances'). For cases where exceptional circumstances were
   found see *Re Holliday (a bankrupt), ex p Trustee of Property of Bankrupt v Holliday* [1981]
   Ch 405, [1980] 3 All ER 385, CA (where a divorced husband filed his own bankruptcy petition
   motivated by a desire to defeat his former wife's application for a property adjustment order;
   sale postponed five years primarily for the benefit of the children); *Re Mott, ex p Trustee of
   Property of Bankrupt v Mott and McQuitty* [1987] CLY 212 (where sale was postponed until
   after the death of a 70-year old widow in poor health likely to deteriorate if she had to move,
   the co-owner being her son, and the creditors in the main being the Commissioners of Inland
   Revenue and the Department of Health and Social Security); *Re Gorman (a bankrupt),*

ex p Trustee of Bankrupt v Bankrupt [1990] 1 All ER 717, [1990] 1 WLR 616 (spouse had actionable claim for negligence against her solicitors which was strong and nearly ready for trial; the court gave her time to raise the funds to purchase the interest of the trustee); *Re Raval (a bankrupt)* [1998] 2 FLR 718, [1998] BPIR 389 (a case decided under the new, amended provisions; wife was a paranoid schizophrenic); *Claughton v Charalamabous* [1998] BPIR 558 (a case decided under the new, amended provisions; seriously ill spouse with special housing needs and reduced life expectancy); *Re Bremner (a bankrupt)* [1999] 1 FLR 912, [1999] BPIR 185 (a case decided under the new, amended provisions; bankrupt terminally ill). In the normal event, the Insolvency Act 1986 s 336(5) (see PARA 673) gives the spouse one year's grace before the trustee may bring an application which will result in a sale postponed for no more than a short time to enable the spouse to make arrangements for any family and, perhaps, to raise sufficient capital to purchase the bankrupt's share of the property. Section 313 (see PARA 413), however, provides a power in the court to impose a charge on the bankrupt's house for the benefit of the estate where the trustee is unable for the time being to realise that property. The bankrupt's house, which will then revert to the bankrupt (see s 313(3); and PARA 413), will remain subject to this charge after the bankrupt obtains his discharge from bankruptcy. Such a charge provides the means whereby the creditors' interests receive some measure of protection without the need to enforce a sale of the house of the bankrupt, his spouse and any children of the family.

8   Insolvency Act 1986 s 335A(3) (as added: see note 4). The term 'creditors' in the Insolvency Act 1986 s 335A(3) refers to both secured and unsecured creditors: *Re Bankrupts (Nos 9587 and 9588 of 1994), Judd v Brown* [1998] 2 FLR 360, [1997] BPIR 470. As to the compatibility of the Insolvency Act 1986 s 335A(3) with the Convention for the Protection of Human Rights and Fundamental Freedoms (Rome, 4 November 1950; TS 71 (1953); Cmd 8969) ('European Convention on Human Rights'), particularly in relation to the courts' interpretation of exceptional circumstances for those purposes, see *Barca v Mears* [2004] EWHC 2170 (Ch), [2005] 2 FLR 1, [2005] BPIR 15; *Donohoe v Ingram (Trustee in Bankruptcy of Kirkup)* [2006] 2 FLR 1084, [2006] Fam Law 733, [2006] All ER (D) 132 (Jan); *Karia v Franses* [2006] BPIR 1226, [2001] All ER (D) 161 (Nov); *Holtham v Kelmanson* [2006] EWHC 2588 (Ch), [2006] BPIR 1422, [2006] All ER (D) 271 (Oct); cf *Official Receiver for Northern Ireland v Rooney* [2008] NI Ch 22, [2009] 2 FLR 1437, [2009] BPIR 536.

673. Rights of occupation of bankrupt's spouse or civil partner. Where a spouse's or civil partner's home rights[1] are a charge on the estate or interest of the other spouse or civil partner, or of trustees for the other spouse or civil partner, and the other spouse or civil partner is adjudged bankrupt:

(1)   the charge continues to subsist notwithstanding the bankruptcy and, subject to the provisions of the Family Law Act 1996, binds the trustee of the bankrupt's estate and persons deriving title under that trustee[2]; and

(2)   any application for an occupation order where the applicant has an estate or interest or has a home right[3] must be made to the court having jurisdiction in relation to the bankruptcy[4].

However, nothing occurring in the initial period of the bankruptcy, that is to say, the period beginning with the day of the presentation of the petition for the bankruptcy order[5] and ending with the vesting of the bankrupt's estate in a trustee[6], is to be taken as having given rise to any home rights[7] in relation to a dwelling house comprised in the bankrupt's estate[8].

On an application for an order for possession under the above provisions[9], the court may make such an order[10] as it thinks just and reasonable having regard to:

(a)   the interests of the bankrupt's creditors;

(b)   the conduct of the spouse or former spouse or civil partner or former civil partner, so far as contributing to the bankruptcy;

(c)   the needs and financial resources of the spouse or former spouse or civil partner or former civil partner;

(d)   the needs of any children; and

(e)   all the circumstances of the case other than the needs of the bankrupt[11].
Where such an application is made after the end of the period of one year
beginning with the first vesting of the bankrupt's estate in a trustee[12], the court
must assume, unless the circumstances of the case are exceptional, that the
interests of the bankrupt's creditors outweigh all other considerations[13].

1   Ie under the Family Law Act 1996: see MATRIMONIAL AND CIVIL PARTNERSHIP LAW vol 72
     (2009) PARA 285 et seq.
2   See *Mekarska v Ruiz* [2011] EWHC 913 (Fam), [2011] 2 FCR 608, [2011] 2 FLR 1351 (wife's
     home rights did not exist in perpetuity but only endured until they were brought to an end by an
     order of the court, whether in the divorce proceedings or by an order in the bankruptcy
     proceedings under the Insolvency Act 1986 s 335A or s 336(2)(b)).
3   Ie under the Family Law Act 1996 s 33: see MATRIMONIAL AND CIVIL PARTNERSHIP LAW vol 72
     (2009) PARA 292.
4   Insolvency Act 1986 s 336(2) (amended by the Family Law Act 1996 s 66(1), Sch 8 para 57; and
     the Civil Partnership Act 2004 s 82, Sch 9 para 21). As to the courts having jurisdiction in
     bankruptcy see PARAS 6, 7. As from a day to be appointed, s 336(1), (2) is amended by the
     Enterprise and Regulatory Reform Act 2013 s 71, Sch 19 paras 1, 29: see PARA 130 note 17.
         In the case of the administration in bankruptcy of the insolvent estate of a deceased person
     dying before the presentation of a bankruptcy petition, the Insolvency Act 1986 s 336 applies:
     Administration of Insolvent Estates of Deceased Persons Order 1986, SI 1986/1999, art 3(1),
     Sch 1 Pt II para 26. As to the administration in bankruptcy of the insolvent estates of deceased
     persons see further PARA 830 et seq.
5   See PARA 130 et seq.
6   See PARA 397 et seq. As to the meaning of 'the bankrupt's estate' see PARA 211.
7   Ie under the Family Law Act 1996 Pt IV (ss 30–63): see MATRIMONIAL AND CIVIL PARTNERSHIP
     LAW vol 72 (2009) PARA 285 et seq.
8   Insolvency Act 1986 s 336(1) (amended by the Family Law Act 1996 Sch 8 para 57; and the
     Civil Partnership Act 2004 Sch 9 para 21). See note 4.
9   Ie under the Insolvency Act 1986 s 336(2).
10   See note 3.
11   Insolvency Act 1986 s 336(4) (amended by the Family Law Act 1996 Sch 8 para 57; the Trusts
     of Land and Appointment of Trustees Act 1996 s 25(2), (4), (5), Sch 4; and the Civil Partnership
     Act 2004 Sch 9 para 21). See *Re Haghighat (a bankrupt)* [2009] EWHC 649 (Ch), [2009] BPIR
     268, [2009] All ER (D) 31 (Jan) (possession order deferred in consideration of needs of disabled
     child). The bankrupt's needs, including his state of health, are not to be taken into account:
     Everitt v Budhram (a bankrupt) [2009] EWHC 1219 (Ch), [2010] Ch 170, [2010] 2 WLR 637.
     See also *Nicholls v Lan* [2006] EWHC 1255 (Ch), [2007] 1 FLR 744, [2006] BPIR 1243.
12   Ie under the Insolvency Act 1986 Pt 9 Ch 4 (ss 305–335): see PARA 397 et seq.
13   Insolvency Act 1986 s 336(5). See *Hosking v Michaelides* [2006] BPIR 1192, [2004] All ER (D)
     147 (May) (spouse's physical and mental circumstances, if out of the ordinary, unusual, special
     or uncommon, may be considered exceptional). See also PARA 672 note 7.

674.   Spouse's or civil partner's equity of exoneration; equitable accounting. If
the property of a spouse or civil partner[1] is mortgaged or charged in order to
raise money for the payment of the other spouse's or civil partner's debts, or
otherwise for the other spouse's or civil partner's benefit, it is presumed, in the
absence of evidence showing an intention to the contrary, that the first spouse or
civil partner meant to charge the property merely by way of security, and in such
case that spouse or civil partner is in the position of surety, and is entitled to be
indemnified by the other spouse or civil partner, and to throw the debt primarily
on that person's estate to the exoneration of his or her own[2]. Where one spouse
or civil partner becomes bankrupt, the other will be able, if the equity is applied,
to throw the burden of any such charge on to the bankrupt's beneficial interest in
any jointly held property[3].

The equity of exoneration is, however, a presumptive right only; it depends on
the intention of the parties, which need not be expressed, that one spouse or civil
partner should be in the position of surety for the other[4]. It may be rebutted by

evidence showing that the first spouse or civil partner intended to make a gift of the property to the other[5]; and it has been held to be rebutted where the money was raised to pay debts which, though legally one party's, had been contracted by reason of the extravagant mode of living of both[6]. No presumption of a right to exoneration arises where the money is raised to discharge the debts or obligations of the party whose property is being mortgaged or charged, or otherwise for that person's benefit[7].

When ordering the sale of the property, the court will direct equitable accounting between the trustee of the co-owner in respect of contributions which have enhanced the value of the property[8].

1 Although the provisions described in this paragraph derive from common law decisions pre-dating the concept of civil partnerships, and are concerned with protecting the property of a wife against her husband's creditors, it is submitted that they must now apply equally to the property of either party to a marriage and also to the property of civil partners.

2 *Earl of Huntingdon v Countess Dowager Huntingdon* (1702) 2 Bro Parl Cas 1, HL; *Pocock v Lee* (1707) 2 Vern 604; *Parteriche v Powlet* (1742) 2 Atk 383; *Aguilar v Aguilar Lousada* (1820) 5 Madd 414; *Re Pittortou (a bankrupt), ex p Trustee of Property of Bankrupt, v Bankrupt* [1985] 1 All ER 285, [1985] 1 WLR 58. As to a spouse's equity of exoneration generally see MATRIMONIAL AND CIVIL PARTNERSHIP LAW vol 72 (2009) PARA 239 et seq.

3 *Re Pittortou (a bankrupt), ex p Trustee of Property of Bankrupt, v Bankrupt* [1985] 1 All ER 285, [1985] 1 WLR 58; and see *Re A Debtor (No 24 of 1971), ex p Marley v Trustee of Property of Debtor* [1976] 2 All ER 1010, [1976] 1 WLR 952, DC.

4 *Paget v Paget* [1898] 1 Ch 470, CA; *Pocock v Lee* (1707) 2 Vern 604; *Aguilar v Aguilar Lousada* (1820) 5 Madd 414; *Gee v Smart* (1857) 8 E & B 313.

5 *Clinton v Hooper* (1791) 3 Bro CC 201.

6 *Paget v Paget* [1898] 1 Ch 470, CA.

7 *Lewis v Nangle* (1752) 1 Cox Eq Cas 240; *Hudson v Carmichael* (1854) Kay 613; *Gray v Dowman* (1858) 27 LJ Ch 702; *Re Pittortou (a bankrupt), ex p Trustee of Property of Bankrupt, v Bankrupt* [1985] 1 All ER 285, [1985] 1 WLR 58 (money used for general household and family living expenses will be treated as used for the joint benefit of the wife and the husband). The court may order an inquiry as to which sums forming part of the money raised under the charge went solely to the benefit of the bankrupt, whether in his business or on his personal account, and which went for the benefit of the spouse or civil partner, either solely or jointly with the bankrupt or children. In respect of the latter sums there was no right of exoneration: see *Re Pittortou (a bankrupt), ex p Trustee of Property of Bankrupt, v Bankrupt* (where such an inquiry was directed).

8 *Re Pittortou (a bankrupt), ex p Trustee of Property of Bankrupt, v Bankrupt* [1985] 1 All ER 285, [1985] 1 WLR 58; *Re Gorman (a bankrupt), ex p Trustee of Bankrupt v Bankrupt* [1990] 1 All ER 717, [1990] 1 WLR 616 (mortgage payments and improvements); *Re Pavlou (a bankrupt)* [1993] 3 All ER 955, [1993] 1 WLR 1046 (mortgage payments and improvements). For the purposes of an equitable accounting between the bankrupt and spouse or civil partner, it makes no difference whether they hold the beneficial interest as joint tenants or tenants in common: *Re Pavlou (a bankrupt)*.

675. Rights of occupation of bankrupt. Where a person who is entitled to occupy a dwelling house[1] by virtue of a beneficial estate or interest is adjudged bankrupt, and any persons under the age of 18 with whom that person had at some time occupied that dwelling house had their home with that person at the time when the bankruptcy petition was presented[2] and at the commencement of the bankruptcy[3], the following provisions apply[4].

Whether or not the bankrupt's spouse or civil partner, if any, has home rights[5]:

    (1)   the bankrupt has the following rights as against the trustee of his estate:

        (a)   if in occupation, a right not to be evicted or excluded from the dwelling house or any part of it, except with the permission of the court;

        (b)   if not in occupation, a right with the permission of the court to enter into and occupy the dwelling house; and

(2)   the bankrupt's rights are a charge, having the like priority as an equitable interest created immediately before the commencement of the bankruptcy, on so much of his estate or interest in the dwelling house as vests in his trustee[6].

1   As to the meaning of 'dwelling house' see PARA 413 note 1.
2   See PARA 130 et seq.
3   As to the commencement of bankruptcy see PARA 209.
4   Insolvency Act 1986 s 337(1). As from a day to be appointed, s 337(1) is amended by the Enterprise and Regulatory Reform Act 2013 s 71, Sch 19 paras 1, 30: see PARA 130 note 17.
    In the case of the administration in bankruptcy of the insolvent estate of a deceased person dying before the presentation of a bankruptcy petition, the Insolvency Act 1986 s 337 applies: Administration of Insolvent Estates of Deceased Persons Order 1986, SI 1986/1999, art 3(1), Sch 1 Pt II para 26. As to the administration in bankruptcy of the insolvent estates of deceased persons see further PARA 830 et seq.
5   Ie under the Family Law Act 1996 Pt IV (ss 30–63): see MATRIMONIAL AND CIVIL PARTNERSHIP LAW vol 72 (2009) PARA 285 et seq.
6   Insolvency Act 1986 s 337(2) (amended by the Family Law Act 1996 s 66(1), Sch 8 para 58; and the Civil Partnership Act 2004 s 82, Sch 9 para 22). The Family Law Act 1996 has effect, with the necessary modifications, as if: (1) the rights conferred by the Insolvency Act 1986 s 337(2)(a) (see text head (1)) were home rights under the Family Law Act 1996; (2) any application for permission there mentioned were an application for an order under s 33 (see MATRIMONIAL AND CIVIL PARTNERSHIP LAW vol 72 (2009) PARA 292); and (3) any charge under the Insolvency Act 1986 s 337(2)(b) (see head (2) in the text) on the estate or interest of the trustee were a charge under the Family Law Act 1996 on the estate or interest of a spouse or civil partner: Insolvency Act 1986 s 337(3) (substituted by the Family Law Act 1996 Sch 8 para 58; and amended by the Civil Partnership Act 2004 Sch 9 para 22).

676.   Application for possession against bankrupt.   The rights of the bankrupt, if in occupation, not to be evicted or excluded from the dwelling house[1] or any part of it, except with the permission of the court and, if not in occupation, with the permission of the court to enter into and occupy the dwelling house[2] take effect as if they were home rights under Part IV of the Family Law Act 1996[3]; and any application for permission takes effect as if it were an application for an order[4] under that Act[5].

Any such application for permission or for an order under the Family Law Act 1996 must be made to the court having jurisdiction in relation to the bankruptcy[6]. On such an application the court must make such order as it thinks just and reasonable having regard to the interests of the creditors, to the bankrupt's financial resources, to the needs of the children and to all the circumstances of the case other than the needs of the bankrupt[7]. Where, however, such an application is made after the end of the period of one year beginning with the first vesting of the bankrupt's estate in a trustee[8], the court must assume, unless the circumstances of the case are exceptional, that the interests of the bankrupt's creditors outweigh all other considerations[9].

1   As to the meaning of 'dwelling house' see PARA 413 note 1.
2   Ie the rights conferred by the Insolvency Act 1986 s 337(2)(a): see PARA 675 head (1).
3   Insolvency Act 1986 s 337(3)(a) (substituted by the Family Law Act 1996 s 66(1), Sch 8 para 58; and amended by the Civil Partnership Act 2004 s 82, Sch 9 para 22).
4   Ie an order under the Family Law Act 1996 s 33: see PARA 673; and MATRIMONIAL AND CIVIL PARTNERSHIP LAW vol 72 (2009) PARA 292. The Family Law Act 1996 has effect, with the necessary modifications, as if any charge under the Insolvency Act 1986 s 337(2)(b) (see PARA 675 head (2)) on the estate or interest of the trustee were a charge under the Family Law Act 1996 on the estate or interest of a spouse or civil partner: Insolvency Act 1986 s 337(3)(c) (substituted by the Family Law Act 1996 Sch 8 para 58; and amended by the Civil Partnership Act 2004 Sch 9 para 22).

As to the application of the Insolvency Act 1986 s 337 in the case of the administration in bankruptcy of the insolvent estate of a deceased person dying before the presentation of a bankruptcy petition see PARA 675 note 4.

5 Insolvency Act 1986 s 337(3)(b) (substituted by the Family Law Act 1996 Sch 8 para 58).

6 Insolvency Act 1986 s 337(4) (amended by the Family Law Act 1996 Sch 8 para 58). As to the courts having jurisdiction in bankruptcy see PARAS 6, 7.

7 Insolvency Act 1986 s 337(5) (amended by the Family Law Act 1996 Sch 8 para 58). Cf the criteria set out in the Family Law Act 1996 s 33: see MATRIMONIAL AND CIVIL PARTNERSHIP LAW vol 72 (2009) PARA 292.

8 Ie under the Insolvency Act 1986 Pt 9 Ch 4 (ss 305–335): see PARA 397 et seq.

9 Insolvency Act 1986 s 337(6). As to 'exceptional circumstances' see PARA 672 note 7; and *Martin-Sklan v White* [2006] EWHC 3313 (Ch), [2007] BPIR 76, [2006] All ER (D) 77 (Nov) (where 'exceptional circumstances' in the Insolvency Act 1986 s 337(6) were the subject of consideration).

677.   Payments in respect of premises occupied by bankrupt. Where any premises comprised in a bankrupt's estate[1] are occupied by him, whether by virtue of the statutory provisions[2] or otherwise, on condition that he makes payments towards satisfying any liability arising under a mortgage of the premises or otherwise towards the outgoings of the premises, the bankrupt does not, by virtue of those payments, acquire any interest in the premises[3].

1 As to the meaning of 'the bankrupt's estate' see PARA 211.

2 Ie by virtue of the Insolvency Act 1986 s 337: see PARA 676.

3 Insolvency Act 1986 s 338. In the case of the administration in bankruptcy of the insolvent estate of a deceased person dying before the presentation of a bankruptcy petition, s 338 applies: Administration of Insolvent Estates of Deceased Persons Order 1986, SI 1986/1999, art 3(1), Sch 1 Pt II para 26. As to the administration in bankruptcy of the insolvent estates of deceased persons see further PARA 830 et seq.

(ii) Adjustment of Prior and Other Transactions

A. TRANSACTIONS AT AN UNDERVALUE AND PREFERENCES

678.   In general. The following provisions[1] relating to transactions[2] at an undervalue and preferences apply where an individual is adjudged bankrupt[3].

1 Ie the provisions set out in PARA 679 et seq. As to the applicability of these provisions where there is a settlement or transfer of property to comply with a property adjustment order see the Matrimonial Causes Act 1973 s 39; the Civil Partnership Act 2004 Sch 5 Pt 14 para 77; and MATRIMONIAL AND CIVIL PARTNERSHIP LAW vol 72 (2009) PARA 505. See also *Mountney v Treharne* [2002] EWCA Civ 1174, [2003] Ch 135, [2002] 3 WLR 1760; *Hill v Haines* [2007] EWCA Civ 1284, [2008] Ch 412, sub nom *Haines v Hill* [2008] 2 All ER 901; and PARA 679 note 3.

2 For these purposes, except in so far as the context otherwise requires, 'transaction' includes a gift, agreement or arrangement; and references to entering into a transaction are to be construed accordingly: Insolvency Act 1986 s 436. As to the recovery of excessive pension contributions see PARA 693 et seq.

3 Insolvency Act 1986 ss 339(1), 340(1). As from a day to be appointed, ss 339(1), 340(1) are amended by the Enterprise and Regulatory Reform Act 2013 s 71, Sch 19 paras 1, 31, 32: see PARA 130 note 17.

In the case of the administration in bankruptcy of the insolvent estate of a deceased person dying before the presentation of a bankruptcy petition, the Insolvency Act 1986 ss 339, 340 apply: Administration of Insolvent Estates of Deceased Persons Order 1986, SI 1986/1999, art 3(1), Sch 1 Pt II para 26. As to the administration in bankruptcy of the insolvent estates of deceased persons see further PARA 830 et seq.

679.   Transactions at an undervalue. An individual enters into a transaction[1] with a person[2] at an undervalue if:

(1)   he makes a gift to that person or he otherwise enters into a transaction with that person on terms that provide for him to receive no consideration;

(2)   he enters into a transaction with that person in consideration of marriage or the formation of a civil partnership; or

(3)   he enters into a transaction with that person for a consideration the value of which, in money or money's worth, is significantly less than the value, in money or money's worth, of the consideration provided by the individual[3].

The creation by an individual of a charge over his assets in favour of a creditor is not a transaction at an undervalue[4].

1   As to the meaning of 'transaction' and references to entering into a transaction see PARA 678 note 2. As to the meaning of 'enter into a transaction' see *Feakins v Department for Environment, Food and Rural Affairs* [2005] EWCA Civ 1513, [2007] BCC 54, sub nom *Department for Environment, Food and Rural Affairs v Feakins* [2006] BPIR 895.

2   In *Re Paramount Airways Ltd (in administration)* [1993] Ch 223, [1992] 3 All ER 1, CA, it was held that the Insolvency Act 1986 s 238, which contains comparable wording to that in s 339, was not territorially limited, nor limited to British citizens. Since, however, the relief to be granted by the court is discretionary, the court would need to be satisfied at the hearing of the application that the defendant was sufficiently connected with England for it to be just and proper to make the order against him despite the foreign element: *Re Paramount Airways Ltd (in administration)* at 239, 240 and at 11, 12. See further COMPANY AND PARTNERSHIP INSOLVENCY vol 17 (2011) PARA 802.

3   Insolvency Act 1986 s 339(3) (amended by the Civil Partnership Act 2004 s 261(1), Sch 27 para 119). Even where, as between transferor and transferee, full consideration is apparently given, there may be a transaction at an undervalue if the interests of a third party are prejudicially affected: *Agricultural Mortgage Corpn plc v Woodward* [1995] 1 BCLC 1, [1994] BCC 688, CA (decided under the Insolvency Act 1986 s 423; husband who had charged his agricultural holding to the plaintiff as security exercised his powers under the Law of Property Act 1925 s 99 and the Agricultural Holdings Act 1986 s 100, Sch 14 para 12 (see AGRICULTURAL LAND vol 1 (2008) PARA 421) to create a lease in favour of his wife, thus reducing the value of the freehold and placing the wife in a 'ransom position' whereby she could bargain with the bank for payment in consideration of her surrendering the lease); cf *Re Martin Coulter Enterprises Ltd* [1988] BCLC 12, 4 BCC 210 (where the court left open the question whether mere detriment could constitute consideration). See also *Barclays Bank plc v Eustice* [1995] 4 All ER 511, [1995] 1 WLR 1238, CA; *Re Kumar (a bankrupt), ex p Lewis v Kumar* [1993] 2 All ER 700, [1993] 1 WLR 224 (wife's assumption of sole liability for a mortgage was transfer at an undervalue because value of her consideration was significantly less than that provided by husband); *Re Brabon, Treharne v Brabon* [2001] 1 BCLC 11, [2000] BPIR 537 (transaction entered into by the debtor's wife as mortgagee of property owned by the debtor was not a transaction 'entered into' by the debtor for the purposes of the Insolvency Act 1986 s 339; on the sale of the mortgaged property by the mortgagor the value of the consideration was the value of the land free of the mortgage and not the value of the mortgagor's equity of redemption). As to the ascertainment of value in connection with property adjustment orders (see PARA 678 note 1) see *Hill v Haines* [2007] EWCA Civ 1284, [2008] Ch 412, sub nom *Haines v Hill* [2008] 2 All ER 901; *Ball v Jones* [2008] 2 FLR 1969, [2008] Fam Law 1184, [2008] BPIR 1051; *Papanicola v Fagan* [2008] EWHC 3348 (Ch), [2009] BPIR 320; *Rubin v Dweck* [2012] BPIR 854.

    A series of transactions may be regarded as a single transaction, if the practical effect of the transactions is as though they were one transaction: *Phillips v Brewin Dolphin Bell Lawrie Ltd* [2001] UKHL 2, [2001] 1 All ER 673, [2001] 1 WLR 143.

    When determining the value of a transaction at the date of the transaction regard can be had to subsequent events affecting the value which are relevant and foreseeable at that date: *Re Thoars; Reid v Ramlort Ltd* [2002] EWHC 2416 (Ch), [2003] 1 BCLC 499, [2003] BPIR 489. The court is not required to calculate the exact values; if the maximum conceivable value for one party is significantly less than the minimum conceivable value for the other party, the transaction is at an undervalue: *Re Thoars (No 2); Reid v Ramlort Ltd (No 2)* [2004] EWCA Civ 800, [2005] 1 BCLC 331, [2004] BPIR 985. The test of value is an objective one, namely what a hypothetical purchaser would be prepared to pay, not what the vendor would be willing to accept: *Hargreaves v Salt* [2010] EWHC 3549 (Fam), [2011] BPIR 656. See also *Re Peppard (a bankrupt); Tomlinson v Harrington* [2009] BPIR 331 (value of property transferred much greater than value of indemnity offered by person of limited means); and *Ailyan and Fry (trustees in bankruptcy of Kevin Foster) v Smith* [2010] EWHC 24 (Ch), [2010] BPIR 289, [2010] All ER (D) 181 (Jun) (payment into pyramid selling scheme constituted transaction at undervalue). See also PARA 689.

As to the application of the Insolvency Act 1986 s 339 in the case of the administration in bankruptcy of the insolvent estate of a deceased person dying before the presentation of a bankruptcy petition see PARA 678 note 3.

4   *Re MC Bacon Ltd* [1990] BCLC 324, [1990] BCC 78; cf *Hill v Spread Trustee Co Ltd* [2006] EWCA Civ 542, [2007] 1 All ER 1106, [2007] 1 WLR 2404.

680.   Remedy in respect of a transaction at an undervalue.   Where an individual has at a relevant time[1] entered into a transaction[2] with any person at an undervalue[3], the trustee of the bankrupt's estate may apply to the court for an order to restore the position to what it would have been if that individual had not entered into that transaction[4]. On such an application, the court may make such order as it thinks fit for achieving this effect[5].

1   As to the meaning of 'relevant time' see PARA 685.
2   As to the meaning of 'transaction' and references to entering into a transaction see PARA 678 note 2.
3   As to the meaning of 'transaction at an undervalue' see PARA 679.
4   Insolvency Act 1986 s 339(1), (2). As to the relevant limitation period see PARA 685 note 5. As to the application of s 339 in the case of the administration in bankruptcy of the insolvent estate of a deceased person dying before the presentation of a bankruptcy petition see PARA 678 note 3.
5   Insolvency Act 1986 s 339(2). As to the orders which may be made see further s 342; and PARA 686. Even if a transaction has been entered into at an undervalue, the court retains an overall discretion which is wide enough to enable it to make no order where justice so requires: *Singla v Brown* [2007] EWHC 405 (Ch), [2008] Ch 357, [2008] 2 FLR 125. The court will fashion the most appropriate remedy with a view to restoring, as far as practicable and just to do so, the position as it would have been if the debtor had not entered into the transaction: *Re Thoars (decd); Reid v Ramlort Ltd* [2004] EWCA Civ 800, [2005] 1 BCLC 331, [2004] BPIR 985.

681.   Preference.   An individual gives a preference to a person if:
(1)   that person is one of the individual's creditors or a surety or guarantor for any of his debts or other liabilities; and
(2)   the individual does anything or suffers anything to be done which, in either case, has the effect of putting that person in a position which, in the event of the individual's bankruptcy, will be better than the position he would have been in if that thing had not been done[1].

1   Insolvency Act 1986 s 340(3). For these purposes, an applicant for ancillary relief in matrimonial proceedings is not a creditor: *Ball v Jones* [2008] 2 FLR 1969, [2008] Fam Law 1184, [2008] BPIR 1051; cf *Re Rich (in bankruptcy)* [2008] BPIR 485. But see now the definition of contingent debts in PARA 510. As to acts done in pursuance of court orders see PARA 684.

As to the application of the Insolvency Act 1986 s 340 in the case of the administration in bankruptcy of the insolvent estate of a deceased person dying before the presentation of a bankruptcy petition see PARA 678 note 3.

682.   Remedy in respect of preference; requisite intention.   Where an individual has at a relevant time[1] given a preference[2] to any person, the trustee of the bankrupt's estate may apply to the court for an order to restore the position to what it would have been if that individual had not given that preference[3]. On such an application, the court may make such order as it thinks fit for achieving this effect[4]; but the court must not make such an order in respect of a preference given to any person unless the individual who gave the preference was influenced in deciding to give it by a desire[5] to produce, in relation to that person, the effect of putting that person into a position which, in the event of the individual's bankruptcy, would be better than the position he would otherwise have been in if the individual's act or sufferance had not been done[6].

1   As to the meaning of 'relevant time' see PARA 685.
2   As to the meaning of 'give a preference' see PARA 681.
3   Insolvency Act 1986 s 340(1), (2). As to the orders which may be made see PARA 686. As to the application of s 340 in the case of the administration in bankruptcy of the insolvent estate of a deceased person dying before the presentation of a bankruptcy petition see PARA 678 note 3.
4   Insolvency Act 1986 s 340(2).
5   The influence and the desire need have been only part of several motives on the part of the bankrupt. The decision need only be demonstrated to have been influenced by the requisite desire (*Re MC Bacon Ltd* [1990] BCLC 324, [1990] BCC 78; *Re Ledingham-Smith (a bankrupt), ex p Trustee of Bankrupt v Pannell Kerr Forster (a firm)* [1993] BCLC 635). There is no need to show dominant intention. See also *Re DKG Contractors Ltd* [1990] BCC 903; *Re Agriplant Services Ltd (in liquidation)* [1997] 2 BCLC 598 at 609–611, [1997] BCC 842 at 851, 852. The relevant time to consider the existence and the extent of the influence is the time when the decision is made to give the preference (*Re MC Bacon Ltd*; *Re Fairway Magazines Ltd, Fairbairn v Hartigan* [1993] BCLC 643, [1992] BCC 924; cf *Wills v Corfe Joinery Ltd (in liquidation)* [1998] 2 BCLC 75, [1997] BCC 511). Case law on the previous statutory provisions is not relevant to the interpretation of the requisite intention under the Insolvency Act 1986 s 340: *Re MC Bacon Ltd*. The state of mind of the creditor being preferred is irrelevant: *Re Stealth Construction Ltd* [2011] EWHC 1305 (Ch), [2012] 1 BCLC 297, [2011] All ER (D) 239 (May). The mere desire to prefer a creditor without an actual preference will not give rise to a claim under the Insolvency Act 1986 s 340: *Re Hawkes Hill Publishing Co Ltd (in liquidation)* [2007] EWHC 3073 (Ch), [2007] BPIR 1035, [2007] All ER (D) 422 (May).
     As to the position where a preference is given to an associate of the bankrupt see the Insolvency Act 1986 s 340(5); and PARA 683.
6   Insolvency Act 1986 s 340(3)(b), (4).

683. Presumed intention in the case of associate. An individual who has given a preference[1] to a person who, at the time the preference was given, was an associate[2] of his, otherwise than by reason only of being his employee, is presumed, unless the contrary is shown, to have been influenced in deciding to give it by a desire to produce, in relation to that person, the effect of putting that person in a position which, in the event of the individual's bankruptcy, would be better than the position he would have been in if the individual's act or sufferance had not been done[3].

1   As to the meaning of 'give a preference' see PARA 681.
2   As to the meaning of 'associate' see PARA 5.
3   Insolvency Act 1986 s 340(4), (5). As to the requisite intention see PARA 682. As to the effect of s 340(5) on the burden of proof see *Re DKG Contractors Ltd* [1990] BCC 903; *Re Beacon Leisure Ltd* [1992] BCLC 565, [1991] BCC 213; *Re Ledingham-Smith (a bankrupt), ex p Trustee of Bankrupt v Pannell Kerr Forster (a firm)* [1993] BCLC 635; *Re Exchange Travel (Holdings) Ltd (in liquidation)* [1997] 2 BCLC 579, [1996] BCC 933; *Phillips v McGregor-Paterson* [2009] EWHC 2385 (Ch), [2010] 1 BCLC 72, [2010] BPIR 239.
     As to the application of the Insolvency Act 1986 s 340 in the case of the administration in bankruptcy of the insolvent estate of a deceased person dying before the presentation of a bankruptcy petition see PARA 678 note 3.

684. Acts pursuant to court orders. The fact that something has been done in pursuance of the order of a court does not, without more, prevent the doing or suffering of that thing from constituting the giving of a preference[1].

1   Insolvency Act 1986 s 340(6). As to the meaning of 'give a preference' see PARA 681. As to setting aside dispositions of property effected pursuant to orders in matrimonial proceedings see PARA 679 note 3.
     As to the effect of the Matrimonial Causes Act 1973 s 24(1)(c) or (d) see *Re Harper (a bankrupt), Harper v O'Reilly* [1998] 3 FCR 475, sub nom *Harper v O'Reilly and Harper*

[1997] 2 FLR 816 (beneficial interest in a matrimonial home transferred to the wife, with the result that it was not part of the estate of a husband who was adjudged bankrupt thereafter). See MATRIMONIAL AND CIVIL PARTNERSHIP LAW vol 72 (2009) PARA 510.

As to the application of the Insolvency Act 1986 s 340 in the case of the administration in bankruptcy of the insolvent estate of a deceased person dying before the presentation of a bankruptcy petition see PARA 678 note 3.

685. The relevant time. In order for there to be a remedy in respect of a transaction at an undervalue or the giving of a preference, the time at which an individual entered into a transaction or gave a preference must be a 'relevant time'[1]. If the transaction is entered into or the preference is given at the following times, it is a 'relevant time' for these purposes:

(1)   in the case of a transaction at an undervalue, at a time in the period of five years ending with the day of the presentation of the bankruptcy petition on which the individual is adjudged bankrupt;

(2)   in the case of a preference which is not a transaction at an undervalue and is given to a person who is an associate[2] of an individual, otherwise than by reason only of being his employee, at a time in the period of two years ending with that day; and

(3)   in any other case of a preference which is not a transaction at an undervalue, at a time in the period of six months ending with that day[3].

Where an individual enters into a transaction at an undervalue or gives a preference at a time mentioned in heads (1), (2) or (3) above, not being, in the case of a transaction at an undervalue, a time less than two years before the end of the period mentioned in head (1) above, that time is not a relevant time unless the individual is insolvent[4] at the time, or becomes insolvent in consequence of the transaction or preference; but these requirements are presumed to be satisfied, unless the contrary is shown, in relation to any transaction at an undervalue which is entered into by an individual with a person who is an associate of his, otherwise than by reason only of being his employee[5].

1   See PARAS 679, 680 (transaction at an undervalue), 681–683 (preference).

2   As to the meaning of 'associate' see PARA 5.

3   Insolvency Act 1986 s 341(1). A transaction entered into or preference given by a person who is subsequently adjudged bankrupt on a petition under s 264(1)(d) (criminal bankruptcy: see PARA 130 head (6)) is to be treated as having been entered into or given at a relevant time for the purposes of ss 339, 340 if it was entered into or given at any time on or after the date specified for the purposes of s 341(4) in the criminal bankruptcy order on which the petition was based: s 341(4). However, no such order may be made under ss 339, 340 by virtue of s 341(4) where an appeal is pending, within the meaning of s 277 (see PARA 130 note 10) against the individual's conviction of any offence by virtue of which the criminal bankruptcy order was made: s 341(5). As to the prospective repeal of ss 277, 341(4), (5) see PARA 1 note 11. As from a day to be appointed, s 341(1) is amended by the Enterprise and Regulatory Reform Act 2013 s 71, Sch 19 paras 1, 33: see PARA 130 note 17.

In the case of the administration in bankruptcy of the insolvent estate of a deceased person dying before the presentation of a bankruptcy petition the Insolvency Act 1986 s 341 applies, save that in s 341(1)(a) (see head (1) in the text) for the words 'day of the presentation of the bankruptcy petition' the words 'date of death of the deceased debtor' are to be substituted: Administration of Insolvent Estates of Deceased Persons Order 1986, SI 1986/1999, art 3(1), Sch 1 Pt II para 27. As to the administration in bankruptcy of the insolvent estates of deceased persons see further PARA 830 et seq.

4   For these purposes, an individual is insolvent if he is unable to pay his debts as they fall due, or the value of his assets is less than the amount of his liabilities, taking into account his contingent and prospective liabilities: Insolvency Act 1986 s 341(3). See further s 123; and COMPANY AND PARTNERSHIP INSOLVENCY vol 16 (2011) PARA 394.

5   Insolvency Act 1986 s 341(2). As to the burden of proof see *Re Calder (in bankruptcy)* [2011] EWHC 3192 (Ch), [2012] BPIR 63. As to the limitation periods applying to transactions at an undervalue and preferences cf *Re Priory Garage (Walthamstow) Ltd* [2001] BPIR 144

(applications to set aside transactions under the Insolvency Act 1986 ss 238–241 are generally actions on a specialty within the meaning of the Limitation Act 1980 s 8(1) and are subject to a 12-year limitation period; but, where the subject of certain applications under the Insolvency Act 1986 ss 238–241 are not to set aside a transaction but to recover a sum recoverable by virtue of ss 238–241, such applications will be governed by the Limitation Act 1980 s 9(1) and are subject to a six-year limitation period). But cf *Giles v Rhind* [2007] EWHC 687 (Ch), [2007] Bus LR 1470, [2007] 2 BCLC 531 (on appeal on another point [2008] EWCA Civ 118, [2009] Ch 191, [2008] 3 All ER 697). It would seem that the limitation period runs from the date of the appointment of the trustee rather than the date of the bankruptcy order: *Hill v Spread Trustee Co Ltd* [2006] EWCA Civ 542, [2007] 1 All ER 1106, [2007] 1 WLR 2404; *Stonham v Ramrattan* [2011] EWCA Civ 119, [2011] 4 All ER 392, [2011] 1 WLR 1617. See LIMITATION PERIODS vol 68 (2008) PARA 975 et seq.

686. Orders which may be made. Without prejudice to the generality of the powers of the court to make orders restoring the position to what it would have been if the individual had not entered into the transaction at an undervalue or given the preference[1], an order with respect to such transactions or preferences entered into or given by an individual may:

(1) require any property transferred as part of the transaction, or in connection with the giving of the preference, to be vested in the trustee of the bankrupt's estate as part of that estate;

(2) require any property to be so vested if it represents in any person's hands the application either of the proceeds of sale of property so transferred or of money so transferred;

(3) release or discharge, in whole or in part, any security given by the individual;

(4) require any person to pay, in respect of benefits received by him from the individual, such sums to the trustee of his estate as the court may direct;

(5) provide for any surety or guarantor whose obligations to any person were released or discharged, in whole or in part, under the transaction, or by the giving of the preference, to be under such new or revived obligations to that person as the court thinks appropriate;

(6) provide for security to be provided for the discharge of any obligation imposed by or arising under the order, for such an obligation to be charged on any property and for such security or charge to have the same priority as a security or charge released or discharged, in whole or in part, under the transaction or by the giving of the preference;

(7) provide for the extent to which any person whose property is vested by the order in the trustee of the bankrupt's estate, or on whom obligations are imposed by the order, is to be able to prove in the bankruptcy for debts or other liabilities which arose from, or were released or discharged, in whole or in part, under or by, the transaction or the giving of the preference[2].

1 Ie under the Insolvency Act 1986 s 339(2) (see PARA 680) or s 340(2) (see PARA 682).
2 Insolvency Act 1986 s 342(1). As from a day to be appointed, s 342(1) is amended by the Enterprise and Regulatory Reform Act 2013 s 71, Sch 19 paras 1, 34: see PARA 130 note 17.
    Any sums required to be paid to the trustee in accordance with an order under the Insolvency Act 1986 s 339 or s 340 are to be comprised in the bankrupt's estate: s 342(3).
    In the case of the administration in bankruptcy of the insolvent estate of a deceased person dying before the presentation of a bankruptcy petition, s 342 applies: Administration of Insolvent Estates of Deceased Persons Order 1986, SI 1986/1999, art 3(1), Sch 1 Pt II para 28. As to the administration in bankruptcy of the insolvent estates of deceased persons see further PARA 830 et seq.

687. Effect of order on third parties. An order made by the court under the above provisions[1] may affect the property of, or impose any obligation on, any person whether or not he is the person with whom the individual in question entered into the transaction or, as the case may be, the person to whom the preference was given; but such an order:

(1) must not prejudice any interest in property which was acquired from a person other than that individual and was acquired in good faith and for value, or prejudice any interest deriving from such an interest; and

(2) must not require a person who received a benefit from the transaction or preference in good faith and for value to pay a sum to the trustee of the bankrupt's estate, except where he was a party to the transaction or the payment is to be in respect of a preference given to that person at a time when he was a creditor of that individual[2].

Where a person has acquired an interest in property from a person other than the individual in question, or has received a benefit from the transaction or preference, and at the time of that acquisition or receipt:

(a) he had notice of the relevant surrounding circumstances[3] and of the relevant proceedings[4]; or

(b) he was an associate of, or was connected with[5], either the individual in question or the person with whom that individual entered into the transaction or to whom that individual gave the preference,

then, unless the contrary is shown, it is to be presumed for the purposes of head (1) above or, as the case may be, head (2) above, that the interest was acquired or the benefit was received otherwise than in good faith[6].

1 Ie an order under the Insolvency Act 1986 s 339 (transactions at an undervalue: see PARAS 678–680) or s 340 (preferences: see PARAS 681–684).

2 Insolvency Act 1986 s 342(2) (amended by the Insolvency (No 2) Act 1994 s 2). The Insolvency Act 1986 s 342(2) has effect only in relation to interests acquired and benefits received on or after 26 July 1994: Insolvency (No 2) Act 1994 s 6(2), (3).

   The amendments of the Insolvency Act 1986 made by the Insolvency (No 2) Act 1994 bind the Crown: s 5(1).

   As to the application of the Insolvency Act 1986 s 342 in the case of the administration in bankruptcy of the insolvent estate of a deceased person dying before the presentation of a bankruptcy petition see PARA 686 note 2.

3 For these purposes, the relevant surrounding circumstances are, as the case may require: (1) the fact that the individual in question entered into the transaction at an undervalue; or (2) the circumstances which amounted to the giving of the preference by the individual in question: Insolvency Act 1986 s 342(4) (substituted by the Insolvency (No 2) Act 1994 s 2(3)). The Insolvency Act 1986 s 342(4) has effect only in relation to interests acquired and benefits received on or after 26 July 1994: Insolvency (No 2) Act 1994 s 6(2), (3).

4 For these purposes, a person has notice of the relevant proceedings if he has notice: (1) of the fact that the petition on which the individual in question is adjudged bankrupt has been presented; or (2) of the fact that the individual in question has been adjudged bankrupt: Insolvency Act 1986 s 342(5) (added by the Insolvency (No 2) Act 1994 s 2(3)). As from a day to be appointed, the Insolvency Act 1986 s 342(5) is amended by the Enterprise and Regulatory Reform Act 2013 s 71, Sch 19 paras 1, 34: see PARA 130 note 17.

5 The Insolvency Act 1986 s 249 (meaning of connected persons and associates: see COMPANY AND PARTNERSHIP INSOLVENCY vol 16 (2011) PARA 5) applies for these purposes as it applies for the purposes and provisions of Pts 1–7 (ss 1–251: see COMPANY AND PARTNERSHIP INSOLVENCY): s 342(6) (added by the Insolvency (No 2) Act 1994 s 2(3)).

6 Insolvency Act 1986 s 342(2A) (added by the Insolvency (No 2) Act 1994 s 2(2)). The Insolvency Act 1986 s 342(2A) has effect only in relation to interests acquired and benefits received on or after 26 July 1994: Insolvency (No 2) Act 1994 s 6(2), (3).

688.   In general.   Transactions at an undervalue entered into by an individual may also be avoided under the statutory provisions[1] whether or not the individual is subject to the insolvency procedures under the Insolvency Act 1986[2], provided that the transaction in question has been entered into with the requisite intention[3]. Whereas victims of the transaction may in certain instances apply for orders avoiding such transactions, there are restrictions on the persons who may apply[4].

1   Ie the Insolvency Act 1986 ss 423–425: see PARA 689 et seq. These provisions also apply, with certain modifications, to transactions entered into by companies: see COMPANY AND PARTNERSHIP INSOLVENCY vol 17 (2011) PARAS 812–813.
2   Cf PARA 678 et seq.
3   See PARA 689. In the case of such transactions there are no restrictions as to the time a transaction at an undervalue may be subject to avoidance such as are referred to in PARA 685.
4   See PARA 690.

689.   Transactions defrauding creditors; requisite intention.   Where a person[1] enters into a transaction at an undervalue, the court[2] may make such order as it thinks fit for restoring the position to what it would have been if the transaction had not been entered into, and[3] protecting the interests of persons who are victims[4] of the transaction[5]. For these purposes, a person enters into such a transaction with another person if:

(1)   he makes a gift to the other person or he otherwise enters into a transaction with the other on terms that provide for him to receive no consideration;

(2)   he enters into a transaction with the other in consideration of marriage or the formation of a civil partnership; or

(3)   he enters into a transaction with the other for a consideration, the value of which, in money or money's worth, is significantly less than the value, in money or money's worth, of the consideration provided by himself[6].

However, in the case of a person entering into such a transaction, an order must only be made if the court is satisfied that it was entered into by him for the purpose:

(a)   of putting assets beyond the reach of a person who is making, or may at some time make, a claim against him; or

(b)   of otherwise prejudicing the interests of such a person in relation to the claim which he is making or may make[7].

Where the respondent has received legal advice in relation to the transaction, the applicant may be able to obtain disclosure of documents which would prima facie be subject to legal professional privilege[8].

1   Unless the contrary intention appears, 'person' includes a body of persons corporate or unincorporate: Interpretation Act 1978 ss 5, 22(1), 23(1), Sch 1, Sch 2 para 4(1)(a). Semble the Insolvency Act 1986 s 423 is extra-territorial in its effect: *Re Paramount Airways Ltd (in administration)* [1993] Ch 223, [1992] 3 All ER 1, CA.
2   For these purposes, 'the court' means the High Court or, if the person entering into the transaction is a body capable of being wound up under the Insolvency Act 1986 Pt 4 (ss 73–219) or Pt 5 (ss 220–229), any other court having jurisdiction to wind it up: s 423(4)(b). See further COMPANY AND PARTNERSHIP INSOLVENCY vol 17 (2011) PARA 812. Where the person entering into the transaction is an individual, 'the court' means the High Court or any other court which would have jurisdiction in relation to a bankruptcy petition relating to him: s 423(4)(a). As to such courts see PARAS 6, 7. The application may be made to any part of the High Court: *TSB Bank plc v Katz* [1997] BPIR 147; cf *Moon v Franklin* [1996] BPIR 196. Where the application

is made to the High Court other than in the exercise of its insolvency jurisdiction, the Insolvency Rules 1986, SI 1986/1925, do not apply to the proceedings: *Aiglon Ltd and L'Aiglon SA v Gau Shan Co Ltd, Gau Shan Co Ltd v Aiglon Ltd* [1993] BCLC 1321; *TSB Bank plc v Katz; Jyske Bank (Gibraltar) Ltd v Spejeldnaes* (1997) Times, 10 October; *Banca Carige SpA Cassa di Risparmio Genova e Imperia v Banco Nacional de Cuba* [2001] 3 All ER 923, sub nom *Re Banco Nacional de Cuba* [2001] 1 WLR 2039 (claim under the Insolvency Act 1986 s 423 does not fall within CPR 6.19(2); permission to serve proceedings out of jurisdiction required).

3   The word 'and' is to be read conjunctively: *Chohan v Saggar* [1994] 1 BCLC 706, [1994] BCC 134, CA.

4   In relation to a transaction at an undervalue, references in the Insolvency Act 1986 ss 423, 424 to a victim of the transaction are to a person who is, or is capable of being, prejudiced by it: s 423(5). A person who cannot demonstrate that he will be worse off as a result of the transaction is not a victim, eg where the only assets of the transferor are fully charged: *Pinewood Joinery (a firm) v Starelm Properties Ltd* [1994] 2 BCLC 412, [1994] BCC 569; cf *Barclays Bank plc v Eustice* [1995] 4 All ER 511, [1995] 1 WLR 1238, CA. A claimant in proceedings who has a chance of success is a 'victim' within the meaning of the Insolvency Act 1986 s 423(5): *Pinewood Joinery (a firm) v Starelm Properties Ltd*. A claimant need not be a creditor but in order to be a victim must be a person who is or is capable of being prejudiced by the transaction: *Clydesdale Financial Services Ltd v Smailes (No 2)* [2009] EWHC 3190 (Ch), [2010] BPIR 77.

    An order protecting the interests of the victims need not restore the position to what it would have been had the transaction not been made: *Moon v Franklin* [1996] BPIR 196.

    In the case of the administration in bankruptcy of the insolvent estate of a deceased person dying before the presentation of a bankruptcy petition, the Insolvency Act 1986 s 423 applies: Administration of Insolvent Estates of Deceased Persons Order 1986, SI 1986/1999, art 3(1), Sch 1 Pt II para 36. As to the administration in bankruptcy of the insolvent estates of deceased persons see further PARA 830 et seq.

5   Insolvency Act 1986 s 423(2). A person 'enters into a transaction' for these purposes if he participates in an arrangement whereby an asset is transferred at an undervalue: *Feakins v Department for Environment, Food and Rural Affairs* [2005] EWCA Civ 1513, [2007] BCC 54, sub nom *Department for Environment, Food and Rural Affairs v Feakins* [2006] BPIR 895. A transaction can be at an undervalue for the purposes of the Insolvency Act 1986 s 423 where it causes prejudice to a single creditor falling within s 423(3), notwithstanding that it did not diminish the debtor's assets and the creditors as a whole were not disadvantaged: *National Westminster Bank plc v Jones* [2001] 1 BCLC 98, [2000] BPIR 1092. In determining whether to grant relief, the court might take into account the mental state of the transferee and the degree of his involvement in the fraudulent scheme to put assets out of the reach of the creditors: *4 Eng Ltd v Harper (No 2)* [2009] EWHC 2633 (Ch), [2010] 1 BCLC 176; *Claridge v Claridge* [2011] EWHC 2047 (Ch), [2012] 1 FCR 388, [2011] BPIR 1529. As to the limitation period for bringing such a claim, see PARA 685 note 5; and *Hill v Spread Trustee Co Ltd* [2006] EWCA Civ 542, [2007] 1 All ER 1106, [2007] 1 WLR 2404 (claims under the Insolvency Act 1986 s 423 will be subject to a 12-year limitation period unless the claim is in essence for a sum of money in which case the claim will be subject to a six-year limitation period).

6   Insolvency Act 1986 s 423(1) (amended by the Civil Partnership Act 2004 s 261(1), Sch 27 para 121). See *Re MC Bacon Ltd* [1990] BCLC 324, [1990] BCC 78 (decided under the Insolvency Act 1986 s 238); *National Bank of Kuwait v Menzies* [1994] 2 BCLC 306, sub nom *Menzies v National Bank of Kuwait SAK* [1994] BCC 119, CA. The incidental detriment accruing to the debtor from the transaction cannot be regarded as consideration: *Agricultural Mortgage Corpn plc v Woodward* [1995] 1 BCLC 1, [1994] BCC 688, CA; cf *Barclays Bank plc v Eustice* [1995] 4 All ER 511, [1995] 1 WLR 1238, CA. Even where, as between transferor and transferee, full consideration is apparently given, there may be a transaction at an undervalue if the interests of a third party are prejudicially affected: *Agricultural Mortgage Corpn plc v Woodward*. See also PARA 679. As to the position where a company enters into a transaction at an undervalue see COMPANY AND PARTNERSHIP INSOLVENCY vol 17 (2011) PARAS 811–814.

7   Insolvency Act 1986 s 423(3). A person cannot contend that his purpose falls outside the relevant purpose of s 423(3) simply by pointing to another purpose, such as the benefit of his family, friends, or the advantage of business associates: *Chohan v Saggar* [1994] 1 BCLC 706, [1994] BCC 134, CA; *Royscot Spa Leasing Ltd v Lovett* [1995] BCC 502, CA; *Barclays Bank plc v Eustice* [1995] 4 All ER 511, [1995] 1 WLR 1238, CA. The applicant must show that the person entering into the transaction had the intention of achieving the relevant purpose: *Hill v Spread Trustee Co Ltd* [2006] EWCA Civ 542, [2007] 1 All ER 1106, [2007] 1 WLR 2404 (contemplation of something as a mere possibility not sufficient); *Chohan v Saggar*; cf *Pinewood Joinery (a firm) v Starelm Properties Ltd* [1994] 2 BCLC 412, [1994] BCC 569;

Midland Bank plc v Wyatt [1997] 1 BCLC 242, [1996] BPIR 288. An applicant under the Insolvency Act 1986 s 423 does not need to prove dishonesty or fraud; even if made after taking legal advice, and with honest motive, it may be set aside if the relevant purpose is established: *Arbuthnot Leasing International Ltd v Havelet Ltd (No 2)* [1990] BCC 636. See also *Re Brabon, Treharne v Brabon* [2001] 1 BCLC 11, [2000] BPIR 537 (it is sufficient for the purposes of the Insolvency Act 1986 s 423 to show that it was a substantial purpose of the debtor to put assets beyond the reach of a person who was making or might at some time have made a claim against him; and it is not necessary to show that this was the dominant purpose); cf *Banca Carige SpA Cassa di Risparmio Genova e Imperia v Banco Nacional de Cuba* [2001] 3 All ER 923, sub nom *Re Banco Nacional de Cuba* [2001] 1 WLR 2039. Putting assets beyond the reach of a potential claimant must be a purpose, rather than a mere consequence, of the transaction, but it does not have to be the dominant purpose: *IRC v Hashmi* [2002] EWCA Civ 981, [2002] 2 BCLC 489, [2002] BPIR 271. See also *Feakins v Department for Environment, Food and Rural Affairs* [2005] EWCA Civ 1513, [2007] BCC 54, sub nom *Department for Environment, Food and Rural Affairs v Feakins* [2006] BPIR 895; *Kali Ltd v Chawla; Advani v Chawla* [2007] EWHC 2357 (Ch), [2008] BPIR 415, [2007] All ER (D) 90 (Sep); *Papanicola v Fagan* [2008] EWHC 3348 (Ch), [2009] BPIR 320.

8   *Barclays Bank plc v Eustice* [1995] 4 All ER 511, [1995] 1 WLR 1238, CA; *Royscot Spa Leasing Ltd v Lovett* [1995] BCC 502, CA.

690. Who may apply. An application for any order under the above provisions[1] may not be made in relation to a transaction except:

(1)   in a case where the debtor[2] has been adjudged bankrupt, by the official receiver, by the trustee of the bankrupt's estate or, with the permission of the court, by a victim[3] of the transaction[4];

(2)   in a case where the victim of the transaction is bound by a voluntary arrangement[5], by the supervisor of the voluntary arrangement or by any person who, whether or not so bound, is such a victim; or

(3)   in any other case, by a victim of the transaction[6].

An application made under any of the above provisions is to be treated as made on behalf of every victim of the transaction[7].

1   Ie the Insolvency Act 1986 s 423: see PARA 689.

2   In relation to a transaction at an undervalue, the person entering into the transaction is referred to in the Insolvency Act 1986 ss 424, 425 as 'the debtor': s 423(5).

     In the case of the administration in bankruptcy of the insolvent estate of a deceased person dying before the presentation of a bankruptcy petition, ss 423, 424 apply: Administration of Insolvent Estates of Deceased Persons Order 1986, SI 1986/1999, art 3(1), Sch 1 Pt II para 36. As to the administration in bankruptcy of the insolvent estates of deceased persons see further PARA 830 et seq.

3   As to the meaning of 'victim' see PARA 689 note 4.

4   In the case where the debtor is a body corporate which is being wound up or is in administration, the application may be made by the official receiver, by the liquidator or the administrator of the body corporate or, with the permission of the court, by a victim of the transaction: see the Insolvency Act 1986 s 424(1)(a) (amended by the Enterprise Act 2002 s 248(3), Sch 17 paras 9, 36); and COMPANY AND PARTNERSHIP INSOLVENCY vol 17 (2011) PARA 813. As from a day to be appointed, s 424(1) is amended by the Enterprise and Regulatory Reform Act 2013 s 71, Sch 19 paras 1, 61: see PARA 130 note 17.

     The requisite permission of the court must be obtained by a victim before initiating proceedings: *National Bank of Kuwait v Menzies* [1994] 2 BCLC 306, sub nom *Menzies v National Bank of Kuwait SAK* [1994] BCC 119, CA. The permission of the court to continue the proceedings is not required where an individual or company against whom the application was made has been adjudged bankrupt or has become insolvent after the commencement of proceedings: *Godfrey v Torpy* [2007] EWHC 919 (Ch), [2007] Bus LR 1203, [2007] BPIR 1538.

5   Ie a voluntary arrangement approved under the Insolvency Act 1986 Pt 8 (ss 252–263G) (see PARA 43 et seq) or, in the case of a body corporate, under Pt 1 (ss 1–7) (see COMPANY AND PARTNERSHIP INSOLVENCY vol 17 (2011) PARA 1212 et seq).

6   Insolvency Act 1986 s 424(1). As to the mode of application and the procedure see PARA 786 et seq; and as to the court to which application should be made see PARA 689 note 2.

7　Insolvency Act 1986 s 424(2). As to the orders which may be made for the benefit of all persons on whose behalf the application for the order is treated as made see PARA 691.

691. Orders which may be made. Without prejudice to the generality of the above provisions[1], an order made with respect to a transaction entered into at an undervalue may[2]:

(1)　require any property transferred as part of the transaction to be vested in any person, either absolutely or for the benefit of all the persons on whose behalf the application for the order is treated as made[3];

(2)　require any property to be so vested if it represents, in any person's hands, the application either of the proceeds of sale of property so transferred or of money so transferred;

(3)　release or discharge, in whole or in part, any security[4] given by the debtor[5];

(4)　require any person to pay to any other person in respect of benefits received from the debtor such sums as the court may direct;

(5)　provide for any surety or guarantor whose obligations to any person were released or discharged, in whole or in part, under the transaction to be under such new or revived obligations as the court thinks appropriate;

(6)　provide for security to be provided for the discharge of any obligation imposed by or arising under the order, for such an obligation to be charged on any property and for such security or charge to have the same priority as a security or charge released or discharged, in whole or in part, under the transaction[6].

1　Ie the Insolvency Act 1986 s 423: see PARA 689 et seq.
2　Ie subject to the Insolvency Act 1986 s 425(2): see PARA 692.
3　See PARA 690.
4　For these purposes 'security' means any mortgage, charge, lien or other security: Insolvency Act 1986 s 425(4).
5　As to the meaning of 'the debtor' see PARA 690 note 2.
6　Insolvency Act 1986 s 425(1). In the case of the administration in bankruptcy of the insolvent estate of a deceased person dying before the presentation of a bankruptcy petition, s 425 applies: Administration of Insolvent Estates of Deceased Persons Order 1986, SI 1986/1999, art 3(1), Sch 1 Pt II para 36. As to the administration in bankruptcy of the insolvent estates of deceased persons see further PARA 830 et seq.

692. Effect on third parties. An order made under the above provisions[1] may affect the property of, or impose any obligation on, any person whether or not he is the person with whom the debtor[2] entered into the transaction; but such an order:

(1)　must not prejudice any interest in property which was acquired from a person other than the debtor and was acquired in good faith, for value and without notice of the relevant circumstances[3], or prejudice any interest deriving from such an interest; and

(2)　must not require a person who received a benefit from the transaction in good faith, for value and without notice of the relevant circumstances to pay any sum unless he was a party to the transaction[4].

1　Ie an order under the Insolvency Act 1986 s 423: see PARA 689.
2　As to the meaning of 'the debtor' see PARA 690 note 2.
3　For these purposes the relevant circumstances in relation to a transaction are the circumstances by virtue of which an order under the Insolvency Act 1986 s 423 (see PARA 689) may be made in respect of the transaction: s 425(3). As to the application of s 425 in the case of the

administration in bankruptcy of the insolvent estate of a deceased person dying before the presentation of a bankruptcy petition see PARA 691 note 6.

4   Insolvency Act 1986 s 425(2). The court is required, as far as possible, to make an order to do justice between victims and third parties: *Chohan v Saggar* [1994] 1 BCLC 706, [1994] BCC 134, CA. See also *Ashe v Mumford* [2001] BPIR 1, CA (whole of property purchased with loan from bankrupt by person benefiting from right to buy at discount ordered to be vested in trustee in bankruptcy, notwithstanding lack of evidence of borrower's state of mind); *Arbuthnot Leasing International Ltd v Havelet Leasing Ltd (No 2)* [1990] BCC 636 (property ordered to be held on trust without prejudice to the claims of subsequent creditors).

C. RECOVERY OF EXCESSIVE PENSION CONTRIBUTIONS

(A) Approved and Unapproved Pension Arrangements

693. Recovery of excessive pension contributions. Where an individual who is adjudged bankrupt has rights under an approved pension arrangement[1] or has excluded rights under an unapproved pension arrangement[2], the trustee of the bankrupt's estate may apply to the court for an order under the following provisions[3].

If the court is satisfied:

(1)   that the rights under the arrangement are to any extent, and whether directly or indirectly, the fruits of relevant contributions[4]; and

(2)   that the making of any of the relevant contributions ('the excessive contributions') has unfairly prejudiced the individual's creditors,

the court may make such order as it thinks fit for restoring the position to what it would have been had the excessive contributions not been made[5].

Where the court is satisfied that the value of the rights under the arrangement is, as a result of the rights of the individual under the arrangement or under any other pension arrangement having at any time become subject to a debit[6] giving effect to pension sharing, less than it would otherwise have been:

(a)   any relevant contributions which were represented by the rights which became subject to the debit are to be taken[7] to be contributions of which the rights under the arrangement are the fruits; and

(b)   where the relevant contributions represented by the rights under the arrangement, including those so represented by virtue of head (a) above, are not all excessive contributions, relevant contributions which are represented by the rights under the arrangement otherwise than by virtue of head (a) above are to be treated as excessive contributions before any which are so represented by virtue of head (a) above[8].

In determining whether it is satisfied under head (2) above, the court must consider, in particular:

(i)   whether any of the contributions were made for the purpose of putting assets beyond the reach of the individual's creditors or any of them; and

(ii)   whether the total amount of any contributions made by or on behalf of the individual to pension arrangements and represented, whether directly or indirectly, by rights under approved pension arrangements or excluded rights under unapproved pension arrangements[9],

is an amount which is excessive in view of the individual's circumstances when those contributions were made[10].

The person responsible[11] for:

(A)   an approved pension arrangement under which a bankrupt has rights; or

(B)   an unapproved pension arrangement under which a bankrupt has excluded rights; or

(C)   a pension arrangement under which a bankrupt has at any time had rights,

must, on the bankrupt's trustee in bankruptcy making a written request, provide the trustee with such information about the arrangement and rights as the trustee may reasonably require for or in connection with the making of an application for an order for the recovery of excessive pension contributions[12]. Where such a request for information has been made to the responsible person by the bankrupt's trustee in bankruptcy and relating to the cash equivalent of a bankrupt's rights or excluded rights, the responsible person must comply with that request within a period of nine weeks beginning with the day on which it is received[13].

Where any sum is required by such an order to be paid to the trustee in bankruptcy, that sum is comprised in the bankrupt's estate[14].

1   For these purposes, 'approved pension arrangement' has the same meaning as in the Welfare Reform and Pensions Act 1999 s 11(2) (see PERSONAL AND OCCUPATIONAL PENSIONS vol 80 (2013) PARA 285): Insolvency Act 1986 s 342A(8) (ss 342A, 342C added by the Pensions Act 1995 s 95(1); substituted by the Welfare Reform and Pensions Act 1999 s 15). See also the Occupational and Personal Pension Schemes (Bankruptcy) (No 2) Regulations 2002, SI 2002/836, reg 2; and PERSONAL AND OCCUPATIONAL PENSIONS vol 80 (2013) PARA 285. For the date on which the Welfare Reform and Pensions Act 1999 s 11(2) and the Occupational and Personal Pension Schemes (Bankruptcy) (No 2) Regulations 2002, SI 2002/836, respectively came into force see PARA 407 note 3. The Welfare Reform and Pensions Act 1999 s 15 entered fully into force on 6 April 2002: see s 89(5); and the Welfare Reform and Pensions Act 1999 (Commencement No 13) Order 2002, SI 2002/153, art 2(e).

2   For these purposes, 'unapproved pension arrangement' has the same meaning as in the Welfare Reform and Pensions Act 1999 s 12 (see PERSONAL AND OCCUPATIONAL PENSIONS vol 80 (2013) PARA 286): Insolvency Act 1986 s 342A(8) (as added and substituted: see note 1). See further the Occupational and Personal Pension Schemes (Bankruptcy) (No 2) Regulations 2002, SI 2002/836, reg 3; and PERSONAL AND OCCUPATIONAL PENSIONS vol 80 (2013) PARA 286.

3   Insolvency Act 1986 s 342A(1) (as added and substituted: see note 1). As from a day to be appointed, s 342A(1) is amended by the Enterprise and Regulatory Reform Act 2013 s 71, Sch 19 paras 1, 35: see PARA 130 note 17.

    In the case of the administration in bankruptcy of the insolvent estate of a deceased person dying before the presentation of a bankruptcy petition, the Insolvency Act 1986 s 342A applies: Administration of Insolvent Estates of Deceased Persons Order 1986, SI 1986/1999, art 3(1), Sch 1 Pt II para 28. As to the administration in bankruptcy of the insolvent estates of deceased persons see further PARA 830 et seq.

4   For these purposes, 'relevant contributions' means contributions to the arrangement or any other pension arrangement which the individual has at any time made on his own behalf or which have at any time been made on his behalf: Insolvency Act 1986 s 342A(5) (as added and substituted: see note 1).

5   Insolvency Act 1986 s 342A(2) (as added and substituted: see note 1). As to the contents of such an order see PARA 694. Nothing in: (1) any provision of the Pension Schemes Act 1993 s 159 or the Pensions Act 1995 s 91 (which prevent assignment and the making of orders that restrain a person from receiving anything which he is prevented from assigning: see PERSONAL AND OCCUPATIONAL PENSIONS vol 80 (2013) PARAS 438, 288 respectively); (2) any provision of any enactment, whether passed or made before or after the passing of the Welfare Reform and Pensions Act 1999, corresponding to any of the provisions mentioned in head (1); or (3) any provision of the arrangement in question corresponding to any of those provisions, applies to a court exercising its powers under the Insolvency Act 1986 s 342A: s 342C(2) (as added and substituted: see note 1).

    In the case of the administration in bankruptcy of the insolvent estate of a deceased person dying before the presentation of a bankruptcy petition, s 342C applies: Administration of Insolvent Estates of Deceased Persons Order 1986, SI 1986/1999, Sch 1 Pt II para 28.

6   Ie under the Welfare Reform and Pensions Act 1999 s 29(1)(a): see PERSONAL AND OCCUPATIONAL PENSIONS vol 80 (2013) PARA 338.

7   Ie for the purposes of the Insolvency Act 1986 s 342A(2).

8   Insolvency Act 1986 s 342A(3), (4) (as added and substituted: see note 1).

9 For these purposes, rights of an individual under an unapproved pension arrangement are excluded rights if they are rights which are excluded from his estate by virtue of regulations under the Welfare Reform and Pensions Act 1999 s 12 (see PERSONAL AND OCCUPATIONAL PENSIONS vol 80 (2013) PARA 286): Insolvency Act 1986 s 342A(7) (added by the Pensions Act 1995 s 95(1); substituted by the Welfare Reform and Pensions Act 1999 s 15).

10 Insolvency Act 1986 s 342A(6) (as added and substituted: see note 1).

11 For these purposes, references to the person responsible for a pension arrangement are to: (1) the trustees, managers or provider of the arrangement; or (2) the person having functions in relation to the arrangement corresponding to those of a trustee, manager or provider: Insolvency Act 1986 s 342C(6) (as added and substituted: see note 1).

12 Insolvency Act 1986 s 342C(1) (as added and substituted: see note 1).

13 Occupational and Personal Pension Schemes (Bankruptcy) (No 2) Regulations 2002, SI 2002/836, reg 10(1)(c)(i).

14 Insolvency Act 1986 s 342C(3) (as added and substituted: see note 1).

694. Contents of orders. An order for the recovery of excessive pension contributions[1] may[2] include provision:

(1) requiring the person responsible for the arrangement[3] to pay an amount to the individual's trustee in bankruptcy;

(2) adjusting the liabilities of the arrangement in respect of the individual[4];

(3) adjusting any liabilities of the arrangement[5] in respect of any other person that derive, directly or indirectly, from rights of the individual under the arrangement;

(4) for the recovery by the person responsible for the arrangement, whether by deduction from any amount which that person is ordered to pay or otherwise, of costs incurred by that person in complying in the bankrupt's case with any relevant requirement[6] or in giving effect to the order[7].

The maximum amount which the person responsible for an arrangement may be required to pay by such an order is the lesser of:

(a) the amount of the excessive contributions[8]; and

(b) the value of the individual's rights under the arrangement, if the arrangement is an approved pension arrangement[9], or of his excluded rights[10] under the arrangement, if the arrangement is an unapproved pension arrangement[11].

An order for the recovery of excessive pension contributions which requires the person responsible for an arrangement to pay an amount ('the restoration amount') to the individual's trustee in bankruptcy must provide for the liabilities of the arrangement to be correspondingly reduced[12].

An order for the recovery of excessive pension contributions in respect of an arrangement is binding on the person responsible for the arrangement and overrides provisions of the arrangement to the extent that they conflict with the provisions of the order[13].

1 Ie an order under the Insolvency Act 1986 s 342A: see PARA 693.

2 Ie without prejudice to the generality of Insolvency Act 1986 s 342A(2): see PARA 693.

3 As to the person responsible for a pension arrangement see PARA 693 note 11.

4 For these purposes, references to adjusting the liabilities of the arrangement in respect of a person include, in particular, reducing the amount of any benefit or future benefit to which that person is entitled under the arrangement: Insolvency Act 1986 s 342B(2) (ss 342B, 342C added by the Pensions Act 1995 s 95(1); and substituted by the Welfare Reform and Pensions Act 1999 s 15). As to the date on which the Welfare Reform and Pensions Act 1999 s 15 entered fully into force see PARA 693 note 1. In the case of the administration in bankruptcy of the insolvent estate of a deceased person dying before the presentation of a bankruptcy petition, the Insolvency Act 1986 s 342B applies: Administration of Insolvent Estates of Deceased Persons Order 1986, SI 1986/1999, Sch 1 Pt II para 28.

5 For these purposes only, the reference to liabilities of the arrangement does not include liabilities in respect of a person which result from giving effect to an order or provision falling within the Welfare Reform and Pensions Act 1999 s 28(1) (pension sharing orders and agreements: see PERSONAL AND OCCUPATIONAL PENSIONS vol 80 (2013) PARA 337): Insolvency Act 1986 s 342B(3) (as added and substituted: see note 4).

6 Ie any requirement under the Insolvency Act 1986 s 342C(1): see PARA 693.

7 Insolvency Act 1986 s 342B(1) (as added and substituted: see note 4).

8 As to the meaning of 'the excessive contributions' see PARA 693.

9 As to the meaning of 'approved pension arrangement' see PARA 693 note 1.

10 As to the meaning of 'excluded rights' see PARA 693 note 9.

11 Insolvency Act 1986 s 342B(4) (as added and substituted: see note 4). As to the meaning of 'unapproved pension arrangement' see PARA 693 note 2. Regulations may make provision about the calculation and verification of any such value as is mentioned in the Insolvency Act 1986 s 342B(4)(b) (see head (b) in the text): s 342C(4)(a) (as added and substituted: see note 4). The power conferred by s 342C(4) includes power to provide for calculation and verification: (1) in such manner as may, in the particular case, be approved by a prescribed person; or (2) in accordance with guidance from time to time prepared by a prescribed person: s 342C(5) (as so added and substituted; and amended by the Pensions Act 2007 s 17, Sch 5 para 3). For these purposes, 'prescribed' means prescribed by regulations; and 'regulations' means regulations made by the Secretary of State: Insolvency Act 1986 s 342C(7) (as so added and substituted). Such regulations may make different provision for different cases and may contain such incidental, supplemental and transitional provisions as appear to the Secretary of State necessary or expedient; and they must be made by statutory instrument subject to annulment in pursuance of a resolution of either House of Parliament: Insolvency Act 1986 s 342C(8), (9) (as so added and substituted). In exercise of the power so conferred the Secretary of State has made the Occupational and Personal Pension Schemes (Bankruptcy) (No 2) Regulations 2002, SI 2002/836.

Accordingly, for the purposes of the Insolvency Act 1986 s 342B(4)(b) (see head (b) in the text), the value of the individual's ('the bankrupt's') rights under an approved pension arrangement, or of his excluded rights under an unapproved pension arrangement, is the cash equivalent of those rights verified in accordance with the following provisions: Occupational and Personal Pension Schemes (Bankruptcy) (No 2) Regulations 2002, SI 2002/836, reg 7(1). In calculating and verifying the cash equivalent of the rights referred to in reg 7(1), the Pensions on Divorce etc (Provision of Information) Regulations 2000, SI 2000/1048, reg 3 (information about pensions and divorce and dissolution of a civil partnership; valuation of pension benefits) has effect for these purposes in like manner to that in which it has effect for the valuation of benefits in connection with the supply of information in connection with domestic and overseas divorce etc and dissolution of a civil partnership in England and Wales and Northern Ireland for the purposes of the Pensions on Divorce etc (Provision of Information) Regulations 2000, SI 2000/1048; and, for these purposes, 'the date on which the request for the valuation was received' is to be read as 'the date on which the trustee in bankruptcy's request for the valuation was received': Occupational and Personal Pension Schemes (Bankruptcy) (No 2) Regulations 2002, SI 2002/836, reg 7(2) (amended by SI 2005/2877).

As to the application of the Insolvency Act 1986 s 342C in the case of the administration in bankruptcy of the insolvent estate of a deceased person dying before the presentation of a bankruptcy petition see PARA 693 note 5.

12 Insolvency Act 1986 s 342B(5) (as added and substituted: see note 4). For these purposes, liabilities are correspondingly reduced if the difference between: (1) the amount of the liabilities immediately before the reduction; and (2) the amount of the liabilities immediately after the reduction, is equal to the restoration amount: Insolvency Act 1986 s 342B(6) (as so added and substituted). Regulations may make provision about the calculation and verification of any such amounts as are mentioned in the Insolvency Act 1986 s 342B(6)(a), (b) (see heads (1), (2)): s 342C(4)(b) (as so added and substituted). At the date at which this volume states the law no such regulations had been made. See also note 11.

13 Insolvency Act 1986 s 342B(7) (as added and substituted: see note 4).

(B) Pension Sharing Cases

695. Recovery of excessive pension contributions in pension sharing cases. A pension sharing transaction[1] is to be taken[2]:

(1)   to be a transaction, entered into by the transferor[3] with the transferee[4], by which the appropriate amount[5] is transferred by the transferor to the transferee; and

(2)   to be capable of being a transaction entered into at an undervalue only so far as it is a transfer of so much of the appropriate amount as is recoverable[6].

A pension sharing transaction is to be taken[7]:

(a)   to be something, namely a transfer of the appropriate amount to the transferee, done by the transferor; and

(b)   to be capable of being a preference given to the transferee only so far as it is a transfer of so much of the appropriate amount as is recoverable[8].

If, on an application to the court on the ground that a transaction is a transaction at an undervalue or a preference[9], any question arises as to whether, or the extent to which, the appropriate amount in the case of a pension sharing transaction is recoverable, the question must be determined in accordance with the following provisions[10].

The court must first determine the extent, if any, to which the transferor's rights under the shared arrangement[11] at the time of the transaction appear to have been, whether directly or indirectly, the fruits of contributions ('personal contributions') which the transferor has at any time made on his own behalf, or which have at any time been made on the transferor's behalf, to the shared arrangement or any other pension arrangement[12].

Where it appears that those rights were to any extent the fruits of personal contributions, the court must then determine the extent, if any, to which those rights appear to have been the fruits of personal contributions whose making has unfairly prejudiced the transferor's creditors ('the unfair contributions')[13].

If it appears to the court that the extent to which those rights were the fruits of the unfair contributions is such that the transfer of the appropriate amount could have been made out of rights under the shared arrangement which were not the fruits under the unfair contributions, the appropriate amount is not recoverable[14].

If it appears to the court that the transfer could not have been wholly so made, the appropriate amount is recoverable to the extent to which it appears to the court that the transfer could not have been so made[15].

In making its determination[16], the court must consider, in particular:

(i)   whether any of the personal contributions were made for the purpose of putting assets beyond the reach of the transferor's creditors or any of them; and

(ii)   whether the total amount of any personal contributions represented, at the time the pension sharing transaction was made, by rights under pension arrangements is an amount which is excessive in view of the transferor's circumstances when those contributions were made[17].

On the transferor's trustee in bankruptcy making a written request to the person responsible for the destination arrangement[18], that person must provide the trustee with such information about the arrangement, the transferee's rights under it and, where the destination arrangement is the shared arrangement, the transferor's rights under it, as the trustee may reasonably require for or in connection with the making of an application to the court on the ground that a transaction is a transaction at an undervalue or a preference[19].

Where the shared arrangement is not the destination arrangement, the person responsible for the shared arrangement must, on the transferor's trustee in bankruptcy making a written request to that person, provide the trustee with such information about the arrangement and the transferor's rights under it as the trustee may reasonable require for or in connection with the making of an application to the court on the ground that a transaction is a transaction at an undervalue or a preference[20].

On the transferor's trustee in bankruptcy making a written request to the person responsible for any intermediate arrangement[21], that person must provide the trustee with such information about the arrangement and the transferor's rights under it as the trustee may reasonable require for or in connection with the making of an application to the court on the ground that a transaction is a transaction at an undervalue or a preference[22].

Where a request for information has been made to the responsible person by the bankrupt's trustee in bankruptcy[23] and relating to the cash equivalent of a transferee's rights under a destination arrangement, the responsible person must comply with that request within a period of nine weeks beginning with the day on which it is received[24].

1   For these purposes, 'pension sharing transaction' means an order or provision falling within the Welfare Reform and Pensions Act 1999 s 28(1) (see PERSONAL AND OCCUPATIONAL PENSIONS vol 80 (2013) PARA 337): Insolvency Act 1986 s 342D(9) (ss 342D, 342F added by the Welfare Reform and Pensions Act 1999 s 84(1), Sch 12 paras 70, 71). The Welfare Reform and Pensions Act 1999 s 84(1), so far as relating to Sch 12 paras 70, 71 came into force on 26 March 2002 for the purpose of making regulations and on 6 April 2002 for all other purposes: Welfare Reform and Pensions Act 1999 (Commencement No 15) Order 2002, SI 2002/818, art 3(a), (b).

     In the case of the administration in bankruptcy of the insolvent estate of a deceased person dying before the presentation of a bankruptcy petition, the Insolvency Act 1986 s 342D applies: Administration of Insolvent Estates of Deceased Persons Order 1986, SI 1986/1999, art 3(1), Sch 1 Pt II para 28. As to the administration in bankruptcy of the insolvent estates of deceased persons see further PARA 823 et seq.

2   Ie for the purposes of the Insolvency Act 1986 ss 339, 341, 342: see PARA 678 et seq. Nothing in: (1) any provision of the Pension Schemes Act 1993 s 159 or the Pensions Act 1995 s 91 (which prevent assignment and the making of orders that restrain a person from receiving anything which he is prevented from assigning: see PERSONAL AND OCCUPATIONAL PENSIONS vol 80 (2013) PARAS 438, 288 respectively); (2) any provision of any enactment, whether passed or made before or after the passing of the Welfare Reform and Pensions Act 1999, corresponding to any of the provisions mentioned in head (1); or (3) any provision of the destination arrangement corresponding to any of those provisions, applies to a court exercising its powers under the Insolvency Act 1986 s 339 or s 340: s 342F(5) (as added: see note 1). As to the meaning of 'the destination arrangement' see PARA 696.

3   For these purposes, 'transferor', in relation to a pension sharing transaction, means the person to whose rights the transaction relates: Insolvency Act 1986 s 342D(9) (as added: see note 1).

4   For these purposes, 'transferee', in relation to a pension sharing transaction, means the person for whose benefit the transaction is made: Insolvency Act 1986 s 342D(9) (as added: see note 1).

5   For these purposes, 'appropriate amount', in relation to a pension sharing transaction, means the appropriate amount in relation to that transaction for the purposes of the Welfare Reform and Pensions Act 1999 s 29(1) (creation of pension credits and debits: see PERSONAL AND OCCUPATIONAL PENSIONS vol 80 (2013) PARA 338): Insolvency Act 1986 s 342D(9) (as added: see note 1).

6   Insolvency Act 1986 s 342D(1) (as added: see note 1).

7   Ie for the purposes of the Insolvency Act 1986 ss 340–342: see PARA 678 et seq.

8   Insolvency Act 1986 s 342D(2) (as added: see note 1).

9   Ie under the Insolvency Act 1986 s 339 or s 340.

10   Insolvency Act 1986 s 342D(3) (as added: see note 1).

11   For these purposes, 'shared arrangement', in relation to a pension sharing transaction, means the pension arrangement to which the transaction relates: Insolvency Act 1986 s 342D(9) (as added: see note 1).

12   Insolvency Act 1986 s 342D(4) (as added: see note 1).

13   Insolvency Act 1986 s 342D(5) (as added: see note 1).

14   Insolvency Act 1986 s 342D(6) (as added: see note 1).

15　Insolvency Act 1986 s 342D(7) (as added: see note 1).
16　Ie under the Insolvency Act 1986 s 342D(5).
17　Insolvency Act 1986 s 342D(8) (as added: see note 1).
18　For these purposes, references to the person responsible for a pension arrangement are to: (1) the trustees or managers or provider of the arrangement; or (2) the person having functions in relation to the arrangement corresponding to those of a trustee, manager or provider: Insolvency Act 1986 s 342F(8) (as added: see note 1).

　　　In the case of the administration in bankruptcy of the insolvent estate of a deceased person dying before the presentation of a bankruptcy petition, the Insolvency Act 1986 s 342F applies: Administration of Insolvent Estates of Deceased Persons Order 1986, SI 1986/1999, Sch 1 Pt II para 28.
19　Insolvency Act 1986 s 342F(1) (as added: see note 1).
20　Insolvency Act 1986 s 342F(2) (as added: see note 1).
21　For these purposes, 'intermediate arrangement' means a pension arrangement, other than the shared arrangement or the destination arrangement, in relation to which the following conditions are fulfilled: (1) there was a time when the transferee had rights under the arrangement that were derived, directly or indirectly, from the pension sharing transaction; and (2) the transferee's rights under the destination arrangement, so far as derived from the pension sharing transaction, are to any extent derived, directly or indirectly, from the rights mentioned in head (1): Insolvency Act 1986 s 342F(4) (as added: see note 1).
22　Insolvency Act 1986 s 342F(3) (as added: see note 1).
23　Ie pursuant to the Insolvency Act 1986 s 342F(1)–(3).
24　Occupational and Personal Pension Schemes (Bankruptcy) (No 2) Regulations 2002, SI 2002/836, reg 10(1)(c)(ii). As to the date on which the Occupational and Personal Pension Schemes (Bankruptcy) (No 2) Regulations 2002, SI 2002/836, came into force see PARA 407 note 3.

696.　Contents of orders.　If the court is making an order on the ground that a transaction is a transaction at an undervalue or a preference[1] in a case where:

(1)　the transaction or preference is, or is any part of, a pension sharing transaction[2]; and

(2)　the transferee[3] has rights under a pension arrangement ('the destination arrangement', which may be the shared arrangement[4] or any other pension arrangement) that are derived, directly or indirectly, from the pension sharing transaction,

the following provisions apply[5].

The order may[6] include provision:

(a)　requiring the person responsible for the destination arrangement[7] to pay an amount to the transferor's[8] trustee in bankruptcy;

(b)　adjusting the liabilities of the destination arrangement[9] in respect of the transferee;

(c)　adjusting any liabilities of the destination arrangement in respect of any other person that derive, directly or indirectly, from rights of the transferee under the destination arrangement;

(d)　for the recovery by the person responsible for the destination arrangement, whether by deduction from any amount which that person is ordered to pay or otherwise, of costs incurred by that person in complying in the transferor's case with any specified requirement[10] or in giving effect to the order;

(e)　for the recovery, from the transferor's trustee in bankruptcy, by the person responsible for a pension arrangement, of costs incurred by that person in complying in the transferor's case with any specified requirement[11].

The maximum amount which the person responsible for the destination arrangement may be required to pay by the order is the smallest of:

(i)　so much of the appropriate amount as is[12] recoverable;

(ii)   so much, if any, of the amount of the unfair contributions[13] as is not recoverable by way of an order[14] containing a requirement that the person responsible for the arrangement pay an amount to the trustee in bankruptcy[15];

(iii)   the value of the transferee's rights under the destination arrangement so far as they are derived, directly or indirectly, from the pension sharing transaction[16].

If the order requires the person responsible for the destination arrangement to pay an amount ('the restoration amount') to the transferor's trustee in bankruptcy, it must provide for the liabilities of the arrangement to be correspondingly reduced[17].

The order is binding on the person responsible for the destination arrangement and overrides provisions of the destination arrangement to the extent that they conflict with the provisions of the order[18].

1   Ie under the Insolvency Act 1986 s 339 or s 340: see PARA 678 et seq.
2   As to the meaning of 'pension-sharing transaction' see PARA 695 note 1.
3   As to the meaning of 'transferee', in relation to a pension-sharing transaction, see PARA 695 note 4.
4   As to the meaning of 'shared arrangement' see PARA 695 note 11.
5   Insolvency Act 1986 s 342E(1) (ss 342E, 342F added by the Welfare Reform and Pensions Act 1999 s 84(1), Sch 12 paras 70, 71). As to the date on which the Welfare Reform and Pensions Act 1999 s 84(1), so far as relating to Sch 12 paras 70, 71, came into force see PARA 695 note 1.
    In the case of the administration in bankruptcy of the insolvent estate of a deceased person dying before the presentation of a bankruptcy petition, the Insolvency Act 1986 s 342E applies: Administration of Insolvent Estates of Deceased Persons Order 1986, SI 1986/1999, Sch 1 Pt II para 28.
6   Ie without prejudice to the generality of the Insolvency Act 1986 s 339(2) (see PARA 680), s 340(2) (see PARA 682) or s 342 (see PARA 686).
7   As to the person responsible for a pension arrangement see PARA 695 note 18.
8   As to the meaning of 'transferor', in relation to a pension-sharing transaction, see PARA 695 note 3.
9   For these purposes, references to adjusting the liabilities of the destination arrangement in respect of a person include, in particular, reducing the amount of any benefit or future benefit to which that person is entitled under the arrangement: Insolvency Act 1986 s 342E(3) (as added: see note 5).
10   Ie any requirement under the Insolvency Act 1986 s 342F(1): see PARA 695.
11   Insolvency Act 1986 s 342E(2) (as added: see note 5). The requirements so specified are requirements under the Insolvency Act 1986 s 342F(2) or (3) (see PARA 695): s 342E(2).
12   Ie in accordance with the Insolvency Act 1986 s 342D: see PARA 695.
13   Ie within the meaning given by the Insolvency Act 1986 s 342D(5): see PARA 695.
14   Ie an order under the Insolvency Act 1986 s 342A: see PARA 693.
15   Ie a provision such as is mentioned in the Insolvency Act 1986 s 342B(1)(a): see PARA 694 head (1).
16   Insolvency Act 1986 s 342E(4) (as added: see note 5). Regulations may, for the purposes of ss 339–342 (see PARA 678 et seq) and ss 342D–324F, make provision about the calculation and verification of any such value as is mentioned in s 342E(4)(c) (see head (iii) in the text): s 342F(6)(a) (as added: see note 5). The power conferred by s 342F(6) includes power to provide for calculation and verification: (1) in such manner as may, in the particular case, be approved by a prescribed person; or (2) in accordance with guidance from time to time prepared by a prescribed person: s 342F(7) (as so added; and amended by the Pensions Act 2007 s 17, Sch 5 para 4). For these purposes, 'prescribed' means prescribed by regulations; and 'regulations' means regulations made by the Secretary of State: Insolvency Act 1986 s 342F(9) (as so added). Such regulations may make different provision for different cases and may contain such incidental, supplemental and transitional provisions as appear to the Secretary of State necessary or expedient; and they must be made by statutory instrument subject to annulment in pursuance of a resolution of either House of Parliament: s 342F(10), (11) (as so added). In exercise of the

power so conferred the Secretary of State has made the Occupational and Personal Pension Schemes (Bankruptcy) (No 2) Regulations 2002, SI 2002/836, reg 9, which came into force on 6 April 2002: reg 1(1).

Accordingly, where the Insolvency Act 1986 s 342E applies, the value of a transferee's rights under a destination arrangement, derived directly or indirectly from a pension-sharing transaction is: (a) the cash equivalent of those rights at the date on which the trustee in bankruptcy's request for that valuation is received by the responsible person; and (b) calculated and verified in accordance with the following provisions: Occupational and Personal Pension Schemes (Bankruptcy) (No 2) Regulations 2002, SI 2002/836, reg 9(1). In calculating and verifying the cash equivalent of the transferee's rights referred to in reg 9(1), the Pension Sharing (Pension Credit Benefit) Regulations 2000, SI 2000/1054, reg 24 (see PERSONAL AND OCCUPATIONAL PENSIONS vol 80 (2013) PARA 341) has effect for these purposes in like manner to that in which it has effect for the calculation and verification of pension credit for the purposes of the Pension Sharing (Pension Credit Benefit) Regulations 2000, SI 2000/1054: Occupational and Personal Pension Schemes (Bankruptcy) (No 2) Regulations 2002, SI 2002/836, reg 9(2).

As to the application of the Insolvency Act 1986 s 342F in the case of the administration in bankruptcy of the insolvent estate of a deceased person dying before the presentation of a bankruptcy petition see PARA 670 note 18.

17 Insolvency Act 1986 s 342E(5) (as added: see note 5). For these purposes, liabilities are correspondingly reduced if the difference between: (1) the amount of the liabilities immediately before the reduction; and (2) the amount of the liabilities immediately after the reduction, is equal to the restoration amount: s 342E(6) (as added: see note 5). Regulations may make provision about the calculation and verification of any such amounts as are mentioned in the Insolvency Act 1986 s 342E(6)(a), (b) (see heads (1), (2)): s 342F(6)(b) (as so added). At the date at which this volume states the law no such regulations had been made. See also note 16.

18 Insolvency Act 1986 s 342E(7) (as added: see note 5).

D. EXTORTIONATE CREDIT TRANSACTIONS

697. In general. Where a person is adjudged bankrupt and he is or has been a party to a transaction for, or involving, the provision to him of credit, the following provisions apply[1].

1 Insolvency Act 1986 s 343(1). As from a day to be appointed, s 343(1) is amended by the Enterprise and Regulatory Reform Act 2013 s 71, Sch 19 paras 1, 36: see PARA 130 note 17.

In the case of the administration in bankruptcy of the insolvent estate of a deceased person dying before the presentation of a bankruptcy petition, the Insolvency Act 1986 s 343 applies: Administration of Insolvent Estates of Deceased Persons Order 1986, SI 1986/1999, art 3(1), Sch 1 Pt II para 28. As to the administration in bankruptcy of the insolvent estates of deceased persons see further PARA 830 et seq.

698. Extortionate credit transaction. A transaction is extortionate if, having regard to the risk accepted by the person providing the credit:

(1) the terms of it are or were such as to require grossly exorbitant payments to be made, whether unconditionally or in certain contingencies, in respect of the provision of the credit[1]; or

(2) it otherwise grossly contravened ordinary principles of fair dealing;

and it is to be presumed, unless the contrary is proved, that a transaction with respect to which an application is made[2] is or, as the case may be, was extortionate[3].

1 For cases considering the acceptability of particular rates of interest for the provision of credit in particular circumstances see CONSUMER CREDIT. See PARA 700.

2 Ie under the Insolvency Act 1986 s 343: see PARA 699.

3 Insolvency Act 1986 s 343(3). As to the application of s 343 in the case of the administration in bankruptcy of the insolvent estate of a deceased person dying before the presentation of a bankruptcy petition see PARA 697 note 1.

699. Orders with respect to extortionate credit transactions. On the application of the trustee of the bankrupt's estate[1], the court may make an order with respect to the transaction if the transaction is or was extortionate[2] and was not entered into more than three years before the commencement of the bankruptcy[3].

An order with respect to any such transaction may contain such one or more of the following provisions as the court thinks fit, that is to say:

(1)   provision setting aside the whole or part of any obligation created by the transaction;

(2)   provision otherwise varying the terms of the transaction or varying the terms on which any security for the purposes of the transaction is held;

(3)   provision requiring any person who is or was a party to the transaction to pay to the trustee any sums paid to that person, by virtue of the transaction, by the bankrupt;

(4)   provision requiring any person to surrender to the trustee any property held by him as security for the purposes of the transaction; and

(5)   provision directing accounts to be taken between any persons[4].

Any sums or property to be paid or surrendered to the trustee in accordance with an order under the above provisions is to be comprised in the bankrupt's estate[5].

1   As to the mode of application and the procedure see PARA 786 et seq.
2   See PARA 698.
3   Insolvency Act 1986 s 343(2). As to the commencement of bankruptcy see PARA 209; and as to the application of s 343 in the case of the administration in bankruptcy of the insolvent estate of a deceased person dying before the presentation of a bankruptcy petition see PARA 697 note 1.
4   Insolvency Act 1986 s 343(4).
5   Insolvency Act 1986 s 343(5).

700. Other remedies. The powers conferred with respect to extortionate credit transactions[1] are exercisable in relation to any transaction concurrently with any powers exercisable under the Insolvency Act 1986 in relation to that transaction as a transaction at an undervalue[2].

1   Ie the powers conferred by the Insolvency Act 1986 s 343: see PARA 699.
2   Insolvency Act 1986 s 343(6) (amended by the Consumer Credit Act 2006 s 70, Sch 4). As to transactions at an undervalue see PARA 678 et seq; and as to the application of the Insolvency Act 1986 s 343 in the case of the administration in bankruptcy of the insolvent estate of a deceased person dying before the presentation of a bankruptcy petition see PARA 697 note 1.

E. ASSIGNMENT OF BOOK DEBTS; CONTRACTS

701. Avoidance of general assignment of book debts. Where a person engaged in any business makes a general assignment[1] to another person of his existing or future book debts[2] or any class of them, and is subsequently adjudged bankrupt, the assignment is void against the trustee of the bankrupt's estate as regards book debts which were not paid before the presentation of the bankruptcy petition[3], unless the assignment has been registered under the Bills of Sale Act 1878[4]. For the purposes of registration under the 1878 Act, an assignment of book debts is to be treated as if it were a bill of sale given otherwise than by way of security for the payment of a sum of money; and the provisions of that Act with respect to the registration of bills of sale apply accordingly with such necessary modifications as may be made by rules under that Act[5].

1	For these purposes, 'assignment' includes an assignment by way of security or charge on book debts, and 'general assignment' does not include: (1) an assignment of book debts due at the date of the assignment from specified debtors or of debts becoming due under specified contracts; or (2) an assignment of book debts included either in a transfer of a business made in good faith and for value or in an assignment of assets for the benefit of creditors generally: Insolvency Act 1986 s 344(3). Where a general equitable assignment of book debts was followed by specific legal assignments of some of the same debts, the latter were valid against the trustee: *Hill v Alex Lawrie Factors Ltd* [2000] BPIR 1038, [2000] All ER (D) 882.

　　In the case of the administration in bankruptcy of the insolvent estate of a deceased person dying before the presentation of a bankruptcy petition, the Insolvency Act 1986 s 344 applies: Administration of Insolvent Estates of Deceased Persons Order 1986, SI 1986/1999, art 3(1), Sch 1 Pt II para 28. As to the administration in bankruptcy of the insolvent estates of deceased persons see further PARA 830 et seq.

2	Ie debts which in the ordinary course of business would be entered in a well-kept trade book: *Shipley v Marshall* (1863) 14 CBNS 566; and see *Blakey v Pendlebury Property Trustees* [1931] 2 Ch 255, CA.

3	See PARA 130 et seq.

4	Insolvency Act 1986 s 344(1), (2). As from a day to be appointed, s 344(1), (2) is amended by the Enterprise and Regulatory Reform Act 2013 s 71, Sch 19 paras 1, 37: see PARA 130 note 17.

　　As to the Bills of Sale Act 1878 see further FINANCIAL SERVICES AND INSTITUTIONS vol 50 (2008) PARA 1620 et seq. As to the procedure for applications under the Insolvency Act 1986 s 344 see *Practice Direction—Alternative Procedure for Claims* PD 8A para 15B.

5	Insolvency Act 1986 s 344(4).

702.　Contracts to which bankrupt is a party. Where a contract has been made with a person who is subsequently adjudged bankrupt, the court may, on the application of any other party to the contract, make an order discharging obligations under the contract on such terms as to payment by the applicant or the bankrupt of damages for non-performance or otherwise as appear to the court to be equitable[1]. Any damages payable by the bankrupt by virtue of such an order of the court are provable as a bankruptcy debt[2].

Where an undischarged bankrupt is a contractor in respect of any contract jointly with any person, that person may sue or be sued in respect of the contract without the joinder of the bankrupt[3].

1	Insolvency Act 1986 s 345(1), (2). As from a day to be appointed, s 345(1) is amended by the Enterprise and Regulatory Reform Act 2013 s 71, Sch 19 paras 1, 38: see PARA 130 note 17.

　　As to the application of the Insolvency Act 1986 s 345 in the case of the administration in bankruptcy of the insolvent estate of a deceased person dying before the presentation of a bankruptcy petition see PARA 447 note 4.

　　Where a contract is unprofitable, from the estate's point of view, the trustee may elect either to adopt or disclaim it: see PARA 430. If the trustee wishes to perform a contract, he must perform the bankrupt's part of the contract, as and when the bankrupt should have done so himself: *Gibson v Carruthers* (1841) 8 M & W 321 at 333. If the trustee does not perform his part of the contract within a reasonable time, the other party may treat the contract as abandoned: *Lawrence v Knowles* (1839) 5 Bing NC 399; *Morgan v Bain* (1874) LR 10 CP 15; *Re Nathan, ex p Stapleton* (1879) 10 ChD 586, CA. The provisions in the Insolvency Act 1986 s 345 enable a party to a contract, presumably one which is not onerous for the estate, to discharge obligations under the contract with suitable orders for compensation to either party in consequence of their discharge: see *Re Potters Oils Ltd (No 2)* [1986] 1 All ER 890, [1986] 1 WLR 201.

2	Insolvency Act 1986 s 345(3). As to proofs of debt see PARA 507 et seq.

3	Insolvency Act 1986 s 345(4). Where one of two joint covenantors has become bankrupt, notice of assignment of the benefit of the contract need not be given to him: *Josselson v Borst, (Gliksten, third party)* [1938] 1 KB 723, [1937] 3 All ER 722, CA.

F. EXECUTION

703.　Rights of execution creditors. Subject to the statutory provisions imposing restrictions on proceedings and remedies[1], and to the following provisions[2], where the creditor of any person who is adjudged bankrupt has, before the commencement of the bankruptcy[3]:

(1)   issued execution against goods or land of that person; or

(2)   attached a debt due to that person from another person,

that creditor is not entitled, as against the official receiver or trustee of the bankrupt's estate, to retain the benefit of the execution or attachment, or any sums paid to avoid it, unless the execution or attachment was completed[4], or the sums were paid, before the commencement of the bankruptcy[5].

Where[6]:

(a)   under an execution in respect of a judgment for a sum exceeding such sum as may be prescribed for these purposes[7], the goods of any person are sold or money is paid in order to avoid a sale; and

(b)   before the end of the period of 14 days beginning with the day of the sale or payment the enforcement officer[8] or other officer charged with the execution is given notice that a bankruptcy petition has been presented in relation to that person; and

(c)   a bankruptcy order is or has been made on that petition,

the balance of the proceeds of sale or money paid, after deducting the costs of the execution, are, in priority to the claim of the execution creditor, comprised in the bankrupt's estate[9].

1   Ie the Insolvency Act 1986 s 285: see PARA 214.

2   See the text and notes 3–9; and PARA 704.

3   As to the commencement of bankruptcy see PARA 209.

4   For these purposes: (1) an execution against goods is completed by seizure and sale or by the making of a charging order under the Charging Orders Act 1979 s 1 (see CIVIL PROCEDURE vol 12 (2009) PARA 1467 et seq); (2) an execution against land is completed by seizure, by the appointment of a receiver or by the making of a charging order under s 1; (3) an attachment of a debt is completed by the receipt of the debt: Insolvency Act 1986 s 346(5). See further PARAS 683–685. The onus of proving that he completed his execution before the date of the bankruptcy order lies on the execution creditor: *Re Matanlè, ex p Schulte* (1874) 9 Ch App 409; *Re Joy, ex p Cartwright* (1881) 44 LT 883, CA. As to the application of the rule that a judicial act was made in the final moment of the day when it was done see *Re Palmer (a debtor)* [1994] Ch 316, [1994] 3 All ER 835, CA. For the purposes of the Insolvency Act 1986 s 346(1), 'execution' does not include distress: *Re Modern Jet Support Centre Ltd* [2005] EWHC 1611 (Ch), [2005] 1 WLR 3880, [2006] STC 808. As to distress see PARA 711.

In the case of the administration in bankruptcy of the insolvent estate of a deceased person dying before the presentation of a bankruptcy petition, the Insolvency Act 1986 s 346 applies: Administration of Insolvent Estates of Deceased Persons Order 1986, SI 1986/1999, art 3(1), Sch 1 Pt II para 28. As to the administration in bankruptcy of the insolvent estates of deceased persons see further PARA 830 et seq.

5   Insolvency Act 1986 s 346(1). As from a day to be appointed, s 346(1), (3) is amended by the Enterprise and Regulatory Reform Act 2013 s 71, Sch 19 paras 1, 39: see PARA 130 note 17.

The rights conferred by the Insolvency Act 1986 s 346(1)–(3) on the official receiver or the trustee may, to such extent and on such terms as it thinks fit, be set aside by the court in favour of the creditor who has issued the execution or attached the debt: s 346(6). See further PARA 706. The court has power under the Charging Orders Act 1979 s 3(5) to set aside a final charging order or final third party debt order at the suit of the trustee in bankruptcy in appropriate circumstances (see *Industrial Diseases Compensation Ltd v Marrons* [2001] BPIR 600) but some additional feature beyond the making of the bankruptcy order must be shown (see *Wright v Nationwide Building Society* [2009] EWCA Civ 811, [2010] Ch 318, [2010] 2 WLR 1097).

6   Ie subject to the Insolvency Act 1986 s 346(6): see note 5.

7   For these purposes, the sum so prescribed is £1,000: Insolvency Proceedings (Monetary Limits) Order 1986, SI 1986/1996, art 3, Schedule Pt II (art 3 amended by SI 2009/465; the Insolvency Proceedings (Monetary Limits) Order 1986, SI 1986/1996, Schedule Pt II substituted by SI 2004/547). As to the Secretary of State's power to prescribe monetary limits see PARA 19 note 9.

8   For these purposes, 'enforcement officer' means an individual who is authorised to act as an
     enforcement officer under the Courts Act 2003: Insolvency Act 1986 s 346(9) (added by the
     Courts Act 2003 s 109(1), Sch 8 para 297). As to enforcement agents see CIVIL PROCEDURE
     vol 12 (2009) PARA 1258 et seq.
9   Insolvency Act 1986 s 346(3) (amended by the Courts Act 2003 Sch 8 para 297). Neither the
     Insolvency Act 1986 s 346(2) (see PARA 704) nor s 346(3) applies in relation to any execution
     against property which has been acquired by or has devolved on the bankrupt since the
     commencement of the bankruptcy, unless, at the time the execution is issued or before it is
     completed: (1) the property has been or is claimed for the bankrupt's estate under s 307 (see
     PARA 458); and (2) a copy of the notice given under s 307 has been or is served on the
     enforcement officer or other officer charged with the execution: s 346(8) (amended by the
     Courts Act 2003 Sch 8 para 297).

704.   Duties of enforcement officer.   Where any goods of a person have been
taken in execution, then, if before the completion of the execution[1] notice is
given to the enforcement officer[2] or other officer charged with the execution that
that person has been adjudged bankrupt:

(1)   the enforcement officer or other officer must on request deliver to the
        official receiver or trustee of the bankrupt's estate the goods and any
        money seized or recovered in part satisfaction of the execution; but
(2)   the costs of the execution are a first charge on the goods or money so
        delivered and the official receiver or trustee may sell the goods or a
        sufficient part of them for the purpose of satisfying the charge[3].

Accordingly, in the case of an execution in respect of a judgment for a sum
exceeding the prescribed sum[4], the enforcement officer or other officer charged
with the execution may not dispose of the balance of the proceeds of any sale of
goods sold under an execution or money paid to avoid a sale after deduction of
the costs of execution[5] within the period of 14 days beginning with the day of
the sale or payment or while there is pending a bankruptcy petition of which he
has been given notice, and must pay that balance, where it is so comprised in the
bankrupt's estate, to the official receiver or, if there is one, to the trustee of that
estate[6].

1   As to completion of an execution against goods see PARA 708.
2   As to the meaning of 'enforcement officer' see PARA 703 note 8.
3   Insolvency Act 1986 s 346(2) (amended by the Courts Act 2003 s 109(1), Sch 8 para 297). The
     Insolvency Act 1986 346(2) is subject to s 346(8) (see PARA 703 note 9): s 346(2). As from a day
     to be appointed, s 346(2), (4) is amended by the Enterprise and Regulatory Reform Act 2013
     s 71, Sch 19 paras 1, 39: see PARA 130 note 17.
        As to the application of the Insolvency Act 1986 s 346 in the case of the administration in
     bankruptcy of the insolvent estate of a deceased person dying before the presentation of a
     bankruptcy petition see PARA 703 note 4.
        The rights conferred by s 346(1)–(3) on the official receiver or the trustee may, to such extent
     and on such terms as it thinks fit, be set aside by the court in favour of the creditor who has
     issued the execution or attached the debt: s 346(6). See further PARA 706.
4   Ie the sum prescribed for the purposes of the Insolvency Act 1986 s 346(3): see PARA 703 note 7.
5   Ie the balance mentioned in the Insolvency Act 1986 s 346(3): see PARA 703.
6   Insolvency Act 1986 s 346(4) (amended by the Courts Act 2003 Sch 8 para 297).

705.   Costs of officers charged with execution of writs or other process.
Where an enforcement officer, or other officer, charged with execution of the
writ or other process is required to deliver up goods or money[1], or has deducted
costs from the proceeds of an execution or money paid to him[2], the office
holder[3] may require in writing that the amount of the enforcement officer's or
other officer's bill of costs be decided by detailed assessment[4]. Where such a
requirement is made, the enforcement officer or other officer must deliver his bill
within three months of the requirement being made, or within such further time

as the court, on application, may grant; and, if he fails to comply with this provision, the office holder may deal with the insolvent estate[5] without regard to any claim by the enforcement officer or other officer, whose claim is forfeited[6].

Where, in the case of a deduction of costs from the proceeds of an execution or money paid to him, any amount is disallowed at the conclusion of the detailed assessment proceedings, the enforcement officer must as soon as reasonably practicable pay a sum equal to that amount to the office holder for the benefit of the insolvent estate[7].

1　Ie under the Insolvency Act 1986 s 346(2): see PARA 704.
2　Ie under the Insolvency Act 1986 s 346(3): see PARA 703.
3　As to the meaning of 'office-holder' see PARA 20 note 7.
4　Insolvency Rules 1986, SI 1986/1925, r 7.36(1) (substituted by SI 1999/1022; and amended by SI 2005/527; and SI 2010/686). As to the general provisions relating to detailed assessment see the Insolvency Rules 1986, SI 1986/1925, rr 7.33A–7.42; and PARA 814 et seq.
5　As to the meaning of 'the insolvent estate' see PARA 53 note 17.
6　Insolvency Rules 1986, SI 1986/1925, rr 7.35(4), 7.36(2) (both substituted by SI 1999/1022; the Insolvency Rules 1986, SI 1986/1925, r 7.35(4) amended by SI 2010/686).
7　Insolvency Rules 1986, SI 1986/1925, r 7.36(3) (substituted by SI 1999/1022; and amended by SI 2005/527; SI 2009/642; and SI 2010/686).

706.　Powers of the court. The rights conferred[1] on the official receiver or the trustee in respect of the benefit of executions or attachments which have not been completed before the commencement of the bankruptcy may, to such extent and on such terms as it thinks fit, be set aside by the court in favour of the creditor who has issued the execution or attached the debt[2].

1　Ie by the Insolvency Act 1986 s 346(1)–(3): see PARAS 703, 704.
2　Insolvency Act 1986 s 346(6). As to the application of s 346 in the case of the administration in bankruptcy of the insolvent estate of a deceased person dying before the presentation of a bankruptcy petition see PARA 703 note 4.

　　The discretionary powers of the court under s 346(6) are extremely wide and of an undefined character. Under the corresponding provisions in ss 183, 184 (formerly the Companies Act 1985 ss 621, 622 (repealed)), the following principles have emerged: (1) it is intended that all creditors, including prima facie all execution creditors who have not 'completed' their execution, should rank pari passu in the distribution of the debtor's assets; (2) an execution creditor who is able to prove that he was unfairly, though not necessarily fraudulently, obstructed in putting in train, or bringing to a conclusion, a process of execution, may qualify for favourable consideration by way of exception to the general rule; (3) in general, however, such a creditor will have to show an extremely strong case before the court will intervene: *Re Grosvenor Metal Co Ltd* [1950] Ch 63, [1949] 2 All ER 948; *Re Suidair International Airways Ltd* [1951] Ch 165, [1950] 2 All ER 920; *Re Rainbow Tours Ltd* [1964] Ch 66, [1963] 2 All ER 820; *Re Redman (Builders) Ltd* [1964] 1 All ER 851, [1964] 1 WLR 541; *Re Caribbean Products (Yam Importers) Ltd, Tickler v Swains Packaging Ltd* [1966] Ch 331, [1966] 1 All ER 181, CA; *Re Aro Co Ltd* [1980] Ch 196, [1980] 1 All ER 1067, CA; *Roberts Petroleum Ltd v Bernard Kenny Ltd (in liquidation)* [1983] 2 AC 192, [1983] 1 All ER 564, HL; *Re Buckingham International plc (in liquidation) (No 2), Mitchell v Buckingham International plc (in liquidation)* [1998] 2 BCLC 369, [1998] BCC 943, CA; *Tagore Investments SA v Official Receiver* [2008] EWHC 3495 (Ch), [2009] BPIR 392, [2009] All ER (D) 63 (Jan). See further COMPANY AND PARTNERSHIP INSOLVENCY vol 17 (2011) PARA 840 et seq.

707.　Rights of third parties. Nothing in the above provisions[1] entitles the trustee of a bankrupt's estate to claim goods from a person who has acquired them in good faith under a sale by an enforcement officer[2] or other officer charged with an execution[3].

1　Ie in the Insolvency Act 1986 s 346: see PARAS 703–706.
2　As to the meaning of 'enforcement officer' see PARA 703 note 8.

3   Insolvency Act 1986 s 346(7) (amended by the Courts Act 2003 s 109(1), Sch 8 para 297). As to
     the application of s 346 in the case of the administration in bankruptcy of the insolvent estate of
     a deceased person dying before the presentation of a bankruptcy petition see PARA 703 note 4.

708.   Completion of execution against goods. An execution against goods is
completed by seizure and sale[1]. An execution is incomplete if the enforcement
officer or other officer charged with an execution has been induced by payment
on account or otherwise to withdraw temporarily, and will, it seems, be
incomplete, even though the officer withdraws permanently, as where, on
payment of part of the debt in order to avoid a sale, he so withdraws with the
execution creditor's assent[2]. Thus, an execution is not completed by the
judgment debtor paying the debt to the judgment creditor[3]. If the sale, for
whatever reason, is not a sale under the execution, the execution is not
completed[4]. Where an execution creditor causes goods to be seized by the
enforcement officer, who, however, is ordered to withdraw in favour of a
receiver, the execution is not completed[5].

An execution against goods is also completed by the making of a charging
order[6] under the Charging Orders Act 1979[7]. The charging order must be
absolute and the bankruptcy of the debtor is a sufficient cause for the court not
to convert an order nisi into an order absolute[8].

1   Insolvency Act 1986 s 346(5)(a). As to the application of s 346 in the case of the administration
     in bankruptcy of the insolvent estate of a deceased person dying before the presentation of a
     bankruptcy petition see PARA 703 note 4. The words 'seizure and sale' are to be strictly
     construed: *Re Andrew, ex p Official Receiver* [1937] Ch 122 at 134, [1936] 3 All ER 450 at
     463, CA; *Re Caribbean Products (Yam Importers) Ltd, Tickler v Swains Packaging Ltd* [1966]
     Ch 331, [1966] 1 All ER 181, CA.
2   *Re Fairley* [1922] 2 Ch 791 at 801. See also *Re Gooding, ex p Trustee* [1914] 2 KB 70: *Re
     Evans, ex p Salaman* [1916] HBR 111.
3   *Re Pollock and Pendle, ex p Wilson and Mathieson Ltd* (1902) 87 LT 238.
4   *Heathcote v Livesley* (1887) 19 QBD 285 at 287 per Wills J.
5   *Mackay v Merritt* (1886) 34 WR 433.
6   Ie under the Charging Orders Act 1979 s 1 (amended by the Administration of Justice Act 1982
     ss 34(3), 37, Sch 3 Pt II paras 2, 3, 6; the County Courts Act 1984 s 148(1), Sch 2 Pt V): see
     CIVIL PROCEDURE vol 12 (2009) PARA 1467 et seq.
7   Insolvency Act 1986 s 346(5)(a).
8   *Roberts Petroleum Ltd v Bernard Kenny Ltd (in liquidation)* [1983] 2 AC 192, [1983] 1 All ER
     564, HL (company case).

709.   Completion of execution against land. An execution against land is
completed by seizure[1], by the appointment of a receiver or by the making of a
charging order[2] under the Charging Orders Act 1979[3]. An execution by the
appointment of a receiver is complete on the making of a final order of
appointment by the court[4], notwithstanding that he has not given any security
and perfected his appointment[5]. An execution by the making of a charging order
is complete on the making of the order absolute[6].

1   As to completing execution and obtaining possession of land see CIVIL PROCEDURE vol 12
     (2009) PARA 1309.
2   Ie under the Charging Orders Act 1979 s 1: see CIVIL PROCEDURE vol 12 (2009) PARA 1467 et
     seq.
3   Insolvency Act 1986 s 346(5)(b). As to the application of s 346 in the case of the administration
     in bankruptcy of the insolvent estate of a deceased person dying before the presentation of a
     bankruptcy petition see PARA 703 note 4.
4   *Roberts Petroleum Ltd v Bernard Kenny Ltd (in liquidation)* [1983] 2 AC 192 at 213, [1983]
     1 All ER 564 at 576, HL (company case).
5   *Re Watkins, ex p Evans* (1879) 13 ChD 252, CA (decided when the relevant statutory provision
     specified that execution was completed by the appointment of a receiver 'in the case of an

equitable interest' in land). Cf *Re Pearce, ex p Official Receiver, Trustee* [1919] 1 KB 354, CA. See also *Re Overseas Aviation Engineering (GB) Ltd* [1963] Ch 24, [1962] 3 All ER 12, CA; *Roberts Petroleum Ltd v Bernard Kenny Ltd (in liquidation)* [1983] 2 AC 192, [1983] 1 All ER 564, HL.

6　*Roberts Petroleum Ltd v Bernard Kenny Ltd (in liquidation)* [1983] 2 AC 192, [1983] 1 All ER 564, HL.

710.　Attachment of debts. An attachment of a debt[1] is completed by actual receipt[2] of the debt by the judgment creditor[3]. Where a judgment creditor has obtained a charging order on the judgment debtor's interest in a partnership[4], and the partners have paid money into court to redeem the judgment debtor's interest and avoid the charging order, there is not a completed execution[5]. Moreover, where the execution takes the form of a writ of sequestration to compel the debtor to pay money into court, and execution has not been completed by a sale before the bankruptcy order, or if, before the bankruptcy order, the money received under the sequestration has merely been paid to the sequestrator's account in court, the execution has not been completed, and the execution creditor is not protected[6].

Execution is completed neither by an order nisi charging securities[7] nor by an order obtained without notice being given to any other party appointing a receiver of a debtor's interest in a residuary estate[8].

As in the case of an execution[9], an attachment, to be protected, must be completed and not merely partly carried out. Where, therefore, a judgment creditor attaches a debt, but agrees not to enforce the attachment against the third party before a certain date, and before this date a bankruptcy order is made against the judgment debtor, the creditor cannot maintain his claim to the debt, and the third party must pay it to the trustee in bankruptcy[10].

1　Ie attachment by third party debt order under CPR Pt 72 or under the Crown Proceedings Act 1947 s 27(1): see CIVIL PROCEDURE vol 12 (2009) PARA 1428.

2　For this purpose, 'receipt' means actual receipt; constructive receipt is not sufficient: *Butler v Wearing* (1885) 17 QBD 182; *Re Trehearne, ex p Ealing Local Board* (1890) 60 LJQB 50, CA; *Re Bagley* [1911] 1 KB 317, CA; *Galbraith v Grimshaw* [1910] AC 508 at 511, HL. See also *George v Tompson's Trustee* [1949] Ch 322, [1949] 1 All ER 554 (where the fact that the creditor had not actually received payment before the receiving order was made was due solely to administrative delay in the court office, but it was held that the attachment was not complete); applied in *Re Lupkovics, ex p Trustee v Freville* [1954] 2 All ER 125, [1954] 1 WLR 1234 (payment by the Crown to the creditor's solicitors did not, in the circumstances, constitute receipt by the creditor).

3　Insolvency Act 1986 s 346(5)(c). As to the application of s 346 in the case of the administration in bankruptcy of the insolvent estate of a deceased person dying before the presentation of a bankruptcy petition see PARA 703 note 4.

4　Ie under the Partnership Act 1890 s 23(2): see PARTNERSHIP vol 79 (2008) PARAS 95–97.

5　*Wild v Southwood* [1897] 1 QB 317.

6　*Re Pollard, ex p Pollard* [1903] 2 KB 41, CA; *Re Hastings, ex p Brown* (1892) 61 LJQB 654 at 659; cf *Re Hoare, ex p Nelson* (1880) 14 ChD 41, CA.

7　See *Re Hutchinson, ex p Hutchinson* (1885) 16 QBD 515.

8　*Re Potts, ex p Taylor* [1893] 1 QB 648, CA; and see *Roberts Petroleum Ltd v Bernard Kenny Ltd* [1983] 2 AC 192, [1983] 1 All ER 564, HL.

9　See PARA 708.

10　*Re Trehearne, ex p Ealing Local Board* (1890) 60 LJQB 50, CA; *George v Tompson's Trustee* [1949] Ch 322, [1949] 1 All ER 554.

G. DISTRESS

711.　Distress. The right of a landlord to distrain for arrears of rent arises at common law[1]. The right to distrain is prospectively abolished by the Tribunals,

Courts and Enforcement Act 2007[2]; but at the date at which this volume states the law the relevant provisions of that Act had not been brought into force.

The right of any landlord or other person to whom rent is payable to distrain on the goods and effects of an undischarged bankrupt for rent due to him from the bankrupt is available, subject to the provisions mentioned below[3], against goods and effects comprised in the bankrupt's estate[4]. Where the distress is levied after the commencement of the bankruptcy[5], the amount of rent accrued due prior to the date of the bankruptcy order for which distress may be levied is limited to six months' rent[6]. As regards rent due after the date of the bankruptcy order, there is no such limitation[7]. Any right to distrain against property comprised in a bankrupt's estate is exercisable notwithstanding that the property has vested in the trustee[8]; and the above provisions are without prejudice to a landlord's right in a bankruptcy to prove for any bankruptcy debt in respect of rent[9].

A landlord's right of distress is lost if he permits the goods to leave the premises[10]. The landlord is not a secured creditor, although he has a preferential right of distress if there are goods on which he can distrain; and, therefore, if he does not distrain, or if at the date when the right of distress arises, no goods available for distress remain on the premises, his only remedy is to prove for his rent[11].

Where a landlord or other person to whom rent is payable has distrained for rent on the goods and effects of an individual to whom a bankruptcy petition relates and a bankruptcy order is subsequently made on that petition, any amount recovered by way of that distress which:

(1)   is in excess of the amount which would have been recoverable after the commencement of the bankruptcy; or

(2)   is in respect of rent for a period or part of a period after the distress was levied,

must be held for the bankrupt as part of his estate[12].

1   As to distress for rent generally see LANDLORD AND TENANT vol 62 (2012) PARA 283 et seq. As to the landlord's right of re-entry see *Cadogan Estates Ltd v McMahon* [2001] 1 AC 378, [2000] 4 All ER 897, HL.

2   See the Tribunals, Courts and Enforcement Act 2007 s 71 (not yet in force); and LANDLORD AND TENANT vol 62 (2012) PARA 283.

3   Ie the Insolvency Act 1986 ss 252(2)(b), 254(1), 347(5): see PARAS 45, 47, 716.

4   Insolvency Act 1986 s 347(1) (amended by the Insolvency Act 2000 s 3, Sch 3 paras 1, 14). As from a day to be appointed the Insolvency Act 1986 s 347(1) is amended by the Tribunals, Courts and Enforcement Act 2007 s 86, Sch 14 para 44 to provide that CRAR (the power of commercial rent arrears recovery under the Tribunals, Courts and Enforcement Act 2007 s 72(1)) is exercisable where the tenant is an undischarged bankrupt against goods and effects comprised in the bankrupt's estate. At the date at which this volume states the law no such day had been appointed. See LANDLORD AND TENANT vol 62 (2012) PARA 288.

Subject to the Insolvency Act 1986 ss 252(2)(b), 254(1) (see PARAS 45, 47) nothing in Pts 7A–11 (ss 251A–385) affects any right to distrain otherwise than for rent; and any such right is at any time exercisable without restriction against property comprised in a bankrupt's estate, even if that right is expressed by any enactment to be exercisable in like manner as a right to distrain for rent: s 347(8) (amended by the Insolvency Act 2000 Sch 3 paras 1, 14).

In the case of the administration in bankruptcy of the insolvent estate of a deceased person dying before the presentation of a bankruptcy petition, the Insolvency Act 1986 s 347 applies: Administration of Insolvent Estates of Deceased Persons Order 1986. SI 1986/1999, art 3(1), Sch 1 Pt II para 28. As to the administration in bankruptcy of the insolvent estates of deceased persons see further PARA 830 et seq.

5   As to the commencement of bankruptcy see PARA 209.

6   Insolvency Act 1986 s 347(1). See note 4.

7 *Re Binns, ex p Hale* (1875) 1 ChD 285; *Re Wells* [1929] 2 Ch 269. As to restrictions on the period for which distress may be levied in the case of an agricultural holding see AGRICULTURAL LAND vol 1 (2008) PARAS 346–348.
8 Insolvency Act 1986 s 347(9).
9 Insolvency Act 1986 s 347(10).
10 *Re MacKenzie, ex p Sheriff of Hertfordshire* [1899] 2 QB 566 at 573, CA. See also *Ex p Descharmes* (1742) 1 Atk 103; *Ex p Plummer* (1739) 1 Atk 103.
11 *Thomas v Patent Lionite Co* (1881) 17 ChD 250, CA. Only rent due to the date of the bankruptcy order is a bankruptcy debt for which the landlord may prove. Where, however, the trustee disclaims a lease, and the landlord sustains loss or damage in consequence of the operation of such disclaimer, he is deemed to be a creditor of the bankrupt to the extent of the loss or damage and accordingly may prove for the loss or damage as a bankruptcy debt: see the Insolvency Act 1986 s 315(5); and PARA 505.
12 Insolvency Act 1986 s 347(2). To avoid distress, the official receiver often undertakes to pay the landlord the rent for which he is entitled to distrain, out of the proceeds of the distrainable goods when sold; this undertaking will bind the official receiver and the trustee: see *Re Chapman, ex p Goodyear* (1894) 10 TLR 449.
   As from a day to be appointed, the Insolvency Act 1986 s 347(2) is amended by the Tribunals, Courts and Enforcement Act 2007 Sch 14 para 44 to provide as follows: Where CRAR (see note 4) has been exercised to recover rent from an individual to whom a bankruptcy petition relates and a bankruptcy order is subsequently made on that petition, any amount recovered by way of CRAR which: (1) is in excess of the amount which by virtue of the Insolvency Act 1986 s 347(1) would have been recoverable after the commencement of the bankruptcy; or (2) is in respect of rent for a period or part of a period after goods were taken control of under CRAR, is to be held for the bankrupt as part of his estate.
   As from a day to be appointed, s 347(2) is further amended by the Enterprise and Regulatory Reform Act 2013 s 71, Sch 19 paras 1, 40: see PARA 130 note 17.

712. Restrictions on right of distress. It appears that a landlord may pursue his claim for rent both by distress and proof until a dividend is declared, after which time he must elect between the two remedies[1]. A landlord who has proved in the bankruptcy of one of two joint tenants may distrain on the goods of the other for the same arrears of rent[2]. The landlord's statutory right of distress[3] is affected neither by the making of the bankruptcy order[4] nor by the fact that the goods have been seized and sold by the enforcement officer, if they still remain on the premises[5].

Where a bankruptcy occurs during a quarter, the landlord may distrain at the end of the quarter for the whole quarter's rent, or for a proportionate part of it accrued due prior to the bankruptcy order[6]. If rent is payable half-yearly, and a bankruptcy order is made against the tenant before the end of the last half-year, the landlord cannot, in respect of rent accrued due prior to the bankruptcy order, obtain by distress levied before the end of the half-year more than six months of the overdue rent[7].

The limitation of the landlord's right is only for the benefit of the creditors, and does not extend to goods not belonging to the bankrupt[8]; but a mortgagee whose goods have been seized and sold may claim to stand in the place of the landlord against other goods of the bankrupt liable to a distress[9].

If a landlord neglects to distrain for his rent, he may be postponed to a solicitor who obtains a charging order in respect of his costs on property recovered or preserved by him[10].

1 See the Insolvency Act 1986 s 347(10); PARA 711; and *Holmes v Watt* [1935] 2 KB 300, CA. Cf *Ex p Grove* (1747) 1 Atk 104. As to the prospective abolition of the right to distrain see the Tribunals, Courts and Enforcement Act 2007 s 71; PARA 711; and LANDLORD AND TENANT vol 62 (2012) PARA 283.
2 *Holmes v Watt* [1935] 2 KB 300, CA. It is not clear whether a landlord who proves and receives a dividend in respect of his claim for rent against a bankrupt joint tenant may also distrain on the goods of the other solvent joint tenant; but it is submitted that, as both joint tenants are

liable for the full amount of the rent, the landlord may pursue whatever remedies are available to him against each of them, so long as he does not receive more than 100 pence in the pound on his claim.

3   See PARA 711.
4   *Re Howell, ex p Mandleberg & Co* [1895] 1 QB 844, DC. See also *Re Mayhew, ex p Till* (1873) LR 16 Eq 97.
5   *Re Davies, ex p Pollen's Trustees* (1885) 3 Morr 27.
6   See the Insolvency Act 1986 s 347(1); PARA 711; *Re Howell, ex p Mandleberg & Co* [1895] 1 QB 844, DC; *Bishop of Rochester v Le Fanu* [1906] 2 Ch 513; *Re Solomon, ex p Dressler* (1878) 9 ChD 252, CA; *Re Leeks* [1902] 2 IR 339.
7   See the judgment of Vaughan Williams J in *Re Wilson, ex p Lord Hastings* (1893) 10 Morr 219 at 226 et seq.
8   *Brocklehurst v Lawe* (1857) 7 E & B 176; *Railton v Wood* (1890) 15 App Cas 363, PC. Cf *Re Collins* (1888) 21 LR Ir 508. Goods of undertenants and lodgers are, however, protected by the Law of Distress Amendment Act 1908: see LANDLORD AND TENANT vol 62 (2012) PARA 326 et seq. As from a day to be appointed the Law of Distress Amendment Act 1908 is repealed by the Tribunals, Courts and Enforcement Act 2007 Sch 14 para 20, Sch 23 Pt 4. At the date at which this volume states the law no such day had been appointed.
9   *Re Stephenson, ex p Stephenson* (1847) De G 586. A person who, at the creditor's request, pays out a distress, after and even with notice of the bankruptcy, may be entitled to claim recoupment out of the estate before the creditors receive a dividend: *Re Humphreys, ex p Kennard* (1870) 21 LT 684; *Re Ayshford, ex p Lovering* (1887) 4 Morr 164. See also *Re Craig & Sons, ex p Hinchcliffe* [1916] 2 KB 497.
10 *Re Suffield and Watts, ex p Brown* (1888) 20 QBD 693, CA.

713. Landlord's rights against execution creditor. The following provisions have effect until a day to be appointed[1].

Where in the case of any execution:

(1)   a landlord is entitled under the Landlord and Tenant Act 1709[2] or the County Courts Act 1984[3] to claim for an amount not exceeding one year's rent; and

(2)   the person against whom the execution is levied is adjudged bankrupt before the notice of claim is served on the enforcement officer or other officer charged with the execution,

the right of the landlord so to claim is restricted to a right to claim for an amount not exceeding six months' rent and does not extend to any rent payable in respect of a period after the notice of claim is so served[4].

Nothing in the above provisions imposes any liability on an enforcement officer or other officer charged with an execution to account to the official receiver or the trustee of a bankrupt's estate for any sums paid by him to a landlord at any time before the enforcement officer or other officer was served with notice of the bankruptcy order in question[5].

1   As from a day to be appointed the Insolvency Act 1986 s 347(6), (7), the Landlord and Tenant Act 1709 s 1 and the County Courts Act 1984 s 102 are repealed by the Tribunals, Courts and Enforcement Act 2007 ss 62(3), 86, 146, Sch 13 paras 68, 76, Sch 14 paras 2, 44, Sch 23 Pts 3, 4. At the date at which this volume states the law no such day had been appointed.
2   Ie under the Landlord and Tenant Act 1709 s 1 (prospectively repealed: see note 1): see LANDLORD AND TENANT vol 62 (2012) PARA 387.
3   Ie under the County Courts Act 1984 s 102 (prospectively repealed: see note 1): see LANDLORD AND TENANT vol 62 (2012) PARA 388.
4   Insolvency Act 1986 s 347(6) (amended by the Courts Act 2003 s 109(1), Sch 8 para 298; prospectively repealed (see note 1)). As to the application of the Insolvency Act 1986 s 347 in the case of the administration in bankruptcy of the insolvent estate of a deceased person dying before the presentation of a bankruptcy petition see PARA 711 note 4.
5   Insolvency Act 1986 s 347(7) (amended by the Courts Act 2003 s 109(1), Sch 8 para 298; prospectively repealed (see note 1)). The Insolvency Act 1986 s 347(7) is without prejudice to the liability of the landlord: s 347(7) (prospectively repealed: see note 1).

714. Landlord's claim against enforcement officer. Where an enforcement officer has seized and sold goods of a debtor in pursuance of a writ of execution in respect of a judgment for a sum exceeding £1,000, and during the 14 days for which he is obliged to hold the proceeds he receives notice of a bankruptcy order made against the debtor, the claim of the official receiver or trustee to the proceeds of sale[1] will be postponed to the landlord's claim against the enforcement officer for rent[2].

Under this provision the landlord may claim from the enforcement officer only rent which accrued due at the time of the taking of the goods in execution, not that which accrued afterwards[3].

1	Ie under the Insolvency Act 1986 s 346(3): see PARA 703.

2	*Re Mackenzie, ex p Sheriff of Hertfordshire* [1899] 2 QB 566, CA. It appears that the same rule will apply where the goods seized under an execution have not been sold, but remain in the enforcement officer's hands, and the official receiver makes a claim under the Insolvency Act 1986 s 346(2) (cited in PARA 704): see *Re Mackenzie, ex p Sheriff of Hertfordshire* at 576. The money which has to be paid to the trustee in bankruptcy is the proceeds of the execution proper, which can only be ascertained after the execution creditor has paid the landlord the amount payable in respect of rent under the Landlord and Tenant Act 1709 (see LANDLORD AND TENANT vol 62 (2012) PARA 387), and the money so paid has been repaid out of the proceeds of the sale to the execution creditor: *Re Craig & Sons, ex p Hinchcliffe* [1916] 2 KB 497. Should the enforcement officer pay over to the trustee in bankruptcy the proceeds of sale without deducting what he has paid to the landlord, the court will make the trustee do what is right and order him to repay the amount to the execution creditor: *Re Craig & Sons, ex p Hinchcliffe*. See also *Re Driver, ex p Sheriff of Lancashire* (1899) 43 Sol Jo 705, CA (where the sheriff sold for the official receiver).

	In short, the express provisions of the Landlord and Tenant Act 1709 in favour of the landlord are not interfered with by the Insolvency Act 1986, except to the extent provided by s 347(6) (see PARA 713). The Landlord and Tenant Act 1709 s 1 does not apply to executions in the county court, which, where there is a claim by the landlord, are regulated by the County Courts Act 1984 s 102: see CIVIL PROCEDURE vol 12 (2009) PARA 1353; LANDLORD AND TENANT vol 62 (2012) PARA 388. As to the prospective repeal of the Insolvency Act 1986 s 347(6), the Landlord and Tenant Act 1709 s 1 and the County Courts Act 1984 s 102 see PARA 713 note 1.

3	*Re Davis, ex p Pollen's Trustees* (1885) 3 Morr 27.

715. Charge for preferential debts. Where any person, whether or not a landlord or person entitled to rent, has distrained on the goods or effects of an individual who is adjudged bankrupt before the end of the period of three months beginning with the distraint, so much of those goods or effects, or of the proceeds of their sale, as is not held for the bankrupt[1] is charged for the benefit of the bankrupt's estate with the preferential debts[2] of the bankrupt to the extent that the bankrupt's estate is for the time being insufficient for meeting those debts[3].

Where, by virtue of any such charge, any person surrenders any goods or effects to the trustee of a bankrupt's estate or makes a payment to such a trustee, that person ranks, in respect of the amount of the proceeds of sale of those goods or effects by the trustee or, as the case may be, the amount of the payment, as a preferential creditor of the bankrupt, except as against so much of the bankrupt's estate as is available for the payment of preferential creditors by virtue of the surrender or payment[4].

1	Ie under the Insolvency Act 1986 s 347(2): see PARA 711.
2	As to preferential debts see PARA 591 et seq.
3	Insolvency Act 1986 s 347(3). As from a day to be appointed, s 347(3) is amended by the Enterprise and Regulatory Reform Act 2013 s 71, Sch 19 paras 1, 40: see PARA 130 note 17.

As to the application of the Insolvency Act 1986 s 347 in the case of the administration in bankruptcy of the insolvent estate of a deceased person dying before the presentation of a bankruptcy petition see PARA 711 note 4.

4 Insolvency Act 1986 s 347(4).

716. No distress after discharge. Until a day to be appointed[1], a landlord or other person to whom rent is payable is not at any time after the discharge of a bankrupt[2] entitled to distrain on any goods or effects comprised in the bankrupt's estate[3].

1 As from a day to be appointed the Insolvency Act 1986 s 347(5) is amended by the Tribunals, Courts and Enforcement Act 2007 s 86, Sch 14 para 44 to provide as follows: CRAR (the power of commercial rent arrears recovery under the Tribunals, Courts and Enforcement Act 2007 s 72(1)) is not exercisable at any time after the discharge of a bankrupt against any goods or effects comprised in the bankrupt's estate. At the date at which this volume states the law no such day had been appointed. See LANDLORD AND TENANT vol 62 (2012) PARA 288.
2 As to discharge from bankruptcy see PARA 629 et seq.
3 Insolvency Act 1986 s 347(5). As to the application of s 347 in the case of the administration in bankruptcy of the insolvent estate of a deceased person dying before the presentation of a bankruptcy petition see PARA 711 note 4.

717. Agreements regarding distress. Where a landlord has agreed to accept a reduced rent if paid punctually and there is a default, his right to distrain for the original rent in the bankruptcy will revive[1].

By agreeing with the tenant after the commencement of his bankruptcy not to distrain, but to take over the goods at a valuation, the landlord cannot become entitled to retain more than six months' rent as against the trustee[2].

1 *Re Smith and Hartogs, ex p Official Receiver* (1895) 2 Mans 400. As to the prospective abolition of the right to distrain see the Tribunals, Courts and Enforcement Act 2007 s 71; PARA 711; and LANDLORD AND TENANT vol 62 (2012) PARA 283.
2 *Re Griffith, ex p Official Receiver* (1897) 4 Mans 217, DC; but see *Re Wilson, ex p Lord Hastings* (1893) 10 Morr 219 (where in special circumstances the landlord was allowed to retain more than six months' rent as against the value of growing crops and other things taken over at a valuation). As to the commencement of bankruptcy see PARA 209.

718. Persons possessing right of distress. The persons to whom the above provisions give priority by way of a right to distrain[1] include not only landlords in the ordinary sense of the term, but also any person who stands in a position analogous to that of a landlord in relation to a person by whom that which is called rent is payable[2].

Thus, a mortgagee to whom the mortgagor has attorned tenant would, where the attornment clause is valid, have a right of distress for rent payable under that clause; but, in effect, owing to certain statutory provisions[3], the exercise of the right of distress by a mortgagee has become practically obsolete[4].

It is no objection that the rent varies from time to time, for example, the arrears payable under a building society's mortgage[5]; or that the mortgagor has already attorned tenant to a prior mortgagee[6].

1 See PARAS 711–715. As to the prospective abolition of the right to distrain see the Tribunals, Courts and Enforcement Act 2007 s 71; PARA 711; and LANDLORD AND TENANT vol 62 (2012) PARA 283.
2 See the Insolvency Act 1986 s 347(1); and *Re Roberts, ex p Hill* (1877) 6 ChD 63, CA.
3 Ie the Bills of Sale Act 1878 s 6: see FINANCIAL SERVICES AND INSTITUTIONS vol 50 (2008) PARA 1652. Where the attornment clause in a mortgage deed is not affected by the Bills of Sale Act 1878, its validity will depend on whether there was a real tenancy at a real and fair rent, or whether it was a sham tenancy and the transaction a device to give the mortgagee, in case of bankruptcy, a security over chattels which belong to the creditors generally. Cf *Re Thompson, ex p Williams* (1877) 7 ChD 138, CA (where the mortgage debt was £55,000, and the

mortgagor attorned tenant at the rent of £20,000 a year, about seven times the letting value of the premises) and *Re Bowes, ex p Jackson* (1880) 14 ChD 725, CA (where the mortgage debt was £7,090 and the rent £8,000), with *Re Stockton Iron Furnace Co* (1879) 10 ChD 335, CA; *Re Knight, ex p Voisey* (1882) 21 ChD 442, CA (where the rent fluctuated in amount). There may be an attornment to more than one mortgagee: *Re Kitchin, ex p Punnett* (1880) 16 ChD 226, CA. An attornment clause will not deprive the mortgagee of his right as a mortgagee to fixtures affixed to the premises after the mortgage: *Re Kitchin, ex p Punnett*.

The proceeds of a distress under such a clause may be applied to payment of principal as well as interest, even though the yearly rent is equal in amount to the interest on the debt: *Re Betts, ex p Harrison* (1881) 18 ChD 127, CA.

Where the parties agreed that a tenancy from year to year should be created, but that the mortgagee should have a right to determine it at any time, it was not thereby made a tenancy at will so as to be determined by liquidation proceedings on the part of the mortgagor under the Bankruptcy Act 1869 s 125 (repealed): *Re Threlfall, ex p Queen's Benefit Building Society* (1880) 16 ChD 274, CA; and see MORTGAGE vol 77 (2010) PARA 343.

4   *Re Willis, ex p Kennedy* (1888) 21 QBD 384, CA.
5   *Re Knight, ex p Voisey* (1882) 21 ChD 442, CA.
6   *Re Kitchin, ex p Punnett* (1880) 16 ChD 226, CA.

719.   Distraint otherwise than for rent.   Subject to the provisions relating to individual voluntary arrangements[1], nothing in the Insolvency Act 1986[2] affects any right to distrain otherwise than for rent; and any such right is at any time exercisable without restriction against property comprised in the bankrupt's estate, even if that right is expressed by any enactment to be exercisable in like manner as a right to distrain for rent[3].

1   Ie subject to the Insolvency Act 1986 ss 252(2)(b), 254(1): see PARAS 45, 47.
2   Ie the Insolvency Act 1986 Pts 7A–11 (ss 251A–385).
3   Insolvency Act 1986 s 347(8) (amended by the Insolvency Act 2000 Sch 3 paras 1, 14). As to the application of the Insolvency Act 1986 s 347 in the case of the administration in bankruptcy of the insolvent estate of a deceased person dying before the presentation of a bankruptcy petition see PARA 711 note 4.

H.   APPRENTICESHIPS

720.   Apprenticeships; articled clerks.   Where a bankruptcy order is made in respect of an individual[1] to whom another individual was an apprentice or articled clerk at the time when the petition on which the order was made was presented[2], and the bankrupt or the apprentice or clerk gives notice to the trustee terminating the apprenticeship or articles, then, subject to the provisions mentioned below[3], the indenture of apprenticeship or, as the case may be, the articles of agreement are discharged with effect from the commencement of the bankruptcy[4].

If any money has been paid by or on behalf of the apprentice or clerk to the bankrupt as a fee, the trustee may, on an application made by or on behalf of the apprentice or clerk, pay such sum to the apprentice or clerk as the trustee thinks reasonable, having regard to:

(1)   the amount of the fee;
(2)   the proportion of the period in respect of which the fee was paid that has been served by the apprentice or clerk before the commencement of the bankruptcy; and
(3)   the other circumstances of the case[5].

The power of the trustee so to make a payment has priority over his obligation to distribute the bankrupt's estate[6]; but, instead of making such a payment, the trustee may, if it appears to him expedient to do so on an application made by or on behalf of the apprentice or clerk, transfer the indenture or articles to a person other than the bankrupt[7]. Where a transfer is so made, the above provisions[8] regarding the effective date of discharge have effect only as between the apprentice or clerk and the bankrupt[9].

If, on an application made to him in writing by an employee, the Secretary of State is satisfied that the employer of that employee has become insolvent, the employee's employment has been terminated and on the appropriate date the employee was entitled to be paid the whole or part of any reasonable sum by way of reimbursement of the whole or part of any fee or premium paid by the apprentice or articled clerk, the Secretary of State must pay the employee out of the National Insurance Fund[10] the amount to which, in the opinion of the Secretary of State, the employee is entitled in respect of that fee or premium[11].

1   See PARA 198 et seq. It appears to be sufficient if the bankrupt has been paid the fee, and the agreement has been made, even though it has not been embodied in an indenture or articles: *Re Donkin, ex p Haynes* (1826) 2 Gl & J 122.

2   See PARA 130 et seq.

3   Ie subject to the Insolvency Act 1986 s 348(6): see the text to notes 8, 9.

4   Insolvency Act 1986 s 348(1), (2). As from a day to be appointed, s 348(1) is amended by the Enterprise and Regulatory Reform Act 2013 s 71, Sch 19 paras 1, 41: see PARA 130 note 17.
    In the case of the administration in bankruptcy of the insolvent estate of a deceased person dying before the presentation of a bankruptcy petition, the Insolvency Act 1986 s 348 applies: Administration of Insolvent Estates of Deceased Persons Order 1986, SI 1986/1999, art 3(1), Sch 1 Pt II para 28. As to the administration in bankruptcy of the insolvent estates of deceased persons see further PARA 830 et seq.

5   Insolvency Act 1986 s 348(3).

6   See PARA 587 et seq.

7   Insolvency Act 1986 s 348(4), (5).

8   Ie the Insolvency Act 1986 s 348(2).

9   Insolvency Act 1986 s 348(6).

10 As to the National Insurance Fund see SOCIAL SECURITY AND PENSIONS vol 44(2) (Reissue) PARA 8.

11 See the Employment Rights Act 1996 ss 182, 184(1)(e); and EMPLOYMENT vol 39 (2009) PARA 557.

I. LIENS ON BOOKS

721. Unenforceability of liens on books etc. A lien or other right to retain possession of any books, papers or other records of a bankrupt is unenforceable to the extent that its enforcement would deny possession of any books, papers or other records to the official receiver or the trustee of the bankrupt's estate[1]; but this provision does not apply to a lien on documents which give a title to property and are held as such[2].

1   Insolvency Act 1986 s 349(1). A trustee in bankruptcy will be entitled to overreach a solicitor's lien over the papers and records of the bankrupt: *Re Aveling Barford Ltd* [1988] 3 All ER 1019, [1989] 1 WLR 360.
    In the case of the administration in bankruptcy of the insolvent estate of a deceased person dying before the presentation of a bankruptcy petition, the Insolvency Act 1986 s 349 applies: Administration of Insolvent Estates of Deceased Persons Order 1986, SI 1986/1999, art 3(1), Sch 1 Pt II para 28. As to the administration in bankruptcy of the insolvent estates of deceased persons see further PARA 823 et seq.

2   Insolvency Act 1986 s 349(2). As to the meaning of 'documents which give a title to property and are held as such' see *Re SEIL Trade Finance Ltd* [1992] BCC 538.

(iii) Disqualification of, and Prohibitions on, Bankrupt

A. DISQUALIFICATION FROM OFFICE

722. Disqualification from Parliament. Before 2004 an individual was disqualified from sitting or voting in Parliament or being elected to the House of Commons if he was adjudged bankrupt[1]. However, since that date only a person in respect of whom a bankruptcy restrictions order[2] or a debt relief restrictions order[3] has effect is disqualified (1) from membership of the House of Commons; (2) from sitting or voting in the House of Lords; and (3) from sitting or voting in a committee of the House of Lords or a joint committee of both Houses[4].

If a member of the House of Commons becomes so disqualified, his seat must be vacated[5], and if a person who is so disqualified is returned as a member of the House of Commons, his return is void[6]. No writ of summons may be issued to a member of the House of Lords who is so disqualified[7].

If a court makes a bankruptcy restrictions order or interim order, or a debt relief restrictions order or an interim debt relief restrictions order[8], in respect of a member of the House of Commons or the House of Lords the court must notify the Speaker[9] of that House[10]. If the Secretary of State accepts a bankruptcy restrictions undertaking or a debt relief restrictions undertaking[11] made by a member of the House of Commons or the House of Lords, the Secretary of State must notify the Speaker of that House[12].

An enactment[13] about insolvency applies in relation to a member of the House of Commons or the House of Lords irrespective of any Parliamentary privilege[14].

1 See the Insolvency Act 1986 s 427 (as originally enacted). However, where a court in Scotland awards sequestration of an individual's estate, the individual is still disqualified for sitting or voting in the House of Lords, for being elected to, or sitting or voting in, the House of Commons and for sitting or voting in a committee of either House until discharged or on the recall or reduction of the award: see s 427 (amended by the Enterprise Act 2002 ss 266(2)(a), 278(2), Sch 26; the Scotland Act 1998 s 125(1), Sch 8 para 23; the Government of Wales Act 1998 s 125, Sch 12 para 24; the Government of Wales Act 2006 s 160(1), Sch 10 para 18; the Northern Ireland Act 1998 s 99, Sch 13 para 6; and SI 2012/1544). If a Member of the House of Commons remains disqualified for more than six months the seat is vacated: see the Insolvency Act 1986 s 427(4) (amended by SI 2012/1544). These restrictions apply also to members of the Scottish Parliament, the National Assembly for Wales and the Northern Ireland Assembly: see the Insolvency Act 1986 s 147(6A), (6B), (6C) (as so amended).
2 As to bankruptcy restrictions orders see PARA 657 et seq.
3 As to debt relief restrictions orders see PARA 125.
4 Insolvency Act 1986 s 426A(1) (ss 426A–426C added by the Enterprise Act 2002 s 266(1); the Insolvency Act 1986 s 426A(1) amended by the Tribunals, Courts and Enforcement Act 2007 s 108(3), Sch 20 para 12).
5 Insolvency Act 1986 s 426A(2) (as added: see note 4).
6 Insolvency Act 1986 s 426A(3) (as added: see note 4).
7 Insolvency Act 1986 s 426A(4) (as added: see note 4).
8 As to interim bankruptcy restrictions orders see PARA 663 et seq. As to interim debt relief restrictions orders see PARA 126.
9 As to the Speakers of the House of Commons and the House of Lords see PARLIAMENT vol 78 (2010) PARAS 850 et seq, 931 et seq.
10 Insolvency Act 1986 s 426A(5) (as added (see note 4); and amended by the Tribunals, Courts and Enforcement Act 2007 Sch 20 para 12). If a court in England and Wales makes a bankruptcy restrictions order or interim order in respect of a member of the Scottish Parliament, the Northern Ireland Assembly or the National Assembly for Wales, or makes a debt relief restrictions order or interim debt relief restrictions order in respect of such a member, the court must notify the presiding officer of that body: Insolvency Act 1986 s 426B(1) (as added (see note 4); and amended by the Tribunals, Courts and Enforcement Act 2007 Sch 20 para 13; and SI 2012/1544). If the High Court in Northern Ireland makes a bankruptcy restrictions order or interim order under the Insolvency (Northern Ireland) Order 1989, SI 1989/2405, Sch 2A, in

respect of a member of the Scottish Parliament or the National Assembly for Wales, the court must notify the presiding officer of that body: Insolvency Act 1986 s 426B(1A) (added by SI 2012/1544). As to the Scottish Parliament, the National Assembly for Wales and the Northern Ireland Assembly see CONSTITUTIONAL LAW AND HUMAN RIGHTS.

11 As to bankruptcy restrictions undertakings see PARAS 668–670. As to debt relief restrictions undertakings see PARA 127.

12 Insolvency Act 1986 s 426A(6) (as added (see note 4); and amended by the Tribunals, Courts and Enforcement Act 2007 Sch 20 para 12). If the Department of Enterprise, Trade and Investment for Northern Ireland accepts a bankruptcy restrictions undertaking made by a member of the House of Commons or the House of Lords under the Insolvency (Northern Ireland) Order 1989, SI 1989/2405, Sch 2A, the Department must notify the Speaker of that House: Insolvency Act 1986 s 426A(7), (8) (added by SI 2012/1544). If the Secretary of State accepts a bankruptcy restrictions undertaking or a debt relief restrictions undertaking made by a member of the Scottish Parliament, the Northern Ireland Assembly or the National Assembly for Wales, the Secretary of State must notify the presiding officer of that body: Insolvency Act 1986 s 426B(2) (as added (see note 4); and amended by the Tribunals, Courts and Enforcement Act 2007 Sch 20 para 13). If the Department of Enterprise, Trade and Investment for Northern Ireland accepts a bankruptcy restrictions undertaking made by a member of the Scottish Parliament or the National Assembly for Wales under the Insolvency (Northern Ireland) Order 1989, SI 1989/2405, Sch 2A, the Department must notify the presiding officer of that body: Insolvency Act 1986 s 426B(3) (added by SI 2012/1544).

13 'Enactment' includes a provision made by or under an Act of the Scottish Parliament or Northern Ireland legislation: Insolvency Act 1986 s 426C(2) (as added: see note 4).

14 Insolvency Act 1986 s 426C(1) (as added: see note 4). As to these privileges see PARLIAMENT vol 78 (2010) PARA 1076 et seq.

723. Local government disqualification. A person is disqualified for being elected or being a member of a local authority if he is the subject of a bankruptcy restrictions order or an interim bankruptcy restrictions order[1], or a debt relief restrictions order or interim debt relief restrictions order[2].

A person who is adjudged bankrupt is disqualified for being elected to or holding the office of Lord Mayor, alderman or common councilman of the City of London[3]; and such disqualification ceases on his discharge from bankruptcy or, if the bankruptcy order is previously annulled, on the date of its annulment[4]. Where a person is adjudged bankrupt while holding any of those offices, his office immediately becomes vacant[5].

A person is disqualified for being elected or being the Mayor or a member of the London Assembly if he is the subject of a bankruptcy restrictions order or an interim bankruptcy restrictions order, or a debt relief restrictions order or interim debt relief restrictions order[6].

An election may be questioned on the ground that the person whose election is questioned was, at the time of the election, disqualified; and may not be so questioned except by an election petition[7]. The continuance in office of a disqualified person may be challenged by proceedings for judicial review for an order restraining such person from acting and a declaration that the office is vacant[8].

1 As to bankruptcy restrictions orders and interim bankruptcy restrictions orders see PARA 657 et seq.

2 See the Local Government Act 1972 s 80(1)(b) (substituted by the Enterprise Act 2002 s 267(1)); and LOCAL GOVERNMENT vol 69 (2009) PARA 119. As to debt relief restrictions orders and interim debt relief restrictions orders see PARA 125 et seq.

3 City of London Municipal Elections Act 1849 s 8B(1) (added by the Statute Law (Repeals) Act 1989 s 1(2), Sch 2 para 1).

4 City of London Municipal Elections Act 1849 s 8B(2) (added by the Statute Law (Repeals) Act 1989 Sch 2 para 1).

5 City of London Municipal Elections Act 1849 s 8B(3) (added by the Statute Law (Repeals) Act 1989 Sch 2 para 1).

6   See the Greater London Authority Act 1999 s 21(1)(c) (substituted by SI 2006/1722; and amended by SI 2012/2404); and LONDON GOVERNMENT vol 71 (2013) PARA 74.
7   See the Representation of the People Act 1983 s 127; and ELECTIONS AND REFERENDUMS vol 15(4) (2007 Reissue) PARA 760.
8   Ie under CPR Pt 54: see JUDICIAL REVIEW vol 61 (2010) PARA 662; CIVIL PROCEDURE vol 12 (2009) PARA 1530. As to judicial review generally see JUDICIAL REVIEW vol 61 (2010) PARA 601 et seq.

724. Other disqualifications of undischarged bankrupt. A person adjudged bankrupt is disqualified for:

(1)   being a charity trustee or trustee for a charity[1];

(2)   being a trustee of a pension scheme[2];

(3)   being appointed as superintendent registrar or registrar of births and deaths or registrar of marriages[3];

(4)   being appointed as donee of a lasting power of attorney in relation to the donor's property and affairs[4];

(5)   engaging in estate agency work of any description except as an employee of another person[5];

(6)   being appointed as a member of a regional flood and coastal committee[6];

(7)   holding a consumer credit licence[7];

(8)   acting as account manager of an account held under the Individual Savings Account Regulations 1998[8];

(9)   exercising the right to buy council property[9];

(10) acting as a fiscal representative for an aircraft operator[10];

(11) holding a public service vehicle operators' licence or road service licence[11];

(12) holding a premises licence[12] or a licence under the Gambling Act 2005[13];

(13) being chairman of a land tribunal[14].

1   See the Charities Act 2011 s 178(1)(b); and CHARITIES vol 8 (2010) PARA 273. A person subject to a bankruptcy restrictions order or an interim order (see PARA 657 et seq) may also not act as trustee (see s 178(1)(b)); nor may a person subject to a moratorium period under a debt relief order under the Insolvency Act 1986 Pt 7A (ss 251A–251X) (see PARA 101 et seq) or to a debt relief restrictions order or interim order under Sch 4ZB (see PARA 125 et seq) (see the Charities Act 2011 s 178(1)(g); and CHARITIES vol 8 (2010) PARA 273).
2   See the Pensions Act 1995 s 29(1)(b); and PERSONAL AND OCCUPATIONAL PENSIONS vol 80 (2013) PARA 218. A person subject to a bankruptcy restrictions order or an interim order (see PARA 657 et seq) may also not act as trustee (see s 29(1)(b)); nor may a person subject to a moratorium period under a debt relief order under the Insolvency Act 1986 Pt 7A (ss 251A–251X) (see PARA 101 et seq) or to a debt relief restrictions order or interim order under Sch 4ZB (see PARA 125 et seq) (see the Pensions Act 1995 s 29(1)(ba); and PERSONAL AND OCCUPATIONAL PENSIONS vol 80 (2013) PARA 218).
3   See the Registration of Births, Deaths and Marriages Regulations 1968, SI 1968/2049, reg 5(a)(i); and REGISTRATION CONCERNING THE INDIVIDUAL vol 88 (2012) PARA 340. A person subject to a bankruptcy restrictions order or an interim order (see PARA 657 et seq) may also not be appointed (see reg 5(a)(i)); nor may a person subject to a moratorium period under a debt relief order under the Insolvency Act 1986 Pt 7A (ss 251A–251X) (see PARA 101 et seq) or to a debt relief restrictions order or interim order under Sch 4ZB (see PARA 125 et seq) (see the Registration of Births, Deaths and Marriages Regulations 1968, SI 1968/2049, reg 5(a)(ia); and REGISTRATION CONCERNING THE INDIVIDUAL vol 88 (2012) PARA 340).
4   See the Mental Capacity Act 2005 s 10(2); and AGENCY vol 1 (2008) PARA 218. This restriction also applies to an individual in respect of whom a debt relief order under the Insolvency Act 1986 Pt 7A (ss 251A–251X) (see PARA 101 et seq) has been made: see the Mental Capacity Act 2005 s 10(2); and AGENCY vol 1 (2008) PARA 218.

5   See the Estate Agents Act 1979 s 23(1); and AGENCY vol 1 (2008) PARA 244. This restriction also
    applies to an individual in respect of whom a debt relief order under the Insolvency Act 1986
    Pt 7A (ss 251A–251X) (see PARA 101 et seq) has been made: see the Estate Agents Act 1979
    s 23(1A); and AGENCY vol 1 (2008) PARA 244.

6   See the Regional Flood and Coastal Committees (England and Wales) Regulations 2011,
    SI 2011/695, reg 11(1)(a), (2)(a); and WATER AND WATERWAYS.

7   See the Consumer Credit Act 1974 s 37(1)(b); and CONSUMER CREDIT vol 21 (2011) PARA 45.
    This restriction also applies to an individual in respect of whom a debt relief order under the
    Insolvency Act 1986 Pt 7A (ss 251A–251X) (see PARA 101 et seq) has been made: see the
    Consumer Credit Act 1974 s 37(1)(b); and CONSUMER CREDIT vol 21 (2011) PARA 45.

8   See the Individual Savings Account Regulations 1998, SI 1998/1870, reg 20(1)(b); and INCOME
    TAXATION vol 23(2) (Reissue) PARA 1208. This restriction also applies to an individual in respect
    of whom a debt relief order under the Insolvency Act 1986 Pt 7A (see PARA 101 et seq) has been
    made: see the Individual Savings Account Regulations 1998, SI 1998/1870, reg 20(1)(ba); and
    INCOME TAXATION vol 23(2) (Reissue) PARA 1208.

9   See the Housing Act 1985 s 121(2)(c); and LANDLORD AND TENANT vol 64 (2012) PARA 1929.
    This restriction also applies if the person has a bankruptcy petition pending against him or is a
    person in relation to whom a moratorium period under a debt relief order applies under the
    Insolvency Act 1986 Pt 7A (ss 251A–251X) (see PARA 101 et seq): see the Housing Act 1985
    s 121(2)(c), (e); and LANDLORD AND TENANT vol 64 (2012) PARA 1929.

10 See the Air Passenger Duty Regulations 1994, SI 1994/1738, reg 7(2)(d); and CUSTOMS AND
    EXCISE vol 31 (2012) PARA 837. A person subject to a bankruptcy restrictions order or an
    interim order (see PARA 657 et seq) may also not act (see reg 7(2)(d)); nor may a person who has
    a debt relief order made in respect of him under the Insolvency Act 1986 Pt 7A (see PARA 101 et
    seq) or who is the subject of a debt relief restrictions order or interim order under Sch 4ZB (see
    PARA 125 et seq): see the Air Passenger Duty Regulations 1994, SI 1994/1738, reg 7(2)(d), (da);
    and CUSTOMS AND EXCISE vol 31 (2012) PARA 837.

11 See the Public Passenger Vehicles Act 1981 s 57(2)(b); and ROAD TRAFFIC vol 90 (2011) PARA
    916. This restriction also applies to an individual in respect of whom a debt relief order under
    the Insolvency Act 1986 Pt 7A (ss 251A–251X) (see PARA 101 et seq) has been made: see the
    Public Passenger Vehicles Act 1981 s 57(2)(b); and ROAD TRAFFIC vol 90 (2011) PARA 916.

12 See the Licensing Act 2003 s 27(1), (3); and LICENSING AND GAMBLING vol 67 (2008) PARA 62.

13 See the Gambling Act 2005 ss 114(1)(c), 194(1)(c), Sch 10 para 15(1)(c), Sch 14 para 15(1)(c);
    and LICENSING AND GAMBLING vol 67 (2008) PARAS 392, 525. This restriction also applies to an
    individual in respect of whom a debt relief order under the Insolvency Act 1986 Pt 7A
    (ss 251A–251X) (see PARA 101 et seq) has been made: see the Gambling Act 2005 ss 114(1)(c),
    194(1)(c), Sch 10 para 15(1)(c), Sch 14 para 15(1)(c); and LICENSING AND GAMBLING vol 67
    (2008) PARAS 392, 525.

14 See the Agriculture Act 1947 Sch 9 para 13(4); and AGRICULTURAL LAND vol 1 (2008) PARA
    671. This restriction also applies to an individual in respect of whom a debt relief order under
    the Insolvency Act 1986 Pt 7A (ss 251A–251X) (see PARA 101 et seq) has been made: see the
    Agriculture Act 1947 Sch 9 para 13(4); and AGRICULTURAL LAND vol 1 (2008) PARA 671.

725. Review of disqualification provisions. The Secretary of State[1] may make
an order[2] in relation to a disqualification provision[3]. A 'disqualification
provision' is a provision[4] which disqualifies, whether permanently or temporarily
and whether absolutely or conditionally[5], a bankrupt[6] or a class of bankrupts
from being elected or appointed to an office or position, holding an office or
position, or becoming or remaining a member of a body[7] or group[8].

An order[9] may repeal or revoke the disqualification provision[10]. An order[11]
may amend, or modify the effect of, the disqualification provision: (1) so as to
reduce the class of bankrupts to whom the disqualification provision applies[12];
(2) so as to extend the disqualification provision to some or all individuals who
are subject to a bankruptcy restrictions regime[13]; (3) so that the disqualification
provision applies only to some or all individuals who are subject to a bankruptcy
restrictions regime[14]; (4) so as to make the application of the disqualification
provision wholly or partly subject to the discretion of a specified person, body or
group[15].

An order by virtue of head (4) may provide for a discretion to be subject to (a) the approval of a specified person or body[16]; (b) appeal to a specified person or body[17]. An order by virtue of head (4) may provide for a discretion to be subject to appeal to a specified court or tribunal; but any such order must if it relates to England and Wales, be made with the concurrence of the Lord Chief Justice of England and Wales[18].

1 For these purposes, a reference to the Secretary of State is to be treated as a reference to the Welsh Ministers in so far as it relates to a disqualification provision which is made by the Ministers, or relates to a function of the Ministers: Enterprise Act 2002 s 268(14); Government of Wales Act 2006 s 162(1), Sch 11 para 30.
2 An order under the Enterprise Act 2002 s 268 may make provision generally or for a specified purpose only, may make different provision for different purposes, and may make transitional, consequential or incidental provision: s 268(12). Such an order must be made by statutory instrument, and may not be made unless a draft has been laid before and approved by resolution of each House of Parliament: s 268(13). See the Enterprise Act 2002 (Disqualification from Office: General) Order 2006, SI 2006/1722 (amended by the Charities Act 2011 s 354(4), Sch 10; and SI 2013/686).
3 Enterprise Act 2002 s 268(1).
4 'Provision' means a provision made by an Act of Parliament passed before or in the same session as the Enterprise Act 2002, and a provision made, before or in the same session as the Enterprise Act 2002, under an Act of Parliament: s 268(11).
5 The reference to a provision which disqualifies a person conditionally includes a reference to a provision which enables him to be dismissed: Enterprise Act 2002 s 268(3).
6 'Bankrupt' means an individual: (1) who has been adjudged bankrupt by a court in England and Wales or in Northern Ireland; (2) whose estate has been sequestrated by a court in Scotland; or (3) who has made an agreement with creditors of his for a composition of debts, for a scheme of arrangement of affairs, for the grant of a trust deed or for some other kind of settlement or arrangement: Enterprise Act 2002 s 268(9).
7 'Body' includes Parliament and any other legislative body: Enterprise Act 2002 s 268(11).
8 Enterprise Act 2002 s 268(2).
9 Ie an order under the Enterprise Act 2002 s 268(1).
10 Enterprise Act 2002 s 268(4).
11 Ie an order under the Enterprise Act 2002 s 268(1).
12 Enterprise Act 2002 s 268(5)(a).
13 Enterprise Act 2002 s 268(5)(b). 'Bankruptcy restrictions regime' means an order or undertaking (1) under the Insolvency Act 1986 Sch 4A (see PARA 657 et seq); or (2) under any system operating in Scotland or Northern Ireland which appears to the Secretary of State to be equivalent to the system operating under Sch 4A: Enterprise Act 2002 s 268(10).
14 Enterprise Act 2002 s 268(5)(c).
15 Enterprise Act 2002 s 268(5)(d).
16 Enterprise Act 2002 s 268(6)(a).
17 Enterprise Act 2002 s 268(6)(b). The Secretary of State may specify himself for the purposes of head (4) or head (a) or (b): s 268(8).
18 Enterprise Act 2002 s 268(7) (amended by the Constitutional Reform Act 2005 ss 15(1), 146, Sch 4 para 305(2)). Provision made by virtue of the Enterprise Act 2002 s 268(7) is subject to any order of the Lord Chancellor under the Access to Justice Act 1999 s 56(1) (see CIVIL PROCEDURE vol 12 (2009) PARA 1658): Enterprise Act 2002 s 268(15). The Lord Chief Justice may nominate a judicial office holder (see COURTS AND TRIBUNALS vol 24 (2010) PARA 961) to exercise his functions under the Enterprise Act 2002 s 268(7): s 268(16) (added by the Constitutional Reform Act 2005 Sch 4 para 305(3)).

726. Bankruptcy of solicitors. An adjudication in bankruptcy of a solicitor or the making of a debt relief order[1] in respect of a solicitor operates immediately to suspend any practising certificate of that solicitor for the time being in force[2]. Where proceedings in bankruptcy have been taken against any solicitor, the Law Society is entitled to inspect the file of those proceedings without payment of any fee, and to be supplied with office copies of those proceedings on payment of the usual charge[3].

1   Ie under the Insolvency Act 1986 Pt 7A (ss 251A–251X) (see PARA 101 et seq).
2   See the Solicitors Act 1974 s 15(1) (amended by SI 2012/2404); and LEGAL PROFESSIONS vol 66
     (2009) PARA 901. The suspension of a practising certificate by virtue of the Solicitors Act 1974
     s 15(1) by reason of an adjudication in bankruptcy terminates if the adjudication is annulled and
     an office copy of the order annulling the adjudication is served on the Law Society: see s 16(2);
     and LEGAL PROFESSIONS vol 66 (2009) PARA 901. As to annulment of bankruptcy orders see
     PARA 620 et seq. The suspension of a practising certificate by virtue of s 15(1) by reason of the
     making of a debt relief order terminates: (1) if the debt relief order is revoked on the ground
     mentioned in the Insolvency Act 1986 s 251L(2)(c) or(d) (see PARA 115 heads (3), (4)) and a
     copy of the notice provided to the debtor under the Insolvency Rules 1986, SI 1986/1925,
     r 5A.16 (see PARA 115) is served on the Law Society or the debt relief order is revoked by the
     court under the Insolvency Act 1986 s 251M(6)(e) (see PARA 116 head (5)) and a copy of the
     court order is served on the Law Society; (2) if the debt relief order is revoked and a period of
     one year has elapsed beginning with the effective date of that order: see the Solicitors Act 1974
     s 16(2A) (added by SI 2012/2404); and LEGAL PROFESSIONS vol 66 (2009) PARA 901.
3   See the Solicitors Act 1974 s 83; and LEGAL PROFESSIONS vol 65 (2008) PARA 625.

B. PROHIBITIONS ON BANKRUPT

727. Prohibition on acting as an insolvency practitioner. A person is not
qualified to act as an insolvency practitioner if at that time: (1) he has been
adjudged bankrupt or sequestration of his estate has been awarded and, in either
case, he has not been discharged[1]; (2) a moratorium period under a debt relief
order applies in relation to him[2]; (3) a bankruptcy restrictions order[3] or a debt
relief restrictions order[4] is in force in respect of him[5]. A person who so acts in
relation to a company or an individual at a time when he is not qualified to do so
is liable to imprisonment or a fine, or to both[6].

1   See the Insolvency Act 1986 s 390(4)(a); and PARA 40. As to insolvency practitioners and their
     qualification see PARA 40; and as to the application of s 390 in the case of the administration in
     bankruptcy of the insolvent estate of a deceased person dying before the presentation of a
     bankruptcy petition see PARA 40 note 3.
2   See the Insolvency Act 1986 s 390(4)(aa); and PARA 40.
3   As to bankruptcy restrictions orders see PARA 657 et seq.
4   As to debt relief orders see PARA 101 et seq.
5   See the Insolvency Act 1986 s 390(5); and PARA 655.
6   Insolvency Act 1986 s 389(1). A person guilty of such an offence is liable on conviction on
     indictment to imprisonment for a term not exceeding two years or a fine, or to both, or on
     summary conviction to imprisonment for a term not exceeding six months or a fine not
     exceeding the statutory maximum, or to both: s 430, Sch 10. As to the statutory maximum see
     SENTENCING AND DISPOSITION OF OFFENDERS vol 92 (2010) PARA 140. Section 389 does not
     apply to the official receiver: s 389(2).

728. Prohibition on acting as receiver or manager. A person commits an
offence if he acts as receiver or manager[1] of the property of a company on behalf
of debenture holders while: (1) he is an undischarged bankrupt; (2) a
moratorium period under a debt relief order applies in relation to him[2]; or (3) a
bankruptcy restrictions order[3] or a debt relief restrictions order[4] is in force in
respect of him[5]. A person guilty of such an offence is liable to imprisonment, a
fine or both[6].

1   This prohibition does not apply to a receiver or a manager acting under an appointment made
     by the court: Insolvency Act 1986 s 31(3) (s 31 substituted by the Enterprise Act 2002 s 257(3),
     Sch 21 para 1).
2   See PARA 109.
3   As to bankruptcy restrictions orders see PARA 657 et seq.
4   As to debt relief restrictions orders see PARA 125 et seq.
5   Insolvency Act 1986 s 31(1) (as substituted (see note 1); and amended by the Tribunals, Courts
     and Enforcement Act 2007 s 108(3), Sch 20 para 2).

6   Insolvency Act 1986 s 31(2) (as substituted: see note 1. A person guilty of such an offence is
     liable on conviction on indictment to imprisonment for a term not exceeding two years or a fine,
     or to both, or on summary conviction to imprisonment for a term not exceeding six months or
     a fine not exceeding the statutory maximum, or to both: see ss 31, 430, Sch 10 (amended by the
     Enterprise Act 2002 Sch 23 para 17(a), Sch 26); and COMPANIES vol 15 (2009) PARA 1346. As to
     the statutory maximum see SENTENCING AND DISPOSITION OF OFFENDERS vol 92 (2010) PARA
     140.

729.   Prohibition on acting as director etc.   It is an offence for a person to act
as director of a company[1] or directly or indirectly to take part in or be concerned
in the promotion, formation or management of a company, without the
permission of the court, at a time when: (1) he is an undischarged bankrupt; (2) a
moratorium period under a debt relief order applies in relation to him[2]; or (3) a
bankruptcy restrictions order[3] or a debt relief restrictions order[4] is in force in
respect of him[5].

In England and Wales, the permission of the court must not be given unless
notice of intention to apply for it has been served on the official receiver; and it
is the latter's duty, if he is of opinion that it is contrary to the public interest that
the application should be granted, to attend on the hearing of the application
and oppose it[6].

A person guilty of an offence under the above provisions is liable on
conviction on indictment to imprisonment for a term not exceeding two years or
a fine, or to both, or on summary conviction to imprisonment for a term not
exceeding six months or a fine not exceeding the statutory maximum, or to
both[7]. The offence is one of strict liability[8].

1   For this purpose, 'company' includes a company incorporated outside Great Britain that has an
     established place of business in Great Britain: Company Directors Disqualification Act 1986
     s 11(4) (added by SI 2009/1941).
2   See PARA 109.
3   As to bankruptcy restrictions orders see PARA 657 et seq.
4   As to debt relief restrictions orders see PARA 125 et seq.
5   See the Company Directors Disqualification Act 1986 s 11(1) (substituted by the Enterprise
     Act 2002 s 257(3), Sch 21 para 5; and amended by the Tribunals, Courts and Enforcement
     Act 2007 s 108(3), Sch 20 para 16); and COMPANY AND PARTNERSHIP INSOLVENCY vol 17
     (2011) PARA 1082. For this purpose, the court is: (1) in the case of a person adjudged bankrupt
     or, in Scotland, whose estate was sequestrated, the court by which the person was adjudged
     bankrupt or sequestration of the person's estate was awarded; (2) in the case of a person in
     respect of whom a court made a debt relief restrictions order (under the Insolvency Act 1986
     Sch 4ZB (see PARA 125)), the court by which the order was made; and (3) in the case of any
     other person, the court to which the person would make an application under s 251M(1), if the
     person were dissatisfied as mentioned there (see PARA 116): Company Directors Disqualification
     Act 1986 s 11(2) (substituted by SI 2012/2404). As to disqualification orders generally see
     COMPANIES vol 15 (2009) PARA 1575 et seq. As to the application for permission see PARAS
     730–732.
6   See the Company Directors Disqualification Act 1986 s 11(3); and COMPANY AND PARTNERSHIP
     INSOLVENCY vol 17 (2011) PARA 1082.
7   See the Company Directors Disqualification Act 1986 s 13. As to the statutory maximum see
     SENTENCING AND DISPOSITION OF OFFENDERS vol 92 (2010) PARA 140.
8   *R v Brockley* [1994] 1 BCLC 606, [1994] BCC 131, CA.

730.   Application for permission to act as director etc.   An application by a
bankrupt[1] for permission to act as director of, or to take part or be concerned in
the promotion, formation or management of, a company[2], must be supported by
a witness statement[3] complying with the following provisions[4].

The witness statement must identify the company and specify:
(1)   the nature of its business or intended business, and the place or places
       where that business is, or is to be, carried on;

(2) in the case of a company which has not yet been incorporated, whether it is, or is to be, a private or a public company;

(3) the persons who are, or are to be, principally responsible for the conduct of its affairs, whether as directors, shadow directors, managers or otherwise;

(4) the manner and capacity in which the applicant proposes to take part or be concerned in the promotion or formation of the company or, as the case may be, its management; and

(5) the emoluments and other benefits to be obtained from the directorship[5].

The court must fix a venue[6] for the hearing of the bankrupt's application, and give notice[7] to him accordingly[8].

1   For these purposes, a reference to a bankrupt includes a reference to a person in respect of whom a bankruptcy restrictions order is in force: see the Insolvency Rules 1986, SI 1986/1925, r 6.202A (added by SI 2003/1730). As to bankruptcy restrictions orders see PARA 657 et seq.
2   Ie under the Company Directors Disqualification Act 1986 s 11: see PARA 729.
3   As to the meaning of 'witness statement' see PARA 161 note 7.
4   Insolvency Rules 1986, SI 1986/1925, r 6.203(1) (amended by SI 2010/686).
5   Insolvency Rules 1986, SI 1986/1925, r 6.203(2) (amended by SI 2010/686).
6   As to the meaning of 'venue' see PARA 46 note 22.
7   As to the mode of giving notice see PARA 808.
8   Insolvency Rules 1986, SI 1986/1925, r 6.203(5).

731.   Report of official receiver.   Not less than 28 days before the date fixed for the hearing, the bankrupt[1] must give to the official receiver and the trustee notice of the venue[2], accompanied by copies of the application and the witness statement[3]. Not less than 14 days before the date fixed for the hearing, the official receiver may file in court[4] a report of any matters which he considers ought to be drawn to the court's attention; and a copy of the report must be sent by him, as soon as reasonably practicable after it is filed, to the bankrupt and to the trustee[5]. Not later than five business days[6] before the date of the hearing, the bankrupt may file in court a notice specifying any statements in the official receiver's report which he intends to deny or dispute; if he so gives notice, he must send copies of it, not less than four days before the date of the hearing, to the official receiver and the trustee[7].

The official receiver and the trustee may appear on the hearing of the application, and may make representations and put to the bankrupt such questions as the court may allow[8].

1   For these purposes, a reference to a bankrupt includes a reference to a person in respect of whom a bankruptcy restrictions order is in force: see the Insolvency Rules 1986, SI 1986/1925, r 6.202A (added by SI 2003/1730). As to bankruptcy restrictions orders see PARA 657 et seq.
2   As to the meaning of 'venue' see PARA 46 note 22.
3   Insolvency Rules 1986, SI 1986/1925, r 6.204(1) (amended by SI 2010/686). As to the meaning of 'witness statement' see PARA 161 note 7. As to the mode of giving notice see PARA 808; and as to the application for permission see PARA 730.
4   As to the meaning of 'file in court' see PARA 57 note 13.
5   Insolvency Rules 1986, SI 1986/1925, r 6.204(2) (amended by SI 2009/642).
6   As to the meaning of 'business day' see PARA 28 note 8.
7   Insolvency Rules 1986, SI 1986/1925, r 6.204(3) (amended by SI 2010/686).
8   Insolvency Rules 1986, SI 1986/1925, r 6.204(4).

732.   Court's order on application.   If the court grants the bankrupt's[1] application for permission to act as director of, or directly or indirectly to take part in or be concerned in the promotion, formation or management of, a company², its order must specify that which by virtue of the order the bankrupt has permission to do³. The court may at the same time, having regard to any representations made by the trustee on the hearing of the application:

(1) include in the order provision varying an income payments order or an income payments agreement⁴ already in force in respect of the bankrupt; or

(2) if no income payments order is in force, make one⁵.

Whether or not the application is granted, copies of the order must be sent by the court to the bankrupt, the trustee and the official receiver⁶.

1 For these purposes, a reference to a bankrupt includes a reference to a person in respect of whom a bankruptcy restrictions order is in force: see the Insolvency Rules 1986, SI 1986/1925, r 6.202A (added by SI 2003/1730). As to bankruptcy restrictions orders see PARA 657 et seq.
2 Ie under the Company Directors Disqualification Act 1986 s 11: see PARA 729. Prior to the enactment of the Enterprise Act 2002, it was held that the policy of the legislature was strongly opposed to a bankrupt being given permission to act as a director or manager of a limited company: *Re McQuillan* (1989) 5 BCC 137.
3 Insolvency Rules 1986, SI 1986/1925, r 6.205(1) (amended by SI 2010/686).
4 As to income payments orders and agreements see PARA 462 et seq.
5 Insolvency Rules 1986, SI 1986/1925, r 6.205(2) (amended by SI 2003/1730).
6 Insolvency Rules 1986, SI 1986/1925, r 6.205(3).

(12) BANKRUPTCY OFFENCES

(i) Offences under the Insolvency Act 1986

733. In general. The following provisions¹ apply where the court has made a bankruptcy order on a bankruptcy petition²; and they apply whether or not the bankruptcy order is annulled, but proceedings for an offence may not be instituted after the annulment³.

Without prejudice to his liability in respect of a subsequent bankruptcy, the bankrupt is not guilty of an offence under the following provisions in respect of anything done after his discharge; but nothing in the Insolvency Act 1986⁴ prevents the institution of proceedings against a discharged bankrupt for an offence committed before his discharge⁵.

It is not a defence in proceedings for an offence under the following provisions that anything relied on, in whole or in part, as constituting that offence was done outside England and Wales⁶.

Proceedings for an offence under the following provisions or under the Insolvency Rules 1986⁷ may not be instituted except by the Secretary of State or by or with the consent of the Director of Public Prosecutions⁸.

1 Ie the Insolvency Act 1986 ss 350–360: see PARA 734 et seq.
2 Insolvency Act 1986 s 350(1). Section 350 is subject to s 360(3) (see PARA 747 note 4): s 350(1). As from a day to be appointed, s 350(1) is amended by the Enterprise and Regulatory Reform Act 2013 s 71, Sch 19 paras 1, 42: see PARA 130 note 17.
   In the case of the administration in bankruptcy of the insolvent estate of a deceased person dying before the presentation of a bankruptcy petition, the Insolvency Act 1986 s 350(1), (2), (4)–(6) applies: Administration of Insolvent Estates of Deceased Persons Order 1986, SI 1986/1999, art 3(1), Sch 1 Pt II para 28. As to the administration in bankruptcy of the insolvent estates of deceased persons see further PARA 830 et seq.
3 Insolvency Act 1986 s 350(2). As to the annulment of bankruptcy orders see PARA 620 et seq. The Insolvency Act 1986 s 350(2) only applies to offences under Pt 9 Ch 6 (ss 350–360) and not to a prosecution under the Company Directors Disqualification Act 1986 (see COMPANY AND PARTNERSHIP INSOLVENCY vol 17 (2011) PARA 1070 et seq) which may not be commenced after annulment: *IRC v McEntaggart* [2004] EWHC 3431 (Ch), [2006] 1 BCLC 476, [2007] BCC 260.

4 Ie nothing in the Insolvency Act 1986 Pts 7A–11 (ss 251A–385).
5 Insolvency Act 1986 s 350(3). As to discharge from bankruptcy see PARA 638 et seq. Section 350(3) is without prejudice to any provision of ss 350–360 which applies to a person in respect of whom a bankruptcy restrictions order (see PARA 657 et seq) is in force: s 350(3A) (added by the Enterprise Act 2002 s 257(3), Sch 21 para 2).
6 Insolvency Act 1986 s 350(4).
7 Ie under the Insolvency Rules 1986, SI 1986/1925.
8 Insolvency Act 1986 s 350(5). As to the Director of Public Prosecutions see CRIMINAL PROCEDURE vol 27 (2010) PARAS 23, 33 et seq.

734. Non-disclosure. The bankrupt is guilty of an offence if:
(1) he does not to the best of his knowledge[1] and belief disclose all the property comprised in his estate[2] to the official receiver or the trustee; or
(2) he does not inform the official receiver or the trustee of any disposal[3] of any property which, but for the disposal, would be so comprised, stating how, when, to whom and for what consideration the property was disposed of[4].

A person who commits such an offence is liable on conviction on indictment to imprisonment for a term not exceeding seven years or a fine, or to both, or on summary conviction to imprisonment for a term not exceeding six months or a fine not exceeding the statutory maximum, or to both[5].

A person is not, however, guilty of such an offence if he proves that, at the time of the conduct constituting the offence, he had no intent to defraud or to conceal the state of his affairs[6].

1 'Knowledge' includes the state of mind of a person who shuts his eyes to the obvious: see *James & Son Ltd v Smee* [1955] 1 QB 78 at 91, [1954] 3 All ER 274 at 278, DC per Parker J; *Westminster City Council v Croyalgrange Ltd* [1985] 1 All ER 740, DC (affd [1986] 2 All ER 353, [1986] 1 WLR 674, HL). Where a person deliberately refrains from making inquiries the result of which he may not wish to have, this can amount to knowledge: *Knox v Boyd* 1941 JC 82 at 86; *Taylor's Central Garages (Exeter) Ltd v Roper* (1951) 115 JP 445 at 449 per Devlin J; and see *Westminster City Council v Croyalgrange Ltd* and *Mallon v Allon* [1964] 1 QB 385 at 394, [1963] 3 All ER 843 at 847, DC. Mere neglect to ascertain what could have been found out by making reasonable inquiries is not tantamount to knowledge: *Taylor's Central Garages (Exeter) Ltd v Roper*; and cf *London Computator Ltd v Seymour* [1944] 2 All ER 11.
2 For these purposes, references to property comprised in the bankrupt's estate or to property possession of which is required to be delivered up to the official receiver or the trustee of the bankrupt's estate include any property which would be such property if a notice in respect of it were given under the Insolvency Act 1986 s 307 (after-acquired property: see PARA 458 et seq), s 308 (personal property and effects of bankrupt having more than replacement value: see PARA 404) or s 308A (vesting in trustee of certain tenancies: see PARA 405): s 351(a) (amended by the Housing Act 1988 s 140(1), Sch 17 para 75).
   In the case of the administration in bankruptcy of the insolvent estate of a deceased person dying before the presentation of a bankruptcy petition, the Insolvency Act 1986 s 351(a) does not apply: Administration of Insolvent Estates of Deceased Persons Order 1986, SI 1986/1999, art 3(1), Sch 1 Pt II para 28. As to the administration in bankruptcy of the insolvent estates of deceased persons see further PARA 830 et seq.
3 'Disposal' includes pledge: see *R v Juston* (1897) 61 JP 505 (decided under the Debtors Act 1869 s 11(15) (repealed)). Cf the Insolvency Act 1986 s 359(5), where references to disposing of property include pawning or pledging it: see PARA 746 note 4.
4 Insolvency Act 1986 s 353(1). Section 353(1)(b) (see head (2) in the text) does not apply to any disposal in the ordinary course of a business carried on by the bankrupt or to any payment of the ordinary expenses of the bankrupt or his family: s 353(2). As to the meaning of 'family' see PARA 211 note 8. An act is done 'in the course of a business' if it is done as part of the activities of that business: *Charles R Davidson & Co v M'Robb (or Officer)* [1918] AC 304 at 321, HL per Lord Dunedin. See also *Havering London Borough v Stevenson* [1970] 3 All ER 609, [1970] 1 WLR 1375, DC; *Wycombe Marsh Garages Ltd v Fowler* [1972] 3 All ER 248, [1972] 1 WLR 1156, DC; and see *Davies v Sumner* [1984] 3 All ER 831, [1984] 1 WLR 1301, HL. 'Business' includes a trade or profession: Insolvency Act 1986 s 436. It is not in the ordinary way of a grocer's business to dispose of goods by bill of sale: *R v Thomas* (1870) 22 LT 138.

5   Insolvency Act 1986 ss 350(6), 353(1), 430, Sch 10. As to the statutory maximum see
     SENTENCING AND DISPOSITION OF OFFENDERS vol 92 (2010) PARA 140. A bankrupt who
     conceals assets and uses them to pay personal debts can expect to receive a custodial sentence:
     R v Mungroo [1997] 25 LS Gaz R 33, CA.
6   Insolvency Act 1986 ss 352, 353(3). As to the compatibility of this provision with the Human
     Rights Act 1998 (see CONSTITUTIONAL LAW AND HUMAN RIGHTS) and as to the burden of proof
     see *A-G's Reference (No 1 of 2004), R v Edwards* [2004] EWCA Crim 1025, [2005] 4 All ER
     457, [2004] 1 WLR 2111; *Sheldrake v DPP; A-G's Reference (No 4 of 2002)* [2004] UKHL 43,
     [2005] 1 AC 264, [2005] 1 All ER 237.

735. Concealment of property. The bankrupt is guilty of an offence if:

(1)   he does not deliver up possession to the official receiver or trustee[1], or
       as the official receiver or trustee may direct, of such part of the property
       comprised in his estate[2] as is in his possession or under his control and
       possession of which he is required by law so to deliver up;

(2)   he conceals any debt due to or from him or conceals[3] any property the
       value of which is not less than the prescribed amount[4] and possession of
       which he is required to deliver up to the official receiver or trustee; or

(3)   in the 12 months before petition[5], or in the initial period[6], he did
       anything which would have been an offence under head (2) above if the
       bankruptcy order had been made immediately before he did it[7].

A person who commits such an offence is liable on conviction on indictment
to imprisonment for a term not exceeding seven years or a fine, or to both, or on
summary conviction to imprisonment for a term not exceeding six months or a
fine not exceeding the statutory maximum, or to both[8].

A person is not, however, guilty of such an offence if he proves that, at the
time of the conduct constituting the offence, he had no intent to defraud[9] or to
conceal the state of his affairs[10].

1   As to the bankrupt's obligation to deliver up possession to the trustee see the Insolvency
     Act 1986 s 312(1); and PARA 408.
2   As to property comprised in the bankrupt's estate see PARA 734 note 2.
3   The bankrupt may be convicted if he is privy to a concealment by someone else, and the
     property need not have come into his hands: *R v Evani* (1825) 1 Mood CC 70. The concealment
     must be wilful, but any secreting is enough, even though a full disclosure is made later:
     Courtivron v Meunier (1851) 6 Exch 74 (decided under 5 & 6 Vict c 122 (1842) s 32
     (repealed)).
4   For these purposes, the amount so prescribed is £1,000: Insolvency Proceedings (Monetary
     Limits) Order 1986, SI 1986/1996, art 3, Schedule Pt II (substituted by SI 2004/547). As to the
     Secretary of State's power to prescribe monetary limits see PARA 19 note 9.
5   For these purposes, a reference to the number of months or years before petition is to that
     period ending with the presentation of the bankruptcy petition: Insolvency Act 1986 s 351(c).
     As from a day to be appointed, s 351(c) is repealed by the Enterprise and Regulatory Reform
     Act 2013 s 71, Sch 19 paras 1, 43: see PARA 130 note 17.
       In the case of the administration in bankruptcy of the insolvent estate of a deceased person
     dying before the presentation of a bankruptcy petition, the Insolvency Act 1986 s 351(c) applies:
     Administration of Insolvent Estates of Deceased Persons Order 1986, SI 1986/1999, art 3(1),
     Sch 1 Pt II para 28. As to the administration in bankruptcy of the insolvent estates of deceased
     persons see further PARA 830 et seq.
6   For these purposes, 'the initial period' means the period between the presentation of the
     bankruptcy petition (see PARA 130 et seq) and the commencement of the bankruptcy (see PARA
     209): Insolvency Act 1986 s 351(b). As from a day to be appointed, s 351(b) is amended by the
     Enterprise and Regulatory Reform Act 2013 s 71, Sch 19 paras 1, 43: see PARA 130 note 17.
       In the case of the administration in bankruptcy of the insolvent estate of a deceased person
     dying before the presentation of a bankruptcy petition, the Insolvency Act 1986 s 351(b) does
     not apply: Administration of Insolvent Estates of Deceased Persons Order 1986, SI 1986/1999,
     Sch 1 Pt II para 28.
7   Insolvency Act 1986 s 354(1). As from a day to be appointed, s 354(1) is amended by the
     Enterprise and Regulatory Reform Act 2013 s 71, Sch 19 paras 1, 44: see PARA 130 note 17.

8 Insolvency Act 1986 ss 350(6), 354(1), 430, Sch 10. As to the statutory maximum see SENTENCING AND DISPOSITION OF OFFENDERS vol 92 (2010) PARA 140.
9 See PARA 734 note 6.
10 Insolvency Act 1986 ss 352, 354(1). See also PARA 734 note 6.

736. Removal of property. The bankrupt is guilty of an offence if he removes[1], or in the initial period[2] removed, any property[3] the value of which was not less than the prescribed amount[4] and possession of which he has or would have been required to deliver up to the official receiver or the trustee[5].

A person who commits such an offence is liable on conviction on indictment to imprisonment for a term not exceeding seven years or a fine, or to both, or on summary conviction to imprisonment for a term not exceeding six months or a fine not exceeding the statutory maximum, or to both[6].

A person is not, however, guilty of such an offence if he proves that, at the time of the conduct constituting the offence, he had no intent to defraud[7] or to conceal the state of his affairs[8].

1 The fact that the trustee may have recovered the property does not in any way affect the bankrupt's criminal liability: *Re Ward, ex p Monkhouse* (1879) 40 LT 296; cf *DPP v Ashley* [1955] Crim LR 565.
2 As to the meaning of 'the initial period' see PARA 735 note 6.
3 As to property comprised in the bankrupt's estate see PARA 734 note 2. As to the bankrupt's obligation to deliver up possession to the trustee see the Insolvency Act 1986 s 312(1); and PARA 408. The property removed must form part of the bankrupt's estate. As to the meaning of 'the bankrupt's estate' see PARA 211. Where a debtor executed an assignment of his property to trustees for the benefit of his creditors which was not registered, and then fraudulently removed part of the assigned stock, a prosecution after a subsequent appointment of a trustee failed because, although the assignment, being unregistered, was void against the new trustee, it was otherwise in force and accordingly, when the debtor fraudulently removed the property, it was not his but belonged to the first trustees: *R v Creese* (1874) LR 2 CCR 105. Where, however, a trustee under an assignment never receives money kept back from him by an absconding debtor, the money is the debtor's property for these purposes: *R v Humphris* [1904] 2 KB 89.
4 For these purposes, the amount so prescribed is £1,000: Insolvency Proceedings (Monetary Limits) Order 1986, SI 1986/1996, art 3, Schedule Pt II (substituted by SI 2004/547). As to the Secretary of State's power to prescribe monetary limits see PARA 19 note 9.
5 Insolvency Act 1986 s 354(2).
6 Insolvency Act 1986 ss 350(6), 354(2), 430, Sch 10. As to the statutory maximum see SENTENCING AND DISPOSITION OF OFFENDERS vol 92 (2010) PARA 140.
7 See PARA 734 note 6.
8 Insolvency Act 1986 ss 352, 354(2). See also PARA 734 note 6.

737. Loss of property. The bankrupt is guilty of an offence if he without reasonable excuse[1] fails, on being required to do so by the official receiver, the trustee or the court:

(1)   to account for the loss of any substantial part of his property[2] incurred in the 12 months before petition[3] or in the initial period[4]; or

(2)   to give a satisfactory explanation of the manner in which such a loss was incurred[5].

A person who commits such an offence is liable on conviction on indictment to imprisonment for a term not exceeding two years or a fine, or to both, or on summary conviction to imprisonment for a term not exceeding six months or a fine not exceeding the statutory maximum, or to both[6].

1 What is a reasonable excuse is primarily a question of fact: see *Leck v Epsom RDC* [1922] 1 KB 383. However, ignorance of the statutory provisions provides no reasonable excuse (see *Aldridge v Warwickshire Coal Co Ltd* (1925) 133 LT 439, CA) nor does a mistaken view of the effect of those provisions (*R v Reid (Philip)* [1973] 3 All ER 1020, [1973] 1 WLR 1283, CA).
    Quaere whether reliance on the advice of an expert can amount to a reasonable excuse: see *Saddleworth UDC v Aggregate and Sand Ltd* (1970) 69 LGR 103. Once evidence of a

reasonable excuse emerges, it is for the prosecution to eliminate the existence of that defence to the satisfaction of the court: see *R v Clarke* [1969] 2 All ER 1008, [1969] 1 WLR 1109, CA.

2   As to property comprised in the bankrupt's estate see PARA 734 note 2.

3   As to references to a number of months before petition see PARA 735 note 5.

4   As to the meaning of 'the initial period' see PARA 735 note 6.

5   Insolvency Act 1986 s 354(3) (amended by the Enterprise Act 2002 s 269, Sch 23 paras 1, 12). As from a day to be appointed, the Insolvency Act 1986 s 354(3) is amended by the Enterprise and Regulatory Reform Act 2013 s 71, Sch 19 paras 1, 44: see PARA 130 note 17.

6   Insolvency Act 1986 ss 350(6), 354(3), 430, Sch 10. As to the statutory maximum see SENTENCING AND DISPOSITION OF OFFENDERS vol 92 (2010) PARA 140. Section 354(3) creates an offence of strict liability which does not breach an accused's right to remain silent or not to incriminate himself: *R v Kearns* [2002] EWCA Crim 748, [2002] 1 WLR 2815, [2003] 1 Cr App Rep 111.

738.   Non-delivery of books and papers.   The bankrupt is guilty of an offence if he does not deliver up possession to the official receiver or the trustee[1], or as the official receiver or trustee may direct, of all books, papers and other records of which he has possession or control and which relate to his estate[2] or his affairs[3].

A person who commits such an offence is liable on conviction on indictment to imprisonment for a term not exceeding seven years or a fine, or to both, or on summary conviction to imprisonment for a term not exceeding six months or a fine not exceeding the statutory maximum, or to both[4].

A person is not, however, guilty of such an offence if he proves that, at the time of the conduct constituting the offence, he had no intent to defraud[5] or to conceal the state of his affairs[6].

1   As to the bankrupt's duty to deliver up to the trustee possession of books, papers or other records see the Insolvency Act 1986 s 312(1) (see PARA 408); and as to the trustee's duty to take possession of books, papers and other records which related to the bankrupt's estate or affairs see s 311(1) (see PARA 408).

2   As to property possession of which is required to be delivered up to the official receiver or the trustee see PARA 734 note 2.

3   Insolvency Act 1986 s 355(1). This provision extends to records kept on a computer: *R v Taylor* [2011] EWCA Crim 728, [2011] 1 WLR 1809, [2011] Bus LR 1011.

4   Insolvency Act 1986 ss 350(6), 355(1), 430, Sch 10. As to the statutory maximum see SENTENCING AND DISPOSITION OF OFFENDERS vol 92 (2010) PARA 140.

5   See PARA 734 note 6.

6   Insolvency Act 1986 ss 352, 355(1). See also PARA 734 note 6.

739.   Concealment of books and papers.   The bankrupt is guilty of an offence if:

(1)   he prevents[1], or in the initial period[2] prevented, the production of any books, papers or other records relating to his estate[3] or affairs;

(2)   he conceals, destroys, mutilates or falsifies, or causes or permits the concealment, destruction, mutilation or falsification of, any books, papers or other records relating to his estate or affairs;

(3)   he makes, or causes[4] or permits[5] the making of, any false[6] entries in any book, document or record relating to his estate or affairs; or

(4)   in the 12 months before petition[7], or in the initial period, he did anything which would have been an offence under head (2) or head (3) above if the bankruptcy order had been made before he did it[8].

A person who commits such an offence is liable on conviction on indictment to imprisonment for a term not exceeding seven years or a fine, or to both, or on summary conviction to imprisonment for a term not exceeding six months or a fine not exceeding the statutory maximum, or to both[9].

A person is not, however, guilty of such an offence if he proves that, at the time of the conduct constituting the offence, he had no intent to defraud[10] or to conceal the state of his affairs[11].

1   'Prevents' means to render impossible: see *Tenants (Lancashire) Ltd v CS Wilson & Co Ltd* [1917] AC 495 at 518, HL.
2   As to the meaning of 'the initial period' see PARA 735 note 6.
3   As to references to property possession of which is required to be delivered up to the official receiver or the trustee see PARA 734 note 2.
4   'Cause' involves some degree of dominance or control, or some express or positive mandate, from the person 'causing': *McLeod (or Houston) v Buchanan* [1940] 2 All ER 179 at 187, HL, per Lord Wright; *Shave v Rosner* [1954] 2 QB 113, [1954] 2 All ER 280; *Lovelace v DPP* [1954] 3 All ER 481, [1954] 1 WLR 1468; *Shulton (Great Britain) Ltd v Slough Borough Council* [1967] 2 QB 471, [1967] 2 All ER 137; *A-G of Hong Kong v Tse Hung-Lit* [1986] AC 876, [1986] 3 All ER 173, PC. A person cannot be said to have 'caused' another to do or omit to do something unless he either knows or deliberately chooses not to know what it is that the other is doing or failing to do: *James & Son Ltd v Smee* [1955] 1 QB 78, [1954] 3 All ER 273; *Ross Hillman Ltd v Bond* [1974] QB 435, [1974] 2 All ER 287.
5   'Permit' denotes a general or particular permission, as distinguishable from a mandate, and the permission may be express or implied: *McLeod (or Houston) v Buchanan* [1940] 2 All ER 179, HL. To permit an offence to be committed involves a knowledge of the facts constituting the offence; but shutting one's eyes to the obvious, or allowing a person to do something in circumstances where a contravention is likely, not caring whether a contravention takes place or not, is sufficient: *James & Son Ltd v Smee* [1955] 1 QB 78 at 91, [1954] 3 All ER 273 at 278 per Parker J; *Gray's Haulage Co Ltd v Arnold* [1966] 1 All ER 896, [1966] 1 WLR 534. Reasonable grounds for suspicion that the offence will be committed may be sufficient but suspicion itself is not enough: *Sweet v Parsley* [1970] AC 132, [1969] 1 All ER 347, HL; *R v Souter* [1971] 2 All ER 1151, [1971] 1 WLR 1187, CA. A person cannot permit unless he is in a position to forbid (*Goodbarne v Buck* [1940] 1 KB 771, [1940] 1 All ER 613, CA; *Lloyd v Singleton* [1953] 1 QB 357, [1953] 1 All ER 291); and no one can permit what he cannot control (*Tophams Ltd v Earl of Sefton* [1967] 1 AC 50, [1966] 1 All ER 1039, HL).
6   A statement may be false on account of what it omits, even though it is literally true: see *R v Lord Kyslant* [1932] 1 KB 442; *R v Bishirgian* [1936] 1 All ER 586; and cf *Curtis v Chemical Cleaning and Dyeing Co Ltd* [1951] 1 KB 805 at 808, 809, [1951] 1 All ER 631 at 634, CA. Whether or not gain or advantage accrues from the false statement is irrelevant: see *Jones v Meatyard* [1939] 1 All ER 140; *Stevens & Steeds Ltd and Evans v King* [1943] 1 All ER 314; *Clear v Smith* [1981] 1 WLR 399; *Barrass v Reeve* [1980] 3 All ER 705, [1981] 1 WLR 408.
7   As to references to a number of months before petition see PARA 735 note 5.
8   Insolvency Act 1986 s 355(2). As from a day to be appointed, s 355(2) is amended by the Enterprise and Regulatory Reform Act 2013 s 71, Sch 19 paras 1, 45: see PARA 130 note 17.
    In its application to a trading record, head (4) in the text has effect as if the reference to 12 months were a reference to two years: Insolvency Act 1986 s 355(4) (s 355(4), (5) added by the Enterprise Act 2002 s 269, Sch 23 para 13). 'Trading record' means a book, document or record which shows or explains the transactions or financial position of a person's business, including: (1) a periodic record of cash paid and received; (2) a statement of periodic stock-taking; and (3) except in the case of goods sold by way of retail trade, a record of goods sold and purchased which identifies the buyer and seller or enables them to be identified: Insolvency Act 1986 s 355(5).
9   Insolvency Act 1986 ss 350(6), 355(2), 430, Sch 10. As to the statutory maximum see SENTENCING AND DISPOSITION OF OFFENDERS vol 92 (2010) PARA 140.
10 See PARA 734 note 6.
11 Insolvency Act 1986 ss 352, 355(2). See also PARA 734 note 6.

740.   Falsification of books etc.   The bankrupt commits an offence if:

(1)   he disposes of, or alters or makes any omission in, or causes[1] or permits[2] the disposal, altering or making of any omission in, any book, document or record relating to his estate[3] or affairs; or

(2)   in the 12 months before petition[4], or in the initial period[5], he did anything which would have been an offence under head (1) above if the bankruptcy order had been made before he did it[6].

A person who commits such an offence is liable on conviction on indictment to imprisonment for a term not exceeding seven years or a fine, or to both, or on summary conviction to imprisonment for a term not exceeding six months or a fine not exceeding the statutory maximum, or to both[7].

A person is not, however, guilty of such an offence if he proves that, at the time of the conduct constituting the offence, he had no intent to defraud[8] or to conceal the state of his affairs[9].

1   As to the meaning of 'cause' see PARA 739 note 4.
2   As to the meaning of 'permit' see PARA 739 note 5.
3   As to references to property possession of which is required to be delivered up to the official receiver or the trustee see PARA 734 note 2.
4   As to references to a number of months before petition see PARA 735 note 5.
5   As to the meaning of 'the initial period' see PARA 735 note 6.
6   Insolvency Act 1986 s 355(3). As from a day to be appointed, s 355(3) is amended by the Enterprise and Regulatory Reform Act 2013 s 71, Sch 19 paras 1, 45: see PARA 130 note 17.
        In its application to a trading record, head (2) in the text has effect as if the reference to 12 months were a reference to two years: Insolvency Act 1986 s 355(4) (added by the Enterprise Act 2002 s 269, Sch 23 para 13). As to the meaning of 'trading record' see PARA 739 note 8.
7   Insolvency Act 1986 ss 350(6), 355(3), 430, Sch 10. As to the statutory maximum see SENTENCING AND DISPOSITION OF OFFENDERS vol 92 (2010) PARA 140.
8   See PARA 734 note 6.
9   Insolvency Act 1986 ss 352, 355(3). See also PARA 734 note 6.

741.   Material omissions.   The bankrupt is guilty of an offence if he makes or has made any material omission in any statement made under any provision of the Insolvency Act 1986[1] and relating to his affairs[2].

A person who commits such an offence is liable on conviction on indictment to imprisonment for a term not exceeding seven years or a fine, or to both, or on summary conviction to imprisonment for a term not exceeding six months or a fine not exceeding the statutory maximum, or to both[3].

A person is not, however, guilty of such an offence if he proves that, at the time of the conduct constituting the offence, he had no intent to defraud[4] or to conceal the state of his affairs[5].

1   Ie the Insolvency Act 1986 Pts 7A–11 (ss 251A–385).
2   Insolvency Act 1986 s 356(1). 'Any statement of affairs' will include a statement under s 256(2)(b) (voluntary arrangement: see PARA 55), s 272(2) (debtor's petition: see PARA 163), s 288(1) (bankruptcy petition made otherwise than on a debtor's petition: see PARA 240) and under the Insolvency Rules 1986, SI 1986/1925, rr 6.66, 6.72 (further statement amplifying, modifying or explaining any matter in statement of affairs: see PARAS 247, 251 respectively). As to the admissibility in evidence of such statements of affairs see the Insolvency Act 1986 s 433; and PARA 802.
3   Insolvency Act 1986 ss 350(6), 356(1), 430, Sch 10. As to the statutory maximum see SENTENCING AND DISPOSITION OF OFFENDERS vol 92 (2010) PARA 140.
4   See PARA 734 note 6.
5   Insolvency Act 1986 ss 352, 356(1). See also PARA 734 note 6.

742.   False statements.   The bankrupt is guilty of an offence if:

(1)   knowing or believing that a false debt has been proved by any person under the bankruptcy, he fails to inform the trustee as soon as practicable;

(2)   he attempts to account for any part of his property[1] by fictitious losses or expenses;

(3)   at any meeting of his creditors in the 12 months before petition[2] or, whether or not at such a meeting, at any time in the initial period[3], he

did anything which would have been an offence under head (2) above if the bankruptcy order had been made before he did it; or

(4) he is, or at any time has been, guilty of any false representation or other fraud for the purpose of obtaining the consent of his creditors, or any of them, to an agreement with reference to his affairs or to his bankruptcy[4].

A person who commits such an offence is liable on conviction on indictment to imprisonment for a term not exceeding seven years or a fine, or to both, or on summary conviction to imprisonment for a term not exceeding six months or a fine not exceeding the statutory maximum, or to both[5].

1   As to the property comprised in the bankrupt's estate see PARA 734 note 2.
2   As to references to a number of months before petition see PARA 735 note 5.
3   As to the meaning of 'the initial period' see PARA 735 note 6.
4   Insolvency Act 1986 s 356(2). As from a day to be appointed, s 356(2) is amended by the Enterprise and Regulatory Reform Act 2013 s 71, Sch 19 paras 1, 46: see PARA 130 note 17.
    As to the modification of the Insolvency Act 1986 s 356(2) by the Insolvent Partnerships Order 1994, SI 1994/2421, in relation to the bankruptcy of an individual member of an insolvent partnership see COMPANY AND PARTNERSHIP INSOLVENCY vol 17 (2011) PARA 1301.
5   Insolvency Act 1986 ss 350(6), 356(2), 430, Sch 10. As to the statutory maximum see SENTENCING AND DISPOSITION OF OFFENDERS vol 92 (2010) PARA 140.

743.   Fraudulent disposal of property.   The bankrupt is guilty of an offence if:

(1) he makes or causes[1] to be made, or has in the period of five years ending with the commencement of the bankruptcy[2] made or caused to be made, any gift or transfer of, or any charge on, his property[3]; or

(2) he conceals or removes, or has at any time before commencement of the bankruptcy concealed or removed, any part of his property after, or within two months before, the date on which a judgment or order for the payment of money has been obtained against him, being a judgment or order which was not satisfied before the commencement of the bankruptcy[4].

A person who commits such an offence is liable on conviction on indictment to imprisonment for a term not exceeding two years or a fine, or to both, or on summary conviction to imprisonment for a term not exceeding six months or a fine not exceeding the statutory maximum, or to both[5].

A person is not, however, guilty of such an offence if he proves that, at the time of the conduct constituting the offence, he had no intent to defraud[6] or to conceal the state of his affairs[7].

1   As to the meaning of 'cause' see PARA 739 note 4.
2   As to the commencement of bankruptcy see PARA 209.
3   As to the property comprised in the bankrupt's estate see PARA 734 note 2. For these purposes, the reference to making a transfer of or charge on any property includes causing or conniving at the levying of any execution against that property: Insolvency Act 1986 s 357(2). 'Conniving' imports knowledge together with acquiescence in the facts constituting the offence. Suspicion may, however, be enough, although mere negligence is not: *Rogers v Rogers* (1830) 3 Hag Ecc 57.
4   Insolvency Act 1986 s 357(1), (3).
5   Insolvency Act 1986 ss 350(6), 357(1), (3), 430, Sch 10. As to the statutory maximum see SENTENCING AND DISPOSITION OF OFFENDERS vol 92 (2010) PARA 140.
6   See PARA 734 note 6.
7   Insolvency Act 1986 ss 352, 357(1), (3). See also PARA 734 note 6.

744.   Absconding.   The bankrupt is guilty of an offence if:

(1) he leaves, or attempts or makes preparations to leave, England and

Wales with any property[1] the value of which is not less than the prescribed amount[2] and possession of which he is required to deliver up to the official receiver or the trustee; or

(2) in the six months before petition[3], or in the initial period[4], he did anything which would have been an offence under head (1) above if the bankruptcy order had been made immediately before he did it[5].

A person who commits such an offence is liable on conviction on indictment to imprisonment for a term not exceeding two years or a fine, or to both, or on summary conviction to imprisonment for term not exceeding six months or a fine not exceeding the statutory maximum, or to both[6].

A person is not, however, guilty of such an offence if he proves that, at the time of the conduct constituting the offence, he had no intent to defraud[7] or to conceal the state of his affairs[8].

1 As to the property comprised in the bankrupt's estate see PARA 734 note 2.
2 For these purposes, the amount so prescribed is £1,000: Insolvency Proceedings (Monetary Limits) Order 1986, SI 1986/1996, art 3, Schedule Pt II (substituted by SI 2004/547). As to the Secretary of State's power to prescribe monetary limits see PARA 19 note 9.
3 As to references to a number of months before petition see PARA 735 note 5.
4 As to the meaning of 'the initial period' see PARA 735 note 6.
5 Insolvency Act 1986 s 358; and see *R v Humphris* [1904] 2 KB 89; *R v Pitchforth* (1908) 1 Cr App Rep 249, CCA. As from a day to be appointed, s 358 is amended by the Enterprise and Regulatory Reform Act 2013 s 71, Sch 19 paras 1, 47: see PARA 130 note 17.
6 Insolvency Act 1986 ss 350(6), 358, 430, Sch 10. As to the statutory maximum see SENTENCING AND DISPOSITION OF OFFENDERS vol 92 (2010) PARA 140.
7 See PARA 734 note 6.
8 Insolvency Act 1986 ss 352, 358. See note 5. See also PARA 734 note 6.

745. Fraudulent dealing with property obtained on credit. The bankrupt is guilty of an offence if, in the 12 months before petition[1], or in the initial period[2], he disposed of any property[3] which he had obtained on credit and, at the time he disposed of it, had not paid for[4].

A person who commits such an offence is liable on conviction on indictment to imprisonment for a term not exceeding seven years or a fine, or to both, or on summary conviction to imprisonment for a term not exceeding six months or a fine not exceeding the statutory maximum, or to both[5].

A person is not, however, guilty of such an offence if:

(1) he proves that, at the time of the conduct constituting the offence, he had no intent to defraud or to conceal the state of his affairs[6]; or

(2) the disposal, acquisition or receipt of the property was in the ordinary course of a business carried on by the bankrupt at the time of the disposal, acquisition or receipt[7].

1 As to references to a number of months before petition see PARA 735 note 5.
2 As to the meaning of 'the initial period' see PARA 735 note 6.
3 As to references to property comprised in the bankrupt's estate see PARA 734 note 2.
4 Insolvency Act 1986 s 359(1). As from a day to be appointed, s 359(1) is amended by the Enterprise and Regulatory Reform Act 2013 s 71, Sch 19 paras 1, 48: see PARA 130 note 17.
     In determining for these purposes whether any property is disposed of, acquired or received in the ordinary course of a business carried on by the bankrupt, regard may be had, in particular, to the price paid for the property: Insolvency Act 1986 s 359(4). As to the meaning of 'in the ordinary course of business' see PARA 734 note 4. In s 359 references to disposing of property include pawning or pledging it; and references to acquiring or receiving property are to be construed accordingly: s 359(5).
     In the case of the administration in bankruptcy of the insolvent estate of a deceased person dying before the presentation of a bankruptcy petition, s 359(1) does not apply, but s 359(3)–(5)

does apply: Administration of Insolvent Estates of Deceased Persons Order 1986, SI 1986/1999, art 3(1), Sch 1 Pt II para 29. As to the administration in bankruptcy of the insolvent estates of deceased persons see further PARA 830 et seq.

5   Insolvency Act 1986 ss 350(6), 359(1), 430, Sch 10.' As to the statutory maximum see SENTENCING AND DISPOSITION OF OFFENDERS vol 92 (2010) PARA 140. As to the application of s 350 in the case of the administration in bankruptcy of the insolvent estate of a deceased person dying before the presentation of a bankruptcy petition see PARA 733 note 2.
6   Insolvency Act 1986 ss 352, 359(1). See PARA 734 note 6.
7   Insolvency Act 1986 s 359(3). See also note 4.

746.   Fraudulent dealing by person with bankrupt.   A person is guilty of an offence if, in the 12 months before petition[1] or in the initial period[2], he acquired or received property[3] from the bankrupt knowing or believing that the bankrupt owed money in respect of the property, and that the bankrupt did not intend, or was unlikely to be able, to pay the money he so owed[4].

A person who commits such an offence is liable on conviction on indictment to imprisonment for a term not exceeding seven years or a fine, or to both, or on summary conviction to imprisonment for a term not exceeding six months or a fine not exceeding the statutory maximum, or to both[5].

A person is not, however, guilty of such an offence if the disposal, acquisition or receipt of the property was in the ordinary course of a business carried on by the bankrupt at the time of the disposal, acquisition or receipt[6].

1   As to references to a number of months before petition see PARA 735 note 5.
2   As to the meaning of 'the initial period' see PARA 735 note 6.
3   As to the property comprised in the bankrupt's estate see PARA 734 note 2.
4   Insolvency Act 1986 s 359(2). As from a day to be appointed, s 359(2) is amended by the Enterprise and Regulatory Reform Act 2013 s 71, Sch 19 paras 1, 48: see PARA 130 note 17.
      In determining, for these purposes, whether any property is disposed of, acquired or received in the ordinary course of a business carried on by the bankrupt, regard may be had, in particular, to the price paid for the property: Insolvency Act 1986 s 359(4). As to the meaning of 'in the ordinary course of business' see PARA 734 note 4. In s 359 references to disposing of property include pawning or pledging it; and references to acquiring or receiving property are to be read accordingly: s 359(5).
      In the case of the administration in bankruptcy of the insolvent estate of a deceased person dying before the presentation of a bankruptcy petition, s 359(2)–(5) applies, save that: (1) in s 359(2) for the words 'petition or initial period' there are to be substituted the words 'the date of death of the deceased debtor'; and (2) in s 359(3) the reference to s 359(1) is to be omitted: Administration of Insolvent Estates of Deceased Persons Order 1986, SI 1986/1999, art 3(1), Sch 1 Pt II para 29. As to the administration in bankruptcy of the insolvent estates of deceased persons see further PARA 830 et seq.
5   Insolvency Act 1986 ss 350(6), 359(2), 430, Sch 10. As to the statutory maximum see SENTENCING AND DISPOSITION OF OFFENDERS vol 92 (2010) PARA 140. As to the application of s 350 in the case of the administration in bankruptcy of the insolvent estate of a deceased person dying before the presentation of a bankruptcy petition see PARA 733 note 2.
6   Insolvency Act 1986 s 359(3). See also note 4.

747.   Obtaining credit; engaging in business.   The bankrupt is guilty of an offence if:

(1)   either alone or jointly with any other person, he obtains credit[1] to the extent of the prescribed amount[2] or more without giving the person from whom he obtains it the relevant information about his status[3]; or

(2)   he engages, whether directly or indirectly, in any business under a name other than that in which he was adjudged bankrupt without disclosing to all persons with whom he enters into any business transaction the name in which he was so adjudged[4].

The offence does not require proof of dishonesty[5].

A person who commits such an offence is liable on conviction on indictment to imprisonment for a term not exceeding two years or a fine, or to both, or on summary conviction to imprisonment for a term not exceeding six months or a fine not exceeding the statutory maximum, or to both[6].

The provisions set out above[7] apply to the bankrupt after discharge while a bankruptcy restrictions order[8] is in force in respect of him[9].

1 For these purposes, the reference to the bankrupt obtaining credit includes the following cases: (1) where goods are bailed to him under a hire-purchase agreement, or agreed to be sold to him under a conditional sale agreement; and (2) where he is paid in advance, whether in money or otherwise, for the supply of goods or services: Insolvency Act 1986 s 360(2). 'Hire-purchase agreement' and 'conditional sale agreement' have the same meanings as in the Consumer Credit Act 1974 (see CONSUMER CREDIT vol 21 (2011) PARAS 64, 66): Insolvency Act 1986 s 436.

As to the application of s 436 in the case of the administration in bankruptcy of the insolvent estate of a deceased person dying before the presentation of a bankruptcy petition see PARA 20 note 6.

A bankrupt who obtains credit for a third party does not commit an offence unless the third party is a company set up for this purpose by the bankrupt: *R v Godwin* (1980) 71 Cr App Rep 97, CA. There need be no agreement to give credit if credit is in fact given: *R v Peters* (1886) 16 QBD 636. Obtaining a cheque in consideration of an immediate dispatch of goods was held not to constitute obtaining credit in *Osborn v Barton* (1949) 66 (pt 1) TLR 115, DC.

2 For these purposes, the amount so prescribed is £500: Insolvency Proceedings (Monetary Limits) Order 1986, SI 1986/1996, art 3, Schedule Pt II (substituted by SI 2004/547). As to the Secretary of State's power to prescribe monetary limits see PARA 19 note 9. The offence is 'obtaining' credit not 'ordering' credit to the extent of the prescribed amount: see *R v Juby* (1886) 55 LT 788 (where the accused, having received goods of a value under the prescribed limit which he had not ordered, then ordered more goods, bringing the aggregate debt over the prescribed limit). The prescribed amount may be reached by aggregating a series of smaller sums and, once that figure is reached, any repayments count only in mitigation of the penalty: *R v Hartley* [1972] 2 QB 1, [1972] 1 All ER 599, CA.

A contract obtained without the required disclosure by which an undischarged bankrupt becomes entitled to credit of the prescribed amount or more is unenforceable: *De Choisy v Hynes* [1937] 4 All ER 54.

3 Insolvency Act 1986 s 360(1)(a). For these purposes, the relevant information about the status of the person in question is the information that he is an undischarged bankrupt or, as the case may be, that his estate has been sequestrated in Scotland and that he has not been discharged: s 360(4).

Disclosure need not necessarily be made at the moment when credit is obtained, provided that it was made at a reasonable time before the transaction took place: *R v Zeitlin* (1932) 23 Cr App Rep 163, CCA. The obligation to disclose bankruptcy is absolute; reasonable belief that such disclosure has been made is no defence: *R v Duke of Leinster* [1924] 1 KB 311, CCA. As to discharge from bankruptcy see PARA 638 et seq.

4 Insolvency Act 1986 s 360(1)(b). As from a day to be appointed, s 360(1)(b) is amended by the Enterprise and Regulatory Reform Act 2013 s 71, Sch 19 paras 1, 49: see PARA 130 note 17.

A person whose estate has been sequestrated in Scotland or who has been adjudged bankrupt in Northern Ireland is guilty of an offence if, before his discharge, he does anything in England and Wales which would be an offence under the Insolvency Act 1986 s 360(1) if he were an undischarged bankrupt and the sequestration of his estate or the adjudication in Northern Ireland were an adjudication under Pt 9 (ss 264–371): s 360(3).

5 *R v Ramzan* [1998] 2 Cr App Rep 328, CA.

6 Insolvency Act 1986 ss 350(6), 360(1), 430, Sch 10. As to the statutory maximum see SENTENCING AND DISPOSITION OF OFFENDERS vol 92 (2010) PARA 140.

7 Ie the Insolvency Act 1986 s 360.

8 As to bankruptcy restrictions orders see PARA 657 et seq.

9 Insolvency Act 1986 s 360(5) (s 360(5), (6) added by the Enterprise Act 2002 Sch 21 para 3). For the purposes of head (1) in the text as it applies to the bankrupt after discharge while a bankruptcy restrictions order is in force in respect of him, the relevant information about his status is the information that a bankruptcy restrictions order is in force in respect of him: Insolvency Act 1986 s 360(6) (as so added).

(ii) Offences under the Debtors Act 1869

748. Offences committed by any debtor. Any person is guilty of an offence[1] and liable on conviction to imprisonment for a term not exceeding one year[2], whether or not he is insolvent[3]:

(1) if he has made or caused to be made any gift, delivery[4], or transfer[5] of, or any charge on, his property, with intent to defraud[6] his creditors[7], or any of them[8];

(2) if he has concealed or removed any part of his property since or within two months before the date of any unsatisfied judgment or order for payment of money obtained against him, with intent to defraud[9] his creditors[10].

1 The offence of obtaining credit by fraud, created by the Debtors Act 1869 s 13(1) (repealed), and by the Bankruptcy Act 1914 s 156(a) (repealed) is now covered by the offences of fraud by false representation (see the Fraud Act 2006 s 2; and CRIMINAL LAW vol 25 (2010) PARA 305 et seq), obtaining services by deception (see s 11; and CRIMINAL LAW vol 25 (2010) PARA 309) and making off without payment (see the Theft Act 1978 s 3; and CRIMINAL LAW vol 25 (2010) PARA 310).

2 Debtors Act 1869 s 13. The Criminal Law Act 1967 s 1(1) abolished the distinction between felonies and misdemeanours; and the Criminal Justice Act 1948 s 1(1) abolished the right to impose hard labour. These offences are triable either summarily or on indictment: see the Magistrates' Courts Act 1980 s 17, Sch 1 para 7; and CRIMINAL PROCEDURE vol 27 (2010) PARA 161.

3 *R v Rowlands* (1882) 8 QBD 530.

4 A debtor does not, however, commit this offence by selling part of his assets below their value, even though his creditors may be prejudiced by it: *Re Cranston, ex p Cranston* (1892) 9 Morr 160.

5 'Transfer' includes a fictitious transfer: *R v Richman* (1910) 4 Cr App Rep 233, CCA.

6 A distinction has been drawn between 'defrauding' and 'deceiving'; there may be deceit without the creditors being cheated out of anything which is what 'defraud' implies: see *R v Ingham* (1859) 8 Cox CC 240; *Re London and Globe Finance Corpn Ltd* [1903] 1 Ch 728 at 732, considered in *R v Wines* [1953] 2 All ER 1497, [1954] 1 WLR 64, CCA, and in *Welham v DPP* [1961] AC 103, [1960] 1 All ER 805, HL. See further CRIMINAL LAW.

7 The person intended to be defrauded must be an actual creditor at the time of the act, not merely a potential creditor: *R v Hopkins* [1896] 1 QB 652 (person who has brought an action against the debtor for unliquidated damages but has not obtained judgment is not a creditor).

8 Debtors Act 1869 s 13(2).

9 See note 6.

10 Debtors Act 1869 s 13(3). The intention proved must be to defraud all creditors generally. In *R v Rowlands* (1882) 8 QBD 530, the debtor, not a bankrupt, had endeavoured to defeat a judgment creditor and was convicted of this offence. As the indictment charged an intent to defraud 'creditors', however, and there was no evidence that there were other creditors, the conviction was quashed. Quaere whether a conviction would have stood if it had been proved that there was only one creditor or that the fraud practised on one was intended to be tried on all.

7. PRACTICE AND PROCEDURE IN INSOLVENCY PROCEEDINGS

(1) ENFORCEMENT PROCEDURES

749. Enforcement of court orders. In any insolvency proceedings[1], orders of the court may be enforced in the same manner as a judgment to the same effect[2]. The High Court and the county courts have jurisdiction throughout England and Wales for the purposes[3] of individual insolvency[4]. For those purposes, a county court has, in addition to its ordinary jurisdiction, all the powers and jurisdiction of the High Court; and the orders of the court may be enforced accordingly in the prescribed manner[5].

Where an order in insolvency proceedings is made, or any process is issued, by a county court ('the primary court'), the order or process may be enforced, executed and dealt with by any other county court ('the secondary court'), as if it had been made or issued for the enforcement of a judgment or order to the same effect made by the secondary court; and this provision applies whether or not the secondary court has jurisdiction to take insolvency proceedings[6].

Where a warrant for the arrest of a person is issued by the High Court, the warrant may be discharged by the county court where the person who is the subject of the warrant: (1) has been brought before a county court exercising insolvency jurisdiction; and (2) has given to the county court an undertaking which is satisfactory to the county court to comply with the obligations that apply[7] to that person[8].

1 As to the meaning of 'insolvency proceedings' see PARA 37 note 9.
2 Insolvency Rules 1986, SI 1986/1925, r 7.19(1). As to orders of the High Court see CPR Sch 1, RSC Ord 45 rr 1–4; and CIVIL PROCEDURE.
3 Ie for the purposes of the Insolvency Act 1986 Pts 7A–11 (ss 251A–385).
4 See the Insolvency Act 1986 s 373(1); and PARA 6. As to the application of s 373 in the case of the administration in bankruptcy of the insolvent estate of a deceased person dying before the presentation of a bankruptcy petition see PARA 6 note 2. As from a day to be appointed, any reference however expressed that is or is deemed to be a reference to a county court held under the County Courts Act 1984 s 1 is to be read as a reference to the county court established by s A1 of that Act: see the Crime and Courts Act 2013 Sch 9 Pt 2 para 11(1)(a), (3)(a). At the date at which this volume states the law no such day had been appointed.
5 See the Insolvency Act 1986 s 373(2); and PARA 6. As from a day to be appointed, the reference to 'a county court' is substituted by a reference to 'the county court': see s 373(2) (amended by the Crime and Courts Act 2013 Sch 9 Pt 3 para 52). At the date at which this volume states the law no such day had been appointed.
6 Insolvency Rules 1986, SI 1986/1925, r 7.19(2). As to enforcing orders in county courts see COURTS AND TRIBUNALS.
7 Ie under the Insolvency Act 1986 or the Insolvency Rules 1986, SI 1986/1925.
8 Insolvency Rules 1986, SI 1986/1925, r 7.19(3) (added by SI 2010/686).

750. Warrants. A warrant issued by the court under any provision of the Insolvency Act 1986 must be addressed to such officer of the High Court or of a county court, whether or not having jurisdiction in insolvency proceedings[1], as the warrant specifies, or to any constable[2].

For the purposes of the court's powers of enforcement[3], the prescribed officers of the court are, in the case of the High Court, the tipstaff and his assistants of the court, and, in the case of a county court, the district judge and the bailiffs[4].

1 As to the meaning of 'insolvency proceedings' see PARA 37 note 9.
2 Insolvency Rules 1986, SI 1986/1925, r 7.21(1). As from a day to be appointed, any reference however expressed that is or is deemed to be a reference to a county court held under the

County Courts Act 1984 s 1 is to be read as a reference to the county court established by s A1 of that Act: see the Crime and Courts Act 2013 Sch 9 Pt 2 para 11(1)(a), (3)(c). At the date at which this volume states the law no such day had been appointed.

3   Ie under the Insolvency Act 1986 s 251N(5) (arrest of debtor who fails to appear before the court and seizure of records or other documents: see PARA 118), s 364(1) (arrest of debtor to whom a bankruptcy petition relates or of an undischarged bankrupt, or of a discharged bankrupt whose estate is still being administered and the seizure of books, papers, records, money or goods in the possession of a person arrested under the warrant: see PARA 217), s 365(3) (search for books, papers or records relating to bankrupt's estate or affairs concealed in premises not belonging to him: see PARA 216), s 366(3) (arrest of bankrupt, bankrupt's spouse or former spouse, any person known or believed to have any property comprised in the bankrupt's estate in his possession or to be indebted to the bankrupt, or any person appearing to the court to be able to give information concerning the bankrupt or the bankrupt's dealings, affairs or property, and the seizure of any books, papers, records, money or goods in that person's possession: see PARA 311).

4   Insolvency Rules 1986, SI 1986/1925, r 7.21(2) (amended by SI 2009/642; and SI 2010/686).

751.   Execution of warrants outside court's district. Where a warrant for a person's arrest has been issued in insolvency proceedings[1] by a county court ('the primary court') and is addressed to another county court ('the secondary court') for execution in its district, the secondary court may send the warrant to the district judge of another county court, whether or not having jurisdiction to take insolvency proceedings, in whose district the person to be arrested is or is believed to be, with a notice to the effect that the warrant is transmitted to that court under this provision for execution in its district at the request of the primary court[2]. The court receiving a warrant so transmitted by the secondary court must apply its seal to the warrant, and secure that all such steps are taken for its execution as would be appropriate in the case of a warrant issued by itself[3].

1   As to the meaning of 'insolvency proceedings' see PARA 37 note 9.
2   Insolvency Rules 1986, SI 1986/1925, r 7.24(1), (2) (r 7.24(2) amended by SI 2010/686). As from a day to be appointed, any reference however expressed that is or is deemed to be a reference to a county court held under the County Courts Act 1984 s 1 is to be read as a reference to the county court established by s A1 of that Act: see the Crime and Courts Act 2013 Sch 9 Pt 2 para 11(1)(a), (3)(c). At the date at which this volume states the law no such day had been appointed.
3   Insolvency Rules 1986, SI 1986/1925, r 7.24(3). As to execution of warrants throughout the United Kingdom see PARA 828.

(2) STAY AND TRANSFER OF PROCEEDINGS

752.   Stay of proceedings; remedies against bankrupt. At any time when proceedings on a bankruptcy petition are pending or an individual has been adjudged bankrupt, the court[1] may stay any action, execution or other legal process against the property or person of the debtor or, as the case may be, of the bankrupt[2]. Any court in which proceedings are pending against any individual may, on proof that a bankruptcy petition has been presented in respect of that individual or that he is an undischarged bankrupt, either stay the proceedings or allow them to continue on such terms as it thinks fit[3].

After the making of a bankruptcy order, no person who is a creditor of the bankrupt in respect of a debt provable in the bankruptcy:

(1)   has any remedy against the property[4] or person of the bankrupt in respect of that debt; or

(2)   may, before the discharge of the bankrupt, commence any action or

other legal proceedings against the bankrupt except with the permission of the court and on such terms as the court may impose[5].

The court may, in advance of the hearing of an application to annul a bankruptcy order, make an interim order staying any proceedings which it thinks ought, in the circumstances of the application, to be stayed[6].

1　Ie the court having jurisdiction in bankruptcy to which bankruptcy proceedings have been allocated (see PARA 6) or transferred (see PARA 756): see the Insolvency Act 1986 s 385(1); and PARA 6 note 8.

As to the application of s 385 in the case of the administration in bankruptcy of the insolvent estate of a deceased person dying before the presentation of a bankruptcy petition see PARA 6 note 8.

2　Insolvency Act 1986 s 285(1). As to the application of s 285 in the case of the administration in bankruptcy of the insolvent estate of a deceased person dying before the presentation of a bankruptcy petition see PARA 214 note 1.

This is no distinction between coercive and punitive proceedings; and the court has power under s 285(1) to make an order staying either type of proceedings: *Smith (a bankrupt) v Braintree District Council* [1990] 2 AC 215, [1989] 3 All ER 897, HL (court made order staying proceedings for the recovery of rates including committal proceedings), overruling *Re Edgcome, ex p Edgcome* [1902] 2 KB 403, CA.

The enforcement by a landlord of his right of peaceable re-entry into leasehold premises on the grounds of arrears of rent does not constitute the enforcement of security or a remedy against the property or the debtor: *Razzaq v Pala* [1997] 1 WLR 1336, [1997] BPIR 726; cf *Exchange Travel Agency Ltd v Triton Property Trust plc* [1991] BCLC 396, [1991] BCC 341. Proceedings for forfeiture and possession on the grounds of non-payment of rent are not a 'remedy against the property or person of the bankrupt': *Harlow District Council v Hall* [2006] EWCA Civ 156, [2006] 1 WLR 2116, [2006] BPIR 712; *Sharples v Places for People Homes Ltd* [2011] EWCA Civ 813, [2012] Ch 382, [2012] 1 All ER 582 (order for possession permissible but not suspended order on condition tenant pays debt provable in the bankruptcy).

3　Insolvency Act 1986 s 285(2). The court may refuse to stay proceedings on terms that all interlocutory applications are to be heard in private and that information and documents acquired in the course of the proceedings are not to be disclosed to third parties: *Polly Peck International plc v Nadir* [1992] BCLC 746. See also *Re Davies (a bankrupt)* [1997] BPIR 619.

4　References in the Insolvency Act 1986 s 285 to property of the bankrupt are to any of his property, whether or not comprised in his estate: s 285(6).

5　Insolvency Act 1986 s 285(3). As to debts provable in a bankruptcy see the Insolvency Rules 1986, SI 1986/1925, r 12.3; and PARA 508. It follows from the fact that any obligation arising under an order made in family proceedings is not provable in a bankruptcy that the order may be enforced against the bankrupt: *Woodley v Woodley (No 2)* [1993] 4 All ER 1010, [1994] 1 WLR 1167, CA. See also *Re X (a bankrupt)* [1996] BPIR 494. Committal to prison is not barred: *Sarkis v Mirza* [2005] EWCA Civ 937, [2006] BPIR 146, [2005] All ER (D) 367 (Jun). No charging order can be made (see *Roberts Petroleum Ltd v Bernard Kenny Ltd* [1983] 2 AC 192, [1983] 1 All ER 564) but a charging order already obtained is not affected (*Wright v Nationwide Building Society* [2009] EWCA Civ 811, [2010] Ch 318, [2010] 2 WLR 1097).

The Insolvency Act 1986 s 285(3) is subject to s 346 (enforcement procedures: see PARA 703 et seq) and s 347 (limited right of distress: see PARA 711 et seq): s 285(3). Subject to s 285(5), (6), s 285(3) does not affect the right of a secured creditor of the bankrupt to enforce his security: s 285(4). See further PARA 214.

6　See the Insolvency Rules 1986, SI 1986/1925, r 6.208(1); and PARA 626.

753. Application for stay of or permission to commence proceedings. An application to stay proceedings against the property or person of the debtor or, as the case may be, the bankrupt, made to the court in which the bankruptcy proceedings are pending must be made by ordinary application[1]. Such an application must be made in the pending proceedings, as may be appropriate[2]. The jurisdiction to stay is discretionary[3]; and in its exercise regard must be had to the primary purpose of bankruptcy, namely the collection of all the assets comprised in the bankrupt's estate, and their distribution pari passu among the bankrupt's creditors after payment of the preferential debts[4].

An application to commence proceedings against the bankrupt after the making of a bankruptcy order must be made by ordinary application to the court in which the bankruptcy proceedings are pending[5].

1 See PARA 787.
2 See CIVIL PROCEDURE vol 11 (2009) PARA 529 et seq.
3 See *Re Manning, ex p Mills* (1871) 6 Ch App 594; *Re Boustead, ex p Rogers* (1881) 16 ChD 665. In *Re Hutton (a bankrupt), Mediterranean Machine Operations Ltd v Haigh* [1969] 2 Ch 201, [1969] 1 All ER 936, Goff J defined the practice of the bankruptcy court under the Bankruptcy Act 1914 (repealed) as leaving to the ordinary tribunals the determination of cases where no points of bankruptcy law were involved, unless the court's own authority, or the necessary protection of its officers, was in issue.
4 *Re Commercial Bank Corpn of India and the East, Smith, Fleming & Co's Case, Gledstanes & Co's Case* (1866) 1 Ch App 538 at 545. Under the Bankruptcy Act 1914 (repealed), after a receiving order was made, a pending action was normally stayed until a trustee was appointed or the receiving order rescinded or discharged: *Franco v Dutton* [1923] WN 40; and see *Hatton v Denison* [1926] WN 80. The court must not restrain any proceedings for a claim from which discharge from bankruptcy would not release the bankrupt: *Re Blake, ex p Coker* (1875) 10 Ch App 652.
5 See PARA 787. The application should be served on the trustee: see *Western and Brazilian Telegraph Co v Bibby* (1880) 42 LT 821.
   Proceedings commenced against a bankrupt after the making of a bankruptcy order without the permission of the court are not null and void for all purposes and are capable of being validated by retrospective permission being granted: *Re Saunders (a bankrupt), Re Bearman (a bankrupt)* [1997] Ch 60, [1997] 3 All ER 992. In considering whether to grant retrospective permission, the court will consider whether the claim would be better resolved by proceedings than by submission of a proof of debt: *Bristol & West Building Society v Trustee of the property of Back (a bankrupt)* [1998] 1 BCLC 485, sub nom *Bristol & West Building Society v Trustee of the property of Back (a bankrupt) and Melinek (a bankrupt)* [1997] BCC 358. The court need not investigate the merits of the claim, provided that it is satisfied that it is not clearly unsustainable: *Bristol & West Building Society v Trustee of the property of Back (a bankrupt)*.

754.   Stay or dismissal of bankruptcy proceedings. If it appears to the court appropriate to do so on the grounds that there has been a contravention of the Insolvency Rules 1986[1] or for any other reason, the court has a general power to dismiss a bankruptcy petition or to stay proceedings on such a petition; and, where it stays proceedings on a petition, it may do so on such terms and conditions as it thinks fit[2].

1 Ie the Insolvency Rules 1986, SI 1986/1925.
2 Insolvency Act 1986 s 266(3). As to the application of s 266 in the case of the administration in bankruptcy of the insolvent estate of a deceased person dying before the presentation of a bankruptcy petition see PARA 130 note 12.
   Where a petition is presented in respect of a judgment and a bona fide serious appeal is pending in respect of the judgment which was being taken seriously by the debtor and has been prosecuted with diligence, bankruptcy proceedings will ordinarily be stayed and the hearing of the petition adjourned: *Re Yeatman, ex p Yeatman* (1880) 16 ChD 283, CA; *Re Noble (a bankrupt), ex p Bankrupt v Official Receiver* [1965] Ch 129, [1964] 2 All ER 522, CA; *Re A Debtor (No 799 of 1994), ex p Cobbs Property Services Ltd* [1995] 3 All ER 723, [1995] 1 WLR 467. In relation to the power of the court on the hearing of a petition to stay or dismiss the petition on the grounds that an appeal is pending from the judgment or order on which the petition is based see further the Insolvency Rules 1986, SI 1986/1925, r 6.25(2); and PARA 199.
   The court may also stay or dismiss a petition on the grounds of want of prosecution (*TSB Bank plc v Platts* [1997] BPIR 151) or on grounds that there is a prior foreign bankruptcy in respect of the debtor or that the debtor has no assets in the jurisdiction (*Re Thulin* [1995] 1 WLR 165). In relation to the court's powers to stay a petition presented for the purpose of preventing a debtor from proceeding with an action see *Re Ross (a bankrupt) (No 2)* [2000] BPIR 636, CA. See further PARA 130.

755.   Stay of advertisement of bankruptcy order. On the application[1] of the bankrupt or a creditor, the court may order the official receiver not to send notice of the making of a bankruptcy order to the Chief Land Registrar, for registration in the register of writs and orders affecting land, not to cause the order to be advertised in such other manner as the official receiver thinks fit, not to cause notice of the order to be gazetted[2] and not to enter the details of the bankruptcy order onto the individual insolvency register[3], pending a further order of the court[4].

1　As to the mode of application and the procedure see PARA 786 et seq.
2　Ie to suspend action under the Insolvency Rules 1986, SI 1986/1925, r 6.46(2): see PARA 207. As to the meaning of 'gazetted' see PARA 165 note 12.
3　Ie to suspend action under the Insolvency Rules 1986, SI 1986/1925, r 6.46(2) and r 6A.4(2) (see PARA 30).
4　See the Insolvency Rules 1986, SI 1986/1925, r 6.46(3) (amended by SI 1999/359; SI 2005/527; and SI 2010/686); and PARA 207. An application for such an order must be supported by a witness statement stating the grounds on which it is made: Insolvency Rules 1986, SI 1986/1925, r 6.46(3A) (added by SI 2010/686). As to the meaning of 'witness statement' see PARA 161 note 7.

756. General power of transfer. The High Court and the county courts have jurisdiction throughout England and Wales for the purposes[1] of individual insolvency[2]. In addition to its ordinary jurisdiction, a county court has all the powers and jurisdiction of the High Court[3]. Jurisdiction is so exercised by the High Court or the Central London County Court in relation to proceedings which are allocated to the London insolvency district[4], and by each county court in relation to the proceedings which are allocated to the insolvency district[5] of that court[6]. Such jurisdiction is without prejudice to the transfer of proceedings from one court to another; and nothing in the above provisions invalidates any proceedings on the grounds that they were initiated or continued in the wrong court[7].

Where bankruptcy proceedings or proceedings relating to a debt relief order[8] are pending in the High Court, the court may order them to be transferred to a specified county court[9]; and, where bankruptcy proceedings or proceedings relating to a debt relief order are pending in a county court, the court may order them to be transferred either to the High Court or to another county court[10]. In any case where bankruptcy proceedings or proceedings relating to a debt relief order are transferred to a county court, the transfer must be to a court which has jurisdiction in bankruptcy[11].

Where bankruptcy proceedings or proceedings relating to a debt relief order are pending in a county court, a judge of the High Court may order them to be transferred to that court[12].

A transfer of proceedings may be so ordered by the court of its own motion, or on the application of the official receiver, or on the application of a person appearing to the court to have an interest in the proceedings[13]; and a transfer of proceedings may be ordered, notwithstanding that the proceedings commenced before 29 December 1986[14].

On a transfer the whole of the relevant bankruptcy proceedings are transferred[15].

1　Ie for the purposes of the Insolvency Act 1986 Pts 7A–11 (ss 251A–385).
2　Insolvency Act 1986 s 373(1). As to the application of s 373 in the case of the administration in bankruptcy of the insolvent estate of a deceased person dying before the presentation of a bankruptcy petition see PARA 6 note 2. As from a day to be appointed, any reference however expressed that is or is deemed to be a reference to a county court held under the County Courts Act 1984 s 1 is to be read as a reference to the county court established by s A1 of that Act: see the Crime and Courts Act 2013 Sch 9 Pt 2 para 11(1)(a), (3)(a), (c). At the date at which this volume states the law no such day had been appointed.

3   Insolvency Act 1986 s 373(2). As from a day to be appointed, the reference to 'a county court' is substituted by a reference to 'the county court': see s 373(2) (amended by the Crime and Courts Act 2013 Sch 9 Pt 3 para 52). At the date at which this volume states the law no such day had been appointed.
4   As to the London insolvency district see PARA 7 note 2.
5   As to insolvency districts outside the London insolvency district see PARA 7.
6   Insolvency Act 1986 s 373(3) (amended by SI 2011/761). As from a day to be appointed, the Insolvency Act 1986 s 373(3) is amended to substitute the reference to the Central London County Court with a reference to the county court; and head (2) in the text is substituted to read 'by the county court in relation to the proceedings which are so allocated to any other insolvency district': see s 373(3) (amended by the Crime and Courts Act 2013 Sch 9 Pt 3 para 93(e), (f)). At the date at which this volume states the law no such day had been appointed.
7   Insolvency Act 1986 s 373(4).
8   As to debt relief orders see PARA 101 et seq.
9   Insolvency Rules 1986, SI 1986/1925, r 7.11(1) (amended by SI 2009/642). See note 2.
10 Insolvency Rules 1986, SI 1986/1925, r 7.11(2) (amended by SI 2009/642); and see *Re Marquis of Huntly, ex p Goldstein* [1917] 2 KB 729, DC; *Re Crossley (a debtor)* [1954] 3 All ER 296, [1954] 1 WLR 1353. In corporate insolvency where two different petitioners present petitions, one in the High Court and one in a county court, and the county court petition is due for virtually immediately hearing, the proceedings should continue as to both petitions, with the High Court to resolve the matter, being informed by affidavit of the facts relating to the county court petition: *Re Filby Bros (Provender) Ltd* [1958] 2 All ER 458, [1958] 1 WLR 683. In *Re Audio Systems Ltd* [1965] 2 All ER 919, [1965] 1 WLR 1096, the High Court petition was due for hearing one month before the county court petition. Pennycuick J made a compulsory order on the High Court petition and transferred the county court petition to the High Court.
      In circumstances where an office-holder holds multiple appointments as trustee in bankruptcy proceedings some of which are in the High Court and some of which are in county courts and it is desired to replace the office-holder, a composite application can be made to the High Court which has jurisdiction to transfer the proceedings from the county courts for the purpose of making an order to replace the office-holder as trustee: see *Supperstone v Auger* [1999] BPIR 152.
11 Insolvency Rules 1986, SI 1986/1925, r 7.11(3A) (added by SI 2009/642); and see *Re Real Estates Co* [1893] 1 Ch 398.
12 Insolvency Rules 1986, SI 1986/1925, r 7.11(4) (amended by SI 2009/642). Solely for the purposes of the Insolvency Rules 1986, SI 1986/1925, r 7.10D (action following application for a block transfer order: see PARA 377), the registrar may transfer to or from the High Court, and the district judge of the county court to which the application is made may transfer to or from that county court, any case in the schedule under r 7.10C(8) (see PARA 377): r 7.11(4A) (added by SI 2010/686). See note 9.
13 Insolvency Rules 1986, SI 1986/1925, r 7.11(5). As to a person 'having an interest' see PARA 346 note 2.
14 Insolvency Rules 1986, SI 1986/1925, r 7.11(6). The Insolvency Rules 1986, SI 1986/1925, came into force on 29 December 1986: r 0.1. As to the mode of application and the procedure see PARA 786 et seq.
      In ordering a transfer, the court takes into account the balance of convenience: see *Re Linton* (1892) 8 TLR 219; on appeal 8 TLR 377, CA. The applicant may be ordered, as a condition of transfer, to give an undertaking to pay the debtor's travelling expenses as and when he may be required to attend the court or the trustee. An appeal may be brought from a refusal to transfer where the judge has refused to exercise his discretion: *Re Walker, ex p Soanes* (1884) 13 QBD 484, DC.
15 *Re Kouyoumdjian (a bankrupt), ex p Trustee of the Property of the Bankrupt v Lord* [1956] 2 All ER 286, [1956] 1 WLR 558; *Re A Debtor (No 26A of 1975)* [1984] 3 All ER 995, [1985] 1 WLR 6.

757.   Application for transfer.   An application by the official receiver for proceedings to be transferred must be made with a report by him setting out the reasons for the transfer, and including a statement either that the petitioner, or the debtor in proceedings relating to a debt relief order[1], consents to the transfer or that he has been given at least 14 days' notice of the official receiver's application[2]. If the court is satisfied from the official receiver's report that the proceedings can be conducted more conveniently in another court, the proceedings must be transferred to that court[3].

Where an application for the transfer of proceedings is made otherwise than by the official receiver, at least 14 days' notice of the application must be given by the applicant to the official receiver attached to the court[4] in which the proceedings are pending, and to the official receiver attached to the court to which it is proposed that they should be transferred[5].

1   As to debt relief orders see PARA 101 et seq.
2   Insolvency Rules 1986, SI 1986/1925, r 7.13(1) (amended by SI 2009/642). As to the general power of transfer see PARA 756.
3   Insolvency Rules 1986, SI 1986/1925, r 7.13(2).
4   As to the attachment of the official receiver to particular courts see PARA 35.
5   Insolvency Rules 1986, SI 1986/1925, r 7.13(3).

758. Proceedings commenced in wrong court.   Where bankruptcy proceedings or proceedings relating to a debt relief order[1] are commenced in a court which is, in relation to those proceedings, the wrong court, that court may order the transfer of the proceedings to the court in which they ought to have been commenced, may order that the proceedings be continued in the court in which they have been commenced, or order the proceedings to be struck out[2].

1   As to debt relief orders see PARA 101 et seq.
2   Insolvency Rules 1986, SI 1986/1925, r 7.12 (amended by SI 2009/642). As to the jurisdiction of the High Court and county courts see PARAS 6, 7; and as to the general power of transfer see PARA 756.

759. Proceedings following order for transfer.   The court making an order for the transfer of bankruptcy proceedings[1] must as soon as reasonably practicable send to the transferee court a sealed copy of the order, and the file of the proceedings[2]. On receipt of these, the transferee court must as soon as reasonably practicable send notice of the transfer to the official receivers attached to that court and the transferor court respectively[3].

Where, however, the order is made by the High Court transferring bankruptcy proceedings to that Court from a county court[4], the High Court must send sealed copies of the order to the county court from which the proceedings are to be transferred, and to the official receivers attached to that court and the High Court respectively; and that county court must send the file of the proceedings to the High Court[5].

1   Ie under the Insolvency Rules 1986, SI 1986/1925, r 7.11: see PARA 756.
2   Insolvency Rules 1986, SI 1986/1925, r 7.14(1) (amended by SI 2009/642).
3   Insolvency Rules 1986, SI 1986/1925, r 7.14(2) (amended by SI 2009/642).
4   Ie under the Insolvency Rules 1986, SI 1986/1925, r 7.11(4): see PARA 756. As from a day to be appointed, any reference however expressed that is or is deemed to be a reference to a county court held under the County Courts Act 1984 s 1 is to be read as a reference to the county court established by s A1 of that Act: see the Crime and Courts Act 2013 Sch 9 Pt 2 para 11(1)(a), (3)(c). At the date at which this volume states the law no such day had been appointed.
5   Insolvency Rules 1986, SI 1986/1925, r 7.14(3).

760. Transfer of other proceedings.   Where a bankruptcy order has been made in the case of an individual by the High Court[1] or an interim receiver has been appointed[2], or bankruptcy proceedings have been transferred to that Court from a county court[3], a judge of any Division of the High Court may, of his own motion, order the transfer to that Division of any such proceedings as are mentioned below and are pending against the individual concerned ('the insolvent') either in another Division of the High Court or in a court in England and Wales other than the High Court[4].

Proceedings which may be so transferred are those brought by or against the insolvent for the purpose of enforcing a claim against the insolvent estate[5], or brought by a person other than the insolvent for the purpose of enforcing any such claim, including proceedings of any description by a mortgagee[6].

Where proceedings are transferred under the above provisions, the registrar may, subject to the directions of the judge, dispose of any matter arising in the proceedings which would, but for the transfer, have been disposed of in chambers or, in the case of proceedings transferred from a county court, by the district judge[7].

1   See PARA 206.
2   See PARA 221.
3   See PARA 756. As from a day to be appointed, any reference however expressed that is or is deemed to be a reference to a county court held under the County Courts Act 1984 s 1 is to be read as a reference to the county court established by s A1 of that Act: see the Crime and Courts Act 2013 Sch 9 Pt 2 para 11(1)(a), (3)(c). At the date at which this volume states the law no such day had been appointed.
4   Insolvency Rules 1986, SI 1986/1925, r 7.15(1), (2) (r 7.15(1) amended by SI 2010/686).
5   As to the meaning of 'the insolvent estate' see PARA 91 note 18. As to restrictions on proceedings and remedies see the Insolvency Act 1986 s 285; and PARAS 218, 758.
6   Insolvency Rules 1986, SI 1986/1925, r 7.15(3). As to the position of secured creditors in the bankruptcy, including mortgagees, see PARA 574 et seq; and as to application to the court by a mortgagee for an order for sale see PARA 428.
7   Insolvency Rules 1986, SI 1986/1925, r 7.15(4) (amended by SI 2010/686).

(3) APPEALS AND REVIEWS OF COURT ORDERS

761. Appeals and reviews of court orders; in general. Every court having jurisdiction under the Insolvency Act 1986 in bankruptcy proceedings[1] may review, rescind or vary any order made by it in the exercise of that jurisdiction[2]. An appeal from a decision made in the exercise of that jurisdiction by a county court or by a registrar in bankruptcy of the High Court lies to a single judge of the High Court; and an appeal from a decision of that judge on such an appeal lies to the Court of Appeal[3].

A county court is not, in the exercise of its jurisdiction in bankruptcy proceedings, subject to be restrained by the order of any other court; and no appeal lies from its decision in the exercise of that jurisdiction except as is mentioned above[4].

1   Ie for the purposes of the Insolvency Act 1986 Pts 7A–11 (ss 251A–385). As to the courts having such jurisdiction see PARAS 6, 7.
2   Insolvency Act 1986 s 375(1). The jurisdiction to review a consent order will only be exercised in an exceptional case where there is serious injustice: *Boorer v Trustee in Bankruptcy of Boorer* [2002] BPIR 21. It is not proper to use the jurisdiction to review under the Insolvency Act 1986 s 375 to circumvent the prohibition in s 255(1)(c) (see PARA 48 head (3)) against second applications for an interim order within a 12-month period: *Hurst v Bennett (No 2)* [2002] BPIR 102.

     The jurisdiction to rehear is unlimited; but, where a decision has been made by a judge after full argument, another judge of co-ordinate jurisdiction presented with the same material on an application to review should substitute his decision only in the most exceptional of circumstances: *Mond v Hammonds Suddards (a firm)* [2000] Ch 40, sub nom *Re RS & M Engineering Ltd, Mond v Hammonds Suddards (a firm) (No 2)* [1999] 2 BCLC 485, CA. In relation to winding-up proceedings see also the Insolvency Rules 1986, SI 1986/1925, r 7.47(1);

Re Thirty-Eight Building Ltd (in liquidation) (No 2), Simms v Saunders [2000] 1 BCLC 201, sub nom *Re Thirty-Eight Building Ltd* [2000] BCC 422; and COMPANY AND PARTNERSHIP INSOLVENCY vol 17 (2011) PARA 991.

It appears that a judge of the High Court has jurisdiction to hear an application to review a decision of a registrar: *O'Brien v IRC* [2000] BPIR 306. See also *Re Piccadilly Property Management* [1999] 2 BCLC 145, [1999] BPIR 260; but cf *Re SN Group plc* [1994] 1 BCLC 319, [1993] BCC 808 (both decisions made in relation to the Insolvency Rules 1986, SI 1986/1925, r 7.47(1)).

The court also has jurisdiction under the Insolvency Act 1986 s 375(1) to rescind a bankruptcy order: *Fitch v Official Receiver* [1996] 1 WLR 242, [1996] BCC 328, CA (bankruptcy order rescinded on application of bankrupt where creditors had changed their mind as to the desirability of an order being made); *Papanicola v Humphreys* [2005] EWHC 335 (Ch), [2005] 2 All ER 418 (something has to have changed to make it appropriate for the court to review its order; otherwise a challenge to an earlier order should be by way of appeal); *Crammer v West Bromwich Building Society* [2012] EWCA Civ 517, [2012] BPIR 963. In exercising its discretion to rescind a bankruptcy order, the court will bear in mind the type of consideration relevant to an applicant to annul a bankruptcy order: *Revenue and Customs Comrs v Cassells* [2008] EWHC 3180 (Ch), [2009] STC 1047, [2009] BPIR 284.

The power of review should only be resorted to in cases where the court is satisfied that there has been something amounting to a miscarriage of justice that cannot be corrected by the ordinary process of appeal: *Scottish & Newcastle Ltd v Raguz* [2010] EWHC 1384 (Ch), [2010] BPIR 945, [2010] All ER (D) 63 (Jun). See also *Haworth v Cartmel* [2011] EWHC 36 (Ch), [2011] BPIR 428, [2011] All ER (D) 23 (Mar) (applicant had not had mental capacity to respond to statutory demand).

As to the application of the Insolvency Act 1986 s 375 in the case of the administration in bankruptcy of the insolvent estate of a deceased person dying before the presentation of a bankruptcy petition see PARA 465 note 4.

3   Insolvency Act 1986 s 375(2) (amended by the Access to Justice Act 1999 s 106, Sch 15 Pt III). See further PARAS 763–764. As to procedure on appeals in bankruptcy proceedings see *Practice Direction—Insolvency Proceedings* Pt 4 (para 19); and PARA 763 et seq. As from a day to be appointed, the reference to 'a county court' is substituted by a reference to 'the county court': see the Insolvency Act 1986 s 375 (amended by the Crime and Courts Act 2013 Sch 9 Pt 3 para 52). At the date at which this volume states the law no such day had been appointed.

4   Insolvency Act 1986 s 375(3). See note 3.

762. Appeal by Secretary of State.
In bankruptcy proceedings, an appeal lies at the instance of the Secretary of State from any order of the court made on an application for the rescission or annulment of a bankruptcy order, or for a bankrupt's discharge[1].

1   Insolvency Rules 1986, SI 1986/1925, r 7.48(1). As to annulment of bankruptcy orders see PARA 620 et seq; and as to discharge from bankruptcy see PARA 638 et seq.

763. Procedure on appeals; in general.
An appeal against a decision at first instance may only be brought with either the permission of the court which made the decision or the permission of the court which has jurisdiction to hear the appeal[1]. An appellant must file an appellant's notice[2] within 21 days after the date of the decision of the court that the appellant wishes to appeal[3]. The procedure set out in CPR Part 52 (Appeals) applies to any appeal in insolvency proceedings[4]. There is also specific provision regarding appeals in insolvency proceedings in Practice Direction–Insolvency Proceedings[5].

1   Insolvency Rules 1986, SI 1986/1925, r 7.49A(1) (added by SI 2010/686).
2   See CPR Pt 52; and CIVIL PROCEDURE vol 12 (2009) PARA 1663.
3   Insolvency Rules 1986, SI 1986/1925, r 7.49A(2) (added by SI 2010/686).
4   Insolvency Rules 1986, SI 1986/1925, r 7.49A(3) (added by SI 2010/686). As to CPR Pt 52 see CIVIL PROCEDURE vol 12 (2009) PARA 1657 et seq.
5   See *Practice Direction–Insolvency Proceedings* Pt 4 (para 19); and PARA 764 et seq.

764. Appeals to and from High Court judge. An appeal from a decision of a county court[1] or of a registrar in insolvency proceedings lies to a judge of the High Court[2]. An appeal from a decision of a Judge of the High Court, whether at first instance or on appeal, lies to the Court of Appeal[3]. For the purposes of insolvency proceedings, such an appeal is termed a 'first appeal'[4].

1　Ie whether made by a district judge, a recorder or a circuit judge.
2　Insolvency Act 1986 s 375(2); *Practice Direction—Insolvency Proceedings* para 19.1; and see PARA 761. As to the application of the Insolvency Act 1986 s 375 in the case of the administration in bankruptcy of the insolvent estate of a deceased person dying before the presentation of a bankruptcy petition see PARA 465 note 4. As from a day to be appointed, the reference to 'a county court' is substituted by a reference to 'the county court': see the Insolvency Act 1986 s 375 (amended by the Crime and Courts Act 2013 Sch 9 Pt 3 para 52). At the date at which this volume states the law no such day had been appointed.
　　An appeal from a decision of a registrar in bankruptcy must be filed at the Royal Courts of Justice in London: *Practice Direction—Insolvency Proceedings* para 19.5.1. An appeal from a decision of a District Judge sitting in a district registry of the High Court may be filed at the Royal Courts of Justice in London or in that district registry: *Practice Direction—Insolvency Proceedings* para 19.5.2.
　　The court centres at which appeals from decisions of county courts on any particular Circuit must be filed, managed and heard (unless the appeal court otherwise orders) are as follows: Midland Circuit: Birmingham; North Eastern Circuit: Leeds or Newcastle upon Tyne; Northern Circuit: Manchester or Liverpool; Wales Circuit: Cardiff, Caernarfon or Mold; Western Circuit: Bristol; South Eastern Circuit: Royal Courts of Justice: *Practice Direction—Insolvency Proceedings* para 19.6.
3　*Practice Direction—Insolvency Proceedings* para 19.2.
4　See *Practice Direction—Insolvency Proceedings* para 19.3.

765. Procedure on first appeal. The procedure and practice for a first appeal[1] are governed by the normal Civil Procedure Rules[2] relating to appeals[3]. A first appeal is subject to the permission requirements of the Civil Procedure Rules[4]. An appeal from a decision of a Judge of the High Court which was made on a first appeal requires the permission of the Court of Appeal[5].

Where the lower court is a county court:

(1)　an appeal or application for permission to appeal from a decision of a District Judge will be heard or considered by a High Court Judge or by any person authorised[6] to act as a judge of the High Court in the Chancery Division;

(2)　an appeal or application for permission to appeal from a decision of a Recorder or a Circuit Judge will be heard or considered by a High Court Judge or by a person authorised[7] to act as a judge of the High Court in the Chancery Division;

(3)　other applications in any appeal or application for permission to appeal may be heard or considered and directions may be given by a High Court Judge or by any person authorised[8] to act as a judge of the High Court in the Chancery Division[9].

In the case of appeals from decisions of Registrars or District Judges in the High Court, appeals, applications for permission to appeal and other applications may be heard or considered and directions may be given by a High Court Judge or by any person authorised[10] to act as a judge of the High Court in the Chancery Division[11].

1　As to the meaning of 'first appeal' see PARA 764.
2　Ie CPR Pt 52: see CIVIL PROCEDURE vol 12 (2009) PARA 1657 et seq.
3　See the Insolvency Rules 1986, SI 1986/1925, r 7.49A; and PARA 763. As to the time for and mode of appeal see COMPANY AND PARTNERSHIP INSOLVENCY vol 17 (2011) PARA 994.

4   *Practice Direction—Insolvency Proceedings* paras 19.3, 19.9. As to the permission requirements see CPR 52.3; and CIVIL PROCEDURE vol 12 (2009) PARA 1660.
5   *Practice Direction—Insolvency Proceedings* para 19.4.
6   Ie under the Senior Courts Act 1981 s 9: see COURTS AND TRIBUNALS vol 24 (2010) PARA 847.
7   Ie under the Senior Courts Act 1981 s 9(1), table item (1), (2) or (4): see COURTS AND TRIBUNALS vol 24 (2010) PARA 847.
8   Ie under the Senior Courts Act 1981 s 9: see COURTS AND TRIBUNALS vol 24 (2010) PARA 847.
9   *Practice Direction—Insolvency Proceedings* para 19.7. As from a day to be appointed, any reference however expressed that is or is deemed to be a reference to a county court held under the County Courts Act 1984 s 1 is to be read as a reference to the county court established by s A1 of that Act: see the Crime and Courts Act 2013 Sch 9 Pt 2 para 11(1)(a), (3)(c). At the date at which this volume states the law no such day had been appointed.
10 Ie under the Senior Courts Act 1981 s 9: see COURTS AND TRIBUNALS vol 24 (2010) PARA 847.
11 *Practice Direction—Insolvency Proceedings* para 19.8.

766.   Interim applications. The following applications relating to insolvent individuals should always be listed before a judge:
(1)   applications for committal for contempt;
(2)   applications for an injunction;
(3)   interim applications and applications for directions or case management after any proceedings have been referred or adjourned to the judge, except where liberty to apply to the registrar has been given[1].

1   See *Practice Direction—Insolvency Proceedings* para 3.3.

767.   Appeal from official receiver. An appeal[1] against a decision of the official receiver must be brought within 28 days of the notification of the decision[2].

In respect of a decision by the official receiver that an investigation of the conduct and affairs of a bankrupt is unnecessary or concluded[3], an appeal must be brought within 14 days of the notification of the decision[4].

An appeal may be made against the official receiver's decision:
(1)   as chairman of a meeting whether a proof should be admitted for the purposes of voting[5];
(2)   as trustee to reject a proof for the purposes of dividend, either in whole or in part[6];
(3)   refusing to release the bankrupt from his duty to submit a statement of affairs or to extend his time for submitting it[7].

1   Ie under the Insolvency Act 1986 or the Insolvency Rules 1986, SI 1986/1925.
2   Insolvency Rules 1986, SI 1986/1925, r 7.50(1) (amended by SI 2003/1730).
3   Ie under the Insolvency Rules 1986, SI 1986/1925, r 6.214A(5)(b): see PARA 638 note 5.
4   Insolvency Rules 1986, SI 1986/1925, r 7.50(2) (added by SI 2003/1730).
5   Ie under the Insolvency Rules 1986, SI 1986/1925, r 6.94: see PARA 287.
6   Ie under the Insolvency Rules 1986, SI 1986/1925, r 6.105: see PARA 551.
7   Ie under the Insolvency Act 1986 s 288(3): see PARA 240.

768.   Appeals from trustee. If a bankrupt or any of his creditors or any other person is dissatisfied[1] by any act, omission or decision of a trustee of the bankrupt's estate, he may apply[2] to the court; and on such an application the court may confirm, reverse or modify any act or decision of the trustee, may give him directions or may make such other order as it thinks fit[3].

In particular, an appeal to the court is allowed from the trustee's decision, as chairman of the meeting, as to a creditor's or class of creditors' entitlement to vote[4], and whether a proof should be admitted for the purposes of voting or rejected[5], and from his decision as to the rejection or admission of a proof for the purpose of dividends[6].

1 As to the meaning of 'person dissatisfied' see PARA 342. Cf the Insolvency Act 1986 s 168(5) (see COMPANY AND PARTNERSHIP INSOLVENCY vol 17 (2011) PARA 1294) where, in corporate insolvency, it is an 'aggrieved' person who may apply to the court against a liquidator's decisions.
2 As to the mode of application and the procedure see PARA 786 et seq.
3 See the Insolvency Act 1986 s 303(1); and PARA 342.
4 Ie under the Insolvency Rules 1986, SI 1986/1925, r 6.93: see PARA 286.
5 Ie under the Insolvency Rules 1986, SI 1986/1925, r 6.94: see PARA 287.
6 Ie under the Insolvency Rules 1986, SI 1986/1925, r 6.105: see PARA 551.

769. Appeal from Secretary of State. There is no general right of appeal to the court from the decisions[1] of the Secretary of State; but a right of appeal is expressly given in the case of any person dissatisfied[2] with the decision of the Secretary of State in respect of a claim to undistributed assets forming part of the bankrupt's estate which have been paid into the Insolvency Services Account[3].

Appeals must be made by application[4]. An appeal against a decision[5] of the Secretary of State must be brought within 28 days of the notification of the decision[6].

1 As to the decisions which the Secretary of State may make see PARA 21.
2 As to the meaning of 'person dissatisfied' see PARA 344.
3 See the Insolvency Regulations 1994, SI 1994/2507, reg 32(2); and PARA 396.
4 As to the mode of application and the procedure see PARA 786 et seq.

5 Ie under the Insolvency Act 1986 or the Insolvency Rules 1986, SI 1986/1925.

6 Insolvency Rules 1986, SI 1986/1925, r 7.50(1) (amended by SI 2003/1730).

770. Appeal from supervisor. If the debtor, any of his creditors or any other person is dissatisfied[1] by any act, omission or decision of the supervisor of a voluntary arrangement or a fast-track voluntary arrangement[2], he may apply[3] to the court; and the court may:

(1) confirm, reverse, or modify any act or decision of the supervisor;

(2) give him directions; or

(3) make such other order as it thinks fit[4].

1 As to the meaning of 'person dissatisfied' see PARA 342.
2 As to voluntary arrangements and fast-track voluntary arrangements see PARA 43 et seq.
3 As to the mode of application and the procedure see PARA 786 et seq.
4 See the Insolvency Act 1986 ss 263(3), 263E; and PARAS 75, 95.

771. Vexatious litigants. A creditor of the bankrupt who has been prohibited from initiating proceedings in the High Court or in any other court without the permission of the High Court[1] may nevertheless prove his debt and, where the proof is rejected by the trustee in bankruptcy, may appeal to the appropriate bankruptcy court[2] against such rejection without first obtaining the permission of the court[3].

1 The High Court has inherent jurisdiction to make an order for the purpose of preventing abuse of its procedures and may make an order restraining a person from instituting proceedings without the permission of the court where those proceedings would be vexatious: see the Senior Courts Act 1981 s 42; and CIVIL PROCEDURE vol 11 (2009) PARAS 244, 258. Such an order may be made on an interim basis: *Ebert v Venvil, Ebert v Birch* [2000] Ch 484, [1999] 3 WLR 670, CA; and see CPR 25.1 (see CIVIL PROCEDURE vol 11 (2009) PARA 315).
2 See PARA 6.

3 *Re Wilson (a bankrupt), ex p Bebbington Easton* [1973] 1 All ER 849, [1973] 1 WLR 314.

(4) MISCELLANEOUS PRACTICE AND PROCEDURE

(i) In general

772. General control of the court. Every bankruptcy is under the general control of the court[1]; and the court has full power[2] to decide all questions of priorities and all other questions, whether of law or fact, arising in any bankruptcy[3]. An undischarged bankrupt or a discharged bankrupt whose estate is still being administered[4] must[5] do all such things as he may be directed to do by the court for the purposes of his bankruptcy or, as the case may be, the administration of that estate[6]; and the official receiver or the trustee may at any time apply to the court for a direction under this provision[7].

If any person without reasonable excuse fails to comply with any obligation so imposed on him, he is guilty of a contempt of court and liable to be punished accordingly, in addition to any other punishment to which he may be subject[8].

1 As to the meaning of 'the court' see PARA 786.
2 Ie subject to the Insolvency Act 1986 Pts 7A–11 (ss 251A–385).
3 Insolvency Act 1986 s 363(1). In *Law Society v Shah* [2007] EWHC 2841 (Ch), [2009] Ch 223, [2008] 3 WLR 1401, the court approved a mechanism using these powers enabling the Law Society to prove its debt without the need for the trustee to adjudicate upon the proof. As to the width of the court's powers see also *Donaldson v O'Sullivan* [2008] EWCA Civ 879, [2009] 1 All ER 1087, [2009] 1 WLR 924. As to the application of the Insolvency Act 1986 s 363 in the case of the administration in bankruptcy of the insolvent estate of a deceased person dying before the presentation of a bankruptcy petition see PARA 215 note 2.
4 Ie under the Insolvency Act 1986 Pt 9 Ch 4 (ss 305–335).
5 Ie without prejudice to any other provision of the Insolvency Act 1986 Pts 7A–11.
6 Insolvency Act 1986 s 363(2).
7 Insolvency Act 1986 s 363(3). As to the mode of application and the procedure see PARA 786 et seq.
8 Insolvency Act 1986 s 363(4). As to contempt of court see CONTEMPT OF COURT vol 22 (2012) PARA 1 et seq; and as to offences see PARA 733 et seq.

773. Rules and regulations; Insolvency Rules Committee. As regards individual insolvency proceedings the practice is, for the most part, regulated by the Insolvency Rules 1986[1] which were made under statutory power[2].

The Insolvency Rules Committee[3] continues to exist for the purposes of being consulted by the Lord Chancellor before he makes rules[4]. The committee must consist of:

(1) a judge of the High Court attached to the Chancery Division;
(2) a circuit judge;
(3) a registrar in bankruptcy of the High Court;
(4) the district judge of a county court[5];
(5) a practising barrister;
(6) a practising solicitor; and
(7) a practising accountant[6].

The Lord Chief Justice must appoint the persons referred to in heads (1) to (4) above, after consulting the Lord Chancellor; and the Lord Chancellor must appoint the persons referred to in heads (5) to (7) above, after consulting the Lord Chief Justice[7].

The Lord Chancellor may appoint as additional members of the committee any person appearing to him to have qualifications or experience that would be of value to the committee in considering any matter with which it is concerned[8]; and he must consult the committee before making any rules[9].

1　Ie the Insolvency Rules 1986, SI 1986/1925. See also the regulations referred to in PARA 2 note 5; and *Practice Direction—Insolvency Proceedings*.

2　The Lord Chancellor, with the concurrence of the Secretary of State and, in the case of rules that affect court procedure, with the concurrence of the Lord Chief Justice, make rules for the purpose of giving effect to the Insolvency Act 1986 Pts 7A–11 (ss 251A–385) or Council Regulation (EC) 1346/2000 (OJ L160, 30.6.2000, p 1) on insolvency proceedings ('European Regulation on Insolvency Proceedings': see PARAS 41, 42): Insolvency Act 1986 s 412(1) (amended by the Constitutional Reform Act 2005 s 15(1), Sch 4 paras 185, 189; the Tribunals, Courts and Enforcement Act 2007 s 108(3), Sch 20 paras 1, 8; and SI 2002/1037). The Lord Chief Justice may nominate a judicial office holder (as defined in the Constitutional Reform Act 2005 s 109(4) (see COURTS AND TRIBUNALS vol 24 (2010) PARA 961)) to exercise his functions under the Insolvency Act 1986 s 412: s 412(6) (added by the Constitutional Reform Act 2005 Sch 4 paras 185, 189).

　　Without prejudice to the generality of the Insolvency Act 1986 s 412(1), or any provision of Pts 7A–11 by virtue of which rules under s 412 may be made with respect to any matter, rules under s 412 may contain: (1) any such provision as is specified in Sch 9 or corresponds to provision contained immediately before 29 December 1986 (see PARA 2) in rules made under the Bankruptcy Act 1914 s 132 (repealed); and (2) such incidental, supplemental and transitional provisions as may appear to the Lord Chancellor necessary or expedient: Insolvency Act 1986 s 412(2). For the purposes of s 412(2), a reference in Sch 9 to doing anything under or for the purposes of a provision of the Insolvency Act 1986 includes a reference to doing anything under or for the purposes of the European Regulation on Insolvency Proceedings, in so far as the provision of the Insolvency Act 1986 relates to a matter to which the European Regulation on Insolvency Proceedings applies: Insolvency Act 1986 s 412(2A) (added by SI 2002/1037). Rules under the Insolvency Act 1986 s 412 for the purpose of giving effect to the European Regulation on Insolvency Proceedings may not create any new criminal offence punishable with imprisonment for more than two years or punishable on summary conviction with imprisonment for more than three months or with a fine of more than level 5 on the standard scale (if not calculated on a daily basis) or with a fine of more than £100 a day: Insolvency Act 1986 s 412(2B) (added by SI 2002/1037); European Communities Act 1972 Sch 2 para 1(1)(d). As to the standard scale see SENTENCING AND DISPOSITION OF OFFENDERS vol 92 (2010) PARA 142.

　　The power to make rules conferred by the Insolvency Act 1986 s 412 is exercisable by statutory instrument subject to annulment in pursuance of a resolution of either House of Parliament: s 412(3). Regulations made by the Secretary of State under a power conferred by rules under s 412 must be made by statutory instrument and, after being made, must be laid before each House of Parliament: s 412(4). Nothing in s 412 prejudices any power to make rules of court: s 412(5).

　　The provisions capable of inclusion in individual insolvency rules are:

(1)　provision with respect to the arrangement and disposition of the business under the Insolvency Act 1986 Pts 7A–11 (ss 251A–385) of courts having jurisdiction for the purpose of Pts 7A–11, including provision for the allocation of proceedings under Pts 7A–11 to particular courts and for the transfer of such proceedings from one court to another (Sch 9 para 1 (amended by the Tribunals, Courts and Enforcement Act 2007 s 108(3), Sch 20 paras 1, 14(1), (2)));

(2)　provision for enabling a registrar in bankruptcy of the High Court or a district judge of a county court having jurisdiction for the purposes of the Insolvency Act 1986 Pts 7A–11 to exercise such of the jurisdiction conferred for those purposes on the High Court or, as the case may be, that county court as may be prescribed (Sch 9 para 2);

(3)　provision for regulating the practice and procedure of any court exercising jurisdiction for the purposes of Pts 7A–11, being any provision that could be made by rules of court (Sch 9 para 3);

(4)　provision conferring rights of audience, in courts exercising jurisdiction for the purposes of Pts 7A–11, on the official receiver and on solicitors (Sch 9 para 4);

(5)　provision requiring notice of any proceedings under Pts 7A–11 or of any matter relating to or arising out of a proposal under Pt 8 (ss 252–263G) (see PARA 43 et seq) or a bankruptcy to be given or published in the prescribed manner (Sch 9 para 5 (amended by the Tribunals, Courts and Enforcement Act 2007 Sch 20 paras 1, 14(1), (3)));

(6)　provision with respect to the form, manner of serving, contents and proof of any petition, application, order, notice, statement or other document required to be presented, made, given, published or prepared under any enactment contained in the Insolvency Act 1986 Pts 7A–11 or subordinate legislation under Pts 7A–11 or Pt 15 (ss 411–422), including provision requiring prescribed matters to be verified by affidavit (Sch 9 para 6 (amended by the Tribunals, Courts and Enforcement Act 2007 Sch 20 paras 1, 14(1), (4)));

(7) provision specifying the persons to whom any notice under the Insolvency Act 1986 Pts 8–11 (ss 252–385) is to be given (Sch 9 para 7);

(8) provision as to the manner in which the official receiver is to carry out his functions under Pt 7A (ss 251A–251X) (Sch 9 para 7A (added by the Tribunals, Courts and Enforcement Act 2007 Sch 20 paras 1, 14(1), (5)));

(9) provision as to the manner in which any requirement that may be imposed by the official receiver on a person under the Insolvency Act 1986 Pt 7A is to take effect (Sch 9 para 7B (added by the Tribunals, Courts and Enforcement Act 2007 Sch 20 paras 1, 14(1), (5)));

(10) provision modifying the application of the Insolvency Act 1986 Pt 7A in relation to an individual who has died at a time when a moratorium period under a debt relief order applies in relation to him (Sch 9 para 7C (added by the Tribunals, Courts and Enforcement Act 2007 Sch 20 paras 1, 14(1), (5)));

(11) provision about debt relief restrictions orders, interim orders and undertakings, including provision about evidence (Insolvency Act 1986 Sch 9 para 7D (added by the Tribunals, Courts and Enforcement Act 2007 Sch 20 paras 1, 14(1), (5)));

(12) provision about the register required to be maintained by the Insolvency Act 1986 s 251W (see PARA 105 note 6) and the information to be contained in it, including provision enabling the amalgamation of the register with another register and enabling inspection of the register by the public (Sch 9 para 7E (added by the Tribunals, Courts and Enforcement Act 2007 Sch 20 paras 1, 14(1), (5)));

(13) provision for the registration of voluntary arrangements approved under the Insolvency Act 1986 Pt 8, including provision for the keeping and inspection of a register (Sch 9 para 8);

(14) provision about the official receiver acting as nominee or supervisor in relation to a voluntary arrangement under Pt 8, including: (a) provision requiring the official receiver to act in specified circumstances; (b) provision about remuneration; (c) provision prescribing terms or conditions to be treated as forming part of a voluntary arrangement in relation to which the official receiver acts as nominee or supervisor; (d) provision enabling those terms or conditions to be varied or excluded, in specified circumstances or subject to specified conditions, by express provision in an arrangement (Sch 9 para 8A (added by the Enterprise Act 2002 s 269, Sch 23 paras 1, 16(1), (3)));

(15) provision as to the manner in which an interim receiver appointed under the Insolvency Act 1986 s 286 (see PARA 218 et seq) is to carry out his functions, including any such provision as is specified in relation to the trustee of a bankrupt's estate in Sch 9 para 21 (see head (27)) or Sch 9 para 27 (see head (34)) (Sch 9 para 9);

(16) provision as to the manner in which the official receiver is to carry out his functions as receiver or manager of a bankrupt's estate under s 287 (see PARA 229), including any such provision as is specified in relation to the trustee of a bankrupt's estate in Sch 9 para 21 (see head (27)) or Sch 9 para 27 (see head (34)) (Sch 9 para 10);

(17) provision with respect to the certification of the appointment of any person as trustee of a bankrupt's estate and as to the proof of that appointment (Sch 9 para 11);

(18) the following provision with respect to meetings of creditors:

    (a) provision as to the manner of summoning a meeting (including provision as to how any power to require a meeting is to be exercised, provision as to the manner of determining the value of any debt for the purposes of any such power and provision making the exercise of any such power subject to the deposit of a sum sufficient to cover the expenses likely to be incurred in summoning and holding a meeting);

    (b) provision specifying the time and place at which a meeting may be held and the period of notice required for a meeting;

    (c) provision as to the procedure to be followed at such a meeting (including the manner in which decisions may be reached by a meeting and the manner in which the value of any vote at a meeting is to be determined);

    (d) provision for requiring a bankrupt or debtor to attend a meeting;

    (e) provision creating, in the prescribed circumstances, a presumption that a meeting has been duly summoned and held; and

    (f) provision as to the manner of proving the decisions of a meeting (Sch 9 para 12);

(19)   provision as to the functions, membership and proceedings of a creditors' committee established under s 301 (see PARA 326 et seq) (Sch 9 para 13);

(20)   provision as to the manner in which any requirement that may be imposed on a person under Pts 8–11 by the official receiver, the trustee of a bankrupt's estate or a special manager appointed under s 370 (see PARA 232 et seq) is to be imposed and, in the case of any requirement imposed under s 305(3) (information etc to be given by the trustee to the official receiver: see PARA 474), provision conferring power on the court to make orders for the purpose of securing compliance with that requirement (Sch 9 para 14);

(21)   provision as to the manner in which any requirement imposed by virtue of s 310(3) (compliance with income payments order: see PARA 462 et seq) is to take effect (Sch 9 para 15);

(22)   provision as to the terms and conditions that may be included in a charge under s 313 (dwelling house forming part of bankrupt's estate: see PARA 413) (Sch 9 para 16);

(23)   provision as to the debts that may be proved in any bankruptcy, as to the manner and conditions of proving a debt and as to the manner and expenses of establishing the value of any debt or security (Sch 9 para 17);

(24)   provision with respect to the manner of the distribution of a bankrupt's estate, including provision with respect to unclaimed funds and dividends (Sch 9 para 18);

(25)   provision modifying the application of Pts 8–11 in relation to a debtor or bankrupt who has died (Sch 9 para 19);

(26)   provision as to the amount, or manner of determining the amount, payable to an interim receiver, the trustee of a bankrupt's estate or a special manager appointed under s 370 by way of remuneration for the performance of functions in connection with or arising out of the bankruptcy of any person (Sch 9 para 20);

(27)   provision with respect to the manner in which moneys received by the trustee of a bankrupt's estate in the course of carrying out his functions as such are to be invested or otherwise handled and with respect to the payment of interest on sums which, in pursuance of rules made by virtue of this head, have been paid into the Insolvency Services Account (see PARA 22) (Sch 9 para 21 (amended by the Insolvency Act 2000 s 13(1)));

(28)   provision enabling the Secretary of State to set the rate of interest paid on sums which have been paid into the Insolvency Services Account (Insolvency Act 1986 Sch 9 para 21A (added by the Enterprise Act 2002 s 271(2)));

(29)   provision as to the fees, costs, charges and other expenses that may be treated as the expenses of a bankruptcy (Insolvency Act 1986 Sch 9 para 22);

(30)   provision as to the fees, costs, charges and other expenses that may be incurred for any of the purposes of Pt 8 or in the administration of any voluntary arrangement approved under Pt 8 (Sch 9 para 23);

(31)   provision requiring registrars and other officers of courts having jurisdiction for the purposes of Pts 8–11:
   (a)   to keep books and other records with respect to the exercise of that jurisdiction and of jurisdiction under the Deeds of Arrangement Act 1914 (see PARA 852 et seq); and
   (b)   to make returns to the Secretary of State of the business of the courts (Insolvency Act 1986 Sch 9 para 24);

(32)   provision requiring a creditor or a committee established under s 301 (see PARA 326 et seq) to be supplied, on payment in prescribed cases of the prescribed fee, with such information and with copies of such documents as may be prescribed (Sch 9 para 25);

(33)   provision as to the manner in which public examinations under s 290 (see PARA 289 et seq) and proceedings under ss 366–368 (see PARA 305 et seq) are to be conducted, as to the circumstances in which records of such examinations and proceedings are to be made available to prescribed persons and as to the costs of such examinations and proceedings (Sch 9 para 26);

(34)   provision imposing requirements with respect to:
   (a)   the preparation and keeping by the trustee of a bankrupt's estate, or the supervisor of a voluntary arrangement approved under Pt 8, of prescribed books, accounts and other records;
   (b)   the production of those books, accounts and records for inspection by prescribed persons;
   (c)   the auditing of accounts kept by the trustee of a bankrupt's estate or the supervisor of such a voluntary arrangement (Sch 9 para 27);

(35)   provision requiring the person who is the supervisor of a voluntary arrangement

approved under Pt 8, when it appears to him that the voluntary arrangement has been fully implemented and that nothing remains to be done by him under it:

(a)   to give notice of that fact to persons bound by the voluntary arrangement; and

(b)   to report to those persons on the carrying out of the functions conferred on the supervisor of it (Sch 9 para 28);

(36)   provision as to the manner in which the trustee of a bankrupt's estate is to act in relation to the books, papers and other records of the bankrupt, including provision authorising their disposal (Sch 9 para 29);

(37)   provision about bankruptcy restrictions orders, interim orders and undertakings (see PARA 657 et seq), including:

(a)   provision about evidence;

(b)   provision enabling the amalgamation of the register mentioned in Sch 4A para 12 with another register;

(c)   provision enabling inspection of that register by the public (Sch 9 para 29A (added by the Enterprise Act 2002 Sch 23 paras 1, 16(1), (3)));

(38)   provision conferring power on the Secretary of State to make regulations with respect to so much of any matter that may be provided for in the rules as relates to the carrying out of the functions of an interim receiver appointed under the Insolvency Act 1986 s 286 (see PARA 218 et seq), of the official receiver while acting as receiver or manager under s 287 (see PARA 229 et seq) or of the trustee of a bankrupt's estate (Sch 9 para 30);

(39)   provision conferring a discretion on the court (Sch 9 para 31);

(40)   provision making non-compliance with any of the rules a criminal offence (Sch 9 para 32);

(41)   provision making different provision for different cases, including different provisions for different areas (Sch 9 para 33).

As from a day to be appointed, Sch 9 para 2 (see head (2) above) is amended to provide that there may be provision for enabling a registrar in bankruptcy of the High Court to exercise such of the jurisdiction conferred for those purposes on the High Court: see Sch 9 para 2 (amended by the Crime and Courts Act 2013 Sch 9 Pt 3 para 93(l)). At the date at which this volume states the law no such day had been appointed.

The Secretary of State may also make regulations for the purpose of giving effect to the Insolvency Act 1986 Pt 13 (ss 388–398) (see PARA 40; and COMPANY AND PARTNERSHIP INSOLVENCY vol 16 (2011) PARAS 9–57): s 419(1). Without prejudice to the generality of s 419(1) or to any provision of Pt 13 by virtue of which regulations may be made with respect to any matter, regulations under s 419 may contain: (i) provision as to the matters to be taken into account in determining whether a person is a fit and proper person to act as an insolvency practitioner; (ii) provision prohibiting a person from so acting in prescribed cases in which a conflict of interest will or may arise; (iii) provision imposing requirements with respect to the preparation and keeping by a person who acts as an insolvency practitioner of prescribed books, accounts and other records, and the production of those books, accounts and records to prescribed persons; (iv) provision conferring power on prescribed persons to require any person who acts or has acted as an insolvency practitioner to answer any inquiry in relation to a case in which he is so acting or has so acted, and to apply to a court to examine such a person or any other person on oath concerning such a case; (v) provision making non-compliance with any of the regulations a criminal offence; and (vi) such incidental, supplemental and transitional provisions as may appear to the Secretary of State necessary or expedient: s 419(2). Any power conferred by Pt 13 or Pt 15 (ss 411–422) to make regulations, rules or orders is exercisable by statutory instrument subject to annulment by resolution of either House of Parliament: s 419(3). Any rule or regulation under Pt 13 or Pt 15 may make different provision with respect to different cases or descriptions of cases, including different provision for different areas: s 419(4).

In the case of the administration in bankruptcy of the insolvent estate of a deceased person dying before the presentation of a bankruptcy petition, ss 412, 419 apply: Administration of Insolvent Estates of Deceased Persons Order 1986, SI 1986/1999, art 3(1), Sch 1 Pt II para 36. As to the administration in bankruptcy of the insolvent estates of deceased persons see further PARA 830 et seq.

3   Ie the committee established under the Insolvency Act 1976 s 10 (repealed).

4   Insolvency Act 1986 s 413(1). In the case of the administration in bankruptcy of the insolvent estate of a deceased person dying before the presentation of a bankruptcy petition, s 413 applies: Administration of Insolvent Estates of Deceased Persons Order 1986, SI 1986/1999, Sch 1 Pt II para 36.

5   As from a day to be appointed, the Insolvency Act 1986 s 413(3)(d) (see head (4) in the text) is substituted with the words 'a district judge': see s 413(3)(d) (substituted by the Crime and

Courts Act 2013 Sch 9 Pt 3 para 93(k)). At the date at which this volume states the law no such day had been appointed. As from a day to be appointed, any reference however expressed that is or is deemed to be a reference to a county court held under the County Courts Act 1984 s 1 is to be read as a reference to the county court established by s A1 of that Act: see the Crime and Courts Act 2013 Sch 9 Pt 2 para 11(1)(a), (3)(a). At the date at which this volume states the law no such day had been appointed.

6   Insolvency Act 1986 s 413(3) (amended by the Constitutional Reform Act 2005 s 15(1), Sch 4 paras 185, 190); Courts and Legal Services Act 1990 s 74(1)(a).

7   Insolvency Act 1986 s 413(3A), (3B) (added by the Constitutional Reform Act 2005 Sch 4 paras 185, 190). The Lord Chief Justice may nominate a judicial office holder (as defined in the Constitutional Reform Act 2005 s 109(4) (see COURTS AND TRIBUNALS vol 24 (2010) PARA 961)) to exercise his functions under the Insolvency Act 1986 s 413: s 413(5) (added by the Constitutional Reform Act 2005 Sch 4 paras 185, 190).

8   Insolvency Act 1986 s 413(4).

9   Insolvency Act 1986 s 413(2). The rules referred to in the text are those made under s 411 (company insolvency: see COMPANY AND PARTNERSHIP INSOLVENCY vol 17 (2011) PARA 1002) and s 412 (see note 2).

774. Application of the Insolvency Rules 1986. The Insolvency Rules 1986[1] apply, save where otherwise expressly provided, to all proceedings under the Insolvency Act 1986 or the Insolvency Rules 1986 commenced on or after 29 December 1986[2].

1   Ie the Insolvency Rules 1986, SI 1986/1925.

2   Insolvency Rules 1986, SI 1986/1925, rr 13.1, 13.14(1)(b), (c). The Insolvency Rules 1986, SI 1986/1925, apply to all insolvency proceedings on and after 11 January 1988 whenever those proceedings were commenced: Insolvency (Amendment) Rules 1987, SI 1987/1919, r 3(1), (2). As to winding-up proceedings see COMPANY AND PARTNERSHIP INSOLVENCY vol 16 (2011) PARA 380 et seq.

775. Use of prescribed forms. The forms contained in the Insolvency Rules 1986[1] must be used in insolvency proceedings[2]. The forms must be used with such variations, if any, as the circumstances may require[3].

The Secretary of State, the official receiver or an insolvency practitioner may incorporate a barcode or other reference or recognition mark into any form a copy of which is received by any of them or is sent to any person by any of them[4].

In any case where information in a prescribed form is required by the Insolvency Rules 1986 to be sent by any person to the Secretary of State, the Chief Land Registrar, or an office-holder, or a copy of a prescribed form is to be sent to the registrar of companies, the requirement is treated as having been satisfied where:

(1)   the information is submitted electronically with the agreement of the person to whom the information is sent;

(2)   the form in which the electronic submission is made satisfies the requirements of the person to whom the information is sent (which may include a requirement that the information supplied can be reproduced in the format of the prescribed form);

(3)   all the information required to be given in the prescribed form is provided in the electronic submission; and

(4)   the person to whom the information is sent can provide in legible form the information so submitted[5].

Where information in a prescribed form is permitted to be sent electronically, any requirement in the prescribed form that the prescribed form be accompanied by a signature is taken to be satisfied: (a) if the identity of the person who is supplying the information in the prescribed form and whose signature is required is confirmed in a manner specified by the recipient; or (b) where no such manner has been specified by the recipient, if the communication contains or is accompanied by a statement of the identity of the person who is providing the information in the prescribed form, and the recipient has no reason to doubt the truth of that statement[6].

Where information in a prescribed form is required by the Insolvency Rules 1986 to be sent by any person to person other than the Secretary of State, the Chief Land Registrar, an office-holder or the registrar of companies, the requirement is treated as having been satisfied where:

(i) the person to whom the information is sent has agreed to receiving the information electronically and to the form in which it is to be sent and to the specified manner in which any requirement for it to be signed is to be satisfied;

(ii) all the information required to be given in the prescribed form is provided in the electronic submission; and

(iii) the person to whom the information is sent can provide in legible form the information so submitted[7].

Any requirement in a prescribed form that it be accompanied by a signature is taken to be satisfied if the identity of the person who is supplying the information and whose signature is required, is confirmed in the specified manner[8].

1 Ie in the Insolvency Rules 1986, SI 1986/1925, Sch 4.
2 Insolvency Rules 1986, SI 1986/1925, r 12A.30(1) (added by SI 2010/686). As to the meaning of 'insolvency proceedings' see PARA 37 note 9.
3 Insolvency Rules 1986, SI 1986/1925, r 12A.30(2) (added by SI 2010/686).
4 Insolvency Rules 1986, SI 1986/1925, r 12A.30(3) (added by SI 2010/686).
5 Insolvency Rules 1986, SI 1986/1925, r 12A.31(1), (2) (added by SI 2010/686). Where information required in prescribed form has been supplied to a person, whether or not it has been supplied electronically, and a copy of that information is required to be supplied to the Secretary of State, the Chief Land Registrar, an office-holder or the registrar of companies, the requirements in heads (1)–(4) in the text apply in respect of the supply of the copy to that other person, as they apply in respect of the original: Insolvency Rules 1986, SI 1986/1925, r 12A.31(4) (added by SI 2010/686). As to the meaning of 'office-holder' see PARA 20 note 7.
6 Insolvency Rules 1986, SI 1986/1925, r 12A.31(3) (added by SI 2010/686).
7 Insolvency Rules 1986, SI 1986/1925, r 12A.32(1), (2) (added by SI 2010/686). The Insolvency Rules 1986, SI 1986/1925, r 12A.32 does not apply in respect of a statutory demand: r 12A.32(5) (added by SI 2010/686). Where information required in prescribed form has been supplied to a person, whether or not it has been supplied electronically, and a copy of that information is required to be supplied to another person, the requirements in heads (i)–(iii) in the text apply in respect of the supply of the copy to that other person, as they apply in respect of the original: Insolvency Rules 1986, SI 1986/1925, r 12A.32(4) (added by SI 2010/686).
8 Insolvency Rules 1986, SI 1986/1925, r 12A.32(3) (added by SI 2010/686).

776. Application of the Civil Procedure Rules. Except as provided[1] and except so far as inconsistent with the Insolvency Rules 1986[2], the Civil Procedure Rules including any Practice Direction[3], apply to insolvency proceedings[4] under the Insolvency Act 1986 and the Insolvency Rules 1986, with any necessary modifications[5].

1 The following provisions of the CPR (including any related practice direction) apply to insolvency proceedings by virtue of the provisions of the Insolvency Rules 1986, SI 1986/1925, specified with any necessary modifications, except so far as inconsistent with the Rules (see r 7.51A(1) (added by SI 2010/686)):
   (1) CPR Pt 6, except CPR 6.30–6.51 (service of documents: see CIVIL PROCEDURE vol 11 (2009) PARA 168 et seq) (applied by the Insolvency Rules 1986, SI 1986/1925, Pt 12A Ch 3 (rr 12A.16–12A.20));

(2)   CPR Pt 18 (further information: see CIVIL PROCEDURE vol 11 (2009) PARAS 611, 612) (applied by the Insolvency Rules 1986, SI 1986/1925, rr 7.60, 9.2(3)(b));

(3)   CPR Pt 31 (disclosure and inspection of documents: see CIVIL PROCEDURE vol 11 (2009) PARA 538 et seq) (applied by the Insolvency Rules 1986, SI 1986/1925, rr 7.60, 9.2);

(4)   CPR Pt 37 (miscellaneous provisions about payments into court: CIVIL PROCEDURE vol 12 (2009) PARA 1553 et seq) (applied by the Insolvency Rules 1986, SI 1986/1925, r 7.59);

(5)   CPR Pts 44, 47 (costs: CIVIL PROCEDURE vol 12 (2009) PARA 1729 et seq) (applied by the Insolvency Rules 1986, SI 1986/1925, Pt 7 Ch 6 (rr 7.33A–7.42));

(6)   CPR Pt 52 (appeals: CIVIL PROCEDURE vol 12 (2009) PARA 1657 et seq) (applied by the Insolvency Rules 1986, SI 1986/1925, r 7.49).

2   Ie the Insolvency Rules 1986, SI 1986/1925.

3   As to the meaning of 'Practice Direction' see PARA 2 note 6.

4   As to the meaning of 'insolvency proceedings' see PARA 35 note 4.

5   Insolvency Rules 1986, SI 1986/1925, r 7.51A(2) (added by SI 2010/686). All insolvency proceedings must be allocated to the multi-track for which CPR Pt 29 (see CIVIL PROCEDURE vol 11 (2009) PARA 293 et seq) makes provision; accordingly those provisions of the CPR which provide for allocation questionnaires and track allocation (see CIVIL PROCEDURE vol 11 (2009) PARA 246 et seq) will not apply: Insolvency Rules 1986, SI 1986/1925, r 7.51A(3) (added by SI 2010/686). CPR Pt 32 (see CIVIL PROCEDURE vol 11 (2009) PARA 749 et seq) applies to a false statement in a document verified by a statement of truth made under the Insolvency Rules 1986, SI 1986/1925, as it applies to a false statement in a document verified by a statement of truth made under CPR Pt 22 (see CIVIL PROCEDURE vol 11 (2009) PARA 613 et seq): Insolvency Rules 1986, SI 1986/1925, r 7.51A(4) (added by SI 2010/686). In general, the CPR does not apply to insolvency proceedings, except to the extent that they are applied to those proceedings by another enactment: see CPR 2.1(2), Table; and CIVIL PROCEDURE vol 11 (2009) PARA 32.

777.   Regulations by Secretary of State. The Secretary of State has power to make regulations with respect to certain matters arising in individual insolvency[1].

1   See PARAS 20, 773 note 2. An example of such regulations is the Insolvency Regulations 1994, SI 1994/2507, relating to books, accounts and records to be kept by the trustee, the handling of moneys etc: see PARA 387 et seq. These regulations were made in exercise of the powers conferred on the Secretary of State by the Insolvency Rules 1986, SI 1986/1925, r 12.1 and the Insolvency Act 1986 s 412, Sch 9: see PARA 773.

778.   Gazetting notices. A copy of the Gazette[1] containing any notice required by the Insolvency Act 1986 or the Insolvency Rules 1986[2] to be gazetted is evidence of any facts stated in the notice[3].

In the case of an order of the court notice of which is required by the Insolvency Act 1986 or the Insolvency Rules 1986 to be gazetted, a copy of the Gazette containing the notice may in any proceedings be produced as conclusive evidence that the order was made on the date specified in the notice[4].

Where an order of the court which is gazetted has been varied, and where any matter has been erroneously or inaccurately gazetted, the person whose responsibility it was to procure the requisite entry in the Gazette must as soon as is reasonably practicable cause the variation of the order to be gazetted or a further entry to be made in the Gazette for the purpose of correcting the error or inaccuracy[5].

1   As to the meaning of 'the Gazette' see PARA 165 note 12.

2   Ie the Insolvency Rules 1986, SI 1986/1925.

3   Insolvency Rules 1986, SI 1986/1925, r 12A.37(1) (added by SI 2010/686).

4   Insolvency Rules 1986, SI 1986/1925, r 12A.37(2) (added by SI 2010/686). However, in the absence of proof of actual notice, gazetting does not amount to notice to all the world: *Fryer v Ewart* [1902] AC 187, HL; *Rooney v Cardona* [1999] 1 WLR 1388, [1999] BPIR 291, CA.

5   Insolvency Rules 1986, SI 1986/1925, r 12A.37(3) (added by SI 2010/686).

779. Contents of notices to be gazetted: 'standard contents'. Where a notice is gazetted[1] under the Insolvency Act 1986 or the Insolvency Rules 1986[2], in addition to any content specifically required, the content of such a notice must be as set out below[3].

All notices published must specify in so far as it is applicable in relation to the particular notice:

(1)   the name and postal address of the office-holder[4] acting in the proceedings;

(2)   the capacity in which the office-holder is acting and the date of appointment;

(3)   either an e-mail address, or a telephone number, through which the office-holder may be contacted;

(4)   the name of any person other than the office-holder, if any, who may be contacted regarding the proceedings;

(5)   the number assigned to the office-holder by the Secretary of State[5]; and

(6)   the court name and any number assigned to the proceedings by the court[6].

In addition to that information a notice relating to a bankrupt must state:

(a)   the bankrupt's full name and residential address;

(b)   any other address at which the bankrupt has resided in the period of 12 months preceding the making of the bankruptcy order;

(c)   the bankrupt's date of birth;

(d)   the bankrupt's occupation;

(e)   any other name by which the bankrupt has been known;

(f)   any name or style (other than the bankrupt's own name) under which the bankrupt carried on business and under which any debt owed to a creditor was incurred[7].

Information required under the provisions above to be included in a notice to be gazetted may be omitted if it is not reasonably practicable to obtain it[8].

1   As to the meaning of 'gazetted' see PARA 165 note 12.
2   Ie the Insolvency Rules 1986, SI 1986/1925.
3   Insolvency Rules 1986, SI 1986/1925, r 12A.33(1) (added by SI 2010/686).
4   As to the meaning of 'office-holder' see PARA 20 note 7.
5   As to the Secretary of State see PARA 19.
6   Insolvency Rules 1986, SI 1986/1925, r 12A.33(2) (added by SI 2010/686).
7   Insolvency Rules 1986, SI 1986/1925, r 12A.35 (added by SI 2010/6863).
8   Insolvency Rules 1986, SI 1986/1925, r 12A.36 (added by SI 2010/686).

780. Notices advertised otherwise than in the Gazette: 'standard contents'. Where under the Insolvency Act 1986 or the Insolvency Rules 1986[1] a notice may be advertised otherwise than in the Gazette[2], in addition to any content specifically required, the content of such a notice must be as set out below[3].

All notices published must specify in so far as it is applicable in relation to the particular notice:

(1)   the name and postal address of the office-holder[4] acting in the proceedings to which the notice relates;

(2)   the capacity in which the office-holder is acting; and

(3)   either an e-mail address, or a telephone number, through which the office-holder may be contacted[5].

In addition to that information, a notice relating to bankruptcy must state:

(a)   the bankrupt's full name and address;

(b)   any other address at which the bankrupt has resided in the period of 12 months preceding the making of the bankruptcy order;

(c)   the bankrupt's date of birth;

(d)   the bankrupt's occupation;

(e)   any other name by which the bankrupt has been known;

(f)   any name or style (other than the bankrupt's own name) under which the bankrupt carried on business and under which any debt owed to a creditor was incurred[6].

The information required to be contained in a notice to which these provisions apply must be included in the advertisement of that notice in a manner that is reasonably likely to ensure, in relation to the form of the advertising used, that a person reading, hearing or seeing the advertisement, will be able to read, hear or see that information[7].

Information required under these provisions to be included in a notice may be omitted if it is not reasonably practicable to obtain it[8].

1   Ie the Insolvency Rules 1986, SI 1986/1925.
2   As to the meaning of 'the Gazette' see PARA 165 note 12.
3   Insolvency Rules 1986, SI 1986/1925, r 12A.38(1) (added by SI 2010/686).
4   As to the meaning of 'office-holder' see PARA 20 note 7.
5   Insolvency Rules 1986, SI 1986/1925, r 12A.38(2) (added by SI 2010/686).
6   Insolvency Rules 1986, SI 1986/1925, r 12A.40 (added by SI 2010/686).
7   Insolvency Rules 1986, SI 1986/1925, r 12A.41(1) (added by SI 2010/686).
8   Insolvency Rules 1986, SI 1986/1925, r 12A.41(2) (added by SI 2010/686).

781.   Insolvency practitioner's security.   Wherever under the Insolvency Rules 1986[1] any person has to appoint, or certify the appointment of, an insolvency practitioner[2] to any office, that person must, before making or certifying the appointment, be satisfied that the person appointed or to be appointed has security for the proper performance of that office[3].

It is the duty of the creditors' committee in bankruptcy[4] to review from time to time the adequacy of the responsible insolvency practitioner's[5] security[6].

In any insolvency proceedings[7] the costs of the responsible insolvency practitioner's security must be defrayed as an expense of the proceedings[8].

1   Ie the Insolvency Rules 1986, SI 1986/1925.
2   As to insolvency practitioners and their qualification see PARA 40; and COMPANY AND PARTNERSHIP INSOLVENCY vol 16 (2011) PARA 14 et seq.
3   Insolvency Rules 1986, SI 1986/1925, r 12A.56(1) (added by SI 2010/686). As to the requirement for security see COMPANY AND PARTNERSHIP INSOLVENCY vol 16 (2011) PARAS 24, 25.
4   See PARA 328 et seq.
5   As to the meaning of 'the responsible insolvency practitioner' see PARA 278 note 4.
6   Insolvency Rules 1986, SI 1986/1925, r 12A.56(2) (added by SI 2010/686).
7   As to the meaning of 'insolvency proceedings' see PARA 37 note 9.
8   Insolvency Rules 1986, SI 1986/1925, r 12A.56(3) (added by SI 2010/686). As to the prescribed order of priority of payment of such expenses see PARA 587 et seq.

782.   Time limits.   The normal rules relating to the calculation of any period of time[1] apply as regards computation of time in respect of anything required or authorised by the Insolvency Rules 1986[2] to be done[3]. The normal rules as to the court's general powers of management[4] apply so as to enable the court to extend or shorten the time for compliance with anything required or authorised to be done by the Insolvency Rules 1986[5]. Where, by any provision of the Insolvency

Act 1986[6] or the Insolvency Rules 1986, the time for doing anything is limited, the court may extend the time, either before or after it has expired, on such terms, if any, as it thinks fit[7].

1 Ie CPR 2.8: see CIVIL PROCEDURE vol 11 (2009) PARA 88.
2 Ie the Insolvency Rules 1986, SI 1986/1925.
3 Insolvency Rules 1986, SI 1986/1925, r 12A.55(1) (added by SI 2010/686).
4 Ie CPR 3.1(2)(a): see CIVIL PROCEDURE vol 11 (2009) PARA 249.
5 Insolvency Rules 1986, SI 1986/1925, r 12A.55(2) (added by SI 2010/686).
6 Ie the Insolvency Act 1986 Pts 7A–11 (ss 251A–385).
7 Insolvency Act 1986 s 376. As to the application of s 376 in the case of the administration in bankruptcy of the insolvent estate of a deceased person dying before the presentation of a bankruptcy petition see PARA 161 note 3.

783. Formal defects in procedure. No insolvency procedings[1] are to be invalidated by any formal defect or by any irregularity, unless the court before which objection is made considers that substantial injustice has been caused by the defect or irregularity, and that the injustice cannot be remedied by any order of the court[2].

1 As to the meaning of 'insolvency proceedings' see PARA 37 note 9.
2 Insolvency Rules 1986, SI 1986/1925, r 7.55. Defective service is within this rule (see *Re Anderson Owen Ltd (in liquidation)* [2009] EWHC 2837 (Ch), [2010] BPIR 37) as is the use of a wrong form of application (see *Phillips v McGregor-Paterson* [2009] EWHC 2385 (Ch), [2010] 1 BCLC 72, [2010] BPIR 239).
   The Insolvency Rules 1986, SI 1986/1925, r 7.55 does not apply to a statutory demand, which is not an insolvency proceeding within r 13.7 (see PARA 37 note 9): *Re A Debtor (No 1 of 1987, Lancaster), ex p Debtor v Royal Bank of Scotland plc* [1989] 2 All ER 46, sub nom *Re a Debtor (No 1 of 1987)* [1989] 1 WLR 271, CA. A formal defect does not, however, invalidate a statutory demand where the debtor is not misled by the mistake: *Re A Debtor (No 190 of 1987)* (1988) Times, 21 May. A debtor applying to set aside a statutory demand under the Insolvency Rules 1986, SI 1986/1925, r 6.5(4)(d) (see PARA 162 text and note 12) on 'other grounds' must do more than show that the demand is perplexing; he must show what is the true position between himself and the creditor or explain why he cannot do so: *Re A Debtor (No 1 of 1987, Lancaster), ex p Debtor v Royal Bank of Scotland plc*. See also *Re McKay (a bankrupt)* [2002] EWHC 2825 (Ch), [2004] BPIR 1272, [2002] All ER (D) 205 (Oct).
   As to the effect of a formal defect in the appointment, election or qualification of a trustee, special manager or member of a creditors' committee see PARA 784; and as to the validation of meetings where notice is not received by all those who are entitled to be summoned see PARA 808.

784. Formal defects in appointment or qualification. The acts of a person as the trustee of a bankrupt's estate[1] or as a special manager[2], and the acts of the creditors' committee[3] established for any bankruptcy, are valid notwithstanding any defect in the appointment, election or qualifications of the trustee or manager or, as the case may be, of any member of the committee[4].

1 See PARA 314 et seq.
2 See PARA 235.
3 See PARA 328.
4 Insolvency Act 1986 s 377. There is no equivalent provision in the case of a formal defect in the appointment or qualification of a supervisor of a voluntary arrangement approved under Pt 8 (ss 252–263G).
   As to the application of s 377 in the case of the administration in bankruptcy of the insolvent estate of a deceased person dying before the presentation of a bankruptcy petition see PARA 235 note 6.

785. Exemption from stamp duty. Stamp duty may not be charged on:
   (1)   any document, being a deed, conveyance, assignment, surrender, admission or other assurance relating solely to property which is

comprised in a bankrupt's estate and which, after the execution of that document, is or remains at law or in equity the property of the bankrupt or of the trustee of that estate;

(2)   any writ, order or certificate or other instrument relating solely to the property of a bankrupt or to any bankruptcy proceedings[1].

1   Insolvency Act 1986 s 378. In the case of the administration in bankruptcy of the insolvent estate of a deceased person dying before the presentation of a bankruptcy petition, s 378 applies: Administration of Insolvent Estates of Deceased Persons Order 1986, SI 1986/1999, art 3(1), Sch 1 Pt II para 30. As to the administration in bankruptcy of the insolvent estates of deceased persons see further PARA 830 et seq.

(ii) Applications to the Court

786.   'The court'; 'the registrar'. Anything to be done under or by virtue of the Insolvency Act 1986 or the Insolvency Rules 1986[1] by, to or before the court may be done by, to or before a judge, district judge or the registrar[2]. The registrar or district judge may authorise any act of a formal or administrative character which is not by statute his responsibility to be carried out by the chief clerk or any other officer of the court acting on his behalf, in accordance with directions given by the Lord Chancellor[3].

'The court', in relation to any matter, means the court to which[4] proceedings with respect to that matter are allocated or transferred[5].

1   Ie the Insolvency Rules 1986, SI 1986/1925.
2   Insolvency Rules 1986, SI 1986/1925, rr 13.1, 13.2(1) (amended by SI 2010/686). 'The registrar' means: (1) a registrar in bankruptcy of the High Court; or (2) where the proceedings are in the district registry of Birmingham, Bristol, Caernarfon, Cardiff, Leeds, Liverpool, Manchester, Mold, Newcastle-upon-Tyne or Preston, a district judge attached to the district registry in question: Insolvency Rules 1986, SI 1986/1925, r 13.2(3A) (added by SI 2010/686). Where CPR 2.4 (see CIVIL PROCEDURE vol 11 (2009) PARAS 49, 61) provides for the court to perform any act, that act may be performed by a registrar in bankruptcy for the purpose of insolvency proceedings in the High Court or a District Judge in a district registry of the High Court and in any county court having insolvency jurisdiction: *Practice Direction—Insolvency Proceedings* paras 1.1(8), 7.1. As from a day to be appointed, any reference however expressed that is or is deemed to be a reference to a county court held under the County Courts Act 1984 s 1 is to be read as a reference to the county court established by s A1 of that Act: see the Crime and Courts Act 2013 Sch 9 Pt 2 para 11(1)(a), (3)(c). At the date at which this volume states the law no such day had been appointed.
       The following applications relating must always be listed before a judge: (a) applications for committal for contempt; (b) applications for an injunction; (c) interim applications and applications for directions or case management after any proceedings have been referred or adjourned to the judge, except where liberty to apply to the registrar has been given: *Practice Direction—Insolvency Proceedings* para 3.3.
       When deciding whether to hear proceedings or to refer or adjourn them to the judge, the registrar should have regard to the following factors: (i) the complexity of the proceedings; (ii) whether the proceedings raise new or controversial points of law; (iii) the likely date and length of the hearing; (iv) public interest in the proceedings: *Practice Direction—Insolvency Proceedings* para 3.4.
3   Insolvency Rules 1986, SI 1986/1925, rr 13.1, 13.2(2) (amended by SI 2010/686). See *Thakerar v Lynch Hall & Hornby* [2005] EWHC 2752 (Ch), [2006] 1 WLR 1513.
4   Ie in accordance with the Insolvency Act 1986 s 373 (see PARA 756) and the Insolvency Rules 1986, SI 1986/1925.
5   Insolvency Act 1986 s 385(1). As to allocation of individual insolvency proceedings see PARAS 6, 7; and as to the transfer of bankruptcy proceedings see PARA 756 et seq. As to the application of s 385 in the case of the administration in bankruptcy of the insolvent estate of a deceased person dying before the presentation of a bankruptcy petition see PARA 6 note 8.
       In the case of the administration in bankruptcy of the insolvent estate of a deceased person dying before the presentation of a bankruptcy petition, 'the court', in relation to any matter, means the court to which, in accordance with s 373 and the Insolvency Rules 1986,

SI 1986/1925, proceedings with respect to that matter are allocated or transferred; and, subject thereto, 'the court' means the court within the jurisdiction of which the debtor resided or carried on business for the greater part of the six months immediately prior to his death: Insolvency Act 1986 s 385(1) (amended by the Administration of Insolvent Estates of Deceased Persons Order 1986, SI 1986/1999, art 3(1), Sch 1 Pt II para 33). As to the administration in bankruptcy of the insolvent estates of deceased persons see further PARA 830 et seq.

787. Applications. The following provisions[1] apply to any application made to the court[2] under the Insolvency Act 1986 or the Insolvency Rules 1986[3] except a petition for a bankruptcy order[4].

1 Ie the Insolvency Rules 1986, SI 1986/1925, Pt 7 Ch 1 (rr 7.3–7.10): see PARAS 788–792.
2 See PARA 786.
3 Ie the Insolvency Rules 1986, SI 1986/1925.
4 Insolvency Rules 1986, SI 1986/1925, r 7.1(c) (amended by SI 2003/1730). The reference to a petition for a bankruptcy order is to such a petition under the Insolvency Act 1986 Pt 9 (ss 264–371: see PARA 129 et seq): Insolvency Rules 1986, SI 1986/1925, r 7.1(c) (as so amended).

788. Form and contents of application. Each application must be in writing and must state:

(1)   that the application is made under the Insolvency Act 1986;
(2)   the names of the parties;
(3)   the name of the bankrupt or the debtor who is the subject of the insolvency proceedings to which the application relates;
(4)   the court and, where applicable, the division or district registry of that court, in which the application is made;
(5)   where the court has previously allocated a number to the insolvency proceedings within which the application is made, that number;
(6)   the nature of the remedy or order applied for or the directions sought from the court;
(7)   the names and addresses of the persons, if any, on whom it is intended to serve the application or that no person is intended to be served;
(8)   where notice of the application is required[1] to be given to specified persons, the names and addresses of all those persons, so far as known to the applicant; and
(9)   the applicant's address for service[2].

The application must be authenticated by the applicant if he is acting in person or, when he is not so acting, by or on behalf of his solicitor[3].

1 Ie by the Insolvency Act 1986 or the Insolvency Rules 1986, SI 1986/1925.
2 Insolvency Rules 1986, SI 1986/1925, r 7.3(1) (amended by SI 2010/686).
3 Insolvency Rules 1986, SI 1986/1925, r 7.3(3) (amended by SI 2010/686). As to authentication see PARA 158 note 2. For these purposes, the reference to a solicitor includes a reference to a body recognised by the Law Society under the Administration of Justice Act 1985 s 9 (see LEGAL PROFESSIONS vol 65 (2008) PARA 515): Solicitors' Recognised Bodies Order 1991, SI 1991/2684, arts 2(1), 3, 4(a), 5, Sch 1 (amended by SI 2009/500).

789. Filing and service of application. An application must be filed with the court[1], accompanied by one copy and a number of additional copies equal to the number of persons who are to be served with the application[2]. Where an application is filed with the court, the court must fix a venue[3] for the application to be heard unless it considers it is not appropriate to do so, the rule under which the application is brought provides otherwise or the case is one that does not require notice[4].

Unless the court otherwise directs, the applicant must serve a sealed copy of the application, indorsed with the venue for the hearing, on the respondent named in the application, or on each respondent, if more than one[5].

The court may give any of the following directions:

(1)   that the application be served on persons other than those specified by the relevant provision[6];

(2)   that the giving of notice to any person may be dispensed with;

(3)   that notice be given in some way other than that specified above[7].

An application must be served at least 14 days before the date fixed for its hearing unless the provision[8] under which the application is made makes different provision or the case is one of urgency[9].

Where the case is one of urgency, the court may, without prejudice to its general power to extend or abridge time limits[10], hear the application immediately, either with or without notice to, or the attendance of, other parties, or authorise a shorter period of service than that mentioned above; and any such application may be heard on terms providing for the filing or service of documents, or the carrying out of other formalities, as the court thinks just[11].

1   As to the meaning of 'file with the court' see PARA 57 note 13.
2   Insolvency Rules 1986, SI 1986/1925, r 7.4(1) (amended by SI 2010/686).
3   As to the meaning of 'venue' see PARA 46 note 22.
4   Insolvency Rules 1986, SI 1986/1925, r 7.4(2) (substituted by SI 2010/686). As to hearings without notice see r 7.5A; and PARA 790.
5   Insolvency Rules 1986, SI 1986/1925, r 7.4(3). Notice of the venue fixed for an application made to the court may be given by service of the sealed copy of the application under r 7.4(3): r 13.3(4) (amended by SI 2009/642).
6   Ie of the Insolvency Act 1986 or the Insolvency Rules 1986, SI 1986/1925.
7   Insolvency Rules 1986, SI 1986/1925, r 7.4(4).
8   Ie of the Insolvency Act 1986 or the Insolvency Rules 1986, SI 1986/1925.
9   Insolvency Rules 1986, SI 1986/1925, r 7.4(5) (substituted by SI 2010/686).
10   See PARA 782.
11   Insolvency Rules 1986, SI 1986/1925, r 7.4(6) (amended by SI 2010/686). The Insolvency Rules 1986, SI 1986/1925, r 7.4(6) enables the court to make an interim ex parte order suspending a bankrupt's automatic discharge from bankruptcy, where it considers that the making of such an order is urgent and appropriate: *Bagnall v Official Receiver* [2003] EWHC 1398 (Ch), [2003] 3 All ER 613, [2003] BPIR 1080.

790.   Other hearings without notice being served on any other party.   Where the relevant provisions[1] do not require service of the application on, or notice of it to be given to, any person the court may hear the application as soon as reasonably practicable without fixing a venue[2] as is otherwise required[3]. Alternatively, the court may fix a venue for the application to be heard in which case the rules as to filing and service[4] apply to the extent that they are relevant[5]. However, nothing in these provisions is to be taken as prohibiting the applicant from giving such notice if the applicant wishes to do so[6].

1   Ie of the Insolvency Act 1986 or the Insolvency Rules 1986, SI 1986/1925.
2   As to the meaning of 'venue' see PARA 46 note 22.
3   Insolvency Rules 1986, SI 1986/1925, r 7.5A(a) (added by SI 2010/686). As to the usual requirement of the court to fix a venue see the Insolvency Rules 1986, SI 1986/1925, r 7.4(2); and PARA 789.
4   Ie the Insolvency Rules 1986, SI 1986/1925, r 7.4: see PARA 789.
5   Insolvency Rules 1986, SI 1986/1925, r 7.5A(b) (added by SI 2010/686).
6   Insolvency Rules 1986, SI 1986/1925, r 7.5A (added by SI 2010/686).

791.   Hearing of application; jurisdiction of district judges and registrars.
Unless the court otherwise directs, the hearing of an application must be in open court[1].

In the county court, the jurisdiction of the court to hear and determine an application may be exercised by the district judge, to whom any application must be made in the first instance, unless a direction to the contrary has been given, or it is not within the district judge's power to make the order required[2].

In the High Court, the jurisdiction of the court to hear and determine an application may be exercised by the registrar, to whom the application must be made in the first instance, unless a direction to the contrary has been given, or it is not within the registrar's power to make the order required[3].

Where the application is made to the district judge in the county court or to the registrar in the High Court, the district judge or the registrar may refer to the judge any matter which the district judge or registrar thinks should properly be decided by the judge, and the judge may either dispose of the matter or refer it back to the district judge or the registrar with such directions as that judge thinks just[4].

Nothing in the provisions set out above precludes an application being made directly to the judge in a proper case[5].

1 Insolvency Rules 1986, SI 1986/1925, r 7.6A(1) (added by SI 2010/686).
2 Insolvency Rules 1986, SI 1986/1925, r 7.6A(2) (added by SI 2010/686). As from a day to be appointed, any reference however expressed that is or is deemed to be a reference to a county court held under the County Courts Act 1984 s 1 is to be read as a reference to the county court established by s A1 of that Act: see the Crime and Courts Act 2013 Sch 9 Pt 2 para 11(1)(a), (3)(c). At the date at which this volume states the law no such day had been appointed.
3 Insolvency Rules 1986, SI 1986/1925, r 7.6A(3) (added by SI 2010/686).
4 Insolvency Rules 1986, SI 1986/1925, r 7.6A(4) (added by SI 2010/686).
5 Insolvency Rules 1986, SI 1986/1925, r 7.6A(5) (added by SI 2010/686).

792. Adjournment of hearing; directions. The court may adjourn the hearing of an application[1] on such terms as it thinks just[2].

The court may at any time give such directions as it thinks just as to:

(1)   service or notice of the application on or to any person;

(2)   whether particulars of claim and defence are to be delivered and generally as to the procedure on the application including whether a hearing is necessary;

(3)   the matters to be dealt with in evidence[3].

The court may give directions as to the manner in which any evidence is to be adduced at a resumed hearing and in particular as to: (a) the taking of evidence wholly or partly by witness statement or orally; (b) the cross-examination of the maker of a witness statement; or (c) any report to be made by an office-holder[4].

1 As to the mode of application and the procedure see PARA 786 et seq.
2 Insolvency Rules 1986, SI 1986/1925, r 7.10(1) (amended by SI 2010/686).
3 Insolvency Rules 1986, SI 1986/1925, r 7.10(2) (amended by SI 2010/686).
4 Insolvency Rules 1986, SI 1986/1925, r 7.10(3) (added by SI 2010/686). As to the meaning of 'office-holder' see PARA 20 note 7.

793. Right of audience. Official receivers and deputy official receivers have right of audience in insolvency proceedings[1], whether in the High Court or a county court[2].

1 As to the meaning of 'insolvency proceedings' see PARA 37 note 9.
2 Insolvency Rules 1986, SI 1986/1925, r 7.52(1). As from a day to be appointed, any reference however expressed that is or is deemed to be a reference to a county court held under the County Courts Act 1984 s 1 is to be read as a reference to the county court established by s A1 of that Act: see the Crime and Courts Act 2013 Sch 9 Pt 2 para 11(1)(a), (3)(c). At the date at which this volume states the law no such day had been appointed.

794. Further information and disclosure. Any party to insolvency proceedings[1] may apply to the court for an order:

(1)   that any other party clarify any matter which is in dispute in the proceedings, or give additional information in relation to any such matter, in accordance with the general rules relating to further information[2]; or

(2)   to obtain disclosure from any other party in accordance with the general rules[3] relating to disclosure and inspection of documents[4].

Any such application may be made without notice being served on any other party[5].

1   As to the meaning of 'insolvency proceedings' see PARA 37 note 9.
2   Ie in accordance with CPR Pt 18: see CIVIL PROCEDURE vol 11 (2009) PARA 611 et seq.
3   Ie in accordance with CPR Pt 31: see CIVIL PROCEDURE vol 11 (2009) PARA 538 et seq.
4   Insolvency Rules 1986, SI 1986/1925, r 7.60(1) (substituted by SI 1999/1022).
5   Insolvency Rules 1986, SI 1986/1925, r 7.60(2) (substituted by SI 1999/1022). As to the mode of application and the procedure see PARA 786 et seq.

795. Payment into court. The general rules relating to payments into court[1] apply to money lodged in court under the Insolvency Rules 1986[2].

1   See CPR Pt 37; and CIVIL PROCEDURE vol 11 (2009) PARA 729 et seq.
2   Insolvency Rules 1986, SI 1986/1925, r 7.59 (substituted by SI 1999/1022; and amended by SI 2010/686).

(iii) Court Records and Returns; Access to Information

796. Court file. The court must open and maintain a file in any case where documents are filed with it under the Insolvency Rules[1] or the Insolvency Act 1986[2]; and any documents which are filed with the court must be placed on the file[3].

The office-holder[4] in the proceedings, the Secretary of State and any person who is a creditor of the individual to whom the proceedings relate, if that person provides the court with a statement in writing by confirming that he is a creditor, may inspect or obtain from the court a copy of, or a copy of any document or documents contained in, that file[5]. The same right to inspect or obtain copies is exercisable in proceedings with respect to a voluntary arrangement[6] or in proceedings relating to a debt relief order[7], by the debtor[8], and in bankruptcy proceedings, by the bankrupt, any person against whom a bankruptcy petition has been presented and any person who has been served[9] with a statutory demand[10]. The right to inspect or obtain a copy of, or a copy of any document or documents contained in, the file may be exercised on that person's behalf by a person authorised to do so by that person[11].

Any person who is not otherwise entitled to inspect or obtain a copy of, or a copy of any document or documents contained in, the file may do so if that person has the permission of the court[12].

On the application of the official receiver, the officer-holder in the proceedings or any person appearing to the court to have an interest, the court may direct that the file, a document (or part of it) or a copy of a document (or part of it) must not be made available[13] without the permission of the court[14].

Where any person wishes to exercise the right to inspect the file[15], if the permission of the court is required, he must file with the court an application notice[16] or, if the permission of the court is not required, he may inspect the file at any reasonable time[17]. Where any person wishes to exercise the right to obtain a copy of a document[18] he must pay any prescribed fee and, if the permission of the court is required, file with the court an application notice or, if the permission of the court is not required, file with the court a written request for the document[19].

If for the purposes of powers conferred by the Insolvency Act 1986 or the Insolvency Rules, the Secretary of State or the official receiver requests the transmission of the file of any insolvency proceedings[20], the court must comply with the request, unless the file is for the time being in use for the court's own purposes[21].

1　Ie the Insolvency Rules 1986, SI 1986/1925.
2　Insolvency Rules 1986, SI 1986/1925, r 7.31A(1) (added by SI 2010/686).
3　Insolvency Rules 1986, SI 1986/1925, r 7.31A(2) (added by SI 2010/686).
4　As to the meaning of 'office-holder' see PARA 20 note 7.
5　Insolvency Rules 1986, SI 1986/1925, r 7.31A(3) (added by SI 2010/686).
6　Ie under the Insolvency Act 1986 Pt 8 (ss 252–263G).
7　As to debt relief orders see PARA 101 et seq.
8　Insolvency Rules 1986, SI 1986/1925, r 7.31A(4)(b), (d) (added by SI 2010/686).
9　Ie in accordance with the Insolvency Rules 1986, SI 1986/1925, Pt 6 Ch 1 (rr 6.1–6.5): see PARA 158 et seq.
10　Insolvency Rules 1986, SI 1986/1925, r 7.31A(4)(c) (added by SI 2010/686).
11　Insolvency Rules 1986, SI 1986/1925, r 7.31A(5) (added by SI 2010/686).
12　Insolvency Rules 1986, SI 1986/1925, r 7.31A(6) (added by SI 2010/686). An application for permission to inspect the file or obtain a copy of a document under the Insolvency Rules 1986, SI 1986/1925, r 7.31A(6) may be made without notice to any other party, but the court may direct that notice must be given to any person who would be affected by its decision: r 7.31A(11) (as so added). The court may require an undertaking restricting the use of information so obtained as a condition of granting permission: *Re Haines Watts* [2004] EWHC 1970 (Ch), [2005] BPIR 798.
13　Ie under the Insolvency Rules 1986, SI 1986/1925, r 7.31A(3), (4), (5).
14　Insolvency Rules 1986, SI 1986/1925, r 7.31A(7), (8) (added by SI 2010/686). An application for a direction under r 7.31A(7) may be made without notice to any other party, but the court may direct that notice must be given to any person who would be affected by its decision: r 7.31A(11) (as so added). See also COMPANY AND PARTNERSHIP INSOLVENCY vol 17 (2011) PARA 1023.
15　Ie under the Insolvency Rules 1986, SI 1986/1925, r 7.31A(3), (4), (5), (6).
16　Ie in accordance with the Insolvency Rules 1986, SI 1986/1925.
17　Insolvency Rules 1986, SI 1986/1925, r 7.31A(9) (added by SI 2010/686).
18　Ie under the Insolvency Rules 1986, SI 1986/1925, r 7.31A(3), (4), (5), (6).
19　Insolvency Rules 1986, SI 1986/1925, r 7.31A(10) (added by SI 2010/686).
20　As to the meaning of 'insolvency proceedings' see PARA 37 note 9.
21　Insolvency Rules 1986, SI 1986/1925, r 7.31A(12) (added by SI 2010/686).

797. Office copies of documents. Any person who[1] has the right to inspect the court file of insolvency proceedings[2] may require the court to provide him with an office copy of any document from the file[3]; and a person's rights under this provision may be exercised on his behalf by his solicitor[4]. An office copy so provided by the court must be in such form as the registrar[5] thinks appropriate, and must bear the court's seal[6].

1　Ie under the Insolvency Rules 1986, SI 1986/1925: see PARA 796.
2　As to the meaning of 'insolvency proceedings' see PARA 37 note 9.
3　Insolvency Rules 1986, SI 1986/1925, r 7.61(1). As to the fee payable where this right is exercised see PARA 799.
4　Insolvency Rules 1986, SI 1986/1925, r 7.61(2). For these purposes, the reference to a solicitor includes a reference to a body recognised by the Law Society under the Administration of Justice Act 1985 s 9 (see LEGAL PROFESSIONS vol 65 (2008) PARA 515): Solicitors' Recognised Bodies Order 1991, SI 1991/2684, arts 2(1), 3, 4(a), 5, Sch 1 (amended by SI 2009/500).
5　As to the meaning of 'the registrar' see PARA 786 note 2.
6　Insolvency Rules 1986, SI 1986/1925, r 7.61(3).

798.   Confidentiality of documents.   Where in insolvency proceedings[1] the office-holder[2] considers that a document forming part of the records of those proceedings:

(1)   should be treated as confidential; or

(2)   is of such a nature that its disclosure would be prejudicial to the conduct of the proceedings or might reasonably be expected to lead to violence against any person,

he may decline to allow it to be inspected by a person who would otherwise be entitled to inspect it[3]. The persons to whom the office-holder may so refuse inspection include the members of a creditors' committee[4].

Where the office-holder determines so to refuse inspection of a document, the person wishing to inspect it may apply to the court for that determination to be overruled; and the court may either overrule it altogether, or sustain it subject to such conditions, if any, as it thinks just[5].

1   As to the meaning of 'insolvency proceedings' see PARA 37 note 9.
2   As to the meaning of 'office-holder' see PARA 20 note 7.
3   Insolvency Rules 1986, SI 1986/1925, r 12A.51(1) (added by SI 2010/686).
4   Insolvency Rules 1986, SI 1986/1925, r 12A.51(2) (added by SI 2010/686).
5   Insolvency Rules 1986, SI 1986/1925, r 12A.51(3) (added by SI 2010/686). As to appeals see PARA 761 et seq; and as to the mode of application and the procedure see PARA 786 et seq.

799.   Right to copy documents.   Where a right is conferred[1] on any person to inspect documents, the right includes that of taking copies of those documents, on payment, in the case of documents on the court's file of proceedings, of the prescribed fee chargeable[2], and in any other case, of the appropriate fee[3].

Except where prohibited[4], a responsible insolvency practitioner[5] or the official receiver is entitled to require the payment of the appropriate fee for the supply of documents requested by a creditor, member, contributory or member of a creditors' committee[6].

1   Ie under the Insolvency Act 1986 or the Insolvency Rules 1986, SI 1986/1925.
2   Ie under any order made under the Courts Act 2003 s 92: see CIVIL PROCEDURE vol 11 (2009) PARA 87.
3   Insolvency Rules 1986, SI 1986/1925, r 12A.52 (added by SI 2010/686). For these purposes, 'the appropriate fee' means 15 pence per A4 or A5 page, and 30 pence per A3 page: Insolvency Rules 1986, SI 1986/1925, r 13.11(b).
4   Ie by the Insolvency Rules 1986, SI 1986/1925.
5   As to the meaning of 'the responsible insolvency practitioner' see PARA 278 note 4.
6   Insolvency Rules 1986, SI 1986/1925, r 12A.53 (added by SI 2010/686).

800.   Right to have list of creditors.   In any proceedings in bankruptcy, a creditor or member state liquidator[1] has the right to require an office-holder[2] to provide a list of the creditors and the amount of their respective debts, except where a statement of affairs has been filed with the court[3]. The office-holder on being required to furnish the list, as soon as reasonably practicable must send it to the person requiring the list, and may charge the appropriate fee[4] for doing so[5]. The name and address of any creditor may be omitted from the list furnished where the office-holder is of the view that its disclosure would be prejudicial to the conduct of the proceedings or might reasonably be expected to lead to violence against any person, provide that the amount of the debt in question is shown in the list and a statement is included in the list that the name and address of the creditor has been omitted in respect of that debt[6].

1   As to the meaning of 'member state liquidator' see PARA 175 note 8.
2   As to the meaning of 'office-holder' see PARA 20 note 7.

3 Insolvency Rules 1986, SI 1986/1925, r 12A.54(1), (2), (5) (added by SI 2010/686).
4 As to the meaning of 'the appropriate fee' see PARA 799 note 3.
5 Insolvency Rules 1986, SI 1986/1925, r 12A.54(3) (added by SI 2010/686).
6 Insolvency Rules 1986, SI 1986/1925, r 12A.54(4) (added by SI 2010/686).

801.   False claim of status as creditor etc. Where provision is made[1] for creditors to have a right to inspect any documents, whether on the court's file or in the hands of an office-holder[2] or other person, it is an offence for a person, with the intention of obtaining a sight of documents which he has no right to inspect, falsely to claim a status which would entitle him to inspect them[3]. A person guilty of an offence under these provisions is liable on conviction on indictment to imprisonment for a term not exceeding two years or a fine, or to both, or on summary conviction to imprisonment for a term not exceeding six months or a fine not exceeding the statutory maximum, or to both[4].

1 Ie under the Insolvency Rules 1986, SI 1986/1925.
2 As to the meaning of 'office-holder' see PARA 20 note 7.
3 Insolvency Rules 1986, SI 1986/1925, r 12.18(1).
4 Insolvency Rules 1986, SI 1986/1925, rr 12.18(2), 12.21(1)–(4), Sch 5. As to the statutory maximum see SENTENCING AND DISPOSITION OF OFFENDERS vol 92 (2010) PARA 140. The Insolvency Act 1986 s 431 has effect in relation to such an offence as it does to offences under the 1986 Act: Insolvency Rules 1986, SI 1986/1925, r 12.21(5).
    In the case of the administration in bankruptcy of the insolvent estate of a deceased person dying before the presentation of a bankruptcy petition, s 431 applies: Administration of Insolvent Estates of Deceased Persons Order 1986, SI 1986/1999, art 3(1), Sch 1 Pt II para 36. As to the administration in bankruptcy of the insolvent estates of deceased persons see further PARA 830 et seq.

(iv) Evidence

802.   Admissibility in evidence of statement of affairs. In any proceedings, whether or not under the Insolvency Act 1986, a statement of affairs prepared for the purpose of any provision of the Insolvency Act 1986 which is derived from the Insolvency Act 1985[1], and any other statement made in pursuance of a requirement imposed by or under such a provision or by or under rules[2] made under the Insolvency Act 1986, may be used in evidence against any person making or concurring in making the statement[3].

However, in criminal proceedings in which any such person is charged with a relevant offence[4] no evidence relating to the statement may be adduced, and no question relating to it may be asked, by or on behalf of the prosecution unless evidence relating to it is adduced, or a question relating to it is asked, in the proceedings by or on behalf of that person[5].

1 Ie the Insolvency Act 1986 s 272 (derived from the Insolvency Act 1985 s 122) (bankrupt's statement of affairs on debtor's petition: see PARA 248); the Insolvency Act 1986 s 288 (derived from the Insolvency Act 1985 s 135) (bankrupt's statement of affairs on creditor's petition: see PARA 240); the Insolvency Act 1986 s 291(4) (derived from the Insolvency Act 1985 s 138) (inventory and information to the official receiver: see PARA 239); and the Insolvency Act 1986 s 333(1) (derived from the Insolvency Act 1985 s 169) (information to trustee: see PARA 343).
2 See the Insolvency Rules 1986, SI 1986/1925, r 6.41 (statement of affairs on debtor's petition: see PARA 163), r 6.66 (further disclosure by creditor to official receiver on creditor's petition, which the official receiver may require to be verified by a statement of truth: see PARA 247) and r 6.72 (further disclosure by creditor to official receiver on debtor's petition, which the official receiver may require to be verified by a statement of truth: see PARA 251).
3 Insolvency Act 1986 s 433(1) (renumbered by the Youth Justice and Criminal Evidence Act 1999 s 59, Sch 3 para 7(1), (2)). The statement may not be used in evidence against third

parties or the trustee: *Re Brunner* (1887) 19 QBD 572; *New, Prance and Garrard's Trustee v Hunting* [1897] 1 QB 607; on appeal [1897] 2 QB 19, CA; affd sub nom *Sharp v Jackson* [1899] AC 419, HL.

In the case of the administration in bankruptcy of the insolvent estate of a deceased person dying before the presentation of a bankruptcy petition, the Insolvency Act 1986 s 433 applies: Administration of Insolvent Estates of Deceased Persons Order 1986, SI 1986/1999, art 3(1), Sch 1 Pt II para 36. As to the administration in bankruptcy of the insolvent estates of deceased persons see further PARA 830 et seq.

4   For these purposes, a relevant offence is any offence other than:
    (1)   an offence under the Insolvency Act 1986 s 353(1) (see PARA 734), s 354(1)(b) or (3) (see PARAS 735, 737) or s 356(1) or (2)(a) or (b) (see PARAS 741, 742) or Sch 7 para 4(3)(a) (see COMPANY AND PARTNERSHIP INSOLVENCY vol 16 (2011) PARA 39);
    (2)   an offence which:
        (a)   is created by rules made under the Insolvency Act 1986; and
        (b)   is designated for these purposes by such rules or by regulations made by the Secretary of State;
    (3)   an offence which is created by regulations made under any such rules and designated for these purposes by such regulations;
    (4)   an offence under the Perjury Act 1911 ss 1, 2 or 5 (false statements made on oath or made otherwise than on oath: see CRIMINAL LAW vol 26 (2010) PARA 668 et seq);
    (5)   an offence under the Criminal Law (Consolidation) (Scotland) Act 1995 (false statements made on oath or otherwise than on oath):
Insolvency Act 1986 s 433(3) (added by the Youth Justice and Criminal Evidence Act 1999 Sch 3 para 7(1), (3)).

Any regulations under head (2)(b) above must be made by statutory instrument and, after being made, must be laid before each House of Parliament: Insolvency Act 1986 s 433(4) (added by the Youth Justice and Criminal Evidence Act 1999 Sch 3 para 7(1), (3)). At the date at which this volume states the law no such regulations had been made.

5   Insolvency Act 1986 s 433(2) (added by the Youth Justice and Criminal Evidence Act 1999 Sch 3 para 7(1), (3)).

803.   Witness statements in general.   Save where a report may be filed in court instead of a witness statement[1], where evidence is required[2] as to any matter, such evidence may be provided in the form of a witness statement unless in any specific case different provision is made[3], or the court otherwise directs[4]. The court may on the application of any party to the matter in question order the attendance for cross-examination of the person making the witness statement[5]. Where, after such an order has been made, the person in question does not attend, the person's witness statement must not be used in evidence without the permission of the court[6].

1   Ie under the Insolvency Rules 1986, SI 1986/1925, r 7.9: see PARA 805. As to the meaning of 'witness statement' see PARA 161 note 7.
2   Ie by the Insolvency Act 1986 or the Insolvency Rules 1986, SI 1986/1925.
3   Ie under the Insolvency Act 1986 or the Insolvency Rules 1986, SI 1986/1925.
4   Insolvency Rules 1986, SI 1986/1925, r 7.7A(1) (added SI 2010/686).
5   Insolvency Rules 1986, SI 1986/1925, r 7.7A(2) (added SI 2010/686). See COMPANY AND PARTNERSHIP INSOLVENCY vol 17 (2011) PARA 1030.
6   Insolvency Rules 1986, SI 1986/1925, r 7.7A(3) (added SI 2010/686).

804.   Filing and service of witness statements.   Unless the provision of the Insolvency Act 1986 or the Insolvency Rules 1986[1] under which the application is made provides otherwise, or the court otherwise allows:
    (1)   if the applicant intends to rely at the first hearing on evidence in a witness statement, he must file the witness statement with the court[2] and serve a copy on the respondent, not less than 14 days before the date fixed for the hearing; and
    (2)   where a respondent to an application intends to oppose it and to rely for that purpose on evidence in a witness statement, he must file the witness

statement with the court and serve a copy on the applicant, not less than five business days[3] before the date fixed for the hearing[4].

1 Ie the Insolvency Rules 1986, SI 1986/1925.
2 As to the meaning of 'file with the court' see PARA 57 note 13.
3 As to the meaning of 'business day' see PARA 28 note 8.
4 Insolvency Rules 1986, SI 1986/1925, r 7.8(1) (amended by SI 2010/686). As to the use of reports instead of affidavits see PARA 805.

805. Use of reports. A report may be filed in court[1] instead of a witness statement in any case:

(1) by the official receiver, whether or not he is acting in any capacity mentioned in head (2) below, or a deputy official receiver; or

(2) unless the application involves other parties or the court otherwise orders, by a trustee in bankruptcy, an interim receiver, a special manager or an insolvency practitioner appointed[2] on a debtor's petition[3].

In any case where a report is so filed instead of a witness statement, the report is to be treated for the purposes of any hearing before the court[4] as if it were a witness statement[5].

Where in insolvency proceedings[6] a witness statement is made by an office-holder[7], the witness statement must state the capacity in which that office-holder is acting and the address at which that office-holder works[8].

1 As to the meaning of 'file in court' see PARA 57 note 13.
2 Ie under the Insolvency Act 1986 s 273(2): see PARA 203.
3 Insolvency Rules 1986, SI 1986/1925, r 7.9(1) (amended by SI 2010/686).
4 Ie under the Insolvency Rules 1986, SI 1986/1925, r 7.8(1): see PARA 804.
5 Insolvency Rules 1986, SI 1986/1925, r 7.9(2) (amended by SI 2010/686).
6 As to the meaning of 'insolvency proceedings' see PARA 37 note 9.
7 As to the meaning of 'office-holder' see PARA 20 note 7.
8 Insolvency Rules 1986, SI 1986/1925, r 7.9(3A) (added by SI 2010/686).

806. Shorthand writers. In the High Court, the judge or registrar and, in a county court, a district judge may in writing nominate one or more persons to be official shorthand writers to the court[1].

At any time in the course of insolvency proceedings[2], the court may appoint a shorthand writer to take down the evidence of a person under examination[3]. Where the official receiver applies to the court for an order appointing a shorthand writer, he must name the person he proposes for appointment[4].

1 Insolvency Rules 1986, SI 1986/1925, r 7.16(1) (amended by SI 2010/686). As to the remuneration of shorthand writers see PARA 304. As from a day to be appointed, any reference however expressed that is or is deemed to be a reference to a county court held under the County Courts Act 1984 s 1 is to be read as a reference to the county court established by s A1 of that Act: see the Crime and Courts Act 2013 Sch 9 Pt 2 para 11(1)(a), (3)(c). At the date at which this volume states the law no such day had been appointed.
2 As to the meaning of 'insolvency proceedings' see PARA 37 note 9.
3 Insolvency Rules 1986, SI 1986/1925, r 7.16(2) (amended by SI 2009/642). The examination is under the Insolvency Act 1986 s 251N (see PARA 118), s 290 (see PARA 289 et seq) or s 366 (see PARA 305 et seq): Insolvency Rules 1986, SI 1986/1925, r 7.16(2) (as so amended).
4 Insolvency Rules 1986, SI 1986/1925, r 7.16(3) (amended by SI 2010/686).

(v) Service of Proceedings and Notices

807. General provisions as to service. Except where different provision is made[1], the Civil Procedure Rules concerned with the service of documents[2] apply in relation to the service of court documents within the jurisdiction with such modifications as the court may direct[3]. Those Rules also apply to the service of court documents outside the jurisdiction with such modifications as the court may direct[4].

Where there are joint office-holders in insolvency proceedings, service on one of them is to be treated as service on all of them[5].

1 Ie under the Insolvency Rules 1986, SI 1986/1925.
2 Ie CPR Pt 6: see CIVIL PROCEDURE vol 11 (2009) PARA 138 et seq.
3 Insolvency Rules 1986, SI 1986/1925, r 12A.17 (rr 12A.16–12A.20 added by SI 2010/686). The Insolvency Rules 1986, SI 1986/1925, rr 12A.17–12A.20 apply in relation to the service of petitions, applications, documents relating to petitions or applications, and court orders, which are required to be served by any provision of the Insolvency Act 1986 or the Insolvency Rules 1986, SI 1986/1925 ('court documents'): r 12A.16(1) (as so added). However, rr 12A.17–12A.19 do not apply to the service of a bankruptcy petition, any document relating to such a petition, or a bankruptcy order: r 12A.16(2) (as so added). See further COMPANY AND PARTNERSHIP INSOLVENCY vol 17 (2011) PARA 1040.
    For the purpose of the application by rr 12A.16–12A.20 of CPR Pt 6 to the service of documents in insolvency proceedings: (1) an application commencing insolvency proceedings (including a bankruptcy petition); or (2) an application within insolvency proceedings against a respondent, is to be treated as a claim form: Insolvency Rules 1986, SI 1986/1925, r 12A.16(3) (as so added). As to the meaning of 'insolvency proceedings' see PARA 37 note 9.
4 Insolvency Rules 1986, SI 1986/1925, r 12A.20 (as added: see note 3). For service within the European Union, compliance is advised with Regulation (EC) 1393/2007 (OJ L324, 10.12.07) of the European Parliament and of the Council on the service in the Member States of judicial and extrajudicial documents in civil or commercial matters (see CIVIL PROCEDURE vol 11 (2009) PARA 157 et seq): *Re Anderson Owen Ltd (in liquidation)* [2009] EWHC 2837 (Ch), [2010] BPIR 37.
5 Insolvency Rules 1986, SI 1986/1925, r 12A.19 (as added: see note 3).

808. The giving of notice and the supply of documents. Save in respect of petitions or applications to the court[1], evidence in support of that petition or application and any order of the court[2], the following provisions[3] apply where a notice or other document is required to be given, delivered or sent[4] by any person, including an office-holder[5].

Personal delivery of a notice or other document is permissible in any case[6].

Unless in any particular case some other form of delivery is required[7] a notice or other document may be sent by post in accordance with the rules for postal service in the Civil Procedure Rules[8] and sending by such means has effect as specified in those rules[9].

Where a meeting of creditors or other persons is summoned by notice[10], the meeting is presumed to have been duly summoned and held, notwithstanding that not all those to whom the notice is to be given have received it[11].

Where a notice or other document is required or authorised to be given, delivered or sent to a person[12], it may be given, delivered or sent instead to a solicitor authorised to accept delivery on that person's behalf[13].

1 See PARA 786 et seq.
2 See PARA 802 et seq.
3 Ie the Insolvency Rules 1986, SI 1986/1925, Pt 12A Ch 1 (rr 12A.1–12A.5): see the text and notes 5–13.
4 Ie under the Insolvency Act 1986 or the Insolvency Rules 1986, SI 1986/1925.
5 Insolvency Rules 1986, SI 1986/1925, r 12A.1 (added by SI 2010/686). As to the meaning of 'office-holder' see PARA 20 note 7.
6 Insolvency Rules 1986, SI 1986/1925, r 12A.2 (added by SI 2010/686).
7 Ie by the Insolvency Act 1986, the Insolvency Rules 1986, SI 1986/1925, or an order of the court.
8 Ie CPR Pt 6: see CIVIL PROCEDURE vol 11 (2009) PARA 138 et seq.
9 Insolvency Rules 1986, SI 1986/1925, r 12A.3 (added by SI 2010/686).

10　Ie in accordance with the Insolvency Act 1986 or the Insolvency Rules 1986, SI 1986/1925.

11　Insolvency Rules 1986, SI 1986/1925, r 12A.4 (added by SI 2010/686). See *Re a Debtor (No 64 of 1992)* [1994] 2 All ER 177, [1994] 1 WLR 264 (decided under the former rules).

12　Ie under the Insolvency Act 1986 or the Insolvency Rules 1986, SI 1986/1925.

13　Insolvency Rules 1986, SI 1986/1925, r 12A.5 (added by SI 2010/686). Where under the Insolvency Act 1986 or the Insolvency Rules 1986 a notice or other document is required or authorised to be given to a person, it may, if he has indicated that his solicitor is authorised to accept service on his behalf, be given instead to the solicitor: Insolvency Rules 1986, SI 1986/1925, rr 13.1, 13.4. For these purposes, the reference to a solicitor includes a reference to a body recognised by the Law Society under the Administration of Justice Act 1985 s 9 (see LEGAL PROFESSIONS vol 65 (2008) PARA 515): Solicitors' Recognised Bodies Order 1991, SI 1991/2684, arts 2(1), 3, 4(a), 5, Sch 1 (amended by SI 2009/500). Where two or more persons are acting jointly as the responsible insolvency practitioner in any proceedings, delivery of a document to one of them is to be treated as delivery to them all: Insolvency Rules 1986, SI 1986/1925, rr 13.1, 13.5. As to the meaning of 'responsible insolvency practitioner' see PARA 278 note 4.

809.　Form of notice, proof of sending and authentication; office holders etc.

The provisions set out below apply where a notice or other document is required to be given, delivered or sent under the relevant insolvency legislation[1].

Subject to any order of the court, any notice or other document required to be given, delivered or sent must be in writing and where electronic delivery is permitted[2] a notice or other document in electronic form is treated as being in writing if a copy of it is capable of being produced in a legible form[3].

Where in any insolvency proceedings[4] a notice or other document is required to be given, delivered or sent by the office-holder[5], the giving, delivering or sending of it may be proved by means of a certificate[6] that the notice or other document was duly given, delivered or sent[7]. In the case of the official receiver the certificate may be given by the official receiver, or a member of the official receiver's staff[8]; and in the case of a responsible insolvency practitioner[9] the certificate may be given by the practitioner, the practitioner's solicitor, or a partner or an employee of either of them[10]. In the case of a notice or other document to be given, delivered or sent by a person other than the official receiver or a responsible insolvency practitioner, the giving, delivering or sending of it may be proved by means of a certificate by that person that the notice or document was given, delivered or sent by that person, or that another person, named in the certificate, was instructed to give, deliver or send it[11].

A document or information given, delivered or sent in hard copy form is sufficiently authenticated if it is signed by the person sending or supplying it[12]. A document or information given, delivered or sent in electronic form is sufficiently authenticated if the identity of the sender is confirmed in a manner specified by the recipient, or where no such manner has been specified by the recipient, if the communication contains or is accompanied by a statement of the identity of the sender and the recipient has no reason to doubt the truth of that statement[13].

1　Insolvency Rules 1986, SI 1986/1925, r 12A.6(1), (2) (added by SI 2010/686). As to the relevant insolvency legislation see the Insolvency Act 1986 and the Insolvency Rules 1986, SI 1986/1925. Where there are joint office-holders in insolvency proceedings, delivery of a document to one of them is to be treated as delivery to all of them: r 12A.15 (added by SI 2010/686).

2　As to electronic delivery see PARA 810.

3　Insolvency Rules 1986, SI 1986/1925, r 12A.7 (added by SI 2010/686).

4　As to the meaning of 'insolvency proceedings' see PARA 37 note 9.

5　As to the meaning of 'office-holder' see PARA 20 note 7.

6　Such a certificate under these provisions may be indorsed on a copy or specimen of the notice or document to which it relates: Insolvency Rules 1986, SI 1986/1925, r 12A.8(5) (added by SI 2010/686).

7　Insolvency Rules 1986, SI 1986/1925, r 12A.8(1) (added by SI 2010/686).

8   Insolvency Rules 1986, SI 1986/1925, r 12A.8(2) (added by SI 2010/686).
9   As to the meaning of 'responsible insolvency practitioner' see PARA 278 note 4.
10   Insolvency Rules 1986, SI 1986/1925, r 12A.8(3) (added by SI 2010/686).
11   Insolvency Rules 1986, SI 1986/1925, r 12A.8(4) (added by SI 2010/686).
12   Insolvency Rules 1986, SI 1986/1925, r 12A.9(1) (added by SI 2010/686).
13   Insolvency Rules 1986, SI 1986/1925, r 12A.9(2) (added by SI 2010/686).

810.   Electronic delivery. The statutory rules relating to electronic delivery[1] do not apply to the filing of any notice or other document with the court or the service of a statutory demand[2].

Subject to this restriction, unless in any particular case some other form of delivery is required[3], a notice or other document may be given, delivered or sent by electronic means provided that the intended recipient of the notice or other document has consented, whether in the specific case or generally, to electronic delivery, and has not revoked that consent, and has provided an electronic address for delivery[4]. In the absence of evidence to the contrary, a notice or other document is presumed to have been delivered where the sender can produce a copy of the electronic message which contained the notice or other document, or to which the notice or other document was attached, and shows the time and date the message was sent; and that electronic message contains the address supplied by the intended recipient[5]. A message sent electronically is deemed to have been delivered to the recipient no later than 9.00 am on the next business day after it was sent[6].

Where an office-holder[7] gives, sends or delivers a notice or other document to any person by electronic means, the notice or document must contain or be accompanied by a statement that the recipient may request a hard copy of the notice or document and specifying a telephone number, e-mail address and postal address which may be used to request a hard copy[8]. Where a hard copy of the notice or other document is requested, it must be sent within five business days[9] of receipt of the request by the office-holder[10]. An office-holder must not require a person making a request for a hard copy of the notice or document to pay a fee for the supply of the document[11].

Except where electronic delivery of documents is otherwise permitted[12], no petition[13], application[14], notice or other document may be delivered or made to a court by electronic means unless the following requirements are met[15]:

(1)   the court provides an electronic working scheme[16] for the proceedings to which the document relates; and

(2)   the electronic communication is delivered[17] and authenticated in a form which complies with the requirements of the scheme, sent to the electronic address provided by the court for electronic delivery of those proceedings, and accompanied by any payment due to the court in respect of those proceedings made in a manner which complies with the requirements of the scheme[18].

Any notice required to be given to an enforcement officer[19] may be given by electronic means to any person who has been authorised to receive such notice on behalf of a specified enforcement officer or on behalf of enforcement officers generally[20].

1   Ie the Insolvency Rules 1986, SI 1986/1925, rr 12A.10–12A.13: see the text and notes 2–11; and PARA 811.
2   Insolvency Rules 1986, SI 1986/1925, r 12A.6(3) (added by SI 2010/686).
3   Ie by the Insolvency Act 1986, the Insolvency Rules 1986, SI 1986/1925, or an order of the court.
4   Insolvency Rules 1986, SI 1986/1925, r 12A.10(1) (added by SI 2010/686).

5   Insolvency Rules 1986, SI 1986/1925, r 12A.10(2) (added by SI 2010/686).
6   Insolvency Rules 1986, SI 1986/1925, r 12A.10(3) (added by SI 2010/686).
7   As to the meaning of 'office-holder' see PARA 20 note 7.
8   Insolvency Rules 1986, SI 1986/1925, r 12A.11(1) (added by SI 2010/686).
9   As to the meaning of 'business day' see PARA 28 note 8.
10 Insolvency Rules 1986, SI 1986/1925, r 12A.11(2) (added by SI 2010/686).
11 Insolvency Rules 1986, SI 1986/1925, r 12A.11(3) (added by SI 2010/686).
12 Ie permitted under another rule of the Insolvency Rules 1986, SI 1986/1925.
13 As to bankruptcy petitions see PARA 129 et seq.
14 As to applications to the court see PARA 786 et seq.
15 Insolvency Rules 1986, SI 1986/1925, r 12A.14(1), (2) (added by SI 2010/686).
16 An electronic working scheme means a scheme permitting insolvency proceedings to be delivered electronically to the court set out in a practice direction: Insolvency Rules 1986, SI 1986/1925, r 12A.14(4) (added by SI 2010/686).
17 An electronic communication is to be treated as delivered to the court at the time it is recorded by the court as having been received: Insolvency Rules 1986, SI 1986/1925, r 12A.14(5) (added by SI 2010/686).
18 Insolvency Rules 1986, SI 1986/1925, r 12A.14(3) (added by SI 2010/686).
19 Ie as provided for under any provision of the Insolvency Act 1986 or the Insolvency Rules 1986, SI 1986/1925.
20 Insolvency Rules 1986, SI 1986/1925, r 12A.29 (added by SI 2010/686).

811.   Use of websites. Where a bankruptcy order is made against an individual or an interim receiver of an individual's property is appointed, or a voluntary arrangement in relation to an individual is proposed or is approved[1], and where the office-holder[2] is required[3] to give, deliver, furnish or send a notice or other document or information to any person, that requirement is satisfied by making the notice, document or information available on a website in accordance with the statutory rules[4] and in such circumstances as may be prescribed[5].

Other than in a case where personal service is required, an office-holder required to give, deliver or send a document to any person may satisfy that requirement by sending that person a notice:

(1)   stating that the document is available for viewing and downloading on a website;

(2)   specifying the address of that website together with any password necessary to view and download the document from that site; and

(3)   containing a statement that the person to whom the notice is given, delivered or sent may request a hard copy of the document and specifying a telephone number, e-mail address and postal address which may be used to request a hard copy[6].

Where a notice is sent, the document to which it relates must be available on the website for a period of not less than three months after the date on which the notice is sent and must be in such a format as to enable it to be downloaded from the website within a reasonable time of an electronic request being made for it to be downloaded[7].

Where a hard copy of the document is requested it must be sent within five business days[8] of the receipt of the request by the office-holder[9], who is not permitted to require the person making the request to pay a fee for the supply of the document[10].

Where a document is given, delivered or sent to a person by means of a website, it is deemed to have been delivered when the document was first made available on the website or, if later, when the notice[11] was delivered to that person[12].

Special provision is made on account of expense as to website use[13].

1   Ie under the Insolvency Act 1986 Pt 8 (ss 252–263G): see PARA 43 et seq.
2   For these purposes, 'the office-holder' means the official receiver, the trustee in bankruptcy, the interim receiver, the nominee or the supervisor of the voluntary arrangement, as the case may be: Insolvency Act 1986 s 379B(1) (s 379B added by SI 2010/18).
3   Ie by any provision of the Insolvency Act 1986 or the Insolvency Rules 1986, SI 1986/1925.
4   Ie in accordance with the Insolvency Rules 1986, SI 1986/1925.
5   Insolvency Act 1986 s 379B(1), (2) (as added: see note 2).
6   Insolvency Rules 1986, SI 1986/1925, r 12A.12(1), (2) (added by SI 2010/686).
7   Insolvency Rules 1986, SI 1986/1925, r 12A.12(3) (added by SI 2010/686).
8   As to the meaning of 'business day' see PARA 28 note 8.
9   Insolvency Rules 1986, SI 1986/1925, r 12A.12(4) (added by SI 2010/686).
10 Insolvency Rules 1986, SI 1986/1925, r 12A.12(5) (added by SI 2010/686).
11 Ie the notice under the Insolvency Rules 1986, SI 1986/1925, r 12A.12(2): see the text to note 6.
12 Insolvency Rules 1986, SI 1986/1925, r 12A.12(6) (added by SI 2010/686).
13 Where the court is satisfied that the expense of sending notices in accordance with the Insolvency Rules 1986, SI 1986/1925, r 12A.12 would, on account of the number of persons entitled to receive them, be disproportionate to the benefit of sending notices in accordance with that provision, it may order that the requirement to give, deliver or send a relevant document to any person may (other than in a case where personal service is required) be satisfied by the office-holder sending each of those persons a notice: (1) stating that all relevant documents will be made available for viewing and downloading on a website; (2) specifying the address of that website together with any password necessary to view and download a relevant document from that site; and (3) containing a statement that the person to whom the notice is given, delivered or sent may at any time request that hard copies of all, or specific, relevant documents are sent to that person, and specifying a telephone number, e-mail address and postal address which may be used to make that request: r 12A.13(1) (added by SI 2010/686). For this purpose, a relevant document means any document which the office-holder is first required to give, deliver or send to any person after the court has made an order under the Insolvency Rules 1986, SI 1986/1925, r 12A.13(1): r 12A.13(6) (added by SI 2010/686).
    A document to which the Insolvency Rules 1986, SI 1986/1925, r 12A.13 relates must be available on the website for a period of not less than 12 months from the date when it was first made available on the website or, if later, from the date upon which the notice was sent, and must be in such a format as to enable it to be downloaded from the website within a reasonable time of an electronic request being made for it to be downloaded: r 12A.13(2) (added by SI 2010/686).
    Where hard copies of relevant documents have been requested, they must be sent by the office-holder: (a) within five business days of the receipt by the office-holder of the request to be sent hard copies, in the case of relevant documents first appearing on the website before the request was received; or (b) within five business days from the date a relevant document first appears on the website, in all other cases: Insolvency Rules 1986, SI 1986/1925, r 12A.13(3) (added by SI 2010/686). An office-holder must not require a person making a request for a hard copy to pay a fee for the supply of the document: Insolvency Rules 1986, SI 1986/1925, r 12A.13(3) (added by SI 2010/686).
    Where a relevant document is given, delivered or sent to a person by means of a website in accordance with this Rule, it is deemed to have been delivered when the relevant document was first made available on the website or, if later, when the notice under the Insolvency Rules 1986, SI 1986/1925, r 12A.13(1) was delivered to that person: r 12.13(5) (added by SI 2010/686).

812. Service of order staying proceedings.

Where in insolvency proceedings[1] the court makes an order staying any action, execution or other legal process against the property or person of an individual debtor or bankrupt[2], service of the order may be effected by sending a sealed copy of the order to whatever is the address for service of the claimant or other party having the carriage of the proceedings to be stayed[3].

1   As to the meaning of 'insolvency proceedings' see PARA 37 note 9.
2   See PARA 752.
3   Insolvency Rules 1986, SI 1986/1925, rr 7.56, 12A.18 (r 7.56 amended, and r 12A.18 added, by SI 2010/686). As to postal delivery of documents see PARA 808.

813. Notices where execution overtaken by individual's insolvency. Where execution has been taken out against property of a judgment debtor, and notice is given to the enforcement officer or other officer charged with the execution[1], the notice must be delivered to the office of the enforcement officer or of the officer charged with the execution by hand or by any other means of delivery which enables proof of receipt of the document at the relevant address[2].

1 Ie under the Insolvency Act 1986 s 346(2) that the judgment debtor has been adjudged bankrupt (see PARA 704), or under s 346(3)(b) that a bankruptcy petition has been presented in respect of him (see PARA 703 head (b)).

2 Insolvency Rules 1986, SI 1986/1925, r 12A.28(1), (2) (added by SI 2010/686). Where the execution is in a county court, and the officer in charge of it is a district judge in that court, then, if: (1) there is filed in that court in respect of the judgment debtor a bankruptcy petition; or (2) there is made by that court in respect of him a bankruptcy order or an order appointing an interim receiver, the Insolvency Act 1986 s 346 is deemed satisfied as regards the requirement of a notice to be served on, or given to, the officer in charge of the execution: Insolvency Rules 1986, SI 1986/1925, r 12A.28(3) (added by SI 2010/686). As from a day to be appointed, any reference however expressed that is or is deemed to be a reference to a county court held under the County Courts Act 1984 s 1 is to be read as a reference to the county court established by s A1 of that Act: see the Crime and Courts Act 2013 Sch 9 Pt 2 para 11(1)(a), (3)(c). At the date at which this volume states the law no such day had been appointed.

(vi) Costs and Detailed Assessment

814. General principles. Civil Procedure Rules stating general rules about costs[1] and the procedure for detailed assessment of costs and default provisions[2] apply to insolvency proceedings[3] with any necessary modifications, except so far as they are inconsistent with the Insolvency Rules 1986[4]. In the Supreme Court, subject to any express provisions and to the rules of court, costs are in the discretion of the court, and the court has full power to determine by whom and to what extent the costs are to be paid[5].

The relevant rules of the Insolvency Rules 1986[6] apply in relation to costs[7] in connection with insolvency proceedings[8].

1 Ie CPR Pt 44 (general rules about costs: see CIVIL PROCEDURE vol 12 (2009) PARA 1737 et seq).
2 Ie CPR Pt 47 (procedure for detailed assessment of costs and default provisions: see CIVIL PROCEDURE vol 12 (2009) PARA 1747 et seq).
3 As to the meaning of 'insolvency proceedings' see PARA 37 note 9.
4 See the Insolvency Rules 1986, SI 1986/1925, r 7.51A; and PARA 776.
5 See the Senior Courts Act 1981 s 51(1), (3); and CIVIL PROCEDURE vol 12 (2009) PARA 1737. However, this does not alter the practice in bankruptcy: see s 51(5). As to the priority of costs in bankruptcy see PARA 588.
6 Ie the Insolvency Rules 1986, SI 1986/1925, Pt 7 Ch 6 (rr 7.33A–7.42): see PARA 816 et seq.
7 For these purposes, costs include charges and expenses: Insolvency Rules 1986, SI 1986/1925, r 7.33A(2) (added by SI 2010/686).
8 Insolvency Rules 1986, SI 1986/1925, r 7.33A(1) (added by SI 2010/686).

815. Costs of proving debts. Unless the court otherwise orders, every creditor bears the cost of proving his own debt, including such as may be incurred in providing documents or evidence[1] the production of which is required by the trustee, or the convener or chairman of any meeting, where he thinks it necessary for the purpose of substantiating the whole or any part of the claim made in the proof[2].

Unless the court otherwise orders, costs incurred by the trustee in estimating the value of a bankruptcy debt[3] which, by reason of its being subject to any contingency or contingencies or for any other reason, does not bear a certain value, fall on the estate, as an expense of the bankruptcy[4].

1　Ie under the Insolvency Rules 1986, SI 1986/1925, r 6.98(3): see PARA 546.

2　Insolvency Rules 1986, SI 1986/1925, r 6.100(1), (3).
3　Ie under the Insolvency Act 1986 s 322(3): see PARA 554.

4　Insolvency Rules 1986, SI 1986/1925, r 6.100(2), (3).

816. Requirement to assess costs by detailed procedure. Where the costs[1] of any person are payable as an expense out of the bankrupt's estate[2] or, as the case may be, the debtor's property, the amount payable must be decided by detailed assessment unless agreed between the office-holder[3] and the person entitled to payment[4]. In the absence of such agreement, the office-holder: (1) may serve notice requiring that person to commence detailed assessment proceedings[5]; and (2) must serve notice where a creditors' committee formed in relation to the insolvency proceedings resolves that the amount of the costs must be decided by detailed assessment[6].

Detailed assessment proceedings must be commenced in the court to which the insolvency proceedings are allocated[7].

Where the costs of any person employed by an office-holder in insolvency proceedings are required to be decided by detailed assessment or fixed by order of the court, the office-holder may make payments on account to such person in respect of those costs provided that person undertakes in writing to repay as soon as reasonably practicable any money which may, when detailed assessment is made, prove to have been overpaid, and to pay interest on any such sum at the specified rate[8] on the date payment was made, and for the period beginning with the date of payment and ending with the date of repayment[9].

In any proceedings before the court, including proceedings on a petition, the court may order costs to be decided by detailed assessment[10].

Unless otherwise directed or authorised, the costs of a trustee in bankruptcy are to be allowed on the standard basis for which provision is made in the Civil Procedure Rules[11].

Where an enforcement officer, or other officer, charged with execution of the writ or other process is required to deliver up goods or money[12] or has deducted costs from the proceeds of an execution or money paid to him[13], the office-holder may require in writing that the amount of the enforcement officer's or other officer's bill of costs be decided by detailed assessment[14]. Where, in the case of a deduction of costs from the proceeds of an execution or money paid to the enforcement or other officer[15], any amount deducted is disallowed at the conclusion of the detailed assessment proceedings, the enforcement officer must as soon as reasonably practicable pay a sum equal to that disallowed to the office-holder for the benefit of the bankrupt's estate[16].

1　As to the meaning of 'costs' see PARA 814 note 7.
2　As to the meaning of 'the bankrupt's estate' see PARA 211.
3　As to the meaning of 'office-holder' see PARA 20 note 7.

4　Insolvency Rules 1986, SI 1986/1925, r 7.34A(1) (added by SI 2010/686); Insolvency Rules 1986, SI 1986/1925, rr 13.1, 13.8(b) (amended by SI 2009/642).
5　Ie in accordance with CPR Pt 47: see CIVIL PROCEDURE vol 12 (2009) PARA 1779 et seq.

6　Insolvency Rules 1986, SI 1986/1925, r 7.34A(2) (added by SI 2010/686). As to the meaning of 'insolvency proceedings' see PARA 37 note 9.

7　Insolvency Rules 1986, SI 1986/1925, r 7.34A(3) (added by SI 2010/686).
8　Ie at the rate specified in the Judgments Act 1838 s 17: see FINANCIAL SERVICES AND INSTITUTIONS vol 49 (2008) PARA 1307.

9　Insolvency Rules 1986, SI 1986/1925, r 7.34A(4) (added by SI 2010/686).

10　Insolvency Rules 1986, SI 1986/1925, r 7.34A(5) (added by SI 2010/686).

11 Insolvency Rules 1986, SI 1986/1925, r 7.34A(6) (added by SI 2010/686). As to the standard basis see CPR 44.3 (basis of assessment: see CIVIL PROCEDURE vol 12 (2009) PARA 1747), CPR 44.4 (factors to be taken into account when deciding the amount of costs: CIVIL PROCEDURE vol 12 (2009) PARA 1748).
12 Ie under the Insolvency Act 1986 s 346(2): see PARA 704.
13 Ie under the Insolvency Act 1986 s 346(3): see PARA 703.
14 Insolvency Rules 1986, SI 1986/1925, r 7.36(1) (substituted by SI 1999/1022; and amended by SI 2005/527; and SI 2010/686). Where such a requirement is made the Insolvency Rules 1986, SI 1986/1925, r 7.35(4) applies (see PARA 817): r 7.36(2) (substituted by SI 1999/1022).
15 Ie a deduction under the Insolvency Rules 1986, SI 1986/1925, r 7.36(1)(b).
16 Insolvency Rules 1986, SI 1986/1925, r 7.36(3) (substituted by SI 1999/1022; and amended by SI 2005/527; SI 2009/642; and SI 2010/686).

817. Procedure where detailed assessment required. Before making a detailed assessment of the costs of any person employed in insolvency proceedings[1] by the office-holder[2], the costs officer must require a certificate of employment, which must be indorsed on the bill and authenticated by the office-holder[3]. The certificate must include the name and address of the person employed, details of the functions to be carried out under the employment, and a note of any special terms of remuneration which have been agreed[4].

Every person whose costs are required to be decided by detailed assessment in insolvency proceedings must, on being required in writing to do so by the office-holder, commence detailed assessment proceedings[5]. If that person does not commence detailed assessment proceedings within three months of that requirement or within such further time as the court, on application, may permit, the office-holder may deal with the bankrupt's estate[6] or, as the case may be, the debtor's property without regard to any claim by that person, whose claim is forfeited by such a failure to commence proceedings[7]; and, where, in any such case, such a claim lies additionally against an office-holder in his personal capacity, that claim is also forfeited by such a failure to commence proceedings[8].

Where costs have been incurred in insolvency proceedings in the High Court and those proceedings are subsequently transferred to a county court, all costs of those proceedings directed by the court or otherwise required to be assessed may nevertheless, on the application of the person who incurred the costs, be ordered to be decided by detailed assessment in the High Court[9].

1 As to the meaning of 'insolvency proceedings' see PARA 37 note 9.
2 As to the meaning of 'office-holder' see PARA 20 note 7.
3 Insolvency Rules 1986, SI 1986/1925, r 7.35(1) (substituted by SI 1999/1022; and amended by SI 2010/686). As to authentication see PARA 158 note 2.
4 Insolvency Rules 1986, SI 1986/1925, r 7.35(2) (substituted by SI 1999/1022).
5 Insolvency Rules 1986, SI 1986/1925, r 7.35(3) (substituted by SI 1999/1022; and amended by SI 2010/686). Detailed assessment proceedings means proceedings in accordance with CPR Pt 47 (procedure for detailed assessment of costs and default provisions: see CIVIL PROCEDURE vol 12 (2009) PARA 1779 et seq): Insolvency Rules 1986, SI 1986/1925, r 7.35(3) (as so substituted and amended).
6 As to the meaning of 'the bankrupt's estate' see PARA 211.
7 Insolvency Rules 1986, SI 1986/1925, r 7.35(4) (substituted by SI 1999/1022; and amended by SI 2010/686); Insolvency Rules 1986, SI 1986/1925, rr 13.1, 13.8(b) (amended by SI 2009/642). As to the mode of application and the procedure see PARA 786 et seq.
8 Insolvency Rules 1986, SI 1986/1925, r 7.35(5) (substituted by SI 1999/1022; and amended by SI 2010/686).
9 Insolvency Rules 1986, SI 1986/1925, r 7.35(6) (substituted by SI 1999/1022). As to the power to transfer see PARA 756. As from a day to be appointed, any reference however expressed that is or is deemed to be a reference to a county court held under the County Courts Act 1984 s 1 is to be read as a reference to the county court established by s A1 of that Act: see the Crime and Courts Act 2013 Sch 9 Pt 2 para 11(1)(a), (3)(c). At the date at which this volume states the law no such day had been appointed.

818. Petitions presented by insolvents. In any case where a petition is presented by an individual ('the insolvent') against himself, any solicitor[1] acting for the insolvent must in his bill of costs give credit for any sum or security received from the insolvent as a deposit on account of the costs and expenses to be incurred in respect of the filing and prosecution of the petition; and the deposit must be noted by the costs officer on the final costs certificate[2].

Where an order is made on a petition presented by an individual against himself and prior to the presentation of that petition a petition had been presented by a creditor, no costs are allowed to the insolvent or that insolvent's solicitor out of that insolvent's estate[3] unless the court considers that the insolvent estate has benefited by the insolvent's conduct or there are otherwise special circumstances justifying the allowance of costs[4].

1 For these purposes, the reference to a solicitor includes a reference to a body recognised by the Law Society under the Administration of Justice Act 1985 s 9 (see LEGAL PROFESSIONS vol 65 (2008) PARA 515): Solicitors' Recognised Bodies Order 1991, SI 1991/2684, arts 2(1), 3, 4(a), 5, Sch 1 (amended by SI 2009/500).
2 Insolvency Rules 1986, SI 1986/1925, r 7.37A(1), (2) (added by SI 2010/686).
3 As to the meaning of 'the insolvent estate' see PARA 53 note 17.
4 Insolvency Rules 1986, SI 1986/1925, r 7.37A(3) (added by SI 2010/686).

819. Costs paid otherwise than out of the insolvent estate. Where the amount of costs is decided by detailed assessment under an order of the court directing that the costs are to be paid otherwise than out of the insolvent estate[1], the costs officer must note on the final costs certificate by whom, or the manner in which, the costs are to be paid[2].

1 As to the meaning of 'the insolvent estate' see PARA 53 note 17.
2 Insolvency Rules 1986, SI 1986/1925, r 7.38 (substituted by SI 1999/1022).

820. Award of costs against official receiver or office-holder. Without prejudice to any provision of the Insolvency Act 1986 or the Insolvency Rules 1986[1] by virtue of which the official receiver is not in any event to be liable for costs and expenses[2], where an office-holder[3] or the official receiver where that official receiver is not acting as an office-holder is made a party to any proceedings on the application of another party to the proceedings, he is not personally liable for costs, unless the court otherwise directs[4].

1 Ie the Insolvency Rules 1986, SI 1986/1925.
2 See PARA 39.
3 As to the meaning of 'office-holder' see PARA 20 note 7.
4 Insolvency Rules 1986, SI 1986/1925, r 7.39 (substituted by SI 1999/1022; and amended by SI 2010/686). See also *Re Mordant (a bankrupt), Mordant v Halls* [1996] BPIR 302, CA.

821. Late applications for costs. Where a party to, or person affected by, any proceedings in an insolvency applies to the court for an order allowing his costs, or part of them, incidental to the proceedings, and that application is not made at the time of the proceedings, the person concerned must serve a sealed copy of his application on the office-holder[1], and, in a bankruptcy or in proceedings relating to a debt relief order, on the official receiver[2].

The office-holder, and where appropriate, the official receiver may appear on the application[3]. The official receiver may appear on an application in proceedings relating to a debt relief order[4].

No costs of or incidental to the application are to be allowed to the applicant unless the court is satisfied that the application could not have been made at the time of the proceedings[5].

1   As to the meaning of 'office-holder' see PARA 20 note 7.
2   Insolvency Rules 1986, SI 1986/1925, r 7.40(1), (2) (r 7.40(1), (2) substituted by SI 2009/642;
    the Insolvency Rules 1986, SI 1986/1925, r 7.40(2) amended by SI 2010/686). As to the mode of
    application and the procedure see PARA 786 et seq. As to debt relief orders see PARA 101 et seq.
3   Insolvency Rules 1986, SI 1986/1925, r 7.40(3) (substituted by SI 2009/642; and amended by
    SI 2010/686).
4   Insolvency Rules 1986, SI 1986/1925, r 7.40(3A) (added by SI 2009/642).
5   Insolvency Rules 1986, SI 1986/1925, r 7.40(4) (substituted by SI 1999/1022).

822.   Costs and expenses of witnesses.   Except as directed by the court, no
allowance as a witness in any examination or other proceedings before the court
may be made to the bankrupt or the debtor[1]. A person presenting any petition in
bankruptcy proceedings is not to be regarded as a witness on the hearing of the
petition; but the costs officer may allow his expenses of travelling and
subsistence[2].

1   Insolvency Rules 1986, SI 1986/1925, r 7.41(1) (substituted by SI 1999/1022; and amended by
    SI 2009/642).
2   Insolvency Rules 1986, SI 1986/1925, r 7.41(2) (substituted by SI 1999/1022; and amended by
    SI 2009/642).

823.   Final costs certificate.   A final costs certificate of the costs officer is final
and conclusive as to all matters which have not been objected to in the manner
provided for under the rules of the court[1]. Where it is proved to the satisfaction
of a costs officer that a final costs certificate has been lost or destroyed, he may
issue a duplicate[2].

1   Insolvency Rules 1986, SI 1986/1925, r 7.42(1) (substituted by SI 1999/1022).
2   Insolvency Rules 1986, SI 1986/1925, r 7.42(2) (substituted by SI 1999/1022).

(vii) Persons who Lack Capacity to Manage their Affairs

824.   Persons who lack capacity to manage their affairs.   Where in insolvency
proceedings[1] it appears to the court that a person affected by the proceedings is
one who lacks capacity[2] to manage and administer his property and affairs either
by reason of lacking capacity[3], or due to physical affliction or disability (the
'incapacitated person'), the court may appoint such person as it thinks just to
appear for, represent or act for the incapacitated person[4]. The appointment may
be made either generally or for the purpose of any particular application or
proceeding, or for the exercise of particular rights or powers which the
incapacitated person might have exercised but for his incapacity[5].

1   As to the meaning of 'insolvency proceedings' see PARA 37 note 9.
2   Ie within the meaning of the Mental Capacity Act 2005: see MENTAL HEALTH AND CAPACITY
    vol 75 (2013) PARA 601 et seq.
3   See note 2.
4   Insolvency Rules 1986, SI 1986/1925, rr 7.43, 7.44(1) (r 7.43(1) amended by SI 2007/1898; the
    Insolvency Rules 1986, SI 1986/1925, r 7.44(1) amended by SI 2010/686). See *De Louville De
    Toucy v Bonhams 1793 Ltd* [2011] EWHC 3809 (Ch), (2011) Times, 10 December, [2011] All
    ER (D) 32 (Nov).
5   Insolvency Rules 1986, SI 1986/1925, r 7.44(2). As to the making of appointments see further
    rr 7.44(3), (4), 7.45A, 7.46; and COMPANY AND PARTNERSHIP INSOLVENCY vol 17 (2011) PARA
    1062. The need for flexibility was emphasised in *Haworth v Cartmel* [2011] EWHC 36 (Ch),
    [2011] BPIR 428, [2011] All ER (D) 23 (Mar); and see also *Hunt v Fylde Borough Council*
    [2008] BPIR 1368 (bankruptcy order annulled where, unknown to the court which made the
    order, the debtor was suffering from Huntington's disease).

(viii) Fees

825. Fees orders. In the Supreme Court and the county court, certain fees are prescribed by the Civil Proceedings Fees Order, which extends to fees in insolvency proceedings before the High Court and county court[1].

Fees orders[2] are in force made under statutory power conferred on the Lord Chancellor to direct, with the sanction of the Treasury, that fees be paid in respect of: (1) the costs of persons acting as approved intermediaries in relation to debt relief orders[3]; (2) proceedings under the Insolvency Act 1986 in relation to individual insolvency[4]; and (3) the performance by the official receiver or the Secretary of State of functions under these provisions, and under the power conferred on the Treasury to direct by whom and in what manner the fees are to be collected and accounted for[5]. The Lord Chancellor may also, with the sanction of the Treasury, by order provide for sums to be deposited, by such persons, in such manner and in such circumstances as may be specified in the order, by way of security for such fees and fees payable to any person who has prepared[6] an insolvency practitioner's report in respect of the debtor[7]. An order made under these powers may contain such incidental, supplemental and transitional provisions as may appear to the Lord Chancellor, or, as the case may be, the Treasury, necessary or expedient[8].

The Secretary of State may by order require a person or body to pay a fee in connection with the grant or maintenance of:

(1)   a designation of that person or body as a competent authority in relation to debt relief orders[9];

(2)   recognition of a professional body[10]; and

(3)   authorisation of a person to act as an insolvency practitioner[11],

and where a fee is not paid the Secretary of State may refuse the application or withdraw an authorisation[12].

The Secretary of State may by order require the payment of fees in respect of the operation of the Insolvency Services Account and in respect of payments into and out of that Account[13].

1   See the Civil Proceedings Fees Order 2008, SI 2008/1053; and CIVIL PROCEDURE vol 11 (2009) PARA 87 et seq. As from a day to be appointed, any reference however expressed that is or is deemed to be a reference to a county court held under the County Courts Act 1984 s 1 is to be read as a reference to the county court established by s A1 of that Act: see the Crime and Courts Act 2013 Sch 9 Pt 2 para 11(1)(a), (3)(c). At the date at which this volume states the law no such day had been appointed.

2   See the Insolvency Proceedings (Fees) Order 2004, SI 2004/593 (amended by SI 2005/544; SI 2006/561; SI 2007/521; SI 2008/714; SI 2009/645; SI 2010/732; SI 2011/1167).

3   See PARA 103.

4   Ie the Insolvency Act 1986 Pts 7A–11 (ss 251A–385).

5   Insolvency Act 1986 s 415(1), (2) (s 415(1) amended by the Tribunals, Courts and Enforcement Act 2007 s 108(3), Sch 20 paras 1, 9). Nothing in the Insolvency Act 1986 s 415 prejudices any power to make rules of court: s 415(7). As from a day to be appointed, s 415(1) is amended by the Enterprise and Regulatory Reform Act 2013 s 71, Sch 19 paras 1, 59: see PARA 130 note 17.

As to the application of the Insolvency Act 1986 s 415 in the case of the administration in bankruptcy of the insolvent estate of a deceased person dying before the presentation of a bankruptcy petition see PARA 39 note 2. The Lord Chancellor's functions under s 415 are protected functions for the purposes of the Constitutional Reform Act 2005 s 19: see s 19(5), Sch 7 para 4. See further CONSTITUTIONAL LAW AND HUMAN RIGHTS.

6   Ie under the Insolvency Act 1986 s 274: see PARA 205.

7   Insolvency Act 1986 s 415(3).

8   Insolvency Act 1986 s 415(4). Orders under these provisions must be made by statutory instrument and, after being made, must be laid before each House of Parliament: s 415(5). Fees payable by virtue of these provisions must be paid into the Consolidated Fund: s 415(6). All

money received by the Secretary of State in respect of proceedings under the Insolvency Act 1986 must be paid into the Insolvency Services Account: see s 403(1); and PARA 22. As to the Consolidated Fund see CONSTITUTIONAL LAW AND HUMAN RIGHTS vol 8(2) (Reissue) PARA 711; PARLIAMENT vol 78 (2010) PARA 1028 et seq.

9   Ie under the Insolvency Act 1986 s 251U: see PARA 103.

10 Ie under the Insolvency Act 1986 s 391: see PARA 40; and COMPANY AND PARTNERSHIP INSOLVENCY vol 16 (2011) PARA 15.

11 Ie under the Insolvency Act 1986 s 393: see PARA 40; and COMPANY AND PARTNERSHIP INSOLVENCY vol 16 (2011) PARA 17.

12 Insolvency Act 1986 s 415A(A1), (1), (2) (s 415A added by the Tribunals, Courts and Enforcement Act 2007 Sch 20 paras 1, 10; the Insolvency Act 1986 s 415A(A1) added by the Enterprise Act 2002 s 270(1)). See the Insolvency Practitioners and Insolvency Services Account (Fees) Order 2003, SI 2003/3363 (amended by SI 2004/476; SI 2005/523; SI 2005/3524; SI 2008/672; SI 2009/487; SI 2009/3081; and SI 2012/2264).

13 See the Insolvency Act 1986 s 415A(3), (4) (as added: see note 12).

8. CROSS BORDER INSOLVENCY

826. Introduction and coverage. The principal sources of the law governing cross border insolvency are:

(1)   in relation to insolvency proceedings in member states of the European Union (except Denmark), the European Regulation on Insolvency Proceedings[1];

(2)   the Cross-Border Insolvency Regulations 2006[2] which give effect in Great Britain to the UNCITRAL model law in a modified form[3];

(3)   the provisions in the Insolvency Act 1986 relating to co-operation between courts having jurisdiction in relation to insolvency[4];

(4)   the common law[5].

In the case of any conflict between British insolvency law[6] and the Cross-Border Insolvency Regulations 2006, the latter will prevail[7]. If any provisions of the UNCITRAL model law conflict with an obligation of the United Kingdom under the European Regulation on Insolvency Proceedings, the requirements of the latter prevail[8].

The provisions relating to cross border insolvency apply to both company and individual insolvency and are set out in detail elsewhere in this work[9].

1   Ie Council Regulation (EC) 1346/2000 (OJ L160, 30.6.2000, p 1) on insolvency proceedings: see PARAS 41, 42.
2   Ie the Cross-Border Insolvency Regulations 2006, SI 2006/1030: see PARA 827.
3   See PARA 827.
4   Ie the Insolvency Act 1986 s 426: see PARA 828.
5   See PARA 829; and COMPANY AND PARTNERSHIP INSOLVENCY vol 17 (2011) PARA 1208.
6   See PARA 827 note 4.
7   See the Cross-Border Insolvency Regulations 2006, SI 2006/1030, reg 3(2).
8   See the Cross Border Insolvency Regulations 2006, SI 2006/1030, Sch 1 art 3.
9   See COMPANY AND PARTNERSHIP INSOLVENCY vol 17 (2011) PARA 1127 et seq.

827. The Cross-Border Insolvency Regulations 2006 and the UNCITRAL Model Law. The Cross-Border Insolvency Regulations 2006[1] have been enacted which give effect to the United Nations Commission on International Trade Law ('UNCITRAL') model law on cross border insolvency[2]. The model law is designed to encourage cooperation and coordination between jurisdictions, rather than attempting the unification of substantive insolvency law. The UNCITRAL model law has the force of law in Great Britain with certain modifications to adapt it for application in Great Britain[3].

The UNCITRAL model law as so modified applies where: (1) assistance is sought in Great Britain by a foreign court or a foreign representative in connection with a foreign proceeding; (2) assistance is sought in a foreign state in connection with a proceeding under British insolvency law; (3) a foreign proceeding and a proceeding under British insolvency law in respect of the same debtor are taking place concurrently; or (4) creditors or other interested persons in a foreign state have an interest in requesting the commencement of, or participating in, a proceeding under British insolvency law[4].

The functions referred to in the modified form of the UNCITRAL model law relating to recognition of foreign proceedings and cooperation with foreign courts are performed by the Chancery Division of the High Court[5]. The court has jurisdiction in relation to those functions in the case of an individual if he has a place of business or a place of residence in England or Wales or has assets situated in England or Wales, or the court considers for any other reason that it is the appropriate forum to consider the question or provide the assistance requested[6].

Foreign representatives and creditors have certain rights of access to courts in Great Britain under the modified model law[7]. A foreign representative may apply for recognition of a foreign proceeding[8]. Provided the conditions for recognition are satisfied, the foreign proceeding will be recognised as a foreign main proceeding if it is taking place in the state where the debtor has the centre of its main interests or as a foreign non-main proceeding if the debtor has an establishment in the foreign state[9]. Upon recognition of a foreign proceeding as a foreign main proceeding certain relief automatically comes into effect[10], whereas the grant of relief on recognition of a foreign proceeding as a foreign non-main proceeding is discretionary[11]. If a foreign proceeding is recognised as a foreign main proceeding, proceedings under British insolvency law must be restricted to assets located in Great Britain and, to the extent necessary to implement coordination and cooperation, to other assets which are required to be administered under the law of Great Britain[12].

Provision is also made in the modified model law for cooperation with foreign courts and foreign representatives[13] and coordination where there are concurrent proceedings[14].

1   Ie the Cross-Border Insolvency Regulations 2006, SI 2006/1030 (amended by SI 2009/1941; and SI 2013/472).

2   See the Insolvency Act 2000 s 14; and COMPANY AND PARTNERSHIP INSOLVENCY vol 17 (2011) PARA 1208. 'Model law on cross-border insolvency' means the model law contained in Annex I of the Report of the 30th session of the United Nations Commission on International Trade Law ('UNCITRAL'): Insolvency Act 2000 s 14(4). See the Report on the work of the 30th session of UNCITRAL, 12–30 May 1997 (*Official Records of the General Assembly of the United Nations, Fifty-second Session, Supplement No 17 (A/52/17) Annex I pp 68–78*). 'UNCITRAL' was established by the UN General Assembly in 1966 (*Resolution 2205(XXI) of 17 December 1966*) to remove or reduce the disparities in national laws which create obstacles to the flow of international trade. As to the United Nations generally see INTERNATIONAL RELATIONS LAW vol 61 (2010) PARA 519 et seq.

3   See the Cross-Border Insolvency Regulations 2006, SI 2006/1030, reg 2(1); and COMPANY AND PARTNERSHIP INSOLVENCY vol 17 (2011) PARAS 1129, 1130. The modified form of the UNCITRAL model law which is given the force of law is contained in the Cross-Border Insolvency Regulations 2006, SI 2006/1030, Sch 1: see COMPANY AND PARTNERSHIP INSOLVENCY vol 17 (2011) PARA 1132 et seq. As to public policy exceptions see COMPANY AND PARTNERSHIP INSOLVENCY vol 17 (2011) PARA 1139.

    Procedural matters in England and Wales are set out in Sch 2: see COMPANY AND PARTNERSHIP INSOLVENCY vol 17 (2011) PARAS 1163–1206.

4   See the Cross-Border Insolvency Regulations 2006, SI 2006/1030, Sch 1 art 1 para 1; and COMPANY AND PARTNERSHIP INSOLVENCY vol 17 (2011) PARA 1132. 'British insolvency law' means, in relation to England and Wales, provision extending to England and Wales and made by or under the Insolvency Act 1986: see the Cross-Border Insolvency Regulations 2006, SI 2006/1030, Sch 1 art 2(a)(i). Certain proceedings are excluded: see Sch 1 art 1 para 2; and COMPANY AND PARTNERSHIP INSOLVENCY vol 17 (2011) PARA 1133. As to third party insurance rights see Sch 1 art 1 para 5; and COMPANY AND PARTNERSHIP INSOLVENCY vol 17 (2011) PARA 1135. As to the protection of proprietary interests see Sch 1 art 1 para 6; and COMPANY AND PARTNERSHIP INSOLVENCY vol 17 (2011) PARA 1136.

5   See the Cross Border Insolvency Regulations 2006, SI 2006/1030, Sch 1 art 4 para 1; and COMPANY AND PARTNERSHIP INSOLVENCY vol 17 (2011) PARA 1137.

6   See the Cross Border Insolvency Regulations 2006, SI 2006/1030, Sch 1 art 4 para 2; and COMPANY AND PARTNERSHIP INSOLVENCY vol 17 (2011) PARA 1137.

7   See the Cross Border Insolvency Regulations 2006, SI 2006/1030, Sch 1 arts 9–14; and COMPANY AND PARTNERSHIP INSOLVENCY vol 17 (2011) PARAS 1140–1143.

8   See the Cross Border Insolvency Regulations 2006, SI 2006/1030, Sch 1 arts 15–24; and COMPANY AND PARTNERSHIP INSOLVENCY vol 17 (2011) PARAS 1144–1154. Notwithstanding

recognition of foreign insolvency proceedings, the model law does not provide for the reciprocal enforcement of judgments: *Rubin v Eurofinance SA* [2012] UKSC 46, [2013] 1 AC 236, [2013] 1 All ER 521.

9 See the Cross Border Insolvency Regulations 2006, SI 2006/1030, Sch 1 art 17; and COMPANY AND PARTNERSHIP INSOLVENCY vol 17 (2011) PARA 1146.

10 See the Cross Border Insolvency Regulations 2006, SI 2006/1030, Sch 1 art 20; and COMPANY AND PARTNERSHIP INSOLVENCY vol 17 (2011) PARA 1150.

11 See the Cross Border Insolvency Regulations 2006, SI 2006/1030, Sch 1 art 21; and COMPANY AND PARTNERSHIP INSOLVENCY vol 17 (2011) PARA 1151.

12 See the Cross Border Insolvency Regulations 2006, SI 2006/1030, Sch 1 art 28; and COMPANY AND PARTNERSHIP INSOLVENCY vol 17 (2011) PARA 1158.

13 See the Cross Border Insolvency Regulations 2006, SI 2006/1030, Sch 1 arts 25–27; and COMPANY AND PARTNERSHIP INSOLVENCY vol 17 (2011) PARAS 1155–1157.

14 See the Cross Border Insolvency Regulations 2006, SI 2006/1030, Sch 1 arts 28–32; and COMPANY AND PARTNERSHIP INSOLVENCY vol 17 (2011) PARAS 1158–1162.

828. Co-operation between courts exercising jurisdiction in relation to insolvency. An order made by a court in any part of the United Kingdom in the exercise of jurisdiction in relation to insolvency law[1] must be enforced in any other part of the United Kingdom as if it were made by a court exercising the corresponding jurisdiction in that other part[2]. Without prejudice to the following provisions, such duty does not, however, require a court in any part of the United Kingdom to enforce, in relation to property situated in that part, any order made by a court in any other part of the United Kingdom[3].

The Secretary of State, with the concurrence, in relation to property situated in England and Wales, of the Lord Chancellor, may by order make provision for securing that a trustee or assignee under the insolvency law of any part of the United Kingdom has, with such modifications as may be specified in the order, the same rights in relation to any property situated in another part of the United Kingdom as he would have in the corresponding circumstances if he were a trustee or assignee under the insolvency law of that other part[4].

The courts having jurisdiction in relation to insolvency law in any part of the United Kingdom must assist the courts having the corresponding jurisdiction in any other part of the United Kingdom or any relevant country or territory[5]. For these purposes, a request made to a court in any part of the United Kingdom by a court in any other part of the United Kingdom or in a relevant country or territory is authority for the court to which the request is made to apply, in relation to any matters specified in the request, the insolvency law which is applicable by either court in relation to comparable matters falling within its jurisdiction; and, in exercising its discretion under this provision, a court must have regard, in particular, to the rules of private international law[6].

The provisions[7] relating to the execution of warrants of arrest throughout the United Kingdom apply to a warrant which, in exercise of any jurisdiction in relation to insolvency law, is issued in any part of the United Kingdom for the arrest of a person as they apply to a warrant issued in that part of the United Kingdom for the arrest of a person charged with an offence[8].

1 For these purposes, 'insolvency law' means: (1) in relation to England and Wales, provision extending to England and Wales and made by or under the Insolvency Act 1986 or the Company Directors Disqualification Act 1986 ss 1A, 6–10, 12–15, 19(c), 20 (with Sch 1) and ss 1–17 as they apply for the purposes of those provisions of that Act; (2) in relation to Scotland, provision extending to Scotland and made by or under the Insolvency Act 1986, the Company Directors Disqualification Act 1986 ss 1A, 6–10, 12–15, 19(c), 20 (with Sch 1) and ss 1–17 as they apply for the purposes of those provisions of that Act, the Companies Act 1985 Pt XVIII (ss 462–487) or the Bankruptcy (Scotland) Act 1985; (3) in relation to Northern Ireland, provision made by or under the Insolvency (Northern Ireland) Order 1989, SI 1989/2405

(NI 19) or the Company Directors Disqualification (Northern Ireland) Order 2002, SI 2002/3150 (NI 4); (4) in relation to any relevant country or territory, so much of the law of that country or territory as corresponds to provisions falling within any of heads (1)–(3); and references to any enactment include, in relation to any time before the coming into force of that enactment, the corresponding enactment in force at that time: Insolvency Act 1986 s 426(10) (amended by the Insolvency Act 2000 s 8, Sch 4 para 16(1), (3)(a), (b); SI 1989/2404 (NI 18); SI 1989/2405 (NI 19); and SI 2002/3150 (NI 4)). As to the meaning of 'relevant country or territory' see note 5. In the application of the Insolvency Act 1986 s 426 to Northern Ireland, for any reference to the Secretary of State there is to be substituted a reference to the Department of Economic Development in Northern Ireland: s 426(12)(a) (added by SI 1989/2405 (NI 19)).

The Banking Act 2009 s 129 provides for provisions of that Act about bank insolvency to be 'insolvency law' for the purposes of the Insolvency Act 1986 s 426; and the Banking Act 2009 s 165 provides for provisions of that Act about bank administration to be 'insolvency law' for the purposes of the Insolvency Act 1986 s 426: s 426(13), (14) (added by the Banking Act 2009 ss 129(2), 165(2)).

The references to insolvency law in the Insolvency Act 1986 s 426 include, in relation to a part of the United Kingdom, the provisions made by or under the Companies Act 1989 Pt VII (ss 154–191) (financial markets and insolvency: see FINANCIAL SERVICES AND INSTITUTIONS vol 48 (2008) PARA 509 et seq) and, in relation to a relevant country or territory so much of the law of that country or territory as corresponds to any provisions made by or under Pt VII: see s 183(1); and FINANCIAL SERVICES AND INSTITUTIONS vol 48 (2008) PARA 537.

'Insolvency law' includes the court's ancillary jurisdiction where it assists in connection with the insolvency proceeding, such as the court's power to grant injunctive relief: *Hughes v Hannover Rückversicherungs-Aktiengesellschaft* [1997] 1 BCLC 497, [1997] BCC 921, CA.

2   Insolvency Act 1986 s 426(1). In the case of the administration in bankruptcy of the insolvent estate of a deceased person dying before the presentation of a bankruptcy petition, s 426 applies: Administration of Insolvent Estates of Deceased Persons Order 1986, SI 1986/1999, art 3(1), Sch 1 Pt II para 36. As to the administration in bankruptcy of the insolvent estates of deceased persons see further PARA 830 et seq. See also COMPANY AND PARTNERSHIP INSOLVENCY vol 17 (2011) PARA 1207.

3   Insolvency Act 1986 s 426(2).

4   Insolvency Act 1986 s 426(3). An order under s 426(3) must be made by statutory instrument subject to annulment in pursuance of a resolution of either House of Parliament: s 426(9). At the date at which this volume states the law no such order had been made.

Where a person who is a trustee or assignee under the insolvency law of any part of the United Kingdom claims property situated in any other part of the United Kingdom, whether by virtue of an order under s 426(3) or otherwise, the submission of that claim to the court exercising jurisdiction in relation to insolvency law in that other part is to be treated in the same manner as a request made by the court for the purpose of s 426(4) (see the text to note 5): s 426(6).

In the application of s 426(3) to Northern Ireland, for the words 'another part of the United Kingdom' and the words 'that other part' there are substituted the words 'Northern Ireland': s 426(12)(b) (added by SI 1989/2405 (NI 19)). In the application of the Insolvency Act 1986 s 426(9) to Northern Ireland, there is substituted the following: An order made under s 426(3) by the Department of Economic Development in Northern Ireland is a statutory rule for the purposes of the Statutory Rules (Northern Ireland) Order 1979 and is subject to negative resolution within the meaning of the Interpretation Act (Northern Ireland) 1954 s 41(6): Insolvency Act 1986 s 426(12)(c) (added by SI 1989/2405 (NI 19)).

5   Insolvency Act 1986 s 426(4). The English court is not bound to accede to a request for assistance from a foreign court, although any such request will always be given great weight and assistance will be granted if it is proper to do so in accordance with the law to be applied: *Hughes v Hannover Rückversicherungs-Aktiengesellschaft* [1997] 1 BCLC 497, [1997] BCC 921, CA; *Re HIH Casualty and General Insurance Ltd* [2008] UKHL 21, [2008] 3 All ER 869, [2008] 1 WLR 852 (assets realised in the course of English insolvency proceedings ordered to be transferred notwithstanding that the distribution under the laws of the requesting court would not be pari passu so as to disadvantage certain creditors). The English courts will grant assistance unless there is a good or compelling reason not to do so, and they might not accede to a request for assistance from a foreign court when the assistance sought would, if granted, interfere with the conduct of insolvency proceedings in England: *Re Focus Insurance Co Ltd* [1997] 1 BCLC 219, [1996] BCC 659.

For these purposes, 'relevant country or territory' means any of the Channel Islands or the Isle of Man, or any country or territory designated for the purposes of this provision by the Secretary of State by order made by statutory instrument: Insolvency Act 1986 s 426(11). The following countries and territories are designated for these purposes: Anguilla, Australia, The Bahamas, Bermuda, Botswana, Brunei Darussalam, Canada, Cayman Islands, Falkland Islands, Gibraltar, Hong Kong, Republic of Ireland, Malaysia, Montserrat, New Zealand, Republic of South Africa, St Helena, Turks and Caicos Islands, Tuvalu, Virgin Islands: Co-operation of Insolvency Courts (Designation of Relevant Countries and Territories) Order 1986, SI 1986/2123, art 2, Schedule; Co-operation of Insolvency Courts (Designation of Relevant Countries) Order 1996, SI 1996/253, art 2, Schedule; Co-operation of Insolvency Courts (Designation of Relevant Country Order) 1998, SI 1998/2766, art 2.

The Insolvency Act 1986 s 426(4), (5), (10), (11) extends to the Bailiwick of Guernsey with certain modifications: see the Insolvency Act 1986 (Guernsey) Order 1989, SI 1989/2409; and PARA 2.

6   Insolvency Act 1986 s 426(5). When faced with a request from a foreign court for assistance, the English court is entitled to apply either English law or the law of the requesting court in determining whether to grant the request for assistance; and, once the English court has chosen to apply foreign law, it must direct itself by reference to that law: *England v Smith* [2001] Ch 419, [2000] 2 WLR 1141, CA. As to the reference in the Insolvency Act 1986 s 426(5) to the application of the rules of private international law see *Re Television Trade Rentals Ltd* [2002] EWHC 211 (Ch), [2002] BCC 807, [2002] BPIR 859 (court will take into account the foreign elements in deciding which law to apply, such as the connection of the parties with England and the requesting country); *Al Sabah v Grupo Torras SA* [2005] UKPC 1, [2005] 1 All ER 871, [2005] 2 WLR 904.

The Insolvency Act 1986 s 426(4), (5) is not concerned with the enforcement of foreign judgments: *Rubin v Eurofinance SA* [2012] UKSC 46, [2013] AC 236, [2013] 1 All ER 521.

Where a company is involved in insolvency proceedings abroad, it has been said that the English courts will do their utmost to co-operate with those proceedings and to avoid any action which might disturb the orderly administration of those proceedings: *Banque Indosuez SA v Ferromet Resources Inc* [1993] BCLC 112; cf *Felixstowe Dock and Rly Co v United States Lines Inc* [1989] QB 360, [1988] 2 All ER 77. But it is not necessary for insolvency proceedings to have been commenced in the jurisdiction of the requesting court in order for the English courts to grant assistance under the Insolvency Act 1986 s 426: *HSBC Bank plc v Tambrook Jersey Ltd* [2013] EWCA Civ 576, [2013] 3 All ER 850, [2013] 2 BCLC 186.

See also *Re Dallhold Estates (UK) Pty Ltd* [1992] BCLC 621, [1992] BCC 394 (English court has jurisdiction to make administration order in relation to a foreign company pursuant to a request made under the Insolvency Act 1986 s 426); *Re Bank of Credit and Commerce International SA (No 9)*, *Re Bank of Credit and Commerce International (Overseas) Ltd* [1994] 3 All ER 764, [1994] 2 BCLC 636 (freezing order granted in support of foreign insolvency proceedings). See further COMPANY AND PARTNERSHIP INSOLVENCY vol 17 (2011) PARA 1207.

7   Ie the Criminal Law Act 1977 s 38 (repealed by the Criminal Justice and Public Order Act 1994 s 168(3), Sch 11).

8   Insolvency Act 1986 s 426(7). Without prejudice to any power to make rules of court, any power to make provision by subordinate legislation for the purpose of giving effect in relation to individuals to the insolvency law of any part of the United Kingdom includes the power to make provision for the purpose of giving effect in that part to any provision made by or under the provisions contained in s 426(1)–(7): s 426(8). As to the meaning of 'subordinate legislation' see the Interpretation Act 1978 s 21(1) (see STATUTES AND LEGISLATIVE PROCESS vol 96 (2012) PARA 608); definition applied by the Insolvency Act 1986 s 436(1).

829. Cooperation under the common law. The English courts have a common law jurisdiction to recognise, and actively assist, a person empowered under foreign insolvency law to act on behalf of a debtor over which a foreign court has jurisdiction. The common law jurisdiction is inherent, and thus independent of any jurisdiction to recognise and assist under statute, subordinate legislation or the European Regulation on Insolvency Proceedings[1], but is subject to certain limits[2].

1   Ie Council Regulation (EC) 1346/2000 (OJ L160, 30.6.2000, p 1) on insolvency proceedings: see PARAS 41, 42.

2   See COMPANY AND PARTNERSHIP INSOLVENCY vol 17 (2011) PARA 1208. As to the limits on the common law jurisdiction see also *Rubin v Eurofinance SA, New Cap Reinsurance Corpn (in liquidation) v Grant* [2012] UKSC 46, [2013] AC 236, [2013] 1 All ER 521 (where *Cambridge*

Gas Transport Corpn v Official Committee of Unsecured Creditors of Navigator Holdings plc [2006] UKPC 26, [2007] 1 AC 508, [2006] 3 All ER 829 was held to have been wrongly decided).

As regards recognition and assistance provided by the English courts to foreign bankruptcies under common law:

(1)   the English courts will recognise that the courts of a foreign state have jurisdiction over a debtor if he was domiciled in that state at the time of the presentation of the petition (*Re Blithman* (1866) LR 2 Eq 23) or if he submitted to the jurisdiction of its courts (*Re Davidson's Settlement Trusts* (1873) LR 15 Eq 383; *Re Anderson* [1911] 1 KB 896; *Bergerem v Marsh* [1921] B & CR 195);

(2)   the vesting of the bankrupt's movable property in his foreign trustee will be given effect by the English courts (*Re Blithman* (1866) LR 2 Eq 23; *Alivon v Furnival* (1834) 1 Cr M & R 277) subject to any existing adverse rights against such property which would be recognised by the English courts (*Galbraith v Grimshaw* [1910] AC 508, HL; *Levasseur v Mason & Barry Ltd* [1891] 2 QB 73, CA); as regards immovable property situated in England and Wales, the English courts, while not recognising the vesting of title in the foreign trustee, may assist him by appointing a receiver over such property with the power to sell and deal with the proceeds (*Re Kooperman* [1928] B & CR 49; *Re Osborn, ex p Trustee* [1931–32] B & CR 189).

9. INSOLVENT ESTATES OF DECEASED PERSONS

(1) IN GENERAL

830. Power to apply statutory provisions. The Lord Chancellor may, by order made with the concurrence of the Secretary of State[1] and the Lord Chief Justice[2], provide that such provisions of the Insolvency Act 1986 as may be specified in the order are to apply in relation to the administration of the insolvent estates of deceased persons[3] with such modifications as may be so specified[4]. Such an order may make different provision for different cases and may contain such incidental, supplemental and transitional provisions as may appear to the Lord Chancellor and the Lord Chief Justice necessary or expedient[5].

1   As to the Secretary of State see PARA 19.
2   The Lord Chief Justice may nominate a judicial office holder, as defined in the Constitutional Reform Act 2005 s 109(4) (see COURTS AND TRIBUNALS vol 24 (2010) PARA 961) to exercise his functions under the Insolvency Act 1986 s 421: s 421(5) (added by the Constitutional Reform Act 2005 Sch 4 Pt 1 paras 185, 192(1), (4)).
3   As to when the estate of a deceased person is insolvent see PARA 831.
4   Insolvency Act 1986 s 421(1) (amended by the Insolvency Act 2000 s 12(2); and the Constitutional Reform Act 2005 Sch 4 Pt 1 paras 185, 192(1), (2)). An order under the Insolvency Act 1986 s 421 must be made by statutory instrument subject to annulment in pursuance of a resolution of either House of Parliament: s 421(3). An order under s 421 may make provision in relation to Council Regulation (EC) 1346/2000 (OJ L160, 30.6.2000, p 1) on insolvency proceedings ('European Regulation on Insolvency Proceedings') (see PARAS 41, 42): Insolvency Act 1986 s 421(1A) (added by SI 2002/1307). However, provision made by virtue of the Insolvency Act 1986 s 421 in relation to the European Regulation on Insolvency Proceedings may not create an offence of a kind referred to in the European Communities Act 1972 Sch 2 para 1(1)(d) (new crimes punishable with more than a specified punishment): Insolvency Act 1986 s 421(1B) (added by SI 2002/1307).

   In exercise of the powers conferred on him by the Insolvency Act 1986 s 421 and of all other powers enabling him in that behalf, with the concurrence of the Secretary of State, the Lord Chancellor made the Administration of Insolvent Estates of Deceased Persons Order 1986, SI 1986/1999, which came into force on 29 December 1986: Administration of Insolvent Estates of Deceased Persons Order 1986, SI 1986/1999, art 1. See further PARA 831 et seq.
5   Insolvency Act 1986 s 421(2) (amended by the Constitutional Reform Act 2005 Sch 4 Pt 1 paras 185, 192(1), (3)). The modifications of the Insolvency Act 1986 which may be made by an order under s 421 include any modifications which are necessary or expedient in consequence of s 421A (see PARA 840): s 421A(6) (added by the Insolvency Act 2000 s 12(1)).

831. Persons dying before presentation of bankruptcy petition. The estate of a deceased person is insolvent[1] if, when realised, it will be insufficient to meet in full all the debts and other liabilities to which it is subject[2]. Certain provisions of the Insolvency Act 1986[3] apply in relation to the administration in bankruptcy of the insolvent estates of deceased persons dying before the presentation of a bankruptcy petition, with any prescribed modifications[4] and with any further such modifications as may be necessary to render them applicable to the estate of a deceased person[5]; and the provisions of the Insolvency Rules 1986[6], the Insolvency Regulations 1994[7] and any other order made with regard to fees and deposits[8] apply accordingly[9].

1   Ie for the purposes of the Insolvency Act 1986 s 421: see PARA 830.
2   Insolvency Act 1986 s 421(4).
3   Ie the provisions of the Insolvency Act 1986 specified in the Administration of Insolvent Estates of Deceased Persons Order 1986, SI 1986/1999, art 3(1), Sch 1 Pts II, III: see PARA 832 et seq.
4   Ie the modifications specified in the Administration of Insolvent Estates of Deceased Persons Order 1986, SI 1986/1999, art 3(1), Sch 1 Pts II, III: see note 3.

5   Ie, in particular, the modifications specified in the Administration of Insolvent Estates of Deceased Persons Order 1986, SI 1986/1999, art 3(1), Sch 1 Pt I, Table. Except in so far as the context otherwise requires: (1) for any reference to the bankrupt or, as the case may be, the debtor, there is to be substituted a reference to the deceased debtor or his personal representative (or, if there is no personal representative, such person as the court may order), as the case may require; (2) for any reference to the bankrupt's estate there is to be substituted a reference to the deceased debtor's estate; (3) for any reference to the commencement of the bankruptcy there is to be substituted a reference to the date of the insolvency administration order; (4) for any reference to a bankruptcy order there is to be substituted a reference to an insolvency administration order; (5) for any reference to an individual being adjudged bankrupt there is to be substituted a reference to an insolvency administration order being made; and (6) for any reference to a debtor's petition there is to be substituted a reference to a petition by the personal representative of a deceased debtor for an insolvency administration order: Sch 1 Pt I. As to the meaning of 'insolvency administration order' see PARA 833 note 1.

6   Ie the Insolvency Rules 1986, SI 1986/1925.

7   Ie the Insolvency Regulations 1994, SI 1994/2507.

8   Ie under the Insolvency Act 1986 s 415: see PARA 825. See further the Department of Trade and Industry (Fees) Order 1988, SI 1988/93; and the Insolvency Proceedings (Fees) Order 2004, SI 2004/593.

9   Administration of Insolvent Estates of Deceased Persons Order 1986, SI 1986/1999, art 3(1). In the case of any conflict between any provision of the Insolvency Rules 1986, SI 1986/1925, and any provision of the Administration of Insolvent Estates of Deceased Persons Order 1986, SI 1986/1999, the latter provision prevails: art 3(2).

(2) INDIVIDUAL VOLUNTARY ARRANGEMENTS

832.   Individual voluntary arrangements.   Where the court has made an interim order[1] in respect of an individual who subsequently dies, the following statutory provisions apply[2]:

(1)   the provisions relating to the nominee's report on the debtor's proposal[3], with the modification that, where the individual dies before he has submitted to the nominee a document setting out the terms of the voluntary arrangement which he is proposing and a statement of his affairs, the nominee must, after the death of the individual comes to his knowledge, give notice to the court that the individual has died[4]; and, after receiving such a notice, the court must discharge the interim order[5];

(2)   the provisions relating to the summoning of a creditors' meeting[6], with the modification that, where the individual dies before a creditors' meeting has been held, no such meeting must be held and, if the individual was at the date of his death an undischarged bankrupt, the personal representative must give notice of the death to the trustee of his estate and the official receiver[7];

(3)   the provisions relating to decisions of the creditors' meeting[8];

(4)   the provisions relating to the report by the chairman of decisions to the court[9];

(5)   the provisions relating to:
    (a)   the effect of the approval of a voluntary arrangement[10];
    (b)   the effect of approval where the debtor was an undischarged bankrupt[11];
    (c)   challenging the meeting's decision[12],
    with the modification that they cease to apply on or after the death of the individual[13];

(6)   the provisions relating to the implementation and supervision of an approved voluntary arrangement[14], with the modification that, where

the individual dies after a voluntary arrangement has been approved, the personal representative of the deceased debtor and any of the deceased debtor's creditors are among the persons who may apply to the court if dissatisfied by any act, omission or decision of the supervisor and the supervisor must give notice to the court that the individual has died[15].

1   Ie under the Insolvency Act 1986 s 252: see PARA 45 et seq.
2   Administration of Insolvent Estates of Deceased Persons Order 1986, SI 1986/1999, Sch 1 Pt III.
3   Ie the Insolvency Act 1986 s 256: see PARA 52 et seq.
4   Insolvency Act 1986 s 256(1A) (added by SI 1986/1999).
5   Insolvency Act 1986 s 256(1B) (added by SI 1986/1999).
6   Ie the Insolvency Act 1986 s 257: see PARA 59.
7   Administration of Insolvent Estates of Deceased Persons Order 1986, SI 1986/1999, Sch 1 Pt III para 2.
8   Ie the Insolvency Act 1986 s 258: see PARA 62.
9   Ie the Insolvency Act 1986 s 259: see PARA 67.
10 Ie the Insolvency Act 1986 s 260: see PARA 69.
11 Ie the Insolvency Act 1986 s 261: see PARA 70.
12 Ie the Insolvency Act 1986 s 262: see PARA 84 et seq.
13 Administration of Insolvent Estates of Deceased Persons Order 1986, SI 1986/1999, Sch 1 Pt III para 4.
14 Ie the Insolvency Act 1986 s 263: see PARA 73 et seq.
15 Administration of Insolvent Estates of Deceased Persons Order 1986, SI 1986/1999, Sch 1 Pt III para 5.

(3) PETITIONS FOR INSOLVENCY ADMINISTRATION ORDER

833. Who may present petition for insolvency administration order. A petition for an insolvency administration order[1] to be made may be presented to the court[2]:

(1) by one of the individual's creditors or jointly by more than one of them[3];

(2) by a temporary administrator[4];

(3) by a liquidator[5];

(4) by the supervisor of, or any person (other than the individual) who is for the time being bound by, a voluntary arrangement proposed by the deceased debtor and approved under Part 8 of the Insolvency Act 1986[6];

(5) where a criminal bankruptcy order has been made against the individual, by the Official Petitioner or by any person specified in the order in pursuance of the Powers of Criminal Courts Act 1973[7].

Subject to the above provisions, the court may make an insolvency administration order on any such petition[8].

1   For these purposes, 'insolvency administration order' means an order for the administration in bankruptcy of the insolvent estate of a deceased debtor, being an individual at the date of his death: Insolvency Act 1986 s 385(1) (definition added by SI 1986/1999); Administration of Insolvent Estates of Deceased Persons Order 1986, SI 1986/1999, art 2. As to when the estate of a deceased person is insolvent see PARA 831.
2   Ie pursuant to the Insolvency Act 1986 s 264 (see PARA 130) (applied with modifications by the Administration of Insolvent Estates of Deceased Persons Order 1986, SI 1986/1999, Sch 1 Pt II para 1).
3   Insolvency Act 1986 s 264(1)(a) (modified by the Administration of Insolvent Estates of Deceased Persons Order 1986, SI 1986/1999, Sch 1 Pt II para 1(a), (b)). As to the prescribed form of petition see the Administration of Insolvent Estates of Deceased Persons Order 1986,

SI 1986/1999, Sch 3 Form 1 (substituted by SI 2002/1309). The Insolvency Act 1986 s 264(1)(b) (see PARA 130 head (2)) is to be omitted: Administration of Insolvent Estates of Deceased Persons Order 1986, SI 1986/1999, Sch 1 Pt II para 1(c).

4   Insolvency Act 1986 s 264(1)(ba) (added by SI 2002/1240; modified by the Administration of Insolvent Estates of Deceased Persons Order 1986, SI 1986/1999, Sch 1 Pt II para 1(ca) (added by SI 2002/1309)). For these purposes, a 'temporary administrator' is one appointed in insolvency proceedings by virtue of Council Regulation (EC) 1346/2000 (OJ L160, 30.6.2000, p 1) ('European Regulation on Insolvency Proceedings') art 38 (see PARAS 41, 42). As to the prescribed form of petition see note 3.

5   Insolvency Act 1986 s 264(1)(bb) (added by SI 2002/1240; modified by the Administration of Insolvent Estates of Deceased Persons Order 1986, SI 1986/1999, Sch 1 Pt II para 1(cb) (added by SI 2002/1309)). For these purposes, a 'liquidator' is one appointed in insolvency proceedings by virtue of the European Regulation on Insolvency Proceedings art 3(1) (see PARA 41 note 7). As to the prescribed form of petition see note 3.

6   Insolvency Act 1986 s 264(1)(c) (modified by the Administration of Insolvent Estates of Deceased Persons Order 1986, SI 1986/1999, Sch 1 Pt II para 1(d)). As to the prescribed form of petition see the Administration of Insolvent Estates of Deceased Persons Order 1986, SI 1986/1999, Sch 3 Form 2 (substituted by SI 2002/1309).

7   Insolvency Act 1986 s 264(1)(d) (modified by the Administration of Insolvent Estates of Deceased Persons Order 1986, SI 1986/1999, Sch 1 Pt II para 1(e)). As to the prescribed form of petition, in any case where a creditor could present such a petition under the Insolvency Act 1986 s 264(1)(a) (as modified: see note 3), see the Administration of Insolvent Estates of Deceased Persons Order 1986, SI 1986/1999, Sch 3 Form 3. See also the Insolvency Act 1986 s 277 (applied by the Administration of Insolvent Estates of Deceased Persons Order 1986, SI 1986/1999, Sch 1 Pt II para 9); and PARA 130 note 10. As to the prospective repeal of the Insolvency Act 1986 s 264(1)(d) and s 277 see PARA 1 note 11; and as to the repeal of the Powers of Criminal Courts Act 1973 s 39 see PARA 1 note 10.

8   Insolvency Act 1986 s 264(2) (modified by the Administration of Insolvent Estates of Deceased Persons Order 1986, SI 1986/1999, Sch 1 Pt II para 1(f)). As to the prescribed form of insolvency administration order see the Administration of Insolvent Estates of Deceased Persons Order 1986, SI 1986/1999, Sch 3 Form 4 (substituted by SI 2002/1309).

834.   Preliminary conditions to be satisfied. An insolvency administration petition[1] must, unless the court otherwise directs, be served on the liquidator[2], if one has been appointed[3] in relation to the deceased debtor, and the personal representative and must be served on such other persons as the court may direct[4]. An insolvency administration petition may not be withdrawn without the permission of the court[5]. If it appears to the court appropriate to do so on the grounds that there has been a contravention of the Insolvency Rules 1986[6] or for any other reason, the court has a general power to dismiss a petition to the court for an insolvency administration order with or without costs or to stay proceedings on such a petition; and, where it stays proceedings on a petition, it may do so on such terms and conditions as it thinks fit[7]. Where a petition for an insolvency administration order is pending at a time when a criminal bankruptcy order is made against an individual, or is presented after such an order has been made, the court may[8], on the application of the Official Petitioner, dismiss the petition if it appears appropriate to do so[9].

1   For these purposes, 'insolvency administration petition' means a petition for an insolvency administration order: Insolvency Act 1986 s 385(1) (added by SI 1986/1999); Administration of Insolvent Estates of Deceased Persons Order 1986, SI 1986/1999, art 2. As to the meaning of 'insolvency administration order' see PARA 833 note 1.

2   Ie a liquidator within the meaning of Council Regulation (EC) 1346/2000 (OJ L160, 30.6.2000, p 1) on insolvency proceedings ('European Regulation on Insolvency Proceedings') art 2(b) (see PARA 41 note 7).

3   Ie appointed in proceedings by virtue of the European Regulation on Insolvency Proceedings art 3(1): see PARA 42.

4   Insolvency Act 1986 s 266(1) (substituted by the Administration of Insolvent Estates of Deceased Persons Order 1986, SI 1986/1999 art 3(1), Sch 1 Pt II para 2(a) (substituted by

SI 2002/1309)). See also PARA 130. As to the procedure for the presentation and filing of petitions generally see PARA 167 et seq. In an appropriate case, the court will dispense with service on the personal representatives or other interested parties: *Re Ballard* [2010] BPIR 149.

5   Insolvency Act 1986 s 266(2) (applied by the Administration of Insolvent Estates of Deceased Persons Order 1986, SI 1986/1999, Sch 1 Pt II para 2); Administration of Insolvent Estates of Deceased Persons Order 1986, SI 1986/1999, Sch 1 Pt I.
6   Ie the Insolvency Rules 1986, SI 1986/1925.
7   Insolvency Act 1986 s 266(3) (modified by the Administration of Insolvent Estates of Deceased Persons Order 1986, SI 1986/1999, Sch 1 Pt II para 2(b)); Administration of Insolvent Estates of Deceased Persons Order 1986, SI 1986/1999, Sch 1 Pt I.
8   Ie without prejudice to the Insolvency Act 1986 s 266(3) (see the text and note 7).
9   Insolvency Act 1986 s 266(4) (applied by the Administration of Insolvent Estates of Deceased Persons Order 1986, SI 1986/1999, Sch 1 Pt II para 2); Administration of Insolvent Estates of Deceased Persons Order 1986, SI 1986/1999, Sch 1 Pt I. As to the prospective repeal of the Insolvency Act 1986 s 266(4) see PARA 1 note 11.

835.   Petition for insolvency administration order.   A creditor's petition must be in respect of one or more debts owed by the deceased debtor; and the petitioning creditor or each of the petitioning creditors must be a person to whom the debt or, as the case may be, at least one of the debts, is owed[1]. A creditor's petition may be presented to the court in respect of a debt or debts only if, had the debtor been alive at the time the petition was presented:

(1)   the amount of the debt, or the aggregate amount of the debts, owed by the debtor would have been equal to or exceeded the bankruptcy level[2]; or

(2)   the debt, or each of the debts, owed by the debtor would have been for a liquidated sum payable to the petitioning creditor, or one or more of the petitioning creditors, either immediately or at some certain future time, and would have been unsecured[3].

A debt which is the debt, or one of the debts, in respect of which a creditor's petition is presented need not be unsecured if either:

(a)   the petition contains a statement by the person having the right to enforce the security that he is willing, in the event of an insolvency administration order[4] being made, to give up his security for the benefit of all the deceased debtor's creditors; or

(b)   the petition is not expressed to be made in respect of the secured part of the debt and contains a statement by that person of the estimated value at the date of the petition of the security for the secured part of the debt[5].

In a case falling within head (b) above the secured and unsecured parts of the debt are to be treated[6] as separate debts[7].

A petition by the personal representative of a deceased debtor for an insolvency administration order may be presented to the court only on the grounds that the estate of the deceased debtor is insolvent[8].

1   Insolvency Act 1986 s 267(1) (applied by the Administration of Insolvent Estates of Deceased Persons Order 1986, SI 1986/1999 art 3(1), Sch 1 Pt II para 3); Administration of Insolvent Estates of Deceased Persons Order 1986, SI 1986/1999, Sch 1 Pt I. As to the procedure on a petition for an insolvency administration order see PARA 836; as to creditors' petitions generally see PARA 132 et seq; and as to the procedure for the presentation and filing of petitions generally see PARA 167 et seq.
2   As to the meaning of 'the bankruptcy level' see PARA 132 note 5.
3   Insolvency Act 1986 s 267(2)(a), (b) (substituted by the Administration of Insolvent Estates of Deceased Persons Order 1986, SI 1986/1999, Sch 1 Pt II para 3(b)). The Insolvency Act 1986 s 267(2)(c), (d) (see PARA 132 heads (3), (4)) does not apply: Insolvent Estates of Deceased Persons Order 1986, SI 1986/1999, Sch 1 Pt II para 3(b).
4   As to the meaning of 'insolvency administration order' see PARA 833 note 1.

5 Insolvency Act 1986 s 269(1) (applied by the Administration of Insolvent Estates of Deceased Persons Order 1986, SI 1986/1999, Sch 1 Pt II para 4); Administration of Insolvent Estates of Deceased Persons Order 1986, SI 1986/1999, Sch 1 Pt I.

6 Ie for the purposes of the Insolvency Act 1986 s 267 (see the text and notes 1–3) and s 269 (see notes 5, 7).

7 Insolvency Act 1986 s 269(2) (modified by the Administration of Insolvent Estates of Deceased Persons Order 1986, SI 1986/1999, Sch 1 Pt II para 4).

8 Insolvency Act 1986 s 272(1) (modified by the Administration of Insolvent Estates of Deceased Persons Order 1986, SI 1986/1999, Sch 1 Pt II para 6); Administration of Insolvent Estates of Deceased Persons Order 1986, SI 1986/1999, Sch 1 Pt I. As to the prescribed form of petition see Sch 3 Form 6 (substituted by SI 2002/1309). As to when the estate of a deceased person is insolvent see PARA 831.

(4) PROCEDURE ON PETITIONS FOR INSOLVENCY ADMINISTRATION ORDER

836. Procedure on a petition for an insolvency administration order. The court may make an insolvency administration order[1] on a petition for an order presented by a person other than a personal representative of the deceased debtor[2] if it is satisfied:

(1) that the debt, or one of the debts, in respect of which the petition was presented is a debt which, having been payable at the date of the petition or having since become payable, has neither been paid nor secured or compounded for or has no reasonable prospect of being paid when it falls due[3]; and

(2) that there is a reasonable probability that the estate will be insolvent[4].

Where an insolvency administration order is made on a petition presented by the supervisor of, or any person who is for the time being bound by, a voluntary arrangement proposed and approved under Part 8 of the Insolvency Act 1986[5], any expenses properly incurred as expenses of the administration of the voluntary arrangement in question are a first charge on the deceased debtor's estate[6].

The statutory provisions[7] relating to a petition based on a criminal bankruptcy order[8] apply in cases where a petition has been presented by the Official Petitioner or by any person specified in the criminal bankruptcy order[9].

On the hearing of a petition presented by a personal representative of a deceased debtor[10], the court must make an insolvency administration order if it is satisfied that the deceased debtor's estate is insolvent[11].

A petition for an insolvency administration order may not be presented to the court after proceedings have been commenced in any court of justice for the administration of the deceased debtor's estate[12]. Where proceedings have been commenced in any such court for the administration of the deceased debtor's estate, that court may, if satisfied that the estate is insolvent, transfer the proceedings to the court exercising jurisdiction in bankruptcy[13]. Where proceedings have been transferred to the court exercising jurisdiction in bankruptcy, that court may make an insolvency administration order as if a petition for such an order had[14] been presented[15].

Nothing in the statutory provisions relating to:

(a) who may present a petition[16];

(b) other preliminary conditions[17];

(c) the grounds of a creditor's petition[18];

(d) creditors with security[19];

(e) proceedings on a creditor's petition[20];

(f)   the appointment of an insolvency practitioner by the court[21],

invalidates any payment made or any act or thing done in good faith by the personal representative before the date of the insolvency administration order[22].

1   As to the meaning of 'insolvency administration order' see PARA 833 note 1.
2   Ie a petition under the Insolvency Act 1986 s 264(1): see PARA 833.
3   Insolvency Act 1986 s 271(1)(a) (s 271 substituted by the Administration of Insolvent Estates of Deceased Persons Order 1986, SI 1986/1999, art 3(1), Sch 1 Pt II para 5). As to the procedure on creditors' petitions generally see PARA 198 et seq.
4   Insolvency Act 1986 s 271(1)(b) (as substituted: see note 3). As to when the estate of a deceased person is insolvent see PARA 831.
5   Ie a petition under the Insolvency Act 1986 s 264(1)(c): see PARA 833 head (4).
6   Insolvency Act 1986 s 276(2) (applied by the Administration of Insolvent Estates of Deceased Persons Order 1986, SI 1986/1999, Sch 1 Pt II para 8); Administration of Insolvent Estates of Deceased Persons Order 1986, SI 1986/1999, Sch 1 Pt I.
7   Ie the Insolvency Act 1986 s 277 (applied by the Administration of Insolvent Estates of Deceased Persons Order 1986, SI 1986/1999, Sch 1 Pt II para 9): see PARA 130 note 10. As to the prospective repeal of the Insolvency Act 1986 s 277 see PARA 1 note 11.
8   Ie pursuant to the Insolvency Act 1986 s 264(1)(d): see PARA 833 head (5). As to the prospective repeal of s 264(1)(d) see PARA 1 note 11.
9   Administration of Insolvent Estates of Deceased Persons Order 1986, SI 1986/1999, Sch 1 Pt I, Pt II para 9.
10   Ie under the Insolvency Act 1986 s 272: see PARA 835.
11   Insolvency Act 1986 s 273 (substituted by the Administration of Insolvent Estates of Deceased Persons Order 1986, SI 1986/1999, Sch 1 Pt II para 7). As to the prescribed form of insolvency administration order see the Administration of Insolvent Estates of Deceased Persons Order 1986, SI 1986/1999, Sch 3 Form 4 (substituted by SI 2002/1309).
12   Insolvency Act 1986 s 271(2) (as substituted: see note 3).
13   Insolvency Act 1986 s 271(3) (as substituted: see note 3).
14   Ie as if a petition for such an order had been presented under the Insolvency Act 1986 s 264: see PARA 833.
15   Insolvency Act 1986 s 271(4) (as substituted: see note 3). As to the prescribed form of insolvency administration order see the Administration of Insolvent Estates of Deceased Persons Order 1986, SI 1986/1999, Sch 3 Form 5 (substituted by SI 2002/1309).
16   Ie the Insolvency Act 1986 s 264: see PARA 833.
17   Ie the Insolvency Act 1986 s 266: see PARA 834.
18   Ie the Insolvency Act 1986 s 267: see PARA 835.
19   Ie the Insolvency Act 1986 s 269: see PARA 835.
20   Ie the Insolvency Act 1986 s 271.
21   Ie the Insolvency Act 1986 s 273.
22   Insolvency Act 1986 s 271(5) (as substituted: see note 3).

(5) INSOLVENCY ADMINISTRATION ORDERS; ADMINISTRATION OTHERWISE THAN IN BANKRUPTCY

837.   Commencement and duration of insolvency administration order. The administration in bankruptcy of the insolvent estate of a deceased debtor commences with the day on which the insolvency administration order[1] is made[2].

The court may annul an insolvency administration order if it at any time appears to the court:

(1)   that, on the grounds existing at the time the order was made, the order ought not to have been made; or

(2)   that, to the extent required by the Insolvency Rules 1986[3], the bankruptcy debts and the expenses of the bankruptcy have all, since the making of the order, been either paid or secured to the satisfaction of the court[4].

Where the court annuls an insolvency administration order:

(a)　　any sale or other disposition of property, payment made or other thing duly done, under any provision of the Insolvency Act 1986, by or under the authority of the official receiver or a trustee of the deceased debtor's estate or by the court is valid; but

(b)　　if any of the deceased debtor's estate is then vested in such a trustee, it vests in such person as the court may appoint or, in default of any such appointment, it reverts to the personal representative of the deceased debtor or, if there is no personal representative, to such person as the court may order, as the case may require, on such terms, if any, as the court may direct[5].

1　As to the meaning of 'insolvency administration order' see PARA 833 note 1.
2　Insolvency Act 1986 s 278(a) (substituted by the Administration of Insolvent Estates of Deceased Persons Order 1986, SI 1986/1999, art 3(1), Sch 1 Pt II para 10). The Insolvency Act 1986 s 278(b) (see PARA 209 head (2)) does not apply: Administration of Insolvent Estates of Deceased Persons Order 1986, SI 1986/1999, Sch 1 Pt II para 10. As to the commencement and duration of bankruptcy orders generally see PARA 209.
3　Ie the Insolvency Rules 1986, SI 1986/1925.
4　Insolvency Act 1986 s 282(1) (applied by the Administration of Insolvent Estates of Deceased Persons Order 1986, SI 1986/1999, Sch 1 Pt II para 11); Administration of Insolvent Estates of Deceased Persons Order 1986, SI 1986/1999, Sch 1 Pt I. As to the annulment of bankruptcy orders generally see PARA 620 et seq.
5　Insolvency Act 1986 s 282(4) (amended by the Enterprise Act 2002 Sch 23 paras 1, 4(a); applied by the Administration of Insolvent Estates of Deceased Persons Order 1986, SI 1986/1999, Sch 1 Pt II para 11); Administration of Insolvent Estates of Deceased Persons Order 1986, SI 1986/1999, Sch 1 Pt I. The court may include in its order such supplemental provisions as may be authorised by the Insolvency Rules 1986, SI 1986/1999: Insolvency Act 1986 s 282(4) (as so amended and applied). As to the effect of the annulment of bankruptcy orders generally see PARA 632 et seq.

838.　Deceased person's estate administered otherwise than in bankruptcy.
Where the estate of a deceased person is insolvent[1] and is being administered otherwise than in bankruptcy, the same provisions as may be in force for the time being under the law of bankruptcy with respect to the assets of individuals adjudged bankrupt apply to the administration of the estate with respect to the respective rights of secured and unsecured creditors[2], to debts and liabilities provable[3], to the valuation of future and contingent liabilities[4] and to the priorities[5] of debts and other payments[6]. However, the reasonable funeral, testamentary and administration expenses have priority over preferential debts[7]; and the statutory prohibition on a person's being appointed as trustee of a bankrupt's estate unless he is, at the time of the appointment, qualified to act as an insolvency practitioner in relation to the bankrupt[8] does not apply[9].

1　As to when the estate of a deceased person is insolvent see PARA 831.
2　As to the effect of bankruptcy on creditors' rights generally see PARA 507.
3　As to provable debts generally see PARA 508.
4　As to contingent debts generally see PARA 510.
5　As to the priority of debts generally see PARA 587 et seq.
6　Administration of Insolvent Estates of Deceased Persons Order 1986, SI 1986/1999, art 4(1).
7　Administration of Insolvent Estates of Deceased Persons Order 1986, SI 1986/1999, art 4(2). For these purposes, 'preferential debts' means the preferential debts listed in the Insolvency Act 1986 s 386, Sch 6 (see PARA 591 et seq): Administration of Insolvent Estates of Deceased Persons Order 1986, SI 1986/1999, art 4(2).
8　Ie the Insolvency Act 1986 s 292(2): see PARA 314.
9　Administration of Insolvent Estates of Deceased Persons Order 1986, SI 1986/1999, art 4(3).

(6) PROTECTION OF DECEASED DEBTOR'S ESTATE; INVESTIGATION OF HIS AFFAIRS

839. Meaning of 'deceased debtor's estate'. The deceased debtor's estate comprises:

(1) all property belonging to or vested in the deceased debtor at the commencement of the administration in bankruptcy of the insolvent estate[1] of the deceased debtor[2]; and

(2) any property which, by virtue of any of the statutory provisions[3], is comprised in that estate or is treated as falling within head (1) above[4].

For these purposes[5], the petition is to be treated as having been presented, and the insolvency administration order[6] is to be treated as having been made, on the date of death of the deceased debtor[7].

The above provisions do not, however, apply to (inter alia) such clothing, bedding, furniture, household equipment and provisions as are necessary for satisfying the basic domestic needs of the family of the deceased debtor[8].

References[9] to property, in relation to a deceased debtor, include:

(a) the capacity to exercise and take proceedings for exercising all such powers over or in respect of property as might have been exercised by his personal representative for the benefit of the estate on the date of the insolvency administration order and as are specified[10] in the Insolvency Act 1986[11];

(b) any power exercisable by him over or in respect of property, except in so far as the power is exercisable over or in respect of property not for the time being comprised in the deceased debtor's estate and is so exercisable at a time after either the official receiver has had his release in respect of that estate[12] or a meeting summoned by the trustee of that estate has been held[13] or cannot be so exercised for the benefit of the deceased debtor's estate; and a power exercisable over or in respect of property is deemed[14] to vest in the person entitled to exercise it at the time of the transaction or event by virtue of which it is exercisable by that person, whether or not it becomes so exercisable at that time[15].

For these purposes[16], property comprised in a deceased debtor's estate is so comprised subject to the rights of any person other than the deceased debtor, whether as a secured creditor[17] of the deceased debtor or otherwise in relation thereto, but disregarding any rights in relation to which a statement[18] by a secured creditor was made in the petition on which an insolvency administration order was made, and any rights which have been otherwise given up in accordance with the Insolvency Rules 1986[19].

The above provisions have effect subject to the provisions of any enactment not contained in the Insolvency Act 1986 under which any property is to be excluded from a bankrupt's estate[20].

1 As to when the estate of a deceased person is insolvent see PARA 831.
2 Insolvency Act 1986 s 283(1)(a) (s 283(1) applied by the Administration of Insolvent Estates of Deceased Persons Order 1986, SI 1986/1999, art 3(1), Sch 1 Pt II para 12); Administration of Insolvent Estates of Deceased Persons Order 1986, SI 1986/1999, Sch 1 Pt I.
3 Ie any of the provisions contained in the Insolvency Act 1986 ss 283–371.
4 Insolvency Act 1986 s 283(1)(b) (as applied: see note 2).
5 Ie for the purposes of the Insolvency Act 1986 s 283.
6 As to the meaning of 'insolvency administration order' see PARA 833 note 1.
7 Administration of Insolvent Estates of Deceased Persons Order 1986, SI 1986/1999, Sch 1 Pt II para 12.

8　Insolvency Act 1986 s 283(2)(b) (modified by the Administration of Insolvent Estates of Deceased Persons Order 1986, SI 1986/1999, Sch 1 Pt II para 12(a)). As to the property excluded from a bankrupt's, or, as the case may be, a deceased debtor's, estate generally see PARA 211 heads (a)–(h).

9　Ie references in the Insolvency Act 1986 Pts 7A–11 (ss 251A–385) (applied by the Administration of Insolvent Estates of Deceased Persons Order 1986, SI 1986/1999, Sch 1 Pt II).

10　Ie in the Insolvency Act 1986 s 283(4) (as applied: see note 15).

11　Insolvency Act 1986 s 283(4A) (added by the Administration of Insolvent Estates of Deceased Persons Order 1986, SI 1986/1999, Sch 1 Pt II para 12(b)).

12　Ie under the Insolvency Act 1986 s 299(2) (applied by the Administration of Insolvent Estates of Deceased Persons Order 1986, SI 1986/1999, Sch 1 Pt II para 18). As to the release of the trustee generally see PARA 380.

13　Ie under the Insolvency Act 1986 s 331 (applied by the Administration of Insolvent Estates of Deceased Persons Order 1986, SI 1986/1999, Sch 1 Pt II para 26). As to the final meeting of creditors generally see PARA 616.

14　Ie for the purposes of the Insolvency Act 1986 Pts 7A–11 (applied by the Administration of Insolvent Estates of Deceased Persons Order 1986, SI 1986/1999, Sch 1 Pt II).

15　Insolvency Act 1986 s 283(4) (applied by the Administration of Insolvent Estates of Deceased Persons Order 1986, SI 1986/1999, Sch 1 Pt II para 12); Administration of Insolvent Estates of Deceased Persons Order 1986, SI 1986/1999, Sch 1 Pt I.

16　Ie for the purposes of any provision in the Insolvency Act 1986 Pts 7A–11 (applied by the Administration of Insolvent Estates of Deceased Persons Order 1986, SI 1986/1999, Sch 1 Pt II).

17　As to the meaning of 'secured creditor' see PARA 574.

18　Ie a statement such as is required by the Insolvency Act 1986 s 269(1)(a) (applied by the Administration of Insolvent Estates of Deceased Persons Order 1986, SI 1986/1999, Sch 1 Pt II para 4). See also PARA 132 note 7.

19　Insolvency Act 1986 s 285(5) (applied by the Administration of Insolvent Estates of Deceased Persons Order 1986, SI 1986/1999, Sch 1 Pt II para 12); Administration of Insolvent Estates of Deceased Persons Order 1986, SI 1986/1999, Sch 1 Pt I.

20　Insolvency Act 1986 s 283(6) (applied by the Administration of Insolvent Estates of Deceased Persons Order 1986, SI 1986/1999, Sch 1 Pt II para 12); Administration of Insolvent Estates of Deceased Persons Order 1986, SI 1986/1999, Sch 1 Pt I.

840. Joint tenancies. Where:

(1)　an insolvency administration order[1] has been made in respect of the insolvent estate of a deceased person[2];

(2)　the petition for the order was presented on or after 2 April 2001[3] and within the period of five years beginning with the day on which he died; and

(3)　immediately before his death he was beneficially entitled to an interest in any property as joint tenant,

then, for the purpose of securing that debts and other liabilities to which the estate is subject are met, the court may, on an application by the trustee appointed pursuant to the insolvency administration order, make an order requiring the survivor[4] to pay to the trustee an amount not exceeding the value lost to the estate[5].

The order may be made on such terms and conditions as the court thinks fit[6]; and, in determining whether to make such an order, and the terms of such an order, the court must have regard to all the circumstances of the case, including the interests of the deceased's creditors and of the survivor; but, unless the circumstances are exceptional, the court must assume that the interests of the deceased's creditors outweigh all other considerations[7]. Any sums required to be paid to the trustee in accordance with such an order are comprised in the estate[8].

1　For these purposes, 'insolvency administration order' has the same meaning as in any order under the Insolvency Act 1986 s 421 (see PARA 833 note 1): s 421A(9) (s 421A added by the

Insolvency Act 2000 s 12(1)). As from a day to be appointed, the Insolvency Act 1986 s 421A(9) is amended by the Enterprise and Regulatory Reform Act 2013 s 71, Sch 19 paras 1, 60: see PARA 130 note 17.

2   As to when the estate of a deceased person is insolvent see PARA 831.

3   Ie the date on which the Insolvency Act 2000 s 12 came into force: see the Insolvency Act 2000 (Commencement No 1 and Transitional Provisions) Order 2001, SI 2001/766, art 2(1)(b). As to the position where the petition for an insolvency administration order was presented before that date see *Re Palmer (a debtor)* [1994] Ch 316, [1993] 4 All ER 812, CA.

4   For these purposes, 'survivor' means the person who, immediately before the death, was beneficially entitled as joint tenant with the deceased or, if the person who was so entitled dies after the making of the insolvency administration order, his personal representatives: Insolvency Act 1986 s 421A(7) (as added: see note 1). If there is more than one survivor, an order may be made against all or any of them, but no survivor may be required to pay more than so much of the value lost to the estate as is properly attributable to him: Insolvency Act 1986 s 421A(8) (as so added). As to the meaning of 'value lost to the estate' see note 5.

5   Insolvency Act 1986 s 421A(1), (2) (as added: see note 1). For these purposes, 'value lost to the estate' means the amount which, if paid to the trustee, would, in the court's opinion, restore the position to what it would have been if the deceased had been adjudged bankrupt immediately before his death: Insolvency Act 1986 s 421A(9) (as so added).

6   Insolvency Act 1986 s 421A(4) (as added: see note 1).

7   Insolvency Act 1986 s 421A(3) (as added: see note 1).

8   Insolvency Act 1986 s 421A(5) (as added: see note 1).

841.   Restrictions on dispositions of property, proceedings and remedies. The statutory provisions relating to:

(1)   the restrictions on dispositions of property[1]; and

(2)   the restrictions on proceedings and remedies[2],

apply to the administration in bankruptcy of the insolvent estate of a deceased debtor[3] dying before the presentation of a bankruptcy petition; but those provisions have effect as if the petition for the insolvency administration order[4] had been presented, and the insolvency administration order had been made, on the date of death of the deceased debtor[5].

1   Ie the Insolvency Act 1986 s 284: see PARA 213.

2   Ie the Insolvency Act 1986 s 285: see PARA 214.

3   As to when the estate of a deceased person is insolvent see PARA 831.

4   As to the meaning of 'insolvency administration order' see PARA 833 note 1.

5   Administration of Insolvent Estates of Deceased Persons Order 1986, SI 1986/1999, Sch 1 Pt II para 12. The Insolvency Act 1986 s 284 as so modified applies so as to render void any appointments made out of the estate of the deceased person from the date of death until the date of the appointment of the trustee of the estate, notwithstanding that the insolvency administration order was not made until many years after the death, subject to ratification of the payment by the court: *Re Vos; Dick v Kendall Freeman* [2006] BPIR 348.

842.   Power to appoint interim receiver. If it is shown to be necessary for the protection of the property[1] of the deceased debtor, the court may at any time after the presentation of a petition for an insolvency administration order and before making an insolvency administration order, appoint the official receiver to be interim receiver of the property of the deceased debtor[2]. The court may by an order appointing any person to be an interim receiver direct that his powers are to be limited or restricted in any respect[3]; but, save as so directed, an interim receiver has, in relation to the property of the deceased debtor, all the rights, powers, duties and immunities of a receiver and manager[4] pending the appointment of a trustee[5]. An order of the court appointing any person to be an interim receiver must require that person to take immediate possession of the property of the deceased debtor or, as the case may be, the part of it to which his powers as interim receiver are limited[6]. Where an interim receiver has been appointed, the personal representative of the deceased debtor, or, if there is no personal representative, such person as the court may order, must give to the interim receiver such inventory of the property of the deceased debtor and such other information, and must attend on the interim receiver at such times, as the latter may reasonably require for the purpose of carrying out his functions[7].

Where an interim receiver is appointed, the statutory restriction on proceedings and remedies[8] applies for the period between the appointment and the making of an insolvency administration order on the petition or the dismissal of the petition, as if the appointment were the making of such an order[9].

A person ceases to be interim receiver of the property of the deceased debtor if the petition for an insolvency administration order relating to the deceased debtor is dismissed, if an insolvency administration order is made on the petition or if the court by order or otherwise terminates the appointment[10].

1 For these purposes, references to the deceased debtor's property are to all his property, whether or not it would be comprised in his estate if an insolvency administration order were made: Insolvency Act 1986 s 286(8) (applied by the Administration of Insolvent Estates of Deceased Persons Order 1986, SI 1986/1999, art 3(1), Sch 1 Pt II para 13); Administration of Insolvent Estates of Deceased Persons Order 1986, SI 1986/1999, Sch 1 Pt I. As to the meaning of 'insolvency administration order' see PARA 833 note 1.

2 Insolvency Act 1986 s 286(1) (applied by the Administration of Insolvent Estates of Deceased Persons Order 1986, SI 1986/1999, Sch 1 Pt II para 13); Administration of Insolvent Estates of Deceased Persons Order 1986, SI 1986/1999, Sch 1 Pt I. As to the appointment of an interim receiver generally see PARA 218 et seq. The Insolvency Act 1986 s 286(2) (see PARA 219) does not apply: Administration of Insolvent Estates of Deceased Persons Order 1986, SI 1986/1999, Sch 1 Pt II para 13.

3 See PARA 841.

4 Ie under the Insolvency Act 1986 s 287: see PARA 843.

5 Insolvency Act 1986 s 286(3) (applied by the Administration of Insolvent Estates of Deceased Persons Order 1986, SI 1986/1999, Sch 1 Pt II para 13); Administration of Insolvent Estates of Deceased Persons Order 1986, SI 1986/1999, Sch 1 Pt I. As to the order of appointment of an interim receiver generally see PARA 221.

6 Insolvency Act 1986 s 286(4) (applied by the Administration of Insolvent Estates of Deceased Persons Order 1986, SI 1986/1999, Sch 1 Pt II para 13); Administration of Insolvent Estates of Deceased Persons Order 1986, SI 1986/1999, Sch 1 Pt I.

7 Insolvency Act 1986 s 286(5) (applied by the Administration of Insolvent Estates of Deceased Persons Order 1986, SI 1986/1999, Sch 1 Pt II para 13); Administration of Insolvent Estates of Deceased Persons Order 1986, SI 1986/1999, Sch 1 Pt I. As to the inquiry into a debtor's dealings and property generally see PARA 224.

8 Ie the Insolvency Act 1986 s 285(3): see PARA 841.

9 Insolvency Act 1986 s 286(6) (applied by the Administration of Insolvent Estates of Deceased Persons Order 1986, SI 1986/1999, Sch 1 Pt II para 13); Administration of Insolvent Estates of Deceased Persons Order 1986, SI 1986/1999, Sch 1 Pt I. As to the restriction on proceedings and remedies generally see PARA 225.

10 Insolvency Act 1986 s 286(7) (applied by the Administration of Insolvent Estates of Deceased Persons Order 1986, SI 1986/1999, Sch 1 Pt II para 13); Administration of Insolvent Estates of Deceased Persons Order 1986, SI 1986/1999, Sch 1 Pt I. As to the termination of the appointment of an interim receiver generally see PARA 228.

843. Receivership pending appointment of trustee. Between the making of an insolvency administration order[1] and the time at which the deceased debtor's estate vests in the trustee[2] the official receiver is the receiver and manager of the deceased debtor's estate and is under a duty to act as such[3]. The statutory provisions relating to the functions of the official receiver and his duties, powers and liabilities[4] apply to the administration in bankruptcy of the insolvent estate of a deceased debtor[5].

1 As to the meaning of 'insolvency administration order' see PARA 833 note 1.
2 As to the vesting of the estate in the trustee see PARA 397 et seq.

3   Insolvency Act 1986 s 287(1) (applied by the Administration of Insolvent Estates of Deceased Persons Order 1986, SI 1986/1999, art 3(1), Sch 1 Pt II para 14); Administration of Insolvent Estates of Deceased Persons Order 1986, SI 1986/1999, Sch 1 Pt I.
4   Ie the Insolvency Act 1986 s 287(2)–(5): see PARAS 230, 231.
5   Administration of Insolvent Estates of Deceased Persons Order 1986, SI 1986/1999, Sch 1 Pt I, Pt II para 14.

844. Statement of affairs. Where an insolvency administration order[1] has been made, the personal representative, or, if there is no personal representative, such person as the court may, on the application of the official receiver, direct, must submit to the official receiver a statement of the deceased debtor's affairs[2] containing particulars of the assets and liabilities of the estate as at the date of the insolvency administration order together with other particulars of the affairs of the deceased debtor in the prescribed form[3] or as the official receiver may require[4]. The statement must be submitted before the end of the period of 56 days beginning with the date of a request by the official receiver for the statement or such longer period as he or the court may allow[5].

If he thinks fit, the official receiver may release the personal representative, or any person directed by the court to submit a statement of the deceased debtor's affairs, from his duty to submit such a statement of affairs, or extend the statutory period for doing so; and, where the official receiver has refused to exercise his statutory power, the court may, if it thinks fit, exercise it[6].

A personal representative, or any person directed by the court, who without reasonable excuse fails to comply with the above obligation or without reasonable excuse submits a statement of affairs that does not comply with the prescribed requirements, is guilty of contempt of court[7] and liable to be punished accordingly, in addition to any other punishment to which he may be subject[8].

1   As to the meaning of 'insolvency administration order' see PARA 833 note 1.
2   As to the bankrupt's statement of affairs generally see PARA 240 et seq.
3   As to the prescribed form of statement of affairs see the Administration of Insolvent Estates of Deceased Persons Order 1986, SI 1986/1999, Sch 3 Form 7.
4   Insolvency Act 1986 s 288(1) (substituted by the Administration of Insolvent Estates of Deceased Persons Order 1986, SI 1986/1999, art 3(1), Sch 1 Pt II para 15).
5   Insolvency Act 1986 s 288(2) (substituted by the Administration of Insolvent Estates of Deceased Persons Order 1986, SI 1986/1999, Sch 1 Pt II para 15).
6   Insolvency Act 1986 s 288(3) (applied by the Administration of Insolvent Estates of Deceased Persons Order 1986, SI 1986/1999, Sch 1 Pt II para 15); Administration of Insolvent Estates of Deceased Persons Order 1986, SI 1986/1999, Sch 1 Pt I. As to the bankrupt's release from his duty to submit a statement of affairs and extension of time generally see PARA 244.
7   As to contempt of court see CONTEMPT OF COURT vol 22 (2012) PARA 1 et seq.
8   Insolvency Act 1986 s 288(4) (applied by the Administration of Insolvent Estates of Deceased Persons Order 1986, SI 1986/1999, Sch 1 Pt II para 15); Administration of Insolvent Estates of Deceased Persons Order 1986, SI 1986/1999, Sch 1 Pt I.

845. Duties in relation to the official receiver. The official receiver is not under any duty to investigate the conduct and affairs of the deceased debtor unless he thinks fit but may make such report, if any, to the court as he thinks fit[1].

Where an insolvency administration order[2] has been made, the personal representative of the deceased debtor, or, if there is no personal representative, such person as the court may order, is under a duty:

(1)   to deliver possession of the deceased debtor's estate to the official receiver; and

(2)   to deliver up to the official receiver all books, papers and other records of which he has possession or control and which relate to the deceased

debtor's estate and its affairs including any which would be privileged from disclosure in any proceedings[3].

In the case of any part of the deceased debtor's estate which consists of things possession of which cannot be delivered to the official receiver, and in the case of any property that may be claimed for the deceased debtor's estate by the trustee, it is the duty of the personal representative, or, if there is no personal representative, such person as the court may order, to do all such things as may reasonably be required by the official receiver for the protection of those things or that property[4].

The personal representative of the deceased debtor, or, if there is no personal representative, such person as the court may order, must give the official receiver such inventory of the deceased debtor's estate and such other information, and must attend on the official receiver at such times, as the official receiver may reasonable require for the purposes of provisions relating to the protection of the deceased debtor's estate and investigation of his affairs[5] or in connection with the making of an insolvency administration restriction order[6].

If the personal representative, or, if there is no personal representative, such person as the court may order, fails without reasonable excuse to comply with any of the above obligations, he is guilty of contempt of court[7] and is liable to be punished accordingly, in addition to any other punishment to which he may be subject[8].

1   Insolvency Act 1986 s 289 (substituted by the Administration of Insolvent Estates of Deceased Persons Order 1986, SI 1986/1999, art 3(1), Sch 1 Pt II para 16). As to the official receiver's duty to investigate generally see PARA 252.

2   As to the meaning of 'insolvency administration order' see PARA 833 note 1.

3   Insolvency Act 1986 s 291(1) (s 291 applied by the Administration of Insolvent Estates of Deceased Persons Order 1986, SI 1986/1999, Sch 1 Pt II para 17); Administration of Insolvent Estates of Deceased Persons Order 1986, SI 1986/1999, Sch 1 Pt I. The Insolvency Act 1986 s 291(1), (2) does not apply where, by virtue of s 297 (see PARA 846), the deceased debtor's estate vests in a trustee immediately on the making of the insolvency administration order: s 291(3) (as so applied); Administration of Insolvent Estates of Deceased Persons Order 1986, SI 1986/1999, Sch 1 Pt I. As to the bankrupt's duties in relation to the official receiver generally see PARA 239.

4   Insolvency Act 1986 s 291(2) (as applied: see note 3); Administration of Insolvent Estates of Deceased Persons Order 1986, SI 1986/1999, Sch 1 Pt I. See also note 3.

5   Ie the Insolvency Act 1986 Pt 9 Ch II (ss 283–291).

6   Insolvency Act 1986 s 291(4) (substituted by the Enterprise Act 2002 Sch 23 paras 1, 5; and as applied (see note 3)); Administration of Insolvent Estates of Deceased Persons Order 1986, SI 1986/1999, Sch 1 Pt I.

7   As to contempt of court see CONTEMPT OF COURT vol 22 (2012) PARA 1 et seq.

8   Insolvency Act 1986 s 291(6) (as applied: see note 3); Administration of Insolvent Estates of Deceased Persons Order 1986, SI 1986/1999, Sch 1 Pt I.

(7)   TRUSTEE IN BANKRUPTCY

846.   Trustee in bankruptcy. The statutory provisions relating to trustees in bankruptcy[1] apply, with the relevant modifications[2], to the administration in bankruptcy of the insolvent estate of a deceased debtor where an insolvency administration order[3] has been made[4]; and, where a meeting of creditors is summoned for the purposes of any provision relating to trustees in bankruptcy, the provisions of the Insolvency Rules 1986[5] relating to the trustee in bankruptcy and the creditors' committee apply accordingly[6].

The statutory provisions relating to the general functions of the trustee[7] apply to the administration in bankruptcy of the insolvent estate of a deceased debtor where an insolvency administration order has been made[8]. In the exercise of those functions, the trustee must have regard to any claim by the personal representative to payment of reasonable funeral, testamentary and administration expenses incurred by him in respect of the deceased debtor's estate, or, if there is no such personal representative, to any claim by any other person to payment of any such expenses incurred by him in respect of the estate, provided that the trustee has sufficient funds in hand for the purpose; and such claims to payment have priority over preferential debts[9].

1 Ie the Insolvency Act 1986 ss 292–304: see PARA 314 et seq.
2 Ie with the general modifications contained in the Administration of Insolvent Estates of Deceased Persons Order 1986, SI 1986/1999, art 3(1), Sch 1 Pt I: see PARA 831 note 5. In addition, the Insolvency Act 1986 s 297 is modified so as to exclude s 297(4) (see PARA 320): Administration of Insolvent Estates of Deceased Persons Order 1986, SI 1986/1999, Sch 1 Pt II para 18.
3 As to the meaning of 'insolvency administration order' see PARA 833 note 1.
4 Administration of Insolvent Estates of Deceased Persons Order 1986, SI 1986/1999, Sch I Pt II paras 18, 19.
5 Ie the Insolvency Rules 1986, SI 1986/1925, rr 6.120–6.166: see PARA 318 et seq.
6 Administration of Insolvent Estates of Deceased Persons Order 1986, SI 1986/1999, Sch 1 Pt II para 18.
7 Ie the Insolvency Act 1986 s 305(1)–(3) (see PARAS 473, 474) and s 305(4) (see PARA 324).
8 Administration of Insolvent Estates of Deceased Persons Order 1986, SI 1986/1999, Sch 1 Pt I, Sch 1 Pt II para 20.
9 Insolvency Act 1986 s 305(5) (added by the Administration of Insolvent Estates of Deceased Persons Order 1986, SI 1986/1999, Sch I Pt II para 20). Preferential debts are those listed in the Insolvency Act 1986 s 386, Sch 6 (see PARA 591 et seq): s 305(5) (as so added).

(8) ADMINISTRATION OF DECEASED DEBTOR'S ESTATE

847. Vesting, acquisition, control, realisation and distribution of deceased debtor's estate. The statutory provisions relating to the vesting, acquisition, control, realisation and distribution of a bankrupt's estate[1] apply, with the relevant modifications[2], to the administration in bankruptcy of the insolvent estate of a deceased debtor[3] where an insolvency administration order[4] has been made[5].

The modifications to those statutory provisions which effect a significant change to them in their application to the estate of a deceased debtor are:

(1) in relation to after-acquired property, the trustee may by notice in writing claim for the deceased debtor's estate any property which has been acquired by, or has devolved on, the deceased debtor or his personal representative since the date of death of the deceased debtor[6];

(2) in relation to the priority of debts, any surplus remaining after the payment of the debts that are preferential or rank equally must be applied in paying interest on those debts in respect of the periods during which they have been outstanding since the date of death of the deceased debtor[7];

(3) in relation to debts to spouses or civil partners, such debts are payable at the specified rate in respect of the period during which they have been outstanding since the date of death of the deceased debtor[8];

(4) in relation to the final distribution, where a surplus remains after payment in full and with interest of all the deceased debtor's creditors and the payment of the expenses of the bankruptcy, the surplus must be paid to the personal representative unless the court orders otherwise[9];

(5) in the case of a transaction at an undervalue, the time at which an

individual enters into a transaction at an undervalue is a relevant time[10] if the transaction is entered into at a time in the period of five years ending with the date of death of the deceased debtor[11].

1   Ie the Insolvency Act 1986 ss 306–349.
2   Ie with the general modifications in the Administration of Insolvent Estates of Deceased Persons Order 1986, SI 1986/1999, art 3(1), Sch I Pt I: see PARA 831 note 5. As to the other modifications see heads (1)–(4) in the text.
3   As to when the estate of a deceased person is insolvent see PARA 831.
4   As to the meaning of 'insolvency administration order' see PARA 833 note 1.
5   Administration of Insolvent Estates of Deceased Persons Order 1986, SI 1986/1999, Pt II paras 21–28.
6   Insolvency Act 1986 s 307(1) (applied and modified by the Administration of Insolvent Estates of Deceased Persons Order 1986, SI 1986/1999, Sch 1 Pt II para 22). As to after-acquired property generally see PARA 458 et seq.
7   Insolvency Act 1986 s 328(4) (applied and modified by the Administration of Insolvent Estates of Deceased Persons Order 1986, SI 1986/1999, Sch 1 Pt II para 24). As to priority of debts generally see PARA 591 et seq.
8   Insolvency Act 1986 s 329(2)(b) (applied and modified by the Administration of Insolvent Estates of Deceased Persons Order 1986, SI 1986/1999, Sch 1 Pt II para 24). As to debts to spouses and civil partners generally see PARA 597.
9   Insolvency Act 1986 s 330(5) (applied and modified by the Administration of Insolvent Estates of Deceased Persons Order 1986, SI 1986/1999, Sch 1 Pt II para 25 (substituted by SI 2002/1309)). This provision is subject to Council Regulation (EC) 1346/2000 (OJ L160, 30.6.2000, p 1) on insolvency proceedings ('European Regulation on Insolvency Proceedings') art 35 (surplus in secondary proceedings to be transferred to main proceedings) (see PARA 42): Insolvency Act 1986 s 330(6) (added by SI 2002/1240; applied and modified by the Administration of Insolvent Estates of Deceased Persons Order 1986, SI 1986/1999, Sch 1 Pt II para 25 (substituted by SI 2002/1309)).
10 As to the meaning of 'relevant time' generally see PARA 685.
11 Insolvency Act 1986 s 341(1)(a) (applied and modified by the Administration of Insolvent Estates of Deceased Persons Order 1986, SI 1986/1999, Sch I Pt II para 27).

848. Application of statutory provisions. The following provisions of the Insolvency Act 1986 apply, with relevant modifications[1], to the administration in bankruptcy of the insolvent estate of a deceased debtor[2] where an insolvency administration order[3] has been made:

(1)   the provisions[4] relating to the powers of the court in bankruptcy[5];
(2)   the general provisions[6] relating to individual insolvency[7];
(3)   the interpretation provisions[8] relating to the insolvency of individuals and bankruptcy[9];
(4)   the provisions[10] relating to preferential debts[11];
(5)   the provisions[12] relating to insolvency practitioners and their qualification[13];
(6)   the provisions[14] relating to public administration (England and Wales)[15];
(7)   the provisions[16] relating to subordinate legislation[17];
(8)   the provisions[18] against debt avoidance[19];
(9)   the miscellaneous and general[20] provisions[21];
(10)   the provisions[22] relating to interpretation[23]; and
(11)   the transitional provisions[24] and savings[25].

1   Ie with the general modifications in the Administration of Insolvent Estates of Deceased Persons Order 1986, SI 1986/1999, art 3(1), Sch 1 Pt I: see PARA 831 note 5.
2   As to when the estate of a deceased person is insolvent see PARA 831.
3   As to the meaning of 'insolvency administration order' see PARA 833 note 1.
4   Ie the Insolvency Act 1986 ss 363–371 (see PARA 215 et seq), other than s 364 (see PARA 217).
5   Administration of Insolvent Estates of Deceased Persons Order 1986, SI 1986/1999, Sch 1 Pt II para 30.

6   Ie the Insolvency Act 1986 ss 372–379B.

7   Administration of Insolvent Estates of Deceased Persons Order 1986, SI 1986/1999, Sch 1 Pt II para 30.

8   Ie the Insolvency Act 1986 ss 380–385. However, in the definition of 'bankruptcy debt' in s 382 (see PARA 508), for the words 'commencement of the bankruptcy', wherever they occur, there are to be substituted the words 'date of death of the deceased debtor' (Administration of Insolvent Estates of Deceased Persons Order 1986, SI 1986/1999, Sch 1 Pt II para 31); and at the end of the definition of 'the court' in the Insolvency Act 1986 s 385 (see PARA 786) there are to be added the words 'and subject thereto 'the court' means the court within the jurisdiction of which the debtor resided or carried on business for the greater part of the six months immediately prior to his death' (Administration of Insolvent Estates of Deceased Persons Order 1986, SI 1986/1999, Sch 1 Pt II para 33).

9   Administration of Insolvent Estates of Deceased Persons Order 1986, SI 1986/1999, Sch 1 Pt II paras 30–33.

10   Ie the Insolvency Act 1986 s 386 and s 387, other than s 387(2)–(4): see COMPANY AND PARTNERSHIP INSOLVENCY vol 17 (2011) PARA 723. However, s 387(6)(a), (b) is modified so that for the reference therein to the making of the bankruptcy order there is to be substituted a reference to the date of death of the deceased debtor: Administration of Insolvent Estates of Deceased Persons Order 1986, SI 1986/1999, Sch 1 Pt II para 35.

11   Administration of Insolvent Estates of Deceased Persons Order 1986, SI 1986/1999, Sch 1 Pt II paras 34, 35.

12   Ie the Insolvency Act 1986 ss 388–398: see PARA 40.

13   Administration of Insolvent Estates of Deceased Persons Order 1986, SI 1986/1999, Sch 1 Pt II para 36.

14   Ie the Insolvency Act 1986 ss 399–410: see PARAS 22 et seq, 35. As to the prospective repeal of s 402 see PARA 1 note 11.

15   Administration of Insolvent Estates of Deceased Persons Order 1986, SI 1986/1999, Sch 1 Pt II para 36.

16   Ie the Insolvency Act 1986 ss 412, 413, 415, 418–420: see PARAS 825, 851.

17   Administration of Insolvent Estates of Deceased Persons Order 1986, SI 1986/1999, Sch 1 Pt II para 36.

18   Ie the Insolvency Act 1986 ss 423–425: see PARA 689 et seq.

19   Administration of Insolvent Estates of Deceased Persons Order 1986, SI 1986/1999, Sch 1 Pt II para 36.

20   Ie the Insolvency Act 1986 ss 426, 428(3), 430, 431 (summary proceedings), s 432 (offences by bodies corporate), s 433 and s 434: see PARAS 3, 4, 20, 802, 828.

21   Administration of Insolvent Estates of Deceased Persons Order 1986, SI 1986/1999, Sch 1 Pt II para 36.

22   Ie the Insolvency Act 1986 s 435 (meaning of 'associate': see PARA 5) and s 436 (expressions used generally).

23   Administration of Insolvent Estates of Deceased Persons Order 1986, SI 1986/1999, Sch 1 Pt II para 36.

24   Ie the Insolvency Act 1986 s 437. However, the Insolvency Act 1986 s 437 only applies so far as it relates to Sch 11 Pt II, except Sch 11 Pt II para 13 (discharge from old bankruptcy: see PARA 638), Sch 11 Pt IV (insolvency practitioners), and Sch 11 Pt V (general transitional provisions and savings): Administration of Insolvent Estates of Deceased Persons Order 1986, SI 1986/1999, Sch 1 Pt II para 36.

25   Administration of Insolvent Estates of Deceased Persons Order 1986, SI 1986/1999, Sch 1 Pt II para 36.

(9) BANKRUPTCY OFFENCES

849. Bankruptcy offences. The following provisions apply where the court has made an insolvency administration order[1]; and they apply whether or not the insolvency administration order is annulled, but proceedings for an offence may not be instituted after the annulment[2].

A person is guilty of an offence if, in the 12 months before the date of death of the deceased debtor[3], he acquired or received property from the deceased debtor knowing or believing that the deceased debtor owed money in respect of the property, and that the deceased debtor did not intend, or was unlikely to be able, to pay the money he so owed[4].

A person who commits such an offence is liable on conviction on indictment to imprisonment for a term not exceeding seven years or a fine, or to both, or on summary conviction to imprisonment for a term not exceeding six months or a fine not exceeding the statutory maximum, or to both[5].

It is not, however, a defence in proceedings for such an offence that anything relied on, in whole or in part, as constituting that offence was done outside England and Wales[6]; but a person is not guilty of such an offence if the disposal, acquisition or receipt of the property was in the ordinary course of a business carried on by the deceased debtor at the time of the disposal, acquisition or receipt[7].

Proceedings for such an offence may not be instituted except by the Secretary of State[8] or by or with the consent of the Director of Public Prosecutions[9].

1 Insolvency Act 1986 s 350(1) (applied by the Administration of Insolvent Estates of Deceased Persons Order 1986, SI 1986/1999, art 3(1), Sch 1 Pt II para 28); Administration of Insolvent Estates of Deceased Persons Order 1986, SI 1986/1999, Sch 1 Pt I. As to the meaning of 'insolvency administration order' see PARA 833 note 1. As to the general provisions relating to bankruptcy offences see PARA 733.

2 Insolvency Act 1986 s 350(2) (applied by the Administration of Insolvent Estates of Deceased Persons Order 1986, SI 1986/1999, Sch 1 Pt II para 28); Administration of Insolvent Estates of Deceased Persons Order 1986, SI 1986/1999, Sch 1 Pt I.

3 For these purposes, a reference to the number of months or years before the date of death of the deceased debtor is to that period ending with the presentation of the petition for an insolvency administration order: Insolvency Act 1986 s 351(c) (applied by the Administration of Insolvent Estates of Deceased Persons Order 1986, SI 1986/1999, Sch 1 Pt II para 28); Administration of Insolvent Estates of Deceased Persons Order 1986, SI 1986/1999, Sch 1 Pt I.

4 Insolvency Act 1986 s 359(2) (modified by the Administration of Insolvent Estates of Deceased Persons Order 1986, SI 1986/1999, Sch 1 Pt II para 29(b)); Administration of Insolvent Estates of Deceased Persons Order 1986, SI 1986/1999, Sch 1 Pt I. As to fraudulent dealing by a person with a bankrupt generally see PARA 746.

5 Insolvency Act 1986 ss 350(6), 359(2), 430, Sch 10 (applied by the Administration of Insolvent Estates of Deceased Persons Order 1986, SI 1986/1999, Sch 1 Pt II paras 28, 29, 36); Administration of Insolvent Estates of Deceased Persons Order 1986, SI 1986/1999, Sch 1 Pt I. As to the meaning of 'the statutory maximum' see SENTENCING AND DISPOSITION OF OFFENDERS vol 92 (2010) PARA 140.

6 Insolvency Act 1986 s 350(4) (applied by the Administration of Insolvent Estates of Deceased Persons Order 1986, SI 1986/1999, Sch 1 Pt II para 28); Administration of Insolvent Estates of Deceased Persons Order 1986, SI 1986/1999, Sch 1 Pt I.

7 Insolvency Act 1986 s 359(3) (modified by the Administration of Insolvent Estates of Deceased Persons Order 1986, SI 1986/1999, Sch 1 Pt II para 29(a)); Administration of Insolvent Estates of Deceased Persons Order 1986, SI 1986/1999, Sch 1 Pt I. In determining, for these purposes, whether any property is disposed of, acquired or received in the ordinary course of business carried on by the deceased debtor, regard may be had, in particular, to the price paid for the property: Insolvency Act 1986 s 359(4) (applied by the Administration of Insolvent Estates of Deceased Persons Order 1986, SI 1986/1999, Sch 1 Pt II para 29). References to the disposing of property include pawning or pledging it; and references to acquiring or receiving property are to be read accordingly: Insolvency Act 1986 s 359(5) (applied by the Administration of Insolvent Estates of Deceased Persons Order 1986, SI 1986/1999, Sch 1 Pt II para 29).

8 As to the Secretary of State see PARA 19.

9 Insolvency Act 1986 s 350(5) (applied by the Administration of Insolvent Estates of Deceased Persons Order 1986 Sch 1 Pt II para 28); Administration of Insolvent Estates of Deceased Persons Order 1986, SI 1986/1999, Sch 1 Pt I. As to the Director of Public Prosecutions see CRIMINAL PROCEDURE vol 27 (2010) PARAS 23, 33 et seq.

(10) PROCEDURE AFTER DEATH OF DEBTOR

850. Procedure after death of debtor. Unless the court otherwise orders, if a debtor by or against whom a bankruptcy petition has been presented dies, the proceedings in the matter are to be continued as if he were alive, subject to the following modifications[1]:

(1)   where a bankruptcy order has been made otherwise than on a debtor's petition and the debtor has subsequently died without submitting a statement of his affairs to the official receiver, the personal representative or such other person as the court, on the application of the official receiver, may direct, must submit to the official receiver a statement of the deceased debtor's affairs containing particulars of the assets and liabilities of the estate as at the date of the order together with other particulars of the affairs of the deceased debtor in the prescribed form[2] or as the official receiver may require and the Insolvency Rules 1986[3] apply to such a statement as they apply to an ordinary statement of affairs[4]; and the statement must be submitted before the end of the period of 56 days beginning with the date of a request by the official receiver for the statement or such longer period as he or the court may allow[5];

(2)   if the trustee intends to declare a final dividend, he must declare and distribute that dividend without regard to the claim of any person in respect of a debt not proved in the bankruptcy and of the personal representative of a debtor dying after the presentation of a bankruptcy petition in respect of reasonable funeral and testamentary expenses of which notice has not already been given to the trustee[6].

The reasonable funeral and testamentary expenses have priority over preferential debts[7].

If a debtor dies after presentation of a bankruptcy petition but before service, the court may order service to be effected on his personal representative or such other person as it thinks fit[8].

1   Administration of Insolvent Estates of Deceased Persons Order 1986, SI 1986/1999, art 5(1).
2   As to the prescribed form of statement of affairs see the Administration of Insolvent Estates of Deceased Persons Order 1986, SI 1986/1999, art 5(1), Sch 3 Form 7.
3   Ie the Insolvency Rules 1986, SI 1986/1925.
4   Insolvency Act 1986 s 288(1) (substituted by the Administration of Insolvent Estates of Deceased Persons Order 1986, SI 1986/1999, art 5(1), Sch 2 para 1). As to the bankrupt's statement of affairs generally see PARA 240.
5   Insolvency Act 1986 s 288(2) (substituted by the Administration of Insolvent Estates of Deceased Persons Order 1986, SI 1986/1999, Sch 2 para 1).
6   Insolvency Act 1986 s 330(4)(b) (modified by the Administration of Insolvent Estates of Deceased Persons Order 1986, SI 1986/1999, Sch 2 para 2). As to final distribution generally see PARA 615.
7   Administration of Insolvent Estates of Deceased Persons Order 1986, SI 1986/1999, art 5(2). The preferential debts are those specified in the Insolvency Act 1986 s 386, Sch 6 (see PARA 591 et seq): Administration of Insolvent Estates of Deceased Persons Order 1986, SI 1986/1999, art 5(2).
8   Administration of Insolvent Estates of Deceased Persons Order 1986, SI 1986/1999, art 5(3).

10. INSOLVENT PARTNERSHIPS

851. Insolvency procedures; application of statutory provisions to insolvent partnerships. The Lord Chancellor[1] may, by order made with the concurrence of the Secretary of State and the Lord Chief Justice[2], provide that such provisions of the Insolvency Act 1986 as may be specified in the order are to apply in relation to insolvent partnerships with such modifications as may be so specified[3]. Such an order may make different provisions for different cases and may contain such incidental, supplemental and transitional provisions as may appear to the Lord Chancellor and the Lord Chief Justice necessary or expedient[4].

The current order is the Insolvent Partnerships Order 1994[5]. Insolvency proceedings in relation to insolvent partnerships are covered in detail elsewhere in this work[6].

1 As to the Lord Chancellor see CONSTITUTIONAL LAW AND HUMAN RIGHTS vol 8(2) (Reissue) PARA 477 et seq. The Lord Chancellor's function under the Insolvency Act 1986 s 420(1) is a protected function for the purposes of the Constitutional Reform Act 2005 s 19: see s 19(5), Sch 7 para 4; and CONSTITUTIONAL LAW AND HUMAN RIGHTS.

2 The Lord Chief Justice may nominate a judicial office holder (as defined in the Constitutional Reform Act 2005 s 109(4) (see COURTS AND TRIBUNALS vol 24 (2010) PARA 961)) to exercise his functions under the Insolvency Act 1986 s 420: s 420(4) (added by the Constitutional Reform Act 2005 s 15(1), Sch 4 Pt 1 paras 185, 191(1), (4)).

3 Insolvency Act 1986 s 420(1) (amended by the Constitutional Reform Act 2005 Sch 4 Pt 1 paras 185, 191(1), (2)). Any such order must be made by statutory instrument subject to annulment in pursuance of a resolution of either House of Parliament: s 420(3).

   An order under s 420 may make provision in relation to the European Regulation on Insolvency Proceedings (ie Council Regulation (EC) 1346/2000 (OJ L160, 30.6.2000, p 1) (see PARAS 41, 42)) but any such provision may not create an offence of a kind referred to in the European Communities Act 1972 Sch 2 para 1(1)(d) (new crimes punishable with more than a specified punishment): Insolvency Act 1986 s 420(1A), (1B) (added by SI 2002/1037).

   In the case of the administration in bankruptcy of the insolvent estate of a deceased person dying before the presentation of a bankruptcy petition, s 420 applies: Administration of Insolvent Estates of Deceased Persons Order 1986, SI 1986/1999, art 3(1), Sch 1 Pt II para 36. As to the administration in bankruptcy of the insolvent estates of deceased persons see further PARA 830 et seq.

4 Insolvency Act 1986 s 420(2) (amended by the Constitutional Reform Act 2005 Sch 4 Pt 1 paras 185, 191(1), (3)).

5 Ie the Insolvent Partnerships Order 1994, SI 1994/2421 (amended by SI 1996/1308; SI 2001/767; SI 2001/3649; SI 2002/1308; SI 2002/1555; SI 2002/2708; SI 2005/1516; SI 2005/2114; SI 2006/622; SI 2006/680).

6 See COMPANY AND PARTNERSHIP INSOLVENCY vol 17 (2011) PARA 1209 et seq.

11. OTHER DEBT MANAGEMENT ARRANGEMENTS

(1) DEEDS OF ARRANGEMENT

(i) General Principles

852. In general. Independently of bankruptcy law, an insolvent debtor, with the general body of his creditors, or with some of his creditors, or with classes of his creditors, may enter into a valid arrangement by which, without paying his debts in full, he obtains release from the claims of the arranging creditors, or temporary or permanent freedom from process of law for the recovery of the debts due to them[1]. These arrangements usually take the form either of a composition with creditors, or an assignment of the arranging debtor's property to a trustee for their benefit, and all constitute contracts between the parties thereto[2].

There are also other forms of arrangement which may be, but are now seldom, used, such as a deed of inspectorship entered into for the purpose of carrying on or winding up a business, or an agreement or letter of licence made or given for the purpose of authorising the debtor, or some other person nominated by his creditors, to manage, carry on, realise or dispose of the debtor's business with a view to the payment of his debts[3]. Many such arrangements will be subject to the provisions of, and will require to be registered under, the Deeds of Arrangement Act 1914[4]. In practice, however, deeds of arrangement are seldom used[5].

Under the Bankruptcy Act 1914 not only the execution of the deed of arrangement but also several of the preliminary procedural steps[6] prior to its execution constituted an act of bankruptcy on which any dissenting creditor could found a bankruptcy petition[7]. Further, creditors who did not assent to the deed were not bound by it and remained free to pursue any remedies available to them[8]. The provisions in the Insolvency Act 1986 relating to personal insolvency do not re-enact the concept of the act of bankruptcy and to this extent deeds of arrangement are now a more satisfactory method for a debtor to compromise with his creditors. The approved voluntary arrangement under the 1986 Act[9] is, however, likely to prove a far more satisfactory procedure for the debtor who wishes to compound with his creditors.

1   As to the effect of a covenant not to sue see *Bateson v Gosling* (1871) LR 7 CP 9.
2   As to assignment and composition see PARAS 854–856.
3   See *Marconi's Wireless Telegraph Co v Newman* [1930] 2 KB 292 (where it was held that a deed of inspectorship did not constitute a partnership between the debtor and his creditors, or between the debtor and the inspector and the committee, and that the debtor did not become the agent of the inspector or of the committee to carry on the business, but it remained the business of the debtor).
4   As to deeds of arrangement to which the Deeds of Arrangement Act 1914 applies see PARA 853.
5   See the *Report of the Review Committee into Insolvency Law and Practice* (Cmnd 8558); and *Consumer credit and personal insolvency review: summary of responses on consumer credit and formal response on personal insolvency* (Department of Business, Innovation and Skills, July 2011) para 5.47 which both recommend the repeal of the Deeds of Arrangement Act 1914.
6   Eg the issue and service of the notice summoning the required meeting of creditors, statements made in the notice, and statements made at the meeting by or on behalf of the debtor.
7   As to acts of bankruptcy see the Bankruptcy Act 1914 s 1 (repealed). Under the Deeds of Arrangement Act 1914 s 24(1) (repealed), where the trustee served a prescribed notice on a creditor of the debtor, that creditor was disentitled to present a bankruptcy petition relying on the execution of the deed or any preparatory act as an act of bankruptcy after the expiration of the period of one month from the service of the notice.

8   As to creditors bound by deeds of arrangement see PARA 878.
9   Ie under the Insolvency Act 1986 Pt 8 (ss 252–263G): see PARA 43 et seq.

853.   Deeds of arrangement to which the Deeds of Arrangement Act 1914 applies.   A deed of arrangement to which the Deeds of Arrangement Act 1914 applies includes any instrument[1] of the classes set out below whether under seal[2] or not:

(1)   made by, for or in respect of the affairs of a debtor for the benefit of his creditors generally[3];

(2)   made by, for or in respect of the affairs of a debtor who was insolvent at the date of the execution of the instrument for the benefit of any three or more of his creditors[4],

otherwise than in pursuance of the law for the time being in force relating to bankruptcy[5]. The classes are:

(a)   an assignment of property[6];

(b)   a deed of or agreement for a composition[7];

and, in cases where creditors of the debtor obtain any control over his property or business:

(c)   a deed of inspectorship entered into for the purpose of carrying on or winding up a business[8];

(d)   a letter of licence authorising the debtor or any other person to manage, carry on, realise or dispose of a business with a view to the payment of debts[9]; and

(e)   any agreement or instrument entered into for the purpose of carrying on or winding up the debtor's business, or authorising the debtor or any other person to manage, carry on, realise or dispose of the debtor's business with a view to the payment of his debts[10].

A deed of arrangement by a limited joint stock company is not registrable under the 1914 Act[11].

1   The Deeds of Arrangement Act 1914 applies only to 'instruments'. It does not apply to oral agreements, and a receipt stating the terms of an oral agreement for a composition is not a deed of arrangement within the 1914 Act so as to require registration: *Hughes and Falconer v Newton* [1939] 3 All ER 869.
      Save as otherwise expressly provided by the Deeds of Arrangement Act 1914, nothing in that Act is to be construed as repealing or affects any provision of the law for the time being in force in relation to bankruptcy or gives validity to any deed or instrument which by law is void or voidable: s 24(3) (amended by the Insolvency Act 1985 Sch 10 Pt III).
2   Any rule of law which required a seal for the valid execution of an instrument as a deed by an individual has, except in relation to a corporation sole, been abolished in relation to instruments delivered as a deed on or after 31 July 1990: see the Law of Property (Miscellaneous Provisions) Act 1989 s 1(1)(b), (10); and DEEDS AND OTHER INSTRUMENTS vol 32 (2012) PARAS 207, 232.
3   Deeds of Arrangement Act 1914 s 1(1)(a). If at the date of execution the debtor was solvent, the deed must be for the benefit of creditors generally. This is a question of fact: *Re Hobbins, ex p Official Receiver* (1899) 6 Mans 212. Such a deed is revocable right up to the time that the fact of execution is communicated to a creditor (*Ellis & Co v Cross* [1915] 2 KB 654) including a creditor who is also trustee (*Beebee & Co v Turner's Successors* (1931) 48 TLR 61).
      'Creditors generally' includes all creditors who may assent to, or take the benefit of, a deed of arrangement: Deeds of Arrangement Act 1914 s 30(1). See *Re Rileys Ltd, Harper v Rileys* [1903] 2 Ch 590; *Re Allix, ex p Trustee* [1914] 2 KB 77 (where a deed signed by 13 out of 20 creditors described as 'hereinafter called the creditors' was held to be a deed for the benefit of creditors generally); *Huddersfield Fine Worsteds Ltd v Todd* (1925) 134 LT 82. See also *Trustee of GR Spink (in bankruptcy) v Dicker* (1978) Times, 26 October (deed was void where it was made in favour of only some of the creditors for an inadequate consideration).
4   Deeds of Arrangement Act 1914 s 1(1)(b). For the purpose of determining the number of creditors for whose benefit a deed is made, any two or more joint creditors are to be treated as a single creditor: s 30(2).

5　Deeds of Arrangement Act 1914 s 1(1). The Deeds of Arrangement Act 1914 does not apply to a voluntary arrangement approved under the Insolvency Act 1986 Pt 8 (ss 252–263G): s 260(3). As to approved voluntary arrangements see PARA 43 et seq.

6　Deeds of Arrangement Act 1914 s 1(2)(a). For these purposes, 'property' has the meaning given by the Insolvency Act 1986 s 436 (see PARA 412): Deeds of Arrangement Act 1914 s 30(1) (definition substituted by the Insolvency Act 1986 Sch 14).

As to whether an instrument is an assignment of property see *Re Halstead, ex p Richardson* [1917] 1 KB 695, CA; *Re Lee, ex p Grunwaldt* [1920] 2 KB 200; *Landsberg v Mendel* [1924] WN 46 (where there was an arrangement by way of assignment of property and also a lump sum composition); *B Lipton Ltd v Bell* [1924] 1 KB 701, CA (where an authority to realise the debtor's property, coupled with a declaration of trust for the application of the proceeds, was held not to be an assignment of property). As to deeds of assignment see PARA 854.

7　Deeds of Arrangement Act 1914 s 1(2)(b); and see *Re Lee, ex p Grunwaldt* [1920] 2 KB 200. As to compositions see PARA 856.

8　Deeds of Arrangement Act 1914 s 1(2)(c).

9　Deeds of Arrangement Act 1914 s 1(2)(d).

10　Deeds of Arrangement Act 1914 s 1(2)(e); and see *Re Wilson* [1916] 1 KB 382 at 398, CA (where it was held that a power of attorney given by the debtor authorising a third party to execute a deed of arrangement under the Deeds of Arrangement Act 1914 was not in itself a deed of arrangement under s 1(2)(e)); *Re Halstead, ex p Richardson* [1916] 2 KB 902; affd [1917] 1 KB 695, CA (assignment of a stockbroker's assets on default to the official assignee of the London Stock Exchange held to be a registrable instrument).

11　*Re Rileys Ltd, Harper v Rileys* [1903] 2 Ch 590. As to voluntary arrangements by companies under the Insolvency Act 1986 Pt 1 (ss 1–7) see COMPANY AND PARTNERSHIP INSOLVENCY vol 17 (2011) PARA 1213 et seq; and as to schemes of arrangement, reconstruction and amalgamation by companies see COMPANIES vol 15 (2009) PARA 1425 et seq.

854. Deeds of assignment. A deed assigning all, or substantially all, of his property to a trustee on trusts declared in the deed, by which the assigned property is to be held and applied for the benefit of the creditors, may be executed by a debtor[1]. The deed may provide for the exercise by the creditors, or by a committee appointed by them, of some control over the trustee's administration of the trust estate, and for the release of the debtor from, or the suspension of, legal proceedings for the recovery of the debts due to the assenting creditors[2].

The assignment of the debtor's property to a trustee is the voluntary act of the arranging creditor[3], and the trusts to which the assignment is subject are those which the debtor himself creates on the vesting by him of the property comprised in the assignment in the trustee[4]. The effect of the deed is to release or suspend the operation of creditors' claims by virtue of the assent of creditors to it, and it binds only those creditors who, in writing or otherwise, expressly or impliedly assent to it[5]. Until a deed of assignment to a trustee has been executed by, or has come to the knowledge of, the creditors, the trustee is only an agent for the debtor under a revocable authority to deal with the estate[6]. The bankruptcy of the debtor, before the deed has become operative by virtue of the creditors' assents so as to create a binding trust, revokes and invalidates the trusts of the deed[7].

In construing a deed of assignment, a special limited condition overrides any general implied condition in the deed[8]; similarly, general words of assignment are controlled by a recital in the deed showing that the assignment was confined to the contents of the schedule[9].

1　A deed of arrangement may be executed by the donee of a power of attorney given by the debtor for that purpose: *Re Wilson* [1916] 1 KB 382, DC.

2　A trustee of a deed of arrangement is a trust corporation and may, therefore, give a valid receipt on the sale of land: see the Law of Property Act 1925 s 27(2); the Trustee Act 1925 s 14(2); and TRUSTS vol 48 (2007 Reissue) PARA 1051.

3　*Wallwyn v Coutts* (1815) 3 Mer 707; *Gibbs v Glamis* (1841) 11 Sim 584.

4　*John v James* (1878) 8 ChD 744, CA; cf *Re LG Clarke, ex p Debtor v S Aston & Son Ltd* [1967] Ch 1121, [1966] 3 All ER 622, DC.

5　*Ilderton v Jewell* (1864) 16 CBNS 142; *Benham v Broadhurst* (1864) 3 H & C 472. See also PARA 878.

6　*Acton v Woodgate* (1833) 2 My & K 492; *Harland v Binks* (1850) 15 QB 713; *Re Douglas, ex p Snowball* (1872) 7 Ch App 534; *Re Ashby, ex p Wreford* [1892] 1 QB 872. The fact that a deed of assignment has been executed in pursuance of previous resolutions of, or at the previous request of, the creditors does not, in the absence of its execution being communicated to them, make the deed irrevocable: *Ellis & Co v Cross* [1915] 2 KB 654.

7　See *Smith v Dresser* (1866) LR 1 Eq 651 at 655; *Johns v James* (1878) 8 ChD 744, CA; *Smith v Keating* (1848) 6 CB 136; *R v Humphris* [1904] 2 KB 89 at 97; *R v Creese* (1874) LR 2 CCR 105 at 113. See also *Siggers v Evans* (1855) 5 E & B 367 (where the trustee was also a beneficiary under the deed, and it was held that assent on his part was not necessary to perfect his title): *Re Waley's Trusts* (1855) 3 Drew 165 at 169; *Garrard v Lord Lauderdale* (1831) 2 Russ & M 451; *Gibbs v Glamis* (1841) 11 Sim 584.

8　See *Re Clement, ex p Goas* (1886) 3 Morr 153, CA (where the trustee was empowered, but failed, to declare the deed void on the debtor's defaulting on instalments; and it was held that the deed was not void until he did so, and that the creditors could not petition in bankruptcy).

9　See *Re Moon, ex p Dawes* (1886) 17 QBD 275, CA. As to the interpretation of deeds generally see DEEDS AND OTHER INSTRUMENTS vol 32 (2012) PARA 364 et seq.

855.　Modes of assignment. Arrangements by means of the assignment of a debtor's property to a trustee for the benefit of his creditors are usually effected in one of two ways, either:

(1)　where the insolvent debtor, before communicating with his creditors, assigns his property to a trustee selected by himself on trust for their benefit, and then obtains the assent of all or some of his creditors to the arrangement[1]; or

(2)　where, before making any assignment, the debtor calls his creditors together to a meeting, or the creditors themselves meet, and the creditors agree to forbear from enforcing their claims, on condition that the debtor assigns his property to a trustee chosen at the meeting, and on trusts of which the creditors approve.

Whichever of these methods is adopted, the assignment becomes operative to create a valid title in the trustee, and validly enforceable trusts for the benefit of the creditors, as soon as the deed has been executed and creditors have assented to it, but subject to the requirements as to registration[2].

1　For an example see *Re Woodroff, ex p Woodroff* (1897) 4 Mans 46. As to revocation of assent before execution of the deed see *Re Jones Bros, ex p Associated Newspapers Ltd* [1912] 3 KB 234. As to when assents can no longer be revoked see *Re LG Clarke, ex p Debtor v S Aston & Son Ltd* [1967] Ch 1121, [1966] 3 All ER 622, DC.

2　As to avoidance of unregistered deeds of arrangement and registration of deeds of arrangement see PARAS 857, 859 et seq.

856.　Compositions. A composition is an agreement between the compounding debtor and all or some of his creditors by which the compounding creditors agree with the debtor, and, expressly or impliedly, with each other, to accept from the debtor payment of less than the amounts due to them in full satisfaction of the whole of their claims[1]. A composition agreement may be made orally or in writing, or partly orally and partly in writing[2]. The consideration supporting the agreement which enables the acceptance of part of a debt to operate as a discharge of the whole debt is the mutual agreement of the creditors to forgo part of their claims[3].

The effect of any particular agreement for a composition depends on its terms[4]. Subject to any statutory provisions, the effect of the composition is that the creditors accept it as a method of paying their debts, failure by the debtor to comply with his obligations under the composition normally entitling the creditors to sue him for the whole of the balance of their debts[5]. Where the effect of the composition is that the creditors accept the debtor's promise with or without a surety in satisfaction of their debts, it seems that, on the debtor's default, the creditors may sue only for the balance of the amount of the composition[6].

1   *Re Hatton* (1872) 7 Ch App 723 at 726; *Slater v Jones, Capes v Ball* (1873) LR 8 Exch 186 at 193, 194. See also *Re Griffith* (1886) 3 Morr 111 at 116.

2   Where, under a deed of composition and release, the debtor is left in possession of his assets and no trustee is appointed, it would seem that the provisions of the Deeds of Arrangement Act 1914, with regard to the giving of security and the duties of trustees under a deed (see PARA 864 et seq), do not apply to the debtor. Compositions may be effected simply by the creditors mutually accepting the composition offered and giving receipts in full.

3   *Norman v Thompson* (1850) 4 Exch 755 at 759 ('it is a good consideration for one to give up part of his claim that another should do the same'); *Carey v Barrett* (1879) 4 CPD 379. See also *Couldery v Bartrum* (1881) 19 ChD 394 at 399, CA. Where the composition is by deed, consideration is not necessary to support it, for the acceptance of less than the amount of a debt in discharge of the whole debt is valid, if made by deed: *Foakes v Beer* (1884) 9 App Cas 605 at 613, HL; applied in *D and C Builders Ltd v Rees* [1966] 2 QB 617, [1965] 3 All ER 837, CA.

4   Sometimes the payment of instalments under a composition is secured by an assignment by the debtor of his property on trust, if the instalments are not paid, to realise the property and to apply it towards the satisfaction of the composition. The deed of composition normally contains a release by the creditors of the debts due to them, or an agreement by the creditors not to enforce their claims by legal proceedings, so long as the instalments are duly paid and the provisions of the agreement are observed by the debtor, with a condition that, on payment of the entire composition, the debtor is released from the whole of the creditors' respective claims. There may also be a proviso that the composition is to be at an end and that the creditors are to regain their original rights if the composition or any instalment is not duly paid or if bankruptcy proceedings are taken against the debtor. Bills of exchange or promissory notes for the amounts payable under the composition might be given to the creditors, or a trustee on their behalf, in which event the agreement to pay the composition should not be by deed, because the obligation of the debtor and sureties on the negotiable instruments might merge in the agreement by deed: *Owen v Homan* (1851) 3 Mac & G 378; affd 4 HL Cas 997.

5   See *Re Hatton* (1872) 7 Ch App 723 (composition under the Bankruptcy Act 1869 (repealed)); cf *Couldery v Bartrum* (1881) 19 ChD 394, CA. See also CONTRACT vol 22 (2012) PARA 610. Time runs against a creditor in respect of his right to sue on the debt only from the date of the debtor's default: *Re Stock, ex p Amos* (1896) 3 Mans 324, following *Irving v Veitch* (1837) 3 M & W 90; and see the Limitation Act 1980 s 29(5) and LIMITATION PERIODS vol 68 (2008) PARA 1184.

6   *Re Hatton* (1872) 7 Ch App 723 at 726.

857. Avoidance of unregistered deeds of arrangement. A deed of arrangement is void[1] unless it is registered[2] within seven clear days[3] after the first execution thereof by the debtor or any creditor, or, if it is executed in any place out of England[4], then within seven clear days after the time at which it would, in the ordinary course of post, arrive in England, if posted within one week after the execution thereof, and unless it bears such stamp as is provided by the Deeds of Arrangement Act 1914[5].

1   If a deed of arrangement is declared void for want of registration, the money in the hands of the trustee under the instrument passes to the trustee in bankruptcy under an order for the administration of the insolvent estate of a deceased debtor, and, if the instrument is declared void, the release it contains is also void: *Re Lee, ex p Grunwaldt* [1920] 2 KB 200. As to the recovery of moneys expended by the trustee see *Re Zakon, ex p Trustee v Bushell* [1940] Ch 253, [1940] 1 All ER 263.

2   The deed of arrangement must be registered with the Registrar of Bills of Sale: Deeds of Arrangement Act 1914 s 2 (amended by the Finance Act 1949 Sch 11). The Registrar of Bills of Sale has been replaced for the purposes of registration under the 1914 Act by a registrar appointed by the Secretary of State: see the Administration of Justice Act 1925 s 22(1). As to

registration see PARA 859 et seq. The Administration of Justice Act 1925 s 22(1) refers to the Board of Trade which now has effect as a reference to the Secretary of State: see PARA 19 note 1.

3 As to the extension of this time limit see PARA 861. Where the time for registering a deed of arrangement expires on a Sunday, or other day on which the registration office is closed, the registration is valid if made on the next following day on which the office is open: Deeds of Arrangement Act 1914 s 8.

4 A deed executed in Scotland under Scots law by a debtor domiciled in England does not require registration in Scotland and is valid in England: *Re Pilkington's Will Trusts* [1937] Ch 574, [1937] 3 All ER 213. See also *Dulaney v Merry & Son* [1901] 1 KB 536.

5 Deeds of Arrangement Act 1914 s 2 (as amended: see note 2).

858. Avoidance of deeds of arrangement unless assented to by a majority of creditors. A deed of arrangement which either is expressed to be or is in fact for the benefit of a debtor's creditors generally[1] is void unless, before or within 21 days after its registration, or within such extended time as may be allowed[2], it has received the assent[3] of a majority[4] in number and value of the creditors of the debtor[5]. The list of creditors annexed to the affidavit of the debtor filed on registration of the deed of arrangement is prima facie evidence of the names of the creditors and the amounts of their claims[6].

The trustee must file[7] at the time of the registration of a deed of arrangement, or in the case of a deed of arrangement assented to after 28 days of registration, within 28 days after registration or within such extended time as may be allowed[8] a statutory declaration by the trustee that the requisite majority of the creditors of the debtor have assented to the deed of arrangement, which declaration is, in favour of a purchaser for value, conclusive evidence, and, in other cases, prima facie evidence, of the fact declared[9].

1 As to the meaning of 'creditors generally' see PARA 853 note 3.

2 Ie by the High Court or the court having jurisdiction for the purposes of the Insolvency Act 1986 Pts 8–11 (ss 252–385) in relation to the district in which the debtor resided or carried on business at the date of the execution of the deed. As to the courts having such jurisdiction see PARAS 6, 7.

3 The assent of a creditor for these purposes is established by his executing the deed of arrangement or sending to the trustee his assent in writing attested by a witness, but not otherwise: Deeds of Arrangement Act 1914 s 3(3).

4 In calculating a majority of creditors for these purposes, a creditor holding security on the property of the debtor is to be reckoned as a creditor only in respect of the balance, if any, due to him after deducting the value of such security; and creditors whose debts amount to sums not exceeding £10 are to be reckoned in the majority in value but not in the majority in number: Deeds of Arrangement Act 1914 s 3(5). In calculating the majority in number of creditors, creditors for debts not exceeding £10 must be eliminated from the total number of creditors as well as from the majority: *Re Wilson* [1916] 1 KB 382, overruled at [1916] 1 KB 382 at 398, CA, purely on the point of jurisdiction of the Divisional Court in entertaining the appeal in the circumstances of that case, the above point not being considered.

5 Deeds of Arrangement Act 1914 s 3(1) (s 3(1), (4) amended by the Insolvency Act 1985 Sch 8 para 2(2); and the Insolvency Act 1986 Sch 14). For the prescribed form of assent see the Deeds of Arrangement Rules 1925, SR & O 1925/795, r 4(1), Appendix, Form 2.

6 Deeds of Arrangement Act 1914 s 3(2).

7 See PARA 857 note 2.

8 See note 2.

9 Deeds of Arrangement Act 1914 s 3(4) (as amended: see note 5). For the prescribed form of statutory declaration see the Deeds of Arrangement Rules 1925, SR & O 1925/795, Appendix, Form 3.

(ii) Registration of Deeds of Arrangement

859. Mode of registration. The registration[1] of a deed of arrangement under the Deeds of Arrangement Act 1914 must be effected by presenting and filing[2] a true copy[3] of the deed, and of every schedule or inventory annexed to it or referred to in it, within seven clear days[4] after the execution of the deed, together with an affidavit[5] verifying the time of execution, and containing a description of the residence and occupation of the debtor, and of the place or places where his business is carried on, and an affidavit by the debtor stating the total estimated amount of property and liabilities included under the deed, the total amount of the composition, if any, payable thereunder, and the names and addresses of his creditors[6].

No deed may be so presented unless the original of the deed, duly stamped with the proper inland revenue duty[7], is produced[8] at the time of such registration[9].

An assignment of property by a debtor to a trustee or assignee for the benefit of his creditors may not be so registered unless it appears from the assignment that it has been or purports to have been executed or, if not made by deed, signed by the trustee or assignee[10].

The prescribed fees must be paid on registration[11].

1   As to the need for registration see PARA 857.

2   See PARA 857 note 2.

3   The Deeds of Arrangement Act 1914 s 5(1) has effect as if it provided that there are to be presented to the registrar such number of copies of the deed and of every schedule or inventory annexed thereto or referred to therein as he may deem to be necessary for the purpose of carrying out the requirements of the 1914 Act: Administration of Justice Act 1925 s 22(2). On every copy of a deed which is presented for filing there must be indorsed, by the person who presents it, the name of the debtor, the date of the deed and of the filing thereof, the total amount of duty with which the deed is stamped and a certificate signed by the solicitor of the debtor or the person who presents the copy for filing certifying that the copy is a correct copy of the deed: Deeds of Arrangements Rules 1925, SR & O 1925/795, r 6. For these purposes, the reference to a solicitor includes a reference to a body recognised by the Law Society under the Administration of Justice Act 1985 s 9 (see LEGAL PROFESSIONS vol 65 (2008) PARA 687): Solicitors' Recognised Bodies Order 1991, SI 1991/2684, arts 2(1), 3, 4(a), Sch 1 (amended by SI 2001/645; and SI 2009/500).

4   As to the position where the time limit expires on a Sunday or other day on which the registration office is closed see PARA 857 note 3; and as to the extension of the time limit see PARA 861.

5   The affidavits to be made pursuant to the Deeds of Arrangement Act 1914 s 5 must be filed with the registrar: Deeds of Arrangement Rules 1925, SR & O 1925/795, r 5. For the prescribed forms of affidavit see r 4(1), Appendix, Form 4 (affidavit of execution by debtor), Form 5 (affidavit of execution where deed is first executed by creditors), Form 6 (debtor's affidavit, with schedule of creditors). The Secretary of State may from time to time alter these forms or substitute new forms, such alterations or substitutions to be published in the London Gazette: r 4(2). Rule 4(2) refers to the Board of Trade, the functions of which are now carried out by the Secretary of State: see PARA 19 note 1.

    These affidavits may not be sworn before the solicitor to the trustee of the deed, or the deed, although registered, will be void: *Re Bagley* [1911] 1 KB 317. The deed will be void if the debtor's affidavit is sworn by a donee of his power of attorney instead of by the debtor personally: *Re Wilson* [1916] 1 KB 382. The affidavit need not include the names and addresses of secured creditors (*Chaplin v Daly* (1894) 71 LT 569); and, if, without fraud, the names and addresses of some of the creditors that should be included are omitted, the registration is not rendered void (*Maskelyne and Cooke v Smith* [1903] 1 KB 671). As to when the debtor's affidavit will be dispensed with see *Re X (An Arranging Debtor)* (1910) 44 ILT 167.

6   Deeds of Arrangement Act 1914 s 5(1) (amended by the Administration of Justice Act 1925 Sch 5). When a deed is so registered, there must be written on the original deed a certificate stating that the deed has been duly registered as prescribed by the Deeds of Arrangement Act 1914, and the date of registration; and such certificate must be sealed with the seal of the registrar: Deeds of Arrangement Rules 1925, SR & O 1925/795, r 8.

7　Stamp duty has been abolished on the conveyance or transfer of property otherwise than on sale in relation to instruments executed on or after 13 March 2008 and not stamped before 19 March 2008: see the Finance Act 2008 s 99, Sch 32 Pt 1 paras 9, 10; and STAMP TAXES vol 96 (2012) PARA 304.

8　See PARA 857 note 2.

9　Deeds of Arrangement Act 1914 s 5(2) (amended by the Finance Act 1949 Sch 11 Pt V).

10　Deeds of Arrangement Rules 1925, SR & O 1925/795, r 7.

11　Deeds of Arrangement Act 1914 s 26(1). Nothing in the 1914 Act makes it obligatory on the registrar to do, or permit to be done, any act in respect of which any fee is specified or prescribed, except on payment of such fee: s 26(1). For the prescribed fees see the Deeds of Arrangement Fees Order 1984, SI 1984/887, art 3(2), Schedule, Fees 4–6 (art 3(2) amended by SI 2009/2748). The fees must be taken in cash: Deeds of Arrangement Fees Order 1984, SI 1984/887, art 3(3).

860.　Procedure on registration.　The registrar must keep a register wherein must be entered, as soon as conveniently may be after the presentation of a deed for registration[1], an abstract of the contents of every deed of arrangement registered, containing the following and any other prescribed particulars:

(1)　the date of the deed;

(2)　the name, address and description of the debtor, and the place or places where his business was carried on at the date of the execution of the deed, and the title of the firm or firms under which the debtor carried on business, and the name and address of the trustee, if any, under the deed;

(3)　the date of registration;

(4)　the amount of property and liabilities included under the deed, as estimated by the debtor[2].

When a deed is so registered, there must be written on the original deed a certificate stating that the deed has been duly registered and the date of registration; and such certificate must be sealed with the seal of the registrar[3].

Where the place of business or residence of the debtor who is one of the parties to a deed of arrangement, or who is referred to therein, is situated in some place outside the London insolvency district[4], the registrar must, within three clear days after registration, and in accordance with the prescribed directions, transmit a copy of the deed to the district judge of the county court in the district of which such place of business or residence is situated; and every copy so transmitted must be filed, kept and indexed by the district judge[5].

1　Ie under the Deeds of Arrangement Act 1914 s 5: see PARA 859.

2　Deeds of Arrangement Act 1914 s 6 (amended by the Administration of Justice Act 1925 s 22(3), Sch 5). For the prescribed form of the register see the Deeds of Arrangement Rules 1925, SR & O 1925/795, r 4(1), Appendix, Form 7.

3　Deeds of Arrangement Rules 1925, SR & O 1925/795, r 8.

4　The Deeds of Arrangement Act 1914 s 10 refers to the London bankruptcy district which is now the London insolvency district: see PARA 7 note 2.

5　Deeds of Arrangement Act 1914 s 10; Deeds of Arrangement Rules 1925, SR & O 1925/795, r 10; Courts and Legal Services Act 1990 s 74(1)(a), (3). On every copy of a deed which is so transmitted to a district judge there must be written copies of every indorsement or certificate written on the original deed or on the filed copy thereof; and such copies must be signed by the registrar or by some other person duly authorised by him: Deeds of Arrangement Rules 1925, SR & O 1925/795, r 11; Courts and Legal Services Act 1990 s 74(1)(a), (3). The copy of a deed which is required to be transmitted to a district judge may be transmitted to him by post: Deeds of Arrangement Rules 1925, SR & O 1925/795, r 12; Courts and Legal Services Act 1990 s 74(1)(a). The district judge must number the copies of deeds received by him in the order in which they are respectively received, and must file and keep them in his office: Deeds of Arrangement Rules 1925, SR & O 1925/795, r 13; Courts and Legal Services Act 1990 s 74(1)(a). Where a debtor who is one of the parties to a deed of arrangement or who is referred to therein has a place of business or residence in some place outside the London bankruptcy district (see note 4), there must be furnished to the registrar sufficient copies of the deed of arrangement to enable him to transmit a copy to the district judge of each district in which such place of business or residence is situated: Deeds of Arrangement Rules 1925, SR & O 1925/795, r 14; Courts and Legal Services Act 1990 s 74(1)(a), (3). The district judge must keep an index, alphabetically arranged, in which he must enter, under the first letter of the surname of the debtor, such surname, with his Christian name, address and description, and the number which has been affixed to the copy: Deeds of Arrangement Rules 1925, SR & O 1925/795, r 15; Courts and Legal Services Act 1990 s 74(1)(a), (3). The Deeds of Arrangement Act 1914 ss 9, 25 (see PARA 862) apply to all documents filed with the registrar pursuant to the 1914 Act or the Deeds of Arrangement Rules 1925, SR & O 1925/795: r 16.

861. Rectification of the register. On being satisfied that the omission to register a deed of arrangement within the time required[1] or that the omission or misstatement of the name, residence or description of any person was accidental, or due to inadvertence, or to some cause beyond the control of the debtor and not imputable to any negligence on his part, the High Court or a judge thereof may, on the application of any party interested, and on such terms and conditions as are just and expedient, extend the time for registration, or order the omission or misstatement to be supplied or rectified by the insertion in the register of the true name, residence or description[2].

1 Ie the time required by the Deeds of Arrangement Act 1914 s 2: see PARA 857.

2 Deeds of Arrangement Act 1914 s 7. Where a debtor becomes mentally incapable of swearing the affidavit leading to registration, the court will order an extension of the prescribed time: *Re X (An Arranging Debtor)* (1910) 44 ILT 167.

   Every application to the court under the Deeds of Arrangement Act 1914 s 7 must be made to a Master of the Queen's Bench Division by claim form under the CPR Pt 8 or by witness statement, setting out the particulars of the deed of arrangement and of the omission or mis-statement and the grounds on which the application is made, and accompanied by payment of the prescribed fee: CPR PD 8A—*Alternative Procedure for Claims* para 12A(2), (4), (5); and CIVIL PROCEDURE vol 11 (2009) PARA 127 et seq. If the application is made by witness statement CPR Pt 23 (see CIVIL PROCEDURE vol 11 (2009) PARA 303 et seq) applies; the witness statement constitutes the application notice under that Part and does not need to be served on any other person; and the application will normally be heard without a hearing: para 12A(3).

862. Searches and office copies. On payment of the prescribed fee, any person is entitled, at all reasonable times, to search the register[1], and, subject to such regulations as may be prescribed, to inspect, examine and make extracts[2] from any registered deed of arrangement, without being required to make a written application or to specify any particulars in reference thereto, on payment of the prescribed fee for each deed of arrangement inspected[3]. On payment of the prescribed fee, the index kept by the district judge of the county court may be searched and the same extracts made from any instrument filed by him as are permitted in the case of registered instruments[4].

On payment of the prescribed fees, any person is entitled to an office copy or extract from any registered instrument or document filed with the registrar, or to an office copy of an instrument filed by the district judge[5].

In all courts and before all arbitrators and other persons an office copy of or extract from a registered instrument is prima facie evidence of the instrument and of the fact and date of registration[6].

1 Ie the register maintained under the Deeds of Arrangement Act 1914 s 6: see PARA 860.

2 The extracts must be limited to the dates of execution and of registration, the names, addresses and descriptions of the debtor and of the parties to the deed, a short statement of the nature and effect of the deed, and any other prescribed particulars: Deeds of Arrangement Act 1914 s 9; Deeds of Arrangement Rules 1925, SR & O 1925/795, r 9.

3   Deeds of Arrangement Act 1914 ss 9, 26(1) (s 9 amended by the Decimal Currency Act 1969
     s 10(1)); Deeds of Arrangement Rules 1925, SR & O 1925/795, r 16. For the prescribed fees see
     the Deeds of Arrangement Fees Order 1984, SI 1984/887, art 3, Schedule, Fee 8 (art 3 amended
     by SI 2009/2718).
4   Deeds of Arrangement Act 1914 s 10; Deeds of Arrangement Rules 1925, SR & O 1925/795,
     r 10; Courts and Legal Services Act 1990 s 74(1)(a), (3). Extracts must be limited as mentioned
     in note 2: see r 9.
5   Deeds of Arrangement Act 1914 ss 10, 25; Deeds of Arrangement Rules 1925,
     SR & O 1925/795, rr 10, 16; Courts and Legal Services Act 1990 s 74(1)(a), (3).
6   Deeds of Arrangement Act 1914 s 25; Deeds of Arrangement Rules 1925, SR & O 1925/795,
     r 16.

863. Registration under other statutes. Where unregistered land is affected by
a deed of arrangement, the deed should be registered in the name of the debtor
under the Land Charges Act 1972[1]; and, if it is not so registered, it is void as
against a purchaser of any land comprised in it or affected by it[2]. A deed of
arrangement may not be entered in the register of title[3].

Deeds of arrangement intended for the benefit of creditors generally are
incapable of registration under the Bills of Sale Acts[4].

1   See the Land Charges Act 1972 s 7(1); and REAL PROPERTY AND REGISTRATION vol 87 (2012)
     PARA 754. Registration may be made on the application of the trustee of the deed or a creditor
     assenting to or taking the benefit of the deed: s 7(1). The registration may be vacated pursuant
     to an order of the High Court: see ss 1(6), 17(1); and REAL PROPERTY AND REGISTRATION vol 87
     (2012) PARA 758. Registration ceases to have effect at the end of the period of five years but may
     be renewed from time to time, and, if so renewed, has effect for five years from the date of
     renewal: see s 8 and REAL PROPERTY AND REGISTRATION vol 87 (2012) PARA 757; cf *Re A
     Receiving Order (in Bankruptcy)* [1947] Ch 498, [1947] 1 All ER 843 (decided under the Land
     Charges Act 1925 s 6 (repealed)).
2   See the Land Charges Act 1972 s 7(2); and REAL PROPERTY AND REGISTRATION vol 87 (2012)
     PARA 756.
3   See the Land Registration Act 2002 s 87(2)(b); and REAL PROPERTY AND REGISTRATION vol 87
     (2012) PARA 537. References to an interest affecting an estate or charge in the Land Registration
     Act 2002 include a deed of arrangement: s 87(1)(d).
4   See the Bills of Sale Act 1878 s 4; the Bills of Sale Act (1878) Amendment Act 1882 s 3; *Johnson
     v Osenton* (1869) LR 4 Exch 107 (where it was held that a deed intended to operate under the
     Bankruptcy Acts, which, owing to irregularity, did not do so, was still a good deed, and for the
     benefit of creditors, and did not come under the Bills of Sale Acts); and FINANCIAL SERVICES AND
     INSTITUTIONS vol 50 (2008) PARA 1620 et seq. See also *General Furnishing and Upholstery Co
     v Venn* (1863) 2 H & C 153 (where the terms of the deed were wide enough to admit all
     creditors, and it was held to fall outside the Bills of Sale Acts).

(iii) Trustees under Arrangements

864. Trustee to be insolvency practitioner. A person who acts as trustee under
a deed which is a deed of arrangement made for the benefit of an individual's
creditors must be qualified to act as an insolvency practitioner in relation to that
individual[1].

1   Insolvency Act 1986 s 388(2)(b). As to insolvency practitioners and their qualification see PARA
     40. Nothing in s 388 applies to anything done (whether in the United Kingdom or elsewhere) in
     relation to insolvency proceedings under Council Regulation (EC) 1346/2000 (OJ L160,
     30.6.2000, p 1) on insolvency proceedings ('European Regulation on Insolvency Proceedings') in
     a member state other than the United Kingdom: Insolvency Act 1986 s 388(6) (added by
     SI 2002/1240). As to the European Regulation on Insolvency Proceedings see PARAS 41, 42.

865. Trustee's duty to give security; bank account. Within seven days[1] from
the date of filing the statutory declaration certifying the creditors' assent[2], the
trustee under a deed of arrangement must give security in the prescribed manner[3]

to the registrar of the court having bankruptcy jurisdiction[4] in relation to the district in which the debtor resided or carried on business as at the date of the execution of the deed, or, if he then resided or carried on business in the London insolvency district[5], to the senior bankruptcy registrar of the High Court, in a sum equal to the estimated assets available for distribution amongst the unsecured creditors as shown by the affidavit filed on registration[6], to administer the deed properly and account fully for the assets which come to his hands[7].

The giving of this security may be dispensed with if a majority in number and value of the creditors[8], either by resolution passed at a meeting convened by notice to all the creditors, or by writing addressed to the trustee, so resolve[9]; and, in that event, the trustee must forthwith file with the registrar a statutory declaration to that effect, which will, in favour of a purchaser for value, be conclusive evidence, and in other cases be prima facie evidence, of the facts declared[10].

If the trustee fails to comply with the above requirements, the court, on the application of any creditor and after hearing such persons as it thinks fit, may declare the deed void or may make an order appointing another trustee[11]. A certificate that the required security has been given, signed by the registrar of the court and filed with the registrar of deeds of arrangement, is conclusive evidence of the fact[12].

The security must be a bond of a guarantee society accepted by the registrar of the court, and a cover note must be accepted by the registrar as a temporary security, pending the preparation of the bond[13]. If the trustee fails to pay the annual premium, or if the society refuses to accept the premium, the society may apply to the registrar of the court to determine its liability under the bond[14].

All money received by the trustee must be banked by him to an account to be opened in the name of the debtor's estate[15].

1   The court cannot extend the seven days' limit: *Re Early, Smith and Pavey, ex p Trustee* (1928) 98 LJ Ch 34.

2   As to filing the statutory declaration see PARA 858.

3   See the Deeds of Arrangement Rules 1925, SR & O 1925/795, rr 24–26, Appendix, Forms 9–11. For the prescribed fee on applying to give security see the Deeds of Arrangement Fees Order 1984, SI 1984/887, art 3, Schedule Fee 1 (art 3 amended by SI 2009/2748).

4   Ie under the Insolvency Act 1986 Pts 8–11 (ss 252–385).

5   As to the meaning of 'the London insolvency district' see PARA 7 note 2.

6   As to registration see PARA 859.

7   Deeds of Arrangement Act 1914 s 11(1) (amended by the Insolvency Act 1985 Sch 8 para 2(3)(a); and the Insolvency Act 1986 Sch 14). For a limitation on this provision see PARA 872.

     A person is not qualified to act as an insolvency practitioner in relation to another person at any time unless there is in force at that time security or, in Scotland, caution for the proper performance of his functions, and that security or caution meets the prescribed requirements with respect to his so acting in relation to that other person: see the Insolvency Act 1986 s 390(3); and COMPANY AND PARTNERSHIP INSOLVENCY vol 16 (2011) PARAS 24, 25. It is apprehended that the obligation to provide such security is concurrent with the obligation under the Deeds of Arrangement Act 1914. When security has been given by a trustee pursuant to s 11(1), the registrar of the court to whom it is given must, within three days after receipt thereof, send to the registrar (see PARA 857 note 2) a certificate signed by him certifying that the security has been given and the registrar must forthwith file the same: Deeds of Arrangement Rules 1925, SR & O 1925/795, r 26.

8   In calculating a majority of creditors for these purposes, a secured creditor is to be reckoned as a creditor only in respect of the balance, if any, due to him after deducting the value of his security, and creditors whose debts amount to sums not exceeding £10 are to be reckoned in the majority in value but not in the majority in number: Deeds of Arrangement Act 1914 s 11(5).

9   Deeds of Arrangement Act 1914 s 11(1) (as amended: see note 7).

10	Deeds of Arrangement Act 1914 s 11(1). For the prescribed form of statutory declaration see the Deeds of Arrangement Rules 1925, SR & O 1925/795, r 4(1), Appendix, Form 8.

11	Deeds of Arrangement Act 1914 s 11(2) (amended by the Insolvency Act 1985 Sch 8 para 2(3); and the Insolvency Act 1986 Sch 14). As to the appointment of a new trustee see PARA 873.

The registrar of the court must send to the registrar (see PARA 857 note 2) within three days after any order made under the Deeds of Arrangement Act 1914 s 11(2) has been perfected a copy of such order: Deeds of Arrangement Rules 1925, SR & O 1925/795, r 26.

12	Deeds of Arrangement Act 1914 s 11(3).

13	Deeds of Arrangement Rules 1925, SR & O 1925/795, r 24. Every trustee, on giving security for the due administration of the deed and for accounting fully for the assets, must produce and hand to the registrar of the court to whom the security is to be given an office copy of the affidavit of the debtor filed on the registration of the deed and the registrar of the court must file such office copy: r 25.

14	Deeds of Arrangement Rules 1925, SR & O 1925/795, r 23. Notice of any such application must be served on the three largest creditors named in the affidavit filed on registration of the deed not less than eight days before the day appointed for the hearing of the application; and any such creditors may appear and be heard thereon: r 23. As to the procedure on such an application see PARA 884.

15	Deeds of Arrangement Act 1914 s 11(4).

866. Trustee's duties towards creditors. When an assignment for the benefit of creditors has become operative and valid, the creditors become the beneficiaries, and the trustee under the deed is to be treated as a trust corporation[1] with the powers provided under the Trustee Act 1925[2]; thus, though not specifically authorised by the deed, he may compromise and treat a creditor as a preferential creditor[3].

His duty is to ascertain all the persons entitled to the benefit of the trusts and the validity of their claims, and to administer the trust estate in accordance with the trusts declared in the deed. If out of the assigning debtor's property he pays to any creditor a sum larger in proportion to the creditor's claim than that paid to other creditors entitled to the benefit of the deed, then, unless the deed authorises him to do so, or unless such payments are either made to a creditor entitled to enforce his claim by distress or are such as would be lawful in a bankruptcy, he is guilty of an offence[4].

Questions arising in the administration of the trust estate are determined by the court having jurisdiction[5] in the district in which the debtor resided or carried on business at the date of the execution of the deed[6].

1	See the Law of Property (Amendment) Act 1926 s 3 (amended by the Constitutional Reform Act 2005 Sch 11 Pt 1 para 1(2)); and TRUSTS AND POWERS vol 98 (2013) PARA 238. See also PARA 854 note 2.

2	See the Trustee Act 1925 s 15 (amended by the Trustee Act 2000 Sch 2, Pt II, para 20); and TRUSTS AND POWERS vol 98 (2013) PARA 518.

3	*Re Shenton* [1935] Ch 651.

4	Deeds of Arrangement Act 1914 s 17. For a limitation on the application of this provision see PARA 872. The Criminal Law Act 1967 s 1(1) abolished the distinction between felonies and misdemeanours. An offence under the Deeds of Arrangement Act 1914 s 17 is triable either summarily or on indictment: see the Magistrates' Courts Act 1980 s 17, Sch 1 para 16; and CRIMINAL PROCEDURE vol 27 (2010) PARA 161.

5	Ie under the Insolvency Act 1986 Pts 8–11 (ss 252–385).

6	See the Deeds of Arrangement Act 1914 s 23; and PARA 883. Where a trustee failed to give priority to preferential creditors according to express trusts in the deed, a declaration of breach of trust was made: *Re Moss, Westminster Corpn v Reubens* [1935] WN 171. A trustee who desires to contract on terms that he is not to be personally liable must clearly express the limitation; a mere description of him as 'trustee' is insufficient: *Hunt Bros v Colwell* [1939] 4 All ER 406, CA.

867. Transmission of accounts to the Secretary of State. At the prescribed times[1] a trustee[2] under a deed of arrangement must send to the Secretary of

State[3], or as he directs, an account, in the prescribed form[4], of his receipts and payments as trustee, verified by affidavit[5] and duly stamped[6]. If any trustee fails to transmit such account, he is liable on summary conviction to a fine not exceeding £5 for each day during which the default continues and, in addition, is guilty of contempt of court[7] and liable to be punished accordingly[8].

The Secretary of State may require a trustee to complete or amend an account which appears to him imperfect, or to furnish an explanation of an account; and the requirement is enforceable in the same manner as the transmission of accounts[9].

If, since becoming trustee or transmitting his last account, a trustee has not received or paid out any money on account of the estate, he must, at the period when he is required to transmit his account, send to the Secretary of State an affidavit of no receipts or payments[10].

As soon as the trustee has realised all the property included in the deed or so much as can probably be realised, and has distributed a final dividend or final instalment of composition, or in any other case as soon as the trusts of the deed and the trustee's obligations have been completely fulfilled, he must transmit his final account and a verifying affidavit[11].

1   The first account must be sent within 30 days from the expiration of 12 months from the date of registration of the deed, and must commence at the date of its execution and be brought down to the end of 12 months from the date of registration; subsequent accounts must be sent at intervals of 12 months and must be brought down to the end of the 12-month period for which they are sent: Deeds of Arrangement Rules 1925, SR & O 1925/795, r 31.

2   In the Deeds of Arrangement Act 1914 s 13, the expression 'trustee' includes any person appointed to distribute a composition or to act in any fiduciary capacity under any deed of arrangement: s 13(4) (amended by the Administration of Justice Act 1925 Sch 5).

3   The Deeds of Arrangement Act 1914 s 13 refers to the Board of Trade, the functions of which are now carried out by the Secretary of State: see PARA 19 note 1.

4   For the prescribed form of trustee's account of receipts and payments see the Deeds of Arrangement Rules 1925, SR & O 1925/795, r 4(1), Appendix, Form 15 (amended by SR & O 1941/1253). See further PARA 868.

5   As to the affidavit verifying the accounts see the Deeds of Arrangement Rules 1925, SR & O 1925/795, r 42, Appendix, Form 17. As to the swearing of affidavits respecting accounts see r 42.

6   Deeds of Arrangement Act 1914 s 13(1). For the prescribed fee see the Deeds of Arrangement Fees Order 1984, SI 1984/887, art 3, Schedule Fee 9 (art 3 amended by SI 2009/2718). As to the submission of a summary or modified statement of accounts see the Deeds of Arrangement Rules 1925, SR & O 1925/795, r 41; and as to inspection of accounts by the debtor or the creditors see PARA 879.

7   As to contempt of court see CONTEMPT OF COURT vol 22 (2012) PARA 1 et seq.

8   Deeds of Arrangement Act 1914 s 13(2) (amended by the Insolvency Act 1985 Sch 8 para 2(4)).

9   See the Deeds of Arrangement Rules 1925, SR & O 1925/795, r 38.

10   See the Deeds of Arrangement Rules 1925, SR & O 1925/795, r 39. Even if there are no assets, the trustee must stamp the account: *Re Hertage* (1896) 3 Mans 297.

11   See the Deeds of Arrangement Rules 1925, SR & O 1925/795, r 40. For the prescribed form of affidavit see r 4(1), Appendix, Form 20.

868. Form of accounts. Each receipt and payment must be entered in the trustee's accounts in such a manner as sufficiently to explain its nature[1]. Where the trustee carries on a business, he must transmit a separate trading account, and only enter the total receipts and payments in his yearly account[2]. He must enter his petty expenses in sufficient detail to show that no estimated charges are made[3]. Where property has been realised, the gross proceeds of sale must be entered under receipts and the necessary disbursements and charges as payments[4].

Where dividends or instalments of composition are distributed, the total amount of each dividend or instalment must be entered in the account as one sum; the trustee must forward to the Secretary of State[5], with each account in which a charge in respect of dividends or composition appears, a statement showing the amount of each creditor's claim and the amount of dividend or composition payable to each creditor, distinguishing in the statement the dividends or instalments paid and those remaining unpaid; with his final account he must forward a complete statement in similar form, showing the amount of the claim and the full amount of the dividend or composition paid to or reserved for each creditor[6].

In the case of a partnership, separate accounts must be kept of the joint and separate estates[7].

1   Deeds of Arrangement Rules 1925, SR & O 1925/795, r 32. For the prescribed form of trustee's account of receipts and payments see r 4(1), Appendix, Form 15 (amended by SR & O 1941/1253).
2   Deeds of Arrangement Rules 1925, SR & O 1925/795, r 33. For the prescribed form of trustee's trading account see r 4(1), Appendix, Form 18.
3   Deeds of Arrangement Rules 1925, SR & O 1925/795, r 34.
4   Deeds of Arrangement Rules 1925, SR & O 1925/795, r 35.
5   These provisions refer to the Board of Trade, the functions of which are now carried out by the Secretary of State: see PARA 19 note 1.
6   Deeds of Arrangement Rules 1925, SR & O 1925/795, r 36. For the prescribed form of list of dividends or compositions see r 4(1), Appendix, Form 19.
7   Deeds of Arrangement Rules 1925, SR & O 1925/795, r 37.

869.   Transmission of accounts to creditors.   At the expiration of six months from the date of the registration of a deed of arrangement, and at the expiration of every subsequent period of six months until the estate has been finally wound up, the trustee must send to each creditor who has assented to the deed a statement in the prescribed form[1] of his accounts and of the proceedings under the deed down to the date of the statement[2]. In his affidavit verifying his accounts he must state whether or not he has duly sent such statements, and the dates on which they were sent; and, if a trustee fails to comply with any of the above provisions, he is guilty of contempt of court[3] and liable to be punished accordingly[4].

1   For the prescribed forms see the Deeds of Arrangement Rules 1925, SR & O 1925/795, r 4(1), Appendix, Form 13 (statement of accounts to be sent to creditors), Form 17 (affidavit verifying trustee's accounts).
2   Deeds of Arrangement Act 1914 s 14 (amended by the Insolvency Act 1985 Sch 8 para 2(5)). For a limitation on the application of this provision see PARA 872.
3   As to contempt of court see CONTEMPT OF COURT vol 22 (2012) PARA 1 et seq.
4   Deeds of Arrangement Act 1914 s 14 (as amended: see note 2).

870.   Audit of accounts.   Where, in the course of the administration of the estate of a debtor who has executed a deed of arrangement, or within 12 months from the date when the final accounts were rendered, written application is made to the Secretary of State[1] by a majority in number and value of the creditors who have assented to the deed for an official audit of the trustee's accounts, the Secretary of State may cause the accounts to be audited[2]. In that case, any rules made under the Insolvency Act 1986[3] relating to the institution and enforcement of an audit of the accounts of a trustee in bankruptcy, including the provisions as to fees, apply with necessary modifications to the audit of the trustee's accounts; and the Secretary of State on the audit has power to require production of a certificate for the assessed costs of any solicitor[4] whose costs have been paid or charged by the trustee, and to disallow the whole or any part of any costs in respect of which no certificate is produced[5].

The Secretary of State may determine how and by what parties the costs, charges and expenses of and incidental to the audit, including any fees[6], are to be borne, whether by the applicants or by the trustee or out of the estate, and, before granting an application for an audit, may require the applicants to give security for those costs[7].

Within seven days of the Secretary of State's order being served on him, by registered post or the recorded delivery service[8], the trustee must deliver to the Secretary of State copies of all his previous accounts transmitted to the Secretary of State, together with a similar account from the date to which the last account extended to the date of the order, and an affidavit verifying the copies and account[9]. The audited accounts and the auditor's certificate or observations must be filed, and must be open to inspection by creditors or the trustee, who may take a copy; and a certified copy of the certificate or observations must be supplied to the trustee or any creditor on application[10].

1   These provisions refer to the Board of Trade, the functions of which are now carried out by the Secretary of State: see PARA 19 note 1.
2   Deeds of Arrangement Act 1914 s 15(1) (amended by the Insolvency Act 1985 Sch 8 para 2(6); and the Insolvency Act 1986 Sch 14). For a limitation on the application of this provision see PARA 872.
3   Ie under the Insolvency Act 1986 s 412: see PARA 773.
4   For these purposes, the reference to a solicitor includes a reference to a body corporate recognised by the Law Society under the Administration of Justice Act 1985 s 9 (see LEGAL PROFESSIONS vol 65 (2008) PARA 687): Solicitors' Recognised Bodies Order 1991, SI 1991/2684, arts 2(1), 3, 4(a), Sch 1 (amended by SI 2009/500; SI 2001/645; and SI 2009/500).
5   Deeds of Arrangement Act 1914 s 15(1).
6   For the prescribed fees see the Deeds of Arrangement Fees Order 1984, SI 1984/887, art 3, Schedule, Fees 11, 12 (art 3 amended by SI 2009/2718).
7   Deeds of Arrangement Act 1914 s 15(2).
8   A reference in the Deeds of Arrangement Rules 1925, SR & O 1925/795, to registered post is to be construed as including a reference to the recorded delivery service: Deeds of Arrangement (Amendment) Rules 1962, SI 1962/297, r 1.
9   Deeds of Arrangement Rules 1925, SR & O 1925/795, r 29.
10 Deeds of Arrangement Rules 1925, SR & O 1925/795, r 30.

871.   Payment of undistributed money into court.   At any time after the expiration of two years from the date of registration of a deed of arrangement, the court having jurisdiction[1] in relation to the district in which the debtor resided or carried on business at the date the deed was executed may, on the application of the trustee or a creditor, or of the debtor, order that all money representing unclaimed dividends and undistributed funds then in the trustee's hands or under his control be paid into the Senior Courts, or, if a county court has jurisdiction in the matter, into that court[2].

1   Ie under the Insolvency Act 1986 Pts 8–11 (ss 252–385). As to the courts having jurisdiction see PARAS 6, 7.
2   Deeds of Arrangement Act 1914 s 16 (amended by the Administration of Justice Act 1965 s 18, Sch 1; the Insolvency Act 1985 Sch 8 para 2(7); the Insolvency Act 1986 Sch 14; and the Constitutional Reform Act 2005 Sch 11 Pt 2 para 4(1), (3)). For a limitation on the application of this provision see PARA 872.

872.   Arrangement not for benefit of creditors generally.   The provisions of the Deeds of Arrangement Act 1914 relating to trustees under deeds of arrangement[1], except such of those provisions:

(1)   as relate to the transmission of accounts to the Secretary of State[2];

(2)   as provide for the protection of trustees under void deeds;

(3)   as require a notice to be given to creditors of avoidance of deeds;

(4)   as provide for the payment of expenses incurred by trustees,

do not apply to a deed of arrangement made for the benefit of any three or more of the debtor's creditors, unless it is in fact for the benefit of the debtor's creditors generally[3].

1   Ie the Deeds of Arrangement Act 1914 Pt IV (ss 11–22).

2   These provisions refer to the Board of Trade, the functions of which are now carried out by the Secretary of State: see PARA 19 note 1.

3   Deeds of Arrangement Act 1914 s 22. As to the meaning of 'creditors generally' see PARA 853 note 3.

873.   Appointment of new deed trustee.   Whenever it is expedient to appoint a new deed trustee, and it is found inexpedient, difficult or impracticable to do so without the court's assistance, the High Court, or the court having bankruptcy jurisdiction in the district in which the debtor resided or carried on business at the date of the execution of the deed, may appoint a new trustee, either in substitution for or in addition to an existing trustee, or even where there is no existing trustee[1]. In particular, and without prejudice to the generality of the above provision, the court may appoint a new trustee in substitution for a trustee who lacks capacity[2] to exercise his functions as trustee, or who is a bankrupt, or who is a corporation which is in liquidation or has been dissolved[3].

If a trustee has failed to comply with the requirements as to the giving of security to administer the deed properly and account fully for the assets[4], the court having jurisdiction[5] in the district in which the debtor resided or carried on business at the date of the execution of the deed may, on the application of any creditor and after hearing such persons as it may think fit, appoint another trustee in place of the trustee appointed by the deed[6].

Where a new trustee has been appointed, he must forthwith send the registrar[7] a notice of his appointment, giving his full name and address, and showing how and when the appointment was made[8].

1   Trustee Act 1925 ss 41(1), (2), 67 (s 41(1) amended by the Mental Health Act 1959 Sch 7 Pt I; the Criminal Law Act 1967 Sch 3 Pt III; and the Mental Capacity Act 2005 Sch 6 para 3(1), (3); the Trustee Act 1925 s 67 amended by the Courts Act 1971 Sch 11 Pt II). An order under the Trustee Act 1925 s 41, and any consequential vesting order or conveyance, does not operate further or otherwise as a discharge to any former or continuing trustee than an appointment of new trustees under any power for that purpose in any instrument would have operated: s 41(3). For the prescribed form of order declaring a deed void or appointing a new trustee see the Deeds of Arrangement Rules 1925, SR & O 1925/795, r 4(1), Appendix, Form 12. As to the appointment of a new trustee generally see TRUSTS AND POWERS vol 98 (2013) PARA 258 et seq.

2   As to persons who lack capacity see MENTAL HEALTH AND CAPACITY vol 75 (2013) PARA 601 et seq.

3   Trustee Act 1925 s 41(1) (as amended: see note 1).

4   See PARA 865.

5   Ie under the Insolvency Act 1986 Pts 8–11 (ss 252–385). As to the courts having jurisdiction see PARAS 6, 7.

6   Deeds of Arrangement Act 1914 s 11(2) (amended by the Insolvency Act 1985 Sch 8 para 2(3); and the Insolvency Act 1986 Sch 14). Where an application to appoint a new trustee is made under the Deeds of Arrangement Act 1914 s 11(2), notice of the application must be served on the existing trustee not less than eight days before the day appointed for the hearing: Deeds of Arrangement Rules 1925, SR & O 1925/795, r 22.

7   See PARA 857 note 2.

8   Deeds of Arrangement Rules 1925, SR & O 1925/795, r 27. The registrar must forthwith file the notice: r 27.

874. Power to ensure continuation of essential supplies by utilities. A trustee under a deed of arrangement for the benefit of an individual's creditors has the like rights as the supervisor of a voluntary arrangement, the official receiver, an interim receiver and a trustee in bankruptcy for ensuring continued supplies of gas, electricity, water and telecommunication services[1].

1 See the Insolvency Act 1986 s 372 (amended by the Gas Act 1995 Sch 4 para 14(3), (4), Sch 6; the Water Act 1989 Sch 25 para 78(1); the Communications Act 2003 Sch 17 para 82(1), (3); and the Utilities Act 2000 Sch 6 Pt III para 47(1), (3)); and PARA 78.

875. Position of trustee where deed void. Where a deed of arrangement is void by reason that the requisite majority of creditors have not assented thereto[1], or, in the case of a deed for the benefit of three or more creditors, by reason that the debtor was insolvent at the time of the execution of the deed and that the deed was not registered as required by the Deeds of Arrangement Act 1914[2], but is not void for any other reason, and a bankruptcy order[3] is made against the debtor on a petition presented after the lapse of three months[4] from the execution of the deed, the trustee under the deed is not liable to account to the trustee in the bankruptcy for any dealings with or payments made out of the debtor's property which would have been proper if the deed had been valid, if he proves that, at the time of such dealings or payments, he did not know, and had no reason to suspect, that the deed was void[5].

If a trustee acts under a deed of arrangement:

(1) after it has, to his knowledge, become void by reason of non-compliance with any of the requirements of the 1914 Act or any enactment repealed by that Act[6]; or

(2) after he has failed to give security within the time and in the manner provided by the 1914 Act[7] or any enactment repealed by that Act[8],

he is liable on summary conviction to a fine not exceeding £5 for every day between the date on which the deed became void or the expiration of the time within which security should have been given, as the case may be, and the last day on which he is proved to have acted as trustee, unless he satisfies the court that his contravention of the law was due to inadvertence, or that his action was confined to taking such steps as were necessary for the protection of the estate[9].

As soon as practicable after a trustee has become aware that a deed is void by virtue of the 1914 Act for any reason other than that, being for the benefit of creditors generally, it has not been registered in time, he must give written notice to each creditor whose name and address he knows, and file a copy of the notice with the registrar; and, if he fails to do so, he is liable on summary conviction to a fine not exceeding level 2 on the standard scale[10].

1 As to avoidance of deeds of arrangement unless assented to by a majority of creditors see PARA 858.
2 As to avoidance of unregistered deeds of arrangements see PARA 857.
3 As to bankruptcy orders see PARA 198 et seq.
4 The period of three months has no significance under the Insolvency Act 1986 but derives from the doctrine of relation back under the Bankruptcy Act 1914 (repealed).
5 Deeds of Arrangement Act 1914 s 19(1) (amended by the Insolvency Act 1985 Sch 8 para 2(8)).
6 Ie in particular the Deeds of Arrangement Act 1887 (repealed) and the Bankruptcy and Deeds of Arrangement Act 1913 (repealed). As to the requirements of the Deeds of Arrangement Act 1914 see PARA 865.
7 See PARA 865.
8 See note 6.
9 Deeds of Arrangement Act 1914 s 12.
10 Deeds of Arrangement Act 1914 s 20; and Criminal Justice Act 1982 ss 37, 46. As to the standard scale see SENTENCING AND DISPOSITION OF OFFENDERS vol 92 (2010) PARA 142.

876. Payment of trustee's expenses where deed avoided. Where a deed of arrangement is avoided by reason of the bankruptcy of the debtor, any expenses properly incurred[1] by the trustee under the deed in the performance of any of the duties imposed on him by the Deeds of Arrangement Act 1914 must be allowed or paid to him by the trustee in the bankruptcy as a first charge on the estate[2]. Where, however, the deed has never become effective because the necessary majority of creditors has not assented[3], the trustee's expenses may be allowed only by the court, and then only if there has been real benefit to the creditors[4].

1　As to the meaning of 'expenses properly incurred' see *Re Green, ex p Parker* [1917] 1 KB 183.
2　Deeds of Arrangement Act 1914 s 21.
3　As to avoidance of deeds of arrangement unless assented to by a majority of creditors see PARA 858.
4　*Re Zakon, ex p Trustee v Bushell* [1940] Ch 253, [1940] 1 All ER 263.

(iv) Creditors under Arrangements

877. Creditors entitled to benefit. Where an arrangement by a debtor is expressed to be with his creditors generally, or with all creditors who assent to it, any creditor who actually, or by his conduct, assents to it and elects to take the benefit of it within the time limit for assent fixed by the instrument, is entitled to share in the benefits of the arrangement, even if he has not signed the instrument[1]. In the exercise of its equitable jurisdiction the court may permit a creditor who has not assented to an arrangement to come in under it and share in its benefits, notwithstanding that the time limited by the instrument for assent has elapsed[2].

A creditor entitled to the benefit of an arrangement must perform fairly all the conditions of the arrangement which apply to the creditors. If he takes any step which is inconsistent with or opposed to those conditions, as, for example, by bringing an action against the debtor to recover his debt, he will be liable to be excluded from the benefit of the arrangement[3]. A creditor who makes any underhand or secret bargain with the debtor, by which he is to receive some payment or advantage in which the other creditors do not share, may be excluded from all the benefits of the arrangement[4].

1　*Re Chambers, ex p Jerrard* (1837) 3 Deac 1 at 7; *Re Baber's Trusts* (1870) LR 10 Eq 554; *Biron v Mount* (1857) 24 Beav 642. In *Baker v Adam* (1910) 102 LT 248, it was held that the words 'according to the law of bankruptcy' in a deed of arrangement were only descriptive of a rateable payment without prejudice or priority and by a series of instalments or dividends, and did not import into the distribution of the money the obligation of allowing a set-off under the Insolvency Act 1986 s 323 (see PARA 561 et seq), to a person who had not signified his assent to the deed. In general, in a case where the deed does not incorporate the bankruptcy rules, a person having only a contingent or future claim against the debtor is not within the deed: *Re Casse* [1937] Ch 405, [1937] 2 All ER 710.
2　*Watson v Knight* (1845) 19 Beav 369; *Raworth v Parker* (1855) 2 K & J 163; *Johnson v Kershaw* (1847) 1 De G & Sm 260; *Brandling v Plummer* (1857) 27 LJ Ch 188; and cf *Re Pilet, ex p Toursier & Co and Berkeley* [1915] 3 KB 519, DC (where creditors, whose debts were provable under a previous composition and which had been discharged, were not allowed to come in under a subsequent arrangement as creditors in respect of those debts).
3　*Field v Lord Donoughmore* (1841) 1 Dr & War 227.
4　*Ilderton v Jewell* (1864) 16 CBNS 142; *Benham v Broadhurst* (1864) 3 H & C 472; *Wood v Barker* (1865) LR 1 Eq 139; *Re Milner, ex p Milner* (1885) 15 QBD 605, CA; *Dauglish v Tennent* (1866) LR 2 QB 49; *Re EAB* [1902] 1 KB 457. As to the consequences of a corrupt bargain see *Knight v Hunt* (1829) 5 Bing 432; *Atkinson v Denby* (1862) 7 H & N 934. For the penalty on the trustee for distributing the funds unequally see the Deeds of Arrangement Act 1914 s 17; and PARA 866.

878. Creditors bound by arrangements. A composition agreement is binding on creditors who execute it or who expressly assent to it, or who by their conduct put themselves in the same situation as if they had executed it[1]; but, if a creditor's assent has been obtained by misrepresentation, he will not be bound by the agreement[2].

If the debtor or some third person acting with his knowledge and on his behalf makes a secret bargain with some of the creditors, giving them an advantage over the other creditors, the arrangement will not be binding on those other creditors[3], and they will not, therefore, be precluded from bringing actions or taking legal proceedings to recover the debts due to them[4]. Where, however, the composition agreement provides that the release contained in it is to be void if the instalments are not duly paid, a creditor who has fraudulently obtained a secret advantage over the other creditors will be bound by the agreement, and his debt will be released, even though default in payment of the instalments has been made by the debtor[5].

Where there is no fraud and no inequality among creditors, the court will not interfere to judge the reasonableness of the arrangement[6].

1 'The principle [is] that, if you put yourself in the situation of having the benefit of a deed, you must bear its obligations, although you have not literally executed the deed': *Forbes v Limond* (1854) 4 De GM & G 298 at 315 per Lord Cranworth LC. An assent by one branch of a company, followed by dissent by another branch, was held to bind the company in respect of all the debts due to the branches from the debtor: *Dunlop Rubber Co v WB Haigh & Son* [1937] 1 KB 347, [1936] 3 All ER 381. For an instance of a creditor's assent by conduct with consequent satisfaction of his right of action see *Victor Weston (Fabrics) Ltd v Morgensterns* [1937] 3 All ER 769, CA.
2 *Cooling v Noyes* (1795) 6 Term Rep 263; *Lewis v Jones* (1825) 4 B & C 506. In *Sier v Bullen* (1915) 84 LJKB 1288, DC, a creditor, the debtor's landlord, was told that, if he assented to a deed of arrangement, he would be paid six months' rent in addition to the dividend in respect of the balance of the rent he would take under the deed; but the other creditors did not assent to the arrangement, and there was no mention of it in the deed; it was held that the creditor had never assented to the deed, his assent being conditional on a bargain which was not enforceable, and that he was not precluded from distraining for rent owing to him.
3 *Dauglish v Tennent* (1866) LR 2 QB 49; *Re Milner, ex p Milner* (1885) 15 QBD 605, CA. As to the consequences of a corrupt bargain see *Knight v Hunt* (1829) 5 Bing 432; and PARA 877.
4 *Re Milner, ex p Milner* (1885) 15 QBD 605, CA.
5 *Re Hodgson, ex p Oliver* (1851) 4 De G & Sm 354. As to the recovery of money paid under a secret bargain see *Atkinson v Denby* (1862) 7 H & N 934.
6 See *Re Richmond Hill Hotel Co, ex p King* (1867) 3 Ch App 10; *Bailey v Bowen* (1868) LR 3 QB 133 at 140.

879. Creditors' rights and position. A creditor may execute a deed of arrangement after its registration[1] without impairing its validity[2]; but, where creditors have attempted to defeat a deed and have failed, they may not claim to come in subsequently and execute it[3].

In the event of bankruptcy supervening and the deed being thereby avoided, creditors who are parties to the deed will not be debarred from proving for their debts in the bankruptcy, unless it is clear from the terms of the deed that they intended to release their debts, whether or not bankruptcy should supervene[4].

If there is a surplus in the hands of the trustee after payment of the debts and expenses, the creditors are not entitled to interest on their debts, unless the deed contains an express or implied provision for payment of interest[5].

The debtor or any creditor or other person interested is entitled, on payment of the prescribed fees[6], to inspect the trustee's accounts and to be furnished with copies of or extracts from them[7].

1 As to registration see PARA 859 et seq.

2 See *Re Batten, ex p Milne* (1889) 6 Morr 110, CA.
3 See *Re Meredith, Meredith v Facey* (1885) 33 WR 778.
4 See *Re Stephenson, ex p Official Receiver* (1888) 20 QBD 540, DC.
5 *Re Rissik* [1936] Ch 68.
6 For the prescribed fees see the Deeds of Arrangement Fees Order 1984, SI 1984/887, art 3, Schedule, Fees 10, 13 (art 3 amended by SI 2009/2718).
7 Deeds of Arrangement Act 1914 s 13(3); see also PARA 867.

880. Rights against persons liable jointly or as sureties. A debtor's creditors often hold rights against sureties as security for their debts, or hold securities over parts of the compounding debtor's property. If a general release in a composition deed or agreement contains also a reservation of the creditors' rights against all persons who are liable to them jointly with or as sureties for the debtor, the release operates only as an obligation not to sue the debtor, and does not operate to discharge or prejudice the creditors' rights against persons liable to them jointly with the debtor or as sureties for him[1]. The reservation by creditors of their rights against sureties imports the continuance of the sureties' rights of indemnity against the debtor[2].

1 *Kearsley v Cole* (1846) 16 M & W 128; *Ex p Gifford* (1802) 6 Ves 805; *Bateson v Gosling* (1871) LR 7 CP 9.
2 *Cole v Lynn* [1942] 1 KB 142, [1941] 3 All ER 502, CA.

881. Secured creditors' rights. If a composition deed or agreement reserves to creditors their rights in respect of securities held by them over the debtor's property, for example by mortgage, charge or lien, a general release contained in the deed or agreement will not prevent them from realising or dealing with and obtaining the benefit of their securities in reduction of the debts due to them[1].

1 *Cullingworth v Loyd* (1840) 2 Beav 385; *Mawson v Stock* (1801) 6 Ves 300. For the rules as to the rights and duties of secured creditors where the trusts of the deed provide for administration according to the rules of bankruptcy law see PARA 574 et seq.

882. Deed must benefit creditors. Each deed must be considered as a whole, to determine whether it is what it appears to be, namely a deed for the benefit of creditors generally, rather than a deed for the debtor's benefit. If it is the latter, the deed may be declared void as being in fraud of the creditors[1] or being a transaction defrauding creditors[2] in spite of being in form a deed for the creditors' benefit[3].

1 In respect of deeds entered into before 29 December 1986 (see PARA 2) see the Law of Property Act 1925 s 172(1) (repealed). An intent to defraud must be established, but whether actual deceit or dishonesty need be shown is doubtful: see *Lloyds Bank Ltd v Marcan* [1973] 3 All ER 754, [1973] 1 WLR 1387, CA.
2 As regards deeds entered into on or after 29 December 1986 see the Insolvency Act 1986 ss 423–425; and PARA 688 et seq.
3 See *Maskelyne and Cooke v Smith* [1903] 1 KB 671 at 676, CA, per Vaughan Williams LJ; *Alton v Harrison, Poyser v Harrison* (1869) 4 Ch App 622; *Evans v Jones* (1864) 3 H & C 423; *Spencer v Slater* (1878) 4 QBD 13; *Boldero v London and Westminster Discount Co* (1879) 5 Ex D 47.

(v) Enforcement; Procedure

883. Enforcement of assignment. Any application by the trustee under a deed of arrangement, which either is expressed to be or is in fact for the benefit of the debtor's creditors generally, or by the debtor or by any creditor entitled to the benefit of such a deed of arrangement, for the enforcement of the trusts or the determination of questions under it, must be made to the court having jurisdiction[1] in relation to the district in which the debtor resided or carried on business at the date of its execution[2]; but any question as to whether any person claiming to be a creditor entitled to the benefit of a deed of arrangement is so entitled may, subject to rules made for the purposes of the Deeds of Arrangement Act 1914[3], be decided either by the court having such jurisdiction or by the High Court[4].

1   Ie under the Insolvency Act 1986 Pts 8–11 (ss 252–385): see PARAS 6, 7.

2   Deeds of Arrangement Act 1914 s 23 (amended by the Insolvency Act 1985 Sch 8 para 2(9); and the Insolvency Act 1986 Sch 14). An application by the debtor for a declaration that a deed of arrangement is void for non-compliance with the provisions of the Deeds of Arrangement Act 1914 is not an application for the enforcement of the trusts or the determination of questions 'under' it, and, therefore, a judge in a county court having bankruptcy jurisdiction has no jurisdiction to entertain such an application: *Re Wilson* [1916] 1 KB 382 at 398, CA. A trustee under a deed of arrangement for the benefit of creditors generally is entitled to obtain a declaration under the Deeds of Arrangement Act 1914 s 23 that certain persons named in a schedule to the deed are not in fact creditors of the assignor, notwithstanding that the trustee is himself a party to the deed: *Re Pilet, ex p Toursier & Co and Berkeley* [1915] 3 KB 519, DC.
    The object of the Deeds of Arrangement Act 1914 s 23 is to provide a trustee or beneficiary under a deed of arrangement with a summary means of obtaining a determination of questions arising in the administration of the trusts of the deed; accordingly, a creditor who has not assented to the deed, but claims adversely to it, cannot avail himself of the summary jurisdiction contained in s 23: *Re Elllis* [1925] Ch 564, CA.

3   See the Deeds of Arrangement Rules 1925, SR & O 1925/795, rr 17–23; and PARAS 884, 885. Power to make rules for the purposes of the Deeds of Arrangement Act 1914, other than s 7 (see PARA 861) is contained in the Administration of Justice Act 1925 s 22(5), (5A) (s 22(5) amended by the Constitutional Reform Act 2005 Sch 4 Pt 1 para 19(1), (2); s 22(5A) added by the Constitutional Reform Act 2005 Sch 4 Pt 1 para 19(1), (3)).

4   Deeds of Arrangement Act 1914 s 23.

884.   Applications.   All applications, other than applications for rectification of the register[1], which are directed or allowed[2] to be made to the High Court or the county court having jurisdiction in bankruptcy in the district in which the debtor resided or carried on business at the date of the execution of the deed are deemed to be proceedings in bankruptcy and must be made in accordance with, and in the manner prescribed for, proceedings under Parts 8 to 11 of the Insolvency Act 1986[3] and the Insolvency Rules 1986[4] for the time being in force, with such variations as the circumstances may require, and must be supported by affidavit[5].

Applications for extension of time for procuring the assent of creditors to a deed[6] or for filing the prescribed statutory declaration[7] may be made without notice being served on any other party and without affidavit unless the court in any case otherwise orders[8].

The application[9] must be made to the registrar of the court who must cause the same, together with the affidavits in support, to be filed, and must appoint a day for the hearing not earlier than 14 days from the filing of the application[10]. The registrar to whom the application is made may direct notice of the application to be served on such person or persons as he thinks fit, but, in the absence of any special direction by him, the notice, together with copies of the affidavits in support, must be served, when the application is made by the trustee, on the debtor and any creditor or other person to be affected thereby, and, when made by the debtor, on the trustee and on any creditor or other person to be affected thereby, and, when made by a creditor, on the trustee and the debtor[11].

All such applications must be heard and determined by the registrar of the court in chambers; but he may in any case, and must at the request of any party thereto, adjourn the application to be heard and determined by the judge in court[12].

1 Ie under the Deeds of Arrangement Act 1914 s 7: see PARA 861.
2 Ie by the Deeds of Arrangement Act 1914 or the Deeds of Arrangement Rules 1925, SR & O 1925/795.
3 Ie the Insolvency Act 1986 Pts 8–11 (ss 252–385): see PARAS 6, 7.
4 Ie the Insolvency Rules 1986, SI 1986/1925.
5 Deeds of Arrangement Rules 1925, SR & O 1925/795, r 17 (amended by SI 1986/2001).
6 Ie under the Deeds of Arrangement Act 1914 s 3(1): see PARA 858.
7 Ie under the Deeds of Arrangement Act 1914 s 3(4): see PARA 858.
8 Deeds of Arrangement Rules 1925, SR & O 1925/795, r 17.
9 Ie except in cases within the proviso contained in the Deeds of Arrangement Rules 1925, SR & O 1925/795, r 17: see the text to notes 6–8. In cases within r 17 proviso the application may be made either to the registrar of the court or to a registrar of the High Court: r 18.
10 Deeds of Arrangement Rules 1925, SR & O 1925/795, r 18.
11 Deeds of Arrangement Rules 1925, SR & O 1925/795, r 18. Notice of any application under the Deeds of Arrangement Act 1914 s 11(2) (see PARA 865) to declare a deed void, or appoint another trustee, must be served on the trustee named in the deed not less than eight days before the day appointed for the hearing: Deeds of Arrangement Rules 1925, SR & O 1925/795, r 22.
12 Deeds of Arrangement Rules 1925, SR & O 1925/795, r 21.

885.   Evidence. Unless the court otherwise orders, the evidence to be used on the application must be given by affidavit[1]; but any opposite party may require, by notice in writing addressed to any deponent or his solicitor[2], the attendance of such deponent for cross-examination[3].

All affidavits intended to be used by any party to such application, other than the applicant, must be filed in the court, and copies served on the applicant not less than four days before the day appointed for the hearing of the application[4].

1 An affidavit required by or for the purposes of the Deeds of Arrangement Act 1914 may be sworn before a master of the Senior Courts or before any person empowered to take affidavits in the Senior Courts or before any other person before whom such an affidavit may, by any law for the time being in force, be sworn: s 29 (amended by the Administration of Justice Act 1925 s 29, Sch 5; and the Constitutional Reform Act 2005 Sch 11 Pt 2 para 4(1), (3)).
2 For these purposes, the reference to a solicitor includes a reference to a body corporate recognised by the Law Society under the Administration of Justice Act 1985 s 9 (see LEGAL PROFESSIONS vol 65 (2008) PARA 687): Solicitors' Recognised Bodies Order 1991, SI 1991/2684, arts 2(1), 3, 4(a), Sch 1 (amended by SI 2009/500; SI 2001/645; and SI 2009/500).
3 Deeds of Arrangement Rules 1925, SR & O 1925/795, r 19.
4 Deeds of Arrangement Rules 1925, SR & O 1925/795, r 20.

(2) ADMINISTRATION ORDERS

(i) Introduction

886.   Introduction and proposed changes to administration orders. Administration orders are a court-administered debt management scheme for those with multiple debts totalling no more than £5,000, one of which must be a judgment debt[1]. Changes have been enacted but not brought into force, first under the Courts and Legal Services Act 1990, which included removal of the need for a judgment debt, an increase in the debt limit, the introduction of a strict three-year limit to the order and power for the court to grant an order restricting enforcement[2]. Second, under the Tribunals, Courts and Enforcement Act 2007, which made a number of changes to the administration orders scheme, including an increase in the debt ceiling and a time limit to orders, in addition to revising the changes proposed by the 1990 Act[3].

Following a government review in 2011, it appears unlikely that the proposed changes will be brought into effect[4]. However, both the existing scheme[5] and the revised scheme[6] have been set out below.

1   See the County Courts Act 1984 Pt VI (ss 112–117); and PARA 887 et seq.
2   See the Courts and Legal Services Act 1990 s 13 (repealed, as from a day to be appointed, by the Tribunals, Courts and Enforcement Act 2007 ss 106(2), 146, Sch 16 para 6, Sch 23 Pt 5).
3   See the Tribunals, Courts and Enforcement Act 2007 s 106, which substitutes the whole of the County Courts Act 1984 Pt 6, as from a day to be appointed.
4   See the Consumer credit and personal insolvency review: summary of responses on consumer credit and formal response on personal insolvency (BIS, July 2011), which states that the government has the 'intention to consult on whether the provisions in relation to County Court administration orders ('CCAOs') should be repealed, as the numbers entering a CCAO are rapidly declining, with just over 5,000 currently in existence'. At the date at which this volume states the law, no consultation had taken place.
5   See PARAS 887–893.
6   See PARAS 894–903.

(ii) Administration Orders under the Current Scheme

887. Power to make administration order. Where a debtor is unable to pay forthwith the amount of a judgment obtained against him, and alleges that his whole indebtedness amounts to a sum not exceeding the county court limit[1], inclusive of the debt for which the judgment was obtained, a county court may make an order providing for the administration of his estate[2].

Before an administration order[3] is made, the appropriate court[4] must[5] send to every person whose name the debtor has notified to the appropriate court as being a creditor of him a notice that that person's name has been so notified[6].

An administration order may provide for the payment of the debts of the debtor by instalment or otherwise, and either in full or to such extent as appears practicable to the court under the circumstances of the case, and subject to any conditions as to his future earnings or income which the court may think just[7].

1   For these purposes, 'the county court limit' means: (1) in relation to any enactment contained in the County Courts Act 1984 for which a limit is for the time being specified by an order under s 145, that limit; and (2) in relation to any enactment contained in the County Courts Act 1984 and not within head (1), the county court limit for the time being specified by any other Order in Council or order defining the limit of county court jurisdiction for the purposes of that enactment: s 147(1). No Order in Council has been made under s 145, specifying the limit for the purposes of s 112(1)(b), (5) but, by virtue of head (2), the limit of £5,000 fixed by the County Courts (Administration Order Jurisdiction) Order 1981, SI 1981/1122, art 2, applies for the purposes of these provisions. See further COURTS AND TRIBUNALS vol 24 (2010) PARA 767. An administration order is not invalid by reason only that the total amount of the debts is found at any time to exceed the county court limit, but in that case the court may, if it thinks fit, set aside the order: County Courts Act 1984 s 112(5).
      Amendments to s 112 were proposed by the Courts and Legal Services Act 1990 s 13 but not brought into force: see PARA 886. As to the new scheme for administration orders proposed under the Tribunals, Courts and Enforcement Act 2007 see PARAS 894–903.
2   County Courts Act 1984 s 112(1).
3   For these purposes, 'administration order' means an order under the County Courts Act 1984 s 112: s 112(2).
4   For these purposes, 'the appropriate court', in relation to an administration order, means the court which has the power to make the order: County Courts Act 1984 s 112(2). Any powers conferred on the court by Pt VI (ss 112–117) may be exercised by the district judge or in certain circumstances by the court officer: CPR Sch 2, CCR Ord 39 r 1. As to the functions of the court officer see PARA 905 note 1.
5   Ie in accordance with rules of court: see CPR Sch 2, CCR Ord 39 r 5; and PARA 904.

6 County Courts Act 1984 s 112(3) (amended by the Civil Procedure Act 1997 s 10, Sch 2 para 2(1), (2)).
7 County Courts Act 1984 s 112(6). A county court administration order may be made in respect of a liability for unpaid community charge: *Preston Borough Council v Riley* [1995] BCC 700, CA.

888. Administration order on application for attachment of earnings order.
Where, on an application to a county court for an attachment of earnings order to secure the payment of a judgment debt[1], it appears to the court that the debtor[2] also has other debts, the court:

(1) must consider whether the case may be one in which all the debtor's liabilities should be dealt with together and that for that purpose an administration order[3] should be made; and

(2) if of opinion that it may be such a case, has power, whether or not it makes the attachment of earnings order applied for, with a view to making an administration order, to order the debtor to furnish to the court a list of all his creditors and the amounts which he owes to them respectively[4].

If, on receipt of such a list, it appears to the court that the debtor's whole indebtedness amounts to not more than the amount which for the time being is the county court limit[5], the court may make such an order in respect of the debtor's estate[6].

However, nothing in the above provisions is to be taken as prejudicing any right of a debtor to apply[7] for an administration order[8].

1 For these purposes, 'judgment debt' means a sum payable under: (1) a judgment or order enforceable by a court in England and Wales, not being a magistrates' court; (2) an order of a magistrates' court for the payment of money recoverable summarily as a civil debt; or (3) an order of any court which is enforceable as if it were for the payment of money so recoverable: Attachment of Earnings Act 1971 ss 2(c), 25(1).

2 For these purposes, 'the debtor', in relation to an attachment of earnings order, or to proceedings in which a court has power to make an attachment of earnings order or to proceedings arising out of such an order, means the person by whom payment is required by the relevant adjudication to be made: Attachment of Earnings Act 1971 ss 2(e), 25(1). 'The relevant adjudication', in relation to any payment secured or to be secured by an attachment of earnings order, means the conviction, judgment, order or other adjudication from which there arises the liability to make the payment: ss 2(d), 25(1). As to the meaning of 'administration order' see note 3.

3 For these purposes, 'administration order' means any order made under, and so referred to in, the County Courts Act 1984 Pt VI (ss 112–117): Attachment of Earnings Act 1971 s 25(1) (amended by the County Courts Act 1984 s 148(1), Sch 2 Pt V). As to the new scheme for administration orders proposed under the Tribunals, Courts and Enforcement Act 2007 see PARAS 894–903.

4 Attachment of Earnings Act 1971 s 4(1) (amended by the Insolvency Act 1976 s 13(2)). For the prescribed form of list of creditors see the County Court (Forms) Rules 1982, SI 1982/586, r 2, Schedule, Form N93. As to the continued use of county court forms see CIVIL PROCEDURE vol 11 (2009) PARA 14.
    Where a county court makes an attachment of earnings order to secure payment of a judgment debt and also, under the Attachment of Earnings Act 1971 s 4(1) orders the debtor to furnish to the court a list of all his creditors, sums paid to the collecting officer in compliance with the attachment of earnings order may not be dealt with by him as mentioned in s 13(1), but must be retained by him pending the decision of the court whether or not to make an administration order and must then be dealt with by him as the court may direct: s 13(3). See further CIVIL PROCEDURE vol 12 (2009) PARA 1452.
    Any powers conferred on the court by the Attachment of Earnings Act 1971 s 4 may be exercised by the district judge or in certain circumstances by the court officer: CPR Sch 2, CCR Ord 39 r 1.

5 As to the meaning of 'the county court limit' see PARA 887 note 1.

6   Attachment of Earnings Act 1971 s 4(2) (amended by the County Courts Act 1984 s 148(1), Sch 2 para 40(a)). The Attachment of Earnings Act 1971 s 4(2) is subject to the County Courts Act 1984 s 112(3) (see PARA 887) and s 112(4) (see PARA 890): Attachment of Earnings Act 1971 s 4(2A) (added by the County Courts Act 1984 Sch 2 para 40(b)).
7   Ie under the County Courts Act 1984 s 112: see PARA 887.
8   Attachment of Earnings Act 1971 s 4(4) (amended by the County Courts Act 1984 Sch 2 para 40(c)).

889.   Attachment of earnings order.   Where a county court makes an administration order[1] in respect of a debtor's estate, it may also make an attachment of earnings order to secure the payments required by the administration order[2]. At any time when an administration order is in force, a county court may, with or without an application, make an attachment of earnings order to secure the payments required by the administration order, if it appears to the court that the debtor has failed to make any such payment[3].

On the revocation of an administration order, any attachment of earnings order made to secure the payments required by the administration order must be discharged[4].

1   As to the meaning of 'administration order' see PARA 888 note 3. As to the new scheme for administration orders proposed under the Tribunals, Courts and Enforcement Act 2007 see PARAS 894–903.
2   Attachment of Earnings Act 1971 s 5(1). The power of a county court under s 5 to make an attachment of earnings order to secure the payments required by an administration order includes, where the debtor is already subject to an attachment of earnings order to secure the payment of a judgment debt, power to direct that the last-mentioned order is to take effect, with or without variation under s 9 (see MATRIMONIAL AND CIVIL PARTNERSHIP LAW vol 73 (2009) PARA 634), as an order to secure the payments required by the administration order: s 5(3). As to the meanings of 'judgment debt' and 'the debtor' see PARA 888 notes 1, 2.
3   Attachment of Earnings Act 1971 s 5(2).
4   CPR Sch 2, CCR Ord 39 r 16. As to revocation of an administration order see PARA 914.

890.   Effect of administration order.   When an administration order[1] is made, no creditor has any remedy[2] against the person or property of the debtor in respect of any debt of which the debtor notified the appropriate court[3] before the administration order was made, or which has been scheduled to the order, except with the permission of the appropriate court, and on such terms as that court may impose[4].

Any county court in which proceedings are pending against the debtor in respect of any debt so notified or scheduled must, on receiving notice of the administration order, stay the proceedings, but may allow costs already incurred by the creditor, and such costs may, on application, be added to the debt[5]. The requirement to stay proceedings does not, however, operate as a requirement that a county court in which proceedings in bankruptcy against the debtor are pending must stay those proceedings[6].

So long as an administration order is in force, a creditor whose name is included in the schedule to the order is not, without the permission of the appropriate court, entitled to present, or join in, a bankruptcy petition against the debtor unless:

(1)   his name was so notified; and

(2)   the debt by virtue of which he presents, or joins in, the petition, exceeds £1,500[7]; and

(3)   the notice given[8] by the appropriate court that his name has been notified was received by the creditor within 28 days immediately preceding the day on which the petition is presented[9].

1   As to the meaning of 'administration order' see PARA 887 note 3. As to the new scheme for administration orders proposed under the Tribunals, Courts and Enforcement Act 2007 see PARAS 894–903.

2   Ie subject to the County Courts Act 1984 s 115 (see PARA 891) and s 116 (see PARA 892).

3   As to the meaning of 'the appropriate court' see PARA 887 note 4.

4   County Courts Act 1984 s 114(1). The object must be to secure equal division of the debtor's available property among all his creditors: *Re Frank* [1894] 1 QB 9.

5   County Courts Act 1984 s 114(2).

6   County Courts Act 1984 s 114(3).

7   The Secretary of State may by regulations increase or reduce the sum for the time being specified in County Courts Act 1984 s 112(4)(b) (see head (2) in the text); but no such increase in the sum so specified affects any case in which the bankruptcy petition was presented before the coming into force of the increase: s 112(7). The power to make such regulations is exercisable by statutory instrument; and no such regulations may be made unless a draft of them has been approved by resolution of each House of Parliament: s 112(8). At the date at which this volume states the law no such regulations had been made.

8   Ie under the County Courts Act 1984 s 112(3): see PARA 887.

9   County Courts Act 1984 s 112(4) (amended by the Insolvency Act 1985 s 220(1), (2)). Amendments to the County Courts Act 1984 s 112(4) were proposed by the Courts and Legal Services Act 1990 s 13 but not brought into force: see PARA 886.

   An application under the County Courts Act 1984 s 112(4) for permission to present or join in a bankruptcy petition must be made on notice to the debtor in accordance with CPR Pt 23 (see CIVIL PROCEDURE vol 11 (2009) PARA 304 et seq); but the court may, if it thinks fit, order that notice be given to any other creditor whose debt is scheduled to the administration order: CPR Sch 2, CCR Ord 39 r 12.

891.   Execution by district judge.   Where it appears to the district judge of the appropriate court[1] at any time while an administration order[2] is in force that property of the debtor exceeds in value the minimum amount[3], he must, at the request of any creditor, and without fee, issue execution against the debtor's goods[4].

1   As to the meaning of 'the appropriate court' see PARA 887 note 4.

2   As to the meaning of 'administration order' see PARA 887 note 3.

3   For these purposes, 'the minimum amount' means £50 or such other amount as the Lord Chancellor may by order specify instead of that amount or the amount for the time being specified in such an order; and any such order must be made by statutory instrument subject to annulment in pursuance of a resolution of either House of Parliament: County Courts Act 1984 s 115(1A) (added by the Insolvency Act 1985 s 220(1), (4)). At the date at which this volume states the law no such order had been made.

4   County Courts Act 1984 s 115(1) (amended by the Insolvency Act 1985 s 220(1), (3); and the Courts and Legal Services Act 1990 s 74(1), (3)). The County Courts Act 1984 s 89 (goods which may be seized: see CIVIL PROCEDURE vol 12 (2009) PARA 1315) applies on an execution under s 115 as it applies on an execution under Pt V (ss 85–111): s 115(2).

892.   Right of landlord to distrain.   A landlord or other person to whom any rent is due from a debtor in respect of whom an administration order[1] is made may at any time, either before or after the date of the order, distrain on the goods or effects of the debtor for the rent due to him from the debtor, with this limitation, that, if the distress for rent is levied after the date of the order, it is available only for six months' rent accrued due prior to the date of the order and is not available for rent payable in respect of any period subsequent to the date when the distress was levied, but the landlord or other person to whom the rent may be due from the debtor may prove under the order for the surplus due for which the distress may not have been available[2].

1   As to the meaning of 'administration order' see PARA 887 note 3.

2   County Courts Act 1984 s 116. The right to distrain is prospectively abolished by the Tribunals, Courts and Enforcement Act 2007: see PARA 711.

893.　Appropriation of money paid. Money paid into court under an administration order[1] must be appropriated first in satisfaction of the costs of administration, which may not exceed ten pence in the pound on the total amount of the debts, and then in liquidation of debts in accordance with the order[2].

1　As to the meaning of 'administration order' see PARA 887 note 3.
2　County Courts Act 1984 s 117(1).

(iii)　Administration Orders under the New Scheme

894.　Power to make administration order. As from a day to be appointed[1], a county court may make an administration order[2] if the following conditions are met[3]:

(1)　the order must be made in respect of an individual who is a debtor under two or more qualifying debts[4];

(2)　that individual ('the debtor') must not be a debtor under any business debts[5];

(3)　the debtor must not be excluded under any of the following: (a) the AO exclusion[6]; (b) the voluntary arrangement exclusion[7]; (c) the bankruptcy exclusion[8];

(4)　the debtor must be unable to pay one or more of his qualifying debts[9];

(5)　the total amount of the debtor's qualifying debts[10] must be less than, or the same as, the prescribed maximum[11];

(6)　the debtor's surplus income[12] must be more than the prescribed minimum[13].

Before making an administration order, the county court must have regard to any representations made by any person about why the order should not be made, or by a creditor under a debt about why the debt should not be taken into account in calculating the total amount of the debtor's qualifying debts[14].

1　See PARA 886.
2　An administration order is an order: (1) to which certain debts are scheduled in accordance with the County Courts Act 1984 ss 112C, 112D (see PARA 896) or s 112Y(3) or (4) (see PARA 903); (2) which imposes the requirement specified in s 112E (see PARA 897) on the debtor; and (3) which imposes the requirements specified in ss 112F–112I (see PARA 897) on certain creditors: ss 112A, 112AA (Pt 6 (ss 112A–112AI) added by the Tribunals, Courts and Enforcement Act 2007 s 106).
3　County Courts Act 1984 s 112B(1) (as added: see note 2). As from a day to be appointed, the reference in s 112B(1) to 'a county court' is replaced by a reference to 'the county court': see s 112B(1) (amended by the Crime and Courts Act 2013 Sch 9 Pt 2 para 47(1), (3)). At the date at which this volume states the law no such day had been appointed.
4　County Courts Act 1984 s 112B(2) (as added: see note 2). All debts are qualifying debts, except for the following: (1) any debt secured against an asset; (2) any debt of a description specified in regulations: s 112AB(1) (as added: see note 2). A business debt is any debt (whether or not a qualifying debt) which is incurred by a person in the course of a business: s 112AB(2) (as so added). Only debts that have already arisen are included in references to debts; and accordingly such references do not include any debt that will arise only on the happening of some future contingency: s 112AB(3) (as so added). As to the making of regulations see s 112AI (as so added). At the date at which this volume states the law no such regulations had been made.
5　County Courts Act 1984 s 112B(3) (as added: see note 2). See note 4.
6　The debtor is excluded under the AO exclusion if: (1) an administration order currently has effect in respect of him; or (2) an administration order has previously had effect in respect of him, and the period of 12 months, beginning with the day when that order ceased to have effect, has yet to finish: County Courts Act 1984 s 112AH(1) (as added: see note 2). In a case that falls within head (2), the debtor is not excluded under the AO exclusion if the previous administration order: (a) ceased to have effect in accordance with any of the provisions listed in

s 112K(7) (effect of enforcement restriction order or debt relief order on administration order: see PARA 898); or (b) was revoked in accordance with s 112U(1)(b) (debtor no longer has any qualifying debts: see PARA 901): s 112AH(2) (as so added).

7 The debtor is excluded under the voluntary arrangement exclusion if: (1) an interim order under the Insolvency Act 1986 s 252 has effect in respect of him (interim order where debtor intends to make proposal for voluntary arrangement: see PARA 45); or (2) he is bound by a voluntary arrangement approved under the Insolvency Act 1986 Pt 8 (ss 252–263G) (see PARA 43 et seq): County Courts Act 1984 s 112AH(3) (as added: see note 2).

8 County Courts Act 1984 s 112B(4) (as added: see note 2). The debtor is excluded under the bankruptcy exclusion if: (1) a petition for a bankruptcy order to be made against him has been presented but not decided; or (2) he is an undischarged bankrupt: s 112AH(4) (as added: see note 2). As to bankruptcy see PARA 129 et seq.

9 County Courts Act 1984 s 112B(5) (as added: see note 2). In a case where an individual is the debtor under a debt that is repayable by a single payment, the debtor is to be regarded as unable to pay the debt only if: (1) the debt has become due; (2) the debtor has failed to make the single payment; and (3) the debtor is unable to make that payment: s 112AC(1) (as so added). In a case where an individual is the debtor under a debt that is repayable by a number of payments, the debtor is to be regarded as unable to pay the debt only if: (a) the debt has become due; (b) the debtor has failed to make one or more of the payments; and (c) the debtor is unable to make all of the missed payments: s 112AC(2) (as so added).

10 The total amount of a debtor's qualifying debts is to be calculated as follows: (1) all of the debtor's qualifying debts which have arisen before the calculation must be taken into account, whether or not the debts are already due at the time of the calculation; and (2) regulations must make further provision about how the total amount of a debtor's qualifying debts is to be calculated: County Courts Act 1984 s 112AD(1)–(3) (as added: see note 2). Regulations may make provision about how the amount of any particular qualifying debt is to be calculated: s 112AD(4) (as so added). That includes the calculation of the amount of a debt for these purposes: (a) calculating the total amount of the debtor's qualifying debts; (b) scheduling the debt to an administration order: s 112AD(5) (as so added). A debt that is repayable by a single payment becomes due when the time for making that payment is reached; and a debt that is repayable by a number of payments becomes due when the time for making the first of the payments is reached: s 112AF (as so added).

11 County Courts Act 1984 s 112B(6) (as added: see note 2). 'Prescribed maximum' means the amount prescribed in regulations for the purposes of s 112B(6): s 112AA(1) (as added: see note 2). At the date at which this volume states the law no such regulations had been made.

12 The debtor's surplus income is to be calculated in accordance with regulations which must, in particular, make provision about what is surplus income and about the period by reference to which the debtor's surplus income is to be calculated: County Courts Act 1984 s 112AE(1), (2) (as added: see note 2). Regulations may, in particular, provide for the debtor's assets to be taken account of when calculating his surplus income: s 112AE(3) (as so added). At the date at which this volume states the law no such regulations had been made.

13 County Courts Act 1984 s 112B(7) (as added: see note 2). 'Prescribed minimum' means the amount prescribed in regulations for the purposes of s 112B(7): s 112AA(1) (as so added). At the date at which this volume states the law no such regulations had been made.

14 County Courts Act 1984 s 112B(8) (as added: see note 2).

895. Administration order on application for attachment of earnings order.
As from a day to be appointed, the following provisions have effect[1]. Where, on an application to a county court for an attachment of earnings order to secure the payment of a judgment debt[2], it appears to the court that the debtor[3] also has other debts, the court:

(1) must consider whether the case may be one in which all the debtor's liabilities should be dealt with together and that for that purpose an administration order[4] should be made; and

(2) if of opinion that it may be such a case, has power, whether or not it makes the attachment of earnings order applied for, with a view to making an administration order, to order the debtor to furnish to the court a list of all his creditors and the amounts which he owes to them respectively[5].

If, on receipt of such a list, the court is satisfied that the conditions as to the power to make administration orders[6] are met in relation to the debtor, the court may make an administration order in respect of the debtor's estate[7].

However, nothing in the above provisions is to be taken as prejudicing any right of a debtor to apply[8] for an administration order[9].

1 See PARA 886. As to administration orders on an application for an attachment of earnings order under the current scheme see PARA 888.
2 As to the meaning of 'judgment debt' see PARA 888 note 1.
3 As to the meaning of 'the debtor' see PARA 888 note 2.
4 As to the meaning of 'administration order' see PARA 888 note 3.
5 Attachment of Earnings Act 1971 s 4(1) (amended by the Insolvency Act 1976 s 13(2)). For the prescribed form of list of creditors see the County Court (Forms) Rules 1982, SI 1982/586, r 2, Schedule, Form N93. As to the continued use of county court forms see CIVIL PROCEDURE vol 11 (2009) PARA 14. See further PARA 888 note 4.
6 Ie the conditions in the County Courts Act 1984 s 112B(2)–(7): see PARA 894.
7 Attachment of Earnings Act 1971 s 4(2) (substituted by the Tribunals, Courts and Enforcement Act 2007 s 106(2), Sch 16 para 1(1), (2)).
8 Ie under the County Courts Act 1984 s 112J: see PARA 898.
9 Attachment of Earnings Act 1971 s 4(4) (amended by the County Courts Act 1984 Sch 2 para 40(c); and the Tribunals, Courts and Enforcement Act 2007 Sch 16 para 1(1), (3)).

896. Scheduling debts. As from a day to be appointed, the following provisions have effect[1]. The following provisions apply to a qualifying debt ('the declared debt') if an administration order[2] is made and, when the order is made, the debt is taken into account[3] in calculating the total amount of the debtor's qualifying debts[4]. If the declared debt is already due at the time the administration order is made, the proper county court[5] must schedule the debt to the order when the order is made[6]. If the declared debt becomes due after the administration order is made, the proper county court must schedule the debt to the order if the debtor, or the creditor under the debt, applies to the court for the debt to be scheduled[7].

If a qualifying debt ('the new debt') arises after an administration order is made, and becomes due during the currency of the order, the proper county court may schedule the new debt to the administration order if: (1) the debtor, or the creditor under the new debt, applies to the court for the debt to be scheduled; (2) the total amount of the debtor's qualifying debts (including the new debt) is less than, or the same as, the prescribed maximum[8].

1 See PARA 886.
2 As to the meaning of 'administration order' see PARA 894 note 2.
3 Ie for the purposes of the County Courts Act 1984 s 112B(6) (see PARA 894 head (5)).
4 County Courts Act 1984 s 112C(1) (Pt 6 (ss 112A–112AI) added by the Tribunals, Courts and Enforcement Act 2007 s 106). As to the meaning of 'qualifying debts' see PARA 894 note 4.
5 In relation to an administration order, references to the proper county court are references to the county court that made the order; but that is subject to rules of court as to the venue for, and transfer of, proceedings in county courts: County Courts Act 1984 s 112AA(3), (4) (as added: see note 4). As from a day to be appointed, s 112AA(3), (4) is repealed and all references to 'proper' in Pt 6 are to be omitted: see the Crime and Courts Act 2013 Sch 9 Pt 2 para 47(1), (2), (8). At the date at which this volume states the law no such day had been appointed.
6 County Courts Act 1984 s 112C(2) (as added: see note 4).
7 County Courts Act 1984 s 112C(3) (as added: see note 4). However, the proper county court must not schedule a debt to an administration order unless the court has had regard to any representations made by any person about why the debt should not be scheduled: ss 112C(4), 112AG(5) (as added: see note 4).
8 County Courts Act 1984 s 112D(1), (2) (as added: see note 4). As to the meaning of 'the prescribed maximum' see PARA 894 note 11.

897. Requirements imposed by administration order. As from a day to be appointed, the following provisions have effect[1]. An administration order[2] must, during the currency of the order[3], impose the following requirements:

(1)　a repayment requirement on the debtor to repay the scheduled debts[4];

(2)　the requirement that no qualifying creditor[5] of the debtor is to present a bankruptcy petition against the debtor in respect of a qualifying debt, unless the creditor has the permission of the proper county court[6];

(3)　the requirement that no qualifying creditor of the debtor is to pursue any remedy for the recovery of a qualifying debt unless regulations[7] provide otherwise, or the creditor has the permission of the proper county court[8];

(4)　the requirement that no creditor under a scheduled debt is to charge any sum by way of interest, fee or other charge in respect of that debt[9];

(5)　the requirement that no domestic utility creditor[10] is to stop the supply of gas or electricity, or the supply of any associated services, except in certain specified cases[11].

1　See PARA 886.

2　As to the meaning of 'administration order' see PARA 894 note 2.

3　References to the currency of an administration order are references to the period which begins when the order first has effect, and ends when the order ceases to have effect: County Courts Act 1984 s 112AA(2) (Pt 6 (ss 112A–112AI) added by the Tribunals, Courts and Enforcement Act 2007 s 106).

4　County Courts Act 1984 s 112E(1), (2) (as added: see note 3). As to the meaning of 'declared debts' see PARA 896. The repayment requirement may provide for the debtor to repay a particular scheduled debt (see PARA 896) in full or to some other extent: s 112E(3) (as so added). It may provide for the debtor to repay different scheduled debts to different extents: s 112E(4) (as so added). In the case of a new debt scheduled to the order in accordance with s 112D (see PARA 896), the repayment requirement may provide that no due repayment in respect of the new debt is to be made until the debtor has made all due repayments in respect of declared debts: s 112E(5) (as so added). The repayment requirement must provide that the due repayments are to be made by instalments: s 112E(6) (as so added). It is for the proper county court to decide when the instalments are to be made; but the proper county court is to determine the amount of the instalments in accordance with repayment regulations: s 112E(7), (8) (as so added). Repayment regulations are regulations which make provision for instalments to be determined by reference to the debtor's surplus income (see PARA 894 note 12): s 112E(9) (as so added). The repayment requirement may provide that the due repayments are to be made by other means (including by one or more lump sums) in addition to the instalments required in accordance with s 112E(6): s 112E(10) (as so added). The repayment requirement may include provision in addition to any that is required or permitted by s 112E: s 112E(11) (as so added). For these purposes, 'declared debt' has the same meaning as in s 112C (and for this purpose it does not matter whether a declared debt is scheduled to the administration order when it is made, or afterwards); and 'due repayments' means repayments which the repayment requirement requires the debtor to make: s 112E(12) (as so added). As to the meaning of 'proper county court' see PARA 896 note 5.

5　'Qualifying creditor' means a creditor under a qualifying debt: County Courts Act 1984 s 112AA(1) (as added: see note 3). As to the meaning of 'qualifying debt' see PARA 894 note 4.

6　County Courts Act 1984 s 112F(1), (2) (as added: see note 3). The proper county court may give permission for these purposes subject to such conditions as it thinks fit: s 112F(3) (as so added).

7　Ie regulations under the County Courts Act 1984 s 112G(3). Regulations may specify classes of debt which are exempted, or exempted for specified purposes, from the restriction imposed by s 112G(2): s 112G(3) (as added: see note 3).

8　County Courts Act 1984 s 112G(1), (2) (as added: see note 3). The proper county court may give permission for these purposes subject to such conditions as it thinks fit: s 112G(4) (as so added). The provisions of s 112G do not have any effect in relation to bankruptcy proceedings: s 112G(5) (as so added). As to bankruptcy proceedings see PARA 129 et seq.

9　County Courts Act 1984 s 112H(1), (2) (as added: see note 3).

10　A domestic utility creditor is any person who: (1) provides the debtor with a supply of mains gas or mains electricity for the debtor's own domestic purposes; and (2) is a creditor under a qualifying debt that relates to the provision of that supply: County Courts Act 1984 s 112I(2) (as added: see note 3). A supply of mains gas is a supply of the kind mentioned in the Gas Act 1986 s 5(1)(b) (see ENERGY AND CLIMATE CHANGE vol 42 (2011) PARA 251); and a supply of mains electricity is a supply of the kind mentioned in the Electricity Act 1989 s 4(1)(c) (see ENERGY AND CLIMATE CHANGE vol 43 (2011) PARA 524): County Courts Act 1984 s 112I(8), (9) (as so added).

11 County Courts Act 1984 s 112I(1), (3) (as added: see note 3). The first specified case is where the reason for stopping a supply relates to the non-payment by the debtor of charges incurred in connection with that supply after the making of the administration order: s 112I(4) (as so added). The second specified case is where the reason for stopping a supply is unconnected with the non-payment by the debtor of any charges incurred in connection with that supply, or any other supply of mains gas or mains electricity, or of associated services, that is provided by the domestic utility creditor: s 112I(5) (as so added). The third specified case is where the proper county court gives permission to stop a supply: s 112I(6) (as so added). The proper county court may give permission for the purposes of s 112I(6) subject to such conditions as it thinks fit: s 112I(7) (as so added).

898. Making an order. As from a day to be appointed, the following provisions have effect[1]. A county court may make an administration order[2] only on the application of the debtor[3]. The debtor may make an application for an administration order whether or not a judgment has been obtained against him in respect of any of his debts[4].

A county court may, at the time it makes an administration order, specify a day on which the order will cease to have effect[5]. The court may not specify a day which falls after the last day of the maximum permitted period, which is the period of five years beginning with the day on which the order is made[6]. If the court specifies a day, the order ceases to have effect on that day[7]. If the court does not specify a day, the order ceases to have effect at the end of the maximum permitted period[8].

1 See PARA 886.
2 As to the meaning of 'administration order' see PARA 894 note 2.
3 County Courts Act 1984 s 112J(1) (Pt 6 (ss 112A–112AI) added by the Tribunals, Courts and Enforcement Act 2007 s 106). As from a day to be appointed, the reference in the County Courts Act 1984 s 112J(1) to 'a county court' is replaced by reference to 'the county court': see s 112J(1) (amended by the Crime and Courts Act 2013 Sch 9 Pt 2 para 47(1), (3)). At the date at which this volume states the law no such day had been appointed.
4 County Courts Act 1984 s 112J(2) (as added: see note 3).
5 County Courts Act 1984 s 112K(1) (as added: see note 3). As from a day to be appointed, the reference in s 112K(1) to 'a county court' is replaced by reference to 'the county court': see s 112K(1) (amended by the Crime and Courts Act 2013 Sch 9 Pt 2 para 47(1), (3)). At the date at which this volume states the law no such day had been appointed.
   The County Courts Act 1984 s 112K is subject to s 112S (variation of duration: see PARA 900) and s 112W (effect of revocation: see PARA 901): s 112K(6) (as so added). It is also subject to s 117I (see PARA 924) and the Insolvency Act 1986 s 251F (see PARA 108 note 15) (effect of enforcement restriction order or debt relief order on administration order): County Courts Act 1984 s 112K(7) (as so added).
6 County Courts Act 1984 s 112K(2), (5) (as added: see note 3).
7 County Courts Act 1984 s 112K(3) (as added: see note 3).
8 County Courts Act 1984 s 112K(4) (as added: see note 3).

899. Effects of order. As from a day to be appointed, the following provisions have effect[1]. If an administration order[2] is made, and immediately before the order is made, other debt management arrangements[3] are in force in respect of the debtor, the other debt management arrangements cease to be in force when the administration order is made[4]. If the proper county court[5] is aware of the other debt management arrangements, the court must give the relevant authority[6] notice that the order has been made[7].

If, and for as long as, an administration order has effect in respect of a debtor, the debtor must, at the prescribed[8] times, provide the proper county court with particulars of his earnings, income, assets and outgoings[9]. A person commits an offence if he fails to provide these particulars[10].

The county court must stay the proceedings if:

(1) an administration order is made;

(2) proceedings in a county court, other than bankruptcy proceedings, are pending against the debtor in respect of a qualifying debt[11];

(3) by virtue of a requirement included in the order[12], the creditor under the qualifying debt is not entitled to continue the proceedings in respect of the debt;

(4) the county court receives notice of the administration order[13].

Money paid into court under an administration order is to be appropriated first in satisfaction of any relevant court fees[14], and then in liquidation of debts[15].

If the debtor repays a scheduled debt to the extent provided for by the administration order, the proper county court[16] must order that the debtor is discharged from the debt and de-schedule the debt[17]. If the debtor repays all of the scheduled debts to the extent provided for by the administration order, the proper county court must revoke the order[18].

1 See PARA 886.

2 As to the meaning of 'administration order' see PARA 894 note 2.

3 'Other debt management arrangements' means any of the following: (1) an enforcement restriction order under the County Courts Act 1984 Pt 6A (ss 117A–117X) (see PARA 916 et seq); (2) a debt relief order under the Insolvency Act 1986 Pt 7A (ss 251A–251X) (see PARA 101 et seq); or (3) a debt repayment plan arranged in accordance with a debt management scheme that is approved under the Tribunals, Courts and Enforcement Act 2007 Pt 5 Ch 4 (ss 109–133) (see PARA 931 et seq): County Courts Act 1984 s 112L(6) (Pt 6 (ss 112A–112AI) added by the Tribunals, Courts and Enforcement Act 2007 s 106). For these purposes, a debt relief order is 'in force' if the moratorium applicable to the order under the Insolvency Act 1986 s 251H has not yet ended: County Courts Act 1984 s 112L(8) (as so added).

4 County Courts Act 1984 s 112L(1), (2) (as added: see note 3).

5 As to the meaning of 'proper county court' see PARA 896 note 5.

6 'The relevant authority' means: (1) in relation to an enforcement restriction order: the proper county court (within the meaning of the County Courts Act 1984 Pt 6A); (2) in relation to a debt relief order: the official receiver (see PARA 35 et seq); (3) in relation to a debt repayment plan: the operator of the debt management scheme in accordance with which the plan is arranged (see PARA 931): s 112L(7) (as added: see note 3). As from a day to be appointed, the words 'within the meaning of the County Courts Act 1984 Pt 6A' in head (1) are omitted: see s 112L(7) (amended by the Crime and Courts Act 2013 Sch 9 Pt 2 para 47(1), (4)). At the date at which this volume states the law no such day had been appointed.

7 County Courts Act 1984 s 112L(3) (as added: see note 3). In a case where the proper county court is aware of other debt management arrangements at the time it makes the order, it must give the notice as soon as practicable after making the order: s 112L(4) (as so added). In a case where the proper county court becomes aware of those arrangements after it makes the order, it must give the notice as soon as practicable after becoming aware of them: s 112L(5) (as so added).

8 In any provision of the County Courts Act 1984 s 112M, 'prescribed' means prescribed in regulations for the purposes of that provision: s 112M(7) (as added: see note 3).

9 County Courts Act 1984 s 112M(1), (2) (as added: see note 3). The debtor must provide particulars of those matters as the matters are at the time the particulars are provided, and as the debtor expects the matters to be at such times in the future as are prescribed: s 112M(3) (as so added). If the debtor intends to dispose of any of his property he must, within the prescribed period, provide the proper county court with particulars of the following matters: (1) the property he intends to dispose of; (2) the consideration, if any, he expects will be given for the disposal; (3) such other matters as may be prescribed; (4) such other matters as the court may specify: s 112M(4) (as so added). This does not apply if the disposal is of: (a) goods that are exempt goods for the purposes of the Tribunals, Courts and Enforcement Act 2007 Sch 12 (see

CIVIL PROCEDURE vol 12 (2009) PARA 1386); (b) goods that are protected under any other enactment from being taken control of under Sch 12; or (c) prescribed property: County Courts Act 1984 s 112M(5) (as so added). The duty to provide the proper county court with particulars of a proposed disposal of property applies whether the debtor is the sole owner, or one of several owners, of the property: s 112M(6) (as so added).

10 A person commits an offence if he fails to comply with the County Courts Act 1984 s 112M(2), (3) or (4) (see note 9): s 112N(1) (as added: see note 3). A person who commits such an offence may be ordered by a judge of the proper county court to pay a fine of not more than £250 or to be imprisoned for not more than 14 days: s 112N(2) (as so added). Where a person is ordered to be imprisoned by a judge of the proper county court, the judge may at any time revoke the order and, if the person is already in custody, order his discharge: s 112N(3) (as so added). As from a day to be appointed, the words 'the judge' are replaced by 'a judge of the county court': see s 112N(3) (amended by the Crime and Courts Act 2013 Sch 9 Pt 2 para 47(1), (5)). At the date at which this volume states the law no such day had been appointed. The County Courts Act 1984 s 129 (enforcement of fines: see CIVIL PROCEDURE vol 12 (2009) PARA 1513) applies to payment of a fine imposed under s 112N(2): s 112N(4) (as so added). For the purposes of the Administration of Justice Act 1960 s 13 (appeal in cases of contempt of court: see CONTEMPT OF COURT vol 22 (2012) PARA 118), the County Courts Act 1984 s 112N(2) is to be treated as an enactment enabling a county court to deal with an offence under s 112N(1) as if it were a contempt of court: s 112N(5) (as so added). A district judge or deputy district judge has the same powers under s 112N as a judge of a county court: s 112N(6) (as so added). As from a day to be appointed, s 112N(6) is repealed by the Crime and Courts Act 2013 Sch 9 Pt 2 para 47(1), (6). At the date at which this volume states the law no such day had been appointed.

11 As to the meaning of 'qualifying debt' see PARA 894 note 4.

12 Ie by virtue of the County Courts Act 1984 s 112G: see PARA 897.

13 County Courts Act 1984 s 112O(1), (2) (as added: see note 3). The court may allow costs already incurred by the creditor: s 112O(3) (as so added). If the court allows such costs, it may on application or of its motion add them: (1) to the debt; or (2) if the debt is a scheduled debt, to the amount scheduled to the order in respect of the debt: s 112O(4) (as so added). The court may not add the costs under head (2) if the court is under a duty under s 112U(6)(b) (see PARA 901) to revoke the order because the total amount of the debtor's qualifying debts, including the costs, is more than the prescribed maximum: s 112O(5) (as so added). As to the meaning of 'the prescribed maximum' see PARA 894 note 11. As to scheduling debts see PARA 896.

14 Relevant court fees are any fees under an order made under the Courts Act 2003 s 92 (see CIVIL PROCEDURE vol 11 (2009) PARA 87) which are payable by the debtor in respect of the administration order: County Courts Act 1984 s 112P(2) (as added: see note 3).

15 County Courts Act 1984 s 112P(1) (as added: see note 3).

16 See PARA 896 note 5.

17 Courts Act 1984 s 112Q(1) (as added: see note 3). The provisions of s 112Q(1), (2) apply to all scheduled debts, including any which, under the administration order, are to be repaid other than to their full extent: s 112Q(3) (as so added).

18 Courts Act 1984 s 112Q(2) (as added: see note 3). See note 17.

900. Variation. As from a day to be appointed, the following provisions have effect[1]. The proper county court[2] may vary an administration order[3] on the application of the debtor or a qualifying creditor[4] or of the court's own motion[5]. This power includes power to vary an administration order so as to specify a day or, if a day has already been specified[6] a different day, on which the order will cease to have effect[7]. This power also includes power to vary an administration order by de-scheduling a debt[8], if it appears to the proper county court that it is just and equitable to do so[9].

1 See PARA 886.

2 As to the meaning of 'proper county court' see PARA 896 note 5.

3 County Courts Act 1984 s 112R(1) (Pt 6 (ss 112A–112AI) added by the Tribunals, Courts and Enforcement Act 2007 s 106). As to the meaning of 'administration order' see PARA 894 note 2.

4 As to the meaning of 'qualifying creditor' see PARA 897 note 5.

5 County Courts Act 1984 s 112R(2) (as added: see note 2).

6 Ie under the County Courts Act 1984 s 112K (see PARA 898) or under s 112S(1).

7　County Courts Act 1984 s 112S(1) (as added: see note 2). The day on which the order will cease
　to have effect in accordance with the variation under s 112S(1) (the 'new termination day') must
　fall on or before the last day of the maximum permitted period, which is the period of five years
　beginning with the day on which the order was originally made: s 112S(2), (4) (as so added). If
　the proper county court varies an administration under s 112S(1), the order ceases to have effect
　on the new termination day: s 112S(3) (as so added). The provisions of s 112S are subject to
　s 112W (effect of revocation: see PARA 901): s 112S(5) (as so added).
8　County Courts Act 1984 s 112T(1) (as added: see note 2). As to the scheduling of debts see PARA
　896.
9　County Courts Act 1984 s 112T(2) (as added: see note 2).

901.　Revocation. As from a day to be appointed, the following provisions
have effect[1]. The proper county court[2] must revoke an administration order[3]:

(1)　where it becomes apparent that, at the time the order was made the
　　　debtor in fact did not have two or more qualifying debts[4];

(2)　where the debtor is no longer a debtor under any qualifying debts[5];

(3)　where it becomes apparent that, at the time the order was made, the
　　　debtor in fact had business debt[6], and he is still a debtor under the
　　　business debt, or any of the business debts, in question[7];

(4)　where the debtor subsequently becomes a debtor under a business debt,
　　　and he is still a debtor under that debt[8];

(5)　where it becomes apparent that, at the time the order was made the
　　　debtor was in fact excluded[9];

(6)　where, after the order is made the debtor becomes excluded under the
　　　voluntary arrangement exclusion[10], or a bankruptcy order is made
　　　against the debtor, and is still in force[11];

(7)　where it becomes apparent that, at the time the order was made, the
　　　debtor was in fact able to pay his qualifying debts[12];

(8)　where the debtor is now able to pay all of his qualifying debts[13];

(9)　where it becomes apparent that, at the time the order was made, the
　　　debtor's qualifying debts in fact amounted to more than the prescribed
　　　maximum[14];

(10)　where the total amount of the debtor's qualifying debts is now more
　　　than the prescribed maximum[15];

(11)　where it becomes apparent that, at the time the order was made, the
　　　debtor's surplus income[16] was in fact less than, or the same as, the
　　　prescribed minimum[17];

(12)　where the debtor's surplus income is now less than, or the same as, the
　　　prescribed minimum[18].

The proper county court may revoke an administration order in any case
where there is no duty to revoke it[19]. The power of revocation may, in particular,
be exercised in any of the following cases: (a) where the debtor has failed to
make two payments, whether consecutive or not, required by the order; (b)
where the debtor has failed to provide the proper county court with the
required[20] particulars[21]. The power of revocation is exercisable on the
application of the debtor or a qualifying creditor[22] or of the court's own
motion[23].

If, under any duty or power, the proper county court revokes an
administration order, the order ceases to have effect in accordance with the terms
of the revocation[24].

If a county court revokes an administration order made in respect of an
individual ('the debtor') on the grounds that:

(a)   the debtor had failed to make two payments, whether consecutive or not, required by the order;

(b)   at the time the order was made the total amount of the debtor's qualifying debts was more than the prescribed maximum, but because of information provided, or not provided, by the debtor, that amount was thought to be less than, or the same as, the prescribed maximum,

the court may, at the time it revokes the administration order, make an order directing that the following provisions[25] and the provisions of the Company Directors Disqualification Act 1986 relating to failure to pay under a county court administration order[26] are to apply to the debtor for such period, not exceeding one year, as may be specified in the order[27]. The individual may not either alone or jointly with another person, obtain credit[28] to the extent of the amount prescribed[29] or more, or enter into any transaction in the course of or for the purposes of any business in which he is directly or indirectly engaged, without disclosing to the person from whom he obtains the credit, or as the case may be, with whom the transaction is entered into, the fact that these provisions apply to him[30].

An individual who contravenes the above provisions is guilty of an offence and liable on conviction on indictment to imprisonment for a term not exceeding two years or a fine, or to both, or on summary conviction to imprisonment for a term not exceeding six months or a fine not exceeding the statutory maximum, or to both[31].

1   See PARA 886.
2   As to the meaning of 'proper county court' see PARA 896 note 5.
3   As to the meaning of 'administration order' see PARA 894 note 2.
4   County Courts Act 1984 s 112U(1)(a) (Pt 6 (ss 112A–112AI) added by the Tribunals, Courts and Enforcement Act 2007 s 106). Head (1) in the text applies where the condition in the County Courts Act 1984 s 112B(2) was not met: see PARA 894. As to the meaning of 'qualifying debts' see PARA 894 note 4.
5   County Courts Act 1984 s 112U(1)(b) (as added: see note 4).
6   Ie the condition in the County Courts Act 1984 s 112B(3) was not met: see PARA 894. As to the meaning of 'business debt see PARA 894 note 4.
7   County Courts Act 1984 s 112U(2)(a) (as added: see note 4).
8   County Courts Act 1984 s 112U(2)(b) (as added: see note 4).
9   County Courts Act 1984 s 112U(3) (as added: see note 4). The debtor is excluded if the condition in s 112B(4) is not met (debtor in fact excluded under AO, voluntary arrangement or bankruptcy exclusion): see PARA 894 text and notes 6–8.
10   See PARA 894 note 7.
11   County Courts Act 1984 s 112U(4) (as added: see note 4). As to bankruptcy see PARA 129 et seq.
12   County Courts Act 1984 s 112U(5)(a) (as added: see note 4). Head (7) applies where the condition in s 112B(5) was not met: see PARA 894.
13   County Courts Act 1984 s 112U(5)(b) (as added: see note 4).
14   County Courts Act 1984 s 112U(6)(a) (as added: see note 4). Head (9) applies where the condition in s 112B(6) was not met: see PARA 894. As to the meaning of 'prescribed maximum' see PARA 894 note 11.
15   County Courts Act 1984 s 112U(6)(b) (as added: see note 4).
16   See PARA 894 note 12.
17   County Courts Act 1984 s 112U(7)(a) (as added: see note 4). Head (11) applies where the condition in s 112B(7) was not met: see PARA 894. As to the meaning of 'prescribed minimum' see PARA 894 note 13.
18   County Courts Act 1984 s 112U(7)(b) (as added: see note 4).
19   County Courts Act 1984 s 112V(1) (as added: see note 4).
20   Ie required by the County Courts Act 1984 s 112M(2), (3), (4): see PARA 899.
21   County Courts Act 1984 s 112V(2) (as added: see note 4).
22   As to the meaning of 'qualifying creditor' see PARA 897 note 5.
23   County Courts Act 1984 s 112V(3) (as added: see note 4).

24 County Courts Act 1984 s 112W(1), (2) (as added: see note 4).

25 Ie the provisions of the Insolvency Act 1986 s 429.

26 Ie the Company Directors Disqualification Act 1986 s 12: see COMPANY AND PARTNERSHIP INSOLVENCY vol 17 (2011) PARA 1083.

27 Insolvency Act 1986 s 429(1), (2), (2A) (s 429(1), (2) substituted, s 429(1A) added, and s 429(3)–(5) amended, by the Tribunals, Courts and Enforcement Act 2007 s 106, Sch 16 para 3). This amendment is not yet in force.

28 Ie the amount prescribed for the purposes of the Insolvency Act 1986 s 360(1)(a): see PARA 747 note 2.

29 For these purposes, the reference to an individual obtaining credit includes: (1) a case where goods are bailed or hired to him under a hire-purchase agreement or agreed to be sold to him under a conditional sale agreement; and (2) a case where he is paid in advance, whether in money or otherwise, for the supply of goods or services: Insolvency Act 1986 s 429(4) (as amended: see note 27). As to the meanings of 'hire-purchase agreement' and 'conditional sale agreement' see PARA 747 note 1.

30 Insolvency Act 1986 s 429(3) (as amended: see note 27).

31 Insolvency Act 1986 ss 429(5), 430, Sch 10 (s 429(5) as amended: see note 27). As to the statutory maximum see SENTENCING AND DISPOSITION OF OFFENDERS vol 92 (2010) PARA 140.

902. Requirement to give notice. As from a day to be appointed, the following provisions have effect[1]. If a notifiable event occurs in relation to an administration order[2], the proper county court[3] must send notice of the event to the creditor under every scheduled debt[4]. There is a notifiable event in any of the following cases:

(1) when the administration order is made[5];

(2) when a debt is scheduled to the administration order at any time after the making of the order;

(3) when the administration order is varied[6];

(4) when the administration order is revoked[7];

(5) when the proper county court is given notice[8] as to the effect of an enforcement restriction order or a debt relief order on the administration order[9].

1 See PARA 886.

2 As to the meaning of 'administration order' see PARA 894 note 2.

3 As to the meaning of 'proper county court' see PARA 896 note 5.

4 County Courts Act 1984 s 112X(1) (Pt 6 (ss 112A–112AI) added by the Tribunals, Courts and Enforcement Act 2007 s 106). As to the scheduling of debts see PARA 896.

5 See PARA 894.

6 See PARA 900.

7 See PARA 901.

8 Ie under the County Courts Act 1984 s 117I (see PARA 924) or the Insolvency Act 1986 s 251F (see PARA 108 note 15): see s 112K(7): and PARA 898 note 5.

9 County Courts Act 1984 s 112X(2) (as added: see note 4).

903. Failure to take account of all qualifying debts. As from a day to be appointed, the following provisions have effect[1]. If an administration order[2] has been made, but it becomes apparent that the total amount of the debtor's qualifying debts[3] was not properly calculated[4], because of an undeclared[5] debt[6], then:

(1) if the undeclared debt is due, whether it became due before or after the making of the order, and the total debt[7] is less than, or the same as, the prescribed maximum[8], then the proper county court[9] must schedule[10] the undeclared debt to the order[11];

(2) if the undeclared debt is not due and the total debt is less than, or the same as, the prescribed maximum, then the proper county court must schedule the undeclared debt to the order when the debt becomes due[12].

If the total debt is more than the prescribed maximum, the proper county court must revoke the administration order, whether or not the undeclared debt is due[13].

1   See PARA 886.
2   As to the meaning of 'administration order' see PARA 894 note 2.
3   As to the meaning of 'qualifying debts' see PARA 894 note 4.
4   Ie for the purposes of the County Courts Act 1984 s 112B(6): see PARA 894.
5   A debt is undeclared if it ought to have been, but was not, taken into account in the calculation for the purposes of the County Courts Act 1984 s 112B(6) (see PARA 894): s 112Y(2) (Pt 6 (ss 112A–112AI) added by the Tribunals, Courts and Enforcement Act 2007 s 106).
6   County Courts Act 1984 s 112Y(1) (as added: see note 5).
7   For this purpose, 'total debt' means the total amount of the debtor's qualifying debts, including the undeclared debt: County Courts Act 1984 s 112Y(6) (as added: see note 5).
8   As to the meaning of 'prescribed maximum' see PARA 894 note 11.
9   As to the meaning of 'proper county court' see PARA 896 note 5.
10 As to the scheduling of debts see PARA 896.
11 County Courts Act 1984 s 112Y(3) (as added: see note 5). The proper county court must not schedule a debt to an administration order under s 112Y(3), (4) unless the court has had regard to any representations made by any person about why the debt should not be scheduled: ss 112Y(7), 112AG(5) (as added: see note 5).
12 County Courts Act 1984 s 112Y(4) (as added: see note 5). See note 11.
13 County Courts Act 1984 s 112Y(5) (as added: see note 5).

(iv) Procedure on Application

904.   Request by debtor for administration order; list of creditors.   A debtor who desires to obtain an administration order[1] must file a request in that behalf in the court for the district in which he resides or carries on business[2].

Where, on his examination[3] or otherwise, a debtor furnishes to the court on oath a list of his creditors and the amounts which he owes to them respectively and sufficient particulars of his resources and needs, the court may proceed as if the debtor had so filed a request[4].

Where a debtor is ordered to furnish a list of creditors in connection with an attachment of earnings order[5], then, unless otherwise directed, the list must be filed within 14 days after the making of the order[6].

1   Ie under the County Courts Act 1984 Pt VI (ss 112–117): see PARA 887 et seq.
2   CPR Sch 2, CCR Ord 39 r 2(1). For the prescribed form of request see the County Court (Forms) Rules 1982, SI 1982/586, r 2, Schedule Form N92 (substituted by SI 1995/2839). The statements in the request mentioned in CPR Sch 2, CCR Ord 39 r 2(1) must be verified by the debtor on oath: CPR Sch 2, CCR Ord 39 r 3. As to the continued use of county court forms see CIVIL PROCEDURE vol 11 (2009) PARA 14.
3   Ie under CPR Pt 71 (see CIVIL PROCEDURE vol 12 (2009) PARA 1251 et seq).
4   CPR Sch 2, CCR Ord 39 r 2(2).
5   Ie under the Attachment of Earnings Act 1971 s 4(1)(b): see PARAS 888 head (2), 895 head (2).
6   CPR Sch 2, CCR Ord 39 r 2(3). The list must be verified by the debtor on oath: CPR Sch 2, CCR Ord 39 r 3.

905.   Orders made by the court officer.   The question whether an administration order should be made, and the terms of such an order, may be decided by the court officer[1] in accordance with the following provisions[2].

On the filing of a request or list[3], the court officer may, if he considers that the debtor's means are sufficient to discharge in full and within a reasonable period the total amount of the debts included in the list, determine the amount and frequency of the payments to be made under such an order ('the proposed rate'); and:

(1)   notify the debtor of the proposed rate requiring him to give written

reasons for any objection he may have to the proposed rate within 14 days of service of notification on him;

(2)   send to each creditor mentioned in the list provided by the debtor a copy of the debtor's request or of the list together with the proposed rate;

(3)   require any such creditor to give written reasons for any objection he may have to the making of an administration order within 14 days of service of the documents mentioned in head (2) above on him[4].

Objections under head (3) above may be to the making of an order, to the proposed rate or to the inclusion of a particular debt in the order[5].

Where no objection under head (1) or head (3) above is received within the time stated, the court officer may make an administration order providing for payment in full of the total amount of the debts included in the list[6].

Where the debtor or a creditor notifies the court of any objection within the time stated, the court officer must fix a day for a hearing at which the district judge will decide whether an administration order should be made and the court must give not less than 14 days' notice of the day so fixed to the debtor and to each creditor mentioned in the list provided by the debtor[7].

Where the court officer is unable to fix a rate[8], whether because he considers that the debtor's means are insufficient or otherwise, he must refer the request to the district judge[9].

Where the district judge considers that he is able to do so without the attendance of the parties, he may fix the proposed rate providing for payment of the debts included in the list in full or to such extent and within such a period as appears practicable in the circumstances of the case[10]. Where the district judge does not so fix the proposed rate, he must direct the court officer to fix a day for a hearing at which the district judge will decide whether an administration order should be made; and the court officer must give not less than 14 days' notice of the day so fixed to the debtor and to each creditor mentioned in the list provided by the debtor[11].

1   The court manager or such other officer of the court as the court making an administration order from time to time appoints has the conduct of the order and must take all proper steps to enforce the order or to bring to the attention of the court any matter which may make it desirable to review the order: CPR Sch 2, CCR Ord 39 r 13(1).
2   CPR Sch 2, CCR Ord 39 r 5(1).
3   Ie under CPR Sch 2, CCR Ord 39 r 2: see PARA 904.
4   CPR Sch 2, CCR Ord 39 r 5(2).
5   CPR Sch 2, CCR Ord 39 r 5(2).
6   CPR Sch 2, CCR Ord 39 r 5(3). Where an administration order is made under CPR Sch 2, CCR Ord 39 r 5(3), the court officer may exercise the power of the court under the Attachment of Earnings Act 1971 s 5 (see PARA 895) to make an attachment of earnings order to secure the payments required by the administration order: CPR Sch 2, CCR Ord 39 r 5(9).
7   CPR Sch 2, CCR Ord 39 r 5(4).
8   Ie under CPR Sch 2, CCR Ord 39 r 5(2).
9   CPR Sch 2, CCR Ord 39 r 5(5).
10 CPR Sch 2, CCR Ord 39 r 5(6). Where the proposed rate is fixed under CPR Sch 2, CCR Ord 39 r 5(6), CPR Sch 2, CCR Ord 39 r 5(2)–(4) applies with the necessary modifications as if the rate had been fixed by the court officer: CPR Sch 2, CCR Ord 39 r 5(7).
11 CPR Sch 2, CCR Ord 39 r 5(8).

906.   Notice of objection by creditor.   Any creditor to whom notice has been given[1] of the appointment of a day for consideration whether an administration order should be made and who objects to any debt included in the list furnished by the debtor must, not less than seven days before the day of hearing, give notice of his objection, stating the grounds thereof, to the court officer[2], to the debtor and to the creditor to whose debt he objects[3]. Except with the permission of the court, no creditor may object to a debt unless he has given notice of his objection[4].

1   Ie under CPR Sch 2, CCR Ord 39 r 5(8): see PARA 905.
2   As to the functions of the court officer see PARA 905 note 1.
3   CPR Sch 2, CCR Ord 39 r 6(1).
4   CPR Sch 2, CCR Ord 39 r 6(2).

907.   Procedure on day of hearing. On the day of the hearing:

(1)   any creditor, whether or not he is mentioned in the list furnished by the debtor[1], may attend and prove his debt or object[2] to any debt included in that list[3];

(2)   every debt included in that list is to be taken to be proved unless it is objected to by a creditor or disallowed by the court or required by the court to be supported by evidence[4];

(3)   any creditor whose debt is required by the court to be supported by evidence must prove his debt[5];

(4)   the court may adjourn proof of any debt and, if it does so, may either adjourn consideration of the question whether an administration order should be made or proceed to determine the question, in which case, if an administration order is made, the debt, when proved, must be added to the debts scheduled to the order[6];

(5)   any creditor whose debt is admitted or proved, and, with the permission of the court, any creditor the proof of whose debt has been adjourned, is entitled to be heard and to adduce evidence on the question whether an administration order should be made and, if so, in what terms[7].

Where an administration order is made[8], the court officer[9] must send a copy to:

(a)   the debtor;

(b)   every creditor whose name was included in the list furnished by the debtor;

(c)   any other creditor who has proved his debt; and

(d)   every other court in which, to the knowledge of the district judge, judgment has been obtained against the debtor or proceedings are pending in respect of any debt scheduled to the order[10].

1   Ie under CPR Sch 2, CCR Ord 39 r 2: see PARA 904.
2   Ie subject to CPR Sch 2, CCR Ord 39 r 6: see PARA 906.
3   CPR Sch 2, CCR Ord 39 r 7(a).
4   CPR Sch 2, CCR Ord 39 r 7(b).
5   CPR Sch 2, CCR Ord 39 r 7(c).
6   CPR Sch 2, CCR Ord 39 r 7(d).
7   CPR Sch 2, CCR Ord 39 r 7(e).
8   For the prescribed form of administration order see the County Court (Forms) Order 1982, SI 1982/586, r 2, Schedule, Form N94 (substituted by SI 1993/712). As to the continued use of county court forms see CIVIL PROCEDURE vol 11 (2009) PARA 14.
9   As to the functions of the court officer see PARA 905 note 1.
10 CPR Sch 2, CCR Ord 39 r 9.

908.   Notice of order and proof of debts. Where an administration order has been made:

(1)   notice of the order must be posted in the office of the county court for

the district in which the debtor resides, and must be sent to every person whose name the debtor has notified to the appropriate court[1] as being a creditor of his or who has proved[2];

(2)   any creditor of the debtor, on proof of his debt before the district judge, is entitled to be scheduled as a creditor of the debtor for the amount of his proof[3];

(3)   any creditor may object in the prescribed manner[4] to any debt scheduled, or to the manner in which payment is directed to be made by instalments[5];

(4)   any person who, after the date of the order, becomes a creditor of the debtor must, on proof of his debt before the district judge, be scheduled as a creditor of the debtor for the amount of his proof, but is not entitled to any dividend under the order until the creditors who are scheduled as having been creditors before the date of the order have been paid to the extent provided by the order[6].

1   As to the meaning of 'the appropriate court' see PARA 887 note 4.
2   County Courts Act 1984 s 113(a) (amended by the Administration of Justice Act 1985 s 67(2) Sch 8 Pt II). As to the requirement to give notice of administration orders under the proposed new scheme see PARA 902.
3   County Courts Act 1984 s 113(b); Courts and Legal Services Act 1990 s 74(1)(a).
4   Ie under CPR Sch 2, CCR Ord 39 r 6(1): see PARA 906.
5   County Courts Act 1984 s 113(c).
6   County Courts Act 1984 s 113(d); Courts and Legal Services Act 1990 s 74(1)(a). All creditors scheduled under the County Courts Act 1984 s 113(d) before an administration order is superseded under s 117(2) (see PARA 915) rank equally in proportion to the amount of their debts subject to the priority given by s 113(d) to those scheduled as having been creditors before the date of the order; but no payment made to any creditor by way of dividend or otherwise may be disturbed by reason of any subsequent proof by any creditor under s 113(d): CPR Sch 2, CCR Ord 39 r 18.

909.   Subsequent objection by creditor.   After an administration order has been made, a creditor who has not received notice[1] of the appointment of a day for consideration whether an administration order should be made and who wishes to object to a debt scheduled to the order, or to the manner in which payment is directed to be made by instalments, must give notice to the court officer[2] of his objection and of the grounds thereof[3]. On receipt of such notice, the court must consider the objection and may allow it, dismiss it, or adjourn it for hearing on notice being given to such persons and on such terms as to security for costs or otherwise as the court thinks fit[4]. The court may[5] dismiss an objection if it is not satisfied that the creditor gave notice of it within a reasonable time of his becoming aware of the administration order[6].

1   Ie under CPR Sch 2, CCR Ord 39 r 5: see PARA 905.
2   As to the functions of the court officer see PARA 905 note 1.
3   CPR Sch 2, CCR Ord 39 r 10(1).
4   CPR Sch 2, CCR Ord 39 r 10(2).
5   Ie without prejudice to the generality of CPR Sch 2, CCR Ord 39 r 10(2).
6   CPR Sch 2, CCR Ord 39 r 10(3).

910.   Subsequent proof by creditor.   Any creditor whose debt is not scheduled to an administration order, and any person who after the date of the order became a creditor of the debtor, must, if he wishes to prove his debt, send particulars of his claim to the court officer[1], who must give notice of it to the debtor and to every creditor whose debt is so scheduled[2].

If neither the debtor nor any creditor gives notice to the court officer, within seven days after receipt of such notice, that he objects to the claim, then, unless it is required by the court to be supported by evidence, the claim is to be taken to be proved[3]. If the debtor or a creditor gives notice of objection within such period of seven days or the court requires the claim to be supported by evidence, the court officer must fix a day for consideration of the claim and give notice of it to the debtor, the creditor by whom the claim was made and the creditor, if any, making the objection, and on the hearing the court may either disallow the claim or allow it in whole or in part[4]. If a claim is taken to be so proved or allowed, the debt must be added to the schedule to the order and a copy of the order must then be sent to the creditor by whom the claim was made[5].

1　As to the functions of the court officer see PARA 905 note 1.
2　CPR Sch 2, CCR Ord 39 r 11(1).
3　CPR Sch 2, CCR Ord 39 r 11(2).
4　CPR Sch 2, CCR Ord 39 r 11(3).
5　CPR Sch 2, CCR Ord 39 r 11(4).

911.　Conduct of order. The court manager or such other officer of the court as the court making an administration order from time to time appoints has the conduct of the order and must take all proper steps to enforce the order[1] or to bring to the attention of the court any matter which may make it desirable to review the order[2]. Any creditor whose debt is scheduled to the order may[3], with the permission of the court, take proceedings to enforce the order[4]; and the debtor or, with the permission of the court, any such creditor, may apply to the court to review the order[5].

The officer having the conduct of the administration order must from time to time declare dividends and distribute them among the creditors entitled to them[6]; and, when a dividend is declared, notice must be sent by the officer to each of the creditors[7].

A debtor who changes his residence must forthwith inform the court of his new address[8]; and, where the debtor becomes resident in the district of another court, the court in which the administration order is being conducted may transfer the proceedings to that other court[9].

1　Ie including exercising the power of the court under the Attachment of Earnings Act 1971 s 5 (see PARA 889) to make an attachment of earnings order to secure payments required by the administration order.
2　CPR Sch 2, CCR Ord 39 r 13(1). When, on a matter being brought to its attention under CPR Sch 2, CCR Ord 39 r 13(1), the court so directs or the debtor or a creditor applies for the review of an administration order, CPR Sch 2, CCR Ord 39 r 8(2) (see PARA 913) applies as if the order were subject to review under CPR Sch 2, CCR Ord 39 r 8(2): CPR Sch 2, CCR Ord 39 r 13(4).
3　Ie without prejudice to the County Courts Act 1984 s 115: see PARA 891.
4　CPR Sch 2, CCR Ord 39 r 13(2).
5　CPR Sch 2, CCR Ord 39 r 13(3). Nothing in CPR Sch 2, CCR Ord 39 r 13 requires the court officer to fix a day for a review under CPR Sch 2, CCR Ord 39 r 13A (see PARA 912): CPR Sch 2, CCR Ord 39 r 13(5).
6　CPR Sch 2, CCR Ord 39 r 17(1).
7　CPR Sch 2, CCR Ord 39 r 17(2).
8　CPR Sch 2, CCR Ord 39 r 19(1).
9　CPR Sch 2, CCR Ord 39 r 19(2).

912.　Review by court officer in default of payment. Where it appears that the debtor is failing to make payments in accordance with an administration order, the court officer[1] must, either on his own initiative or on the application of a creditor whose debt is scheduled to the order, send a notice to the debtor informing him of the amounts which are outstanding and requiring him, within 14 days of service of the notice on him:

(1)   to make the payments as required by the order; or

(2)   to explain his reasons for failing to make the payments; and

(3)   to make a proposal for payment of the amounts outstanding; or

(4)   to make a request to vary the order[2].

If the debtor does not comply with any such notice within 14 days of service, the court officer must revoke the administration order[3]. The court officer must refer any notice given by a debtor under heads (2), (3) or (4) above to the district judge who may:

(a)   without requiring the attendance of the parties:

    (i)   revoke the administration order or vary it so as to provide for payment of the debts included in the order in full or to such extent and within such a period as appears practicable in the circumstances of the case; or

    (ii)   suspend the operation of the order for such time and on such terms as he thinks fit[4]; or

(b)   require the court officer to fix a day for the review of the administration order and to give to the debtor and to every creditor whose debt is scheduled to the order not less than eight days' notice of the day so fixed[5].

Any party affected by an order so made[6] may, within 14 days of service of the order on him and giving his reasons, apply on notice for the district judge to consider the matter afresh; and the court officer must fix a day for the hearing of the application before the district judge and give to the debtor and to every creditor whose debt is scheduled to the administration order not less than eight days' notice of the day so fixed[7]. On hearing such an application, the district judge may confirm the order or set it aside and make such new order as he thinks fit and the order so made must be entered in the records of the court[8].

1   As to the functions of the court officer see PARA 905 note 1.
2   CPR Sch 2, CCR Ord 39 r 13A(1).
3   CPR Sch 2, CCR Ord 39 r 13A(2).
4   CPR Sch 2, CCR Ord 39 r 13A(3)(a).
5   CPR Sch 2, CCR Ord 39 r 13A(3)(b).
6   Ie under CPR Sch 2, CCR Ord 39 r 13A(2) or (3)(a).
7   CPR Sch 2, CCR Ord 39 r 13A(4).
8   CPR Sch 2, CCR Ord 39 r 13A(5).

913.   Review of order.   On making an administration order or at any subsequent time, the court may direct that the order is to be subject to review at such time or at such intervals as the court may specify[1]. The debtor or, with the permission of the court, any creditor whose debt is scheduled to the administration order may apply to the court to review the order[2]. Where the court has directed that an administration order is to be subject to review, or where the debtor or a creditor applies to the court to review the order, the court officer[3] must give to the debtor and to every creditor who appeared when the order was made not less than seven days' notice of any day appointed for such review[4].

On the review of an administration order, the court may:

(1)   if satisfied that the debtor is unable from any cause to pay any

instalment due under the order, suspend the operation of the order for such time and on such terms as it thinks fit;

(2)   if satisfied that there has been a material change in any relevant circumstances since the order was made, vary any provision of the order[5];

(3)   if satisfied that the debtor has failed without reasonable cause to comply with any provision of the order or that it is otherwise just and expedient to do so, revoke the order, either forthwith or on failure to comply with any condition specified by the court; or

(4)   make an attachment of earnings order[6] to secure the payments required by the administration order or vary or discharge any such attachment or earnings order already made[7].

The court officer must send a copy of any order[8] varying or revoking an administration order to the debtor, to every creditor whose debt is scheduled to the administration order and, if the administration order is revoked, to any other court to which a copy of the administration order was[9] sent[10].

1   CPR Sch 2, CCR Ord 39 r 8(1).
2   CPR Sch 2, CCR Ord 39 r 13(3).
3   As to the functions of the court officer see PARA 905 note 1.
4   CPR Sch 2, CCR Ord 39 rr 8(2), 13(4). Nothing in CPR Sch 2, CCR Ord 39 rr 8 or 13 requires the court officer to fix a day for a review under CPR Sch 2, CCR Ord 39 r 13A (see PARA 912): CPR Sch 2, CCR Ord 39 rr 8(3), 13(5).
5   Ie made by virtue of the County Courts Act 1984 s 112(6): see PARA 887.
6   As to attachment of earnings orders see PARA 889.
7   CPR Sch 2, CCR Ord 39 r 14(1).
8   For the prescribed form of order revoking an administration order see the County Court (Forms) Rules 1982, SI 1982/586, r 2, Schedule, Form N95 (substituted by SI 1993/712); and for the prescribed form of order suspending or varying an administration order see the County Court (Forms) Rules 1982, SI 1982/586, Schedule, Form N95A (added by SI 1993/712; and amended by SI 1997/1838).
9   Ie pursuant to CPR Sch 2, CCR Ord 39 r 9: see PARA 907.
10   CPR Sch 2, CCR Ord 39 r 14(2).

914. Revocation of administration order. Where a person fails to make any payment which he is required to make by virtue of an administration order under Part VI of the County Courts Act 1984[1], the court which is administering that person's estate under the order may, if it thinks fit, revoke the administration order, and make an order directing that the following provisions[2] and the provisions of the Company Directors Disqualification Act 1986 relating to failure to pay under a county court administration order[3] are to apply to that person for such period, not exceeding one year, as may be specified in the order[4].

A person to whom these provisions apply may not:

(1)   either alone or jointly with another person, obtain credit[5] to the extent of the prescribed amount[6] or more; or

(2)   enter into any transaction in the course of, or for the purposes of, any business in which he is directly or indirectly engaged,

without disclosing to the person from whom he obtains the credit, or, as the case may be, with whom the transaction is entered into, the fact that these provisions apply to him[7].

A person who contravenes the above provisions is guilty of an offence and liable on conviction on indictment to imprisonment for a term not exceeding two years or a fine, or to both, or on summary conviction to imprisonment for a term not exceeding six months or a fine not exceeding the statutory maximum, or to both[8].

On the revocation of an administration order an attachment of earnings order[9] made to secure the payments required by the administration order must be discharged[10].

1 Ie under the County Courts Act 1984 Pt VI (ss 112–117): see PARA 887 et seq. As to the revocation of administration orders under the proposed new scheme see PARA 901.

2 Ie the provisions of the Insolvency Act 1986 s 429.

3 Ie the Company Directors Disqualification Act 1986 s 12: see COMPANY AND PARTNERSHIP INSOLVENCY vol 17 (2011) PARA 1083.

4 Insolvency Act 1986 s 429(1), (2) (amended by the Tribunals, Courts and Enforcement Act 2007 s 269, Sch 23 paras 1, 15).

5 Ie the amount prescribed for the purposes of the Insolvency Act 1986 s 360(1)(a): see PARA 747 note 2.

6 For these purposes, the reference to a person obtaining credit includes: (1) a case where goods are bailed or hired to him under a hire-purchase agreement or agreed to be sold to him under a conditional sale agreement; and (2) a case where he is paid in advance, whether in money or otherwise, for the supply of goods or services: Insolvency Act 1986 s 429(4). As to the meanings of 'hire-purchase agreement' and 'conditional sale agreement' see PARA 747 note 1.

7 Insolvency Act 1986 s 429(3).

8 Insolvency Act 1986 ss 429(5), 430, Sch 10. As to the statutory maximum see SENTENCING AND DISPOSITION OF OFFENDERS vol 92 (2010) PARA 140.

9 As to attachment of earnings orders see PARA 889.

10 CPR Sch 2, CCR Ord 39 r 16.

915. Discharge of administration order. Where money is paid into court and the amount received is sufficient to pay:

(1) each creditor scheduled to the administration order to the extent provided by the order;

(2) the costs of the claimant in the action in respect of which the order was made; and

(3) the costs of the administration,

the order is superseded, and the debtor must be discharged from his debts to the scheduled creditors[1].

1 County Courts Act 1984 s 117(2). As to the discharge of administration orders under the new scheme see PARA 899.

(3) ENFORCEMENT RESTRICTION ORDERS

(i) In general

916. Enforcement restriction order. As from a day to be appointed, the following provisions have effect[1]. An enforcement restriction order is an order that imposes specified requirements[2] on certain creditors[3]. An enforcement restriction order may also impose a repayment requirement[4] on the debtor[5].

1 Enforcement restriction orders were introduced by the Tribunals, Courts and Enforcement Act 2007 s 107 (not yet in force) which added the County Courts Act 1984 Pt 6A (ss 117A–117X) from a day to be appointed.

2 Ie the requirements in the County Courts Act 1984 ss 117C–117E: see PARAS 918–920.

3 County Courts Act 1984 ss 117A(1), 117T(1) (ss 117A–117X added by the Tribunals, Courts and Enforcement Act 2007 s 107).

4 Ie in accordance with the County Courts Act 1984 s 117F: see PARA 921.

5 County Courts Act 1984 s 117A(2) (as added: see note 3).

917. Power to make order. As from a day to be appointed, the following provisions have effect[1]. A county court may make an enforcement restriction order[2] if the following conditions are met[3]:

(1)   the order must be made in respect of an individual who is a debtor under two or more qualifying debts[4];

(2)   that individual ('the debtor') must not be a debtor under any business debts[5];

(3)   the debtor must not be excluded under any of the following: (a) the ERO exclusion[6]; (b) the voluntary arrangement exclusion[7]; or (c) the bankruptcy exclusion[8];

(4)   the debtor must be unable to pay[9] one or more of his qualifying debts[10];

(5)   the debtor must be suffering from a sudden and unforeseen deterioration in his financial circumstances[11];

(6)   there must be a realistic prospect that the debtor's financial circumstances will improve within the period of six months beginning when the order is made[12];

(7)   it must be fair and equitable to make the order[13].

Before making an enforcement restriction order, the county court must have regard to any representations made by any person about why the order should not be made[14].

1   See PARA 916 note 1.
2   As to the meaning of 'enforcement restriction order' see PARA 916.
3   County Courts Act 1984 s 117B(1) (ss 117A–117X added by the Tribunals, Courts and Enforcement Act 2007 s 107). As from a day to be appointed, the reference in the County Courts Act 1984 s 117B(1) to 'a county court' is replaced by reference to 'the county court': see s 117B(1) (amended by the Crime and Courts Act 2013 Sch 9 Pt 2 para 48(1), (2)). At the date at which this volume states the law no such day had been appointed.
4   County Courts Act 1984 s 117B(2) (as added: see note 3). All debts are qualifying debts, except for the following: (1) any debt secured against an asset; (2) any debt of a description specified in regulations: s 117U(1) (as so added). A business debt is any debt, whether or not a qualifying debt, which is incurred by a person in the course of a business: s 117U(2) (as so added). Only debts that have already arisen are included in references to debts; and accordingly such references do not include any debt that will arise only on the happening of some future contingency: s 117U(3) (as so added).
5   County Courts Act 1984 ss 117B(3), 117T(1) (as added: see note 3). See note 4.
6   The debtor is excluded under the ERO exclusion if: (1) an enforcement restriction order currently has effect in respect of him; or (2) an enforcement restriction order has previously had effect in respect of him, and the period of 12 months, beginning with the day when that order ceased to have effect, has yet to finish: County Courts Act 1984 s 117W(1) (as added: see note 3). In a case that falls within head (2), the debtor is not excluded under the ERO exclusion if the previous enforcement restriction order: (a) ceased to have effect in accordance with any of the provisions listed in s 117H(7) (effect of administration order or debt relief order on enforcement restriction order: see PARA 923 note 3); or (b) was revoked in accordance with s 117O(1)(b) (debtor no longer has any qualifying debts: see PARA 929): s 117W(2) (as so added).
7   The debtor is excluded under the voluntary arrangement exclusion if: (1) an interim order under the Insolvency Act 1986 s 252 has effect in respect of him (interim order where debtor intends to make proposal for voluntary arrangement: see PARA 45); or (2) he is bound by a voluntary arrangement approved under the Insolvency Act 1986 Pt 8 (ss 252–263G) (see PARA 43 et seq): County Courts Act 1984 s 117W(3) (as added: see note 3).
8   County Courts Act 1984 s 117B(4) (as added: see note 3). The debtor is excluded under the bankruptcy exclusion if: (1) a petition for a bankruptcy order to be made against him has been presented but not decided; or (2) he is an undischarged bankrupt: s 117W(4) (as so added). As to bankruptcy see PARA 129 et seq.
9   In a case where an individual is the debtor under a debt that is repayable by a single payment, the debtor is to be regarded as unable to pay the debt only if: (1) the time for making the payment has been reached; (2) the debtor has failed to make the single payment; and (3) the debtor is unable to make that payment: County Courts Act 1984 s 117V(1) (as added: see note 3). In a case where an individual is the debtor under a debt that is repayable by a number of payments, the debtor is to be regarded as unable to pay the debt only if: (a) the time for

making the first of the payments has been reached; (b) the debtor has failed to make one or more of the payments; and (c) the debtor is unable to make all of the missed payments: s 117V(2) (as so added).

10   County Courts Act 1984 s 117B(5) (as added: see note 3).
11   County Courts Act 1984 s 117B(6) (as added: see note 3).
12   County Courts Act 1984 s 117B(7) (as added: see note 3).
13   County Courts Act 1984 s 117B(8) (as added: see note 3).
14   County Courts Act 1984 s 117B(9) (as added: see note 3). This is subject to Civil Procedure Rules: County Courts Act 1984 s 117B(10) (as so added). As to the Civil Procedure Rules see generally CIVIL PROCEDURE.

(ii) Requirements imposed by Enforcement Restriction Order

918.   Presentation of bankruptcy petition.   As from a day to be appointed, the following provisions have effect[1]. An enforcement restriction order[2] must, during the currency of the order[3], impose the requirement that no qualifying creditor[4] of the debtor[5] is to present a bankruptcy petition[6] against the debtor in respect of a qualifying debt, unless the creditor has the permission of the proper county court[7]. The proper county court may give permission subject to such conditions as it thinks fit[8].

1   See PARA 916 note 1.
2   As to the meaning of 'enforcement restriction order' see PARA 916.
3   References to the currency of an enforcement restriction order are references to the period which begins when the order first has effect and ends when the order ceases to have effect: County Courts Act 1984 s 117T(2) (ss 117A–117X added by the Tribunals, Courts and Enforcement Act 2007 s 107).
4   'Qualifying creditor' means a creditor under a qualifying debt: County Courts Act 1984 s 117T(1) (as added: see note 3). As to the meaning of 'qualifying debt' see PARA 917 note 4.
5   As to the debtor see PARA 917.
6   As to bankruptcy petitions see PARA 129 et seq.
7   County Courts Act 1984 s 117C(1), (2) (as added: see note 3). In relation to an enforcement restriction order, references to the proper county court are references to the county court that made the order (s 117T(3) (as so added)); but that is subject to rules of court as to the venue for, and transfer of, proceedings in county courts (s 117T(4) (as so added)). As from a day to be appointed, s 117T(3), (4) is repealed and all references to 'proper' in Pt 6A (ss 117A–117X) are to be omitted: see the Crime and Courts Act 2013 Sch 9 Pt 2 para 48(1), (3), (9). At the date at which this volume states the law no such day had been appointed.
8   County Courts Act 1984 s 117C(3) (as added: see note 3).

919.   Remedies other than bankruptcy.   As from a day to be appointed, the following provisions have effect[1]. An enforcement restriction order[2] must, during the currency of the order[3], impose the requirement that no qualifying creditor[4] of the debtor[5] is to pursue any remedy for the recovery of a qualifying debt[6] unless regulations[7] provide otherwise, or the creditor has the permission of the proper county court[8]. The proper county court may give permission subject to such conditions as it thinks fit[9].

1   See PARA 916 note 1.
2   As to the meaning of 'enforcement restriction order' see PARA 916.
3   As to the currency of the order see PARA 918 note 3.
4   As to the meaning of 'qualifying creditor' see PARA 918 note 4.
5   As to the debtor see PARA 917.
6   As to the meaning of 'qualifying debt' see PARA 917 note 4.
7   Regulations may specify classes of debt which are exempted, or exempted for specified purposes, from any requirement imposed by the County Courts Act 1984 s 117D(2) (see the text and note 8): s 117D(3) (ss 117A–117X added by the Tribunals, Courts and Enforcement Act 2007 s 107). At the date at which this volume states the law no such regulations had been made.
       It is for the Lord Chancellor to make regulations under the County Courts Act 1984 Pt 6A (ss 117A–117X): s 117X(1) (as so added). Any power to make regulations under Pt 6A is

exercisable by statutory instrument: s 117X(2) (as so added). A statutory instrument containing regulations under Pt 6A is subject to annulment in pursuance of a resolution of either House of Parliament: s 117X(3) (as so added).

8   County Courts Act 1984 s 117D(1), (2) (as added: see note 7). As to the proper county court see PARA 918 note 7. The provisions of s 117D do not have any effect in relation to bankruptcy proceedings: s 117D(4) (as so added). As to bankruptcy proceedings see PARA 129 et seq.

9   County Courts Act 1984 s 117D(3) (as added: see note 7). See note 8.

920. Stopping supplies of gas or electricity. As from a day to be appointed, the following provisions have effect[1]. An enforcement restriction order[2] must, during the currency of the order[3], impose the requirement that no domestic utility creditor[4] is to stop the supply of gas or electricity, or the supply of any associated services, except in the following cases[5]:

(1)   where the reason for stopping a supply relates to the non-payment by the debtor of charges incurred in connection with that supply after the making of the enforcement restriction order[6];

(2)   where the reason for stopping a supply is unconnected with the non-payment by the debtor of any charges incurred in connection with either that supply, or any other supply of mains gas or mains electricity, or of associated services, that is provided by the domestic utility creditor[7];

(3)   where the proper county court[8] gives permission to stop a supply[9].

The proper county court may give permission subject to such conditions as it thinks fit[10].

1   See PARA 916 note 1.
2   As to the meaning of 'enforcement restriction order' see PARA 916.
3   As to the currency of the order see PARA 918 note 3.
4   For this purpose, a domestic utility creditor is any person who: (1) provides the debtor with a supply of mains gas or mains electricity for the debtor's own domestic purposes; and (2) is a creditor under a qualifying debt that relates to the provision of that supply: County Courts Act 1984 s 117E(2) (ss 117A–117X added by the Tribunals, Courts and Enforcement Act 2007 s 107). A supply of mains gas is a supply of the kind mentioned in the Gas Act 1986 s 5(1)(b) (see ENERGY AND CLIMATE CHANGE vol 42 (2011) PARA 251): County Courts Act 1984 s 117E(8) (as so added). A supply of mains electricity is a supply of the kind mentioned in the Electricity Act 1989 s 4(1)(c) (see ENERGY AND CLIMATE CHANGE vol 43 (2011) PARA 524): County Courts Act 1984 s 117E(9) (as so added). As to the meaning of 'qualifying debt' see PARA 917 note 4.
5   County Courts Act 1984 s 117E(1), (3) (as added: see note 4).
6   County Courts Act 1984 s 117E(4) (as added: see note 4). As to the debtor see PARA 917.
7   County Courts Act 1984 s 117E(5) (as added: see note 4).
8   As to the proper county court see PARA 918 note 7.
9   County Courts Act 1984 s 117E(6) (as added: see note 4).
10   County Courts Act 1984 s 117E(7) (as added: see note 4).

921. Repayment requirement. As from a day to be appointed, the following provisions have effect[1]. An enforcement restriction order[2] may impose a repayment requirement on the debtor[3]. A repayment requirement is a requirement that the debtor make payments, in respect of one or more of his qualifying debts[4], to the person or persons to whom he owes the debt or debts[5].

A county court may include a repayment requirement in an order only if: (1) the debtor has surplus income[6] at the time of the inclusion of the requirement; and (2) the inclusion of the requirement would be fair and equitable[7].

The county court may include the requirement in the order at the time it makes the order[8]. The proper county court[9] may, at any time after an enforcement restriction order has been made, vary the order so as to include a repayment requirement[10]. The proper county court may, at any time when an enforcement restriction order includes a repayment requirement, vary the order so as to remove the repayment requirement or include a different repayment requirement[11].

The proper county court may vary an enforcement restriction order of its own motion, on the application of the debtor or on the application of a qualifying creditor[12].

1   See PARA 916 note 1.
2   As to the meaning of 'enforcement restriction order' see PARA 916.
3   County Courts Act 1984 s 117F(1) (ss 117A–117X added by the Tribunals, Courts and Enforcement Act 2007 s 107). As to the debtor see PARA 917.
4   As to the meaning of 'qualifying debt' see PARA 917 note 4.
5   County Courts Act 1984 s 117F(5) (as added: see note 3).
6   The debtor's surplus income is to be calculated in accordance with regulations: County Courts Act 1984 s 117F(7) (as added: see note 3). As to the making of regulations see PARA 919 note 7. Regulations under s 117F(7) must make the following provision: (1) provision about what is surplus income; (2) provision about the period by reference to which the debtor's surplus income is to be calculated: s 117F(8) (as so added). The regulations may, in particular, provide for the debtor's assets to be taken account of for the purpose of calculating his surplus income: s 117F(9) (as so added).
7   County Courts Act 1984 s 117F(6) (as added: see note 3). As from a day to be appointed, the reference in s 117F(6) to 'a county court' is replaced by a reference to 'the county court': see s 112F(6) (amended by the Crime and Courts Act 2013 Sch 9 Pt 2 para 48(1), (2)). At the date at which this volume states the law no such day had been appointed.
8   County Courts Act 1984 s 117F(2) (as added: see note 3).
9   As to the proper county court see PARA 918 note 7.
10 County Courts Act 1984 s 117F(3) (as added: see note 3).
11 County Courts Act 1984 s 117F(4) (as added: see note 3).
12 County Courts Act 1984 s 117F(10) (as added: see note 3). As to the meaning of 'qualifying creditor' see PARA 918 note 4.

(iii) Making of Enforcement Restriction Order

922.   Application for enforcement restriction order.   As from a day to be appointed, the following provisions have effect[1]. A county court may make an enforcement restriction order[2] only on the application of the debtor[3]. The debtor may make an application for an enforcement restriction order whether or not a judgment has been obtained against him in respect of any of his debts[4].

1   See PARA 916 note 1.
2   As to the meaning of 'enforcement restriction order' see PARA 916.
3   County Courts Act 1984 s 117G(1) (ss 117A–117X added by the Tribunals, Courts and Enforcement Act 2007 s 107). As to the debtor see PARA 917. As from a day to be appointed, the reference in s 117G(1) to 'a county court' is replaced by a reference to 'the county court': see s 112G(1) (amended by the Crime and Courts Act 2013 Sch 9 Pt 2 para 48(1), (2)). At the date at which this volume states the law no such day had been appointed.
4   County Courts Act 1984 s 117G(2) (as added: see note 3).

923.   Duration of enforcement restriction order.   As from a day to be appointed, the following provisions have effect[1]. A county court may, at the time it makes an enforcement restriction order[2], specify a day on which the order will cease to have effect[3]. The court may not specify a day which falls after the last day of the maximum permitted period, which is the period of 12 months beginning with the day on which the order is made[4]. If the court specifies a day, the order ceases to have effect on that day[5]. If the court does not specify a day, the order ceases to have effect at the end of the maximum permitted period[6].

1   See PARA 916 note 1.
2   As to the meaning of 'enforcement restriction order' see PARA 916.

3 County Courts Act 1984 s 117H(1) (ss 117A–117X added by the Tribunals, Courts and Enforcement Act 2007 s 107). As from a day to be appointed, the reference in s 117H(1) to 'a county court' is replaced by a reference to 'the county court': see s 112H(1) (amended by the Crime and Courts Act 2013 Sch 9 Pt 2 para 48(1), (2)). At the date at which this volume states the law no such day had been appointed.

The County Courts Act 1984 s 117H is subject to s 117N (variation of duration: see PARA 928) and s 117Q (effect of revocation: see PARA 929): s 117H(6) (as so added). Section 117H is also subject to s 112L (see PARA 899) and the Insolvency Act 1986 s 251F (see PARA 108 note 15) in relation to the effect of an administration order or a debt relief order on an enforcement restriction order: County Courts Act 1984 s 117H(7) (as so added).

4 County Courts Act 1984 s 117H(2), (5) (as added: see note 3).
5 County Courts Act 1984 s 117H(3) (as added: see note 3).
6 County Courts Act 1984 s 117H(4) (as added: see note 3).

(iv) Effects of Enforcement Restriction Order

924. Effect on other debt management arrangements. As from a day to be appointed, the following provisions have effect[1]. If an enforcement restriction order[2] is made and, immediately before the order is made, other debt management arrangements[3] are in force in respect of the debtor[4] then:

(1)   the other debt management arrangements cease to be in force when the enforcement restriction order is made[5];

(2)   if the proper county court[6] is aware of the other debt management arrangements, the court must give the relevant authority[7] notice that the order has been made[8];

(3)   in a case where the proper county court is aware of those arrangements at the time it makes the order, it must give the notice as soon as practicable after making the order[9];

(4)   in a case where the proper county court only becomes aware of those arrangements after it makes the order, it must give the notice as soon as practicable after becoming aware of them[10].

1   See PARA 916 note 1.
2   As to the meaning of 'enforcement restriction order' see PARA 916.
3   'Other debt management arrangements' means any of the following: (1) an administration order under the County Courts Act 1984 Pt 6 (ss 112A–112AI) (see PARA 894 et seq); (2) a debt relief order under the Insolvency Act 1986 Pt 7A (see PARA 101 et seq); (3) a debt repayment plan arranged in accordance with a debt management scheme that is approved under the Tribunals, Courts and Enforcement Act 2007 Pt 5 Ch 4 (ss 109–133) (see PARA 931 et seq): County Courts Act 1984 s 117I(6) (ss 117A–117X added by the Tribunals, Courts and Enforcement Act 2007 s 107).
4   County Courts Act 1984 s 117I(1) (as added: see note 3). As to the debtor see PARA 917. For these purposes, a debt relief order is 'in force' if the moratorium applicable to the order under the Insolvency Act 1986 s 251H (see PARA 109) has not yet ended: County Courts Act 1984 s 117I(8) (as so added).
5   County Courts Act 1984 s 117I(2) (as added: see note 3).
6   As to the proper county court see PARA 918 note 7.
7   'The relevant authority' means: (1) in relation to an administration order, the proper county court (within the meaning of the County Courts Act 1984 Pt 6 (see PARA 896 note 5)); (2) in relation to a debt relief order, the official receiver (see PARA 35 et seq); (3) in relation to a debt repayment plan, the operator of the debt management scheme in accordance with which the plan is arranged: s 117I(7). As from a day to be appointed, the words 'within the meaning of Pt 6' in head (1) are repealed: see s 117I(7) (amended by the Crime and Courts Act 2013 Sch 9 Pt 2 para 48(1), (4)). At the date at which this volume states the law no such day had been appointed.
8   County Courts Act 1984 s 117I(3) (as added: see note 3).
9   County Courts Act 1984 s 117I(4) (as added: see note 3).
10 County Courts Act 1984 s 117I(5) (as added: see note 3).

925. Duty to provide information. As from a day to be appointed, the following provisions have effect[1]. If, and for as long as, an enforcement restriction order[2] has effect in respect of a debtor[3], the debtor must, at the prescribed[4] times, provide the proper county court[5] with particulars of his earnings, income, assets and outgoings[6]. The debtor must provide particulars of those matters both as the matters are at the time the particulars are provided, and as the debtor expects the matters to be at such times in the future as may be prescribed[7]. If the debtor intends to dispose of any of his property he must, within the prescribed period, provide the proper county court with particulars of the following matters: (1) the property he intends to dispose of; (2) the consideration, if any, he expects will be given for the disposal; (3) such other matters as may be prescribed; and (4) such other matters as the court may specify[8]. The duty to provide the proper county court with particulars of a proposed disposal of property applies whether the debtor is the sole owner, or one of several owners, of the property[9].

A person commits an offence if he fails to comply with the requirements[10] to provide information[11].

1 See PARA 916 note 1.
2 As to the meaning of 'enforcement restriction order' see PARA 916.
3 County Courts Act 1984 s 117J(1) (ss 117A–117X added by the Tribunals, Courts and Enforcement Act 2007 s 107). As to the debtor see PARA 917.
4 In any provision of the County Courts Act 1984 s 117J, 'prescribed' means prescribed in regulations for the purposes of that provision: s 117J(7) (as added: see note 3). At the date at which this volume states the law no such regulations had been made. As to the making of regulations see PARA 919 note 7.
5 As to the proper county court see PARA 918 note 7.
6 County Courts Act 1984 s 117J(2) (as added: see note 3).
7 County Courts Act 1984 s 117J(3) (as added: see note 3).
8 County Courts Act 1984 s 117J(4) (as added: see note 3). This requirement does not apply if the disposal is of: (1) goods that are exempt goods for the purposes of the Tribunals, Courts and Enforcement Act 2007 Sch 12 (see CIVIL PROCEDURE vol 12 (2009) PARA 1389); (2) goods that are protected under any other enactment from being taken control of under Sch 12; or (3) prescribed property: County Courts Act 1984 s 117J(5) (as so added).
9 County Courts Act 1984 s 117J(6) (as added: see note 3).
10 Ie the requirements under the County Courts Act 1984 s 117J(2), (3) or (4): see the text and notes 4–8.
11 County Courts Act 1984 s 117K(1) (as added: see note 3). A person who commits such an offence may be ordered by a judge of the proper county court to pay a fine of not more than £250 or to be imprisoned for not more than 14 days: s 117K(2) (as so added). Where a person is ordered to be imprisoned by a judge of the proper county court, the judge may at any time revoke the order and, if the person is already in custody, order his discharge: s 117K(3) (as so added). As from a day to be appointed, the words 'the judge' are substituted with the words 'a judge of the county court': see s 117K(3) (amended by the Crime and Courts Act 2013 Sch 9 Pt 2 para 48(1), (5)). At the date at which this volume states the law no such day had been appointed.
   The provisions of the County Courts Act 1984 s 129 (enforcement of fines: see CIVIL PROCEDURE vol 12 (2009) PARA 1513) apply to payment of a fine imposed under s 117K(2): s 117K(4) (as so added). For the purposes of the Administration of Justice Act 1960 s 13 (appeal in cases of contempt of court: see CONTEMPT OF COURT vol 22 (2012) PARA 118), the County Courts Act 1984 s 117K(2) is to be treated as an enactment enabling a county court to deal with an offence under s 117K(1) as if it were a contempt of court: s 117K(5) (as so added). A district judge or deputy district judge has the same powers under s 117K as a judge of a county court: s 117K(6) (as so added). As from a day to be appointed, s 117K(6) is repealed, and the words 'a county court' in s 117K(5) are substituted with the words 'the county court': see s 117K(5), (6) (amended by the Crime and Courts Act 2013 Sch 9 Pt 2 para 48(1), (6), (7)). At the date at which this volume states the law no such day had been appointed.

926.   Existing county court proceedings to be stayed.   As from a day to be appointed, the following provisions have effect[1]. If : (1) an enforcement restriction order[2] is made; (2) proceedings in a county court, other than bankruptcy proceedings[3], are pending against the debtor[4] in respect of a qualifying debt[5]; (3) by virtue of a requirement included in the order[6] the creditor under the qualifying debt is not entitled to continue the proceedings in respect of the debt; and (4) the county court receives notice of the enforcement restriction order[7], then the county court must stay the proceedings[8].

The county court may allow costs already incurred by the creditor and, if the court allows such costs, may on application or of its own motion add them to the debt owed to the creditor[9].

1   See PARA 916 note 1.
2   As to the meaning of 'enforcement restriction order' see PARA 916.
3   As to bankruptcy proceedings see PARA 129 et seq.
4   As to the debtor see PARA 917.
5   As to the meaning of 'qualifying debt' see PARA 917 note 4.
6   Ie by virtue of the County Courts Act 1984 s 117D: see PARA 919.
7   County Courts Act 1984 s 117L(1) (ss 117A–117X added by the Tribunals, Courts and Enforcement Act 2007 s 107). As from a day to be appointed, the words 'a county court' in head (2) in the text are substituted with the words 'the county court': see s 117L(1) (amended by the Crime and Courts Act 2013 Sch 9 Pt 2 para 48(1), (6)). At the date at which this volume states the law no such day had been appointed.
8   County Courts Act 1984 s 117L(2) (as added: see note 7).
9   County Courts Act 1984 s 117L(3) (as added: see note 7).

927.   Charges.   As from a day to be appointed, the following provisions have effect[1]. During, and after, the currency[2] of an enforcement restriction order[3], a qualifying creditor[4] may not make any charge in respect of a protected qualifying debt[5], unless the charge is interest, or is not interest but relates to a time before or after the currency of the order[6]. A charge made in breach of these restrictions is not recoverable[7].

1   See PARA 916 note 1.
2   As to the currency of the order see PARA 918 note 3.
3   County Courts Act 1984 s 117M(1) (ss 117A–117X added by the Tribunals, Courts and Enforcement Act 2007 s 107). As to the meaning of 'enforcement restriction order' see PARA 916.
4   As to the meaning of 'qualifying creditor' see PARA 918 note 4.
5   'Protected qualifying debt' means any qualifying debt under which the debtor was a debtor at some time during the currency of the enforcement restriction order: County Courts Act 1984 s 117M(4) (as added: see note 3). As to the meaning of 'qualifying debt' see PARA 917 note 4. As to the debtor see PARA 917.
6   County Courts Act 1984 s 117M(2) (as added: see note 3).
7   County Courts Act 1984 s 117M(3) (as added: see note 3).

(v)   Variation of Duration; Revocation; Notification

928.   Variation of duration.   As from a day to be appointed, the following provisions have effect[1]. The proper county court[2] may vary an enforcement restriction order[3] so as to specify a day or, if a day has already been specified[4], a different day, on which the order will cease to have effect[5]. The new termination day must fall on or before the last day of the maximum permitted period, which is the period of 12 months beginning with the day on which the order was originally made[6]. If the proper county court varies an enforcement restriction order, the order ceases to have effect on the new termination day[7].

The power to vary the duration is exercisable on the application of the debtor[8], on the application of a qualifying creditor[9] or of the court's own motion[10].

1   See PARA 916 note 1.
2   As to the proper county court see PARA 918 note 7.
3   As to the meaning of 'enforcement restriction order' see PARA 916.
4   Ie under the County Courts Act 1984 s 117H (see PARA 923) or s 117N.
5   County Courts Act 1984 s 117N(1) (ss 117A–117X added by the Tribunals, Courts and Enforcement Act 2007 s 107). The County Courts Act 1984 s 117N is subject to s 117Q (effect of revocation: see PARA 929): s 117N(6) (as so added).
6   County Courts Act 1984 s 117N(2), (5)(b) (as added: see note 5).
7   County Courts Act 1984 s 117N(3) (as added: see note 5). 'New termination day' means the day on which the order will cease to have effect in accordance with the variation under s 117N(1): s 117N(5)(b) (as so added).
8   As to the debtor see PARA 917.
9   As to the meaning of 'qualifying creditor' see PARA 918 note 4.
10   County Courts Act 1984 s 117N(4) (as added: see note 5).

929.   Revocation of order. As from a day to be appointed, the following provisions have effect[1]. The proper county court[2] must revoke an enforcement restriction order[3]:

(1)   where it becomes apparent that, at the time the order was made, the debtor[4] in fact did not have two or more qualifying debts[5];

(2)   where the debtor is no longer a debtor under any qualifying debts[6];

(3)   where it becomes apparent that, at the time the order was made, the debtor in fact had business debt[7], and he is still a debtor under the business debt, or any of the business debts, in question[8];

(4)   where the debtor subsequently becomes a debtor under a business debt, and he is still a debtor under that debt[9];

(5)   where it becomes apparent that, at the time the order was made, the debtor was in fact excluded under an ERO exclusion, a voluntary arrangement exclusion or a bankruptcy exclusion[10];

(6)   where the debtor becomes excluded under the voluntary arrangement exclusion[11];

(7)   where a bankruptcy order is made against the debtor, and is still in force[12];

(8)   where it becomes apparent that, at the time the order was made, the debtor was in fact able to pay his qualifying debts[13];

(9)   where the debtor is now able to pay all of his qualifying debts[14];

(10)   where it becomes apparent that, at the time the order was made, the debtor was in fact not suffering from a sudden and unforeseen deterioration in his financial circumstances[15];

(11)   where the debtor is no longer suffering from the deterioration in financial circumstances which was taken into account when the order was made[16], even if he is suffering from some other sudden and unforeseen deterioration in his financial circumstances[17];

(12)   where it becomes apparent that, at the time the order was made, there was in fact no realistic prospect of improvement in debtor's financial circumstances[18];

(13)   where there is no longer a realistic prospect that the debtor's financial circumstances will improve during the period within which the order would continue to have effect, if not revoked[19];

(14)   where it becomes apparent that, at the time the order was made, it was not in fact fair and equitable to make the order[20];

(15)   where it is not fair and equitable for the order to continue to have effect[21].

The proper county court may revoke an enforcement restriction order in any case where there is no duty[22] to revoke it[23]. The power of revocation may, in particular, be exercised in any of the following cases: (a) where the order includes, or has previously included, a repayment requirement[24], and the debtor has failed to comply with that requirement; and (b) where the debtor has failed to provide the proper county court with the required[25] information[26]. The power of revocation is exercisable on the application of the debtor or a qualifying creditor[27] or of the court's own motion[28].

If, under any duty or power[29], the proper county court revokes an enforcement restriction order, the order ceases to have effect in accordance with the terms of the revocation[30].

1   See PARA 916 note 1.
2   As to the proper county court see PARA 918 note 7.
3   As to the meaning of 'enforcement restriction order' see PARA 916.
4   As to the debtor see PARA 917.
5   County Courts Act 1984 s 117O(1)(a) (ss 117A–117X added by the Tribunals, Courts and Enforcement Act 2007 s 107). This provision applies where the condition in the County Courts Act 1984 s 117B(2) is not met: see PARA 917. As to the meaning of 'qualifying debt' see PARA 917 note 4.
6   County Courts Act 1984 s 117O(1)(b) (as added: see note 5).
7   Ie the condition in the County Courts Act 1984 s 117B(3) was not met: see PARA 917. As to business debts see PARA 917 note 4.
8   County Courts Act 1984 s 117O(2)(a) (as added: see note 5).
9   County Courts Act 1984 s 117O(2)(b) (as added: see note 5).
10 County Courts Act 1984 s 117O(3) (as added: see note 5). This provision applies where the condition in s 117B(4) is not met: see PARA 917. As to the exclusions see PARA 917 notes 6–8.
11 County Courts Act 1984 s 117O(4)(a) (as added: see note 5).
12 County Courts Act 1984 s 117O(4)(b) (as added: see note 5).
13 County Courts Act 1984 s 117O(5)(a) (as added: see note 5). This provision applies where the condition in s 117B(5) is not met: see PARA 917.
14 County Courts Act 1984 s 117O(5)(b) (as added: see note 5).
15 County Courts Act 1984 s 117O(6)(a) (as added: see note 5). This provision applies where the condition in s 117B(6) is not met: see PARA 917.
16 Ie for the purposes of the County Courts Act 1984 s 117B(6): see PARA 917.
17 County Courts Act 1984 s 117O(6)(b) (as added: see note 5).
18 County Courts Act 1984 s 117O(7)(a) (as added: see note 5). This provision applies where the condition in s 117B(7) is not met: see PARA 917.
19 County Courts Act 1984 s 117O(7)(b) (as added: see note 5).
20 County Courts Act 1984 s 117O(8)(a) (as added: see note 5). This provision applies where the condition in s 117B(8) is not met: see PARA 917.
21 County Courts Act 1984 s 117O(8)(b) (as added: see note 5).
22 Ie under the County Courts Act 1984 Pt 6A (ss 117A–117X).
23 County Courts Act 1984 s 117P(1) (as added: see note 5).
24 As to the repayment requirement see PARA 921.
25 Ie the information required by the County Courts Act 1984 s 117J(2), (3) or (4): see PARA 925.
26 County Courts Act 1984 s 117P(2) (as added: see note 5).
27 As to the meaning of 'qualifying creditor' see PARA 918 note 4.
28 County Courts Act 1984 s 117P(3) (as added: see note 5).
29 Ie under the County Courts Act 1984 Pt 6A.
30 County Courts Act 1984 s 117Q(1), (2) (as added: see note 5).

930. Requirement to give notice. As from a day to be appointed, the following provisions have effect[1]. If a notifiable event occurs in relation to an enforcement restriction order[2], the proper county court[3] must give notice of the event to every identified qualifying creditor[4] of the debtor[5]. There is a notifiable event in any of the following cases:

(1)   when the enforcement restriction order is made[6];

(2)   when the enforcement restriction order is varied[7];

(3)   when the enforcement restriction order is revoked[8];

(4)   when the proper county court is given notice[9] as to the effect of an enforcement restriction order or a debt relief order on the administration order[10].

1   See PARA 916 note 1.

2   As to the meaning of 'enforcement restriction order' see PARA 916.

3   As to the proper county court see PARA 918 note 7.

4   A person is an identified qualifying creditor of the debtor if: (1) the debtor has notified the proper county court, or another court whilst it was previously the proper county court, that the person is a qualifying creditor; or (2) the proper county court is satisfied that the person is a qualifying creditor: County Courts Act 1984 s 117R(3) (ss 117A–117X added by the Tribunals, Courts and Enforcement Act 2007 s 107). As to the meaning of 'qualifying creditor' see PARA 918 note 4. As from a day to be appointed, the words 'or another court whilst it was previously the proper court' in head (1) are repealed: see the County Courts Act 1984 s 117R(3) (amended by the Crime and Courts Act 2013 Sch 9 Pt 2 para 48(1), (8)). At the date at which this volume states the law no such day had been appointed.

5   County Courts Act 1984 s 117R(1) (as added: see note 4). As to the debtor see PARA 917.

6   See PARA 917.

7   See PARA 928.

8   See PARA 929.

9   Ie under the County Courts Act 1984 s 112L (see PARA 899) or the Insolvency Act 1986 s 251F (see PARA 108 note 15): see the County Courts Act 1984 s 117H(7): and PARA 923 note 3.

10   County Courts Act 1984 s 117R(2) (as added: see note 4).

(4) DEBT MANAGEMENT SCHEMES

(i) In general

931.   Debt management schemes.   One option for a person falling into debt is to enter into a debt management arrangement with creditors under which it is agreed that the debtor is to pay reduced monthly payments without incurring extra charges or fees. Such an arrangement is intended to allow the debtor time to become financially stable and eventually be in a position to pay off the debts in full. At present, such arrangements are non-statutory, although providers of debt management advice are required to be licensed under the Consumer Credit Act 1974[1]. The Tribunals, Courts and Enforcement Act 2007 introduced a statutory debt management scheme but this has not yet been brought into effect[2].

Under the 2007 Act, a debt management scheme is a scheme that meets the following conditions[3]:

(1)   the scheme must be open to some or all non-business debtors[4];

(2)   the scheme must provide that, if such a request is made, a decision must be made about whether a debt repayment plan is to be arranged for the non-business debtor, and such a plan must be arranged, if that is the decision made[5];

(3)   the scheme must be operated by a body of persons, whether a body corporate or not[6].

A debt repayment plan is a plan that specifies all of the debtor's qualifying debts[7] and requires the debtor to make payments in respect of each of the specified debts[8]. It does not matter if the plan requires payments of different amounts to be made in respect of a specified debt at different times, or if the payments that the plan requires to be made in respect of a specified debt would, if all made, repay the debt only in part[9].

1 See the Consumer Credit Act 1974 s 145; and CONSUMER CREDIT vol 21 (2011) PARA 292.
2 See the Tribunals, Courts and Enforcement Act 2007 Pt 5 Ch 4 (ss 109–133) (not yet in force).
3 Tribunals, Courts and Enforcement Act 2007 ss 109(1), 131(1).
4 Tribunals, Courts and Enforcement Act 2007 s 109(2). 'Non-business debtor' means any individual who: (1) is a debtor under one or more qualifying debts; but (2) is not a debtor under any business debts: s 131(1). A scheme is open to a non-business debtor if it allows him to make a request to the scheme operator for a debt repayment plan to be arranged for him: s 109(3). 'Scheme operator' means the body that operates a debt management scheme: s 131(1).
5 Tribunals, Courts and Enforcement Act 2007 s 109(4).
6 Tribunals, Courts and Enforcement Act 2007 s 109(5). As to bodies corporate see CORPORATIONS vol 24 (2010) PARA 301 et seq.
7 All debts are qualifying debts, except the following: (1) any debt secured against an asset; (2) in relation to a debt repayment plan which has been requested or arranged, any debt which could not, by virtue of the terms of the debt management scheme, be specified in the plan: Tribunals, Courts and Enforcement Act 2007 s 132(1). A business debt is any debt, whether or not a qualifying debt, which is incurred by a person in the course of a business: s 132(2).
8 Tribunals, Courts and Enforcement Act 2007 ss 110(1)–(3), 131(1).
9 Tribunals, Courts and Enforcement Act 2007 s 110(4).

(ii) Approval of Debt Management Schemes

932. Approval by supervising authority. As from a day to be appointed, the following provisions have effect[1]. The supervising authority[2] may approve one or more debt management schemes[3].

Regulations may make provision about any or all of the following:

(1) conditions that must be met before the supervising authority may approve a debt management scheme;

(2) considerations that the supervising authority must, or must not, take into account in deciding whether to approve a debt management scheme[4].

Regulations may, in particular, make provision about conditions or considerations that relate to any of the following matters[5]:

(a) the scheme operator[6];
(b) the terms of a debt management scheme[7];
(c) the operation of a debt management scheme[8];
(d) changes that affect the scheme operator[9];
(e) changes to the terms of a debt management scheme or the operation of a debt management scheme[10];
(f) the transfer of the operation of a debt management scheme to another body[11].

The supervising authority may approve a debt management scheme whether a body is operating the scheme at the time of the approval, or is proposing to operate the scheme from a time in the future[12].

1 See PARA 931.
2 The supervising authority is: (1) the Lord Chancellor; or (2) any person that the Lord Chancellor has authorised to approve debt management schemes under the Tribunals, Courts and Enforcement Act 2007 s 111: ss 129(1), 131(1). In any case where an authorisation under head (2) starts or ends, the start or end of the authorisation does not affect the validity of an approval that is in force at the relevant time: s 129(2), (3). The new supervising authority may exercise all of its functions in relation to an approval that is in force at the relevant time as though it had given the approval itself: s 129(2), (4). 'Approval' means an approval of a debt management scheme given under s 111; and 'relevant time' means the time when an

authorisation starts or ends: s 129(5). As to the Lord Chancellor see CONSTITUTIONAL LAW AND HUMAN RIGHTS vol 8(2) (Reissue) PARA 477 et seq.

3   Tribunals, Courts and Enforcement Act 2007 s 111(1). As to the meaning of 'debt management scheme' see PARA 931. 'Approved scheme' means a debt management scheme that is approved under s 111: s 131(1).

4   Tribunals, Courts and Enforcement Act 2007 s 111(2). At the date at which this volume states the law no regulations had been made under s 111.

The power to make regulations under Pt 5 Ch 4 (ss 109–133) is given to the Lord Chancellor: see s 130(1), (9). The power to make regulations is exercisable by statutory instrument: s 130(2). A statutory instrument containing regulations is subject to annulment in pursuance of a resolution of either House of Parliament: s 130(3). However, this does not apply in the case of a statutory instrument that contains any of the following: (1) the first regulations under a particular provision of Pt 5 Ch 4; (2) any regulations under s 118(6) (stopping supplies of gas or electricity: see PARA 939); (3) any regulations under s 120 that amend the Courts Act 2003 s 98 (see PARA 941); (4) any regulations that amend s 122 or s 123 (appeals: see PARAS 943, 944): s 130(4). In such a case the statutory instrument may not be made unless a draft of the instrument has been laid before, and approved by a resolution of, each House of Parliament: s 130(5). Regulations may make different provision in relation to different cases: s 130(6). Regulations may make supplementary, incidental or consequential provision or transitory, transitional or saving provision if the Lord Chancellor thinks it is necessary or expedient: s 130(7). Provision under s 130(7) may, in particular, amend s 122 or s 123 (see PARAS 943, 944), including by making provision for further grounds of appeal: s 130(8).

5   Tribunals, Courts and Enforcement Act 2007 s 111(3).

6   Provision may be made in relation to the following aspects: (1) the constitution of the scheme operator; (2) the governance of the scheme operator; (3) the size of the scheme operator's undertaking; (4) the financial standing of the scheme operator; and (5) whether or not a scheme operator is a profit-making organisation: Tribunals, Courts and Enforcement Act 2007 Sch 21 paras 1, 2 table item 1. As to the meaning of 'scheme operator' see PARA 931 note 4.

7   Provision may be made in relation to the following aspects: (1) the non-business debtors to whom the scheme is open; (2) the kinds of debts which may be specified in a plan arranged in accordance with the scheme: Tribunals, Courts and Enforcement Act 2007 Sch 21 paras 1, 2 table item 2.

8   Provision may be made in relation to the following aspects: (1) how decisions are made about whether debt repayment plans are to be arranged; (2) how debt repayment plans are arranged; (3) how decisions are made about the terms of debt repayment plans, including decisions about what payments will be required in relation to the specified debts, the amounts, times and recipients of payments and the duration of the plan; (4) the format of debt repayment plans; (5) when debt repayment plans begin to have effect; (6) how changes are to be made to debt repayment plans, including the specification of debts after a plan has been arranged; (7) how decisions are made about whether debt repayment plans are to be terminated and (8) how debt repayment plans are terminated: Tribunals, Courts and Enforcement Act 2007 Sch 21 paras 1, 2 table item 3. As to the meaning of 'debt repayment plan' see PARA 931.

9   Tribunals, Courts and Enforcement Act 2007 Sch 21 paras 1, 2 table item 4.

10   Provision may be made in relation to the following aspects: (1) whether changes may be made; (2) how changes are made: Tribunals, Courts and Enforcement Act 2007 Sch 21 paras 1, 2 table item 5.

11   Provision may be made in relation to the following aspects: (1) whether the operation of the scheme may be transferred; (2) how the operation of the scheme is transferred: Tribunals, Courts and Enforcement Act 2007 Sch 21 paras 1, 2 table item 6.

12   Tribunals, Courts and Enforcement Act 2007 s 111(4).

933. Applications for approval. As from a day to be appointed, the following provisions have effect[1]. Regulations may specify a procedure for making an application for approval of a debt management scheme[2]. Such regulations may, in particular, specify a procedure that requires any or all of the following: (1) an application to be made in a particular form; (2) information to be supplied in support of an application; (3) a fee to be paid in respect of an application[3].

1   See PARA 931.

2   Tribunals, Courts and Enforcement Act 2007 s 112(1). At the date at which this volume states the law no such regulations had been made. As to the making of regulations see PARA 932 note 4. As to the meaning of 'debt management scheme' see PARA 931.

3   Tribunals, Courts and Enforcement Act 2007 s 112(2).

934. Terms of approval. As from a day to be appointed, the following provisions have effect[1]. The approval of a debt management scheme[2] has effect subject to any relevant terms[3], which are the terms, if any, specified in regulations that relate to the approval, and the terms, if any, that the supervising authority[4] includes in the approval[5]. Relevant terms may, in particular, deal with all or any of the following: (1) the start of the approval; (2) the expiry of the approval; (3) the termination of the approval, including termination because of the breach of some other term[6]. Relevant terms may, in particular, impose requirements on the scheme operator[7] or may relate to any of the following matters[8]:

  (a)   the scheme operator[9];

  (b)   the terms of a debt management scheme[10];

  (c)   the operation of a debt management scheme[11];

  (d)   changes that affect the scheme operator[12];

  (e)   changes to the terms of a debt management scheme or the operation of a debt management scheme[13];

  (f)   the transfer of the operation of a debt management scheme to another body[14].

Regulations may also make provision about terms that the supervising authority must, or must not, include in an approval[15].

1   See PARA 931.

2   As to the meaning of 'debt management scheme' see PARA 931.

3   Tribunals, Courts and Enforcement Act 2007 s 113(1).

4   As to the meaning of 'supervising authority' see PARA 932 note 2.

5   Tribunals, Courts and Enforcement Act 2007 s 113(2). At the date at which this volume states the law no such regulations had been made. As to the making of regulations see PARA 932 note 4.

6   Tribunals, Courts and Enforcement Act 2007 s 113(3). As to termination see PARAS 946, 947.

7   Tribunals, Courts and Enforcement Act 2007 s 113(4). As to the meaning of 'scheme operator' see PARA 931 note 4.

8   Tribunals, Courts and Enforcement Act 2007 s 113(5). The matters are those mentioned in Sch 21: see PARA 932 heads (a)–(f).

9   See the Tribunals, Courts and Enforcement Act 2007 Sch 21 paras 1, 2 table item 1; and PARA 932 note 6.

10 See the Tribunals, Courts and Enforcement Act 2007 Sch 21 paras 1, 2 table item 2; and PARA 932 note 7.

11 See the Tribunals, Courts and Enforcement Act 2007 Sch 21 paras 1, 2 table item 3; and PARA 932 note 8.

12 See the Tribunals, Courts and Enforcement Act 2007 Sch 21 paras 1, 2 table item 4; and PARA 932 note 9.

13 See the Tribunals, Courts and Enforcement Act 2007 Sch 21 paras 1, 2 table item 5; and PARA 932 note 10.

14 See the Tribunals, Courts and Enforcement Act 2007 Sch 21 paras 1, 2 table item 6; and PARA 932 note 11.

15 Tribunals, Courts and Enforcement Act 2007 s 113(6).

(iii) Effect of Plans

935. Discharge from specified debts. As from a day to be appointed, the following provisions have effect[1]. If a debt repayment plan[2] is arranged for a non-business debtor[3] in accordance with an approved scheme[4], and the plan comes into effect, then the debtor is discharged from the debts that are specified in the plan[5]. The discharge from a particular specified debt[6] takes effect at the time when all the required payments[7] have been made[8].

1   See PARA 931.
2   As to the meaning of 'debt repayment plan' see PARA 931.
3   As to the meaning of 'non-business debtor' see PARA 931 note 4.
4   As to the meaning of 'approved scheme' see PARA 932 note 3.
5   Tribunals, Courts and Enforcement Act 2007 s 114(1), (2).
6   'Specified debt' means a debt specified in a debt repayment plan: Tribunals, Courts and Enforcement Act 2007 s 131(1).
7   The required payments are the payments in respect of the debt that are required by the provision included in the plan in accordance with the Tribunals, Courts and Enforcement Act 2007 s 110(3) (see PARA 931): s 114(4).
8   Tribunals, Courts and Enforcement Act 2007 s 114(3).

936. Presentation of bankruptcy petition. As from a day to be appointed, the following provisions have effect[1]. During the currency of a debt repayment plan[2] arranged in accordance with an approved scheme[3], no qualifying creditor[4] of the debtor is to present a bankruptcy petition[5] against the debtor in respect of a qualifying debt, unless regulations provide otherwise[6], or the creditor has the permission of a county court[7]. A county court may give permission subject to such conditions as it thinks fit[8].

1   See PARA 931.
2   The reference to the currency of a debt repayment plan is a reference to the period which begins when the plan first has effect, and ends when the plan ceases to have effect: Tribunals, Courts and Enforcement Act 2007 s 115(4). As to the meaning of 'debt repayment plan' see PARA 931.
3   Tribunals, Courts and Enforcement Act 2007 s 115(1). As to the meaning of 'approved scheme' see PARA 932 note 3.
4   'Qualifying creditor' means a creditor under a qualifying debt: Tribunals, Courts and Enforcement Act 2007 s 131(1). As to the meaning of 'qualifying debt' see PARA 931 note 7.
5   As to bankruptcy petitions see PARA 129 et seq.
6   At the date at which this volume states the law no such regulations had been made. As to the making of regulations see PARA 932 note 4.
7   Tribunals, Courts and Enforcement Act 2007 s 115(2). Any reference to a county court is subject to rules of court as to the venue for, and transfer of, proceedings in county courts: s 131(2). As to transfer of proceedings see CIVIL PROCEDURE vol 11 (2009) PARA 66 et seq. As from a day to be appointed, s 131(2) is repealed, and the words 'a county court' in s 115(2), (3) are substituted with the words 'the county court': see the Crime and Courts Act 2013 Sch 9 Pt 3 paras 52, 136(b). At the date at which this volume states the law no such day had been appointed.
8   Tribunals, Courts and Enforcement Act 2007 s 115(3).

937. Remedies other than bankruptcy. As from a day to be appointed, the following provisions have effect[1].

A period of protection[2], in relation to a non-business debtor[3], begins if, and when, the debtor makes a request to the operator of an approved scheme[4] for a debt repayment plan[5] to be arranged in accordance with the scheme[6]. The period ends as follows: (1) if a debt repayment plan is not arranged in consequence of the request: when the decision is made not to arrange the plan; (2) if a debt repayment plan is arranged in consequence of the request: when that plan ceases to have effect[7]. However, if other debt management arrangements[8] are in force in relation to the debtor immediately before he makes the request, the period does not begin unless, and until, a debt repayment plan is arranged in consequence of the request, and comes into effect[9].

In relation to a non-business debtor during a period of protection, no qualifying creditor[10] of the debtor is to pursue any remedy for the recovery of a qualifying debt[11], unless regulations provide otherwise[12], or the creditor has the permission of a county court[13]. A county court may give such permission subject to such conditions as it thinks fit[14].

1   See PARA 931.
2   A 'period of protection' is a period which begins and ends as specified in the Tribunals, Courts and Enforcement Act 2007 s 133: s 133(1).
3   As to the meaning of 'non-business debtor' see PARA 931 note 4.
4   As to the meaning of 'approved scheme' see PARA 932 note 3.
5   As to the meaning of 'debt repayment plan' see PARA 931.
6   Tribunals, Courts and Enforcement Act 2007 s 133(2).
7   Tribunals, Courts and Enforcement Act 2007 s 133(3).
8   For this purpose, the reference to other debt management arrangements which are in force has the same meaning as such references in the Tribunals, Courts and Enforcement Act 2007 s 121 (see PARA 942): s 133(5).
9   Tribunals, Courts and Enforcement Act 2007 s 133(4). Such arrangements come into effect in accordance with s 121(2): see PARA 942.
10 As to the meaning of 'qualifying creditor' see PARA 936 note 4.
11 As to the meaning of 'qualifying debt' see PARA 931 note 7.
12 At the date at which this volume states the law no such regulations had been made. As to the making of regulations see PARA 932 note 4.
13 Tribunals, Courts and Enforcement Act 2007 s 116(1), (2). The provisions of s 116 do not have any effect in relation to bankruptcy proceedings: s 116(4). As from a day to be appointed, the references in s 116(2), (3) to 'a county court' are replaced by references to 'the county court': see s 116(2), (3) (amended by the Crime and Courts Act 2013 Sch 9 Pt 3 para 52). At the date at which this volume states the law no such day had been appointed.
14 Tribunals, Courts and Enforcement Act 2007 s 116(3). See note 13.

938.   Charging of interest. As from a day to be appointed, the following provisions have effect[1]. In relation to a non-business debtor[2] during a period of protection[3], no qualifying creditor[4] is to charge any sum by way of interest, fee or other charge in respect of a qualifying debt[5], unless regulations provide otherwise[6], or the creditor has the permission of a county court[7]. A county court may give such permission subject to such conditions as it thinks fit[8].

1   See PARA 931.
2   As to the meaning of 'non-business debtor' see PARA 931 note 4.
3   As to the meaning of 'period of protection' see PARA 937 note 2.
4   As to the meaning of 'qualifying creditor' see PARA 936 note 4.
5   As to the meaning of 'qualifying debt' see PARA 931 note 7.
6   At the date at which this volume states the law no such regulations had been made. As to the making of regulations see PARA 932 note 4.
7   Tribunals, Courts and Enforcement Act 2007 s 117(1), (2). As from a day to be appointed, the references in s 117(2), (3) to 'a county court' are replaced by references to 'the county court': see s 117(2), (3) (amended by the Crime and Courts Act 2013 Sch 9 Pt 3 para 52). At the date at which this volume states the law no such day had been appointed.
8   Tribunals, Courts and Enforcement Act 2007 s 117(3). See note 7.

939.   Stopping supplies of gas or electricity. As from a day to be appointed, the following provisions have effect[1]. In relation to a non-business debtor[2] during a period of protection[3], no domestic utility creditor[4] is to stop the supply of gas or electricity, or the supply of any associated services, except in the following cases[5]:

(1)   where the reason for stopping a supply relates to the non-payment by the debtor of charges incurred in connection with that supply after the start of the period of protection[6];

(2)   where the reason for stopping a supply is unconnected with the non-payment by the debtor of any charges incurred in connection with

that supply, or any other supply of mains gas or mains electricity, or of associated services, that is provided by the domestic utility creditor[7];
 (3)   where regulations allow the supply to be stopped[8];
 (4)   where a county court gives permission to stop a supply[9].
A county court may give permission subject to such conditions as it thinks fit[10].

1   See PARA 931.
2   As to the meaning of 'non-business debtor' see PARA 931 note 4.
3   As to the meaning of 'period of protection' see PARA 937 note 2.
4   In relation to the debtor, a domestic utility creditor is any person who: (1) provides the debtor with a supply of mains gas or mains electricity for the debtor's own domestic purposes; and (2) is a creditor under a qualifying debt that relates to the provision of that supply: Tribunals, Courts and Enforcement Act 2007 s 118(2). A supply of mains gas is a supply of the kind mentioned in the Gas Act 1986 s 5(1)(b) (see ENERGY AND CLIMATE CHANGE vol 42 (2011) PARA 251); and a supply of mains electricity is a supply of the kind mentioned in the Electricity Act 1989 s 4(1)(c) (see ENERGY AND CLIMATE CHANGE vol 43 (2011) PARA 524): Tribunals, Courts and Enforcement Act 2007 s 118(9), (10).
5   Tribunals, Courts and Enforcement Act 2007 s 118(1), (3).
6   Tribunals, Courts and Enforcement Act 2007 s 118(4).
7   Tribunals, Courts and Enforcement Act 2007 s 118(5).
8   Tribunals, Courts and Enforcement Act 2007 s 118(6). At the date at which this volume states the law no such regulations had been made. As to the making of regulations see PARA 932 note 4.
9   Tribunals, Courts and Enforcement Act 2007 s 118(7). As from a day to be appointed, the references in s 118(7), (8) to 'a county court' are replaced by references to 'the county court': see s 118(7), (8) (amended by the Crime and Courts Act 2013 Sch 9 Pt 3 para 52). At the date at which this volume states the law no such day had been appointed.
10 Tribunals, Courts and Enforcement Act 2007 s 118(8). See note 9.

940. Existing county court proceedings to be stayed. As from a day to be appointed, the following provisions have effect[1]. If (1) a debt repayment plan[2] is arranged for a non-business debtor[3] in accordance with an approved scheme[4]; (2) proceedings in a county court, other than bankruptcy proceedings[5], are pending against the debtor in respect of a qualifying debt[6]; (3) the creditor under the qualifying debt is not entitled to continue the proceedings[7] in respect of the debt; and (4) the county court receives notice of the debt repayment plan[8], the county court must stay the proceedings[9].

The court may allow costs already incurred by the creditor[10]. If the court allows such costs, and the qualifying debt is a specified debt[11], the operator of the approved scheme may, if requested to do so by the non-business debtor or the creditor under the qualifying debt, add the costs to the amount specified in the plan in respect of the debt[12]. However, the operator may not add the costs if, under the terms of the approved scheme, the operator is under a duty to terminate the plan[13].

1   See PARA 931.
2   As to the meaning of 'debt repayment plan' see PARA 931.
3   As to the meaning of 'non-business debtor' see PARA 931 note 4.
4   As to the meaning of 'approved scheme' see PARA 932 note 3.
5   As to bankruptcy proceedings see PARA 129 et seq.
6   As to the meaning of 'qualifying debt' see PARA 931 note 7.
7   Ie by virtue of the Tribunals, Courts and Enforcement Act 2007 s 116: see PARA 937.
8   Tribunals, Courts and Enforcement Act 2007 s 119(1). As from a day to be appointed, the reference in s 119(1)(b) (see head (2) in the text) to 'a county court' is replaced by a reference to 'the county court': see s 119(1)(b) (amended by the Crime and Courts Act 2013 Sch 9 Pt 3 para 52). At the date at which this volume states the law no such day had been appointed.
9   Tribunals, Courts and Enforcement Act 2007 s 119(2).
10 Tribunals, Courts and Enforcement Act 2007 s 119(3).

11 Tribunals, Courts and Enforcement Act 2007 s 119(4). As to the meaning of 'specified debt' see PARA 935 note 6.
12 Tribunals, Courts and Enforcement Act 2007 s 119(5).
13 Tribunals, Courts and Enforcement Act 2007 s 119(6). As to termination see PARAS 946, 947.

941.   Registration of plans. As from a day to be appointed, the following provisions have effect[1]. Regulations may make provision about the registration[2] of either or both of the following: (1) any request made to the operator of an approved scheme[3] for a debt repayment plan[4] to be arranged in accordance with the scheme; (2) any debt repayment plan arranged for a non-business debtor[5] in accordance with an approved scheme[6].

1 See PARA 931.
2 For these purposes, 'registration' means registration in the register maintained under the Courts Act 2003 s 98 (the register of judgments and orders etc: see CIVIL PROCEDURE vol 12 (2009) PARA 1147): Tribunals, Courts and Enforcement Act 2007 s 120(2). Regulations under s 120 may amend the Courts Act 2003 s 98: Tribunals, Courts and Enforcement Act 2007 s 120(3). At the date at which this volume states the law no such regulations had been made. As to the making of regulations see PARA 932 note 4.
3 As to the meaning of 'approved scheme' see PARA 932 note 3.
4 As to the meaning of 'debt repayment plan' see PARA 931.
5 As to the meaning of 'non-business debtor' see PARA 931 note 4.
6 Tribunals, Courts and Enforcement Act 2007 s 120(1). At the date at which this volume states the law no such regulations had been made.

942.   Other debt management arrangements in force. As from a day to be appointed, the following provisions have effect[1]. If a debt repayment plan[2] is arranged for a debtor in accordance with an approved scheme[3], and immediately before the plan is arranged, other debt management arrangements[4] are in force in respect of the debtor[5], then the plan is not to come into effect unless the other debt management arrangements cease to be in force[6].

If the operator of the approved scheme is aware of the other debt management arrangements, the operator must give the relevant authority[7] notice that the plan has been arranged[8]. In a case where the operator is aware of other debt management arrangements at the time the plan is arranged, it must give the notice as soon as practicable after the plan is arranged[9]. In a case where the operator becomes aware of those arrangements after the plan is arranged, it must give the notice as soon as practicable after becoming aware of them[10].

1 See PARA 931.
2 As to the meaning of 'debt repayment plan' see PARA 931.
3 As to the meaning of 'approved scheme' see PARA 932 note 3.
4 'Other debt management arrangements' means any of the following: (1) an administration order under the County Courts Act 1984 Pt 6 (ss 112A–112AI) (see PARA 886 et seq); (2) an enforcement restriction order under the County Courts Act 1984 Pt 6A (ss 117A–117X) (see PARA 916 et seq); (3) a debt relief order under the Insolvency Act 1986 Pt 7A (ss 251A–251X) (see PARA 101 et seq): Tribunals, Courts and Enforcement Act 2007 s 121(7). For the purposes of s 121, a debt relief order is 'in force' if the moratorium applicable to the order under the Insolvency Act 1986 s 251H has not yet ended (see PARA 109): Tribunals, Courts and Enforcement Act 2007 s 121(9).
5 Tribunals, Courts and Enforcement Act 2007 s 121(1).
6 Tribunals, Courts and Enforcement Act 2007 s 121(2). Any provision, whether in the plan or elsewhere, about when the plan is to come into effect is subject to s 121(2): s 121(3).
7 'The relevant authority' means: (1) in relation to an administration order: the proper county court (within the meaning of the County Courts Act 1984 Pt 6 (see PARA 896 note 5)); (2) in relation to an enforcement restriction order: the proper county court (within the meaning of Pt 6A (see PARA 918 note 7)); (3) in relation to a debt relief order: the official receiver (see PARA 35 et seq): Tribunals, Courts and Enforcement Act 2007 s 121(8). As from a day to be appointed, heads (1) and (2) above are repealed and replaced by a new head which provides that

the relevant authority in relation to an administration order or an enforcement restriction order is the county court: see s 121(8) (amended by the Crime and Courts Act 2013 Sch 9 Pt 3 para 136(a)). At the date at which this volume states the law no such day had been appointed.
8   Tribunals, Courts and Enforcement Act 2007 s 121(4).
9   Tribunals, Courts and Enforcement Act 2007 s 121(5).
10 Tribunals, Courts and Enforcement Act 2007 s 121(6).

(iv) Appeals

943. Right of appeal. As from a day to be appointed, the following provisions have effect[1]. If a debt repayment plan[2] is arranged for a debtor in accordance with an approved scheme[3], an affected creditor[4] may appeal to a county court against any of the following: (1) the fact that the plan has been arranged; (2) the fact that a debt owed to the affected creditor has been specified in the plan; (3) the terms of the plan, including any payment provision[5] included in the plan[6]. However, head (3) above does not allow an affected creditor to appeal against the fact that a debt owed to any other creditor has been specified in the plan[7].

1   See PARA 931.
2   As to the meaning of 'debt repayment plan' see PARA 931.
3   As to the meaning of 'approved scheme' see PARA 932 note 3.
4   For these purposes, 'affected creditor' means the creditor under any debt which is specified in the plan: Tribunals, Courts and Enforcement Act 2007 ss 122(4), 131(1).
5   Ie any payment provision included in the plan in accordance with the Tribunals, Courts and Enforcement Act 2007 s 110(3): see PARA 931.
6   Tribunals, Courts and Enforcement Act 2007 s 122(1), (2). As from a day to be appointed, the reference in s 122(2) to 'a county court' is replaced by a reference to 'the county court': see s 122(2) (amended by the Crime and Courts Act 2013 Sch 9 Pt 3 para 52). At the date at which this volume states the law no such day had been appointed.
7   Tribunals, Courts and Enforcement Act 2007 s 122(3).

944. Dealing with appeals. As from a day to be appointed, the following provisions have effect[1]. If an appeal is made to a county court[2], the county court may determine the appeal in any way that it thinks fit[3]. The county court may make such orders as may be necessary to give effect to the determination of the appeal[4]. The county court may, in particular, order the scheme operator[5] to do any of the following:
   (1)   to reconsider the decision to arrange the plan;
   (2)   to reconsider any decision about the terms of the plan;
   (3)   to modify the debt repayment plan[6];
   (4)   to revoke the debt repayment plan[7].
The county court may make such interim provision as it thinks fit in relation to the period before the appeal is determined[8].

1   See PARA 931.
2   Ie under the Tribunals, Courts and Enforcement Act 2007 s 122: see PARA 943. The county court is the county court to which the appeal is made: s 123(6). As from a day to be appointed, s 123(6) is repealed: see the Crime and Courts Act 2013 Sch 9 Pt 3 para 136(b). At the date at which this volume states the law no such day had been appointed.
3   Tribunals, Courts and Enforcement Act 2007 s 123(1), (2). As from a day to be appointed, the reference in s 123(1) to 'a county court' is replaced by a reference to 'the county court': see s 123(1) (amended by the Crime and Courts Act 2013 Sch 9 Pt 3 para 52). At the date at which this volume states the law no such day had been appointed.
4   Tribunals, Courts and Enforcement Act 2007 s 123(3).
5   As to the meaning of 'scheme operator' see PARA 931 note 4.
6   As to the meaning of 'debt repayment plan' see PARA 931.
7   Tribunals, Courts and Enforcement Act 2007 s 123(4).
8   Tribunals, Courts and Enforcement Act 2007 s 123(5).

(v) Charging

945. Charges by operator of approved scheme. As from a day to be appointed, the following provisions have effect[1]. The operator of an approved scheme[2] may recover its costs[3] by charging debtors[4] or affected creditors[5], or both[6].

1   See PARA 931.
2   As to the meaning of 'approved scheme' see PARA 932 note 3.
3   'Costs' means the costs which the operator incurs, taking one year with another, in connection with the approved scheme, so far as those costs are reasonable: Tribunals, Courts and Enforcement Act 2007 s 124(2).
4   'Debtors' means: (1) debtors who make requests for debt repayment plans to be arranged in accordance with the approved scheme; and (2) debtors for whom debt repayment plans are arranged in accordance with the approved scheme: Tribunals, Courts and Enforcement Act 2007 s 124(2).
5   As to the meaning of 'affected creditor' see PARA 943 note 4.
6   Tribunals, Courts and Enforcement Act 2007 s 124(1).

(vi) Termination of Approval

946. Procedure for termination. As from a day to be appointed, the following provisions have effect[1]. Regulations may specify a procedure for terminating the approval of a debt management scheme[2]. The regulations may, in particular, specify a procedure that requires any or all of the following:

(1)   notice of, or the reasons for, an intended termination to be given, whether to the supervising authority[3], the scheme operator[4], the Lord Chancellor[5] or any other person[6];
(2)   conditions to be met before a termination takes effect[7];
(3)   a particular period of time to elapse before a termination takes effect[8].

1   See PARA 931.
2   Tribunals, Courts and Enforcement Act 2007 s 125(1). As to the meaning of 'debt management scheme' see PARA 931. At the date at which this volume states the law no such regulations had been made. As to the making of regulations see PARA 932 note 4.
3   As to the meaning of 'supervising authority' see PARA 932 note 2.
4   As to the meaning of 'scheme operator' see PARA 931 note 4.
5   As to the Lord Chancellor see CONSTITUTIONAL LAW AND HUMAN RIGHTS vol 8(2) (Reissue) PARA 477 et seq.
6   Tribunals, Courts and Enforcement Act 2007 s 125(2)(a).
7   Tribunals, Courts and Enforcement Act 2007 s 125(2)(b).
8   Tribunals, Courts and Enforcement Act 2007 s 125(2)(c).

947. Terminating an approval. As from a day to be appointed, the following provisions have effect[1]. The approval of a debt management scheme[2] may be terminated only if the termination is in accordance with all of the following, so far as they are relevant:

(1)   any terms to which the approval is subject[3];
(2)   any provision made in regulations as to the procedure for termination[4];
(3)   any other provision made in other regulations[5] in relation to debt management schemes[6].

1   See PARA 931.
2   As to the meaning of 'debt management scheme' see PARA 931.
3   Ie by virtue of the Tribunals, Courts and Enforcement Act 2007 s 113: see PARA 934.
4   Ie under the Tribunals, Courts and Enforcement Act 2007 s 125: see PARA 946.
5   Ie under the Tribunals, Courts and Enforcement Act 2007 Pt 5 Ch 4 (ss 109–133).
6   Tribunals, Courts and Enforcement Act 2007 s 126.

948. Alternatives to termination. As from a day to be appointed, the following provisions have effect[1]. Regulations may make provision to allow the supervising authority[2] to deal with a termination case other than by terminating the approval[3]. A termination case is a case in which the supervising authority would be entitled to terminate the approval of a debt management scheme[4]. The regulations may, in particular, make provision to allow the supervising authority to transfer the operation of the scheme to itself or to any other body[5].

1 See PARA 931.
2 As to the meaning of 'supervising authority' see PARA 932 note 2.
3 Tribunals, Courts and Enforcement Act 2007 s 127(1). At the date at which this volume states the law no such regulations had been made. As to the making of regulations see PARA 932 note 4.
4 Tribunals, Courts and Enforcement Act 2007 s 127(2). As to the meaning of 'debt management scheme' see PARA 931. As to termination see PARAS 946, 947.
5 Tribunals, Courts and Enforcement Act 2007 s 127(3).

949. Effects of end of approval. As from a day to be appointed, the following provisions have effect[1]. Regulations may make provision about the effects if the approval of a debt management scheme[2] comes to an end[3]. The regulations may, in particular, make provision about the treatment of debt repayment plans[4] arranged for non-business debtors[5] before the scheme came to an end[6]. This includes provision to treat a plan as though the approval had not come to an end, or as though the plan had been made in accordance with a different approved scheme[7].

The regulations may also, in particular, make provision about cases where, at the time the scheme comes to an end, the scheme operator is in breach of a relevant obligation[8]. This includes provision to ensure that the operator is not released from the relevant obligation by virtue of the termination[9].

1 See PARA 931.
2 As to the meaning of 'debt management scheme' see PARA 931.
3 Tribunals, Courts and Enforcement Act 2007 s 128(1). At the date at which this volume states the law no such regulations had been made. As to the making of regulations see PARA 932 note 4.
4 As to the meaning of 'debt repayment plan' see PARA 931.
5 As to the meaning of 'non-business debtor' see PARA 931 note 4.
6 Tribunals, Courts and Enforcement Act 2007 s 128(2).
7 Tribunals, Courts and Enforcement Act 2007 s 128(3).
8 Tribunals, Courts and Enforcement Act 2007 s 128(4). For the purposes of s 128(4), (5), 'relevant obligation' means any obligation, including a requirement or condition, however arising, that relates to: (1) the scheme in question, including its operation; (2) the approval of that scheme; or (3) the termination of that approval: s 128(6).
9 Tribunals, Courts and Enforcement Act 2007 s 128(5). See note 8.

INDEX

Bankruptcy and Individual Insolvency

References are to paragraph numbers; superior figures refer to notes

References are to paragraph numbers; superior figures refer to notes

References are to paragraph numbers; superior figures refer to notes

References are to paragraph numbers; superior figures refer to notes

References are to paragraph numbers; superior figures refer to notes

References are to paragraph numbers; superior figures refer to notes

References are to paragraph numbers; superior figures refer to notes

References are to paragraph numbers; superior figures refer to notes

References are to paragraph numbers; superior figures refer to notes

TRUSTEE IN BANKRUPTCY—*continued*
  removal of—*continued*
    meeting of creditors, by—
      notice of, 364
      power of court to regulate, 365
      resolutions, 364
      summoning of, 362
    notice of, 367
    order of court, by, 362
    procedure on, 366
    release on, 379
    Secretary of State, by, 369
  remuneration—
    court, recourse to, 352
    creditors' meeting, recourse to, 351
    entitlement to, 348
    excessive, creditors claiming, 353
    factors taken into account, 348, 349
    fixing, 348
    joint trustees, of, 350
    matters effecting, 350
    new trustee, of, 355
    review of, 354
    services, for, 349
    set fee, apportionment of, 356
  resignation—
    action following acceptance of, 359
    creditors' meeting to receive, 358
    notice of, 357, 362
    permission of court for, 360
    prescribed circumstances, in, 357
    release on, 379
  right or cause of action vesting in—
    after-acquired property, as, 448
    bankrupt, pending by or against, 452
    compromise, power of, 456
    damage to person or property,
        involving, 449
    functions of, 448
    litigant, bringing or defending as, 455
    personal injury, etc, relating to, 448
    personal services, contracts for, 450
    personal torts, 451
    proceedings—
      expenditure, limits of, 454
      powers, as to, 453
    property, as, 447
  sale, power of, 476
  sanction, powers exercisable with, 478
  sanction, powers exercisable without,
      479

TRUSTEE IN BANKRUPTCY—*continued*
  second bankruptcy, functions on, 489
  stocks and shares, transfer of, 476
  utilities, power to ensure continuation
      of essential supplies by, 485
  vacancy in office, filling, 370
  vacation of office—
    annulment of bankruptcy order, on,
        373
    block transfer of cases on, 377
    disbursements etc, repayment of, 394
    duties on, 376
    final creditors' meeting, after, 372
    intention of, notice to official
        receiver, 375
    loss of qualification as insolvency
        practitioner, on, 371
  vesting of property in—
    company books, transferable on, 409
    confiscation order discharged or
        quashed, subject to orders of,
        403
    detention, property released from,
        400
    documents and records, taking
        possession of, 408
    excess value, items of, 404
    generally, 325, 397
    object of, 397
    property exempt from, 407
    realisation order, subject to, 402
    receivership or administration order,
        subject to, 401
    restraint order, property subject to,
        399
    security, goods held as, 411
    tenancies, of, 405
    things in action, 410
    time of, 398
    title acquired on, 406
VOLUNTARY ARRANGEMENTS
  individual. *See* INDIVIDUAL VOLUNTARY
      ARRANGEMENTS
  insolvency procedure, as, 1
WARRANT
  cross border insolvency, relating to, 828
  insolvency provisions, under—
    execution outside court's district, 751
    issue of, 750
WOMEN
  bankruptcy law, subject to, 10

Words and Phrases

Words in parentheses indicate the context in which the word or phrase is used